www.wadsworth.com

wadsworth.com is the World Wide Web site for Wadsworth Publishing Company and is your direct source to dozens of online resources.

At *wadsworth.com* you can find out about supplements, demonstration software, and student resources. You can also send e-mail to many of our authors and preview new publications and exciting new technologies.

wadsworth.com
Changing the way the world learns®

Lovers of Wisdom

An Introduction to Philosophy with Integrated Readings

Second Edition

Daniel Kolak

William Paterson University of New Jersey

WADSWORTH

THOMSON LEARNING

Australia • Canada • Mexico • Singapore • Spain • United Kingdom • United States

WADSWORTH
THOMSON LEARNING

Philosophy Editor: *Peter Adams*
Assistant Editor: *Kara Kindstrom*
Editorial Assistant: *Mark Andrews*
Marketing Manager: *David Garrison*
Print Buyer: *April Reynolds*
Permissions Editor: *Stephanie Keough*
Production Service: *Ruth Cottrell*

Copy Editor: *Ruth Cottrell*
Cover Designer: *Bill Stanton*
Cover Image: *Planet Art*
Compositor: *Ruth Cottrell Books*
Text and Cover Printer: *Custom/ Von Hoffmann*

Library of Congress Cataloging-in-Publication Data

Kolak, Daniel.
  Lovers of wisdom : an introduction to philosophy with integrated readings / Daniel Kolak.—2nd ed.
    p. cm.
  Includes index
  ISBN 0-534-54146-1
    1. Philosophy—Introductions. I. Title.
BD21 .K64 2000
190—dc21   00-043338

Wadsworth/Thomson Learning
10 Davis Drive
Belmont, CA 94002-3098
USA

For information about our products, contact us:
Thomson Learning Academic Resource Center
1-800-423-0563
http://www.wadsworth.com

International Headquarters
Thomson Learning
International Division
290 Harbor Drive, 2nd Floor
Stamford, CT 06902-7477
USA

UK/Europe/Middle East/South Africa
Thomson Learning
Berkshire House
168-173 High Holborn
London WC1V 7AA
United Kingdom

Asia
Thomson Learning
60 Albert Street, #15-01
Albert Complex
Singapore 189969

Canada
Nelson/Thomson Learning
1120 Birchmount Road
Toronto, Ontario M1K 5G4
Canada

For Julia and Sophia

Contents

PART III: THE MODERN RATIONALISTS   195

Chapter 9: Prelude to Modern Philosophy: The Copernican Revolution   196

Chapter 10: Descartes   224

PART VII: THE 20TH CENTURY 441

Chapter 23: The Birth of Analytic Philosophy: Frege, Russell, Wittgenstein, and Quine   503

Chapter 24: The Postmodernists: Gadamer, Merleau-Ponty, Foucault, and Derrida   538

Topical Contents

III. A BRIEF COURSE IN METAPHYSICS: IN SEARCH OF REALITY

IV. A BRIEF COURSE IN EPISTEMOLOGY: IN SEARCH OF KNOWLEDGE

V. A Brief Course in the Philosophy of Mind: In Search of Consciousness, Self, and Identity

VI. A Brief Course in Ethics: In Search of Morality

VII. A BRIEF COURSE IN SOCIAL AND POLITICAL PHILOSOPHY: IN SEARCH OF SOCIAL JUSTICE AND FAIRNESS

Preface

Lovers of Wisdom: An Introduction to Philosophy with Integrated Readings connects you directly to the wonder, profundity, and excitement of philosophy by introducing you to the philosophers themselves. Intended primarily as a textbook for one- and two-semester introductory classes, it is a complete, self-contained, and self-sufficient course in itself, requiring no special skills or background knowledge.

One common obstacle to doing philosophy is that, in many cases, the writings that contain the most potent and germane philosophical substance are inaccessible to contemporary readers. The solution offered in this book is a new approach to an old idea: a text with integrated readings. The text selections are long. The integration is substantial. If two decades of teaching philosophy at a variety of institutions and in a variety of settings has taught me anything, it is that philosophy is best introduced to students not as a series of oppositions divided into movements and schools but as an integrated activity. My overarching goal has been to strengthen the similarities among even the most diverse thinkers so that beginning philosophers—at whatever age they enter the portal—have an integrated experience that will stimulate and play upon their own insights and wonder.

One common obstacle to teaching philosophy is that whereas textbooks and anthologies generally do an adequate job of presenting the issues, they fail to capture the intellectual and emotional passion typical of most philosophical inquiry. Students tend to perceive the theories as dry, overly technical, and more concerned with defending this or that position rather than discovering truth. By presenting the philosophy in the way that philosophers would have presented it if they themselves were here, I have tried to capture some of the genuine excitement of the art of philosophical dialog. I have a story to tell. It is the story of the world, of existence, of the quest for wisdom, of enlightenment; it is full of unexpected surprises.

Because the focus is on the individual philosophers themselves—their writings, their insights, their ideas, the contexts in which they lived and worked—*Lovers of Wisdom* is suitable for any introductory philosophy course regardless of philosophical orientation. It is inclusive: analytic and continental, Western and non-Western, religious and secular. It is expansive: ancient, medieval, modern, nineteenth and twentieth centuries, contemporary. It spans all aspects of philosophy: metaphysics, epistemology, ethics, religion, mind, logic, critical thinking. Having the full philosophical spectrum allows you to choose your own best path to wisdom.

To the Instructor

Today, when we all know so much more than was ever dreamt possible, philosophy is more important than ever. Often, philosophy is introduced as if it were simply another subject matter. Students are presented with various tidbits that try to introduce them to the "issues" and "problems" in the hope that they will gain some abstract idea about what philosophy is. But philosophy divorced from the philosophers and from its own historical development tends to produce merely a vague, general feeling of skepticism and relativism about knowledge. For this reason, this book starts at the beginning. It evolves with the reader. The philosophy emerges with the philosophers. It is not everything, but it is intact. Each of the original readings touches upon some central philosophical issue that has been pivotal in the discovery, development, and evolution of philosophy. In becoming wise about these developments, students will be doing philosophy, not just reading about it.

Note that there are two tables of contents. The first is for those wishing to use the book from cover to cover, chronologically. This order brings out in full force the rich development of ideas in their historical contexts. The second is for those who take a topical rather than a historical approach. It is organized as nine "brief courses": logic, philosophy of religion, metaphysics, epistemology, philosophy of mind, ethics, social and political philosophy, philosophy of language, and philosophy of mathematics and science. These features should also help students not only with their studying but also with their writing.

Users of this book seeking a deeper immersion into the original texts should consider *The Philosophy Source on CD-ROM*, which contains more than 100 masterworks. It is available for less than the cost of a typical workbook and can be bundled with this book at an additional discount. Finally, Joe Salerno's free student's companion that is already bundled with this book provides much additional pedagogy, including sample tests and help with writing papers.

Introduction

Of all the courses students take during their undergraduate education, philosophy is the only subject in which they have probably never had a course before college. Courses in English, chemistry, physics, psychology, physical education, history, and so on, tend to differ from high school courses primarily in level of difficulty and method of approach. Not so with philosophy. To most students philosophy is completely new—which is ironic since of all the disciplines philosophy is the oldest.

And yet, when experts in the various scholarly fields attain a doctorate they have a Ph.D. behind their name, which stands for "Doctor of Philosophy." So, while a philosophy course is something most students have never had before college, philosophy has something in common with every discipline. Philosophy is, in that sense, a discipline that knows no boundaries. Philosophy courses, typically, involve the other disciplines directly—such as philosophy of science, philosophy of language, philosophy of art, philosophy of music, philosophy of physics, political and social philosophy, philosophy of biology, philosophy of mathematics, philosophy of mind, philosophy of history, philosophy of psychology, and so on, each of which we will touch upon in this book. But all courses in all other disciplines at least indirectly, and often directly, involve philosophy.

But what is philosophy, in and of itself? Philosophers disagree about that question. Nevertheless, there is some agreement that there are at least three vastly different but closely related and equally important senses of what philosophy is. The word philosophy is often used publicly in only the first of its senses, when people say "My philosophy is . . . ," which means something like, "in my view," "according to my beliefs," "according to my theory," and so on. This is a valid but easily misunderstood sense, especially since one of the most important functions of philosophy is just the opposite: to question any and all accepted views and beliefs, to show up the weaknesses and gaps in all theories, even one's own. This requires expertise in a given area. But it also requires the philosopher's stamina of not being seduced by the prevailing views and theories, to understand but to remain critical and skeptical—not for the purpose of being destructive (usually) but, rather, for being instructive, for keeping a wise Socratic eye on the broader historical sweep of the knowledge seeking enterprises each of whose unquestionable contributions are tempered by an unquestioning tendency toward pretense, confabulation, self-deception, and errors. Someone who is a philosopher in a particular area of knowledge must be able to draw up a map of that discipline, show where the peaks and valleys are, where the different roads lead, and then, pointing, show exactly where the map falls off into a dark abyss of unknowing and why: *Knowledge goes this way, then that way, winds around here and ends there.*

So the first sense—in which philosophy means having a particular view, or having a system of beliefs, or a theory, as in "my philosophy is . . . "—the discipline of philosophy ought better to be called "philosophies." For, in this first sense, philosophy is the study of views—a sort of "view of views."[1] This is one of its positive aspects. Its second, negative, aspect—vastly different from yet closely related to the first—consists in critically pointing out the inconsistencies and gaps (what is wrong, incoherent, or missing) within some particular view, system of beliefs, or theory. Its third aspect, another "positive" one, which is different from yet closely related to the other two, consists in the presentation of a new view, system of beliefs, or theory in contrast to some prevailing view.

Nobody likes philosophers. Physicists don't like them. Mathematicians don't like them. Psychologists don't like them. Not because the philosopher doesn't know enough—though sometimes it is true that the philosopher doesn't—nor because the philosopher knows more than they do—though sometimes the philosopher does. On the contrary, the reason experts in other areas don't like philosophers is because often the philosopher knows what they do not know: not in the sense of having some knowledge that the expert lacks but, rather, in the sense of knowing that there is some knowledge that the expert lacks and, what is even worse for anyone in a position of authority, being able to point knowingly to the holes in the expert's expertise.

It would, however, be wrong to think of philosophy as being somehow opposed to the different disciplines to which it is both originating mother and stern, hypercritical father. Like a good parent, philosophy not only loves its children but also tries to understand and sometimes perhaps even guide them.

Early Greek philosophers before the time of Socrates and Plato (often called "pre-Socratics," some of whom you will meet shortly) made no sharp divisions between the various disciplines of knowledge. By the end of the fifth century B.C.E., however, they realized that arithmetic, geometry, astronomy, and music were related but distinct fields. They called these fields *mathemata*, meaning "disciplines," from which the word "mathematics" descends. Throughout the Middle Ages, these first separate disciplines were grouped together at the universities as the quadrivium. But already from the start, the philosophers recognized the importance of seeing the limitations of knowledge in all its forms. Following Socrates, they called this knowledge, about the limitations of knowledge, "wisdom."

We all know many things and so everyone is to some degree knowledgeable. But there are many more things we don't know than things we do know. The problem, however, is not just that we don't know; we are ignorant, in the sense that we use what we do know to obscure—that is, ignore, what we do not know. In other words, the more we know, the more we are in danger of being blinded by our knowledge. So from Socrates on, the goal of philosophy has been not just knowledge per se—which by itself can be blinding—but wisdom. Philosophical wisdom means knowing and, at the same time, actually seeing the limitations of that very knowledge.

This, of course, is to a certain degree my personal view of what philosophy is. It is not the only view and in this book you will see many other views. But my view is not just a made-up view. It comes from having considered what other philosophers have said, studying their works, and thinking. The degree to which these three activities can bring not just knowledge but wisdom will be measured by the degree to which this book inspires you to do not just the first two but all three.

Lastly, and most importantly, philosophy is a very personal activity. Although there have been various "movements," which we shall look at, philosophy is mainly done by individuals. Therefore, we shall begin at the beginning and move forward through time until the present century, taking each philosopher in turn. Rather than studying the systems or movements within philosophy per se, we shall be entering into the life of each philosopher and trying to see the philosophy through the philosopher's eyes, to think as the philosopher thinks, to commune with the philosopher within ourselves.

Acknowledgments

I thank Peter Adams, David Bohm, Bill Boos, Noam Chomsky, Daniel Dennett, Umberto Eco, David Goloff, Saul Kripke, David Lewis, Ray Martin, Hope May, Marshall Missner, Thomas Nagel, Robert Nozick, John O'Connor, Derek Parfit, Willard Quine, Mike Russo, Joe Salerno, Steve Stitch, Bill Styron, Garrett Thompson, Horst Ungerer, Victor Velarde, John Archibald Wheeler, John White, and Wendy Zentz. I thank William Paterson College for providing continuous support for my writing projects over the past several years. I thank Cunard for sailing my wife and me to the ancient birthplaces of philosophy. I thank the reviewers: Daniel Campana, University of La Verne; Michael Clifford, Mississippi State University; Theodore Guleserian, Arizona State University; Edward Johnson, University of New Orleans; Tracy Lounsbury, Loyola University of Chicago; Scott Lowe, Bloomsburg University of Pennsylvania; Ann Pirruccello, University of San Diego; Michael Potts, Methodist College; Daniel Silber, Florida Southern College; Michael Potts, University of South Florida; and Paul Tang, California State University, Long Beach. I thank the many students whose eyes have been my windows. And I thank the great lovers of wisdom without whom there would be no book.

NOTE

1. Philosophers sometimes call this a "second-order" discipline: beliefs about beliefs, thinking about thinking, knowledge about knowledge, wonder about wonder, theory of theories, and so on.

0 ✿ The Dawn of Philosophy

0.0 The Birth of Wisdom

You wake up one morning from uneasy dreams and find yourself an overnight celebrity: reporters at your door, your face on the front page, your friends and relatives on the talk shows. It's all over the news. A secret national commission, specially appointed by the president to find the wisest person in the country, has completed its search. Their answer is *you*.

You can't believe it. It must be a mistake, a joke. Surely there are lots of people far wiser than you. Scientists, doctors, educators, inventors, artists, the list is endless: winners of the Nobel prize; discoverers of DNA; astronauts who have walked on the moon; computer scientists; Ph.D.'s in quantum physics, microbiology, mathematics, history, literature, music . . . How could you possibly be wiser than any of them?

You explain that this must be some kind of bizarre mistake. Everyone thinks you're just being humble—exactly what one would expect from someone wise! You ask, Why did they pick me? Nobody knows. You're perplexed. You know for a fact that you know hardly anything at all. The president's commission must simply be wrong. *You*, wiser than all the doctors? Wiser than all the scientists? Wiser than all the philosophers?

But now suddenly everyone wants to know anything and everything about you. You're hounded everywhere you go. Your opinions, your advice, your suggestions for how to solve personal problems, national problems, global problems—people hang on your every word. You tell them you don't know anything. They think you're being coy, secretive. Finally, you decide once and for all to prove that you are not what they think you are. The task, you think, will be simple. All you have to do is seek out some of the people who are acknowledged authorities in their areas of expertise and question them. It will then quickly become apparent to everyone that others know much more than you do and that therefore they are far wiser.

You seek out leading scientists, religious leaders, educators, artists, and politicians. Initially, they are very happy to talk to you because, of course, they would like your endorsement. You ask them questions. At first you seem to be making your point, but then things don't go as you imagined. You find that many experts like to talk but few of them like to be *questioned*. They answer you only up to a point and then they begin to evade. Often, they end up pointing you in the direction of another authority, such as some other expert or a book. But, because you have something to prove, you persist. When they use terms you don't understand, you ask them to clarify their language. This they can do only up to a point beyond which it seems even they do not fully understand their own words or, if they do, they cannot make their meanings clear. Soon you begin to get a strange, nagging suspicion that somehow they are trying to pull the wool over your eyes, that there are some fundamental unknowns that they are covering up. But why would all these knowledgeable experts be covering up their unknowns? Yet that's the way it seems to you.

You go from expert to expert, authority to authority. When they fail to convince, or to demonstrate, or to justify, or to explain, you demand that they do so. They can't. You keep questioning. They make statements they cannot justify. Soon they seem to be going beyond what they know, yet they speak with the same authority. No, now they sound even more certain! The more you persist, the more angry they become. Finally, they refuse to talk with you anymore.

In the end, you draw an inexorable conclusion. Certainly, many experts do know more than you. They can describe in great detail a variety of views and theories. You do not have anything like that under your command. But then, at some point, invariably the experts seem to go beyond what they know. They make statements that are not known by them to be true and they do so with the same air of authority as when they talk about what they do know. Past a certain point they seem to you to become defensive. That's when you begin to suspect that they *pretend to know more than they actually know.*

How strange, you think, how ironic. It's not that they don't know anything. Far from it. It's as if their very knowing has somehow corrupted them. You've heard it said that power corrupts and absolute power corrupts absolutely. Maybe something like that is true with knowledge?

Knowledge corrupts and absolute knowledge corrupts absolutely? Could something like that really be true? You wonder.

Perhaps the secret commission was not wrong after all! You simply assumed that wisdom and knowledge were the same thing. But maybe wisdom and knowledge are only somehow related and not the same thing at all. Unlike all the great knowers with whom you spoke, you know perfectly well what you do not know and—unlike them (at least that's how it seems to you)—you do not pretend to know more than you actually do know. Might *that* be wisdom? Knowing how little you know? Knowing the *limitations* of knowledge?

0.1 The Legend of Socrates (470–399 B.C.E.): Knowing the Unknown

The story you've just read is no mere make-believe. It is based on actual events that happened more than two thousand years ago to a young Greek named Socrates.

It has often been pointed out that what the character of Jesus is to Christendom, the character of Socrates is to Western philosophy. Both became tidal forces for opposing sides of a revolutionary sea change. Some have gone so far as to claim that the Jesus story is just a rewriting of the Socrates story. (Christianity has been called, by Bertrand Russell and others, "Platonism for the masses.") Certainly, the similarity of themes is striking: both supposedly sacrificed themselves for their respective causes, having been sentenced to death for crimes against their respective states. Neither Socrates nor Jesus wrote an autobiography, leaving it to oral historians and subsequent writers to interpret their lives.

Socrates came first. He lived in Athens, a city-state in ancient Greece, from 470 through 399 B.C.E. (Before the Common Era). He was the teacher of Plato who was the teacher of Aristotle who was the teacher of Alexander the Great who by the age of 33 conquered the known world.[1]

According to Plato, the unexpected events that turned Socrates into a philosopher began at the temple at Delphi. Plato tells the story like this. While still a young man, Socrates—like many a young person at the time—traveled about seeking wisdom by asking questions of everyone who would talk to him, questions about anything and everything. Socrates thereby, to his own surprise, got a reputation for being extremely wise. One day, a friend of his went to the official oracle (the high priestess through whom supposedly the gods spoke) and asked whether anyone in Athens was wiser than Socrates; "the Delphic prophetess answered that there was no one wiser."

How did Socrates react to this? According to his testimony as told to us by Plato, Socrates did not believe the oracle. So he set out to prove the gods wrong. His method was simple: go to those who you think are wiser than you and question them until you demonstrate to yourself their superiority. In the following passage from the *Apology* he gives a moving and eloquent statement telling of how he stumbled upon the true meaning of wisdom. All the supposedly "wise" people whom Socrates questioned invariably pretended to know more than they actually knew:

⚎

Apology

[A] friend of mine . . . went to Delphi and boldly asked the oracle to tell him whether . . . there was anyone wiser than I was, and the Pythian prophetess answered that there was no one wiser . . .

. . . When I heard the answer, I said to myself, What can God mean? and what is the interpretation of this riddle? For I know that I have no wisdom, small or great. What can she mean when she says that I am the wisest of men? And yet she is a god and cannot lie; that would be against her

From Plato, "Apology," in *The Dialogues of Plato*, B. J. Jowett trans. (London: The Clarendon Press, 1892) with emendations by the author.

nature. After a long consideration, I at last thought of a method of trying the question. I reflected that if I could only find someone wiser than myself, then I might go to the god with a refutation in my hand. I should say to her, "Here is someone who is wiser than I am; but you said that I was the wisest." Accordingly I went to one who had the reputation of wisdom, and observed him—his name I need not mention; he was a politician whom I selected for examination—and the result was as follows: When I began to talk with him, I could not help thinking that he was not really wise, although he was thought wise by many, and wiser still by himself; and I went and tried to explain to him that he thought himself wise, but was not really wise; and the consequence was that he hated me, and his enmity was shared by several who were present and heard me. So I left him, saying to myself, as I went away: Well, although I do not suppose that either of us knows anything really beautiful and good, I am better off than he is—for he knows nothing, and thinks that he knows. I neither know nor think that I know. In this latter particular, then, I seem to have slightly the advantage of him. Then I went to another, who had still higher philosophical pretensions, and my conclusion was exactly the same. I made another enemy . . . and . . . many others.

After this I went to one person after another, being not unconscious of the enmity which I provoked, and I lamented and feared this: but necessity was laid upon me—the word of God, I thought, ought to be considered first. And I said to myself, Go I must to all who appear to know, and find out the meaning of the oracle. And . . . the result of my mission was just this: I found that those most in repute were all but the most foolish; and that some inferior ones were really wiser and better. I will tell you the tale of my wanderings and of the Herculean labors, as I may call them, which I endured only to find at last the oracle irrefutable. When I left the politicians, I went to the poets; tragic, dithyrambic, and all sorts. And there, I said to myself, you will be detected; now you will find out that you are more ignorant than they are. Accordingly, I took them some of the most elaborate passages in their own writings, and asked what was the meaning of them—thinking that they would teach me something. Will you believe me? I am almost ashamed to speak of this, but still

I must say that there is hardly a person present who would not have talked better about their poetry than they did themselves. That showed me in an instant that not by wisdom do poets write poetry, but by a sort of genius and inspiration; they are like diviners or soothsayers who also say many fine things, but do not understand the meaning of them. And the poets appeared to me to be much in the same case; and I further observed that upon the strength of their poetry they believed themselves to be the wisest . . . in other things in which they were not wise. So I departed, conceiving myself to be superior to them for the same reason that I was superior to the politicians.

At last I went to the artisans, for I was conscious that I knew nothing at all, as I may say, and I was sure that they knew many fine things; and in this I was not mistaken, for they did know many things of which I was ignorant, and in this they certainly were wiser than I was. But I observed that even the good artisans fell into the same error as the poets; because they were good workers they thought that they also knew all sorts of high matters, and this defect in them overshadowed their wisdom—therefore I asked myself on behalf of the oracle, whether I would like to be as I was, neither having their knowledge nor their ignorance, or like them in both; and I made answer to myself and the oracle that I was better off as I was.

This investigation has led to my having many enemies of the worst and most dangerous kind, and has given occasion also to many calumnies, and I am called wise, for my hearers always imagine that I myself possess the wisdom which I find wanting in others.

※

Notice that the pretense of the authorities whom Socrates questioned is not even conscious. That is, in pretending to know more than they knew, the politicians, poets, philosophers, and artists—the "experts," the "authorities"—weren't merely lying to Socrates. *They were lying to themselves.* And they were lying to themselves *successfully.* In other words, they did not just lie that they knew what they did not know, they actually believed it. They were self-deceived. Socrates, on the other hand, realized

that he knew perfectly well how little he knew. He did not pretend to know more. He was not self-deceived about what he knew and what he didn't know. Socrates calls this "wisdom."

0.2 The Wisdom of Unknowing

What, then, did the original Socrates actually mean by *wisdom?* Suppose we give the following criteria of wisdom:

1. knowing how little you know
2. not pretending to know more than you know
3. not being self-deceived

But notice that in the *Apology* Socrates says at one point that he doesn't know anything at all. At another point he says he doesn't know anything "really worth knowing." So which is it? Part of the problem may be that it isn't clear what Socrates may have thought versus what Plato thought. We simply don't know; there's no way to tell. Socrates didn't write anything down. All we have is what Plato says. And Plato apparently changed his mind, not merely about what wisdom is but even about what philosophy is and how it should be practiced. Another problem may be that Socrates said many different things and changed his mind throughout his life—at least once, significantly, when he went from being a *sophist* (meaning, literally, "wiseman," see Chapter 1) to calling himself a *philosopher* (meaning, literally, "lover of wisdom"). Moreover, scholars disagree vehemently about what Socrates really meant, even what Plato really meant; there are lots of different interpretations of each philosopher's views. In fact, as you shall see, there are almost as many views of what wisdom is, what knowledge is, and whether (and how) we can get either—even what philosophy is—as there are philosophers.

I therefore want to make very clear here at the outset what I think philosophy is *not.* Philosophy is *not* the study of what this or that philosopher has said. Philosophy simply *can't* be that because there is *no agreement among philosophers what philosophy is or how it should be done.* Reading and studying the works of philosophers can on some views of philosophy be important. I think it is not very important. In fact, I think it is almost insignificant. Why then am I adding yet another philosophy book to the pile, one that contains and discusses all the major great written works of philosophers? The reason is that *reading philosophy is the most important insignificant aspect of philosophy to which a mind can have access.* Why?

Well, all this should become clear to you once you have worked through some of the ideas in this book. For now, let me just say this. If Socrates is right about the top experts and the best authorities being self-deceived, *what about you?* If the so-called "wisest" are self-deceived, are you self-deceived? And if you are, can you trust yourself—that is, can you trust your opinions and beliefs? Are your beliefs and opinions true or are they part of an elaborate self-deception? *How do you know?* Are your beliefs and opinions even *yours,* or are most of the things you believe simply the opinions of others *internalized* through conditioning by authority? That is, are your beliefs and opinions yours not just in the psychological sense that you identify with them but yours in the philosophical sense, that you came to them through critical inquiry, ques-

tioning, and examination? (Or, even, that they came to you from within, mysteriously, through some hidden insight?) Or are "your" beliefs simply the opinions of others that have been thrust upon you by the very authorities and experts whom Socrates says are themselves self-deceived? If so, then everything you believe—your entire view of the world—is a second-order deception. That is, if you have been deceived through conditioning by authority to believe you know things that you do not know, and the majority of those who conditioned you are themselves self-deceived, then you have been deceived by the deceived. You are a puppet of puppets, the slave of slaves, the derivative of an illusion.

NOTE

1. Sometimes details stand in the way of the telling of a really good story; thus, the poetic phrase "known world" merely refers to most of Asia Minor. As King of Macedonia, Alexander overthrew the entire Persian empire except for Paphlagonia, Cappadocia, and Armenia, which retained some independence. He is in any case regarded as one of the greatest generals in history and the Hellenistic, Roman, Christian, and Byzantine empires all owe much to Alexander's achievements.

Part I ⚘ The Legacy of the Ancients

1 ✳ The First Philosophers

Socrates was not the first philosopher. By the time he came upon the scene in the fifth century B.C.E. he was as far removed from the first philosophers as, say, a twentieth-century philosopher like Bertrand Russell (see Chapter 23) is from his modern (eighteenth-century) predecessors. Socrates does, however, provide an opening doorway through which to step even farther back, all the way to the beginning, not just of philosophy but of recorded history itself. Henceforth, we shall commence our journey chronologically.

If what you are after is knowledge of a certain sort—say medical, or scientific, or technological—you would tend to look to the latest, most recent sources available. Today a nineteenth-century scientific journal has mainly historical value. Even a scientific journal that is more than a few decades old—or even just a few years old!—is outdated. For instance, if you were about to undergo some complicated medical procedure and you noticed the doctor prescribing your medication using a drug manual from the 1950s, you would probably become suspicious and worried. However, there are other sorts of knowledge, the seeking of which requires just the opposite. You look to the past,

for instance, when seeking ultimate answers to life's questions—say, the meaning of life—or various sorts of religious inquiry, questions having to do not only with "spiritual" but even purely historical matters, questions having to do with who and what we are. In such cases looking at the latest up-to-date materials seems superficial and out of place. One easily suspects that the latest "spiritual fads," "pop philosophies," and "intellectual fashions" are not the right sources for seeking wisdom. And it is in this respect that philosophical inquiry has much in common with religious and spiritual inquiry. One has the sense or hunch that somehow what one is looking for is not to be found in the present. Indeed, that which is given to us in the present and seems most vividly and importantly urgent may itself obscure something hidden, something sacred, something timeless and universal. Isn't that why our own deep intuitions direct us one way with certain types of inquiry (such as the scientific and technological) and another when it comes to matters religious or philosophical?

There is another important similarity between philosophy and religion. Most of the philosophy that we shall study in this book can be attributed to the particular individuals or groups of individuals who originated it. This is true of religion as well as philosophy. Usually there is some extraordinary individual—such as a Buddha or a Christ—who expresses ideas and thoughts in a new way that profoundly affects the course of subsequent thought. You could of course emphasize the differences between figures like Christ, Buddha, Mohammed, etc., on the one hand and Plato, Descartes, Kant, etc., on the other. It all depends on the sort of story you want to tell. That's not the story I want to tell. At this point I would rather the important similarity between religion and philosophy.

When we study philosophy, in nearly every case what we are looking at is the work of a particular philosopher. This fact usually confuses beginning students, who sometimes wonder why in philosophy—unlike in mathematics or science, for instance (disciplines that nevertheless owe much to and have a lot in common with philosophy, as we shall see)—we don't just study the latest results of the collective enterprise of philosophy. The reason is that, according to this philosopher at least, this would be as fruitless an enterprise as trying to study the latest results of the collective enterprise of religion. There simply are no such results. You end up with a hodgepodge of nonsense—not because there aren't any truths contained therein but because when you mush it all together you lose all the colors, textures, and styles in which the great lovers of wisdom have tried to express all the truths and insights they could muster. In that respect, philosophy and religion both have much in common with great art.

1.0 Indian Philosophy: The *Vedas* and the *Upanishads* (2500–600 B.C.E.)

Indian philosophy—perhaps because it is the oldest in recorded history—is unusual in that its origins can no longer be traced to a particular individual (which is also the case with some other old religions, such as Judaism). What we do know about it is based on books written as far

back as four thousand years ago, some time before 1,000 B.C.E. There are four collections of such "Books of Knowledge," called *Vedas* (Sanskrit for *knowledge*): the *Rg-Veda,* the *Sāma-Veda,* the *Yajur-Veda,* and the *Athar-Veda.* Each of the *Vedas* is divided into four subsections: the *Samhitās* (sacred hymns, prayers, and sacrificial incantations), the *Brāhmanas* (commentaries on the *Samhitās*), the *Āranyakas* (the so-called "forest books"), and the *Upanishads.* Collectively, these sacred books contain some of the most ancient writings about the nature of existence, the self, life, death, and the meaning of it all supposedly as revealed to sages who had attained a super-conscious state of awareness.

1.0.1 The Vedas (2500–600 B.C.E.)

The *Rg-Veda* is the oldest of these vast anthologies. It was composed over many generations and contains more than a thousand hymns (*mantras*) addressed to the principal Vedic gods. These gods can themselves be traced back to ancient religious traditions of nature-worship, where the powers of nature—such as fire (*agni*), wind and air (*vāyu*), etc.—are personified into divine forces to whom the texts themselves were addressed. Like most ancient religions, early Hinduism is extremely polytheistic; the gods number in the hundreds of thousands. Although there is no single supreme God or ruler of the Gods (such as the Greek god Zeus, the king of the gods), a theme that runs throughout all the *Vedas* is that there exists some hidden, common power behind all the gods. This unstated force is the single primal cause of everything, including all the gods, a "being beyond all being" that divided itself into and became all the many individual aspects of the universe. This ancient Hindu conception of the Absolute is called, simply, *Tat Ekam,* meaning, literally, "That One."

In the *Rg-Veda,* the gods and the Absolute One are not talking to us; we are talking to them. Thus the sorts of titles one finds to the various poems are "To Visnu" (one of the deities of the Hindu trinity Brahma-Vishnu-Shiva—the metaphysical forces of creation, maintenance, and destruction, respectively), "To the Waters," "To the Dawn," "To Goddess Earth," "To the Soul of Man," etc. Here, for instance, is "The Song of Creation":

✦

The Song of Creation

Then was not non-existent nor existent: there was no realm of air, no sky beyond it.
What covered in, and where? and what gave shelter? Was water there, unfathomed depth of water?

Death was not then, nor was there aught immortal: no sign was there, the day's and night's divider.
That one thing, breathless, breathed by its own nature: apart from it was nothing whatsoever.

Darkness there was: at first concealed in darkness, this All was indiscriminated chaos.
All that existed then was void and formless: by the great power of warmth was born that unit.

Thereafter rose desire in the beginning, Desire, the primal seed and germ of spirit.
Sages who searched with their heart's thought discovered the existent's kinship in the non-existent.

Transversely was their severing line extended: what was above it then, and what below it?
There were begetters, there were mighty forces, free action here and energy up yonder.

Who verily knows and who can here declare it, whence it was born and whence came this creation?
The gods are later than this world's production. Who knows, then, whence it first came into being?

He, the first origin of this creation, whether he formed it all or did not form it,
Whose eye controls this world in highest heaven, he verily knows it, or perhaps he knows not.

✦

Here we see the idea that the origin of all things, the entire universe and everything in it, comes from a primordial state that neither existed nor did not exist—"then was not non-existent nor existent."

The question of where everything, the universe included, comes from is a deep and profound one that we shall encounter time and again in this book. One possibility of course is that everything has always existed. According to the latest quantum-cosmology, the universe originated from nothing in a "big bang" (see pp. 378–382). The "big bang" theory is of very recent vintage; it was put forth in the twentieth century, and until recently (about fifty years ago) astronomers and physicists were divided as to whether they believed in the big bang hypothesis or the steady-state theory, according to which the universe is eternal. Nearly all of cosmologists today (but not all) believe in the big bang. The difficulty for them and for us is to understand how something could possibly come from nothing, a notion that many find troubling and, on the face of it, unsatisfactory. But notice that the notion that the universe has existed forever is equally troubling and unsatisfying, since in that case the question is *why* the universe has always existed. Or, to suppose that God created the universe may satisfy some of us regarding the question of the existence of the universe, but then there is the question of why God exists rather than no God. And many find it no less puzzling and unsatisfactory to suppose that God has always existed because, say, that is God's nature, than the notion that the universe has always existed because that is its nature.

We shall discuss these ideas again in due course. I bring them up now only because it may help us to see how insightful and brilliant the

From Nicol Macnicol, ed., *Hindu Scriptures* (London: J. M. Dent, 1938).

ancient "Song of Creation" is. It taunts us with an idea that surely must strike us as wise indeed, namely, that the beginning of everything came from a state that neither existed nor did not exist.

The origin of existence itself neither exists nor does not exist. The universe (the totality of everything that exists) came neither from something (which would itself be paradoxical, if what we are inquiring into is why there is something at all rather than nothing) nor from nothing, but from a "not-something, not-nothing." In other words, to think about the origin of everything we must, according to this ancient wisdom, stretch the categories of our thinking beyond what we are accustomed to ordinarily. We might not like to engage in such an exercise. We might find it pointless, incomprehensible, even nonsensical. Or it might give us goose bumps to try and grapple with the mystery. Perhaps we are connecting to some deep, primordial truth. Or perhaps we are connecting to some human being who wrote a poem four thousand years ago. In either case, we are connecting. And that is what matters. As one great writer put it, ". . . only connect."[1]

1.0.2 *The* Upanishads *(800–600* B.C.E.*)*

The *Upanishads* were written between 700 and 600 B.C.E. Because they form the concluding part of the *Vedas*, they are also known as the *Vedānta* (literally, "the ending of the *Vedas*") philosophy. Whereas in the *Samhitās* and *Brāhmanas* the emphasis is on acting in accordance to rituals steeped in tradition (*Karma-mārga*), in the *Upanishads* the focus is on secret knowledge, the teaching of which produces liberation and enlightenment. Insofar as the *Samhitās* and *Brāhmanas* look outward to nature and the gods, the *Upanishads* are remarkable for their turning inward, into the self, directing the mind to look at itself, into thought and consciousness, seeking within itself insights about the ultimate nature of reality, the Universe, and beyond.

Today when people think of "Eastern phi-

losophy," especially of the Indian variety, they usually associate it with images of a *guru* (Sanskrit for *teacher*) imparting wisdom or secret teaching to disciples who sit around listening, meditating, and so on. The word "Upanishad" itself is formed from the Sanskrit words *upa* (near), *ni* (down), and *sad* (sit). The *Upanishads*, a collection of "secret" teachings that are supposed to be imparted in this way, are remarkable for several reasons, not the least of which is the spectrum of philosophical topics ranging from knowledge, metaphysics, and ethics to the self, God, death, immortality, and enlightenment. Its authors are unknown, but its doctrines can be attributed to a number of sages—Aruni, Yājñavalkya, Bālāki, Śvetaketu, Sāndilya— whose teachings were a distinct break with the traditions of the past insofar as they spoke from their own "enlightened experience." Furthermore, they applied their teachings and techniques of meditation for the purpose of liberating the minds of their students from their illusions and false beliefs, until they too attained such states of "inner illumination." To seek God, truth, and reality outside yourself is the greatest of all illusions. You must turn away from the deceptive appearances and seek salvation, not through obedience to traditional religious doctrines or the performance of some sort of "right action" (*Karma-mārga*), but from within, through spiritual illumination based on inner knowledge (*Jñāna-mārga*).

The key to understanding the *Upanishads* lies in the concepts of the *Ātman* and the *Brāhman*, and the nature of the relationship between the two. The themes already expressed in the *Rg-Veda* here take on a new and vivid form. *Brāhman* is the name given to an impersonal, pantheistic[2] world-soul that is experienced objectively as the world outside oneself. *Ātman* is the name give to the self, soul, ego, or I, which ultimately is nothing less than the world-soul incarnate. The two are identical. *Ātman* is *Brāhman* and *Brāhman* is *Ātman*.

You are the world and the world is you: *tat tvam Asi*, "That thou art," and *Aham Brāhman asmi*, "I am Brāhman."

⚹

Unmoving, the One is swifter than the mind.
The sense-powers reached not It, speeding on
     before.
Past others running, This goes standing. . . .
It moves. It moves not.
It is far, and It is near.
It is within all this,
And It is outside of all this.
Now, he who on all beings
Looks as just in the Self (*Ātman*),
And on the Self as in all beings—
He does not shrink away from Him.
In whom all beings
Have become just the Self of the discerner—
Then what delusion, what sorrow is there,
Of him who perceives the unity!
He has environed. The bright, the bodiless, the
     scatheless,
The sinewless, the pure, unpierced by evil!
Wise, intelligent, encompassing, self-existent,
Appropriately he distributed objects through the
     eternal years.
Into blind darkness enter they
That worship ignorance;
Into darkness greater than that, as it were, they
That delight in knowledge.
Other, indeed, they say, than knowledge!
Other, they say, than non-knowledge!
—Thus we have heard from the wise
Who to us have explained It.
Knowledge and non-knowledge—
He who this pair conjointly knows,
With non-knowledge passing over death,
With knowledge wins the immortal.
Into blind darkness enter they
Who worship non-becoming;
Into darkness greater than that, as it were, they
Who delight in becoming.
Other, indeed—they say—than origin!

Other—they say—than non-origin!
—Thus have we heard from the wise
Who to us have explained It.
Becoming and destruction—
He who this pair conjointly knows,
With destruction passing over death,
With becoming wins the immortal.
With a golden vessel
The Real's face is covered o'er.
That do thou, O Pūṣan, uncover
For one whose law is the Real to see.
O Nourisher, the sole Seer, O Controller, O Sun, off-
     spring of Prajāpati, spread forth thy rays!
     Gather thy brilliance! What is thy fairest form—
     that of thee I see. He who is yonder, yonder
     Person—I myself am he!

⚹

This selection, taken from *Īśāvāsyam*, the shortest of the *Upanishads* (its name is simply the first word of the text), is truly remarkable in the boldness of its assertions. You are Self, *Ātman*, the world-soul that is everyone and everything, the source of the world, the ultimate ground of being. Furthermore, your identity with the ultimate and absolute unity that underlies all things is beyond comprehension as ordinarily conceived, and to understand how it is possible that you are the world and that the world is you is impossible unless the mind can transcend its own illusions. This is achieved by identifying the unidentifiable *Ātman* through the method of *Neti, Neti*, (*not this, not this*), thereby demonstrating to yourself the indemonstrable truth that All is One and that you are that One. "It is not understood by those who understand It: It is understood by those who understand It not:"

⚹

The *Kena Upanishad*

By whom impelled soars forth the mind projected?
By whom enjoined goes forth the earliest
     breathing?

From Nicol Macnicol, ed., *Hindu Scriptures* (London: J. M. Dent, 1938).

The Thirteen Principal Upanishads, R. E. Hume, trans. (London: Oxford University Press, 1921).

By whom impelled this speech do people utter?
The eye, the ear—what god, pray, them enjoineth?

That which is the hearing of the ear, the thought
   of the mind,
The voice of speech, as also the breathing of the
   breath,
And the sight of the eye! Past these escaping, the
   wise,
On departing from this world, become immortal.
There the eyes go not;
Speech goes not, nor the mind.
We know not, we understand not
How one would teach It.
Other, indeed, is It than the known,
And moreover above the unknown.
—Thus have we heard of the ancients
Who to us have explained It.

It is conceived of by him by whom It is not con-
   ceived of.
He by whom It is conceived of, knows It not.
It is not understood by those who [say they] under-
   stand It.
It is understood by those who [say they] under-
   stand It not.
When known by an awakening, It is conceived of; . . .

⁂

   The notion that mind cannot know the
mind—that you can neither know nor see your
true self—through the senses, nor by reason, nor
through learning, but that this can only be
achieved directly through deep, intuitive insight,
is again expressed in the *Katha Upanishads*. The
image of the body as being like a chariot driven
by the self is the one we shall see again in the
work of one of the greatest Western philosophers, Plato.

⁂

The wise one . . . is not born, nor dies.
This one has not come from anywhere, has not
   become anyone.

The Thirteen Principal Upanishads, R. E. Hume,
Trans. London: Oxford University Press, 1921.

Unborn, constant, eternal, primeval, this one
Is not slain when the body is slain.
If the slayer think to slay,
If the slain think himself slain,
Both these understand not.
This one slays not, nor is slain.
More minute than the minute, greater than the
   great,
Is the Self that is set in the heart of a creature here.
One who is without the active will beholds Him,
   and becomes freed from sorrow—
When through the grace of the Creator he beholds
   the greatness of the Self.
Him who is the bodiless among bodies,
Stable among the unstable,
The great, all-pervading Self—
On recognizing Him, the wise man sorrows not.
This Self is not to be obtained by instruction,
Nor by intellect, nor by much learning.
He is to be obtained only by the one whom he
   chooses;
To such a one that Self reveals his own person.
Not he who has not ceased from bad conduct,
Not he who is not tranquil, not he who is not
   composed,
Not he who is not of peaceful mind
Can obtain Him by intelligence (*prajñā*).
He for whom the priesthood and the nobility
Both are as food,
And death is as a sauce—
Who really knows where He is? . . .

Know thou the self (*ātman*) as riding in a chariot,
The body as the chariot.
Know thou the intellect (*buddhi*) as the
   chariot-driver,
And the mind as the reins.
The senses, they say, are the horses;
The objects of sense, what they range over.
The self combined with senses and mind
Wise men call "the enjoyer."
He, however, who has not understanding,
Who is unmindful and ever impure,
Reaches not the goal,
But goes on to transmigration [rebirth].
He, however, who has understanding,
Who is mindful and ever pure,
Reaches the goal
From which he is born no more. . . .
Higher than the senses are the objects of sense.

Higher than the objects of sense is the mind;
And higher than the mind is the intellect (*buddhi*).
Higher than the intellect is the Great Self (*Ātman*).
Higher than the Great is the Unmanifest (*avyakta*).
Higher than the Unmanifest is the Person.
Higher than the Person there is nothing at all.
That is the goal. That is the highest course.
Though He is hidden in all things,
That Self shines not forth.
But He is seen by subtle seers
With superior, subtle intellect.
An intelligent man should suppress his speech and
   his mind.
The latter he should suppress in the
   Understanding-Self (*jñāna ātman*).
The understanding he should suppress in the Great
   Self.
That he should suppress in the Tranquil Self. . . .
Arise ye! Awake ye!
Obtain your boons and understand them!
A sharpened edge of a razor, hard to traverse,
A difficult path is this—poets declare!
What is soundless, touchless, formless,
   imperishable,
Likewise tasteless, constant, odorless,
Without beginning, without end, higher than the
   great, stable—
By discerning That, one is liberated from the
   mouth of death. . . .

He who is awake in those that sleep,
The Person who fashions desire after desire—
   That indeed is the Pure. That is *Brahman*.
   That indeed is called the Immortal.
   On it all the worlds do rest;
   And no one soever goes beyond it.
This, verily, is That!
As the one fire has entered the world
And becomes corresponding in form to every form,
So the one Inner Self (*antarātman*) of all things
Is corresponding in form to every form, and yet is
   outside.
As the one wind has entered the world
And becomes corresponding in form to every
   form,
So the one Inner Self of all things
Is corresponding in form to every form, and yet is
   outside.
As the sun, the eye of the whole world,
Is not sullied by the external faults of the eyes,

So the one Inner Self of all things
Is not sullied by the evil in the world, being
   external to it.
The Inner Self of all things, the One Controller,
Who makes his one form manifold—
The wise who perceive Him as standing in
   oneself,
They, and no others, have eternal happiness!

⚹

We shall encounter the ideas expressed in these most ancient texts again in the works of some of the greatest philosophers, separated by great gulfs of space and time, in different cultures. The theme of the One and the Many—that the multiplicity of the appearances is an illusion and resolves into some underlying unity—is a recurring one. The ancient Greeks grappled with it, and we shall see it as one of the great paradigms of Western philosophy and science, which in that respect can be seen to have something in common with both Eastern and Western forms of mysticism. The ancient Vedic notion that what we see as the world external to ourselves is ultimately the creation of the mind is also the cornerstone of one of the most pervasive of all themes in both Western and Eastern philosophy, which has found expression in the many varieties of *idealism*. Even the view that the world-soul is identical to each and every one of us—that we are each a manifestation of the same cosmic mind—will find a number of adherents in different times and places (Bruno, Averroës, Royce).

1.1 Thales (624–546 B.C.E.): The First Greek Philosopher

As the influence of the *Upanishads* spread throughout India, forming the basis of all subsequent philosophy in the East, remarkably similar ideas that became the foundation for all subsequent Western philosophy began to take root in Greece three thousand miles to the west.

Entire epochs in human history have been

named after the raw materials that have subsequently come to be viewed as definitive of the age—stone, iron, atomic. It is therefore entirely appropriate that in the West philosophy was born in what subsequent ages have called the Age of the Seven Wise Men. There have been some variations as to who they were,[3] but Thales makes every list. He lived in the early part of the sixth century B.C.E. (more than 2,600 years ago, several generations before Socrates and Plato), in Miletus, a sprawling seacoast city of white stone and olive groves, with labyrinthine streets of villas overlooking a harbor full of ships. In its heyday Miletus was the leading seaport on the west coast of Ionia in Asia Minor (present-day Turkey). Its cobbled highways stretched north and south and east as far as the eye could see; one could walk, or ride, all the way to the Orient, where the four great eastern sages of antiquity—Gautama Buddha, Confucius, Lao Tzu, and Chaung Tzu—were all alive at the same time. (We shall meet them shortly.) Why philosophy should have blossomed with such synchronicity in these vastly different civilizations remains an unsolved mystery. Some have speculated that it is merely a historical accident. Others have supposed that there must have been open lines of communications between these vastly separated geographic regions, perhaps along some trade routes. A few—such as, most notably, Hegel (see pp. 374–384)—have argued that ideas evolve through historical necessity, that they are themselves the evolution of a cosmic mind of which the world and everything in it is a manifestation.

In riddle, in anecdote, in epigram, with "winged words" the ancient wise men traveled throughout the ancient world, espousing wisdom to anyone who would listen. What they said varied, but there are at least two sayings that we know they had in common:

"Know Thyself" (or, "know your selves")[4]

and

"Nothing in excess," or, "Everything in good measure."

One wonders whether the first imperative, "Know Thyself," prompted the warning comprising the second. Can there be such a thing as too much self-knowledge? One wouldn't think so. But perhaps too much philosophy was too much even for these early wise men. Certainly, philosophy was not all they did. Thales was no exception. He was both a metaphysician concerned with the question of what reality in and of itself consisted and a natural scientist who revolutionized nautical science. His understanding of geometry and the laws of nature were astounding. He showed how to calculate the height of a pyramid by measuring its shadow at the time of day when a man's shadow is equal to his height and even predicted the solar eclipse of May 28, 585 B.C.E. During the Persian war he showed the army how to cross a wide river by building a dam and diverting its flow into two narrower rivers across which bridges could then be built. Indeed, in most of his work one finds the underlying theme of water and navigating beyond the limits of the seen into the dark, steering through the unknown.

Due in part to the achievements of Thales and others like him, Miletus became the most powerful center of commercial activity of the ancient Grecian world. Riches and knowledge poured in from Europe and Egypt and the Orient. Private and public wealth acquired from trade gave the citizens of Miletus an unprecedented amount of leisure. Perhaps for the first time in the history of the world, ordinary people were freed from the pressures of daily needs long enough to turn their hearts and minds to art and science, to speculate about themselves and the world, to discuss, argue, and wonder about everything. Religious, political, social, and scientific beliefs were openly discussed without the primitive bloodshed that was going on at the time on the European continent because business was the rule of the day. Milesian courts drew poets from all over the world; its leaders founded libraries and supported every movement in art and science. Lyric poetry replaced old universal religious and political sentiments, giving way to new forms of personal and individual expression. Satirical poetry arose alongside the lyric, expressing keen and cleverly developed individualism, often critical of the lyrical passions and excitement, even of one's own traditions and culture; it was no less than the birth of self-criticism. There also emerged at this time the so-called Gnomic poetry, wise sayings and reflections on moral, practical, and metaphysical principles. These poetic wisdoms advocated moderation between the passions and the intellect through the establishment of enlightened rules about life, derived not from obedience to and worship of the gods as espoused by religious authorities, but achieved through independent, personal, individual reflection. In thus signaling a move away from the external to the internal world, these works had much in common thematically with the *Upanishads*.

The extraordinary revolution started by Thales, rightly regarded today as the first philosopher on record, has become such an integral part of our thinking that it is almost impossible to fully comprehend its scope. So let us try to see things from the point of view of his contemporaries.

It's the early part of the sixth century B.C.E., more than 2,600 years ago, several generations before the birth of Socrates and Plato. You're an ordinary citizen of Miletus. What is your view of the world? What sorts of things do you believe? How do you live your life?

Like most Milesians, you accept without question the answers you've been given by your religious authorities. You trust them completely the way young children trust their parents. It's not that you merely *believe* what the priests say, it never even occurs to you to *question* their authority. As far as you are concerned, their knowledge comes directly from the gods. One day, a priest who is famous throughout the whole of Asia Minor for his wisdom and great deeds announces that he will reveal the ultimate truth about all things to anyone who dares to listen. Naturally, you go. The square is teeming with the devout and the curious. A robed figure

appears. It is Thales. A silence falls upon the crowd.

"I have come to enlighten you," he says, "about the world, about yourselves, about all things. Gather round. Listen."

You feel a strange excitement. You know this man; everyone knows him as one of the wisest among you. So what does this wise man, Thales, have to say about the world? What is his great truth that will enlighten all of mankind?

"Everything is made of water," he pronounces.

Really try to put yourself in the shoes of our ancient Milesian who has just heard these words for the first time. What is your reaction? What do you think about this statement? What do you feel? *Everything is made of water.* How do you respond? Try projecting yourself via your imagination into the soul of our ancient Milesian standing in the square listening to Thales. If you say to yourself something like, "Well, yes, I can see how that might make sense to someone back then—you live by the sea, water everywhere, everyone must drink water to survive—people back then didn't know any better," then think again. First, notice that when you say something like that to yourself, in the back of your mind—subtly, just beneath the surface of conscious perception—you're quietly, innocently, reassuring yourself that our present state of knowledge is an advance over the past. You're quietly telling yourself that today's understanding of ourselves and the world so outstrips our ancestors that, compared with contemporary wisdom, their ancient views are laughably naive, even absurd. Second, notice that Thales didn't say, "Many things are made of water," "Water is very important for our survival," or anything remotely like that. Presumably, figuring out how best to put it would have been a small feat for someone who could calculate the height of a pyramid by measuring its shadow, figure out *apparently from scratch* how to navigate at night at sea using the stars, and accurately predict solar eclipses. (Can you, thousands of years later, with all your sophisticated education, access to hundreds of thousands of books on all subjects which then did not even exist, do *any* of the sorts of things that Thales did, or anything even remotely like them?)

Let us assume that you, the Milesian standing in the square listening to Thales, know perfectly well what the word *everything* means. It doesn't mean "many things" or even "most things." It means all things that exist. *And you also know perfectly well what water is.* You see water. You swim. You drink. You've just been told that everything—*everything*—is made of the one substance you probably are more familiar with than any other: *water.* Rocks are made of water. Air is made of water. Light is made of water. Fire is made of water. . . .

Suppose you are told by a religious authority that there exists a God who made the first man out of *clay, breathed* life into him, and then took one of the fellow's *ribs* and out of that *rib* made the first *woman.* You either accept this or reject it. In the same way, people 2,600 years ago could simply have accepted or rejected the statement that "Everything is made of water." But notice something. Let's say somebody gives you the "God made Adam from clay and Eve from Adam's rib" story. Let's say it sounds plausible to you. Or maybe it sounds completely crazy. It doesn't much matter how it affects you. Either way, *what can you do about it?* Not much. Oh, you could perhaps go into the question of the reliability of scriptural accounts of miracles, of historical interpretations of Bible stories, and of current scientific theories and how they measure up against religious accounts of the origin of humanity. You could raise questions about human ribs, about magic, about truth and allegory, and so on. It quickly becomes quite complicated. There is no simple way of trying to prove or disprove the Adam and Eve story. But now consider, on the other hand, how very different the case is with the statement "Everything is made of water." Here you can do something right away. Anyone can. And you can do it yourself. You don't have to defer to some other authority. No faith required. No special training.

You can try to find out for yourself whether the statement "Everything is made of water" is true or false simply by *testing it using your own experience and reason.*

I thus conjecture that the first and immediate effect Thales's statement had on his listeners was nothing like what common sense might suppose. Rather, it went something like this. *A great and wise priest, the voice of the gods, has just uttered an obviously false statement.* You, our ordinary Milesian citizen, went home after having heard one simple declarative sentence from Thales, and nothing would ever be the same again. All your life you've accepted the wisdom of the priests. You believe in the God. You also believe that God does not lie. Everything, made of water? You think, suppose you locked Thales in a room and when he got thirsty and asked for water you gave him a cup of pebbles. Would he thank you and drink it? Or would he ask for some *water*? Does Thales wash himself using fire? Hardly. No, something profound has just been made perfectly clear to you. Thales didn't just say something profound and enlightening. *He showed you something.* What, though? Well, in a sense, he sacrificed himself as your authority so that you might begin thinking for yourself. His words could not simply be accepted at face value—except by a fool at his own peril. I know that an obvious way to respond would be to say that Thales spoke only "metaphorically," that he was just trying to communicate in a way that ordinary people would understand. But I think such a response misses the point. The first philosopher is indeed trying to communicate some profound truth to others, but he is also trying to make them profoundly aware that no one has a perfect monopoly on the truth.

In other words, once you—our ancient Milesian—have really thought about what you've just heard one of the most respected priests say, you realize that even if God does exist, you cannot know for certain whether any priest or oracle has direct access to God. Thales said he would enlighten you. What a revolutionary way of enlightening you—not by telling but by *showing.*

I believe that's the first thing to be learned by Thales's statement: a person in authority is showing you that to be wise you cannot simply be a follower of truth; you must yourself become a seeker of truth. Second, not only has Thales evoked in you the desire to prove him wrong, *you, an ordinary person, can do so*. This second point is as revolutionary as the first. Instead of being given a monologue that you are expected to accept obediently, you are given a chance to enter into a dialogue; you are, by your own wits, forced into reacting, thinking, responding, debating, disagreeing. Can you see what a profound shift this is? Usually, even today, when you are in the presence of someone who is deemed very knowledgeable, a great expert in something, or wise, and you want to get the benefit of the knowledge or wisdom, you *listen* and try to *remember*. Suppose a physicist tells you "$F = ma$." That's a very important statement, a formula linking force with mass and acceleration. You learn the formula and you apply it—that's the purpose of the physicist telling it to you in the first place. Or, the doctor tells you that your blood pressure is way too high; you had better remember to do something about it. As a child, you learned what to eat and what not to eat. In most cases, the purpose of making statements about things is to tell you things you need to remember, to record those statements in the back of your mind. Statements made in science, mathematics, geography, and so on, are designed for that purpose. They have something important in common with philosophical statements: they can be checked as to whether they are true. In the case of $F = ma$, for instance, there are a number of experiments you could do with billiard balls, hockey pucks, etc. These experiments would help you to understand Newton's second law, which can be translated from its mathematical expression into an English sentence by saying that for every action there is an equal and opposite reaction. But let's also notice an important difference between the *purpose* of philosophical statements and scientific statements. The purpose of philosophical statements is not merely to give you an answer that you are then

supposed to record and remember (though sometimes that can be the intent), or even to try and verify whether it is true (though, again, that too might be required). The ultimate purpose is to awaken your awareness, to make you wonder, to make you look for yourself, not just for the right answer but in order to see and appreciate the unknowns within and beyond the known. The goal is to see the invisible framework of beliefs and methods within which our questions are asked and our answers given—in a word, to understand through *questioning*. Because it is the art of questioning, philosophy is a dialogue—with ourselves, with the world, with everything.

Scientific and mathematical statements often lead to the same result. Great scientists and mathematicians often engage in philosophy when they begin to question the statements they have been taught to accept as true. Often, such activity leads to new breakthroughs in science and mathematics, to overturning long-standing theories with revolutionary new ones, creating whole new areas of inquiry. In other words, physics and mathematics were not invented by physicists and mathematicians per se, any more than the English language was invented by the British or the German language was invented by the Germans. Rather, as history bears out, physics and mathematics were invented by philosophers. Sometimes, as in the case of Pythagoras, Descartes, Leibniz, and Russell (each of whom you will meet in subsequent chapters), they were philosophers first who came to the other disciplines with specific questions that brought new insights and developments. At other times, they were scientists or mathematicians first who became true philosophers when they began to question their systems of knowledge and frameworks of understanding (what "systems" and "frameworks" are and how they "work" is one major aspect of philosophy that we shall explore throughout this book).

Thales's statement provides two more lessons, so profoundly important that in many ways these overshadow the first two. Look again at the statement: "Everything is made of water." Now that we have explored the first two responses, both of which are mainly negative and predicated on the observation that the statement is obviously false, we might try turning to its positive aspect. That is, let us now assume for the moment that Thales knows what he is doing and so, besides evoking in us the desire to find out for ourselves and to question, there may be some truth in what he says about the world. After all, Thales was by all accounts not just wise but also very clever. For instance, besides the feats already mentioned, he once—apparently, just to make a point—gained control over the entire economy of Miletus. Plato writes in the *Theaetetus* that this happened after a young woman laughed at Thales when he "was looking up to study the stars and tumbled down a well. She scoffed at him for being so eager to know what was happening in the sky that he could not see what lay at his feet." Aristotle, too, tells the story in his *Politics,*

❧

There is . . . the story which is told of Thales of Miletus. It is a story about a scheme for making money, which is fathered on Thales owing to his reputation for wisdom. . . . He was reproached for his poverty, which was supposed to show the use-lessness of philosophy. According to the story, observing from his knowledge of meteorology while it was yet winter that there would be a great harvest of olives in the coming year, he gave deposits for all the olive-presses in Miletus and Chios, which he hired at a low price because no one bid against him. When the harvest time came, and there was a sudden and simultaneous demand for the olive presses, he let out the stock he had collected at any rate he chose to fix; and making a considerable fortune, he succeeded in proving that it is easy for philosophers to become rich if they like, but that their ambition lies elsewhere.

❧

Aristotle goes on to identify Thales as the originator of the idea that some underlying *material* substance forms the basis of the existence of all things.

❧

Aristotle on Thales

Now, most of the earliest philosophers regarded principles of a *material* kind as the only principles of all things. That of which all things consist, from which they are originally generated, and into which they are finally dissolved, is substance persisting though its attributes change; this, they affirm, is an element and first principle of Being. Hence, too, they hold that nothing is ever generated or annihilated, since this primary entity always persists. Similarly, we do not say of Socrates that he comes into being, in an absolute sense, when he becomes handsome or cultivated, nor that he is annihilated when he loses these qualifications, because their *substrate,* viz., Socrates himself, persists. In the same way, they held, nothing else absolutely comes into being or perishes. For there must be one or more entities which persist, and out of which all other things are generated. They do not, however, all agree as to the number and character of these prin-ciples. Thales, the founder of this type of philoso-phy, says it is *water.* Hence, he also put forward the view that the earth floats on the water. Perhaps he was led to this conviction by observing that the nutriment of all things is moist, and that even heat is generated from moisture, and lives upon it. (Now, that from which anything is generated is in every case a first principle of it.) He based his conviction, then, on this, and on the fact that the germs of all things are of a moist nature, while water is the first principle of the nature of moist things. There are also some who think that even the men of remote antiquity who first speculated about the gods, long before our own era, held this same view about the primary entity. For they represented Oceanus and Tethys as the progenitors of creation, and the oath of the gods as being by water, or, as they [the poets] call it, Styx. Now, the most ancient of things is most venerable, while the most venerable thing is taken to swear by. Whether this opinion about the pri-mary entity is really so original and ancient is very possibly uncertain; in any case, Thales is said to have put forward this doctrine about the first cause.

From A. E. Taylor. *Aristotle on His Predecessors* (La Salle, IL: Open Court, 1962, first printed in 1907), pp. 80–82.

⊥

Thinking along those lines, it quite naturally occurs to us that, in whatever sense the statement is true, *it certainly does not seem to be the case that everything is made of water.* In other words, playing along with Thales for the moment, it seems that his third lesson is that *appearances are deceiving.* But more than that. In what way are they deceiving?

Well, looking around, you see many different sorts of things: tables, chairs, rocks, stars, people, air, fire, and so on. The ancient philosophers whom you will meet in the upcoming pages will often talk about this aspect of the world by referring, simply and directly, to *the many.* In speaking of "the many," they are referring to all the multiplicity you see around you. They also will speak of *the appearances.* In speaking of "the appearances," they are referring to the way things appear to you when you are looking at them. For instance, standing on railroad tracks, appearances tell you that the tracks converge in the distance, which you know by walking along the tracks is false. Appearances tell you that things that are closer are bigger than things that are farther, which is not always true. They tell you that grass is green and that the sky is blue; whether either of these statements is true is a matter we shall take up later when we look at the philosophy of Locke, Berkeley, and Hume. The point for now is that what Thales is saying is that appearances are deceiving and the *least obvious and most deceptive way in which the appearances are deceiving is that they do not appear to be appearances!* They appear to be *things.* But things don't shrink and grow as you move closer and farther from them! Only the appearances do. (Of course, as always in philosophy, language is especially tricky here in that the word *appearance* is ambiguous; for there is the sense in which my hand [that is, the image of my hand] appears to get smaller as I move it farther from my eyes and there is the sense in which my hand does *not* "appear" to change in size at all: that is, only by paying special attention do I notice relative size differences. Under ordi-

nary circumstances there is what is called "object constancy," the mind's ability to interpret varying image relations in such a way as to make the visual appearances appear more constant than as given by their actual visual geometries.) So there is an important sense in which what you're looking at when you look at "things" can't be the *things themselves* as they exist "out there" in the world independently of the mind but, rather, only the way the things appear to the mind. Most things don't appear to be water. Thales is saying that the way things appear is not the way they are.

Thales's fourth lesson is that an aspect of the appearances that he is drawing to your attention is that they appear as a *many.* In saying that everything is made of water, he is implying that what may appear to be many different things may really be just different aspects of one and the same thing. So, why water? Water has no shape, no "form" of its own. Pour it in a round container, the water takes on a round form. Pour it in a square container, it takes on a square form. And so on. So the idea Thales is trying to communicate is that behind the appearances, which present themselves to us as many, there is an underlying unity. Ultimately, all things are made of one single substance. That one underlying substance he identifies as "water."

Thales is not merely trying to play guessing games with us or to engage in clever tricks. I don't believe Thales knew what the one underlying substance beneath all things is. I don't know whether anybody does, or even if that idea is true. What I do know is that for the next twenty-five centuries, the whole history and development of philosophy and science has altered Thales's statement by only one word! That history goes something like this:

Everything is made of water.
Everything is made of air.
Everything is made of the infinite boundless.
Everything is made of fire.
Everything is made of numbers.
Everything is made of atoms.
Everything is made of quarks.

That last statement, made by physicists in the latter part of the twentieth century, is a powerful testimony of the great things that can happen when a philosopher gets it right and knows he's wrong. Indeed, that's not such a bad initial formulation of a first principle for would-be lovers of wisdom.

Get it right and know you're wrong. That is *my* "paradoxical" definition of wisdom.

Oh, and by the way—I almost forgot—Thales also said, "Everything is full of gods." Now, what do you suppose he could have meant by *that*? And why didn't I make that the focal point of this section?

1.2 Anaximander (d. 546 B.C.E.): The Infinite Boundless

The first and most notable response on record to Thales came from one of his young students, Anaximander of Miletus. We don't know when he was born, but he died around 546 B.C.E. Most of our historical information about him comes from Theophrastus (370–287 B.C.E.), a student of Aristotle (see Chapter 3) who produced voluminous writings of which only a few fragments remain. In them, he quotes directly from Anaximander's otherwise lost book:

The Infinite

Anaximander of Miletos, son of Praxiades, a fellow-citizen and associate of Thales, said that the material cause and first element of things was the Infinite, he being the first to introduce this name of the material cause. He says it is neither water nor any other of the so-called elements, but a substance different from them which is infinite, from which arise all the heavens and the worlds within them.

He says that this is "eternal and ageless," and that it "encompasses all the worlds."

And into that from which things take their rise they pass away once more, "as is meet: for they make reparation and satisfaction to one another for their injustice according to the ordering of time," as he says in these somewhat poetical terms.

And besides this, there was an external motion, in which was brought about the origin of the worlds.

He did not ascribe the origin of things to any alteration in matter, but said that the oppositions in the substratum, which was a boundless body, were separated out.

Anaximander thus agreed with Thales that all individual things derive their existence from one eternal, indestructible universal something into which they ultimately return when they cease to exist as individual things. But, he disagreed about what that ultimate source of existence is. How and why the Milesians came to think that everything in the world reduced to some single, underlying substance is as mysterious as the question of where any ideas—right or wrong, true or false, important or unimportant—come from. And that question is one we shall explore in more detail again later (in the seventeenth century, for instance, John Locke will ask this question; see Chapter 13). But we can to a certain degree trace the reasoning by which he moved away from Thales's conception of water as the ultimate substance to the infinite boundless, through Anaximander's argument, preserved by Aristotle in his *Physics*:

Further, there cannot be a single, simple body which is infinite, either, as some hold, one distinct from the elements, which they then derive from it, or without this qualification. For there are some who make this (*i.e.* a body distinct from the elements) the infinite, and not air or water, in order that the other things may not be destroyed by their infinity. *They are in opposition one to another*—air is cold, water moist, and fire hot—and therefore, *if any one of them*

From John Burnet, *Early Greek Philosophy*, 2d. ed. (London: A & C Black, Ltd., 1902; New York: Barnes & Noble, Inc.). Footnotes omitted.

*were infinite, the rest would have ceased to be
by this time.* Accordingly they say that what is
infinite is something other than the elements,
and from it the elements arise.

⁂

Thus, in a way that would become a pivotal
bone of contention among philosophers up to
the present day, Anaximander disagreed with
Thales regarding the degree to which truth can
be expressed using the terms of ordinary language. Language, after all, evolved as a way of
making noises consistently to refer to various
things among our perceptions. The sounds,
"water," "fire," "air," and so on, are noises we
make consistently to stand for something we
wish to refer to in our experience. Our experience consists of appearances. If the appearances are deceiving, if there is an underlying
reality beyond appearances that is radically different from things as they appear to us through
our senses, then to what degree can we use language—which evolved to describe the appearances—to get at what is beyond mere appearance? That is what Anaximander wondered.

Anaximander concluded that philosophy
must create new terms to stand for new concepts, ones that are not simply an attempt to
refer to immediate appearances. He took what
he thought to be the essential aspects of water,
which Thales had used in purely allegorical ways,
and abstracted from them their underlying concept. In a way, Anaximander tried to capture the
abstract "form" of water and he came up with
the concept of what he called the "infinite
boundless." That is the key aspect of the type of
thing that water is that makes it such a good
metaphor for the underlying substance, the
"stuff of reality." Whereas individual things have
a specific, finite shape, water has none; whereas
individual things have an intrinsic, built-in
boundary, water has none. The basic idea, then,
is that the world is an undifferentiated, infinite
substance, a sort of cosmic, frothing ocean in
which the various parts separate out due to the
various motions.

1.3 Anaximenes (585–528 B.C.E.): A Question of Language

Anaximander's young student Anaximenes
(585–528 B.C.E.) found the notion of an "infinite
boundless" unintelligible. He argued that Thales
had originally been on the right track.
Philosophers, according to him, ought to stick to
known terms as they arise in common language
and not invent new ones as abstractions. In other
words, he thought that moving away from ordinary language into abstract terms should be
avoided because such terms are *meaningless*. Only
words as they arise in reference to specific things
in our experience were legitimate. Furthermore,
he used his simple, ordinary terms in an unpre-
tentious, lean writing style very different from
the lyrical, poetical prose of Anaximander. His
book, which has since been lost, was celebrated
for the lucidity of its prose. Theophrastus devoted a long passage to the work, which gives us
a glimpse into Anaximenes' ideas.

⁂

The Breath of the World

Anaximenes of Miletos, son of Eurystratos, who
had been an associate of Anaximander, said, like
him, that the underlying substance was one and
infinite. He did not, however, say it was indeterminate, like Anaximander, but determinate; for he
said it was Air.

From it, he said, the things that are, and have
been, and shall be, the gods and things divine, took
their rise, while other things come from its offspring.

"Just as," he said, "our soul, being air, holds us
together, so do breath and air encompass the
whole world."

And the form of the air is as follows. Where it is
most even, it is invisible to our sight; but cold and
heat, moisture and motion, make it visible. It is
always in motion; for, if it were not, it would not
change so much as it does.

From John Burnet, *Early Greek Philosophy*, 2d. ed.
(London: A & C Black, Ltd., 1902; New York:
Barnes & Noble, Inc.). Footnotes omitted.

It differs in different substances in virtue of its rarefaction and condensation.

When it is dilated so as to be rarer, it becomes fire; while winds, on the other hand, are condensed Air. Cloud is formed from Air by felting; and this, still further condensed, becomes water. Water, condensed still more, turns to earth; and when condensed as much as it can be, to stones.

⁂

Anaximenes chose to refer to the primary, infinite substance underlying all things as "air." He thought this was a great improvement over both of his predecessors, with the best aspects of both. Air, like water, has properties that also evoke even more strongly the abstract idea of a substance that is an "infinite boundless" because air is invisible. You cannot *see* air, you can only see its effects. Yet "air" is a perfectly ordinary term, familiar to all. Whereas Anaximander used the concept of motion to explain differentiation within the single primary substance underlying all things, Anaximenes used ideas like "rarefaction" and "condensation," explaining, for instance, that "air that is condensed forms winds . . . if this process goes further, it gives water, still further earth, and the greatest condensation of all is found in stones."

So here at the very beginnings of philosophy we see immediately the emergence of *methods of inquiry* that have remained central themes to the present day not just in philosophy but also in science and mathematics. The idea that all the things in the world reduce to some one underlying substance (whatever it may be, whether physical, metaphysical, or mental ["spiritual"]) is a form of *reductionism*. (In philosophy this term has several different usages and quite different meanings. On the one hand there is "theoretical reduction," as, for instance, in Carnap's "reduction sentences," and there is "phenomenological reduction," as for instance in Husserl's phenomenology (see Section 21.1).) The question of what sort of language to use to describe truth—whether it is legitimate to create new terms and concepts or whether one must stick to the familiar terms of ordinary language, and what constitutes *meaningful* vs.

meaningless expressions and theories—has been debated, as we shall see, up to the present day.

1.4 Confucius (557–479 B.C.E.): The Moral Way

As Thales and his students began the revolution in thinking that heralded the coming Golden Age of Greece, as Indian sages sat with their students in the forests of India to engage with the *Upanishads*, in China—separated from these two ancient cultures by the Himalayan mountains—there appeared a young sage named Confucius. According to some accounts he was born to a poor family in the state of Lu, present-day Shangtung. If you look at a map you will see that it is about as far away as you can get from Greece and India and still be in Asia. It is a province on the eastern seacoast of the East China Sea, where Japan lies about 500 miles away to the northeast. Other accounts make him the son of nobility. In either case, it is fairly agreed upon that Confucius's father died shortly after he was born and that he experienced great hardships growing up at a time when China itself was in a great state of inner turmoil. As a young man he supported himself by working in a granary, then as a herder—first of cattle, then of sheep. How he became Grand Secretary of Justice and then Chief Minister in his native state is unknown. But as a young man he had already achieved his reputation as a person of such great wisdom that throughout China princes, lords, and scholars consulted him and craved to hear him speak. He became the first teacher in Chinese history to offer education to anyone who cared to listen, whether they paid tuition or not. Yet, unlike most Chinese sages who had the ears of the political and social leaders at that time, Confucius did not say the things that people—the leaders especially—wanted to hear. As one recent commentator put it, "Everyone wanted to hear him but no one wanted to listen."

In that respect Confucius had much in common with a gadfly we have already met—Socrates. What was it that Confucius taught that people so wanted to hear, even though they did not like what they heard? "He who learns, but does not think, is lost," he says in his *Analects;* "He who thinks but does not learn, is in grave danger." He was banished from Ch'I; in Sung he was threatened with execution. They drove him out of Sung and Wei. In Ch'en and Ts'ai he was arrested. They invited him, then they booed him. When the Sung head of state, Huan Tuei, threatened to have him killed if he did not recant what he said, here is what Confucius had to say about it:

> Heaven has endowed me with a moral destiny. What can Huan Tuei do to me?

So, what did Confucius say? Let us peek into his *Analects.* Like Socrates and like Christ, Confucius did not write down his philosophy. The *Analects* contains a series of sayings written between 475 and 220 B.C.E. by unknown authors, probably his students, who compiled it mainly for the purpose of instructing others. Confucius appears in these dialogs as a teacher of virtue who tries to impart a new and different dimension to the moral, social, and political values raised by some other teacher or sage. Here are some of my favorite of his sayings:

⚹

At fifteen, I set my heart on learning. At thirty, I had already a good grasp of the rites and morals. At forty, I could form my own judgments of things. At fifty, I began to know the objective laws of nature. At sixty, I could know a man from his words and make a clear distinction between right and wrong. At seventy, I could follow my inclinations without any of my words or deeds ever running counter to the rules.

Do bear in mind, You, what I am now teaching you: when you know a thing, say that you know it; when you do not know a thing, admit you do not know it. That is wisdom.

When you have met a virtuous person, try to fol-

Book XV. All excerpts are from *The Analects of Confucius,* Lao An, trans., Jinan, China: Shandong Friendship Press, 1992. With minor emendations by the author.

low that person as an example; when you have met an immoral person, try to examine yourself inwardly.

The superior person is even-tempered and good-humored but never self-important. The inferior person is self-important but never even-tempered and good-humored.

Do not do to others what you would not want others to do to you.

Those who are capable of sweet words and fine appearances are rarely people of true virtue.

The superior person may not be observed and tested in small matters, but can be entrusted with great concerns. The inferior person cannot be entrusted with great concerns, but can be observed and tested in small matters.

⚹

Consider the simple, clear insights here. Some of them you have heard before, such as the golden rule—which he espoused many centuries before its reappearance in Judaism and Christianity. What is truly remarkable about these sayings is not only how they still ring true today, but also that they *still*—after three thousand years—have the power to wake us up, to make us question what we might have come to take for granted.

What, after all, is Confucius telling us here? He is saying to watch out, to be careful, to not be unduly guided by appearances. You can test for certain sorts of things and not others. What is truly great cannot be put to the test. Those among us who are the most fastidious and puritanical in their behavior may not be the most moral. Those who make a big show of how moral they are may be doing it for the sake of what other people think. If you are truly a virtuous person, what do you care what other people think of you? Are you so insecure in your knowledge of your self that your image in the mind of another can disturb you?

> I do not worry about people not knowing me; I am worrying that I myself do not know others.

1.5 Lao Tzu (6th Century B.C.E): The Way of Tao

Part of what we are trying to do in this book is to see the greatness of the great lovers of wisdom. One of the greatest and most important lessons that we must learn, if we ourselves are to succeed in understanding wisdom and becoming wise, is that wisdom is not some one-dimensional set of "great truths" or principles to which we must ourselves be true. On the contrary. A mind that requires that kind of simplicity can never appreciate the beauty and power of the sort of complex understanding wisdom requires. It is the ability to see things from more than one point of view that is the hallmark of wisdom. Wisdom requires a big mind in which there is room enough for many points of view. It requires a multiperspectival vision. We shall see this time and again, and here is a perfect example.

In the time of Confucius there lived a man who in many respects was just his opposite, an antithesis to just about everything that Confucius taught. Yet he too was wise. To feel the contradiction between these two great sages, consider the following famous story about a meeting between Confucius and Lao Tzu that supposedly took place in Chu (present-day Honan), a province in the south of China. Lao Tzu was a little-known teacher-priest. He had gotten in trouble with the authorities for teaching the Yin people, who lived under the suppressive authority of the ruling people of Chou, the method of "inaction" as a way of becoming free. Lao Tzu happened to be the custodian of old documents that Confucius, who was working hard at the time trying to promote the disintegrating culture of the Chou people, went to consult about certain rituals.

Lao Tzu was an old man at the time. Confucius was twenty or thirty years younger. *Lao Tzu* means "the old guy." Nobody knew his real name and he simply went by that. Supposedly, the topic of morality came up. Confucius was someone who, as you can quickly gather from the passages from his *Analects*, talked a great deal about how to become a superior human being. He taught us how to attain moral excellence and virtue through cultivating correct principles of action to which one must always be true, to follow rules from which one must never veer. In that respect he had much in common with the great eighteenth-century German philosopher Immanuel Kant (Chapter 16). Lao Tzu, on the other hand, taught just the opposite: "If you are immoral," he supposedly said to Confucius, "only then the question of morality arises. And if you don't have any character, only then you think about character. A man of character is absolutely oblivious of the fact that anything like character exists. A man of morality does not know what the word 'moral' means. So don't be foolish! And don't try to cultivate. Just be natural."

Lao Tzu and Confucius did not like each other. Indeed, by some accounts they had a great argument and ended up hating each other. Lao Tzu saw Confucius as a pompous, self-righteous disciplinarian; Confucius saw Lao Tzu as a dangerous, undisciplined radical. Often, as we shall see, some of the greatest lovers of wisdom in history had some of the greatest disagreements! But that should not prevent us from trying to understand their wisdom. Indeed, we should draw a great lesson from it.

Let us take a look at some of Lao Tzu's actual writing. He wrote only one book, a short compilation of verses, called the *Tao Te Ching*. It has been translated into nearly every language and has become one of the most influential literary-philosophical works in the world.

✦

1.

Tao that can be described is not the universal and
    eternal Tao;
Name that can be named is not the universal and
    eternal name.
The beginning of Heaven and Earth is nameless;

From *On Lao Tzu*, by David Hong Cheng (Belmont, CA: Wadsworth, 2000).

The mother of everything is naming.
Thus:
    Be always objective, one may discover the
        wonders;
    Be always subjective, one only sees the
        manifestations.
    Both emerge from the same source, but with
        different names.
    Both are mysterious.
    The mystery hidden inside of mysteries
    Is the door to all wonders.

2.

When the world knows what beauty is, then there
    is ugliness;
When the world knows what good is, then there is
    evil.
Thus:
    Being and Non-being produce each other,
    Difficult and easy complement each other,
    Long and short calibrate each other,
    High and low contrast each other,
    Music and noise harmonize each other, and
    Front and back accompany each other.
Therefore the sage chooses to:
    Manage affairs by taking no action;
    Teach without words;
    Allow all things to develop, but not to start;
    Produce, but not to possess;
    Care for, but not to master;
    Complete work, but not to claim credit,
    By not claiming credit, his credit will not be
        lost. . . .

4.

Tao is empty, yet forever inexhaustible.
It is so far-reaching, the source of everything.
Blunting sharpnesses, resolving conflicts, softening
    lights.
It thus harmonizes the dusty world.
So deep and profound,
It has forever existed.
I do not know whose child it is,
It has existed before the notion of god. . . .

8.

The ultimate good is like water.
Water benefits all things without competing with
    them.

It stays at places where all people disdain,
Therefore it is close to Tao.

A habitat is good because of its location;
A mind is good because of its profundity;
A friend is good because of his kindness;
A statement is good because of its credibility;
A government is good because of its excellent
    management;
A worker is good because of his productivity; and
A move is good because of its timeliness.

Only by being not contentious,
Will there be no ill will.

9.

Holding a cup to fill it to brim,
It is better to stop in time.
Making a sword extremely sharp,
It is hard to keep its sharpness for long.
Filling up a hall with gold and jade;
It cannot be securely guarded.
He who becomes arrogant with wealth and
    power,
Sows the seeds of his own misfortune.
Retire once the work is successfully
    completed.
This is the way of heaven.

10.

Command your body and soul to embrace the One,
Can there be no separation?
Concentrate your vital energy to achieve complete
    softness,
Can you be like an infant?
Cleanse your thoughts and purify your insight,
Can you be flawless?

In loving your people and governing your
    state,
Can you be without preconception?
In opening and closing the gate of Heaven,
Can you behave like a female?
In comprehending and penetrating the truth,
Can you be mindful of taking no action against
    Tao?

In producing and in nurturing lives, you are:
    To produce, but not to possess;
    To care for, but not to control;
    To lead, but not to subjugate.
This is known as the profound virtue.

Here we see again some of the perennial ideas of ancient wisdom, except central is the mystical, ineffable, inexpressible notion of the *Tao*. What is it? It is like water—Thales would agree!—it is the One, it is the great ineffable source of everything to which the *Upanishads* in their own way elude, which philosophers will try to express in numerous ways up to the present day, which theologians would call God. The religion of Taoism is based on it.

Lao Tzu openly rejects the Confucian teachings based on rules and discipline. His book is a great mystical ode against books and against teaching, in fact, much in the way that we will encounter again in the case of Socrates and Plato. The *tao*—the ultimate "way" everything is—cannot be understood through lecture or dialog but must be experienced directly. The word itself is ambiguous in meaning and there is no good translation of it. The Chinese symbol, which is supposed to be based on an impressionistic depiction of a moving head, looks like this:

Tao has been translated, variously, as "the way," "truth," and even "reason," but *the way* is closest to the Chinese, where it can be used, variously, to say "he has his own *way* of doing things," "that's *the way* I judge it," and so on. The idea is that there is some way that things go in the world that parallels the way we ourselves are, think, or act; in that respect, the *tao* has something in common with the Greek concept of *logos*, which we shall study later in the chapter.

According to Lao Tzu, knowledge of *tao* cannot be achieved by any sort of ritual but can be attained only through a sort of mystical revelation, through meditation. The truth is ineffable, it cannot be expressed in words, it can only be

experienced. This perennial theme was the source of another philosophical and religious revolution taking place at this time on the other side of the Himalayas, in India, where a young sage had begun to attract numerous followers. His name was Gotama Buddha.

1.6 Gotama Buddha (563–483): The Way of Enlightenment

In his definitive work on the Buddha, contemporary American philosopher Bart Gruzalski provides the following introduction that is as brief as it is lucid:

The name "Buddha" refers to a person who has awakened from the delusions of ordinary life and has discovered the nature of reality. The particular Buddha whose ideas we are to explore was born into the Sakya clan and was named Siddhattha Gotama. Gotama (Sanskrit is Gautama) came to see that life, for all its promise and hope, ended with dying and inevitably contained irritation, disappointment, and loss. Rather than being overwhelmed and depressed by the suffering in life, Gotama set out to discover a solution to it. This book is a reflective summary of his discovery.

The historical person whom we call the Buddha was a prince who was no more divine than any other human being. He was born in North India in the 6th century BC. According to legend, an oracle told his parents that their child would be either a great king or a great spiritual leader. His father, wanting him to be a great king, asked what might cause his son to turn from being a great king into becoming a spiritual leader. The oracle told him that if his son saw the four signs that often cause people to be reflective about the human condition (old age, disease, death, and a wandering ascetic) he would retire from the

From Bart Gruzalski; *On the Buddha* (Belmont, CA: Wadsworth, 2000).

worldly life. The king surrounded his son Gotama with luxury and gave orders that his son should not come in contact with any of the four signs. Despite his father's best attempts to keep his son distracted by luxury, Gotama conspired with his charioteer to explore beyond the palace walls and, in the course of these excursions, came upon a very elderly person, an extremely ill person, and a corpse. He came to realize that sickness, old age, and death were an inevitable part of human life. After he saw wandering ascetics who had retired from the worldly life to seek liberation, he determined that he would do the same. Seeking to discover a solution to the problem of suffering, Gotama left the comforts of the princely life, leaving his wife and his son in the care of his parents.

Gotama began practicing meditation under meditation master Alara Kalama. Having reached the highest attainment that Alara Kalama himself had reached, Gotama left when he found that this attainment did not lead to peace, to direct realization, or to Nibbana (M: 26, 15). He next practiced with Uddaka Ramaputta and reached an even higher meditative state but left for the same reason (M: 26, 17). Going off on his own, he practiced the severest of yogic austerities for six years. During this period five ascetics joined him.

At the end of this six-year period Gotama almost died because of the severity of his practice. He came to the conclusion that an excessively emaciated body was not a means to enlightenment. He ate a meal of boiled rice and bread. When the five ascetics saw him eating rice and bread, they left in disgust thinking "Gotama now lives luxuriously; he has given up his striving and reverted to luxury" (M: 36, 33).

Gotama again went off on his own. He was thirty-five years old. He determined he would sit under a tree on the bank of the river Neranjara at the place now called Buddh Gaya until he had seen through delusion and solved the problem of suffering. During a night of intense and deep meditation he "woke up" and understood the nature of reality. The problem of suffering was solved. He was an awakened one, a "Buddha."

At first he believed he could not successfully convey his realization to others. The Buddha saw anything he taught would go against the worldly stream because most people live pursuing what is pleasurable and avoiding what they take to be unpleasant (M: 26, 19). Part of the problem, too, was that the Buddha's deepest insights were inca-

pable in principle of being fully conveyed in words. Nonetheless, the Buddha realized that there were beings with "little dust in their eyes" whom he might try to teach. His first two choices were the meditation masters with whom he had practiced, Alara Kalama and Uddaka Ramaputta. Unfortunately, both had died. He chose, therefore, to try to convey what he could to the five ascetics who had left him when he ate the bread and boiled rice.

The Buddha walked to Benares, to the Deer Park at Isipatana, and approached the group of five. Although they were still uncertain about him because he had succumbed to the luxury of ordinary food, they greeted him warmly. He told them that he was enlightened. They did not believe it. After all, from their perspective he was living a life of luxury. Gotama told them he was not living luxuriously—was he not living the homeless life? They were still unbelieving, since his practice was not the strenuous asceticism to which they were accustomed. Finally he said to them, "Have you ever known me to speak like this before?" They agreed that they had not and so he began teaching them. What he taught that day in Deer Park at Benares has become the foundation of one of the oldest philosophical and religious traditions on earth.

The basic teachings of the Buddha point only to what can be experienced. The Buddha did not encourage beliefs in transcendental or metaphysical dogmas. He rejected all speculative reasoning and theorizing. He articulated no belief in a personal creator deity. The beginning and end of his teachings point to what each human being can experience. Throughout his life the Buddha emphasized direct realization by the individual. Even as he was dying, at the age of eighty years old, his last words to his disciples were that they should strive on tirelessly. . . .

✦

I have already pointed out the similarity between Socrates and Jesus. There are equally striking parallels between Jesus and the Buddha. Jesus was a Jew, probably a rabbi, raised on the so-called "Old Testament," to which his teachings were such a strong and powerful reaction that they became the source for a completely new religion—Christianity. Gotama Buddha was raised as a Hindu and he so completely overturned the Vedanta philosophy of the *Upanishads* that he became the founder of a new religion: Buddhism. Ironically, what Christ gave to the old Judaic philosophy was what Buddha took away from the old Hindu philosophy: the soul. For central to Buddha's teachings is the doctrine of *anatta*, which means, literally, "no soul" or "not self."

The view itself is one that will be echoed in the West by the great modern philosopher David Hume (see Chapter 15), who also argued persuasively and on the basis of direct experience that the Self we *think* we have (or are) is but an *illusion*. We are not who and what we think we are; in fact, in one sense we do not even exist. There is no continuous self in experience, no metaphysical soul to provide permanence; the mind is but an ever-changing flux of experience that belongs, ultimately, to no one. Not only do you not have an immortal soul that will survive your bodily death, you do not even have a permanent self that will survive the night. That is what David Hume will try to teach us. And it is what Buddha taught.

Here again we see a stark difference between the Hindu wisdom of the *Upanishads* and the *Vedas*, on the one hand, and the Buddhist wisdom that seems on the surface of it to deny what the other affirms. According to one philosophy, not only do you have a permanent self, you have a permanent self that is an immortal, metaphysical soul that is one with the Godhead: the world-soul. According to the other, the very notion that there is any kind of permanence to you is an illusion that must be dispelled if there is to be enlightenment and liberation from suffering. (We shall see similar sorts of deep disagreements between Hume and, for instance, Immanuel Kant.) So who is correct? What is the truth?

If what you are looking for is answers, you will be frustrated because the right answer depends on whom you ask. If what you seek is wisdom, then you must try to understand *why* a Buddha or Hume thinks and believes as he does, *why* a Kant disagrees so strongly with them, what the basis is for the *Upanishads*, or for the New Testament, or for any great book of wisdom. You can do this in a number of ways.

You might try to identify the (often unstated, or hidden) *presuppositions* of a particular view. This means asking yourself what truths are being taken for granted. Buddha, for instance, puts great stock in experience. He believes experience can reveal the truth, that thinking, theorizing, and intellectual pursuits in general are the cause of great illusion and much suffering. The sages who wrote and taught the *Upanishads*, on the other hand, consider experience itself to be the major source of illusion. Like the great philosopher Plato, whom we shall meet in the next chapter, they believe that one must look beyond the appearances, through the light of reason or intuition or mystical insight. So, which approach is right?

Wrong question—for now. The right question is the one that brings to light the *philosophical* insight that there are two very different ways of looking at things—two different points of view, two perspectives—that can give rise to very different systems of thought. One is what philosophers have dubbed *empiricism*, the other *rationalism*. The *philosophical* debate about which, if either, method is better is itself a philosophical question that we shall see debated time and again by leading philosophers. And our task in this book is not to become Buddhists or Hindus or Christians; empiricists or rationalists or Kantians; utilitarians, deontologists, or phenomenologists—the list is endless—which is not to say that there is anything wrong with adopting any of these sorts of perspectives on ourselves and the world. On the contrary. Part of the goal of this book is to help you form your own views, not through indoctrination into a particular system of thought but by becoming wise about such things so that you can better choose, create, explore, and embark on intellectual, emotional, spiritual adventures. Here, in fact, is a marked difference between philosophy and religion (we've already noted some of the similarities). It is a difference that *itself* can be applied to what goes on within the auspices of "philosophy" or "religion." Once you "become" a Christian—or a Buddhist or a Humean or a Kantian, for that matter—you may no longer be a philosopher (assuming, of course, that you ever were one). But not necessarily. It all depends. Can you still see, understand, and know the presuppositions behind what you so ardently believe? Can you still see and explain the presuppositions and limitations of the view through which you see yourself and the world? Does discussing and exploring up to the edge of the known and beyond invigorate and excite you? Do you love questioning and being questioned? If so, then regardless of whether you regard yourself as religious, or a particular sort of philosopher, you are a true lover of wisdom.

There is another very important point to be made. In most cases the lovers of wisdom discussed in this book are great in part because when you approach their work carefully, seriously, without attachment to the need for simple answers, in most cases you will find that the views themselves cannot be put into a simple mold. In other words, the very sort of disagreements we have been discussing—the polarities of thought expressed by the various philosophers and philosophical systems—are very difficult to put into straightforward yes or no, simple, black and white terms. This is most clearly seen when one tries to explain what exactly a Hume, a Kant, or a Buddha—or Jesus, for that matter—really meant by what he said. When one studies their writings carefully, as scholars do, often one is led to a variety of extremely different interpretations. Take, for example, the case of the great sage in whose shadow we still are in this section—Buddha. Take, in particular, the cornerstone of Buddhist philosophy, the *anatta* doctrine. Here, for instance, is a dialogue between Vacchagotta, a student-wonderer, and Buddha:

❖

"Now, master Gotama, is there a self?"
At these words the Exalted One was silent.

_____

From *Sanyutta-nikaya*, trans. A. F. Rhys Davis and F. L. Woodward.

"How, then, master Gotama, is there not a Self?"
For a second time also the Exalted One was silent.
Then Vacchagotta the Wanderer rose from his seat and went away.
Now not long after the departure of the Wanderer, the venerable
Ananda said to the Exalted One:
"How is it, lord, that the Exalted One gave no answer... ?"
"If, Ananda, when asked by the Wanderer: 'Is there a self?' I had replied to him: 'There is a self,' then, Ananda, that would be siding with the recluses and brahmins who are eternalists. But if, Ananda, when asked: 'Is there not a self?' I had replied that it does not exist, that, Ananda, would be siding with those recluses and brahmins who are annihilationists. Again, Ananda, when asked by the Wanderer: 'Is there a self?' had I replied that there is, would my reply be in accordance with the knowledge that all things are notself?"
"Surely not, lord."
"Again, Ananda, when asked by Vacchagotta the Wanderer: 'Is there not a self?' had I replied that there is not, it would have been more bewilderment for the bewildered Vacchagotta. For he would have said: 'Formerly indeed I had a self, but now I have not one anymore'" (S: XLIV, X, 10).

❖

Different interpretations of what Buddha meant have led to different forms of Buddhism. There are even disagreements within each of the interpretations as to whether, for instance, Buddha really denied the existence of the Self and as to his true purpose. In some cases, some philosophers have even lamented that *they themselves* are not quite clear about what they actually mean to say—such as, most notably, David Hume on this very topic of the Self! (Hume, as we shall see, realizes that what he says is not quite consistent and yet, at the same time, that he can see no way out of the labyrinth.) In the case of Buddha, however, it seems fairly clear that—in marked distinction with Hume's stated purposes—the purpose in going through the thinking, experiencing, and questioning process is not to reach some "metaphysical truth." The goal, rather, is to be liberated from the suffering caused by the confusion of muddled thinking.

⋆

The Four Noble Truths

Now this, monks, is the noble truth of suffering: Birth is suffering, aging is suffering, death is suffering; sorrow, lamentation, pain, dejection, and despair are suffering; association with the disliked is suffering, separation from the loved is suffering, not to obtain what we desire is suffering. In short, the five aggregates affected by clinging are suffering.

And this, monks, is the noble truth of the origination of suffering: the craving which causes the renewal of becoming, is accompanied by sensual delight and seeks satisfaction now here, now there: that is to say, the craving for sensual pleasure, the craving for becoming, the craving for non-becoming.

And this, monks, is the noble truth of the cessation of suffering: the remainderless fading and cessation, renunciation, relinquishment, release, and letting go of craving.

And this, monks, is the noble truth of the way of practice leading to the cessation of suffering, the Noble Eightfold Path: right understanding, right attitude, right speech, right action, right livelihood, right effort, right mindfulness, and right concentration (S: LVI, XII, ii).

⋆

This "therapeutic" aspect of Buddha's philosophy has something in common with one of the greatest twentieth-century philosophers, Ludwig Wittgenstein, whom you will meet him in Chapter 23. As Gruzalski puts it:

⋆

From *Sanyutta-nikaya*, trans. A. F. Rhys Davis and F. L. Woodward.

The student of philosophy will recognize in the conversations of the Buddha with Malunkyaputta, Vacchagotta, and the king a clarity and precision of speech that illustrates what Ludwig Wittgenstein described as the only correct method in philosophy:

> The right method in philosophy would be to say nothing except what can be said using sentences such as those of natural science—which of course has nothing to do with philosophy—and then, to show those wishing to say something metaphysical that they failed to give any meaning to certain signs in their sentences. Although they would not be satisfied—they would feel you weren't teaching them any philosophy—*this* would be the only right method."[5]

Wittgenstein ends the book from which the above quote is drawn with the statement: "What we cannot speak about we must pass over in silence." For the Buddha, anatta is a reflection on all that we can experience, on all about which we can speak. It is a tool a person may use in search of truth and insight. Every phenomenon that one notices, every thing or title or position or process with which one might identify or in terms of which one thinks of himself, each is anatta. A feeling, the process of thinking, the body, a vocation, an occupation—each is not me, not mine, and I am not it. Beyond that, the Buddha is silent.

⋆

1.7 Pythagoras (c. 572–497 B.C.E.): Form, Limit, and Number as the Basis of All Things

In the Aegean Sea between Miletus and Athens lies a small island called Samos, which during ancient Greece was the main commercial rival of Miletus. Samos also happened to be the birthplace of its leading philosophical rival, Pythagoras (572–497 B.C.E.). Expelled by Polycrates, the tyrant of Samos, he migrated to

From Bart Gruzalski, *On the Buddha* (Belmont, CA: Wadsworth, 2000).

Crotona, a Dorian colony in southern Italy where he became the leader of a religious brotherhood based on ancient Orphic rites. Similar to the Hindu religious tradition, its practices were designed to purify the soul to free it from the "wheel of birth." His method, however, relied on mathematics and music to achieve enlightenment.

Pythagoras's philosophy grew out of the same foundation as that of the Milesians and yet in sharp contrast to it. It is a unique blend of what today would be considered opposites: a mathematical system based on demonstrative deductive argument, which Pythagoras himself invented and which is still the foundation of mathematical thinking even today, and mysticism, which became the basis of a new religion. Pythagoras even seems to have invented the Western musical scale, which is based on his discovery that by measuring the appropriate lengths of string on a monochord, one finds that musical intervals correspond to simple numerical ratios between the first four integers. The lengths in the ratio 2:3:4 emit a tonic, its fifth, and its octave, respectively, and the major triad has relative frequencies expressible in the ratio 4:5:6. Pythagoras not only invented new string instruments (some of which became the basis for the guitar) but showed empirically that these ratios hold for vibrating strings as well as for resonating air columns, thereby laying the foundation for the subsequent construction of pipe organs. His followers, sworn to secrecy about his musical, mathematical, and philosophical discoveries, swore oaths on the tetractys, a series of dots summarizing the musical harmonies:

octave (2:1)   .

                         .   .   fifth (3:2)

fourth (4:3)   .   .   .

                   .   .   .   .

The Pythagoreans were so impressed by the tetractys that they saw in it the secret insight that all of nature can be understood through mathematics—an idea that would influence later thinkers for centuries to come and still today is accepted by most scientists. Pythagoras showed how numbers explained musical harmonies and that the first four integers were essential in that they could be represented in an equilateral triangle of ten dots as arranged above. The secret oath of his students began: "By him that gave to our generation the tetractys which contains the fountain and root of eternal nature . . ."

Pythagoras and his disciples were also deeply concerned with discovering the nature of how the mind works and developing ways to perfect its intellectual and perceptual abilities by "purifying" it of its many deceptions and errors. They considered philosophy, mathematics, and science to be the chief instruments of enlightenment. As we are about to see in our discussion of his famous theorem that still today bears the name of Pythagoras, in discovering the relationship between arithmetic and geometry, the Pythagoreans were the first to see the intimate relationship between number and magnitude. They lay the foundation for subsequent philosophers and scientists to create systems based on the Pythagorean premise that the structure and order of the universe could be understood by the human mind, provided that it could perfect both its logical reasoning ability and powers of mystical insight. And mathematics was the point of contact between the rational and the mystical. The universe itself, according to the Pythagoreans, revealed itself as consisting of numbers.

Whereas Thales said that "Everything is made of water," Pythagoras claimed that "Everything is made of numbers." What could he have meant by this? There is both a striking difference between the two statements and a striking similarity. Obviously, it's a variation of the same formula. All separately existing individual things in the universe—"the many"—ultimately consist of the same sort of thing, though numbers are not "things." Similarly, it certainly doesn't *seem* as if everything is made of numbers—so, again, the idea is that appearances must be extremely and fundamentally deceiving. But, first, the underlying oneness is not some sort of *stuff* or *matter,* as the Milesians (Thales, Anaximander, and Anaximenes) thought. Rather, ultimate reality is not a *thing* at all. This is probably one of the most important ideas of all time—namely, the recognition that there is a distinction to be made between tangible *things* and intangible *ideas*. For if numbers are not things and everything is made of numbers, then everything is ultimately not made of *things* but of some sort of *ideas* or abstract relations (whatever numbers are—which we shall consider shortly).

Let us make sure we understand this. What is a number?

Here we might pause and reflect a moment on the difference between, say, a book trying to teach you some mathematics and a book trying to teach you some philosophy. This book is an example, I hope, of the latter. And this is a perfect place to see precisely why. Mathematics, of course, has a great deal to do with numbers, just as literature has a great deal to do with words. But the question "What is a number?" will hardly ever, if at all, come up in the course of the study of mathematics, just as "What is a word?" will hardly ever come up in the course of the study of literature. This is because you don't have to know what a word is to learn language any more than you have to know what a number is to learn mathematics. Some would say such questions even get in the way of learning and are therefore impractical. (Some would also say such questions only get in the way of studying mathematics and language. I would say they only get in the way of not properly understanding them.) Philosophy, however, is extremely impractical in this way. It won't necessarily help you to be a better mathematician (though it might) any more than it will help you better to learn language (though it might do that too). What it will do is connect you to questions that you might otherwise never think to ask. For instance, you would never think to ask, "What is a number?" while adding numbers in your checkbook. Nor would you ever, while turning excitedly from page to page as you read an exciting mystery story, ask, "What

are these little inkblots so arranged that give me such great pleasure?" While we're on this topic, we might as well add that you would probably never, while watching a beautiful sunset, ask, "What is *watching*?" "What is *seeing*?" "What is *is*?" (Ouch!) Of course I might as well point out that numbers and words are not unique in this way. The question "What is a thing?" is equally mysterious, as is the question "What is a rock?"

So, what is a number? Unfortunately, as we shall see, it is notoriously difficult to make any progress on such questions. This question doesn't have to do with just Pythagoras, although this is as good a place as any to talk about it. It has to do with the distinction between, on the one hand, physical things and abstract things and, on the other, between things of any kind and the symbols used to represent them.

Here's a riddle: What do two apples and a pair of shoes have in common? You may be tempted to say, "nothing." But let's add to the list a married couple, a bull's horns, and your hands. What do these all have in common? The more examples we put into this riddle, the easier it is to solve. For, of course, what two apples, a pair of shoes, a married couple, a bull's horns, and your hands have in common is *the number 2*. But what is that? These objects have nothing physical in common, not color nor shape nor weight. Well, what, then?

Once again, this question may seem either too trivial or too obvious. But what do the things in this list really have in common? You might say, "twoness," "duality," "twinness," "pairing," and so on—but to what exactly do such words refer? Look at any two things, for instance, two chairs. Where is the twoness? Can you point to it? There is just the chair on the left and the chair on the right. Certainly, the two chairs don't know they are two. It is you who knows this about them. Nor *are* they two. If you remove the two chairs from the room you do not remove the number 2 from the room. The number 2 was not in the room to begin with.

Furthermore, many other chairs exist. What makes *any* chairs *two* in number? Do they have to be near each other? No. Put a chair out on a street corner in Beijing and put one out on a street corner in Washington, DC. Those chairs, though at opposite ends of the earth, are two in number. Perhaps, then, it is only because your mind singles some two chairs out as such that makes them two in number. Yet aren't *those* chairs *two*, even if you weren't thinking about them, for the same reason that the earth is the third planet from the sun whether anybody thinks about it or not? But where then is this "number" property? What is it? What *is* the number 2?

A strange question indeed, perhaps even perplexing because no easy answer is forthcoming, and yet few things are as familiar to us as the concept of number. Without numbers there would be no mathematics, no science, no economy, not even something as simple as counting 1, 2, 3. . . . Without numbers, life as we know it would end; civilization would grind to a halt. Indeed, without numbers civilization would never have begun.

Even before Pythagoras, the ancient Greeks, as well as the neighboring Hindu and Arab cultures, were so enamored with numbers that they ascribed to them a religious significance. For instance, they believed the number 1 was somehow the generator of the entire cosmos, and the number of the length of the hypotenuse of a unit square was evil and dangerous to think about. Why such fanciful thoughts about something that to us seems so ordinary and commonplace? Were they crazy? Superstitious? Naive fanatics? Hardly. The architects of civilization perceived numbers with the awe and wonder of cosmic mysticism for the simple reason that they experienced directly, within themselves, something that today we take for granted. They experienced the birth of abstract reasoning. They experienced in their lifetimes the birth of philosophy, science, and mathematics.

When a young couple experiences the birth of their first child, they feel awe and mystery, as if their child were a gift from the gods. The child gets older, diapers need to be changed, hungry mouths need to be fed. The child does not do what the parents want but goes its own way. The practical concerns and pressures of life easily diminish the initial wonder. It is the same with the birth of new ideas. Numbers to the Greeks were truly like gifts from the gods, so much so that the Pythagoreans created a powerful church for the study and worship of numbers that gained control over many Western Greek colonies. They considered numbers to be the light of knowledge, thrown forth into the world of ignorance from within the soul by the gods to illuminate the darkness, a divine revelation of the secrets of the universe. We may find this strange, but remember that part of the excitement for them was finding in the realm of pure thought a way of distinguishing themselves from animals and the rest of nature. We have the divine number sense. Animals, trees, rocks, and plants do not. Most important of all: *numbers have an existence apart from our physical bodies.* It thus comes as no surprise that the very heart of the concept of human spirituality—the soul—was invented by Pythagoras and perfected by his most famous student (though he came a generation later), Plato. (Note that the Old Testament makes no explicit use or mention of the human soul, whereas the New Testament, written four to six centuries after Pythagoras and Plato did their work, makes the soul the cornerstone of its worldview.)

Today we may know so much more than any of our ancestors ever dreamed possible, yet in our society numbers are mostly thought of as dry, uninteresting, and definitely unspiritual. Part of the reason is that mathematics is usually delivered up as a set of inherited answers, which we then take for granted. Also, the focus on the practical utility of mathematics, where we are only interested in problem solving, puts us in the practical frame of mind, which the inventors of mathematics warned hinders, rather than helps, our understanding. Philosophy, however, can help return us to an intimate understanding of numbers in a way that not only unlocks the essence of abstract thinking so essential to philosophical activity, but also even helps us glimpse into the hearts and minds of those ancient philosophers like Pythagoras who, having arisen at the first dawn of humanity to look out across the unknown horizon, boldly proclaimed: "Everything is made of numbers!"

1.7.1 Where Is the Number 2?

Suppose you are given an assignment: find the number 2. What do you do? You point to two chairs. But those things are not numbers! They're chairs. Take the chair apart and you will not find any numbers there—only wood, plastic, and other parts. So where is the number 2? You open up a book and point to the second page. There it is: in the corner of the page, a printed "2." But that is no more the number 2 than the word *dog* is a dog! To see why, consider another riddle: How many numbers are inside the following box?

$$\boxed{2}$$

You might say "one." Or, you might say "two." Or, you might even say "three"—thinking, for instance, that the numbers "0," "1," and "2" are all in the box. The correct answer, however, is that there are no numbers in the box, *none*. What you're looking at is not a number but a *representation* of a number: a *numeral*. The numeral *2* is not the number that it represents, any more than the words *New York* are the city that they represent. New York consists of buildings, people, Central Park, and so on and is many miles long. The words *New York* are very small by comparison and contain not one building.

The mystery does not end there. We can point to what the words "New York" refer; we *cannot* point to what "the number 2" refers.

Nowhere in the whole universe could anyone ever, even in principle, point to the number 2 or to any other number. Small wonder that the twentieth-century, Nobel-prize winning philosopher Bertrand Russell remarked, "It must have required many ages to discover that a brace of pheasants and a couple of days were both instances of the number two."

Numbers exist neither in space nor in time. They are *abstract concepts*. But they nevertheless do exist. Numbers are real. Compare, for instance, the concept of the positive whole number between 1 and 3, "2," and the concept of the positive whole number between 1 and 3 other than 2, call it "sigma." Sigma does not exist; it is not real. Two does exist; it is real.

Not all concepts are real. "Unicorn," for instance, belongs to the same category as sigma: it denotes a nonexistent object. Just because we can conceive of something and name it does not mean it exists. On the other hand, just because something is a concept does not mean it is not real. Indeed, not only is the reality of numbers independent of the existence of any physical objects in time and space, in an important sense numbers are uncreated, indestructible, and exist independently of the mind. That is, numbers don't just refer to "mental entities" that exist "only in the mind." When dinosaurs roamed the earth, for instance, the earth was still the third planet from the sun, not the second or fourth—even though no minds existed who knew this. So numbers would exist even if there were no minds to conceive of them. In fact, we can imagine how it is possible that the sum of 2 and 2 would still be 4 even if the universe did not exist—if there was absolutely nothing. Nobody would *know* that 2 + 2 = 4, but nevertheless 2 + 2 would still equal 4. Numbers, it seems, are thus the sorts of entities that can exist without having ever been created. Suppose we erased the 2 from the pictured box. Have we destroyed the number 2? Suppose we erased all representations of the number 2. Would we have wiped the number 2 out of existence?

The mysterious, uncreated, and eternal nature of numbers is one reason why the Greeks thought so highly of them and ascribed various mystical properties to them. Pythagoras and his students worshipped them as the soul of the world because they were eternal and immortal guides to absolute and irrefutable truth. Small wonder that Plato (whom you will meet in the next chapter), who founded the first university, put a sign above it which read: "Let no one ignorant of mathematics enter here."

1.7.2 Numbers Without Numerals

Let us see how abstract concepts like numbers are conceived in the mind. In particular, let us see the distinction between the numeral used to represent a number and the number being represented. We have already noted that "2" is not the number two; rather it is a symbol. Such a symbol is called a numeral. Other numerals have been used to denote the number two. For instance, in the Roman numeral system, "II" denotes the number two. Our usual numeral system, the Hindu-Arabic, uses "2" to denote the number two. The question still stands: What is the number 2? that exists independently of any minds using any sort of numerals to represent it. We will now approach this question by seeing how the properties of numbers can be expressed without using any numerals.

That is not to say that numerals (how we represent individual numbers) are not important. They are. If you have direct access to the thing represented by the symbol, the symbol does not really matter. With numbers, however, we cannot access the individuals without the numerals. That is why in philosophy, as well as in mathematics, *how we represent what we wish to refer to in part defines what we are able to refer to and what we are then able to do with it.* That is why *definitions* are so extremely important. And that is why getting a sense of the difference between numbers and numerals is doubly important: it reveals the properties of the numbers independently of the numerals and the properties of the numerals (the system of representation) independently of the numbers. In many ways, mathematics is a superabstract form of abstract painting, where even the paintbrushes, the canvas, and the paint must be painted before the work begins. (But with what? We don't know! This is part of what mystified the Greeks.) That is one reason why the historical development of numeral systems—the actual symbols used to represent numbers—goes hand in hand with the most important scientific, philosophical, social, and political advances of Western civilization. The techniques of mathematics have painted some of our most important concepts into existence, those we use to understand ourselves and the world.

To discover the properties of numbers themselves rather than of the numeral system used to represent them, it sometimes helps tremendously to be able to refer not to individual numbers but to *any* numbers. The numbers you are already most familiar with—1, 2, 3, . . . ,—are called the *natural numbers* or *counting numbers.* "God created the natural numbers; all else is the work of man," wrote mathematician Leopold Kronecker (1823–1891). For a long time, the positive counting numbers were the only numbers known, but they revealed certain general properties of all such numbers (even ones the early mathematicians didn't know about yet!) that can be expressed as laws. When we make a specific statement about numbers using numerals, such as "3 + 4 = 7," we make a true statement limited to only *those* numbers referred to in *that* statement using *those* numerals. Notice, however, that simply by using letters of the alphabet as shorthand (usually a, b, c, and d) to refer to the numbers, we can make statements about them, such as "$a + b = b + a$," which says simply that it doesn't matter in what order you add two numbers, the sum will be the same (one of the Laws of Arithmetic, the commutative law of addition). Each of a and b is saying, "I am a number." Each refers to each and every one of the counting numbers. Substitute any counting number for *a* and *b* and the equation "*a* + *b* = *b* + *a*" will be true. Like all laws, Laws of Arithmetic are *general statements about particular entities*. In this case, the entities being referred to are *numbers,* and they are a specific type of number—counting numbers (1, 2, 3, and so on). So we can represent something about numbers and the relationship between them without using any particular numbers or saying anything about what any particular number is. This too is in part why the Greeks were so fascinated with numbers; mathematics seems able to reveal truths about an otherwise completely invisible and unknowable world of pure *forms* (an extremely important concept in subsequent Platonic philosophy, to be discussed in Chapter 2).

The reason we are for the moment focusing on numbers and certain mathematical relations is that it is a perfectly precise and clear way of pinning down our talk about *abstract terms*. It gives you definite examples. This will be very important when we try to move from what I call *automatic* thinking to what I call *philosophical* thinking. The points made earlier about thinking about what words are, what perception is, and so on, don't happen automatically. What happens automatically is that you think, "Oh, what a pretty sunset," or "Where did I park my car?" It is like breathing. Ordinarily you do it automatically. But breathing can also be done with attention; you can learn to direct your breathing. This can give you great power over your body as well as your emotions; there are, for instance, a slew of relaxation techniques based on mastering breathing techniques, such as those used in Lamaze birthing classes. Thinking too can be done automatically or with attention. You can learn to direct your thinking. What meditation is to breathing, philosophy is to thinking. There may even be similar benefits. The Pythagoreans certainly thought so.

Now that we are a bit clearer (but perhaps more *puzzled!*) about what numbers are in and of themselves (as opposed to numerals, their symbolic representations), we are ready to appreciate Pythagoras's excitement over his discovery that anything that has shape and size must be based on definite numerical relations. The importance of this notion can best be understood in contrast to the Milesians' view that the world is some sort of undifferentiated, unified, single substance—"water," "the indeterminate boundless," "air," and so on. Thales, Anaximander, and Anaximenes could only allude to what then accounted for the differentiation observed among all things. Pythagoras explained the observed differences among things with the concept of *form,* by which he meant *limit* and *proportion* as understood in purely numerical terms. It is extremely important for us to understand this if we are to comprehend the key notion in the philosophy of Plato. For it is numbers that represent the application of a specific *limit,* or *form,* to the *unlimited* stuff of the world (matter or substance). It is this specific line of Pythagoras's thought that paved the way for the philosophy of Plato, one of the greatest philosophers of all time. Before moving on, however, if you would like to try to understand Pythagoras's revolutionary ideas in more detail, you may wish to work through one central aspect of Pythagoras's thought as presented in his famous theorem.

1.7.3 The Pythagorean Theorem

Today, Pythagoras is most famous for having discovered the theorem that still bears his name. The Pythagorean theorem exhibits a formula expressing an algebraic relationship between the lengths of the sides of a right triangle. Algebraic relationships are purely intellectual representations of proportions and ratios, without any visual pictures. Geometric representations, like triangles and squares, are based on visual pictures. The fundamental Pythagorean argument, the model for all subsequent demonstrative deductive arguments in mathematics, not only illustrates the Pythagorean theorem but also is one of the world's best examples of the Pythagorean discovery of the unique relationship between perception and the intellect. This relationship between seeing and thinking influenced all subsequent thinking in philosophy, mathematics, and the sciences. As you learn the following picture argument, reflect upon the way your thought process involves an interplay of your own mind's visual and intellectual faculties.

Here is a right triangle; the lengths of its sides are labeled *a*, *b*, and *c*.

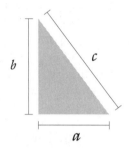

The side opposite the right (90 degree) angle, called the *hypotenuse*, has length *c*. The other two sides, having lengths *a* and *b*, are called *legs*. We will now consider four identical copies of this right triangle obtained from 0-, 90-, 180-, and 270-degree turns.

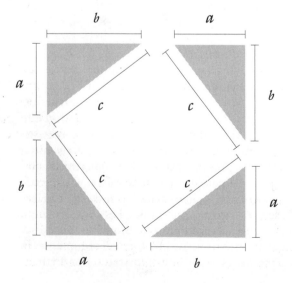

Putting these four copies together, we form Figures 1 and 2.

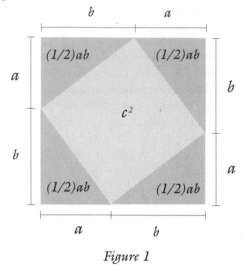

Figure 1

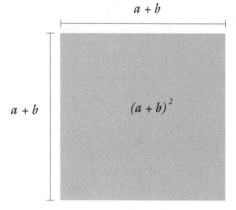

Figure 2

The trick now is to look at and think about the original figure in two ways: First, in Figure 1 we account for the area of each part separately. There are four identical right triangles, each of whose area is $\frac{1}{2} ab$. There is also one square in the middle, whose area is c^2. Thus, if A denotes the area of the big square made up from the smaller figures, then we have

$$A = 4(\tfrac{1}{2} ab) + c^2 = 2ab + c^2$$

Second, in Figure 2 we ignore the distinct parts and regard the figure as one big square.

Since the length of its side is $a + b$, this square's area is $(a + b)^2$. This, if A denotes the area of the big square, then we have

$$A = (a + b)^2$$

Now we have two different expressions to represent one and the same area, A. Since the two expressions represent the same quantity A, the two expressions are equal to each other:

$$(a + b)^2 = 2ab + c^2$$

Simplifying the left side of the equation, we have

$$a^2 + 2ab + b^2 = 2ab + c^2$$

Canceling the common term $2ab$ from both sides, we have

$$a^2 + b^2 = c^2$$

We have derived the formula of the Pythagorean theorem, which can now be formally stated as follows:

DEFINITION	Let a triangle in the plane have sides of length a, b, and c. Then this triangle is a right triangle whose hypotenuse has length c if and only if $$a^2 + b^2 = c^2$$

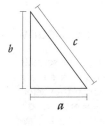

Expressing this formula in words, the sum of the squares of the lengths of the legs equals the square of the length of the hypotenuse.

Now, what's so great about that? Of course, it's nice to have an additional tool to calculate distances. Thales was able to do this and probably Pythagoras was able to formalize his predecessor's methods. But there is nothing especially

philosophically astounding or remarkable about that. Yet the impact this proof has had on philosophers over the last twenty-five centuries has been immense. Consider, for instance, the response of the great early modern philosopher Thomas Hobbes (1588–1679, see Chapter 9) when he first came upon the theorem. His friend John Aubrey writes that Hobbes

✦

was 40 years old before he looked on geometry; which happened accidentally. Being in a gentleman's library Euclid's *Elements* lay open, and it was the Theorem of Pythagoras. Hobbes read the proposition. "By God," said he, "this is impossible!" So he reads the demonstration of it, which referred him back to such a proposition, which proposition he read. That referred him back to another, which he also read. *Et sic deincepts,* that at last he was demonstratively convinced of the truth.

✦

Why the excitement? Well, notice, first, that the proposition "The sum of the squares of adjoining perpendicular lines having length a and b, respectively, is the square of the line connecting their endpoints, length c" is not intuitively true. That is, you cannot determine the ratio of the length of the hypotenuse to the sum of the two sides just by looking at the two sides of a right triangle. In calling such ratios "squared" numbers (a number raised to the power of 2, like x^2), Pythagoras tried to evoke the sense that numbers, which have no shape or form, are somehow related to things that do have form and shape, like two-dimensional areas. That is why still today we speak in terms of *square feet*, as when counting the tiles in a room to determine the area. Likewise, we speak of the cubes of numbers (x^3) that represent three-dimensional areas. Once the squares of lengths a, b, and c are known to correspond according to Pythagoras's equation $a^2 + b^2 = c^2$, this relationship can be expressed geometrically, as shown in the figure on page 40.

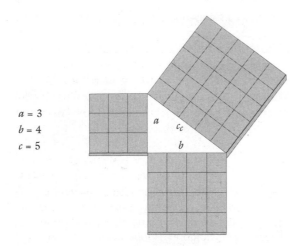

$a = 3$
$b = 4$
$c = 5$

But why should this be so? One can *see* no reason for it. Hence Hobbes's (and everyone else who has been taken by Pythagoras's theorem) initial disbelief that this could be so. For what is a theorem? A theorem is a type of proposition. Propositions are statements that are either true or false (see the discussion on pages 509–513). Some propositions, like "Two points determine a line," are accepted as true without proof because they are intuitively obvious. (Just try and draw any two points that cannot be connected by a line—impossible.) When the authors of the U.S. constitution wrote that "We take these truths to be self-evident," they were evoking this idea. In mathematics these are called *axioms*. Some propositions are proven to be true by using what is called the *axiomatic method*. They are called *theorems*. The *axiomatic method* begins with propositions that are axioms and moves step by step, using other axioms or combinations thereof, to derive some new proposition, called the *conclusion*. The whole procedure is called an *argument*. And the type of argument that Pythagoras gave to the world, which has been the foundation of mathematical thought for the last twenty-five centuries, is the *demonstrative deductive argument*. Notice in Hobbes's reaction to the proof that he is amazed that each proposition leading up to the conclusion is intuitively obvious, while the conclusion is not. This is the cornerstone of this method of reasoning and no

doubt gave impetus to Pythagoras's mysticism. Take one intuitively obvious step after another and you end up with an intuitively unobvious conclusion known with perfect certainty to be true! In other words, you have a method for looking very carefully at what you can see to see what cannot be seen. This will have a profound effect, as we shall see, on all subsequent Western thought founded upon the work of Plato.

It is interesting—perhaps even an ominous portent of philosophical things to come—that as Pythagoras neared the end of his life his students and many devoted followers split into two rival factions. The "Akousmatics," or "Pythagorists," followed the mystical and ritual side of his teachings. To them, Pythagoras was more of a divine guru than a teacher in the Western sense. The other group, who called themselves "the Mathematicians," went on to develop his scientific interests; they believed that the universe was mathematical (in particular, arithmetical) and seem to have believed literally in Pythagoras's statement that everything is made of numbers. And the bombshell that started their philosophical war came with the discovery by one of Pythagoras's most devoted students, Hippasus, that—to anachronistically quote Shakespeare— "there are more things in heaven and earth than can be dreamt of in your [Pythagorean] philosophy." It is to this shocking discovery that we shall turn in the next section.

⚹

Aristotle on the Pythagoreans

At the same time, and even earlier, the so-called Pythagoreans attached themselves to the mathematics and were the first to advance that science by their education, in which they were led to suppose that the principles of mathematics are the principles of all things. So as *numbers* are logically first among these principles, and as they fancied they could perceive in numbers many analogues of

From A. E. Taylor, *Aristotle and His Predecessors* (La Salle, IL: Open Court, 1907).

what is and what comes into being, much more readily than in fire and earth and water (such and such a property of number being *justice*, such and such another *soul* or *mind*, another *opportunity*, and so on, speaking generally, with all the other individual cases), and since they further observed that the properties and determining ratios of *harmonies* depend on numbers—since, in fact, everything else manifestly appeared to be modeled in its entire character on numbers, and numbers to be the ultimate things in the whole Universe, they became convinced that the elements of numbers are the elements of everything, and that the whole "Heaven" is harmony and number. So, all the admitted analogies they could show between numbers and harmonies and the properties or parts of the "Heaven" and the whole order of the universe, they collected and accommodated to the facts; if any gaps were left in the analogy, they eagerly caught at some additional notion, so as to introduce connection into their system as a whole. I mean, e.g., that since the number 10 is thought to be perfect, and to embrace the whole essential nature of the numerical system, they declare also that the number of revolving heavenly bodies is ten, and as there are only nine visible, they invent the Antichthon as a tenth. But I have discussed this subject more in detail elsewhere. I only enter on it here for the purpose of discovering from these philosophers as well as from the others what principles they assume, and how those principles fit into our previous classification of causes. Well, they, too, manifestly regard number as a principle, both in the sense that it is the *material* of things, and in the sense that it constitutes their *properties and states*. The elements of number are, they think, the Even and the Odd, the former being unlimited, the latter limited. Unity is composed of both factors, for, they say, it is both even and odd. Number is derived from unity, and numbers, as I have said, constitute the whole "Heaven."

Other members of the same school say that the principles are ten, which they arrange in a series of corresponding pairs:

Limit—the Unlimited.	Rest—Motion.
Odd—Even.	Straight—Curved.
Unity—Multitude.	Light—Darkness.
Right—Left.	Good—Evil.
Male—Female.	Square—Oblong.

1.8 The Rational Versus the Irrational

The long-standing historical division between "rational" philosophical methods (exemplified in the disciplines of mathematics, science, and logic) and "irrational" philosophical methods (exemplified in the disciplines of mysticism, religion, and art) is perhaps as misleading and confusing as it is important and profound. *Irrational* has often been used pejoratively to mean "crazy" or "deluded," and *rational* has often been used to mean "correct," "intelligent," and so on. But this naive and destructive usage covers up much that it is extremely important to understand if we are going to open our minds to what philosophy is. Fortunately, we have already arrived at a perfect point where we can illustrate a very precise and meaningful distinction between these two broadly sketched categories, using the Pythagorean distinction between rational and irrational *numbers*.

The Pythagoreans knew about square roots of certain numbers because of the Pythagorean theorem, which states that the square of the hypotenuse of a right triangle is equal to the sum of the squares of the other two sides: $x^2 + y^2 = z^2$. Thus, one needs to take a square root in order to solve for z. The numbers fitting this relation are still today called "Pythagorean numbers," triples in the form (3,4,5), (5,12,13), (6,8,10), (7,24,25), and so on: ($3^2 + 4^2 = 5^2 = 9 + 16 = 25$).

Armed with this knowledge, Hippasus, Pythagoras's student, raised a problem with Pythagoras's numbers that turned out to be one of the most important puzzles in history. Suppose we have a unit square, that is, a square whose sides each have length 1. From the Pythagorean theorem, we know that the length of the hypotenuse will be the sum of the lengths of the sides: $1^2 + 1^2 = ?^2$. Taking the square root of both sides, we get: $\sqrt{1^2 + 1^2} = \sqrt{?^2}$. Simplifying, we get

$$\sqrt{1+1} = ?$$

$$\sqrt{2} = ?$$

Two problems immediately present themselves. First, the number represented by $\sqrt{2}$ *cannot be expressed as the ratio of two numbers.* In other words, it is not a rational number! Under the domain of rational numbers, the expression $\sqrt{2}$ is *meaningless.* Yet, as if this weren't bad enough, we can construct its exact position on the number line by bringing down the hypotenuse:

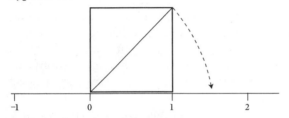

And yet the value of this number is a nonterminating and nonrepeating decimal, 1.4142135 62373 . . . . This means that if you were to compute the decimal representation you would never stop having to compute more decimal places (there will be no final term) and you would never find a perpetually repeating pattern of digits. From the point of view of the rational numbers, there is no such number. Pythagoras's student proved this as follows. The method of proof is another one of the most useful in history. Called *reductio ad absurdum* (literally, "reduction to the absurd"), it works by assuming that what you're trying to prove is false and then illiciting a contradiction that must have resulted from the fact that what you're trying to prove is actually true. So let us do this by assuming that $\sqrt{2}$ is rational. If this is so, then we can write $\sqrt{2}$ as a rational number, the ratio of two integers in reduced form. That would mean that there is some rational number, $\frac{a}{b}$, reduced to its lowest terms, such that

$$\frac{a}{b} = \sqrt{2} \qquad (1)$$

In that case, squaring both sides, we get:

$$\frac{a^2}{b^2} = \sqrt{2} \qquad (2)$$

Multiplying both sides by b^2, we get:

$$a^2 = 2b^2 \qquad (3)$$

This tells us that 2 must be part of the unique prime factorization of a^2. This means that a^2 must be even, since $2b^2$ is divisible by 2. If a^2 is even, then since the square of an odd number would have to be odd, a must also be even. If a is even, it must contain 2 as a factor; that is,

$$a = 2c$$

for some number, c. Substituting this value of a into equation 3, we get

$$2b^2 = (2c)^2 = 2c \times 2c = 4c^2 \qquad (4)$$

Thus, since

$$2b^2 = 4c^2$$

we can divide both sides by 2 to get:

$$b^2 = 2c^2 \qquad (5)$$

which proves that b^2, too, is an even number, and so therefore b is an even number. But then both a and b are even. *This contradicts the original assumption that $\frac{a}{b}$ was a rational number reduced to simplest terms.* Therefore, there is no such number. Why not reduce $\frac{a}{b}$? Because we could take that reduced fraction and derive the same contradiction. The number represented by $\sqrt{2}$ is not rational.

Here now comes the astounding part of the story. Since there was no way to represent this as a rational number, the Greeks called it "irrational." According to some, this revealed a religious, mystical truth: the human mind and reason are inadequate for understanding the world. Knowledge cannot be attained through reason because, according to these religious mystics, our best and most precise concepts—numbers—fail us. They are irreparably incomplete. We must therefore content ourselves with the bitter realization that, ultimately, true knowledge of the world is beyond the reach of the mind; the world is incomprehensible. The gods, perhaps, can know the truth and comprehend the world; the gods and perhaps a few chosen holy persons have the capacity for religious mystical experiences and insights that link them directly to unmitigated, nonrepresentational reality. In other words, because the human mind has access only to its own representations of things (that is, only to its own concepts and ideas), not to things in themselves, and these representations are inadequate, human concepts are ultimately inadequate tools for apprehending reality. Knowledge through reason is impossible. True knowledge and understanding of reality must therefore be attained, if at all, through some sort of religious faith or mystical revelation. Reason, according to the religious mystics, ought to be discarded as a path to knowledge in favor of religion.

The immediate opposition to this idea came from those scientifically minded rationalists who wanted to save rationality against the mystics. True knowledge of reality could, according to the scientists, be attained through reason. Partly because the Greeks were so clever, they were able to make a very close rational approximation of $\sqrt{2}$ that worked for all practical purposes. The rational number $\frac{289}{144}$ differs from the value of $\sqrt{2}$ by less than $\frac{1}{7}$ of 1%! It is precisely the mind's ability to make do with close approximations that almost doomed the evolution of philosophy from the start because it made it easy for the rational scientists to defend reason against the religious mystics by digging in their heels and resisting any tampering with the conceptual framework.

However, the beginnings of a philosophical alternative to both religious mysticism and rational science were already in place. As mentioned above, a shift had already taken place in which what might be thought of as a calculation problem to be performed (such as $\sqrt{4}$, whose "answer" is 2) could instead be seen as the number that it is, and what is called "the answer" is just another way to represent it. That is, had the mystics prevailed in a similar controversy about allowing ratio problems to be numbers, they would not now have had an even better example to reinforce their position, $\sqrt{2}$. Note that to prove that $\sqrt{2}$ is irrational, you need to work with a rational number form ($\frac{a}{b}$) which, on the assumption for the sake of illiciting a contradiction, is not just a square root to be found but a number that can be manipulated in the proof whether or not it has been calculated. They would not have allowed rational numbers, or $\sqrt{2}$ which they needed to make the case for how deficient human concepts are for understanding the world. On the other hand, had the practically minded rational scientists prevailed, we would have remained with the status quo of rational numbers and not have today's more complete real line and everything that goes with it, including a method for locating, logically and precisely, $\sqrt{2}$ on the number line.

It was the dogged determination of the *philosophical* rationalists who were willing to balance between the two extremes of *scientific* rationalism and religious mysticism that saved Western philosophy and paved the way for the subsequent evolution of Western thought. They agreed with the mystics that $\sqrt{2}$ cannot really be expressed by $\frac{289}{144}$, but they also agreed with the scientists that our concepts are the most valuable tools we have for understanding and should not simply be discarded. They felt that both the religious and scientific extremes were static in their own way. In either case, they were stuck. And so the philosophers, unwilling to give up the ghost to religious mysticism or compromise the truth with the fictional approximations of the rational scientists, continued the evolution of the conceptual framework, making possible the advances of not only philosophy but mathematics and science as well.

Picture it this way. You've got the mystics standing on the point where the diagonal of the square falls on the line, saying, "If you're not here, at this point, then you're not here." The practical, rational scientists are saying, "Look, we're standing close enough." The philosophers, on the other hand, are saying, "Let's start where the scientists are standing, use where the mystics are standing as a beacon and then slowly, carefully, let us start building a bridge." *Philosophy thus evolved on the razor's edge between religion and science.*

In other words, the philosophically minded Pythagorean mathematicians, instead of giving up and deciding that the world was irrational or that our concepts were not good enough, chose to invent symbols for the incomprehensible and treat them like ordinary numbers. They called these new numbers *irrational numbers.* Combining the irrational numbers and rational numbers, they called their new conceptual universe the set of *real numbers.*

Think of it this way. The power of the idea of rational numbers is that the "thing"—the place, if you like, or the actual point in space—is a *ratio* between two numbers. Numbers are concepts. In that case, "all (reality) is full" and the mind's picture, its representation, is complete. It leaves nothing out. You can get from any number to any other number, and by representing points as numbers you can get from any point to any other point. So, literally, Pythagoras could claim that "Everything is numbers." Everything is accessible to our basic number concept. But now what Hippasus's demonstration shows is that there is a number that is not a number! That is, there is a place—the point on the number line where the diagonal of the unit square falls—that (on the view that all places can be accessed by numbers) is not a place. The new alternative, proposed by the mathematical philosophers, was that the "real" was not merely a conglomerate of ratios but, in addition, consisted of "irratios," that is, places that could not be expressed using finite proportions.

How many irrational numbers are there? There are an infinite number of integers (the counting numbers 1, 2, 3, . . . ,). Consider, then, the following numbers:

$$. . . , \sqrt{2} - 3, \sqrt{2} - 2, \sqrt{2} - 1, \sqrt{2},$$
$$\sqrt{2} + 1, \sqrt{2} + 2, \sqrt{2} + 3, . . .$$

This is an infinite list of numbers. Let us show that they are irrational. Each of them is of the form $\sqrt{2} + n$. Let us use reductio ad absurdum. Suppose

$$\sqrt{2} + n = \frac{a}{b}$$

where a, b, and n are integers. Then

$$\sqrt{2} = \frac{a}{b} - n = \frac{a - bn}{b}$$

which is rational since $a - bn$ and b are integers but $\sqrt{2}$ isn't. Thus, we have constructed an infinite list of irrationals. Do not be misled by this; the list does not include all the irrationals. But it is infinite.

Suddenly a whole new universe has opened up: in the gaps between the natural (counting) numbers, or positive integers, we find irrational numbers whose numerical representations seem to imply that they continue getting bigger by smaller and smaller increments but forever and yet don't exceed a particular number. For instance, although $\sqrt{2} = 1.414213562373$ (keep adding digits *forever*), we see that the concept of *number* is not static but somehow dynamic; any rational approximation in terms of a terminating decimal can only be improved by adding more digits and as we do this each successive approximation is greater than the last. Our representation "keeps growing," even though we know the number itself never exceeds a particular magnitude. This seems deeply paradoxical. After all, how can you keep growing forever toward a certain point and never go past that point? It is precisely with such paradoxical entities that the continuum of the numbers, like the continuum of the number line, is filled in—a sort of "flowing cement of the universe." We're used to thinking of numbers as static things. What we're beginning to see is that numbers are *dynamic* concepts.

But that, of course, is what they were to begin with. The problem is that we came to conceive of numbers as static rather than dynamic concepts only because we were fooled by our representations scheme. This sounds complicated but is as simple to demonstrate as it is revealing. To see this, recall that, with the exception of zero, all real numbers (consisting both of rational and irrational numbers) can be expressed as infinite decimal fractions. Some can be expressed using finite expressions—that is,

$$\frac{1}{10} = .1, \quad \frac{58}{10} = 5.8, \quad \frac{2}{5} = \frac{4}{10}, \quad \frac{1}{25} = .04,$$

while others require infinite decimal fractions, such as

$$\frac{1}{3} = 0.333333333333333\ldots,$$

$$\frac{7}{6} = 1.16666666666666666\ldots,$$

$$\frac{1}{11} = 0.09999999999999\ldots,$$

and so on. Well, but what actually is the difference between the infinite decimal representations and the finite decimal representations? In reality, the difference is in large part illusory, generated by the symbols we use to express them. Even "finite" fractions such as 1.26 and 0.08 are expressible in infinite decimal form. One way to do this is by writing 1.26000 000000000000, . . . , and 0.0800000 00000000000000 . . . , which seems innocent enough. One can also do it by writing

$$1.26 = 1.25999999999999999999\ldots,$$

and

$$0.08 = 0.79999999999999999\ldots,$$

and so on. Rigorous proofs exist of this surprising conclusion, but a simple way to demonstrate it is by showing that

$$\frac{1}{3} = 0.3333333333333333$$

can be reduced as follows: Multiply both sides of the equation by 3 to get

$$\frac{1}{3} \times 3 = 1$$

on the left and

$$0.33333333\ldots \times 3 = 0.9999999999999\ldots$$

on the right. Therefore,

$$1 = 0.999999999999999\ldots.$$

The concept we are here beginning to generate (which would take many centuries after the pioneering work of the Greek thinkers to achieve) is, once again, approaching the modern concept of *limit.* This is a careful philosophical balancing act between practical science and religious mysticism. It puts the paradox into a precise concept, thereby increasing the power of the mind to engage with reality in an ever-evolving sequence of more and more elaborate concepts. For the early Greeks the key idea that thus presented itself came to be called the *forms* of things, that conceptual realm that allows the mind to look beyond the appearances to apprehend the ever-elusive truth behind them. We shall discuss this again in the next chapter.

The Greek philosophers thus opened up a Pandora's box of mysteries. In deciding to forge ahead with new concepts into the unknown, the numbers that kept emerging "out of the gap" led to many of the most important mathematical innovations, such as calculus. By the time the twentieth century rolled around, the ultimate issues of space, time, and reality came to be graspable using the extensions of the concept of number begun by those ancient seekers of wisdom. As you will see in the next section, those Pythagoreans who began calling themselves "Mathematicians" were criticized by the philosophers Parmenides and Zeno. However, both the mystical and scientific aspects of Pythagoras's philosophy lived on through the centuries. Plato wrote about him extensively in the *Republic* and always held mathematical truths to be the paradigm of rational knowledge. Many centuries later, when Galileo wrote, "The book of nature is written in the language of mathematics," he was echoing Pythagoras. And we shall see these ideas reemerge again in a powerful new form in the nineteenth and twentieth centuries with Frege (Section 23.0), Russell (Section 23.1), and Wittgenstein (Section 23.2). Small wonder that the twentieth-century Nobel-prize winning philosopher Bertrand Russell called Pythagoras "intellectually one of the most important men that ever lived . . . one of the most interesting and puzzling men in history."

1.9 Heraclitus (540–480 B.C.E.): The Way of Logos

The term used by ancient Greek philosophers to refer to the world in its totality, to the universe as a whole, was *kosmos,* which meant "ordered whole." It is not difficult to imagine why. Looking at the world around you, what do you see? In varying degrees, things seem to persist in an orderly and predictable fashion. Things don't just pop in and out of existence haphazardly. The seasons come and go; the sun rises and sets; children are born; you leave a room and unless someone rearranged the things in it, when you return the objects are all still there exactly as you left them, and so on. The list goes on forever. Yet every time you look at something the images you see are never exactly as they were before; the perspective is always a bit different, the colors not the same, the shapes and forms are constantly changing. As you walk across a room the images you see of the walls grow and shrink along with the perspectival shifting of all you see. Furthermore, you can never compare one image of something (say, the one you are having now of this book) with another (say, one you had only a few moments ago). Your memory says the image you see now and the image you saw then are images of the same book, but you cannot compare these images to make sure. One image replaces another, the appearances come and go in a rapid succession of flickering happenings, appearing from the ceaselessly unfolding future as if from out of nowhere and disappearing instantly and forever into the ever-receding past.

And yet the human mind, guided by the logic of its own operations, can apprehend through reason the underlying logic of existence, a mental mirror of the cosmic *logos.* It learns to perceive regularities from out of the flux of ever-changing and ephemeral sensations; it can think and speak about them. This was proof positive to Heraclitus that nature and mind were inextricably linked by the same principles. The reflective human mind and the cosmos were linked by the same laws, guided by the same principles, affected by the same causes: this was the basis for Heraclitus's philosophy, according to which all the many individual, separately existing things in the world are united by the same underlying principles of reason, the logos. The appearances, which themselves are in constant flux and show the individual things of the world to be many, can also reveal through reason that beneath this diversity operates a hidden and cosmic unity. This insight cannot be seen directly; it must be intuited. Furthermore, this ultimate truth transcends the varying subjective opinions of unreflected thought when we sleepwalk through life, barely conscious of the existence of the world and of ourselves:

> To those who are awake the world-order is one, common to all; but the sleeping turn aside each into a world of his own. We ought not to act and speak like men asleep. We ought to follow what is common to all; but though the *logos* is common to all, the many live as though their thought were private to themselves.

Logos, the word Heraclitus used to refer to the unifying aspect conjoining the mind to the world as well as sustaining them both, is derived from a verb meaning "to speak." *Logos* meant several different things in ancient Greek. It referred simultaneously both to the words used by a speaker and to the thought, or meaning, thereby expressed, which exists independently of the words. It is the latter sense that Heraclitus relied upon:

> Listening not to me but to the logos, it is wise to acknowledge that all things are one.

In Heraclitus's philosophy, the term came to signify reason or order both in words (which makes language and thought possible) and in things (which makes existence and the world possible). It could be used to refer to discourse, definition, formula, principle, and mathematical ratio, but the most important sense that Heraclitus gave to it was to the cosmic unity operating according to reason. Thus, it is logos that both guides the world and makes it intelligible to the mind. It is at once the source of all natural processes and of human reason. As we shall see, the Stoics (Chapter 4) relied on this concept as the basis for their view of the world as a living, breathing unity, supremely perfect in its conjoinment of parts to the whole, imbibed by order and reason. The logos, which according to Heraclitus regulates all things, became for the Stoics the concept of Fate, and insofar as it directed everything toward the good (as we shall explore in more detail in the philosophies of Plato and Aristotle, especially in regard to the concept of the Good in the former and *teleology* in the latter), the logos gives rise to the concept of divine Providence as well as to the idea of Nature conceived as an ordered course of events. We shall see how subsequent thinkers interpret logos as an immaterial instrument, the personal agency through which the creative power of God forms and directs the course of events and even the origin of the world. In Christian philosophy, for instance, the logos became the second person of the Trinity, identified primarily with the creative, illuminating, and redemptive nature of Jesus Christ. Thus, the fourth Gospel of the New Testament begins with the cryptic statement, "In the beginning was the Word," where "Word" is a translation of "Logos."

Heraclitus was born in Ephesus, a town between Miletus and Colophon, on the west coast of Ionia (today's Turkey), a generation after the first three great Milesian philosophers (Anaximenes, the youngest of the three, was already an old man). A descendant from earlier kings of Ephesus, Heraclitus was a rich nobleman who gave up any pretense to the throne and all family privileges to his brother so that he could pursue philosophy. Whereas Thales, Anaximander, and Anaximenes were by and large in consort with the societies that made them figures of authority and in which they lived more or less as priests, Heraclitus by all accounts was one of the first of a long tradition of philosophers (culminating in the character of Socrates and deeply influential to the present day) who was deeply critical of his fellow citizens, includ-

ing other philosophers. There has rarely in history been a more explicit and eloquent expression of this sentiment than the one Heraclitus makes of his fellow Ephesians when, in a foreshadowing of the similar fate awaiting the future Socrates, they put one of Heraclitus's teachers, Hermodorus, on trial for corrupting the youth and raising questions in people's minds about the accepted gods:

> The Ephesians would do well to hang themselves, every adult man, and bequeath their City-State to adolescents.

He urges the elders—presumably because he sees them as people in power who are half-asleep and full of ignorance and pretense—to give way to the youth, presumably because the youth have not yet been corrupted. These themes will be taken up again shortly by Socrates and Plato.

Heraclitus's ideas about the nature of the world and the mind's attempt to comprehend it have been monumentally influential, especially in the thought of Plato, the Stoics, Kant, Hegel, and Nietzsche. What remains of Heraclitus's major philosophical work, published around 500 B.C.E. (about one hundred fragments as quoted by subsequent writers) reveals the vivid, cryptic, and prophetic style that earned him the nickname, "the Obscure." Because we have no continuous narrative, we must rely solely on brief statements taken from his surviving aphorisms to glimpse his thoughts. Consider, for instance, his definition of wisdom. Once again we see a philosophy emerge from the Milesian's premise of cosmic unity:

> Wisdom is one thing: to understand the thought which steers all things through all things.

There is, as with his Milesian predecessors, some underlying oneness in the world; the difference for Heraclitus is that the permanence and unity hidden behind the appearances is not some abiding substance, some stuff conceived of in terms of physical matter, as the Milesians thought. We don't know to what extent he might have had discourse with Pythagoras and his followers, but if we were to try to understand the differences between the Pythagorean and Heraclitean approaches to the problem of understanding the world, I would say that the method of the former is to reduce everything to mathematics, whereas the method of the latter is to reduce everything to logic. What logic—understood in its later Aristotelian, modern, and contemporary forms—is, we shall explore in due course, including the twentieth-century attempt by Bertrand Russell to reduce mathematics to logic. For now, let us simply note that for Heraclitus the appearances are in constant flux and the stuff of the world is itself undergoing constant change. All things, mental phenomena as well as physical phenomena, correspondingly come into being and pass away. The view that one or the other sort of phenomena—either physical (as for later atomists) or mental (as for later idealists)—was itself an enduring object over time, perhaps even a primary aspect of being itself, would become the foundation for the complementary view of Heraclitus's great contemporary, Parmenides (whom we shall meet in the next section). The difference between these two thinkers, often exaggerated as polar opposites, is mainly a question of emphasis: for Parmenides, what needs to be explained away as illusory are the apparent changes observed in experience; the ephemeral, the transient must give way to some unchanging, permanent substance. For Heraclitus, what needs to be explained away as illusory are the apparent permanencies observed in experience; the fixed, the identical over time must give way to some flux in which the only permanence is the impermanence of all things understood in terms of eternal, fixed laws of change and motion. Though this is a gross oversimplification, until the twentieth century modern science was in many ways fundamentally Parmenidean. The twentieth century, which brought the revolution of quantum mechanics, saw a return to a fundamentally Heraclitean perspective captured in one of his most famous

aphorisms, "You can't step into the same river twice." Heraclitus couches this in terms of unity found through the discovery of the world order via a uniting of opposites:

> All things come into being through opposition, and all are in flux like a river.
> Upon those who step into the same rivers flow other and yet other waters.

Like Anaximander and Anaximenes, Heraclitus claims that the order of the world comes about through the continual changes brought about by movement:

> Cool things become warm; what is warm cools; what is wet dries out; what is dry becomes moist.

Essential to this process is the coming together of opposites which, when properly understood, reveal the hidden cosmic unity, not in things, which are ephemeral, but in the form expressed through universal laws of change that cannot be understood except in terms of opposites:

> Sea water is very pure and very impure; drinkable and healthful for fishes, but undrinkable and destructive to humans. The path traced by the pen is straight and crooked. In a circle, beginning and end are common. The way up and the way down are the same.

Once such opposites are understood as manifestations of common principles through reason, the mind learns that the world itself was neither created nor can it be destroyed, for it is itself ceaselessly coming into being and passing away according to the laws of chaos and chance:

> This world-order, the same for all, no god made or any man, but it always was and is and will be an ever-living fire, kindling by measure and going out by measure.

Thus, the physical world as represented in the appearances is described by Heraclitus allegorically as an "ever-living, all-consuming fire." The only orderliness among the succession of appearances and of things, the only thing that does not change, is change itself, manifested by the underlying laws governed by "reason," the logos itself, an eternal pattern of cosmic flux. In an important way, Heraclitus thus foreshadowed the modern concept of uniform law.

Therefore, the most important thing for human beings to understand, according to Heraclitus, is the logos, the universal formula of change, structuring not only the cosmos and all things in it but also the operations of the human mind. (This idea—that both the inner workings of the human mind and the inner workings of the world [cosmos] are structured by the same underlying reality—will find its fullest expression in the work of Immanuel Kant.) Unfortunately, according to Heraclitus, the majority of people ignore the logos, even after it has been explained to them. The problem is that the human mind, not fully awake or enlightened to its own presence in the world, tends to constantly divide itself with a sort of black-and-white thinking, disagreeing with itself because of its own naive conceptualizations according to which things are one way or the other, not both. In other words, we tend to think in simplistic, rigid terms using words that are themselves limited and incapable of expressing the whole except through very careful reasoning. The truth is that the world will not be cast in too simple a mold because our concepts, divisive in their simplicity, cannot render the world as it really is. We must learn to make room for what will seem like utterly perplexing contradictions to the unenlightened mind. That is the purpose of philosophy. Let us now consider some of Heraclitus's aphorisms to see if we can find these ideas among his thoughts.

⚴

Heraclitean Aphorisms

For the many do not understand such things when they meet with them; nor having learned do they comprehend, though they think they do.

Though the *logos* is as I have said, people always fail to comprehend it, both before they hear it and when they hear it for the first time. For though all things come into being in accordance with this *logos,* they seem like people without experience, though in fact they do have experience both of words and deeds such as I have set forth, distinguishing each thing in accordance with its nature and declaring what it is. But other people are as unaware of what they do when awake as they are when they are asleep.

Though they are in daily contact with the *logos* they are of variance with it, and what they meet with appears alien to them.

Listening not to me but to the *logos,* it is wise to acknowledge that all things are one.

To those who are awake the world-order is one, common to all; but the sleeping turn aside each into a world of his own.

We ought not to act and speak like people asleep.

We ought to follow what is common to all, but though the *logos* is common to all, the many live as though their thought were private to themselves.

If you do not expect the unexpected you will not find it; for it is hard to find and difficult.

Nature loves to hide.

Eyes and ears are bad witnesses to people if they have souls that do not understand their language.

People do not comprehend how, though it is at variance with itself, it agrees with itself. It is a harmony of opposed tensions, as in the bow and the lyre.

In opposition there is agreement; between unlike, the fairest harmony.

The hidden harmony is stronger than the apparent.

Aggregations are wholes, yet not wholes, brought together, yet carried asunder; in accord, yet not in accord. From all, one; from one, all.

Changing, it rests.

The soul has a *logos* which increases itself.

I searched out myself.

You would not find out the boundaries of the soul though you traveled every road, so deep is its *logos.*

Life is a child moving pieces in a game. The kingship is in the hands of a child.

The Ephesians ought to hang themselves—every adult amongst them—and leave their city to adolescents.

From Kathleen Freeman, *Ancilla to the Pre-Socratic Philosophers* (Cambridge, MA: Harvard University Press, 1948).

There await us, after death, such things as we neither hope nor imagine.

⚶

To the question, then, of whether the world is in its totality—the cosmos, the whole of reality—is fundamentally *one* or *many*, Heraclitus would most likely answer: it is both one and many. From the point of view of our perceptions—the appearances, the images the mind makes in response to its senses—what we see is *many*. It consists of opposites: small and large, infinite and finite, hot and cold, dead and living, wet and dry, and so on, all of which constantly undergo change, going from one to the other. But why does it not all vanish? There must be something to it all: the way it goes, the mysterious, ever-present, but nowhere to be seen logos. And also, at the same time, reason corrects our ever-flickering view of the world due to our constantly changing perceptions, for reason reveals that in spite of all the change, something must nevertheless remain the same. Again, the logos: the mind is attuned to the same reasoning principles guiding the being of the world.

1.10 Parmenides (c. 515–445 B.C.E): The Way of Truth

Parmenides was born in Elea, a Greek city in southern Italy (today called Velia) that lay at the other end of the known world from where Heraclitus and the other Ionians lived. But he almost certainly studied in Athens (situated just about at the center of the then-known world), and there is ample evidence that he was a student of Anaximander and deeply influenced by the teachings of the Pythagoreans, whose religious and philosophical brotherhood he joined at their school in Crotona. All we have left of his writings are about 160 lines of a poem called "Nature," written for his illustrious student Zeno (whom you will meet in the next section) and preserved in the writings of later philosophers such as

Sextus Empiricus. His style, no doubt influenced by Pythagorean mysticism, owes more to earlier myths and allegories designed as much to stupefy and mislead the uninitiated as to pass on to other initiates the secret teachings of the wise and enlightened masters.

Thus in the prologue to the poem, written in hexameters, he describes a journey from darkness upward into the light; beyond both realms he finds the goddess who instructs him into the ultimate truth:

⚶

Nature (Prologue)

The mares that draw me as far as my heart would go escorted me, when the goddesses who were driving set me on the renowned road that leads through all cities the man who knows. Along this I was borne; for along it the wise horses drew at full stretch the chariot, and maidens led the way. The axle, urged round by the whirling wheels at either end, shrilled in its sockets and glowed, as the daughters of the sun, leaving the house of night and pushing the veils from their heads, hastened to escort me towards the light.

There are the gates of the ways of night and day, enclosed by a lintel and a threshold of stone; and these, high in the ether, are fitted with great doors, and avenging Justice holds the keys which control these ways. The maidens entreated her with gentle words, and wisely persuaded her to thrust back quickly the bolts of the gate. The leaves of the door, swinging back, made a yawning gap as the brazen pins on either side turned in their sockets. Straight through them, along the broad way, the maidens guided mares and chariot; and the goddess received me kindly, and taking my right hand in hers spoke these words to me:

"Welcome, youth, who come attended by immortal charioteers and mares which bear you on your journey to our dwelling. For it is no evil fate that has set you to travel on this road, far from the beaten paths of men, but right and justice. It is meet that

From *An Introduction to Early Greek Philosophy*, J. M. Robinson (New York: Houghton Mifflin, 1968).

you learn all things—both the unshakable heart of well-rounded truth and the opinions of mortals in which there is no true belief. But these, too, you must learn completely, seeing that appearances have to be acceptable, since they pervade everything."

The unnamed goddess (identified by his students variously as "Wisdom" and "Nature") has instructed Parmenides to learn all things, both truth, which is absolutely certain, and the varying opinions among human beings among which there can be no truth. There are, she tells him, only three ways mortals have of getting at the truth. The first is to assert that, "*It is not,* and there must be not-being." But this is impossible and forbidden, for what is not cannot even be thought of. The second way open to unwise mortals is to say of being—to speak of "what is"—that both "it is and is not," "is the same and not the same." (This presumably is the Heraclitean way.) The third and correct path to truth is to start from the proposition "*It is,* and not-being is impossible."

The Way of Truth

Come now, and I will tell thee—and do thou hearken and carry my word away—the only ways of enquiry that can be thought of: the one way, that it is and cannot not-be, is the path of Persuasion, for it attends upon Truth; the other, that it *is-not* and needs must not-be, that I tell thee is a path altogether unthinkable. For thou couldst not know that which is-not (that is impossible) nor utter it; for the same thing can be thought as can be [construction as above, literally the same thing exists for thinking and for being].

That which can be spoken and thought needs must be: for it is possible for it, but not for nothing, to be; that is what I bid thee yonder. This is the first way of enquiry from which I hold thee

From G. S. Kirk and J. E. Raven, *The Presocratic Philosophers* (New York: Cambridge University Press, 1957).

back, and then from that way, also on which mortals wander knowing nothing, two-headed; for helplessness guides the wandering thought in their breasts; they are carried along, deaf and blind at once, altogether dazed—hordes devoid of judgment, who are persuaded that to be and to be-not are the same, yet not the same, and that of all things the path is backward-turning.

For never shall this be proved, that things that are not are; but do thou hold back thy thought from this way of enquiry, nor let custom, born of much experience, force thee to let wander along this road thy aimless eye, thy echoing ear or thy tongue; but do thou judge by reason the strife-encompassed proof that I have spoken.

One way only is left to be spoken of, that it *is*; and on this way are full many signs that what *is* is uncreated and imperishable, for it is entire, immovable and without end. It *was* not in the past, nor *shall* it be, since it *is* now, all at once, one, continuous; for what creation wilt thou seek for it? how and whence did it grow? Nor shall I allow thee to say or to think, "from that which is not"; for it is not to be said or thought that it is not. And what need would have driven it on to grow, starting from nothing, at a later time rather than an earlier? Thus it must either completely be or be not.

The central idea here is that while it seems we can start out by thinking either about what is or about what is not, in truth we cannot think about what is not. We can only think about what is. Whatever we think about is, itself, an object of thought. That is what Parmenides means when he identifies *thought* and *being* as one and the same. Thoughts—even the thought, "Unicorns exist"— have being, regardless of whether the things we think about exist independently of our thoughts. When we think that unicorns exist, we are merely thinking something false about what exists; we are not thereby thinking of not-being. The point is that not-being is not a possible object of thought. So, since nothing is not, we must reject the first of the three possible ways of inquiry into truth.

Likewise, we must reject the second possible way of inquiry, advocated by Heraclitus, that to say of "what is" that it is "the same and not the same." This erroneous way of thinking is brought about by seduction of the mind by the appearances, which are illusory. We must instead, Parmenides urges, go beyond the sense in which Heraclitus evoked reason, to rely solely on reason and to deny the reality of what our senses tell us is true of the world:

🐦

The Way of Truth (*Continued*)

Nor will the force of credibility ever admit that anything should come into being, beside Being itself, out of Not-Being. So far as that is concerned, justice has never released (*Being*) in its fetters and set it free either to come into being or to perish, but holds it fast. The decision on these matters depends on the following: IT IS, or IT IS NOT. It is therefore decided—as is inevitable—(*that one must*) ignore the one way as unthinkable and inexpressible (for it is no true way) and take the other as the way of Being and Reality. How could Being perish? How could it come into being? If it came into being, it Is Not; and so too if it is about-to-be at some future time. Thus Coming-into-Being is quenched, and Destruction also into the unseen.

Nor is Being divisible, since it is all alike. Nor is there anything (*here or*) there which could prevent it from holding together, nor any lesser thing, but all is full of Being. Therefore it is altogether continuous; for Being is close to Being.

But it is motionless in the limits of mighty bonds, without beginning, without cease, since Becoming and Destruction have been driven very far away, and true conviction has rejected them. And remaining the same in the same place, it rests by itself and thus remains there fixed; for powerful Necessity holds it in the bonds of a Limit, which constrains it round about, because it is decreed by divine law that Being shall not be without boundary. For it is not lacking; but if it were (*spatially infinite*), it would be lacking everything.

To think is the same as the thought that It Is; for

From *Ancilla to the Pre-Socratic Philosophers*, Kathleen Freeman, trans. (Oxford: Basil Blackwell, 1947).

you will not find thinking without Being, in (*regard to*) which there is an expression. For nothing else either is or shall be except Being, since Fate has tied it down to be a whole and motionless; therefore all things that mortals have established, believing in their truth, are just a name: Becoming and Perishing, Being and Non-Being, and Change of position, and alteration of bright colour.

But since there is a (*spatial*) Limit, it is complete on every side, like the mass of a well-rounded sphere, equally balanced from its centre in every direction; for it is not bound to be at all either greater or less in this direction or that; nor is there Not-Being which could check it from reaching to the same point, nor is it possible for Being to be more in this direction, less in that, than Being, because it is an inviolate whole. For, in all directions equal to itself, it reaches its limits uniformly.

At this point I cease my reliable theory (*Logos*) and thought, concerning Truth; from here onwards you must learn the opinions of mortals, listening to the deceptive order of my words.

🐦

So the true character of the Cosmos, of the world as a whole, reality as it exists in and of itself, is revealed in Parmenides' vision in the following terms:

1. It is uncreated.
2. It is permanent and unchangeable.
3. It is whole, indivisible, and everywhere continuous.
4. It is identical with the thought that recognizes it.

Thus all the things that our ordinary, common-sense conception predicates of reality—generation and destruction, being and not-being, change of position, change in qualities—are nothing more than illusions. It is to this strange possibility that we now turn.

1.11 Zeno of Elea (490–430 B.C.E.): The Way of Paradox

Enter Zeno of Elea. It is one thing to come down off the mountaintop or out of the desert and make mystical proclamations to your fellow human beings about the world, truth, and the nature of ultimate reality—especially when much of what you have to say flies in the face of common sense. It is quite another to offer *proof*—not in terms of miracles, holy scriptures, reliance on any kind of authority, or hearsay, but in terms of explicit, logical, rational, even mathematical, demonstration. We already encountered such a method when we considered the explicit example of Pythagoras's famous theorem. Parmenides, who for a time was initiated into both the Pythagorean mysteries and their mathematical methods, no doubt passed on his teachings to his leading student, Zeno (who may or may not have been part of the Pythagorean training). In any case, Zeno came armed not with allegory or myth but with a mathematically precise demonstration that things were not as they seemed.

Observe the world around you and you find yourself automatically engaged in concepts like place or position, time, distance, size or measurement, and a combination of these concepts called *motion*. Motion, in turn, involves the concept of identity: *one and the same* object is thought to occupy different *places* at different *times*. Thus, your most simple, commonsense beliefs about ordinary objects moving from one place to another involve some of the most complex and deepest philosophical concepts: space, time, and identity. Ordinarily, however, you do not think about these concepts. You just use them.

It is important to point out that *all* of these are concepts. Probably you do not think of space, time, and identity as concepts at all but as "realities." That is, you think of them as realities that exist "out there" in the world independently of the mind. This, however, is a belief that you will see questioned and even explicitly denied, philosopher after philosopher, century after century. Not all philosophers deny that there exists a mind-independent reality. Only some do, and usually they are called "idealists" or "phenomenalists." But even most of those

who don't (that is, those who are not idealists or phenomenalists) will acknowledge in no uncertain terms that the objects of your perceptions—the things *seen* (that is, the images you are aware of but which you take to be objects outside you)—are not things as they exist in themselves but, at most, visual and tactile representations of things as they exist outside the mind. We shall explore all these things in much more detail as we progress through the history and development of these ideas over the last two and a half millennia. For now, let us merely focus on that aspect of this strange and intriguing idea as it was evoked, probably for the first time, in a demonstrative form by Zeno. The world has never been the same. Indeed, Zeno's arguments have confounded philosophers, mathematicians, and scientists to the present day.

Zeno supported Parmenides' philosophy with several arguments against the possibility of the key central concept of *motion*. The influence of these paradoxes on philosophical, mathematical, and scientific thought has been significant and continuous. As the twentieth-century philosopher Alfred North Whitehead notes, "No one has ever touched Zeno without refuting him, and every century thinks it worthwhile to refute him." This is deeply ironic since once something is refuted, we do not need to keep refuting it. As Albert Einstein once wrote in response to the book *100 Authors Against Einstein,* "If I were wrong, then one would have been enough!" Indeed, more solutions have been offered to Zeno's paradoxes than just about any other; some rely on philosophical argument, some on scientific theories about the nature of space and time, and some on mathematical methods such as summing infinite series, calculus, and even (in the latest form) something called "nonstandard set theory." All of these attempted solutions, I think, fail. But let us first see exactly what the problem is.

We have seen Parmenides assert that the world ultimately consists not of individual things but that, in reality, "all is one." When we use the light of reason to glimpse behind the shimmering, illusory veil of appearance, we apprehend the cosmos as one undifferentiated, unchanging, eternal whole. Even the simplest change, such as one thing moving from one place to another, is but an illusion. One of Parmenides' main arguments was: if the whole of existence is *not* one (if the cosmos is made of different things), then what separates one thing from another? Parmenides concluded that the supposed separation between one thing and another would have to consist in something that does not exist—that is, nothing—and that this would be an absurdity. If we suppose that there are two things between which there is nothing, then these are not two things but one thing.

Zeno tried to *prove* Parmenides right. Zeno focused on the fundamental concepts previously mentioned. He presented about forty paradoxes, each of which was designed to show that those who claimed Parmenides' view was absurd were starting from an even *more* absurd view! Only a handful of his paradoxes have survived the twenty-five centuries since Zeno posed them, and here we discuss only the "Dichotomy," one of his paradoxes of motion.

1.11.1 The Dichotomy

Zeno begins by assuming, for the sake of argument, that things are pretty much as they seem to you right now: there exist different places and objects at those places, and objects can move from one place to another. He then poses the following puzzle:

Achilles starts running from a starting position toward a finish line. Before he reaches the finish line he must go half the distance. Achilles must then also go half of the remaining distance. And then he must go half of the distance that still remains. And so on. This is pictured in Figure 3.

Suppose Achilles starts running at a constant speed toward the finish line one mile away. Obviously, before he runs the whole mile he must run $\frac{1}{2}$ mile. After he has gone $\frac{1}{2}$ mile, he cannot just suddenly appear at the finish line without first crossing half the *remaining* $\frac{1}{2}$ mile—that is, he must go $\frac{3}{4}$ of the distance from the starting point. When he has run $\frac{3}{4}$ mile, there is $\frac{1}{4}$ mile remaining but, again, he can't just appear at the finish line without going halfway between the mark and the finish line. When Achilles is only $\frac{1}{8}$ mile away from the finish line, he must still run halfway between where he is at the moment and the finish line. At that point Achilles will be only $\frac{1}{16}$ mile from the finish line. But, again, he can't run $\frac{1}{16}$ mile without first going one-half of that $\frac{1}{16}$ mile. And so on. "To say it once," as Zeno was fond of putting it, "is to say it forever."

Is there any remaining distance, at *any* point in the run, where Achilles can reach the finish

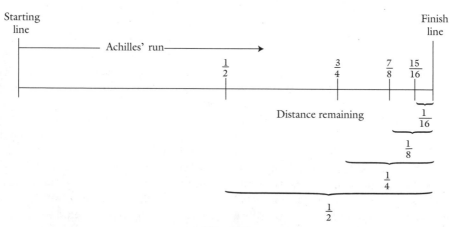

Figure 3

line *without first running halfway between wherever he is and where the finish line is?* Of course not. How *long* can he proceed this way? Forever! Wherever Achilles is between the starting line and the finish line, there will always be some distance remaining between him and the finish line. So: *How is it possible for Achilles to ever reach the finish line?*

Achilles *does* appear at the finish line. Things *do* get from one place to another. That's what our eyes tell us! Reason says otherwise. If we think carefully about what we are seeing, we will understand that what *seems* to be going on can't *really* be going on—at least not in the way we think!

To address this paradox we must give it a precise formulation so that instead of merely intuitively feeling that there is a paradox (a psychological sense of dissonance), we can precisely identify the discrepancy. Let us therefore restate the problem more formally. Let A denote any starting point, and let B denote the endpoint—in this case, the finish line. We know that Achilles must, before he appears at the finish line, be at the point halfway between A and B. Call this halfway point between A and B, B_1. To say this is not to divide the space between A and B, nor to "halve the distance"; it is merely to give a name to a point that must be there. B_1 is there whether we name it or not. That is, we are not performing some loaded manipulative move; we are not in any way changing the distance between A and B; we are merely bringing out of our conceptual framework that which, implicitly, already is there in the path between any two points, A and B.

Our concept of the path taken by Achilles involves an ordering of the path between Achilles at the starting position at A and the finish line at B, as follows. There is a point halfway between A and B, B_1, such that Achilles' path is ordered so that B_1 comes after A and before B. There is a point, halfway between B_1 and B, and let us call this point B_2. There is a point halfway between B_2 and B, B_3. And so on (Figure 4) forever.

Suppose Achilles is at B_{1099}, the point halfway between B_{1098} and B. Between B_{1099} and B is a point, B_{1100}; Achilles at B_{1099} cannot just suddenly, without cause and for no reason, vanish out of existence and pop into existence at B! He must move along a continuous path through the midpoint. But there is *always* another midpoint remaining!

That Achilles could never arrive at B is implied in our description of how he arrives at the finish line, which evokes the necessity of an *infinite process*. To get from any point to any other he must have gone through an infinite number of halfway points. Thus, there are infinitely many B_n: B_1, B_2, B_3, . . . , B_{1099}, B_{1100}, · . . , B_n, ...

If you are not sufficiently puzzled yet, then note that even if B_1 were eliminated from the discussion and all the other B_n were kept in the discussion, it would have no effect whatsoever on Zeno's paradox: none! Similarly, for any finite number of B_n: no matter where he begins prior to B, Achilles only reaches the finish line at B after passing through infinitely many B_n. For instance, if Achilles starts at B_{1786} and starts running toward B, you would have exactly the same paradox as before. But we should also note that where before we had a mere psychological sense of puzzlement concerning Achilles running toward a finish line, we now have a specific set of concepts within our conceptual framework to which this paradox can be addressed and to

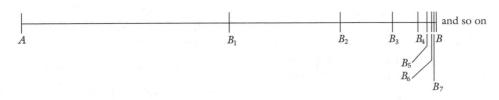

Figure 4

which we must turn our rational attention. For this applies to *any* distance between *any* two points. Note that what we are seeing here is not merely that "there is something wrong with our conceptual framework." We see exactly what parts of the conceptual framework appear to be out of whack (as opposed to the general feeling that "something is out of whack").

You probably believe things move and runners reach finish lines. Zeno is not claiming that experience is not that way. He is claiming that the nature of our experience is conceptually problematic. For instance, if you tried to refute Zeno by running across the room, he would probably just shake his head and tell you that you have misunderstood his paradox, for had you *not* been able to run across the room *then there would be no paradox!* The point is that what you (think you) *see* and what you (think you) think lead you to form particular beliefs about the way things actually are, but that a closer examination of the concepts behind your beliefs contradicts those very beliefs! Thus, Zeno's paradox is an argument against your ordinary beliefs about the way things are. Indeed, the word *paradox* means, literally, "beyond (*para*) belief (*doxa*)." And it is your own (often hidden) conceptions of the way things are that generate this paradox.

Note that Zeno's paradox directly examines the question of what there is between one place (the starting point) and another (the finish line). Thus, this addresses Parmenides' question of what separates one thing from another in a specific way. Notice, too, that this question is posed precisely and in mathematical terms: Zeno discusses *quantified* distances.

Zeno's paradox makes us question whether our beliefs regarding what is going on in the world can be made coherent using our concepts of motion, points, continuous lines, space, time, change, identity, and so on. In implying that you don't know how motion is possible, what is at issue, ultimately, in Zeno's paradox, is the entire basis of the concepts we use in developing our knowledge of the world.

1.11.2 A False Solution

One of the most common types of solutions to this paradox relies on trying to apply sophisticated mathematical techniques of calculation to the problem of the ever-remaining gap between wherever Achilles is at any moment and wherever he is at the next moment. For instance, one solution commonly offered relies on a method based on techniques developed by the brilliant nineteenth-century mathematical wizard J. C. F. Gauss (1777–1855). The series of terms expressed in Zeno's paradox can be expressed as a series of ever-decreasing lengths, whose sum, S, is:

$$S = \tfrac{1}{2} + \tfrac{1}{4} + \tfrac{1}{8} + \tfrac{1}{16} + \tfrac{1}{32} + \tfrac{1}{64} + \cdots$$

$$2S = 1 + \tfrac{1}{2} + \tfrac{1}{4} + \tfrac{1}{8} + \tfrac{1}{16} + \tfrac{1}{32} + \cdots$$

$$2S - 1 = \tfrac{1}{2} + \tfrac{1}{4} + \tfrac{1}{8} + \tfrac{1}{16} + \cdots$$

But notice that on the right side of the equation we have exactly what we started with. Therefore,

$$S = 2S - 1$$

and so $S = 1$. So what's the problem?

Well, one problem is that this mathematical solution works only by a sort of clever accident. Many writers on this topic do not realize that Zeno could have made things much more difficult by posing his questions in terms of going $\tfrac{1}{3}$ of the distance instead of going $\tfrac{1}{2}$ the distance. Then one must go a distance as long as the previous distance traveled, $\tfrac{1}{9}$ of the full distance, and so on. In the $\tfrac{1}{2}$s case, each increment is $\tfrac{1}{2}$ of the previous increment. This is the same as going $\tfrac{1}{2}$ of the remaining distance. In the $\tfrac{1}{3}$'s case, it is not the same as going $\tfrac{1}{2}$ of the remaining distance. For instance, at the second increment, Achilles goes $\tfrac{1}{3}$ of the previous distance but only $\tfrac{1}{6}$ of the remaining distance. Thus, going by $\tfrac{1}{3}$'s would have forced us to consider the following infinite sum:

$$S = \tfrac{1}{3} + \tfrac{1}{9} + \tfrac{1}{27} + \tfrac{1}{81} + \cdots$$

Here, if we follow the same procedure as earlier, we get $S = 3S - 1$ and thus: $S = \frac{1}{2}$. This means that the runner gets only $\frac{1}{2}$ of the way to the finish line! The $\frac{1}{2}$ marks, even though there are an infinite number of them, would not extend to the finish line. Thus, we see that Zeno posed an infinite series problem of minimum difficulty! If you pose one of greater difficulty (or refine the paradox slightly differently, as I shall do shortly) Zeno's paradox cannot be solved in this way.

Other, even more sophisticated types of mathematical solutions have been offered, from calculus to the latest versions of nonstandard set theory (we cannot fully go into them in this book, since refuting such solutions often requires equally sophisticated mathematical techniques).[6] What we can do, however, is perform the following thought experiment to focus our attention even further into the question of what separates one thing from another and illustrate in an intuitively clear way exactly why Zeno's paradox cannot ever, even in principle, be solved.

Let us begin by taking a look at our Zeno diagram in Figure 5. As the n in the B_n get larger and larger the B_n get closer and closer to B and it becomes increasingly more difficult to draw, see, or imagine (the final endpoint) the tiny gaps between B_n and B for the successively larger n. Let us assume that we are drawing our Zeno diagram with a pencil of thickness 1 millimeter (mm). Then, when the gaps between B_n and B are smaller than 1 mm, we do the following. Through our conceptual microscope we take a picture of the 1-mm remaining part of the Zeno diagram—say at B_5. We now have an enlarged picture of the gap between B_5 and B. If the length of the remaining interval between Achilles and the finish line at B is 1 meter, the enlargement is also 1 meter and to scale: It is a

"blowup" (like the "blowup" feature used in photo enlargements).

Now that the picture is blown up, we can continue to use our 1-mm pencil to mark off further B_n until once again—this time at B_{10}—we will have to use our conceptual microscope to take another picture that will be a blowup of the gap between B_{10} and B. It should be intuitively obvious that we can continue this process forever; since there are infinitely many B_n, we can make infinitely many diagrams. Our Zeno diagram was constructed to examine the path of any moving object: in this case Achilles. When we used the infinite series our attention was focused on the distance traveled, that is, what was being added up. Let us focus our attention now on the gap itself, that is, on the distance between Achilles and the finish line.

Our story begins back in the Lyceum. Zeno has just finished posing his paradox of motion to a group who have been ridiculing Parmenides' view that all is one. Turning to Achilles, their leader, Zeno says:

"You make fun of Parmenides because you think you are so wise. You think you know where space, time, and motion are; but I have just shown that you merely *think* you know! You say Parmenides' views are absurd because they contradict what your eyes tell you. But your view is the far more absurd view, for you contradict yourself! If a wise man is someone who knows how little he knows, obviously, Achilles, you are anything but wise—you are just the opposite!"

Insulted, Achilles orders his men to seize Zeno.

"Enough," cries Achilles. "I will now defeat both you and your arguments, Zeno!"

Achilles orders his strongest warriors to form a gauntlet, or corridor, that ends at a wall, with Zeno in the middle. Achilles begins at one end

Figure 5

and starts running after Zeno, who, when he reaches the wall, will be crushed between the wall and Achilles' shield.

Unbeknown to any of them, however, Zeus has been watching the proceedings from a cloud:

"Hera, come and watch how these brutes think to dismiss the magical query, which against my wishes you have thrown down to the mortal philosophers. You said it would make them think, but look! Our poor Zeno's skull is about to be crushed. What a shame. I was hoping we would have millennia of long and lasting amusement at the mortals' attempt to reconcile their contradictory points of view. You have overestimated these foolish mortals. How often have you heard them dismiss the greatest mysteries as simply being mysteries? How their poets go on and on, ad nauseum, about their wonderful lack of explanation! Your game will end up but a beautifully unenlightening poem, and Zeno will be crushed."

"I have already taken care of it."

"What have you done, my dear and clever wife?"

"Watch, dear, and be amazed."

Achilles takes up his shield and begins running toward the wall with Zeno between the shield and the wall. When Achilles is 1 meter away from the wall, Zeno puts his right hand up to block against the shield and his left hand up to brace himself against the wall, thinking this might help prevent him from being crushed when, suddenly, he begins to shrink! When the distance between Achilles' shield and the wall has halved, Zeno has shrunk by one-half. When the distance between the shield and the wall is $\frac{1}{4}$ meter, Zeno has shrunk by one-quarter. And so on. When the distance between the shield and the wall is $\frac{1}{128}$ meter, Zeno has shrunk down to $\frac{1}{128}$ scale. And Zeno keeps shrinking such that as the distance is $\frac{1}{2}^n$ meters, Zeno has shrunk down to $\frac{1}{2}^n$ scale. By the moment Achilles has smashed his shield into the wall, Zeno is nowhere to be seen!

Up in the clouds, Zeus turns to Hera and says, "You must feel very little for your bold young student Zeno, my dear wife, that you should wish him to suffer so sincerely for your folly."

"Bold indeed, but why so certain that he suffers? That mighty warrior's shield did not crush him. Nor was there suffering upon his countenance while he was visible. And this is exactly all that is certain, for he is no longer visible! It is your gloating that hides suffering so insincerely. Were you sincere you would surely recognize that I have bequeathed us all a query worthy of great deliberation and which I am certain will only vindicate my Zeno and make your gloating but a fool's solution to a mystery worthy of even us gods."

Let us look at the situation more closely. We begin with Achilles' shield at point A 1 meter from the wall and Zeno standing between the shield at A and the wall at B, his arms extended between the shield and the wall (see Figure 6).

Let us examine the situation from Zeno's point of view between the shield and the wall. Doing so will help us discover the source of Hera's confidence.

As Hera pointed out in our story, from the point of view of the outside observers the shield never crushes Zeno. What about from Zeno's point of view? As he begins to shrink he sees Achilles' shield getting larger and larger. By the time Achilles' shield is at, say, $B_{11,000}$, the surface of the shield is still only just barely touching the surface of Zeno's right hand, but the shield is now so big compared with Zeno's body that it looks to him like a giant wall reaching all the way up and all the way down as far as he can see. At the same time, the wall that his left palm is just barely touching seems to go upward forever and downward forever. From Zeno's point of view, the spectators in the Lyceum are even farther away than the already unseen receding base of Achilles' shield; thus they are virtually infinitely far away. Therefore, at this point, *Zeno will observe no further changes in his visual field whatsoever.* From Zeno's point of view, nothing is happening! Nothing else is moving. There is a virtually infinite shield on his right and a virtually infinite wall on his left. If there ever was some process going on, from his point of view it has stopped (see Figure 7).

Let us now go back to the point of view of the gloating spectators and the unworried Hera. When Achilles' shield first touches Zeno's right hand, the spectators see Zeno shrink. As Achilles' shield approaches the wall they still see Zeno getting smaller and smaller until at some instant before the shield hits the wall Zeno virtually disappears from their sight. At that point they conclude that Zeno must have been crushed when the shield smashed into the wall. Since the spectators see the shield smash into the wall, from their point of view there is no gap. There is no space in which Zeno's extended body can extend and therefore no space in which for him to exist as a real entity. Where, then, is Zeno?

The spectators conclude that Zeno has disappeared and, in some sense, they are right. They cannot see him. And no physical microscope, regardless of how powerful, could allow Zeno to be seen because, after all, his size is 0. Zero multiplied by any (finite) number is still 0. An (extensionless) point magnified by any (finite)

magnification is still an extensionless point. From the spectators' point of view alone, Zeno has indeed disappeared.

Since we are aware that there are two points of view here—the spectators' and Zeno's—we should address the question of their (in)commensurability. For it is the question of the (in)commensurability of these two points of view that *refines* Zeno's paradox.

Does it make sense, from Zeno's point of view, that at some moment *he* disappears? As we have seen at all moments during which the process is still happening from his point of view, (1) he still exists as an extended being, (2) except for Achilles' shield and the wall, which still exist in their virtually infinitely enlarged form, the spectators, the Lyceum, and all the rest of the world have disappeared, and (3) nothing is happening in that the picture is static

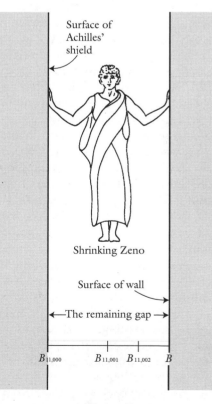

Figure 7

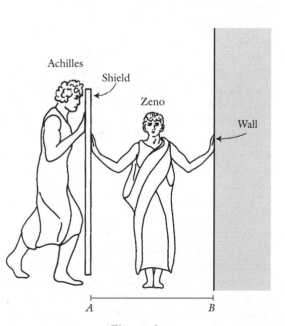

Figure 6

for Zeno, just as the picture is static for the spectators once Achilles' shield hits the wall. So Zeno's understanding of the suggestion that he disappeared would have to be described, from his point of view, as a "popping out of the universe" *for no reason whatsoever*; that is, no reasons from within his point of view could possibly explain a popping out of the universe. For Zeno to understand how it is possible that he disappears he not only would have to favor the spectators' point of view—which would be a strange thing given that from within his point of view it is they who have disappeared, not him—he would have to give up the reasons available to him within his point of view and accept reasons from a point of view to which he has no access.

That is, we can imagine Zeno thinking, as he is shrinking: "My friend Hera has saved me by enlarging the spectators and the universe out of existence!" The idea of something that shrinks continuously (and self-similarly, retaining its same shape) shrinking suddenly and spontaneously out of existence and the idea of something that enlarges continuously (and self-similarly) being suddenly and spontaneously enlarged out of existence are equally unjustified (or, even, equally justified) but (in either case) they are incommensurate. They are incommensurate because the only way it would make sense for Zeno to think that he ever disappears from the universe is for him to think that from the point of view of the spectators at some point he disappears. But, once again, from his point of view it is they who at some point do in fact disappear.

These "popping out of existence" alternatives are incommensurate. To himself, Zeno still exists and from his point of view there can be no reason to simply decree that he suddenly and spontaneously stops existing. It is also as equally unjustified to decree that the spectators in the Lyceum spontaneously vanish from the universe, just to make things consistent with Zeno's point of view. Someone could say that, from each other's point of view, the other disappears. But how then would we reconcile these two appar-

ently irreconcilable, noncommensurate points of view?

If from each point of view, taken separately, it is true to say that the other pops out of existence, then a fundamental revision of our most basic concept of existence is required; it would entail that Zeno's paradox reaches into the very heart of existence—that existence itself is somehow paradoxical.

If the shrinking Zeno paradox is to be successfully addressed, we must reconcile the two apparently incommensurate points of view, and not simply and arbitrarily pick one point of view over the other. Either we take the spectators' point of view and conclude for no sufficient reason that Zeno's body has become an extensionless point, B, or we can take Zeno's point of view and conclude without sufficient reason that the spectators occupy no position on the floor of the Lyceum, since they are infinitely far away from Zeno.[7] Each alternative makes sense relative to the relevant points of view considered separately. But the two points of view are incommensurate and mutually exclusive.

Let us therefore instead of dismissing Zeno from the realm of existence rejoin him on his journey. More than a second of time has gone by and he knows that, since Achilles is traveling at 1 meter per second, Achilles' shield relative to the spectators' point of view has indeed reached the wall. From Zeno's point of view, now after a second, he is there with the (now not merely virtually but *actually*) infinitely large shield touching his right palm, the wall touching his left palm. From his own point of view Zeno knows that the spectators seem to have disappeared but have not actually disappeared. He reasons as follows. "I know it is my own point of view that dictates that the spectators will become infinitely far away from me when I become (from their point of view) an extensionless point. I also know when the spectators become infinitely far away from me, Achilles' shield will have grown infinitely large and therefore any part of it will be infinitely large. But, by Zeus, how then could I possibly continue to see a shield, or myself for that matter, or anything at all?"

I will now, as Zeno did, ask a perplexing question: How can it be that Achilles' moving shield ever makes contact with the wall at *B*? I want to focus your attention on what the gap is like from our shrinking Zeno's point of view. Immediately we notice that from his point of view Achilles' shield is not moving. Indeed, within the gap, *nothing is happening whatsoever.* This is because as the shield (from Achilles' point of view) gets closer to the wall, from Zeno's point of view they always remain an arm's length apart. If he were to look up and to the sides he would see the lines extending farther and farther upward. However, he does not see or feel the walls moving.

If we construct blowups as before, the pictures will be exactly the same except the shield and wall get taller. Note, too, that there is a (virtual) variant from picture to picture. If each picture were a movie of the moving Achilles, then if Achilles moves at the constant velocity of 1 meter per second (as described in the original Zeno diagram) then his shield would be seen through the microscope to be traveling 32 times faster in each subsequent diagram. For example, the surface of the shield facing Zeno would be seen to be moving at 32 meters per second in the first enlargement, 32^2 meters per second in the second enlargement, 32^3 meters per second in the third enlargement, and 32^n meters per second in the nth enlargement.

When n is sufficiently large, Achilles' shield will *seem* to be moving faster than light. Technically, this is neither an illusion nor a hallucination, since the image being seen is an actual image; it is *not* like the case of the drunk who sees pink elephants. And yet what is being seen is not the actual motion of the shield which, after all, is at any point in its journey from *A* to *B* traveling at 1 meter per second. It is the motion of one part of an image relative to other parts of the image. This raises the philosophical question of what makes some images virtual, or only images, and some images the images of things that are seen and therefore "real." The problem, in other words, is that supposedly one kind of motion we are seeing is real motion of real things, while other motions we are seeing are only the motions of images that—while they

do correspond, by the rule of enlargement, to something real—are themselves not real. The virtual motion of Achilles' shield in our enlargements, however, does not in actuality exceed the speed of light.

It is obvious that we are beginning our journey deep into the tail end of the sequence of B_n. In a sense, we have constructed a conceptual microscope through which we can see something that we understand as a place beyond all the halfway marks and yet before the wall. Our conceptual microscope is already in place through our consideration of enlargement diagrams that picture our shrinking Zeno. The problem here is that these intervals collapse to a point in the limit. But a point does not fit conceptually into the pattern of our diagrams. That is, a point is obviously qualitatively different from an interval in that a point is not the sort of thing that can be further divided.

But how can this be? We know that since Achilles is moving at 1 meter per second, and the wall is 1 meter away, that from Achilles' point of view after exactly one second the shield makes contact with the wall (that is, there is no space between them). We also know that from Zeno's point of view there is no reason whatsoever that the shield and the wall should *ever* make contact. This is the very essence of our refined paradox. We know, from one point of view, that it is absolutely *necessary* that contact happens and that, from the other point of view, it is *impossible* that contact ever happens!

Our shrinking Zeno paradox does not *add* anything to the distance between *A* and *B*. It merely illuminates, via a sort of conceptual microscope, what is already there and what is already paradoxical. It does, however, in a sense add something to the *conceptual* space between *A* and *B*. It forces us to add that strange place where our shrinking Zeno is to our conception of space. An infinitesimal calculus would offer some solution to this paradox by adding the place where Zeno now is to our concept of space, thereby creating a new mathematical spatial object. And though the shrinking Zeno paradox alters Zeno's original form of his paradoxes, the key issues remain the same. The solution offered to the original paradox had eliminated the issue of infinite process—finite distance. The shrinking Zeno paradox does not depend on the infinite–finite issue. However, the key issue that the gap between two things is paradoxical—Parmenides' question of what separates one thing from another—is preserved. Thus, it is indeed right to call the shrinking Zeno paradox Zeno's paradox. *And it cannot be solved by summing the series nor by standard calculus.*

We now have a real problem on our hands! The problem is this. From his own point of view, Zeno has not disappeared; therefore, he is somewhere. From the spectators' point of view, he has disappeared. Therefore, as far as they are concerned, he is nowhere. What does it mean to say that *X* is somewhere? It means that *X* is in a containing space. To have a location is to be embedded in a space. Well, what about shrinking Zeno? Where is he? How can we attribute to him the kind of somewhereness that we usually attribute to things? Can we say that he is in the Lyceum? From his point of view, he is infinitely far away from anything in the Lyceum. Furthermore, if you looked through the Lyceum for him, even armed with the most (finitely) powerful microscope in the world, you would not find him there.

Yet, we could say that his hand is near the rest of his body and that it is on the wall rather than, say, on his forehead. This is puzzling because the people in the Lyceum are also near the wall! One problem with the idea that Zeno is somewhere is that the surface of the wall and the surface of the shield are in contact—so how can Zeno's right hand be on Achilles' shield and his left hand be on the wall? If the shield and the wall are in contact, there is no space between them!

Asking where shrinking Zeno is, is in some ways like asking: *Where are the points of space?* Even with our most powerful microscope, you will not be able to find them. Yet they are somewhere: there, in *that* location and not in some other.

Obviously, the shrinking Zeno paradox examines the idea of motion differently from the paradox of Achilles running the racecourse. Instead of looking at a distance and examining what happens across a distance, the shrinking Zeno paradox focuses on motion at one instant of time in one point of space—as does Zeno's original paradox of the arrow. If an arrow is moving, then it is moving at each instant of time and at each point along a path. Time is conceived of as being made of moments and space is conceived of as being made of points (places). How can you find the motion in each instant and place occupied at that instant? You can't. At each moment the arrow is where it is. At each moment the arrow is the same as a stationary arrow at the same instant in the same place. Zeno's paradox of the arrow is that if you can't find the motion in the units of which time and space are made, then how can it be possible to find it in time and space? If John is not at any place in this room, then how can he be in this room?

Calculus (see pages 270–273) addresses the problem of instantaneous motion through the idea of a derivative. The concept of a derivative depends on the idea of intervals collapsing on a point—*as in our shrinking Zeno paradox.* Thus, the shrinking Zeno paradox shows that Zeno's original paradoxes of motion have not really been solved. Asking where our shrinking Zeno is, is to ask where the points of space are and, ultimately, to inquire into the deeply mysterious question of what space is made of.

After all, where are the spectators in the Lyceum? If you ask our shrinking Zeno, he cannot see them and he could not see them through any telescope, no matter how powerful. From Zeno's point of view they are nowhere! Again, each could say "I am here where I am." They would point to things available to their point of view and say they are near those things. But once again there is a problem with the idea of where things are with respect to the two incommensurate points of view.

Ever since Zeno posed his original paradoxes, subsequent philosophical reflection on this puzzling gap separating one thing from another has over the centuries challenged both mathematicians and scientists to try and conceptualize the place where our shrinking Zeno is.[8] To thus recognize that Zeno's paradoxes are not solved does not mean that our concepts of space, time, motion, and identity are *worthless* and that we should therefore give up rationality and the pursuit of knowledge. Sometimes the Eleatics are interpreted that way, as extreme skeptics. The point here is to try and understand that narrow path—"thin as a razor"—between, science and mathematics on the one hand, and, on the other, religion, that is the way of philosophy. The philosophical method used by Zeno draws our attention to the paradox, just as the demonstration of the incommensurability of the unit square forced the Pythagoreans to invent new, irrational numbers. This philosophical method gives a precise new way of focusing our attention on the discrepancy both between reality and our concepts and between reality and our perception of reality. To function as rational beings we must have concepts, which are the medium of rational consciousness. Without concepts, there can be no paradox. At the same time, while we must rely on perceptions, we must remember the philosophical wisdom of knowing that our eyes are not windows. That is the point that all the ancient Greek philosophers, from the Ionians and Eleatics to Protagoras and the Sophists, and even Plato (as you shall see in the next chapter), in their various ways tried to make clear. No aspect of our minds, they realized—neither our concepts nor our perceptions—gives us direct access to reality (at least not in the way that we ordinarily think). We must always interpret our experience according to our concepts. Zeno's paradox thus examines the puzzling, unsolved nature of the mysterious relationship between our minds and the world.

Since what is inside our minds is not, and never can be, exactly identical to reality,[9] there will always be paradoxes that must be addressed to improve our understanding of our relationship (or lack thereof) to reality. That is part of the *philosophy* passed down to us from the ancient Greeks.

And yet, at the same time, Zeno intended to use his paradoxes to defend Parmenides. In other words, he apparently believed in the posi-

tive thesis that "all is one," that the world in its entirety consists not in a collection of many things but in one, single, indivisible unity. What, then, in light of Zeno's paradoxes not being solved, ought we to make of Parmenides' claim that "all is one"? Well, Zeno's paradox has just shown us why the commonsense notion of the universe as an ever-changing collection of many things, separated from other things, all constantly moving about in space is, itself, *deeply paradoxical.* And if we were to accept Parmenides' view, then there is still a paradox: namely, why does the world not appear as it is? That is, why do we experience the world as a *many* (or at least *think* we do) instead of as a *one*?

The problem, then, is this. There is what we might call "our *experience* of reality." This is just our experience as it unfolds and which we take (rightly or wrongly) to be *of* reality (*except,* of course, when we are dreaming—a problem that will again jolt the mind in the work of René Descartes). When we think about what reality really is like, even when we do so on the basis of our experience, we often come to the conclusion that reality is vastly different from how it appears to us in experience. Let us call this our "*view* of reality." Thus, one way of stating our current state of philosophical puzzlement, based on our working through Zeno's paradox, is that even if we accept the paradox as a true refutation of our "*experience* of reality," and we accept Zeno's and Parmenides' "*view* of reality," there appears to be no way to reconcile these two opposites. In the next section, we shall consider the first of many subsequent attempts to do exactly that.

1.12 Protagoras (480–410 B.C.E.) and the Sophists: The Way of Relativism

At this point in history the human mind found itself facing a dilemma (literally, "two-forked path") over which philosophers genuinely divided themselves for the next twenty-five centuries, up to the present day. Many superficial philosophical divisions have been drawn by various commentators who, using broad, sweeping generalizations, have relied on labels that artificially accentuate the differences among philosophers in a way that only confounds philosophy. This division has elements of sophism. Ironically, such accentuated divisions tend to give an impression that the sophists were right after all in contending that there is no absolute truth—truth is relative to systems of belief—and that philosophy is impotent when it comes to achieving true and certain knowledge. Such sophomoric thinking (even if it turned out ultimately to be true) only hinders understanding the genuine differences among the philosophers which, as we shall see time and again in this book, are much rarer than is ordinarily believed and tend to be extremely subtle. (The old adage "divide and conquer" is hauntingly appropriate here: the philosophical taxonomy provides a convenient surrogate to philosophical understanding.) The two fundamentally different types of philosophical responses to the problems considered thus far, however, are an example of an unusually unsubtle, extremely monumental, philosophical division.

The first response, taken by the sophists, was to look at all the different and apparently contradictory things the philosophers had said thus far about the world and to conclude on the basis of their differences that there is no single truth about the way that the world is, or that knowledge is impossible, or both. The second response, taken by Democritus and Plato, was to surmise, on the basis of what the philosophies thus far had in common, some new solution to the problems raised that would pave a path to certain, undoubtable knowledge of the truth. Let us look first at the way of the sophists.

The word *sophist* appears in the word *philosophy,* which consists of the Greek *philein*—to love—and *sophia*—wisdom. The word *philosophy* means, literally, "love of wisdom," and *philosopher* means "lover of wisdom." Thus, the early "sophists" were, literally, "wise men." They appeared in the Greek city-states during the fifth century B.C.E. as "traveling teachers for hire," who taught the youth of the aristocracy who aspired to power. With the advent of

democracy in that century, a new and profound power shift had occurred among the ruling class, one that had a definite and positive effect on the birth of philosophy. Whereas before to attain power you had merely to have inherited a political position, wealth, or land, now to attain positions of political authority you had to demonstrate your intellectual skills and earn the right to power. This required skills of argumentation and rhetoric; you had to win your case in open debate. The sophists came from all over the known world—often from non-democratic localities where their brand of disputation had more often than not gotten them in trouble with the authorities—to take advantage of these new freedoms by seeking employment for their knowledge and abilities.

Thus, the word "sophist" did not originally have the pejorative connotation it has today, that of someone who uses a superficial grasp of knowledge and truth to confuse, confound, and manipulate. This connotation is due mainly to the influence of their great adversary, Plato. The sophists came to Athens at a time when no formal education existed, and no provisions were made on the part of the state for the education of the youth. It was not until Plato's Academy—built in part as an alternative to the way of the sophists—that the first university was born. It is still the model of most institutions of higher learning today (see Chapter 2). Up to the time of Plato, education in ancient Greece was for the privileged and the few; the sophists, however, had already begun to tip the balance by teaching anyone—noble or commoner—who could afford their rates. Since success in Athenian society depended on oratory skills and appealing to the masses, the sophists—much like the lawyers of today—became highly sought after by everyone who sought a position of power.

All the sophists had in common the belief that any philosophical position could be argued for persuasively and that the difference between the better and the worse argument depended not on reaching the truth but on the skills of the rhetorician. Their belief, no doubt inspired at least in part by the recent flurry of wildly opposing philosophical viewpoints on everything, was thus predicated on what I will call *epistemological relativism.* Epistemology is that branch of philosophy that deals with the question of what knowledge is, what distinguishes true knowledge from mere true belief, and if and how knowledge can be attained (I shall have a lot more to say about this important and, in many ways, central aspect of philosophy throughout this book). *By epistemological relativism* I simply mean the view that objective, absolute knowledge cannot be had by us and that, at best, who is right and who is wrong is relative to beliefs, persuasion, and so on, rather than being determined solely by the criterion of objective truth.

Small wonder that the greatest opponent to the sophists, Plato, who tried to build a philosophy based on the notion of a single, objective truth along with a system for attaining absolute knowledge, so despised and ridiculed the sophists on exactly this point. Plato was in many ways the founder of what I will call *epistemological objectivism,* the view that there is but one true way that things are and that the truth can be known by us. However, Plato's own teacher, Socrates, was educated by the sophists and originally made his living as one, distinguishing himself at a young age as the most skilled of all the sophists. The one sophist for whom Plato seemed to have great respect, however, probably because of his theory of perception, which in many ways was very similar to Plato's, was Protagoras, to whom Plato devoted an entire dialogue.

Protagoras was born in Abdera, a coastal town in the northernmost hub of the Aegean Sea. Along with Anaxagoras and Zeno of Elea, he enjoyed the patronage of Pericles (495–429 B.C.E.), the enlightened political leader and military general most responsible for the development of the Athenian democracy and the rise of the Greek empire. Protagoras spent most of his adult life traveling throughout the empire, teaching anyone for a fee. His exposure to many different societies, with lots of different customs, laws, and religions, no doubt impressed upon him the vast latitude of ideas that the human

mind could accept as true. Himself a teacher of Pericles, he showed the great leader the extent to which religious and moral codes were based not upon nature or some god-given truth but on socially constructed conventions. Rhetoric, the art of persuasive speech, could and should therefore, according to him, be used to influence people's opinions and change them in ways that great leaders like Pericles could see would be best, at least relative to the interests of the society. In that way he anticipated Plato's concept of the philosopher king.

As the oldest and generally regarded as the wisest of the sophists who came to Athens, Protagoras wielded a huge influence. Like his most famous student Socrates, Protagoras raised doubts in the minds of the youth about the gods, which they had come by tradition to accept, saying, "About the gods, I am not able to know whether they exist or do not exist, nor what they are like in form; for the factors preventing knowledge are many: the obscurity of the subject, and the shortness of human life." What influenced Protagoras more than anything else was the ancient's discovery that we do not directly perceive the external word, something he learned from the Ionians who preceded him. From Thales to Zeno, one point that had been driven home, time and again, was that the mind did not have direct access to the world but only to its own images of the world. Keenly aware of this, and not yet able to try to find a way of transcending such limitations, as Plato and subsequent epistemologists would do, Protagoras summed up his philosophy in his famous proposition: "Man is the measure of all things." This idea was expressed and developed in his book *On Truth,* of which only the first sentence remains: "Of all things the measure is man; of existing things, that they exist; of nonexistent things, that they do not exist."

In Plato's dialogue *Cratylus,* Socrates ponders Protagoras's cryptic meaning. The dialogue is named after another of Socrates' enigmatic sophist teachers, Cratylus, who was such a nihilist (see Gorgias) that not only did he, like Socrates, refuse to write anything down, he refused even to speak. He merely wagged his finger occasionally to acknowledge that it seemed to him that sensations were occurring.

> Socrates: So what is true of existing things, according to Protagoras, is this: what each thing itself is depends on the individual perceiving it. This is what Protagoras means when he says "Man is the measure of all things." The way things appear to me is the way they are for me; the way things appear to you is the way they are for you.

The idea is this. Each of us exists in our own world of appearances. If there are thirty of us in a room, the room each of us sees may to some degree be similar to the room seen by the others, but the images themselves that each of us sees are in each case different. There are, in effect, among our thirty minds, thirty different visual impressions of the room. For some it may be too cold, for others too warm; some find it beautiful, some ugly, some too crowded, and so on. There may be a certain degree of verbal agreement we could reach, but this agreement, Protagoras points out, is subject to alteration through verbal persuasion. In saying that man is the measure of all things, he is saying that your knowledge of the world is based on your knowledge of your own perceptions; the world you see is your world and no one else's. The problem is that there is no objective test to find out which person, if any, perceives things correctly, as they really are. It is thus impossible to discover the true nature of anything.

In other words, Protagoras is not saying that there is no reality. Rather, he is saying that appearance *is* reality, at least subjectively for the one who is experiencing those appearances. Nor is he saying that knowledge cannot be had by anyone. Knowledge is possible, but its domain is the personal experience of each individual. Knowledge is thus relative to each person. For instance, I could be mistaken about the objects of my own perception; it may take some soul-searching for me to correct my false opinions (false relative to my own perceptions) and make them true (again, relative to my own perceptions). I could believe that I was very happy and

content in life without knowing that in reality I was very unhappy and discontented, as some soul-searching or guidance by a wise man might reveal to me. This is an extremely important idea, one that contrasts Protagoras's response to epistemological relativism with that of the other leading sophists of the time, Gorgias and Thrasymachus. Each agreed with him concerning epistemological relativism but drew very different conclusions on the basis of that conviction. To distinguish his view from theirs, I will call this type of philosophy *conventionalism*.

Conventionalism, then, is the view that while there is no objective truth (epistemological relativism), there is truth relative to each individual person. In other words, truth is man-made. Truth exists solely by human convention. In other words, in Protagoras's view there is an important sense in which *everything is true*. That is, anything that is subjectively true for anyone, regardless of how different it may be for someone else, is true because there is no objective truth. All opposing viewpoints, insofar as they are each held properly by their individuals and correspond in the right way to their individual perceptions, are thus true.

On the basis of epistemological relativism, Protagoras constructed a theory of *moral relativism,* according to which what is right and what is wrong also is merely the result of human conventions. This view, however, was far from destructive. It certainly was not demoralizing. In fact, this view influenced and inspired Pericles and other democratically minded thinkers of the time to pass laws granting freedom to multiple and conflicting viewpoints within their society, much in the way that contemporary American society gives, at least in principle, a voice to all opposing viewpoints.

Protagoras's epistemological conventionalsim had important *pragmatic* repercussions for his theory of education, which is remarkably similar to nineteenth-century American pragmatists William James and John Dewey (whom you will meet in Chapter 20) and their German avatar F. C. S. Schiller. This pragmatist slant comes out of Plato's dialogue *Protagoras,* in which

Protagoras responds to Socrates' criticism that if truth and knowledge are relative in they way Protagoras is claiming, then no one is wiser than anyone else. But Protagoras denies this, saying that in fact there is a special responsibility that the wise man has, due to the *freedom* which the understanding that truth is man-made confers upon the enlightened.

⚘

Protagoras

Each of us is the measure of what is and of what is not, but people differ from one another in this: that different things appear and are to different people. . . .

Don't quibble with my use of language, but try to understand what I mean. Remember what was said earlier: to the man who is sick his food seems bitter and is bitter; to the man who is well it is and seems just the opposite. Now neither of these men is to be made wiser, for that is impossible; nor should it be claimed that the sick man is ignorant because he believes what he does, or the well man wise because he believes otherwise. But a change must be brought about from the one condition to the other, because the other is better. So it is with education: a change must be brought about from a worse condition to a better; but whereas the physician produces this change by drugs, the sophist does it by words. No one has ever yet made anyone who previously had false beliefs have true ones; for it is impossible to believe what is not, nor anything but what one experiences, and this is always true. But I believe that one can make a man who is in a depraved condition of soul and has beliefs of a like nature good, so that he has different beliefs. These appearances some, through inexperience, call "true"; but I say that some are "better" than others, but not "truer." And the wise, friend Socrates, I am very far from calling frogs, but when they have to do with the body I call them physicians, and when they have to do with plants, farmers.

_____

From Plato's *Protagoras*, J. M. Robinson, Trans., *An Introduction to Early Greek Philosophy* (Boston: Houghton Mifflin, 1968).

For I maintain that the latter induce in sickly plants good and healthy and true sensations instead of bad, and that wise and good orators make good things instead of wicked things appear just to their cities. For I believe that whatever *seems* right or wrong to each city *is* right or wrong for it, so long as it continues to think so. But the wise man causes the good things instead of the bad to appear and to be for them in each case.

⚘

The idea is that philosophy can and should be used as therapy: instead of drugs, words. But what is it that the sophist, or "wiseman," uses words to do? The answer is deceptively simple. Change attitudes. Affect beliefs. Open closed minds. The idea that this is good for you and can help you lead a better life is a theme we shall encounter again; we shall see such thinking applied in force by philosophers as diverse as the pre-Medieval Pyrhonnian skeptics, Gotama Buddha, and the twentieth-century philosophical genius, Ludwig Wittgenstein. The Skeptics, for instance, believed that the right measure of doubt can free up a mind from attachment to the "bad" beliefs that prevent it from functioning properly in the world. Buddha believed that particular sorts of illusory beliefs about the self and reality are the source of much suffering and that once one gives up those false beliefs suffering ends. But what is the insight that Protagoras thinks is the source of enlightenment and liberation?

It is the realization that the world I live in is to a large extent one of my own making. But I am not conscious of this—I am blind, ignorant of the contributions my own mind makes to its experience at all levels. Once I am brought by the sophist to see the degree to which I am the source of my own meaning I am given the opportunity to choose freely, to make my life my own.

1.12.1 Protagoras's Bucket Experiment

It is extremely important to note that the sophists, especially the three we shall discuss in this section, while propounding their negative views about truth and knowledge, laid the foundation for much of subsequent philosophy because they all relied on perfecting their *methods of demonstration and argument.*

To demonstrate his point, Protagoras devised an experiment. He would assemble his audience before a stage and then take three volunteers. The first he would take to a secluded area behind the stage and put his hand in a bucket of cold water. He would take the second one to another secluded area and immerse his hand in hot water. The third would place his hand in the bucket of lukewarm water on the stage. After a few minutes, the other two would join him and put their hands in the bucket with the lukewarm water.

"Tell us the temperature of the water," Protagoras would say.

"It is very hot," said the first.

"It is very cold," said the second.

"It is lukewarm," said the third.

Now of course one could say to Protagoras that the only reason the water felt differently was because the three people had gotten used to three different temperatures. But Protagoras's argument was much deeper and more subtle than that. He openly revealed what accounted for the differences. His point wasn't that he was "manipulating" what each person felt, but rather that the words *hot, cold,* and *lukewarm* refer to sensations -that the mind conjures up among its perceptions in response to some stimulus. That stimulus is neither hot nor cold nor lukewarm.

This is an incredibly advanced insight about the nature of perception and its relation to the world. Today, science tells us that temperature is really a measure of the relative motion of molecules. But *the motion of particles,* by itself, is not the *feeling* of warmth or coldness. What Protagoras was claiming is something we will see many later philosophers argue with much more precision: the hotness of heat and the coldness of cold are mental *phenomena,* not physical things. And insofar as our perceptions consist of mental phenomena, they are not a direct apprehension of objective reality but constructions by the

mind relative to the observer. It is to Proagoras's credit that he could make such a sophisticated type of argument using something as simple as three buckets of water. Throughout this book I shall sum up Protagoras's type of theory of perception with the following reminder: *your eyes are not windows.*

1.12.2 Gorgias

What is most remarkable about all the sophists is that whereas they agreed on the principle of epistemological relativism, they drew radically different conclusions from it. Gorgias (480–375 B.C.E.), who came to Athens from Sicily as an ambassador of the city of Leontini, started out as a philosopher in the tradition of Thales and Parmenides. He was, however, so taken by the other sophists that he gave up his former views, becoming the most radical of all the sophists. Whereas Protagoras argued that everything is true in that truth is relative to the perceptive world of each individual mind, Gorgias argued from the same premise of epistemological relativism that there is no truth. Relying on the reasoning methods developed by the Eleatic philosophers, especially Zeno, Gorgias claimed:

1. nothing exists
2. if anything did exist it would be incomprehensible and unknowable
3. even if it were comprehensible or knowable, it could not be communicated to others

Just as Pythagoras had pointed out the difference between numerals and numbers—numerals are the symbols used to denote, or refer to, the (intangible) numbers—and the previous philosophers had pointed out the difference between our perceptions (the appearances) and the things perceived (the things out there in the world), so Gorgias painstakingly pointed out that words, which were only symbols or signs for the thing represented, could never properly be used to denote the objects they stand for. True communication is therefore impossible. This view I shall call *epistemological nihilism.* This is even stronger than *epistemological skepticism,* which holds only that we cannot know anything but *not*, as Gorgias and the epistemological nihilists supposed, that there is nothing there to be known at all.

1.12.3 Thrasymachus

The third of the three great sophists, Thrasymachus, appears in Plato's dialogue the *Republic* as the defender of yet a third type of response to the same principle of epistemological relativism. Instead of arguing the nihilistic position that there is no truth, as Gorgias did, or the conventionalist position that truth is man-made and so everything that anyone believes is true, as Protagoras did, Thrasymachus argued for what I will call *epistemological authoritarianism*. This is the view that "might is right." Just as laws are made by rulers for their own interest, and just as the rulers then define what is right in that society, so the most powerful are the ones who can determine by their authority what is "true." This extends to the moral realm: there is no morality beyond the subjugating of truth and right for one's own personal gain and interest; whether one succeeds is determined in a competitive struggle against all other contenders for the truth and the law. Thrasymachus's philosophy would achieve its most eloquent and sophisticated exposition in the nineteenth century in the brilliant and influential writings of Friedrich Nietzsche (see Chapter 18).

Disgusted with the sophists' abandonment of the pure and disinterested search for truth, Socrates left the sophists in search of higher wisdom. His greatest contribution, no doubt, came in the form of his greatest student, Plato, who almost single-handedly ended the influence of the sophists and for the next several centuries put philosophy on the path to certain and absolute knowledge. But before turning to Plato we must first look at another great master of the time whose belief in ultimate truth and the search for a method to attain it not only paralleled Plato's but became the paradigm for all subsequent physical science: Democritus, who invented both Democracy and the view that everything is made of individual, indivisible entities that he called *atoms*.

1.13 Democritus (460–360 B.C.E.): The Way of Materialism

Plato, it has often been said, was the first full-fledged *idealist* philosopher. Democritus, it has likewise often been said, was the first full-fledged *materialist*. For the time being we can think of these categories, which I have already suggested can be as misleading as they are helpful, in the following terms. Idealism and materialism are by and large artificial categories denoting opposing metaphysical systems whose conceptual differences are often easily misunderstood, and so it would be good to try to get them right from the start.

Idealism is characterized by placing as primary and fundamental the nonspatial, nonvisual, incorporeal, nonsensuous, normative, or valuational. Materialism stresses the spatial, visual, corporeal, sensuous, nonvaluational, factual, and mechanistic. Notice that these distinctions can be counterintuitive, especially insofar as idealism broadly construed emphasizes the nonspatial and nonvisual, whereas materialism emphasizes the spatial and visual. That this is so will become much clearer once we see why Plato so vehemently objected to visual, pictorial representations of reality; for Plato, as for many subsequent idealists, the primary reality itself consists of *ideas,* which are nonspatial (that is, are unextended in space) and mental, rather than *matter*, which is essentially spatial (that is, extended in space) and nonmental. But there are so many more types of "idealism" than there are types of "materialism" that these distinctions are by no means carved in stone and should be regarded only as signposts rather than formal definitions and, if used at all, must always be carefully revised according to each different type of philosophical system. (Indeed, pure, physical, materialism as naively understood has been such a rarity among major thinkers that the history of philosophy could easily be regarded as mainly a history of idealism.)[10]

On the other hand, it should also be noted that these two supposedly opposing metaphysical systems, idealism and materialism, have one deeply fundamental common principle: *rationalism*. Each system in its own way tries to encompass the entire scope of the scientific and philosophical knowledge of the time. Although Democritus agreed with Plato (whose views you will encounter in greater detail in the next chapter) concerning the Protagorean theory of perception, he held steadfastly to the more ancient form of rationalism as espoused by the Eleatic philosophers (Parmenides and Zeno). This type of rationalism must be contrasted with yet another type, the natural science theory of sense perception.

Recall the Greek notion of "rational" exemplified in the concept of *rational number.* A number is rational if it can be expressed as a ratio, or measured proportion, of other numbers. Similarly, a thought or idea is rational if it can be expressed as a ratio, or measured proportion, of other ideas (Aristotle will rely on a similar idea when he defines virtue and excellence in terms of a rational *mean* between various extremes). In other words, what Democritus had in mind in forging the concept of rationality was something along the following lines, as is well evidenced by his attempt at creating a balanced synthesis of all opposing philosophical viewpoints. Unlike Protagoras and the sophists, who viewed philosophical differences as incommensurable and each subjectively valid, Democritus tried to find *a ratio* among them by, in effect, holding them all up for view at the same time. It is almost as if the multiperspectival view that he was after came about as a sort of intellectual and conceptual interference pattern from a multiplicity of apparently opposing viewpoints.

Like perception, thinking in Democritus's view consists ultimately of nothing more than the motion of atoms. This too was a pivotal idea in that it suggested there may be logical mechanisms underlying our thought processes, themselves ultimately the result of atoms in motion. Remarkably, Democritus's elaborate theory about perception and the nature of thought is in many ways similar to modern theories of the electrochemical functioning of the brain. In his

view, the influence of external things upon us can come about only through contact among various types of atoms via mechanical principles. He distinguished the ordinary atoms constituting nonminded physical objects from the even finer, "fiery" atoms responsible for thoughts and perceptions. Inspired no doubt by Heraclitean ideas about the fundamental role of fire in the cosmic scheme of things, Democritus viewed sensations as the effect of fire atoms upon the sense organs. Sensation, he claimed, cannot give us true knowledge of the external world because our perceptions as such consist only of subjective qualities like color, taste, and temperature, not of the objective quantities of true reality. We see colors and shapes, not atoms; likewise, when we pay attention to our minds we experience images and sensations, not the firing of atoms. Sense experience thus cannot present objective truth as it really is, only indirectly, through an obscure, subjective view of the actual world consisting of visual, tactile, and auditory images that are not the actual things out there in the world but, at best, imperfect representations of them. True, objective, knowledge, which would mean *knowledge of the atoms,* which are themselves as imperceptible to our senses as empty space is, can only be arrived at by *thought.* And only thought that is fundamentally *rational,* in the sense of being properly balanced with full knowledge of all views, is the key. This is very different from taking an *empirical* approach to epistemology, and so it must be stressed that Democritus's brand of materialism had much more in common with the rational epistemology of Plato than with the later, empirical materialists (see Section 14.4).

Plato forged his rational idealism based not on a theory of physical reality but on Socrates' view of the *concept.* Keep in mind that although Plato's philosophy was the dominant force in Greek thinking and became the most influential philosophy of all time, modern scientific philosophy since Galileo, Bacon, and Gassendi (see Chapter 8) returned to an explicitly Democritean type of materialistic view of nature, though slightly more empirically based. This

Democritean view has once again, in turn, been overturned in the twentieth century in favor of a Pythagorean/Platonic framework buttressed by a new synthesis of Parmenidean and Heraclitean thought and the paradoxical blend of idealist and materialist metaphysics found in quantum mechanics (see Chapter 14).

Democritus, like Protagoras, was born in Abdera, Thrace. He was about twenty years younger than Protagoras and ten years younger than Socrates. Although he lived to be 100 years old and overlapped with the young Plato, the latter makes no mention of him in any of his work. (Democritus was seventy-five when Plato wrote his *Symposium*.) Not only does Democritus's name not appear anywhere in Plato's work, Plato makes no mention of the atomic theory. This is especially odd since Plato's star pupil and philosophical successor, Aristotle (who, like Democritus, was a northern Ionian), wrote knowingly about him. Democritus wrote that whereas Protagoras received a great welcome upon his arrival in Athens, "I went to Athens, and no one knew me." One possible clue comes from the ancient biographer Diogenes Laertius (on whom most of the biographical and source material on the pre-Socratic philosophers is based), who claimed that Plato so despised Democritus that he would have liked to see all his books burned.

What we do know with some confidence is that Democritus was as prolific a writer as Plato. He had more than fifty books to his credit, all of which were destroyed between the third and fifth centuries C.E. (Common Era). After traveling about the ancient world, Democritus went to study with Leucippus at his highly influential School of Abdera at about the same time as Protagoras. At his school, Leucippus took what he regarded as the primary aspects of being that Parmenides had ascribed to the whole of reality and applied them not to the whole (that is, not to the world entire) but to the ultimate *parts*. Recall that Parmenides argued that if there is a separation between two beings (between two existent *any*things), it cannot be nothing (for that is *no* separation) for that is nonbeing; so

nonbeing cannot be ascribed to it. *Being* has the following properties:

1. unity
2. indivisibility
3. indestructibility
4. eternity

For Parmenides and Zeno, *being,* the world in its totality—the entire cosmos—is one complete totality without any parts and everywhere completely full. *Non*being, in the sense of some sort of void between things, is according to them impossible, for the following logical reason. To say that there is a "void" is to say that the "void" has existence; if it has existence, then it is a type of being. Of course *void* means something like "emptiness" or "lack of being," but the Greeks realized the importance of not using a term that means, in effect, "not *X*" to refer to "*X*" (substitute "being" for "*X*")—a lesson that has often been *cleverly* forgotten by philosophers, mathematicians, and scientists as a way of ignoring a deep philosophical problem. In a nutshell, Parmenides and Zeno thought it absurd to say that a *nothing* (the void) exists. It is this sort of logical precision and correctness of language that leads to the startling paradoxes of Zeno discussed in Section 1.11.

The sophists, demoralized by the inability of logic, reason, and language to make sense of the world, inspired by the extreme differences between the various philosophies that had thus far developed, gave up the search for truth and turned instead to the practice of rhetoric and the attainment of power through persuasion. The idea that there was some ultimate truth about the way the world is and the nature of human existence became subjugated to ancient myths, legends, and religious imagery that drew sharply divisive lines between the worldly affairs of the human intellect and the cosmic truths accessible only to the divine. But a glimmer of hope that the human knowledge-seeking enterprise would not come to an end in its infancy came from the school founded by Leucippus. There, both the epistemological positivism of the Ionian philosophers (Thales, Anaxagoras, Anaximenes, Pythag-

oras, Heraclitus) and the epistemological nega-
tivism of the Eleatic philosophers (Parmenides,
Zeno) were studied with great seriousness.
Leucippus guided the research that could be
summed up as the quest for a synthesis of apparently irreconcilable philosophical differences
into a system that would enlighten the human
mind to its own operations in a way that would
give us a heretofore unimaginable power to
understand ourselves and the world.

To this formidable task, Democritus devoted
his entire, century-long life. His solution was a
synthesis of all that had come before him,
inspired on the one hand by the atomic physical
theory of Leucippus and, on the other, by
Protagoras's representational theory of the mind
and the indirect nature of perception. Leucippus
had already begun the project of philosophical
synthesis by, in effect, giving the Parmenidean
properties of being not the whole of existence
but only its ultimate, indivisible, eternal, units,
which he called *atoms* (literally, *a*[non]*tom*[divis-
ible]). The concept of *nothing,* or nonbeing,
became at his school the concept of *space.*
Whereas Parmenides had claimed that reality
consists of a single, undifferentiated and indivisible One, which was completely full, Democritus
claimed that there were an *infinite* number of
separate, individual, things—atoms—each one
completely full, containing no void (no empty
space), and indivisible. Because they are so small,
the atoms are invisible; because they are eternal,
they are neither created nor destroyed. So reality consists not of one thing but of *two* very different things—one which is a thing proper, the
atom, and the other which is a nonthing, space.
Space, a vacuum, has only the property of extension, so the atoms can freely move about. Their
motions give rise to the various constellations of
physical objects as well as to the visual objects of
our perceptions.

Democritus used the atomic theory to try to
circumvent the problems posed by Zeno's paradoxes, especially those of motion. Motion is possible because everything consists of numberless,
self-moving, qualitatively similar atoms that
combine themselves in various shapes and forms

in empty space. Whereas Pythagoras used numbers, represented as dots, to form various shapes,
Democritus put in place of these ideal objects
(numbers conceived as "abstract dots") the minimal physical dots of existence: atoms. By thus
combining Leucippus's atomic theory with
mathematics and Protagoras's theory of perception, Democritus argued that the different
arrangements that the indistinguishable atoms
could take and their various motions accounted
for the qualitative differences among perceived
objects. These perceived qualities do not belong
to things in themselves, which consist solely of
differently arranged atoms, but are only the
result of the manner in which the mind of the
perceiving subject (the observer) constructs the
representation. Likewise the behavior of the
atoms themselves is purely mechanical, the result
of laws of motion which are always and everywhere the same.

Democritus's philosophy thus had a new,
multidimensional aspect to it; there is an
absolute reality (beyond the perceptions), and
this reality is partly responsible for the relative
reality that we perceive. He also thought that
with a fully developed atomistic theory of matter
and the void, he could answer Zeno's objections
to the possibility of motion and provide a solution raised by the Parmenidean problem of how
to reconcile appearances with ultimate reality so
that we could have true knowledge of the world.
Democritus's brilliant response was to make the
Heraclitean (Ionian) and Parmenidean (Eleatic)
philosophies—as Democritus's colleague Protagoras would similarly claim—both true, but
not simply in the subjective way that Protagoras
and other sophists claimed. Rather, the
Parmenidean and Heraclitean views were both
objectively true of the world. It was just that the
objective world contained *both* material reality
("the physical world") *and* ideal reality ("the
ideal world"). Thus, the first *multiperspectival*
philosophy was born.

Thus, too, was born a view of the world that
has persisted to this day, one in which there is an
objective, external, physical reality consisting of
atoms in motion through empty space, and the

subjective, internal, mental world of perceptions, ideas, and thoughts. According to Democritus, the mental world is to be explained in terms of the mind-independent reality of the physical world. In that regard, he was the first thoroughgoing materialist: the mind and all its phenomena are ultimately of derivative reality, to be explained the same way that the physical phenomena of nature are explained, by the movement of atoms. The materialist worldview, overshadowed for centuries by the emerging philosophies of Plato and Aristotle, came into its own again in Epicurus (341–270 B.C.E., Epictetus (55–135 C.E.), and the Stoics (see Sections 4.0, 4.1, and 4.2). It vanished during the Middle Ages and then resurfaced in the seventeenth century. Wrote Sir Isaac Newton (1642–1727) in his famous *Principia*, where he deduced the universal force accounting for the motion of all things in the universe:

> I wish we could devise the rest of the phenomena of Nature by the same kind of reasoning from mechanical principles, for I am induced by many reasons to suspect that they may all depend upon certain forces by which the particles of bodies, by some causes hitherto unknown, are either mutually impelled towards one another and cohere in regular figures, or are repelled and recede from one another.

Materialism thus eventually became the dominant world view until the early part of the twentieth century, when Albert Einstein's revolutionary theory of spacetime (see Section 17.2) paved the way for the next philosophical synthesis of idealist and materialist thought in which mind and world are inextricably linked (as we shall see when we explore the strange world of quantum mechanics, Section 17.2).

Before we turn to Plato and the subsequent developments in philosophy, let us end on the following unifying, rather than divisive, note. In Democritus's theory, the atoms were primarily distinguished from each other by their *form*, of which there are an infinite number. The Greek term for this, ιδεα, standardly translated as *form* or *idea*, is the same as that used by Anaxagoras,

Democritus, and Plato, where it is translated both as *form* and *idea*. In pre-Socratic philosophy, *idea* was used variably to mean form, nature, fashion, mode, class, or species. After Plato the term came to mean a timeless essence or universal (see Chapter 2), a sort of dynamic, creative pattern out of which individually existent things are formed. After the Stoics (Chapter 4), ideas came to be regarded as class concepts in the human mind. Neoplatonists (Chapter 5), on the other hand, regarded the ideas as archetypes of individual things subsisting within the cosmic mind (*nous* or *logos*). In the seventeenth century we shall see René Descartes (Chapter 10) identify the ideas with subjective but logically pure concepts of the human mind, whereas John Locke (Chapter 13) identifies them with all objects of consciousness. For George Berkeley (Chapter 14), ideas are but the sense objects of our perceptions, operating either as modes of the human mind or as a type of mind-dependent being (ideas derived from objects of intuitive introspection he calls "notions"). On the other hand, when David Hume (Chapter 15) uses the term *idea*, he means a "faint image" or memory copy of sense impressions. And, finally, for Immanuel Kant (Chapter 16), ideas are but concepts that are *representations* incapable of being known via the categories of the understanding, which are beyond the limits of cognition.

So it obviously behooves us to pay extra careful attention to the *context* in which the philosophers use terms like *idea*, rather than wedding ourselves to some abstract notion in our own heads that never quite fits and unnecessarily exaggerates the differences among great thinkers. Often, even when philosophers use the same words, they are using them in a technical sense specific to their own theories, thereby speaking of various aspects of similar but often slightly different things; more often than not, the major philosophers we are considering in this book tend to agree with the substance of the views of those philosophers who have been popularly depicted throughout history as their philosophical adversaries.[11] This must be kept in mind for much of what follows in our study of

Plato, since the term used by Anaxagoras, Democritus, and Plato to refer to absolute reality is none other than ιδεα.

NOTES

1. E. M. Forster, *Howard's End*.
2. From *pan*, all, and *theos*, god, meaning that everything that exists is a manifestation of God.
3. The lists vary somewhat, but four names appear on all of them, including Plato's (Protagoras, 343a): Bias of Priene, who saved the Ionians during the Persian invasion with a migration to Sardinia; Pittacus, the tyrant of Mitylene; Solon, a gnomic poet who became the "lawgiver" of Athens; and Thales.
4. The original Greek is *gnothi s'afton*, and it can be translated into English either as the old formal address (such as the French *vous*) "Know Thyself," which is of course no longer in use in English, or it can be interpreted as the informal plural. I have used the latter in *In Search of Myself: Life, Death and Personal Identity* (Belmont, CA: Wadsworth, 1999).
5. From *Wittgenstein's Tractatus*, Daniel Kolak, trans. (Mountain View, CA: Mayfield, 1999).
6. For a more detailed discussion, see Daniel Kolak and David Goloff, "The Incredible Shrinking Zeno," on which this section is based, in *The Experience of Philosophy*, 3d ed., D. Kolak & R. Martin, eds., Belmont: Wadsworth 1996, pp. 41–55.
7. For instance, if he were holding a ruler in his hand, the ruler would not be visible to the spectators through any finite microscope, no matter how powerful. Therefore, the distance between him and the spectators would be infinite compared to that ruler. Furthermore, if he laid that ruler side to side any finite number of times, he would never reach the spectators.
8. In fact the idea of a derivative in calculus involves exactly this type of image. The infinitesimal calculus and quantum physics both try to offer theories that move us beyond the realm of object spaces as ordinarily conceived. In standard calculus, the real numbers are used. In infinitesimal calculus, new types of quantities are used that mark and conceptualize the place where our shrinking Zeno is when he has shrunk out of sight. Quantum mechanics postulates that the ordinary concept of space and time completely breaks down where our shrinking Zeno is.
9. Again, at least not in the way we naively think. We shall encounter several philosophers—Absolute Idealists such as Hegel and "presentationalists" such as Ernst Mach, William James, and John Dewey—who each in their own way believe that we do in fact experience reality directly, but not in the way we naively think! In Hegel's view, for instance, the whole world is but an idea; in the views of Mach and James, the whole world consists in sensations (Mach) or pure experience (James).
10. Rather than trying to memorize these labels, the reader will fare better by simply using them as conceptual categories and then letting the ideas get gradually filled in, as they will of their own accord, once the reader becomes more familiar with the different metaphysical systems as espoused by the various philosophers.
11. Though of course there are exceptions, often the big difference between "opposing" philosophers is in some ways not unlike the difference in today's United States between, say, a Republican political candidate who argues with great bravado that those leftist, liberal Democrats are idiots, while the Democratic opponent argues with equally great bravado that those right-wing conservative Republicans are idiots when the positions of the candidates are in reality quite close. The public is then, of course, given the "freedom" to "choose" whichever "side" it prefers.

2 ✹ Plato

2.0 Plato (428–348 B.C.E.)

Born into a prominent aristocratic Athenian family, Plato grew up during the twenty-seven-year Peloponnesian War between Athens and Sparta. The war ended in 404 B.C.E. with the surrender of Athens and the overthrow of the world's first democracy. Instead of taking up the political life for which his family had prepared him, Plato became a disciple of Socrates and went on to become one of the greatest and most influential philosophers of all time. Among his many achievements, he founded what would become the avatar of today's university, the Academy, a center for the advancement of wisdom and a training ground for philosophers that lasted nearly a thousand years. Under Plato's direction, the Academy also spawned a slew of scientific and mathematical innovations, linking fifth-century B.C.E. Pythagorean mathematics with Egyptian geometry and Alexandrian arithmetic.

Unlike his beloved mentor Socrates, who wrote nothing, Plato was a prolific writer. He produced more than two dozen dialogues that cover nearly every topic. Their impact upon Western thought has been so great that the twentieth-century philosopher Alfred North Whitehead called the entire history of Western philosophy "a series of footnotes to Plato."

Why Plato wrote his dialogues is a mystery, especially since Socrates apparently not only shunned the written word but claimed that to try to write down philosophy would be unphilosophical. Indeed, some of Plato's own works, such as *The Republic*, contain explicit arguments against the very types of books that he wrote. There is, however, good reason to believe that he began writing the dialogues shortly after Socrates was executed by his fellow Athenians for "corrupting" its youth and raising doubts in their minds about accepted "gods." The infamous trial and death of Socrates had a profound effect on young Plato and may well have changed his mind about the role of writing. Disgusted by the ineptitudes and injustices of Athenian democracy, not the least of which was Socrates' death, Plato left Athens for about ten years and traveled in southern Italy and Sicily. During this time he began writing his early dialogues.

In them, Socrates appears as a philosophical gadfly who seeks human excellence, not by offering solutions to life's vexing problems but by goading adversaries into offering a definition of some term, such as *justice, courage, intelligence,* or *piety.* By drawing inferences from his opponents' responses and eliciting contradictions, Socrates demonstrates their profound ignorance, unmasks their pretense, and ultimately frustrates them into his own befuddled state of puzzlement and unknowing. Regardless of whether this method was used by Socrates, or whether it is Plato's own invention (or, more likely, some combination of the two), the significance of such adversarial intellectual activity to the advent and development of Western thought cannot be overestimated. Instead of forging beliefs through agreement or disagreement against a fixed system of dogma (as in orthodox religious traditions) or through extraordinary experience usually codified by special, typically secret, ritual (as in mystical religious traditions), the measure of correctness in the Socratic tradition as passed down to us by Plato consists in the consistency and accuracy of one's own statements tempered by one's own reason through free and open discourse. The result: instead of fixity, a flow of ideas; instead of the stagnant stability of inculcated opinion that has steered many a civilization into a secure dead end, Socrates and his philosophical descendants empowered the Western mind with a profound insecurity about all things, freeing it to change, to grow, to evolve, to live.

The method is as profound as it is simple. If you anchor yourself to some external dogma, you can force yourself to be consistent in relation to that dogma. There is some set of principles, rules, fundamental propositions, scriptural truths, and so on, and they become permanent fixtures that give guidance and structure to the mind. This is also true of internal dogma. Propositions, any propositions, any set of written "truths"—*unlike thoughts*—can stand still. I believe this may well be the reason why Socrates did not want philosophy to be written down: *thinking does not stand still.* It is very difficult, perhaps impossible, for us to remain absolutely consistent in our thinking about anything for very long. One of the most frustrating things,

not just about thinking but reasoning in general and the whole process of philosophy itself, is that if you think long enough, reason carefully enough, and philosophize enough, you will, almost *invariably,* change your mind about whatever it is that you are trying to make up your mind about! The made-up mind is not just an *unphilosophical* mind, it is an *imaginary* or *fictitious* mind. And that is why, when the mind engages in the type of mental *activity,* or philosophical thinking *process* as espoused by Socrates and Plato, it continually shifts, grows, creates, and transcends its own systems. And that is why Western civilization, insofar as it has embodied the philosophy to which this book pays homage, has in my opinion been unmatched by any other known civilization. Ours is a unique ability to generate and hold on high radically different, often mutually exclusive, views of ourselves and the world juxtaposed, grating cacophonously against each other within us in one glorious symphony of intellectual disagreement, perpetual argument, debate, irresolution of all things most fundamental. To put the point in a nutshell and somewhat paradoxically: to have *a* philosophy is to have no philosophy.

This is the sense in which (as has already been suggested in Chapter 0) Western philosophy truly begins with Socrates. Reverent of neither the external authority of orthodoxy nor the internal authority of mystical experience, the Socrates of Plato's early dialogues questions both internal and external types of authority by literally forcing the mind to see—typically, against its own wishes—its inconsistencies, inaccuracies, and fabrications. Masked under the guise of an externally sanctioned, absolute authority—such as the "gods"—or an internally sanctioned absolute authority—such as "mystical" experience—the unphilosophical mind deceives itself into thinking it has arrived at some final, certain knowledge, when in truth the mind has not arrived because there is no arrival; there is no authority; there is just the ever-evolving, living path called wisdom. It is better for the mind to know how little it knows with absolute certainty and live wisely in its insecurity, Plato's Socrates argues, than for the mind to not know how little it knows and live self-deceived, safely in the prison of its own ignorance.

2.1 Plato's *Euthyphro*

To actually see some of the weaves of Plato's thought, let's take a close look at the first dialogue, the *Euthyphro*, which takes place shortly before Socrates' infamous trial and subsequent execution in 399 B.C.E. Plato presents Euthyphro as a wise religious prophet, so highly pious that he has come to court to prosecute his own father, a rich landowner, for causing the death of a slave who had murdered another slave in some brawl. Euthyphro's father bound the murderer and left him in a ditch while he went to fetch the authorities, during which time the slave died. Going against the wishes of all the rest of his family, Euthyphro accuses his father of murder and comes to court seeking justice. If we are to take Socrates' words here at face value, he is so impressed by the lengths to which Euthyphro has gone in the name of moral justice that he says he wants to become Euthyphro's "disciple" and learn from *him* the true meaning of piety so that he can better defend himself against the charge of impiety.

⚓

Euthyphro

EUTHYPHRO: Why have you left the Lyceum, Socrates? And what are you doing in the Porch of the King Archon? Surely you cannot be involved in a suit before the King, like myself?

SOCRATES: Not in a suit, Euthyphro: impeachment is the word which the Athenians use.

EUTH.: What! I suppose that some one has been

From Plato, "Euthyphro," in *The Dialogues of Plato*, Benjamin Jowett, trans. (Oxford: Oxford University Press, 1920), with emendations by the author.

prosecuting you, for I cannot believe that you are the prosecutor of another.

SOC.: Certainly not.

EUTH.: Then some one else has been prosecuting you?

SOC.: Yes.

EUTH.: And who is he?

SOC: A young man who is little known, Euthyphro: and I hardly know him: his name is Meletus, and he is of the deme of Pitthis. Perhaps you may remember his appearance: he has a beak, and long straight hair, and a scraggly beard.

EUTH.: No, I do not remember him, Socrates. But what is the charge which he brings against you?

SOC.: What is the charge? Well, a very serious charge, which shows a good deal of character in the young man, and for which he is certainly not to be blamed. He says he knows how the youth are corrupted and who are their corruptors. I fancy that he must be a wise man, and seeing that I am the reverse of a wise man, he has found me out, and is going to accuse me of corrupting his young friends. And of this our mother the state is to be the judge. Of all our political men he is the only one who seems to me to begin in the right way, with the cultivation of virtue in youth; like a good gardner, he makes the young shoots his first care, and clears away us who are the destroyers of them. This is only the first step; he will afterwards attend to the elder branches; and if he goes on as he has begun, he will be a very great public benefactor.

EUTH.: I hope that he may; but I rather fear, Socrates, that the opposite will turn out to be the truth. My opinion is that in attacking you he is simply aiming a blow at the foundation of the state. But in what way does he say that you corrupt the young?

SOC.: He brings a wonderful accusation against me, which at first hearing excites surprise: he says that I am a poet or maker of gods, and that I invent new gods and deny the existence of old ones; this is the ground of his indictment.

EUTH.: I understand, Socrates; he means to attack you about the familiar sign which occasionally, as you say, comes to you. He thinks that you are a neologian, and he is going to have you up before the court for this. He knows that such a charge is readily received by the world, as I myself know too well; for when I speak in the assembly about divine things, and foretell the future to them, they laugh at me and think me a madman. Yet every word that I say is true. But they are jealous of us all; and we must be brave and go at them.

SOC.: Their laughter, friend Euthyphro, is not a matter of much consequence. For a man may be thought wise; but the Athenians, I suspect, do not much trouble themselves about him until he begins to impart his wisdom to others; and then for some reason or other, perhaps, as you say, from jealousy, they are angry.

EUTH.: I am never likely to try their temper in this way.

SOC.: I dare say not, for you are reserved in your behaviour, and seldom impart your wisdom. But I have a benevolent habit of pouring out myself to everybody, and would even pay for a listener, and I am afraid that the Athenians may think me too talkative. Now if, as I was saying, they would only laugh at me, as you say that they laugh at you, the time might pass gaily enough in the court; but perhaps they may be in earnest, and then what the end will be you soothsayers only can predict.

EUTH.: I dare say that the affair will end in nothing, Socrates, and that you will win your cause; and I think that I shall win my own.

SOC.: And what is your suit, Euthyphro? Are you the prosecutor or the defendant?

EUTH.: I am the prosecuter.

SOC.: Of whom?

EUTH.: You will think me mad when I tell you.

SOC.: Why, has the fugitive wings?

EUTH.: Nay, he is not very volatile at his time of life.

SOC.: Who is he?

EUTH.: My father.

SOC.: Your father! . . .

EUTH.: Yes.

SOC.: And of what is he accused?

EUTH.: Of murder, Socrates.

SOC.: . . . Euthyphro! how little does the common herd know of the nature of right and truth. A man must be an extraordinary man, and have made great strides in wisdom, before he could have seen his way to bring such an action.

EUTH.: Indeed, Socrates. He must.

SOC.: I suppose that the man whom your father murdered was one of your relatives—clearly he was; for if he had been a stranger you would never have thought of prosecuting him.

EUTH.: I am amused, Socrates, at your making a distinction between one who is a relation and one who is not a relation; for surely the pollution is the same in either case, if you knowingly associate with the murderer when you ought to clear yourself and him by proceeding against him. The real question is whether the murdered man has been justly slain. If justly, then your duty is to let the matter alone; but if unjustly, then even if the murderer lives under the same roof with you and eats at the same table, proceed against him. Now the man who is dead was a poor dependant of mine who worked for us as a field laborer on our farm in Naxos, and one day in a fit of drunken passion he got into a quarrel with one of our domestic servants and slew him. My father bound him hand and foot and threw him into a ditch, and then sent to Athens to ask of a diviner what he should do with him. Meanwhile he never attended to him and took no care about him, for he regarded him as a murderer; and thought that no great harm would be done even if he did die. Now this was just what happened. For such was the effect of cold and hunger and chains upon him, that before the messenger returned from the diviner, he was dead. And my father and family are angry with me for taking the part of the murderer and prosecuting my father. They say that he did not kill him, and that if he did, the dead man was but a murderer, and I ought not to take any notice, for that a son is impious who prosecutes a father. Which shows, Socrates, how little they know what the gods think about piety and impiety.

SOC.: Good heavens, Euthyphro! And is your knowledge of religion and of things pious and impious so very exact, that, supposing the circumstances to be as you state them, you are not afraid lest you too may be doing an impious thing in bringing an action against your father?

EUTH.: The best of Euthyphro, and that which distinguishes him, Socrates, from other men, is his exact knowledge of all such matters. What should I be good for without it?

SOC.: Rare friend! I think that I cannot do better than be your disciple. Then before the trial with Meletus comes on I shall challenge him, and say that I have always had a great interest in religious questions, and now, as he charges me with rash imaginations and innovations in religion, I have become your disciple. You, Meletus, as I shall say to him, acknowledge Euthyphro to be a great theologian, and sound in his opinions; and if you approve of him you ought to approve of me and not have me into court; but if you disapprove, you should begin by indicting him who is my teacher, and who will be the ruin, not of the young, but of the old; that is to say, of myself whom he instructs, and of his old father whom he admonishes and chastises. And if Meletus refuses to listen to me, but will go on, and will not shift the indictment from me to you, I cannot do better than repeat this challenge in the court.

EUTH.: Yes, indeed, Socrates; and if he attempts to indict me I am mistaken if I do not find a flaw in him; the court shall have a great deal more to say to him than to me.

SOC.: And I, my dear friend, knowing this, am desirous of becoming your disciple. For I observe that no one appears to notice you—not even this Meletus; but his sharp eyes have found me out at once, and he has indicted me for impiety. And therefore, I beg you to tell me the nature of piety and impiety, which you said that you knew so well, and of murder, and of other offences against the gods. What are they? Is not piety in every action always the same? And impiety, again—is it not always the opposite of piety, and also the same with itself, having, as impiety, one notion which includes whatever is impious?

EUTH.: To be sure, Socrates.

SOC.: And what is piety, and what is impiety?

If anyone knows what piety is, then surely Euthyphro—an acknowledged prophet who has gone to such extreme lengths in the name of piety—knows. Under Socrates' persistent questioning, however, each of Euthyphro's answers fails *not* because it is in disagreement with Socrates' beliefs *but because Euthyphro, guided by his own reasoning ability, ultimately disagrees with it.*

EUTH.: Piety is doing as I am doing; that is to say, prosecuting any one who is guilty of murder, sacrilege, or of any similar crime—whether he be your father or mother, or whoever he may be—that makes no difference; and not to prosecute them is impiety. And please to consider, Socrates, what a notable proof I will give you of the truth of my

words, a proof which I have already given to others: of the principle, I mean, that the impious, whoever he may be, ought not to go unpunished. For do not men regard Zeus as the best and most righteous of the gods? And yet they admit that he bound his father [Cronos] because he wickedly devoured his sons, and that he too had punished his own father [Uranus] for a similar reason, in a nameless manner. And yet when I proceed against my father, they are angry with me. So inconsistent are they in their way of talking when the gods are concerned, and when I am concerned.

SOC.: May not this be the reason, Euthyphro, why I am charged with impiety—that I cannot away with these stories about the gods? And therefore I suppose that people think me wrong. But, as you who are well informed about them approve of them, I cannot do better than assent to your superior wisdom. What else can I say, confessing as I do, that I know nothing about them? Tell me, for the love of Zeus, whether you really believe that they are true.

EUTH.: Yes, Socrates; and things more wonderful still, of which the world is in ignorance.

SOC.: And do you really believe that the gods fought with one another, and had dire quarrels, battles, and the like, as the poets say, and as you may see represented in the works of great artists? The temples are full of them; and notably the robe of Athene, which is carried up to the Acropolis at the great Panathenaea, is embroidered with them. Are all these tales of the gods true, Euthyphro?

EUTH.: Yes, Socrates; and, as I was saying, I can tell you, if you would like to hear them, many other things about the gods which would quite amaze you.

SOC.: I dare say; and you shall tell me them at some other time when I have leisure. But just at present I would rather hear from you a more precise answer, which you have not as yet given, my friend, to the question, What is "piety"? When asked, you only replied, Doing as you do, charging your father with murder.

EUTH.: And what I said was true, Socrates.

SOC.: No doubt, Euthyphro; but you would admit that there are many other pious acts?

EUTH.: There are.

SOC.: Remember that I did not ask you to give me two or three examples of piety, but to explain the general idea which makes all pious things to be pious. Do you not recollect that there was one idea which made the impious impious, and the pious pious?

EUTH.: I remember.

SOC.: Tell me what is the nature of this idea, and then I shall have a standard to which I may look, and by which I may measure actions, whether yours or those of any one else, and then I shall be able to say that such and such an action is pious, such another impious.

EUTH.: I will tell you, if you like.

SOC.: I should very much like.

EUTH.: Piety, then, is that which is dear to the gods, and impiety is that which is not dear to them.

SOC.: Very good, Euthyphro; you have now given me the sort of answer which I wanted. But whether what you say is true or not I cannot as yet tell, although I make no doubt that you will prove the truth of your words.

EUTH.: Of course.

SOC.: Come, then, and let us examine what we are saying. That thing or person which is dear to the gods is pious, and that thing or person which is hateful to the gods is impious, these two being the extreme opposites of one another. Was not that said?

EUTH.: It was.

SOC.: And well said?

EUTH.: Yes, Socrates, I thought so; it was certainly said.

SOC.: And further, Euthyphro, the gods were admitted to have enmities and hatreds and differences?

EUTH.: Yes, that was also said.

SOC.: And what sort of difference creates enmity and anger? Suppose for example that you and I, my good friend, differ about a number; do differences of this sort make us enemies and set us at variance with one another? Do we not go at once to arithmetic, and put an end to them by a sum?

EUTH.: True.

SOC.: Or suppose that we differ about magnitudes, do we not quickly end the differences by measuring?

EUTH.: Very true.

SOC.: And we end a controversy about heavy and light by resorting to a weighing machine?

EUTH.: To be sure.

SOC.: But what differences are there which cannot be thus decided, and which therefore make us angry and set us at enmity with one another? I dare say the answer does not occur to you at the moment, and therefore I will suggest that these enmities arise when the matters of difference are the just and unjust, good and evil, honourable and dishonourable. Are not these the points about which men differ, and about which when we are unable satisfactorily to decide our differences, you and I and all of us quarrel, when we do quarrel?

EUTH.: Yes, Socrates, the nature of the differences about which we quarrel is such as you describe.

SOC.: And the quarrels of the gods, noble Euthyphro, when they occur, are of a like nature?

EUTH.: Certainly they are.

SOC.: They have differences of opinion, as you say, about good and evil, just and unjust, honourable and dishonourable: there would have been no quarrels among them, if there had been no such differences—would there now?

EUTH.: You are quite right.

SOC.: Does not every man love that which he deems noble and just and good, and hate the opposite of them?

EUTH.: Very true.

SOC.: But, as you say, people regard the same things, some as just and others as unjust,—about these they dispute; and so there arise wars and fightings among them.

EUTH.: Very true.

SOC.: Then the same things are hated by the gods and loved by the gods, and are both hateful and dear to them?

EUTH.: True.

SOC.: And upon this view the same things, Euthyphro, will be pious and also impious?

EUTH.: So I should suppose.

SOC.: Then, my friend, I remark with surprise that you have not answered the question which I asked. For I certainly did not ask you to tell me what action is both pious and impious: but now it would seem that what is loved by the gods is also hated by them. And therefore, Euthyphro, in thus chastising your father you may very likely be doing what is agreeable to Zeus but disagreeable to Cronos or Uranus, and what is acceptable to Hephaestus but unacceptable to Herè, and there may be other gods who have similar differences of opinion.

EUTH.: But I believe, Socrates, that all the gods would be agreed as to the propriety of punishing a murderer: there would be no difference of opinion about that.

soc.: Well, but speaking of men, Euthyphro, did you ever hear any one arguing that a murderer or any sort of evil-doer ought to be let off?

euth.: I should rather say that these are the questions which they are always arguing, especially in courts of law: they commit all sorts of crimes, and there is nothing which they will not do or say in their own defence.

soc.: But do they admit their guilt, Euthyphro, and yet say that they ought not to be punished?

euth.: No; they do not.

soc.: Then there are some things which they do not venture to say and do: for they do not venture to argue that the guilty are to be unpunished, but they deny their guilt, do they not?

euth.: Yes.

soc.: Then they do not argue that the evil-doer should not be punished, but they argue about the fact of who the evil-doer is, and what he did and when?

euth.: True.

soc.: And the gods are in the same case, if as you assert they quarrel about just and unjust, and some of them say while others deny that injustice is done among them. For surely neither God nor man will ever venture to say that the doer of injustice is not to be punished?

euth.: That is true, Socrates, in the main.

soc.: But they join issue about the particulars—gods and men alike; and, if they dispute at all, they dispute about some act which is called in question, and which by some is affirmed to be just, by others to be unjust. Is not that true?

euth.: Quite true.

soc.: Well then, my dear friend Euthyphro, do tell me, for my better instruction and information, what proof have you that in the opinion of all the gods a servant who is guilty of murder, and is put in chains by the master of the dead man, and dies because he is put in chains before he who bound him can learn from the interpreters of the gods what he ought to do with him, dies unjustly; and that on behalf of such an one a son ought to proceed against his father and accuse him of murder. How would you show that all the gods absolutely agree in approving of his act? Prove to me that they do, and I will applaud your wisdom as long as I live.

euth.: It will be a difficult task; but I could make the matter very clear indeed to you.

soc.: I understand; you mean to say that I am not so quick of apprehension as the judges: for to them you will be sure to prove that the act is unjust, and hateful to the gods.

euth.: Yes indeed, Socrates; at least if they will listen to me.

soc.: But they will be sure to listen if they find that you are a good speaker. There was a notion that came into my mind while you were speaking; I said to myself: "Well, and what if Euthyphro does prove to me that all the gods regarded the death of the serf as unjust, how do I know anything more of the nature of piety and impiety? for granting that this action may be hateful to the gods, still piety and impiety are not adequately defined by these distinctions, for that which is hateful to the gods has been shown to be also pleasing and dear to them." And therefore, Euthyphro, I do not ask you to prove this; I will suppose, if you like, that all the gods condemn and abominate such an action. But I will amend the definition so far as to say that what all the gods hate is impious, and what they love pious or holy; and what some of them love and others hate is both or neither. Shall this be our definition of piety and impiety?

euth.: Why not, Socrates?

soc.: Why not! Certainly, as far as I am concerned, Euthyphro, there is no reason why not. But whether this admission will greatly assist you in the task of instructing me as you promised, is a matter for you to consider.

euth.: Yes, I should say that what all the gods love is pious and holy, and the opposite which they all hate, impious.

Euthyphro first claims that piety means doing what he is doing—namely, prosecuting an unjust person, in this case, his own father, for some wrongdoing. Socrates asks whether an example of piety—even if a good one—would, on Euthyphro's own understanding, be sufficient to provide a general meaning of piety. Euthyphro comes to see that an example is not a definition; what is needed is some general statement delineating the character of impiety that can then be used to ascertain whether *any* particular action is pious or impious. Clearly, to know a general concept like piety, justice, intelligence, or courage, one would have to do more than merely cite examples of pious, just, intelligent, or courageous actions. The meaning of the general concept is necessary for the understanding of the particular examples. Euthyphro thus gives a more general statement and a fairly straightforward one: pious actions please the gods; impious actions displease them. We now have a *definition* instead of an *example*, which is the right *type* of answer. But is the answer *right*? Socrates asks whether, on Euthyphro's own understanding of the nature of the gods, the gods sometimes disagree. Clearly, they do—not about matters of fact but of value. Socrates then points out that an action that pleases some gods will anger others, so that a particular action can on Euthyphro's definition be both pious and impious, which is contradictory. Euthyphro responds by suggesting that on some things all gods agree.

At this point Socrates could take issue with Euthyphro in one of several ways; he could raise questions about whether the gods really do agree on anything universally, or how we could know whether they do and what it is that they agree on. He could even have ridiculed Euthyphro's acceptance of what the gods say on faith. But this would be to rely on factors external to Euthyphro's own point of view. Had the author been a lesser philosopher, the dialogue might well have taken such a turn. The result would have been a clash between systems—in this case, between a religious-based ethical system and a secular one—which probably could not have been resolved by reason at that time. What we get instead is one of the most devastating assaults ever mounted against a religious-based ethics, in the form of one simple, piercing question: Is an action pious, or holy, because it pleases all the gods, or does it please all the gods because it is holy? In other words, *Is it right because God says so or does God say so because it is right?* This question cuts so deeply to the heart of the issue that contemporary philosopher Anthony Flew has remarked that "one good test of a person's aptitude for

philosophy is to discover whether he can grasp its force and point."

⚹

SOC.: Ought we to inquire into the truth of this Euthyphro, or simply to accept the mere statement on our own authority and that of others? What do you say?

EUTH.: We should inquire; and I believe that the statement will stand the test of inquiry.

SOC.: We shall know better, my good friend, in a little while. The point which I should first wish to understand is whether the pious or holy is beloved by the gods because it is holy, or holy because it is beloved of the gods.

EUTH.: I do not understand your meaning, Socrates.

SOC.: I will endeavor to explain: we speak of carrying and we speak of being carried, of leading and being led, seeing and being seen. You know that in all such cases there is a difference, and you know also in what the difference lies?

EUTH.: I think that I understand.

SOC.: And is not that which is beloved distinct from that which loves?

EUTH.: Certainly.

SOC.: Well; and now tell me, is that which is carried in this state of carrying because it is carried, or for some other reason?

EUTH.: No; that is the reason.

SOC.: And the same is true of what is led and of what is seen?

EUTH.: True.

SOC.: And a thing is not seen because it is visible, but conversely, visible because it is seen; nor is a thing led because it is in the state of being led, or carried because it is in the state of being carried, but the converse of this. And now I think, Euthyphro, that my meaning will be intelligible; and my meaning is, that any state of action or passion implies previous action or passion. It does not become because it is becoming, but it is in a state of becoming because it becomes; neither does it suffer because it is in a state of suffering, but it is in a state of suffering because it suffers. Do you not agree?

EUTH.: Yes.

SOC.: Is not that which is loved in some state either of becoming or suffering?

EUTH.: Yes.

SOC.: And the same holds as in the previous instances; the state of being loved follows the act of being loved, and not the act the state.

EUTH.: Certainly.

SOC.: And what do you say of piety, Euthyphro: is not piety, according to your definition, loved by all the gods?

EUTH.: Yes.

SOC.: Because it is pious or holy, or for some other reason?

EUTH.: No, that is the reason.

SOC.: It is loved because it is holy, not holy because it is loved?

EUTH.: Yes.

SOC.: And that which is dear to the gods is loved by them, and is in a state to be loved of them because it is loved of them?

EUTH.: Certainly.

SOC.: Then that which is dear to the gods, Euthyphro, is not holy, nor is that which is holy loved of God, as you affirm; but they are two different things.

EUTH.: How do you mean, Socrates?

SOC.: I mean to say that the holy has been acknowledged by us to be loved of God because it is holy, not to be holy because it is loved.

EUTH.: Yes.

SOC.: But that which is dear to the gods is dear to them because it is loved by them, not loved by them because it is dear to them.

EUTH.: True.

SOC.: But, friend Euthyphro, if that which is holy is the same with that which is dear to God, and is loved because it is holy, then that which is dear to God would have been loved as being dear to God; but if that which is dear to God is dear to him because loved by him, then that which is holy would have been holy because loved by him. But now you see that the reverse is the case, and that they are quite different from one another. For one is of a kind to be loved because it is loved, and the other is loved because it is of a kind to be loved. Thus you appear to me, Euthyphro, when I ask you what is the essence of holiness, to offer an attribute only, and not the essence—the attribute of being loved by all the gods. But you still refuse to explain to me the nature of holiness. And therefore, if you please, I will ask you not to hide your treasure, but to tell me once more what holiness or

piety really is, whether dear to the gods or not (for that is a matter about which we will not quarrel); and what is impiety?

EUTH.: I really do not know, Socrates, how to express what I mean. For somehow or other our arguments, on whatever ground we rest them, seem to turn round and walk away from us.

SOC.: Your words, Euthyphro, are like the handiwork of my ancestor Daedalus; and if I were the sayer or propounder of them, you might say that my arguments walk away and will not remain fixed where they are placed because I am a descendant of his. But now, since these notions are your own, you must find some other gibe, for they certainly, as you yourself allow, show an inclination to be on the move.

EUTH.: Nay, Socrates, I shall still say that you are the Daedalus who sets arguments in motion; not I, certainly, but you make them move or go round, for they would never have stirred, as far as I am concerned.

SOC.: Then I must be greater than Daedalus: for whereas he only made his own inventions to move, I move those of other people as well. And the beauty of it is, that I would rather not. For I would give the wisdom of Daedalus, and the wealth of Tantalus, to be able to detain them and keep them fixed. But enough of this. As I perceive that you are lazy, I will myself endeavor to show you how you might instruct me in the nature of piety; and I hope that you will not grudge your labour. Tell me, then, Is not that which is pious necessarily just?

EUTH.: Yes.

SOC.: And is, then, all which is just pious? Or, is that which is pious all just, but that which is just, only in part and not all, pious?

✺

Socrates' famous question forces Euthyphro into a dilemma, literally, a "two-forked path." Each fork leads to disaster, *even from within Euthyphro's own point of view.* If an action is right because it pleases all the gods, then it is not the merits of the action that make it right or wrong, but the collective moods of the gods. This would make the difference between right and wrong ultimately arbitrary, which Euthyphro feels cannot be the case. (If, for instance, it pleased all the gods to see innocent children tortured and then sacrificed, then on such a definition it would be wrong for us not to do so.) Recognizing the problem, Euthyphro takes the second horn of the dilemma, stating that obviously it must be something about the characteristics of a pious act itself that make all the gods love it, not their love for that act that makes it pious; in other words, the love of the gods is itself an *effect*, not the *cause*, of some action being a pious one. But now on Euthyphro's own view this makes the approval of the gods irrelevant to the definition of the essential characteristics of piety! Again, prompted by Socrates, this is something that Euthyphro can reason out for himself.

⚹

EUTH.: I do not understand you, Socrates.

SOC.: And yet I know that you are as much wiser than I am, as you are younger. But, as I was saying, revered friend, the abundance of your wisdom makes you lazy. Please to exert yourself, for there is no real difficulty in understanding me. What I mean I may explain by an illustration of what I do not mean. The poet (Stasinus) sings—

"Of Zeus, the author and creator of all these things,
You will not tell: for where there is fear there is also reverence."

Now I disagree with this poet. Shall I tell you in what respect?

EUTH.: By all means.

SOC.: I should not say that where there is fear there is also reverence; for I am sure that many persons fear poverty and disease, and the like evils, but I do not perceive that they reverence the objects of their fear.

EUTH.: Very true.

SOC.: But where reverence is, there is fear; for he who has a feeling of reverence and shame about the commission of any action, fears and is afraid of an ill reputation.

EUTH.: No doubt.

SOC.: Then we are wrong in saying that where there is fear there is also reverence; and we should say, where there is reverence there is also fear. But

there is not always reverence where there is fear; for fear is a more extended notion, and reverence is a part of fear, just as the odd is a part of number, and number is a more extended notion than the odd. I suppose that you follow me now?

EUTH.: Quite well.

SOC.: That was the sort of question which I meant to raise when I asked whether the just is always the pious, or the pious always the just; and whether there may not be justice where there is not piety; for justice is the more extended notion of which piety is only a part. Do you disagree?

EUTH.: No. I think that you are quite right.

SOC.: Then, if piety is a part of justice, I suppose that we should inquire what part? If you had pursued the inquiry in the previous cases; for instance, if you had asked me what is an even number, and what part of number the even is, I should have had no difficulty in replying, a number which represents a figure having two equal sides. Do you not agree?

EUTH.: Yes. I quite agree.

SOC.: In like manner, I want you to tell me what part of justice is piety or holiness that I may be able to tell Meletus not to do me injustice or indict me for impiety, as I am now adequately instructed by you in the nature of piety or holiness, and their opposites.

EUTH.: Piety or holiness, Socrates, appears to me to be that part of justice which attends to the gods, as there is the other part of justice which attends to men.

SOC.: That is good, Euthyphro; yet still there is a little point about which I should like to have further information. What is the meaning of "attention"? For attention can hardly be used in the same sense when applied to the gods as when applied to other things. For instance, horses are said to require attention, and not every person is able to attend to them, but only a person skilled in horsemanship. Is it not so?

EUTH.: Certainly.

SOC.: I should suppose that the art of horsemanship is the art of attending to horses?

EUTH.: Yes.

SOC.: Nor is every one qualified to attend to dogs, but only the huntsman?

EUTH.: True.

SOC.: And I should also conceive that the art of the huntsman is the art of attending to dogs?

EUTH.: Yes.

SOC.: As the art of the oxherd is the art of attending to oxen?

EUTH.: Very true.

SOC.: In like manner holiness or piety is the art of attending to the gods?—that would be your meaning, Euthyphro?

EUTH.: Yes.

SOC.: And is not attention always designed for the good or benefit of that to which the attention is given? As in the case of horses, you may observe that when attended to by the horseman's art they are benefited and improved, are they not?

EUTH.: True.

SOC.: As the dogs are benefited by the huntsman's art, and the oxen by the art of the oxherd, and all other things are tended or attended for their good and not for their hurt?

EUTH.: Certainly, not for their hurt.

SOC.: But for their good?

EUTH.: Of course.

SOC.: And does piety or holiness, which has been defined to be the art of attending to the gods, benefit or improve them? Would you say that when you do a holy act you make any of the gods better?

EUTH.: No, no; that was certainly not what I meant.

SOC.: And I, Euthyphro, never supposed that you did. I asked you the question about the nature of the attention, because I thought that you did not.

EUTH.: You do me justice, Socrates; that is not the sort of attention which I mean.

SOC.: Good: but I must still ask what is this attention to the gods which is called piety?

EUTH.: It is such, Socrates, as servants show to their masters.

SOC.: I understand—a sort of ministration to the gods.

EUTH.: Exactly.

SOC.: Medicine is also a sort of ministration or service, having in view the attainment of some object—would you not say of health?

EUTH.: I should.

SOC.: Again, there is an art which ministers to the ship-builder with a view to the attainment of some result?

EUTH.: Yes, Socrates, with a view to the building of a ship.

SOC.: As there is an art which ministers to the housebuilder with a view to the building of a house?

EUTH.: Yes.

SOC.: And now tell me, my good friend, about the art which ministers to the gods: what work does that help to accomplish? For you must surely know if, as you say, you are of all men living the one who is best instructed in religion.

EUTH.: And I speak the truth, Socrates.

SOC.: Tell me then, oh tell me—what is that fair work which the gods do by the help of our ministrations?

EUTH.: Many and fair, Socrates, are the works which they do.

SOC.: Why, my friend, and so are those of a general. But the chief of them is easily told. Would you not say that victory in war is the chief of them?

EUTH.: Certainly.

SOC.: Many and fair, too, are the works of the gardner, if I am not mistaken; but his chief work is the production of food from the earth?

EUTH.: Exactly.

SOC.: And of the many and fair things done by the gods, which is the chief or principal one?

EUTH.: I have told you already, Socrates, that to learn all these things accurately will be very tiresome. Let me simply say that piety or holiness is learning how to please the gods in word and deed, by prayers and sacrifices. Such piety is the salvation of families and states, just as the impious, which is unpleasing to the gods, is their ruin and destruction.

SOC.: I think that you could have answered in much fewer words the chief question which I asked, Euthyphro, if you had chosen. But I see plainly that you are not disposed to instruct me—clearly not: else why, when we reached the point, did you turn aside? Had you only answered me I should have truly learned of you by this time the nature of piety. Now, as the asker of a question is necessarily dependent on the answerer, whither he leads I must follow; and can only ask again, what is the pious, and what is piety? Do you mean that they are a sort of science of praying and sacrificing?

EUTH.: Yes, I do.

SOC.: And sacrificing is giving to the gods, and prayer is asking of the gods?

EUTH.: Yes, Socrates.

SOC.: Upon this view, then, piety is a science of asking and giving?

EUTH.: You understand me capitally, Socrates.

SOC.: Yes, my friend; the reason is that I am an attendant of your science, and give my mind to it, and therefore nothing which you say will be thrown away upon me. Please then to tell me, what is the nature of this service to the gods? Do you mean that we prefer requests and give gifts to them?

EUTH.: Yes, I do.

SOC.: Is not the right way of asking to ask of them what we want?

EUTH.: Certainly.

SOC.: And the right way of giving is to give to them in return what they want of us. There would be no meaning in an art which gives to any one that which he does not want.

EUTH.: Very true, Socrates.

SOC.: Then piety, Euthyphro, is an art which gods and men have of doing business with one another?

EUTH.: That is an expression which you may use, if you like.

SOC.: But I have no particular liking for anything but the truth. I wish, however, that you would tell me what benefit accrues to the gods from our gifts. There is no doubt about what they give to us; for there is no good thing which they do not give; but how we can give any good thing to them in return is far from being equally clear. If they give everything and we give nothing, that must be an affair of business in which we have very greatly the advantage of them.

EUTH.: And do you imagine, Socrates, that any benefit accrues to the gods from our gifts?

SOC.: But if not, Euthyphro, what is the meaning of gifts which are conferred by us upon the gods?

EUTH.: What else, but tributes of honour; and, as I was just now saying, what pleases them?

SOC.: Piety, then, is pleasing to the gods, but not beneficial or dear to them?

EUTH.: I should say that nothing could be dearer.

SOC.: Then once more the assertion is repeated that piety is dear to the gods?

EUTH.: Certainly.

SOC.: And when you say this, can you wonder at your words not standing firm, but walking away? Will you accuse me of being the Daedalus who makes them walk away, not perceiving that there is another and far greater artist than Daedalus who makes them go round in a circle, and he is yourself; for the argument, as you will perceive, comes round to the same point. Were we not saying that the holy or pious was not the same with that which is loved of the gods? Have you forgotten?

EUTH.: I quite remember.

SOC.: And are you not saying that what is loved of the gods is holy; and is not this the same as what is dear to them—do you see?

EUTH.: True.

SOC.: Then either we were wrong in our former assertion; or, if we were right then, we are wrong now.

EUTH.: One of the two must be true.

SOC.: Then we must begin again and ask, What is piety? That is an inquiry which I shall never be weary of pursuing as far as in me lies; and I entreat you not to scorn me, but to apply your mind to the utmost, and tell me the truth. For, if any man knows, you are he; and therefore I must detain you, like Proteus, until you tell. If you had not certainly known the nature of piety and impiety, I am confident that you would never, on behalf of a serf, have charged your aged father with murder. You would not have run such a risk of doing wrong in the sight of the gods, and you would have had too much respect for the opinions of men. I am sure, therefore, that you know the nature of piety and impiety. Speak out then, my dear Euthyphro, and do not hide your knowledge.

EUTH.: Another time, Socrates, for I am in a hurry, and must go now.

SOC.: Alas! My companion, and will you leave me in despair? I was hoping that you would instruct me in the nature of piety and impiety; and then I might have cleared myself of Meletus and his indictment. I would have told him that I had been enlightened by Euthyphro, and had given up rash innovations and speculations, in which I indulged only through ignorance, and that now I am about to lead a better life.

⁂

Thus we come full circle, with Euthyphro having to see the gaps and inconsistencies in his own system of beliefs, forced under Socratic cross-examination to face what he had been hiding from all along: the unknown behind the mask of the known, hidden from him by his own ignorance. But the point is not just about Euthyphro. Keep in mind the kind of person that Euthyphro is: someone so concerned with justice, fair play, and the rights of all individuals that he would defend a poor (and even murderous) slave, not just against his master but against a master who is Euthyphro's own father. This is *not* a bad and corrupt man! Indeed, if you think about it, few of us would have such high moral scruples as to bring similar charges against our own parents under similar circumstances. Furthermore, Euthyphro is an acknowledged prophet through whom the gods speak (note, however, that Euthyphro prophesies how well Socrates' trial will go and that he will be found innocent—Plato is cleverly here mocking the prophets). So in effect the point here is that even those recognized experts whose thoughts and actions are of the highest caliber cannot ultimately know with absolute certainty that they are right. But, if not them, who? *How?* By what *method?*

2.2 The Trial and Death of Socrates

The *Apology* and *Crito* describe Socrates' trial and imprisonment. Socrates was in his seventies at the time and already famous throughout the Hellenic world. Even plays had been written about him. The most famous, *The Clouds* by Aristophanes, satirized Socrates and his students and made them the objects of public ridicule. Socrates' trial, described by Plato in the *Apology* (the Greek word means "defense," not "request for forgiveness"), began, as was traditional at the time, with a defense by the accused. It opened with the prosecution having already made its case; Socrates repeated the charges against him and then went on to insult his audience, ridicule his accusers, and suggest that his appropriate punishment should be a lifelong pension! Along the way we learn of the unexpected events that began at the holy temple at Delphi and helped turn Socrates into a philosopher. By the end of his apology, however, Socrates is found guilty by a vote of 281 to 220. He is sentenced to prison to await execution by drinking hemlock (a poisonous plant). In *Crito*, we find out that the citizens of Athens appar-

ently had no wish for him actually to die. They seem to have gone along with Socrates' students in bribing the guards and arranging for his escape to another country. Socrates' students fully expected that he would do this. However, Socrates, always the gadfly, found a way of pulling the rug out from under even his own followers at the very end. Socrates did not flee. He stayed.

Crito ends with Socrates fearlessly drinking the hemlock. He chose death rather than to retract the principles at the root of his philosophy. In a sense, by killing Socrates the Athenian democracy voted to preserve obedience and unquestioning reverence for its gods and for its own authority by banishing the irreverent questioning of the philosopher. A few years later it lost the war with Sparta, a totalitarian city-state; the first known experiment in democracy ended in an overthrow by a totalitarian regime. When democracy was restored a year later, it was plagued by so much corruption that it too lasted only briefly. Thus ended the golden age of Greece, the first democratic society; there followed utter disarray and then the Roman Empire. After this came centuries of the so-called Dark Ages, where religious repression was rampant and the scale of human suffering, under the iron hand of religious fascism, immeasurable. One can only wonder what might have happened had the Athenians voted differently. Perhaps it would have made no difference. Or it might have made all the difference in the world. Certainly, the mere *possibility* that choosing life for Socrates might have made a tremendous difference is enough to give one pause.

2.3 Plato's Epistemology and Metaphysics: The Myth of the Cave

In the *Meno*, another early dialogue, Plato gives a detailed argument (again through the character of Socrates) for his view that not only is knowledge possible, but you already had it but lost it at birth: knowledge is in fact *recollection*. He uses a slave to show that even someone completely une-ducated has the capacity for understanding and that this capability demonstrates that the soul once knew what it has now forgotten. Otherwise, such a feat would, according to him, be impossi-ble. This theory—that knowledge ultimately comes from within, that it is already in you, waiting to be discovered—will become one of the most recurrent themes in subsequent philosophy.

Starting with the *Phaedrus*, probably an early middle dialogue, Plato uses the examples of love and beauty to present his theory of the immor-tality of the soul and of the ideas, or forms. As the ultimate constituents of reality and the proper objects of mystical contemplation, the ideal forms make possible the evolution and enlightenment of the soul. It is extremely important to note that all the subsequent dia-logues of Plato's so-called middle and late periods carry this more "positive" theme forward. Written at the Academy, they focus on many of the same questions as the earlier ones, but instead of the dialectical cross-examination by Socrates that leaves his interlocutors, as well as the reader, perplexed and frustrated without any solution to the questions posed, the Socrates of the middle and late dialogues is much less adversarial; the main characters often end up in agreement with positive answers to even the most vexing questions. Relying on the Parmenidean distinction between reality and appearance, armed with the demonstrability of Pythagorean mathematics (see Section 1.7), Plato shifts focus in these dialogues from the state of Socratic unknowing to the attainment of knowledge of the forms. Ignorance, which comes from living in the realm of appearances and mistaking them for realities, can be dis-pelled by attending instead to the ideal forms behind the appearances as seen in the "mind's eye"—that is, through the light of reason.

None of the objects of knowledge, according to Plato's dialogues written during his middle period, can be found in the world of appear-ances; our senses only obscure them. What this ultimately means in terms of our understanding of reality, the relationship between the mind and the world, the nature of knowledge, and the lim-itations of language in which we describe this, Plato himself likens to the realization that we live in a cave and that appearance is to reality as shadows are to things that cast shadows. This aspect of Plato's thought—exemplified in the allegory of the cave, the simile of the sun, and the divided line—contains some of the most famous passages in all of philosophy. They appear in *The Republic*, the major work from his middle period, which Plato kept revising for the rest of his life. It describes a conversation that supposedly took place during a pause in the Peloponnesian War, about ten years before Socrates' fateful drinking of the hemlock. Athens was still a democracy. Among the characters are Plato's older brothers, Glaucon and Adeimantus. The "I" of the narrator is Socrates.

As you read, keep your mind's focus on the word *idea* as it appears in the text; this is the word that is sometimes translated as *form*. Try to see if you can imbue the word with some other, perhaps deeper, sense than common sense would give it by reading it in this doubled way.

✦

The Republic

The many, as we say, are seen but not known, and the ideas are known but not seen.

Exactly.

And what is the organ with which we see the visible things?

The sight, he said.

And with the hearing, I said, we hear, and with the other senses perceive the other objects of sense?

True.

But have you remarked that sight is by far the most costly and complex piece of workmanship which the originator of the senses ever contrived?

From *The Dialogues of Plato*, Benjamin Jowett, trans. (London: The Clarendon Press, 1892), with emen-dations by the author.

No, I never have, he said.

Then reflect: has the ear or voice need of any third or additional nature in order that the one may be able to hear and the other to be heard?

Nothing of the sort.

No, indeed, I replied; and the same is true of most, if not all, the other senses—you would not say that any of them requires such an addition?

Certainly not.

But you see that without the addition of some other nature there is no seeing or being seen?

How do you mean?

Sight being, as I conceive, in the eyes, and he who has eyes wanting to see; color being also present in them, still unless there be a third nature specially adapted to the purpose, the owner of the eyes will see nothing and the colors will be invisible.

Of what nature are you speaking?

Of that which you term light, I replied.

True, he said.

Noble, then, is the bond which links together sight and visibility, and great beyond other bonds by no small difference of nature; for light is their bond, and light is no ignoble thing?

Nay, he said, the reverse of ignoble.

And which, I said, of the gods in heaven would you say was the lord of this element? Whose is that light which makes the eye to see perfectly and the visible to appear?

You mean the sun, as you and all mankind say.

May not the relation of sight to this deity be described as follows?

How?

Neither sight nor the eye in which sight resides is the sun?

No.

Yet of all the organs of sense the eye is the most like the sun?

By far the most like.

And the power which the eye possesses is a sort of effluence which is dispensed from the sun?

Exactly.

Then the sun is not sight, but the author of sight who is recognized by sight.

True, he said.

And this is he whom I call the child of the good, whom the good begat in his own likeness, to be in the visible world, in relation to sight and the things of sight, what the good is in the intellectual world in relation to mind and the things of mind.

Will you be a little more explicit? he said.

Why, you know, I said, that the eyes, when a person directs them towards objects on which the light of day is no longer shining, but the moon and stars only, see dimly, and are nearly blind; they seem to have no clearness of vision in them?

Very true.

But when they are directed towards objects on which the sun shines, they see clearly and there is sight in them?

Certainly.

And the soul is like the eye: when resting upon that on which truth and being shine, the soul perceives and understands and is radiant with intelligence; but when turned towards the twilight of becoming and perishing, then she has opinion only, and goes blinking about, and is first of one opinion and then of another, and seems to have no intelligence?

Just so.

Now, that which imparts truth to the known and the power of knowing to the knower is what I would have you term the idea of good, and this you will deem to be the cause of science, and of truth in so far as the latter becomes the subject of knowledge; beautiful too, as are both truth and knowledge, you will be right in esteeming this other nature as more beautiful than either; and, as in the previous instance, light and sight may be truly said to be like the sun, and yet not to be the sun, so in this other sphere, science and truth may be deemed to be like the good, but not the good; the good has a place of honour yet higher.

What a wonder of beauty that must be, he said, which is the author of science and truth, and yet surpasses them in beauty; for you surely cannot mean to say that pleasure is the good?

God forbid, I replied; but may I ask you to consider the image in another point of view?

In what point of view?

You would say, would you not, that the sun is not only the author of visibility in all visible things, but of generation and nourishment and growth, though he himself is not generation?

Certainly.

In like manner the good may be said to be not only the author of knowledge to all things known, but of their being and essence, and yet the good is not essence, but far exceeds essence in dignity and power.

Glaucon said, with a ludicrous earnestness: By the light of heaven, how amazing!

Yes, I said, and the exaggeration may be set down to you; for you made me utter my fancies.

And pray continue to utter them; at any rate let us hear if there is anything more to be said about the similitude of the sun.

Yes, I said, there is a great deal more.

Then omit nothing, however slight.

I will do my best, I said; but I should think that a great deal will have to be omitted.

You have to imagine, then, that there are two ruling powers, and that one of them is set over the intellectual world, the other over the visible. I do not say heaven, lest you should fancy that I am playing upon the name. May I suppose that you have this distinction of the visible and intelligible fixed in your mind?

I have.

Now take a line which has been cut into two unequal parts, and divide each of them again in the same proportion, and suppose the two main divisions to answer, one to the visible and the other to the intelligible, and then compare the subdivisions in respect of their clearness and want of clearness, and you will find that the first section in the sphere of the visible consists of images. And by images I mean, in the first place, shadows, and in the second place, reflections in water and in solid, smooth and polished bodies and the like: Do you understand?

Yes, I understand.

Imagine, now, the other section, of which this is only the resemblance, to include the animals which we see, and everything that grows or is made.

Very good.

Would you not admit that both the sections of this division have different degrees of truth, and that the copy is to the original as the sphere of opinion is to the sphere of knowledge?

Most undoubtedly.

Next proceed to consider the manner in which the sphere of the intellectual is to be divided.

In what manner?

Thus:—There are two subdivisions, in the lower of which the soul uses the figures given by the former division as images; the inquiry can only be hypothetical, and instead of going upwards to a principle descends to the other end; in the higher of the two, the soul passes out of hypotheses, and goes up to a principle which is above hypotheses, making no use of images as in the former case, but proceeding only in and through the ideas themselves.

I do not quite understand your meaning, he said.

Then I will try again; you will understand me better when I have made some preliminary remarks. You are aware that students of geometry, arithmetic, and the kindred sciences assume the odd and the even and the figures and three kinds of angles and the like in their several branches of science; these are their hypotheses, which they and every body are supposed to know, and therefore they do not deign to give any account of them either to themselves or others; but they begin with them, and go on until they arrive at last, and in a consistent manner, at their conclusion?

Yes, he said, I know.

And do you not know also that although they make use of the visible forms and reason about them, they are thinking not of these, but of the ideals which they resemble; not of the figures which they draw, but of the absolute square and the absolute diameter, and so on—the forms which they draw or make, and which have shadows and reflections in water of their own, are converted by them into images, but they are really seeking to behold the things themselves, which can only be seen with the eye of the mind?

That is true.

And of this kind I spoke as the intelligible, although in the search after it the soul is compelled to use hypotheses; not ascending to a first principle, because she is unable to rise above the region of hypothesis, but employing the objects of which the shadows below are resemblances in their turn as images, they having in relation to the shadows and reflections of them a greater distinctness, and therefore a higher value.

I understand, he said, that you are speaking of the province of geometry and the sister arts.

And when I speak of the other division of the intelligible, you will understand me to speak of that other sort of knowledge which reason herself attains by the power of dialectic, using the hypotheses not as first principles, but only as hypotheses—that is to say, as steps and points of departure into a world which is above hypotheses, in order that she may soar beyond them to the first principle of the whole; and clinging to this and then to that which depends on this, by successive steps she descends again without the aid of any sensible object, from ideas, through ideas, and in ideas she ends.

I understand you, he replied; not perfectly, for you seem to me to be describing a task which is really tremendous; but, at any rate, I understand you to say that knowledge and being, which the science of dialectic contemplates, are clearer than the notions of the arts, as they are termed, which proceed from hypotheses only: these are also contemplated by the understanding, and not by the senses: yet, because they start from hypotheses and do not ascend to a principle, those who contemplate them appear to you not to exercise the higher reason upon them, although when a first principle is added to them they are cognizable by the higher reason. And the habit which is concerned with geometry and the cognate sciences I suppose that you would term understanding and not reason, as being intermediate between opinion and reason.

You have quite conceived my meaning, I said; and now, corresponding to these four divisions, let there be four faculties in the soul—reason answering to the highest, understanding to the second, faith (or conviction) to the third, and perception of shadows to the last—and let there be a scale of them, and let us suppose that the several faculties have clearness in the same degree that their objects have truth.

I understand, he replied, and give my assent, and accept your arrangement.

⁂

Let us focus for just a few moments on the first line: "The many, as we say, are seen but not known, and the ideas are known but not seen." By *the many*, Plato simply refers to all the various things that appear before you as a multitude. In referring to them as "many" rather than as "things," or "objects," and so on, he is trying to refer to the world you see around you (but notice how loaded that way of putting it is?) in as neutral a way as possible. Clearly, what all this before you *is*, it *appears* as a many. Although your "field of vision" doesn't have any noticeable "gaps" in it, there are borders and boundaries making themselves apparent: the color gradations, changes in

shape, and so on, which you automatically interpret as "a many" different things: books, people, furniture, rocks, and so on.

Now, in saying that the many are seen but not known, Plato is drawing your attention to the fact that all these appearances presently before you—whatever they are—do indeed *appear*. They are seen by you to exist as a variegated multitude of *somethings*, but they are not *known*. In what sense are they not known? You see tables, chairs, people, and so on, so you do know these things in the sense of being able to name them, distinguish them, and so on. But what are all these things that seem so familiar that even to question whether you know what they are seems, on the face of it, absurd. But if you reflect a moment you will realize that you "know" these things only in some very superficial way; you are *acquainted with their presence*, so to speak. You make the same noises that others do in referring to them. *But what are they really?* Why do they exist? How did they come to be? What are they made of?

The moment you begin to engage with such questions you have moved away, in thought, from the appearances themselves (as they appear) and have entered the realm of what Plato is calling *ideas*. This book that you hold in your hand, for instance: Why does it exist? If you ask yourself this question, the answer that appears within you has to do with the idea of an author, a printing press, a publishing company, and so on. Have you ever met me? Ever been to any publishing house, much less the one that is responsible for this book? Whichever the case may be, most certainly at this very moment as you are reading, your thoughts relate you, not to anything that is in your immediate presence, but rather, to your own ideas. For instance, you may have an idea of me as the author of this book, but you do not at present see me. Likewise, you may have an idea of the printing press. Or, to shift directions slightly, you may have an idea of what this book is made of, such as atoms, but presently you do not see them. And yet these ideas are *known*. Well, but what, exactly, is it that is known?

Your idea of me is an idea of an author. *That* you know; you know that this book has an author. *This is an idea*. It is an abstract entity, a concept that *as such* is nowhere to be seen! Suppose you meet me. Have you now met an idea? Have you even *really* met an author? No, Plato would say: even if I am in your presence it is an idea of an author that somehow is involved in my being, in my existence, but *authorship* is not, itself, an appearance like colors, temperatures, shapes, and so on. So right from the start Plato has us reflecting beyond what is merely given. Why should knowledge be of things that are not seen and not of things seen? This is the very foundation of Plato's *rationalist* epistemology, in which he bases knowledge in a realm utterly removed from experience, in pure reason.

The next question to which he directs our attention is about as profound as any in the whole of philosophy. It has two related parts. First, *what do you see the appearances with* and, second, *with what organ, or faculty, do you apprehend the ideal forms?* Plato's point about the sun is that there is something other than the seen objects themselves—the cause of light—which makes vision possible; likewise, there is something other than the known items themselves— the cause of knowledge. This is the mental faculty of *understanding*. And it is this faculty that is responsible *both* for the items you see and the ideal forms you know and understand, because what you are looking at has an immediate cause nowhere apparent among the appearances. It is like when you are dreaming. What do you see the objects in your dreams with? What imbues them with light? What makes you understand that in your dream it is a dog chasing you rather than a dragon? The objects in your dreams are apprehended as particular objects they seem as they seem rather than some other way. What makes that possible?

There is something within you analogous to the sun; indeed, it is what gives light to everything within what you call your world. But you do not see this thing any more than you see any of the things as they really are in themselves. For, as Plato describes in the next section, you live in a cave of darkness; the objects you see are but shadows of real things, inaccurate and illusory representations of real things: the ideal forms.

⬥

And now, I said, let me show in a figure how far our nature is enlightened or unenlightened: Behold! Human beings living in an underground cave, which has a mouth open towards the light and reaching all along the cave; here they have been from their childhood, and have their legs and necks chained so that they cannot move, and can only see before them, being prevented by the chains from turning round their heads. Above and behind them a fire is blazing at a distance, and between the fire and the prisoners there is a raised way; and you will see, if you look, a low wall built along the way, like the screen which marionette players have in front of them, over which they show the puppets.

I see.

And do you see, I said, men passing along the wall carrying all sorts of vessels, and statues and figure of animals made of wood and stone and various materials, which appear over the wall? Some of them are talking, others silent.

You have shown me a strange image, and they are strange prisoners.

Like ourselves, I replied; and they see only their own shadows, or the shadows of one another, which the fire throws on the opposite wall of the cave?

True, he said; how could they see anything but the shadows if they were never allowed to move their heads?

And of the objects which are being carried in like manner they would only see the shadows?

Yes, he said.

And if they were able to converse with one another, would they not suppose that they were naming what was actually before them?

Very true.

And suppose further that the prison had an echo which came from the other side, would they not be sure to fancy when one of the passers-by spoke that the voice which they heard came from the passing shadow?

No question, he replied.

To them, I said, the truth would be literally nothing but the shadows of the images.

That is certain.

And now look again, and see what will naturally follow if the prisoners are released and disabused of their error. At first, when any of them is liberated and compelled suddenly to stand up and turn his neck round and walk and look towards the light, he will suffer sharp pains; the glare will distress him, and he will be unable to see the realities of which in his former state he had seen the shadows; and then conceive some one saying to him, that what he saw before was an illusion, but that now, when he is approaching nearer to being and his eye is turned towards more real existence, he has a clearer vision—what will be his reply? And you may further imagine that his instructor is pointing to the objects as they pass and requiring him to name them—will he not be perplexed? Will he not fancy that the shadows which he formerly saw are truer than the objects which are now shown to him?

Far truer.

And if he is compelled to look straight at the light, will he not have a pain in his eyes which will make him turn away to take refuge in the objects of vision which he can see, and which he will conceive to be in reality clearer than the things which are now being shown to him?

True, he said.

And suppose once more, that he is reluctantly dragged up a steep and rugged ascent, and held fast until he is forced into the presence of the sun himself, is he not likely to be pained and irritated? When he approaches the light his eyes will be dazzled, and he will not be able to see anything at all of what are now called realities.

Not all in a moment, he said.

He will require to grow accustomed to the sight of the upper world. And first he will see the shadows best, next the reflections of men and other objects in the water, and then the objects themselves; then he will gaze upon the light of the moon and the stars and the spangled heaven; and he will see the sky and the stars by night better than the sun or the light of the sun by day?

Certainly.

Last of all he will be able to see the sun, and not mere reflections of him in the water, but he will see him in his own proper place, and not in another; and he will contemplate him as he is.

Certainly.

He will then proceed to argue that this is he who gives the season and the years, and is the guardian of all that is in the visible world, and in a certain way the cause of all things which he and his fellows have been accustomed to behold?

Clearly, he said, he would first see the sun and then reason about him.

And when he remembered his old habitation, and the wisdom of the den and his fellow-prisoners, do you not suppose that he would felicitate himself on the change, and pity them?

Certainly, he would.

And if they were in the habit of conferring honors among themselves on those who were quickest to observe the passing shadows and to remark which of them went before, and which followed after, and which were together; and who were therefore best able to draw conclusions as to the future, do you think that he would care for such honors and glories, or envy the possessors of them? Would he not say with Homer,

"Better to be the poor servant of a poor master,"

and to endure anything, rather than think as they do and live after their manner?

Yes, he said, I think that he would rather suffer anything than entertain these false notions and live in this miserable manner.

Imagine once more, I said, this person coming suddenly out of the sun to be replaced in his old situation; would he not be certain to have his eyes full of darkness?

To be sure, he said.

And if there were a contest, and he had to compete in measuring the shadows with the prisoners who had never moved out of the cave, while his sight was still weak, and before his eyes had become steady (and the time which would be needed to acquire this new habit of sight might be very considerable), would he not be ridiculous? Men would say of him that up he went and down he came without his eyes; and that it was better not even to think of ascending; and if any one tried to loose another and lead him up to the light, let them only catch the offender, and they would put him to death.

No question, he said.

This entire allegory, I said, you may now attach, dear Glaucon, to the previous argument; the cave is the world of sight, the light of the fire is the sun, and you will not misapprehend me if you interpret the journey upwards to be the ascent of the soul into the intellectual world according to my poor belief, which, at your desire, I have expressed—whether rightly or wrongly God knows. But, whether true or false, my opinion is that in the world of knowledge the idea of good appears last of all, and is seen only with an effort; and, when seen, is also inferred to be the universal author of all things beautiful and right, parent of light and of the lord of light in this visible world, and the immediate source, of reason and truth in the intellectual; and that this is the power upon which he who would act rationally either in public or private life must have his eye fixed.

I agree, he said, as far as I am able to understand you.

Moreover, I said, you must not wonder that those who attain to this beatific vision are unwilling to descend to human affairs; for their souls are ever hastening into the upper world where they desire to dwell; which desire of theirs is very natural, if our allegory may be trusted.

Yes, very natural.

And is there anything surprising in one who passes from divine contemplations to the evil state of man, misbehaving himself in a ridiculous manner; if, while his eyes are blinking and before he has become accustomed to the surrounding darkness, he is compelled to fight in courts of law, or in other places, about the images or the shadows of images of justice, and is endeavouring to meet the conceptions of those who have never yet seen absolute justice?

Anything but surprising, he replied.

Any one who has common sense will remember that the bewilderments of the eyes are of two kinds, and arise from two causes, either from coming out of the light or from going into the light, which is true of the mind's eye, quite as much as of the bodily eye; and he who remembers this when he sees any one whose vision is perplexed and weak, will not be too ready to laugh; he will first ask whether that soul of man has come out of the brighter life, and is unable to see because unaccustomed to the dark, or having turned from darkness to the day is dazzled by excess of light. And he will count the one happy in his condition and state of being, and he will pity the other; or, if he have a mind to laugh at the soul which comes from below into the light, there will be more reason in this than in the laugh which greets him who returns from above out of the light into the den.

That, he said, is a very just distinction.

But then, if I am right, certain professors of education must be wrong when they say that they can put a knowledge into the soul which was not there before, like sight into blind eyes.

They undoubtedly say this, he replied.

Whereas, our argument shows that the power and capacity of learning exists in the soul already; and that just as the eye was unable to turn from darkness to light without the whole body, so too the instrument of knowledge can only by the movement of the whole soul be turned from the world of becoming into that of being, and learn by degrees to endure the sight of being, and of the brightest and best of being, or in other words, of the good.

Very true.

And must there not be some art which will effect conversion in the easiest and quickest manner; not implanting the faculty of sight, for that exists already, but has been turned in the wrong direction, and is looking away from the truth?

Yes, he said, such an art may be presumed.

And whereas the other so-called virtues of the soul seem to be akin to bodily qualities, for even when they are not originally innate they can be implanted later by habit and exercise, the virtue of wisdom more than anything else contains a divine element which always remains, and by this conversion is rendered useful and profitable; or, on the other hand, hurtful and useless.

☙

Notice what happens when the philosopher leaves the cave. He becomes, literally, enlightened. But he has lived so long in the darkness, among the shadows, that his eyes have grown accustomed to the dark and so now he cannot see the truth, the real sun; reality blinds rather than illuminates him. At first. But then if he does not give in to fear but remains in the blinding light that obliterates everything—if he can stand being surrounded by an apparent nothingness until he, literally, comes to his senses—a new and brilliant world of absolute truth and ultimate being reveals itself. What then?

The philosopher, if he is a true lover of wisdom, is unselfish and does not remain outside the cave. He must go back into the cave and try to enlighten the others. So he stumbles back into the dark. He tries to tell the others but they think he is a fool; they want him to prove that he has attained true wisdom and enlightenment by, for instance, predicting the patterns of the shadows on the cave wall. He cannot even see them! He clumsily knocks into things; the philosopher is blind in the darkness they call light.

2.4 Plato's Next Step: The Birth of Self-Criticism

As if all his many achievements were not enough, Plato brought to philosophy something that had been virtually unthinkable to just about all of his predecessors, for nearly all philosophers before him were in one respect not unlike religious priests: *they used all the means available to them to defend their positions.* Plato, however, in the dialogues written in the third and final period of his life, questions his own theories. Unlike most old men who get set in their ways, Plato kept questioning even his own views. Rather than spending the last of his energies shoring up clever defenses for his many views, he turned his critical eye to his own theories and became self-critical.

This ability to be self-critical is an important characteristic that sharply distinguishes many philosophers from most nonphilosophically minded people, including—and especially—religious thinkers. Suppose you have a set of beliefs. Obviously, you think that your beliefs are true, or else you would not believe them. Suppose I asked you, "What's wrong with your beliefs?" Probably you would respond with a shrug. Suppose I asked you to point out all the gaps in your beliefs or the holes in your theories, and to explain precisely what is wrong with your opinions. Would you be able to do it?

This may seem like an odd thing to try and do. After all, if there is something wrong with your beliefs, if they are questionable, then you would not hold them. But Plato, like most great philosophers after him, is painfully aware that all beliefs, even his own, no matter how certain he may feel about them, and all views, no matter how true they may seem, are open to criticism. He does not hide from this. Many philosophers after him have taken this to be a defining characteristic of a philosopher. This skill has come to be called, in popular usage, *critical distance.*

Plato's dialogue *Parmenides* is a perfect example of the philosophical power of having an open mind, not just about the views of others but even your own. It describes a meeting that supposedly took place, years before Plato's birth, between Socrates as a young man and a very old Parmenides accompanied by his most famous pupil, Zeno of Elea. Recall that, according to Parmenides, existence is not made up of individual things; in reality, "all is one." The totality of existence is one undifferentiated, unchanging, eternal whole. Even the simplest change, such as one thing moving from one place to another, is but an illusion. Zeno tried to prove Parmenides right (Section 1.11), using his famous paradoxes that have lasted more than two thousand years.

The narrator of the dialogue is supposed to be Cephalus describing a conversation told to him by Plato's older half-brother Antiphon. Socrates tries to solve one of Zeno's paradoxes using Plato's theory of forms. As is often the case with the dialogues from Plato's later period, there is a detailed examination of philosophical logic directed toward a critical and often unflattering scrutiny of Plato's own theory of forms. Parmenides thus counters Socrates' attempt at solving one of Zeno's paradoxes with a devastating *reductio ad absurdum* of Plato's theory.

⚖

Parmenides

What is your meaning, Zeno? Do you maintain that if being is many, it must be both like and unlike, and that this is impossible, for neither can the like be unlike, nor the unlike like—is that your position?

Just so, said Zeno.

And if the unlike cannot be like or the like unlike, then, according to you, being could not be many; for this would involve an impossibility. In all that you say have you any other purpose except to disprove the being of the many? And is not each division of your treatise intended to furnish a separate proof of this, there being in all as many proofs of the not-being of the many as you have composed arguments? Is that your meaning, or have I misunderstood you?

No, said Zeno; you have correctly understood my general purpose.

I see, Parmenides, said Socrates, that Zeno would like to be not only one with you in friendship but your second self in his writings too; he puts what you say in another way, and would fain make believe that he is telling us something which is new. For you in your poems say "The All is one," and of this you adduce excellent proofs; and he on the other hand says that it is not many, and on behalf of this he offers overwhelming evidence. You affirm unity, he denies plurality. And so you deceive the world into believing that you are saying different things when really you are saying much the same. This is a strain of art beyond the reach of most of us. . . .

While Socrates was speaking, Pythodorus thought that Parmenides and Zeno were not altogether pleased at the successive steps of the argument;* but still they gave the closest attention, and often looked at one another, and smiled as if in admiration of him. When he had finished, Parmenides expressed their feelings in the following words:

Socrates, he said, I admire the bent of your mind towards philosophy; tell me now, was this your own distinction between ideas in themselves and the things which partake of them? And do you think that there is an idea of likeness apart from the likeness which we possess, and of the one and many, and of the other things which Zeno mentioned?

I think that there are such ideas, said Socrates.

Parmenides proceeded: And would you also make absolute ideas of the just and the beautiful and the good, and of all that class?

Yes, he said, I should.

And would you make an idea of man apart from us and from all other human creatures, or of fire and water?

I am often undecided, Parmenides, as to whether I ought to include them or not.

And would you feel equally undecided, Socrates, about things of which the mention may provoke a smile? I mean such things as hair, mud, dirt, or anything else which is vile and paltry; is it hard to decide whether each of these has an idea distinct from the actual objects with which we come into contact, or not?

Certainly not, said Socrates; visible things like these are such as they appear to us, and I am afraid that there would be an absurdity in assuming any idea of them, although I sometimes get disturbed, and begin to think that there is nothing without an idea; but then again, when I have taken up this position, I run away, because I am afraid that I may fall into a bottomless pit of nonsense, and perish; and so I return to the ideas of which I was just now speaking, and occupy myself with them.

Yes, Socrates, said Parmenides; that is because you are still young; the time will come, if I am not mistaken, when philosophy will have a firmer grasp of you, and then you will not despise even the meanest things; at your age, you are too much disposed to regard the opinions of men. But I should like to know whether you mean that there are certain ideas of which all other things partake, and from which they derive their names; that similars, for example, become similar, because they partake of similarity; and great things become great, because they partake of greatness; and that just and beautiful things become just and beautiful, because they partake of justice and beauty?

Yes, certainly, said Socrates, that is my meaning.

Then each individual partakes either of the whole of the idea or else of a part of the idea? Can there be any other mode of participation?

There cannot be, he said.

Then do you think that the whole idea is one, and yet, being one, is in each one of the many?

What objection is there, Parmenides? said Socrates.

The result will be that one and the same thing

---

*See Section 1.11 on Zeno and his paradoxes.

will exist as a whole at the same time in many separate individuals, and will therefore be in a state of separation from itself.

Nay, but the idea may be like the day which is one, and the same in many places at once, and yet continuous with itself; in this way each idea may be one and the same in all at the same time.

I like your way, Socrates, of making one in many places at once. You mean to say, that if I were to spread out a sail and cover a number of men, there would be one whole including many—is not that your meaning?

I think so.

And would you say that the whole sail includes each man, or a part of it only, and different parts different men?

The latter.

Then, Socrates, the ideas themselves will be divisible, and things which participate in them will have a part of them only and not the whole idea existing in each of them?

That seems to follow.

Then would you like to say, Socrates, that the one idea is really divisible and yet remains one?

Certainly not, he said.

Suppose that you divide absolute greatness, and that of the many great things each one is great in virtue of a portion of greatness less than absolute greatness—is that conceivable?

No.

Or will each equal thing, if possessing some small portion of equality less than absolute equality, be equal to some other thing by virtue of that portion only?

Impossible.

Or suppose one of us to have a portion of smallness; this is but a part of the small, and therefore the absolutely small will be greater; while that to which the abstracted part of the small is added will be smaller and not greater than before.

That, indeed, can scarcely be.

Then in what way, Socrates, will all things participate in the ideas, if they are unable to participate in them either as parts or wholes?

Indeed, he said, you have asked a question which is not easily answered.

Well, said Parmenides, and what do you say of another question?

What question?

I imagine that your reason for assuming one idea of each kind is as follows: Whenever a number of objects appear to you to be great there doubtless seems to you to be one and the same idea (or nature) visible in them all; hence you conceive of greatness as one.

Very true, said Socrates.

But now, if you allow your mind in like manner to embrace in one view this real greatness and those other great things, will not one more greatness arise, being required to account for the semblance of greatness in all these?

It would seem so.

Then another idea of greatness now comes into view over and above absolute greatness and the individuals which partake of it; and then another, over and above all these, by virtue of which they will all be great, and so you will be left not with a single idea in every case, but with an infinite number. . . .

☨

Because Plato offers no response to the problems posed to his theory of ideal forms in the *Parmenides*, some scholars have interpreted this to signify a final move by Plato away from his dualism, that is, an abandonment of the separation between the world of ideal forms and the sensible world of appearances. It is precisely this aspect of Plato's dualism that Aristotle, the most famous of Plato's formidable students at the Academy, criticized most severely.

The many themes raised by Plato will emerge and reemerge, sometimes through the counterpoint of ideas influenced by his most famous pupil, Aristotle, throughout the rest of this book. It has been called the Great Conversation. That, I think, is an understatement. Western philosophy is not just talk. It is an awakening.

NOTE

1. Another reminder: "B.C.E." stands for "Before the Common Era," and "C.E." stands for "Common Era," in accordance with "B.C." and "A.D."

3 ⚘ Aristotle

3.0 Aristotle (384–322 B.C.E.): The Birth of Logic

Aristotle was born at Stagira, in Macedonia, a Greek colonial town settled by the Ionians. The son of Nicomachus, the personal physician of King Amyntas of Macedonia, Aristotle entered Plato's Academy at the age of seventeen and quickly became Plato's most prodigious pupil. Besides absorbing Plato's philosophy, Aristotle developed a method for systematizing all knowledge. He wrote on virtually every subject, including physics, astronomy, meteorology, taxonomy, psychology, biology, ethics, politics, aesthetics, metaphysics, and logic.

At the time Aristotle entered the Academy, Plato—then sixty and in the final period of his philosophical creativity—was involved in the division of ideal forms further and further down until the *infinia species*, the final unit of division—the indivisible—could be reached. This influenced Aristotle's early work, especially his development of metaphysics and logic. Whereas Plato considered the world of appearances as illusory, seeking instead knowledge through pure reason that could be communicated only abstractly, through myths and metaphors such as the cave, Aristotle became convinced that the knowledge acquired through the senses, though not sufficient in itself, was the true path to wisdom. Although the two thinkers remained friends until Plato's death at the age of eighty-one, they continued to disagree about whether reason or experience was primary, as well as about the nature of ideal forms—a debate that would continue into the twentieth century. Under the influence of Pythagoras, Plato's development of ideas was based on geometric forms and the abstract rules of numbers and a love of mathematics, whereas Aristotle's classifications of genera and species led him away from pure mathematics and toward natural science, especially organic biology and the study of physiology.

Aristotle classified knowledge into three main categories: (1) *theoretical*, whose aim is impartial and disinterested knowledge; (2) *practical*, whose aim is to influence and guide human conduct; and (3) *productive*, whose aim is to offer guidance to the various arts. Fundamental to all three is the primary science that he called *analytic*, now known as logic. The purpose of the analytic, or logic, is to set down the necessary and sufficient conditions for any discipline that has truth as its aim. He defined *science* as the demonstrated knowledge of the causes of things, of which there are four types: (1) the *material* cause, "that from which, as its constitutive material, something comes, for example the bronze of the statue"; (2) the *formal,* or ideal, cause, what the particular statue is, its essence or nature, such as its being a bust of Plato; (3) the *efficient* cause, that by which it initially comes into existence, "the source of the first beginning of change," as in "the father is the cause of the child"; and (4) the *final* cause, its "end" or purpose, "that for the sake of which" something is done, such as "health is [the final cause] of walking around."

Aristotle's method for attaining knowledge of these causes of things is by syllogistic deduction from premises known to be certain. This is in marked contrast to the other two prevailing methods of discourse at the time: *dialectic,* which starts from probable premises, and *eristic,* whose purpose is rhetorical victory, not truth. A syllogism is the simplest unit of reasoning. It says, if something is so and something is so, then something else *must* be so. It consists of three propositions—sentences that assert something is so (as contrasted with imperatives, such as "Shut the door!")—the first two which are called "premises" and the third, which must necessarily be true if the first two are, called the "conclusion." Syllogistic inference works on the principle that the term common to both premises, the "middle term," must be related (either as subject or predicate) to each of the other two terms such that a conclusion is necessarily forced regarding the relation of the two terms to one another. For instance, consider the famous

All men are mortal.

Socrates is a man.

Therefore, Socrates is mortal.

"Man," the middle term, is related (as subject) to "mortal" and (as object) to "Socrates" in such a way that *Socrates* and *mortal* must necessarily be conjoined as in the conclusion.

Aristotle not only invented syllogistic reasoning but also gave such a thorough analysis of the subject-predicate relation and all syllogistic forms that this method, now called deductive logic, has virtually remained unchanged to this day. Aristotle also developed the method of logical *induction,* in which knowledge is attained even when the conclusion cannot be known to be true with absolute certainty but only probably. It involves passing from the individuals (particulars) of sense experience (things knowable to us) to the universal, necessary principles involved in sense experience (things knowable in themselves), a thinking process that later would reach its peak in extremely dramatic ways in the work of Immanuel Kant.

In the centuries following Aristotle, his principles of matter and form were further developed, especially by the medieval thinkers, in terms of his fundamental distinction between "potential" and "actual" existence. The main problem for Aristotle was to explain change. To the pre-Socratics, whom Aristotle discusses at length in the first selection from his *Metaphysics,* change was to be interpreted as a passage from nonbeing to being. To them this seemed absolutely absurd and incomprehensible: if ever there was nothing, then still there would be nothing, since nothing can come from nothing! Aristotle thought he solved this problem as follows. What at first has only potential being is transformed, through its ideal form, into actual being, what Aristotle called *entelechy.* Thus, existence becomes in Aristotle's cosmology a dynamic evolutionary system in which change is not illusory but real, spontaneous, continuous, and teleological.

At forty-two, Aristotle accepted an invitation from King Philip of Macedonia to become private tutor to his thirteen-year-old crown prince, Alexander. Less than six years later, when Alexander became Alexander the Great, conqueror of the whole ancient world from Greece to India, Aristotle returned to Athens and set up his own school, the Lyceum (also called Peripatos, hence Aristotelians are sometimes called "Peripatetics"). It lasted eight hundred years. Whereas Plato's Academy led in the development of mathematics and geometry, the Lyceum focused on applied scientific research, especially in the natural sciences. Not being an Athenian citizen, Aristotle had to rent the land on which the Lyceum operated. Although he was widely regarded as one of the greatest minds of the time, many Athenians resented him for having trained the Macedonian who had become their conqueror. So when in 323 B.C.E. Alexander suddenly died and the Macedonians were ousted from power, Athens turned against Aristotle. Ironically, Plato's greatest pupil, like Plato's teacher Socrates, also ended up being arrested by the Athenian government and charged—like Socrates—with atheism and impiety. Sentenced to death or exile, Aristotle—unlike Socrates—chose exile. A year later, he died on the island of Euboea.

3.1 Aristotle's Epistemology: Knowledge for Its Own Sake

Of the dialogues and expository works Aristotle published in his lifetime, only fragments remain, but many of his unpublished writings have survived in the form of lecture notes or texts used by his students. In his *Metaphysics*, Aristotle develops his view of individuals as composites of ideal forms and physical substance along with his dynamic theory of change. It begins with the famous passage, "All men by nature desire to know." This desire is not something you have been conditioned by authorities to have. It is *innate*; you are born with it. Indeed, the implication is that the human mind must be conditioned *away* from its natural desire to know through seduction.

Furthermore, this innate desire is not merely the wish to know how to do or make something. It's not just practical knowledge we seek. Rather, the knowledge we by nature seek is knowledge for its own sake. What is knowledge for knowledge's sake? He gives the example of our own senses. Besides being useful, there is the "delight we take in our senses; for even apart from their usefulness

they are loved for themselves." The aesthetic sense of beauty, for instance, has value in and of itself.

He distinguishes different levels of knowledge, only the highest form of which is wisdom. Unlike Plato, he allows that knowledge can be attained through the senses but, like Plato, he does not regard this as wisdom. For such knowledge can only tell us the "that" of a thing, not the "why." For instance, to know *that* aspirin can help your headache is knowledge without wisdom; to know *why* is altogether another thing. To be able to explain *why* aspirin works as it does requires much more than merely seeing that it does. It requires reasoning and deeper understanding of causes. Wisdom requires that we go beyond sense experience and reach the truth about the *causes* of things through reason.

For Aristotle, therein lies the true foundation of *wisdom*: the *first principles and causes*, which give us knowledge not of appearances but of that which is behind the appearances and makes them as they are.

⁂

Metaphysics

Book A

All men by nature desire to know. An indication of this is the delight we take in our senses; for even apart from their usefulness they are loved for themselves; and above all others the sense of sight. For not only with a view to action, but even when we are not going to do anything, we prefer seeing (one might say) to everything else. The reason is that this, most of all the senses, makes us know and brings to light many differences between things.

By nature animals are born with the faculty of sensation, and from sensation memory is produced in some of them, though not in others. And therefore the former are more intelligent and apt at learning than those which cannot remember; those which are incapable of hearing sounds are intelli-

From Aristotle, *Metaphysics*, W. D. Ross, trans. (Oxford: Oxford University Press, 1908).

gent though they cannot be taught, e. g. the bee, and any other race of animals that may be like it; and those which besides memory have this sense of hearing can be taught.

The animals other than man live by appearances and memories, and have but little of connected experience; but the human race lives also by art and reasonings. Now from memory experience is produced in men; for the several memories of the same thing produce finally the capacity for a single experience. And experience seems pretty much like science and art, but really science and art come to men *through* experience; for "experience made art," as Polus says, "but inexperience luck." Now art arises when from many notions gained by experience one universal judgment about a class of objects is produced. For to have a judgment that when Callias was ill of this disease this did him good, and similarly in the case of Socrates and in many individual cases, is a matter of experience; but to judge that it has done good to all persons of a certain constitution, marked off in one class, when they were ill of this disease, e. g. to phlegmatic or bilious people when burning with fever,—this is a matter of art.

With a view to action experience seems in no respect inferior to art, and men of experience succeed even better than those who have theory without experience. (The reason is that experience is knowledge of individuals, art of universals, and actions and productions are all concerned with the individual; for the physician does not cure *man*, except in an incidental way, but Callias or Socrates or some other called by some such individual name, who happens to be a man. If, then, a man has the theory without the experience, and recognizes the universal but does not know the individual included in this, he will often fail to cure; for it is the individual that is to be cured.) But yet we think that *knowledge* and *understanding* belong to art rather than to experience, and we suppose artists to be wiser than men of experience (which implies that Wisdom depends in all cases rather on knowledge); and this because the former know the cause, but the latter do not. For men of experience know that the thing is so, but do not know why, while the others know the "why" and the cause. Hence we think also that the master-workers in each craft are more honorable and know in a truer sense and are wiser than the manual workers, because they know the causes of the things that are done (we think

the manual workers are like certain lifeless things which act indeed, but act without knowing what they do, as fire burns,—but while the lifeless things perform each of their functions by a natural tendency, the laborers perform them through habit); thus we view them as being wiser not in virtue of being able to act, but of having the theory for themselves and knowing the causes. And in general it is a sign of the man who knows and of the man who does not know, that the former can teach, and therefore we think art more truly knowledge than experience is; for artists can teach, and men of mere experience cannot.

Again, we do not regard any of the senses as Wisdom; yet surely these give the most authoritative knowledge of particulars. But they do not tell us the "why" of anything—e. g. why fire is hot; they only say *that* it is hot. . . .

Evidently we have to acquire knowledge of the original causes (for we say we know each thing only when we think we recognize its first cause), and causes are spoken of in four senses. In one of these we mean the substance, i. e. the essence (for the "why" is reducible finally to the definition, and the ultimate "why" is a cause and principle); in another the matter or substratum, in a third the source of the change, and in a fourth the cause opposed to this, the purpose and the good (for this is the end of all generation and change). . . .

⚹

The central goal of the Aristotelian philosophy is to transform the Socratic–Platonic conceptual philosophy into a theory capable of explaining the phenomenal (mental) world of the appearances. Plato's philosophy could account only for the relationship between the conceptual reality of the ideas, or forms, and the perceptual reality of perceived objects using allegories like the cave. To say that the perceived objects are but shadows of the forms, ideas, or even their representations is not to give an account in Aristotle's sense of *first principles*, that is, in terms of explaining the causes of such phenomena. This is the goal of what he calls *first philosophy*, or *metaphysics*, the most abstract and at the same time the most exact of all the sciences. The purpose of metaphysics, then, is to discover those first principles from which all the other various sciences are derived. Unlike the secondary sciences, like physics, which ask what things are and why, metaphysics asks the more general question: What does it mean to be anything whatsoever? What does it mean to *be*? It is "the science of any existent, as existent." In other words, what is the cause of being? Why is there existence—any type of existence—at all?

In the book *Metaphysics*, from which both selections in this section are taken, Aristotle argues that Platonic ideas, or forms, cannot explain the existence of empirical facts (like the fact that I see a table in front of me). Nor can they explain their own existence. To simply claim that the ideas, or forms, are eternal is not a sufficient explanation; *why* are they eternal? What causes them to be so? To hypothesize some higher level of being, even to think of ideas or forms in some theological terms like God-made entities, would not satisfy Aristotle. If God exists the metaphysical problem is the same as if God does not exist. The problem is with being—*any* being. Why? *Why anything at all?*

⚹

The investigation of the truth is in one way hard, in another easy. An indication of this is found in the fact that no one is able to attain the truth adequately, while, on the other hand, we do not collectively fail, but every one says something true about the nature of things, and while individually we contribute little or nothing to the truth, by the union of all a considerable amount is amassed. Therefore, since the truth seems to be like the proverbial door, which no one can fail to hit, in this respect it must be easy, but the fact that we can have a whole truth and not the particular part we aim at shows the difficulty of it.

Perhaps, too, as difficulties are of two kinds, the cause of the present difficulty is not in the facts but in us. For as the eyes of bats are to the blaze of day, so is the reason in our soul to the things which are by nature most evident of all.

It is just that we should be grateful, not only to those with whose views we may agree, but also to those who have expressed more superficial views;

for these also contributed something, by developing before us the powers of thought. It is true that if there had been no Timotheus we should have been without much of our lyric poetry; but if there had been no Phrynis there would have been no Timotheus. The same holds good of those who have expressed views about the truth; for from some thinkers we have inherited certain opinions, while the others have been responsible for the appearance of the former.

It is right also that philosophy should be called knowledge of the truth. For the end of theoretical knowledge is truth, while that of practical knowledge is action (for even if they consider how things are, practical men do not study the eternal, but what is relative and in the present). Now we do not know a truth without its cause; and a thing has a quality in a higher degree than other things if in virtue of it the similar quality belongs to the other things as well (e. g. fire is the hottest of things; for it is the cause of the heat of all other things); so that that which causes derivative truths to be true is most true. Hence the principles of eternal things must be always most true (for they are not merely sometimes true, nor is there any cause of their being, but they themselves are the cause of the being of other things), so that as each thing is in respect of being, so is it in respect of truth.

But evidently there *is* a first principle, and the causes of things are neither an infinite series nor infinitely various in kind. For (1) neither can one thing proceed from another, as from matter, *ad infinitum* (e. g. flesh from earth, earth from air, air from fire, and so on without stopping), nor can the sources of movement form an endless series (man for instance being acted on by air, air by the sun, the sun by Strife, and so on without limit). Similarly the final causes cannot go on *ad infinitum*,—walking being for the sake of health, this for the sake of happiness, happiness for the sake of something else, and so one thing always for the sake of another. And the case of the essence is similar. For in the case of intermediates, which have a last term and a term prior to them, the prior must be the cause of the later terms. For if we had to say which of the three is the cause, we should say the first; surely not the last, for the final term is the cause of none; nor even the intermediate, for it is the cause only of one. (It makes no difference whether there is one intermediate or more, nor whether they are infinite or finite in number.) But of series which are infinite in this way, and of the infinite in general, all the parts down to that now present are alike intermediates; so that if there is no first there is no cause at all.

Nor can there be an infinite process downwards, with a beginning in the upward direction, so that water should proceed from fire, earth from water, and so always some other kind should be produced. For one thing comes *from* another in two ways—not in the sense in which "from" means "after" (as we say "from the Isthmian games come the Olympian"), but either (i) as the man comes from the boy, by the boy's changing, or (ii) as air comes from water. By "as the man comes from the boy" we mean "as that which has come to be from that which is coming to be, or as that which is finished from that which is being achieved" (for as becoming is between being and not being, so that which is becoming is always between that which is and that which is not; for the learner is a man of science in the making, and this is what is meant when we say that *from* a learner a man of science is being made); on the other hand, coming from another thing as water comes from air implies the destruction of the other thing. This is why changes of the former kind are not reversible, and the boy does not come from the man (for it is not that which comes to be something that comes to be as a result of coming to be, but that which exists after the coming to be; for it is thus that the day, too, comes from the morning—in the sense that it comes after the morning; which is the reason why the morning cannot come from the day); but changes of the other kind are reversible. But in both cases it is impossible that the number of terms should be infinite. For terms of the former kind, being intermediates, must have an end, and terms of the latter kind change back into *one another*; for the destruction of either is the generation of the other.

At the same time it is impossible that the first cause, being eternal, should be destroyed; for since the process of becoming is not infinite in the upward direction, that which is the first thing by whose destruction something came to be must be non-eternal.

Further, the *final cause* is an end, and that sort of end which is not for the sake of something else, but for whose sake everything else is; so that if there is to be a last term of this sort, the process will not be infinite; but if there is no such term, there will be no final cause, but those who main-

tain the infinite series eliminate the Good without knowing it (yet no one would try to do anything if he were not going to come to a limit); nor would there be reason in the world; the reasonable man, at least, always acts for a purpose, and this is a limit; for the end is a limit.

But the *essence*, also, cannot be reduced to another definition which is fuller in expression. For the original definition is always more of a definition, and not the later one; and in a series in which the first term has not the required character, the next has not it either.—Further, those who speak thus destroy science; for it is not possible to have this till one comes to the unanalyzable terms. And knowledge becomes impossible; for how can one apprehend things that are infinite in this way? For this is not like the case of the line, to whose divisibility there is no stop, but which we cannot think if we do not make a stop (for which reason one who is tracing the infinitely divisible line cannot be counting the possibilities of section), but the whole line also must be apprehended by something in us that does not move from part to part.—Again, nothing infinite can exist; and if it could, at least the notion of infinity is not infinite.

But (2) if the *kinds* of causes had been infinite in number, then also knowledge would have been impossible; for we think we know, only when we have ascertained the causes, but that which is infinite by addition cannot be gone through in a finite time.

The effect which lectures produce on a hearer depends on his habits; for we demand the language we are accustomed to, and that which is different from this seems not in keeping but somewhat unintelligible and foreign because of its unwontedness. For it is the customary that is intelligible. The force of habit is shown by the laws, in which the legendary and childish elements prevail over our knowledge about them, owing to habit. Thus some people do not listen to a speaker unless he speaks mathematically, others unless he gives instances, while others expect him to cite a poet as witness. And some want to have everything done accurately, while others are annoyed by accuracy, either because they cannot follow the connexion of thought or because they regard it as pettifoggery. For accuracy has something of this character, so that as in trade so in argument some people think it mean. Hence one must be already trained to know how to take each sort of argument, since it is absurd to seek at the same time knowledge and the way of attaining knowledge; and it is not easy to get even one of the two.

The minute accuracy of mathematics is not to be demanded in all cases, but only in the case of things which have no matter. Hence its method is not that of natural science; for presumably the whole of nature has matter. Hence we must inquire first what nature is: for thus we shall also see what natural science treats of [and whether it belongs to one science or to more to investigate the causes and the principles of things].

⚓

Thus, Aristotle's solution to the problem of metaphysics is to claim that Plato's ideas are merely a duplication of the empirical, phenomenal world of appearances. The distinction between the two different realities, one of which is more fundamental and more real than the other, is, according to Aristotle, Plato's big mistake. The fundamental thought in Aristotle's metaphysics is that the world of ideas and the world of sense are identical. There is just one world.

3.2 Aristotle's Criticism of Plato's Ideal Forms

Aristotle criticized Plato's theory of ideal forms by raising the "third man argument" and several other difficulties, such as that the ideal forms ultimately fail to explain anything and that Plato cannot prove their existence with his arguments, which can be used to prove the existence of problematic ideal forms such as negations and relations. In the end what remains primarily real for Aristotle is substance—individual entities, like you and me, tables and chairs, rocks, and planets. Since the essence of things is known by means of class concepts like "man," "horse," "table," and so on, the fundamental problem of Aristotle's philosophy and his solution to the problems posed by Plato concern an explanation of the relationship of the *universal* to the *particular*.

⚓

Categories

When one thing is predicated of another, all that which is predicable of the predicate will be predicable also of the subject. Thus, "man" is predicated of the individual man; but "animal" is predicated of "man"; it will, therefore, be predicable of the individual man also: for the individual man is both "man" and "animal."

If genera are different and co-ordinate, their differentiae are themselves different in kind. Take as an instance the genus "animal" and the genus "knowledge." "With feet," "two-footed," "winged," "aquatic," are differentiae of "animal"; the species of knowledge are not distinguished by the same differentiae. One species of knowledge does not differ from another in being "two-footed."

But where one genus is subordinate to another, there is nothing to prevent their having the same differentiae: for the greater class is predicated of the lesser, so that all the differentiae of the predicate will be differentiae also of the subject.

Expressions which are in no way composite signify substance, quantity, quality, relation, place, time, position, state, action, or affection.

⚓

According to Aristotle, the key notion is that universals, like "man," or "blueness," do not exist independently of particular individuals. Each individual thing in the world is a "primary substance" whose species and genera are "secondary substances" that make the thing what it is rather than some other thing. It may help to understand what Aristotle means if we note that the actual word used by Aristotle, *ouisa*, usually translated as "substance," is also sometimes translated as "reality." To argue that particular individuals, such as you and I, tables and chairs, and rocks, are a type of primary substance—that is, a primary *reality*—contradicts Plato's theory

From "Categories," E M. Edghill, trans., *The Oxford Translation of Aristotle*, W D. Ross, ed. (Oxford: Clarendon Press, 1928).

that the objects of sense experience are at best only partly real reflections of the ideal forms.

So whereas "man" and "horse" are examples of substances, phrases like "is six feet tall" and "weighs 165 pounds" are examples of the category of *quantity*. "Greater," "smaller," and "double" are examples of the category of *relation*. "In the room" and "on the moon" fall under the category of *place*, whereas "yesterday," "now," and "tomorrow" fall under the category of *time*. "Lying" and "sitting" are examples of *position*; "happy," "hungry," and "armed" are examples of the category of *state*. "To kill" and "to run" fall under the category of *action*. "To be wounded" is an example of the category of *affection*. Aristotle claims that,

⚘

No one of these terms, in and by itself, involves an affirmation; it is by the combination of such terms that positive or negative statements arise. For every assertion must, as is admitted, be either true or false, whereas expressions which are not in any way composite, such as "man," "white," "runs," "wins," cannot be either true or false.

Substance, in the truest and primary and most definite sense of the word, is that which is neither predicable of a subject nor present in a subject; for instance, the individual man or horse. But in a secondary sense those things are called substances within which, as species, the primary substances are included; also those which, as genera, include the species. For instance, the individual man is included in the species "man," and the genus to which the species belongs is "animal"; these, therefore—that is to say, the species "man" and the genus "animal"—are termed secondary substances.

It is plain from what has been said that both the name and the definition of the predicate must be predicable of the subject. For instance, "man" is predicated of the individual man. Now in this case the name of the species "man" is applied to the individual, for we use the term "man" in describing the individual; and the definition of "man" will also be predicated of the individual man, for the individual man is both man and animal. Thus, both the name and the definition of the species are predicable of the individual.

⚘

Thus, instead of the a priori analysis of ideal forms that Plato envisioned as the true function of the philosopher, Aristotle focused on an empirical study of the structure of the individual objects of the sensible world. At the same time, Aristotle denied that the soul, or mind, exists as a separately existing substance from the body but, rather, that it is itself part of the living process. He then analyzed the concepts of ideal form and physical substance from the perspective of language and gave the first logical definition of substance, one that would influence philosophers throughout the Middle Ages and for many generations to come.

3.3 Aristotle's Theory of Mind

Plato argued in the *Phaedo* that the soul, or individual mind, is eternal and immortal; like the eternal Platonic ideal forms, the soul can exist without the body and is even more real. However, in the next selection, taken from *On the Soul*, Aristotle argues to the contrary: the soul is not an entity that exists separately from the body, and it cannot exist without the body.

⚘

On the Soul

Let us . . . make a fresh start and try to determine what soul is and what will be its most comprehensive definition. Now there is one class of existent things which we call substance, including under the term, firstly, matter, which in itself is not this or that; secondly, shape or form, in virtue of which the term this or that is at once applied; thirdly, the whole made up of matter and form. Matter is identical with potentiality, form with actuality. And there are two meanings of actuality: knowledge

From "On the Soul," translated by R. D. Hicks, in *Aristotle: De Anima* (Cambridge University Press, 1907), pp. 51–59.

illustrates the one, exercise of knowledge the other. Now bodies above all things are held to be substances, particularly such bodies as are the work of nature; for to these all the rest owe their origin. Of natural bodies some possess life and some do not: where by life we mean the power of self-nourishment and of independent growth and decay. Consequently every natural body possessed of life must be substance, and substance of the composite order. And since in fact we have here body with a certain attribute, namely, the possession of life, the body will not be the soul: for the body is not an attribute of a subject, it stands rather for a subject of attributes, that is, matter. It must follow, then, that soul is substance in the sense that it is the form of a natural body having in it the capacity of life. Such substance is actuality. The soul, therefore, is the actuality of the body above described. But the term "actuality" is used in two senses; in the one it answers to knowledge, in the other to the exercise of knowledge. Clearly in this case it is analogous to knowledge: for sleep, as well as waking, implies the presence of soul; and, whilst waking is analogous to the exercise of knowledge, sleep is analogous to the possession of knowledge without its exercise; and in the same individual the possession of knowledge comes in order of time before its exercise. Hence soul is the first actuality of a natural body having in it the capacity of life. And a body which is possessed of organs answers to this description. We may note that the parts of plants, as well as those of animals, are organs, though of a very simple sort: for instance, a leaf is the sheath of the pod and the pod of the fruit. The roots, again, are analogous to the mouths of animals, both serving to take in nourishment. If, then, we have to make a general statement touching soul in all its forms, the soul will be the first actuality of a natural body furnished with organs. Hence there is no need to enquire whether soul and body are one, any more than whether the wax and the imprint are one; or, in general, whether the matter of a thing is the same with that of which it is the matter. For, of all the various meanings borne by the terms unity and being, actuality is the meaning which belongs to them by the fullest right.

It has now been stated in general terms what soul is, namely, substance as notion or form. And this is the quiddity of such and such a body. Suppose, for example, that any instrument, say, an axe, were

a natural body, its axeity would be its substance, would in fact be its soul. If this were taken away, it would cease, except in an equivocal sense to be an axe. But the axe is after all an axe. For it is not of a body of this kind that the soul is the quiddity, that is, the notion or form, but of a natural body of a particular sort, having in itself the origination of motion and rest.

Further, we must view our statement in the light of the parts of the body. For, if the eye were an animal, eyesight would be its soul, this being the substance as notion or form of the eye. The eye is the matter of eyesight, and in default of eyesight it is no longer an eye, except equivocally, like an eye in stone or in a picture. What has been said of the part must be understood to apply to the whole living body; for, as the sensation of a part of the body is to that part, so is sensation as a whole to the whole sentient body as such. By that which has in it the capacity of life is meant not the body which has lost its soul, but that which possesses it. Now the seed in animals, like the fruit in plants, is that which is potentially such and such a body. As, then, the cutting of the axe or the seeing of the eye is full actuality, so, too, is the waking state; while the soul is actuality in the same sense as eyesight and the capacity of the instrument. The body, on the other hand, is simply that which is potentially existent. But, just as in the one case the eye means the pupil in conjunction with the eyesight, so in the other soul and body together constitute the animal.

Now it needs no proof that the soul—or if it is divisible into parts, certain of its parts—cannot be separated from the body, for there are cases where the actuality belongs to the parts themselves. There is, however, no reason why some parts should not be separated, if they are not the actualities of any body whatever. Again, it is not clear whether the soul may not be the actuality of the body as the sailor is of the ship. This, then, may suffice for an outline or provisional sketch of soul.

But, as it is from the things which are naturally obscure, though more easily recognized by us, that we proceed to what is clear and, in the order of thought, more knowable, we must employ this method in trying to give a fresh account of soul. For it is not enough that the defining statement should set forth the fact, as most definitions do; it should also contain and present the cause: whereas in practice what is stated in the definition is usually no more than a conclusion. For example, what is quadrature? The construction of an equilateral rectangle equal in area to a given oblong. But such a definition expresses merely the conclusion. Whereas, if you say that quadrature is the discovery of a mean proportional, then you state the reason.

We take, then, as our starting-point for discussion that it is life which distinguishes the animate from the inanimate. But the term life is used in various senses; and, if life is present in but a single one of these senses, we speak of a thing as living. Thus there is intellect, sensation, motion from place to place and rest, the motion concerned with nutrition and, further, decay and growth. Hence it is that all plants are supposed to have life. For apparently they have within themselves a faculty and principle whereby they grow and decay in opposite directions. For plants do not grow upwards without growing downwards; they grow in both directions equally, in fact in all directions, as many as are constantly nourished and therefore continue to live, so long as they are capable of absorbing nutriment. This form of life can be separated from the others, though in mortal creatures the others cannot be separated from it. In the case of plants the fact is manifest: for they have no other faculty of soul at all.

It is, then, in virtue of this principle that all living things live, whether animals or plants. But it is sensation primarily which constitutes the animal. For, provided they have sensation, even those creatures which are devoid of movement and do not change their place are called animals and are not merely said to be alive. Now the primary sense in all animals is touch. But, as the nutritive faculty may exist without touch or any form of sensation, so also touch may exist apart from the other senses. By nutritive faculty we mean the part of the soul in which even plants share. Animals, however, are found universally to have the sense of touch: why this is so in each of the two cases will be stated hereafter.

For the present it may suffice to say that the soul is the origin of the functions above enumerated and is determined by them, namely, by capacities of nutrition, sensation, thought, and by motion. But whether each one of these is a soul or part of a soul and, if a part, whether it is only logically distinct or separable in space also is a question, the answer to which is in some cases not hard to see: other cases present difficulties. For, just as

in the case of plants some of them are found to live when divided and separated from each other (which implies that the soul in each plant, though actually one, is potentially several souls), so, too, when insects or annelida are cut up, we see the same thing happen with other varieties of soul: I mean, each of the segments has sensation and moves from place to place, and, if it has sensation, it has also imagination and appetency. For, where there is sensation, there is also pleasure and pain: and, where these are, desire also must of necessity be present. But as regards intellect and the speculative faculty the case is not yet clear. It would seem, however, to be a distinct species of soul, and it alone is capable of separation from the body, as that which is eternal from that which is perishable. The remaining parts of the soul are, as the foregoing consideration shows, not separable in the way that some allege them to be: at the same time it is clear that they are logically distinct. For the faculties of sensation and of opinion taken in the abstract are distinct, since to have sensation and to opine are distinct. And so it is likewise with each of the other faculties above mentioned. Again, while some animals possess all these functions, others have only some of them, others only one. It is this which will differentiate animal from animal. The reason why this is so must be investigated hereafter. The case is similar with the several senses: some animals have all of them, others some of them, others again only one, the most indispensable, that is, touch.

⚘

The soul, then, according to Aristotle is the principle of life, "the primary actualization of a natural organic body." Souls are individuated from one another by the variety and complexity of their functions, which in turn correspond to individuating differences in the organic structures that embody them. The fundamental functions, common both to all living things including plants and animals, are nutrition, growth, and reproduction. At the next level are sensations, desires, and locomotion. Finally, at the highest level, unique to human beings, is rationality, which in turn has several faculties, the most important of which is perception—the faculty of receiving the sensible form of outward objects without their matter (phenomena). He also coined the term *common sense* as a sense common to the five senses of perception, which makes possible the unity of data by the five separate senses into a single apperception and also accounts for the soul's awareness of its own activity of perception as well as all its other states. Hence, it is directly responsible for the activity of consciousness. Reason, as a separate faculty from perception that allows the soul to apprehend the universals and first principles necessary for all knowledge, while useless without sense perception, is not limited to what can be experienced but can through understanding grasp the universal, ideal forms.

⚹

On the Soul (*continued*)

Now "that by which we live and have sensation" is a phrase with two meanings, answering to the two meanings of "that by which we know" (the latter phrase means, firstly, knowledge and, secondly, soul, by either of which we say we know). Similarly that by which we have health means either health itself or a certain part, if not the whole, of the body. Now of these knowledge and health are the shape and in some sort form, the notion and virtual activity, of that which is capable of receiving in the one case knowledge, in the other health: that is to say, it is in that which is acted upon or conditioned that the activity of the causal agencies would seem to take effect. Now the soul is that whereby primarily we live, perceive, and have understanding: therefore it will be a species of notion or form, not matter or substratum. Of the three meanings of substance mentioned above, form, matter and the whole made up of these two, matter is potentiality and form is actuality. And, since the whole made up of the two is endowed with soul, the body is not the actuality of soul, but soul the actuality of a particular body. Hence those are right who regard the soul as not independent of body and yet at the same time as not itself a species of body. It is not body, but something belonging to body, and therefore resides in body

and, what is more, in such and such a body. Our predecessors were wrong in endeavouring to fit the soul into a body without further determination of the nature and qualities of that body: although we do not even find that of any two things taken at random the one will admit the other. And this result is what we might expect. For the actuality of each thing comes naturally to be developed in the potentiality of each thing: in other words, in the appropriate matter. From these considerations, then, it is manifest that soul is a certain actuality, a notion or form, of that which has the capacity to be endowed with soul.

⚹

3.4 The Nichomachean Ethics

Aristotle's masterpiece on the purpose of human life, the *Nichomachean Ethics*, is named after his son Nichomachus. It is widely regarded as one of the greatest works ever written on moral philosophy. Aristotle's teleological view of the world—that each and every thing exists for some purpose toward which it tends by its own special and unique nature—permeates throughout. He defines the final end, or good, of one's life in terms of the fulfillment of human nature. This means fulfilling the essence, or unique defining characteristic, of humanity: the rational soul. Therefore, the good for human beings necessarily consists in the actualization of those faculties unique to the human mind, namely, the further exercise and development of the rational soul (in contrast to its vegetative and sense-perceptive aspects).

It should not be surprising, given the development of Aristotle's views regarding knowledge, reality, and human nature, that his view of the good life should be different from Plato's. Their disagreement is not over particular goods; both argue for moderation, justice, virtue, courage, and so on, as defining characteristics of the good person. Both claim that knowledge of what is good can be attained by rational means. Moreover, both Plato and Aristotle conceive of the good and virtuous person as an essentially *happy* person. The difference between their approach to ethics is based on Aristotle's rejection of Plato's ideal forms. In effect, Aristotle's system makes central the notion that absolute knowledge cannot be had in the sphere of morality and ethics.

⁂

Nichomachean Ethics

Every art and every inquiry, and similarly every action and pursuit, is thought to aim at some good; and for this reason the good has rightly been declared to be that at which all things aim. But a certain difference is found among ends; some are activities, others are products apart from the activities that produce them. Where there are ends apart from the actions, it is the nature of the products to be better than the activities. Now as there are many actions, arts, and sciences, their ends also are many; the end of the medical art is health, that of shipbuilding a vessel, that of strategy victory, that of economics wealth. But where such arts fall under a single capacity—as bridle-making and the other arts concerned with the equipment of horses fall under the art of riding, and this and every military action under strategy, in the same way other arts fall under yet others— in all of these the ends of the master arts are to be preferred to all the subordinate ends; for it is for the sake of the former that the latter are pursued. It makes no difference whether the activities themselves are the ends of the actions, or something else apart from the activities, as in the case of the sciences just mentioned.

If, then, there is some end of the things we do, which we desire for its own sake (everything else being desired for the sake of this), and if we do not choose everything for the sake of something else (for at that rate the process would go on to infinity, so that our desire would be empty and vain), clearly this must be the good and the chief good. Will not the knowledge of it, then, have a great influence on life? Shall we not, like archers who have a mark to aim at, be more likely to hit

upon what is right? If so, we must try, in outline at least, to determine what it is, and of which of the sciences or capacities it is the object. It would seem to belong to the most authoritative art and that which is most truly the master art. And politics appears to be of this nature; for it is this that ordains which of the sciences should be studied in a state, and which each class of citizens should learn and up to what point they should learn them; and we see even the most highly esteemed of capacities to fall under this, e. g. strategy, economics, rhetoric; now, since politics uses the rest of the sciences, and since, again, it legislates as to what we are to do and what we are to abstain from, the end of this science must include those of the others, so that this end must be the good for man. For even if the end is the same for a single man and for a state, that of the state seems at all events something greater and more complete whether to attain or to preserve; though it is worth while to attain the end merely for one man, it is finer and more godlike to attain it for a nation or for city-states. These, then, are the ends at which our inquiry aims, since it is political science, in one sense of that term. . . .

Let us resume our inquiry and state, in view of the fact that all knowledge and every pursuit aims at some good, what it is that we say political science aims at and what is the highest of all goods achievable by action. Verbally there is very general agreement; for both the general run of men and people of superior refinement say that it is happiness, and identify living well and doing well with being happy; but with regard to what happiness is they differ, and the many do not give the same account as the wise. For the former think it is some plain and obvious thing, like pleasure, wealth, or honor; they differ, however, from one another— and often even the same man identifies it with different things, with health when he is ill, with wealth when he is poor; but, conscious of their ignorance, they admire those who proclaim some great ideal that is above their comprehension. Now some thought that apart from these many goods there is another which is self-subsistent and causes the goodness of all these as well. To examine all the opinions that have been held were perhaps somewhat fruitless; enough to examine those that are most prevalent or that seem to be arguable. . . .

The question might be asked, what we mean by

From *Nichomachean Ethics*, W. D. Ross, trans. (Oxford: Oxford University Press, 1915).

saying that we must become just by doing just acts, and temperate by doing temperate acts; for if men do just and temperate acts, they are already just and temperate, exactly as, if they do what is in accordance with the laws of grammar and of music, they are grammarians and musicians.

Or is this not true even of the arts? It is possible to do something that is in accordance with the laws of grammar, either by chance or at the suggestion of another. A man will be a grammarian, then, only when he has both done something grammatical and done it grammatically; and this means doing it in accordance with the grammatical knowledge in himself.

Again, the case of the arts and that of the virtues are not similar; for the products of the arts have their goodness in themselves, so that it is enough that they should have a certain character, but if the acts that are in accordance with the virtues have themselves a certain character it does not follow that they are done justly or temperately. The agent also must be in a certain condition when he does them; in the first place he must have knowledge, secondly he must choose the acts, and choose them for their own sakes, and thirdly his action must proceed from a firm and unchangeable character. These are not reckoned in as conditions of the possession of the arts, except the bare knowledge; but as a condition of the possession of the virtues knowledge has little or no weight, while the other conditions count not for a little but for everything, i. e. the very conditions which result from often doing just and temperate acts.

Actions, then, are called just and temperate when they are such as the just or the temperate man would do; but it is not the man who does these that is just and temperate, but the man who also does them *as* just and temperate men do them. It is well said, then, that it is by doing just acts that the just man is produced, and by doing temperate acts the temperate man; without doing these no one would have even a prospect of becoming good.

But most people do not do these, but take refuge in theory and think they are being philosophers and will become good in this way, behaving somewhat like patients who listen attentively to their doctors, but do none of the things they are ordered to do. As the latter will not be made well in body by such a course of treatment, the former will not be made well in soul by such a course of philosophy. . . .

⚓

Aristotle characterizes virtue in terms of traits that help individuals to achieve happiness and live well (*eudaimonia*, usually translated as happiness) in communities; he argues that social institutions are therefore necessary for human happiness. Truly moral individuals cannot exist independently of the political setting that enables them to develop the virtues for the good life. He distinguishes between moral virtues and intellectual virtues: the latter can be taught, the former must be lived to be learned. Finally, Aristotle defines the ideal of human happiness and explains what he takes to be the nature of the fundamental relationship between politics and ethics.

Part II ⚘ The Middle Period

4 ✿ The Epicureans, Stoics, and Skeptics

4.0 Epicurus (341–270 B.C.E.)

In the Hellenistic and Roman periods after Plato and Aristotle, philosophy branched into three distinct movements: Epicureanism, Stoicism, and Skepticism. The first of these is named after its founder, Epicurus. Born on the Greek island of Samos, Epicurus came to Athens in 323 B.C.E., the same year that Aristotle escaped. An early proponent of the view still widely held today that the universe consists ultimately of physical particles called "atoms" (literally, "indivisibles") moving about in a void, Epicurus used his version of atomism as the basis for his moral theory. He founded his own school of philosophy in Athens in 306, which—unlike Plato's Academy and Aristotle's Lyceum—accepted women. There, teaching in his garden, Epicurus and his students created a unique theory of life that integrated their atomistic view of the physical world with ethical principles designed to liberate humanity from the superstitious terrors of religion.

According to Epicurus, the soul, which like the rest of nature is made of physical atoms, is born, grows, and dies with the body. Like the Greek credited with the invention of atomism, Democritus (see Section 1.13), Epicurus did not believe that God created the universe, nor that—contra Aristotle—human life (or anything else, for that matter) existed for some purpose. Though in Epicurus's view gods do exist, they cannot exert any causal influence whatsoever upon human affairs. We therefore need not fear death or the gods. Epicurus argued that seeing the sober truth about ourselves and accepting it, rather than hiding behind a veil of spiritualism or religious faith, liberate us from the fears imposed by religion and allow us to live, without fear or postponement of gratification, in a way that maximizes pleasure and minimizes pain, here and now, in this world, in this life.

Unlike Democritus, whose atoms behaved as Newton would someday imagine, with perfect determinism, Epicurus's atoms moved partly by pure chance; a random swerve ("clinamen") in their path brought indeterminism and chance into the universe by making the atoms change their course. Strict causality from one part of the universe to another could therefore not hold; the future did not come about through fate but was a random occurrence. Putting stock in metaphysical and religious theories to guide one's actions was therefore pointless, since everything could and would change haphazardly, guided by nothing more than pure chance.

Except for a few letters and some fragments, most of Epicurus's voluminous writings have been lost. The following selection is from his *Letter to Herodotus*, in which Epicurus explains how everything comes about through the random collisions of atoms falling through empty space. This knowledge has the power not only to free us from the misery imposed on us by religious conditioning, but also to spare us from fear of death. According to Epicurus, the gods themselves are merely collections of physical atoms in empty space, and they have no effect whatsoever on our lives unless we are led by fear of them to act in ways we think will please them. According to the common wisdom of the time, the gods not only ruled over all human affairs but also directly caused human happiness and misery alike. Epicurus denied this, claiming—as would the atomist Hobbes in the sixteenth century—that it is we who are responsible for all our misery as well as our happiness. Unlike Democritus, who believed in strict determinism, Epicurus held that whereas some events necessarily happen by chance, some are within our causal control. Belief in destiny, he argued, is more repressive than belief in the myths about the gods; the former at least gives us hope, whereas determinism leads only to despair. Once you understand that neither gods nor destiny affects our lives, you "shall live like a god among men."

⊥

Letter to Herodotus

Furthermore, the motions . . . must not be thought to be due to any being who controls and ordains

or has ordained them and at the same time enjoys perfect bliss together with immortality. . . . Otherwise this . . . will cause the greatest disturbance in men's souls. Therefore we must believe that it is due to the original inclusion of matter in such agglomerations during the birth-process of the world that this law of regular succession is also brought about.

Furthermore, we must believe that to discover accurately the cause of the most essential facts is the function of the science of nature, and that blessedness for us in the knowledge of celestial phenomena lies in this and in the understanding of the nature of the existences seen in these celestial phenomena, and of all else that is akin to the exact knowledge requisite for our happiness . . . nothing which suggests doubt or alarm can be included at all in that which is naturally immortal and blessed. Now this we can ascertain by our mind is absolutely the case. . . .

And besides all these matters in general we must grasp this point, that the principal disturbance in the minds of men arises because they think that these celestial bodies are blessed and immortal, and yet have wills and actions and motives inconsistent with these attributes; and because they are always expecting or imagining some everlasting misery, such as is depicted in legends, or even fear the loss of feeling in death as though it would concern them themselves; and, again, because they are brought to this pass not by reasoned opinion, but rather by some irrational presentiment, and therefore, as they do not know the limits of pain, they suffer a disturbance equally great or even more extensive than if they had reached this belief by opinion. But peace of mind is being delivered from all this, and having a constant memory of the general and most essential principles.

Wherefore we must pay attention to internal feelings and to external sensations in general and in particular, according as the subject is general or particular, and to every immediate intuition in accordance with each of the standards of judgment. For if we pay attention to these, we shall rightly trace the causes whence arose our mental disturbance and fear, and, by learning the true causes of celestial phenomena and all other occurrences that come to pass from time to time, we shall free ourselves from all which produces the utmost fear in other men.

From Epicurius: *The Extant Remains*, Cyril Bailey, trans. (Oxford: The Clarendon Press, 1926).

⚜

In his *Letter to Menoeceus,* from which the following selection is taken, we find Epicurus's major ethical theme: everyone should always seek plea-sure. According to him, this is not just some cavalier formula; it requires great skill and wisdom. One must be virtuous and prudent, knowing the values of various sorts of pleasures—how to weigh them, how to attain them, how to forgo some pleasures to achieve greater pleasures, and so on. However, contrary to subsequent popular belief, he did not tolerate the gluttony that has come to be symbolized by his name. In fact, he argued just the opposite: prudence in life frees us from the ills brought about by desire. This, in turn, requires learning philosophy so that one can be free of moral anxiety and superstitious fears brought about by religious worship of the gods. Having supposedly himself attained the ideal life in which the soul is released from its anxieties into real happiness, he was worshipped by his followers as "a god among men." Many regarded him as the founder of a new religion. His school, which lasted into the fourth century C.E., had a number of influential and devout followers, among them Metrodorus, Hermarchus, Colotes of Lampsacus, Appolodorus, Demetrius Lacon, Zeno of Sidon (Cicero's teacher), and the great Latin poet Lucretius (99–55 B.C.E.). Lucretius's *De Rerum Natura* (*On the Nature of Things*) is widely regarded as one of the greatest didactic poems ever written. In rendering Epicurus's atomic theory from the abstract Greek prose into Latin hexameters, Lucretius made Epicurus's ideas about the role of pleasure in the realm of ethics especially poignant; these ideas would later influence the utilitarians, especially Bentham and Mill.

⚜

Letter to Menoeceus

Let no one when young delay to study philosophy, nor when he is old grow weary of his study. For no one can come too early or too late to secure the health of his soul. And the man who says that the age of philosophy has either not yet come or has gone by is like the man who says that the age for happiness is not yet come to him, or has passed away. Wherefore both when young and old a man must study philosophy, that as he grows old he may be young in blessings through the grateful recollection of what has been, and that in youth he may be old as well, since he will know no fear of what is to come. We must then meditate on the things that make our happiness, seeing that when that is with us we have all, but when it is absent we do all to win it. . . .

Become accustomed to the belief that death is nothing to us. For all good and evil consists in sensation, but death is deprivation of sensation. And therefore a right understanding that death is nothing to us makes the mortality of life enjoyable, not because it adds to it an infinite span of time, but because it takes away the craving for immortality. For there is nothing terrible in life for the man who has truly comprehended that there is nothing terrible in not living. So that the man speaks but idly who says that he fears death not because it will be painful when it comes, but because it is painful in anticipation. For that which gives no trouble when it comes is but an empty pain in anticipation. So death, the most terrifying of ills, is nothing to us, since so long as we exist, death is not with us; but when death comes, then we do not exist. It does not then concern either the living or the dead, since for the former it is not, and the latter are no more.

But the many at one moment shun death as the greatest of evils, at another yearn for it as a respite from the evils in life. But the wise man neither seeks to escape life nor fears the cessation of life, for neither does life offend him nor does the absence of life seem to be any evil. And just as with food he does not seek simply the larger share and nothing else, but rather the most pleasant, so he seeks to enjoy not the longest period of time, but the most pleasant. . . .

When, therefore, we maintain that pleasure is the end, we do not mean the pleasures of profligates and those that consist in sensuality, as is supposed

From "Epicurus to Menoeceus" in *The Extant Remains*, C. Bailey, trans. (Oxford: The Clarendon Press, 1926).

by some who are either ignorant or disagree with us or do not understand, but freedom from pain in the body and from trouble in the mind. For it is not continuous drinkings and revelings, nor the satisfaction of lusts, nor the enjoyment of fish and other luxuries of the wealthy table, which produce a pleasant life, but sober reasoning, searching out the motives for all choice and avoidance, and banishing mere opinions, to which are due the greatest disturbance of the spirit.

⚜

4.1 Epictetus (55–135 C.E.)[1]

Stoic philosophy originated with Zeno from Citium[2] (334–262 B.C.E.), a native of Cyprus who came to Athens as a young man to study philosophy. He developed a pantheistic system according to which the whole of reality is a rational order within the world-soul, subject to laws of reason fully accessible to the human intellect and thus making revelations from the gods superfluous. Around 300 B.C.E., Zeno and his students began teaching their views from a *stoa,* or porch, in the marketplace. This is how their philosophical movement, which lasted six centuries and continues to exert influence today, got its name.

Early Stoics developed all Platonic and Aristotelian fields of philosophy, including logic, physics, and ethics. The only good, according to Stoic doctrine, is virtue, which is attainable not by faith but through knowledge, as Socrates had taught. The result is happiness. The truly wise use knowledge to achieve independence from both the external world of social and political forces and the internal world of their own passions and emotions. Stoic views appealed to all classes and found wide support, even among rulers, and exerted great influence upon the Roman Empire; one of its greatest adherents was Roman Emperor Marcus Aurelius (see Section 4.2).

Although the Stoics developed their philosophy in opposition to Epicurean hedonism, they agreed with Epicurus that the way to the good and happy life is through the pursuit and practice of philosophy. Their claim that nothing whatso-ever could possibly disturb the happiness of a true philosopher grew out of the views of Socrates, Plato, and Aristotle. According to Socrates, a good man cannot be harmed. Happiness for Plato consisted in a "harmony of the soul." In Aristotle's view "the good is something proper to the person and cannot be taken away." Epictetus likewise argued that "Men are disturbed not by things, but by the views they take of things."

Epictetus was born a Roman slave in Hierapolis, in Asia Minor (the peninsula that is most of modern Turkey). While still a slave, he began studying with the Stoic Musonius Rufus. Shortly after his master freed him, Epictetus founded his own school in Nicopolis, Epirus. Like Socrates, Epictetus wrote nothing. His teaching, based on early, rather than late, Stoic doctrines, has been preserved by one of his students, Arrian (known also for writing the history of Alexander the Great). In *The Enchiridion,* or *Manual,* and *The Discourses,* Arrian transcribed Epictetus's lectures. In *The Enchiridion,* from which the first selection is taken, Epictetus argues that both happiness and unhappiness are completely under our control.

⚜

The Enchiridion, or Manual

Of things, some are in our power and others not. In our power are opinion, pursuit, desire, aversion, and, in one word, whatever are our own actions. Not in our power are body, property, reputation, command, and, in one word, whatever are not our own actions.

Now, the things in our power are by nature free, unrestrained, unhindered; but those not in our power, weak, slavish, restrained, belonging to others. Remember, then, that if you suppose things by nature slavish to be free, and what belongs to others your own, you will be hindered; you will lament; you will be disturbed; you will find fault both with gods and men. But if you suppose that

---

From *The Discourse of Epictetus,* Elizabeth Carter, trans. (London, J. M. Dent, 1910).

only to be your own which is your own, and what belongs to others such as it really is, no one will ever compel you; no one will restrain you; you will find fault with no one; you will accuse no one; you will do no one thing against your will; no one will hurt you; you will not have an enemy, for you will suffer no harm. . . .

Study therefore to be able to say to every harsh appearance, "You are but an appearance, and not absolutely the thing you appear to be." And then examine it by those rules which you have, and first, and chiefly, by this: whether it concerns the things which are in our own power, or those which are not; and, if it concerns anything not in our power, be prepared to say that it is nothing to you.

Remember that desire promises the attainment of that of which you are desirous; and aversion promises the avoiding of that to which you are averse; that he who fails of the object of his desire is disappointed, and he who incurs the object of his aversion wretched. If, then, you confine your aversion to those objects only which are contrary to the natural use of your faculties, which you have in your own power, you will never incur anything to which you are averse. But if you are averse to sickness, or death, or poverty, you will be wretched. Remove aversion, then, from all things that are not in our power, and transfer it to things contrary to the nature of what is in our power. But, for the present, totally suppress desire: for, if you desire any of the things not in our own power, you must necessarily be disappointed; and of those which are, and which it would be laudable to desire, nothing is yet in your possession. Use only [the requisite acts] of pursuit and avoidance; and even these lightly, and with gentleness and reservation. . . .

Men are disturbed, not by things, but by the principles and notions which they form concerning things. Death, for instance, is not terrible, else it would have appeared so to Socrates. But the terror consists in our notion of death that it is terrible. When therefore we are hindered, or disturbed, or grieved, let us never impute it to others, but to ourselves; that is, to our own principles. It is the action of an uninstructed person to lay the fault of his own bad condition upon others; of one entering upon instruction to lay the fault on himself; and of one perfectly instructed, neither on others nor on himself.

. . .

Be not elated on any excellence not your own. If a horse should be elated and say, "I am handsome," it would be supportable. But when you are elated, and say, "I have a handsome horse," know that you are elated on what is, in fact, only the good of the horse. What, then, is your own? The use of the appearances of things. So that when you behave conformably to nature in the use of these appearances, you will be elated with reason; for you will be elated on some good of your own. . . .

Require not things to happen as you wish, but wish them to happen as they do happen, and you will go on well.

Never say of anything, "I have lost it"; but, "I have restored it." Is your child dead? It is restored. Is your wife dead? She is restored. Is your estate taken away? Well, and is not that likewise restored? "But he who took it away is a bad man." What is it to you by whose hands he, who gave it, hath demanded it back again? While he gives you to possess it, take care of it; but as of something not your own, as passengers do of an inn.

If you wish your children, and your wife, and your friends to live forever, you are stupid; for you wish things to be in your power which are not so, and what belongs to others to be your own. So likewise, if you wish your servant to be without fault, you are a fool; for you wish vice not to be vice, but something else. But, if you wish to have your desires undisappointed, this is in your own power. Exercise, therefore, what is in your power. He is the master of every other person who is able to confer or remove whatever that person wishes either to have or to avoid. Whoever, then, would be free, let him wish nothing, let him decline nothing, which depends on others else he must necessarily be a slave.

Remember that you must behave [in life] as at an entertainment. Is anything brought round to you? Put out your hand and take your share with moderation. Doth it pass by you? Do not stop it. Is it not yet come? Do not stretch forth your desire towards it, but wait till it reaches you. Thus do with regard to children, to a wife, to public posts, to riches, and you will be some time or other a worthy partner of the feasts of the gods. And if you do not so much as take the things which are set before you, but are able even to despise them, then you will not only be a partner of the feasts of the gods, but of their empire also. For, by thus doing, Diogenes and

Heraclitus, and others like them, deservedly became, and were called, divine.

. . .

When you see any one weeping for grief, either that his son is gone abroad, or dead, or that he hath suffered in his affairs, take heed that the appearance may not hurry you away with it. But immediately make the distinction within your own mind, and have it ready to say, "It is not the accident that distresses this person, for it [does] not distress another man; but the judgment which he forms concerning it." As far as words go, however, do not disdain to condescend to him, and even, if it should so happen, to groan with him. Take heed, however, not to groan inwardly too.

. . .

Remember that you are an actor in a drama, of such a kind as the author pleases to make it. If short, of a short one; if long, of a long one. If it be his pleasure you should act a poor man, a cripple, a governor, or a private person, see that you act it naturally. For this is your business, to act well the character assigned you; to choose it is another's.

If you have an earnest desire of attaining to philosophy, prepare yourself from the very first to be laughed at, to be sneered by the multitude, to hear them say, "He is returned to us a philosopher all at once," and "Whence this supercilious look?" Now, for your part, do not have a supercilious look indeed; but keep steadily to those things which appear best to you as one appointed by God to this station. For remember that, if you adhere to the same point, those very persons who at first ridiculed will afterwards admire you. But if you are conquered by them, you will incur a double ridicule.

. . .

If you ever happen to turn your attention to externals, so as to wish to please any one, be assured that you have ruined your scheme of life. Be contented, then, in everything with being a philosopher; and, if you wish to be thought so likewise by any one, appear so to yourself, and it will suffice you.

Never call yourself a philosopher, nor talk a great deal among the unlearned about theorems, but act conformably to them. Thus, at an entertainment, do not talk how persons ought to eat, but eat as you ought. For remember that in this manner Socrates

also universally avoided all ostentation. And when persons came to him and desired to be recommended by him to philosophers, he took and recommended them, so well did he bear being overlooked. So that if ever any talk should happen among the unlearned concerning philosophic theorems, be you, for the most part, silent. For there is great danger in immediately throwing out what you have not digested. And, if any one tells you that you know nothing, and you are not nettled at it, then you may be sure that you have begun your business. For sheep do not throw up the grass to show the shepherds how much they have eaten; but, inwardly digesting their food, they outwardly produce wool and milk. Thus, therefore, do you likewise not show theorems to the unlearned, but the actions produced by them after they have been digested.

✤

Epictetus relies on the Stoic distinction between what is within our power—"the use of the phenomena of existence"—and what is not, namely, the phenomena of existence themselves. In other words, although we have no control over the objects of existence, we can to a certain limited extent control their *use* because we have the power to view objects as we choose, to form opinions about them, to fear or desire them. This can be achieved only if we learn "how it is possible to employ desire and aversion without hindrance."

The main purpose of philosophy, according to Epictetus, is to help us achieve inner peace through a proper understanding of the world. Like most Stoics, he had a Heraclitean philosophy of nature, according to which change, the fundamental force of the universe, is governed by Logos or Reason. Inner peace comes from conforming to the way the world is rather than to our own prejudice and then following reason in three stages: master your desires, perform your duties, and think correctly about yourself and the world.

Notice that he warns against boasting about philosophy or knowledge so as not to draw attention to one's self; in fact, he even suggests that the wise ought not indiscriminately teach their wisdom to whomever would have it. And note, too, that he explicitly warns against revealing *theorems*. A theorem is a proposition that has been proved to be true.

In the second selection, taken from *The Discourses*, Epictetus begins by arguing, following Plato, that you cannot make yourself believe something simply by wishing it. For instance, if you try to make yourself believe on a bright day that it is the middle of the night, you will fail. Or, try to make yourself believe that right now as you are reading this book there are exactly 1,720 other people reading this book (there might be—you don't know). Still, you can't do it. In other words, our beliefs and ideas about ourselves and the world are not of our own conscious choosing. We cannot simply believe what we wish, nor can we wish whatever ideas we want into our own minds. We therefore, according to Epictetus, are not responsible for the way the world is nor for our own ideas. All that we are responsible for is reduced by Epictetus to the *use* we make of the ideas that present themselves to our minds: "Two maxims we must ever bear in mind—that apart from the will there is nothing good or bad, and that we must not try to anticipate or to direct events, but merely to accept them with intelligence."

⋆

The Discourses

That We Are Not to Be Angry with Mankind.

What is the cause of assent to anything?

Its appearing to be true.

It is not possible, therefore, to assent to what appears to be not true.

Why?

Because it is the very nature of the understanding to agree to truth, to be dissatisfied with falsehood, and to suspend its belief in doubtful cases.

What is the proof of this?

Persuade yourself, if you can, that it is now night.

Impossible.

Unpersuade yourself that it is day.

Impossible.

Persuade yourself that the stars are, or are not, even.

Impossible.

When any one, then, assents to what is false, be assured that he [does] not wilfully assent to it as false (for, as Plato affirms, the soul is never voluntarily deprived of truth); but what is false appears to him to be true. Well, then, have we, in actions, anything correspondent to true and false in propositions?

Duty, and contrary to duty: advantageous, and disadvantageous: suitable and unsuitable; and the like.

A person, then, cannot think a thing advantageous to him, and not choose it.

He cannot. . . .

. . . Now, since you think that you make a suitable application of your pre-conceptions to particular cases, tell me whence you derive this.

From its seeming so to me.

But it [does] not seem so to another, and [does] not he too form a conceit that he makes a right application?

He [does].

Is it possible, then, that each of you should apply your pre-conceptions right, on the very subjects about which you have contradictory opinions?

It is not.

Have you anything to show us, then, for this application, preferable to its seeming so to you? And [does] a madman act any [other way] than seems to him right? Is this, then, a sufficient criterion to him too?

It is not.

Come, therefore, to something preferable to what seems.

What is that?

The beginning of philosophy is this: The being sensible of the disagreement of men with each other; an inquiry into the cause of this disagreement, and a disapprobation and distrust of what merely seems. . . .

Of Freedom

He is free who lives as he likes; who is not subject either to compulsion, to restraint, or to violence;

From *The Moral Discourses of Epictetus*, Elizabeth Carter, trans. (London: J. M. Dent, 1910), with emendations by the author.

whose pursuits are unhindered, his desires success-ful, his desires unincurred. Who, then, would wish to lead a wrong course of life?—"No one." Who would live deceived, prone to mistake, unjust, dissolute, discontented, dejected?—"No one." No wicked man, then, lives as he likes; therefore neither is he free. And who would live in sorrow, fear, envy, pity; with disappointed desires, and incurred aversions?—"No one." Do we then find any of the wicked exempt from sorrow, fear, disap-pointed desires, incurred aversions?—"Not one." Consequently, then, not free.

If a person who [has] been twice consul should hear this, provided you add, "But you are a wise man; this is nothing to you," he will forgive you. But if you tell him the truth—that in point of slavery he doth not differ from those who have been thrice sold,—what must you expect but to be beaten? "For how," says he, "am I a slave? My father was free, my mother free. Besides, I am a senator, too, and the friend of Caesar, and have been twice consul, and have myself many slaves." In the first place, most worthy sir, perhaps your father too was a slave of the same kind, and your mother, and your grandfather, and all your ances-tors successively. But even if they were ever so free, what is that to you? For what if they were of a generous, you of a mean spirit; they brave, and you a coward; they sober, and you dissolute? . . .

Consider in animals what is our idea of freedom. Some keep tame lions, and feed and even carry them about with them; and who will say that any such lion is free? Nay, [does] he not live the more slavishly the more he lives at ease? And who, that had sense and reason, would wish to be one of those lions? Again, how much do birds, which are taken and kept in a cage, suffer by trying to fly away? Nay, some of them starve with hunger rather than undergo such a life; then, as many of them as are saved, it is scarcely and with difficulty and in a pining condition, and the moment they find any hole, out they hop. Such a desire have they of natural freedom, and to be at their own disposal and unrestrained.—"And what harm [does] this confinement do you?"—"What say you? I was born to fly where I please, to live in the open air, to sing when I please. You deprive me of all this, and say, What harm [does] it do you?"

Hence we will allow those only to be free who do not endure captivity; but, as soon as they are

taken, die, and escape. Thus Diogenes somewhere says, that the only way to freedom is to die with ease. And he writes to the Persian king, " You can no more enslave the Athenians than you can fish."—"How? What, shall not I take them?"—"If you do take them," says he, "they will leave you, and be gone like fish. For take a fish, and it dies. And, if the Athenians too die as soon as you have taken them, of what use are your war-like prepara-tions?" This is the voice of a free man, who had examined the matter in earnest, and, as it might be expected, found it out. But, if you seek it where it is not, what wonder if you never find it?

A slave wishes to be immediately set free. Think you it is because he is desirous to pay his fine to the officer? No; but because he fancies that, for want of acquiring his freedom, he [has] hitherto lived under restraint and unprosperously. "If I am once set free," says he, "it is all prosper-ity; I care for no one, I speak to all as their equal, and on a level with them. I go where I will, I come when and how I will." He is at last made free; and presently, having nowhere to eat, he seeks whom he may flatter, with whom he may sup. He then either submits to the basest and most infamous prostitution, and, if he can obtain admission to some great man's table, falls into a slavery much worse than the former; or, if the creature, void of sense and right taste, happens to acquire an afflu-ent fortune, he doats upon some girl, laments, and is unhappy, and wishes for slavery again. "For what harm did it do me? Another clothed me, another shod me, another fed me, another took care of me when I was sick. It was but in a few things, by way of return, I used to serve him. But now, miserable wretch! what do I suffer in being a slave to many instead of one! Yet, if I can obtain the equestrian rings, I shall live with the utmost prosperity and happiness." In order to obtain them he first suffers what be deserves, and, as soon as he hath obtained them, it is all the same again. "But, then," says he, "if I do but get a military command, I shall be delivered from all my troubles." He gets a military command. He suffers as much as the vilest rogue of a slave; and, nevertheless, he asks for a second command, and a third; and, when he [has] put the finishing hand and is made a senator, then he is a slave indeed. When he comes into the assembly, it is then that he undergoes his finest and most splendid slavery.

⚹

Lame and physically weak from the time he had been a slave, Epictetus worked arduously in making his views known. He developed a large following, even among early Christians, and in 90 C.E. Emperor Domitian expelled him from Rome along with many other philosophers whose teachings he saw as dangerous to his tyranny. In the latter part of the selection from *The Discourses,* you have found Epictetus's powerful and ironical polemic against the illusion of freedom, no doubt inspired by his own experience of having been "freed" from slavery and then attaining fame and even power. Thinking that because you are not a slave you are free can be especially deceptive, he says, because unlike the slave who knows he is not the master of his own life, a "free" man is in the even graver danger of being a slave without even knowing it. You are then powerless to act against your oppressor for you do not realize you are oppressed. How can you be a slave and not even know it? By being a slave to greed, vanity, and desire and thinking that these are in your own self-interest. According to Epictetus, true freedom, the greatest good, can be attained only in a way similar to that espoused five centuries later by the Indian sage Gautama Buddha: free yourself from your desires and the greedy corruption of the self, or ego, so that you can attain that rare freedom from the self that eludes the mass of humanity. The Stoic philosopher seeks freedom through surrender to what is, taking as a guide neither the illusory reins of the internal authority of self nor the illusory whip of the external authority of society but rather the correct principles that make the philosopher one with the actual world—fearless, incorruptible.

4.2 Marcus Aurelius (121–180): Philosopher King

According to Plato, "philosophers must become kings or kings must become philosophers before the world will have peace." The fourteenth Roman emperor (from 161 to 180), Marcus Aurelius was probably the closest thing to a philosopher king the world has ever known. Born to a prominent Spanish family in Rome, he became an orphan at a young age and devoted himself to a life of study. By the age of twelve he was mastering geometry, music, mathematics, painting, and literature. Under the mentorship of private tutors he learned fluent Greek and Latin and the whole of philosophy from the ancients through the Stoics, whom he most admired. By the age of fourteen he received the *toga virilis,* the white robe signifying adulthood and full citizenship in Rome.

A series of events that brought him to the throne began when Emperor Hadrian picked Marcus's uncle Antoninus as his successor but only on the condition that Antoninus designate Marcus to be the next emperor. Thus, by the age of seventeen, Marcus Aurelius had become the heir apparent to the imperial throne of Rome. He began preparing himself for the job. By the time he became emperor at the age of thirty-nine, he had earned a reputation as a great statesman and philosophical visionary. During his subsequent nineteen-year reign he brought about more political, social, educational, and economic reforms than any other emperor. He became known as a champion of the poor and of children—especially orphans—and brought about many reforms with the idea of improving the condition of slaves. By all accounts he resisted what he saw as the corrupting trappings of power, remaining a sincere and simple human being capable of great kindness but a powerful and resolute leader. As the commander-in-chief of the Roman legions, he also successfully defended Rome against more invasions than any other emperor; he fought back invasions from Syria, Spain, Egypt, Britain, Italy, and the Germanic tribes along the Rhine-Danube frontier. He regarded Christians as the most subversive and dangerous elements within the Roman Empire and violently persecuted them. He warned that if Christianity were allowed to corrupt the intellects and souls of the citizens, the entire Roman Empire would fall and be destroyed in the end, not by physical assault from external enemies, but from within, ruined by the mental deterioration of its own people.

In Athens he financed all four great philosophical schools: the Academy, the Lyceum, the Garden, and the Stoa. *Meditations,* written to himself during military campaigns, is a twelve-volume compendium of his ruminations on life. It reveals the mind of a Stoic philosopher of great eloquence, laying out his own path of self-discovery and enlightenment. He rejected, for instance, the Stoic doctrine of absolute truth, holding instead that we can at best have *probable* knowledge and that therefore to be virtuous we must always keep an open mind. His overarching theme throughout *Meditations* is that there is but one thing that can keep the *"daemon* within a man free"* through the tumultuous trials and tribulations of life: philosophy.

⁎

Meditations

Book II

Begin the morning by saying to thyself, I shall meet with the busybody, the ungrateful, arrogant, deceitful, envious, unsocial. All these things happen to them by reason of their ignorance of what is good and evil. But I who have seen the nature of the good that it is beautiful, and of the bad that it is ugly, and the nature of him who does wrong, that it is akin to me, not only of the same blood or seed, but that it participates in the same intelligence and the same portion of the divinity. I can neither be injured by any of them, for no one can fix on me what is ugly, nor can I be angry with my kinsman, nor hate him. For we are made for co-operation, like feet, like hands, like eyelids, like the rows of the upper and lower teeth. To act against one another

From *The Meditations of Marcus Aurelius,* George Long, trans. (New York: C. P. Putnam's Sons, 1862).

then is contrary to nature; and it is acting against one another to be vexed and to turn away. . . .

This thou must always bear in mind, what is the nature of the whole, and what is my nature, and how this is related to that, and what kind of a part it is of what kind of a whole; and that there is no one who hinders thee from always doing and saying the things which are according to the nature of which thou are a part. . . .

The soul of man does violence to itself, first of all, when it becomes an abscess and, as it were, a tumor on the universe, so far as it can. For to be vexed at anything which happens is a separation of ourselves from nature, in some part of which the natures of all other things are contained. In the next place, the soul does violence to itself when it turns away from any man, or even moves towards him with the intention of injuring, such as are the souls of those who are angry. In the third place, the soul does violence to itself when it is overpowered by pleasure or by pain. Fourthly, when it plays a part, and does or says anything insincerely and untruly. Fifthly, when it allows any act of its own and any movement to be without an aim, and does anything thoughtlessly and without considering what it is, it being right that even the smallest things be done with reference to an end; and the end of rational animals is to follow the reason and the law of the most ancient city and polity.

Of human life the time is a point, and the substance is in a flux, and the perception dull, and the composition of the whole body subject to putrefaction, and the soul a whirl, and fortune hard to divine, and fame a thing devoid of judgment. And, to say all in a word, everything which belongs to the body is a stream, and what belongs to the soul is a dream and vapour, and life is a warfare and a stranger's sojourn, and after-fame is oblivion. What then is that which is able to conduct a man? One thing and only one, philosophy. But this consists in keeping the daemon within a man free from violence and unharmed, superior to pains and pleasures, doing nothing without a purpose, nor yet falsely and with hypocrisy, not feeling the need of another man's doing or not doing anything; and besides, accepting all that happens, and all that it allotted, as coming from thence, wherever it is, from whence he himself came; and, finally, waiting for death with a cheerful mind, as being nothing else than a dissolution of the elements of which every living being is compounded. But if there is no harm to the elements themselves in each continually changing into another, why should a man have any apprehension about the change and dissolution of all the elements? For it is according to nature, and nothing is evil which is according to nature. . . .

If our intellectual part is common, the reason also, in respect of which we are rational beings, is common: if this is so, common also is the reason which commands us what to do, and what not to do; if this is so, there is a common law also; if this is so, we are fellow-citizens; if this is so, we are members of some political community; if this is so, the world is in a manner a state. For of what other common political community will any one say that the whole human race are members? And from thence, from this common political community comes also our very intellectual faculty and reasoning faculty and our capacity for law; or whence do they come? For as my earthly part is a portion given to me from certain earth, and that which is watery from another element, and that which is hot and fiery from some peculiar source (for nothing comes out of that which is nothing, as nothing also returns to non-existence), so also the intellectual part comes from some source.

Everything harmonizes with me, which is harmonious to thee, O Universe. Nothing for me is too early nor too late, which is in due time for thee. Everything is fruit to me which thy seasons bring, O Nature: from thee are all things, in thee are all things, to thee all things return.

⚹

4.3 Sextus Empiricus (c. 175–225): The Way of Skepticism

The only writings that have survived from the Pyrrhonean skeptics, named after the followers of Pyrrho of Elis (367–275 B.C.E.), are those of Sextus Empiricus. The Pyrrhonists argued that it is impossible to attain knowledge about anything and that, therefore, we should suspend judgment about whether any statement is true or false—including the statement that it is impossible to attain knowledge about anything! This supposedly leads not to insecurity and anxiety,

but to a tranquil, liberating state of indifference about the world.

Probably the most extreme skeptic of all time, and one of the first, was one of Socrates' teachers, Cratylus (450–385 B.C.E.), whom we already encountered in Chapter 1. Cratylus claimed that no knowledge can be had about reality and that no one can ever say anything true about anything. His reasoning was the same type used later by the modern Skeptic David Hume (see Chapter 15). Before he stopped speaking altogether, Cratylus taught that all things are in perpetual change and that even the language used to talk about the ephemeral state of things continually changes because the meanings and ideas change even as one thinks and speaks. Whereas Heraclitus (Section 1.9) claimed that you can't step into the same river twice because the river is always changing, Cratylus claimed that you can't step into the same river twice, not only because the river is constantly changing but also because you, too, are always changing. Cratylus ended up merely wagging his finger to indicate that he was responding to various, fleeting stimuli.

The word *skepticism* comes from the Greek *skeptesthai*, which means "to consider" or "to examine carefully" and *skepsis*, which means "to seek." Like the early Sophists (such as Cratylus) and their successor Socrates, who in the *Apology* declares "All that I know is that I know nothing," the early Skeptics claimed that before you accept anything as true, you should subject it to careful, rigorous scrutiny, seeking proof based on clear and undoubtable evidence. Such strict adherence to absolute certainty as a necessary condition for knowledge led them to extremely negative views about the possibility of there being any knowledge whatsoever. As a philosophical method, the Pyrrhonean movement grew out of the form of Skepticism that had developed in Plato's Academy under its leaders Arcesilas (315–241 B.C.E.) and Carneades (213–129 B.C.E.). They presented a series of devastating arguments designed to show why nothing at all can be known except one thing: that nothing can be known. One ought therefore to live only by probabilities—a principle the Pyrrhonists regarded as too dogmatic, arguing that even the previous Skeptical position that "nothing can be known" itself cannot be known. The Pyrrhonists were thus led to suspend judgment about everything, never affirming or denying anything. Things appear a certain way and the Pyrrhonean Skeptics accepted this at face value without knowing whether the appearances were as they seem. The Pyrrhonists suspended judgment about everything that was not immediately evident and lived by following the laws and customs of society (just as their predecessor Socrates did), with peace of mind that came from not having ever to judge anything.

Sextus Empiricus, a medical doctor and teacher, was the last leader of the Pyrrhonean movement. His written works are copies of lectures consisting of arguments worked out by previous Skeptics. His *Against the Mathematicians* and *Against the Dogmatists* contain detailed arguments against each area of knowledge: the liberal arts (grammar, rhetoric, geometry, arithmetic, astronomy, and music) and what then were the three branches of philosophy—logic, physics, and ethics. Ironically, these works are two of our most important sources of knowledge about the early history of astronomy, geometry, grammar, and the prevailing Stoic theology of the time.

His *Outlines of Pyrrhonism*, from which the next selection is taken, is a general summary of the various Pyrrhonean arguments organized into a specific and precise philosophical method. Just as doctors use varying remedies of different strengths to cure the sick, depending on the severity of their illness, so the skeptical philosopher must use arguments of appropriate strength and measure to cure the dogmatic ills of dogmatic belief. The more entrenched you are in your beliefs, the stronger the skeptical argument should be applied to you until you see that you don't really know what you think you know.

Sextus Empiricus distinguishes the Pyrrhonean position both from the dogmatists, such as Aristotle and Epicurus who think they have discovered the truth, and from those who think it cannot be found. The purpose of his skeptical arguments is to cure people from both types of dogmatism—the dogmatism of those who believe they have attained knowledge and the dogmatism of those who believe that knowledge cannot be attained. The philosophically healthy position, according to Empiricus and as advocated by the Pyrrhonists, is to always and forever keep seeking. To this end Empiricus developed what he called a "skeptical grammar," in which every sentence must always end in "so it seems to me at the moment."

⚓

Outlines of Pyrrhonism—Book I

Chapter IV—What Skepticism Is

Skepticism is an ability, or mental attitude, which opposes appearances to judgments in any way whatsoever, with the result that, owing to the equipollence of the objects and reasons thus opposed, we are brought firstly to a state of mental suspense and next to a state of "unperturbedness" or quietude. Now we call it an "ability" not in any subtle sense, but simply in respect of its "being able." By "appearances" we now mean the objects of sense-perception, whence we contrast them with the objects of thought or "judgments." . . .

The originating cause of skepticism is, we say, the hope of attaining quietude. Men of talent, who were perturbed by the contradictions in things and in doubt as to which of the alternatives they ought to accept, were led on to inquire what is true in things and what false, hoping by the settlement of this question to attain quietude. The main basic principle of the skeptic system is that of opposing to every proposition an equal proposition; for we believe that as a consequence of this we end by ceasing to dogmatize.

When we say that the skeptic refrains from dogmatizing we do not use the term "dogma," as some do, in the broader sense of "approval of a thing" (for the skeptic gives assent to the feelings which

_____

From *Outlines of Pyrrhonism* by Sextus Empiricus, R. G. Bury, trans.

are the necessary results of sense-impressions, and he would not, for example, say when feeling hot or cold "I believe that I am not hot or cold"); but we say that "he does not dogmatize" using "dogma" in the sense, which some give it, of "assent to one of the non-evident objects of scientific inquiry"; for the Pyrrhonean philosopher assents to nothing that is non-evident. Moreover, even in the act of enunciating the skeptic formulae concerning things non-evident—such as the formula "No more (one thing than another)," or the formula "I determine nothing," or any of the others which we shall presently mention,—he does not dogmatize. For whereas the dogmatizer posits the things about which he is said to be dogmatizing as really existent, the skeptic does not posit these formulae in any absolute sense; for he conceives that, just as the formula "All things are false" asserts the falsity of itself as well as of everything else, as does the formula "Nothing is true," so also the formula "No more" asserts that itself, like all the rest, is "No more (this than that)," and thus cancels itself along with the rest. And of the other formulae we say the same. If then, while the dogmatizer posits the matter of his dogma as substantial truth, the skeptic enunciates his formulae so that they are virtually canceled by themselves, he should not be said to dogmatize in his enunciation of them. And, most important of all, in his enunciation of these formulae he states what appears to himself and announces his own impression in an undogmatic way, without making any positive assertion regarding the external realities. . . .

That we adhere to appearances is plain from what we say about the Criterion of the Sceptic School. The word "Criterion" is used in two senses: in the one it means "the standard regulating belief in reality or unreality," (and this we shall discuss in our refutation); in the other it denotes the standard of action by conforming to which in the conduct of life we perform some actions and abstain from others; and it is of the latter that we are now speaking. The criterion, then, of the skeptic school is, we say, the appearance, giving this name to what is virtually the sense-presentation. For since this lies in feeling and involuntary affection, it is not open to question. Consequently, no one, I suppose, disputes that the underlying object has this or that appearance; the point in dispute is whether the object is in reality such as it appears to be.

Adhering, then, to appearances we live in accordance with the normal rules of life, undogmatically, seeing that we cannot remain wholly inactive. And it would seem that this regulation of life is fourfold, and that one part of it lies in the guidance of nature, another in the constraint of the passions, another in the instruction of the arts. Nature's guidance is that by which we are naturally capable of sensation and thought; constraint of the passions is that whereby hunger drives us to food and thirst to drink; tradition of customs and laws, that whereby we regard piety in the conduct of life as good, but impiety as evil; instruction of the arts, that whereby we are not inactive in such arts as we adopt. But we make all these statements undogmatically.

Our next subject will be the end of the skeptic system. Now an "end" is "that for which all actions or reasonings are undertaken, while it exists for the sake of none"; or, otherwise, "the ultimate object of appetency." We assert still that the skeptic's end is quietude in respect of matters of opinion and moderate feeling in respect of things unavoidable. For the skeptic, having set out to philosophize with the object of passing judgment on the sense-impressions and ascertaining which of them are true and which false, so as to attain quietude thereby, found himself involved in contradictions of equal weight, and being unable to decide between them suspended judgment; and as he was thus in suspense there followed, as it happened, the state of quietude in respect of matters of opinion. For the man who opines that anything is by nature good or bad is forever being disquieted: when he is without the things which he deems good he believes himself to be tormented by things naturally bad and he pursues after the things which are, as he thinks, good; which when he has obtained he keeps falling into still more perturbations because of his irrational and immoderate elation, and in his dread of a change of fortune he uses every endeavour to avoid losing the things which he deems good. On the other hand, the man who determines nothing as to what is naturally good or bad neither shuns nor pursues anything eagerly; and, in consequence, he is unperturbed.

The skeptic, in fact, had the same experience which is said to have befallen the painter Apelles. Once, they say, when he was painting a horse and wished to represent in the painting the horse's foam, he was so unsuccessful that he gave up the attempt and flung at the picture the sponge on which he used to wipe the paints off his brush, and the mark of the sponge produced the effects of the horse's foam. So, too, the skeptics were in hopes of gaining quietude by means of a decision regarding the disparity of the objects of sense and thought, and being unable to effect this they suspended judgment; and they found that quietude, as if by chance, followed upon their suspense, even as a shadow follows its substance. We do not, however, suppose that the skeptic is wholly untroubled; but we say that he is troubled by things unavoidable; for we grant that he is old at times and thirsty, and suffers various affections of that kind. But even in these cases, whereas ordinary people are afflicted by two circumstances—namely, by the affections themselves and in no less a degree, by the belief that these conditions are evil by nature—the skeptic, by his rejection of the added belief in the natural badness of all these conditions, escapes here too with less discomfort. Hence we say that, in regard to matters of opinion the skeptic's end is quietude, in regard to things unavoidable it is "moderate affection." But some notable skeptics have added the further definition "suspension of judgment in investigations."

Now that we have been saying that tranquillity follows on suspension of judgment, it will be our next task to explain how we arrive at this suspension. Speaking generally, one may say that it is the result of setting things in opposition. We oppose either appearances to appearances or objects of thought to objects of thought or *alternando.* For instance, we oppose appearances to appearances when we say "The same tower appears round from a distance, but square from close at hand"; and thoughts to thoughts, when in answer to him who argues the existence of providence from the order of the heavenly bodies we oppose the fact that often the good fare ill and the bad fare well, and draw from this the inference that providence does not exist. And thoughts we oppose to appearances, as when Anaxagoras countered the notion that snow is white with the argument, "Snow is frozen water, and water is black; therefore snow also is black." With a different idea we oppose things present sometimes to things present, as in the foregoing examples, and sometimes to things past or future, as, for instance, when someone propounds to us a theory which we are unable to refute, we say to him in reply, "Just as, before the birth of the

founder of the school to which you belong, the theory it holds was not as yet apparent as a sound theory, although it was really in existence, so likewise it is possible that the opposite theory to that which you now propound is already really existent, though not yet apparent to us, so that we ought not as yet to yield assent to this theory which at the moment seems to be valid."

⚓

4.4 Nagarjuna (2nd Century C.E.): The Way of Nirvana

We've already seen some remarkable cases of how the same ideas can take root simultaneously in vastly diverse areas of the world. The parallel between the Pyrrhonian skeptics in Greece and the Buddhism that was blossoming in India and China at the same time is another such case. Nagarjuna lived several thousand miles away in northern India at the same time as Sextus Empiricus. He was a Buddhist sage who traveled throughout the land teaching people how to attain *nirvana*, a term which can be traced all the way back to the *Upanishads* (see pp. 11–14), denoting a state of mind which in the original Sanskrit means, literally, "blown out." One is supposed to be able to achieve such a state only through the complete annihilation of the individual self but without loss of consciousness. In such a state all pain, suffering, and mental anguish vanish. It is the ending of *samsara* (Sanskrit, "going about"), which refers to the transit of the soul through the cycle of birth, death, and rebirth. According to the Buddhist philosophy, however, this refers not to the metaphysical transmigration of the soul from one physical body lifetime to another, but within the series of births, deaths, and rebirths that occurs within the lifetime of an individual—the moment to moment annihilation of each self, so that consciousness sees itself as always and eternally new.

What is unique about Nagarjuna's approach is that it is strictly rationalistic in approach, requiring precision of language and logical reasoning.

He uses the same methods as his Greek contemporaries to argue for the unreality of the objects in experience. He does this in much the way as Zeno did, by showing that just about all of our most cherished beliefs about ourselves and the world are so inconsistent and paradoxical that our ordinary view of ourselves and the world cannot possibly be true.

In particular Nagarjuna attacks our most fundamental concepts, such as causality, in ways similar to the methods that will be employed by the great modern skeptic David Hume. If each cause precedes each effect, then the cause does not exist when the effect exists. But then it can't be the real cause of that effect, since the real cause must exist presently to produce the effect. If, on the other hand, the cause and effect are related by identity, then everything produces itself, which is absurd. Therefore, all such relations, Nagarjuna argues, are illusory. The only real relation is that of identity. Once again, like Zeno and Parmenides, Nagarjuna uses such conclusions to show that each individual thing is the same as all other things—that "All is One."

The One according to Nagarjuna is an immeasurable, incomprehensible, Void that can only be known through the experience of nirvana.

⚹

The Unity of Being

The Perfect Buddha,
The foremost of all Teachers I salute.
He has proclaimed
The principle of relativity,
'Tis like blissful [nirvāṇa],
Quiescence of plurality.
There nothing disappears,
Nor anything appears;
Nothing has an end,
Nor is anything eternal;
Nothing is identical [with itself],
Nor is there anything differentiated;
Nothing moves, Neither hither nor thither.

───────────

Trans. by Th. Stcherbatsky.

I.   There absolutely are no things,
     Nowhere and none, that arise
     Neither out of themselves, nor out of
          non-self,
     Nor out of both, nor at random.

II. Four can be the conditions
     [Of everything produced],
     Its cause, its object, its foregoing
          moment,
     Its most decisive factor.

III. In these conditions we can find
     No self-existence of the entities.
     Where self-existence is deficient,
     Relational existence also lacks.

IV. No energies in causes,
     Nor energies outside them.
     No causes without energies,
     Nor causes that possess them.

V.   Let those facts be causes
     With whom coordinated other facts
          arise.
     Non-causes will they be,
     So far the other facts have not arisen.

VI. Neither non-*ens* nor *ens*
     Can have a cause.
     If non-*ens*, whose the cause?
     If *ens*, what for the cause?

VII. Neither an *ens* nor a non-*ens*,
     Nor any *ens-non-ens*,
     No element is really turned out.
     How can we then assume
     The possibility of a producing cause?

VIII. A mental *ens* is reckoned as an element,
     Separately from its objective [counter-
          part].
     Now, if it [begins] by having no objec-
          tive counterpart,
     How can it get one afterward?

IX. If [separate] elements do not exist,
     Nor is it possible for them to disappear.
     The moment which immediately
          precedes

Is thus impossible. And if 'tis gone,
How can it be a cause?

X.   If entities are relative,
They have no real existence.
The [formula] "this being, that appears"
Then loses every meaning.

XI.   Neither in any of the single causes
Nor in all of them together
Does the [supposed] result reside.
How can you out of them extract
What in them never did exist?

XII.   Supposing from these causes does
appear
What never did exist in them,
Out of non-causes, then,
Why does it not appear?

XIII.   The result is cause-possessor,
But causes are not even self-possessors.
How can result be cause-possessor,
If of non-self-possessors it be a result?

XIV.   There is, therefore, no cause-possessor,
Nor is there an effect without a cause.
If altogether no effect arises,
[How can we then distinguish]
Between the causes and non-causes?

Examination of Nirvāna

I.   If every thing is relative,
No [real] origination, no [real] annihila-
tion,
How is *nirvāna*, then, conceived?
Through what deliverance, through
what annihilation?

II.   Should every thing be real in substance,
No [new] creation, no [new] destruction,
How would *nirvāna*, then, be reached?
Through what deliverance, through
what annihilation?

III.   What neither is released, nor is it ever
reached,
What neither is annihilation, nor is it
eternality,

What never disappears, nor has it been
created,
This is *nirvāna*. It escapes precision.

IV.   *Nirvāna*, first of all, is not a kind of *ens*,
It would then have decay and death.
There altogether is no *ens*
Which is not subject to decay and death.

V.   If *nirvāna* is *ens*,
It is produced by causes,
Nowhere and none the entity exists
Which would not be produced by causes.

VI.   If *nirvāna* is *ens*,
How can it lack substratum?
There whatsoever is no *ens*
Without any substratum.

VII.   If *nirvāna* is not an *ens*,
Will it be, then, a non-*ens*?
Wherever there is found no *ens*,
There neither is a [corresponding]
non-*ens*.

VIII.   Now, if *nirvāna* is a non-*ens*,
How can it, then, be independent?
For sure, an independent non-*ens*
Is nowhere to be found.

IX.   Coordinated here or caused are [sepa-
rate things],
We call this world phenomenal;
But just the same is called *nirvāna*,
When from causality abstracted.

X.   The Buddha has declared
That *ens* and non-*ens* should be both
rejected.
Neither as *ens* nor as a non-*ens*
Nirvāna therefore is conceived.

XI.   If *nirvāna* were both *ens* and non-*ens*,
Final deliverance would be also both
Reality and unreality together.
This never could be possible!

XII.   If *nirvāna* were both *ens* and non-*ens*,
Nirvāna could not be uncaused.
Indeed the *ens* and the non-*ens*
Are both dependent on causation.

XIII.   How can *nirvāṇa* represent
An *ens* and a non-*ens* together?
Nirvāṇa is, indeed, uncaused;
Both *ens* and non-*ens* are productions.

XIV.   How can *nirvāṇa* represent
[The place] of *ens* and of non-*ens*
together,
As light and darkness [in one spot]
They cannot simultaneously be present.

XV.   If it were clear, indeed,
What an *ens* means, and what a non-
ens,
We could then understand the doctrine
About *nirvāṇa* being neither *ens* nor
non-*ens*.

XVI.   If *nirvāṇa* is neither *ens* nor
non-*ens*,
No one can really understand
This doctrine which proclaims at once
Negation of them both together.

XVII.   What is the Buddha after his *nirvāṇa*?
Does he exist or does he not exist,
Or both, or neither?
We never will conceive it!

XVIII.   What is the Buddha, then, at lifetime?
Does he exist, or does he not exist,
Or both, or neither?
We never will conceive it!

XIX.   There is no difference at all Between
nirvāṇa and *saṁsāra*.
There is no difference at all
Between *saṁsāra* and *nirvāṇa*.

XX.   What makes the limit of *nirvāṇa*
Is also then the limit of *saṁsāra*.
Between the two we cannot find
The slightest shade of difference.

XXI.   [Insoluble are antinomic] views
Regarding what exists beyond *nirvāṇa*,
Regarding what the end of this world is,
Regarding its beginning.

XXII.   Since everything is relative [we do not
know],
What is finite and what is infinite?
What means finite and infinite at once?
What means negation of both issues?

XXIII.   What is identity, and what is difference?
What is eternity, what non-eternity?
What means eternity and non-eternity
together?
What means negation of both issues?

XXIV.   The bliss consists in the cessation of all
thought,
In the quiescence of plurality.
No [separate] reality was preached at all,
Nowhere and none by Buddha!

NOTES

1. Common Era.
2. Not to be confused with Zeno of Elea (490–430
B.C.E.), inventor of the famous paradoxes of motion.

5 ❧ Catholic Philosophy

5.0 The Fragmentation of Philosophy: Fear of the Known

Forget for a moment about history and think just about the ideas raised thus far by the philosophers we've considered. Let us assume you are an ordinary person in today's world, immersed in the commonsense view of reality. Maybe you've thought about philosophical questions before. Maybe you think religion provides answers. Whatever the case may be, put aside for the moment whatever defenses you may have, take stock of what the philosophers have said, and ask: can the world—existence—really be as strange as all that? Suppose the philosophers are somehow right. What does it mean to you?

We don't need to answer these questions right now. We need only to ask them. For the moment let's simply assume that the philosophers are in some sense right. You've been living your life without ever really stopping to think seriously about how all this came to be, what the world is, why it exists, who and what you are, what consciousness is, and so on. Again, you may think that these questions fall under the domain of religion or are beyond your reach. In any case, let's just try to draw our full attention to the strangeness of finding ourselves existing, wondering, and not knowing. The strangeness is compounded by the things we have learned, such as that you do not directly perceive things in themselves, that the images you see are at best accurate facsimiles of reality—that is, representations of the world. Let's really take this seriously. How does it make you feel?

Perhaps the best word to describe it is *strange*. Before one begins to think philosophically, the world and one's own existence in it are nothing if not familiar, even intimately so; we feel as if we have always existed, as if the world has always been here, as if we belong here. Now suddenly after reading some philosophy the trees are not just trees. The dark is not just the dark. The light is not just light. A thought—what is that? The present moment—what is this? How? Why? You hold up your hand. How did you do that? What are these images? What is this *stuff*?

The point of this exercise is that with the advent of philosophy in one's life, things can start seeming a bit spooky. It's not that there are monsters or demons lurking about (though you never know) or that there are magical beings behind everything (or that maybe everything is full of gods). It's more like everything suddenly seems magical, but not necessarily in a friendly way—unexplained, doubtful, uncertain. There is a certain new edge to it all, a discomfort maybe, a growing insecurity about the existence of the world and one's own place in it.

As it is with us, so perhaps it was with the ancients at the sudden advent of philosophy. One wants to go back, only now there's no going back. The security of childhood is gone. If you think about it, you'll realize it's not the *unknown* we fear. Socrates said so himself on his deathbed: how can you fear it, if it is unknown? We fear the known.

This, of course, is contrary to Aristotle, who said, "All people by their nature desire to know." If Aristotle was right, why is the earth not a planet populated by the wise—a world of scientists and philosophers? Is it because most people are too *dumb*? As we shall see when we look at recent advances in the branch of philosophy known as cognitive science, all the evidence suggests that no healthy human brain is different from any other. We may each think different thoughts, but we all think the same way; the operating system in our brains is the same, with the same basic hardware. There are of course differences due to education and other factors, but as we shall see, even a brain that has had no education whatsoever has the awesome ability to make representations of the world, to use language, and so on, each of which is so complex that *any learned mental activity, regardless of its sophistication, pales by comparison*. The myth of I.Q. The myth of genius. The myth of *experts and authorities*. How convenient! Sound radical? New? Think again. Reread Plato's Socrates.

Beginning philosophy students often worry, usually secretly, that if they keep thinking "about this stuff" they may go "crazy." There is a parallel with beginning psychology students who often worry, usually in secret, that they may have some (or just about all) the scary disorders they are now reading about for the first time. The answer in both cases is the same: if you haven't

had cause to worry before, *then don't start now*. And people who do go "crazy" and do crazy things like hurting other people rarely do so as a result of wondering about themselves, the world, the nature of existence, and so on. Usually, it's the people who have stopped wondering and think they have all the answers that end up doing the most heinous things imaginable. But the suggestion I am making here is that thinking about the sorts of things philosophers think about will drive you crazy, feeling that you are not intelligent enough to understand yourself and the world, and fearing that experts and authorities will make a fool of you *are all part of the same self-deceiving mechanism*. We fear knowledge.

In other words, we must acknowledge that the human mind does not, at this point in its evolution, seem to want to come naturally to philosophy. Perhaps this itself is for evolutionary reasons. We need not speculate. The fact is that although the inscription at the temple at Delphi still reads, "Know Thyself," few, if any, of us do. Again, just think of the extent to which the human mind is not even aware of its own existence as such—that is, the extent to which the human mind is not at all consciously aware of its own operations. (Are you now consciously aware of how your brain-mind complex is actively processing the sensory data and constructing just the visual field of your perceptions? how the language you are using is structured and operating within you? and so on.) It may be that we can't—at least not yet. Maybe we never will be able to. But the point I am raising here for you to think about is that maybe *we don't want to*. We shall explore this last possibility in due course when we consider a variety of great philosophers who have thought that something very much like that is true. For now, we need but raise the real possibility that *perhaps*—for whatever reasons—we don't want to know ourselves. We might even speculate whether religion arises specifically for the purpose of preventing us from inquiring into the very questions that philosophers insist are keys for unlocking the secrets to understanding ourselves and the world.

Musing on this possibility may help us to understand in a more personal and vivid way why suddenly, at the culmination of all the great philosophy we have thus far considered from Thales to Sextus Empiricus, philosophy ground to a screeching halt. Indeed, what happened next has a strange and similar parallel to developments at the early part of our own century. One can well imagine enlightened Roman citizens at the height of the empire wondering: where do we go from here? With the Hellenic philosophical genius behind them and the emerging political, social, and cultural advances before them, it must have seemed as if some great, cosmic awakening was about to happen, as if the next level of enlightenment within human consciousness was just around the corner. What they got instead were the Dark Ages: the burning of books, the closing of the philosophy schools, the collapse of the empire.

The only other time in recorded history that humanity suffered a similarly sudden setback after centuries of great intellectual development occurred in our own century, when the great scientific, philosophical, technological, and moral advances of the last several hundred years seemed to unravel all at once and humanity plunged into the deadliest wars in its history—wars that brought us several times to the brink of global destruction. Indeed, some of the greatest philosophical, scientific, and political—even moral—achievements of all time had recently occurred in none other than Germany.

By the third century C.E., the cities that once were the cultural centers of the empire—home to philosophers, artists, and political leaders—began to unravel economically because of economic pressure from the constant military campaigns. Large numbers of wealthier citizens fled to escape the steadily rising taxes, health conditions began to deteriorate, and within a fairly short period about a third of the population died from either wars or the plague. The militaristic elements of the Roman Empire gained supreme power, even over the emperors. This was in part the result of growing attacks by Germans from the north and Persians from the east, who sought to capitalize on what they perceived as a growing weakness within the empire. Meanwhile, from inside there came a growing movement among the citizens who began to turn away from culture and education, seeking instead personal prestige and amassing wealth from within an ever-widening class system.

The distinctly antireligious sentiments of the Epicurean and Stoic philosophers, which had developed along with the rise of the Roman Empire, gave way to a slew of cults and emerging religions vying for people's beliefs. Among them, various Christian cults began for the first time to gain large numbers of followers. The Roman leaders, concerned more by the threat of external enemies than by internal fragmentation within their own society, ignored the danger signs that Marcus Aurelius had warned about. Superstition became rampant, along with a growing syncretism in which philosophies and religions were assembled haphazardly, like a collage of prevailing opinions without a philosophical center. Furthermore, instead of trying to lay a substantial foundation for its philosophical principles and methods, the Roman aristocracy began to worship its emperors as gods. Meanwhile, people divided themselves among the cults: Isis, which combined Greek and Egyptian gods into a sort of unitarian religion; the Mithraic cult, which worshipped the sun; and the Phrygian cult, which worshipped the Mother of the Gods. The Christians, no longer persecuted as they had been under Marcus Aurelius, were beginning to win more converts than all the other cults combined.

It is against this backdrop that the last of the great ancient philosophers, Plotinus, appeared on the scene. He tried to rekindle the flame amid the growing darkness. The dawn of philosophy had long since come and gone. Its first day, which had lasted six hundred years, was rapidly drawing to a close. Plato's sun had begun to set. Philosophy's first twilight descended rapidly across the known world. It was the beginning of the six-hundred-year night.

5.1 Plotinus (205–270): The Twilight of Philosophy

Plotinus, born and raised in Egypt, studied philosophy in Alexandria. After briefly joining the Roman expedition against the Persians in 244 with the idea of learning about Eastern philosophies, he settled in Rome where he single-handedly tried to revive the classical Hellenistic philosophy as an antidote to the ruin and misery of the crumbling world around him. Because it was based on the views of Plato, the philosophical movement that Plotinus founded came to be called Neoplatonism.

Under the auspices of Emperor Gallienus, Plotinus became extremely influential throughout the Roman Empire, and for a time it seemed as if his mission would succeed. At one point the emperor agreed to let him build near Rome a second city, based on Plato's *Republic,* to be called Platonopolis. It would have been the center for the new philosophical revival. But then, suddenly, for reasons unknown, the emperor withdrew the offer. Plotinus turned instead to writing.

Plotinus stands at the crossroads between the Greek tradition spanning the seven centuries from Thales to Sextus Empiricus and the beginning of Christendom. Although he did not begin writing until he was forty-nine, his works, edited posthumously by his student Porphyry into fifty-four books called the *Enneads,* covered every major branch of philosophy except politics. In them, under the influence of all the ancient thinkers, especially Parmenides and Pythagoras, Plotinus tried to resurrect Plato's philosophy. He used Plato's ideas to attack what he saw as the materialism of the Stoics and atomists, as well as to argue against the whole of Epicurean philosophy. He thought that, for all their practical wisdom, the Epicureans were incapable of dealing with the base instincts driving the superstitious beliefs that suddenly seemed to be making philosophy irrelevant. Plotinus's works had an important influence on the Catholic theology that came with the end of the Roman Empire and the subsequent Christian era of the Middle Ages.

Plotinus's distinction among three levels of reality became an avatar for later views of the Holy Trinity. First, there is the Parmenidean One, sometimes called "God," which transcends Being and which Plotinus often equates with Plato's *good*. Sometimes he writes as if the One precedes the good, but always the One is essentially undefinable and therefore no predicates can be attributed to it; all we can say about this highest level of reality is that "It is." At the second level, below the One, is its image, *nous* (variously translated as mind, spirit, or intellectual principle). *Nous* exists because the One, in its quest to understand itself, attains the power of seeing, or vision; in a sense, *nous* is the "light" by which the One sees itself. Finally, the third and lowest level of reality is the soul, which in Plotinus's view is the creator of all living things, including the sun, moon and stars, and the visible world itself. The soul has two parts: the inner soul, which faces the *nous,* and the outer soul, which faces the external. The three metaphysical levels—the One, the *nous,* and the soul—correspond, respectively, to three distinct levels of consciousness: mystical awareness, intuitive thought, and discursive thought—the soul, the *nous,* and the One, respectively.

Relying on Aristotle's notion that contemplation receives the form of the object contemplated, Plotinus argues that the soul—which forgets that it is but an emanation of the One—can through contemplation transcend itself and glimpse that which it is the reflection of—the *nous*—and that which the *nous* is the reflection of—the One. Since, unlike the *nous* and the One, the soul can contemplate its objects only in succession, it gives rise to time, space, and matter; this quasi-reality of nature in turn contemplates, but in a dreamlike state, ultimately deteriorating into the nonconscious level of matter. Going in the other, "inward" direction, when the soul is "divinely possessed and inspired," it sees the next higher level, where there is the fragmented image of the One—"thought thinking itself"—the *nous*, a "unity-in-diversity," where all ideas are present in each and every idea, and the soul then is able to have direct, mystical contact with the One.

⚜

The Enneads

. . . It has appeared to us that the nature of *the good* is simple and the first; for every thing which is not the first is not simple; and since it has nothing in itself, but is one alone, and the nature of what is called *the one,* is the same with *the good*; for it is not first something else, and afterwards one,—nor is *the good* something else, and afterwards *the good*; this being the case, when we say *the one*, and when we say *the good*, it is necessary to think that we speak of one and the same nature; not predicating any thing of it, but manifesting it to ourselves as much as possible. It is also called *the first*, because it is most simple; and sufficient to itself, because it does not consist of many things. For if it did, it would be suspended from the things of which it consists. It likewise is not in any thing else, because every thing which is in another, is also derived from another. If, therefore, it is neither from, nor in another, and has not had any composition in its nature, it is necessary that there should not be any thing superior to it. Hence, it is not [necessary] to proceed to other principles, but having admitted this, and next to this intellect which is primarily intellect, we ought afterwards to place soul, as the next in rank. For this is the order according to nature, neither to admit more, nor fewer than these in the intelligible. For those who admit fewer than these, must either say that soul and intellect are the same, or that intellect and that which is first are the same. It has, however, been frequently demonstrated by us, that these are different from each other.

It remains, therefore, that we should consider at present, if there are more than these three, what the natures are which exist besides these. For since

From *Select Works of Plotinus*, T. Taylor, trans. (London: George Bell & Sons, 1985), with emendations by the author.

the principle of all things subsists in the way we have shown, it is not possible for any one to find a more simple and elevated principle. . . .

When, therefore, that which is truly intellect intellectually perceives itself in its intellections, and the intelligible of it is not externally posited, but intellect itself is also the intelligible, it necessarily follows that in intellectual perception it possesses itself, and sees itself. But seeing itself, it perceives itself not to be void of intelligence, but intelligent. So that in primarily energizing intellectually, it will also have a perception that it sees intellectually, both being as one; nor can there be any conception of duplicity there. If, likewise, always perceiving intellectually it is that which it is, what place can there be for the conception which separates intellectual perception from the perceiving that it sees intellectually? If, however, someone should introduce a third conception to the second, which asserts that it perceives that it sees intellectually, and should say that it understands (*i.e.*, sees intellectually), that what understands understands, the absurdity is still more apparent. And why may not assertions of this kind be made to infinity? The reason, likewise, proceeding from intellect which may be adduced, and from which afterwards another reason is generated in the soul, so as to become a medium between intellect and soul, deprives the soul of intellectual perception, if it does not derive this reason from intellect, but from some other intermediate nature. Hence it would possess an image of reason, but not reason itself. And in short, it would not have a knowledge of intellect, nor would it be intelligent.

Hence it must not be admitted that there are more principles than these, nor must these superfluous conceptions be adopted, which have no place there; but it must be said that there is one intellect always subsisting with invariable sameness, and in every respect without fluctuation, which imitates as much as possible its father; and with respect to our soul, that one part of it always abides on high, that another part of it is conversant with sensibles, and that another has a subsistence in the middle of these. For as there is one nature in many powers, at one time the whole soul tends upward in conjunction with the most excellent part, of itself, and of the universe, but at another time, the worst part being drawn down, draws together with itself the middle part. For it is not lawful that the whole of it should be drawn downward. This passion also happens to the soul, because it did not abide in that which is most beautiful, where the soul which does not rank as a part abiding, and of which we are not a part, imparts to the whole body of the universe, as much as it is able to receive from it. At the same time also, this soul remains free from all solicitude, not governing the world by the discursive energy of reason, nor correcting any thing but by the vision of that which is prior to itself, adorning the universe with an admirable power. For the more it looks to itself, the more beautiful and powerful it becomes, and possessing these excellencies from the intelligible world, it imparts them to that which is posterior to itself, and as it is always illuminated, it always illuminates.

Being therefore always illuminated, and continually possessing light, it imparts it to the natures that are in a consequent order. And these are always contained and irrigated by this light, and enjoy life through it, as far as they are able. . . .

⚓

In the following passages, however, Plotinus formally raises for the first time the question (alluded to in Section 5.0): Why is the mind not aware of itself? He puts this in the form of the soul being oblivious to itself:

⚓

What is the reason that souls become oblivious of divinity, being ignorant both of themselves and him, though their allotment is from thence, and they in short partake of God? The principle therefore of evil to them is audacity, generation, the first difference, and the wish to exercise an unrestrained freedom of the will. [The five genera of being are, essence, sameness, *difference*, motion and permanency. This *difference*, therefore, which ranks as the first, and which is the source of all diversity, causes souls by predominating in them to be forgetful of deity, and themselves.] When, therefore, [souls] began to be delighted with this unbounded liberty, abundantly employing the power of being moved from themselves, they ran

in a direction contrary to their [origin], and thus becoming most distant from their source, they were at length ignorant that they were thence derived. Just as children who are immediately torn from their parents, and have for a long time been nurtured at a great distance from them, become ignorant both of themselves and their parents. Hence, souls neither seeing their father, nor themselves, despise themselves through ignorance of their race, but honor other things, and admiring every thing rather than themselves, being vehemently astonished about, and adhering to sensible natures, they as much as possible hurl themselves and thus despise the beings from which they have become [estranged]. Hence, the honor which they pay to sensible objects, and the contempt of themselves, happen to be the causes of their [complete] ignorance. For at the same time they pursue and admire something else, and acknowledge themselves to be inferior to that which they admire and pursue. But the soul admitting that it is something subordinate to [ephemeral] things . . . and apprehending that it is the most ignoble and mortal of every thing which it honors, neither believes in the nature nor power of God. . . .

⚓

In saying that without the soul there is no sun, he is relying on the idealist worldview, which began with Plato and will find its culmination among the modern British philosophers in Berkeley; among the Germans in Hegel, Fichte, and Schelling; and among the nineteenth-century American idealists in Royce. As has already been suggested, the very latest science, as exemplified by twentieth-century physics, will once more echo these ancient voices from the past. And by the time we near the end of our philosophical journey through the historical development of pivotal ideas that have shaped Western thought, we may find ourselves having to revise the words of the great twentieth-century physicist Niels Bohr, who wrote, "Those who think that modern quantum mechanics makes sense have not understood it." We can ask: makes sense (or not) *compared to what*? That is, we might instead say, "Those who think the latest, mind-boggling theories of twentieth-century science do not make sense—or think they are completely new—have not read the history of philosophy."

5.2 Augustine (354–430): The Beginning of Christendom

Catholic philosophy developed in part from philosophical views derived from Plato, the Stoics, and the Neoplatonists. It dominated Western thought for a thousand years, from the time of Augustine to the Renaissance. Of its four main Latin Church founders—St. Ambrose, St. Jerome, St. Augustine, and Pope Gregory the Great—Augustine (Aurelius Augustinus of Hippo) had the deepest and most lasting influence.

Born at Tagaste (in North Africa near Carthage) during the final years of the decline and fall of the Roman Empire, Augustine studied and then taught rhetoric—"the art of persuasion"—in Carthage, Rome, and Milan. As a young man he joined a movement known as Manichaenism, a synthesis of Christianity and Zoroastrianism that had spread throughout the Roman Empire and exerted the most influence during the third and seventh centuries. For a time it rivaled the growing Christian religion. Its Magian founder, Mani (Greek Manes, Latinized Manichaeus), converted to Chris-tianity from Zoroastrianism, an Indo-Iranian movement (also known as Mazdaism, Bah Din, and Parsiism) based on the teachings of Zarathustra. An ancient figure who lived in the sixth century B.C.E., Zarathustra taught that the human struggle between good and evil is itself a manifestation of a cosmic duel between the angelic forces of light and the demonic forces of darkness. Each individual human spirit must, according to Zarathustra, fight a personal battle between light and darkness, truth and falsehood, moral right and wrong, in order to gain either the salvation of eternal bliss or eternal agony. Mani sought to synthesize Zoroastrian ideas with Christianity, claiming that Christ was an incarnation of the same spirit as Buddha and Zarathustra—the original soul of the first man created by the "mother of light" to help the rest of humanity become a major force in the combat against the overpowering darkness.

Under the influence of the Skeptics, Augustine eventually rejected Manichaenism as a religion and then discovered Plotinus, through whose writings he became a devout Neoplatonist, arguing on behalf of Plotinus's semireligious interpretation of Plato. Zoroastrian and Manichean influences, however, especially those concerning the human struggle between good and evil, sin and salvation, remained the focal point of his thought even after his conversion to Christianity. Through Augustine's powerfully persuasive writings these ideas became a central aspect of later Christian dogma.

In Carthage and Rome, where he taught rhetoric, Augustine was highly regarded for his abilities to train young lawyers in the art of pleading unpopular cases. He became a leading professor of rhetoric at the University of Milan until 387 when, at the age of thirty-two, he converted to Christianity. He returned to Africa where he established many monasteries, becoming a priest in 391. In 396 the papacy appointed him bishop of Hippo, a city near Carthage, a post he retained until the end of his life.

It has often been pointed out that the history of philosophy consists in variations on the themes of Plato and Aristotle. Similarly, the history of Christian thought consists in variations on the themes of Augustine and Aquinas. Since Aquinas was primarily an Aristotelian and Augustine primarily a Platonist, the primal influence of Plato and Aristotle has thus remained central in Western thought. Augustine's main concern, however, is not with metaphysics and epistemology for their own sakes, as they were for Plato, but with a more Socratic interest in the evolutionary development of the individual soul—salvation from suffering and the attainment of happiness, both in this world and in the next world. From the Epicureans, Stoics, and Skeptics, Augustine thus took as fundamental the maxim that the various purposes of philosophy have but one main ultimate aim: the attainment of happiness. In addition, in the Neoplatonists he found "all things but one—the *Logos* made flesh." He took their views, especially those of Plotinus, and made them the basis for his philosophy, which became the foundation for subsequent Christianity. This includes a Christian reinterpretation of the Neoplatonic view (itself a reinterpretation of Platonism) that ultimate knowledge can be obtained by only a select few individuals via mystical intuition of supreme reality (that is, "the supreme Form of the Good," "Being," "God," and so on). In the process, Augustine developed a rich and vast metaphysics driven by a unique dialectic method in which philosophy begins with a study of the sensations of the external world, proceeds to an *inward* empiricism—a careful, rigorous, introspective psychology of the self—and moves finally upward to God.

In his own dramatic conversion experience, Augustine sees both the key role that the desire for happiness plays in the mind's desire (or lack thereof) to know, and its solution. Influenced by the Manichean doctrine that final salvation comes through ascetic living, itself derived from the views of the Stoics and Skeptics, Augustine argues that the path to salvation lies in turning away from the worldly pleasures—but not through to the abstract detachment of the Stoics nor the belief-free disinterestedness of the Skeptics. Augustine's answer is predicated on the understanding, provided in the philosophies of his Platonic predecessors, that what we call "the world" is not the real world but only our idea of it. But more than that: what you call your "self" is also but an idea in your mind and not your real soul. In other words, Augustine views the Stoics as caught up in reaction to what is not real and the Skeptics as merely noting the unreality of the appearances and blinded by their inability to see beyond. It is in the ability to see beyond both the external and internal world of appearances that

one attains knowledge of ultimate reality, which he calls *God*.

Whenever a philosopher uses this word it is prudent to stop and ask: *what does the philosopher mean by this word*? That is, what *concept* does the word "God" stand for in this philosopher's system? More often than not, the answer to this question is not readily apparent. Certainly, there is by no means a universal usage of this word among philosophers. (That there is no universal usage among theologians is obvious in the fact that there are so many different religions.) Augustine was both a philosopher *and* a theologian. Were he a theologian only and not a philosopher, he would not have been included in this book. A theologian can be a philosopher (and vice versa) just as a physicist or mathematician can. This has already been explained (Chapters 0 and 1). The most important thing to keep in mind is this: *don't assume that what the philosopher means is what the contemporary, bible-thumping minister, evangelist, or priest means.* Typically, what religious writers and speakers mean by inviting you to "come to God" or to "accept God," for instance, or when they speak of having themselves found "God," is, ultimately, but *a call to, or an expression of, their religion.* Thus what they mean when they say, for instance, that you ought to "accept God," is that you ought to accept the creeds of their religion. This most certainly is *not* what the philosopher *qua* philosopher means.[1] And Augustine most certainly is no exception, as we shall see shortly when we experience some of his writings.

Before we do so, however, let us consider a second note of warning. Augustine's *arguments* for his views do not rest on faith. Under the philosophical influence of Plato, and distinctly *unlike* much of the Christianity of today, Augustine's view is grounded, he claims, in reason.[2] Faith[3] plays a subordinate but important role. This fact is important because he is asking for the kind of critical engagement with his arguments that, typically, has little in common with the religious rhetoric you are familiar with today.

These two warnings aside, let us proceed to some more general comments, and then we shall focus more closely on the text. Augustine criticizes the ancient Greek philosophers on grounds that to know the truth does not guarantee *doing* the truth. The problem is that the essence of humanity is not, as Aristotle had supposed, rationality but *will*. According to Augustine, no one can believe in the true God (whatever *that* is—we don't know yet what he means by this word) without first willing it. This is because no amount of rational argument can affect the will. Self-centeredness corrupts us away from truth and the "true reality" (the "true God") so that we fashion reality in our own image. Only when we are touched by "Divine Grace" can we will the true God—true reality—to be God made real for *us*. In other words, the true reality can be understood as real only when we understand that what we take to be true reality—the world of appearances, for instance—is false. Augustine's view, then, is that the sort of inner, transcendental revelation of truth, which he calls "faith," cannot be approached by reason. Rather, one must start with inner insights and reason from them to the truth (this will be exactly the procedure that Descartes will later use). One cannot reason *to* faith; one must reason *from* faith. The cornerstone of his position is the famous dictum, "I believe in order to understand."

Thus, as you read Augustine, remember that he did not simply *accept* and *follow* the dogmatic creed of a particular religion. This is easy to forget. He calls himself a Christian, of course, but the Christianity he is referring to is not the Christianity that existed before him but the one *he invented*! This is not as controversial as it may sound; few theologians today would disagree with this statement which says just this: *Augustine's* theology—the "view" of religion *invented* by *him* (remember, this is one of the proper functions of philosophy—see pp. 1–4)— replaced the previous theology and dominated subsequent Christian thought for more than nine centuries, until the advent of Aquinas's scholastic philosophy. So here are *at least* three

different systems of belief that fall under the name "Christianity": that which preceded Augustine, that which came after him for nine centuries, and that which came after Aquinas. *Religions—in spite of any claims to the contrary— are themselves evolving systems whose evolutions have often been achieved through the work of philosophers.*

So then what are some of the truths that Augustine found by his method of reasoning from inner insight ("faith")? First, he held that the mind cannot grasp reality on its own: that is, without special conditioning into states of illumination, we simply cannot ever know God. God must first illuminate the mind through inner revelation so that the truth can then be grasped. Knowledge of God is thus predestined by God and there is nothing any of us can do to attain such knowledge. No amount of study will help, no amount of learning—not even prayer makes any difference whatsoever. This is the actual view of one of the founders of Christian dogma, one of the religion's own "saints." Few, if any, professing Christians believe this today; Christianity today is in large part a religion that preaches that what you do can affect whether or not you attain knowledge of God. According to Augustine, however, such "illumination" either will or will not happen to you as preordained, in advance of anything you do, by God's own "grace." The idea, in other words, is that this can be *bequeathed* only by God *for no rational reason whatsoever*, and it cannot under any circumstances be earned. Nor can the human intellect dispel the mystery of God's wisdom in choosing some human beings over others. We are, however, obliged, according to Augustine, to seek God even though we cannot know whether we will ever receive true knowledge or salvation.

The idea, then, is that in Augustine's view we must seek the truth, enlightenment, ultimate reality, God, but we cannot ever know whether this will lead us on a correct path; there is no "correct path." This sounds contradictory but it is the seed of a very powerful idea that gripped

and inspired minds of both religious and antireligious persuasions for generations to come.

Let us now turn to some of his writings. The
first selection is from his *Confessions*. Written in
400 when he was forty-three, it begins with a
description of the events of his life that led to his
conversion.

⚓

Confessions

What then have I to do with men, that they should
hear my confessions—as if they could *heal all my
infirmities*—a race, curious to know the lives of
others, slothful to amend their own? Why seek
they to hear from me what I am; who will not hear
from Thee what themselves are? And how know
they, when from myself they hear of myself,
whether I say true; seeing *no man knows what is in
man, but the spirit of man which is in him*? But if
they hear from Thee themselves, they cannot say,
"The Lord lies." For what is it to hear from Thee of
themselves, but to know themselves? and who
knows and says, "It is false," unless himself lies?
But because *charity believes all things* (that is,
among those whom knitting unto itself it makes
one), I also, O Lord, will in such wise confess unto
Thee, that men may hear, to whom I cannot
demonstrate whether I confess truly; yet they
believe me, whose ears charity opens unto me. . . .

. . . With what objective then, O Lord my God,
to Whom my conscience daily confesses, trusting
more in the hope of Thy mercy than in her own
innocency, with what objective, I pray, do I by this
book confess to men also in Thy presence what I
now am, not what I have been? For that other
objective I have seen and spoken of. But what I
now am, at the very time of making these confessions, divers desire to know, who have or have not
known me, who have heard from me or of me; but
their ear is not at my heart, where I am, whatever I
am. They wish then to hear me confess what I am
within; whither neither their eye, nor ear, nor
understanding can reach: they wish it, as ready to

From *The Confessions of St. Augustine*, E. B. Pusey,
trans. (New York: Collier & Son, 1909), with emendations by the author.

believe—but will they know? For charity, whereby
they are good, tells them that in my confessions I
lie not; and she in them, believes me. . . .

This is the objective of my confessions of what I
am, not of what I have been, to confess this, not
before Thee only, in a secret *exultation with trembling,* and a secret sorrow with hope; but in the
ears also of the believing sons of men, sharers of
my joy, and partners in my mortality, my fellow-
citizens, and fellow-pilgrims, who are gone before,
or are to follow on, companions of my way. . . .

⚓

He now turns to the following, deep, philosophical question: "When I think of God, *what
is the object of my thought*?" Before we go on to
see exactly what he does with this question, let us
pause a moment, as a good philosopher should,
on the word *object*. There is a dual sense of this
word, a duality which subsequent philosophers[4]
will use much to their advantage.

To see the point, suppose I am thinking about
my death. You ask me, "What is the object of
your thought?" This would be an analogous
puzzle to what Augustine is here raising.[5] My
death, like God, is not an object present before
my mind the way a table or a chair is. It's not
even so much a question of what I am thinking *of*
or *about* as it is a question of what, exactly, is
present to my mind at the moment when my
thinking *about that* is going on. *God* is not
present (at least not the way the chair is) any
more than *death* (my own death) is present.
What, then, *is* present? A concept? An idea?
Whatever *these* are, they are present before the
mind. Thus, the mind is thereby engaging with a
concept or an idea, each of which is present to
consciousness (it is at that moment the "object"
of consciousness), of a something *beyond* (both in
the case of God and of death) that which is
immediately grasped by the mind. At the same
time, however, there is operating within the mind
a second sense of *object*, as an *intention*. You can
ask "What is the object of this thought (of God
or of death)," to mean *what is being intended by
your mind when it is having such thoughts*?

What might be intended is something completely different from anything of which I am consciously aware. Augustine, like many subsequent philosophers, goes to great lengths to point out this double function of the objects present to the mind. This second sense, "What is the object of your thought?" is like asking, "What is the function of this idea within the overall system of beliefs within which you operate?" In other words, Augustine here—as philosophers so often do—engages in what we previously identified as a *second-order* activity. So here, then, is how Augustine puts the question of what the actual *object* of his thinking, desiring, worshipping, and so forth *is* when he contemplates God:

⚓

. . . But what do I love, when I love Thee? not beauty of bodies, nor the fair harmony of time, nor the brightness of the light, so beautiful to our eyes, nor sweet melodies of varied songs, nor the fragrant smell of flowers, and ointments, and spices, not manna and honey, not limbs acceptable to embracements of flesh. None of these I love, when I love my God; and yet I love a kind of light, and melody, and fragrance, and meat, and embracement when I love my God, the light, melody, fragrance, meat, embracement of my inner man: where there shines unto my soul what space cannot contain and there sounds what time bears not away, and there smells what breathing disperses not, and there tastes what eating diminishes not, and there clings what satiety divorces not. This is it which I love when I love my God.

And what is this? I asked the earth, and it answered me, "I am not He"; and whatsoever are in it confessed the same. I asked the sea and the depths, and the living creeping things, and they answered, "We are not Thy God, seek above us." I asked the moving air; and the whole air with his inhabitants answered, "Anaximenes was deceived, I am not God." I asked the heavens, sun, moon, stars, "Nor (say they) are we the God whom thou seeks." And I replied unto all the things, which encompass the door of my flesh: "You have told me of my God, that you are not He: tell me something of Him." And they cried out with a loud voice, "He made us." My questioning them, was my thoughts on them: and their form of beauty gave the answer. And I turned myself unto myself, and said to myself, "Who are you?" And I answered, " A man." And behold, in me there present themselves to me soul, and body, one without, the other within. By which of these ought I to seek my God? I had sought Him in the body from earth to heaven, so far as I could send messengers, the beams of mine eyes. But the better is the inner, for to it as presiding and judging, all the bodily messengers reported the answers of heaven and earth, and all things therein, who said, "We are not God, but He made us." These things did my inner man know by the ministry of the outer: I the inner knew them; I, the mind, through the senses of my body. I asked the whole frame of the world about my God; and it answered me, "I am not He, but He made me."

⚓

It should now be a little clearer to you that when Augustine talks of "God" he most definitely is *not* evoking some image as suggested, for instance, by various holy books, including the Christian bibles. This can be seen most vividly when he returns to a distinctly pre-Socratic perspective to ask "what everything is" and explicitly mentions Anaximenes: in addressing the objects which he perceives to be the items of the world—the mountains, the sky, the air—he asks, "Are you God?" Imagine standing before a tree and asking, "Are you God?" The tree does not answer. Augustine understands the tree to be but a mental imagine within his own mind. So really, what is he asking? He is using his own mind to inquire into what this, the object of his attention, is, and asking his own mind to reveal to him, through thinking, whether this thing he is looking at—the tree, the mountain, the air before him—is ultimate reality. It is a most profound philosophical activity in which he is engaged. And from within himself he gets his answer: "The whole air with his inhabitants answered, 'Anaximenes was deceived, I am not God.'"

Augustine had the same access to Aristotle's commentaries and the fragmentary writings of Anaximenes that we do. Anaximenes nowhere uses the term "God." Thus, in putting it this way, Augustine makes his intentions quite clear. Like most philosophers from Thales to Plato, he seeks to understand what *ultimate,* or *absolute,* reality is. Augustine's God is the age-old quest for the ultimate ground, or source, of Being—the primary case, or essence, of existence.[6]

Just as Plato argued that the objects of our perceptions are not real things in themselves but have only derivative existence (that is, the "shadows"), Augustine argues that the things we see "are not God," meaning that they are not in and of themselves real. Without that which gives to the appearances their derivative reality—without *God*—the appearances (the objects we see, the world that we mistakenly call real, which in reality is but illusion) could not exist at all, not even as a figment of someone's imagination.

If you still don't get a clear sense of what Augustine is saying or how it connects with previous or later thinkers, try substituting the word *brain* for the word *God.* Augustine's argument consists mainly in a vivid demonstration that something other than the objects of our perception is responsible for structuring the appearances as they present themselves to us. It is an argument that we shall see again and again, most notably in the work of Bishop George Berkeley. This part of the argument, by itself (divorced from its explicitly religious implications), most philosophers before him and after him would accept. Images don't control or cause images. Images are but the effects of something higher ("higher" here meaning merely that the latter causes the former but not vice versa). This, in Augustine's view, leads one to infer the existence of God: only God could be responsible for this being so. But the same form of argument can and will be used to claim that what is beyond (or behind, or the cause of) the appearances is a "transcendental" self, or nonconscious and superconscious mental structures or even just the physical brain.

Augustine now reiterates the Protagorean point that each of us has access to only our own points of view on the world, not to the world as it exists in and of itself. What, then, accounts for the possibility of connecting our many different, often conflicting, perspectives? The following passages highlight the way in which Augustine *argues* for the existence of God (that is, the existence of some supreme, higher being of which this reality is only an image or imperfect representation):

Is not this corporeal figure apparent to all whose senses are perfect? why then speaks it not the same to all? Animals small and great see it, but they cannot ask it: because no reason is set over their senses to judge on what they report. But men ask, so that *the invisible things of God are clearly seen, being understood by the things that are made*, but by love of them, they are made subject unto them: and subjects cannot judge. Nor yet do the creatures answer such as ask, unless they can judge: nor yet do they change their voice (*i.e.,* their appearance), if one man only sees, another seeing asks, so as to appear one way to this man, another way to that; but appearing the same way to both, it is dumb to this, speaks to that; . . . rather it speaks to all; but they only understand, who compare its voice received from without, with the truth within. For truth says to me, "Neither heaven, nor earth, nor any other body is your God." This, their very nature says to him that sees them: "They are a mass; a mass is less in a part thereof than in the whole." Now to you I speak, O my soul, you are my better part: for you quicken the mass of my body, giving it life, which no body can give to a body: but your God is even unto you the Life of your life.

What then do I love, when I love my God? who is He above the head of my soul? By my very soul will I ascend to Him. I will pass beyond that power whereby I am united to my body, and fill its whole frame with life. Nor can I by that power find my God; for so *horse and mule that have no understanding*, might find Him; seeing it is the same power, whereby even their bodies live. But another power there is, not that only whereby I animate, but that too whereby I imbue with sense my flesh, which the Lord has framed for me: commanding the eye not to hear, and the ear not to see; but the eye, that through it I should see, and the ear, that through it I should hear; and to the other senses severally, what is to each their own peculiar seats and offices; which, being diverse, I the one mind, do through them enact. I will pass beyond this power of mine also; for this also have the horse and mule, for they also perceive through the body.

✠

Augustine's main philosophical concern now is with what *faculty* of the mind can we know God? This is a deep question, not just about a religious concept per se, but about how it could be possible that the mind can reach out beyond itself, either via its percepts or its concepts, to gain some sort of access to what is beyond the mind. This is a question that many philosophers, mathematicians, and scientists continue to address to the present day. Thus, Augustine here enters upon what is probably the first introspective psychological analysis ever of the nature and function of awareness, consciousness, language, and memory, from both an analytic and phenomenological perspective. He is trying to see what it is about the mind's own structures that allow it by inner extension to "reach out" beyond itself and thereby apprehend structures as they exist in themselves, outside the mind's own *actual* reach. That this is even possible will be denied by many idealist philosophers, and so here we see that Augustine is squarely a *realist,* a position from which all subsequent Christian thought, even post-Thomistic (Aquinas), never veered.

✠

I will pass then beyond this power of my nature also, rising by degrees unto Him who made me. And I come to the fields and spacious palaces of my memory, where are the treasures of innumerable images, brought into it from things of all sorts perceived by the senses. There is stored up, whatsoever besides we think, either by enlarging or

diminishing, or any other way varying those things which the sense has come to; and whatever else has been committed and laid up, which forgetfulness has not yet swallowed up and buried. When I enter there, I require what I will to be brought forth, and something instantly comes; others must be longer sought after, which are fetched, as it were, out of some inner receptacle; others rush out in troops, and while one thing is desired and required, they start forth, as who should say, "Is it perchance I?" These I drive away with the hand of my heart, from the face of my remembrance; until what I wish for is unveiled, and appears in sight, out of its secret place. Other things come up readily, in unbroken order, as they are called for; those in front making way for the following; and as they make way, they are hidden from sight, ready to come when I will. All which takes place when I repeat a thing by heart.

There are all things preserved distinctly and under general heads, each having entered by its own avenue: as light, and all colors and forms of bodies by the eyes; by the ears all sorts of sounds; all smells by the avenue of the nostrils; all tastes by the mouth; and by the sensation of the whole body, what is hard or soft; hot or cold; smooth or rugged; heavy or light; either outwardly or inwardly to the body. All these does that great harbor of the memory receive in her numberless secret and inexpressible windings, to be forthcoming, and brought out at need; each entering in by his own gate, and there laid up. Nor yet do the things themselves enter in; only the images of the things perceived are there in readiness, for thought to recall. Which images, how they are formed, who can tell, though it does plainly appear by which sense each has been brought in and stored up? For even while I dwell in darkness and in silence, in my memory I can produce colors, if I will, and discern between black and white, and what others I will: nor yet do sounds break in and disturb the image drawn in by my eyes, which I am reviewing, though they also are there, lying dormant, and laid up, as it were, apart. For these too I call for, and . . . they appear. And though my tongue be still, and my throat mute, so can I sing as much as I will; nor do those images of colors, which notwithstanding be there, intrude themselves and interrupt, when another store is called for, which flowed in by the ears. So the other things, piled in and up by the other senses, I recall at my pleasure. Yes, I discern the breath of lilies from violets, though smelling nothing; and I prefer honey to sweet wine, smooth before rugged, at the time neither tasting nor handling, but remembering only.

These things do I within, in that vast court of my memory. For there are present with me, heaven, earth, sea, and whatever I could think on therein, besides what I have forgotten. There also meet I with myself, and recall myself, and when, where, and what I have done, and under what feelings. There be all which I remember, either on my own experience, or others' credit. Out of the same store do I myself with the past continually combine fresh and fresh likenesses of things which I have experienced, or, from what I have experienced, have believed: and thence again infer future actions, events and hopes, all these again I reflect on, as present. "I will do this or that," say I to myself, in that great receptacle of my mind, stored with the images of things so many and so great, "and this or that will follow." "O that this or that might be!" "God avert this or that!" So speak I to myself: and when I speak, the images of all I speak of are present, out of the same treasury of memory; nor would I speak of any thereof, were the images wanting.

Great is this force of memory, excessive great, O my God; a large and boundless chamber! who ever sounded the bottom thereof? yet is this a power of mine, and belongs unto my nature; nor do I myself comprehend all that I am. Therefore is the mind too strait to contain itself. And where should that be, which it contained not of itself? Is it without it, and not within? how then does it not comprehend itself? A wonderful admiration surprises me, amazement seizes me upon this. And men go abroad to admire the heights of mountains, the mighty billows of the sea, the broad tides of rivers, the compass of the ocean, and the circuits of the stars, and pass themselves by; nor wonder that when I spoke of all these things, I did not see them with my eyes, yet could not have spoken of them, unless I then actually saw the mountains, billows, rivers, stars which I had seen, and that ocean which I believe to be, inwardly in my memory, and that, with the same vast spaces between, as if I saw them abroad. Yet did not I by seeing draw them into myself, when with my eyes I beheld them; nor are they themselves with me, but their images only. And I know by what sense of the body each was impressed upon me. . . .

Lord, I, truly, toil therein, yes and toil in myself; I am become a heavy soil requiring over much *sweat of the brow.* For we are not now searching out the regions of heaven, or measuring the distances of the stars, or enquiring the balancings of the earth. It is I myself who remember, I the mind. It is not so wonderful, if what I myself am not, be far from me. But what is nearer to me than myself? And lo, the force of mine own memory is not understood by me; though I cannot so much as name myself without it.

※

Notice how Augustine carefully examines what is and what is not within the power of the mind; you ask yourself questions and answers come forth, as if from out of nowhere; you direct your attention to ideas, events past and present, and the mind goes where the attention is directed by the words you use when you think. But where do the words that you call your own come from? Twentieth-century philosopher Ludwig Wittgenstein (see Chapter 23) will remark, "Thinking is not something I do but something that happens to me." Augustine would agree. When we pay close attention to our own minds we see ourselves, not as the causal agents of our own mental activities, but as their effects. In other words, as he concludes in the preceding passage, "what is nearer to me than myself? And lo, the force of mine own memory is not understood by me; though I cannot so much as name myself without it." It is exactly this kind of careful consideration of the actual functioning of the conscious mind that leads Augustine to give up the selfish life of the ego and to contemplate, instead, the acceptance of the supreme reality of what is beyond the ego, which he calls God.

It is deeply interesting to note that at about this time religion in general, which had been regarded by the Roman commanding authorities as mere superstition, and Christianity in particular, which they tended to regard as a form of what today we might call mental illness, were beginning to be seen in a new light. Why? Nobody knows.

We can, however, speculate. The activities of conscious reason had constructed a world system in which regard of all powers came to be associated with conscious human activity and social engagement through social institutions. This, however, was leading to a decline in those very structures. Something had gone wrong somewhere. For centuries people had come to believe that no higher powers, other than the conscious human mind and its domain, existed; now there came a resurgence of belief in occult forces, of powers beyond the grasp of human consciousness and reason.

In 313, Emperor Constantine granted Christians—whom previous emperors, such as Marcus Aurelius, had persecuted as a dangerous degeneracy in the empire—the right to worship. There were so many widely differing sects, however, that in 325 the Council of Nicaea defined an "official" Christian orthodoxy and declared all other sects to be heresies. Once he had himself converted to Christianity from the Manicheans, Augustine used his rhetorical skills to exert a powerful influence in putting down the nonorthodox religions as heresies. The following selection is taken from his *Writings Against the Manicheans*, which presents his criticism of the Manichean version of Zoroastrianism to which he had once belonged. Here he outlines his call to an acceptance of the very forces and powers, beyond the grasp of the conscious mind and the intellect, that the Epicureans and Stoics had claimed were but illusory beliefs responsible for human suffering—that which is beyond the world we see, beyond ourselves: God.

⚹

How then, according to reason, ought man to live? We all certainly desire to live happily; and

From Augustine, in *The Writings against the Manicheans and against the Donatists* (a Select Library of the Nicene and post-Nicene Fathers), First Series, edited by Philip Schaff, vol. 4, The Christian Literature Publishing Co., New York, 1886–1890, with emendations by the author.

there is no human being but assents to this statement almost before it is made. But the title happy cannot, in my opinion, belong either to him who has not what he loves, whatever it may be, or to him who has what he loves if it is hurtful, or to him who does not love what he has, although it is good in perfection. For one who seeks what he cannot obtain suffers torture, and one who has got what is not desirable is cheated, and one who does not seek for what is worth seeking for is diseased. Now in all these cases the mind cannot but be unhappy, and happiness and unhappiness cannot reside at the same time in one man: so in none of these cases can the man be happy. I find, then, a fourth case, where the happy life exists—when that which is man's chief good is both loved and possessed. For what do we call enjoyment but having at hand the objects of love? And no one can be happy who does not enjoy what is man's chief good, nor is there any one who enjoys this who is not happy. We must then have at hand our chief good, if we think of living happily. . . . Now if we ask what is the chief good of the body, reason obliges us to admit it is that by means of which the body comes to be in its best state. But of all the things which invigorate the body, there is nothing better or greater than the soul. The chief good of the body, then, is not bodily pleasure, not absence of pain, not strength, not beauty, not swiftness, or whatever else is usually reckoned among the goods of the body, but simply the soul. For all the things mentioned the soul supplies to the body by its presence, and, what is above them all, life. Hence I conclude that the soul is not the chief good of man, whether we give the name of man to soul and body together, or to the soul alone. For as, according to reason, the chief good of the body is that which is better than the body and from which the body receives vigor and life, so whether the soul itself is man, or soul and body both, we must discover whether there is anything which goes before the soul itself, in following which the soul comes to the perfection of good of which it is capable in its own kind. If such a thing can be found, all uncertainty must be at an end, and we must pronounce this to be really and truly the chief good of man.

. . . But if it follows, as it does, that the body which is ruled over by a soul possessed of virtue is ruled both better and more honorably, and is in its greatest perfection in consequence of the perfection of the soul which rightfully governs it, that which gives perfection to the soul will be man's chief good, though we call the body man. For if my coachman, in obedience to me, feeds and drives the horses he has charge of in the most satisfactory manner, himself enjoying the more of my bounty in proportion to his good conduct, can any one deny that the good condition of the horses, as well as that of the coachman, is due to me? So the question seems to me to be not, whether soul and body is man, or the soul only, or the body only, but what gives perfection to the soul; for when this is obtained, a man cannot but be either perfect, or at least much better than in the absence of this one thing. . . . The peace of the body . . . consists in the duly proportioned arrangement of its parts. The peace of the irrational soul is the harmonious repose of the appetites, and that of the rational soul the harmony of knowledge and action. The peace of body and soul is the well-ordered and harmonious life and health of the living creature. Peace between man and God is the well-ordered obedience of faith to eternal law. Peace between man and man is well-ordered concord. Domestic peace is the well-ordered concord between those of the family who rule and those who obey. Civil peace is a similar concord among the citizens. The peace of the celestial city is the perfectly ordered and harmonious enjoyment of God, and of one another in God. The peace of all things is the tranquillity of order. Order is the distribution which allots things equal and unequal, each to its own place.

⚹

A natural question to ask is why, if the true cause of everything in the world is through the design of God, the world we experience is so imperfect. If the world is merely the result of random chance, as the Stoics and Democritan materialists supposed, that any of it works at all is then a lucky coincidence, and evil, pain, and suffering should be par for the course. What else but imperfection should one expect to come out of chaos? If, on the other hand, the world is the result of divine design, then why is there

evil, pain, and suffering? One way to respond would be to claim that God is evil, that the purpose of existence is itself negative. Apparently, some medieval theologians believed this to be the case and traveled through the land inflicting pain on others and each other, thinking that this is what God wanted.[7] Or, one could claim that what we take to be evil, pain, and suffering are but an elaborate type of illusion. Augustine does not take either of these ways out. He claims, instead, that evil and suffering are themselves necessary tools by which God carries out God's plan.

Furthermore, in the next selection, taken from the *Enchiridion*, Augustine claims that whereas God is perfectly good, not all the things God creates—such as human beings—are perfectly good. God created us knowing we would sometimes choose evil so that, through our evil acts, God's perfectly good will could be fulfilled in ways that we, in our finite wisdom, cannot understand. The subtle but, again, deeply influential implication is that God needs human beings because we can do what God cannot; we are a necessary ingredient in the fabric of reality. We make it possible for God to carry out what otherwise God could not achieve.

⚹

Enchiridion

All beings were made good, but not being made perfectly good, are liable to corruption: All things that exist, therefore, seeing that the Creator of them all is supremely good, are themselves good. But because they are not, like their Creator, supremely and unchangeably good, their good may be diminished and increased. But for good to be diminished is an evil, although, however much it may be diminished, it is necessary, if the being is

---

From Saint Augustine, *Enchiridion*, J. F. Shaw, trans., from *The Works of Aurelius Augustine*, M. Dods, ed. (Edinburgh, T&T. Clark, 1892), with emendations by the author.

to continue, that some good should remain to constitute the being. For however small or of whatever kind the being may be, the good which makes it a being cannot be destroyed without destroying the being itself. An uncorrupted nature is justly held in esteem. But if, still further, it be incorruptible, it is undoubtedly considered of still higher value. When it is corrupted, however, its corruption is an evil, because it is deprived of some sort of good. For if it be deprived of no good, it receives no injury; but it does receive injury, therefore it is deprived of good. Therefore, so long as a being is in process of corruption, there is in it some good of which it is being deprived; and if a part of the being should remain which cannot be corrupted, this will certainly be an incorruptible being, and accordingly the process of corruption will result in the manifestation of this great good. But if it does not cease to be corrupted, neither can it cease to possess good of which corruption may deprive it. But if it should be thoroughly and completely consumed by corruption, there will then be no good left, because there will be no being. Wherefore corruption can consume the good only by consuming the being. Every being, therefore, is a good; a great good, if it cannot be corrupted; a little good, if it can: but in any case, only the foolish or ignorant will deny that it is a good. And if it be wholly consumed by corruption, then the corruption itself must cease to exist, as there is no being left in which it can dwell. . . .

The omnipotent God does well even in the permission of evil: Nor can we doubt that God does well even in the permission of what is evil. For He permits it only in the justice of His judgment. And surely all that is just is good. Although, therefore, evil, insofar as it is evil, is not a good; yet the fact that evil as well as good exists, is a good. For if it were not a good that evil should exist, its existence would not be permitted by the omnipotent God, who without doubt can as easily refuse to permit what He does not wish, as bring about what He does wish. And if we do not believe this, the very first sentence of our creed is endangered, wherein we profess to believe in God the Father Almighty. For He is not truly called Almighty if He cannot do whatsoever He pleases, or if the power of His almighty will is hindered by the will of any creature whatsoever. . . .

The will of God is never defeated, though much is done that is contrary to His will: These are the great works of the Lord, sought out according to all His pleasure, and so wisely sought out, that when the intelligent creation, both angelic and human, sinned, doing not His will but their own, He used the very will of the creature which was working in opposition to the Creator's will as an instrument for carrying out His will, the supremely Good thus turning to good account even what is evil, to the condemnation of those whom in His justice He has predestined to punishment, and to the salvation of those whom in His mercy He has predestined to grace. For, as far as relates to their own consciousness, these creatures did what God wished not to be done: but in view of God's omnipotence, they could in no wise effect their purpose. For in the very fact that they acted in opposition to His will, His will concerning them was fulfilled. And hence it is that "the works of the Lord are great, sought out according to all His pleasure," because in a way unspeakably strange and wonderful, even what is done in opposition to His will does not defeat His will. For it would not be done did He not permit it (and of course His permission is not unwilling, but willing); nor would a Good Being permit evil to be done that in His omnipotence He can turn evil into good.

The will of God, which is always good, is sometimes fulfilled through the evil will of man: Sometimes, however, a man in the goodness of his will desires something that God does not desire, even though God's will is also good, nay, much more fully and more surely good (for His will never can be evil): for example, if a good son is anxious that his father should live, when it is God's goodwill that he should die. Again, it is possible for a man with evil will to desire what God wills in His goodness: for example, if a bad son wishes his father to die, when this is also the will of God. It is plain that the former wishes what God does not wish, and that the latter wishes what God does wish; and yet the filial love of the former is more in harmony with the goodwill of God, though its desire is different from God's, than the want of filial affection of the latter, though its desire is the same as God's. So necessary is it, in determining whether a man's desire is one to be approved or disapproved, to consider what it is proper for man, and what it is proper for God, to desire, and what is in each case the real motive of the will. For God accomplishes some of His purposes, which of course are all good, through the evil desires of wicked men.

⚑

Augustine's *City of God*, from which the next selection is taken, was written after the fall of Rome in 410. In large part a synthesis of Plato's *Republic* and the theology of St. Paul, it was an attempt to respond to critics who had claimed that the weakening of the Roman Empire was—as Marcus Aurelius had warned—brought about directly by Christianity. Many religious thinkers of the time claimed that belief in Christ had brought the vengeance of the "pagan" gods, whereas secular philosophers claimed that Christian belief in otherworldliness had ruined the minds of the citizens and weakened their hold on practical reality. Indeed, more than fifteen hundred years later, the same charge is echoed by Bertrand Russell in his *History of Western Philosophy*. Speaking of Jerome, Ambrose, and Augustine, he writes, "It is no wonder that the Empire fell into ruin when all the best and most vigorous minds of the age were so completely remote from secular concerns." Russell does, however, acknowledge the powerful emotional appeal of Augustine: "On the other hand, if ruin was inevitable, the Christian outlook was admirably fitted to give men fortitude, and to enable them to preserve their religious hopes when earthly hopes seemed vain. The expression of this point of view, in *The City of God*, was the supreme merit of Saint Augustine."

In The *City of God*, Augustine depicts the entire spiritual history of humanity from the "fall of Adam and Eve" to the "Last Judgment" as a struggle between the "City of God" and the "City of Man." The latter is founded upon the principle of self-love and its citizens are greedy materialists in pursuit of carnal pleasure; the former is founded upon the love of God and the contempt of self and its citizens live as a "mystical and unanimous society of saints in Heaven and believers on Earth."

⚑

The City of God

[I]t does not follow that, though there is for God a certain order of all causes, there must therefore be nothing depending on the free exercise of our own wills, for our wills themselves are included in that order of causes which is certain to God, and is embraced by His foreknowledge, for human wills are also causes of human actions; and He who foreknew all the causes of things would certainly among those causes not have been ignorant of our wills. . . .

If that is to be called *our necessity* which is not in our power, but even though we be unwilling, effects what it can effect,—as, for instance, the necessity of death,—it is manifest that our wills by which we live uprightly or wickedly are not under such a necessity; for we do many things which, if we were not willing, we should certainly not do. This is primarily true of the act of willing itself,—for if we will, it *is*; if we will not, it *is* not,—for we should not will if we were unwilling. But if we define necessity to be that according to which we say that it is necessary that anything be of such or such a nature, or be done in such and such a manner, I know not why we should have any dread of that necessity taking away the freedom of our will. For we do not put the life of God or the foreknowledge of God under necessity if we should say that it is necessary that God should live forever, and foreknow all things; as neither is His power diminished when we say that He cannot die or fall into error,—for this is in such a way impossible to Him, that if it were possible for Him, He would be of less power. But assuredly He is rightly called omnipotent, though He can neither die nor fall into error. For He is called omnipotent on account of His doing what He wills, not on account of His suffering what He wills not; for if that should befall Him, He would by no means be omnipotent. Wherefore, He cannot do some things for the very reason that He is omnipotent. . . .

Let no one, therefore, look for an efficient cause of the evil will; for it is not efficient, but deficient, as the will itself is not an effecting of something, but a defect. For defection from that which supremely is,

---

From Saint Augustine, *City of God*, M. Dods, trans. (Edinburgh: T.&T. Clark, 1881), with emendations by the author.

to that which has less of being,—this is to begin to have an evil will. Now, to seek to discover the causes of these defections,—causes, as I have said, not efficient, but deficient,—is as if someone sought to see darkness, or hear silence. Yet both of these are known by us, and the former by means only of the eye, the latter only by the ear; but not by their positive actuality, but by their want of it. Let no one, then, seek to know from me what I know that I do not know; unless he perhaps wishes to learn to be ignorant of that of which all we know is, that cannot be known. . . . For when the eyesight surveys objects that strike the sense, it nowhere sees darkness but where it begins not to see. And so no other sense but the ear can perceive silence, and yet it is only perceived by not hearing. Thus, too, our mind perceives intelligible forms by understanding them; but when they are deficient, it knows them by not knowing them; for who can understand defects?

. . . And I know likewise, that the will could not become evil, were it unwilling to become so; and therefore its failings are justly punished, being not necessary, but voluntary. For its defections are not to evil things, but are themselves evil; that is to say, are not towards things that are naturally and in themselves evil, but the defection of the will is evil, because it is contrary to the order of nature, and an abandonment of that which has supreme being for that which has less. For avarice is not a fault inherent in gold, but in the man who inordinately loves gold, to the detriment of justice, which ought to be held in incomparably higher regard than gold. Neither is luxury the fault of lovely and charming objects, but of the heart that inordinately loves sensual pleasures, to the neglect of temperance, which attaches us to objects more lovely in their spirituality, and more delectable by their incorruptibility. Nor yet is boasting the fault of human praise, but of the soul that is inordinately fond of the applause of men, and that makes light of the voice of conscience. Pride, too, is not the fault of him who delegates power, nor of power itself, but of the soul that is inordinately enamored of its own power, and despises the more just dominion of a higher authority. Consequently he who inordinately loves the good which any nature possesses, even though he obtain it, himself becomes evil in the good, and wretched because deprived of a greater good. . . .

Though there are very many and great nations all over the earth, whose rites and customs, speech, arms, and dress are distinguished by marked differences, yet there are no more than two kinds of human society, which we may justly call two cities, according to the language of our Scriptures. The one consists of those who wish to live after the flesh, the other of those who wish to live after the spirit; and when they severally achieve what they wish, they live in peace, each after their kind. . . .

⚜

In the final selection, "Self-Knowledge and the Nature of Mind," from *On the Trinity*, Augustine displays his philosophical gifts in a context where it can be viewed outside of the religious framework of most of the rest of his writings. Turning to the difficult question of how self-knowledge is possible and why it is so difficult to attain, he claims that most of the mind's own beliefs about itself are false. Arguing against the Skeptics, according to whom we cannot know ourselves with certainty, he points out that even if one is a Skeptic and doubts everything, the act of doubting requires thought and a thinker and therefore affirms the existence of the self. Augustine thus anticipates Descartes's famous argument of more than a thousand years later that the proposition, "I think, therefore I am," can be known with absolute certainty. Indeed, the following passages were so influential to the thinking of Descartes, generally regarded as the founder of modern philosophy, that studying them gives us a unique opportunity to understand firsthand the source of much subsequent thinking about the relationship between our minds and world and the nature of knowledge.

⚜

Self-Knowledge and the Nature of Mind

Book X: Opinion Which the Mind Has of Itself Is Deceitful.

8. But the mind errs, when it so lovingly and intimately connects itself with these images, as

From *History of the Christian Church*, Vol. III, *Nicene and Post-Nicene Fathers*, Philip Schaff, ed. (New York: Charles Scribner's Sons, 1884), with emendations by the author.

even to consider itself to be something of the same kind. For so it is conformed to them to some extent, not by being this, but by thinking it is so: not that it thinks itself to be an image, but outright that very thing itself of which it entertains the image. For there still lives in it the power of distinguishing the corporeal thing which it leaves without, from the image of that corporeal thing which it contains therefrom within itself; except when these images are so projected as if felt without and not thought within, as in the case of people who are asleep, or mad, or in a trance. . . .

9. When, therefore, it thinks itself to be something of this kind, it thinks itself to be a corporeal thing; and since it is perfectly conscious of its own superiority, by which it rules the body, it has hence come to pass that the question has been raised what part of the body has the greater power in the body; and the opinion has been held that this is the mind, nay, that it is even the whole soul altogether. And some accordingly think it to be the blood, others the brain, others the heart; . . . Others, again, have believed the soul to be made up of very minute and individual corpuscles, which they call atoms, meeting in themselves and cohering. Others have said that its substance is air, others fire. Others have been of opinion that it is no substance at all, since they could not think any substance unless it is body, and they did not find that the soul was body; but it was in their opinion the tempering together itself of our body, or the combining together of the elements, by which that flesh is as it were conjoined. And hence all of these have held the soul to be mortal; since, whether it were body, or some combination of body, certainly it could not in either case continue always without death. But they who have held its substance to be some kind of life the reverse of corporeal, since they have found it to be a life that animates and quickens every living body, have by consequence striven also, according as each was able, to prove it immortal, since life cannot be without life. . . .

10. Now, in the case of all these opinions, any one who sees that the nature of the mind is at once substance, and yet not corporeal,—that is, that it does not occupy a less extension of place with a less part of itself, and a greater with a greater,—must needs see at the same time that they who are of opinion that it is corporeal, do not err from defect of knowledge concerning mind,

but because they associate with it qualities without which they are not able to conceive any nature at all. For if you bid them conceive of existence that is without corporeal phantasms, they hold it merely nothing. And so the mind would not seek itself, as though wanting to itself. For what is so present to knowledge as that which is present to the mind? Or what is so present to the mind as the mind itself? . . .

11. It is then a wonderful question, in what manner the soul seeks and finds itself; at what it aims in order to seek, or whither it comes, that it may come into or find out. For what is so much in the mind as the mind itself? But because it is *in* those things which it thinks of with love, and is wont to be in sensible, that is, in corporeal things with love, it is unable to be in itself without the images of those corporeal things. And hence shameful error arises to block its way, whilst it cannot separate from itself the images of sensible things, so as to see itself alone. For they have marvelously cohered with it by the close adhesion of love. And herein consists its uncleanness; since, while it strives to think of itself alone, it fancies itself to be that, without which it cannot think of itself. When, therefore, it is bidden to become acquainted with itself, let it not seek itself as though it were withdrawn from itself; but let it withdraw that which it has added to itself. For itself lies more deeply within not only than those sensible things, which are clearly without, but also than the images of them; which are indeed in some part of the soul, *viz.*, that which beasts also have, although these want understanding, which is proper to the mind. As therefore the mind is within, it goes forth in some sort from itself, when it exerts the affection of love towards these, as it were, footprints of many acts of attention. And these footprints are, as it were, imprinted on the memory, at the time when the corporeal things which are without are perceived in such way, that even when those corporeal things are absent, yet the images of them are at hand to those who think of them. Therefore let the mind become acquainted with itself, and not seek itself as if it were absent; but fix upon itself the act of [voluntary] attention, by which it was wandering among other things, and let it think of itself. So it will see that at no time did it ever not love itself, at no time did it ever not know itself; but

by loving another thing together with itself it has confounded itself with it, and in some sense has grown one with it. And so, while it embraces diverse things, as though they were one, it has come to think those things to be one which are diverse.

Chapter 9. The Mind Knows Itself, by the Very Act of Understanding the Precept to Know Itself.

12. Let it not therefore seek to discern itself as though absent, but take pains to discern itself as present. Nor let it take knowledge of itself as if it did not know itself, but let it distinguish itself from that which it knows to be another. For how will it take pains to obey that very precept which is given it, "Know thyself," if it knows not either what "know" means or what "thyself" means? But if it knows both, then it knows also itself. Since "know thyself" is not so said to the mind as is "Know the cherubim and the seraphim": for they are absent, and we believe concerning them, and according to that belief they are declared to be certain celestial powers. Nor yet again as it is said, Know the will of that man: for this it is not within our reach to perceive at all, either by sense or understanding, unless by corporeal signs actually set forth; and this in such a way that we rather believe than understand. Nor again as it is said to a man, Behold thy own face; which he can only do in a looking-glass. For even our own face itself is out of the reach of our own seeing it; because it is not there where our look can be directed. But when it is said to the mind, Know thyself; then it knows itself by that very act by which it understands the word "thyself"; and this for no other reason than that it is present to itself. . . .

13. Let it not then add anything to that which it knows itself to be, when it is bidden to know itself. For it knows, at any rate, that this is said to itself; namely, to the self that is, and that lives, and that understands. . . .

14. But since we treat of the nature of the mind, let us remove from our consideration all knowledge which is received from without, through the senses of the body, and attend more carefully to the position which we have laid down, that all minds know and are certain concerning themselves. For men certainly have doubted whether the power of living, of remembering, of understanding, of willing, of thinking, of knowing, of judging, be of air, or of

fire, or of the brain, or of the blood, or of atoms, or besides the usual four elements of a fifth kind of body, I know not what; or whether the combining or tempering together of this our flesh itself has power to accomplish these things. And one has attempted to establish this, and another to establish that. Yet who ever doubts that he himself lives, and remembers, and understands, and wills, and thinks, and knows, and judges? Seeing that even if he doubts, he lives; if he doubts, he remembers why he doubts; if he doubts, he understands that he doubts; if he doubts, he wishes to be certain; if he doubts, he thinks; if he doubts, he knows that he does not know; if he doubts, he judges that he ought not to assent rashly. Whosoever therefore doubts about anything else, ought not to doubt of all these things; which if they were not, he would not be able to doubt of anything. . . .

16. . . . And therefore, when the mind knows itself, it knows its own substance; and when it is certain about itself, it is certain about its own substance. But it is certain about itself, as those things which are said above prove convincingly; although it is not at all certain whether itself is air, or fire, or some body, or some function of body. Therefore it is not any of these. And to that whole which is bidden to know itself, belongs this, that it is certain that it is not any of those things of which it is uncertain, and is certain that it is that only, which only it is certain that it is. For it thinks in this way of fire, or air, and whatever else of the body it thinks of. Neither can it in any way be brought to pass that it should so think that which itself is, as it thinks that which itself is not. Since it thinks all these things through an imaginary fantasy, whether fire, or air, or this or that body or that part or combination and tempering together of the body: nor assuredly is it said to be all those things, but some one of them. But if it were any one of them, it would think this one in a different manner from the rest, *viz.* not through an imaginary fantasy, as absent things are thought, which either themselves or some of like kind have been touched by the bodily sense; but by some inward, not feigned, but true presence (for nothing is more present to it than itself); just as it thinks that itself lives, and remembers, and understands, and wills. For it knows these things in itself, and does not imagine them as though it had touched them by the sense outside itself, as corporeal things are touched. And if it attaches nothing to itself from the thought of these things, so as to

think itself to be something of the kind, then what-soever remains to it from itself, that alone is itself. . . .

⚘

Notice Augustine's answer to Plotinus's question about why the soul is not fully aware of itself. According to Augustine, the reason the mind is not readily known to itself is because, in order to function properly in the world, the mind must have images of things and take them to be not images but things; hence, through deceiving itself into taking its own representations as being not of its own self but of things in the world, the mind must operate under a false view of its own operations. To become illuminated to its own existence, the mind must detach itself—in the manner of the Buddhist, Stoic, and Skeptic—from its own perceptions and the things to which it is attracted by desire. The mind must remove itself from the seduction of its own images, reminiscent of the path of the philosopher who leaves the darkness of Plato's cave for the light of the sun. This the mind attains when it becomes aware of its three distinct faculties as separately functioning aspects of one entity of the mind. These three faculties—memory, understanding, and will—are, he claims, the direct image within us of the Holy Trinity.

5.3 Anselm (1033–1109): The New Scholasticism

Though he served as archbishop of Canterbury in England, Anselm was not English but Italian; he was born in Piedmont (Aosta), a town in the Italian Alps that was of strategic importance as a crossroads throughout Roman and medieval times. As a young man, Anselm rejected the political career for which his father, an Italian nobleman, had prepared him. Instead, he traveled about Europe for many years as a wandering scholar. Eventually, he joined a Benedictine monastery at Bec, Normandy, where he studied philosophy and theology with its famous prior,

Lanfranc. Three years later, when Lanfranc left to become archbishop of Canterbury, Anselm became the new abbott. In 1093, after Lanfranc's death, Anselm again succeeded to his former mentor's position and became the next archbishop. However, partly because of Anselm's devotion to Greek rationalism and partly because he was not servile to King William II and his successor, Henry I, both kings found cause to exile him on several occasions.

Besides his three main theological works, *Molologion, Proslogion,* and *Cur Deus Homo* (Why God Became Man), he wrote studies on semantics (*De Grammatico*), truth (*De Veritate*), and freedom (*De Libertate Arbitrii*). In his final, unfinished work, *On Power and Powerlessness, Possibility and Impossibility, Necessity and Liberty,* he tried to unravel the mystery of how a soul could come into existence. Upon learning that he would soon die, he wrote, "If it is His will I shall gladly obey, but if He should prefer me to stay with you just long enough to solve the question of the origin of the soul which I have been turning over in my mind, I would gratefully accept the chance, for I doubt whether anybody else will solve it when I am gone."[8]

Anselm's influential writings helped build a foundation for Scholasticism, a method and system of thought primarily based on the works of Plato and Aristotle. It embraced all the intellectual, artistic, philosophical, and theological activities carried on in various medieval schools as taught by its proponents, called *doctores scholastici.* Unlike ancient Greek philosophy, which was essentially the work of individuals, Scholasticism was an attempt to build philosophy as part of a "Christian society" whose purpose in turn was to transcend both individuals and nations. As the corporate product of social thought, scholastic reasoning depended on obedience to authority as espoused by the traditional forms of thought codified within the supposedly "revealed" Christian religion under the auspices of the church. As a result, philosophy was subjugated to theology and rigidly controlled by the authoritarian hierarchy of the church.

Anselm pioneered the technique for using linguistic analysis to "solve" philosophical problems. For instance, in his *De Veritate (On Truth)* he showed that there are different senses of the concept of "truth," while in *De Libertate Arbitrii (On Free Will)* he identified the necessary conditions for the concept of free will. In *De Casu Diaboli (On the Devil's Fall)* he used the idea of the fall from grace by a God-created Satan to argue that the existence of evil is compatible with the existence of an all-good God. In all his works he relied on Aristotelian logic as developed by Boethius,[9] along with a variety of Neoplatonist ideas, to argue that the existence of God can be known rationally.

Anselm's facility with linguistic analysis paved the way for his most famous work, *Proslogion,* from which the next selection is taken. In it, Anselm originates the famous ontological argument for the existence of God. Later thinkers were vehemently divided over it. Those inclined toward a Platonic or Neoplatonic realism about universals in which the role of essences is emphasized over materialism—such as Descartes, Spinoza, Leibniz, and Hegel—each accepted some form of the ontological argument as valid and profound. Those under the influence of Aristotelian nominalism—such as the Empiricists—rejected the argument as mere verbal trickery; thus Aquinas, Hume, and Kant all dismissed it.

Anselm quotes from Psalms 14:1, "The fool has said in his heart, There is no God," in an attempt to equate the denial of God with a self-contradiction, something only a fool would do. According to Anselm God's existence can be derived from the very meaning of "God," which he defines as the greatest conceivable being "a greater than which" cannot be conceived. He then claims that since existence is greater than nonexistence, to say that "God does not exist" is tantamount to saying something like, "A being that cannot be conceived as anything other than existing does not exist," or "A being that exists necessarily does not exist," which according to Anselm is self-contradictory. Paramount to understanding Anselm's thinking here is the distinction between an idea that exists in reality—*in re*—and an idea that exists only in conception—*in intellectu.* Anselm's argument is that if an idea is the greatest then it must exist *in re*, not just *in intellectu*, since it is greater to exist in reality than merely in the conception. That is why any supreme or perfect idea, such as Being, exists *in re*, why reality itself has existence in actuality not just in concept (for instance, merely *in intellectu* in the mind of God). This line of argument—based on Plato's realistic metaphysics and buttressed by Augustine's Neoplatonic reinterpretation of Christian dogma—was inspired by a question that had puzzled many medieval Christian thinkers, namely why God would have to create a world at all; that is, why was the world not merely a dream in the mind of God? If the world was in some important sense a dream in the mind of God, then it was in no sense an independent entity from God, implying a sort of pantheism incompatible with orthodox Christianity doctrine, which required as a fundamental distinction things that were God from things that were not God.

Anselm's ontological argument is followed by objections from another Benedictine monk, Gaunilon, from the Abbey of Marmoutier near Tours. Gaunilon claims, on behalf of "the fool," that Anselm's proof is bogus for two main reasons: first, we cannot properly form the concept of a necessarily existent being since there is nothing in experience on which to base such a concept; second, we can imagine lots of perfect things defined as "perfect" but that in fact do not exist. Gaunilon's criticism is followed by Anselm's rebuttal.

⚓

Proslogion: The Ontological Argument

. . . I began to ask myself whether there might be found a single argument which would require no

---

From the *Proslogium*, translated by Sidney Norton Deane (La Salle, IL: Open Court, 1903), with emendations by the author.

other for its proof than itself alone; and alone would suffice to demonstrate that God truly exists, and that there is a supreme good requiring nothing else, which all other things require for their existence and well-being; and whatever we believe regarding the divine Being.

Although I often and earnestly directed my thought to this end, and at some times that which I sought seemed to be just within my reach, while again it wholly evaded my mental vision, at last in despair I was about to cease, as if from the search for a thing which could not be found. But when I wished to exclude this thought altogether, lest, by busying my mind to no purpose, it should keep me from other thoughts, in which I might be successful; then more and more, though I was unwilling and shunned it, it began to force itself upon me, with a kind of importunity. So, one day, when I was exceedingly wearied with resisting its importunity, in the very conflict of my thoughts, the proof of which I had despaired offered itself, so that I eagerly embraced the thoughts which I was strenuously repelling. . . .

And so Lord, do thou, who dost give understanding to faith, give me, so far as thou knowest it to be profitable, to understand that thou art as we believe; and that thou art that which we believe. And, indeed, we believe that thou art a being than which nothing greater can be conceived. Or is there no such nature, since the fool hath said in his heart, there is no God? But, at any rate, this very fool, when he hears of this being of which I speak—a being than which nothing greater can be conceived—understands what he hears, and what he understands is in his understanding; although he does not understand it to exist.

For, it is one thing for an object to be in the understanding, and another to understand that the object exists. When a painter first conceives of what he will afterwards perform, he has it in his understanding, but he does not yet understand it to be, because he has not performed it. But after he has made the painting, he both has it in his understanding, and he understands that it exists, because he has made it.

Hence, even the fool is convinced that something exists in the understanding, at least, than which nothing greater can be conceived. For, when he hears of this, he understands it. And whatever is understood, exists in the understanding. And

assuredly that, than which nothing greater can be conceived, cannot exist in the understanding alone. For, suppose it exists in the understanding alone: then it can be conceived to exist in reality; which is greater.

Therefore, if that, than which nothing greater can be conceived, exists in the understanding alone, the very being, than which nothing greater can he conceived, is one, than which a greater can be conceived. But obviously this is impossible. Hence, there is no doubt that there exists a being, than which nothing greater can be conceived, and it exists both in the understanding and in reality. . . .

And it assuredly exists so truly, that it cannot be conceived not to exist. For, it is possible to conceive of a being which cannot be conceived not to exist, and this is greater than one which can be conceived not to exist. Hence, if that, than which nothing greater can be conceived, can be conceived not to exist, it is not that, than which nothing greater can be conceived. But this is an irreconcilable contradiction. There is, then, so truly a being than which nothing greater can be conceived to exist, that it cannot even be conceived not to exist; and this being thou art, O Lord, our God.

So truly, therefore, dost thou exist, O Lord, my God, that thou canst not be conceived not to exist; and rightly. For if a mind could conceive of a being better than thee, the creature would rise above the Creator; and this is most absurd. And, indeed, whatever else there is, except thee alone, can be conceived not to exist. To thee alone, therefore, it belongs to exist more truly than all other beings, and hence in a higher degree than all others. For, whatever else exists does not exist so truly, and hence in a less degree it belongs to it to exist. Why, then, has the fool said in his heart, there is no God, since it is so evident, to a rational mind, that thou dost exist in the highest degree of all? Why, except that he is dull and a fool? . . .

In Behalf of the Fool

AN ANSWER TO THE ARGUMENT OF ANSELM BY GAUNILON, A MONK OF MARMOUTIER

. . . if it should be said that a being which cannot be even conceived in terms of any fact, is in the understanding. I do not deny that this being is, accordingly, in my understanding. But since through this fact it can in no wise attain to real existence also, I do not yet concede to it that existence at all, until some certain proof of it shall be given.

For he who says that this being exists, because otherwise the being which is greater than all will not be greater than all, does not attend strictly to what he is saying. For I do not yet say, no, I even deny or doubt that this being is greater than any real object. Nor do I concede to it any other existence than this (if it should be called existence) which it has when the mind, according to a word merely heard, tries to form the image of an object absolutely unknown to it.

How, then, is the veritable existence of that being proved to me from the assumption, by hypothesis, that it is greater than all other beings? For I should still deny this, or doubt your demonstration of it, to this extent, that I should not admit that this being is in my understanding and concept even in the way in which many objects whose real existence is uncertain and doubtful, are in my understanding and concept. For it should be proved first that this being itself really exists somewhere; and then, from the fact that it is greater than all, we shall not hesitate to infer that it also subsists in itself.

For example: it is said that somewhere in the ocean is an island, which, because of the difficulty, or rather the impossibility, of discovering what does not exist, is called the lost island. And they say that this island has an inestimable wealth of all manner of riches and delicacies in greater abundance than is told of the Islands of the Blest; and that having no owner or inhabitant, it is more excellent than all other countries, which are inhabited by mankind, in the abundance with which it is stored.

Now if someone should tell me that there is such an island, I should easily understand his words, in which there is no difficulty. But suppose that he went on to say, as if by a logical inference: "You can no longer doubt that this island which is more excellent than all lands exists somewhere, since you have no doubt that it is in your understanding. And since it is more excellent not to be in the understanding alone, but to exist both in the understanding and in reality, for this reason it must exist. For if it does not exist, any land which really exists will be more excellent than it; and so the island already understood by you to be more excellent will not be more excellent."

If a man should try to prove to me by such reasoning that this island truly exists, and that its existence should no longer be doubted, either I should believe that he was jesting, or I know not which I ought to regard as the greater fool: myself, supposing that I should allow this proof; or him, if he should suppose that he had established with any certainty the existence of this island. For he ought to show first that the hypothetical excellence of this island exists as a real and indubitable fact, and in no wise as any unreal object, or one whose existence is uncertain, in my understanding.

ANSELM'S REPLY

But, you say, it is as if one should suppose an island in the ocean, which surpasses all lands in its fertility, and which, because of the difficulty, or rather the impossibility, of discovering what does not exist, is called a lost island; and should say that there can be no doubt that this island truly exists in reality, for this reason, that one who hears it described easily understands what he hears.

Now I promise confidently that if any man shall devise anything existing either in reality or in concept alone (except that than which a greater cannot be conceived) to which he can adapt the sequence of my reasoning, I will discover that thing, and will give him his lost island, not to be lost again.

But it now appears that this being than which a greater is inconceivable cannot be conceived not to be, because it exists on so assured a ground of truth; for otherwise it would not exist at all.

Hence, if any one says that he conceives this being not to exist, I say that at the time when he conceives of this either he conceives of a being than which a greater is inconceivable, or he does not conceive at all. If he does not conceive, he does not conceive of the nonexistence of that of which he does not conceive. But if he does conceive, he certainly conceives of a being which cannot be even conceived not to exist. For if it could be conceived not to exist, it could be conceived to have a beginning and an end. But this is impossible.

He, then, who conceives of this being conceives of a being which cannot be even conceived not to exist; but he who conceives of this being does not conceive that it does not exist; else he conceives what is inconceivable. The nonexistence, then, of that than which a greater cannot be conceived is inconceivable.

NOTES

1. The expression, "philosopher *qua* philosopher" is commonly used in philosophy to distinguish the philosopher writing or speaking as (*qua*) a philosopher rather, than, say, a layperson, human being, citizen, and so forth.

2. That is *not* to say that rationality is somehow par for the course in philosophy, or even essential to it. We shall see many examples of philosophers who have argued, asserted, or even just expressed (without any rational argument whatsoever) that *nothing* can be argued for rationally, that *everything* rests on faith—not just one's views of God.

3. And there are many different meanings of this word, too, as used in different systems of thought.

4. Most notably Brentano and those influenced by his notion of intentionality; see Section 21.0.

5. We shall see Josiah Royce raise this in exactly the same way, even using similar examples (see Chapter 20).

6. And, like most philosophers, he is assuming that *essence precedes existence*. We shall see several more recent philosophers deny this, most notably the nineteenth- and twentieth-century existentialist philosophers such as Jean-Paul Sartre, who claimed that "existence precedes essence" (see Section 21.3).

7. Ingmar Bergman's film *The Seventh Seal* is a classic that poignantly explores this theme.

8. M. Charlesworth, *St. Anselm's Proslogion* (Oxford, 1965), p. 21.

9. An influential commentator (470–525) on Aristotle reflecting a strong influence of Neoplatonism and Augustinianism.

6 ⚘ The Islamic Influence

6.0 Averroës (ibn-Rushd) (1126–1198): The Unity of All Minds

In 529 C.E., two centuries after the fall of the Roman Empire and the rise of Christianity, Emperor Justinian sought to secure the new religion by shutting down the philosophical schools of Athens. The thousand-year tenure of Platonic and Aristotelian wisdom thus came to an end. Within a generation, Greek learning—denounced by papal authorities as pagan heresies punishable by death—virtually disappeared from Europe.

A number of philosophers, most of them Neoplatonists, escaped to Persia where classical and ancient Greek works, translated first into Syriac and then into Arabic, had already begun to exert wide influence among Islamic and Jewish thinkers. Over the next five hundred years, while the Dark Ages of Christendom ruled Europe, the Platonic and Aristotelian systems survived and continued to evolve on the other side of the Mediterranean. Schools in Alexandria, Syria, and Persia became centers for the translation and study of Greek texts. After the Arab conquest of Spain, philosophy migrated back across North Africa into Europe through Spain, where in Toledo and Córdova a group of brilliant Islamic philosophers rekindled the flame of the golden age of Greece within Christendom.

Two of the most important Islamic philosophers were Avicenna (ibn-Sina, 980–1037) and Averroës. Both considered themselves followers solely of Aristotle, due in part to a confusion of Platonic and Aristotelian ideas as espoused in an influential work of the time, the *Theology of Aristotle*. This Neoplatonic work was really a compilation of Plotinus's *Enneads*. Averroës saw Avicenna's interpretations of Aristotle as colored by religion on the one hand and by Stoic and Neoplatonist influences on the other. He tried to purge these influences from his own interpretations of Aristotle, whom he regarded not only as the greatest of all philosophers but also as the "model of human perfection."

Born in Córdova, Spain, Averroës (Muhammad ibn-Rushd) was the son of a qadi (judge). He studied theology, law, medicine, mathematics, and philosophy, which under Islamic protection centered on the masterworks of Plato and Aristotle as preserved by an evolving series of lengthy and often innovative commentators. By now these ideas had been banned for centuries and virtually forgotten in the adjoining Holy Roman Empire. Like his father and his grandfather, Averroës too became a judge, first in Seville and then in Córdova, though his main love was philosophy. Supposedly, one night over dinner, he entered into a discussion with the Almohad prince Abu Ya'qub Yusuf over the origin of the world and the nature of mind. Averroës's ruminations on Aristotle's account of existence and the nature of the soul so impressed the ruler that he commissioned Averroës to write an entire set of commentaries. A few years later the prince appointed Averroës as his personal physician. Under the prince's auspices, Averroës spent the rest of his life writing commentaries on virtually all of Aristotle's works, producing detailed and original reconstructive commentaries on Aristotle's *Metaphysics, Physics, Posterior Analytics, De Caelo,* and *De Anima,* as well as Plato's *Republic.*

Averroës's chief concern was not with the subtle reinterpretations of ancient Greek wisdom according to then-current religious tenets to which most previous Islamic commentators (and most subsequent Christian commentators) were prone; rather he wished to reawaken philosophy's slumbering soul. In his commentaries, Averroës argues persistently and with painstaking precision that all previous commentators, including and especially the widely admired Avicenna, had completely misunderstood and corrupted the ideas of Aristotle by surrendering the great philosopher's ideas to theological concerns. Consequently, after the death of Abu Ya'qub Yusuf, Averroës was accused by his enemies of promoting the "pagan" philosophy of the ancients instead of following the accepted Muslim faith. He spent many of his last years in exile, first outside Córdova and then finally in Morocco. Just as five centuries earlier Justinian had purged Christendom of philosophy, the caliph al-Mansur burned all books on logic and metaphysics and published an edict that anyone who believed that truth can be known by unaided reason, independently of divine revela-

tion, would be sentenced by God to hell. As the wars between Christians and Muslims gradually pushed the Muslims out of Spain, the censorship of Averroës by the Islamic rulers marked the end of Muslim philosophy and its banishment from the Mohammedan world by a rigid orthodoxy. Ironically, just as the Islamic authorities once welcomed works banned by their Christian enemies, the conquering Christians were quick to seize works banned by the Muslims. Thus, in one of the greatest of all historical twists, philosophy safely passed hands from one opposing religion to another and then back again, gradually finding a way back to its ancient European roots.

As Avicenna's philosophical rival and critic of the Muslim theologian al-Ghazali (1058–1111), Averroës defended Aristotelian philosophy and "purified" it of its Stoic and Neoplatonic elements so well that Scholastic writers called him "The Commentator." Thomas Aquinas, for instance (see Section 7.0), used Averroës as a constant source while writing his own commentaries on Aristotle and the *Summa contra Gentiles.* During his lifetime, Averroës courageously, openly, and successfully defended philosophy from various assaults by the Mohammedan orthodoxy found in works such as the widely read *Destruction of the Philosophers,* in which the theologian Algazel argues that because all necessary truth is revealed in the Koran, philosophical speculation is completely unnecessary. Averroës responded by brazenly publishing his *Destruction of the Destruction,* in which he shows that religious dogmas are at best philosophical truths presented in allegorical form and thus amenable to an Aristotelian interpretation. Averroës's *Tahafut al-Tahafut* (*The Incoherence of the Incoherence*) was a response to al-Ghazali's attack on philosophy in *The Incoherence of the Philosophers.* Al-Ghazali had criticized philosophers, especially Avicenna, for advocating views incompatible with religious faith. In his defense of the philosophers, Averroës brilliantly attacks al-Ghazali's book without having to deny any of the doctrines of

Islam by evoking a distinction between "revealed" theology and "natural" theology. Many later medieval philosophers would rely upon this distinction to keep themselves out of direct conflict with the Christian counterparts of the orthodox Muslim authorities.

According to Averroës, philosophy and theology each has a legitimate but distinct function based on a three-tiered class division of human beings, much like the Golden Lie espoused by Plato in *The Republic* about the three different classes of souls ("gold," "silver," and "bronze"). Like Plato's cave dwellers, the lowest class of people—the vast majority—live by imagination, not reason. Unable to comprehend philosophy, they need the security of religious answers forced by obedience to an orthodox dogma into which they must be indoctrinated by eloquent or charismatic priests. The next, slightly higher, class—much smaller than the first—lives by the same sorts of beliefs as the lowest class but with more intelligence. They do not accept dogma merely because it is taught but instead try to establish intellectual justification for their beliefs. Theologians come from this class. However, since they too are ultimately prejudiced (they seek only justification for commonly accepted beliefs), they can never attain the truth, which requires complete impartiality from all orthodoxy. The third, and highest, level of intelligence allows one to see that religion does not and cannot ever provide a connection to truth. This highest level of intelligence is found only among a few extraordinary individuals—the philosophers—who can discover directly for themselves the awesome truths that the rational theologians and the irrational believers can only go on seeking.

According to Averroës, philosophers know that to know the truth one must know it not by faith nor by rationalization from premises accepted as true by faith but directly on the basis of premises first tested by experience and justified by careful and logical reasoning. And the most difficult of all truths, known by only a select few philosophers, is that the active part of the mind of each human being is not a distinct and separately existing individual but is the same, numerically identical unity. The greatest of all truths, hidden in the tradition passed down to us from Plato and Aristotle as revealed through Averroës's commentaries, is that each individual mind is numerically identical to all other individual minds, identical to the Agent Intellect, the mind of God.

Throughout his works Averroës argues that the existence of God, along with complete knowledge of God's attributes, can be known directly by philosophers and demonstrated through reason. Following Aristotle, however, he argues against the individual immortality of the soul, at least of that aspect which he and Aristotle call the passive intellect. Like Avicenna before him, Averroës claims that the individual human intellect, activated from without by the Agent Intellect (God), is itself the emanation of the Agent Intellect (God). But it has both an active and a passive part. The passive intellect, brought into existence through interaction with the Agent Intellect via the active intellect, does not survive the body. Only the active intellect, which is immortal, survives. It is this active intellect that is numerically identical (one and the same entity) within all sentient beings.

The active intellect, described in this selection presented from his *Commentary on De Anima* (*the Soul*), is not a personal faculty but is itself numerically identical to the Agent Intellect, the One which individuates itself into the Many by illuminating the passive intellects within individual human beings.

⟟

Commentary on De Anima

Text 4. It is necessary, therefore, that, if [the intellect] understands all things, it be not mixed,

Philosophy in the Middle Ages, A. Hyman and J. Walsh, eds., from "Long Commentary on *De Anima*," A. Hyman, trans. (New York: Harper & Row, 1967). Used by permission of Arthur Hyman.

as Anaxagoras has said, in order that it may dominate, that is in order that it may understand. For if [something] were to appear in it, that which appears would prevent something foreign [from appearing in it], since it is something other.

Commentary. After [Aristotle] has set down that the material, receiving intellect must belong to the genus of passive powers, and, that in spite of this, it is not altered by the reception [of that which it receives], for it is neither a body nor a power within a body, he provides a demonstration for this [opinion]. And he says: *It is necessary, therefore, that, if the intellect understands,* etc. That is, it is necessary, therefore, that, if the [intellect] understands all those things which exist outside the soul, it be described—prior to its understanding—as belonging to the genus of passive, not active, powers, and [it is necessary] that it be not mixed with bodies, that is, that it be neither a body nor a power within a body, be it a natural or animate [power], as Anaxagoras has said. Thereafter [Aristotle] says: *in order that it may understand* etc. That is, it is necessary that it be not mixed, in order that it may understand all things and receive them. For if it were mixed, then it would be either a body or a power within a body, and if it were one of these, it would have a form proper to itself, which form would prevent it from receiving some foreign form.

This is what he has in mind when he says: *For if something were to appear in it* etc. That is, if [the passive intellect] were to have a form proper to itself, then that form would prevent it from receiving the various external forms, which are different from it. Thus, one must inquire into those propositions by means of which Aristotle shows these two things about the intellect, namely [1] that it belongs to the genus of passive powers, and [2] that it is not alterable, since it is neither a body nor a power within a body. For these two [propositions] are the starting point of all those things which are said about the intellect. As Plato said, the most extensive discussion must take place in the beginning; for the slightest error in the beginning is the cause of the greatest error in the end, as Aristotle says.

We say: That conception by the intellect belongs in some way to a passive power, just as in the case of a sensory power [perception by a sense belongs to a passive power], becomes clear through the following [considerations]. Now, the passive powers are moveable by that to which they are related (*attribuuntur*), while active powers move that to which they are related (*attribuuntur*). And since it is the case that something moves something else only insofar as it exists in actuality and [something] is moved insofar as it exists in potentiality, it follows necessarily, that since the forms of things exist in actuality outside the soul, they move the rational soul insofar as it understands them, just as in the case of sensible things it is necessary that they move the senses insofar as they are things existing in actuality and that the senses are moved by them. Therefore, the rational soul must consider the forms (*intentiones*) which are in the imaginative faculty, just as the senses must inspect sensible things. And since it appears that the forms of external things move this power in such a way that the mind abstracts these forms from material things and thereby makes them the first intelligibles in actuality, after they had been intelligibles in potentiality—it appears from this that this soul [the intellect] is [also] active, not [only] passive. For insofar as the intelligibles move [the intellect], it is passive, but insofar as they are moved by it, it is active. For this reason Aristotle states subsequently that it is necessary to posit in the rational soul the following two distinct [powers], namely, an active power and a passive power. And he states clearly that each one of [the rational soul's] parts is neither generable nor corruptible. In the present discussion, however, he begins to describe the nature (*substantiam*) of this passive power, to the extent to which it is necessary in this exposition. Therefore he states that this distinct [power], namely, that which is passive and receptive, exists in the rational faculty. . . .

Text 5. And thus [the material intellect] has no other nature but that which is possible. Therefore that [part] of the soul which is called intellect (and I call intellect that [part] by means of which we distinguish and think) is not something existing in actuality before it thinks.

Commentary. After [Aristotle] has shown that the material intellect does not possess any of the forms of material things, he begins to define it in the following manner. And he says that it has no nature but the nature of the possibility for receiving the material intelligible forms. And he states: *And thus [the material intellect] has no other nature,* etc. That is, that [part] of the soul which is called the material intellect has no nature and essence, through which it exists (*constituatur*) insofar as it is material but the nature of possibility, for it is devoid of all material and intelligible forms.

Thereafter he says: *and I call intellect,* etc. That is, and I intend by *intellect* that faculty of the soul which is truly called intellect, not that faculty which is called intellect in a general sense, that is, the imaginative faculty (in the Greek language), but [I intend] that faculty by means of which we distinguish speculative things and by means of which we think about things to be done in the future. Thereafter he says: *it is not something existing in actuality before it thinks.* That is, it is the definition of the material intellect that it is that which is in potentiality all the concepts (*intentiones*) of the universal material forms and it is not something in actuality before it understands them.

Since this is the definition of the material intellect, it is clear that it differs in respect to itself from prime matter in that it is in potentiality all the concepts (*intentiones*) of the universal material forms, while prime matter is in potentiality all these sensible forms, not [as] knowing and comprehending. And the reason why this nature, that is, the material intellect, distinguishes and knows, while prime matter does not distinguish or know, is that prime matter receives differentiated, that is, individual and particular forms, while [the material intellect] receives universal forms. . . .

As for the question stating: in what way are the speculative intelligibles generable and corruptible, while [the intellect] producing them and that receiving them are eternal (and what need would there be to posit an agent intellect and a receiving [intellect] were there not something that is generated)—this question would not arise would there not exist something which is the cause of the generation of the speculative intelligibles. But what has been said concerning the fact that these [speculative] intelligibles consists of two [principles], one of which is generated, the other of which is not generated is according to the course of nature. For, since conception by the intellect, as Aristotle says, is like perception by the senses—but perception by a sense is accomplished through two principles, one of which is that object through which sense perception becomes true (and this is the sensible outside the soul), and the other is that subject through which sense perception is an existing form (and this is the first actuality of the sense organ), it

is likewise necessary that the intelligibles in actuality have two principles, one of which is the object (*subiectum*) through which they are true, namely, the forms which are the true images, the other one of which is that subject (*subiectum*) through which the intelligibles are one of the things existing in the world, and this is the material intellect. But there is no difference between sense and intellect except that the object through which sense-perception is true exists outside the soul, while the object through which conception by the intellect is true exists within the soul. As will be seen subsequently, this is what was said by Aristotle about this intellect. . . .

But the second question which states: in what way is the material intellect numerically one in all individual human beings, not generable nor corruptible, while the intelligibles existing in it in actuality (and this is the speculative intellect) are numbered according to the numeration of individual human beings, and generable and corruptible through the generation and corruption of individual [human beings]—this question is extremely difficult and one that has the greatest ambiguity.

If we posit that this material intellect is numbered according to the numeration of individual human beings, it follows that it is some individual thing, either a body or a power in a body. And if it were some individual thing, it would be the intelligible form (*intentio*) in potentiality. But the intelligible form in potentiality is an object which moves the receiving intellect, not a subject which is moved. For, if the receiving subject were assumed to be some individual thing, it would follow, as we have said, that something receives itself, and this is impossible. . . .

[On the other hand], were we to assert that [the material intellect] is not numbered according to the numeration of individual [human beings], it would follow that its relation to all individual human beings who possess its ultimate perfection through generation would be the same. . . .

And regardless whether you assert that the ultimate perfection which is generated in some individual [human being]—that is, that perfection through which the material intellect is joined [to human beings] and through which it is as a form separable from the subject to which it is joined—inheres in the intellect, if something like that should be the case, or whether you assert that this perfection belongs to one of the faculties of the soul or to one of the faculties of the body, each of these assumptions leads to an absurd conclusion.

Therefore one must be of the opinion that if there exist some beings having a soul whose first perfection is a substance existing in separation from their subjects, as it is thought about the celestial bodies, it is impossible that there exist in each of their species more than one individual. For if there would exist in these, that is, in each of their species more than one individual, for example, in the body moved by the same mover, then the existence of these individuals would be unnecessary and superfluous, since their motion would result from the form (intentio) which is one in number. For example, it is unnecessary that one sailor [captain] should have more than one ship at the same time, and it is likewise unnecessary that one artisan should have more than one instrument of the same kind. . . .

Since it is clear from the previously mentioned difficulties that it is impossible that the intelligible be joined to each individual human being and that it be numbered according to their numeration through that part which is to it as matter, that is, through the material intellect, it remains that the conjunction of the intelligibles with us human beings takes place through the conjunction of the intelligible forms (and they are the imaginative forms) with us, that is, through that part which is in us in respect to them in some way like a form. . . .

Since as a result of this discussion we are of the opinion that the material intellect is a single one for all human beings and since we are also of the opinion that the human species is eternal, as has been shown in other places, it follows that the material intellect is never devoid of the natural principles which are common to the whole human species, namely, the first propositions and individual concepts which are common to all. For these intelligibles are one according to the recipient [the material intellect], and many according to the received form [the imaginative form].

Hence according to the manner in which they are one, they are necessarily eternal, for existence does not depart from the received object, namely the moving principle which is the form (intentio) of the imaginative forms, and there is nothing on part of the recipient which prevents [its reception]. For generation and corruption belongs to them only according to the multitude which befalls

them, not according to the manner according to which they are one. Therefore, when in respect to some individual human being, some knowledge of the things first known is destroyed through the destruction of the object through which it is joined to us and through which it is true, that is, the imaginative form, it does not follow that this knowledge is destroyed absolutely, but it is [only] destroyed in respect to some individual human being. Because of this we can say that the speculative intellect is one in all [human beings].

This escaped many modern philosophers, so that they deny what Aristotle said in the eleventh treatise of the First Philosophy, namely, that it is necessary, that the incorporeal forms which move the celestial bodies are [numbered] according to the number of the celestial bodies. Therefore, knowledge about the soul is necessary for the knowledge of First Philosophy. It is necessary that the receiving intellect knows the intellect which exists in actuality. For if [this intellect] understands the material forms, it is more fitting that it understands immaterial forms, and that which it knows of the incorporeal forms, for example, of the agent intellect, does not hinder it from knowing the material forms.

. . . The manner in which we have described the essence of the material intellect answers all the questions arising about our statement that this intellect is one and many. For if something which is known by me and by you were one in all respects, it would follow that, if I know something, you would also know it, and many other absurdities [would also follow]. And if we were to assert that the material intellect is many, it would follow that something known by me and by you is one in respect to species and two in respect to individual, and thus something known would possess something else known and this would go on to infinity. Thus it will be impossible that a student learns from a teacher if the knowledge which exists in the teacher is not a force generating and producing the knowledge which is in the student, in the same manner as one fire produces another fire alike to it in species, which is absurd. The fact that something known by the teacher and the student is the same in this manner made Plato believe that learning is remembering. But if we assert that something known by me and by you is many in respect to that object (in subiecto) according to which it is true, that is in respect to the imaginative forms, and one in respect to the subject through which it is an existing intellect (and this is the material intellect), these questions are resolved completely.

⚹

The distinction between the active and the passive intellect is based on the observation that to represent objects to itself the mind does not consciously do anything; you go into a room and if a chair is there, your mind will represent to itself, in the form of a visual perception, a chair. (Later thinkers, such as Bishop Berkeley [see Chapter 14], would take this fact as evidence for the existence of God even in modern times.) We can, as Stoics such as Epictetus took great pains to point out, actively reflect upon our given (passive) perceptions. The two easily recognizable faculties of the mind, referred to by all Aristotelian metaphysicians as the "passive" and "active" intellects, often present an unnecessary source of confusion which a little reflection can make intuitively quite clear. According to Aristotle, the main function of the active intellect is to abstract the forms from things. The passive or potential intellect is but a mental repository whose main function is to receive the forms as concepts or ideas represented in conscious perception. These active and passive intellects come together in individual human beings: the active intellect produces, through its contact with the passive intellect, a combined intellect that Averroës called the *material* intellect. The material intellect, however, is not a substance but an activity; as he explains near the end of the selection, it is the activity of the active intellect within each individual human. It is both one and many. That is why the same things aren't known by all minds even though they are the same mind in action. The passive intellect differentiates us and is not immortal, while the active intellect—*nous*—is not only immortal but everywhere identical: *nous* is numerically one and the same being manifested in all of us. As one twentieth-century philosopher put it, "We are all the same person."[1]

Averroës's monopsychism was completely antithetical both to Christian dogma and the Mohammedan theology within which Averroës presented it. Averroës's response to his Mohammedan rulers was to claim that whereas reason compelled him to assert the unity of the intellect among all human beings, the belief in separate individual human intelligences could be accepted by faith. But he persisted in arguing that the ultimate culmination of reason led to what he took to be Aristotle's secret teaching as passed down through his cryptic remarks in *On the Soul*: the intellectual unity of all mankind.

During the time that the Islamic theologians tried to reinterpret their understanding of Greek philosophy away from Averroës's monopsychism and, lacking any good argument, quickly banned it, as a Muslim heresy the idea was much discussed within Christendom, and it managed to excite great attention, especially among secular thinkers in northern Europe. Monopsychism developed a large following that culminated in the thirteenth century in a philosophical movement known as the "Averroists," or "integral Aristotelians." Its main proponents consisted of members of the faculty of arts in Paris who argued, following Averroës, that the ultimate conclusion of reason and the correct understanding of Plato and Aristotle led to the same inexorable truth: the numerical unity of the active intelligences of all conscious beings. Christian theologians of the time, notably St. Albert and St. Thomas, saw in this idea the end, not just of Islam but of Christianity as well, and so like their Islamic counterparts they united as a front against Averroism until monopsychism was also proclaimed a Christian heresy, condemned by the church in Paris in 1270 and formally added to the list of Forbidden Propositions. In the same year Thomas's *On the Unity of the Intellect Against the Averroists* was published. The idea thus had the added distinction of being declared heresy in two opposing religions. Although the Averroists continued to teach in secret what they took to be the only correct understanding of the ancient Greek wisdom—the unity of the active intellect within all minds—the idea was successfully repressed from Western philosophy.

6.1 Maimonides (Moses ben Maimon) (1135–1204): Guide for the Perplexed

A contemporary of Averroës, also born in Córdova, Spain, Maimonides came from a prominent Jewish family. In 1148, when the Almohads conquered Córdova and life became difficult for the Jews, his family moved to Morocco (then Palestine), finally settling in Fostat (old Cairo), Egypt. Trained both as a physician and a rabbi, Maimonides became such a good doctor that he was appointed royal physician to the King of Egypt. As rabbi he became *nagid,* or head of the Egyptian Jewish community in Fostat.

Among his philosophical works are *Sharh al-Mishnah* (*Commentary on the Mishnah*); the Mishnah, also known as *Siraj* (*Luminary*), *1168; Mishnah Torah* (*Code of Jewish Law*), 1178; and *Treatise on Resurrection*, 1191. His most famous work, generally regarded as one of the greatest philosophical works of the Middle Ages, *Dalalat al-Ha'rin* (*Guide for the Perplexed,* 1190), is an attempt to bring Judaism in line with Neoplatonic Aristotelianism as taught by al-Farabi (Abu Nasr, 870–950) and Avicenna. Written in Arabic for philosophers and theologians, not for the general public, and often deliberately obscure, the work presents metaphysics as the supreme level of human activity, attainable only by those with a sufficiently high intellect. Unlike Averroës, however, who implied that the different classes of intellectual ability among people were predetermined, Maimonides offers a pedagogy by which individuals can evolve through the different stages of intellectual ability up to the highest level. This evolution requires careful guidance through education. His work had a tremendous influence over both Jewish and Christian Scholasticism, especially Albertus Magnus and Thomas Aquinas, as well as, in subsequent centuries, Spinoza, Mendelssohn, and Leibniz.

One of the most important methodological innovations in the *Guide for the Perplexed* was Maimonides's further development of John Scotus Erigena's (810–877) method *via negativa* (literally, "the negative way"). This involved relating a thing's attributes not by stating its essence in positive terms but by what is left after the deficiency of all positive statements about its essence is exhausted. This method *via negativa* could be used, according to Maimonides, to transcend the limitations of the human mind and attain knowledge of things beyond the direct reach of the senses or the intellect, such as God.

The *Guide for the Perplexed* was written for his favorite disciple, Iknin of Syria. It is divided into three parts. The first deals with problems of Biblical anthropomorphisms and application of the *via negativa* method to discovering the divine attributes of God, along with criticisms of the Muslim Scholastic theology according to the method of *Kalam,* in which philosophical proof is used to justify religious propositions already accepted in advance to be true. The second part offers proofs of God's existence, an Aristotelian analysis of the relationship between matter and form, and an explanation of the role of prophecy. The third part contains studies of the problems of free will and determinism, evil, the nature of rationality, and an original defense of how to reconcile reason with divine revelation. If on some point the Old Testament is perfectly clear and no obvious philosophical arguments can be adduced to the contrary, we ought to accept the word of the Bible. If, on the other hand, the point seems dubious and a contrary philosophical argument easily presents itself, the Biblical statement ought to be reinterpreted according to the dictates of rationality so it could be understood in only allegorical terms. At the time this was an extremely revolutionary idea that paved the way for subsequent Jewish philosophers to emphasize reason over scripture.

The selection from the *Guide for the Perplexed* begins with an explanation of why one ought *not* to begin with the study of metaphysics. There are certain things that the undisciplined mind simply cannot accurately represent to itself, either as a perception or as a concept. Trying to do so without the proper training is like trying to lift too heavy a weight or running too far before one is in the proper physical condition. The highest form of knowledge consists in the truths of metaphysics, but these cannot be comprehended by unaided perception or unaided reason without causing psychological and intellectual harm. The methods of religion and of science are themselves insufficient for representing metaphysical truths, but Maimonides reconciles their function in human society as preparation for metaphysics as practiced by philosophy—the only way by which human beings can attain a true understanding of God and the world.

In this way Maimonides offers to reconcile not just religion and philosophy but also science and metaphysics. These are but different ways of inquiry suited to the different aspects of the human mind, and they must function together in the proper order until the mind is ready to attain full intellectual illumination through true wisdom, which Maimonedes defines as "consciousness of self." This illumination must take place through a gradual evolution, from the particular to the abstract, relying on faith where reason fails, but always being prepared to give the upper hand to reason. In this way we can transcend the natural limitations of our own minds and attain complete knowledge of ourselves, the world, and God. As he puts it, "When you understand Physics, you have entered the hall; and when, after completing the study of Natural Philosophy, you master Metaphysics, you have entered the innermost court, and are with the king in the same palace."

※

Guide for the Perplexed

Know that for the human mind there are certain objects of perception which are within the scope

---

From Maimonides, *Guide for the Perplexed*, M. Friedländer, trans. (London: Routledge & Kegan Paul, 1904).

of its nature and capacity; on the other hand, there are, amongst things which actually exist, certain objects which the mind can in no way and by no means grasp: the gates of perception are closed against it. Further, there are things of which the mind understands one part, but remains ignorant of the other; and when man is able to comprehend certain things, it does not follow that he must be able to comprehend everything. This also applies to the senses: they are able to perceive things, but not at every distance; and all other powers of the body are limited in a similar way. A man can, e.g., carry two kikkar, but he cannot carry ten kikkar. How individuals of the same species surpass each other in these sensations and in other bodily faculties is universally known, but there is a limit to them, and their power cannot extend to every distance or to every degree. . . .

. . . You must consider, when reading this treatise, that mental perception, because connected with matter, is subject to conditions similar to those to which physical perception is subject. That is to say, if your eye looks around, you can perceive all that is within the range of your vision; if, however, you overstrain your eye, exerting it too much by attempting to see an object which is too distant for your eye, or to examine writings or engravings too small for your sight, and forcing it to obtain a correct perception of them, you will not only weaken your sight with regard to that special object, but also for those things which you otherwise are able to perceive: your eye will have become too weak to perceive what you were able to see before you exerted yourself and exceeded the limits of your vision.

The same is the case with the speculative faculties of one who devotes himself to the study of any science. If a person studies too much and exhausts his reflective powers, he will be confused, and will not be able to apprehend even that which had been within the power of his apprehension. For the powers of the body are all alike in this respect.

The mental perceptions are not exempt from a similar condition. If you admit the doubt, and do not persuade yourself to believe that there is a proof for things which cannot be demonstrated, or to try at once to reject and positively to deny an assertion the opposite of which has never been proved or attempt to perceive things which are beyond your perception, then you have attained the highest degree of human perfection, . . . If, on the other hand, you attempt to exceed the limit of your intellectual power, or at once to reject things as impossible which have never been proved to be impossible, or which are in fact possible, though their possibility be very remote, then you will . . . not only fail to become perfect, but you will become exceedingly imperfect. Ideas founded on mere imagination will prevail over you, you win incline toward defects, and toward base and degraded habits, on account of the confusion which troubles the mind, and of the dimness of its light, just as weakness of sight causes invalids to see many kinds of unreal images, especially when they have looked for a long time at dazzling or at very minute objects.

You must know that it is very injurious to begin with this branch of philosophy, viz., Metaphysics; or to explain [at first] the sense of the similes occurring in prophecies, and interpret the metaphors which are employed in historical accounts and which abound in the writings of the Prophets. Oh the contrary, it is necessary to initiate the young and to instruct the less intelligent according to their comprehension; those who appear to be talented and to have capacity for the higher method of study, i.e., that based on proof and on true logical argument, should be gradually advanced towards perfection, either by tuition or by self-instruction. He however, who begins with Metaphysics, will not only become confused in matters of religion, but will fall into complete infidelity. I compare such a person to an infant fed with wheaten bread, meat and wine; it will undoubtedly die, not because such food is naturally unfit for the human body, but because of the weakness of the child, who is unable to digest the food, and cannot derive benefit from it. . . .

⚓

Maimonides turns next to a critical dismissal of commonly accepted notions of faith. True faith is neither the acceptance of taught beliefs nor verbal or even psychological affirmation of dogma. Rather, it is the leap of faith that truths represented in *experience* and supported by *reason* correspond to things as they actually are

in the world—something that cannot ever be known. He criticizes both Christian notions of faith and the Christian concept of God as having certain attributes. God, according to Maimonides, is absolute Unity—a pure One without any form, indivisible, and everywhere identical. The doctrines of the Trinity and the corporeal embodiment of God in Christ are dismissed by him as utter absurdities that lead the intellect into depravity and corruption. A true understanding of God shows that there can be no relation between any aspect of the world, including the human intellect, and the absolute unity of God. People who think they have a relationship of any sort with God are utterly deluded, for there can be no such relationship between the relative world of potentiality and the absolute actuality. Even to say of God that "God exists" or that "God is One" must, according to Maimonides, be tempered with the knowledge that God exists without having the attribute of existence, and that God is one without having the attribute of unity. God has no positive attributes at all.

Yet God is not nothing. And in some mysterious way the universe does not exist independently of God but ultimately is itself a reflection of God. The universe, like God, is one individual being, everywhere identical to itself even though its parts are differentiated. He likens the unity of the universe to the unity of the body, in which through a joint activity the parts constitute one integrated whole whose characteristics are nowhere to be found in any of its individual elements. The selection concludes with a brief passage in which he explains what he calls the "mysteries of the Law." The true secrets of the universe must be kept secret, never revealed in writing, and passed on, if at all, *"vivâ voce"*—by word of mouth—to only those worthy disciples who have demonstrated that they have attained the highest levels of intellectual maturity.

⚓

When reading my present treatise, bear in mind that by "faith" we do not understand merely that which is uttered with the lips, but also that which is apprehended by the soul, the conviction that the object [of belief] is exactly as it is apprehended. If as regards real or supposed truths, you content yourself with giving utterance to them in words, without apprehending them or believing in them, especially if you do not seek real truth, you have a very easy task as, in fact, you will find many ignorant people professing articles of faith without connecting any idea with them.

If, however, you have a desire to rise to a higher state, viz., that of reflection, and truly to hold the conviction that God is One and possesses true unity, without admitting plurality or divisibility in any sense whatever, you must understand that God has no essential attribute in any form or in any sense whatever, and that the rejection of corporeality implies the rejection of essential attributes. Those who believe that God is One, and that He has many attributes, declare the unity with their lips, and assume plurality in their thoughts. This is like the doctrine of the Christians, who say that He is one and He is three, and that the three are one. Of the same character is the doctrine of those who say that God is One, but that He has many attributes; and that He with His attributes is One, although they deny corporeality and affirm His most absolute freedom from matter; as if our object were to seek forms of expression, not subjects of belief. For belief is only possible after the apprehension of a thing; it consists in the conviction that the thing apprehended has its existence beyond the mind [in reality] exactly as it is conceived in the mind. If in addition to this we are convinced that the thing cannot be different in any way from what we believe it to be, and that no reasonable argument can be found for the rejection of the belief or for the admission of any deviation from it, then the belief is true. Renounce desires and habits, follow your reason, and study what I am going to say in the chapters which follow on the rejection of the attributes; you will then be fully convinced of what we have said; you will be of those who truly conceive the Unity of God. . . .

. . . There cannot be any belief in the unity of God except by admitting that He is one simple substance, without any composition or plurality of elements; one from whatever side you view it, and by whatever test you examine it; not divisible into two parts in any way and by any cause, nor

capable of any form of plurality either objectively or subjectively, as will be proved in this treatise.

Some thinkers have gone so far as to say that the attributes of God are neither His essence nor anything extraneous to His essence. This is like the assertion of some theorists, that the ideals, i.e., the *universalia,* are neither existing nor non-existent, and like the views of others, that the atom does not fill a definite place, but keeps an atom of space occupied; that man has no freedom of action at all, but has acquirement. Such things are only said; they exist only in words, not in thought, much less in reality. But as you know, and as all know who do not delude themselves, these theories are preserved by a multitude of words, by misleading similes sustained by declamation and invective, and by numerous methods borrowed both from dialectics and sophistry. If after uttering them and supporting them by such words, a man were to examine for himself his own belief on this subject, he would see nothing but confusion and stupidity in an endeavour to prove the existence of things which do not exist, or to find a mean between two opposites that have no mean. Or is there a mean between existence and non-existence, or between the identity and non-identity of two things? . . .

Therefore we, who truly believe in the Unity of God, declare, that as we do not believe that some element is included in His essence by which He created the heavens, another by which He created the [four] elements, a third by which He created the ideals, in the same way we reject the idea that His essence contains an element by which He has power, another element by which He has will, and a third by which He has a knowledge of His creatures. On the contrary, He is a simple essence, without any additional element whatever; He created the universe, and knows it, but not by any extraneous force. There is no difference whether these various attributes refer to His actions or to relations between Him and His works; in fact, these relations, as we have also shown, exist only in the thoughts of men. . . .

This chapter is even more [obscure] than the preceding. Know that the negative attributes of God are the true attributes: they do not include any incorrect notions or any deficiency whatever in reference to God, while positive attributes imply polytheism, and are inadequate, as we have already shown. It is now necessary to explain how negative expressions can in a certain sense be employed as attributes, and how they are distinguished from positive attributes. Then I shall show that we cannot describe the Creator by any means except by negative attributes. An attribute does not exclusively belong to the one object to which it is related; while qualifying one thing, it can also be employed to qualify other things, and is in that case not peculiar to that one thing. . . .

Know that this Universe, in its entirety, is nothing else but one individual being; that is to say, the outermost heavenly sphere, together with all included therein, is as regards individuality beyond all question a single being. . . . The variety of its substances—I mean the substances of that sphere and all its component parts—is like the variety of the substances of a human being: just as, e.g., Said is one individual, consisting of various solid substances, such as flesh, bones, sinews, of various humors, and of various spiritual elements.

The living being as such is one through the action of its heart, although some parts of the body are devoid of motion and sensation, as, e.g., the bones, the cartilage, and similar parts. The same is the case with the entire universe; although it includes many beings without motion and without life, it is a single being living through the motion of the sphere, which may be compared to the heart of an animated being. You must therefore consider the entire globe as one individual being which is endowed with life, motion, and a soul. This mode of considering the universe is, as will be explained, indispensable, that is to say, it is very useful for demonstrating the unity of God; it also helps to elucidate the principle that He who is One has created only one being.

Again, it is impossible that any of the members of a human body should exist by themselves, not connected with the body, and at the same time should actually be organic parts of that body, that is to say, that the liver should exist by itself, the heart by itself, or the flesh by itself. In like manner, it is impossible that one part of the Universe should exist independently of the other parts in the existing order of things as here considered. . . .

In man there is a certain force which unites the members of the body, controls them, and gives to each of them what it requires for the conservation of its condition, and for the repulsion of injury— the physicians distinctly call it the leading force in the body of the living being; sometimes they call it "nature." The Universe likewise possesses a force which unites the several parts with each other, protects the species from destruction, maintains the individuals of each species as long as possible, and endows some individual beings with permanent existence. Whether this force operates through the medium of the sphere or otherwise remains an open question. . . .

NOTE

1. Daniel Kolak, *I Am You: The Metaphysical Foundations for Global Ethics,* The Netherlands: Kluwer Academic Publishers, 2000. See, also, Daniel Kolak, *In Search of Myself: Life, Death and Personal Identity*, Belmont, CA: Wadsworth, 1999.

7 ⚹ The Medievals

7.0 Aquinas (1225–1274): The Godhead

The son of the Count of Aquino, Thomas Aquinas was born in Italy at the Roccasecca castle of his father near Aquino, between Rome and Naples. Until the age of fourteen he was educated at the Benedictine abbey at Monte Cassino. He then went to the University of Naples to study liberal arts. In 1244, to his family's horror, he joined the Dominican Order of mendicant (begging) friars who espoused complete poverty and traveled the country spreading the Gospel as living examples of Jesus's teaching. His affluent family, which had expected him to join the Benedictines (a powerful, prestigious order with great corporate wealth) was appalled; when he wouldn't take their advice, his father locked him up in the castle where he had been born. According to legend, his family offered him all sorts of bribes, including a beautiful prostitute, whose services Aquinas supposedly refused, much to his father's dismay.

Aquinas escaped from his father's castle to Paris and Cologne where he studied philosophy and theology under the tutelage of Albertus Magnus (1200–1280), the great Scholastic philosopher and theologian (known as "Doctor Universlis," and "Albert the Great" because of his immense knowledge). Magnus, a Dominican, was largely responsible for transmitting Greek and Islamic philosophy, especially in the natural sciences, to the philosophers of the Middle Ages. In Paris, the Dominicans had fallen under the suspicion of the conservative university authorities because of their "heretical sympathy" with Averroist doctrine that, contrary to Christian doctrine, it is not the human personality as exemplified by the individual soul that is immortal but only the active intellect, which is numerically identical in all sentient beings. Aquinas helped defend the Dominicans with his Averroist arguments that there were two different sorts of truths, one based on reason and the other based on revelation,, and that only through revelation could one know the "real" truth. Since Christian dogma was foundationally embedded in views antithetical to Averroës's monopsychism, its truths must supersede the cosmic unity of all mankind as espoused by the internal Aristotelian philosophers of the Averroës school. Ten years later, in 1245, Aquinas became a lecturer and then a regent master (full professor) at Paris; in subsequent years he served under the popes at Orvieto, Rome, and Vitergo in Italy, and continued teaching in Paris and Naples.

Aristotle's main works had been lost to the non-Arabic world until the early part of the thirteenth century. Conservative Christian theologians feared their return to the philosophical scene, especially after the Islamic philosophers had put their own spins and interpretations on them through their commentaries; the theologians saw his works as a pagan and infidel threat to their Christian dogma. Aquinas took the opposite approach. He saw Aristotle as the greatest of all philosophers—calling him *The* Philosopher—and he also saw an opportunity to put Christian doctrine on a solid intellectual foundation through Aristotle's metaphysics, cosmology, and epistemology, provided that an account of the soul could be given that preserved individual human egos as surviving, personalities intact, as separately existing entities beyond the grave.

Aquinas's early work consisted largely of commentaries on his friend William of Moerbeke's translations of Aristotle. In them Aquinas tried to put the conservative theologians' fears to rest by showing how Aristotelian philosophy could be made consistent with Christian belief; he sometimes did it by simply rejecting whatever parts of Aristotle's philosophy did not fit with Christian revelation. In most cases, however, when there was an outright conflict between the two worldviews, Aquinas went to great lengths to show that reason could not force either conclusion, implying that one needed faith to decide. This position would be taken again and again by conflicting systems, including that of Copernicus. For instance, whereas Christian belief has it that God created the universe, Aristotle argued that the universe was eternal and uncreated. Aquinas, in a sense anticipating the Kantian antinomies, argued that neither the creation of the universe nor the eternity of the universe could be confirmed or denied by reason; we thus *need* revelation to know the truth. Similarly, instead of simply declaring Averroist monopsychism to be a false heresy, he argued that whether the individual human soul was mortal or immortal could not be settled by reason; one needs revelation to know the truth. Aristotelian arguments against the immortality of the soul according to Aquinas only help make the point that without divine revelation there can be no knowledge. This line of thought pleased church leaders and at the same time, ironically, made the arguments of the philosophers part of the church's "proof" of the need for nonphilosophical ways of knowing truth—not by reason but directly from God, through revelation.

In this way, Aquinas either advertently or inadvertently managed to appease the conservative critics of philosophy and revive Greek philosophy within the Christian domain. Like his antithesis Averroës, his early work consisted mostly of commentaries on Aristotle, the most famous of which are on the *Analytics, De Anima, De Caelo, Ethics, De Interpretatione, Metaphysics, Physics,* and *Politics.* Among his best original writings are *De Ente et Essentia,* which explores the nature of being and essence, the *De Principiis Naturae* on the principles and causes of change in nature, and *De Unitate Intellectus* in which he explicitly argues against the Averroist position that all human beings share one and the same, numerically identical, intellect. His two most important works are the encyclopedic *Summa contra Gentiles* and *Summa Theologica.* The former, written between 1259 and 1264, attempts to speak to readers who are not already believing Christians and uses arguments without assuming, in advance, that Christianity is true. The latter, from which the selection is taken, was written between 1265 and 1274 and contains his famous "five proofs" for the existence of God.

Summma Theologica

The First Way:
The Argument from Change

The existence of God can be shown in five ways. The first and clearest is taken from the idea of motion. (1) Now it is certain, and our senses corroborate it, that some things in this world are in motion. (2) But everything which is in motion is moved by something else. (3) For nothing is in motion except in so far as it is in potentiality in relation to that towards which it is in motion. (4) Now a thing causes movement in so far as it is in actuality. For to cause movement is nothing else than to bring something from potentiality to actuality; but a thing cannot be brought from potentiality to actuality except by something which exists in actuality, as, for example, that which is hot in actuality, like fire, makes wood, which is only hot in potentiality, to be hot in actuality, and thereby causes movement in it and alters it. (5) But it is not possible that the same thing should be at the same time in actuality and potentiality in relation to the same thing, but only in relation to different things; for what is hot in actuality cannot at the same time be hot in potentiality, though it is at the same time cold in potentiality. (6) It is impossible, therefore, that in relation to the same thing and in the same way anything should both cause movement and be caused, or that it should cause itself to move. (7) Everything therefore that is in motion must be moved by something else. If therefore the thing which causes it to move be in motion, this too must be moved by something else, and so on. (8) But we cannot proceed to infinity in this way, because in that case there would be no first mover, and in consequence, neither would there be any other mover; for secondary movers do not cause movement except they be moved by a first mover, as, for example, a stick cannot cause movement unless it is moved by the hand. Therefore it is necessary to stop at some first mover which is moved by nothing else. And this is what we all understand God to be.

From *Summa Theologica*, Laurence Shapcote, trans. (London: O. P Benziger Brothers, 1911).

The Second Way:
The Argument from Causation

The Second Way is taken from the idea of the Efficient Cause. (1) For we find that there is among material things a regular order of efficient causes. (2) But we do not find, nor indeed is it possible, that anything is the efficient cause of itself, for in that case it would be prior to itself, which is impossible. (3) Now it is not possible to proceed to infinity in efficient causes. (4) For if we arrange in order all efficient causes, the first is the cause of the intermediate, and the intermediate the cause of the last, whether the intermediate be many or only one. (5) But if we remove a cause the effect is removed; therefore, if there is no *first* among efficient causes, neither will there be a last or an intermediate. (6) But if we proceed to infinity in efficient causes there will be no first efficient cause, and thus there will be no ultimate effect, nor any intermediate efficient causes, which is clearly false. Therefore it is necessary to suppose the existence of some first efficient cause, and this men call God.

The Third Way:
The Argument from Contingency

The Third Way rests on the idea of the "contingent" and the "necessary" and is as follows: (1) Now we find that there are certain things in the Universe which are capable of existing and of not existing, for we find that some things are brought into existence and then destroyed, and consequently are capable of being or not being. (2) But it is impossible for all things which exist to be of this kind, because anything which is capable of not existing, at some time or other does not exist. (3) If therefore *all* things are capable of not existing, there was a time when nothing existed in the Universe. (4) But if this is true there would also be nothing in existence now; because anything that does not exist cannot begin to exist except by the agency of something which has existence. If therefore there was once nothing which existed, it would have been impossible for anything to begin to exist, and so nothing would exist now. (5) This is clearly false. Therefore all things are not contingent, and there must be something which is necessary in the Universe. (6) But everything which is necessary either has or has not the cause of its necessity from an outside source. Now it is not possible to proceed to infinity in necessary things which have a cause of their necessity, as has been proved in the case of efficient causes. Therefore it is necessary to suppose the existence of something which is necessary in itself, not having the cause of its necessity from any outside source, but which is the cause of necessity in others. And this "something" we call God.

The Fourth Way: The Argument from Degrees of Excellence

The Fourth Way is taken from the degrees which are found in things. (1) For among different things we find that one is more or less good or true or noble; and likewise in the case of other things of this kind. (2) But the words "more" or "less" are used of different things in proportion as they approximate in their different ways to something which has the particular quality in the highest degree—e.g., we call a thing hotter when it approximates more nearly to that which is hot in the highest degree. There is therefore something which is true in the highest degree, good in the highest degree and noble in the highest degree; (3) and consequently there must be also something which has being in the highest degree. For things which are true in the highest degree also have being in the highest degree (see Aristotle, *Metaphysics*, 2). (4) But anything which has a certain quality of any kind in the highest degree is also the cause of all the things of that kind, as, for example, fire which is hot in the highest degree is the cause of all hot things (as is said in the same book). (5) Therefore there exists something which is the cause of being, and goodness, and of every perfection in all existing things; and this we call God.

The Fifth Way: The Argument from Harmony

The Fifth Way is taken from the way in which nature is governed. (1) For we observe that certain things which lack knowledge, such as natural bodies, work for an End. This is obvious, because they always, or at any rate very frequently, operate in the same way so as to attain the best possible result. (2) Hence it is clear that they do not arrive at their goal by chance, but by purpose. (3) But those things which have no knowledge do not

move towards a goal unless they are guided by someone or something which does possess knowledge and intelligence—e.g., an arrow by an archer. Therefore, there does exist something which possesses intelligence by which all natural things are directed to their goal; and this we call God.

※

7.1 Duns Scotus (1266–1308): The Logical Analysis of Being

John Duns Scotus was born in the village of Duns, Berwickshire. At the age of fourteen he entered a Franciscan seminary in Scotland at Haddington, Dumfries. After being ordained in 1291 he continued his studies in theology and philosophy at Oxford and Paris. Through his mentor at Paris, Peter of Spain, he was influenced by Islamic philosophy, especially Avicenna and Averroës. He received his doctorate from Paris in 1305 and became a professor at Cologne where he remained until his premature death.

Nicknamed the "Subtle Doctor," Duns Scotus originated many subtle but important distinctions that have continued to influence philosophers as diverse as Leibniz, Heidegger, and Peirce. Yet he also concocted an idea that has since become one of the central tenets of Roman Catholic dogma and believed by hundreds of millions of people: the Immaculate Conception. After much subsequent debate among Christian theologians, the councils of Basel (1439) and Trent (1546) finally sided with what came to be called the "Scotist opinion," and some years later Pius IX issued the bull *Ineffabilis Deus* declaring Duns Scotus's notion of the Immaculate Conception to be a divine revelation that must under threat of hell be believed without question.

Although Duns Scotus's contributions to philosophy are somewhat less dramatic, he is generally regarded as the most important of the British medieval thinkers. His voluminous writings, organized from lectures, drafts, and marginal notes passed down by his highly devoted students and numerous followers, make for extremely difficult reading because of Duns Scotus's reliance on obscure Latin terms and technical words of his own invention. So reading even a brief selection from his *Ordinatio* (also called the *Oxford Commentary on the Sentences of Peter Lombard*) requires us to make clear several terms in his vastly influential philosophy. Of primary importance is his complicated sounding notion of the *univocality* of the world (as opposed to its *equivocality,* multiplicity of interpretation and meaning). The world according to Duns Scotus is not merely One (as Parmenides and so many others have already claimed); it has an unmistakable, unambiguous *single meaning* discoverable by the human intellect through our own experience and reason.

⚚

Ordinatio

And lest there should be a dispute about the "univocity," I call that a univocal concept whose unity suffices for contradiction when it is affirmed and denied of the same thing. It also suffices as a syllogistic middle term; so that the extremes, united without the fallacy of equivocation in a middle term which is one in this way, may be concluded to be unified among themselves.

And I prove univocity so understood in three ways. First: every intellect certain about one concept and doubtful about different ones has a concept of that of which it is certain which is different from the concepts about which it is doubtful. But the subject includes the predicate, and the intellect of the wayfarer can be certain of something (God) that it is being while at the same time doubting whether that is finite or infinite, created or uncreated being. Therefore, the concept of the being of anything (God) is different from this concept or that one, and so it is neither in itself and is included in both. Therefore, it is univocal.

From *Philosophy of the Middle Ages*, Arthur Hyman & James Walsh, eds., J. Walsh, trans. (New York: Harper & Row, 1967). Used by permission of Arthur Hyman.

The proof of the major is that since no self-same concept is certain and doubtful, therefore either there is another one, which is the proposed position, or else there is none; and then there will be no certitude concerning any concept. I prove the minor: every philosopher was certain that what he held as first principle is being—for instance, one was certain that fire is being and another that water is being. But he was not certain whether it is created or uncreated being, first or not first. He was not certain that it is first, since then he would have been certain about what is false, and what is false cannot be known. Nor was he certain that it is not the first being, since then he would not have been able to maintain the opposite.

The argument is confirmed, for anyone seeing the philosophers disagree could be certain concerning any of them that he held the first principle to be being, and yet, because of the contrariety of their opinions, he could doubt whether it is this being or that. And such a doubter, if he should make a demonstration affirming or destroying some lower concept, for instance that fire was not the first being, but some being posterior to the first being, that first certain concept which he had of being would not be destroyed, but it would be preserved in that particular concept proved of fire. And though this is proved the proposition assumed in the last consequence of the argument, which was that that certain concept which is of itself neither of the doubtful ones, is preserved in both of them.

But if you do not care for this authority accepted from the diversity of the opinions of the philosophizers, but you say that any one has two neighboring concepts in the intellect which seem to be one concept because of the nearness of the analogy, it seems to be against this that from this evasion there seems to be destroyed every way for proving the unity of any univocal concept. For if you say that man has one concept for Socrates and Plato, it will be denied, and it will be said that they are two, but they seem one because of the great similarity.

I argue the second principal proof thus: No concept of what is real is naturally produced in the intellect of the wayfarer unless by what naturally activates our intellect. But that is a phantasm or an object reflected in the phantasm, as well as the active intellect. Thus no simple concept is now naturally produced in our intellect except what can be produced by virtue of these. But a concept which would not be univocal with an object reflected in a phantasm, but rather would be altogether different from and prior to that to which it has analogy, could not be produced by virtue of the active intellect and a phantasm, as I shall prove. Thus there never will be such a different and analogous concept which is posited as occurring naturally in the intellect of the wayfarer; and in this way no concept of God could ever be naturally possessed, which is false. Proof of the assumption: Any object, whether reflected in a phantasm or in an intelligible species, with the active or possible intellect acting coordinately to the limit of its forces, produces in the intellect as an effect adequate to itself its own concept and every concept essentially or virtually included in it. But that other concept, which is held to be analogous, is neither essentially nor virtually included in this, nor is it this very concept. Therefore, it is not produced by any such activator. . . .

⚹

He thus sides with Aquinas against both Averroës and Maimonides that the world can be fully understood by the human mind; no special mystical or divine illumination is needed. Instead, a new more precise language is needed. In Duns Scotus's view, the philosopher is free, like the mathematician, to invent new distinctions and terms as needed to capture subtle differences and thereby increase the resolution power of the mind until it can correctly apprehend being. According to Duns Scotus, knowledge is not based on innate ideas (through which the forms might be directly intuited) but must begin from individual experience. He thus turns away from Platonic dualism (as captured, for instance, by the allegory of the cave, where the real world—being as it truly is—exists independently of the mind's representational images and ideas that are, at best, copies of reality).

According to Duns Scotus, the primary object of the intellect—that is, what the mind directly apprehends when it is conscious of something of which it has knowledge (that is, the "shadows on the walls of the cave")—is not a mere representation of some universal idea, as Plato and Aristotle had each in his own way thought. Nor is it the divine essence, as Augustine had claimed (and Berkeley will in his own way reclaim), nor material objects, as Aquinas had suggested. Duns Scotus instead takes a brilliant and innovative stance on the doctrine of *hylomorphism,* the view that existent things are a combination of Aristotelian forms and primordial matter. He explains the existence of various individual things known by us—the objects in our immediate presence—in terms of a formal principle which he calls *haecceity* (literally, "thisness"), of the same logical type as a universal. In many ways this idea anticipates the sort of metaphysical move that would eventually find its culmination in Kant's synthesis of empirical and rational thought (see Chapter 16), wherein empirical objects exist through a combination of the activity of mind (that is, as representations in the phenomenal world) and the activity of things-in-themselves (*ding-an-sich* in the noumenal world). Thus, while rejecting universal hylomorphism, Duns Scotus argues that material things exist as a conjunction of matter and form but that these are different principles. Each individual object—including the primary objects to which the intellect has access (perceptions, thoughts, ideas, and so on)—is itself *esse,* being as such. Everything that exists has *esse*—it can be predicated "univocally" of all things—and without it nothing is comprehensible. In other words, whereas for Aquinas "to be" means "to have being," for Duns Scotus being as such is in reality always and everywhere.

Aquinas argued that individual things cannot be known directly by the mind because the primary object of human knowledge is an idea abstracted from matter and revealed through the universal concept. The universal or common term (for instance, "man"), because it is essentially conjoined to a "this," makes the singular term intrinsically intelligible. So for Aquinas the mind apprehends individual things only indirectly, via representations such as visual perception, so as to preclude intellectual intuition (that is, perception) of the thing in itself. According to Duns Scotus, however, the mind has a primary intellectual intuition of the individual thing in itself. His argument, basically, is that it would be impossible to abstract the universal idea from the individual thing unless we possessed a previous intellectual intuition of the individual thing; the abstraction is from the individual, not the universal. Thus *being,* which can be predicated univocally of everything, provides universal meaning to all things even though it is really separate. This is accomplished in Duns Scotus's system with a subtle distinction among distinctions: a *real* distinction, between things, versus a merely *logical* distinction, between aspects of the same thing made by the intellect.

To illustrate, consider that Socrates is human and that Plato is human. As distinct individuals they are different humans and yet there must be some amorphous aspect of their being—"humanness"—that allows of distinct individuations—"Socraticity" and "Platoness"—the "thisness" (*haecceity*) of each of them as a numerically distinct individual. Duns Scotus painstakingly argues that it is possible to distinguish the individual concepts such as "Socraticity" and "Platoness" from general concepts such as "humanness." On what, then, is the distinction based? In no way is "Socraticity"—Socrates' individual essence, or nature—separable in actuality from his existence as a human being—his "humanness." Remove the human being from existence and you remove the individual Socrates. Destroy the individual Socrates and you destroy the human being. According to Duns Scotus, not even God could separate the two. Yet the distinction is not merely verbal or a mental conundrum. It is what he called a "formal objective distinction."

Crucial for understanding Duns Scotus's subtle metaphysics is his notion of being, which for him involves not a genus but the concept of opposition to nonbeing, or nothingness. There are various types of oppositions to nothingness, from God to human to inanimate objects. It is

partly manifested in the will, both divine and human; neither God nor individual human beings are bound by necessity to act according to the dictates, either of a deterministic providence or logically guided reason, as the Arabic Neoplatonic and Aristotelian intellectualist philosophers held. They both exist as autonomous individual agents in the universe. The world is apprehended through the primacy of being itself, for being is known directly, as such, by all conscious beings who are aware of anything. Being itself is something apprehended immediately and directly along with whatever else is known by whatever means it is known. Its method and domain is metaphysics.

7.2 Ockham (1280–1349): The Razor's Edge

Born in the village of Ockham in Surrey, near London, England, William of Ockham studied first the arts and then theology at Oxford University. We know hardly anything about his family and little of his early life, except that he was a Franciscan monk completing his doctorate at the University of Oxford when suddenly he was accused of heresy. He had been lecturing on the Bible and the *Books of Sentences* by Peter Lombard (1100–1160), the official textbook of theology at nearly all universities well into the sixteenth century. Hundreds of philosophers and theologians wrote commentaries on the *Sentences* and so did Ockham, but although his contained fairly standard sorts of disputations (formal questions with replies and rebuttals) according to the style of the time, the chancellor of Oxford—an ardent follower of Aquinas—brought Ockham before the Holy See at Avignon on more than fifty charges of heresy. Instead of retracting his opinion, Ockham took the opportunity to present explicit criticisms of current orthodoxy (such as whether Jesus and his followers possessed property, one of the "major" issues of the day) and to raise questions about the nature of the relation of the papacy to secular authority. He wrote:

In these so-called pronouncements I found a great many things that are heretical, erroneous, stupid, ridiculous, fantastic, insane and defamatory. They are patently perverse and equally contrary to orthodox faith, good morals, natural reason, certain experience, and brotherly love.[1]

Reprimanded for his publicist views but not officially condemned, Ockham went on to write half a dozen politically charged works, such as *Dialogus de Potestate Papae et Imperatoris* (*Dialogue on the Power of the Emperor and the Pope,* 1339–1342), in which he argued against the temporal supremacy of the pope in favor of the idea of a secular state, laying the foundations for modern theories of government. Ockham continued his criticism of Pope John XXII in favor of the Franciscan General Michael of Cesena, with whom in 1328 he joined a branch of the Franciscans called the Spirituals and fled from Avignon to Pisa. But the Franciscans also found him too independent of mind, expelling Ockham from their order, and he took refuge in Munich with Ludwig of Bavaria.

As a philosopher Ockham is best known as the originator of "Ockham's razor," a principle of ontological economy: "multiplicity ought not to be posited without necessity." That is, according to Ockham, as few entities as possible should be regarded as real and the rest should be dismissed as mere *ficta* (fictions), terms that have only intentional meaning without reference or extension. This principle led Ockham to abandon the view of universals as mind-independently real entities. Taking as his starting point the views of Duns Scotus, whom he regarded as a realist about universals, Ockham offered an alternative view that has come to be known as *nominalism.* His fellow nominalists (sometimes called "terminists") called it the *via moderna* ("the modern way") versus *via antiqua* ("the ancient way"). Ockham paved the way for terminist logic by taking an analytical, critical, and empiricist approach to the analysis of the functions of individual terms within propositions. Central to this effort was his

pivotal distinction, which has remained influential to this day, between a term's meaning and that which it stands for, which he called *suppositio* ("standing for").

In the first book of the *Prior Analytics,* Aristotle defines terms by stating, "I call a term that into which a proposition is resolved (viz. the predicate, or that of which something is predicated) when it is affirmed or denied that something *is* or *is not* something." But what is the nature of the existence of such terms, especially when they seem to involve universal rather than particular entities? Ockham says that a term can stand for something in three different ways. In "This man Socrates is a philosopher," the term "this man" stands for a specific individual; in "Socrates is a mortal man," the term "man" stands for a class; and in "Man is a noun," the term "man" stands for the word. If I write the word down, it exists on paper; if I say it, it exists as an audible sound; but the third and most important aspect of the word is the concept. Concepts are to written and spoken words that express them as numbers are to numerals; they are not the symbols themselves. Rather, according to Ockham, a symbol expresses a concept that is itself the mental concept or impression possessing signification. In no case, such as in "Man is mortal," does the term "man" stand for some mind-independent universal entity that all the individual instances have in common, as Plato and the Neoplatonists claimed. Only the meanings of terms themselves—names as such— have the property of being universal, not that to which they refer (not to any actual things themselves). All things exist only as individuals. Names that seem to stand for universals in reality are but signs for classes of individuals.

Thus, in the following passage from his *Logic,* Ockham identifies conceptual terms and propositions as "mental words" that do not belong to any language. He claimed that,

There is no universal outside the mind really existing in individual substances or in the essences of things. . . . The reason is that everything that is not many things is necessarily one thing in number and consequently a singular thing.[2]

In other words, universals exist only in the mind and cannot be uttered, they are but signs subordinated to mental concepts or contents.

⚹

Logic

. . . Because it was said in the preceding chapter that some names are those of the first intention and some of the second intention, and because the ignorance of words is for many people an occasion to err, for that reason, it is to be incidentally noted, what is intention, what is first and second intention, and how they are distinguished. First, then, we have to know that "intention of the soul" is the name given to an entity in the soul which is meant to signify something. And as was said before in connection with writing, which was found to be a secondary sign of the word, in the same manner, words, which are foremost of all arbitrarily instituted signs, are secondary signs, of those things of which the intentions of the soul are primary signs. It is with reference to this that Aristotle says that words are marks of those passions which are in the soul. Now this something subsisting in the soul, which is a sign of the thing, and out of which the mental proposition is composed as the vocal proposition is composed out of the words, is called sometimes the intention of the soul, sometimes the concept of the soul, sometimes the passion of the soul, and sometimes a likeness of the thing. Boethius in his Commentary on the book *On Interpretation* calls it the meaning (*intellectus*). And he adds that the mental proposition is composed of "meanings," not of such meanings as are actually identical with the intellectual soul, but of intentions, which are certain signs in the soul signifying some things, I mean intentions, out of which mental propositions are composed. Therefore, when somebody pronounces a vocal proposition, he first formulates internally a mental proposition which is of no language, as is evidenced by the fact that many people frequently form inner

From Stephen C. Tornay, *Ockham: Studies and Selections* (La Salle, IL: Open Court, 1938)).

propositions which, however, they cannot express because of linguistic shortcomings. The parts of such mental propositions are called concepts, intentions, similitudes, and meanings. But what is that in the soul which is such a sign? It must be said that there are various opinions about this question. Some say that it is nothing else than some fictitious entity produced by the soul; some say that it is a certain quality subsisting psychologically in the soul, distinct from the act of understanding; again some say that it is the act of understanding itself. And for this latter view the following reason may be shown: it is needless to have recourse to many entities when we can get along with fewer ones. Everything, however, that can be saved by admitting something distinct from the act of understanding, could be saved without such a distinct thing. For to stand for something and to signify something can be attributed just as well to the act of understanding as to that fictitious entity; therefore, there is no need to posit anything else beyond the act of understanding.

⚹

Ockham does not mean by this that spoken words are signs of mental concepts, but simply that they signify the same things signified by mental concepts. A concept signifies something "primarily and naturally," whereas the word signifies it "secondarily," a distinction that would later be used by Locke in his explanation of the relationship between mind and world (see Chapter 13). He claims that this is what Aristotle really meant when he said that "Words are signs of the impressions in the soul." Thus, for Ockham and all subsequent nominalists influenced by him, to say that words signify, or are signs of, impressions in the mind means simply that they are signs that signify secondarily what the impressions of the mind import primarily. Whereas the designation of a spoken or written term can be changed at will, the designation of the conceptual term cannot be changed at anybody's will. In thus continuing the medieval tradition of advancing Aristotelian logic into a science of language capable of revealing what the mind is thinking about and how it is representing the world to itself, ever since Ockham one of the central tasks of philosophy has involved precise formulation of what words signify along with the mode of their signification.

In the following selection from his *Theory of Knowledge and Metaphysics,* he lays the foundation for his empiricism, arguing that all knowledge must ultimately come from the senses and cannot be had without them. Whereas for Plato things outside the mind must correspond exactly to things inside the mind in order for there to be knowledge, and for Aristotle universals in the mind are based on the thing existing in reality independently of the mind but do not correspond exactly, for Ockham only individual, particular things exist such that each has its own nature. This means that there can be no identity among things, only similarity.

♁

Theory of Knowledge and Metaphysics

Any imaginable thing which exists by itself without any addition, is singular and numerically one. Every science begins with individuals. From sensation, which gives only singular things, arises memory, from memory experience, and through experience, we obtain the universal which is the basis of art and science. As all our knowledge derives from the senses, every science, too, originates from individual objects, although no doctrine should treat of singular things. Properly speaking, that is, there is no science of individuals but of universals standing for individuals.

I say that no intellectual act is without a phantasm, for the reason that all intellectual cognition necessarily presupposes in our present status sensitive imagination both of the exterior and interior senses. Nothing can be an object of the interior sense without having been an object of the exterior sense. Intuitive cognition is cognition by virtue of which it can be known that a thing is when it is, and that a thing is not when it is not. When

From Stephen C. Tornay, *Ockham: Studies and Selections* (La Salle, IL: Open Court, 1938).

someone sees Socrates intuitively and whiteness as inherent in Socrates, he can know plainly that Socrates is white.

♁

This is in marked contrast to Duns Scotus's position that a common nature exists in things that is distinct from the individual things yet somehow contained in them. Thus, the problem of individuation has no meaning in his view, since each thing is singular in itself. Ultimately, for Ockham, the distinction between essence and existence is itself fictitious: "Existence and Essence signify one and the same thing."

♁

To conclude, I say that there is no such a thing as a universal, intrinsically present in the things to which it is common. No universal, except that which is such by voluntary agreement, is existent in any way outside of the soul, but everything which can be predicated of many things, is by its nature in the mind either psychologically or logically. Nothing of that sort is of the essence or quiddity of any substance.

It seems to some, nevertheless, that the universal is somehow outside of the soul and present in individuals not as distinct from them really, but yet formally. Accordingly, they say that there is in Socrates a human nature which is contracted to Socrates by an individual differentia, being distinguished not really but formally from that nature. Hence, there are no two things together, yet one is not the other formally. This is the opinion, as I understand, of the Subtle Doctor, who excelled others in incisiveness of judgment. In the view of this doctor, there is besides the numerical unity another real unity less than the numerical unity. This entity is neither the matter nor the form nor their composite, inasmuch as every one of these is the nature, but it is the ultimate reality of being.

Against this opinion one can argue in a double manner: first, by saying that it is impossible to admit that in created things any thing differs formally without being distinguished really. Secondly, granting this distinction, the aforesaid view is still untrue. If nature were common in that manner, it follows that there would be just as many species and genera as there are individuals. Therefore, it is not to be imagined that in Socrates there is a humanity or human nature distinct in some way from Socrates, to which an individual differentia is to be added, thereby contracting that nature. Contrarily, whatever imaginable substantial thing exists in Socrates is either the particular matter or the particular form, or something composed of these. Therefore, all essence and quiddity and whatever belongs to the substance, if it is real outside of the soul, is either without qualification and absolutely the matter, or the form, or a composite of the two. According to the opinion which I assert as true, there is in man more than one substantial form—at least the forms of corporeity and of the intellectual soul.

⚹

Ockham uses his concept of *intellectual intuition* to make explicitly clear that the perceptions you are now having are not of things in themselves but exist only in the mind; he calls it the "intuitive vision," much in the way that Kant will later talk of intuitions (see Chapter 16). Following Augustine, he further paves the way for the Cartesian method of finding certainty by finding certain propositions that cannot be doubted, such as one's own existence, based on the having of mental events regardless of whether they are *of* anything actual or not; the

mere fact that one is thinking is evidence for one's existence as *something*. He also provides the first clear statement of a theory of the mind in terms of *intention*, distinguishing two sorts: the first intention—"the sign of something not itself a sign," a "mental name meant to stand for its signified object"—and the second intention, "something in the soul which is applicable to things and is predicable of the names of things when they do not stand in personal supposition but in a simple one" (as already discussed in the previous selection from his *Logic*). Universals are thus to be understood as second intentions. They have only "logical being." That is, they exist in the logical realm, which for Ockham subsists in the soul but not as psychological entities such as sensations, images, or figments of the imagination. They exist in the logical realm just as external objects exist in the ontological realm and are thus real without existing independently of the mind.

NOTES

1. OPol III; K 3–4., quoted in Sharon Kaye and Robert Martin, *On Ockham* (Belmont, CA: Wadsworth, 2000).
2. PPh II 11–2, quoted in Sharon Kaye and Robert Martin, *On Ockham* (Belmont, CA: Wadsworth, 2000).

8 ⚜ The Renaissance

The term *Renaissance* has generally come to signify the period of sudden intellectual and artistic growth that took place in Italy and Europe during the fifteenth and sixteenth centuries.[1] Philosophically, this was a period of transition between the medieval, theologically centered worldview and the modern, scientific one. The emphasis in literature, art, science, and philosophy shifted from the relationship between God and the world to the nature of the relationship between the human mind and the rest of nature. Buttressed by the remarkable developments in logic and reason of the Middle Ages, each of the three philosophers of the period that we shall study now rejects in his own way medieval standards and methods of inquiry in favor of a return to ancient, pre-Christian thought enlivened by the advent of a new style and literary form.

8.0 Nicholas of Cusa (1401–1464): Everything Is Everything

Nicholas Krebs took the name Nicholas of Cusa (also known as Nicholas Cusanus) in honor of his birthplace, the small German village of Cusa on the Moselle River. He showed such high promise as a boy that at the age of twelve he received a scholarship to study with the Brothers of the Common Life at Deventer in the Lowlands. This mystical group was devoted to experiencing unity with God as inspired by a widely influential book of the time, *Imitation of Christ,* written by one of their fellows. Over the next twelve years he went on to study the arts, philosophy, law, mathematics, the sciences, and theology at the universities of Heidelberg, Rome, Cologne, and Padua. He received a doctorate in law from the latter. In 1433, at the age of twenty-nine, he became an ordained priest and pursued a series of ecclesiastical appointments culminating in his becoming cardinal in 1448 and bishop of Brixen in 1450.

One of the leading church conciliators of the fifteenth century, Cusa used his knowledge of theology, law, and philosophy to negotiate among widely differing religious and political factions whose main bone of contention was whether the church, the council, or the pope was the highest authority. Called a "mystic on horseback" because of his extensive travels in the cause of political and religious unity, he rode into Byzantium to help end the centuries-old rift between Latin and Greek churches. His earliest written work, *De Concordantia Catholica* (*On Catholic Concordance*, 1433), dedicated to his colleagues at the council of Basel, argues for a global harmony of the church conceived as the supreme form of human society.

Amid all his political and theological activities, Cusa worked continuously on behalf of the advancement of philosophy, where his achievements are so impressive that he is generally regarded as a key transitional figure between the Middle Ages and the Renaissance. As in his political and religious work, he created a philosophical synthesis of widely differing views. In his major philosophical work, *De Docta Ignorantia* (*Of Learned Ignorance*, 1440), the key element in his thinking is the concept of the identity of opposites (*coincidentia oppositorun*), according to which the distinctions and oppositions among finite beings resolve into unity at the absolute level. For instance, draw a series of bigger and bigger circles, all touching a line at the same point (see Figure 8.1). Notice that as the circles get bigger and bigger, the more the curve "flattens out" and approaches the straightness of the

line. If you drew an *infinitely large* circle and placed it against the line, there would no longer be any difference between the "curved" line of the circle and the straight line. In this precise way Cusa argues that in the infinite all the opposites become one: "an infinite line . . . would be at once a straight line, a triangle, a circle, a sphere; similarly, if there were an infinite sphere, it would at once be a circle, a triangle, and a line; and it would be likewise with the infinite triangle and infinite circle." And thus his thesis that "everything is everything":

⚹

Everything Is Everything

From a keen study of what has already been said we come to understand easily enough, perhaps even more fully than Anaxagoras himself, the depth of the truth he expressed in the words "everything is everything." For from the First Book we learned that God is in all things in such a way that all things are in him; in the previous chapter we discovered that God is in all things by the medium, as it were, of the universe; so it follows that all is in all, and each in each. As if by nature's order it was that the most perfect—the universe—came into being before all things, so that anything might be in anything. In fact, in every creature the universe is the creature; consequently each creature receives all, so that in any creature all creatures are found in a relative way. Since all creatures are finite, no creature could be all things in fact; but all things are contracted in order to form each creature. If then, all things are in all, it is clear that all is prior to the individual; and all here does not signify plurality, for prior to the individual there is no plurality. For that reason all without plurality has preceded the individual in the order of nature with the consequence that in any actual individual there is not more than one: all without plurality is that one.

Only by way of contraction is the universe in things; in fact it is restricted by each actually existing thing to be actually what each thing is. Every-

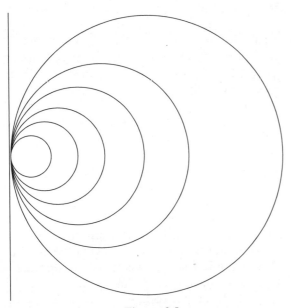

Figure 8.1

From *Of Learned Ignorance*, G. Heron, trans. (London: Routledge & Kegan Paul, 1954).

thing actually existing is in God, for He is the act of all. Act means perfection and the realization of what was possible. Since the universe restricted is in each actually existing individual, then evidently God, Who is in the universe, is in every individual and every individual actually existing is, like the universe, immediately in God. To Say that "everything is in everything" is in all things and that the universe, by the intermediary of all things, is in God. How God is without any diversity in all, since everything is everything, and how all is in God, because all is in all, are truths of a very high order which are clearly understood by keen minds. The universe is in each individual in such a way that each individual is in it, with the result that in each individual the universe is by contraction what the particular individual is; and every individual in the universe is the universe, though the universe is in each individual in a different way and each thing is in the universe in a different way.

⚒

In other words, whereas essence and existence are distinct among finite objects, in God they are identical. This concept owes much to the previous doctrines of Thomas Aquinas, and it will later influence Schelling's "philosophy of identity" (see Chapter 17), in which Schelling views individual differences as vanishing points of the Absolute. Indeed, in many ways one can see in Cusa the early stages of the philosophy that would find its full force in German Idealism.

A blend of Neoplatonic philosophy and thirteenth-century mysticism, this aspect of Cusa's thought grew out of an opposition to scholastic Aristotelianism. In creating a synthesis of, on the one hand, mathematical and experimental knowledge and, on the other, mysticism and knowledge, he continuously makes use of analogies from mathematics, claiming much in the way that Kant would later that the categories of reason, with their opposites and contradictions, can give us at best only a limited and inadequate representation of reality which in itself is beyond our direct access and understanding. He thus relies on a version of the medieval "negative way" (see Chapter 6), in combination with what

he calls "learned ignorance," a concept so important to his overall vision that he gives it the name of his book. This should not be confused with the idea of "learned incompetence" or some such anti-authoritarian stance toward intellectual orthodoxy. Rather, what Cusa means by this is very similar to, and is basically an elaboration of, what Socrates meant when he defined wisdom as knowing how little you know. He means, in effect, something like "wise ignorance"; that is, only through struggling in our efforts to understand the world do we realize precisely how and why the absolute truth about God, the world, and even our own natures, transcends our understanding. Each and all of these things—even the mind—are infinities; the items of our understanding are finitudes. Never can the infinite things in themselves properly be understood by the finite terms in which we are forced by our language and our thought to represent them.

The problem is that reason (*ratio*) is by its very nature *discursive* (Latin: *discurrere,* "to run about"). This means that because our thinking is discursive, any conclusions drawn upon it are attained through a series of inferences and not by direct insight. Although the intellect (*intellectus*) transcends this limitation insofar as it is capable of intuitive cognitions (apprehended all at once), such as insights, our language cannot adequately express these intuitions because it relies necessarily on categories, oppositions, and contradictions that exist only at the finite, relative level of immediate appearances. Thus, the unity of opposites in ultimate reality can never be directly attained by us; however, when the mind sees that it cannot do this, it is then already enlightened, at which point it can mystically transcend its limitations. In other words, during the brief instant that the mind can *see* (not just believe in) its own limits, it transcends its own limits; it moves beyond itself toward the infinite. That is the learned ignorance that according to Cusa is the main goal of philosophy.

In studying the world we study God. This is an idea that would reverberate throughout the

Renaissance, from scientists like Galileo, who sought to study the world directly rather than through official Scriptures to learn about God (which was the real reason the church sought to censor him), to modern philosophers like Berkeley who argued that at each and every moment in which you experience anything you are having, at that and every other moment, the direct experience of God. The world is a theophany, an appearance of God. Like Giordano Bruno (Section 8.2) and Baruch Spinoza (Chapter 11), Cusa speaks of the world as an endless unfolding of God; the present existence is the result of a divine "contraction" from which the unity of God unfolds into multiplicity. The world is therefore itself infinite, which leads Cusa to reject the idea of fixed points in space and time in a way that anticipates twentieth-century developments in the relativity of space and time as pioneered by Albert Einstein. No body in the universe—neither the earth nor the sun—has a privileged position. All judgments about location must be relative. He even went so far as to declare that the geocentric view of the solar system expressed by the Old Testament was false, written for the people of the time in terms that they could understand.

All individual things, too, are contractions of the divine infinity. Stimulated no doubt by the forbidden views of Averroës, he argues that each individual is a manifestation of God, forming a harmonious system in which each is both unique and part of the whole. Thus, his revival of the key phrase from Anaxagoras, "everything is in everything," states that everything in some way mirrors the entire universe. God is in everything and everything is in God: "all is in all, and each in each . . . each creature receives all, so that in any creature all creatures are found in a relative way." And anticipating both Spinoza and Leibniz still further, he concludes: "all things are what they are, because they could not be otherwise nor better."

Unlike all of his contemporaries, Cusa did not belong to, nor did he try to make his thought adhere to, any particular school of philosophy or theology. He saw no orthodox or institutional path to knowledge. Ultimately, the mind must through its own efforts transcend the limitations of sensory knowledge and attain through intellectual intuition a vision that goes beyond reason, logic, and language. The finite is thus returned to the infinite, and the philosopher through learned ignorance achieves a mystical union with God. As he described in his final work, *De Visione Dei* (*Vision of God*, 1453), the enlightened are then free to live out the rest of their lives in mystical contemplation of the oneness of all things, forging between the relative, finite world and the absolute, infinite world, a living bridge.

8.1 Bacon (1561–1626): The Idols of the Mind

Francis Bacon was born in London to a family of high-ranking civil servants. After studying law at Trinity College, Cambridge, he began an illustrious political and legal career, becoming Lord Chancellor (attorney general) under King James I. A prolific and brilliant writer, he produced a body of highly revolutionary philosophical works that made him a pivotal figure in the ensuing transition from medieval to modern philosophy and influenced subsequent British empiricist philosophers Locke, Berkeley, Hume, Mill, and Russell.

Bacon's philosophical works shifted the entire focus of the knowledge-seeking enterprise away from the medieval concerns with predominantly religious themes. He introduced a new way of gathering scientific knowledge, the "Baconian Method," in which one moves from particular facts to more general knowledge of forms using experimentally discovered laws. He shunned what he saw as a vain craving for psychological satisfaction under the guise of a search for truth: "I find that even those that have sought knowledge for itself, and not for benefit or ostentation, or any practical enablement in the course of their life, have nevertheless propounded to themselves a wrong mark, namely statistician (which men call Truth) and not operation." According to Bacon the purpose of knowledge is not the attainment of bliss or happiness but the technological mastery of nature. Philosophers should focus on practical concerns, not the abstract contemplations about the ultimate natures of things that so interested medieval theologians, nor the attainment of inner tranquillity sought by the Stoics and ancients. Philosophy should "endow the condition and life of man with new powers or works," and "extend more widely the limits of the power and greatness of man." Philosophers must stop "prostituting" themselves by supporting or establishing religious or even scientific dogma. Nor should they seek inner bliss or any other manner of "delight only and not of discovery." The Baconian method is thus a shift away from metaphysical abstraction and psychological satiation toward a concrete, practical, utilitarian conception of wisdom.

Critical both of Skeptics who claim that knowledge is impossible and of the dogmatists who claim that knowledge must be based on the authority of ancient Greek learning, Bacon seeks a balanced middle ground between the present and the past. His method, explicitly designed to be used by individuals to make sound judgments and to find out the truth for themselves, provides a purely mechanical procedure for attaining knowledge that is openly available to anyone. Just as a person untrained in geometry could construct a circle by using a pair of compasses, anyone using Bacon's method could construct knowledge. Before this method can be learned or applied, however, the mind must be cleared of all the falsehoods it has been conditioned to believe and carefully directed away from its false notions and erroneous ways.

In the following selection, taken from his most celebrated work, the *Novum Organum*, Bacon exposes the psychological motives and covert personal interests hiding behind earlier philosophies and standing in the way of real progress. These fallacies come in four types,

which he labels *idols of the tribe, idols of the cave, idols of the marketplace, and idols of theater.*

The Idols of the Mind

The idols and false notions which are now in possession of the human understanding, and have taken deep root therein, not only so beset men's minds that truth can hardly find entrance, but even after entrance obtained, they will again in the very instauration of the sciences meet and trouble us, unless men being forewarned of the danger fortify themselves as far as may be against their assaults.

There are four classes of Idols which beset men's minds. To these for distinction's sake I have assigned names,—calling the first class *Idols of the Tribe*; the second, *Idols of the Cave*; the third, *Idols of the Marketplace*; the fourth, *Idols of the Theatre*.

The formation of ideas and axioms by true induction is no doubt the proper remedy to be applied for the keeping off and clearing away of idols. To point them out, however, is of great use; for the doctrine of Idols is to the Interpretation of Nature what the doctrine of the refutation of Sophisms is to common Logic.

The Idols of the Tribe have their foundation in human nature itself, and in the tribe or race of men. For it is a false assertion that the sense of man is the measure of things. On the contrary, all perceptions as well of the sense as of the mind are according to the measure of the individual and not according to the measure of the universe. And the human understanding is like a false mirror, which, receiving rays irregularly, distorts and discolours the nature of things by mingling its own nature with it.

The Idols of the Cave are the idols of the individual man. For every one (besides the errors common to human nature in general) has a cave or den of his own, which refracts and discolours the light of nature; owing either to his own proper and peculiar nature; or to his education and

From *The Philosophical Works of Francis Bacon*, R. L. Ellis and J. Spedding, eds., J. Spedding, trans., with emendations by the author.

conversation with others; or to the reading of books, and the authority of those whom he esteems and admires; or to the differences of impressions, accordingly as they take place in a mind preoccupied and predisposed or in a mind indifferent and settled; or the like. So that the spirit of man (according as it is meted out to different individuals) is in fact a thing variable and full of perturbation, and governed as it were by chance. Whence it was well observed by Heraclitus that men look for sciences in their own lesser worlds, and not in the greater or common world.

There are also Idols formed by the intercourse and association of men with each other, which I call Idols of the Marketplace, on account of the commerce and consort of men there. For it is by discourse that men associate; and words are imposed according to the apprehension of the vulgar. . . .

⚹

In other words, *the idols of the tribe* are fallacies based on a sort of "wishful thinking." For instance, most people delude themselves into thinking that nature exhibits a far greater regularity than it actually does; this is the result of the mind generalizing from affirmative instances while neglecting negative instances through an elaborate but socially sanctioned self-deception. Because our perceptions of the world are neither veridical nor even adequately accurate, we learn to ignore what we cannot grasp by painting the world in our own false image.

The idols of the cave are personal prejudices stemming from one's own individual temperament, beliefs, upbringing, and education. Bacon puts a new twist on Plato's allegory of the cave by suggesting that we do not even all live in the same cave—we are each individually encased in our own private illusion. We thus cannot simply by reasoning see the truth "as if through a glass darkly," as Plato imagined; the mind, in Bacon's words, is not the window but a "false mirror" of reality. Unfit to trust our own sensibilities, we naively use our eccentricities, emotions, and cravings to imprison ourselves. He warns that,

"In general, let every student of nature take this as a rule, that whatever his mind seizes and dwells upon with particular satisfaction is to be held in suspicion."

The idols of the marketplace are ideas, rumors, and beliefs passed along in social settings, through work and play; they result from our not taking the time to define our words properly. Even though we may not be consciously aware of it, words exert a deep and seductive power over the mind. Bacon saw as philosophically blinding the trappings rampant in a society of merchants and consumers, defined by persuasive advertising, rumors, and hearsay. According to Bacon, the idols of the marketplace are the worst of all the fallacies for two reasons: first, so many words in our vocabulary are but names for nonexistent things; second, most of our words are concepts abstracted from a few instances and then applied in a haphazard and sloppy manner to a whole range of things. This process, he says, has been particularly devastating for philosophy because it has led to arguments about literally nothing, as for instance when philosophers have taken part in empty religious debates.

The idols of the theater are fallacious modes of thinking that have come about through blind acceptance of tradition and authority, including—and especially—bad philosophy. The worst perpetrator of such bad philosophy, according to Bacon, was none other than Aristotle, whom he accuses of trying to force nature into his own vain abstractions and then using them to try to explain things away merely through the use of clever definitions. According to Bacon theology has similarly been the result of this fourth type of fallacy that infected the mind with superstition and glorified ignorance.

These four intellectual and emotional idolatries, as the main obstacles to objective knowledge, have kept humanity in the dark for centuries. Bacon urges people to dispense with them so that they can apply his new method and thereby pave the way for new thinking. Once freed from these old fallacies, humanity would be free to establish a natural philosophy, which he divides into theoretical and practical, physical and metaphysical. This leads him to his concept of forms, the central aspect of his theory, which is supposed to solve both the theoretical and practical problems of science.

In the next selection, he describes his method.

✻

On Induction

But by far the greatest obstacle to the progress of science and to the undertaking of new tasks and provinces therein, is found in this—that men despair and think things impossible. For wise and serious men are wont in these matters to be altogether distrustful; considering with themselves the obscurity of nature, the shortness of life, the deceitfulness of the senses, the weakness of the judgment, the difficulty of experiment and the like; and so supposing that in the revolution of time and of the ages of the world the sciences have their ebbs and flows: that at one season they grow and flourish, at another wither and decay, yet in such sort that when they have reached a certain point and condition they can advance no further. If therefore any one believes or promises more, they think this comes of an ungoverned and unripened mind, and that such attempts have prosperous beginnings, become difficult as they go on, and end in confusion. . . .

Those who have handled sciences have been either men of experiment or men of dogmas. The men of experiment are like the ant; they only collect and use: the reasoners resemble spiders, who make cobwebs out of their own substance. But the bee takes a middle course; it gathers its material from the flowers of the garden and of the field, but transforms and digests it by a power of its own. Not unlike this is the true business of philosophy; for it neither relies solely or chiefly on the powers of the mind, nor does it take the matter which it gathers from natural history and mechani-

From *The Philosophical Works of Francis Bacon*, R. L. Ellis and J. Spedding, eds., J. Spedding, trans., with emendations by the author.

cal experiments and lay it up in the memory whole, as it finds it; but lays it up in the understanding altered and digested. Therefore from a closer and purer league between these two faculties, the experimental and the rational (such as has never yet been made), much may be hoped.

We have as yet no natural philosophy that is pure; all is tainted and corrupted; in Aristotle's school by logic; in Plato's by natural theology; in the second school of Platonists, such as Proclus and others, by mathematics, which ought only to give definiteness to natural philosophy, not to generate or give it birth. From a natural philosophy pure and unmixed, better things are to be expected.

No one has yet been found so firm of mind and purpose as resolutely to compel himself to sweep away all theories and common notions, and to apply the understanding, thus made fair and even, to a fresh examination of particulars. Thus it happens that human knowledge, as we have it, is a mere medley and ill-digested mass, made up of much credulity and much accident, and also of the childish notions which we at first imbibed. . . .

Now if any one of ripe age, unimpaired senses, and well-purged mind, apply himself anew to experience and particulars, better hopes may be entertained of that man. In which point I promise to myself a like fortune to that of Alexander the Great; and let no man tax me with vanity till he have heard the end; for the thing which I mean tends to the putting off of all vanity. For of Alexander and his deeds Æschines spoke thus: "Assuredly we do not live the life of mortal men; but to this end were we born, that in after ages wonders might be told of us." . . .

The understanding must not however be allowed to jump and fly from particulars to remote axioms and of almost the highest generality (such as the first principles, as they are called, of arts and things), and taking stand upon them as truths that cannot be shaken, proceed to prove and frame the middle axioms by reference to them; which has been the practice hitherto; the understanding being not only carried that way by a natural impulse, but also by the use of syllogistic demonstration trained and inured to it. But then, and then only, may we hope well of the sciences, when in a just scale of ascent, and by successive steps not interrupted or broken, we rise from particulars to lesser axioms; and then to middle axioms, one above the other; and last of all to the most general. For the lowest axioms differ but slightly from bare experience, while the highest and most general (which we now have) are notional and abstract and without solidity. But the middle are the true and solid and living axioms, on which depend the affairs and fortunes of men; and above them again, last of all, those which are indeed the most general; such I mean as are not abstract, but of which those intermediate axioms are really limitations.

The understanding must not therefore be supplied with wings, but rather hung with weights, to keep it from leaping and flying. Now this has never yet been done; when it is done, we may entertain better hopes of the sciences.

In establishing axioms, another form of induction must be devised than has hitherto been employed; and it must be used for proving and discovering not first principles (as they are called) only, but also the lesser axioms, and the middle, and indeed all. For the induction which proceeds by simple enumeration is childish; its conclusions are precarious, and exposed to peril from a contradictory instance; and it generally decides on too small a number of facts, and on those only which are at hand. But the induction which is to be available for the discovery and demonstration of sciences and arts, must analyse nature by proper rejections and exclusions; and then, after a sufficient number of negatives, come to a conclusion on the affirmative instances: which has not yet been done or even attempted, save only by Plato, who does indeed employ this form of induction to a certain extent for the purpose of discussing definitions and ideas. But in order to furnish this induction or demonstration well and duly for its work, very many things are to be provided which no mortal has yet thought of; insomuch that greater labour will have to be spent in it than has hitherto been spent on the syllogism. And this induction must be used not only to discover axioms, but also in the formation of notions. And it is in this induction that our chief hope lies.

But in establishing axioms by this kind of induction, we must also examine and try whether the axiom so established be framed to the measure of those particulars only from which it is derived, or whether it be larger and wider. And if it be larger and wider, we must observe whether by indicating

to us new particulars it confirm that wideness and largeness as by a collateral security; that we may not either stick fast in things already known, or loosely grasp at shadows and abstract form; not at things solid and realised in matter. And when this process shall have come into use, then at last shall we see the dawn of a solid hope.

⚹

Bacon's method, then, is as follows. Always begin with as clear and unambiguous a description of the facts as possible. Next, all generalizations from these facts must be checked by a search for (1) positive instances of the phenomenon in question, (2) negative instances of its absence, and (3) instances of its presence in varying degrees. Finally, one must eliminate whatever is not directly connected with the phenomenon under investigation. Points (1), (2), and (3) are essentially an anticipation of the methods of agreement, the joint method and the method of concomitant variations as used in modern science.

Although Bacon is sometimes labeled an empiricist who anticipated Locke and Hume, it should be noted that he says "the Empirical school of philosophy gives birth to dogmas more deformed and monstrous than the Sophistical or Rational school." He is as suspicious of experience as of blind reason and though he insists that experience must always be put to the test through experiment, he is also as deeply critical of the "experimentalists" as he is of the rationalists:

> The men of experiment are like the ant; they only collect and use: the reasoners resemble spiders, who make cobwebs out of their own substance. But the bee takes a middle course; it gathers its material from the flowers of the garden and of the field, but transforms and digests it by a power of its own. Not unlike this is the true business of philosophy. . . . Therefore from a closer and purer league between these two faculties, the experimental and the rational (such as has never yet been made), much may be hoped.

A complete system based on exactly such a synergy between experience and reason, as

Bacon is here clearly anticipating, would have to wait many more centuries, until the ground-breaking work of Immanuel Kant (Chapter 16).

It has also been suggested by some scholars that Bacon may have been the real author of the plays bearing the name of William Shakespeare. Their reasoning is based on clues found in old letters to Bacon stored in the University of London library, the fact that many references in Shakespeare's plays are to works by Bacon unpublished at the time, and the fact that both authors used so many of the same quotes from biblical, legal, and classical sources. They also point to numerous ciphered messages throughout the plays, such as the word *honorificabilitudinitatibus* in *Love's Labour's Lost*, which forms the anagram *Hi ludi F. Baconis nati tuiti orbi*, "These plays, the offspring of F. Bacon, are preserved for the world."

In any case, Bacon's influence on the subsequent revolution in modern thought has been pivotal and often unappreciated. Early twentieth-century philosopher John Dewey (Section 20.2), himself inspired by Bacon's views (as summed up in the aphorism "Knowledge Is Power") to invent the philosophy known as American pragmatism, wrote "Francis Bacon of the Elizabethan age is the great forerunner of the spirit of modern life," who as "a prophet of new tendencies," "hardly receives his due as the real founder of modern thought."

8.2 Giordano Bruno (1548–1600): The World-Soul Is You

One of the most controversial and certainly the most persecuted of the late Renaissance philosophers, Giordano Bruno was born in Nola, Italy. At the age of fourteen he went to Naples to study with a leading member[2] of a secret Averroist circle of philosophers. The group had continued teaching Averroist ideas in spite of the fact that they were banned on the list of Forbidden Propositions. After learning logic from an Augustinian friar, in 1565 he continued

his studies at the Neapolitan convent of San Domenico Maggiore, where he became a Dominican. Early on he got into trouble for his anti-ascetic and anti-Christian views. In 1576, after being suspected of heresy, he fled to Rome where he got involved in a murder case and had to flee again, first to Liguria and then Venice. In 1578 he had to leave the Dominican order and fled across the Alps to Geneva, where he made his living as a proofreader. He converted to Calvinism and, as soon as he was in favor with the authorities, he published a devastating criticism of leading Calvinist Antoine de la Faye. Charged with impiety and heresy once again, he went to prison until he retracted his views. After his release he moved to Toulouse, earned a master of arts degree, and secured a lecturing position in philosophy.

It is well worth pointing out that most, if not all, philosophers who have been accused of impiety and heresy—from Socrates onward (even the case of Galileo, as we shall see)—were *not* accused of being atheists. Rather, the problem, as the church authorities saw it, was that these philosophers claimed to be able to know God or ultimate reality themselves, directly, on the basis of their own reason or experience. (We shall see that Spinoza will find himself in the same predicament.) In other words, that what got them in trouble with the religious authorities was *not* the proposition "God does not exist," but the proposition "God can be known independently of church-sanctioned revelation." And the case of Giordano Bruno is no exception. What got him in trouble was what the church considered to be the most heretical and dangerous idea ever to have come along: the idea that the universe is the living God and everything in it is a manifestation of God. This view has come to be called *pantheism*.

Bruno's pantheistic philosophy developed out of the metaphysics of Averroës and the festering Copernican revolution. A precursor of Spinoza, Bruno thus conceived of God in ways that church officials saw as the most heretical of all, which they feared far more than atheism: the identification of God with the world. That is, according to Bruno, "God" and "world" were but two names for one and the same reality. As God, *natura naturans,* the universe is one unified whole, transcendent and ineffable; as *natura naturata* it is the infinity of worlds, things, and events. The idea is that Being, which is a cosmic, Parmenidean unity, divides itself into a Many to display all infinite potentialities of the One. This leads to an eternal process of outgoing creative activity into the Many and a return into the One, the divine unity. The supreme achievement of this activity is the human mind, whose search for the One within the Many—unity among diversity, simplicity in complexity, the changeless within the eternal, and so on—is the expression of the divine mind returning to itself. In Bruno's philosophy the human mind functions as the fulcrum of the cosmic process of existence, which is in many ways suggestive of the philosophy of Hegel (Chapter 17).

But let us pause a moment. Before we go further into this sort of view, let us once again try to put ourselves in the shoes of the philosophers and see what such thinking really entails in a way that we can understand it. Otherwise, what you've just read sounds like an elaborate fairy tale, exotic thinking of a very strange variety indeed! Often, not just students but philosophers become so entrenched in our "commonsense" view of things that it becomes next to impossible to really excavate and reconstruct the original impetus behind the thinking behind the philosopher! For instance, to take but one notable example, here is what the president of the American Philosophical Association (APA), Larry Laudan, said in his 1995 Presidential Address before the annual Pacific Division meeting:

> Viewed from an only slightly jaundiced perspective, the history of philosophy is a tale of the artful contriving of counterintuitive and outlandish stories about the world. Thus, we might all be extensions of the divine mind, living in an immaterial world. An evil genie

might be deceiving us with respect to all our perceptual and conceptual judgments. We could be brains in a vat, wired to have precisely the mental life that we do. There might be a twin earth, perceptibly indistinguishable from this one. Perhaps physical objects are nothing but complex bundles of sensations, etc., etc. Philosophy is a bit like a think tank for turning out story-lines for B-grade Hollywood horror movies. "The Evil Genie Meets the Brain in a Vat," "War of the Worlds Part II: Earth vs. Twin Earth," and so on.*

He could just as well have been addressing Giordano Bruno, who in fact believed that we are all "extensions of the divine mind, living in an immaterial world." And the phrase "physical objects are nothing but complex bundles of sensations, etc." is perhaps meant to ridicule the views of nearly every philosopher who has been called an *idealist* or a *phenomenalist.* But let us take stock of what exactly might be motivating such philosophers (idealists have, in fact, historically been in the majority). Let us put it in simple and straightforward, scientific terms that may grab you. Science, after all, is all the vogue today, and most people accept the scientific terminology with which we construct our views (or have them constructed for us) in the same way that people once accepted theological terminology. To see the full power and force of a philosopher like Bruno, who is speaking within the theological vocabulary of his day, all we have to do is translate it into the scientific vocabulary of our own day, which I shall now do.

Consider this book, which you can see yourself, and the other objects you see around you. *What sense* can we make of the proposition that the book you see and the other objects you see are the same object? The thought seems preposterous, as preposterous as propositions like "Everything is made of water" and "Everything

*Presidential address delivered before the sixty-ninth annual Pacific Division Meeting of the APA in San Francisco, California, March 31, 1995.

is made of numbers." But on several occasions we've discussed the problem of perception and trying to understand the relationship between the *visual images that you see* and the "physical objects" that exist "out there," independently of your mind. We are perhaps familiar enough with why a philosopher who is focusing on the appearances themselves, rather than on what the appearances are supposed to be *of,* might wish to point out that although the appearances *look different*, they are in a more fundamental and basic sense *the same thing.* Imagine a television set showing lots of different pictures, or one of those electronic billboards like the one at Times Square in New York. If what you want to talk about is what the images *look like* or *what they represent* or what they *refer to,* and so on, then you will want to highlight the differences among them. If what you want to talk about is what the images *consist in* or what makes them appear as they do while they are appearing, then you will want to find some means of drawing attention to the level at which they are happening. In the case of the television set or the electronic billboard, if you look very closely at them you will see the same picture tube "be" something different—at one moment that surface of the picture tube *is* "Lucy," until she "moves," at which point that very same part of the surface of the picture tube "becomes" "Ricky."

Likewise with the electronic billboard. The very same electric lightbulb that lights up as part of a face now becomes a box, now a hand, now a cloud. That is not to say that clouds and boxes and hands, or Ricky and Lucy in the case of the television set, are the same thing. Rather, it is to draw attention to the television set or to the billboard. What happens when we do this is that we cease paying attention to the show or to the advertisements and start attending to something different. That is what the philosopher is doing. Some may not like this activity because it disrupts the show, and people don't want it to be interrupted. "The show must go on." "Do not draw attention away from the images; let them happen so that we can attend to them, etc."

Practicality or the desire to make the central focus of one's philosophy *the content of the show* rather than *what is behind the content* is partly at issue here, and some philosophers have viewed the former as more important than the latter. But the point is not thereby dismissed.

More *to* the point, consider the most recent and most sophisticated answers to the question, "What am I looking at when I am seeing the images that I am now seeing?" That answer, from cognitive philosophers of the brain, is "I am looking at the surface of my brain." Well, in that case there is a very real sense in which the *types of things* that those things (which we "take to be physical objects existing independently of us") are, as we consciously attend to the appearances, are really *the same single thing:* the surface of the brain.

Now, this is *not* Bruno's philosophy, but it is relevant in case you do not see the relevance of his philosophy. For in both cases—whether Bruno's view is true or whether the most recent and most scientifically sophisticated philosophy of perception is true—Bruno's view and the most recent view are *closer to the truth* than the commonsense, unreflective, preanalytic, "natural" view. Do you see the significance of this? Bruno's very old and dated "outlandish story" (to use Laudan's phrase) is *closer* to the "best available current view" than the "natural," commonly accepted view! If you do see this point, then you will understand instantly the importance and relevance of understanding philosophy. For there is an aspect of it, regardless of the vicissitudes of the practical and scientific evolution of thought, that is *timeless.*

The fact that particular propositions offered to the world by the great philosophers we are considering in this book, from Thales on, turn out to be false is not by itself detrimental. Recall, after all, Thales's famous "Everything is made of water." There is an obvious sense in which he was wrong, but there is also an unobvious sense in which he was right.

There is another, even subtler point that we can make here. What is being denied is *the world as it is understood by the conscious human ego.* In fact, in a way, such philosophy is a direct affront to the ego! Perhaps that is why the world in which we live as constructed by our own institutions, themselves in many ways extensions of our own egos, seems intent on repressing this activity of philosophy. For in either case—whether in Bruno's vision or in the current view from neuroscience—the ego is obviously not what it appears to be: the sum and substance of reality. Even the way you present yourself to yourself (or, the way you are to yourself presented by the brain or God or whatever is *really* doing it) is illusory and self-deceiving—*in ways even Socrates could never have imagined.*

Yet of course most philosophers persist. Bruno was no exception. In spite of warnings from the authorities, Bruno continued teaching and publishing his controversial views, and just when he was in danger French king Henry III read his works and was so impressed that he offered Bruno his protection, brought him to Paris, and appointed him official court lecturer. Two years later Bruno got in trouble again, this time at Oxford, for his unorthodox views about the immortality of the soul and the unity of the intellect among all human beings.

During his stay in England he published *Ars Reminiscendi* (1583) and *La Cena de le Ceneri* (1584), in which he accepts Copernicus's view of the solar system and argues for an infinite universe composed of an infinite number of worlds. In addition, the works criticize English society in general and the Oxford philosophers and theologians as unenlightened pedants. His *De la Causa, Principio et Uno* (*Concerning the Cause, the Principle and the One*, 1585), from which the next selection is taken, is an Averroës-inspired attempt to demonstrate the fundamental unity of all substances including, and especially, the human intellect. Let us see how he attempts this.

You may notice right off the bat how apt the comparison with Thales is; Bruno draws attention to the world *as it appears to us* as described within the current Scholastic terminology and the traditional Aristotelian distinctions: form and matter, cause and principle, final and efficient

cause, and *potentia* (possibility) and *actus* (actuality). Keep these distinctions in mind as you read and remember that Bruno uses them for a single purpose: to express the unity of the universal world-form and of the world-soul. Thus, he uses the distinctions to show that they are but relative and only of partial significance.

中

Concerning the Cause, the Principle, and the One

PERSONAGES { AURELIUS DIXON
THEOPHILUS
GERVASIUS
POLYHYMNIUS

Dixon. Have the kindness, Master Polyhymnius, and you too, Gervasius, not to interrupt our discourse further.

Polyhymnius. So be it.

Gervasius. If he who is the master speaks, surely I shall be unable to keep silence.

Dix. Then you say, Theophilus, that everything which is not a first principle and a first cause, has such a principle and such a cause?

Theo. Without doubt and without the least controversy.

Dix. Do you believe, accordingly, that whoever knows the things thus caused and originated must know the ultimate cause and principle?

Theo. Not easily the proximate cause or the proximate principle; it would be extremely difficult to recognize even the traces of an ultimate cause and creative principle.

Dix. Then how do you think that those things which have a first and a proximate cause and principle can be really known, if their efficient cause (which is one of the things which contribute to the true cognition of things) is hidden?

Theo. I grant you that it is easy to set forth the theory of proof, but the proof itself is difficult. It is very practicable to set forth the causes, circumstances, and methods of sciences; but afterward

Translated from the Italian by Josiah Royce and Katherine Royce (London: Routledge, 1902).

our method-makers and analytical scholars can use but awkwardly their *organum*, the principles of their methods, and their arts of arts.

Gerv. Like those who know how to make fine swords, but do not know how to use them.

Poly. Aye, aye.

Gerv. May your eyes be closed so that you may never be able to open them.

Theo. I should say, then, that one should not expect the natural philosopher to make plain all causes and principles; but only the physical, and only the principal and most essential of these. And although these depend upon the first cause and first principle, and can be said to possess such a cause and principle, this is, in any case, not such a necessary relation that from the knowledge of the one the knowledge of the other would follow; and therefore one should not expect that in the same science both should be set forth.

Dix. How is that?

Theo. Because from the cognition of all dependent things, we are unable to infer other knowledge of first cause and principle, than by the somewhat inefficacious method of traces. All things are, indeed, derived from the Creator's will or goodness, which is the principle of His works, and from which proceeds the universal effect. The same consideration arises in the case of works of art, in so much as he who sees the statue does not see the sculptor; he who sees the portrait of Helen does not see Apelles: but he sees only the result of the work which comes from the merit and genius of Apelles. This work is entirely an effect of the accidents and circumstances of the substance of that man, who, as to his absolute essence, is not in the least known.

Dix. So that to know the universe is like knowing nothing of the being and substance of the first principle, because it is like knowing the accidents of the accidents.

⚹

Let us pause to interject some questions at this point. What is this dialogue about? What is being discussed? If you've just read this and can't make heads or tails of it, then you (1) read it too quickly or (2) did not try to relate Bruno's words to what I said in the preceding pages.

Remember: one of the conditions of understanding something is that you can put it in your own words or recognize it within a different setting as the same idea presented in different words. The *unfamiliarity* of terms like "first cause" and "efficient cause" are not as apocryphal as they may seem. They are convenient placeholders for you to pause and think, to see if your mind will fill in the blanks for you.

Here is what is going on. The issue is as timeless as philosophy. It is absolutely fundamental, and you will see it again and again in so many different ways in this book that it would be pointless to point out all the philosophers who will again raise it. The people in Bruno's dialogue are discussing the relationship between that which you see—the immanent images of things—and that which is their *efficient* cause—that is, whatever it is that causes them to appear as they do. Now, the physical tables and chairs "out there" in the world may be the first or initiating cause, the first domino, of a long series of causes that finally ends up causing the images you see. But notice that you don't see either of the causes. That is, even if there is a physical object "out there" that corresponds to the visual image you see, what is responsible for the creation of the visual image as such? Just pause a moment and really try to meditate on this question. *The physical object out there can't be the direct cause of the image.* Think about it!

Tables and chairs don't reach into your brain and grab your neurons; they don't take hold of your mind! Your own mind/brain must be doing it, at least as the final cause of the whole series of events, starting with the "stuff" out there (like atoms and lightwaves or whatever it is). *The immediate cause is you.* But you are not aware of this! You do not see this. But you can infer it. Let us go on:

⚹

Dixon. Behold, then, of the divine substance, as well because it is infinite as because it is extremely remote from its effects (while these effects are the furthest boundary of the source of our reasoning faculties), we can know nothing,—unless through the means of traces, as the Platonists say, of remote effects, as the Peripatetic philosophers say, of the dress or outer covering, as say the Cabalists, of the mere shoulders and back, as the Talmudists say, or of the mirror, the shadow, the enigma, as the Apocalyptic writers say.

Theophilus. All the more is this the case because we do not see perfectly this universe whose substance and principle are so difficult of comprehension. And thus it follows that with far less ground can we know the first principle and cause through its effect, than Apelles may be known through the statue he has made. For the statue all may see and examine, part by part; but not so the grand and infinite effect of the Divine Power. Therefore our simile should be understood not as a matter of close comparison.

Now, what does he mean by *divine substance?* He means things in themselves as they actually are—the originating, first cause of all the things that we see: the ultimate reality of which the appearances are merely a secondary effect. In calling it "divine" he is as much claiming that it is *transcendental* to experience (rather than immanent) as he is claiming that it is God. On both the "thing in itself" and the "transcendental" nature of it, Kant, as we shall see, will agree; whether or not to call it God is another question.

Indeed, in that regard it is well worth pointing out that one of the translators of this Bruno selection, Josiah Royce (along with his wife Katharine), is a (nineteenth- and early twentieth-century) highly influential American philosopher whom we shall consider in due course (Chapter 20). Royce will express essentially the same ideas as Bruno, whom he is here translating, but in a more contemporary context far removed from the theological and scholastic language in which Bruno states it.

Keep this in mind (and file it away in the back of your mind as one of the originating foundations of what shall come to be known as a form of *idealism*) as we go on. In the following section, Dixon asks Theophilus to explain the difference between the cause and the principle and how the distinction resolves itself into unity in the concept of the world-soul which exists as the same individual in each one of us:

Dix. Since, then, we have come to an understanding concerning the difference between those things, I wish you to devote your attention first to the Causes and then to the Principles. And as to the Causes, I desire first to know about the first efficient cause, about the formal cause, which you say is conjoined to the efficient; and, lastly, about the final cause, which is understood to be the power which moves this.

Theo. The order of discourse which you propose pleases me much. Now as to the efficient cause: I assert that the universal physical efficient cause is the universal Intellect, which is the first and principal faculty of the world-soul and which is the universal form of the Cosmos.

Dix. Your thought appears to me to be not only in agreement with that of Empedocles, but more certain, more distinct, and more explicit, and also (in so far as I can see from the above) more profound, yet you will give me pleasure if you will explain the whole more in detail, beginning by informing me just what is that universal intellect.

Theo. The universal intellect is the most intimate, real, and essential faculty and effective part of the world-soul. This is one and the same thing which fills the whole, illumines the universe and directs nature to produce the various species as is fitting, and has the same relation to the production of natural things as our intellect to the parallel production of our general ideas.* This is called by the Pythagoreans the moving spirit and pro-

*The reference is to a well-known scholastic parallel of the universals present *in things* and the universals present *in our minds* when we form our ideas of natural classes. The universal Intellect is related to the production of natural forms, or species, as our mind is related to the production of our ideas of these species.

pelling power of the universe; as saith the poet, "Infused through the members, mind vitalizes the whole mass and is mingled with the whole body." This is called by the Platonic philosophers the world-builder. This builder (they say) proceeds from the higher world (which is, in fact, one) to this world of sense, which is divided into many, and in which not only harmony but also discord reigns, because it is sundered into parts. This intellect, infusing and extending something of its own into matter, restful and moveless in itself, produces all things. By the Magi this intelligence is called most fruitful of seeds, or even the seed-sower, since it is He who impregnates matter with all its forms, and according to the type and condition of these succeeds in shaping, forming, and arranging all in such admirable order, as cannot be attributed to chance, or to any principle which cannot consciously distinguish or arrange. Orpheus calls this Intellect the eye of the world, because it sees all natural objects, both within and without, in order that all things may succeed in producing and maintaining themselves in their proper symmetry, not only intrinsically but also extrinsically. By Empedocles it is called the Distinguisher, since it never wearies of unfolding the confused forms within the breast of matter or of calling forth the birth of one thing from the corruption of another. Plotinus calls it the father and progenitor, because it distributes seeds throughout the field of nature, and is the proximate dispenser of forms. By us this Intellect is called the inner artificer, because it forms and shapes material objects from within, as from within the seed or the root is sent forth and unfolded the trunk, from within the trunk are put forth the branches, from within the branches the finished twigs, and from within the twigs unfurl the buds, and there within are woven like nerves, leaves, flowers and fruits; and inversely, at certain times the sap is recalled from the flowers and fruits to the twigs, from the twigs to the branches, from the branches to the trunk, and from the trunk to the root. Just so it is with animals; its work proceeding from the original seed, and from the center of the heart, to the external members, and from these finally gathering back to the heart the unfolded powers, it behaves as if again knotting together spun-out threads. Now, since we believe that even inanimate works, such as we know how to produce with a certain order, imitatively working on the surface of matter, are not produced without forethought and mind,—as when, cutting and sculpturing a piece of wood, we bring forth the effigy of a horse: how much greater must we believe is that creative intelligence which, from the interior of the germinal matter, brings forth the bones, extends the cartilage, hollows out the arteries, breathes into the pores, weaves the fibres, forms the branching nerves, and with such admirable mastery arranges the whole? I say, how much greater an artificer is He who is not restricted to one sole part of the material world, but operates continually throughout the whole. . . .

Dix. You show me the seemingly true way in which the opinion of Anaxagoras may be maintained, who held that all things are in all things. For since spirit, or soul, or universal form, exists in all things, all may be produced from all.

Theo. I do not say seemingly true, but true. For spirit is found in all things, those which are not living creatures are still vitalized, if not according to the perceptible presence of animation and life, yet they are animate according to the principle and, as it were, primal being of animation and life. . . . On other occasions, I shall be able to discuss more at length the mind, the spirit, the soul, the life, which penetrates all, is in all, and moves all matter, fills the lap of that matter and dominates it rather than is dominated by it. For the spiritual substance cannot be overpowered by the material, but rather embraces it.

Dix. That appears to me to conform not only to the sense of Pythagoras, whose opinion the Poet rehearses when he says,—

In the beginning the sky, the earth and the fields of the waters, Glistening orb of the moon, and also the radiant sunlight,
All is inspired with life, and trembling through every member,
Mind vitalizes the mass, and with the whole body is mingled.

Virgil's Aeneid, VI 724

but also it conforms to the Theologian who says, "The spirit rules over and fills the earth, and that it is which contains all things." And another, speaking perchance of the dealings of form with matter and with potentiality, says that the latter is dominated by actuality and by form.

Theo. If then, spirit, mind, life, is found in all things, and in various degrees fills all matter, it must certainly follow, that it is the true actuality, and the true form of all things. The soul of the world, then, is the formal, constitutive principle of the universe, and of that which is contained within it. I say that if life is found in all things, the soul must be the form of all things; that which through everything presides over matter, holds sway over composite things, effects the composition and consistency of their parts. And therefore such form is no less enduring than matter. This I understand to be One in all things, which, however, according to the diversity of the disposition of matter, and according to the power of the material principle, both active and passive, comes to produce diverse configurations, and to effect different faculties, sometimes showing the effects of life without sense, sometimes the effects of life and sensation without intellect, and sometimes it appears that all the faculties are suppressed or repressed either by weakness, or by other conditions of matter. While this form thus changes place and circumstance, it is impossible that it should be annulled; because the spiritual substance is not less real than the material. Then only external forms can change and even be annulled, because they are not things but of things; they are not substances; they are accidents and circumstances.

Dix. Then you approve, in some sort, the opinion of Anaxagoras who calls the particular forms of Nature latent, and in a sense that of Plato who deduces them from ideas, and in a manner that of Empedocles who makes them proceed from intelligence, and in some sort that of Aristotle who makes them, as it were, issue from the potentiality of matter?

Theo. Yes. Because, as we have said, where there is form, there is, in a certain manner, everything. Where there is soul, spirit, life, there is everything, for the creator of ideal forms and varieties is intellect. And even if it does not obtain forms from matter, it nevertheless does not go begging for them outside of matter, because this spirit fills the whole.

. . . Know, then, in brief, that the Soul of the World, and the Divinity are not omnipresent through all and through every part, in the way in which material things could be there: because this is impossible to any sort of body, and to any sort of spirit; but in a manner which is not easy to explain to you if not in this way. You should take notice that if the Soul of the World and the universal form are said to be everywhere, we do not mean *corporeally* and *dimensionally,* because such things cannot be; and just so they cannot be in any part. But they are *spiritually* present in everything—as, for example (perhaps a rough one), you can imagine a voice which is throughout a whole room and in every part of the room; because, through all, it is completely heard: just as these words which I utter are heard completely by all, even were there a thousand present, and my voice, could it reach throughout the whole world, would be everywhere through everything. I tell you then, Master Polyhymnius, that the soul is not indivisible like a point, but in some sort like the voice. And I answer you, Gervasius, that the Divinity is not everywhere in the sense that the God of Grandazzo was in the whole of the chapel, because, although he was present throughout the church, yet all of him was not present everywhere, but his head was in one part, his feet in another, his arms and his chest in yet other parts. But that other is in its entirety in every part, as my voice is heard completely in every part of this room.

⁂

Notice that in the dialogue the idea of the ultimate and fundamental unity of all things— the immanence of the world-soul and of the world-form in everything—is expressed as an *intuition* rather than as some sort of demonstrable proposition. Bruno's motive is not just the impartial search for *truth*. He claims that intuiting the truth has two *practical* benefits. If the individual soul (you) learns to view itself as being one with the world-soul, this alleviates within it all fear of death. Furthermore, what is most valuable about any individual being is that it can itself come to express the meaning expressed by the whole world and all its parts.

In his subsequent writings, such as *De l'Infinito, Universo et Mondi* (1585), he continued using the arguments of pre-Socratic philosophers against Aristotle. Ironically, whereas Averroës argued for such a numerical identity of all minds on the basis of his interpretation of Aristotle, Bruno considers Aristotle's views in particular and the language imposed upon philosophy by the prevailing Scholasticism as unduly constraining. That is one of the reasons why he presents the immanence of the world-soul and of the world-form in every being as incapable of logical demonstration but nevertheless graspable as an intellectual, or rational, intuition. This ultimate and secret truth, he argues, has the power to relieve individuals from fear of death and liberates the mind to contemplate its nature and the nature of the world unencumbered by the constraining concepts brought upon its craving for religion as a result of its ignorant fears.

Bruno also wrote works on ethics in which he urges social reforms along anti-Christian lines but which had obvious parallels: treat others as yourself not because God says this is the way you should be kind to others, "*as if* they were you," but *because they are you*. Once again the church, which held as sacred the division of human beings into good and evil, sinners and saved, could not withstand such an assault on its authority; for if Bruno was right, everyone had the same relationship to God, indeed, in a very important sense *was* God. The person who follows obediently the rules of the church is no closer to God than the person who rebels against them; they are equally close; they are one. Bruno was ordered burned at the stake.

Upon his return to Paris, he continued his criticisms of Aristotle in his *Fuguratio Aristotelici Physici Auditus* (1586) and presented

his own heretical views, for which even the king's favors could not help him, and he was forced to leave. The only place that allowed him to teach was in Wittenberg, Germany, where he continued to publish until the Calvinists came to power and he was once again exiled, this time finding a brief haven in Prague, Czechoslovakia. Among his works the greatest is *De Immenso* (1588), in which his theory of psychic monism, based on Averroist philosophy, explicitly argues for the single identity view of the human intellect. As a result, the local Protestant church excommunicated him. He fled this time to Frankfurt, was denounced, and fled to Venice under the protection of the same Venetian nobleman who shortly thereafter denounced him to the Inquisition. The nobleman helped them bring Bruno to Rome where, after seven years in prison and a long trial for heresy, he still refused to take back any aspect of his views. He continued to espouse the unity of the universal world-form and of the numerical identity within each human being of the world-soul—that we are all the same person—until he was finally burned at the stake.

NOTES

1. It was first coined in 1860 by J. Burckhardt.
2. G. V. de Colle ("il Sarnase").

Part III ⚹ The Modern Rationalists

9 ✽ Prelude to Modern Philosophy: The Copernican Revolution

9.0 The Copernican Revolution: Start of the Second Dawn

The year is 1543. A seventy-year-old Polish cler-gyman named Mikolaj Kopernik (Latinized "Nicolaus Copernicus") publishes his lifelong work, *Concerning the Revolutions of the Celestial Spheres*. In it, he offers an explanation of the pos-sibility that the sun, not the earth, is at the center of the solar system. He receives the first published copy on his deathbed.

The public is shocked, astounded, amazed—perhaps as shocked and amazed as when the ancient Greek philosopher Thales made the unbelievably absurd statement that everything is made of water (Section 1.1)! How could anyone think that anything like that is possible? How could anyone claim that the earth moves, that it is not at the center of the universe?

Before Copernicus (1473–1543) just about everyone believed that the earth does *not* move and that the sun, moon, planets, and stars all revolve around the earth. Most people today believe just the opposite: the earth moves around the sun (the modern heliocentric view). Furthermore, most people today believe that *the*

reason they believe this about the solar system is because Copernicus, Galileo, and other great sci-entists were able to dispel the old "religious" myth that the earth does not move and that everything revolves around the earth (the ancient geocentric view). That is, most of us today have been taught to believe that people before Copernicus and Galileo believed that the earth was at the center of the solar system because the geocentric view was written into the Bible, and people were conditioned by religious authorities to take the word of the Bible as truth. People who dared question what is in the Bible were tortured or put to death, like Giordano Bruno, who was burned at the stake or Galileo Galilei, who was put under house arrest for putting forth a "Copernican view" of the solar system. According to the "official" story that most of us have been taught at school, this is why people before us stupidly and out of super-stitious fear blinded themselves to the truth that the earth goes around the sun and believed, instead, what the church wanted them to believe: that the sun goes around the earth.

It is true that the church did have that kind of power and it did exercise it. But that is *not* why people believed that the earth is at the center of the solar system and that it does not move! In fact, neither religion nor superstition had anything to do with it. They believed it because that's what their senses told them. That's what their eyes told them. And their reason confirmed it. "No one in his senses," wrote the sixteenth-century philosopher Jean Bodin, "or imbued with the slightest knowledge of physics, will ever think that the earth, heavy and unwieldy from its own weight and mass, staggers up and down around its own center and that of the sun; for at the slightest jar of the earth, we would see cities and fortresses, towns and mountains thrown down."

Look up at the sky on a clear night. The first thing you will notice, if you keep on looking, is that everything up there appears to be moving around the earth. Meanwhile, you certainly don't see or feel the earth move, do you? You see all the other heavenly objects move. Nothing is more natural than the idea of a stationary earth around which all the heavenly bodies revolve. So why do *you* believe that the earth moves around the sun? Is that what *your* eyes tell you? Is that the "truth" that you arrived at through experience and reason?

Hardly. It is *you,* not those people who for more than a thousand years believed what their eyes told them, who on this question blindly submits to authority. This by itself is philosophically revealing. It suggests that the age we are living in, in spite of all our great advances in "knowledge," is one of great philosophical ignorance.

Philosophical Ignorance Versus Philosophical Enlightenment

The shift from the religious authority of the church to the secular authority of science did little to dispel what we might call, for lack of a better term, *"the ignorance of philosophy."* What is *philosophical ignorance?* In a nutshell, it has two complementary components: an experiential component, in which we mistake our eyes for windows onto reality, and an intellectual compo-

nent, in which we mistake our theories for reality. The experiential component consists mainly in what we've called "naive realism," the view described by the phrase "our eyes our windows," the almost universally accepted misconception that our experience consists of items in the physical world. The truth is that our experience consists not of physical items[1] but of mental items that are, at best, representations of items in the physical world.[2] The intellectual component, which consists mainly in mistaking theories for reality, treats (accepted) theories (that is, ones we've grown up with) as if they were the only view to reality, when the profound philosophical truth is that there is *always* an alternative view available. As we shall see time and again, for any theory, T_1, about the way the world is, there is always another theory, T_2, which contradicts T_1 but "fits the facts" just as well. Which is *not* to say that we don't know anything or that skepticism is true (a view that many sixteenth-century thinkers, partly on the basis of Copernicus's argument, accepted as the only viable alternative). It is just to say that the job of the philosopher is never done.[3]

We have once again arrived at a point in our historical discovery of philosophy where we can perfectly well illustrate the subtle but all important difference between, on the one hand, philosophy and, on the other, religion and science. We have already pointed out in what sense philosophy is a narrow path between the two (pp. xvi–xviii). And one of the recurring themes of this book is that most of humanity lives in philosophical ignorance. Occasionally, perhaps as need arises, there occur individuals in whom this ignorance is lifted, for one reason or another (or perhaps even just by chance).

We must point out, however, that in this respect there is nothing especially unique about philosophy. Take something much more practical, like medicine. Just as the British did not invent the English language and philosophers did not invent philosophy, so physiologists did not invent physiology. The human body was already there. We had bodies with circulating systems, hearts, brains, and so on, for many millions of years before we ever *knew* that we had them! Does the brain know that it is a brain, the heart that it is a heart? Not in the linguistic, propositional sense. It is *minds* that know things like that. Even if the mind turns out to be just the brain, the "knowledge" that is already there in the operating system of your neurons at a functional machine level is not of the sort that we speak about in the philosophical sense, which involves the use of (natural) language and the offering of philosophical explanations using sentences (propositions). So the point about philosophy not being especially unique in terms of the notion of *philosophical ignorance* is just that most of us, as human beings, exist in ignorance about most things having to do with knowledge in the propositional sense, and have successfully done so for millions of years. *Philosophical ignorance* is no different from *physiological ignorance* or *medical ignorance*. Nobody "knew" about recombinant DNA methods even as their cells were doing it. Cave dwellers did not "know" about immunology, even as their bodies successfully fought off invading germs. Just as most of us today do not know that our eyes are not windows, or that the theory of reality ("folk physics," "folk astronomy," "folk religion," "folk psychology," and so on,) that we absorbed and were taught growing up and now accept as reality is not reality but only a transparent theory (transparent because we do not see it as such).

The concept of philosophical ignorance is thus not a conspiratorial concept, nor is it merely a question of something lacking in us as functional human beings. We can and do function perfectly well in philosophical ignorance, just as we have evolved successfully to biologically dominate this entire planet both in philosophical and biological ignorance. It is the "illumination" of these processes within the sphere of conscious thought that involves the advent of the various disciplines of the knowledge-seeking enterprise, such as physics, physiology, chemistry, and so on. Philosophy is no exception. The *construction* of perceived reality is a process that precedes the advent of philosophy by millions, perhaps billions, of years; any animal that has a mental representational system has something like that going on within itself as a process. This is also true for the construction of beliefs, concepts, and so on. The *conscious human activity* of philosophy is in that sense like any other sphere of conscious human knowledge: it is the attempt to make perspicuous processes that are already functioning within us at some automatic (or at least nonconscious[4]) level. And *philosophical enlightenment,* as a conscious realization that, for instance, one's eyes are not windows and one's theory or belief system is not the same as reality, is but the making clear to one's self of an unclear process that is already going on at a preconscious or unconscious level of activity. Thus, it is making it *known* to one's self. It involves the organism becoming consciously aware of itself and of its own activities, as such, within its own representational system of the world, containing now a representation of itself and of the entire system.

Nowhere is the persistence of philosophical ignorance more clearly evident than in the supposed intellectual, scientific, and philosophical sea change from a geocentric view to a heliocentric view of the solar system. The shift from the religiously sanctioned geocentric view to the scientifically sanctioned heliocentric view merely passed the job of successfully implementing, *en masse,* philosophical ignorance from one system of authority to another. In fact, as we are about to discover, one reason why genuine philosophy must by its very nature exist in opposition to authority is that the *philosophical function* (but not a positive one) of authority is to force a single worldview onto the mind when real philosophy itself is the knowledge that no such single worldview is ever authentically possible. But these are just abstractions. To see this in concrete terms, let us now inquire into the origins of the idea that the earth goes around the sun and how and why the issue became so pivotal in the developments leading up to the truly *philosophical* revolution begun shortly thereafter by René Descartes—a revolution so profound that it is marked as the beginning of *modern* philosophy.

Plato's Homework Problem

We know where the idea that the earth does not move comes from. Our senses. It was Aristotle who formalized what we see when we look up into the sky, putting the apparent motions of the heavenly bodies into a coherent explanation of the surrounding cosmos. He took as his starting point the appearances (what we actually see when we look up at the night sky) and then extrapolated, or generalized, from these appearances. This was no simple feat. At the Academy, which Aristotle entered as a teenager (Section 3.0), Plato regularly assigned to his advanced students the following homework problem in philosophy: create a geometric pattern that accounts for and accurately predicts the observed motion of the sun, moon, and planets.

These motions are not nearly as regular as you might at first glance suppose. First, the sun has three different motions—its daily movement from east to west, its eastward movement against the background stars, and its yearly north-south motion which causes the change of seasons in the middle-northern and middle-southern latitudes (Figure 9.1). (You've probably noticed, if you live in the Northern Hemisphere, that the sun is higher in the sky in summer and lower in winter.) Any geometric pattern must show why the sun repeats these three motions exactly to return to any given position in slightly more than 365 days. The moon not only moves east to west nightly and eastward monthly, but also its

north-south motion is even greater than the sun's; in addition, it shows phases. Further, successive phases (such as the full moon) do not occur in the same place in the sky. Finally, what makes the problem especially difficult is the "retrograde motion" of the planets, a sudden *backward* loop that ancient astronomers had noted as early as 1900 B.C.E.

The five planets visible to the naked eye of the ancients move nightly east to west. During the year they slack off against the background stars in an eastwardly direction, just as the sun does. Their overall motion in the eastward relation is constant, but the individual retrograde motions in the western directions are different for each planet. Saturn is the slowest in its eastward movement, and it makes 28 retrogressive backward loops. Jupiter is faster and makes 11 retrogressive motions, about one every 200 earth days. Mercury is much faster and shows only 1 retrograde motion every 116 earth days. No wonder Plato placed this sign over the entrance to the Academy: "Let no one ignorant of mathematics enter here!"

Ancient astronomers kept extremely accurate records of all these apparent motions. Ancient philosophers, from Thales to Parmenides, from Pythagoras to Plato, all argued that the appearances—both in the sky and on the earth—are deceiving. Reality must be apprehended, if at all, through the inner light of reason. And the world that we intuit through reason is very different from the world as it appears to the senses. The world as it appears to the senses is highly irregular, constantly changing, and so on. But beneath (or beyond) the ephemeral appearances there is

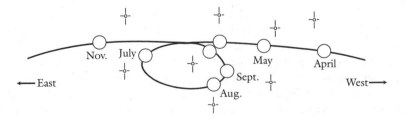

Figure 9.1

the permanent and well-ordered reality. But wait: where did *that* idea come from?

"The *world* that we *intuit* through *reason?*" *Which* world is that? Reason leads to many different views of the world; most of the ancient philosophers we studied made a very big point of that. So which alternative view (recall, for instance, the arguments of Protagoras) is the *real* view? The view, perhaps, that *fits* the world that we perceive through our senses? But, first—again, the ancient philosophers pointed this out time and again—there were always a multiplicity of "rational" views, that is, models based on intellectual intuitions or "arrived at" (derived) by logical reasoning. Some ancient philosophers, most notably Heraclitus and Democritus, believed that ultimate reality—the way the world really is—is the result of random chaos. They believed this not for religious reasons but based on what they took to be evidently sound reason and verified experience. Others, most notably Pythagoras and Plato, believed that ultimate reality is not just a haphazard, random chaos or even some irregular hodgepodge: the real world is continuous and balanced in its essential properties, ruled by order and reason. They believed this not for religious reasons (in fact, most of the religions at the time presented the gods as extremely volatile, irrational, and often very corrupt). They believed it based on what they knew about the nature of reason, logic, and especially mathematics, buttressed by what they also knew about the ephemeral and often illusory nature of experience.

Second, the *real* view is *not* reality, is it? It is only, at most, the *correct* view, meaning that it represents reality correctly. But then there is the additional problem of how we can know that it does. What do we check our view of reality against? One is tempted to say, "check it against reality," but the problem with that is that, again, we don't have direct access to reality but, at best, a *view*, a *perception*, or an *interpretation* of reality.

For the Platonists, the perceived irregularities observed in the sky thus posed an interesting philosophical problem. Looking up we see the whole rest of the universe, or at least a large portion of it. If the lawful regularities that the Platonic philosophers, under the influence of the Pythagorean mathematicians, believed to be the underlying clockwork, or operating system, of the cosmos, were not in evidence in our cosmic view of the heavens, then where? Hence, the motives for Plato's homework problem. Explain the irregularities seen in the appearances with some underlying, hidden regularities revealed to the mind's inner eye, "through a glass darkly," the *inner* light of reason, and you will know the true reality.

Several mathematical models were offered as explanations. Some at the Academy put the earth not at the center but moving around the sun. Others, most notably, Heraclides, had the earth rotating while the stars were stationary. Others had the sun revolving around the earth but the planets Mercury and Venus revolving around the sun. One of the best solutions to the problem was offered by Eudoxus (408–355 B.C.E.), who drew a series of homocentric spheres that each carried the sun, moon, planets, and stars around the earth. His model contained 27 perfect circles: 1 for the fixed stars, 3 each for the sun and moon, and 4 each for the 5 visible planets. By having each sphere move at a different rate in opposite directions, Eudoxus could account for just about all the observed motions. Aristotle added 22 more spheres. By doing so, he could make all "real" motions perfectly circular, perfectly uniform (all moving at exactly the same speed), and with the earth perfectly at the center. And, *for all practical purposes,* it worked!

We've encountered this sort of phenomenon before, with the Pythagorean response to "irrational ratios" such as the square root of 2. Recall how one group tried to suppress this by inventing increasingly more accurate fractional (but imperfect) representations *that worked for all practical purposes.* Another group tried to use the demonstration of the possibility that there are more numbers than all the numbers thus far known (the rationals) as a way to move from one then-currently accepted "theory of numbers" to a new theory of numbers that would contain the new "irrational numbers." But whereas in the case of the "discovery" of irrational numbers the rationalists won over the pragmatically minded "scientists," in the case of the alternative models of the solar system the Aristotelian pragmatists won over the Platonic rationalists. The universe in which they decided they lived was an Aristotle-inspired confabulation of "fudge factors," which *worked for all practical purposes.*

Small wonder Plato called Aristotle "the brain." Just try to do the same thing yourself, using all the advancements available in the subsequent 2,500 years of development. Use anything you want—drawing instruments, slide rules, calculators, computers—and see how far you get! In any case, what Aristotle presented was a system that accounted for the way things appear *and* explained away *all the apparent irregularities* using the tools of reason and mathematics to explain away the gaps, inconsistencies, and irregularities in our experience. *And Ptolemy (85–165) improved it until it worked so well that it was accepted as reality.*

You've heard it said that power corrupts, and absolute power corrupts absolutely. Well, in the case of knowledge, something like that is true too; knowledge corrupts *philosophically* and "absolute knowledge" (that is, the belief that one has it) corrupts *absolutely.* For the perfected model accounted for the appearances so perfectly well that it was forgotten that this was only a philosophical interpretation of reality, a model, a theory. In other words, like religion before and after, the science of the time *led to philosophical ignorance.*

Copernicus Versus Ptolemy

It would be grossly unfair to blame the church of the sixteenth century (or, indeed, of the preceding thousand years) for the existence of philosophical ignorance. As we've pointed out, philosophical ignorance is something we human beings inherited as part of our emergence into the cosmos. Nor would it be correct to suppose

that either religion or science *suppresses* philosophical activity as such (though they do tend to limit it, by way of the proliferation of systems of orthodoxy, to the select few). Indeed, one way of trying to understand what philosophy is, in the sense presented in this book, is this: philosophy is that activity which, in varying times, religion or science usually has under its employ and which, in brief periods and very rarely, is done by philosophers who are neither theologians nor scientists (though even these philosophers, too, tend to pledge allegiance to the religion or science of their time, often to both; the present century is no exception).

Up until the time of Copernicus and Galileo (1564–1642), what is generally called "religion" (in contrast to "science") but what really ought to be called "religious faith,"[5] contained philosophy in the following way. First, it was the social system, or structure, within which the practice of philosophy occurred. It was within the auspices of religion that philosophy was taught; its literature preserved; the rules, procedures, and innovations developed; and so on. Second, that's also where it was kept under control and supervision by a hierarchical structure of intellectual authority.[6]

Copernicus's work, and even that of Galileo, was part of a long tradition within the church-sanctioned philosophical activity of offering alternative explanations, or models, of reality that contained, in effect, the essence of what we have been calling philosophical enlightenment: the realization that eyes are not windows on reality, that our received theories (like *any* theories) are not reality. (Thus, *philosophical enlightenment* is the opposite of *philosophical ignorance*). To give but one paradigm, in the fourteenth century Nicole Oresme (1320–1382), a French bishop and Aristotelian scholar, used the hypothesis that the earth rotates to show that one cannot tell that the earth is still just by looking! Back then arguments had already begun to arise over whether one needed divinely inspired revelation to know the true nature of reality. Some developing "scientists" were beginning to make the claim that one could discover the truth by doing experiments. Thus, for instance, these fourteenth-century scientists (who were called "astrologers," "alchemists," and "diabolists") claimed to be able to prove that the earth is still by using the following procedure (Figure 9.2). Drop a rock from a high tower. If the earth moves, it will move out from under the rock. Thus, the rock will fall not on a perfectly perpendicular line with the earth and hit at *X,* it will fall slightly at an angle (as the earth moves out from under it) and hit at *X'.* But when we do this experiment, we see that the rock hits at *X,* not at *X'.* Therefore, we can indeed tell that the earth is not moving. Two points. First, the physics used here is that of Aristotle. It is the physics of commonsense appearances (remember: the Greek word for *physics* means *reality*). Aristotle had no concept of *inertia.* The puzzle that needed to be

explained, within his philosophy, was why things kept moving when there was no direct contact force. Everything in Aristotle's physics has its natural place. It is a teleological system where all things have a purpose, function, or essence. In today's post-Newtonian physics, which has adopted the concept of *inertia,* the puzzle that needs to be explained is not why things keep moving when there is no direct contact force but why they stop. Once pushed, why don't they keep going forever? We shall return to this point about the concept of inertia in a moment. Second, lest you think the Aristotelian perspective unduly ignorant, keep in mind that most people today accept it quite readily (again, as with the Ptolemaic system, because it accords with experience). Consider, for instance, what happens on the popular science fiction series *Star Trek* when the spaceship Enterprise, flying through outer space, runs out of fuel. It stops!

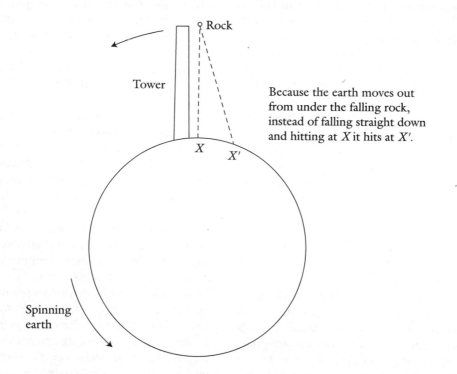

Figure 9.2

The engineer has to scuttle to fix the engines. But why did the spaceship grind to a halt? When astronauts fly to the moon, once they have propelled themselves in the right direction, they use the rockets only to steer themselves into moon orbit, to break orbit, and so on; the rest of the time the ship does not need to be pushed. It is being carried along by *inertia*. So the Enterprise should keep on going when it runs out of fuel. But it doesn't. It stops. Because it is conceived within an Aristotelian universe.

So where did our concept of inertia come from? We return once more to our fourteenth-century bishop, Oresme, who invented the concept (he called it "impetus") *as a fictional force*. No one at the time took it seriously as a *real* force because it is completely invisible and you cannot see it directly; you would know it only (if at all) by its *effects*. So if there were such invisible forces, Oresme argued, the moving earth could impart an "impetus" onto the rock while it was in contact with the hand holding it at the top of the tower, and this impetus kept the rock moving at the same rate as the earth. Thus, the rock would hit at X, not at X', exactly as observed (Figure 9.3 on page 204). So *you can't determine the truth just by doing the experiment.* You need something called "divine revelation," given only to the great initiates of the church. They reveal that the truth is that there are no invisible forces. (Why would God trick us like that?) And the earth is exactly as it appears to us to be. Motionless.

Galileo would take this invented concept of "impetus" and use it within his own theory to his own ends. But that's another story. The point we are focusing on at present is that what Copernicus and Galileo did as philosopher-mathematician-scientists under the employ of the church was to generate alternative hypotheses and theories. The authoritarian hierarchy of the church picked its official line from the various philosophical alternatives and then enforced it. Part of the *reasoning* (or perhaps it was only *rationalization*) on the part of the philosophers in high position under church employ was that the general public needed the security of a *resolved reality*. The mind of the public could not tolerate the metaphysical ambiguity that is the sum and substance of true philosophy. Ambiguity, indecision, the unknown— all are socially disruptive. Hence, philosophy was kept under lock and key.

No one knows the real reason for the shift in power over the intellectual universe from church authority to secular authority, nor is this the place to try to do such philosophical anthropology, interesting and revealing though it may be. What is most important for our purposes is to realize that the shift from the religiously enforced Ptolemaic universe to a scientifically enforced Copernican one was not really a *philosophical* shift at all. Philosophical "shifts" are what we are trying to become aware of through the works of the great philosophers in this book. The transition from church authority to secular authority was merely the replacement of one theory as the true picture of reality for another. This is not philosophy at all. This is, in both cases, the enforcement of philosophical ignorance through the displacement of alternative views by an intellectual authority—in the one case, the authority of religion and, in the other, the authority of science. Without the authority you are back in the anti-authoritarian universe of enlightened unknowing, better known as Socratic philosophy, the love of wisdom. The deep philosophical irony is that then you are back in a state of nature, where philosophical ignorance is par for the course except for unexplained, mysterious enlightened individuals who are not *made* but born, much in the way that Augustine imagined was the case with salvation. In that case, as Socrates taught (paradoxically), philosophy cannot really be taught at all. It must just happen, like everything else. Or not. To try to teach it would be as mistaken and as great a fall from the true way as other artificial ways in which the conscious ego tries to usurp reality to its own means and ends. And when one realizes that the conscious ego is more an effect than a cause, as we shall see many subsequent philosophers take great pains to show, we are back full

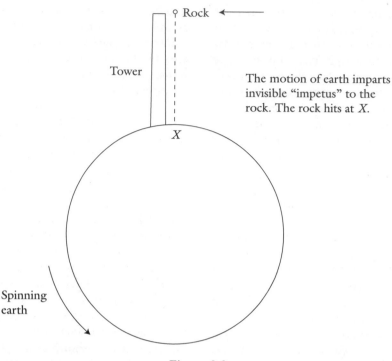

Figure 9.3

circle to the doubly paradoxical philosophical standpoint of having painted ourselves into a corner from which no movement is possible. We shall return to such perplexing puzzles in due course. Let us return for now to the specific issues at hand.

Before Copernicus, Kepler, and Galileo, the single picture of the earth according to the official church doctrine, which answered in an absolutely incontrovertible way the ultimately unanswerable question—*which way is it really going*, was that the earth does not move, period. What you see (when you look up) is what you get: that's the way it really is. There is always an alternative view available; alternative pictures were on display in the secret church gallery for those who would not be driven mad by their confusing sights, in which that which one sees is *not* true, but then one is confused, unknowing, lost in uncertainty. Thus, the one truth is selected from among the many truths through

"revelation." It is as if God gets us out of the eternal purgatory that is philosophy by telling us what we cannot otherwise know. (Notice that this intellectual "evolution" seems to have been experienced, within one individual, in the mind of Plato as he shifted from a Socratic state of unknowing to his view of certainty through understanding of the forms.)

Since the time of Copernicus, Kepler, and Galileo, what is generally called "science," but what ought really to be called "scientific faith,"[7] the single picture of the earth according to the official scientific doctrine that answers in an absolutely incontrovertible way the ultimately unanswerable question—*which way is it really going*—is that the earth moves. That's the answer, the only true and correct answer. And now even the secret gallery is no more! We do not need God to identify for us the *one* "true" truth among the many "truths." We have no more need for the alternative pictures because we now know them, thanks to science, to be *false* pictures. And we know this in an absolutely incontrovertible way, through "experiment," "evidence," and "reason." The Oresmes and Copernicuses, the philosophers—the painters of alternative pictures—are no longer needed.

That is the true philosophical irony. It is as if the ultimate seduction away from philosophy is not the naive "eyes are windows" perspective on reality. *It is the sophisticated "paintings (theories) are not just pictures (theories)" perspective on reality.* In other words, in the view of philosophy that we are developing, the true lover of wisdom is never seduced through the power of our renditions of reality—the "paintings" that the great works of philosophy are—into mistaking the art for the real thing.

Thus, ultimately, the world according to the secular intellectual authority of science is very much the same world as that of the religious authority of theology: it is a one true reality that is accessible directly, somehow, by our renderings of it. The difference between the religious picture (theory) and the scientific picture (theory) is in the nature of the connection to reality (through revelation, reason, experience, and so on). According to philosophy *the world* is not really a *world* at all, in the sense of being the one true reality. What we call the "world" exists only in our philosophy. That is not to say that there is no real world. It is just to say that one cannot get to it without philosophy. And philosophy consists, within the conscious sphere, in *philosophical enlightenment.* This means that the philosopher must always keep in mind that the world is not a given thing, it is not a mind-independent reality accessible in *any* way whatsoever. The world is, rather, something created through the activity of mind. But, again, that is *not* to say that idealism is true! It is merely to say, at most, that we don't have any direct and immediate access to the world as such but only to our pictures of the world, to our theories, and to our perceptions, which are themselves reconstructions of reality and not a passive receptacle of the truth.[8] The ultimate truth in philosophy—and this is as hard

to admit as it is to swallow—is that the world is always an uncertainty, an approximation to the truth; it is *my* world. According to church canons, the pope, speaking as the pope, has the right of infallibility. By virtue of the knowledge that any world in which there is no need for philosophy is but a fictional world, the philosopher has the *duty of fallibility.* That is, once again, in philosophy *neither experience nor theory is taken to be the avatar of reality.* The philosopher is alone. Ultimately, the philosopher knows not only what he does not know but also that which he does not *want* to know, that the world to which the mind has access (and it may be the *only* world, *in which case* idealism is true) in some ultimate sense is of "his own" making. Except this truth is almost unbearable because he is not the constructor, the dreamer, but part of the construction, the picture, the dream. The philosopher lives as a figment in the philosopher's own imagination, in utter aloneness. There is no reward in that. It is impractical. Unthinkable.

Yet the philosopher keeps thinking the unthinkable. Nevertheless, the temptation is always there, *real* temptation, the *temptation of the real.* So seductive is the world of appearance, our manifold of perception, that one can only through elaborate theory, argument, or experiential analysis of experience force one's self to accept the first and most fundamental philosophical insight, that our eyes are not windows. And so doubly seductive is the world of theory, our storehouse of concepts that both generate and then interpret our manifold of perceptive experience, that we do not even realize that the world, which in our naive imaginations we think our eyes open into, is but a world created by our elaborate, received theories! It is only the theories that are not being used at the moment to structure our experience that can, with great effort, be understood for what they are, how they work, and how they arise. (In a very important sense, theories too are no more invented by theoreticians than languages such as English or German were invented by their language users.) The power afforded by theory, especially a theory that for a time at least works better than any other, is tremendous. The temptation to be seduced is overpowering.

Copernicus seemed well aware that his heliocentric view was but an alternative account of how things appear to the senses, as described in the received Ptolemaic theory. In the telling preface to his *On the Revolutions of the Heavenly Spheres*,[9] he writes,

⚒

I may well presume, most Holy Father, that certain people, as soon as they hear that in this book I ascribe movement to the earthly globe, will cry out that, holding such views, I should at once be hissed off the stage. . . . That I allow the publication of these my studies may surprise your Holiness the less in that, having been at such travail to attain them, I had already not scrupled to commit to writing my thoughts upon the motion of the Earth. How I came to dare to conceive such motion of the Earth, contrary to the received opinion of the Mathematicians and indeed contrary to the impression of the senses, is what your Holiness will rather expect to hear. So I should like your Holiness to know that I was induced to think of a method of computing the motions of the spheres by nothing else than the knowledge that the Mathematicians are inconsistent in these investigations.

For, first, the Mathematicians are so unsure of the movements of the Sun and Moon that they cannot even explain or observe the constant length of the seasonal year. Secondly, in determining the motions of these and of the five other planets, they do not even use the same principles and hypotheses as in their proofs of seeming revolutions and motions.

⚒

Thus, it seems, Copernicus was not seduced by the heliocentric model into mistaking a theory for reality. He did not succumb to the tempta-

tion. But Kepler so improved the theory that, finally, Galileo did.

9.1 From the Religious Authority of the Church to the Secular Authority of Science

One thing we do know about the origin of Copernicus's model of the solar system is that his basic picture was already rendered two thousand years earlier by Aristarchus of Samos, the so-called Copernicus of antiquity. He, in the middle of the third century B.C.E., had proposed, in answer to the question posed by Plato's homework problem, a sun-centered model of the solar system. Copernicus had come across it in his translations of the works of Aristotle and had at first rejected it as absurd, not because he dogmatically believed in whatever the church said about the solar system, but because it flew against the senses and against the elaborate reasonings of the mathematician-astronomers. He at first rejected the viability of the heliocentric view for the same reason that most people did. As the contemporary philosopher and historian of science, Thomas Kuhn, notes in *The Copernican Revolution*:

⚒

The reasons for the rejection were excellent. These alternative cosmologies violate the first and most fundamental suggestions provided by the senses about the structure of the universe. Furthermore, this violation of common sense is not compensated for by any increase in the effectiveness with which they account for the appearances. At best they are no more economical, fruitful, or precise than the two-sphere universe, and they are a great deal harder to believe. . . .

─────────────

From Nicholas Copernicus, *On the Revolutions of the Heavenly Spheres*, A. M. Duncan, trans. (New York: Barnes and Noble, 1976).

─────────────

Thomas S. Kuhn, *The Copernican Revolution: Planetary Astronomy in the Development of Western Thought* (Cambridge, MA: Harvard University Press, 1957).

All of these alternative cosmologies take the motion of the earth as a premise, and all (except Heraclides' system) make the earth move as one of a number of heavenly bodies. But the first distinction suggested by the senses is that separating the earth and the heavens. The earth is not part of the heavens; it is the platform from which we view them. And the platform shares few or no apparent characteristics with the celestial bodies seen from it. The heavenly bodies seem bright points of light, the earth an immense nonluminous sphere of mud and rock. Little change is observed in the heavens: the stars are the same night after night. . . . In contrast the earth is the home of birth and change and destruction. . . . It seems absurd to make the earth like celestial bodies whose most prominent characteristic is that immutable regularity never to be achieved on the corruptible earth.

The idea that the earth moves seems initially equally absurd. Our *senses* tell us all we know of motion, and they indicate no motion for the earth. Until it is reeducated, common sense tells us that, if the earth is in motion, then the air, clouds, birds, and other objects not attached to the earth must be left behind. A man jumping would descend to the earth far from the point where his leap began, for the earth would move beneath him while he was in the air. Rocks and trees, cows and men must be hurled from a rotating earth as a stone flies from a rotating sling. Since none of these effects is seen, the earth is at rest. . . . The Greeks could only rely on observation and reason, and neither produced evidence for the earth's motion. Without the aid of telescopes or of elaborate mathematical arguments that have no apparent relation to astronomy, no effective evidence for a moving planetary earth can be produced. The observations available to the naked eye fit the two-sphere universe very well (remember the universe of the practical navigator and surveyor), and there is no more natural explanation of them. It is not hard to realize why the ancients believed in the two-sphere universe. The problem is to discover why the conception was given up.

※

The Copernican hypothesis was no more based on *observation* than was the atomic hypothesis of Democritus (Section 1.9).

Remember: just as Democritus, who came up with the idea of the atom, had no microscope, Copernicus, who came up with the idea of the solar system as such, had no telescope. So where, then, did such an idea come from, and why was it accepted as the one "true" truth about the solar system over the previously one "true" view?

Well, in terms of where such ideas—or, in fact, *any* ideas—come from, all we can say at this point is that we don't really know where they come from, any more than we know where reality comes from. Indeed, we can no more explain how theories come about than we can explain how languages come about. Part of the problem, as we shall see when we explore the developments in the philosophy of language in the twentieth century, is that we are already involved in using a language (and, likewise, a theory) when we begin such a process of analysis, and this affects how far we can get. Thus, in answer to the question, "Where do such ideas come from?" we must admit, perhaps with some embarrassment, that in many ways the concept that most seems to fit is that of "revelation!"

But there is much more to it than that. This question is often asked by philosophers as, "Is there a logic of discovery?" To suppose "yes" is to suppose that there is some definite way in which the mind is forced (that is, the *logic* of discovery) to think, hypothesize, deduce, infer, extrapolate, and so on, along some more-or-less linear path toward an ever-improving approximation of the truth. This would make philosophy, as such, eventually unnecessary—a view that has been held by many philosophers. In my view, such philosophers have succumbed to the seduction we previously discussed—the same seduction as imposed by religion and by science. In any case, the actual history of science does not fare well for this popular scientific view of the knowledge-seeking enterprise, so closely tied to the popular philosophical view, as we are about to see. This popular misconception is related to the second aspect of our question as to why the

Ptolemaic view was rejected in favor of the Copernican. The commonly accepted belief, part of the scientific mythology surrounding the Copernican "revolution," is that Copernicus's idea was an improvement over the previous model—that it works better and is more accurate. But this is just not true. Let us see why.

Aristotle's original conception was further improved by the Alexandrine mathematician, philosopher, and astronomer Claudius Ptolemy (85–165 C.E.), who applied to it an extended version of the epicycle-deferent system first developed by Apollonius (third century B.C.E.) and Hipparchus (190–120 B.C.E.). (See Figure 9.4.)

We should note at this point that one leading criticism from the start of this system of epicycles and deferents—made even before Ptolemy's application—was that a planet is carried in its eastward motion by the deferent (the large circle), the actual planet revolves along the epicycle (the smaller circle), and there is *no actual (physical) object at the center of the epicycle*. There is only a mathematical point. This is extremely important, given that Galileo's "improvement" of the Copernican heliocentric system *also* does not put the sun

exactly at the center (as it is according to commonly accepted beliefs) but off to one side (the path of the planets becomes an ellipse, with once again *nothing* but a mathematical point strictly in the center). In any case, Ptolemy added two additional curves, *eccentrics* and *equants*, to the epicycles and deferents invented by Apollonius and Hipparchus. By using eccentric circles he displaced the earth slightly off the center of a circle, and the central point was placed on a circular orbit revolving around the earth (Figure 9.5). In that way a planet revolved on an epicycle around a central point on yet another circle, which revolved around a center, which revolved around the earth. The equant made the motion of the planets uniform, relative not to the center of the earth but to a displaced point. This was so accurate in accounting for and predicting the motions of the sun, moon, and planets that in fact the U.S. Coast Guard still uses it because the calculations are simpler and more precise than the Copernican-based model as improved by Galileo. The overall system looked like Figure 9.5.

Figure 9.6 details the earth's equant point.

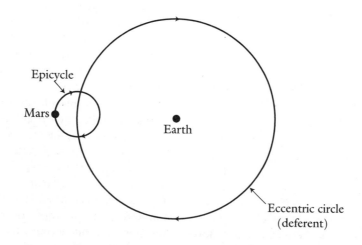

Figure 9.4

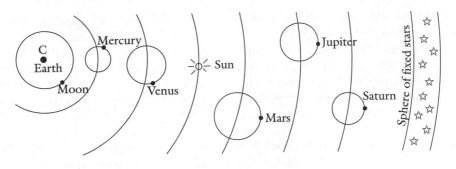

Figure 9.5

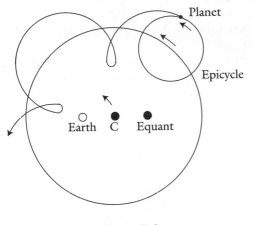

Figure 9.6

In the words of Thomas Kuhn,

🌿

Ptolemy's contribution is the outstanding one, and this entire technique of resolving the problem of the planets is appropriately known by his name, because it was Ptolemy who first put together a particular set of compounded circles to account . . . for the observed quantitative regularities and irregularities in the apparent motions of all the seven planets (Sun, Moon, and five planets). His *Algamest,* the book that epitomizes the greatest achievement of ancient astronomy, was the first systematic mathematical treatise to give a *complete, detailed,* and quantitative account of all the celestial motions. . . . For its subtlety, flexibility, complexity, and power the epicycle-deferent technique . . . has no parallel in the history of science until quite recent times. In its most developed form the system of compounded circles was an astounding achievement.

🌿

So why then was Ptolemy's view given up in favor of Copernicus's? Another prevalent idea today is that with our modern telescopes and with our spaceships that go to the moon, we are in a much more secure position than the people of the sixteenth century, who were thrown into such turmoil by the Copernican hypothesis. Surely, we need not be troubled with the question of whether Ptolemy or Copernicus is right, of whether the sun goes around the earth or the earth goes around the sun! Well, let us see.

How did *you* come to believe that the earth goes around the sun? Nineteenth-century schoolhouses in the United States had ominous signs over the blackboard which read, "Fear God!" Religious pictures, such as scenes from heaven, various saints, and the hierarchy of the angels, were not uncommon in nearly every school across the country. These religious icons have since been replaced with pictures of great scientists like Albert Einstein, Thomas Edison, Madame Curie, George Washington Carver, and so on, and various charts such as the hierarchy of the elements. And what elementary school classroom today does not have at least one picture of

From Thomas Kuhn, *The Copernican Revolution.*

the solar system, with the sun at the center and all the planets revolving around the sun?

Probably it was some such image that introduced you to the Copernican-based heliocentric view of the solar system. How convenient for the teacher in charge of indoctrinating you with this belief; all she had to do was point to the great mural on the wall and say, "There . . . *see?*" This pointing is just a ritual that simplifies having to go outside, and it demonstrates how in fact this is known to be true, right? Because, in principle, one could go outside and verify this, right? One just doesn't have to, right?

After all, can't we, in principle, go outside and look directly at the solar system and *see* whether the earth goes around the sun or the sun goes around the earth? Probably you believe some scientist must have had some such experience, or else surely this view would not be so widely disseminated with such absolute authority. Galileo must have looked in his telescope, an astronaut must have looked out the window, or *something*. Surely, somebody must have actually looked and seen the great truth that the greats, like Copernicus and Galileo, discovered—namely, that the earth indeed can be observed to move and to go around the sun.

Well, but let's think about it. Could we, if we wanted to and had all our technology at our disposal, go and *see* whether the sun goes around the earth or the earth goes around the sun? Of course, it would be silly and we'd be laughed at if we actually went to anyone, doubting what everybody obviously knows, and said we just want to see for ourselves. It would be like going to pull on Santa's beard in the department store to try to verify whether that is the real Santa. You'd have to be a little crazy to do it. So let's be a little crazy—even though we're all certain that the earth has been seen by somebody to move around the sun. Let's doubt the obvious; let's pretend we really are crazy enough to doubt what is so obviously true. How could we see the truth for ourselves? Science, after all, is based on experience. Surely the empirical method will allow us to see that the earth goes around the sun.

We step outside and look up. What do we see? The sun rises, then sets. The moon rises, then sets. The stars move across the heavens . . . so far, everything seems to be moving around the earth. Not very convincing for the sun-centered view! We had better go up in a spaceship.

We go to Florida, we get in a rocket, and we lift off. We go straight up until we are in a synchronous orbit around the earth. Many satellites are in such a synchronous orbit, meaning that (according to the heliocentric theory) they move at the same speed that the earth revolves, thus remaining in the same position over the earth. Like tall radio and television towers, these satellites are used to bounce signals from one side of the earth to the other.

Now, inside our spaceship, looking down from our synchronous orbit, what do we see? Below us is the earth, with the Florida coastline visible beneath a layer of clouds. The earth is perfectly motionless. We look up. The sun, the moon, all the planets, and all the stars are seen to move around the earth!

Well, of course, we are in earth's reference frame. It's like being on a moving train; throw a coin up in the air. It doesn't just fly away and smash against the back wall because the momentum of the train has been imparted to the coin. If the train is moving 70 miles an hour westward, the coin is moving 70 miles an hour westward and continues to do so even when you toss it up; that's why it lands back down in your hand, which also is moving 70 miles an hour westward.

So, obviously, up in our spaceship above the earth, what we must do is start moving about. We fire our thrusters and start orbiting the earth. We look up. What do we see? The sun, the moon, and all the stars—*still going about the spinning earth below.* Well, obviously, then, to see with our own eyes what the *real* movement of the solar system is, we must leave earth's reference frame and go to the sun. We fire our thrusters and retrorockets and fly away until we are in a synchronous orbit around the sun (the air conditioning is very good). What do we see?

Lo and behold, we now see the sun perfectly

still beneath us and all the planets and stars moving about the sun. Finally! Copernicus and Galileo vindicated! But hold on. We now fly to Mars. From our orbit around Mars, what do we see? Earth, the other planets, the sun, and all the stars revolving around Mars. So Mars is at the center. No, wait . . . What is going on?

Well, the truth must then be this: whatever reference point in the solar system you're looking from, that place will seem to be still and everything else will seem to be moving around it. But what, then, are the *true* motions of the planets and the sun? Do they even have a *true* motion in some absolute sense? Even if they did, *you can't—even in principle—see it just by looking.*

We are now in a position to understand the true *philosophical* nature and significance of the revolutionary developments that helped contribute to the advent of modern philosophy. The real philosophical shock of the Copernican-Galilean model was that *there is no way to discover, just by looking, what the truth is about a simple, basic fact such as whether the earth goes around the sun or the sun goes around the earth.*

In other words, the problem wasn't that, at the time, you couldn't go up to have a look—as some scientists and historians today may have led you to believe (and may even themselves, wrongly, believe to be the case). The problem wasn't that back then people didn't have airplanes and spaceships. We can go up and look all we want! The problem is that looking doesn't settle it: there is no position in the universe from which to look.

You might think the problem is that what really is needed is a better vantage point. We would have to leave the solar system. All right, well, let's lift off from Florida and never stop; we just keep going up, up, up . . . finally, we're beyond the orbit of Pluto. We look back at earth. What do we see?

We see the earth as a stationary dot, and all the other planets, including the sun and the stars, revolving around the earth! Unless we shifted our reference frame to some other position—say, Alpha Centauri, which then will be the one and

only still object in the whole cosmos—our point of view will remain locked into the earth's position and everything else will be seen to move around that point. Indeed, as Einstein showed, there is no absolute vantage point in the universe where we could stand to see what the "true" motions of anything are. (That is why his picture is in all the schools.) The only absolute thing about motion is that it is relative.

At this point, one is apt to wonder: well, how then did we ever come to accept the Copernican picture as the one true view in preference to the Ptolemaic view? As already explained, the most commonly accepted answer—that the Copernican model is the more accurate—is simply false. The next most widely accepted answer is that Copernicus's system is the simpler and more elegant of the two and should therefore be preferred on grounds of simplicity. But that, too, is false. Either system can get you just as well from the earth to the moon. As already mentioned, not only does the U.S. Coast Guard still use Ptolemaic calculations because they are simpler, it is not even clear *which system uses fewer epicycles!* What, you say? That's preposterous! Isn't Ptolemy's system the ugly one with all the crazy epicycles?

Here once again the popular myth turns out to be false. Not just because Copernicus's system also had epicycles. Because the best scientific, historical, and philosophical experts, the great knowers who have access to and have studied the actual scientific documents, cannot even agree as to who had how many! Let's check a few sources and see, for ourselves, what the experts actually do say:

"Copernicus reduced the number of epicycles from 80 to 34." [Burtt, *Metaphysical Foundations of Modern Science*]

"Copernicus uses altogether 48 epicycles—if I counted them correctly . . . Brought up to date by Peurbach in the 15th century, the number of circles required in the Ptolemaic system was not 80, as Copernicus said, but 40. In other words, contrary to popular, and even academic belief, Copernicus did not reduce the number of circles, but increased them (from 40 to 48)" [Koestler *The Sleepwalkers*]

"[Copernicus's] full system was little if any less cumbersome than Ptolemy's had been. Both employed over thirty circles; there was little to choose between them in economy." [Kuhn, *The Copernican Revolution*]

"[Copernicus] used 34." [Crombie, *Ancient and Medieval Science*]

"Copernicus reduced the number of circles required to explain the movements of the heavens from the 80 or so used in the elaborate versions of the Ptolemaic system to 48." [Mason, *History of Science*]

"Copernicus used 17 epicycles." [Margenau, *The Nature of Physical Reality*]

"Copernicus used 80 epicycles." [Harre, *The Anticipation of Nature*]

"Copernicus used no epicycles." [Bohm, *The Special Theory of Relativity*]

"[Copernicus] used 40, as opposed to 240 for Ptolemy." [Motz and Duveen, *Essentials of Astronomy*]

"Copernicus succeeded in reducing by more than half the number of arbitrary circular motions which Ptolemy had been obliged to postulate." [Armitage, *Copernicus*]

"The introduction of the revolution of the earth about the sun never managed to do away with more than five epicycles." [Dijksterhuis, *The Mechanization of the World Picture*]

"Copernicus used no epicycles." [Kaplan, "Sociology Learns the Language of Mathematics" in Wiener, *Readings in the Philosophy of Science*]

May I please have the envelope? And . . . the winner is:

"The popular belief that Copernicus' heliocentric system constitutes a significant simplification of the Ptolemaic system is *obviously* wrong. . . . The Copernican models themselves require about twice as many circles as

the Ptolemaic models and are far less elegant and adaptable." [Neugebauer, *The Exact Sciences in Antiquity,* my emphasis]

Really reinforces your faith in science and history, doesn't it? But look: we're not talking here about superstring theory, quantum electrodynamics, wormholes, virtual vacuum fluctuations, the many-worlds interpretation of quantum mechanics—to mention but a few of some of the latest "scientific sobrieties"—that help science to "see the truth." We're talking about something as simple and supposedly as incontrovertible as whether the earth goes around the sun or the sun goes around the earth—a question of "brute scientific fact" supposedly settled centuries ago and taught to school children as "straightforward, scientific facts" that were settled centuries ago in a land far, far away . . .

Right now, at this moment, do you have an answer to the puzzling, perhaps even disturbing, questions presently being raised? Probably you don't. Are you going to rush to the library to examine the preceding sources or even the originals? You probably won't, any more than you'll pull on Santa's beard next time you see him at the mall. You might repeat what you've just read without checking any of it. Even if you did go look up the sources would your feeling of certainty change? Hasn't it been so indoctrinated into you, the "scientific facts" so driven into your mind by persuasive authorities, that questioning such "obvious" and "incontrovertible" facts as the movement of the earth seems ultimately preposterous, a waste of time, perhaps a bit like intellectual blasphemy?

Small wonder some critics of science, such as the philosopher Paul Feyerabend, have remarked:

⚓

How to Defend Society Against Science

Scientific "facts" are taught at a very early age and in the very same manner in which religious "facts" were taught only a century ago. There is no attempt to waken the critical abilities of the pupil so that he may be able to see things in perspective. At the universities the situation is even worse, for indoctrination is here carried out in a much more systematic manner. Criticism is not entirely absent. Society, for example, and its institutions, are criticized most severely and often most unfairly and this already at the elementary school level. But science is excepted from this criticism. In society at large the judgment of bishops and cardinals was accepted not too long ago. The move towards "demythologization," for example, is largely motivated by the wish to avoid any clash between Christianity and scientific ideas. If such a clash occurs, then science is certainly right and Christianity wrong. Pursue this investigation further and you will see that science has now become as oppressive as the ideologies it had once to fight.*

⚹

We are finally in a position to understand what the real "Copernican revolution" was about. In and of itself, Copernicus's demonstration that one cannot tell, just by looking at the appearances, what is really going on in the universe around us, was *not* a new development. To show how it is possible that everything we see around us is not reality and that the world is not necessarily the way it appears, and that everything we think might be wrong in such a way that we wouldn't or couldn't *know that,* is not even merely a return to early Socratic Platonism; it is the starting point of any good philosophy.

Indeed, it is extremely interesting to note that Giordano Bruno, whose death at the stake for heresy brought in the century of Descartes, criticized the "new scientists" of the time who were beginning to claim—contrary to Copernicus's own disclaimer in his preface—that the Copernican picture could be known to be true

with absolute certainty on grounds of mathematical "simplicity and elegance." Bruno had conceived of an infinity of possible worlds that could be grasped in their entirety neither through reason nor empiricism; one could only "with magic and divine rites . . . ascended to . . . the divinity by that same scale of nature by which the divinity descends to the smallest things by the communication of itself." (It was *this* that got Bruno in so much trouble with the church, for in his view each individual human being was, in a sense, the direct emanation of God and could know truth directly through connection to God rather than through the socially sanctioned authority of the church.)

The popular myth surrounding the "Copernican revolution" is mostly fiction. Like most myths, it serves mainly a social function—in this case, to redirect people's faith from the external authority of religion to the external authority of science *at the expense of the awareness that our eyes are not windows and that our theories are not reality.* The real Copernican revolution was not about the disproof of a religious hypothesis in favor of a scientific hypothesis, as you may have been led to believe, but the replacing of a view based primarily on an Aristotelian philosophy with a new view based primarily on a Platonic philosophy *with no clear way of distinguishing which, if either, view, was the true view.* It was no less than the beginning of the reawakening, after the thousand-year night, of the realization that we live not just in a universe but also inside a *philosophy.*

Plato's sun had begun once more to rise. Descartes would soon awaken to the second dawn. The modern era was about to begin.

9.2 Thomas Hobbes (1588–1679): Materialism, the New Science, and the Quest for Secular Ethics

One of the first philosophers who tried to develop a complete system of thought based on the new mechanical view of nature emerging

---

*Paul Feyerabend, "How to Defend Society Against Science," in Kolak and Martin, eds., *Self, Cosmos, God* (Fort Worth: Harcourt Brace Jovanovich, 1992).

from the Copernican-Galilean revolution was Thomas Hobbes (1588–1679). He was a forty-two year old at the time, struggling but failing to make sense of all the disagreements among the philosophers and the different systems developed by the various schools. In the library he happened to come across a book—Euclid's *Elements*—that someone had left open to the page showing the proof of the Pythagorean theorem, much like the one in this book (see pp. 31–41). The theorem struck him as probably false and certainly undemonstrable. Incredulous, he followed the proof to its inexorable conclusion. He realized, in a flash of insight, the obvious connection between geometry and the Copernican revolution. Geometry, in Galileo's words, had achieved "a rape of the senses" to pierce the veil of illusion, to move the mind beyond the realm of appearance, to show what cannot be seen. Profoundly moved by seeing how the power of reason could attain such absolute certainty, not only in geometry but to provide knowledge about the world, Hobbes began thinking about how—and whether—one could achieve the same level of certainty within philosophy.

Hobbes was born near Malmesbury, England. His father, the vicar of Westport and Charlton, enrolled him in the church school at Westport at the age of four, intending for his son to follow in his footsteps. A few years later his father got into a vicious fight at the church door and then disappeared, leaving his three children to be brought up by his uncle, a glover in Malmesbury. When Hobbes turned fourteen, his uncle sent him to Magden Hall of Oxford University. Bored and even repulsed by the prevailing Oxfordian scholasticism, Hobbes spent most of his time reading travel books and studying charts and maps.

The event described above—his epiphany with geometry—was the culmination of a series of gradual awakenings to philosophy. The first of these occurred after he graduated at the age of twenty, when he was hired by the noble Cavendish family as a sort of travel companion

and tutor to a young man only a few years his junior, William Cavendish, who would later become the second earl of Devonshire. The two took the opportunity to travel throughout continental Europe, and there Hobbes was surprised to find himself defending the Oxfordian philosophy which, much to his surprise, was treated with great contempt, especially by the French, Germans, and Italians. This contempt inspired him, upon their return, to study more carefully the philosophy which had not in the least bit stirred his interest earlier.

The second event came as a stroke of luck when between 1622 and 1625 he was hired by Francis Bacon to transcribe his lectures and oral notes and to translate some of his essays into Latin. Thus, although he was already in his late thirties, by coincidence and almost without his own will he happened to become a personal student of one of the greatest living philosophers of the time. This association further stoked his growing interest in philosophy and science that culminated with the third event, described above, of his discovery of geometry at the age of forty-two.

Armed with an avid aversion to the religiously tainted views of his immediate philosophical predecessors and a mathematical model of knowledge, Hobbes set out to purge philosophy of its scholastic influence and to develop a method for attaining absolutely certain knowledge to which end all the subsequent modern philosophers aspired.

Hobbes tried to understand the world in its entirety and as a unity. What perplexed him most of all is this: if the world is ultimately all one substance, how can there ever be a distinction between one thing and another? How can there even be perception (in addition to the thing perceived)?

It is with this burning question that Hobbes approached the leading thinkers of the time. His support from the Cavendish family continued after William died, and Hobbes became tutor to William Cavendish Jr., whom he took on a prolonged trip to France and Italy. During this trip he met with Marin Mersenne's circle in Paris, and in Florence he visited Galileo. Impressed by Galileo's mechanics, he saw in his method a key to developing a new mechanical philosophy. Especially influential at the time was Galileo's distinction between constant and accelerated motion as a replacement of the Aristotelean paradigm of motion versus rest. Whereas for Aristotle rest was simply the fulfillment of an object's natural inclination or goal (teleology), for Galileo rest was but the limiting case of motion, which means that there is no absolute center to the universe, no natural state of things, no "essence" required to explain why everything is as it is. There are just matter and motion to be explained, not in terms of final causes or essences, as in Aristotle's system, but purely mechanically. Hobbes took this model and applied it not just to nature but to the human mind itself.

According to Hobbes everything can be explained in terms of the motion of bodies, from sense perception to the imagination. Yet unlike the experimental scientists of the time, Hobbes was moved by his insights into geometry to develop a purely a priori, mathematical system that was in sharp contrast with the prevailing inductive approaches based on the methods of Francis Bacon. IIc thus formulated the major philosophical insight that would propel his thinking on all subjects for the rest of his life— namely, that all things must be understood just as the ancient Greek Democritus had once supposed, in terms of bodies in motion. He embarked on a philosophical trilogy that would explain everything. In *De corpore* he would show that all physical phenomena could be explained using geometry and mechanics. In *De homine* he would show that specific bodily motions were the specific causes of all human mental activity, including thinking and willing. In *De cive* he would explain how the ideal human society should be formed and sustained to be in harmony with the way the world is.

Upon his return to England, however, he found that instead of embarking on his philo-

sophical quest he had to deal with the political turmoil of civil war. Having just turned fifty, he thought he should give up his philosophical dream and help his country, and so he used his knowledge and growing influence to heal the two sides that had begun to fight over the divine right of kings versus the rule of constitutional government. His views, however, ended up antagonizing both sides; those loyal to the king saw him as a traitor for arguing that the sovereignty of law ought to be based on the social contract, whereas the parliamentarians were threatened by his advocacy of the rule of many by one single individual. In 1440 he was thus forced to flee to Paris, and during the next 11 years spent in exile he not only began work on his trilogy but also joined the Mersenne circle where, by lucky coincidence, there happened to be circulating a new and unpublished work that would become one of the most influential documents in the history of philosophy, the *Meditations* by none other then René Descartes (Chapter 10). Hobbes wrote brilliant objections to the *Meditations*. The work looked to him so derivative of Plato that his first response was to say, "I am sorry that so excellent an author of new speculations should publish this old stuff." Descartes published all of Hobbes's objections, along with Descartes's rebuttal, in his edition of the *Meditations* (see the next section). But Hobbes's continued criticisms so angered Descartes that after several exchanges he refused to have anything more to do with "the Englishman."

Because of the political turmoil across Europe, stemming from the beginning of the end of the great monarchies, *De Cive* (1642) was the first of Hobbes's trilogy to appear. In 1651 he published his masterpiece, *Leviathan, or the Matter, Form and Power of a Commonwealth, Ecclesiastical and Civil*. At the end of that year, though still exiled from the British court and now under suspicion by Paris authorities for his attack on the papacy, Hobbes returned to London and made peace with the new regime. Now 63, he began work on *De corpore* (1655).

He had by now further alienated the philosophers at Oxford for his attack in *Leviathan* of the university system as functioning mainly to covertly sustain papal against civil authority and to confound the people by their adherence to "old learning." In 1658 he completed his *De homine*, which presented a new theory of vision and an account of psychology.

In 1660, at the age of 72, Hobbes published a severe and brilliant attack on the prevailing methods of mathematical analysis (*Examinatio et emendatio mathematicae hodiernae qualis explicatur in libris Johannis Wallisii*) and then one upon current trends in natural philosophy, what would come to be called physics (*Dialogus physicus, sive De Naura aeris*), in which he argued against both Wallis and Robert Boyle, as well as the other scholars who were just then beginning to form the Royal society—the famous British group of scientists and scholars that still meets today. In spite of an onslaught of severe criticism and even slanderous propaganda levied against him by his many enemies, Hobbes continued his attacks against what he saw as errors and misdirections of the new trends in philosophy; he was 88 years old when he published *De principiis et ratiocinatione geometrarum* (1666), in which he argued that the geometricians and their supposedly "certain" works, as Descartes and other mathematically and scientifically inclined philosophers had claimed, were no more certain than the faulty speculations of the physicists, and as full of errors as the works of the ethicists.

From his seventies on, Hobbes enjoyed the protection and patronage of the new King Charles II, who it turned out had been a pupil of Hobbes while Hobbes was in exile in Paris and Charles was still the Prince of Wales. Thus while Hobbes was widely regarded as a freethinker and for his attacks on the church as a subversive atheist against all religion, the king bequeathed to him a lifelong pension and much enjoyed his presence in court, precisely because it scandalized the bishops. The only proviso that the king made was that in the interest of not further inflaming the public, Hobbes would not be allowed to publish in England regarding anything relating to human conduct.

In the selection from the *Leviathan* that follows, Hobbes considers knowledge as fundamentally empirical in nature, yet he insists that the appropriate method for inferring the causes of things from their effects and vice versa must be done via an a priori mathematical method. By carefully analyzing the elements of experience, one finds the concepts of matter and motion to be the least common denominators, and that is why Hobbes claims that physical bodies and their movements, as understood by geometric laws, are the only valid subject matter of philosophy.

⚼

Leviathan

Part 1. Of Man

CHAPTER 1: OF SENSE

Concerning the thoughts of man, I will consider them first singly, and afterwards in train, or dependence upon one another. Singly, they are every one a *representation* or *appearance*, of some quality, or other accident of a body without us, which is commonly called an *object*. Which object works on the eyes, ears, and other parts of a man's body; and by diversity of working, produces diversity of appearances.

The original of them all, is that which we call SENSE, for there is no conception in a man's mind, which has not at first, totally or by parts, been begotten upon the organs of sense. The rest are derived from that original. . . .

The cause of sense, is the external body, or object, which presses the organ proper to each sense, either immediately, as in the taste and touch; or mediately, as in seeing, hearing, and smelling; which pressure, by the mediation of the nerves, and other strings and membranes of the body, continued inwards to the brain and heart, causes there a

---

Leviathan, first edition, London, 1651. From Hobbes's *English Works*, collected and edited by Sir William Molesworth, London, 1839, vol. iii. With emendations by the author.

resistance, or counterpressure or endeavour of the heart to deliver itself, which endeavour, because *outward*, seems to be some matter without. And this *seeming*, or fancy, is that which men call *sense;* and consists, as to the eye, in a *light*, or *colour figured;* to the ear, in a *sound;* to the nostril, in an *odour;* to the tongue and palate, in a *savour;* and to the rest of the body, in *heat, cold, hardness, softness,* and such other qualities as we discern by *feeling*. All which qualities, called *sensible*, are in the object, that causes them, but so many several motions of the matter, by which it presses our organs diversely. Neither in us that are pressed, are they anything else, but diverse motions; for motion produces nothing but motion. But their appearance to us is fancy, the same waking, that dreaming. And as pressing, rubbing, or striking the eye, makes us fancy a light; and pressing the ear, produces a din; so do the bodies also we see, or hear, produce the same by their strong, though unobserved action. For if those colours and sounds were in the bodies, or objects that cause them, they could not be severed from them, as by glasses, and in echoes by reflection, we see they are; where we know the thing we see is in one place, the appearance in another. And though at some certain distance, the real and very object seem invested with the fancy it begets in us; yet still the object is one thing, the image or fancy is another. So that sense, in all cases, is nothing else but original fancy, caused, as I have said, by the pressure, that is, by the motion, of external things upon our eyes, ears, and other organs thereunto ordained.

But the philosophy-schools, through all the universities of Christendom, grounded upon certain texts of Aristotle, teach another doctrine, and say, for the cause of *vision*, that the thing seen, sends forth on every side a *visible species*, in English, a *visible show, apparition*, or *aspect*, or *a being seen;* the receiving whereof into the eye is *seeing*. And for the cause of *hearing*, that the thing heard, sends forth an *audible species*, that is an *audible aspect*, or *audible being seen;* which entering at the ear, makes *hearing*. Nay, for the cause of *understanding* also, they say the thing understood, sends forth an *intelligible species,* that is, an *intelligible being seen;* which, coming into the understanding, makes us understand. I say not this, as disproving the use of universities; but because I am to speak hereafter of their office in a commonwealth, I must let you see on all occasions by the way, what things would be amended in them; amongst which the frequency of insignificant speech is one.

⁂

Hobbes' theory of consciousness is surprisingly similar to many contemporary theories in cognitive science. He claims that consciousness in both its sensitive aspects—the ability to attain percepts—and its cognitive aspects—the ability to form mental models and to think—are but two different aspects resulting from the jarring of the nervous system by the surrounding environment. Both physical and psychological events are covered by four subdivisions within philosophy. Geometry describes the spatial motions of physical objects. Physics describes the effects of moving bodies on each other. Ethics describes the movements of the nervous system. Even politics merely describes the effects of nervous systems upon each other.

Like Descartes (see Chapter 10), Hobbes calls for a specific method of inquiry that will lead to certain knowledge in philosophy, but along a slightly different path. He called the method, which in many ways grew as much out of Bacon as it did out of Descartes and Galileo, "resolution and composition." Like Descartes's second rule for the direction of the mind, itself based on Plato's division of ideas, resolution is analysis of complex wholes into simpler elements. Like Descartes's third rule, composition consists in synthesis, or putting back together, the parts into a whole. But the similarities end there. Whereas Descartes argued that the mind is something completely separate and distinct from the body, and not reducible to physical elements, Hobbes takes the opposite position, arguing not only that the mind is not something separate from the body but also that, like the body, the mind is itself a purely physical thing.

Although *Leviathan* was supposed to be mainly a treatise on the philosophy of politics, it remains a fundamental work in metaphysics and epistemology, as well as the philosophy of language and philosophical psychology. Paramount to both aspects is Hobbes's distinction between two different functions of the mind. On the one hand there is sense, imagination, and the movements arising from them; on the other, there is ratiocination—calculation, using words—into the causes of phenomena. The former is natural, the latter artificial in that it depends on the manipulation of language and the naming of things. Philosophy's main concern is with the latter. Following Galileo and the emerging physical science of the time, which involved a new synthesis of empiricism and mathematics, Hobbes here developed in precise modern terms the ancient Democritan and Epicurean atomistic materialist philosophy according to which everything that exists reduces to ultimate physical particles moving in accordance with physical laws. Thus, for instance, the first law of motion appears in every body as a tendency toward self-preservation and self-assertion, which becomes a natural right. On this basis he argued that both organic as well as inorganic bodies exist in the primary condition of collision, conflict, and war. Similarly, the second law of motion manifests itself in organic things and impels us to relinquish a portion of our natural rights in purely self-interested acts in return for being guaranteed that others will do the same. This is how the antagonistic forces of diverse individual wills can exist in harmony through a social contract that forms the basis of the political state.

⚓

CHAPTER XIV: OF THE FIRST AND SECOND NATURAL LAWS, AND OF CONTRACTS

The RIGHT OF NATURE, which writers commonly call *jus naturale,* is the liberty each man has, to use his own power, as he will himself, for the preservation of his own nature; that is to say, of his own life; and con-

Leviathan, first edition, London, 1651. From Hobbes's *English Works,* collected and edited by Sir William Molesworth, London, 1839, vol. iii. With emendations by the author.

sequently, of doing anything which in his own judgment and reason he shall conceive to be the aptest means thereunto.

By LIBERTY is understood, according to the proper signification of the word, the absence of external impediments: which impediments, may oft take away part of a man's power to do what he would; but cannot hinder him from using the power left him, according as his judgment and reason shall dictate to him.

A LAW OF NATURE, *lex naturalis,* is a precept or general rule, found out by reason, by which a man is forbidden to do that, which is destructive of his life, or takes away the means of preserving the same; and to omit that, by which he thinks it may be best preserved. For though they that speak of this subject use to confound *jus* and *lex, right* and *law*: yet they ought to be distinguished; because RIGHT consists in liberty to do, or to forbear; where LAW, determines, and binds to one of them: so that law, and right, differ as much as obligation, and liberty; which in one and the same matter are inconsistent.

And because the condition of man, as has been declared in the precedent chapter, is a condition of war of every one against every one; in which case every one is governed by his own reason; and there is nothing he can make use of, that may not be a help unto him in preserving his life against his enemies; it follows, that in such a condition, every man has a right to everything; even to one another's body. And therefore, as long as this natural right of every man to everything endures, there can be no security to any man, how strong or wise soever he be, of living out the time which Nature ordinarily allows men to live. And consequently it is a precept, or general rule of reason, *that every man ought to endeavour peace, as far as he has hope of obtaining it; and when he cannot obtain it, that he may seek, and use, all helps and advantages of war.* The first branch of which rule contains the first and fundamental law of Nature; which is *to seek peace, and follow it.* The second, the sum of the right of Nature: which is, *by all means we can, to defend ourselves.*

From this fundamental law of Nature, by which men are commanded to endeavour peace, is derived this second law; *that a man be willing, when others are so too, as far-forth, as for peace, and defence of himself he shall think it necessary to lay down this right to all things; and be contented with so much liberty against other men as be would allow other men against himself.* For as long as every man holds this right of doing anything he likes; so long are all men in the condition of war. But if other men will not lay down their right, as well as he; then there is no reason for any one to divest himself of his: for that were to expose himself to prey, which no man is bound to, rather than to dispose himself to peace. This is that law of the Gospel; *whatsoever you require that others should do to you, that do ye to them.* And that law of all men, *quod tibi fieri non vis, alteri ne feceris.*

To *lay down* a man's *right* to anything is to *divest* himself of the *liberty* of hindering another of the benefit of his own right to the same. For he that renounces, or passes away his right, gives not to any other man a right which he had not before; because there is nothing to which every man had not right by Nature: but only stands out of his way, that he may enjoy his own original right, without hindrance from him; not without hindrance from another. So that the effect which redounds to one man, by another man's defect of right is but so much diminution of impediments to the use of his own right original.

Right is laid aside, either by simply renouncing it; or by transferring it to another. By *simply* RENOUNCING; when he cares not to whom the benefit thereof redounds. By TRANSFERRING; when he intends the benefit thereof to some certain person or persons. And when a man has in either manner abandoned, or granted away his right; then is he said to be OBLIGED, or BOUND, not to hinder those, to whom such right is granted, or abandoned, from the benefit of it: and that he *ought*, and it is his DUTY, not to make void that voluntary act of his own: and that such hindrance is INJUSTICE, and INJURY, as being *sine jure*; the right being before renounced, or transferred. So that *injury*, or *injustice*, in the controversies of the world is somewhat like to that, which in the disputations of scholars is called *absurdity*. For as it is there called an absurdity, to contradict what one maintained in the beginning: so in the world it is called injustice, and injury, voluntarily to undo that, which from the beginning he had voluntarily done. The way by which a man either simply renounces, or transfers his right, is a declaration, or signification, by some voluntary and sufficient sign, or signs, that he

does so renounce, or transfer; or has so renounced, or transferred the same, to him that accepts it. And these signs are either words only, or actions only: or, as it happens most often, both words and actions. And the same are the BONDS, by which men are bound, and obliged: bonds that have their strength, not from their own nature, for nothing is more easily broken than a man's word, but from fear of some evil consequence upon the rupture.

Whensoever a man transfers his right, or renounces it; it is either in consideration of some right reciprocally transferred to himself, or for some other good he hopes for thereby. For it is a voluntary act; and of the voluntary acts of every man, the object is some *good to himself*. And therefore there be some rights, which no man can be understood by any words, or other signs, to have abandoned, or transferred. As first a man cannot lay down the right of resisting them, that assault him by force, to take away his life; because he cannot be understood to aim thereby, at any good to himself. The same may be said of wounds, and chains, and imprisonment; both because there is no benefit consequent to such patience; as there is to the patience of suffering another to be wounded, or imprisoned: as also because a man cannot tell, when he sees men proceed against him by violence, whether they intend his death or not. And lastly the motive and end for which this renouncing and transferring of right is introduced, is nothing else but the security of a man's person, in his life, and in the means of so preserving life, as not to be weary of it. And therefore if a man by words, or other signs, seems to despoil himself of the end, for which those signs were intended; he is not to be understood as if he meant it, or that it was his will; but that he was ignorant of how such words and actions were to be interpreted.

The mutual transferring of right is that which men call CONTRACT.

There is difference between transferring of right to the thing and transferring, or tradition, that is delivery of the thing itself. For the thing may be delivered together with the translation of the right; as in buying and selling with ready-money; or exchange of goods, or lands; and it may be delivered some time after.

Again, one of the contractors may deliver the thing contracted for on his part, and leave the other to perform his part at some determinate time after, and in the meantime be trusted; and then the contract on his part is called PACT, or COVENANT: or both parts may contract now, to perform hereafter; in which cases, he that is to perform in time to come, being trusted, his performance is called *keeping of promise*, or faith; and the failing of performance, if it be voluntary, *violation of faith*.

When the transferring of right is not mutual: but one of the parties transfers, in hope to gain thereby friendship, or service from another, or from his friends; or in hope to gain the reputation of charity; or magnanimity; or to deliver his mind from the pain of compassion; or in hope of reward in heaven; this is not contract, but GIFT, FREEGIFT, GRACE: Which words signify one and the same thing. . . .

CHAPTER XV: OF OTHER LAWS OF NATURE

From that law of Nature, by which we are obliged to transfer to another, such rights, as being retained, hinder the peace of mankind, there follows a third; which is this, *that men perform their covenants made*. without which, covenants are in vain, and but empty words; and the right of all men to all things remaining, we are still in the condition of war.

And in this law of Nature consists the fountain and original of JUSTICE. For where no covenant has preceded, there has no right been transferred, and every man has right to everything; and consequently, no action can be unjust. But when a covenant is made, then to break it is *unjust*: and the definition of INJUSTICE is no other than *the not performance of covenant*. And whatsoever is not unjust is *just*.

But because covenants of mutual trust, where there is a fear of not performance on either part, as has been said in the former chapter, are invalid; though the original of justice be the making of covenants; yet injustice actually there can be none, till the cause of such fear be taken away; which while men are in the natural condition of war, cannot be done. Therefore before the names of just and unjust can have place, there must be some coercive power, to compel men equally to the performance of their covenants, by the terror of some punishment, greater than the benefit they expect by the breach of their covenant; and to make good that propriety, which by mutual contract men

acquire, in recompense of the universal right they abandon: and such power there is none before the erection of a commonwealth. And this is also to be gathered out of the ordinary definition of justice in the Schools: for they say, that *justice is the constant will of giving to every man his own*. And therefore where there is no *own*, that is no propriety, there is no injustice; and where there is no coercive power erected, that is, where there is no commonwealth, there is no propriety; all men having right to all things: therefore where there is no commonwealth, there nothing is unjust. So that the nature of justice consists in keeping of valid covenants: but the validity of covenants begins not but with the constitution of a civil power, sufficient to compel men to keep them; and then it is also that propriety begins. . . .

Part II: Of Commonwealth

CHAPTER XVII: OF THE CAUSES, GENERATION, AND DEFINITION OF A COMMONWEALTH

The final cause, end, or design of men, who naturally love liberty, and dominion over others, in the introduction of that restraint upon themselves, in which we see them live in commonwealths, is the foresight of their own preservation, and of a more contented life thereby; that is to say, of getting themselves out from that miserable condition of war, which is necessarily consequent, as has been shown in chapter xiii, to the natural passions of men, when there is no visible power to keep them in awe, and tie them by fear of punishment to the performance of their covenants, and observation of those laws of Nature set down in the fourteenth and fifteenth chapters.

For the laws of Nature, as *justice, equity, modesty, mercy*, and, in sum, *doing to others, as we would be done to*, of themselves, without the terror of some power, to cause them to be observed, are contrary to our natural passions, that carry us to partiality, pride, revenge, and the like. And covenants, without the sword, are but words, and of no strength to secure a man at all. Therefore notwithstanding the laws of nature, which every one has then kept, when he has the will to keep them, when he can do it safety, if there be no power erected, or not great enough for our security, every man will, and may lawfully rely on his own strength and art, for caution against all other men. And in all places, where men have lived by small families, to rob and spoil one another, has been a trade, and so far from being reputed against the law of Nature, that the greater spoils they gained, the greater was their honour; and men observed no other laws therein, but the laws of honour; that is, to abstain from cruelty, leaving to men their lives, and instruments of husbandry. And as small families did then; so now do cities and kingdoms, which are but greater families, for their own security, enlarge their dominions, upon all pretences of danger, and fear of invasion, or assistance that may be given to invaders, and endeavour as much as they can, to subdue, or weaken their neighbours, by open force and secret arts, for want of other caution, justly; and are remembered for it in after ages with honour.

Nor is it the joining together of a small number of men, that gives them this security; because in small numbers, small additions on the one side or the other, make the advantage of strength so great, as is sufficient to carry the victory; and therefore gives encouragement to an invasion. The multitude sufficient to confide in for our security, is not determined by any certain number, but by comparison with the enemy we fear; and is then sufficient when the odds of the enemy is not of so visible and conspicuous moment, to determine the event of war, as to move him to attempt.

And be there never so great a multitude; yet if their actions be directed according to their particular judgments, and particular appetites, they can expect thereby no defence, nor protection, neither against a common enemy, nor against the injuries of one another. For being distracted in opinions concerning the best use and application of their strength, they do not help but hinder one another; and reduce their strength by mutual opposition to nothing: whereby they are easily, not only subdued by a very few that agree together; but also when there is no common enemy, they make war upon each other, for their particular interests. For if we could suppose a great multitude of men to consent in the observation of justice, and other laws of Nature, without a common power to keep them all in awe; we might as well suppose all mankind to do the same; and then there neither would be, nor need to be any civil government or commonwealth at all; because there would be peace without subjection.

Nor is it enough for the security, which men desire should last all the time of their life, that they be governed, and directed by one judgment, for a limited time; as in one battle, or one war. For though they obtain a victory by their unanimous endeavour against a foreign enemy; yet afterwards, when either they have no common enemy, or he that by one part is held for an enemy, is by another part held for a friend, they must needs by the difference of their interests dissolve, and fall again into a war amongst themselves.

It is true that certain living creatures, as bees and ants, live sociably one with another, which are therefore by Aristotle numbered amongst political creatures; and yet have no other direction, than their particular judgments and appetites; nor speech, whereby one of them can signify to another, what he thinks expedient for the common benefit: and therefore some man may perhaps desire to know, why mankind cannot do the same. To which I answer,

First, that men are continually in competition for honour and dignity, which these creatures are not; and consequently amongst men there arises on that ground, envy and hatred, and finally war; but amongst these not so.

Secondly, that amongst these creatures, the common good differs not from the private; and being, by nature inclined to their private, they procure thereby the common benefit. But man, whose joy consists in comparing himself with other men, can relish nothing but what is eminent.

Thirdly, that these creatures, having not, as man, the use of reason, do not see, nor think they see any fault, in the administration of their common business; whereas amongst men, there are very many that think themselves wiser, and abler to govern the public, better than the rest; and these strive to reform and innovate, one this way, another that way; and thereby bring it into distraction and civil war.

Fourthly, that these creatures, though they have some use of voice, in making known to one another their desires and other affections; yet they want that art of words, by which some men can represent to others, that which is good, in the likeness of evil; and evil, in the likeness of good; and augment, or diminish the apparent greatness of good and evil; discontenting men, and troubling their peace at their pleasure.

Fifthly, irrational creatures cannot distinguish between *injury*, and *damage*; and therefore as long as they be at ease, they are not offended with their fellows: whereas man is then most troublesome, when he is most at ease; for then it is that he loves to show his wisdom, and control the actions of them that govern the commonwealth.

Lastly, the agreement of these creatures is natural; that of men is by covenant only, which is artificial; and therefore it is no wonder if there be somewhat else required, besides covenant, to make their agreement constant and lasting; which is a common power, to keep them in awe, and to direct their actions to the common benefit.

The only way to erect such a common power, as may be able to defend them from the invasion of foreigners, and the injuries of one another, and thereby to secure them in such sort, as that by their own industry, and by the fruits of the earth, they may nourish themselves, and live contentedly; is to confer all their power and strength upon one man, or upon one assembly of men, that may reduce all their wills, by plurality of voices, unto one will: which is as much as to say, to appoint one man, or assembly of men, to bear their person; and every one to own, and acknowledge himself to be author of whatsoever he that so bears their person, shall act, or cause to be acted, in those things which concern the common peace and safety; and therein to submit their wills, every one to his will, and their judgments, to his judgment. This is more than consent, or concord; it is a real unity of them all, in one and the same person, made by covenant of every man with every man, in such manner, as if every man should say to every man, *I authorize and give up my right of governing myself, to this man, or to this assembly of men, on this condition, that thou give up thy right to him, and authorize all his actions in like manner.* This done, the multitude so united in one person is called a COMMONWEALTH, in Latin CIVITAS. This is the generation of that great LEVIATHAN, or rather, to speak more reverently, of that *mortal god,* to which we owe under the *immortal God,* our peace and defence. For by this authority, given him by every particular man in the Commonwealth, he has the use of so much power and strength conferred on him, that by terror thereof, he is enabled to perform the wills of them all, to peace at home, and mutual aid against their enemies abroad. And in him consists the essence of the Commonwealth; which, to define it, is *one person, of whose acts a great multitude, by mutual covenants one with another, have made themselves every one the author, to the end be may use the strength and means of them all, as be shall think expedient, for their peace and common defence.*

And he that carries this person is called SOVEREIGN, and said to have *sovereign power;* and every one besides, his SUBJECT.

The attaining to this sovereign power is by two ways. One, by natural force; as when a man makes his children to submit themselves, and their children, to his government, as being able to destroy them if they refuse; or by war subdues his enemies to his will, giving them their lives on that condition. The other is when men agree amongst themselves to submit to some man or assembly of men, voluntarily, on confidence to be protected by him against all others. This latter may be called a political commonwealth, or commonwealth by *institution;* and the former, a commonwealth by *acquisition.*

⁂

Hobbes was unabashedly pessimistic about human nature. This is not surprising, given that he lived in a century of great social and political upheaval, one of the most violent in British history. He viewed human beings as being inherently selfish and hedonistic, such that "of the voluntary acts of every man, the object is some good to himself." Life is a "war of every man against every man." Without obedience to the social contract and the sovereign, which is ultimately for everyone's good, life is "solitary, poor, nasty, brutish and short." Thus the state, which is formed through the selfish and hedonistic actions of its individuals, is the "individual writ large," a "Leviathan," guided from within and without by the principles of natural law. He thus had a lasting influence on the natural law philosophers of the seventeenth and eighteenth centuries, as well as on subsequent British political and economic theorist. Bentham's hedonistic calculus, for instance, owed much to Hobbes's view of human nature. Adam Smith's ideas about how an economy can and should sustain social equilibrium between contradictory self-interests is rooted in Hobbesian ideas that continue to influence world political and economic systems to this day.

NOTES

1. At least not in some straightforward, direct way, even if some strong version of physical reductionism is true, such as that all perceptions are physical events on the surface of my brain. The items that appear to me as "things on my desk" do not *appear* to me to be "events on my brain." I can only know this, if I know it, in theory.

2. Or, at best, direct apprehension of items in the mental world which might be the only world there is, a view we shall discuss when we consider various "presentationalist" theories (see Chapter 20).

3. Unfortunately, many of the strongest proponents of philosophical ignorance have been philosophers— a theme we shall return to again. For now, it may be merely enough to remind ourselves of Plato's warning in *The Republic* that most philosophers are "errant rogues" while the rest are "mostly useless!"

4. In the *ordinary* sense of *conscious*.

5. By "faith" I mean the belief in something that cannot be seen to be so, or cannot be demonstrated incontrovertibly to be so.

6. To put it slightly differently and with philosophical tongue in cheek: unlike the citizens of Athens, the church does not make Socrates drink the hemlock but takes him up on his substitute offer of free meals and monetary payments. That is, it does not kill Socrates; like today's computer hackers who are employed by the companies whose security codes they have broken instead of being sent to jail, it gives Socrates a job.

7. Again, by "faith" I mean belief in what cannot be seen to be so or demonstrated incontrovertibly to be so.

8. Or, even, if it somehow *is* reality, as the presentationalists (in contrast to "representationalists") of the nineteenth century will argue, this cannot be known without philosophy.

9. This work has been so (mis)reinterpreted into the commonly accepted scientific mythology that, lacking a cogent understanding of the real issues behind these developments, some are so perplexed by what they read here that they have gone so far as to attribute it to another author trying to "save" the seventy-year-old Copernicus from the wrath of the church.

10 ✤ Descartes

10.0 Descartes (1596–1650): The Founder of Modern Philosophy

René Descartes was born in La Haye in Touraine, France. His mother died shortly after his birth and he was raised by his father, a councilor of the *parlement* of Rennes in Brittany. His father enrolled him in the celebrated Jesuit college of La Flèche at the age of eight. When Descartes refused to get up in the mornings, complaining of ill health, his teachers allowed him to study in bed until noon, a practice he continued for the rest of his life.

During his eight years at La Flèche, Descartes was exposed to the latest developments in science, philosophy, literature, and mathematics by some of the best minds of the time. It was a period of great transition. Scholasticism was already drawing to a close after centuries of church-dominated Aristotelianism. The challenge of the Copernican revolution, compounded by the Protestant Reformation begun by Martin Luther (1483–1546), had set the stage for the revival of Skepticism fueled still further by

the republication, between 1562 and 1569, of all of Sextus Empiricus's writings (Section 4.3). By the close of the sixteenth century the Catholic "Counter-Reformation" was in full swing, and Catholic theologians began using the newly rediscovered Pyrrhonean Skepticism against Protestants, Calvinists, and Lutheran opponents, arguing that they could not use reason to come to know what they professed to know. Indeed, as we saw, the work of Copernicus and even Galileo was, at least initially, part of their method of demonstration. Thus, ironically, during Descartes's school years Skepticism had aligned itself with religion in the exact way it once had opposed it, creating a climate in which it was generally believed that no certainty could be found in the teachings of science and philosophy and that even the methods of mathematics were not infallible. Such ideas are often attributed to Descartes, but they were already "in the air" during his upbringing and his own teachers taught Skepticism.

Thus by the time he graduated from La Flèche at the age of sixteen, Descartes, like many of his contemporaries, found that

⚹

as soon as I had finished the whole course of studies at the end of which one is normally admitted among the ranks of the learned . . . I found myself embarrassed by so many doubts and errors, that it seemed to me that the only profit I had had from my efforts to acquire knowledge was the progressive discovery of my own ignorance. And yet I was in one of the most celebrated schools in Europe; and I thought there must be learned men there, if there were such in any part of the globe. I had learned everything that the others were learning there; and, not content with the studies in which we were instructed, I had even perused all the books that came into my hands, treating of the studies considered most curious and recondite. At the same time . . . I did not find myself considered inferior to my fellow-students, although there were some among them already marked out to fill the places of our masters. Moreover, our age seemed to me to be flourishing, and as fertile in powerful minds, as any preceding one. This made me take the liberty of judging of all other men by myself, and of holding that there was no such learning in the world as I had been previously led to hope for. . . .

That was why, as soon as my age allowed me to pass from under the control of my instructors, I entirely abandoned the study of letters, and resolved not to seek after any science but what might be found within myself or in the great book of the world. So I spent the rest of my life's youth in travel, in frequenting courts and armies, in mixing with people of various dispositions and ranks, in collecting a variety of experiences . . . and in reflecting always on things as they came up, in a way that might enable me to derive some profit from them.

⚹

He turned to gambling, fencing, horsemanship, and a series of tempestuous love affairs that

From René Descartes, "Discourse on Method" in *Descartes: Philosophical Writings*, E. Anscombe and P. Geach, trans. (Indianapolis: Bobbs-Merrill, 1971).

led him to fight a duel over a woman. To say that he found the "book of the world" as full of uncertainty as books made of letters would be an understatement. Though a citizen of France, he ended up fighting as a soldier in the armies of three foreign countries: the Netherlands, Bavaria, and Hungary.

What, though, does Descartes mean by saying that he abandoned "the study of *letters*"? What was generally meant by the phrase is, literally, the study of *letters!* These little inkblots on the page that *you yourself are right now studying*. If Descartes could send you a message from beyond the grave, he might well say: don't be fooled by this Kolak fellow into thinking that you are here studying *Descartes*. Only I, Descartes, could study Descartes. You must study yourself. What you are studying, directly, is not me nor my thoughts *but little letters on a page that are supposed to represent me and my thoughts.*

So why are you doing this? You've been instructed to do it, of course, just as Descartes was instructed by his teachers. In the present case, you're trying to learn about things like *reality, truth, existence, the mind, knowledge, philosophy,* and so on, as expressed through the learned thoughts, ideas, and opinions of one René Descartes. And how are you going to accomplish this? By looking at inkblots? Do such concepts consist of letters? Do people?

Well, what else are you to do? Stare at your reflection in the bathroom mirror?

Now there's a crazy idea. *But not crazy enough.* Maybe you need to do something even crazier. How about staring at your reflection in the bathroom mirror with the door closed and the lights off and the windows boarded up, completely in the dark? Actually, that's quite close to what Descartes ended up doing *for the purpose of discovering some ultimate truth on which to base all thought.*

The idea, then, which Descartes goes to great lengths to make in his *Discourse on Method,* is that you cannot come to know truths about the world nor about yourself by studying letters!

That's not a new idea. Socrates argued vehemently that philosophy ought not to be written down. He claimed it would deceive everyone into thinking that the words were the thing. Indeed, Socrates might well be conceived as summing up his view, to mirror that famous phrase from his metaphysically reversed double, Jesus, "In the beginning was the word," with the phrase "In the end was the word." The end of philosophy.

Indeed, if we want to understand the developments in religion, science, and philosophy during the entire time from Plato and Aristotle to Descartes, we must realize that during those two thousand years philosophy in general, as well as religion and science, became derivative activities predicated on a variety of conformities and disputations on the written word. In ending this process, Descartes reawakens philosophy as it was done before the advent of letters as such, before the main object of study came to be the written word.

And so Descartes, after more than two millennia of learning, knowledge, and wisdom since the time of Socrates, seems to be essentially reviving the activity of philosophy as it was actually practiced by Socrates, Plato, and Aristotle. It is, after all, important and eye-opening to remember that the founders of philosophy were not men of letters. Thus, he writes that

> after spending some years thus in the study of the book of the world, and in trying to gain experience, there came a day when I resolved to make my studies within myself, and use all my powers of mind to choose the paths I must follow. This undertaking, I think, succeeded much better than it would have if I had never left my country or my books.*

What happened to Descartes next has not only elements of high drama but a certain aura of mysterious fatefulness. In the *Discourse,* he tells us how one night, while returning from the emperor's coronation to his military post in Germany (where some three centuries later the

twentieth-century philosophical genius Ludwig Wittgenstein [Chapter 23] would write another one of the greatest masterpieces of philosophy from the trenches of World War I):

> the winter held me up in quarters in which I found no conversation to interest me; and since, fortunately, I was not troubled by any cares or passions, I spent the whole day shut up alone in a stove-heated room, and was at full liberty to discourse with myself about my own thoughts.

These, "my own thoughts," became the basis for the revolutionary ruminations expressed in his *Meditations on First Philosophy,* which we shall read in the final section.

Descartes tried out his new ideas on the philosophy club in Paris headed by Marin Mersenne, a former fellow pupil at La Flèche, who would eventually oversee the publication of the work. These influential thinkers became convinced that Descartes possessed the key to a new method in philosophy. They beseeched him to publish. It is rarely, if ever, pointed out that *he refused.* In fact, he went into hiding, keeping his residence a secret, changing it frequently whenever someone (usually, a new lover) chanced to find it.

In 1629, having in his own words grown disillusioned with "the book of the world," Descartes fled to Holland where he could continue developing his iconoclastic philosophy in solitude. In 1630 he began writing *Le Monde* (*The World*), which he divided into two parts, "Light" and "Man." When his old friend from La Flèche, now Father Marsenne, chanced to read it, he urged him to publish. The standard historical rumor has it that upon hearing about the condemnation of Galileo in 1632, Descartes feared a similar fate from the still powerful church and that *that* is why he suspended publication. But the historical facts suggest otherwise. Father Marsenne had *The Meditations* read by the Faculty of Theology in Paris, and the leading theologian on the committee approved of it. In fact, it wasn't until twenty-two years after Descartes's death that the Roman Catholic Church put the work on the

---

* *Discourse on Method*, John Veritch, trans.

Index Librorum Prohibiorum, the dreaded list of books dangerous to read begun by Pope Pious V back in 1571 and approved by the Council of Trent.[1]

In any case, *Le Monde* was not published in his lifetime; only fragments of the work and a brief summary of it appeared after his death. But he subsequently did publish the groundbreaking *Discourse on the Method of Properly Guiding the Reason in the Search for Truth in the Sciences* (1637). In it, he writes that "The greatest minds, as they are capable of the highest excellencies, are open likewise to the greatest aberrations; and those who travel very slowly may yet make far greater progress, provided they keep always to the straight road, than those who, while they run, forsake it." Seeking to correct the "aberrations of the mind," he directs rationality to follow four fundamental rules, to which we now turn.

10.1 The Cartesian Method: The Axioms of Rationality

Inspired by Francis Bacon's proposition that "the entire work of the understanding must be begun afresh, and the mind itself be, from the start, not left to take its own course, but be guided step by step," the straight road that Descartes says must be followed without ever veering from it consists in four fundamental principles. Here is how he came to them:

⚓

Discourse on Method

[L]ike one walking alone and in the dark, I resolved to proceed so slowly and with such circumspection, that if I did not advance far, I would at least guard against falling. I did not even choose to dismiss

---

From *Discourse on Method*, John Veritch, trans. (La Salle, IL: Open Court, 1901), with emendations by the author.

summarily any of the opinions that had crept into my belief without having been introduced by Reason, but first of all took sufficient time carefully to satisfy myself of the general nature of the task I was setting myself, and ascertain the true Method by which to arrive at the knowledge of whatever lay within the compass of my powers.

Among the branches of Philosophy, I had, at an earlier period, given some attention to Logic, and among those of the Mathematics to Geometrical Analysis and Algebra,—three Arts or Sciences which ought, as I conceived, to contribute something to my design. But, on examination, I found that, as for Logic, its syllogisms and the majority of its other precepts are of avail rather in the communication of what we already know, or even as the Art of Lully, in speaking without judgment of things of which we are ignorant, than in the investigation of the unknown; and although this Science contains indeed a number of correct and very excellent precepts, there are, nevertheless, so many others, and these either injurious or superfluous, mingled with the former, that it is almost quite as difficult to effect a severance of the true from the false as it is to extract a Diana or a Minerva from a rough block of marble. Then as to the Analysis of the ancients and the Algebra of the moderns, besides that they embrace only matters highly abstract, and, to appearance, of no use, the former is so exclusively restricted to the consideration of figures, that it can exercise the Understanding only on condition of greatly fatiguing the Imagination;*and, in the latter, there is so complete a subjection to certain rules and formulas, that there results an art full of confusion and obscurity calculated to embarrass, instead of a science fitted to cultivate the mind. By these considerations I was induced to seek some other Method which would comprise the advantages of the three and be exempt from their defects. And as a multitude of laws often only hampers justice, so that a state is best governed when, with few laws, these are rigidly administered; in like manner, instead of the great number of precepts of which Logic is composed, I believed that the four following would prove perfectly sufficient for me,

---

*The imagination must here be taken as equivalent simply to the representative faculty.

provided I took the firm and unwavering resolution never in a single instance to fail in observing them.

The *first* was never to accept anything for true which I did not clearly know to be such; that is to say, carefully to avoid precipitancy and prejudice, and to comprise nothing more in my judgment than what was presented to my mind so clearly and distinctly as to exclude all ground of doubt.

The *second,* to divide each of the difficulties under examination into as many parts as possible, and as might be necessary for its adequate solution.

The *third*, to conduct my thoughts in such order that, by commencing with objects the simplest and easiest to know, I might ascend by little and little, and, as it were, step by step, to the knowledge of the more complex; assigning in thought a certain order even to those objects which in their own nature do not stand in a relation of antecedence and sequence.

And the *last*, in every case to make enumerations so complete, and reviews so general, that I might be assured that nothing was omitted.

The long chains of simple and easy reasonings by means of which geometers are accustomed to reach the conclusions of their most difficult demonstrations, had led me to imagine that all things, to the knowledge of which man is competent, are mutually connected in the same way, and that there is nothing so far removed from us as to be beyond our reach, or so hidden that we cannot discover it, provided only we abstain from accepting the false for the true, and always preserve in our thoughts the order necessary for the deduction of one truth from another. And I had little difficulty in determining the objects with which it was necessary to commence, for I was already persuaded that it must be with the simplest and easiest to know, and, considering that of all those who have hitherto sought truth in the sciences, the mathematicians alone have been able to find any demonstrations, that is, any certain and evident reasons, I did not doubt but that such must have been the rule of their investigations. I resolved to commence, therefore, with the examination of the simplest objects, not anticipating, however, from this any other advantage than that to be found in accustoming my mind to the love and nourishment of truth, and to a distaste for all such reasonings as were unsound.

 ⚹

Let us first consider the first of his four principles, restating it again:

The *first* was never to accept anything for true which I did not clearly know to be such; that is to say, carefully to avoid precipitancy and prejudice, and to comprise nothing more in my judgment than what was presented to my mind so clearly and distinctly as to exclude all ground of doubt.

There it is: the beginning of modern philosophy, the foundation of modern thought. Few statements have such eloquence and power, a simplicity that allows anyone to see the fundamentals. You can see it clearly and distinctly, everyone can—that is why it caused such a revolution. That much seems obvious. Right?

Well, if that's what you think, then think again. All you got were the inkblots, the words (but maybe not even that), not that which is represented by them. Most students simply accept what they (half) read in that statement with hardly any conscious action on their part. Here, let me show you: what is *precipitancy*? Well, but if you don't understand the word you don't understand the phrase; if you don't understand the phrase you don't understand the sentence; if you don't understand the sentence you don't understand the paragraph.

Of course, the words are not the thing. But if you don't even get the words, how are you even going to attempt to get at the concepts represented by the words? Here's a suggestion from Descartes: avoid *precipitancy*.

Precipitancy is what we do just about all of the time, accepting things *rashly, hastily, without due skeptical and critical inquiry*. But even translating the concept into other, perhaps more familiar concepts, does not guarantee that you *actually see this process of precipitancy in your own mental activity*. Do you? To actually *see* that within yourself, the actual conscious experience of your own superficial acceptance of things without question, is altogether a different thing from merely having an understanding of the meaning of the word. It is, in part, to attend to the understanding of the mind and how it makes meaning out of its own symbols.

The same is true when Descartes warns us to avoid prejudice. He is noting another common psychological occurrence. When you *prejudge* something to be true you affirm it to yourself to be so without having actually *judged* it. What does it mean to judge something? Well, what does a judge do, if not consider all sides to an issue? So whenever we don't consider *reasons why something we think is so might not be so*, we are in fact acting not rationally but through *prejudice.*

Now, what does it mean to *clearly know* something to be so? This is a common word: "clear." Explain to yourself, right now, then, what it means to *clearly* know something! For that matter, what does it mean to *know* something? Do you notice what the problem is? We're trying to make *definitions,* which require more definitions, and so on. We're not really getting at anything. *And this is exactly the pseudo-understanding that Descartes is attacking.* As we shall see, he is trying to replace the notion of defining concepts with the direct experience, through insight, of the actuality, the *being,* residing in the concept.

Most people can't answer questions such as, "What is mental *clarity?*" They strive for definitions, which require further definitions, and soon one is lost in obscurity. Descartes is looking not for a definition but an *experience*—albeit an internal experience of one's own consciousness. Thus most people, when they read Descartes's first principle, accept on blind faith that they understand what is being said because they think a definition is being offered. Descartes is not offering a definition but asking you to inquire with him into the conscious experience of what he is talking about. To accept what he is saying as merely a definition is to act in complete prejudice which, if you really understand what he is saying, leads you to not accept any such statements without first embarking upon a philosophical inquiry on your own, in terms of your own conscious experience. Thales—and just about every other great philosopher we have thus far encountered—would agree.

I will now restate Descartes's four principles in my own words, breaking up the all-important first one into several steps:

1. Never accept as true any proposition that is not clearly recognized by you to be true.
   a. Avoid precipitancy: don't be too hasty in accepting a new proposition.
   b. Avoid prejudice: don't be too dogmatic in holding on to a previously accepted proposition.
   c. If you use a proposition as a basis from which you derive some others, make sure that the fundamental proposition is presented to your mind so clearly and so distinctly that you cannot possibly doubt it.
2. Divide each complex problem requiring many steps into more basic parts, each of which involves only a single step.[2]
3. Start with absolutely the simplest and the easiest known propositions and move very slowly, step by step, to the more complex.
4. Always make a complete list of all your steps so that you can review them to make absolutely certain that you have omitted nothing.

The impetus driving his conviction that one must start from premises known to be certain beyond any doubt stems from the axiomatic method in mathematics. An axiom is a proposition known to be true, not by empirical evidence but accepted as true from the beginning simply because it is seen so clearly and distinctly to be so that it is beyond doubt. The classical example is the geometric system of Euclid. His axioms, such as that two points determine a line, are so clearly etched in the mind that demonstration is superfluous. Mathematics[3] then proceeds by a deductive method in which each new proposition is simply derived from the axioms with clear and distinct certainty, each step perspicuous and accounted for. Only when such perfection can be attained in all the sciences and even philosophy can humanity be certain that it is on the path to true knowledge. With this goal in mind he set out to create a universal mathematics. The result would be not a "collection of curiosities" or a disarray of separate sciences and methods of inquiry but a universal science.

This task of the philosopher, which Descartes admitted was "incredibly ambitious," requires our making a careful and deep analysis of the way the mind works, not just "what it says," and the ways and methods of reason. Once again Descartes is taking the activity of mathematics as his model, where thoughts are not the guide but the guided (see note 3).

Now, what do you suppose would happen if you actually tried to apply Descartes's method? Could you even do it? Would you want to?

Often students respond to such thoughts with the idea that this would be an awfully constraining way of thinking, that it would lessen our freedom, or that it would be a task so arduous and artificial that it would lead us to ruin. But if you think about it a little, you will realize that what we call "freedom of thought" can itself be extremely constraining. Why? Because when we can think anything we "want," then we are open to seduction by our own thoughts into believing things, not because they are true but because we would like them to be true. That is no path to freedom but a self-imposed slavery of ignorance.

Ask yourself this: how many things have you accepted as true that you do not "clearly know" to be so? *Probably most of the things you think you know are not really known by you to be so.* They may be known by others (such as those who conditioned you to think that way). Or not. In that case, your position and standing in the world is weakened, insofar as you are not the master of your own knowledge. Or, even worse, you live in a prison of false truths and half-truths, subordinate to those who are in the know. But *who is that?* Anyone who cares to find out for himself or herself, using the Cartesian method, what is true and actual. I suggested that what Descartes means by "clearly know" is related to what Plato meant and so I used the more familiar term "recognize." For Plato, you will recall, all knowledge is recollection. There is a point, as with the example of Meno the slave learning the Pythagorean theorem (Section 1.7), at which something strikes you as true in a way that it seems you already have known it to be so; there is an "aha," the way you recognize, say, something unfamiliar as really being familiar. One can always quibble, intellectually, with such a notion. The point, however, at least initially, is to focus on that conscious experience until it becomes clear and distinct—that is, until it stands out from all other ideas in a unique way.

This might end up being merely a psychological illusion, but Descartes is suggesting that you already have a built-in, extremely accurate, internal mechanism for discriminating the true from the false. There may be cases where that feeling is mistaken, but there are some clear and distinct cases where this inner sense is veridical (accurate). Descartes is inviting you to look inside yourself to find this inner faculty inside your own mind.

Instead of appealing to external authority, the Cartesian method *appeals to internal "authority" in terms of a specific and clearly defined conscious mental state.* Think, by analogy, of the concept of learning pitch in music; there is a certain conscious state in which something "being in tune" is clearly and distinctly recognized as such. Once you are attuned to this inner tuning, you cannot be wrong. This is actually true. Unless you are "tone deaf," you can tell, perfectly clearly, whether someone is in tune or not. And what Descartes is claiming is that, intellectually, most people are "tone deaf." They cannot hear the truth. Their minds must be tuned. *And they must be tuned to themselves.*

Part of the problem, according to Descartes, is that minds have lost their inner tuning due to the fallacy of tuning ourselves to the thoughts of others. This does not make us in tune with the truth and, furthermore, it makes us out of tune with ourselves.

Descartes is *not* just saying, "whatever seems true to you, is true," or anything like that. Let's take an empirical example (but keep in mind that he is explicitly *not* an empiricist). You probably couldn't pick me out of a crowd. My wife could. Why? Because she, unlike you, recognizes me. What is that recognition? What does it consist in? Well, when she sees me she doesn't have any sort of double vision—that is, she is not comparing her present image of me with some past image. That (or something like that) is being done automatically for her by her brain. She simply has the sense of familiarity associated with the image of me that she sees. There is no conscious interpretation necessary. Her entire cognitive apparatus is doing it for her. As we shall see shortly when we look at his *Meditations,* Descartes suggests that visual appearances in the empirical world are easily deceiving in ways that *propositions* in the rational realm are not.

What are propositions? They are the "meanings" of which thoughts are internal experiences.[4] Ordinarily, the activity of *thinking* involves the use of *language.* Stop reading for a few moments and think about something else. Listen to yourself think. What do you hear? A string of words composing sentences, fragments, questions, single words, and so on. In other words, conscious thinking consists of stringing together words, the most important of which—in terms of *knowledge*—has to do with *propositions.* Propositions are expressed by sentences that are either true or false. At a later point, especially when we consider some of the philosophy of the twentieth century, we shall focus more closely on propositions, what they are, in what sense they can be distinguished from sentences, and so on (much in the same way that numbers can be distinguished from the numerals that represent them). For Descartes, knowledge consists of true propositions—but not just that. For instance, the proposition "There are 559 numbered pages in this book," is *true,* but it is not at this moment known by you to be true. It is, however, known by me to be true. Once you look on the last page and verify that there has not been some typo or some trick, then you can claim to be on the way to knowing that this proposition is true. Why? Because you are then *evidently justified* in your belief. Descartes is thus

laying down a *justified true belief* theory of knowledge, an epistemological theory (we shall return to this again when we consider various subsequent epistemologies). But the evidence is not in terms of some *external* experience. It is your own internal experience, what he calls a "rational insight," itself a clear and distinct occurrence within the human mind, that is the key to knowledge and on the basis of which he will attempt to construct a new and absolutely solid foundation for all subsequent philosophy: objectivity found hidden in the last place where anyone would have thought to look, inside the dark and hidden heart of one's own *subjectivity.*

10.2 The Cartesian Coordinate System and the Invention of Analytic Geometry: Toward the Unification of Perception and the Intellect

In his profound and original works, Descartes rejects scholastic Aristotelianism in favor of a return to a type of classical Platonism by formulating a new system of universal knowledge founded on undoubtable premises. As in mathematics, he proceeds with straightforward deductions in which each step is as clear as the starting proposition. It was in his attempt to construct a "universal mathematics," a complete system of absolute validity regarding not just the nature of numbers and figures but the whole world, that he found for the first time a way to link geometry and algebra, thereby inventing a new branch of mathematics known today as analytic geometry.

Lest this seem like just so many words, let us actually take a look at the philosophical implications of this revolutionary mathematical development. Understanding its significance can help us to see how what Descartes did returned philosophy to its Platonic foundations. Look at the drawing in Figure 10.1. You can see that the drawing has smooth lines and sharp corners, but

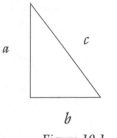

Figure 10.1

this is only because you are not looking very closely. Under a microscope, we would see that the lines are not perfectly straight, the corners are not precise, and the whole thing is a fuzzy representation of a triangle and not, itself, a perfect triangle. You will recall that this is a point that Plato made over and over about how the objects we perceive are not themselves the thing but only representations of the thing. That, too, is why Plato, like Descartes, considered mathematics the highest form of knowledge. The mathematics Plato had in mind was geometry, but his argument had to be allegorical; he claimed that the seen triangle is only a "reflection" of a perfect triangle, which is not an appearance but an "idea," leaving it rather mysterious as to what these ideas, or "forms," are.

Like his teacher Pythagoras (Section 1.7), Plato was inspired by the view that everything could be explained in terms of numbers (which Pythagoras pictured geometrically). For Plato, trying to express the concept of a triangle perfectly in the world (the world of appearances) would be like trying to draw a perfect triangle using a felt tip pen on tissue paper; everything gets very blotchy and only the vaguest, fuzzy resemblance to a perfect triangle is possible. It was not until Descartes showed exactly how to express what a geometric figure like a triangle is in terms of a perfectly precise algebraic formula that Plato's ideas could further be developed. What Descartes managed to do using his now famous coordinate system that still bears his name ("Cartesian coordinates"), in which the x and y axes are number lines that serve like crosshairs in translating the figure into an abstract formula, is to translate the *image* into a formal relationship among variables

such that one can simply plug in the appropriate numbers. He showed that the preceding drawing describes a geometric figure: a (right) triangle. Here is the equation:

$$a^2 + b^2 = c^2$$

You can see that the equation contains variables (a,b,c), exponents (^{2}), a plus sign, and an equal sign. The equation is neither smooth nor does it have any sharp corners. The equation describes a geometric figure: a (right) triangle.

If you look through a microscope at the geometric figure, you will see that its lines are not very smooth at all and that there are lots of tiny variations due to the fuzziness of the inkblots. And you will also see that the angle that represents a right angle is not exactly a right angle. The drawn figure is therefore not a right triangle but a *geometric representation* of a right triangle. What, then, is the type of thing being represented? What is a right triangle? Or, for that matter, what is a triangle?

A triangle is the name of a *concept*. One can represent one such type of concept (that is, right triangle) with the algebraic equation, $a^2 + b^2 = c^2$. This equation, too, is obviously not a type of triangle but an *algebraic representation* of a type of triangle. That one can make either a geometric or an algebraic representation of the same type of concept—"right triangle"—shows that the two different representations are different *sorts* of representations. We say that one *looks like* the type of concept it represents whereas the other does not. But in neither case is the representation the thing represented.

This is exactly the point we made in Sections 1.3 and 1.4, where we distinguished the *numerical representations* of numbers with those which are represented by them—the numbers. Numbers, as such, are purely abstract conceptual entities. And what Descartes showed is that purely abstract formal relations, such as the ones studied by algebraic equations, can contain (or represent) all the information contained by a visual figure. In other words, he showed that there is an *intimate and fundamental relationship between our perceptions—the world of appear-*

ance—and our intellect—the world of pure reason. This idea will reach its culmination in the work of Immanuel Kant.

How far can we take Descartes's unification of perception and the intellect? Well, why not to *everything,* including ourselves? So, for instance, just as geometric representation visually resembles the thing it represents, whereas the algebraic representation does not, so too the visual representation of your hand—the perceived object you see when you are looking at your hand—is not your hand. What confuses you into thinking that it is your hand is that—just as the seen geometric triangle looks like the thing it represents—the visual representation looks like a hand. But it is not a hand! A hand is a physical object. What you are looking at is just an image. It is not the thing in itself. It is only a representation.

In the case of the triangle, the concept represented in perception resembles (looks like) what it represents. The drawing of the type of concept called "right triangle" is that representation. The algebraic equation of the right triangle, on the other hand, describes what it represents without perceptually resembling what it describes. A little reflection thus reveals the surprising fact that both the triangle drawn on the page that you see with your eyes and the triangle you apprehend intellectually in your mind via an algebraic equation are both representations of a concept. One is visual, in that it appeals directly to perception. The other is not, in that it appeals directly to the intellect. Both are symbolic representations! (You can also, of course, with your eyes closed, imagine a right triangle by "drawing" a mental picture of a triangular shape. But imagining a right triangle is very different from describing the properties of a right triangle via the algebraic equation $a^2 + b^2 = c^2$.

In the case of the drawn triangle, it is easy to forget that what one sees is only a representation because the drawn triangle looks like what it represents—a right triangle. We forget that *the representation is not the thing represented.* Just as the symbol "3" is not a number but a numeral (a symbol), and just as the "=" in an equation is not equality but the symbol for equality, so too the

drawn triangle is not a triangle but a *symbol* representing a triangle. And just as the Roman numeral "III" may look to you more like the number (a concept) that it represents (because you can count the "I"s) than does the numeral "3" (a symbol), so too the geometric figure may look more like the right triangle (a type of concept) it represents than does the algebraic equation $a^2 + b^2 = c^2$. In neither case is the symbol the thing it represents any more than the word *dog* is a dog or the word *hand* is a hand. And likewise, the images you see when you are looking at your hands are not your hands but images of your hands.

What this ultimately means in terms of our understanding of reality, the relationship between percepts and concepts, the nature of knowledge, and the limitations of language in which we describe all this, is that two thousand years prior to Descartes, Plato had likened the fact that the things we see (the perceived objects) are to actualities (the objects perceived) as shadows are to the things that cast the shadows (Plato's allegory of the cave, Section 2.3). This realization comes in many forms, from the myth in which Plato presented it to the contemporary scientific terms in which we can say that the brain lives in darkness; the skull lets no light in. It is as dark inside your brain as it is inside a computer mainframe. Where then is this light you are looking at? Well, contemporary neurophysiology says it is in the calcarine fissure of the key part of the brain in which perception occurs. This is deep within the brain. It is dark! The light you see is, at best, a representation of the light "out there."

Descartes, in discovering that geometric representations can be represented algebraically, became convinced that all aspects of reality were ultimately mathematical and therefore accessible—perfectly, clearly, and distinctly—to the mind. Since size, figure, volume, and so on—representations of the objects we find in nature—are geometric representations that, by Descartes's method, can be purely represented mathematically, it should be possible for us in principle to understand *everything.* All we need is a universal language that can represent things in themselves perfectly, just as Descartes showed how algebraic equations can represent geometric objects perfectly.

Geometry has to do with the shape of space. It deals with *extended* things. Thought, as such, like intellectual activity, is *unextended*—that is, it does not exist in space as such (but perhaps in time—many later philosophers will identify thinking with time). Descartes in fact understood the thinking mind as a *res cogitans*—an unextended, "thinking thing"—and the rest of the universe of space in which it exists as a *res extensa*—an "extended" thing. Although the *res cogitans* as the thinking substance and the *res extensa* as the extended substance constitute what has been dubbed the "Cartesian dualism," his lifelong project was to reduce one to the other. Key to this was his contention that the *res cogitans* is not only the individual mind that thinks but also the substance that pervades *all* individual minds. We encountered this notion before in the philosophies of Averroës and Bruno, and we shall encounter it again, near the beginning of our own century, in the work of the American philosopher Josiah Royce.

10.3 How to Become a Genius: Descartes's *Rules for the Direction of the Mind*

Such grand and eloquent ideas! How can we—how can *you*—ever even feign to approach a real understanding of them? This is a question that continually strikes not just beginning philosophy students but most philosophers in their quest for wisdom. And this is a perfect point at which to raise this question because of all the philosophers we shall study in this book, Descartes is the only one who wrote a manual outlining his method in perfect detail for anyone who should wish to follow in his footsteps. It's called *Rules for the Direction of the Mind.*

I still remember the day when I—a perplexed, confused, and overanxious undergraduate student—happened in despair to come upon this little book. What was I in despair about? I was studying physics, trying to write the greatest novel ever written, playing in a band, and hoping to direct some plays and movies . . . not to mention trying to rethink mathematics from the ground up and teach it to myself because I was convinced that my professors didn't understand it! Can you imagine? My problem was that I was doing what seemed very natural to me, which was to do and learn everything, and everyone told me that this was a path to ignorance, misery, starvation . . . except Descartes. I found his *Rules for the Direction of the Mind* and suddenly, for the first time, felt as if somebody understood me, what I was feeling and thinking, a voice from many centuries ago. It actually encouraged me to keep right on doing what I was doing, which was just about everything!

You too have probably heard lots of advice on how to become a "learned" person, the most important of which is to pick *one* area of study and then to learn *it* to the exclusion of other areas. For instance, if you are a student in college, you are invited to pick a major; furthermore, you are asked things like whether you are a "humanities" type or a "mathematics and science" type, and so on. Trying to "learn everything" or "understand everything" is the mark of the dilettante. Well, if that's so, then Descartes, like Plato and Aristotle before him, was certainly one of the greatest dilettantes of all time! For the founder of modern philosophy made profound and original contributions, not just to mathematics but also to physics; his scientific work inspired Newton to develop his own groundbreaking theory of mechanics and gravity.

And yet, one of the most revolutionary aspects of the Cartesian path to knowledge is that it is a path open and accessible to *everyone*. You don't have to be special. You don't have to be gifted. You don't have to be chosen by God. Indeed, as we saw by his own testimony in the previous section, Descartes did not regard himself in any way special or gifted. This is, for us, an extremely important bit of self-revelation. Often, the history of great philosophers, scientists, and artists presents them as great geniuses capable of unique and unusual feats of brilliance that no ordinary person could ever hope to achieve. If you think about it, you will realize that such views are deeply inconsistent with the themes of *philosophical enlightenment* we have been developing in this book. So what is Descartes's secret?

His secret is that there is no secret. He offers clear and explicit rules which anyone can follow and which, he claims, have the power to lead to similar, far-reaching results in anyone who applies them. *The key is to study and learn everything you can about as many different, even nonconnected, areas, teaching yourself the skills in those areas even if they seem completely unrelated.*

With this in mind, let us see how he actually puts it in his *Rules for the Direction of the Mind,* written in 1628 but not published until more than half a century after his death in 1701. Descartes formulated in explicit detail rules for philosophical thought—rules designed to lead to clear and distinct ideas via a method modeled on the precision of mathematical thought. The purpose is not mathematical theory per se but the foundation of a perfect and complete understanding of ourselves and the world.

⚹

Rules for the Direction of the Mind

Rule I

The end of study should be to direct the mind towards the enunciation of sound and correct judgments on all matters that come before it.

Whenever men notice some similarity between two things, they are wont to ascribe to each, even in those respects in which the two differ, what they have found to be true of the other. Thus they erroneously compare the sciences, which entirely consist in the cognitive exercise of the mind, with the arts, which depend upon an exercise and disposition of the body. They see that not all the arts can be

From René Descartes, *Rules for the Direction of the Mind,* Elizabeth S. Haldane and G. R. T. Ross, trans. (Cambridge: Cambridge University Press, 1911).

acquired by the same man, but that he who restricts himself to one, most readily becomes the best executant, since it is not so easy for the same hand to adapt itself both to agricultural operations and to harp-playing, or to the performance of several such tasks as to one alone. Hence they have held the same to be true of the sciences also, and distinguishing them from one another according to their subject matter, they have imagined that they ought to be studied separately, each in isolation from all the rest. But this is certainly wrong. For since the sciences taken all together are identical with human wisdom, which always remains one and the same, however applied to different subjects, and suffers no more differentiation proceeding from them than the light of the sun experiences from the variety of the things which it illumines, there is no need for minds to be confined at all within limits; for neither does the knowing of one truth have an effect like that of the acquisition of one art and prevent us from finding out another, it rather aids us to do so. Certainly it appears to me strange that so many people should investigate human customs with such care, the virtues of plants, the motions of the stars, the transmutations of metals, and the objects of similar sciences, while at the same time practically none bethink themselves about good understanding, or universal Wisdom, though nevertheless all other studies are to be esteemed not so much for their own value as because they contribute something to this. Consequently we are justified in bringing forward this as the first rule of all, since there is nothing more prone to turn us aside from the correct way of seeking out truth than this directing of our inquiries, not towards their general end, but towards certain special investigations. I do not here refer to perverse and censurable pursuits like empty glory or base gain; obviously counterfeit reasonings and quibbles suited to vulgar understanding open up a much more direct route to such a goal than does a sound apprehension of the truth. But I have in view even honorable and laudable pursuits, because these mislead us in a more subtle fashion. For example take our investigations of those sciences conducive to the conveniences of life or which yield that pleasure which is found in the contemplation of truth, practically the only joy in life that is complete and untroubled with any pain. There we may indeed expect to receive the legitimate fruits of scientific inquiry; but if, in the course of our study, we think of them, they frequently cause us to omit many facts which are necessary to the understanding of other matters, because they seem to be either of slight value or of little interest. Hence we must believe that all the sciences are so inter-connected, that it is much easier to study them all together than to isolate one from all the other. If, therefore, anyone wishes to search out the truth of things in serious earnest, he ought not to select one special science; for all the sciences are conjoined with each other and interdependent: he ought rather to think how to increase the natural light of reason, not for the purpose of resolving this or that difficulty of scholastic type, but in order that his understanding may light his will to its proper choice in all the contingencies of life. In a short time he will see with amazement that he has made much more progress than those who are eager about particular ends, and that he has not only obtained all that they desire, but even higher results than fall within his expectation.

Rule III

In the subjects we propose to investigate, our inquiries should be directed, not to what others have thought, nor to what we ourselves conjecture, but to what we can clearly and perspicuously behold and with certainty deduce; for knowledge is not won in any other way.

To study the writings of the ancients is right, because it is a great boon for us to be able to make use of the labors of so many men; and we should do so, both in order to discover what they have correctly made out in previous ages, and also that we may inform ourselves as to what in the various sciences is still left for investigation. But yet there is a great danger lest in a too absorbed study of these works we should become infected with their errors, guard against them as we may. For it is the way of writers, whenever they have allowed themselves rashly and credulously to take up a position in any controverted matter, to try with the subtlest of arguments to compel us to go along with them. But when, on the contrary, they have happily come upon something certain and evident, in displaying it they never fail to surround it with ambiguities, fearing, it would seem, lest the simplicity of their explanation should make us respect their discovery less, or because they grudge us an open vision of the truth.

Further, supposing now that all were wholly open and candid, and never thrust upon us doubtful opinions as true, but expounded every matter in good faith, yet since scarce anything has been asserted by any one man the contrary of which has not been alleged by another, we should be eternally uncertain which of the two to believe. It would be no use to total up the testimonies in favor of each, meaning to follow that opinion which was supported by the greater number of authors; for if it is a question of difficulty that is in dispute, it is more likely that the truth would have been discovered by few than by many. But even though all these men agreed among themselves, what they teach us would not suffice for us. For we shall not, e.g. all turn out to be mathematicians though we know by heart all the proofs that others have elaborated, unless we have an intellectual talent that fits us to resolve difficulties of any kind. Neither, though we have mastered all the arguments of Plato and Aristotle, if yet we have not the capacity for passing a solid judgment on these matters, shall we become Philosophers; we should have acquired the knowledge not of a science, but of history. . . .

⚹

Descartes echoes Plato's warning, placed above the Academy, "Let no one ignorant of mathematics enter here." But he suggests, first, that the mathematics done by the great ancient philosophers such as Pythagoras and Plato was of a wholly different kind from that practiced by the pedants of Descartes's own time. Indeed, his description of mathematics education seems to be hauntingly appropriate for our own times. He suggests that the mathematicians are either of a mind that has forgotten what mathematics is all about, or else they are like the great inventors who jealously guard their secrets; in either case, *the function of their "education" is to make you ignorant.* His remedy is therefore to follow a method that would make your mind incorruptible to their manipulations, distractions, and ignorances. For he also claims that the knowledge to be thus gained is made to look difficult and incomprehensible when in reality it is involved in the very operations of the mind all the time, hidden behind the veil of appearances.

Descartes's method simply unveils it before the mind's eye.

Put simply, Descartes—the inventor of one of the most important branches of mathematics—would claim that *you already know mathematics.* Indeed, his overall epistemological theme is that you already have knowledge but have become deceived away from it; the ego has been made to forget. We encountered this view before in the work of Plato. But what is remarkable is that Descartes, unlike Plato, communicates not via myths, mysteries, and allegories but directly, by revealing his method in simple, clear rules that anyone can follow.

This is extremely important: Descartes is claiming that *anyone* can know everything there is to know. This would, on the views of other philosophers such as Bruno and Averroës, be possible through mystical intuitions, unity with the divine, the transcendental self, and so on; it does not require divine grace or genius or any sort of special talent. What makes it possible for the mind to attain such knowledge is explained in the very first rule, in which he claims that one of the greatest mistakes we make is to limit the mind in the ways that we limit the physical body.

Thus, right from the start, Descartes's distinction between the mind and the body is not merely metaphysical. The body, as part of the extended universe, has certain limitations due to its finitude. Being a great violin player necessitates your not being, say, a great wrestler or bricklayer; your fingers simply weren't made for such diversity of action. The mistake, however, according to Descartes, is that *people assume that the limitations of the body are the limitations of the mind!* And this is an egregious error, the source of much of our self-imposed limitation among human beings. Thus, in the first rule he insists that

> since . . . human wisdom, which always remains one and the same, however applied to different subjects, and suffers no more differentiation proceeding from them than the light of the sun experiences from the variety of the things which it illuminates, there is no need for minds to be confined at all within

limits; for neither does the knowing of one truth have an effect like that of the acquisition of one art and prevent us from finding out another, it rather aids us to do so.

No need for minds to be confined at all within limits. Yet think about all the limits imposed upon it by authorities from the outside and by its own images of itself from the inside! And so,

> If, therefore, anyone wishes to search out the truth of things in serious earnest, he ought not to select one special science; for all the sciences are conjoined with each other and interdependent: he ought rather to think how to increase the natural light of reason, not for the purpose of resolving this or that difficulty of scholastic type, but in order that his understanding may light his will to its proper choice in all the contingencies of life. *In a short time he will see with amazement that he has made much more progress than those who are eager about particular ends, and that he has not only obtained all that they desire, but even higher results than fall within his expectation.*

I know from personal experience that he is correct.

10.4 The Revival of Skepticism: Descartes's First Meditation

Descartes's *Meditations on First Philosophy, in Which the Existence of God and the Distinction Between Mind and Body Are Demonstrated* is among the most influential philosophical works of all time. By "first philosophy," Descartes means the same thing as Aristotle's first *principles of things,* or metaphysics. "Thus the whole of philosophy," Aristotle wrote, "is like a tree; the roots are metaphysics, the trunk is physics, and the branches that rise from the trunk are all the other sciences."

The Meditations have the distinction of being reprinted more times than just about any other work of philosophy in introductory anthologies and texts, along with Plato's *Euthyphro.* In it, Descartes dispenses with the foundations laid by all previous philosophical and scientific systems built upon external authority and attempts to reconstruct philosophy and the entire knowledge-seeking enterprise anew. While many philosophers objected to it furiously at the time, others praised it as a great achievement. Instead of ignoring his critics, Descartes published in the same volume all the most prominent objections and criticisms, including those of Pierre Gassendi, Antoine Arnauld, and even the great English philosopher Thomas Hobbes. To Hobbes the work looked so derivative of Plato that his first response, which Descartes published exactly as written, was, "I am sorry that so excellent an author of new speculations should publish this old stuff."

Before you begin reading, you might pause a moment and reflect upon all the sorts of things you believe to be true. Make a list. Now ask yourself *how you know that these things are true.* Or, you might ask *how you came to believe the things you believe.*

You believe so many things that it would be virtually impossible to individually examine each one of your beliefs. But notice that there are only a few *methods* by which *you* acquired *your* beliefs. Perhaps most of your beliefs come about through conditioning by various people in a position of authority: parents, teachers, religious leaders, politicians, celebrities, and so on. Descartes now asks: *Have you ever been deceived by any of these methods?* If so, then *throw out all beliefs derived by that method.*

The idea, then, is that instead of considering each belief individually, find the principles on the basis of which the beliefs were acquired, test the general principles rather than the particular beliefs, and throw out any and all principles that led to any erroneous beliefs. Descartes's suggestion may seem rather drastic. But what Descartes is after calls for drastic means; he wants absolute certainty. And if there is some method by which you acquired *a false* belief, that method is *unreliable.*

Suppose you have a friend. You confide in this friend some most intimate secret about yourself. You ask your friend never to tell a soul about it, never to betray you. The friend then betrays you.

Is this friend trustworthy? No. A friend who has betrayed you in this way even once is *not* trustworthy. You can never really trust this friend again. It is the same with beliefs. What Descartes is saying, in the first Meditation, about any supposed method of knowledge, is this: if the method has betrayed you even once, it is not trustworthy. Throw out all beliefs based on that method. If that leaves you with nothing, then so be it.

He first considers the senses. The senses often mislead us: appearances are deceiving. But even if our senses mislead us only sometimes, that is enough to make them unreliable. Therefore, throw out any beliefs derived from the senses. But what about *general* beliefs derived from the senses? There may be optical illusions, visual deceptions, and so on, but what about the most general sorts of information revealed to us through the senses—such as that there is a table in front of me (even though I may be wrong about some of its particular aspects such as its color, exact shape, and so on)?

Here Descartes evokes one of the Skeptics' most powerful questions: how do you know right now that you are not dreaming, or that an evil demon (or God) is not deceiving you? These may seem like far-fetched possibilities. But let us now read the first Meditation and then we shall see that what may at first glance strike you as not very possible is in fact very, very real.

⚓

Meditations on the First Philosophy, in Which the Existence of God, and the Real Distinction of Mind and Body, Are Demonstrated.

Meditation I.

OF THE THINGS OF WHICH WE MAY DOUBT.

Several years have now elapsed since I first became aware that I had accepted, even from my youth,

---

From René Descartes, *Meditations on First Philosophy,* 1641 (2d ed., Amsterdam: 1642).

many false opinions for true, and that consequently what I afterwards based on such principles was highly doubtful; and from that time I was convinced of the necessity of undertaking once in my life to rid myself of all the opinions I had adopted, and of commencing anew the work of building from the foundation, if I desired to establish a firm and abiding superstructure in the sciences. But as this enterprise appeared to me to be one of great magnitude, I waited until I had attained an age so mature as to leave me no hope that at any stage of life more advanced I should be better able to execute my design. On this account, I have delayed so long that I should henceforth consider I was doing wrong were I still to consume in deliberation any of the time that now remains for action. To-day, then, since I have opportunely freed my mind from all cares, [and am happily disturbed by no passions], and since I am in the secure possession of leisure in a peaceable retirement, I will at length apply myself earnestly and freely to the general overthrow of all my former opinions. But, to this end, it will not be necessary for me to show that the whole of these are false—a point, perhaps, which I shall never reach; but as even now my reason convinces me that I ought not the less carefully to withhold belief from what is not entirely certain and indubitable, than from what is manifestly false, it will be sufficient to justify the rejection of the whole if I shall find in each some ground for doubt. Nor for this purpose will it be necessary even to deal with each belief individually, which would be truly an endless labour; but, as the removal from below of the foundation necessarily involves the downfall of the whole edifice, I will at once approach the criticism of the principles on which all my former beliefs rested.

All that I have, up to this moment, accepted as possessed of the highest truth and certainty, I received either from or through the senses. I observed, however, that these sometimes misled us; and it is the part of prudence not to place absolute confidence in that by which we have even once been deceived.

But it may be said, perhaps, that, although the senses occasionally mislead us respecting minute objects, and such as are so far removed from us as to be beyond the reach of close observation, there are yet many other of their informations (presentations), of the truth of which it is manifestly impossible to doubt; as for example, that I am in this

place, seated by the fire, clothed in a winter dressing-gown, that I hold in my hands this piece of paper, with other intimations of the same nature. But how could I deny that I possess these hands and this body, and withal escape being classed with persons in a state of insanity, whose brains are so disordered and clouded by dark bilious vapours as to cause them pertinaciously to assert that they are monarchs when they are in the greatest poverty; or clothed [in gold] and purple when destitute of any covering; or that their head is made of clay, their body of glass, or that they are gourds? I should certainly be not less insane than they, were I to regulate my procedure according to examples so extravagant.

Though this be true, I must nevertheless here consider that I am a man, and that, consequently, I am in the habit of sleeping, and representing to myself in dreams those same things, or even sometimes others less probable, which the insane think are presented to them in their waking moments. How often have I dreamt that I was in these familiar circumstances,—that I was dressed, and occupied this place by the fire, when I was lying undressed in bed? At the present moment, however, I certainly look upon this paper with eyes wide awake; the head which I now move is not asleep; I extend this hand consciously and with express purpose, and I perceive it; the occurrences in sleep are not so distinct as all this. But I cannot forget that, at other times, I have been deceived in sleep by similar illusions; and, attentively considering those cases, I perceive so clearly that there exist no certain marks by which the state of waking can ever be distinguished from sleep, that I feel greatly astonished; and in amazement I almost persuade myself that I am now dreaming.

Let us suppose, then, that we are dreaming, and that all these particulars—namely, the opening of the eyes, the motion of the head, the forth-putting of the hands—are merely illusions; and even that we really possess neither an entire body nor hands such as we see. Nevertheless, it must be admitted at least that the objects which appear to us in sleep are, as it were, painted representations which could not have been formed unless in the likeness of realities; and, therefore, that those general objects, at all events,—namely, eyes, a head, hands, and an entire body—are not simply imaginary, but really existent. For, in truth, painters themselves, even when they study to represent sirens and satyrs by forms the most fantastic and extraordinary, cannot bestow upon them natures absolutely new, but can only make a certain medley of the members of different animals; or if they chance to imagine something so novel that nothing at all similar has ever been seen before, and such as is, therefore, purely fictitious and absolutely false, it is at least certain that the colours of which this is composed are real.

And on the same principle, although these general objects, viz. [a body], eyes, a head, hands, and the like, be imaginary, we are nevertheless absolutely necessitated to admit the reality at least of some other objects still more simple and universal than these, of which, just as of certain real colours, all those images of things, whether true and real, or false and fantastic, that are found in our consciousness (*cogitatio*), are formed.

To this class of objects seem to belong corporeal nature in general and its extension; the figure of extended things, their quantity or magnitude, and their number, as also the place in, and the time during, which they exist, and other things of the same sort. We will not, therefore, perhaps reason illegitimately if we conclude from this that Physics, Astronomy, Medicine, and all the other sciences that have for their end the consideration of composite objects, are indeed of a doubtful character; but that Arithmetic, Geometry, and the other sciences of the same class, which regard merely the simplest and most general objects, and scarcely inquire whether or not these are really existent, contain somewhat that is certain and indubitable: for whether I am awake or dreaming, it remains true that two and three make five, and that a square has but four sides; nor does it seem possible that truths so apparent can ever fall under a suspicion of falsity [or incertitude].

Nevertheless, the belief that there is a God who is all-powerful, and who created me, such as I am, has, for a long time, obtained steady possession of my mind. How, then, do I know that he has not arranged that there should be neither earth, nor sky, nor any extended thing, nor figure, nor magnitude, nor place, providing at the same time, however, for [the rise in me of the perceptions of all these objects, and] the persuasion that these do not exist otherwise than as I perceive them? And further, as I sometimes think that others are in error respecting matters of which they believe themselves to

possess a perfect knowledge, how do I know that I am not also deceived each time I add together two and three, or number the sides of a square, or form some judgment still more simple, if more simple indeed can be imagined? But perhaps Deity has not been willing that I should be thus deceived, for He is said to be supremely good. If, however, it were repugnant to the goodness of Deity to have created me subject to constant deception, it would seem likewise to be contrary to his goodness to allow me to be occasionally deceived; and yet it is clear that this is permitted. Some, indeed, might perhaps be found who would be disposed rather to deny the existence of a Being so powerful than to believe that there is nothing certain. But let us for the present refrain from opposing this opinion, and grant that all which is here said of a Deity is fabulous: nevertheless in whatever way it be supposed that I reached the state in which I exist, whether by fate, or chance, or by an endless series of antecedents and consequents, or by any other means, it is clear (since to be deceived and to err is a certain defect) that the probability of my being so imperfect as to be the constant victim of deception, will be increased exactly in proportion as the power possessed by the cause, to which they assign my origin, is lessened. To these reasonings I have assuredly nothing to reply, but am constrained at last to avow that there is nothing of all that I formerly believed to be true of which it is impossible to doubt, and that not through thoughtlessness or levity, but from cogent and maturely considered reasons; so that henceforward, if I desire to discover anything certain, I ought not the less carefully to refrain from assenting to those same opinions than to what might be shown to be manifestly false.

But it is not sufficient to have made these observations; care must be taken likewise to keep them in remembrance. For those old and customary opinions perpetually recur—long and familiar usage giving them the right of occupying my mind, even almost against my will, and subduing my belief; nor will I lose the habit of deferring to them and confiding in them so long as I shall consider them to be what in truth they are, viz., opinions to some extent doubtful, as I have already shown, but still highly probable, and such as it is much more reasonable to believe than deny. It is for this reason I am persuaded that I shall not be doing wrong, if, taking an opposite judgment of deliberate design, I become my own deceiver, by supposing, for a time, that all those opinions are entirely false and imaginary, until at length, having thus balanced my old by my new prejudices, my judgment shall no longer be turned aside by perverted usage from the path that may conduct to the perception of truth. For I am assured that, meanwhile, there will arise neither peril nor error from this course, and that I cannot for the present yield too much to distrust, since the end I now seek is not action but knowledge.

I will suppose, then, not that Deity, who is sovereignly good and the fountain of truth, but that some malignant demon, who is at once exceedingly potent and deceitful, has employed all his artifice to deceive me; I will suppose that the sky, the air, the earth, colours, figures, sounds, and all external things, are nothing better than the illusions of dreams, by means of which this being has laid snares for my credulity; I will consider myself as without hands, eyes, flesh, blood, or any of the senses, and as falsely believing that I am possessed of these: I will continue resolutely fixed in this belief, and if indeed by this means it be not in my power to arrive at the knowledge of truth, I shall at least do what is in my power, viz., [suspend my judgment], and guard with settled purpose against giving my assent to what is false, and being imposed upon by this deceiver, whatever be his power and artifice.

But this undertaking is arduous, and a certain indolence insensibly leads me back to my ordinary course of life; and just as the captive, who, perchance, was enjoying in his dreams an imaginary liberty, when he begins to suspect that it is but a vision, dreads awakening, and conspires with the agreeable illusions that the deception may be prolonged; so I, of my own accord, fall back into the train of my former beliefs, and fear to arouse myself from my slumber, lest the time of laborious wakefulness that would succeed this quiet rest, in place of bringing any light of day, should prove inadequate to dispel the darkness that will arise from the difficulties that have now been raised.

※

You've just read the first Meditation. Suppose you don't understand what you've read. You want to know what it means; you want a better or deeper understanding. Beethoven was once asked after playing one of his piano sonatas what it meant. He responded by playing it again. What I suggest you do if you've read this and don't understand it is what I or any other philosopher I know does: read it again. In fact, I'd like to throw in another personal anecdote, this one about another philosopher, my friend and sometime coauthor Ray Martin. When he was an undergraduate he had to take an introduction to philosophy course that he hated because he didn't understand much of it. It was a large class and he sat in the back of the auditorium and never said a word. When they were assigned Descartes's *Meditations* Ray read it. He didn't understand any of it, either. Frustrated, he decided that he had had enough: he was going to just reread the same book over and over again until either he got it or else he would drop the class and maybe drop out of college. Upon the fifth or sixth reading, as he now tells the story, "something went off inside my head. I understood it. I understood *everything*. It was like a great darkness had been lifted from me and I realized I'd been living my life up to that moment as if in a dream, accepting everything, not questioning anything. Suddenly I craved the truth because I think for a moment I glimpsed what it was. Nothing was certain. Everything was floating on sand. Everything. Except my own existence. *But maybe not even that.*"

Let us try, then, and reflect a bit on that first Meditation. Note, first, that not since Augustine's *Confessions* in the fourth century has a work been written so explicitly in the first person. It is a personal philosophical account of a journey that Descartes invites you to attempt yourself. And he begins by no less than an "overthrow of all my former opinions."

We have already encountered the axioms, or principles, of Descartes's method for attaining certainty. Before applying this method, he wanted to start afresh, for he realized that most of his opinions entered his mind, not through any such method but simply through uncritical acceptance of conditioning by authority. He would therefore throw them all away to see what, if anything, is indubitable.

In the doubting process, Descartes got to the question, *how do you know that you are not right now dreaming?* This question, which philosophers are often apt to ask, is often and easily misunderstood. Typically, when presented with such a question, most people can recall situations when they were having especially vivid dreams in which they believed, at the time, that what was happening was not a dream but reality. They then woke up with much surprise to find that it was only a dream. What these people fail to realize is that just about *every* one of your dreams, no matter how "crazy," "discontinuous," and so on, *is taken by you while it is occurring to be reality.* The proof? While you're having a dream—*any* dream—you don't say to yourself, hey, gee, look, here I am dreaming again! Look at those imaginary images I see! Isn't this fun?

No, regardless of how strange the dream, it is usually the case that as you experience the dream you take it to be reality. Why? Because Descartes's demon is not imaginary. It's real. It's running just about all the time, able to deceive you quite vividly about all sorts of things and make you believe that what you are experiencing is not a mental construction but mind-independently real objects outside your head. Today, we call it your *brain.*

Or have you already forgotten all about philosophical enlightenment? Have you forgotten what you have supposedly learned in many different ways from many different philosophers—for instance, that eyes are not windows, that in a very important sense you are *always* dreaming, even with your eyes open, because the appearances are themselves mental constructions? The objects you see may to some degree be accurate representations of the things "out there," outside your head, but they are not numerically identical—that is, they are not one and the same things. Just as the word *dog* is not a dog, so the image of the chair in front of you is not a chair. Cross your eyes! The one chair becomes two? Hardly. The one image of the chair becomes two images.

And that's why you can't tell, just by *looking*, that what you are seeing is actually the way it appears. What Descartes is here pointing out in the first Meditation is that you cannot even be absolutely sure that the object you see is there *at all.* You've been deceived before, when the object you were looking at existed only as a dream image, into believing that what you were looking at was a mind-independent object outside your head. The appearances are therefore, by themselves, not trustworthy.

But it's worse than that. Even when you are not dreaming—that is, when you are wide awake—you are not directly aware of what Kant will call the "transcendental illusion" (Section 16.2), the philosophical insight that we have tried to capture in the most simple way with the phrase "eyes are not windows." So you are still being deceived by your own perceptual-cognitive apparatus—your brain!

Again, light stops at the back of the retina, where an impulse (actually, a bunch of potassium ions bouncing back and forth) goes along the optic "nerve" (it's not really a nerve as such, nor does anything *optical* travel along it in the sense of visual images as such) to the brain. (We discussed this at length on pages 186–189.) Say you're looking at a chair: an image of that chair appears upside down on the back of your retina and then this "information" is translated into a sort of numerical code that is then used by your brain to construct the image that you see when you see a chair. The chair "out there" doesn't cause the image you see, nor does the brain passively receive any such image; the brain creates such an image from scratch using its own active processing. The information from the optic nerve just tells it, in effect, what sort of mental picture to paint, but that information does not, itself, come in the form of a visual image.

So you see, even with all our advanced science and neuroscience of perception, Descartes's *epistemological* question stands as vividly as ever. What we call "reality" is already a sort of "virtual reality," and so how do we know that what we are looking at is real? For all you know, given the way that perception works, you might be a brain in a vat on a planet in the Alpha Centauri system being stimulated by electrodes into experiencing an imaginary virtual reality film called *Life on Earth*. The Alpha Centaurians are running experiments to see what kinds of imaginary worlds they can create. *Any* experience you try to verify that something like that is *not* so can itself, for all you know, be an induced, virtual reality experience!

So we don't need the perhaps antiquated concept of a deceiving demon or a god to get the point of Descartes's first Meditation. Everything we have learned in the meantime about the operations of our own eyes and brains makes such extraordinary, supernatural concepts unnecessary; we can now, thanks to the "advances" of science, raise exactly the same problem with our ordinary, natural concepts, such as *the brain* and *the eye*.

Will we fare as well with the *solution* to this devastating problem of Skepticism raised by the first Meditation? Let us see.

10.5 The New Rationalism: "I Think, Therefore I Am": Descartes's Second Meditation

The second *Meditation* begins with Descartes literally drowning in doubt. He has doubted everything that can be doubted—whether he knows anything at all, whether the world or anyone else exists—and now he wants to see what, if anything, is left. He went in search of some ultimate bedrock, a firm foundation, upon which to erect a new structure for philosophy from the ground up. But this far he has found only layers of quicksand, followed by a maelstrom of sinking uncertainty. Yet he does not stop. In the second *Meditation* he continues doubting ever more!

Le us now rejoin him in the depths of darkness from within which he will emerge victorious, the bearer of one of the most profound rational insights of all time. Pay close attention to where and exactly how his doubt ends. Why can Descartes go no further? Here at the dead end of doubt you can see hidden in plain sight the beginning of something so completely new and different from all the philosophizing that went on before him that it has come to be known as "modern philosophy." With the stroke of a pen the thousand-year night ends. First light: Plato's sun is about to rise again. Witness philosophy's second dawn.

⋆

Meditation II.

OF THE NATURE OF THE HUMAN MIND; AND THAT IT IS MORE EASILY KNOWN THAN THE BODY.

The Meditation of yesterday has filled my mind with so many doubts, that it is no longer in my power to forget them. Nor do I see, meanwhile, any principle on which they can be resolved; and, just as if I had fallen all of a sudden into very deep water, I am so greatly disconcerted as to be unable either to plant my feet firmly on the bottom or sustain myself by swimming on the surface. I will, nevertheless, make an effort, and try anew the same path on which I had entered yesterday, that is, proceed by casting aside all that admits of the slightest doubt, not less than if I had discovered it to be absolutely false; and I will continue always in this track until I shall find something that is certain, or at least, if I can do nothing more, until I shall know with certainty that there is nothing certain. Archimedes, that he might transport the entire globe from the place it occupied to another, demanded only a point that was firm and immoveable; so also, I shall be entitled to entertain the highest expectations, if I am fortunate enough to discover only one thing that is certain and indubitable.

I suppose, accordingly, that all the things which I see are false (fictitious); I believe that none of those objects which my fallacious memory represents ever existed; I suppose that I possess no senses; I believe that body, figure, extension, motion, and place are merely fictions of my mind. What is there, then, that can be esteemed true? Perhaps this only, that there is absolutely nothing certain.

But how do I know that there is not something different altogether from the objects I have now enumerated, of which it is impossible to entertain the slightest doubt? Is there not a God, or some being, by whatever name I may designate him, who causes these thoughts to arise in my mind? But why suppose such a being, for it may be I myself am capable of producing them? Am I, then, at least not something? But I before denied that I possessed senses or a body; I hesitate, however, for what follows from that? Am I so dependent on the body and the senses that without these I cannot exist? But I had the persuasion that there was absolutely nothing in the world, that there was no sky and no earth, neither minds nor bodies; was I not, therefore, at the same time, persuaded that I did not exist? Far from it; I assuredly existed, since I was persuaded. But there is I know not what being, who is possessed at once of the highest power and the deepest cunning, who is constantly employing all his ingenuity in deceiving me. Doubtless, then, I exist, since I am deceived; and let him deceive me as he may, he can never bring it about that I am nothing, so long as I shall be conscious that I am something. So that it must, in fine, be maintained, all things being maturely and carefully considered, that this proposition (*pronunciatum*) I am, I exist, is necessarily true each time it is expressed by me, or conceived in my mind.

But I do not yet know with sufficient clearness what I am, though assured that I am; and hence, in the next place, I must take care, lest perchance I inconsiderately substitute some other object in room of what is properly myself, and thus wander from truth, even in that knowledge (cognition) which I hold to be of all others the most certain and evident. For this reason, I will now consider anew what I formerly believed myself to be, before I entered on the present train of thought; and of my previous opinion I will retrench all that can in the least be invalidated by the grounds of doubt I have adduced, in order that there may at length remain nothing but what is certain and indubitable. What then did I formerly think I was? Undoubtedly I judged that I was a man. But what is a man? Shall I say a rational animal? Assuredly not; for it would be necessary forthwith to inquire into what is meant by animal, and what by rational, and thus, from a single question, I should insensibly glide into others, and these more difficult than the first; nor do I now possess enough of

leisure to warrant me in wasting my time amid subtleties of this sort. I prefer here to attend to the thoughts that sprung up of themselves in my mind, and were inspired by my own nature alone, when I applied myself to the consideration of what I was. In the first place, then, I thought that I possessed a countenance, hands, arms, and all the fabric of members that appears in a corpse, and which I called by the name of body. It further occurred to me that I was nourished, that I walked, perceived, and thought, and all those actions I referred to the soul; but what the soul itself was I either did not stay to consider, or, if I did, I imagined that it was something extremely rare and subtle, like wind, or flame, or ether, spread through my grosser parts. As regarded the body, I did not even doubt of its nature, but thought I distinctly knew it, and if I had wished to describe it according to the notions I then entertained, I should have explained myself in this manner: By body I understand all that can be terminated by a certain figure; that can be comprised in a certain place, and so fill a certain space as therefrom to exclude every other body; that can be perceived either by touch, sight, hearing, taste, or smell; that can be moved in different ways, not indeed of itself, but by something foreign to it by which it is touched [and from which it receives the impression]; for the power of self-motion, as likewise that of perceiving and thinking, I held as by no means pertaining to the nature of body; on the contrary, I was somewhat astonished to find such faculties existing in some bodies.

But as to myself, what can I now say that I am, since I suppose there exists an extremely powerful, and, if I may so speak, malignant being, whose whole endeavours are directed towards deceiving me? Can I affirm that I possess any one of all those attributes of which I have lately spoken as belonging to the nature of body? After attentively considering them in my own mind, I find none of them that can properly be said to belong to myself. To recount them were idle and tedious. Let us pass, then, to the attributes of the soul. The first mentioned were the powers of nutrition and walking; but, if it be true that I have no body, it is true likewise that I am capable neither of walking nor of being nourished. Perception is another attribute of the soul; but perception too is impossible without the body: besides, I have frequently, during sleep, believed that I perceived objects which I afterwards observed I did not in reality perceive. Thinking is another attribute of the soul; and here I discover what properly belongs to myself. This alone is inseparable from me. I am—I exist: this is certain; but how often? As often as I think; for perhaps it would even happen, if I should wholly cease to think, that I should at the same time altogether cease to be. I now admit nothing that is not necessarily true: I am therefore, precisely speaking, only a thinking thing, that is, a mind (*mens sive animus*), understanding, or reason,—terms whose signification was before unknown to me. I am, however, a real thing, and really existent; but what thing? The answer was, a thinking thing. The question now arises, am I aught besides? I will stimulate my imagination with a view to discover whether I am not still something more than a thinking being. Now it is plain I am not the assemblage of members called the human body; I am not a thin and penetrating air diffused through all these members, or wind, or flame, or vapour, or breath, or any of all the things I can imagine; for I supposed that all these were not, and, without changing the supposition, I find that I still feel assured of my existence.

But it is true, perhaps, that those very things which I suppose to be non-existent, because they are unknown to me, are not in truth different from myself whom I know. This is a point I cannot determine, and do not now enter into any dispute regarding it. I can only judge of things that are known to me: I am conscious that I exist, and I who know that I exist inquire into what I am. It is, however, perfectly certain that the knowledge of my existence, thus precisely taken, is not dependent on things, the existence of which is as yet unknown to me: and consequently it is not dependent on any of the things I can feign in imagination. Moreover, the phrase itself, I frame an image (*effingo*), reminds me of my error; for I should in truth frame one if I were to imagine myself to be anything, since to imagine is nothing more than to contemplate the figure or image of a corporeal thing; but I already know that I exist, and that it is possible at the same time that all those images, and in general all that relates to the nature of body, are merely dreams [or chimeras]. From this I discover that it is not more reasonable to say, I will excite my imagination that I may know more distinctly what I am, than to express myself as follows: I am now awake, and perceive something real; but because my perception is not suffi-

ciently clear, I will of express purpose go to sleep that my dreams may represent to me the object of my perception with more truth and clearness. And, therefore, I know that nothing of all that I can embrace in imagination belongs to the knowledge which I have of myself, and that there is need to recall with the utmost care the mind from this mode of thinking, that it may be able to know its own nature with perfect distinctness.

But what, then, am I? A thinking thing, it has been said. But what is a thinking thing? It is a thing that doubts, understands, [conceives], affirms, denies, wills, refuses, that imagines also, and perceives. Assuredly it is not little, if all these properties belong to my nature. But why should they not belong to it? Am I not that very being who now doubts of almost everything; who, for all that, understands and conceives certain things; who affirms one alone as true, and denies the others; who desires to know more of them, and does not wish to be deceived; who imagines many things, sometimes even despite his will; and is likewise percipient of many, as if through the medium of the senses. Is there nothing of all this as true as that I am, even although I should be always dreaming, and although he who gave me being employed all his ingenuity to deceive me? Is there also any one of these attributes that can be properly distinguished from my thought, or that can be said to be separate from myself? For it is of itself so evident that it is I who doubt, I who understand, and I who desire, that it is here unnecessary to add anything by way of rendering it more clear. And I am as certainly the same being who imagines; for, although it may be (as I before supposed) that nothing I imagine is true, still the power of imagination does not cease really to exist in me and to form part of my thought. In fine, I am the same being who perceives, that is, who apprehends certain objects as by the organs of sense, since, in truth, I see light, hear a noise, and feel heat. But it will be said that these presentations are false, and that I am dreaming. Let it be so. At all events it is certain that I seem to see light, hear a noise, and feel heat; this cannot be false, and this is what in me is properly called perceiving (*sentire*), which is nothing else than thinking. From this I begin to know what I am with somewhat greater clearness and distinctness than heretofore.

But, nevertheless, it still seems to me, and I cannot help believing, that corporeal things, whose images are formed by thought, which fall under the senses, and are examined by the same, are known with much greater distinctness than that I know not what part of myself which is not imaginable; although, in truth, it may seem strange to say that I know and comprehend with greater distinctness things whose existence appears to me doubtful, that are unknown, and do not belong to me, than others of whose reality I am persuaded, that are known to me, and appertain to my proper nature; in a word, than myself. But I see clearly what is the state of the case. My mind is apt to wander, and will not yet submit to be restrained within the limits of truth. Let us therefore leave the mind to itself once more, and, according to it every kind of liberty, [permit it to consider the objects that appear to it from without], in order that, having afterwards withdrawn it from these gently and opportunely, [and fixed it on the consideration of its being and the properties it finds in itself], it may then be the more easily controlled.

Let us now accordingly consider the objects that are commonly thought to be the most easily, and likewise the most distinctly known, viz., the bodies we touch and see; not, indeed, bodies in general, for these general notions are usually somewhat more confused, but one body in particular. Take, for example, this piece of wax; it is quite fresh, having been but recently taken from the bee-hive; it has not yet lost the sweetness of the honey it contained; it still retains somewhat of the odour of the flowers from which it was gathered; its colour, figure, size, are apparent (to the sight); it is hard, cold, easily handled; and sounds when struck upon with the finger. In fine, all that contributes to make a body as distinctly known as possible, is found in the one before us. But, while I am speaking, let it be placed near the fire—what remained of the taste exhales, the smell evaporates, the colour changes, its figure is destroyed, its size increases, it becomes liquid, it grows hot, it can hardly be handled, and, although struck upon, it emits no sound. Does the same wax still remain after this change? It must be admitted that it does remain; no one doubts it, or judges otherwise. What, then, was it I knew with so much distinctness in the piece of wax? Assuredly, it could be nothing of all that I observed by means of the senses, since all the things that fell under taste, smell, sight, touch, and hearing are changed, and yet the same wax

remains. It was perhaps what I now think, viz., that this wax was neither the sweetness of honey, the pleasant odour of flowers, the whiteness, the figure, nor the sound, but only a body that a little before appeared to me conspicuous under these forms, and which is now perceived under others. But, to speak precisely, what is it that I imagine when I think of it in this way? Let it be attentively considered, and, retrenching all that does not belong to the wax, let us see what remains. There certainly remains nothing, except something extended, flexible, and movable. But what is meant by flexible and movable? Is it not that I imagine that the piece of wax, being round, is capable of becoming square, or of passing from a square into a triangular figure? Assuredly such is not the case, because I conceive that it admits of an infinity of similar changes; and I am, moreover, unable to compass this infinity by imagination, and consequently this conception which I have of the wax is not the product of the faculty of imagination. But what now is this extension? Is it not also unknown? for it becomes greater when the wax is melted, greater when it is boiled, and greater still when the heat increases; and I should not conceive clearly and according to truth, the wax as it is, if I did not suppose that the piece we are considering admitted even of a wider variety of extension than I ever imagined. I must, therefore, admit that I cannot even comprehend by imagination what the piece of wax is, and that it is the mind alone (*mens*, Lat., *entendement*, F.) which perceives it. I speak of one piece in particular; for, as to wax in general, this is still more evident. But what is the piece of wax that can be perceived only by the understanding or mind? It is certainly the same which I see, touch, imagine; and, in fine, it is the same which, from the beginning, I believed it to be. But (and this it is of moment to observe) the perception of it is neither an act of sight, of touch, nor of imagination, and never was either of these, though it might formerly seem so, but is simply an intuition (*inspectio*) of the mind, which may be imperfect and confused, as it formerly was, or very clear and distinct, as it is at present, according as the attention is more or less directed to the elements which it contains, and of which it is composed.

But, meanwhile, I feel greatly astonished when I observe [the weakness of my mind, and] its proneness to error. For although, without at all giving expression to what I think, I consider all this in my own mind, words yet occasionally impede my progress, and I am almost led into error by the terms of ordinary language. We say, for example, that we see the same wax when it is before us, and not that we judge it to be the same from its retaining the same colour and figure: whence I should forthwith be disposed to conclude that the wax is known by the act of sight, and not by the intuition of the mind alone, were it not for the analogous instance of human beings passing on in the street below, as observed from a window. In this case I do not fail to say that I see the men themselves, just as I say that I see the wax; and yet what do I see from the window beyond hats and cloaks that might cover artificial machines, whose motions might be determined by springs? But I judge that there are human beings from these appearances, and thus I comprehend, by the faculty of judgment alone which is in the mind, what I believed I saw with my eyes.

The man who makes it his aim to rise to knowledge superior to the common, ought to be ashamed to seek occasions of doubting from the vulgar forms of speech: instead, therefore, of doing this, I shall proceed with the matter in hand, and inquire whether I had a clearer and more perfect perception of the piece of wax when I first saw it, and when I thought I knew it by means of the external sense itself, or, at all events, by the common sense (*sensus communis*), as it is called, that is, by the imaginative faculty; or whether I rather apprehend it more clearly at present, after having examined with greater care, both what it is, and in what way it can be known. It would certainly be ridiculous to entertain any doubt on this point. For what, in that first perception, was there distinct? What did I perceive which any animal might not have perceived? But when I distinguish the wax from its exterior forms, and when, as if I had stripped it of its vestments, I consider it quite naked, it is certain, although some error may still be found in my judgment, that I cannot, nevertheless, thus apprehend it without possessing a human mind.

But, finally, what shall I say of the mind itself, that is, of myself? for as yet I do not admit that I am anything but mind. What, then! I who seem to possess so distinct an apprehension of the piece of wax,—do I not know myself, both with greater truth and certitude, and also much more distinctly and clearly? For if I judge that the wax exists because I see it, it assuredly follows, much more

evidently, that I myself am or exist, for the same reason: for it is possible that what I see may not in truth be wax, and that I do not even possess eyes with which to see anything; but it cannot be that when I see, or, which comes to the same thing, when I think I see, I myself who think am nothing. So likewise, if I judge that the wax exists because I touch it, it will still also follow that I am; and if I determine that my imagination, or any other cause, whatever it be, persuades me of the existence of the wax, I will still draw the same conclusion. And what is here remarked of the piece of wax, is applicable to all the other things that are external to me. And further, if the [notion or] perception of wax appeared to me more precise and distinct, after that not only sight and touch, but many other causes besides, rendered it manifest to my apprehension, with how much greater distinctness must I now know myself, since all the reasons that contribute to the knowledge of the nature of wax, or of any body whatever, manifest still better the nature of my mind? And there are besides so many other things in the mind itself that contribute to the illustration of its nature, that those dependent on the body, to which I have here referred, scarcely merit to be taken into account.

But, in conclusion, I find I have insensibly reverted to the point I desired; for, since it is now manifest to me that bodies themselves are not properly perceived by the senses nor by the faculty of imagination, but by the intellect alone; and since they are not perceived because they are seen and touched, but only because they are understood [or rightly comprehended by thought], I readily discover that there is nothing more easily or clearly apprehended than my own mind. But because it is difficult to rid one's self so promptly of an opinion to which one has been long accustomed, it will be desirable to tarry for some time at this stage, that, by long continued meditation, I may more deeply impress upon my memory this new knowledge.

⁂

So, just as Archimedes showed how he could move the entire earth if only he had a firm place to put his fulcrum, Descartes found a firm place to put his absolutely indubitable proposition, which he then used to move the whole of philosophy. After allowing himself the liberty of doubting everything that could be doubted, throwing out anything that could even *in principle* be doubted, he finally found solid ground. For even if he was dreaming, even if an evil demon, God, or a scientist on some planet in the Alpha Centauri system was manipulating his brain into having the experiences it was having, *nobody, not even his own brain, not even God, could deceive him into believing falsely that he existed*. At the very least, even in the case where he was being deceived about everything, *deception* was going on and so there was something, someone, being deceived.

I think, therefore I am.

This principle was not intended and should not be considered as a deduction of the conclusion, "I am," from the premise, "I think" (see the discussion on Aristotelian logic and syllogisms, Section 3.0). Rather, it comes about as an insight at the tail end of a series of apparently endless doubts: I doubt that the world is what it appears, that there is a God, that external objects exist, that I have a body, that twice two is four (even *that* can be doubted!). But it is impossible for me to doubt that I, who am involved in this activity of doubting, exist. So here is this one single point at which the apparently endless series of doubts comes to an abrupt end: at the doubter, at the self-existence of the thinker who thinks such thoughts. I can doubt everything except that I doubt and that, in thus doubting, I am. Even if a being superior to me tried to deceive me in all my thinking, such a being could not succeed unless I already existed; the deceiver could not cause me *not* to exist as long as I thought. To be deceived means to think falsely, but that something even in that moment of false thinking is being thought, no matter what it is, is itself *not* a deception. It might be true that nothing at all exists, but then there would be no one to conceive of this nonexistence. Even if every thought I ever had is a mistaken thought, the state of being mistaken, the activity of thinking, is itself not a mistake: even when everything is denied the denier remains. Undermine the whole content of consciousness by making its assertions false, still that consciousness itself—the doubting activity, the *being* of the thinker—is not thereby undermined but affirmed, acknowledged, realized. This, then, is the absolute point of departure necessary for knowledge, found in the *self-certitude of the thinking ego*.[5] In other words, from the fact that I doubt—that is, from the fact that I think—it follows not as a logical deduction that I, the doubter, the thinker, am, but as an *insight* or philosophical *realization*. Thus Descartes's Latin phrase, *Cogito, ergo sum*—literally, "Thinking, therefore existing"—is the most certain of all truths, the first axiom of Cartesian rationality.

So, again, this axiom is *not* a deduction. Once I realize in my own experience that, as a thinking being, I exist, I can then reach the general conclusion that thought and existence are in this specific sense *inseparable*. This fundamental truth is thus not a syllogism but a self-evident, immediate cognition, a *pure intuition: sum cogitans*.

In other words, my existence *is revealed by my activity of thought*. My thought is my being: in me thought and existence are identical. I am a being whose essence consists in thinking. I am a mental entity, an ego, a rational mind. The existence of the mind is therefore not only the most certain of all things, not only the basis for the possibility of finding certainty among all other things, *mind is itself identical to being*.

Thus, the method of "Cartesian doubt," according to which a solid foundation for philosophy must begin by doubting everything that can be doubted, raises a question that would be a major preoccupation for all the philosophers we shall consider in Chapters 13 through 15—Locke, Berkeley, and Hume—and which continues today. Is knowledge attained through rational intuition or sense experience? Descartes's answer, in marked contrast to the preceding three subsequent British Empiricists, was a forerunner of Kant's critique of dogmatic metaphysics, planting the seeds of idealism with his argument that we know our own minds more immediately than we know the material world.

For the sum and substance of the Cartesian philosophy is not a skeptical renunciation of the unattainable any more than it is a dogmatic doctrine. It is the precept, the starting point of philosophy, *not* its conclusion: The *cogito* is, in other words, a methodological instrument for the knowledge-seeking enterprise that uses doubt to find the indubitable.

Let me put it still slightly differently. Descartes's method is *not* aimed at the *possibility* of knowledge, as it is sometimes presented (and in which case it obviously fails to do what is supposedly intended). Rather, its method is taken on the assumption *that knowledge has already been attained.* In Descartes's view, part of the problem, not only with his contemporaries but also with most thinkers today, is that we confuse the acquisition and handing down of information with knowledge of the truth. The only *certain* knowledge according to Descartes is that which is self-attained and self-tested and this, just as Socrates so wisely taught, *cannot* be learned and *cannot* be handed down. It can be rediscovered only through one's own examination and experience. That is, the real "secret" of the search for truth is to become utterly independent of one's own or any other age, to think for one's self instead of taking one's own unsupported opinions or the opinions of others as a guide. Only this independence will remedy the dangers of self-deception involved in other "false" systems of *un*philosophical attempts at knowledge.

One way to try to understand the Cartesian revolution is to compare it with the way Aristotle answers Descartes's question, "Who am I?" Aristotle, as we saw, claimed that all knowledge must proceed on the basis of definition. So how do you define what you are? You first give its *genus*—that part of the essence of anything that belongs also to other things differing from it in species—and then its *differentia*—that part of its essence that can be possessed by, or predicated of, members of only its own class, or species. (The *species* is the subclass of the more general class, genus.) Thus, for instance, according to

Aristotle's definition, the genus of the term *human being* is *animal,* whereas its *differentia* is *rational.* Descartes raises a very Socratic type of objection to this method of acquiring knowledge; you don't then know what a human being is unless you can also define *animal* and *rational.* And then whatever you define those as will, in turn, require more definitions, *ad infinitum.* The process, Descartes claimed, must come to an end—but where? Certainly not on a definition. Remember Euclid's axioms. They are definitions in a sense but they are *self-evident* truths, like "any two points define a line." Descartes wanted to find terms that did not need Aristotelian definitions, whose meanings could be seen directly by the conscious mind: the "clear and distinct" ideas that then became the elements out of which to construct more complex terms. This is in fact the direct application of the second and third axioms of his system (Section 10.1). Thus metaphysics, like mathematics, must derive its conclusions by deduction from *self-evident* principles.

It is also fruitful to compare Descartes's notion of *ideas* with that of Plato. Indeed, Descartes is the first philosopher to use the word *idea* in its modern sense. This will be extremely important when we come to the British Empiricists. What Descartes means by *idea* is "whatever the mind directly perceives." That is, *anything* that is itself directly an event in consciousness is an idea. This goes for the tables and chairs that you *see*—that is, the items of your perceptions (remember, eyes are not windows)—as well as for the tables and chairs that you imagine. The latter sorts of ideas exist only as modes of thought, whereas the former exist as *representations* of reality. In other words, when you're imagining a chair in a dream there is no chair at that moment in front of your eyes of which the image is a representation. When you are "looking" at a chair—that is, in a sense, when you're "dreaming with your eyes open"—the image is a representation of the chair "out there," the one that exists outside the mind. Now, even in dreams, we cannot deny the reality of ideas *as ideas,* that is, as presentations of the mind. What we can take issue with—what is, itself, the deepest question of epistemology—is whether the ideas that are supposed to be representations of "objective reality," and our judgments based on them, are *accurate.* That is, is there any aspect of our sense-images that is *unmistakably* an aspect of objective reality? Do any of our ideas, or any aspect of them, truly correspond to reality?

Obviously, not in the case of dreams. *Maybe* in the case of those that come "from without," that is, which are at least in part covariant with the outside world. But, as Descartes takes great pains to argue, this can never be known by us with certainty. This was in part his argument in *Meditations* based on the fact that we are often mistaken as to sounds and sights. As *methods,* sights and sounds are not trustworthy avatars of the truth.

But there is, according to Descartes, another class of ideas that neither originate in ourselves, such as dreams, nor are imparted to us as a result of our interaction with the external world. These are the ideas with which we are born, the fundamental concepts akin to the Aristotelian categories or the Platonic Ideas. These innate, a priori ideas are themselves known to us as the truths of *mathematics.* For whether asleep or awake, three and two make five, and so on: ideas of numbers therefore are more than just modes of thought. They have objective reality. However, even in mathematics we are not free from error because mathematical ideas are no more self-authenticating than are our sense-images. Our faith in the ideas of mathematics is like our habitual faith in our own senses. A malicious demon who has access to the innermost workings of our minds, or God, could deceive us even as to what we take to be the fundamental truths of mathematics; that is, *mathematics as we know it* might be an elaborate *construction* of the mind.[6] This is an aspect of Descartes's philosophy that is often overlooked, for it makes the possibility of certain knowledge about things other than one's self dependent on the existence

of a benevolent God. Unless such a benevolent God exists, Cartesian certainty cannot extend beyond one's own mind, and each one of us is caught within a solipsistic universe in which only *I exist* can be known with absolute certainty, a world in which the existence of a mind-independent "external world" is fundamentally and deeply called into question.

After its publication, *Meditations* attracted a wide following, not just among philosophers, scientists, artists, and leading intellectuals of the time, but even among royalty. The daughter of the titular king of Bohemia, Princess Elizabeth, began writing to him and Descartes wrote back that her understanding of both his *Discourse* and his *Meditations* was "incomparable." A few years later, in 1649, Queen Christina of Sweden urged him to come to Sweden to become her private tutor so that she could become enlightened by his new philosophy. At first he turned down her offer "to live in the land of bears among rocks and ice," but the French ambassador persuaded him to go. In Stockholm the queen requested her lessons to be held while much of the court was still asleep, at 5:00 A.M. Within four months, Descartes caught pneumonia and died.

NOTES

1. The Council of Trent, the Roman Catholic church council created to deal with the crisis created by the Protestant Reformation, started the Catholic Counter-Reformation and the *Index* was one of its main tools.
2. We just did that with principle (1).
3. Mathematics is derived from the ancient Greek *mathemata,* meaning thoughts occurring not in random but guided by clear and distinct principles, like a logical machinery or a computer program. So in that sense mathematics can be thought of as philosophy done in a way where the driving force is not the thoughts (the meaning, or semantics) but, rather, the thoughts are driven by some rule (rule-governed structure, or syntax).
4. Leibniz and Kant will use the word *apperception* to distinguish experience of one's own mental states

as such in contrast to *perception*, experience of things (still within one's own representational mental states, of course, but not as such). Thus, propositions can be thought of as the *apperception of meaning*.

5. The Latin "ego" just means "I."

6. In the twentieth century, mathematical *intuitionism*, also known as *constructionism*, was developed by Brower and others as a replacement for traditional mathematics deductively conceived.

11 ✻ Spinoza

11.0 Spinoza (1632–1677): The Philosophers' Philosopher

Baruch (Latin name, "Benedictus") Spinoza was born in Amsterdam to a prosperous Jewish merchant family that had come to Holland from their native Portugal to escape persecution. He attended the local school for Jewish boys where at a young age he had already begun arguing with his students and teachers, telling them that the Bible offered no reason for believing in angels or the immortality of the soul and that its authors were as ignorant about physics as they were about theology. When his rabbi and teachers failed to silence him with arguments, they tried to bribe him but he persisted, until finally the entire Jewish community excommunicated him in 1656; he was even banished from Amsterdam.

During this time he learned through his Christian acquaintances about the "new philosophy" of Descartes. He started a philosophy club for the study of religious and philosophical problems and supported himself mainly by grinding and polishing lenses. Privately, he worked to develop his vast metaphysical system that subse-quently came to deeply influence philosophers as diverse as Hegel and Leibniz.

In 1670 Spinoza published his *Tractatus Theologico-Politicus* (Treatise on Theology and Politics); Christian theologians banned it, calling it a work "forged in Hell by a renegade Jew and the devil." As a result, his masterpiece, *Ethics*, did not appear in print until after his death. He thus has the distinction of being banned by both Christian and Jewish theologians.

As one of the three so-called Continental Rationalists—Descartes and Leibniz were the other two—Spinoza was influenced by the sudden success of mathematics and geometry in physics. His *Ethics* was designed according to a strictly rational geometric system with definitions, axioms, and propositions arranged in a deductive system. He began with a discussion of God's nature, on which all the rest of existence, as well as our understanding of it, is based. Spinoza's conception of God, however, was not the traditional theistic one but pantheistic. Instead of using the concept of God as something separate and distinct from the world to explain existence, Spinoza's God is in everything; the world itself is God and whatever is true of God is to some extent true of each and every existent thing in the world. This is, essentially, an elaboration of a Parmenidean view of the world in which there exists but one substance; even mind and matter—thought and extension—are but attributes of the one infinite and universal substance, God. Individual persons do not have separate identities nor are they individual things; we are each merely aspects of one infinite being, God. According to Spinoza this pantheistic view of the universe can be seen to be true independently of any belief in a personal God, through the sort of introspection begun by Descartes. Indeed, Spinoza's methods of introspective analysis of the mind are so detailed and thorough that they anticipate many twentieth-century developments in psychology and psychiatry.

Starting with Descartes's logical presuppositions, Spinoza built an essentially Cartesian metaphysics into a geometric method even more rigorous than Descartes's; indeed, it is the technical precision of his *Ethics* that led many to refer to him as "the philosophers' philosopher." According to Spinoza, absolutely everything is knowable with perfect certainty through reason. Through its pure concepts (that is, unfiltered by experience) and intuitions, the intellect can grasp the world entire. The human mind is epistemologically omnipotent.

Spinoza also accepted the Cartesian notion of substance: "By substance," wrote Descartes, "we can conceive nothing else than a thing which exists in such a way as to stand in need of nothing beyond itself." And yet even though he is typically regarded as a substance dualist, the monistic (one substance) view of Spinoza was already anticipated when Descartes said that "And in truth, there can be conceived but one substance which is absolutely independent, and that is God," which he equated with "infinite substance." Descartes's mistake—a deep and fundamental contradiction in the Cartesian system, according to Spinoza—was to distinguish between infinite and finite substances. The body—corporeal substance—is finite, whereas the mind—incorporeal substance—is infinite.

Spinoza took the Cartesian definition of substance as that which is absolutely independent and then showed why there can be only one such substance. Essentially, the idea is that it would be logically impossible for there to be two such substances, for the two would limit each other's independence.

Thus, the Cartesian "mind–body" problem is solved; the assumed interaction between mind and body is as unnecessary as it is impossible. Body and mind do not need to act on each other because they are not two things but one thing. What explains the apparent duality, according to Spinoza, is that when the one universal substance (reality) is viewed from the perspective of its attribute of extension, it becomes *body,* whereas when it is viewed from the perspective of its attribute of thought, it becomes *mind*. It is impossible for two real substances to affect each other because by having influence on each other, indeed, by their very duality, they would lose their independence and therefore their substantiality as such.

Therefore, in Spinoza's metaphysics there can be no plurality of substances, but only one, infinite, Parmenidean substance. This is the centerpiece of his system of thought. Material and spiritual being form but two sides of one and the same world: particular extended beings and particular thinking beings are but the ephemeral and transitory states of the eternal, unified world-being, its *modes*. All multiplicity, the apparent self-substance of particular objects, free will, and evolution are but illusions.

11.1 Spinoza's *Ethics*: The World Is God

The three so-called Continental Rationalists—Descartes, Leibniz, and Spinoza—based their philosophies on mathematical systems of thought designed as methods to correct and improve the understanding, the inner light of reason, so that pure knowledge of reality could be attained. But, unlike Descartes, Spinoza began with definitions, added to them axioms, and derived further propositions or theorems until he had in every case provided a proof by demonstration for his conclusions.

⊀

Ethics, Book I: On God

Definitions

I. By cause of itself I understand that whose essence involves existence, or that whose nature cannot be conceived unless existing.

II. That thing is called finite in its own kind (*in suo genere*) which can be limited by another thing of the same nature. For example, a body is called finite because we always conceive another which is greater. So a thought is limited by another thought; but a body is not limited by a thought, nor a thought by a body.

III. By substance I understand that which is in itself and is conceived through itself; in other words, that the conception of which does not need the conception of another thing from which it must be formed.

IV. By attribute I understand that which the intellect perceives of substance as constituting its essence.

V. By mode I understand the modifications of substance, or that which is in another thing through which also it is conceived.

VI. By God I understand Being absolutely infinite, that is to say, substance consisting of infinite attributes, each one of which expresses eternal and infinite essence.

Explanation. I say absolutely infinite but not infinite in its own kind (*in suo genere*), for of whatever is infinite only in its own kind (*in suo genere*), we can deny infinite attributes; but to the essence of that which is absolutely infinite pertains whatever expresses essence and involves no negation.

VII. That thing is called free which exists from the necessity of its own nature alone and is determined to action by itself alone. That thing, on the other hand, is called necessary or rather compelled which by another is determined to existence and action in a fixed and prescribed manner.

VIII. By eternity I understand existence itself, so far as it is conceived necessarily to follow from the definition alone of the eternal thing.

Explanation. For such existence, like the essence of the thing, is conceived as an eternal truth. It cannot therefore be explained by duration or time, even if the duration be conceived without beginning or end.

Axioms

I. Everything which is, is either in itself or in another.

II. That which cannot be conceived through another must be conceived through itself.

III. From a given determinate cause an effect necessarily follows; and, on the other hand, if no determinate cause be given it is impossible that an effect can follow.

IV. The knowledge (*cognitio*) of an effect depends upon and involves the knowledge of the cause.

V. Those things which have nothing mutually in common with one another cannot through one another be mutually understood, that is to say, the conception of the one does not involve the conception of the other.

VI. A true idea must agree with that of which it is the idea (*cum suo ideato*).

VII. The essence of that thing which can be conceived as not existing does not involve existence.

Propositions

Proposition I. *Substance is by its nature prior to its modifications.*

Demonstration. This is evident from Defs. 3 and 5.

Proposition II. *Two substances having different attributes have nothing in common with one another.*

Demonstration. This is also evident from Def. 3. For each substance must be in itself and must be conceived through itself, that is to say, the conception of one does not involve the conception of the other.—Q.E.D.

Proposition III. *If two things have nothing in common with one another, one cannot be the cause of the other.*

Demonstration. If they have nothing mutually in common with one another, they cannot (Ax. 5) through one another be mutually understood, and therefore (Ax. 4) one cannot be the cause of the other.—Q.E.D.

Proposition IV. *Two or more distinct things are distinguished from one another, either by the difference of the attributes of the substances or by the difference of their modifications.*

Demonstration. Everything which is, is either in itself or in another (Ax. I), that is to say (Defs. 3 and 5), outside the intellect there is nothing but substances and their modifications. There is nothing therefore outside the intellect by which a number of things can be distinguished one from another, but substances or (which is the same thing by Def. 4) their attributes and their modifications.—Q.E.D.

Proposition V. *In nature there cannot be two or more substances of the same nature or attribute.*

Demonstration. If there were two or more distinct substances, they must be distinguished one from the other by difference of attributes or difference of modifications (Prop. 4). If they are distinguished only by difference of attributes, it will be granted that there is but one substance of the same attribute. But if they are distinguished by difference of modifications, since substance is prior by nature to its modifications (Prop. I), the modifications therefore being placed on one side, and the substance being considered in itself, or, in other words (Def. 3 and Ax. 6), truly considered, it cannot be conceived as distinguished from another substance, that is to say (Prop. 4), there cannot be two or more substances, but only one possessing the same nature or attribute.—Q.E.D.

Proposition VI. One *substance cannot be produced by another substance.*

Demonstration. There cannot in nature be two substances of the same attribute (Prop. 5), that is to say (Prop. 2), two which have anything in common with one another. And therefore (Prop. 3), one cannot be the cause of the other, that is to say, one cannot be produced by the other.—Q.E.D.

Corollary. Hence it follows that there is nothing by which substance can be produced, for in Nature there is nothing but substances and their modifications (as is evident from Ax. I and Defs. 3 and 5). But substance cannot be produced by substance (Prop. 6). Therefore absolutely there is nothing by which substance can be produced.—Q.E.D.

Another Demonstration. This corollary is demonstrated more easily by the *reductio ad absurdum.* For if there were anything by which substance could be produced, the knowledge of substance would be dependent upon the knowledge of its cause (Ax. 4), and therefore (Def. 3) it would not be substance.

Proposition VII. *It pertains to the nature of substance to exist.*

Demonstration. There is nothing by which substance can be produced (Corol. Prop. 6). It will therefore be the cause of itself, that is to say (Def. I), its essence necessarily involves existence, or, in other words, it pertains to its nature to exist.—Q.E.D.

Proposition VIII. *Every substance is necessarily infinite.*

Demonstration. Substance which has only one attribute cannot exist except as one substance (Prop. 5), and to the nature of this one substance it pertains to exist (Prop. 7). It must therefore from its nature exist as finite or infinite. But it cannot exist as finite substance, for (Def. 2) it must (if finite) be limited by another substance of the same nature, which also must necessarily exist (Prop. 7), and therefore there would be two substances of the same attribute, which is absurd (Prop. 5). It exists therefore as infinite substance.—Q.E.D.

. . .

Proposition XXV. *God is not only the efficient cause of the existence of things, but also of their essence.*

Demonstration. Suppose that God is not the cause of the essence of things, then (Ax. 4) the essence of things can be conceived without God, which (Prop. 15) is absurd. Therefore, God is the cause of the essence of things.—Q.E.D.

Note. This proposition more clearly follows from Prop. 16. For from this proposition it follows that, from the existence of the divine nature, both the essence of things and their existence must necessarily be concluded, or, in a word, in the same sense in which God is said to be the cause of Himself He must be called the cause of all things. This will appear still more clearly from the following corollary.

Corollary. Individual things are nothing but modifications or modes of God's attributes, expressing those attributes in a certain and determinate manner. This is evident from Prop. 15 and Def. 5.

. . .

Proposition XXXII. *The will cannot be called a free cause, but can only be called necessary.*

Demonstration. The will is only a certain mode of thought, like the intellect, and therefore (Prop. 28) no volition can exist or be determined to action unless it be determined by another cause, and this again by another, and so on *ad infinitum*. And if the will be supposed infinite, it must be determined to existence and action by God, not in so far as He is substance absolutely infinite, but in so far as He possesses an attribute which expresses the infinite and eternal essence of thought (Prop. 23). In whatever way, therefore, the will be conceived, whether as finite or infinite, it requires a cause by which it may be determined to existence and action, and therefore (Def. 7) it cannot be called a free cause, but only necessary or compelled.—Q.E.D.

Corollary. I. Hence it follows, first, that God does not act from freedom of the will.

Corollary. 2. It follows, secondly, that will and intellect are related to the nature of God as motion and rest, and absolutely as all natural things, which (Prop. 29) must be determined by God to existence and action in a certain manner. For the will, like all other things, needs a cause by which it may be determined to existence and action in a certain manner, and although from a given will or intellect infinite things may follow, God cannot on this account be said to act from freedom of will, any more than He can be said to act from freedom of motion and rest by reason of the things which follow from motion and rest (for from motion and rest infinite numbers of things follow). Therefore, will does not appertain to the nature of God more than other natural things, but is related to it as motion and rest and all other things are related to it—these all following, as we have shown, from the necessity of the divine nature, and being determined to existence and action in a certain manner.

Proposition XXXIII. *Things could have been produced by God in no other manner and in no other order than that in which they have been produced.*

Demonstration. All things have necessarily followed from the given nature of God (Prop. 16), and from the necessity of His nature have been determined to existence and action in a certain manner (Prop. 29). If, therefore, things could have been of another nature or could have been determined in another manner to action, so that the order of nature would have been different, the nature of God might then be different to that which it now is, and hence (Prop. II) that different nature would necessarily exist, and there might consequently be two or more Gods, which (Corol. I, Prop. 14) is absurd. Therefore, things could be produced by God in no other manner and in no other order than that in which they have been produced.—Q.E.D.

⚓

Thus he begins, in Book I of *Ethics,* "On God," with the traditional distinction between that which requires no external cause to exist and that which owes its existence to some other being. Something that is its own cause, because it has no external cause (is not *contingent*) exists *necessarily;* it needs nothing but itself to be conceived. This he called *substance.* It possesses infinite attributes; this is why you seem to be seeing so many different things that in reality are just one thing.

Spinoza also relies on a classical, fundamentally Aristotelian definition of knowledge, according to which we can know something only if we understand it through its causes. Thus, his proofs for the one substance that is absolutely infinite and its own cause is a modern version of the ancient Parmenidean argument for the One. Like Zeno, he claims that the one infinite substance cannot be divided, nor can the existence of any second such substance be conceived without contradiction. And that is why he concludes, at the end of the preceding section, what has probably been the most often popularized aspect of his philosophy, namely, that whatever is, is in God, and that nothing can either be or be conceived without God. This is the view of reality traditionally known as *pantheism.*

In the Appendix to Book I, Spinoza presents an elaborate refutation of Christian and Jewish theology, especially those aspects adapted from

Aristotelian *teleology*, the philosophy of final purposes—the view that all things exist for a preordained purpose. Thus Spinoza was, in a sense, the first existentialist philosopher. Existentialism, as we shall see when we get to the nineteenth- and twentieth-century philosophies, is the view summarized by twentieth-century philosopher Jean-Paul Sartre with the famous phrase, "existence precedes essence." According to Judeo-Christian doctrine, God acts so as to achieve certain ends, for otherwise the fundamental theological doctrines of sin and redemption make no sense. According to Spinoza, however, everything that happens does so through absolute necessity. Thus, the enlightened philosopher transcends the various perspectival views on reality and experiences reality itself, *sub specie aeternitatis*, meaning from the perspective of reality itself:

⚹

. . . everyone judges things by the constitution of his brain, or rather accepts the modifications of his imagination in the place of things. It is not, therefore, to he wondered at, as we may observe in passing, that all those controversies which we see have arisen amongst men, so that at last scepticism has been the result. For although human bodies agree in many things, they differ in more, and therefore that which to one person is good will appear to another evil, that which to one is well arranged to another is confused, that which pleases one will displease another, and so on in other cases which I pass by both because we cannot notice them at length here, and because they are within the experience of everyone. For everyone has heard the expressions: So many heads, so many ways of thinking; everyone is satisfied with his own way of thinking; differences of brains are not less common than differences of taste—all which maxims show that men decide upon matters according to the constitution of their brains, and imagine rather than understand things. If men understood things, they would, as mathematics prove, at least be all alike convinced if they were not all alike attracted. We see, therefore, that all those methods by which the common

people are in the habit of explaining Nature are only different sorts of imaginations, and do not reveal the nature of anything in itself, but only the constitution of the imagination; and because they have names as if they were entities existing apart from the imagination, I call them entities not of the reason but of the imagination. All argument, therefore, urged against us based upon such notions can be easily refuted. Many people, for instance, are accustomed to argue thus: If all things have followed from the necessity of the most perfect nature of God, how is it that so many imperfections have arisen in Nature—corruption, for instance, of things till they stink; deformity, exciting disgust; confusion, evil, crime, etc.? But, as I have just observed, all this is easily answered. For the perfection of things is to be judged by their nature and power alone; nor are they more or less perfect because they delight or offend the human senses, or because they are beneficial or prejudicial to human nature. But to those who ask why God has not created all men in such a manner that they might be controlled by the dictates of reason alone, I give but this answer: because to Him material was not wanting for the creation of everything, from the highest down to the very lowest grade of perfection; or, to speak more properly, because the laws of His nature were so ample that they sufficed for the production of everything which can be conceived by an infinite intellect, as I have demonstrated in Prop. 16.

These are the prejudices which I undertook to notice here. If any others of a similar character remain, they can easily be rectified with a little thought by anyone.

⚹

11.2 *Ethics*, Book II: The Origin and Nature of the Mind

Becoming "one" with reality, that is, viewing it *sub specie aeternitatis*, is made possible in Spinoza's philosophy through his understanding of the origin and nature of the mind, which form the central topics of Book II, to which we now turn.

⚴

The Origin and Nature of the Mind

Definitions

I. By body I understand a mode which expresses in a certain and determinate manner the essence of God in so far as He is considered as the thing extended. (See Corol. Prop. 25, pt. I.)

II. I say that to the essence of anything pertains that, which being given, the thing itself is necessarily posited, and, being taken away, the thing is necessarily taken; or, in other words, that without which the thing can neither be nor be conceived, and which in its turn cannot be nor be conceived without the thing.

III. By idea I understand a conception of the mind which the mind forms because it is a thinking thing.

Explanation. I use the word "conception" rather than "perception" because the name perception seems to indicate that the mind is passive in its relation to the object. But the word conception seems to express the action of the mind.

IV. By adequate idea I understand an idea which, in so far as it is considered in itself, without reference to the object, has all the properties or internal signs (*denominationes intrinsecas*) of a true idea.

Explanation. I say internal, so as to exclude that which is external, the agreement, namely, of the idea with its object.

V. Duration is the indefinite continuation of existence.

Explanation. I call it indefinite because it cannot be determined by the nature itself of the existing thing nor by the efficient cause, which necessarily posits the existence of the thing but does not take it away.

VI. By reality and perfection I understand the same thing.

VII. By individual things I understand things which are finite and which have a determinate existence; and if a number of individuals so unite in one action that they are all simultaneously the cause of one effect, I consider them all, so far, as one individual thing.

Axioms

I. The essence of man does not involve necessary existence; that is to say, the existence as well as the non-existence of this or that man may or may not follow from the order of nature.

II. Man thinks.

III. Modes of thought, such as love, desire, or the emotions of the mind, by whatever name they may be called, do not exist unless in the same individual exists the idea of a thing loved, desired, etc. But the idea may exist although no other mode of thinking exist.

IV. We perceive that a certain body is affected in many ways.

V. No individual things are felt or perceived by us except bodies and modes of thought.

The postulates will be found after Proposition 13.

Propositions

Proposition I. *Thought is an attribute of God, or God is a thinking thing.*

Demonstration. Individual thoughts, or this and that thought, are modes which express the nature of God in a certain and determinate manner (Corol. Prop. 25, pt. I). God therefore possesses an attribute (Def. 5, pt. I) the conception of which is involved in all individual thoughts, and through which they are conceived. Thought, therefore, is one of the infinite attributes of God which expresses the eternal and infinite essence of God (Def. 6, pt. I), or, in other words, God is a thinking thing.—Q.E.D.

Note. This proposition is plain from the fact that we can conceive an infinite thinking Being. For the more things a thinking being can think, the more reality or perfection we conceive it to possess, and therefore the being which can think an infinitude of things in infinite ways is necessarily infinite by his power of thinking. Since, therefore, we can conceive an infinite Being by attending to thought alone, thought is necessarily one of the infinite attributes of God (Defs. 4 and 6, pt. I), which is the proposition we wished to prove.

Proposition II. *Extension is an attribute of God, or God is an extended thing.*

Demonstration. The demonstration of this proposition is of the same character as that of the last.

Proposition III. *In God there necessarily exists the idea of His essence and of all things which necessarily follow from His essence.*

Demonstration. For God (Prop. I, pt. 2) can think an infinitude of things in infinite ways, or (which is the same thing, by Prop. 16, pt. I) can form an idea of His essence and of all the things which necessarily follow from it. But everything which is in the power of God is necessary (Prop. 35, pt. I), and therefore this idea necessarily exists, and (Prop. 15, pt. I) it cannot exist unless in God.—Q.E.D.

Note. The common people understand by God's power His free will and right over all existing things, which are therefore commonly looked upon as contingent; for they say that God has the power of destroying everything and reducing it to nothing. They very frequently, too, compare God's power with the power of kings. That there is any similarity between the two we have disproved in the first and second Corollaries of Prop. 32, pt. I; and in Prop. 16, pt. I, we have shown that God does everything with that necessity with which He understands Himself, that is to say, as it follows from the necessity of the divine nature that God understands Himself (a truth admitted by all), so by the same necessity it follows that God does an infinitude of things in infinite ways. Moreover, in Prop. 34, pt. I, we have shown that the power of God is nothing but the active essence of God, and therefore it is as impossible for us to conceive that God does not act as that He does not exist. If it pleased me to go further, I could show besides that the power which the common people ascribe to God is not only a human power (which shows that they look upon God as a man or as being like a man), but that it also involves weakness. But I do not care to talk so much upon the same subject. Again and again I ask the reader to consider and reconsider what is said upon this subject in the first part, from Prop. 16 to the end. For it is not possible for anyone properly to understand the things which I wish to prove unless he takes great care not to confound the power of God with the human power and right of kings. . . .

Proposition XI. *The first thing which forms the actual being of the human mind is nothing else than the idea of an individual thing actually existing.*

Demonstration. The essence of man is formed (Corol. Prop. 10, pt. 2) by certain modes of the attributes of God, that is to say (Ax. 2, pt. 2), modes of thought, the idea of all of them being prior by nature to the modes of thought themselves (Ax. 3, pt. 2); and if this idea exists, other modes (which also have an idea in nature prior to them) must exist in the same individual likewise (Ax. 3, pt. 2). Therefore an idea is the first thing which forms the being of the human mind. But it is not the idea of a non-existent thing, for then the idea itself (Corol. Prop. 8, pt. 2) could not be said to exist. It will, therefore, be the idea of something actually existing. Neither will it be the idea of an infinite thing, for an infinite thing must always necessarily exist (Props. 21 and 22, pt. 1), and this (Ax. 1, pt. 2) is absurd. Therefore, the first thing which forms the actual being of the human mind is the idea of an individual thing actually existing.—Q.E.D.

Corollary. Hence it follows that the human mind is a part of the infinite intellect of God, and therefore, when we say that the human mind perceives this or that thing, we say nothing else than that God has this or that idea; not indeed in so far as He is infinite, but in so far as He is manifested through the nature of the human mind, or in so far as He forms the essence of the human mind; and when we say that God has this or that idea, not merely in so far as He forms the nature of the human mind, but in so far as He has at the same time with the human mind the idea also of another thing, then we say that the human mind perceives the thing partially or inadequately.

Note. At this point many of my readers will no doubt stick fast, and will think of many things which will cause delay; and I therefore beg of them to advance slowly, step by step, with me, and not to pronounce judgment until they shall have read everything which I have to say.

Notice that, by proposition XI, he proves that when you perceive something, say right now this book, that this is really nothing more than God having that idea. You reading right now is nothing less than the world-soul, the divine mind, contemplating one of its infinite modes!

However, neither the mind of man nor the mind of God has anything akin to the illusion we call "freedom of choice." As he so eloquently argues in Book III:

⚓

The Origin and Nature of the Emotions

. . . [H]uman affairs would be much more happily conducted if it were equally in the power of men to be silent and to speak; but experience shows over and over again that there is nothing which men have less power over than the tongue, and that there is nothing which they are less able to do than to govern their appetites, so that many persons believe that we do those things only with freedom which we seek indifferently, as the desire for such things can easily be lessened by the recollection of another thing which we frequently call to mind; it being impossible, on the other hand, to do those things with freedom which we seek with such ardor that the recollection of another thing is unable to mitigate it. But if, however, we had not found out that we do many things which we afterwards repent, and that when agitated by conflicting emotions we see that which is better and follow that which is worse, nothing would hinder us from believing that we do everything with freedom. Thus the infant believes that it is by free will that it seeks the breast; the angry boy believes that by free will he wishes vengeance; the timid man thinks it is with free will he seeks flight; the drunkard believes that by a free command of his mind he speaks the things which when sober he wishes he had left unsaid. Thus the madman, the chatterer, the boy, and others of the same kind, all believe that they speak by a free command of the mind, whilst, in truth, they have no power to restrain the impulse which they have to speak, so that experience itself, no less than reason, clearly teaches that men believe themselves to be free simply because they are conscious of their own actions, knowing nothing of the causes by which they are determined; it teaches, too, that the decrees of the mind are nothing but the appetites themselves, which differ, therefore, according to the different temper of the body. For every man determines all things from his emotion; those who are agitated by contrary emotions do not know what they want, whilst those who are agitated by no emotion are easily driven hither and thither. All this plainly shows that the decree of the mind, the appetite, and determination of the body are coin-

cident in Nature, or rather that they are one and the same thing which, when it is considered under the attribute of thought and manifested by that, is called a "decree," and when it is considered under the attribute of extension and is deduced from the laws of motion and rest is called a "determination." This, however, will be better understood as we go on, for there is another thing which I wish to be observed here—that we cannot by a mental decree do a thing unless we recollect it. We cannot speak a word, for instance, unless we recollect it. But it is not in the free power of the mind either to recollect a thing or to forget it. It is believed, therefore, that the power of the mind extends only thus far—that from a mental decree we can speak or be silent about a thing only when we recollect it. But when we dream that we speak, we believe that we do so from a free decree of the mind, and yet we do not speak, or, if we do, it is the result of a spontaneous motion of the body. We dream, again, that we are concealing things, and that we do this by virtue of a decree of the mind like that by which, when awake, we are silent about things we know. We dream, again, that, from a decree of the mind, we do some things which we should not dare to do when awake. And I should like to know, therefore, whether there are two kinds of decrees in the mind—one belonging to dreams and the other free. If this be too great nonsense, we must necessarily grant that this decree of the mind which is believed to be free is not distinguishable from the imagination or memory, and is nothing but the affirmation which the idea necessarily involves in so far as it is an idea (Prop. 49, pt. 2). These decrees of the mind, therefore, arise in the mind by the same necessity as the ideas of things actually existing. Consequently, those who believe that they speak or are silent or do anything else from a free decree of the mind dream with their eyes open.

⚓

Take a look even at your own activity of speaking; where do the words you say come from? Did you choose them? Select them? Pay close attention to the actual activity of your own conscious mind in the act of speaking or thinking and you will find the words appearing as if from out of nowhere, much as the words that you are reading here are not created by your conscious activity (nor by mine).

Once it is realized that everything that happens occurs not by conscious free choice but of metaphysical necessity, the mind attains a Stoiclike state of blissful joy, in which even the most negative of our emotions are transformed into a clear and distinct idea of divine blessedness. It is a philosophy that Spinoza tried to realize and insofar as he attained it, the great twentieth-century philosopher Bertrand Russell called him "the noblest and most lovable of the great philosophers."

When Spinoza finished *Ethics* in 1675, he decided not to publish what would subsequently be regarded as one of the greatest metaphysical systems in the history of philosophy because of his previous difficulties with the various theological and political authorities. He lived out his life in exile in The Hague in south Holland. Works such as his *Tractatus Theologico-Politicus,* in which he argued in defense of complete liberty of thought and the right of each individual to criticize any and all biblical writings, had been published anonymously; thus, except for his friends and a few intellectual acquaintances, he was largely unknown.

In 1676, however, a year before his death, he was visited by Leibniz, who came to Spinoza to learn not his philosophy but his techniques for grinding lenses! Leibniz had heard of Spinoza as one of the greatest lens makers in Europe and had sent him one of his own research articles on optics. In his reply, Spinoza included the *Tractatus Theologico-Politicus,* which deeply influenced Leibniz's own philosophical development. From that point on, according to Leibniz's account, he "conversed with him often and at great length," until Spinoza died a year later, his lungs having been destroyed by years of inhaling glass from the grinding of lenses.

12 ⚹ Leibniz

12.0 Leibniz (1646–1716): The Great Calculator

Gottfried Wilhelm Leibniz—philosopher, mathematician, logician, and historian—was one of the great systematic thinkers of modern times. Like Descartes, he too invented an entirely new branch of mathematics: the differential and integral calculus, which he published several years before Newton. As a lifelong project, he, like Descartes and Spinoza, sought to invent a universal language based not on geometry but on his calculus perfected down to the level of logic. This language would then provide a common mathematical, philosophical, logical, and scientific foundation to all thought. In Leibniz's ideal system, all philosophical, scientific, and mathematical disagreements could be resolved the same way: by a series of rigorous calculations. Perhaps most remarkably, he invented and constructed the very first mechanical calculator—a machine that could add, subtract, and do square roots. In his belief that in principle such a calculating machine could do everything that the human mind does, he was probably the first thinker to have conceived the possibility of modern-day computers.

Son of a philosophy professor of Slavic descent (the family name was originally Lubeniecz), Leibniz learned Greek and Latin by the age of twelve. At fifteen he entered the University of Leipzig to study law where, under the guidance of a neo-Aristotelian philosophy professor, Jakob Thomasius, he devoted most of his time to the works of Bacon, Kepler, Galileo, and Descartes. His undergraduate thesis, written when he was only twenty, *De Principio Individui* (1663), presented a nominalistic view of individuation and identity.

After taking his doctorate in law, Leibniz worked for the elector of Mainz in Frankfurt until 1672. He then went to Paris for five years where he met and worked with Malebranche, Arnauld, and Huygens.[1] It was on his way home that he visited Spinoza in The Hague. He then traveled to Hanover to work as a librarian and historian at the House of Brunswick. In Berlin he directed the founding of the Academy and served as its first college president. During his life he continued trying to apply philosophy and mathematics to everyday affairs. For instance, he once tried to demonstrate, using logic and mathematics, why a German candidate should succeed the Polish monarchy, and he used his calculus to try and make peace between Catholic and Protestant theologies.

The last years of Leibniz's life were tormented by the controversy over whether he or Isaac Newton had first invented the calculus. By then he had already fallen out of favor with the princes of Brunswick who viewed his philosophy and academic propaganda as impractical and no longer useful. He died in virtual obscurity. Unlike most great philosophers, however, he left no single great work, not even, like Spinoza, one that was published posthumously. Some of his original and powerful writing can be found in his two main books, *New Essays on the Human Understanding* (1705) and *Theodicy* (1710). But his most important contributions lie in his many shorter works, most of which were not published until this century and many of which for reasons not quite understood still exist only in manuscript form.

One of the most important ideas in Leibniz's philosophy is *individual substance*. Derived from the Aristotelian doctrine of true predication, wherein the predicate is contained in the subject, an individual substance is complete in itself such that an all-knowing being could derive all true propositions about it simply by pure reason and without having to contemplate any other individual substances. According to Leibniz reality thus consists not of one substance, as Spinoza and other types of monists believed, nor in some finite number of different substances, as Descartes and other mind–body dualists believed, but in an *infinite* number of individual substances![2] As the ultimate constituents of the whole of reality, these individual substances (realities), which he called *monads,* are—like the Parmenidean whole—simple (without parts); "What is not truly *one* being," he wrote in his letter to Arnauld in 1687, "is not truly one *being*." Furthermore, monads are neither created nor destroyable; viewed abstractly, they are like physical points but, being unextended

(nonspatial), their only essential attribute is *thought*.

Following the Cartesian argument that substances cannot interact, Leibniz held that monads cannot interact with each other nor can they be causally related; each monad exists in a preestablished harmony with all other monads, each one a "windowless" mirror of the entire universe. (Remember our various discussions about how eyes are not windows?) Monads form a hierarchy according to the clearness and distinctness with which they mirror the universe. The perceptions of monads vary in levels of confusion from minute perceptions so tenuous or mixed up that they exist at a threshold below consciousness to clear and distinct, fully conscious perceptions, which Leibniz calls *apperception*. Relying on concepts from his infinitesimal calculus, he seems to suggest that the rational determination of an individual substance is a derivative of the infinite universe of space and time. Just as any infinitesimal part of a curve—the differential quotient of a curve derived from its analytic equation—contains virtually the entire curve, each individual monad contains virtually the entire universe. Thus, it should in principle be possible to deduce all knowledge about all aspects of the universe from within a single monad.

Although Leibniz's work in pure logic anticipated many later developments in mathematical logic, including versions of a calculus similar to Boolean algebra, he never completed his lifelong goal of developing a formal language that could be used to both describe and discover all aspects of the universe. His idea was to create a universal encyclopedia of all knowledge expressed in a natural language; the words would then be properly defined (as in binary arithmetic, where the infinite integers can be defined with only two signs, 1 and 0, so that the sign could be put in a machine—that is, a computer) with each symbol standing for only one idea. Just as all words in English are composed using only twenty-six letters, all the words in Leibniz's universal encyclopedia would be analyzed into undefinable primitives. All that would then be required is a syntax for the new ideal language; one could then algorithmatize without reasoning the effect of reasoning, and the whole thing would be so simple it could be programmed into a machine. That is how we could then calculate everything we needed to know about anything.

Though he never completed it, Leibniz's systematic program for all knowledge got its start, after his death, in the form of cooperative academies of learning in Berlin, Leipzig, Vienna, and Petersburg. Other collective institutions, such as the Royal Society in London and the French Academy in Paris, were founded for the systematization of all knowledge based on his ideas. Leibniz himself was involved with the first of these institutions, the Prussian Academy of the Sciences in Berlin, where he served as its first president. During his tenure there he pursued both the goal of inventing a formal system for the undefinable primitives, into which the meanings of all words and the operational rules for their combination resolved. Not only did Leibniz inspire the subsequent attempts of Gottlob Frege, Alfred N. Whitehead, and Bertrand Russell to invent a system of mathematical logic as the grammar of all science, his dream of a universal calculating machine was eventually realized in the form of the modern-day computer.

12.1 Leibniz and the Origin of the Modern Worldview

Before the American nineteenth- and early twentieth-century pragmatist philosopher John Dewey (Section 20.2) became a great philosopher in his own right, he wrote a doctoral dissertation and then a spectacular book on Leibniz, *Leibniz's New Essays Concerning Human Understanding: A Critical Exposition* (1888), when Dewey was only twenty-eight. It so well describes several important aspects of Leibniz's thought that one can do no better than turn to Dewey, one of the important founders of an influential movement in early twentieth-

century philosophy, to see for ourselves what has been called "the great conversation"—philosophers communicating with each other across centuries through their great works.

⚖

Leibniz's New Essays Concerning Human Understanding

His philosophy is the dawning of consciousness of the modern world. In it we see the very conception and birth of the modern interpretation of the world. The history of thought is one continuous testimony to the ease with which we become hardened to ideas through custom. Ideas are constantly precipitating themselves out of the realm of ideas into that of ways of thinking and of viewing the universe. The problem of one century is the axiom of another. What one generation stakes its activity upon investigating is quietly taken for granted by the next. And so the highest reach of intellectual inspiration in the sixteenth century is to-day the ordinary food of thought, accepted without an inquiry as to its source, and almost without a suspicion that it has a recent historic origin. We have to go to Bacon or to Leibniz to see the genesis and growth of those ideas which to-day have become materialized into axiomatic points of view and into hard-and-fast categories of thought. In reading Leibniz the idea comes over us in all its freshness that there was a time when it was a discovery that the world is a universe, made after one plan and of one stuff. The ideas of inter-relation, of the harmony of law, of mutual dependence and correspondence, were not always the assumed starting-points of thought; they were once the crowning discoveries of a philosophy aglow and almost intoxicated with the splendor of its far-reaching generalizations. I take these examples of the unity of the world, the continuity and interdependence of all within it, because these are the ideas which come to their conscious and delighted birth in the philosophy of Leibniz. We do not put ourselves into the right attitude for understanding his thought until

From John Dewey, *Leibniz's New Essays Concerning Human Understanding: A Critical Exposition.* First published in 1880.

we remember that these ideas—the commonest tools of our thinking—were once new and fresh, and in their novelty and transforming strangeness were the products of a philosophic interpretation of experience. Except in that later contemporary of Leibniz, the young and enthusiastic Irish idealist, Berkeley, I know of no historic thinker in whom the birth-throes (joyous, however) of a new conception of the world are so evident as in Leibniz. But while in Berkeley what we see is the young man carried away and astounded by the grandeur and simplicity of a "new way of ideas" which he has discovered, what we see in Leibniz is the mature man penetrated throughout his being with an idea which in its unity answers to the unity of the world, and which in its complexity answers, tone to tone, to the complex harmony of the world.

The familiarity of the ideas which we use hides their grandeur from us. The unity of the world is a matter of course with us; the dependent order of all within it a mere starting-point upon which to base our investigations. But if we will put ourselves in the position of Leibniz, and behold, not the new planet, but the new universe, so one, so linked together, swimming into our ken, we shall feel something of the same exultant thrill that Leibniz felt,—an exultation not indeed personal in its nature, but which arises from the expansion of the human mind face to face with an expanding world. The spirit which is at the heart of the philosophy of Leibniz is . . . a spirit which feels that the secret of the universe has been rendered up to it, and which breathes a buoyant optimism. And if we of the nineteenth century have chosen to bewail the complexity of the problem of life, and to run hither and thither multiplying "insights" and points of view till this enthusiastic confidence in reason seems to us the rashness of an ignorance which does not comprehend the problem, and the unity in which Leibniz rested appears cold and abstract beside the manifold richness of the world, we should not forget that after all we have incorporated into our very mental structure the fundamental thoughts of Leibniz,—the thoughts of the rationality of the universe and of the "reign of law."

☙

Dewey makes several important notes about Leibniz. First, as we have noted time and again,

it is often difficult to see from our contemporary perspective the profundity of the achievements made by great philosophers of the past; think, for instance, back to our very first philosopher, Thales. In marked contrast to Descartes, who regarded history as not only irrelevant but also deceptive in its inability to offer us philosophical insight, Leibniz is first to offer an interpretation of the historical developments in thought as a view of the development and gradual enlightenment of the mind, much in the way that, and on the basis of which, Hegel would later construct an entire metaphysical system.

12.2 Infinite Realities: *The Monadology*

Like Spinoza, Leibniz sought to improve Cartesian metaphysics. But whereas the geometrical labyrinth of Spinoza's thought everywhere closes in upon itself until it reveals a world of pantheistic monism, Leibniz's logical calculus is an open labyrinth of endless paths, each leading into a different universe, a separate world, another reality. We are still in Plato's cave but now it opens to an infinity of suns.[3]

Leibniz's improvement over the Cartesian system begins with a marriage between the Cartesian concept of extended, continuous substance and the atomists' concept of ultimate, indivisible individual units of reality. The atomists explain reality in terms of simple, indivisible eternal units—atoms—but according to their essentially materialist conception, the atoms are lifeless lumps of matter. These two lines of thought combine in Leibniz's concept of the monad. Indeed, Leibniz called Cartesianism "the antechamber" of the true philosophy, and atomism the preparation for his theory of monads. The monads, as Cartesian substances, are not lifeless atoms but self-acting forces and *immaterial*. The monads are fundamentally *representative forces*. There is nothing truly real in the world save the monads and their representations, which are ideas and perceptions.

⚚

The Monadology

1. The Monad, of which we will speak here, is nothing else than a simple substance, which goes to make up composites; by simple, we mean without parts.

2. There must be simple substances because there are composites; for a composite is nothing else than a collection or *aggregatum* of simple substances.

3. Now, where there are no constituent parts there is possible neither extension, nor form, nor divisibility. These Monads are the true Atoms of nature, and, in fact, the Elements of things.

4. Their dissolution, therefore, is not to be feared and there is no way conceivable by which a simple substance can perish through natural means.

5. For the same reason there is no way conceivable by which a simple substance might, through natural means, come into existence, since it can not be formed by composition.

6. We may say then, that the existence of Monads can begin or end only all at once, that is to say, the Monad can begin only through creation and end only through annihilation. Composites, however, begin or end gradually.

7. There is also no way of explaining how a Monad can be altered or changed in its inner being by any other created thing, since there is no possibility of transposition within it, nor can we conceive of any internal movement which can be produced, directed, increased or diminished there within the substance, such as can take place in the case of composites where a change can occur among the parts. The Monads have no windows through which anything may come in or go out. The Attributes are not liable to detach themselves and make an excursion outside the substance, as could *sensible species* of the Schoolmen. In the same way neither substance nor attribute can enter from without into a Monad.

8. Still Monads must needs have some qualities,

From Gottfried Wilhelm Leibniz, *The Monadology*, George Montgomery, trans. (La Salle, IL: Open Court, 1902).

otherwise they would not even be existences. And if simple substances did not differ at all in their qualities, there would be no means of perceiving any change in things. Whatever is in a composite can come into it only through its simple elements and the Monads, if they were without qualities, since they do not differ at all in quantity, would be indistinguishable one from another. For instance, if we imagine *a plenum* or completely filled space, where each part receives only the equivalent of its own previous motion, one state of things would not be distinguishable from another.

9. Each Monad, indeed, must be different from every other. For there are never in nature two beings which are exactly alike, and in which it is not possible to find a difference either internal or based on an intrinsic property.

10. I assume it as admitted that every created being, and consequently the created Monad, is subject to change, and indeed that this change is continuous in each.

11. It follows from what has just been said, that the natural changes of the Monad come from an internal principle, because an external cause can have no influence upon its inner being.

12. Now besides this principle of change there must also be in the Monad a manifoldness which changes. This manifoldness constitutes, so to speak, the specific nature and the variety of the simple substances.

13. This manifoldness must involve a multiplicity in the unity or in that which is simple. For since every natural change takes place by degrees, there must be something which changes and something which remains unchanged, and consequently there must be in the simple substance a plurality of conditions and relations, even though it has no parts.

14. The passing condition which involves and represents a multiplicity in the unity, or in the simple substance, is nothing else than what is called Perception. This should be carefully distinguished from Apperception or Consciousness, as will appear in what follows. In this matter the Cartesians have fallen into a serious error, in that they treat as nonexistent those perceptions of which we are not conscious. It is this also which has led them to believe that spirits alone are Monads and that there are no souls of animals or other Entelechies, and it has led them to make the

common confusion between a protracted period of unconsciousness and actual death. They have thus adopted the Scholastic error that souls can exist entirely separated from bodies, and have even confirmed ill-balanced minds in the belief that souls are mortal.

15. The action of the internal principle which brings about the change or the passing from one perception to another may be called Appetition. It is true that the desire (*l'appetit*) is not always able to attain to the whole of the perception which it strives for, but it always attains a portion of it and reaches new perceptions.

16. We, ourselves, experience a multiplicity in a simple substance, when we find that the most trifling thought of which we are conscious involves a variety in the object. Therefore all those who acknowledge that the soul is a simple substance ought to grant this multiplicity in the Monad, and Monsieur Bayle should have found no difficulty in it, as he has done in his *Dictionary,* article "Rorarius."

17. It must be confessed, however, that Perception, and that which depends upon it, are inexplicable by mechanical causes, that is to say, by figures and motions. Supposing that there were a machine whose structure produced thought, sensation, and perception, we could conceive of it as increased in size with the same proportions until one was able to enter into its interior, as he would into a mill. Now, on going into it he would find only pieces working upon one another, but never would he find anything to explain Perception. It is accordingly in the simple substance, and not in the composite nor in a machine that the Perception is to be sought. Furthermore, there is nothing besides perceptions and their changes to be found in the simple substance. And it is in these alone that all the internal activities of the simple substance can consist.

18. All simple substances or created Monads may be called Entelechies, because they have in themselves a certain perfection. There is in them a sufficiency which makes them the source of their internal activities, and renders them, so to speak, incorporeal Automatons.

19. If we wish to designate as soul everything which has perceptions and desires in the general sense that I have just explained, all simple substances or created Monads could be called souls.

But since feeling is something more than a mere perception I think that the general name of Monad or Entelechy should suffice for simple substances which have only perception, while we may reserve the term Soul for those whose perception is more distinct and is accompanied by memory.

20. We experience in ourselves a state where we remember nothing and where we have no distinct perception, as in periods of fainting, or when we are overcome by a profound, dreamless sleep. In such a state the soul does not sensibly differ at all from a simple Monad. As this state, however, is not permanent and the soul can recover from it, the soul is something more.

21. Nevertheless it does not follow at all that the simple substance is in such a state without perception. This is so because of the reasons given above; for it cannot perish, nor on the other hand would it exist without some affection and the affection is nothing else than its perception. When, however, there are a great number of weak perceptions where nothing stands out distinctively, we are stunned; as when one turns around and around in the same direction, a dizziness comes on, which makes him swoon and makes him able to distinguish nothing. Among animals, death can occasion this state for quite a period.

22. Every present state of a simple substance is a natural consequence of its preceding state, in such a way that its present is big with its future.

23. Therefore, since on awakening after a period of unconsciousness we become conscious of our perceptions, we must, without having been conscious of them, have had perceptions immediately before; for one perception can come in a natural way only from another perception, just as a motion can come in a natural way only from a motion.

24. It is evident from this that if we were to have nothing distinctive, or so to speak prominent, and of a higher flavor in our perceptions, we should be in a continual state of stupor. This is the condition of Monads which are wholly bare.

25. We see that nature has given to animals heightened perceptions, having provided them with organs which collect numerous rays of light or numerous waves of air and thus make them more effective in their combination. Something similar to this takes place in the case of smell, in that of taste and of touch, and perhaps in many other

senses which are unknown to us. I shall have occasion very soon to explain how that which occurs in the soul represents that which goes on in the sense-organs.

26. The memory furnishes a sort of consecutiveness which imitates reason but is to be distinguished from it. We see that animals when they have the perception of something which they notice and of which they have had a similar previous perception, are led by the representation of their memory to expect that which was associated in the preceding perception, and they come to have feelings like those which they had before. For instance, if a stick be shown to a dog, he remembers the pain which it has caused him and he whines or runs away.

27. The vividness of the picture, which comes to him or moves him, is derived either from the magnitude or from the number of the previous perceptions. For, oftentimes, a strong impression brings about, all at once, the same effect as a long-continued habit or as a great many re-iterated, moderate perceptions.

28. Men act in like manner as animals, in so far as the sequence of their perceptions is determined only by the law of memory, resembling the *empirical physicians* who practice simply, without any theory, and we are empiricists in three-fourths of our actions. For instance, when we expect that there will be day-light to-morrow, we do so empirically, because it has always happened so up to the present time. It is only the astronomer who uses his reason in making such an affirmation.

29. But the knowledge of eternal and necessary truths is that which distinguishes us from mere animals and gives us reason and the sciences, thus raising us to a knowledge of ourselves and of God. This is what is called in us the Rational Soul or the Mind.

30. It is also through the knowledge of necessary truths and through abstractions from them that we come to perform Reflective Acts, which cause us to think of what is called the I, and to decide that this or that is within us. It is thus, that in thinking upon ourselves we think of *being* of *substance*, or the *simple* and *composite*, of a *material* thing and of *God* himself, concerning that what is limited in us is in him without limits. These Reflective Acts furnish the principal objects of our reasonings.

31. Our reasoning is based upon two great principles: first, that of Contradiction, by means of which we decide that to be false which involves contradiction and that to be true which contradicts or is opposed to the false.

32. And second, the principle of Sufficient Reason, in virtue of which we believe that no fact can be real or existing and no statement true unless it has a sufficient reason why it should be thus and not otherwise. Most frequently, however, these reasons cannot be known by us.

33. There are also two kinds of Truths: those of Reasoning and those of Fact. The Truths of Reasoning are necessary, and their opposite is impossible. Those of Fact, however, are contingent, and their opposite is possible. When a truth is necessary, the reason can be found by analysis in resolving it into simpler ideas and into simpler truths until we reach those which are primary.

34. It is thus that with mathematicians the Speculative Theorems and the practical Canons are reduced by analysis to Definitions, Axioms, and Postulates.

35. There are finally simple ideas of which no definition can be given. There are also the Axioms and Postulates or, in a word, the primary principles which cannot be proved and, indeed, have no need of proof. These are identical propositions whose opposites involve express contradictions.

36. But there must be also a sufficient reason for contingent truths or truths of fact; that is to say, for the sequence of the things which extend throughout the universe of created beings, where the analysis into more particular reasons can be continued into greater detail without limit because of the immense variety of the things in nature and because of the infinite division of bodies. There is an infinity of figures and of movements, present and past, which enter into the efficient cause of my present writing, and in its final cause there are an infinity of slight tendencies and dispositions of my soul, present and past.

37. And as all this detail again involves other and more detailed contingencies, each of which again has need of a similar analysis in order to find its explanation, no real advance has been made. Therefore, the sufficient or ultimate reason must needs be outside of the sequence or series of these details of contingencies, however infinite they may be.

38. It is thus that the ultimate reason for things must be a necessary substance, in which the detail of the changes shall be present merely potentially, as in the fountain-head, and this substance we call God.

⚶

Let us pause here to reflect on what we have just read. Especially important in Leibniz's work and in much of the philosophy that follows is his notion of the activity of *representation*. Leibniz distinguishes representation that happens at a nonconscious level from *conscious* representation, which he calls "perception" and "apperception," respectively (see paragraph 14). Consider the proverbial tree falling in the forest. If you are there in the forest near the tree, the sound you hear consists of a series of numerous waves, each too small to be heard:

))

Yet each individual sound wave (represented by each arc) must make an impression on us, albeit a very small one, since otherwise their total—a sum of mere nothings—would not be audible. That is, your eardrum responds to each single wave but you do not hear it. The sensations that the motion of the single wave causes is a weak, confused, unconscious, infinitesimal *perception* that must then be combined with many similar minute sensations so as to become strong and distinct and thereby rise above the unconscious level to the bare minimal threshold of consciousness. The sound of the single wave, Leibniz points out, is felt but not distinguished: *it is perceived but not apperceived.*

Apperception is thus the name that Leibniz gives to any perception that occurs as a conscious mental state. You could, of course, call *everything* that occurs in the world of our sensations "perception," as the unreflecting mind has been conditioned to do, but this misses the point entirely: first, that some perceptions occur as conscious events and others do not and, second, that the former must consist of the latter.

This all-important distinction between nonconscious *perception* and conscious *apperception*, so often glossed over or not properly understood even by philosophers of note, is crucial for any true understanding of Leibniz and subsequent developments, especially in the German traditions, most notably Kant and even the neo-Kantian movements including phenomenology. This is not merely a psychological point. In stating that obscure states of unconscious representation, which are present in the mind along with states of clear consciousness, give rise to the whole life of each individual monad, Leibniz is avoiding both the dualism of atomistic materialism, in which the mind arises out of individual inert substances, and the monism of pantheistic idealism, in which the entire universe is one mind. The former leads to incoherent scientism, the latter to incoherent mysticism, both of which according to Leibniz are unphilosophical in that they deny the possibility of true understanding.

Thus, perception is defined as the *representation of the external in the internal, of multiplicity in unity.* It is a mechanical process. The representing being, without any loss of its absolute simplicity, bears in itself a multitude of relations to external things. What now is the manifold, which is expressed, perceived, or represented, in the unit—the monad? *It is the whole world.* Every monad represents all others in itself, a concentrated all, the universe in miniature. Each individual monad contains an infinity in itself. A supreme intelligence, for which every obscure idea would at once become distinct, would be able to read in a single monad the whole universe and its entire history. All that is, has been, or will be; for the past has left its traces behind it in the monad, and the future will bring nothing not founded in the present. The monad is the bearer of the past and the forebearer of the future.

Every monad is thus a mirror of the universe. And it is a *living* mirror, meaning that it generates the images of things by its own activity or develops them from within itself. All monads represent the same universe, but each one represents it differently, that is, from its particular point of view. In other words, each monad represents that which is near at hand distinctly, and that which is distant confusedly. Since they all reflect the same content or object, their difference consists only in the energy or degree of clearness in their representations.

When a group of monads appears as a body it is indistinctly perceived. No monad represents the common universe and its individual parts exactly as do any others; neither is any one better or worse—there are as many different degrees of clearness and distinctness as there are monads. The natures of the .monads consist in nothing else than the sum of relations in which the individual monad stands to all other monads, wherein each one takes account of all others and at the same time is considered by them, and thus exerts influence as well as suffers it. The essence of each monad is simply the position that it occupies in the organic whole of the cosmos; each monad is related in a preestablished harmony to every other monad and shares actively and passively in the life of all the rest. The history of the universe is a single great process in numberless reflections, each of which is an entire and complete universe unto itself, the totality of which is God:

⚹

53. Now as there are an infinity of possible universes in the ideas of God, and but one of them can exist, there must be a sufficient reason for the choice of God which determines him to select one rather than another.

54. And this reason is to be found only in the fitness or in the degree of perfection which these worlds possess, each possible thing having the right to claim existence in proportion to the perfection which it involves.

55. This is the cause for the existence of the greatest good; namely, that the wisdom of God permits him to know it, his goodness causes him to choose it, and his power enables him to produce it.

56. Now this interconnection, relationship, or this adaptation of all things to each particular one, and of each one to all the rest, brings it about that every simple substance has relations which express all the others and that it is consequently a perpetual living mirror of the universe.

57. And as the same city regarded from different sides appears entirely different, and is, as it were multiplied respectively, so, because of the infinite number of simple substances, there are a similar infinite number of universes which are, nevertheless, only the aspects of a single one as seen from the special point of view of each monad.

58. Through this means has been obtained the greatest possible variety, together with the greatest order that may be; that is to say, through this means has been obtained the greatest possible perfection.

59. This hypothesis, moreover, which I venture to call demonstrated, is the only one which fittingly gives proper prominence to the greatness of God.

⚹

The metaphysics of Leibniz thus began with the concept of representation and ended with the harmony of the universe. The representations were multiplicity in unity; the harmony is unity in multiplicity. All monads represent the same universe. But each one mirrors it differently. The unity, as well as the difference, cannot be greater than it is; every possible degree of distinctness of representation is present in each single monad, and yet there is a single harmonic accord in which the infinite tones unite.

12.3 The Calculus: The Mathematics of Reality

Some of the ideas we just discussed no doubt sound ethereal, metaphysical, and downright mystical. It may therefore come as a surprise that the inventor of this metaphysics is also the inventor of the most precise, practical, and powerful mathematical tool of all time: the calculus. Moreover, he invented it as a means of making such metaphysical understanding comprehensible to the human mind.

When most students are confronted with a mathematics course in calculus, they find it almost impossible to understand because of the tediousness of its rigor. Similarly, when most students are confronted with the philosophy of Leibniz, they find his complex metaphysics one of the most challenging to understand. Ironically, according to Leibniz, it is only when you put the two together that you can understand both with perfect ease.

Yet, typically, these two aspects of Leibniz's thought—his philosophy and his mathematics—are separated as if they belonged to someone with multiple personality disorder. *Never* are they properly integrated! The point isn't just to talk about the calculus in abstract terms but to understand it in clear and distinct terms as presented by Leibniz, as an aid to understanding metaphysics. This is *exactly* what the mathematical machinery was designed for by its inventor. It behooves the philosopher to learn such a precise language in which to do philosophy so as to move beyond the constraints of ordinary language. Leibniz was thus one of the first philosophers to suggest an alternative way for the knowledge-seeking enterprise in general and philosophy in particular to proceed by using an artificial, formal language to extend the limitations of the conscious mind. Here, however, we can take only the briefest excursion into the calculus and its relevance to the problems of metaphysics.

You may have noticed in several passages of *The Monadology* that something, such as *apperception,* consists of smaller quantities of something else, in this case *perceptions,* such that these two distinct levels of one continuous type of thing become, from the other's perspective, two very different sorts of things. In other words, you get differences in *type* from differences of *degree.* Thus, the individual sound waves in our earlier example are for all practical purposes nonexistent from the point of view of apperception (the heard sound). You don't experience air pressure or air waves but sounds. Everything in Leibniz's system of metaphysics understood

through the methods of mathematics and logic depends on these distinct levels of relative minuteness; the calculus allows one to make a formal bridge between such levels, extending the precision of language and thought beyond the resolution power of the concepts of which the words of ordinary language are a representation.

Take the familiar example of time. There are 60 minutes in an hour, 24 hours in a day, 7 days in a week. There are therefore 1440 minutes in a day and 10,080 minutes in a week. Obviously, 1 minute is a very small quantity of time compared with a whole week. Indeed, the term *minute* historically entered the language in precisely this way, which has by now been forgotten: people considered the minute as small compared with 1 hour and so they called it "1 minute," meaning a minute (small) fraction—one-sixtieth of an hour. When they came to require still smaller subdivisions of time, they divided each minute into 60 still smaller parts which they called "second minutes," meaning small quantities of the second order of minuteness. Since then, this phrase has been shortened to just "seconds," meaning "second minutes," or a second order of magnitude.

Now, if a minute is a tiny interval as compared with a whole day, how much smaller is 1 second! Thus, if we define some numerical fraction as constituting the proportion which for some purpose we can call relatively small, we can define other fractions of a higher degree of smallness. Thus, if 1/60 is a small fraction, then 1/60 of 1/60—a small fraction of a small fraction—may be regarded as a *small quantity of the second order of smallness.* When mathematicians today speak about the "second order of *magnitude*" (which means, literally, "greatness"), what they really mean is just the opposite—the second order of *smallness.* Similarly, if we take 1 percent (1/100) as a small fraction, then 1 percent of 1 percent (1/10,000) is a small fraction of the second order of smallness; and 1/1,000,000 is a small fraction of the third order of smallness, being 1 percent of 1 percent of 1 percent. Likewise, suppose that we regard 1/1,000,000 as small for the purpose of making a great watch. If a watch is not going to lose or gain more than half a minute in a year, it must keep time with an accuracy of 1 part in 1,051,200. If, for this purpose, we regard 1/1,000,000 (one millionth) as a small quantity, then 1/1,000,000 of 1/1,000,000, that is, 1/1,000,000,000,000 (one thousand billionth) will be a small quantity of the second order of smallness and may be utterly disregarded by comparison.

Thus, Leibniz realized that although we can proceed with the process of analysis (meaning, literally, breaking down something into its smaller and smaller constituents) *forever*, the tools of analysis—the concepts we use to get at what we are trying to comprehend, understand, or see—bring a certain structure to our study in such a way that we can proceed beyond the limitations of those tools and extract information. For instance, we see that the smaller a small quantity is, the more negligible the corresponding small quantity of the *second* order becomes. Hence, we know that perspectives come and go, absorbing each other in such a way that if we begin at a certain level of analysis as our starting point, we are justified in neglecting the small quantities of the second (or third or higher) orders, because from that perspective they do not exist, if we make the small quantity of the first order small enough in itself.

This was the first of Leibniz's insights, one that made it possible for him to perform calculations where no one had dared calculate before. Things are made of smaller things which are made of smaller things still, and the mind has concepts by which it can remove or retain information about these structures of decreasing magnitude in a perfectly ordered manner, thereby seeing into the unseen. What, after all, is *metaphysics* about, if not the study of the way things are *beyond the appearances*? "Meta," meaning *beyond*, and "physics," meaning in this case reality as it manifests itself in the material world perceived by the senses. To have knowledge of metaphysics is to have knowledge of the way things are in themselves, in reality as they

exist beyond mere appearance. To use the phrase that will be evoked by the post-Leibnizian philosopher Immanuel Kant—the study of *things in themselves*. But you can't *see* them! So how? *By calculating*. That's Leibniz's method. But what are the things being studied? They are the *monads*, the ultimate individual point elements of existence that cannot ever be experienced directly but only through varying degrees and levels of conceptual representation.

Now, rather than using Leibniz's original symbolic terminology, we shall rephrase his system of calculus in terms of the way calculus is done today to help you to understand calculus in the way it is currently taught. It has not changed very much at all. We write dx for a little bit of x. The symbol X can represent anything that is in the process of change. The world is constantly changing and so is everything in it, at least from the temporal, momentary perspective of experiencing minds. So let X be any variable, which is at any moment some specific (but never perfectly quantifiable) changing quantity. The symbol X could represent the human population, your blood pressure, the amount of money in your savings account growing at compound interest, and so on. The things symbolized by dx and dy, called "differentials," are the *differential* of x, or of u, or of y, as the case may be (you read them as "dee-eks," "dee-you," or "dee-why"), meaning that they are a little bit of some variable x, u, or y. If dx is a small bit of x, and relatively small of itself, it does not follow that such quantities as x multiplied by dx, or $x^2 dx$, or $a^x dx$ don't exist or are negligible; however, dx multiplied by dx would then be negligible, or nonexistent from the point of view of x, being a small quantity of the second order. That is how, in principle, one can construct a metaphysical method of dealing with the concept of something being made up of nothings in a perfectly orderly way, accessible to the logical language of mathematics.

Again, think of points. Monads are points. Lines, space, *extension* are made up of points, which are extensionless entities. They are zeros.

So how do you get something from nothing? How do a bunch of unextended elements add up to an extended thing? (You may recall that this was one of Zeno's paradoxes; see Section 1.11.) Moreover, since we exist at the extended level (as creatures "in" space), how are we to be able to even think about the unextended elements in which we consist? What one needs, Leibniz believed, is the technical formal language of his calculus, following the laws of deterministic logic, that would bridge the world between the seen and the unseen, the visible and the invisible, the extended and the unextended.

Again, this is not the place to learn calculus; any good introductory mathematics text with lots of examples and problems will do, as long as you keep in mind that there you are learning the bare technique *with all the philosophy censored.* That may be putting it too strongly, but I think that is exactly how Leibniz would put it if he saw the textbooks today that teach the method he invented. I can merely offer, in broad strokes, some symbolic language in which Leibniz's system works. In addition to the *differential* calculus there is also the *integral* calculus.

A lot of the mystery surrounding the symbol ∫ can be removed if you keep in mind that it is only an elongated S, which has become a shorthand way (a code) for writing "the sum of," or, more precisely, "the sum of all the quantities of" whatever follows it. Thus, ∫ means "the sum of all the quantities of little bits of *y*." It is related to another Greek symbol, Σ, sigma, which is also a sign of summation. The crucial difference is that while Σ is generally used to indicate the sum of a number of finite quantities, the integral sign ∫ is generally used to indicate the summing up of a vast number of small quantities of *indefinitely minute magnitude.* Thus,

$$\int dy = y$$

and

$$\int dx = x$$

In this way, the whole of anything can be conceived of as made up of a lot of little bits. The smaller the bits, the more of them there will be. Thus, a line 1-inch long may be conceived as made up of 10 line segments each 1/10-inch long, or of 100 line segments each 1/100-inch long, or of 1,000,000 parts each 1/1,000,000-inch long. Or, pushing the thought to the limits of conceivability, the 1-inch line may be conceived as made up of an infinite number of elements each of which is *infinitesimally* small.

So what is the use of thinking of things in this way? Why not think of them as wholes to begin with? The reason is that there are a vast number of cases in which one cannot calculate the bigness of the thing as a whole without reckoning with the sum of a lot of small parts. The process of *integrating* enables us to calculate totals that we would otherwise be unable to estimate directly because we cannot ever see the whole. In fact, if you think about it, you will realize that you *never* "see" the whole of anything, you only see one little bit of it anyway. Leibniz's calculus provides a machinery, a sort of conceptual microscope into the very small and a conceptual telescope for the very large, so we can see *conceptually,* within our mathematical computations, beyond the limitations of the appearances.

12.4 The Machine Within the Machine Within the Machine

In *The Monadology* (paragraph 17), Leibniz asks what would happen if you stepped inside a "machine whose structure produced thought, sensation, and perception"—for instance, the brain. Suppose we shrink down, as in Isaac Asimov's science fiction film *Fantastic Voyage,* to microscopic size and enter. When this happens to the scientists in the movie, they travel into the brain and see electrical discharges along the neurons which they conclude must be the thoughts occurring in that brain. But thoughts *as thoughts*, images *as images* are *not* flashes of electrical discharge along neurons! If we looked inside your brain and saw neurons firing, we would not see the images you see or hear the thoughts you hear. Likewise, if we shrank even further, until we saw the atoms out of which the neurons are composed, what we would see, according to such a materialist picture of reality, are lifeless clumps of atoms floating in empty space. They would look like a constellation of stars. *Where are the thoughts, ideas, and images* that are supposed to exist at some macroscopic level, where these lifeless little pieces of matter give rise to them? Impossible! That is part of Leibniz's argument for his thesis that unless the ultimate constituents of the world are, themselves, living minds, minds as we know them could never emerge into existence as such.

But what does it mean to say that the world consists not of lifeless, immaterial atoms but of monads, each of which is a living individual mind? *Especially* since Leibniz refers to the human body as a machine in several passages! Here, in one of his most powerful and original images, he explains why. Starting with composites of simple substances, he distinguishes *divine* machines, or *natural automata,* which is what we are, from artificial automata, that is, *artificial* machines such as those made by us: the difference is that we, unlike the machines we make, *are an infinity of machines within machines, forever, all the way down.* And the only reason why each monad is not God—why you are not identical with the world-soul, as in Bruno's and Averroës's philosophy—is that you are confused.

⚶

The Monadology

60. . . . If the representation were distinct as to the details of the entire universe, each monad would be a Deity. It is not in the object represented that the monads are limited, but in the modifications of their knowledge of the object. In a confused way they reach out to infinity or to the whole, but are limited and differentiated in the degree of their distinct perceptions.

61. In this respect composites are like simple substances, for all space is filled up; therefore, all

matter is connected. And in a plenum or filled space every movement has an effect upon bodies in proportion to this distance, so that not only is every body affected by those which are in contact with it and responds in some way to whatever happens to them, but also by means of them the body responds to those bodies adjoining them, and their intercommunication reaches to any distance whatsoever. Consequently every body responds to all that happens in the universe, so that he who saw all could read in each one what is happening everywhere, and even what has happened and what will happen. He can discover in the present what is distant both as regards space and as regards time; "All things conspire" as Hippocrates said. A soul can, however, read in itself only what is there represented distinctly. It cannot all at once open up all its folds, because they extend to infinity.

62. Thus although each created monad represents the whole universe, it represents more distinctly the body which specially pertains to it and of which it constitutes the entelechy. And as this body expresses all the universe through the interconnection of all matter in the plenum, the soul also represents the whole universe in representing this body, which belongs to it in a particular way.

63. The body belonging to a monad, which is its entelechy or soul, constitutes together with the entelechy what may be called a *living being,* and with a soul what is called an *animal.* Now this body of a living being or of an animal is always organic, because every monad is a mirror of the universe is regulated with perfect order there must needs be order also in what represents it, that is to say in the perceptions of the soul and consequently in the body through which the universe is represented in the soul.

64. Therefore every organic body of a living being is a kind of divine machine or natural automaton, infinitely surpassing all artificial automatons. Because a machine constructed by man's skill is not a machine in each of its parts; for instance, the teeth of a brass wheel have parts or bits which to us are not artificial products and contain nothing in themselves to show the use to which the wheel was destined in the machine. The machines of nature, however, that is to say, living bodies, are still machines in their smallest parts *ad infinitum.* Such is the difference between nature and art, that is to say, between divine art and ours.

65. The author of nature has been able to employ this divine and infinitely marvelous artifice, because each portion of matter is not only, as the ancients recognized, infinitely divisible, but also because it is really divided without end, every part into other parts, each one of which has its own proper motion. Otherwise it would be impossible for each portion of matter to express all the universe.

66. Whence we see that there is a world of created things, of living beings, of animals, of entelechies, of souls, in the minutest particle of matter.

67. Every portion of matter may be conceived as like a garden full of plants and like a pond full of fish. But every branch of a plant, every member of an animal, and every drop of the fluids within it, is also such a garden or such a pond.

68. And although the ground and air which lies between the plants of the garden, and the water which is between the fish in the pond, are not themselves plants or fish, yet they nevertheless contain these, usually so small however as to be imperceptible to us.

69. There is, therefore, nothing uncultivated, or sterile or dead in the universe, no chaos, no confusion, save in appearance; somewhat as a pond would appear at a distance when we could see in it a confused movement, and so to speak, a swarming of the fish, without however discerning the fish themselves.

70. It is evident, then, that every living body has a dominating entelechy, which in animals is the soul. The parts, however, of this living body are full of other living beings, plants and animals, which in turn have each one its entelechy or dominating soul.

71. This does not mean, as some who have misunderstood my thought have imagined, that each soul has a quantity or portion of matter appropriated to it or attached to itself for ever, and that it consequently owns other inferior living beings destined to serve it always; because all bodies are in a state of perpetual flux like rivers, and the parts are continually entering in or passing out.

72. The soul, therefore, changes its body only gradually and by degrees, so that it is never deprived all at once of all its organs. There is frequently a metamorphosis in animals, but never metempsychosis or a transmigration of souls.

Neither are there souls wholly separate from bodies, nor bodiless spirits. God alone is without body.

73. This is also why there is never absolute generation or perfect death in the strict sense, consisting in the separation of the soul from the body. What we call generation is development and growth, and what we call death is envelopment and diminution.

74. Philosophers have been much perplexed in accounting for the origin of forms, entelechies, or souls. To-day, however, when it has been learned through careful investigations made in plant, insect and animal life, that the organic bodies of nature are never the product of chaos or putrefaction, but always come from seeds in which there was without doubt some preformation, it has been decided that not only is the organic body already present before conception, but also a soul in this body, in a word, the animal itself; and it has been decided that, by means of conception the animal is merely made ready for a great transformation, so as to become an animal of another sort. We can see cases somewhat similar outside of generation when grubs become flies and caterpillars butterflies.

75. These little animals, some of which by conception become large animals, may be called spermatic. Those among them which remain in their species, that is to say, the greater part, are born, multiply, and are destroyed, like the larger animals. There are only a few chosen ones which come out upon a greater stage.

76. This, however, is only half the truth. I believe, therefore, that if the animal never actually commences by natural means, no more does it by natural means come to an end. Not only is there no generation, but also there is no entire destruction or absolute death. These reasonings, carried on *a posteriori* and drawn from experience, accord perfectly with the principles which I have above deduced *a priori*.

⚓

By *a posteriori* he means truths (true propositions) that are known *after the fact of experience* to be so, versus *a priori* truths (true propositions) that are known prior to there being any conscious experience. All truths in his system are derived a priori, as he makes perfectly clear in another of his great works, *Discourse on Metaphysics,* where he declares himself to be an explicit Platonist in opposition to the Aristotelians of his time.

⚓

Discourse on Metaphysics

XXVI. Ideas are all stored up within us. Plato's doctrine of reminiscence.

In order to see clearly what an idea is, we must guard ourselves against a misunderstanding. Many regard the idea as the form or the differentiation of our thinking, and according to this opinion we have the idea in our mind, in so far as we are thinking of it, and each separate time that we think of it anew we have another idea although similar to the preceding one. Some, however, take the idea as the immediate object of thought, or as a permanent form which remains even when we are no longer contemplating it. As a matter of fact our soul has the power of representing to itself any form or nature whenever the occasion comes for thinking about it, and I think that this activity of our soul is, so far as it expresses some nature, form or essence, properly the idea of the thing. This is in us, and is always in us, whether we are thinking of it or no. (Our soul expresses God and the universe and all essences as well as all existences.) This position is in accord with my principles that naturally nothing enters into our minds from outside.

It is a bad habit we have of thinking as though our minds receive certain messengers, as it were, or as if they had doors or windows. We have in our minds all those forms for all periods of time because the mind at every moment expresses all its future thoughts and already thinks confusedly of all that of which it will ever think distinctly. Nothing can be taught us of which we have not already in our minds the idea. This idea is as it

From Gottfried Wilhelm Leibniz, *Discourse on Metaphysics,* G. R. Montgomery, trans. (La Salle, IL: Open Court, 1902), with emendations by the author.

were the material out of which the thought will form itself. This is what Plato has excellently brought out in his doctrine of reminiscence, a doctrine which contains a great deal of truth, provided that it is properly understood and purged of the error of pre-existence, and provided that one does not conceive of the soul as having already known and thought at some other time what it learns and thinks now. Plato has also confirmed his position by a beautiful experiment. He introduces a small boy, whom he leads by short steps, to extremely difficult truths of geometry bearing on incommensurables, all this without teaching the boy anything, merely drawing out replies by a well arranged series of questions. This shows that the soul virtually knows those things, and needs only to be reminded (animadverted) to recognize the truths. Consequently it possesses at least the idea upon which those truths depend. We may say even that it already possesses those truths, if we consider them as the relations of the ideas.

XXVII. In what respect our souls can be compared to blank tablets and how conceptions are derived from the senses.

Aristotle preferred to compare our souls to blank tablets prepared for writing, and he maintained that nothing is in the understanding which does not come through the senses. This position is in accord with the popular conceptions as Aristotle's positions usually are. Plato thinks more profoundly. Such tenets or practicologies are nevertheless allowable in ordinary use somewhat in the same way as those who accept the Copernican theory still continue to speak of the rising and setting of the sun. I find indeed that these usages can be given a real meaning containing no error, quite in the same way as I have already pointed out that we may truly say particular substances act upon one another. In this same sense we may say that knowledge is received from without through the medium of the senses because certain exterior things contain or express more particularly the causes which determine us to certain thoughts. Because in the ordinary uses of life we attribute to the soul only that which belongs to it most manifestly and particularly, and there is no advantage in going further. When, however, we are dealing with the exactness of metaphysical truths, it is important to recognize the powers and independence of the soul which extend infinitely further than is commonly supposed. In order, therefore, to avoid misunderstandings it would be well to choose separate terms for the two. These expressions which are in the soul whether one is conceiving of them or not may be called ideas, while those which one conceives of or constructs may be called conceptions, *conceptus*. But whatever terms are used, it is always false to say that all our conceptions come from the so-called external senses, because those conceptions which I have of myself and of my thoughts, and consequently of being, of substance, of action, of identity, and of many others came from an inner experience.

⊀

Crucial to his reasoning here is the Principle of Sufficient Reason, which we already encountered in our first selection from *The Monadology* (pp. 274–275), and his advance toward our understanding of the traditional distinction between two types of truths. Kant and all subsequent philosophers will call them *analytic* versus *synthetic* truths.

Whereas the *a priori/a posteriori* distinction is concerned with *how we know* whether a proposition is true, the *analytic/synthetic* distinction is concerned with *what makes a proposition true*. "All bachelors are unmarried," "2 + 3 = 5," and "Either it is raining or it is not raining" are all examples of analytically true propositions. To suppose, for instance, that John is a married bachelor would be to contradict yourself; once you know the meaning of the word *bachelor*— "unmarried male of a marriageable age"—it is impossible that John is both a bachelor and married. Why? Because it is not possible to be an *un*married married man. To suppose otherwise is self-contradictory. Furthermore, when we consider analytically true propositions like "Either it is raining or it is not raining," we see that it is not possible that they could be false. It is *always and everywhere* true that either it is raining or it isn't. In other words, as Leibniz would put it, *analytically true propositions are*

true in all possible worlds, they are *necessarily true*.

Thus, in calling a proposition *analytic*, we are saying something about *what makes it true*. Notice that all analytic propositions, such as the preceding three, are a priori; that is, they are known to be true independently of experience. While I could in principle discover that all bachelors are unmarried males by taking a survey of all men, the whole empirical procedure would be a ridiculous waste of time and an elaborate self-deception; all I have to do is understand, from the inside, the meaning of the terms.

On the other hand, propositions such as "The sky is blue," "Kolak has blond hair," and "George Washington was the first president of the United States" are all examples of *synthetically* true sentences. Their truth depends not on meanings but on the facts of the world, and they are in no sense necessary. It is possible for them to be false; that they are true is what Aristotle called "accidents" of nature or of some aspect of the world. Thus, for instance, if there were less moisture in the air or if the refractive properties of oxygen were different or if our brains responded differently to particular wavelengths of light, the sky would be a different color; indeed, on Mars the sky *is* a different color (or would be seen as such if someone were there to see it). Likewise, I might have been born with brown or black hair. And so on. To say that "George Washington was the first president of the United States" is synthetically true because someone other than George Washington might have been the first president of the United States. This is not so with the proposition "George Washington was the first president of the United States or George Washington was not the first president of the United States," which is true in all possible worlds—even in possible worlds where George Washington never existed and in which there are no countries. In such a world, it would still *have* to be true that either Washington was or was not president. In the latter case, it would be true that he wasn't, just as in "our" world (what is ordinarily taken to be the actual world) "Either Snerdly Goofelbumbs Derogjebe was first president of Atlantis or he was not" is true. It is *necessarily* true.

These may seem like fine points or trivialities of language. But Leibniz's elaborate and precise clockwork metaphysics is constructed on exactly such precision and shows the way his mind worked, extracting giant truths from little subtleties. Think about it: a statement that is true *in all* possible worlds? Whether we are dreaming or awake? Whether we are gods or madmen? This is precisely the sort of certainty that Descartes craved. *And what accounts for this fact?* That is, what "forces" make it so? What could possibly account for such facts of the world? In basing his system on such logical underpinnings, Leibniz is painting a picture of a God that is itself an elaborate, perfect, absolutely precise infinite machine, a logical space of infinite possibilities *that must itself exist not by design nor by cause but of itself.* For, as we have discussed before, what makes 2 + 3 = 5? What makes "*p* or not *p*" true? *Nothing.*

Yet it is so.

The problem is that it seems the propositions that are necessarily true—the analytic propositions—are of the sort that do not give us information about the actual world we live in. Here, however, Leibniz makes one of his boldest metaphysical moves, one that anticipates a move made by the great twentieth-century philosopher W. V. O. Quine.[4] But whereas we shall see Quine question the validity of the analytic synthetic distinction, Leibniz argues in no uncertain terms that *all synthetic sentences are really analytic.* That is, *sub specie aeternitatis*—from "God's point of view"—all true propositions are *necessarily* true. If ever we were shocked by propositions such as "Everything is made of water" or "Everything is made of numbers" or "All is one," *this* statement—that all true propositions are necessarily true—once understood, is more shocking than all such propositions put together! For in Leibniz's system of the world, "Kolak has blond hair" is as necessarily true as

"Bachelors are not married." In saying that all synthetic propositions are really analytic, Leibniz is saying, in a nutshell, that *there are no accidents. Everything that is, must be exactly as it is and it is impossible for it to be any other way.* Everything you are doing right now. Everything you have ever done or will do. And so for *everything.*

There is, however, an important qualification. We must distinguish *absolutely necessary* propositions from those that are "accidentally" necessary, that is, ones that are in an obtuse way dependent upon the way the world is. Once the world gets going there will be a certain class of world-dependent (world-relative) necessities in addition to the absolute, transworld necessities, based on utter *incomplete inaccessibility and freedom,* such as is enjoyed only in the sum total of being, in the mind of God. Thus, Leibniz's God, unlike Spinoza's, is free:

⚓

XIII. As the individual concept of each person includes once for all everything which can ever happen to him, in it can be seen, *a priori* the evidences or the reasons for the reality of each event, and why one happened sooner than the other. But these events, however certain, are nevertheless contingent, being based on the free choice of God and of his creatures. It is true that their choices always have their reasons, but they incline to the choices under no compulsion of necessity.

But before going further it is necessary to meet a difficulty which may arise regarding the principles which we have set forth in the preceding. We have said that the concept of an individual substance includes once for all everything which can ever happen to it and that in considering this concept one will be able to see everything which can truly be said concerning the individual, just as we are able to see in the nature of a circle all the properties which can be derived from it. But does it not seem that in this way the difference between contingent and necessary truths will be destroyed, that there will be no place for human liberty, and that an absolute fatality will rule as well over all our actions as over all the rest of the events of the world? To this I reply that a distinction must be made between that which is certain and that which is necessary. Every one grants that future contingencies are assured since God foresees them, but we do not say just because of that that they are necessary. But it will be objected, that if any conclusion can be deduced infallibly from some definition or concept, it is necessary; and now since we have maintained that everything which is to happen to anyone is already virtually included in his nature or concept, as all the properties are contained in the definition of a circle, therefore, the difficulty still remains. In order to meet the objection completely, I say that the connection or sequence is of two kinds; the one, absolutely necessary, whose contrary implies contradiction, occurs in the eternal verities like the truths of geometry; the other is necessary only *ex hypothesi,* and so to speak by accident, and in itself it is contingent since the contrary is not implied. This latter sequence is not founded upon ideas wholly pure and upon the pure understanding of God, but upon his free decrees and upon the processes of the universe. Let us give an example. Since Julius Caesar will become perpetual Dictator and master of the Republic and will overthrow the liberty of Rome, this action is contained in his concept, for we have supposed that it is the nature of such a perfect concept of a subject to involve everything, in fact so that the predicate may be included in the subject *ut possit inesse subjecto.* We may say that it is not in virtue of this concept or idea that he is obliged to perform this action, since it pertains to him only because God knows everything. But it will be insisted in reply that his nature or form responds to this concept, and since God imposes upon him this personality, he is compelled henceforth to live up to it. I could reply by instancing the similar case of the future contingencies which as yet have no reality save in the understanding and will of God, and which, because God has given them in advance this form, must needs correspond to it. But I prefer to overcome a difficulty rather than to excuse it by instancing other difficulties, and what I am about to say will serve to clear up the one as well as the other. It is here that must be applied the distinction in the kind of relation, and I say that that which happens conformably to these decrees is assured, but that it is not therefore necessary, and if anyone did the contrary, he would do nothing impossible in itself, although it is impossible *ex*

hypothesi that that other happen. For if anyone were capable of carrying out a complete demonstration by virtue of which he could prove this connection of the subject, which is Caesar, with the predicate, which is his successful enterprise, he would bring us to see in fact that the future dictatorship of Caesar had its basis in his concept or nature, so that one would see there a reason why he resolved to cross the Rubicon rather than to stop, and why he gained instead of losing the day at Pharsalus, and that it was reasonable and by consequence assured that this would occur, but one would not prove that it was necessary in itself, nor that the contrary implied a contradiction, almost in the same way in which it is reasonable and assured that God will always do what is best although that which is less perfect is not thereby implied. For it would be found that this demonstration of this predicate as belonging to Caesar is not as absolute as are those of numbers or of geometry, but that this predicate supposes a sequence of things which God has shown by his free will. This sequence is based on the first, free decree of God which was to do always that which is the most perfect and upon the decree which God made following the first one, regarding human nature, which is that men should always do, although freely, that which appears to be the best. Now every truth which is founded upon this kind of decree is contingent, although certain, for the decrees of God do not change the possibilities of things and, as I have already said, although God assuredly chooses the best, this does not prevent that which is less perfect from being possible in itself. Although it will never happen, it is not its impossibility but its imperfection which causes him to reject it. Now nothing is necessitated whose opposite is possible. One will then be in a position to satisfy these kinds of difficulties, however great they may appear (and in fact they have not been less vexing to all other thinkers who have ever treated this matter), provided that he considers well that all contingent propositions have reasons why they are thus, rather than otherwise, or indeed (what is the same thing) that they have proof *a priori* of their truth, which render them certain and show that the connection of the subject and predicate in these propositions has its basis in the nature of the one and of the other, but he must further remember that such contingent propositions have not the demonstrations of necessity, since their reasons are founded only on the principle of contingency or of the existence of things, that is to say, upon that which is, or which appears to be the best among several things equally possible. Necessary truths, on the other hand, are founded upon the principle of contradiction, and upon the possibility or impossibility of the essences themselves, without regard here to the free will of God or of creatures.

⚓

Such a divine perspective on everything, however, is not reserved for God but is open to each and every mind; for the key to each mind is also the key to metaphysics. That key is logic, which through Leibniz's philosophy allows us to infer conclusions about the real world from studying the grammar of our propositions! This is because you already contain all your predicates, so that if you (or anyone else) comprehended yourself, that is, had a *complete individual notion* of you, we could deduce each and every event of your life and every one of your personal characteristics, in the same way that "the quality of king . . . belongs to Alexander the Great." Furthermore, you are as you are and cannot be any different any more than the world itself, indeed, the totality of all possible worlds, can be any different; nothing can be any other way than it actually is. The actual world, which Leibniz argues is the best of all possible worlds, is one in which everything has a necessary reason for why it is as it is rather than some other way; this is his Principle of Sufficient Reason. It is impossible, according to this principle, that something could exist without any explanation, cause, or reason; this is the main principle of his metaphysical rationality.

For instance, let us assume that at this moment you are wearing some clothes; why those clothes rather than some others? You did not pop into existence fully dressed. You may say you don't know what the reason is. But there nevertheless must be some reasons why those clothes are on you right now.

It may be the case that only God's perspective can clearly and distinctly reveal all the reasons until the necessity is itself made explicit, but the inquiry into the reasons is in principle open to human scientific inquiry. The answer consists of facts such as your predilections, available clothes, the causes of your thoughts and actions at each moment (even if they are not readily apparent), and so on.

What is true of your clothes is true of the whole of existence; there must be a reason why the universe in its totality and everything in it exists at all. Why is there something at all rather than nothing? Because everything exists of necessity. Like Thomas Aquinas, whom he greatly admires, Leibniz answers this biggest question of all time in terms of an uncaused cause, an all-perfect being whose being is itself necessary. He calls this being "God."

Again, unlike Spinoza's God, Leibniz's God is free, but not in any ordinary sense. God must act so as to create the maximum amount of existence—metaphysical perfection—and the maximum amount of possible activity—moral perfection. But God is free in the absolute sense—that is, the absolute necessities, which are world-independent, come into existence with the actual world, realized by God through "free choice." Thus, the logic of existence, the infinity of possibilities and actualities, is so large as to contain more room than is contained within itself; that is, *existence itself contains no boundaries.* There is a certain *meta*logical incompleteness to the complete totality of the whole, an openness to reality. Such thinking would have to await many subsequent developments before it could be articulated in the twentieth century, subsequent to the work of Frege and Russell, in the famous incompleteness theorems of Kurt Gödel.

NOTES

1. Nicolas Malebranche (1638–1715) was a Cartesian from Paris who believed that mind and body cannot possibly interact. Antoine Arnauld

(1560–1619) was the noble Parisian lawyer who demolished the entire Jesuit case against the University of Paris in one of the first and most forceful defenses of academic freedom against political and religious authority. Christian Huygens (1629–1695) was the great Dutch mathematician, astronomer, and physicist who invented the wave theory of light.

2. Remember, "substances" can be thought of as "realities"; thus Leibniz was the first thinker to conceive of a many-worlds view of the world, an infinity of existences each of which is equally and fully real.

3. I owe this image to Bill Boos.

4. In his famous article, "The Analytic-Synthetic Distinction," see Sect. 23.3.

Part IV ✤ The Modern Empiricists

13 ❧ Locke

13.0 Locke (1632–1704): In Search of the Mind's Eye

John Locke was born in Somerset, England. After attending the Westminster school he studied philosophy at Oxford University, which was then still under the influence of medieval Scholasticism. He became deeply interested in both medical research and the experimental science of Robert Boyle and Isaac Newton, having met the two as a member of the Royal Society. Although he became a medical doctor, he turned his full attention to philosophy after reading Descartes's *Meditations* and seeing how a method that could accommodate the progress being made in the newly emerging sciences might be worked out. Whereas Descartes, Spinoza, and Leibniz were all rationalists who, like Plato, held that knowledge must be attained by the light of reason, Locke was an empiricist who claimed, as did Aristotle, that knowledge could be attained only by the light of experience. Locke fully agreed with Descartes, however, that the mind and our ideas are better and more directly known than physical objects, which are known only indirectly through our ideas.

In many ways, Locke's *Essay Concerning Human Understanding* (1690) is a critical response to, and further development of, the views of Descartes, but taken in the opposite direction from that of Leibniz. Locke attacks the idea of innate knowledge, arguing that all ideas in the mind can be accounted for through experience—either via sensation (mental events derived from the outer senses) or reflection (mental events evoked through introspection). He further differentiates simple ideas like red, cold, and salty (which are atomic in that they cannot be further divided) from complex compound ideas, put together by the mind, which do not correspond to the real world (like fictional objects). He tries to explain the origin of all our ideas by an analysis of complex ideas into simpler ones. In the first book he paves the way for his account of the nature and origin of the mind and our ideas. The second book, from which the next selection is taken, begins with a criticism of the commonsense distinction between our perceptions and our ideas.

For Locke, as for Descartes, *perception* and *having ideas* are one and the same thing (Bk. II, Ch. 1, para. 9). That is, although it is obvious that all mental events—anything that occurs in the mind—are ideas, it is clear to Locke that perceptions, too, are mental events. All the philosophers of his time, even those who are "divided" into categories of "rationalist" and "empiricist," including Descartes, Leibniz, Berkeley, Hume, and Kant, shared this view. We've been over this point many times but it is one of the most difficult philosophical lessons to learn. What you are perceiving right now (for instance, a book, hands holding a book) are not the things in themselves as they exist "out there" beyond your mind but, rather, ideas that at best resemble those things to a certain degree and in certain limited ways. Locke explains that the objects "out there" make impressions on some part of the body such as on your physical hands and on your physical eyes. These impressions are then transmitted to the mind which, in turn, creates perceptions and, subsequently, reasons, remembers, and makes judgments about them. So when you are aware of having a particular perception, such as of this book, it is not with your eyes that this perception is apprehended. With what, then?

Let me put it to you in no uncertain terms. You're at home, in bed, asleep, dreaming. Say in your dream you find yourself at the beach. You're sitting under an umbrella looking out across the water at a boat. Here's a question: *What are you seeing that boat with?* The boat exists only in your dream. Your eyes are closed. Yet you see a boat (it's not a *fish* or a *skyscraper* but a boat). Right? So why are you seeing a boat if your eyes are closed? Aren't eyes necessary for vision? No, they're not. As we've been saying over and over in this book, your eyes are not windows. When you are experiencing images— with your eyes open, when awake, or with your eyes closed, when asleep—*what then are you apprehending those images with?*

Obvious answer: your mind. But that's just a word! What does it mean to say that? Can you look inside yourself and see how that is happening, how you're doing it, what you're doing it *with*? Furthermore, there are aspects of your mind that *don't* do that, which are not involved in the having of perceptions. So, again, what, exactly, is it within your mind that makes seeing, as a visual event, possible?

It's not the things out there in the world! The real boat on the real water doesn't care what goes on in your mind; it doesn't make images. Your mind does that. But how? With what faculty?

What was only implicit before Locke is now made explicit. The all-important mental faculty, as Locke defines it, is *the faculty of the understanding*. The understanding is to perception what the eyes are to objects out there in the world. Locke has found Plato's sun. It is not outside the cave. It is there, within you:

☙

Since it is the *understanding* that sets man above the rest of sensible beings, and gives him all the advantage and dominion which he has over them; it is certainly a subject, even for its nobleness, worth our labour to inquire into. The understanding, like the eye, whilst it makes us see and perceive all other things, takes no notice of itself; and it requires art and pains to set it at a distance and make it its own object. But whatever be the difficulties that lie in the way of this inquiry; whatever it be that keeps us so much in the dark to ourselves; sure I am that all the light we can let in upon our minds, all the acquaintance we can make with our own understandings, will not only be very pleasant, but bring us great advantage, in directing our thoughts in the search of other things.*

☙

Furthermore, just as the eyes are "transparent" to themselves—the looking eye does not see itself, the eye, looking—so too the understanding does not notice itself. More, it is a feeble and weak light, not a sun but a candle, that must be made brighter:

☙

If we can find out how far the understanding can extend its view; how far it has faculties to attain certainty; and in what cases it can only judge and

---

*From John Locke, *Essay Concerning Human Understanding*. First published in 1690.

guess, we may learn to content ourselves with what is attainable by us in this state. . . . It will be no excuse to an idle and untoward servant, who would not attend his business by candle light, to plead that he had not broad sunshine. The Candle that is set up in us shines bright enough for all our purposes.

***

Thus, in explicit counterpoint to Descartes's attempt to begin at the beginning and doubt everything, he retorts that

***

If we will disbelieve everything, because we cannot certainly know all things, we shall do much what as wisely as he who would not use his legs, but sit still and perish, because he had not wings to fly.

***

Nevertheless, his first chapter begins from a Cartesian standpoint, that is, from the certainty of his own existence.

***

Of Ideas in General and Their Original*

Every man being conscious to himself that he thinks; and that which his mind is applied about whilst thinking being the *ideas* that are there, it is past doubt that men have in their minds several ideas,—such as are those expressed by the words *whiteness, hardness, sweetness, thinking, motion, man, elephant, army, drunkenness,* and others: it is in the first place then to be inquired, *How he comes by them?*

I know it is a received doctrine, that men have native ideas, and original characters, stamped upon their minds in their very first being. This opinion I have at large examined already; and, I suppose what I have said in the foregoing Book will be much more easily admitted, when I have shown

_____

*From John Locke, *Essay Concerning Human Understanding.* First published in 1690.

whence the understanding may get all the ideas it has; and by what ways and degrees they may come into the mind;—for which I shall appeal to every one's own observation and experience.

Let us then suppose the mind to be, as we say, white paper, void of all characters, without any ideas:—How comes it to be furnished? Whence comes it by that vast store which the busy and boundless fancy of man has painted on it with an almost endless variety? Whence has it all the *materials* of reason and knowledge? To this I answer, in one word, from EXPERIENCE. In that all our knowledge is founded; and from that it ultimately derives itself. Our observation employed either, about external sensible objects, or about the internal operations of our minds perceived and reflected on by ourselves, is that which supplies our understandings with all the *materials* of thinking. These two are the fountains of knowledge, from whence all the ideas we have, or can naturally have, do spring.

***

This is the famous passage of which it has often been said that Locke claims that at birth the mind is exactly what Leibniz claimed it was *not,* namely, a *tabula rasa,* a blank slate. This is the so-called empirical view of knowledge acquired from the "external world," "through the senses," according to which the newborn mind knows nothing and is thereby ready to learn anything and everything, which it can do only through experience. But if you read the passage carefully you will find that Locke does *not* claim that all our ideas are derived from experience. Only those ideas which he calls *perceptions!* The *other* category of ideas, which he calls *reflection,* by which he means not "yellow, white, heat, cold," and so on, as in the case of perceptions, but "perception, thinking, doubting, believing, reasoning, knowing," and so on. *"This* source of ideas every man has wholly in himself; and though it be not sense, as having nothing to do with external object, yet it is very like it, and might properly enough be called *internal sense."*

In other words, as you are about to see for yourself, the so-called empirical view of the knowledge-seeking enterprise and the world in general, and the "scientific" worldview that such an "empirical philosophy" is supposed to afford, has much in common with those enlightened philosophers who, typically, have been drawn into an "opposing" camp.[1] He then gives a detailed account of the history and origin of our ideas on which our understanding of ourselves and the world is based:

⚹

First, our Senses, conversant about particular sensible objects, do convey into the mind several distinct perceptions of things, according to those various ways wherein those objects do affect them. And thus we come by those *ideas* we have of *yellow, white, heat, color, soft, hard, bitter, sweet,* and all those which we call sensible qualities; which when I say the senses convey into the mind, I mean, they from external objects convey into the mind what produces there those perceptions. This great source of most of the ideas we have, depending wholly upon our senses, and derived by them to the understanding, I call SENSATION.

Secondly, the other fountain from which experience furnisheth the understanding with ideas is,—the perception of the operations of our own mind within us, as it is employed about the ideas it has got;—which operations, when the soul comes to reflect on and consider, do furnish the understanding with another set of ideas, which could not be had from things without. And such are *perception, thinking, doubting, believing, reasoning, knowing, willing,* and all the different actings of our own minds;—which we being conscious of, and observing in ourselves, do from these receive into our understandings as distinct ideas as we do from bodies affecting our senses. This source of ideas every man has wholly in himself; and though it be not sense, as having nothing to do with external objects, yet it is very like it, and might properly enough be called *internal sense.* But as I call the other Sensation, so I call this REFLECTION, the ideas it affords being such only as the mind gets by reflecting on its own operations within itself. By reflection then, in the following part of this discourse, I would be understood to mean, that notice which the mind takes of its own operations, and the manner of them, by reason whereof there come to be ideas of these operations in the understanding. These two, I say, viz.

external material things, as the objects of SENSATION, and the operations of our own minds within, as the objects of REFLECTION, are to me the only originals from whence all our ideas take their beginnings. The term *operations* here I use in a large sense, as comprehending not barely the actions of the mind about its ideas, but some sort of passions arising sometimes from them, such as is the satisfaction or uneasiness arising from any thought.

The understanding seems to me not to have the least glimmering of any ideas which it doth not receive from one of these two. *External objects* furnish the mind with the ideas of sensible qualities, which are all those different perceptions they produce in us; and *the mind* furnishes the understanding with ideas of its own operations.

These, when we have taken a full survey of them, and their several modes, [combinations, and relations,] we shall find to contain all our whole stock of ideas; and that we have nothing in our minds which did not come in one of these two ways. Let any one examine his own thoughts, and thoroughly search into his understanding; and then let him tell me, whether all the original ideas he has there, are any other than of the objects of his senses, or of the operations of his mind, considered as objects of his reflection. And how great a mass of knowledge soever he imagines to be lodged there, he will, upon taking a strict view, see that he has not any idea in his mind but what one of these two have imprinted;—though perhaps, with infinite variety compounded and enlarged by the understanding, as we shall see hereafter.

⚹

Having thus distinguished *perception* from *reflection*—the mind's reaction to "external objects," the mind's reaction to its own perceptive states—he uses the word *idea* to refer to any and all perceptions.

⚹

To ask, at what *time* a man has first any ideas, is to ask, when he begins to perceive;—*having ideas* and *perception* being the same thing . . . the perception of ideas being (as I conceive) to the soul, what motion is to the body; not its essence, but one of its operations.

⚹

In other words, what Leibniz calls *apperception* applies both to Locke's "ideas" (perceptions) and his "reflections" (apperceptions). In effect, Locke is denying the existence of what Leibniz is implying by the Leibnizian notion of perceptions as existing below the threshold of consciousness. And this is all happening simply at the level of the language that these philosophers are using to describe what they take to be the incontrovertible facts about their experience (a point that George Berkeley will use in the next chapter with great insight and advantage in constructing the first fully "idealist" philosophy, in which *nothing* exists but ideas).

In the next excerpt, Locke explains how, just as the eye cannot actively choose how it reacts to the light hitting upon it but is passive, so too the understanding is completely passive. Thus, "the mind is forced to receive the impressions"; further, it cannot "avoid the perception of those ideas that are annexed to them."

⚹

In time the mind comes to reflect on its own operations about the ideas got by sensation, and thereby stores itself with a new set of ideas, which I call ideas of reflection. These are the impressions that are made on our senses by outward objects that are extrinsical to the mind; and its own operations, proceeding from powers intrinsical and proper to itself, which, when reflected on by itself, become also objects of its contemplation—are, as I have said, the original of all knowledge. Thus the first capacity of human intellect is,—that the mind is fitted to receive the impressions made on it; either through the senses by outward objects, or by its own operations when it reflects on them. This is the first step a man makes towards the discovery of anything, and the groundwork whereon to build all those notions which ever he shall have naturally in this world. All those sublime thoughts which tower above the clouds, and reach as high as heaven itself, take their rise and footing here: in all that great extent wherein the mind wanders, in those remote speculations it may seem to be elevated with, it stirs not one jot beyond those

ideas which *sense* or *reflection* have offered for its contemplation.

In this part the understanding is merely passive; and whether or no it will have these beginnings, and as it were materials of knowledge, is not in its own power. For the objects of our senses do, many of them, obtrude their particular ideas upon our minds whether we will or not; and the operations of our minds will not let us be without, at least, some obscure notions of them. No man can be wholly ignorant of what he does when he thinks. These simple ideas, when offered to the mind, the understanding can no more refuse to have, nor alter when they are imprinted, nor blot them out and make new ones itself, than a mirror can refuse, alter, or obliterate the images or ideas which the objects set before it do therein produce. As the bodies that surround us do diversely affect our organs, the mind is forced to receive the impressions; and cannot avoid the perception of those ideas that are annexed to them.

⚹

What causes impressions and the subsequent perceptions based on them is that objects out there in the world have *qualities,* by which Locke means *powers:* the power of objects to affect our minds. Ideas (that is, perceptions) in the mind are the effect, the qualities of objects are the cause. Ideas of primary qualities, which resemble objects out there in the world, are solidity, extension, figure, mobility, and number. Ideas of secondary qualities, which do not resemble objects out there in the world, exist only in the mind, giving rise to complex ideas (such as colors, smells, and textures). As a result, our perceptions do not render an accurate and perfect picture of the world but, rather, are imperfect representations of reality. As in Leibniz's philosophy, each is an individual "mirror" of a part of reality, albeit a distorted and imperfect one:

⚹

To discover the nature of our *ideas* the better, and to discourse of them intelligibly, it will be convenient to distinguish them *as they are ideas or per-*

ceptions in our minds; and as they are modifications of matter in the bodies that cause such perceptions in us: that so we may not think (as perhaps usually is done) that they are exactly the images and resemblances of something inherent in the subject; most of those of sensation being in the mind no more the likeness of something existing without us, than the names that stand for them are the likeness of our ideas, which yet upon hearing they are apt to excite in us.

Whatsoever the mind perceives *in itself,* or is the immediate object of perception, thought, or understanding, that I call *idea*; and the power to produce any idea in our mind, I call *quality* of the subject wherein that power is. Thus a snowball having the power to produce in us the ideas of white, cold, and round,—the power to produce those ideas in us, as they are in the snowball, I call qualities; and as they are sensations or perceptions in our understandings, I call them ideas; which *ideas*, if I speak of sometimes as in the things themselves, I would be understood to mean those qualities in the objects which produce them in us.

Qualities thus considered in bodies are,

First, such as are utterly inseparable from the body, in what state soever it be;] and such as in all the alterations and changes it suffers, all the force can be used upon it, it constantly keeps; and such as sense constantly finds in every particle of matter which has bulk enough to be perceived; and the mind finds inseparable from every particle of matter, though less than to make itself singly be perceived by our senses: v.g. Take a grain of wheat, divide it into two parts; each part has still solidity, extension, figure, and mobility: divide it again, and it retains still the same qualities; and so divide it on, till the parts become insensible; they must retain still each of them all those qualities. For division (which is all that a mill, or pestle, or any other body, does upon another, in reducing it to insensible parts) can never take away either solidity, extension, figure, or mobility from any body, but only makes two or more distinct separate masses of matter, of that which was but one before; all which distinct masses, reckoned as so many distinct bodies, after division, make a certain number. These I call *original* or *primary qualities* of body, which I think we may observe to produce simple ideas in us, viz. solidity, extension, figure, motion or rest, and number.

Secondly, such qualities which in truth are nothing in the objects themselves but powers to produce various sensations in us by their primary qualities, i.e. by the bulk, figure, texture, and motion of their insensible parts, as colours, sounds, tastes, &c. These I call *secondary qualities.* To these might be added a *third* sort, which are allowed to be barely powers; though they are as much real qualities in the subject as those which I, to comply with the common way of speaking, call qualities, but for distinction, secondary qualities. For the power in fire to produce a new colour, or consistency, in *wax* or *clay,*—by its primary qualities, is as much a quality in fire, as the power it has to produce in *me a* new idea or sensation of warmth or burning, which I felt not before,—by the same primary qualities, viz. the bulk, texture, and motion of its insensible parts.

᠅

Thus, according to Locke, these representations that we ordinarily call "perceptions," and which he calls "ideas," ultimately consist in primary qualities only: colorless, odorless, tasteless, extended solid particles—the atoms of Newtonian mechanics. But since we can have no clear and distinct idea of physical substances, we cannot have genuine knowledge about the real nature of things; all we can see is that they are an "I know not what." What allows us to have knowledge to the extent that we do have it, however, is that all our simple ideas are real: the mind cannot create them but receives them, passively, from the primary qualities in the things in themselves that exist out there independently of the mind. Ideas of secondary qualities are also real but represent only partially and imperfectly things out there beyond the mind.

13.1 Locke's Political Philosophy

Locke was an equally important political philosopher. The selection in this section is from the second of his *Two Treatises of Civil Government* (1690, published the same year as his *Essays Concerning Human Understanding*). Though motivated in part to justify the ascendancy of

King William after the "Glorious Revolution" of 1688, it is widely regarded as among the greatest political works of modern times.

Locke begins, like Hobbes, with an analysis of the "state of nature" as it existed prior to the formation of a political state. But Locke takes a much less pessimistic view than Hobbes. According to Locke all human beings are created equal "within the bounds of the law of nature," which is *reason* itself: "reason, which is that law, teaches all mankind who will but consult it, that, being all equal and independent, no one ought to harm another in his life, health, liberty or possessions."

Since in Locke's view empirical inquiry furnishes no certain universal knowledge, and since assumptions such as like bodies will in the same circumstances have like effects are only conjectures from analogy, natural science does not exist in the strict sense. Both mathematics and ethics, however, belong in the sphere of the demonstrative knowledge of relations. Thus, according to Locke, the principles of ethics are as capable of exact demonstration as those of arithmetic and geometry, although their underlying ideas are more complex, more involved, and hence more exposed to misunderstanding. Furthermore, though lacking the visible symbols of mathematics, these principles should be made explicit through careful and strictly consistent definitions. Moral principles such as "where there is no property there is no injustice," and "no government allows absolute liberty," are as certain as any propositions in Euclid.

For Locke, the advantage of the mathematical and moral sciences over the physical sciences consists in the fact that, in the former, the real and nominal essences, or qualities, of their objects coincide, whereas in the latter they do not. That is, the true inner constitution of objects in terms of their primary qualities is completely unknown to us, and we can deduce nothing from them. Moral ideas, however, like mathematical ideas and their relations, are entirely accessible because they are the products

of our own voluntary operations. They are not copied from things in themselves but are archetypal for reality and need no confirmation whatsoever from experience.

For instance, the connection constituted by our understanding between the ideas *crime* and *punishment,* such as is expressed by the proposition, "Crime deserves punishment," would be valid even if it were the case that no crimes had ever been committed and none ever punished. In other words, existence is not at all involved in universal propositions: "general knowledge lies only in our own thoughts, and consists barely in the contemplation of our own abstract ideas" and their relations. Therefore the truths of ethics, like the truths of mathematics, are both universal and certain, whereas in the natural sciences single observations and experiments are most certain, but not general, and general propositions are only more or less probable. Both the particular experiments and the general conclusions are of great value, but they do not meet the requirements of comprehensive and certain knowledge. This certain knowledge can be attained only in the moral and mathematical realms.

In this way, Locke constructs one of the most influential political philosophies of all time, in which exactly those propositions usually taken to be most subjective and least certain become the most incontrovertible and best known. What is brewing in such a new and revolutionary philosophy, in part, is the idea that society can be constructed in such a way that its functioning can become an absolute arbiter, not just of justice but of truth and knowledge. A just political system must be constructed so that it reflects and amplifies the natural state of the world. Majority rule, the separation of church and state, the right of a people to change governments, the natural right of a people to overthrow unjust governments, and the separation of powers within a government are all ideas central to Locke's system that influenced political philosophy in the eighteenth century, including, and especially, the founders of the United States.

⊥

Two Treatises of Civil Government (Second Treatise)

VII. Of the Beginning of Political Societies

Men being, as has been said, by nature all free, equal, and independent, no one can be put out of his estate and subjected to the political power of another without his own consent, which is done by agreeing with other men, to join and unite into a community for their comfortable, safe, and peaceable living, one amongst another, in a secure enjoyment of their properties, and a greater security against any that are not of it. This any number of men may do, because it injures not the freedom of the rest; they are left, as they were, in the liberty of the state of nature. When any number of men have so consented to make one community or government, they are thereby presently incorporated, and make one body politic, wherein the majority have a right to act and conclude the rest.

For, when any number of men have, by the consent of every individual, made a community, they have thereby made that community one body, with a power to act as one body, which is only by the will and determination of the majority. For that which acts any community, being only the consent of the individuals of it, and it being one body, must move one way, it is necessary the body should move that way whither the greater force carries it, which is the consent of the majority, or else it is impossible it should act or continue one body, one community, which the consent of every individual that united into it agreed that it should; and so everyone is bound by that consent to be concluded by the majority. And therefore we see that in assemblies empowered to act by positive laws where no number is set by that positive law which empowers them, the act of the majority passes for the act of the whole, and of course determines as having, by the law of nature and reason, the power of the whole.

From John Locke, *Two Treatises of Civil Government.* First published in 1690.

And thus every man, by consenting with others to make one body politic under one government, puts himself under an obligation to everyone of that society to submit to the determination of the majority, and to be concluded by it; or else this original compact, whereby he with others incorporates into one society, would signify nothing, and be no compact if he be left free and under no other ties than he was in before in the state of nature. For what appearance would there be of any compact? What new engagement if he were no farther tied by any decrees of the society than he himself thought fit and did actually consent to? This would be still as great a liberty as he himself had before his compact, or anyone else in the state of nature hath, who may submit himself and consent to any acts of it if he thinks fit.

For if the consent of the majority shall not in reason be received as the act of the whole, and conclude every individual, nothing but the consent of every individual can make any thing to be the act of the whole, which, considering the infirmities of health and avocations of business, which in a number though much less than that of a commonwealth, will necessarily keep many away from the public assembly; and the variety of opinions and contrariety of interests which unavoidably happen in all collections of men, 'tis next impossible ever to be had. And, therefore, if coming into society be upon such terms, it will be only like Cato's coming into the theatre, *tantum ut exiret*. Such a constitution as this would make the mighty *Leviathan* of a shorter duration than the feeblest creatures, and not let it outlast the day it was born in, which cannot be supposed till we can think that rational creatures should desire and constitute societies only to be dissolved. For where the majority cannot conclude the rest, there they cannot act as one body, and consequently will be immediately dissolved again.

Whosoever therefore out of a state of nature unite into a community, must be understood to give up all the power necessary to the ends for which they unite into society to the majority of the community, unless they expressly agreed in any number greater than the majority. And this is done by barely agreeing to unite into one political society, which is all the compact that is, or needs be, between the individuals that enter into or make up a commonwealth. And thus, that which begins and actually constitutes any political society is nothing but the consent of any number of freemen capable of a majority, to unite and incorporate into such a society. And this is that, and that only, which did or could give beginning to any lawful government in the world. . . .

To conclude, the power that every individual gave the society when he entered into it, can never revert to the individuals again as long as the society lasts, but will always remain in the community, because without this there can be no community, no commonwealth, which is contrary to the original agreement; so also when the society hath placed the legislative in any assembly of men to continue in them and their successors, with direction and authority for providing such successors, the legislative can never revert to the people whilst that government lasts, because having provided a legislative with power to continue for ever, they have given up their political power to the legislative and cannot resume it. But if they have set limits to the duration of their legislative, and made this supreme power in any person or assembly only temporary; or else when by the miscarriages of those in authority it is forfeited; upon the forfeiture, or at the determination of the time set, it reverts to the society, and the people have a right to act as supreme, and continue the legislative in themselves; or place it in a new form, or new hands as they think good.

His argument can be summed up as follows. All people are born free and with like capacities and rights to preserve their own interests, without injuring those of others. The right to be treated by everyone as a rational being holds even prior to the founding of a state, but then there is no authoritative power to decide conflicts. The state of nature is not in itself a state of war, but it would lead to war if each person attempted to exercise the right of self-protection. To prevent such acts of violence the civil community is constructed based on a free contract to which all individual members transfer their natural freedom and power. Submission to the authority of the state is thus defined by Locke as a free act; by this "contract" natural rights are not

destroyed but guarded. Political freedom is thus an obedience to self-imposed law, the subordination to the common will expressing itself in the majority. Political power should therefore be neither tyrannical, since arbitrary rule is no better than the state of nature; nor should it be paternal, since rulers and their subjects are all equally rational, which is not the case in a parent-child relationship. The supreme power is the legislative power, entrusted by the community to its chosen representatives, whose laws should aim at the general good. Subordinate to the legislative power, and to be kept separate from it, are the two executing powers, the executive and the federative—best united in a single hand under a king or monarch. The executive power (administrative and judicial) carries the laws into effect, and the federative power defends the community against external enemies.

The ruler is subject to the same law as the citizens. If the government, through violation of the law, has become unworthy of the power entrusted to it, sovereign authority reverts to the source from which it was derived—the people—who then must decide whether its representatives and leader have deserved the confidence placed in them. The people then have the right to depose their leaders. The sworn obedience of the subjects is to the law alone, not to the ruler; so a ruler who acts contrary to the law has lost the right to govern. Revolution is then necessary.

Philosophy of Education

In his *Thoughts Concerning Education*, Locke presented one of the first comprehensive philosophies of education. Derived from his moral and political views, themselves derived from his theory of knowledge, his philosophy of education continues to exert a powerful influence, especially in the United States. Locke argues that the aim of education should not be to instill anything into the student but, rather, to develop everything *from* the student. Serving as a gentle guide, not a master, education should develop the student's capacities in a natural way, encouraging intellectual and emotional independence instead of drilling the student into the rigid mindset of a scholar. Rousseau (Section 16.5) was greatly influenced by Locke's ideas in general and his philosophy of education in particular. But whereas Locke insisted on the need to raise the students' sense of self-esteem, Rousseau ignored such psychological pandering to individual egos, claiming that raising students' self-esteem would actually repress them, albeit subtly. Rousseau thought that making students feel good about themselves was but a surrogate for real learning, which often requires doing battle with the ego and self-deception, through which, in our self-imposed ignorance, we avoid taking responsibility for ourselves and for the world.

NOTE

1. The phrase "divide and conquer" comes to mind; for a fuller reference to what is here being asserted, see Chapter 9 on the "Copernican Revolution."

14 ✿ Berkeley

14.0 Berkeley (1685–1753): The Modern Idealist

Born in Kilkenny, Ireland, George Berkeley entered Trinity College, in Dublin, at the age of fifteen. He studied the philosophical luminaries of the time—Locke, Newton, and Malebranche—as well as previous philosophers such as Bacon, Descartes, Hobbes, and Leibniz. He learned mathematics, physics, and optics from the works of Kepler, Descartes, and Newton. Plato, however, had the greatest influence on him.

Deeply critical of both Descartes and Newton, Berkeley saw the scientific revolution of his day as the starting symptoms of the decline of the philosophical mind, on its way toward being seduced away from real philosophical inquiry, blinded by its own knowledge to the awe and mystery of existence. According to Berkeley, science and mathematics were both ultimately on par with religion, none of which could dispel the mystery. In his criticism of the calculus of Newton and Leibniz, he wrote, "He who can digest a second or third fluxion[1] . . . need not, methinks, be squeamish about any point in divinity." By showing the presence of insoluble paradoxes at the center of scientific and mathematical thought, he argued vehemently that neither science nor mathematics could do any better than religious thought. He was less a Skeptic than, by his own reckoning, a true philosopher who pointed to the hidden holes in the conceptual framework—not for the purpose of destroying knowledge but rather for improving and revising it.

Berkeley remained at Trinity for thirteen years, where he produced his most important works: *Essays Towards a New Theory of Vision* (1709), *Three Dialogues Between Hylas and Philonous* (1713), and *A Treatise Concerning Human Knowledge* (1710), written when he was only twenty-five. All three works were either ignored or vehemently disliked, mostly because they were completely misunderstood. Philosophers, scholars, and theologians alike labeled him a Skeptic, a label he tried to refute; nevertheless, his views were for the most part regarded as being patently absurd.

His books having, in his eyes, failed, Berkeley journeyed to the American colonies with the idea of founding a new university in the style of Plato's Academy, where he could be an "educator," not a "re-educator," as he saw himself in England. "The savage Americans," he wrote, "if they are in a state purely natural and unimproved by education, they are also unencumbered with all that rubbish of superstition and prejudice, which is the effect of a wrong one." He moved to Newport, Rhode Island, and awaited the monetary support he had been promised to begin building his academy in Bermuda. The money never came, forcing him to give up the project and return to London where three years later he received a position as bishop of Cloyne. He continued to write, but his works were largely ignored.

Subsequent philosophers, however, have held Berkeley in great esteem. David Hume called his pioneering work on the nature of the mind—particularly his analysis of the complex, bundled nature of our ideas, and the elaborate argument against the existence of abstract ideas—"one of the greatest and most valuable discoveries that has been made of late years in the republic of letters." American idealists considered Berkeley their founder; among them was Josiah Royce (1855–1916) at Harvard who developed his own brand of absolute idealism. The American pragmatist Charles Sanders Peirce (1839–1914) claimed that Berkeley paved the way for the development of pragmatism. Immanuel Kant (1724–1804), though supposedly a critic of Berkeley's idealism, relied heavily on Berkeley's views, especially Berkeley's criticism of materialism. Kant's transcendental idealism incorporates Berkeley's famous dictum, *esse is percipi*, "to be is to be perceived," tailored according to Kant's transcendental philosophy. Arthur Schopenhauer (1788–1860) credited Berkeley as being the first to put forth the view that the world is but an idea in the mind. Ernst Mach (1838–1916), influential physicist and philosopher, claims to have been guided in his criticisms of absolute space, time, and motion by the work of Berkeley, which led him toward laying the foundations for the revolutionary idea in physics that the conscious observer plays a fundamental role in structuring reality. Indeed, Einsteinian relativity as well as contemporary quantum mechanics can be viewed as the ultimate vindication of Berkeley's ideas.

Berkeley's views developed in part as a reaction to Locke. Whereas Locke showed that secondary qualities exist only in the mind, Berkeley pushes the empiricist analysis of ideas to the extreme by arguing that even primary qualities exist only in the mind. Locke's mistake, according to Berkeley, is that he derived the objective existence of extension, hardness, weight, motion, and the other primary qualities of sensible objects through the (bogus) principle of abstraction. Also according to Berkeley, Locke mistakenly thinks he has an abstract idea of substance and extension—matter—as a something "I know not what" to which the mind adheres the secondary qualities of color, texture, and so on. A closer scrutiny of such notions and careful inspection of the actual contents of the mind, along with an analysis of language—the "curtain of words" that deceives us—reveal, Berkeley argues, that there really are no such things as abstract ideas. If we do not allow ourselves to be deceived by our language and instead analyze the actual notions, we shall see that the mind contains only *particular* ideas.

What Locke called the "primary qualities" of sensible objects thus have no existence beyond the conscious mind. Each and every property of a sensible object exists only as a sensation within the perception of a conscious being. In Berkeley's view, once we realize the truth about the nature of perception and the inner working of the mind, we will see that "all the choir of heaven and furniture of the earth, in a word, all those bodies which compose the mighty frame of the world, have not any subsistence without a mind—that their *being* is to be perceived or know, that, consequently so long as they are not actually perceived by me or do not exist in my mind or that of any other created spirit, they must either have no existence at all or else subsist in the mind of some eternal spirit."[2] The entire universe, and all things within it, cannot exist without being perceived by a mind.

14.1 The Role of Language

Berkeley is one of the most misunderstood of all philosophers. This is deeply ironic, given his own warning to his readers. He prefaces his master-piece, *A Treatise*, with the words,

🟊

I make it my request that the reader suspend his judgment till he has once at least read the whole through with that degree of attention and thought which the subject matter shall seem to deserve. For as there are some passages that, taken by themselves, are very liable (nor could it be remedied) to gross misinterpretation, and to be charged with most absurd consequences which, nevertheless, upon an entire perusal will appear not to follow from them, so likewise, through the whole should be read over, yet, if this be done transiently, it is very probable my sense may be mistaken; but to a thinking reader, I flatter myself, it will be throughout clear and obvious.

🟊

These words have turned out to be prophesy. No philosopher has been more butchered and explained away into incoherence than Berkeley. With that in mind, let us read, slowly and patiently and with great care, a portion of his treatise and see what he says for ourselves. Indeed, we should find his philosophy especially poignant in light of the very first and most essential bit of wisdom, which we have identified as part of our meaning of the term *philosophical enlightenment*. For no philosopher has gone to greater lengths to make it clear that your eyes are not windows than Berkeley.

Right at the start he identifies the two major obstacles that we have erected in the way of clear understanding. The first has to do with the nature and abuse of language. The second has to do with the false opinion that "the mind has the power of framing *abstract ideas* or notions of things."

🟊

A Treatise Concerning the Principles of Human Knowledge

In order to prepare the mind of the reader for the easier conceiving what follows, it is proper to premise somewhat, by way of introduction, concerning the nature and abuse of language. But the unraveling this matter leads me in some measure to anticipate my design by taking notice of what seems to have had a chief part in rendering speculation intricate and perplexed and to have occasioned innumerable errors and difficulties in almost all parts of knowledge. And that is the opinion that the mind has a power of framing *abstract ideas* or notions of things. He who is not a perfect stranger to the writings and disputes of philosophers, must needs acknowledge that no small part of them are spent about abstract ideas. These are in a more especial manner thought to be the object of those sciences which go by the name of logic and metaphysics, and of all that which passes under the notion of the most abstracted and sublime learning, in all which one shall scarce find any question handled in such a manner as does not suppose their existence in the mind, and that it is well acquainted with them.

It is agreed on all hands that the qualities or modes of things do never really exist each of them apart by itself and separated from all others, but are mixed, as it were, and blended together, several in the same object. But we are told the mind, being able to consider each quality singly, or abstracted from those other qualities with which it is united, does by that means frame to itself abstract ideas. For example, there is perceived by sight an object extended, colored, and moved: this mixed or compound idea the mind, resolving into its simple, constituent parts and viewing each by itself, exclusive of the rest, does frame the abstract ideas of extension, color, and motion. Not that it is possible for color or motion to exist without extension, but only that the mind can frame to itself by *abstraction* the idea of color exclusive of extension, and of motion exclusive of both color and extension.

🟊

From *The Works of George Berkeley*, A. C. Fraser, ed. (Oxford: Clarendon Press, 1901).

In his *Essay*, Locke asked, "Since all things that exist are only particulars, how come we by general terms?" His answer was, "Words become general by being made the signs of general ideas," Berkeley responds:

☨

By observing how ideas become general we may the better judge how words are made so. And here it is to be noted that I do not deny absolutely there are general ideas, but only that there are any *abstract* general ideas; for, in the passages above quoted, wherein there is mention of general ideas, it is always supposed that they are formed by abstraction. . . . Now, if we will annex a meaning to our words and speak only of what we can conceive, I believe we shall acknowledge that an idea which, considered in itself, is particular, becomes general by being made to represent or stand for all other particular ideas of the same sort. To make this plain by an example, suppose a geometrician is demonstrating the method of cutting a line in two equal parts. He draws, for instance, a black line of an inch in length: this, which in itself is a particular line, is nevertheless with regard to its signification general, since, as it is there used, it represents all particular lines whatsoever; for that which is demonstrated of it is demonstrated of all lines or, in other words, of a line in general. And, as that *particular* line becomes general by being made a sign, so the *name* "line," which taken absolutely is particular, by being a sign is made general. And as the former owes its generality not to its being the sign of an abstract or general line, but of all particular right lines that may possibly exist, so the latter must be thought to derive its generality from the same cause, namely, the various particular lines which it indifferently denotes. . . .

We have, I think, shown the impossibility of abstract ideas . . . and endeavored to show they are of no use for those ends to which they are thought necessary. And lastly, we have traced them to the source from whence they flow, which appears to be language.—It cannot be denied that words are of excellent use, in that by their means all that stock of knowledge which has been purchased by the joint labors of inquisitive men in all ages and nations may be drawn into the view and made the possession of one single person. But at the same time it must be owned that most parts of knowledge have been strangely perplexed and darkened by the abuse of words, and general ways of speech wherein they are delivered. Since therefore words are so apt to impose on the understanding, whatever ideas I consider, I shall endeavor to take them bare and naked into my view, keeping out of my thoughts so far as I am able those names which long and constant use has so strictly united with them; from which I may expect to derive the following advantages:

First, I shall be sure to get clear of all controversies purely verbal—the springing up of which weeds in almost all the sciences has been a main hindrance to the growth of true and sound knowledge. *Secondly,* this seems to be a sure way to extricate myself out of that fine and subtle net of *abstract ideas* which has so miserably perplexed and entangled the minds of men; and that with this peculiar circumstance, that by how much the finer and more curious was the wit of any man, by so much the deeper was he likely to be ensnared and faster held therein. *Thirdly,* so long as I confine my thoughts to my own ideas divested of words, I do not see how I can easily be mistaken. The objects I consider I clearly and adequately know. I cannot be deceived in thinking I have an idea which I have not. It is not possible for me to imagine that any of my own ideas are alike or unlike that are not truly so. To discern the agreements or disagreements there are between my ideas, to see what ideas are included in any compound idea and what not, there is nothing more requisite than an attentive perception of what passes in my own understanding.

But the attainment of all these advantages does presuppose an entire deliverance from the deception of words, which I dare hardly promise myself—so difficult a thing it is to dissolve a union so early begun and confirmed by so long a habit as that betwixt words and ideas. Which difficulty seems to have been very much increased by the doctrine of *abstraction.* For so long as men thought abstract ideas were annexed to their words, it does not seem strange that they should use words for ideas—it being found an impracticable thing to lay aside the word and retain the *abstract* idea in the mind, which in itself was perfectly inconceivable. This seems to me the principal cause why those men who have so emphatically recommended to others the laying aside all use of words in their meditations, and contemplating their bare ideas, have yet failed to perform it themselves. Of late many have been very sensible of the absurd opinions and insignificant disputes which grow out of the abuse of words. And, in order to remedy these evils, they advise well that we attend to the ideas signified and draw off our attention from the words which signify them. But, how good soever this advice may be they have given others, it is plain they could not have a due regard to it themselves so long as they thought the only immediate use of words was to signify ideas, and that the immediate signification of every general name was a determinate abstract idea.

But, these being known to be mistakes, a man may with greater ease prevent his being imposed on by words. He that knows he has no other than *particular* ideas will not puzzle himself in vain to find out and conceive the *abstract* idea annexed to any name. And he that knows names do not always stand for ideas will spare himself the labor of looking for ideas where there are none to be had. It were, therefore, to be wished that everyone would use his utmost endeavors to obtain a clear view of the ideas he would consider, separating from them all that dress and encumbrance of words which so much contribute to blind the judgment and divide the attention. In vain do we extend our view into the heavens and pry into the entrails of the earth, in vain do we consult the writings of learned men and trace the dark footsteps of antiquity—we need only draw the curtain of words, to behold the fairest tree of knowledge, whose fruit is excellent and within the reach of our hand.

Unless we take care to clear the first principles of knowledge from the embarrassment and delusion of words, we may make infinite reasonings upon them to no purpose; we may draw consequences from consequences, and be never the wiser. The further we go, we shall only lose ourselves the more irrecoverably, and be the deeper entangled in difficulties and mistakes. Whoever, therefore, designs to read the following sheets, I entreat him to make my words the occasion of his own thinking and endeavor to attain the same train of thoughts in reading that I had in writing them. By this means it will be easy for him to discover the truth or falsity of what I say. He will be out of all danger of being deceived by my words, and I do not see how he can be led into an error by considering his own naked, undisguised ideas.

⚹

Now, what exactly is Berkeley's point about the role of language in our philosophizing? And what does language have to do with the question of whether the *chair* in my study is *there* whether or not I am looking at it? Let's start with the words *chair* and *there* and work our way backward.

I am in my study. I am sitting on my chair. I get up and leave the room. Is that *chair* that I was sitting on still *there*? Berkeley's first and foremost point in the introduction is that you can't answer that question without first specifying exactly what you mean by the words *chair* and *there*.

Let's talk first about the meaning of the word *chair*. But wait—what about the meaning of *meaning*? This is not a joke. There are two, perhaps equally important, senses of the word *meaning*. There is the *general term* "chair," as a sign for all chairs, meaning something like "things to sit on," but that's not quite right; it's too general. Maybe "a thing with legs and a seat that usually goes with a table." But what about armchairs? This is a problem with this first sense of the word "chair," where it is a general term referring to a whole class of things in which, ultimately, it is rather arbitrary where we draw boundaries between chairs and nonchairs. For instance, an elephant is not a chair, but it has four legs and Sabu is sitting on it. Well, but the elephant is alive. So we kill the elephant and stuff it and now Sabu sits on it in his (large) living room. Is it now a chair? It's sort of up to us to decide how we wish to classify it. But clearly, this abstract sense of the word *chair* does not refer explicitly to any actual, particular, real chair. Do you see this? It's easy to miss. Berkeley doesn't miss it. He wants you not to miss it too and so he spends a great deal of time on what may seem trivial and pedantic to you, but it is like trying to corner a notorious self-deceiving mechanism that is driven by your language and which holds power over even the things to which your conscious mind attends, even to what it considers "sense" and "nonsense." It's like trying to win an argument with your own brain, where it can literally put words in your mouth and thoughts in your mind and feelings in your emotions.

But let us try to stay focused on the chair. To repeat: the first sense of the meaning of the word *chair does not refer to a particular real object*. It's like the phrase *United States of America*. Or the word *humanity*. Or the word *philosophy*. Are any of these *real*? Well, there may be a whole class of *real things* that such names and general terms refer to, but *there is no entity, as such, that is any one of those things*. The United States of America exists only as an idea in people's heads. So does humanity. Why? Because that term, that symbol, is a tool of classification; there is no actual thing in the real world, Berkeley would remind us, that is, itself, *humanity*. Like "United States of America," this phrase is a noise we make consistently in referring to a concept that exists only in our minds to help us with the classification of real things. And what are those real things?

The real things are the things that you and I experience. It's as simple as that. For the word *real*, too—like the word *philosophy*, like the preceding words discussed—has this double meaning, or function. One is to serve as a general term, which gets reified into what Berkeley calls *abstract ideas*, and the other is to designate actual things as they exist. But now the same is true of the word *exist*. And to what does the word *exist* refer, not in its mistaken role as a designator of an *abstract idea* (that is, not as something existing beyond the realm of actual experience, beyond the mind), but as an ostensive designator for something that we can touch, see, feel, taste?

Do you now see why Berkeley wants to say that the *chair*, the *real* chair—*not* the abstract generalization as a class concept to which there is no actual designated object, but the chair that actually *exists*—is not *there* when no one is in the room seeing, touching, or feeling it? You can't sit on an abstract concept! Even the word *there* does not designate—in Berkeley's attempt to achieve *realism* within the domain of language—an abstract idea (an idea of something that exists beyond the realm of mind, that is, an *idea that is*

not an idea, an absurd contradiction). *Space* is that which is right now being seen by you as the manifold within which objects exist. It is, as such, a mental phenomenon. The *there*, the *actual phenomenon*, is not inside a stone room but inside the mind. The reference of *stone room* is something that exists, in the sense of being *tangibly*, actually *there*, as an idea. Not an abstract idea! Even space is not an abstract idea. Think of what the word *abstract* means. It means, literally, "to exist not in space and time." And what Berkeley clearly acknowledges, and what will be one of the firm foundations for the philosophy of Immanuel Kant (Chapter 16), is that space and time are categories of the mind. For Berkeley, they are not just categories in the sense of some transcendental (beyond experience) necessary condition for the having of experience as such, as it will be in Kant's view; rather, space and time are existent things only insofar as the experience called space and time is going on. In a nutshell: to exist not in space and time is to not exist.

But we shall go over this again. And Berkeley has not yet even gotten started. So let us see, now that we have some sense of the important role that language plays in his philosophy, how Berkeley develops his extraordinary worldview.

14.2 To Be Is to Be Perceived: A Treatise Concerning the Principles of Human Knowledge

⚓

That neither our thoughts, nor passions, nor ideas formed by the imagination exist without the mind is what everybody will allow. And it seems no less evident that the various sensations or ideas imprinted on the sense, however blended or combined together (that is, whatever objects they compose), cannot exist otherwise than in a mind

From *The Works of George Berkeley*, A. C. Fraser, ed. (Oxford: Clarendon Press, 1901).

perceiving them.—I think an intuitive knowledge may be obtained of this by anyone that shall attend to what is meant by the term "exist" when applied to sensible things. The table I write on I say exists, that is, I see and feel it; and if I were out of my study I should say it existed—meaning thereby that if I was in my study I might perceive it, or that some other spirit actually does perceive it. There was an odor, that is, it was smelled, there was a sound, that is to say, it was heard; a color or figure, and it was perceived by sight or touch. This is all that I can understand by these and the like expressions. For as to what is said of the absolute existence of unthinking things without any relation to their being perceived, that seems perfectly unintelligible. Their *esse* is *percipi*, nor is it possible they should have any existence out of the minds or thinking things which perceive them.

⁂

"*Their esse is percipi.*" You will find this phrase quoted again and again in various places, translated, now world famously, as "to be is to be perceived." But that all-important first word is usually, and notoriously, left out. Without the *their* as a reference point, the phrase becomes exactly the sort of abstraction that Berkeley's philosophy was designed to eradicate from the enlightened mind.

Let anyone try to demonstrate the falsity of Berkeley's statement with the word *their* intact. It is impossible. The full statement of Berkeley's thesis is incontrovertible. He derives it without reference to science or experience or experiment, a priori. In fact, though this may be a gross oversimplification, what Berkeley is saying is actually a tautology—a logically necessary truth that cannot possibly be false—"That which is mental is mental." Or, "Events in the mind are events in the mind." He doesn't just stay with that, any more than Descartes stays with his *cogito*, "I think therefore I am." Like Descartes, Berkeley attempts to erect a whole philosophy upon the certainty of his true statement. And their subsequent philosophies aside, the starting points of their philosophies are themselves sufficient to produce philosophical enlightenment. If you

understood nothing more in this entire book than the full meaning of the starting propositions of Descartes's and Berkeley's philosophies, you would have gone a long way—perhaps even all the way—to becoming a lover of wisdom.

But since we have lots of time and nowhere to go, let's see where he goes with it.

⁂

It is indeed an opinion strangely prevailing amongst men that houses, mountains, rivers, and, in a word, all sensible objects have an existence, natural or real, distinct from their being perceived by the understanding. But with how great an assurance and acquiescence soever this principle may be entertained in the world, yet whoever shall find in his heart to call it in question may, if I mistake not, perceive it to involve a manifest contradiction. For what are the forementioned objects but the things we perceive by sense? And what do we perceive besides our own ideas or sensations? And is it not plainly repugnant that any one of these, or any combination of them, should exist unperceived?

If we thoroughly examine this tenet it will, perhaps, be found at bottom to depend on the doctrine of *abstract ideas*. For can there be a nicer strain of abstraction than to distinguish the existence of sensible objects from their being perceived, so as to conceive them existing unperceived? Light and colors, heat and cold, extension and figures—in a word, the things we see and feel—what are they but so many sensations, notions, ideas, or impressions on the sense? And is it possible to separate, even in thought, any of these from perception? For my part, I might as easily divide a thing from itself. I may, indeed, divide in my thoughts, or conceive apart from each other, those things which, perhaps, I never perceived by sense so divided. Thus I imagine the trunk of a human body without the limbs, or conceive the smell of a rose without thinking on the rose itself. So far, I will not deny, I can abstract—if that may properly be called "abstraction" which extends only to the conceiving separately such objects as it is possible may really exist or be actually perceived asunder. But my conceiving or imagining power does not extend beyond the possibility of real existence or perception. Hence, as it is impossible for me to see or feel anything without an actual sensation of that thing, so it is impossible for me to conceive in my thoughts any sensible thing or object distinct from the sensation or perception of it.

Some truths there are so near and obvious to the mind that a man need only open his eyes to see them. Such I take this important one to be, to wit, that all the choir of heaven and furniture of the earth, in a word, all those bodies which compose the mighty frame of the world, have not any subsistence without a mind—that their *being* is to be perceived or known, that consequently, so long as they are not actually perceived by me or do not exist in my mind or that of any other created spirit, they must either have no existence at all or else subsist in the mind of some external spirit— it being perfectly unintelligible, and involving the absurdity of abstraction, to attribute to any single part of them an existence independent of a spirit. To be convinced of which, the reader need only reflect, and try to separate in his own thoughts, the *being* of a sensible thing from its *being perceived.*

From what has been said it follows there is not any other substance than *spirit,* or that which perceives. But, for the fuller proof of this point, let it be considered the sensible qualities are color, figure, motion, smell, taste, and such like—that is, the ideas perceived by sense. Now, for an idea to exist in an unperceiving thing is a manifest contradiction, for to have an idea is all one as to perceive; that, therefore, wherein color, figure, and the like qualities exist must perceive them; hence it is clear there can be no unthinking substance or *substratum* of those ideas.

But, say you, though the ideas themselves do not exist without the mind, yet there may be things like them, whereof they are copies or resemblances, which things exist without the mind in an unthinking substance. I answer, an idea can be like nothing but an idea; a color or figure can be like nothing but another color or figure. If we look but ever so little into our thoughts, we shall find it impossible for us to conceive a likeness except only between our ideas. Again, I ask whether those supposed originals or external things, of which our ideas are the pictures or representations, be themselves perceivable or no? If they are, then they are ideas and we have gained our point; but if you say they are not, I appeal to anyone whether it be

sense to assert a color is like something which is invisible; hard or soft, like something which is intangible; and so of the rest.

Some there are who make a distinction betwixt primary and secondary qualities. By the former they mean extension, figure, motion, rest, solidity or impenetrability, and number; by the latter they denote all other sensible qualities, as colors, sounds, tastes, and so forth. The ideas we have of these they acknowledge not to be the resemblances of anything existing without the mind, or unperceived, but they will have our ideas of the primary qualities to be patterns or images of things which exist without the mind, in an unthinking substance which they call "matter." By "matter," therefore, we are to understand an inert, senseless substance, in which extension, figure, and motion do actually subsist. But it is evident from what we have already shown that extension, figure, and motion are only ideas existing in the mind, and that an idea can be like nothing but another idea, and that consequently neither they nor their archetypes can exist in an unperceiving substance. Hence it is plain that the very notion of what is called "matter" or "corporeal substance" involves a contradiction in it.

They who assert that figure, motion, and the rest of the primary or original qualities do exist without the mind in unthinking substances do at the same time acknowledge that colors, sounds, heat, cold, and such—like secondary qualities do not—which they tell us are sensations existing in the mind alone, that depend on and are occasioned by the different size, texture, and motion of the minute particles of matter. This they take for an undoubted truth which they can demonstrate beyond all exception. Now, if it be certain that those original qualities are inseparably united with the other sensible qualities, and not, even in thought, capable of being abstracted from them, it plainly follows that they exist only in the mind. But I desire anyone to reflect and try whether he can, by any abstraction of thought, conceive the extension and motion of a body without all other sensible qualities. For my own part, I see evidently that it is not in my power to frame an idea of a body extended and moved, but I must withal give it some color or other sensible quality which is acknowledged to exist only in the mind. In short, extension, figure, and motion, abstracted from all other qualities, are inconceivable. Where therefore the other sensible qualities are, there must these be also, to wit, in the mind and nowhere else.

Again, *great* and *small, swift* and *slow* are allowed to exist nowhere without the mind, being entirely relative, and changing as the frame or position of the organs of sense varies. The extension, therefore, which exists without the mind is neither great nor small, the motion neither swift nor slow; that is, they are nothing at all. But, say you, they are extension in general, and motion in general: thus we see how much the tenet of extended movable substances existing without the mind depends on that strange doctrine of *abstract ideas.* And here I cannot but remark how nearly the vague and indeterminate description of matter or corporeal substance, which the modern philosophers are run into by their own principles, resembles that antiquated and so much ridiculed notion of *materia prima,* to be met with in Aristotle and his followers. Without extension, solidity cannot be conceived; since, therefore, it has been shown that extension exists not in an unthinking substance, the same must also be true of solidity.

⊼

If you've followed the argument (if you haven't, read it again), then you realize the main thrust of Berkeley's assault on the (abstract) idea of a world out there "existing" (a meaningless term when divorced from experienceable perception) comes down to a very specific (not abstract), clear point: *the so-called primary qualities are just as much mind-dependent for their existence (that is, are themselves "secondary") as so-called secondary qualities.* It may interest you to know, especially if you read Chapter 9 on the "Copernican revolution," that the distinction between primary and secondary qualities did not originate with Locke, though that is where we first read about it. It actually originated in none other than Galileo. Here is how Galileo put it:

⊼

I feel myself impelled by the necessity, as soon as I conceive a piece of matter or corporeal substance, of conceiving that *in its own nature* it is bounded and figured in such and such a figure, that in rela-

tion to others it is large or small, that it is in this or that place, in this or that time, that it is in motion or remains at rest [the primary qualities] . . . but that it must be white or red, bitter or sweet, sounding or mute, of a pleasant or unpleasant odor [the secondary qualities], I do not perceive my mind forced to acknowledge it necessarily accompanied by such conditions. . . . Hence I think that these tastes, odors, colors, etc., on the side of the object in which they seem to exist, are nothing else but mere names, but hold their residence solely in the sensitive body; *so that if the animal were removed, every such quality would be abolished and annihilated.* *

⊼

In other words, remove the lone cat sitting on the chair in the red room and drinking the leftover sweet and sour milk, and you have removed from real existence the redness, the sweetness, and the sourness, which existed only as long as the cat was creating those qualities within its mind. Those are secondary qualities. But the roominess of the room, the impenetrability of the mahogany walls, the hardness of the chair, and so on, were not thereby destroyed when the cat was crushed. These are the primary qualities. Or so says Galileo. And so says Newton. Berkeley is denying what they are saying, but more than that, he is asking you to reflect upon those primary qualities and the meaning of the words in those statements because doing so will make it perfectly clear to you that Galileo and Newton are dead wrong in the worst possible way: their statements are self-contradictory. As an exercise, try making clear what that contradiction is. If you have trouble doing so, reread Berkeley. In the meantime, let us take a peek at Newton's "philosophy of nature," which so influenced the popular conception of things (what is often called by philosophers "the received view").

---

*Opere Complete di Galilei, in *Science and the Human Prospect* by Ronald C. Pine (Belmont, CA: Wadsworth, 1989).

14.3 Newton (1642–1727): The World According to Modern Physical Science

One of the most remarkable things about Newton's worldview, which even a mild understanding of some of the issues within the philosophy and history of science makes perfectly clear, is that the world according to Newton is not, by itself, in any sense obvious; nor does it, in any clear way, make much sense. This is a hard thing to say, given that much of our so-called commonsense view of reality is predicated on it. Lest we find too much difficulty with the idea, you will no doubt recall that *that* world, Newton's world, has since been turned upside down and inside out (*literally*) by twentieth-century relativity and quantum physics. But even before then, in the nineteenth-century work of eminent physicists such as Ernst Mach, Newton's world revealed itself to be but a figment of his imagination *in exactly the way that Berkeley had claimed*.[3]

One of the most famous figures in the entire history of science, Newton was born at Woolsthorpe, near Grantham in Lincolnshire. By age 26 he had developed the binomial theorem and the method of fluxions, an early form of differential calculus that many regard, along with Leibniz's calculus, as the most important innovation in mathematical thought since the time of the ancient Greeks. Newton also formalized Galilean mechanics. He discovered the inverse square law of universal gravitation. He made fundamental contributions to the theory of light and invented the Newtonian reflecting telescope that bears his name. He also claimed that his law of universal gravity, the most comprehensive system of mechanics ever developed, provided clear evidence for the existence of God!

In 1672, at the age of thirty, Netwon was appointed Lucasian Professor of Mathematics at Cambridge University, the prestigious position presently held by Stephen Hawking. Much of Newton's empirical and inductive method grew out of an extended response to and reac-tion against the philosophical and scientific views of Descartes. In turn, most seventeenth- and eighteenth-century philosophers, as well as scientists, were deeply influenced by Newton, especially the British empiricists Locke, Berkeley, and Hume. Locke's distinction between primary and secondary qualities (themselves derived from Galileo) and his causal theory of perception, for instance, were the direct result of his trying to work out the philosophical implications of Newtonian mechanics. Among Newton's most notable adversaries was Leibniz, with whom he had a prolonged debate. They disagreed vehemently about which of them was the first to invent calculus (which most probably happened independently), about the absolute versus relative conceptions of space and time (Leibniz arguing for the latter), and the question of whether God was above mathematics and logic or whether logic and mathematics were above God (Newton arguing for the former).

Newton's most famous principle is, "Abandon substantial forms and occult qualities and reduce natural phenomena to mathematical laws." This he tried to achieve through a union of Bacon's experimental induction (Section 8.1) with the mathematical deduction of Descartes, a combination of the analytic and synthetic methods that would lead to the establishment of mathematically formulated natural laws *provided that we presuppose that nature as it exists in itself is deprived of all inner life*. This is what he means by his call for the abandonment of substantial forms and "occult" qualities:

⁎

II. Fundamental Principles of Natural Philosophy

Since the ancients (as we are told by Pappus) esteemed the science of mechanics of greatest importance in the investigation of natural things, and the moderns, rejecting substantial forms and

From Isaac Newton, Preface to the first edition of the *Principia* (Cambridge, 1686).

occult qualities, have endeavored to subject the phenomena of nature to the laws of mathematics, I have in this treatise cultivated mathematics as far as it relates to philosophy. The ancients considered mechanics in a twofold respect: as rational, which proceeds accurately by demonstration, and practical. To practical mechanics all the manual arts belong, from which mechanics took its name. But as artificers do not work with perfect accuracy, it comes to pass that mechanics is so distinguished from geometry that what is perfectly accurate is called geometrical; what is less so is called mechanical. However, the errors are not in the art, but in the artificers. He that works with less accuracy is an imperfect mechanic; and if any could work with perfect accuracy, he would be the most perfect mechanic of all; for the description of right lines and circles, upon which geometry is founded, belongs to mechanics. Geometry does not teach us to draw these lines, but requires them to be drawn; for it requires that the learner should first be taught to describe these accurately before he enters upon geometry, then it shows how by these operations problems may be solved. To describe right lines and circles are problems, but not geometrical problems. The solution of these problems is required from mechanics, and by geometry the use of them, when so solved, is shown; and it is the glory of geometry that from those few principles, brought from without, it is able to produce so many things. Therefore geometry is founded in mechanical practice and is nothing but that part of universal mechanics which accurately proposes and demonstrates the art of measuring. But since the manual arts are chiefly employed in the moving of bodies, it happens that geometry is commonly referred to their magnitude, and mechanics to their motion. In this sense rational mechanics will be the science of motions resulting from any forces whatsoever and of the forces required to produce any motions, accurately proposed and demonstrated. This part of mechanics, as far as it extended to the five powers which relate to manual arts, was cultivated by the ancients, who considered gravity (it not being a manual power) not otherwise than in moving weights by those powers. But I consider philosophy rather than arts, and write not concerning manual but natural powers, and consider chiefly those things which relate to gravity, levity, elastic force, the resistance of fluids, and the like forces, whether attractive or impulsive; and therefore I offer this work as the mathematical principles of philosophy, for the whole burden of philosophy seems to consist in this: from the phenomena of motions to investigate the forces of nature, and then from these forces to demonstrate the other phenomena; and to this end the general propositions in the First and Second Books are directed. In the Third Book I give an example of this in the explication of the System of the World; for by the propositions mathematically demonstrated in the former books, in the third I derive from the celestial phenomena the forces of gravity with which bodies tend to the sun and the several planets. Then from these forces, by other propositions which are also mathematical, I deduce the motions of the planets, the comets, the moon, and the sea. I wish we could derive the rest of the phenomena of Nature by the same kind of reasoning from mechanical principles, for I am induced by many reasons to suspect that they may all depend upon certain forces by which the particles of bodies, by some causes hitherto unknown, are either mutually impelled toward one another and cohere in regular figures, or are repelled and recede from one another. These forces being unknown, philosophers have hitherto attempted the search of Nature in vain; but I hope the principles here laid down will afford some light either to this or some truer method of philosophy.

The single most fundamental presumption in the world according to Newton is this: the *physical* (real) world does not in any way require *mind* for its existence. In other words, he takes as an absolute starting point the belief that there exists a mind-independent reality. Even the mind of God—in whom the universe is what Newton called the "sensorium" of experience, a divine theater just like the human mind is the "sensorium" of the brain—does not disturb the universe through knowing it, sensing it, experiencing it:

> In him are all things contained and moved, yet neither affects the other; God suffers nothing from the motion of bodies, bodies find no resistance from the omnipresence of God.

Thus the physical world exists independently of any perceiving minds, even independently of the mind of God.

Such a conception, in which there is an absolute independence between mind and reality, accords with much of today's common-sense view of the way things are. When you look at, say, a chair, you believe that your looking does not in any way affect the physical chair, that your observation is a passive activity, like you're peeking into the universe from out of your head (or, out of Plato's cave) through a keyhole, an epistemological voyeur. This explains why, regardless of how hard you wish that the chair would be other than it is, your wishes do not change anything. Your point of view on the chair does not alter in any way any of the chair's qualities, such as its shape, position, how long it has existed, and so on. Your measurements of the chair's spatial and temporal locations, while they may be due to differences of viewing angles, margin of error, and so on, may differ from mine, but the differences between our points of view are irrelevant to the facts of existence. The *differences* within our views of things are not *real*. There exists but one space, one time, one world: the physical universe. Or so you believe.

Insofar as the mind exists in such a universe, it is an objective, passive observer. Its intellectual activity, which includes seeing, thinking, believing, and so on, does not influence the physical reality that is the object of our mental activity. Subjective mental states have no effect upon objective physical states. Thus, I cannot by thinking turn the chair into a table or a cat.

Few people, even today, recognize the hidden *presuppositions* behind such a Netwonian worldview. It is a world in which philosophy, as such, is not necessary. That is, words like *thing, object, world, reality,* and so on refer not to constructions (or interpretations) of the mind but to existences "in themselves." This view of things came to be known as modern scientific materialism. It is a view that has come and gone; the world of twentieth-century physics is anything but Newton's world. It is the world of Einstein and quantum mechanics, in which the mind has once again returned to center stage as a necessary ingredient to reality, a world in which science can only exist, as such, within a philosophy.

14.3.1 Newton's God Versus Spinoza's God

Although God did not exist in Newton's world, Newton's world existed inside Newton's God, an essentially Christian notion, in which God exists as something separate from the universe: a divine creator to be found nowhere in the world or any aspect of it, but existing beyond the world, a transcendent supreme being. Compare this divine being with the God of Spinoza (Chapter 11), who is not transcendent but *immanent*. Spinoza's God is in no sense a Christian God, as conceived in popular Christianity as a fatherly figure on a gold throne in some heavenly world, nor as conceived in sophisticated, scientifically, and intellectually inspired Christianity as some sort of transcendental superforce existing beyond the cosmos. Rather, Spinoza's God, like the God of Bruno and Averroës, is *immanent*. God is a mystical, rational force that is not just *in* the universe but is, itself, *the* universe. God is everything, including you. The physical world according to Newton is for Spinoza but one of God's "modes," just as the mental, spiritual world is another. In Spinoza's philosophy we saw that the language that best describes this immanent force of existence, insofar as it can be captured within the sphere of our limited human understanding, is the very same mathematical laws discovered by science. Thus, in studying the cosmos mathematically, one studies God, the object of our "intellectual love." Interestingly enough, in the twentieth century when Albert Einstein was asked whether he believed in God, he replied that he believed in "Spinoza's God." When the church held political power, belief in such a God got you burned at the stake.

What is at issue here for us is not anyone's concept of God but the nature of the relationship between mind and reality. Berkeley's philosophy is difficult to make sense of from inside the perspective of Newton's world. But we no longer live in Newton's world. We live in the world of Einstein and quantum mechanics. Common sense has just not caught up with it. In the world of twentieth-century physics, the notion of physical reality as such has itself become subordinate to the concept of mind; it has come to question the fundamental presuppositions accepted without question as true within the Newtonian perspective. They were not even recognized as presuppositions at the time, except for the fact that philosophers like Berkeley went to great lengths to try to make these hidden assumptions apparent. When the assumptions are apparent, the universe as such (the one universe consisting of the one true reality as it exists independently of any minds) literally disappears, replaced by an infinity of worlds. Science and religion both must once again give way to philosophy.

14.4 Will the Real World Please Reveal Itself?

Let us see exactly how Berkeley pulls the material world right out from under Newton's feet. The tiny, precise key to understanding the gross and abominable error that led not only to Newton's physical materialism but also to the subsequent myth of modern science which coexists (contrary to popular conceptions) perfectly well with modern religion, consists in drawing a boundary between primary and secondary qualities by which the realm of single, determined, absolute, interpretation-free, mind-independent *facts* exist. Philosophy is needed only here, on the inside of the border, where things are messy and unresolved; beyond that boundary there is no need for philosophy because there all things are just exactly the one way that they are and cannot be any other way:

⚘

I shall further add that, after the same manner as modern philosophers prove certain sensible qualities to have no existence in matter, or without the mind, the same thing may be likewise proved of all other sensible qualities whatsoever. Thus, for instance, it is said that heat and cold are affections only of the mind, and not at all patterns of real beings existing in the corporeal substances which excite them, for that the same body which appears cold to one hand seems warm to another. Now, why may we not as well argue that figure and extension are not patterns or resemblances of qualities existing in matter, because to the same eye at different stations, or eyes of a different texture at the same station, they appear various and cannot, therefore, be the images of anything settled and determinate without the mind? Again, it is proved that sweetness is not really in the sapid thing, because, the thing remaining unaltered, the sweetness is changed into bitter, as in case of a fever or otherwise vitiated palate. Is it not as reasonable to say that motion is not without the mind, since if the succession of ideas in the mind become swifter, the motion, it is acknowledged, shall appear slower without any alteration in any external object?

In short, let anyone consider those arguments which are thought manifestly to prove that colors and tastes exist only in the mind, and he shall find they may with equal force be brought to prove the same thing of extension, figure, and motion. Though it must be confessed this method of arguing does not so much prove that there is no extension or color in an outward object as that we do not know by sense which is the true extension or color of the object. But the arguments foregoing plainly show it to be impossible that any color or extension at all, or other sensible quality whatsoever, should exist in an unthinking subject without the mind, or, in truth, that there should be any such thing as an outward object.

But let us examine a little the received opinion.— It is said extension is a mode or accident of matter, and that matter is the *substratum* that supports it. Now I desire that you would explain what is meant by matter's "supporting" extension. Say you, I have no idea of matter and, therefore, cannot explain it. I answer, though you have no positive, yet, if you have any meaning at all, you must at least have a relative idea of matter; though you know not what it is, yet you must be supposed to know what relation it bears to accidents, and what is meant by its supporting them. It is evident "support" cannot here be taken in its usual or literal sense—as when we say that pillars support a building; in what sense therefore must it be taken?

If we inquire into what the most accurate philosophers declare themselves to mean by "material substance," we shall find them acknowledge they have no other meaning annexed to those sounds but the idea of being in general together with the relative notion of its supporting accidents. The general idea of being appears to me the most abstract and incomprehensible of all other; and as for its supporting accidents, this, as we have just now observed, cannot be understood in the common sense of those words; it must, therefore, be taken in some other sense, but what that is they do not explain. So that when I consider the two parts or branches which make the signification of the words "material substance," I am convinced there is no distinct meaning annexed to them. But why should we trouble ourselves any further in discussing this material *substratum* or support of figure and motion and other sensible qualities? Does it not suppose they have an existence without the mind? And is not this a direct repugnancy and altogether inconceivable?

But, though it were possible that solid, figured, movable substances may exist without the mind, corresponding to the ideas we have of bodies, yet how is it possible for us to know this? Either we must know it by sense or by reason. As for our senses, by them we have the knowledge only of our sensations, ideas, or those things that are immediately perceived by sense, call them what you will; but they do not inform us that things exist without the mind, or unperceived, like to those which are perceived. This the materialists themselves acknowledge. It remains therefore that if we have any knowledge at all of external things, it must be by reason, inferring their existence from what is immediately perceived by sense. But what reason can induce us to believe the existence of bodies without the mind, from what we perceive, since the very patrons of matter themselves do not pretend there is any necessary connection betwixt them and our ideas? I say it is granted on all hands (and what happens in dreams, frenzies, and the like, puts it beyond dispute) that it is possible we might be affected with all the ideas we have now,

though no bodies existed without resembling them. Hence it is evident the supposition of external bodies is not necessary for the producing our ideas; since it is granted they are produced sometimes, and might possibly be produced always in the same order we see them in at present, without their concurrence.

But though we might possibly have all our sensations without them, yet perhaps it may be thought easier to conceive and explain the manner of their production by supposing external bodies in their likeness rather than otherwise; and so it might be at least probable there are such things as bodies that excite their ideas in our minds. But neither can this be said, for, though we give the materialists their external bodies, they by their own confession are never the nearer knowing how our ideas are produced, since they own themselves unable to comprehend in what manner body can act upon spirit, or how it is possible it should imprint any idea in the mind. Hence it is evident the production of ideas or sensations in our minds can be no reason why we should suppose matter or corporeal substances, since that is acknowledged to remain equally inexplicable with or without this supposition. . . .

I am afraid I have given cause to think me needlessly prolix in handling this subject. For to what purpose is it to dilate on that which may be demonstrated with the utmost evidence in a line or two to anyone that is capable of the least reflection? It is but looking into your own thoughts, and so trying whether you can conceive it possible for a sound, or figure, or motion, or color to exist without the mind or unperceived. This easy trial may make you see that what you contend for is a downright contradiction. Insomuch that I am content to put the whole upon this issue: if you can but conceive it possible for one extended movable substance, or, in general, for any one idea, or anything like an idea, to exist otherwise than in a mind perceiving it, I shall readily give up the cause. And, as for all that compages of external bodies which you contend for, I shall grant you its existence, though you cannot either give me any reason why you believe it exists, or assign any use to it when it is supposed to exist. I say the bare possibility of your opinion's being true shall pass for an argument that it is so.

But, say you, surely there is nothing easier than to imagine trees, for instance, in a park, or books existing in a closet, and nobody by to perceive them. I answer you may so, there is no difficulty in it; but what is all this, I beseech you, more than framing in your mind certain ideas which you call books and trees, and at the same time omitting to frame the idea of anyone that may perceive them? But do not you yourself perceive or think of them all the while? This therefore is nothing to the purpose; it only shows you have the power of imagining or forming ideas in your mind; but it does not show that you can conceive it possible the objects of your thought may exist without the mind. To make out this, it is necessary that you conceive them existing unconceived or unthought of, which is a manifest repugnancy. When we do our utmost to conceive the existence of external bodies, we are all the while only contemplating our own ideas. But the mind, taking no notice of itself, is deluded to think it can and does conceive bodies existing unthought of or without the mind, though at the same time they are apprehended by or exist in itself. A little attention will discover to anyone the truth and evidence of what is here said, and make it unnecessary to insist on any other proofs against the existence of *material substance*.

It is very obvious, upon the least inquiry into our own thoughts, to know whether it be possible for us to understand what is meant by "the absolute existence of sensible objects in themselves, or without the mind." To me it is evident those words mark out either a direct contradiction or else nothing at all. And to convince others of this, I know no readier or fairer way than to entreat they would calmly attend to their own thoughts; and if by this attention the emptiness or repugnancy of those expressions does appear, surely nothing more is requisite for their conviction. It is on this, therefore, that I insist, to wit, that "the absolute existence of unthinking things" are words without a meaning, or which include a contradiction. This is what I repeat and inculcate, and earnestly recommend to the attentive thoughts of the reader.

Let us put Berkeley's explanatory thesis once again in the following explicit terms. Consider the "things" you are right now "looking" at. Do

they exist when you are not looking at them? Forget now about anything and everything not having to do explicitly with *those* things that you are looking at. Forget your *theory* about the way the world is. Forget about everything you tacitly assume to be so about what you are looking at and focus just on what you are looking at. *What is that? What are those things?* And *do those things, the very things that you are looking at, exist when you are not looking at them?*

Well, why don't you close your eyes and find out? Do it, close your eyes. What happened? Everything that you were looking at disappeared. This is so obvious that we should ask ourselves why it is that we are even writing this in a book or reading it or thinking about it. You see a chair. You close your eyes. The chair disappears. Well, you say, the chair didn't disappear. Well, all right, *what* then disappeared, if not the chair?

One is tempted to say that *your viewing* disappeared, or your *image* of the chair disappeared, and so on, but not *the* chair. Now, what Berkeley would ask you to do at this point is to reflect upon what—*within the sphere of your knowledge*—the word *chair* refers to. Because what Berkeley has just tried to teach you in the reading is that you are confused about language; or, more precisely, your language—the way it automatically interprets your experience for you—confuses you about what is going on right now and at each waking moment of your life. By "chair" Berkeley means the *actual* chair that you are looking at, whereas what *you* mean by "chair" is not the actual chair that you are looking at but the theoretical chair that you *imagine* is there whether you are looking at it or not! (But not even really that, since there is no *imaging* of *that* chair which *you* say is the real referent of the word *chair*.)

If this is not clear, I would suggest that you reread the substantive sections quoted from Berkeley, especially the part about language. Read the whole thing again (and again, if necessary) until you get a sense of what is being said, for it makes perfect sense once you understand what Berkeley is referring to. He is referring to those things that you actually see. Those are the things of which your world consists, and those are the referents of your object terms such as *chairs, books, rocks, stars, mountains,* and so on.

In other words, even if there is a world beyond this world that you actually see—the world of tables, chairs, colors, shapes, and so on—*those things that you are looking at are not those things*. Again, we've done this before, but let's do it again, just because it is such a crazy demonstration of what is so obvious that it is bizarre to realize, once you do realize it, to what lengths we have to go to make this clear to ourselves. Look at this page. Find a particular word and look at it. Now cross your eyes. What happens? You can make the word split in two, move about, blur, get bigger and smaller, and so on. Now how are you doing that? Mind over matter? Hardly. It's mind over mind. You can do that because what you're looking at is *not* inkblots but images. Images are not made out of ink and paper! They're made out of the stuff that dreams are made of.

Now forget every bizarre thing you may have heard about what has been dubbed "idealism," or "Berkeley's philosophy." Any way you look at it, the immediate *stuff* with which you are acquainted among your perceptions is not *nonmental matter*. This is what Berkeley is saying. He eventually goes beyond saying just that. *But do you get that first point?* People who take issue with what Berkeley is saying typically move very quickly beyond that first point, which is merely that what you are *immediately* and *directly* experiencing when you are looking at these objects, whatever they may be, are *not* made out of rocks and nails! First, are there rocks and nails in your head? No. At most there are images of rocks and nails in your head. (But where are *they*? Hume will answer: Nowhere.) Rocks don't swell up and shrink depending on your movements. The rock you're looking at does. Now, you may say it's just a matter of your perspective on the rock. But take a look at that rock (or that pencil, or this book, or whatever) that you are actually looking

at. Bring "it" closer to your "eyes." *What* has just "grown"? Your *perspective*? But what is that? Do objects have perspective? No. Viewers in a space have perspective. And where is that space within which all this is being seen?

Let me put it to you still another way. One reason why it may be so difficult for us to really see what is being said here is that no matter how you look at it, it is incontrovertible proof that you are not in direct control of what you call *your* images. Berkeley makes this perfectly clear:

⚹

All our ideas, sensations, or the things which we perceive, by whatsoever names they may be distinguished, are visibly inactive—there is nothing of power or agency included in them. So that one idea or object of thought cannot produce or make any alteration in another. To be satisfied of the truth of this, there is nothing else requisite but a bare observation of our ideas. For since they and every part of them exist only in the mind, it follows that there is nothing in them but what is perceived; but whoever shall attend to his ideas, whether of sense or reflection, will not perceive in them any power or activity; there is, therefore, no such thing contained in them. A little attention will discover to us that the very being of an idea implies passiveness and inertness in it, insomuch that it is impossible for an idea to do anything or, strictly speaking, to be the cause of anything; neither can it be the resemblance or pattern of any active being. . . . Whence it plainly follows that extension, figure, and motion cannot be the cause of our sensations. To say, therefore, that these are the effects of powers resulting from the configuration, number, motion, and size of corpuscles must certainly be false.

We perceive a continual succession of ideas, some are anew excited, others are changed or totally disappear. There is, therefore, some cause of these ideas, whereon they depend and which produces and changes them. That this cause cannot be any quality or idea or combination of ideas is clear from the preceding section. It must therefore be a substance; but it has been shown that there is no corporeal or material substance: it remains, therefore, that the cause of ideas is an incorporeal, active substance or spirit.

A spirit is one simple, undivided, active being— as it perceives ideas it is called "the understand- ing," and as it produces or otherwise operates about them it is called "the will." Hence there can be no *idea* formed of a soul or spirit; for all ideas whatever, being passive and inert, they cannot rep- resent unto us, by way of image or likeness, that which acts. A little attention will make it plain to anyone that to have an idea which shall be like that active principle of motion and change of ideas is absolutely impossible. Such is the nature of *spirit*, or that which acts, that it cannot be of itself per- ceived, but only by the effects which it produces. If any man shall doubt of the truth of what is here delivered, let him but reflect and try if he can frame the idea of any power or active being, and whether he has ideas of two principal powers marked by the names "will" and "understanding," distinct from each other as well as from a third idea of substance or being in general, with a rela- tive notion of its supporting or being the subject of the aforesaid powers—which is signified by the name "soul' or "spirit." This is what some hold; but, so far as I can see, the words "will," "soul," "spirit" do not stand for different ideas or, in truth, for any idea at all, but for something which is very different from ideas, and which, being an agent, cannot be like unto, or represented by, any idea whatsoever. . . .

But, whatever power I may have over my own thoughts, I find the ideas actually perceived by sense have not a like dependence on my will. When in broad daylight I open my eyes, it is not in my power to choose whether I shall see or no, or to determine what particular objects shall present themselves to my view; and so likewise as to the hearing and other senses; the ideas imprinted on them are not creatures of my will. There is there- fore some *other* will or spirit that produces them.

⚵

So right now you're seeing things. How are *you* making these images happen? Well, on the common view, it's the stuff out there in the world imposing itself upon your eyes, which then transmit what you are looking at to you inside your brain. Or something like that. But

the generation, the immediate cause, of what you are seeing, is coming from "you." Why "you" and not *you?* Because "you" are as much a projected image as all these other things that you see—all the things that your language tells you are real things that exist independently of "you." "You" are neither the direct cause of *you* nor of the things you are seeing, the images. It is all happening somewhere behind the scenes, in the workings of your brain or whatever it is beyond the reach of your conscious awareness, what Berkeley calls "some *other* will," which ulti- mately he identifies with God. But that there is some intermediary *will* running your world, controlling your images (even in the case where they conform veridically to some external objects!), an absolute "other" insofar as your own conscious access goes, that is the insight that Berkeley is suggesting it is possible for us, as conscious egos, to have. The ego does not like being exposed for what it is: a fiction. But the ego, as a psychological appearance, cannot do anything! *Except be what it is: a deception, the ultimate deception, a willful act of self-deception.* I am not the deceiver. I am the deceived. And behind the deception there is *nothing*, a void, utter insubstantiality.

Descartes was wrong: *I can be mistaken about my own existence.* Hume will now make this clear for us.

NOTES

1. That is, "derivative," see Section 12.4.
2. George Berkeley, "A Treatise Concerning the Principles of Human Knowledge." In *The Works of George Berkeley,* ed. A. C. Fraser (Oxford, Clarendon Press, 1901).
3. We might wonder why *that* view became the pub- licly accepted (not to mention publicly conditioned and enforced) rather than the alternative view, espe- cially when the alternative is on far more solid ground *at least at the starting gate.* No one has ever given an account of this, or, as far as I know, even tried to.

15 ✿ Hume

15.0 Hume (1711–1776): The Skeptical Inquirer

David Hume was born in Edinburgh, Scotland. His family pushed him to study law but he preferred to read and write philosophy. He worked for awhile in a merchant's office in Bristol and then moved to France. He spent most of his time at La Flèche, the same school Descartes attended, writing his *Treatise of Human Nature*. When he published it in England three years later, the work was almost completely ignored; in his words, "It fell dead-born from the press." When he tried to get a teaching position in philosophy nobody would take him, and those who had read the *Treatise* accused him of heresy and atheism. Hume thus had to support himself first by tutoring a marquess and then by working as a secretary, first to a general and then to an ambassador. After failing yet again in 1752 to get hired as a philosopher in Glasgow, he got a job as head librarian at the Advocates' library at Edinburgh.

During those years Hume continued to write and further develop his views. He recast much of Book I of the *Treatise* into his *Inquiry Concern-*ing Human Understanding* (1748) and the material from Book III into his *Inquiry Concerning the Principles of Morals*. By the time he was in his late forties his writings began to attract a steadily growing audience; by 1762, James Boswell declared him to be "the greatest writer in Britain." Fearing that his *Dialogues Concerning Natural Religion* would again get him into trouble with church authorities, he left instructions to his nephew to publish them posthumously, which he did in 1777.

Hume had a tremendous influence on nearly all the philosophers who came after him. He inspired August Comte in his development of positivism, an antitheological and antimetaphysical system of scientific knowledge. His moral philosophy influenced Jeremy Bentham and John Stuart Mill. Immanuel Kant claimed that Hume awoke him from his "dogmatic slumbers." And Hume probably had more influence on twentieth-century analytic philosophy than any other modern philosopher.

One of Hume's major goals was to develop the empirical philosophy of Locke and Berkeley to its logical conclusion. Whereas Locke's views were tempered by commonsense notions of reality, often inconsistently, and Berkeley made an exception to his empiricist principles by relying on the concept of a transcendental other (God), Hume refused to make his philosophy bow either to common sense—for which he was criticized by Thomas Reid (1710–1796)—or to transcendental metaphysics. He wanted to create a fully consistent but purely empirical philosophy. Bertrand Russell, a sympathetic critic of Hume, remarked that by making the empirical philosophy of Berkeley and Locke consistent, Hume "made it incredible." Indeed, not only does Hume deny the existence of a Berkeleyian or Cartesian self, he also provides devastating empirical criticisms of many metaphysical concepts, such as causation, morality, space, time, and freedom—formulating skeptical objections to all inferences that go beyond immediate experience. Even impressions of the "external" senses exist only in the sensing mind, and he rejects all attempts to argue from the senses to the existence of continuing physical substances outside the mind.

In his earliest philosophical work, *A Treatise of Human Nature,* Hume pushes Berkeley's criticism of abstract ideas and general entities to their extreme and ends up dissolving the idea of a continuously existing mental substance. He replaces the notion of a unified, continuously existing soul with the famous "bundle theory" of the mind that has so influenced twentieth-century personal identity theorists, most notably Derek Parfit. According to Hume, the mind is an aggregate, or bundle, of discreet and discontinuous experiences; our minds seem continuous to us only because our imaginations smooth out the borders, bumps, and ceaseless changes.

In the preface to his *Treatise,* Hume claims that he will apply Newton's experimental method to the human mind in an effort to develop a "science of man." In Book I, "Of the Understanding" (an obvious reference to Locke's *Essay Concerning Human Understanding*), Hume analyzes the mind into a bundle of perceptions, of which there are but two kinds: *impressions* and *ideas.* He claims to be restoring

"the word *idea* to its original sense, from which Mr. Locke had perverted it, in making it stand for all our perceptions."

15.1 Hume's Theory of Ideas

Recall the question we asked in Chapter 13 on Locke: with what faculty does the mind apprehend its own visual images? Locke's answer, and Hume's, is *the understanding.* This often overlooked aspect of their philosophical systems carries with it the implication that although I do not see the world, it is possible, through philosophy, to *understand* it. But understanding for these empirically minded philosophers is an *empirical* notion; that is, it is cast in terms of perceptions. The having of perceptions is, itself, an understanding of the things that are perceived, provided that one is aware of the origin and nature of our ideas.

Thus, in Section I, Part I of Hume's *Treatise,* appropriately called "Of the Origin of Our Ideas," Hume sets out, as did Berkeley, to improve Locke's theory of knowledge. In some ways he does not go as far as Berkeley; in others he goes even farther. Like Berkeley, Hume is an ultranominalist, in that he denies the possibility of there being any sorts of abstract ideas. He does not, however, deny the existence of an "external" reality, although he does claim that it cannot be known with certainty. On the other hand, he goes to much greater extremes in removing fictional, imagined, or theoretically implied but nowhere experienced (ghostly) elements from our immediate sensations. That is, Hume's astute and often intense introspections lead him to point out that our immediate sensations are even more ephemeral and contain many fewer phenomena than unenlightened common sense ordinarily ascribes to them. Most important, there is no causality whatsoever among phenomena. Finally, and in many ways most radically, he will conclude that there is no need whatsoever for the supposition that there must be something underlying the various perceived qualities: he will thereby deny substantiality to immaterial as well as to material beings.

🟊

A Treatise of Human Nature

Section I: Of the Origin of Our Ideas

All the perceptions of the human mind resolve themselves into two distinct kinds, which I shall call IMPRESSIONS and IDEAS. The difference betwixt these consists in the degrees of force and liveliness with which they strike upon the mind, and make their way into our thought or consciousness. Those perceptions, which enter with most force and violence, we may name *impressions:* and under this name I comprehend all our sensations, passions and emotions, as they make their first appearance in the soul. By *ideas* I mean the faint images of these in thinking and reasoning; such as, for instance, are all the perceptions excited by the present discourse, excepting only, those which arise from the sight and touch, and excepting the immediate pleasure or uneasiness it may occasion. I believe it will not be very necessary to employ many words in explaining this distinction. Every one of himself will readily perceive the difference betwixt feeling and thinking. The common degrees of these are easily distinguished; tho' it is not impossible but in particular instances they may very nearly approach to each other. Thus in sleep, in a fever, in madness, or in any very violent emotions of soul, our ideas may approach to our impressions: As on the other hand it sometimes happens, that our impressions are so faint and low, that we cannot distinguish them from our ideas. But notwithstanding this near resemblance in a few instances, they are in general so very different, that no-one can make a scruple to rank them under distinct heads, and assign to each a peculiar name to mark the difference.

🟊

What, exactly, does he mean by *impressions* versus *ideas?* Impressions are perceptions that

_____

From David Hume, *A Treatise of Human Nature.* First published in 1738.

enter most immediately and vividly by way of the senses, whereas ideas are perceptions that are dim facsimiles of impressions. But what is an *impression?* In a footnote he states that there is actually no ordinary word to refer to that aspect of phenomenal experience to which, with reluctance, he chooses to apply the word *impression:*

🟊

By the term of "impression" I would not be understood to express the manner, in which our lively perceptions are produced in the soul, but merely the perceptions themselves; for which there is no particular name either in the *English* or any other language that I know of.

🟊

All ideas originate from impressions—each of which is distinct, exists only for a brief moment, and is disconnected from any other. How, then, can we justify any of our beliefs that reach beyond the contents of our present consciousness? Ultimately, we can't, which will bring us to Hume's problem of induction (which we shall discuss in the next section).

Two things must be noted. First, Berkeley was right in drawing our attention to the nature, function, and power of language, for look what has begun to happen here; in making claims such as that Locke is misusing the word *idea*, that there is no ordinary common word for that which he will designate using the word *impression,* and so on, he too is drawing our attention to the language we use when we are philosophizing. Something remarkable and subtle has happened, as important to our understanding of what philosophical enlightenment is as the realization that our eyes are not windows: that to which the proverbial ocular windows open is not reality but theory. In other words, language is yet another intermediary layer between us and reality.

There is a deep irony here. Without eyes we

are blind. With eyes we no longer seem to be blind. There is now a sense in which we are no longer blind but also a sense in which we are still blind, because the things we see (that is, the perceptions constructed by our mind or brain or whatever is doing it) are not things as they exist in themselves but only appearances that, at best, in some sense and in some degree inform us as to what there really is. The situation has gotten better but more complicated; furthermore, and this is where philosophy comes in, we are in danger of becoming entrapped in the beautiful, luminous cocoon called vision. We don't want to get rid of it; that would be stupid. We just want to remain aware of it for what it is, which is very, very difficult. Likewise with our theories. We need them. We cannot do without them. With them we are smart, intelligent; we can do what other animals cannot because we can extend, to some degree reliably, our beliefs beyond our immediate perceptions into realms of which we cannot even form images. Theories are thus intellectual extensions of the eyes. How wonderful! How important that we not lose ourselves in our knowledge. (Perhaps there is a wise Socratic warning to all this.)

But likewise with our language. We can talk, communicate, ask questions, preserve our beliefs, form written procedures so that others can follow in our footsteps when we have discovered something. Language is a tremendous acquisition on the part of the human mind— some would even say the greatest one. But, again, and perhaps most ominously, language, like our eyes and our theories, becomes yet another double-edged tool, bringing us closer to the world while at the same time severing our consciousness from it, for we become as seduced by our language as we do by our images and our theories. And so now philosophy has a triple function: to keep us wise about perception, theory, and language. We must remember, too, what it means to be *wise* versus being "in the *know*." It is very difficult to know how to proceed here. Yet Hume proceeds, with caution.

One way to get an experiential sense of his distinction between impressions and ideas is to listen to a few bars of a popular song and then to shut the music off and recall what you have just heard. What you heard when the stereo was blaring—an auditory image—is an impression; what you heard when the stereo was off and you were recalling the song—also an auditory image—is an idea. Thus, both impressions and ideas are *mental images*—in this case *auditory images*—that is, sound images. Similarly, look at the cover of this book and then close your eyes and remember it. The first visual image consists of *impressions;* the second visual image consists of *ideas;* and so on for the other contents of your mind. Run your fingers along the edge of the book; that tactile image consists of impressions. Now recall it. That tactile image consists of ideas.

So what is the difference between impressions and ideas? First, again, notice that it really doesn't make much sense to ask this question independently of a particular philosopher. One reason why philosophers today spend a lot of time talking about other philosophers is not because they don't want to do their own original work. Nor is it because they are interested, per se, in what other people who are taken to be authorities have said (at least not usually). Rather, the reason has to do with the specificity of language. When nonphilosophers talk about "ideas," the discussion is, typically, very boring to a philosopher. The philosopher usually gets impatient. In general, it's because the word *idea* is used in all sorts of vague and ambiguous senses. There is no clear notion of what, exactly, is under discussion; even worse, nonphilosophers are not even aware of this. Yet they keep talking, whereas philosophers today will, for instance, preface their discussion about ideas by making it as clear as possible what is actually under discussion and analysis. The easiest and quickest way to do this is with words such as "Locke," "Berkeley," "Hume," or "Hegel," and so on, where the name is but a sort of philosophical shorthand. It gets us right to the point. Each name refers not to a person as such but to a particular philosophy. Let us thus proceed with the philosophy that now goes under the name of *Hume.* We return to our discussion of the difference between impressions and ideas. Both, in Hume, are mental images: auditory images, visual images, tactile images, and so on. Ideas are fainter than impressions. That's the first and major difference. It is, if you like, a fact about your experience that this is the case.

The second thing to notice about ideas and impressions is that ideas are themselves representations of impressions. This is about as important an insight as one can have. What Hume is saying is that your ideas are not representations of things in themselves, of objects "out there in the world"; like Berkeley, he is deeply critical of Locke's supposition that that is what all ideas are. Rather, ideas are representations of impressions. What, then, are impressions? Are they representations of things out there in the world? We'll get to that. For now, let us be perfectly clear that thus far we are on the inside of our own minds, trying to fine-tune our language so as to be able to communicate with ourselves about what is actually going on within us.

So, here is what we have thus far: the mind consists of perceptions of which there are two kinds, impressions and ideas. But there is yet another distinction among our perceptions, which carries over into both impressions and ideas: the division into simple and complex:

⚹

There is another division of our perceptions, which it will be convenient to observe, and which extends itself both to our impressions and ideas. This division is into SIMPLE and COMPLEX. Simple perceptions or impressions and ideas are such as admit of no distinction nor separation. The complex are the contrary to these, and may be distinguished into parts. Tho' a particular colour, taste, and smell are qualities all united together in this apple, 'tis easy to perceive they are not the same, but are at least distinguishable from each other.

Having by these divisions given an order and arrangement to our objects, we may now apply ourselves to consider with the more accuracy their qualities and relations. The first circumstance, that strikes my eye, is the great resemblance betwixt our impressions and ideas in every other particular, except their degree of force and vivacity. The one seem to be in a manner the reflexion of the other: so that all the perceptions of the mind are double, and appear both as impressions and ideas. When I shut my eyes and think of my chamber, the ideas I form are exact representations of the impressions I felt; nor is there any circumstance of the one, which is not to be found in the other. In running over my other perceptions, I find still the same resemblance and representation. Ideas and impressions appear always to correspond to each other. This circumstance seems to me remarkable, and engages my attention for a moment.

Upon a more accurate survey I find I have been carried away too far by the first appearance, and that I must make use of the distinction of perceptions into *simple and complex,* to limit this general decision, *that all our ideas and impressions are resembling.* I observe, that many of our complex ideas never had impressions, that corresponded to them, and that many of our complex impressions never are exactly copied in ideas. I can imagine to myself such a city as the *New Jerusalem,* whose pavement is gold and walls are rubies, tho' I never saw any such. I have seen *Paris;* but shall I affirm I can form such an idea of that city, as will perfectly represent all its streets and houses in their real and just proportions?

I perceive, therefore, that tho' there is in general a great resemblance betwixt our *complex* impressions and ideas, yet the rule is not universally true, that they are exact copies of each other. We may next consider how the case stands with our *simple* perceptions. After the most accurate examination, of which I am capable, I venture to affirm, that the rule here holds without any exception, and that every simple idea has a simple impression, which resembles it; and every simple impression a correspondent idea. That idea of red, which we form in the dark, and that impression, which strikes our eyes in sun-shine, differ only in degree, not in nature. That the case is the same with all our simple impressions and ideas, 'tis impossible to prove by a particular enumeration of them. Every one may satisfy himself in this point by running over as many as he pleases. But if any one should deny this universal resemblance, I know no way of convincing him, but by desiring him to show a simple impression, that has not a correspondent idea, or a simple idea, that has not a correspondent impression. If he does not answer this challenge, as 'tis certain he cannot, we may from his silence and our own observation establish our conclusion.

Thus we find, that all simple ideas and impressions resemble each other; and as the complex are formed from them, we may affirm in general, that these two species of perception are exactly correspondent. Having discover'd this relation, which requires no farther examination, I am curious to find some other of their qualities. Let us consider how they stand with regard to their existence, and which of the impressions and ideas are causes, and which effects.

The *full* examination of this question is the subject of the present treatise: and therefore we shall here content ourselves with establishing one general proposition, *That all our simple ideas in their first appearance are deriv'd from simple impressions, which are correspondent to them, and which they exactly represent.*

In seeking for phænomena to prove this proposition, I find only those of two kinds; but in each kind the phænomena are obvious, numerous, and conclusive. I first make myself certain, by a new review, of what I have already asserted, that every simple impression is attended with a correspondent idea, and every simple idea with a correspondent impression. From this constant conjunction of resembling perceptions I immediately conclude, that there is a great connexion betwixt our correspondent impressions and ideas, and that the existence of the one has a considerable influence upon that of the other. Such a constant conjunction, in such an infinite number of instances, can never arise from chance; but clearly proves a dependence of the impressions on the ideas, or of the ideas on the impressions. That I may know on which side this dependence lies, I consider the order of their *first appearance;* and find by constant experience, that the simple impressions always take the precedence of their correspondent ideas, but never appear in the contrary order. To give a child an idea of scarlet or orange, of sweet or bitter, I present the objects, or in other words, convey to

him these impressions; but proceed not so absurdly, as to endeavour to produce the impressions by exciting the ideas. Our ideas upon their appearance produce not their correspondent impressions, nor do we perceive any colour, or feel any sensation merely upon thinking of them. On the other hand we find, that any impressions either of the mind or body is constantly followed by an idea, which resembles it, and is only different in the degrees of force and liveliness. The constant conjunction of our resembling perceptions, is a convincing proof, that the one are the causes of the other; and this priority of the impressions is an equal proof, that our impressions are the causes of our ideas, not our ideas of our impressions.

To confirm this I consider another plain and convincing phænomenon; which is, that where-ever by any accident the faculties, which give rise to any impressions, are obstructed in their operations, as when one is born blind or deaf; not only the impressions are lost, but also their correspondent ideas; so that there never appear in the mind the least traces of either of them. Nor is this only true, where the organs of sensation are entirely destroy'd, but likewise where they have never been put in action to produce a particular impression. We cannot form to ourselves a just idea of the taste of a pine-apple, without having actually tasted it.

⚘

First, what does he mean by simple versus complex impressions and ideas? Take, for example, the following auditory image: shut the book. That was an impression and it was simple. Recall it: that is an idea, a simple one. Listen to music: those impressions are complex. Recall the melody: that is an idea, a complex one. Thus, complex impressions consist of simple impressions and complex ideas consist of simple ideas.

Second, in noticing "the great resemblance betwixt our impressions and ideas," we must be careful to not be deceived into thinking that "all the perceptions of the mind are double, and appear both as impressions and ideas." This is true only of simple ones; that is, *every simple idea corresponds to a simple impression that resembles it.*

Therefore, there is a "constant conjunction" between them. And the impression always appears first, the idea later. This is what makes us think that there is a relation of dependence between them, insofar as every simple idea is a copy of a simple impression.

What, then, is the origin of all our ideas? Our impressions. No impressions, no ideas. This is the first principle of his philosophical method.

⚹

Inquiry Concerning Human Understanding

Here, therefore, is a proposition, which not only seems, in itself, simple and intelligible; but, if a proper use were made of it, might render every dispute equally intelligible, and banish all that jargon, which has so long taken possession of metaphysical reasonings, and drawn disgrace upon them. All ideas, especially abstract ones, are naturally faint and obscure: the mind has but a slender hold of them: they are apt to be confounded with other resembling ideas; and when we have often employed any term, though without a distinct meaning, we are apt to imagine it has a determinate idea annexed to it. On the contrary, all impressions, that is, all sensations, either outward or inward, are strong and vivid: The limits between them are more exactly determined: nor is it easy to fall into any error or mistake with regard to them. When we entertain, therefore, any suspicion that a philosophical term is employed without any meaning or idea (as is but too frequent), we need but enquire, *from what impression is that supposed idea derived?* And if it be impossible to assign any, this will serve to confirm our suspicion.

⚹

Notice that Hume has, once again, just made a point about *language*. A term is meaningless unless it is associated with an idea. Some terms have no idea to which they are thus associated.

_____
From David Hume, *Inquiry Concerning Human Understanding* (London, 1748).

Yet we get used to using them because they are in our language. We are thereby deceived.

How can we discover which of our terms are thus merely false reifications from our language or if they really mean something? Notice the parallel with our previous discussions having to do with the representational nature of perception. Once it is discovered that some of our images (that is, colors, warmth, and so on) exist in our minds and are perceived as if they exist in the object out there in the world when they do not (that is, when they exist only in the mind), the question becomes how to distinguish those aspects of our perceptions that correspond to reality and those that do not. Hume is asking the same question, as did Berkeley, with the terms in our language. To miss this aspect of their philosophies is to miss a great deal; in fact, it keeps us from taking the next philosophical step, the one leading to subsequent developments into the twentieth century.

There is but one way to find out whether a particular term really means something or not. We must trace the associated idea back to an impression. If we can do this, then the term is meaningful insofar as it expresses a real idea. If we can't, then the term is just so much noise in our heads or blots of ink on paper.

15.2 Hume's Fork: The Analytic-Synthetic Distinction

Thus far, then, Hume has analyzed the mind into *perceptions*. Remember that *analysis* means, literally, to break apart or divide something into its simpler components. He then further analyzed the perceptions into impressions and ideas. Next, he proceeds to the stage of *synthesis*, that is, putting these together by offering an explanation in terms of the *principles* that bind these elements together into a fully functioning mind. At this point all the elements of the mind are conjoined, or bound together, by various principles of *association*.

⚹

Of the Association of Ideas

It is evident, that there is a principle or connexion between the different thoughts or ideas of the mind, and that, in their appearance to the memory or imagination, they introduce each other with a certain degree of method and regularity. In our more serious thinking or discourse this is so observable that any particular thought, which breaks in upon the regular tract or chain of ideas, is immediately remarked and rejected. And even in our wildest and most wandering reveries, nay in our very dreams, we shall find, if we reflect, that the imagination ran not altogether at adventures, but that there was still a connexion upheld among the different ideas, which succeeded each other. Were the loosest and freest conversation to be transcribed there would immediately be observed something which connected it in all its transitions. Or where this is wanting, the person who broke the thread of discourse might still inform you, that there had secretly revolved in his mind a succession of thought, which had gradually led him from the subject of conversation. Among different languages, even where we cannot suspect the least connexion or communication, it is found, that the words, expressive of ideas, the most compounded, do yet nearly correspond to each other: a certain proof, that the simple ideas, comprehended in the compound ones, were bound together by some universal principle, which had an equal influence on all mankind.

Though it be too obvious to escape observation, that different ideas are connected together; I do not find that any philosopher has attempted to enumerate or class all the principles of association; a subject, however, that seems worthy of curiosity, To me, there appear to be only three principles of connexion among ideas, namely, *Resemblance*, *Contiguity* in time or place, and *Cause* or *Effect*.

That these principles serve to connect ideas will not, I believe, be much doubted. A picture naturally leads our thoughts to the original [resemblance]: the mention of one apartment in a building naturally introduces an enquiry or discourse concerning the others [contiguity]: and if we think of a wound, we can scarcely forbear reflecting on the pain which follows it [cause and effect]. But that this enumeration is complete, and that there are no

From David Hume, *Inquiry Concerning Human Understanding* (London, 1748).

other principles of association except these, may be difficult to prove to the satisfaction of the reader, or even to a man's own satisfaction. All we can do, in such cases, is to run over several instances, and examine carefully the principle which binds the different thoughts to each other, never stopping till we render the principle as general as possible. The more instances we examine, and the more care we employ, the more assurance shall we acquire, that the enumeration, which we form from the whole, is complete and entire.

✦

So there are three principles of association among our ideas: (1) *resemblance*, (2) *contiguity*, and (3) *cause and effect*. Just as Newton's theory of universal gravity governs the elements of the entire physical universe, so the "gentle force" of association governs the entire mind. It is "a kind of Attraction, which in the mental world will be found to have as extraordinary effects as in the natural, and to show itself in as many as various forms." The most startling thing about it is that this gentle force within the mind, the force of association, operates entirely without any conscious willing on our part. It is not something that we control, any more than natural objects control the force of gravity; rather, it controls *us*.

Now that we have a sense of what the mind is, what it consists of, and how it works, we can turn to the question of *how knowledge might be possible*. We can't just plunge into the knowledge-seeking enterprise. We must first understand the tools—especially since what we are studying when we look at things is not the world directly but an experience mediated by our perceptions, which themselves exist within and are subservient to mental activity. But, given Hume's analysis of the mind, what is that activity? Here Hume invokes his famous distinction, now called "Hume's fork," between (1) inquiry into *relations of ideas* and (2) *inquiry into matters of fact:*

✦

All the objects of human reason or enquiry may naturally be divided into two kinds, to wit, *Relations of Ideas,* and *Matters of Fact.* Of the first kind are the sciences of Geometry, Algebra, and Arithmetic; and in short, every affirmation which is either intuitively or demonstratively certain. *That the square of the hypotenuse is equal to the squares of the two sides,* is a proposition which expresses a relation between these figures. *That three times five is equal to the half of thirty,* expresses a relation between these numbers. Propositions of this kind are discoverable by the mere operation of thought, without dependence on what is anywhere existent in the universe. Though there never were a circle or triangle in nature, the truths demonstrated by Euclid would for ever retain their certainty and evidence.

Matters of fact, which are the second objects of human reason, are not ascertained in the same manner; nor is our evidence of their truth, however great, of a like nature with the foregoing. The contrary of every matter of fact is still possible; because it can never imply a contradiction, and is conceived by the mind with the same facility and distinctness, as if ever so conformable to reality. *That the sun will not rise tomorrow* is no less intelligible a proposition, and implies no more contradiction than the affirmation, *that it will rise.* We should in vain, therefore, attempt to demonstrate its falsehood. Were it demonstratively false, it would imply a contradiction, and could never be distinctly conceived by the mind.

It may, therefore, be a subject worthy of curiosity, to enquire what is the nature of that evidence which assures us of any real existence and matter of fact, beyond the present testimony of our senses, or the records of our memory. This part of philosophy, it is observable, has been little cultivated, either by the ancients or moderns; and therefore our doubts and errors, in the prosecution of so important an enquiry, may be the more excusable; while we march through such difficult paths without any guide or direction. They may even prove useful, by exciting curiosity, and destroying that implicit faith and security, which is the bane of all reasoning and free enquiry. The discovery of defects in the common philosophy, if any such there be, will not, I presume, be a discouragement, but rather an incitement, as is usual, to attempt something more full and satisfactory than has yet been proposed to the public.

⚔

We've encountered Hume's distinction between "relations of ideas" and "matters of fact" before, in Leibniz's analytic-synthetic distinction. Recall that analytic propositions are expressed by a priori sentences whose negation leads to a self-contradiction. They are true by definition and are therefore necessarily true. Synthetic propositions, on the other hand, are expressed by a posteriori sentences that are not necessarily true and whose negation is not a self-contradiction; they are not necessarily true. Following Leibniz, Spinoza, and Descartes, Hume accepts that there are a priori necessary truths, but he argues that they are *tautological.* Tautologies are empty, merely verbal truths that provide information about only the conventional meanings of words. They do not provide any new information about the world. Consider, for instance, the proposition "I am me." This just tells us that the words "I" and "me" are synonyms. It doesn't tell you who I am. Or, consider, "All brothers are siblings." This sentence doesn't tell us anything about any particular brother that wasn't already known to be so by the word *brother.* Similarly, once we understand the concepts "thirty," "fifteen," "twice," and "equal," we already know that twice fifteen is thirty.

The upshot of this is that a priori truths, not being descriptions of anything real, cannot give us knowledge of reality. Only "matters of fact," or synthetic propositions, can possibly do that. Synthetic truths can be known only a posteriori. Therefore, if there is any true knowledge about the world, it must be based on observation. But does observation, which consists of nothing but perceptions—which are representations not of things in the world but of our impressions—connect us to reality?

Not directly. But notice what Hume has done; in distinguishing analytic from synthetic propositions he has created a whole category in which to dump the contents of the mind that we know are *not* even possible contenders for giving us knowledge of reality. It is a category called *nonsense.* Any proposition will be either analytic or synthetic, or else it will be nonsense. Thus, although we may not be able to perceive reality directly, we *may* be able, perhaps, to make true statements that are at least *meaningful*.

We come upon a proposition that we would like to test for truth. We ask, Is it analytic? The answer is decided by negating the sentence expressing the proposition. If the result is a self-contradiction, the original sentence is analytic. If the answer is yes, the proposition is analytic, then the proposition is true but trivial. It is a mere tautology, empty of information about reality. If the answer is no, the proposition is not analytic. We ask, Is it synthetic? How can we tell? Hume has already given us the answer:

> When we entertain . . . any suspicion that a philosophical term is employed without any meaning or idea (as is but too frequent), we need but inquire, *from what impression is that supposed idea derived?* And if it be impossible to assign any, this will serve to confirm our suspicion.

So a proposition can be synthetic only if we can trace the idea back to some impressions. For example, if "Fire is hot," can be traced back to some impressions, then it is a synthetically true proposition. If, on the other hand, some particular idea cannot be traced back to an impression, then it is vacuous and we know that we are dealing with *nonsense*.

Whereas Descartes started out by doubting whether all of his beliefs are true, Hume does something much more radical. He starts out by showing that most of his beliefs are neither true nor false; they are not even capable of being true. They are not even *contenders*; they are *nonsense*.

The concept of *self* is nonsense. *God* is nonsense. And so is *the world*.

15.3 Cause and Effect: Dissolving the Cement of the Universe

The world of Hume was Newton's world, a world in which one supposedly knew the true causes of the phenomena one saw. The science of the time, which was Newtonian mechanics, provided the method by which the true causes could be known, through such universal concepts as gravity. The Copernican-Keplerian-Galilean model came to be accepted, not as a theory but as the truth, in which the true cause of the motion of the planets was known. That cause was gravity.

Many of the greatest minds of the time went along with the program, declaring, along with the influential French mathematician Jean Le Rond d'Alembert, "The true system of the world has been recognized, developed and perfected." Scientist Hermann von Helmholtz likewise declared that thanks to Newton the new science would bring an end to the knowledge-seeking enterprise; soon we would know *everything:* "[science] will be ended as soon as the reduction of natural phenomena to simple forces is complete and the proof given that this is the only reduction of which phenomena are capable."

Like nearly every epoch in which great advances occurred, it was a time in which people believed that it was no longer possible that we could all be completely wrong about everything. Indeed, the idea that there is a world in which it is not possible that everyone (even a God if God existed in that world) could be completely wrong about everything is nothing less than the idea that it is possible for there to be a world without need of philosophy. If there is anything we have learned thus far, it is that such a world is not possible. It is *always* possible that we could all be not just *a little* bit off, or that merely some of us are grossly mistaken, but that everyone in the whole world is completely wrong about everything!

That's what Hume showed to his contemporaries. At the very height of all the successes of the Newtonian scientific achievements, Hume showed in no uncertain terms that everybody, including and especially Newton, could still be wrong about completely everything. How? He didn't do it with science. That would have to await the work of Einstein, who showed that

Newton's *gravity* was *not* the true cause of anything because it was *a fiction*, and that Newton's *space* and Newton's *time* did not exist. It would have to await the advent of quantum mechanics to show that minds were not passive observers of reality, as in Newton's world, but intimately involved in the game of existence. So how *did* Hume do it?

To understand how Hume did it is another wonderful opportunity to see how the activity of philosophy differs from the activity of science. Hume did it by showing that each and every one of Newton's major concepts, including gravity, was exactly what it would take science centuries more to discover: *a fiction*. And he did it not by doing any experiments or creating elaborate contraptions with which to measure physical phenomena, but by a philosophical analysis of the key concept in Newton's world: *causality*.

⚹

All reasonings concerning matter of fact seem to be founded on the relation of *Cause and Effect*. By means of that relation alone we can go beyond the evidence of our memory and senses. If you were to ask a man, why he believes any matter of fact, which is absent; for instance, that his friend is in the country, or in France; he would give you a reason; and this reason would be some other fact; as a letter received from him, or the knowledge of his former resolutions and promises. A man finding a watch or any other machine in a desert island, would conclude that there had once been men in that island. All our reasonings concerning fact are of the same nature. And here it is constantly supposed that there is a connexion between the present fact and that which is inferred from it. Were there nothing to bind them together, the inference would be entirely precarious. The hearing of an articulate voice and rational discourse in the dark assures us of the presence of some person: Why? because these are the effects of the human make and fabric, and closely connected with it. If we anatomize all the other rea-

From *Inquiry Concerning Human Understanding*.

sonings of this nature, we shall find that they are founded on the relation of cause and effect, and that this relation is either near or remote, direct or collateral. Heat and light are collateral effects of fire, and the one effect may justly be inferred from the other.

If we would satisfy ourselves, therefore, concerning the nature of that evidence, which assures us of matters of fact, we must enquire how we arrive at the knowledge of cause and effect.

I shall venture to affirm, as a general proposition, which admits of no exception, that the knowledge of this relation is not, in any instance, attained by reasonings a priori; but arises entirely from experience, when we find that any particular objects are constantly conjoined with each other. Let an object be presented to a man of ever so strong natural reason and abilities; if that object be entirely new to him, he will not be able, by the most accurate examination of its sensible qualities, to discover any of its causes or effects. Adam, though his rational faculties be supposed, at the very first, entirely perfect, could not have inferred from the fluidity and transparency of water that it would suffocate him, or from the light and warmth of fire that it would consume him. No object ever discovers, by the qualities which appear to the senses, either the causes which produced it, or the effects which will arise from it; nor can our reason, unassisted by experience, ever draw any inference concerning real existence and matter of fact.

⚹

In each of the cases he considers, when someone claims to know something not present in his perceptions, it is the idea of cause and effect that supposedly allows the knower to extend beyond his immediate experience to the object of his knowledge. In each case, an impression—reading a letter, seeing a watch, hearing a voice in the dark—is associated with an idea—a friend being in France, someone dropping the watch, someone speaking, respectively. Each idea is an idea of something not present to the mind at that moment. That's how beliefs about matters of fact beyond our senses arise: they are grounded in our sense of cause and effect. The letter is the effect of someone writing it and mailing it, which are the causes; the presence of the watch is the effect of someone having dropped it, which is the cause; the heard voice in the dark is the effect of someone speaking, which is the cause; and so on. In every one of these cases it is the idea of *causation* that supposedly extends the mind beyond the narrow limits of the present moment, allowing us to reach beyond our immediate conscious experience: "By means of that relation alone we can go beyond the evidence of our memory and senses."

But now Hume asks a devastating question: *From what impression is the idea of cause and effect derived?* As he already explained, the cause and effect relation cannot be known a priori. Consider the sentence, "*A* causes *B*," where *A* and *B* are both events. *A* is the event of billiard ball *a* striking billiard ball *b*, and *B* is the event of billiard ball *b* moving after having been struck by *a*. Is this sentence analytic? No, because its negation, "It is not the case that *A* causes *B*" is not a self-contradiction. We can easily conceive *a* striking *b*, where *b* doesn't move. Here's why. Suppose we knew everything there is to know about the two billiard balls—their size, shape, weight, moment, and so on—but never had any experience of one thing striking another. Could we still predict that when *a* strikes *b, b* will move? Hardly. If we never had any prior experience of billiard balls hitting each other, for all we know they might stick together (think of silly putty), or get absorbed into one another (think of water drops), or explode (think of grenades). The belief that when ball *a* strikes *b, a* will bounce off or stop (depending on the angle and momentum) while *b* keeps moving, is entirely dependent on our having observed that sort of thing before.

So is then the sentence "*A* causes *B*" synthetic? It should be. But is it? Well, applying our method, we must now see if we can trace back the idea of "cause" to an impression. Can we do that? No. But let's try anyway.

I certainly do notice that I have the expectation that *b* will move when *a* strikes it. This

clearly is the result of my having seen that sort of thing before. My expectation at least seems like a reasonable one to have in this circumstance. But is it really?

It isn't. Hume gives two devastating reasons why. First, in analyzing the concept of "*A* causes *B*," we find it consists of three components: (1) "*A* is prior to *B*," (2) "*A* is contiguous to *B*," and (3) "the connection between *A* and *B* is *necessary*." The first two conditions can be traced back to impressions. *But not the third,* and that's the crucial one. Why? Because no matter how many times I've observed billiard ball *a* strike billiard ball *b*—no matter how many such impressions I've had—I will never *observe* anything like *necessary connection*; that is, I will never have any *impression,* as such, of necessity. What does necessity *look* like? Is it red? Colored? What shape does it have? Is it hard? Soft? No.

But the problem is worse than that. The turkey sees the farmer. Food follows. The next day, the turkey sees the farmer. Food follows. This happens 99 days in a row. On the 100th day, the turkey, being a very good scientist, runs to the farmer, expecting that food will follow. Food does not follow, though it has 99 times in the past. Today the axe follows. Thanksgiving!

How do we know we're not in *that* sort of situation with whatever we observe in the world—indeed, with the entire world? Remember, what we have to go on is not *the things out there* but our *impressions.* And we might merely have mistaken *covariation* for *causality.* Event *A* covaries in a certain constant way with event *B*; whenever *A*, there is *B. But this does not establish causality.* In the case of the turkey, a psychological expectation was set up in the turkey's mind between one set of impressions—the farmer—and another set of impressions—the food. But this psychological expectation connecting the first set of impressions with the second set is just a covariation among the two sets of events, *not the cause* of any necessary link between them; the psychological expectation in the turkey's mind is not any sort of necessary link between the farmer and the food!

But this problem extends to *everything*. Let's go back, for instance, to our so-called Copernican revolution. For thousands of years people had watched the covariation of the sun moving from east to west every single day. They assumed that the cause of what they were seeing was the movement of the sun. The cause of what they were seeing was *not* the sun. But nor was the *cause* of what they were seeing the motion of the earth. I repeat: the *cause* of the motion of the sun across the sky was *not* the motion of the earth. Can you guess what that cause was?

Their own minds. Or did you already forget? You don't have direct access to the motions of *anything!* It all comes to you by way of your mind's own habits of drawing its world.

Perhaps we could try to bridge the gap between the idea and the impression (or, more accurately, make up for the lack of there being any impression) with an argument. That is, we could try to justify the proposition "*A* causes *B*" with a rational argument by making it the conclusion of a syllogism. Let's give it a try.

1. I have seen *a* strike *b* 100 times.

2. Each time *a* strikes *b*, *b* moves.

Therefore, 3. *b* will move the next time when *a* strikes it.

This simply will not work. Clearly, (3) does not *follow* from (1) and (2); the conclusion is not forced. The argument is not valid.

We might try to add another premise, such as

1a. The future will in relevant ways resemble the past.

But this only sinks us deeper into an ever-widening abyss; we have just fallen into an epistemological black hole, better known as Hume's notorious *problem of induction*.

15.4 The Problem of Induction

Our idea of causality—the principle of cause and effect, the cornerstone of Newtonian physics—is not analytic. It is not synthetic. It is, literally, *non*sense.

As if that weren't enough, proposition (1a) is another cornerstone, not only of the scientific worldview but of every philosophy we have thus far considered. It is called the principle of the uniformity of nature. Is it true?

Oh-oh. We now know what to do with such questions. Is (1a) an analytic statement? No. Is it synthetic?

Well, what impression is it based on? Can we trace the idea of the uniformity of nature back to some impression? Forget it. There isn't any such impression. There's nothing even close.

Take all the information scientists have gathered, from light waves and radio waves, about all the rest of the universe. All their telescopes, optical and radio alike, have thus far examined the energy equivalent to one snowflake hitting the ground. Compare that with the mass-energy of the entire universe and you'll have an impression (that's right) of how solid and incontrovertible all the currently accepted laws, principles, and so-called universal constants of science are. Not very. And just how long have scientists been checking *them* (that is, the current ones, not the previously accepted ones which were just about all completely different, even completely different *concepts*, having to do with things like phlogiston and ether)? A few decades. How much of the *temporal* extension of the universe have they checked? The universe is, supposedly, fifteen billion years old. What percentage of that is twenty years? One-billionth of one percent. You now have an *impression* of the flimsiness of the so-called scientific worldview.

By the way, do you see that Hume's destruction is not just *negative*—that is, it is not merely a Skeptical attack—but gives *positive affirmations* of his thesis, in terms of actual *impression*? This philosophical fact is often overlooked by philosophers who have themselves been corrupted, as many philosophers in Newton's time were, by the current scientific paradigms (not to mention previous philosophers who were corrupted by the prevailing religious ones). Hume was not corrupted.

So, how do we know that the so-called laws of

nature work everywhere in the universe? How do we know they have worked all the way back into the past and will continue to do so into the future? We don't.

Again, you can check this yourself. Is the statement analytic? No. Is it synthetic? No. Then it's nonsense.

Really, once you start thinking about it even a little bit, you will realize, as Hume did, that there are no *necessary* connections between any two events in the world. Well then why on earth (and this is not meant just as a figure of speech) do we—and why do all the so-called scientists—believe in the uniformity of nature? Here is Hume's unflattering answer:

⚘

It must certainly be allowed, that nature has kept us at a great distance from all her secrets, and has afforded us only the knowledge of a few superficial qualities of objects; while she conceals from us those powers and principles on which the influence of those objects entirely depends. Our senses inform us of the colour, weight, and consistence of bread; but neither sense nor reason can ever inform us of those qualities which fit it for the nourishment and support of a human body. Sight or feeling conveys an idea of the actual motion of bodies; but as to that wonderful force or power, which would carry on a moving body for ever in a continued change of place, and which bodies never lose but by communicating it to others; of this we cannot form the most distant conception. But notwithstanding this ignorance of natural powers and principles, we always presume, when we see like sensible qualities, that they have like secret powers, and expect that effects, similar to those which we have experienced, will follow from them. If a body of like colour and consistence with that bread, which we have formerly eat, be presented to us, we make no scruple of repeating the experiment, and foresee, with certainty, like nourishment and support. Now this is a process of the mind or thought, of which I would willingly know the foundation. It is allowed on all hands that there is no known connexion between the sensible qualities

and the secret powers; and consequently, that the mind is not led to form such a conclusion concerning their constant and regular conjunction, by anything which it knows of their nature. As to past *Experience,* it can be allowed to give *direct* and *certain* information of those precise objects only, and that precise period of time, which fell under its cognizance: but why this experience should be extended to future times, and to other objects, which, for aught we know, may be only in appearance similar; this is the main question on which I would insist. The bread, which I formerly eat, nourished me; that is, a body of such sensible qualities was, at that time, endued with such secret powers: but does it follow, that other bread must also nourish me at another time, and that like sensible qualities must always be attended with like secret powers? The consequence seems nowise necessary. At least, it must be acknowledged that there is here a consequence drawn by the mind; that there is a certain step taken; a process of thought, and an inference, which wants to be explained. These two propositions are far from being the same, *I have found that such an object has always been attended with such an effect,* and *I foresee, that other objects, which are, in appearance, similar, will be attended with similar effects.* I shall allow, if you please, that the one proposition may justly be inferred from the other: I know, in fact, that it always is inferred. But if you insist that the inference is made by a chain of reasoning, I desire you to produce that reasoning. The connexion between these propositions is not intuitive. There is required a medium, which may enable the mind to draw such an inference, if indeed it be drawn by reasoning and argument. What that medium is, I must confess, passes my comprehension; and it is incumbent on those to produce it, who assert that it really exists, and is the origin of all our conclusions concerning matter of fact.

⚘

Let us make sure we are clear about what Hume is doing here. He is inquiring into our ideas that go beyond the contents of our present consciousness. On what are they based? They all depend on relations of cause and effect. That is, such ideas are effects caused by impressions. Notice that Hume has not

_____

From *Inquiry Concerning Human Understanding.*

inquired into where those impressions come from or what *they* are based on. It is a brilliant philosophical move, akin to Socrates being too wise to get drawn into a debate with Euthyphro about how he knows that what the gods say is true. Socrates just gives him that. Because of course that argument can go on *forever*. Hume doesn't want to get into the endless dialectic about impressions. He just lets you have them. You can assume what you want about them, even that they are perfect representations of the external world. This is incredible! Because even if they are, the problem is as awful and devastating as before. It is just like it was with Socrates and Euthyphro; let Euthyphro have his direct knowledge of what God loves. Big deal! The problem is so much deeper than that. What is the nature of the connection between God's *love* and a thing being *good*? Is God's love *the cause*? No. So even if Euthyphro truly knows what God loves, he does not know the *cause* of good.

It is the same with our impressions. Let them be as veridical as you like. Look at your impressions. How far do they extend? The life of individual impressions is extremely short. Everything else—your entire knowledge of the world, including yourself—must be based on the impressions you are right now having at this moment—then, a moment later, on *those* impressions. Do you see that this is impossible? You have ideas, which are of more than just the immediate impressions, *but what is the nature of the connection between those ideas and whatever impressions gave rise to them?* That is, what is the foundation of the causal inference? It can only be experience. But *experience cannot provide sufficient reason in any particular case*. For instance, in Hume's examples, I don't have sufficient reason to believe that my friend is in France on the basis of the impression that I hold in my hand a letter with a Paris postmark. The gulf between premise and conclusion remains because it is always possible that the premise is true while the conclusion is false. *Reason* itself cannot bridge the gap.

So *why* then do we all believe in the unifor-mity of nature? Let us make sure we understand a revolutionary subtlety in Hume's answer. It is this: the "reason" we all believe as we do is not, itself, a *reason*. It is just a *fact*. This goes contrary to just about all previous philosophies, both Platonic and Aristotelian, which assumed that the universe and the mind each function in a certain way. Each may function differently, but there is some way that the universe is and there is some way that the mind is—meaning that there are certain *stabilities, continuities, laws, tendencies,* and so on. Human rationality and natural functionality, regardless of to what degree they are in sync, have a certain stable way of going on; even if there is a Heraclitean insta-bility, there is a certain way that this flux is, rather than some other way, in which the *logos* (reason, breath, thought, logic, in all its multif-erous meanings) participates or is even cause. In other words, not just our belief in cause and effect, but all our beliefs about the world and ourselves based on it, are not merely irrational! They are *nonrational* beliefs.

This overturns both Aristotelian tradition and common sense, according to which the relation of cause and effect is the foundation of all beliefs that go beyond immediate conscious-ness. Under the sharp knife of Hume's analysis, however, cause and effect dissolve into a psy-chological construction based on habit: it is a fiction without any reason or evidence behind it. We can never, even in principle, reach beyond the fleeting, momentary, chaotic experience of the present moment to infer truths about the world that reach beyond the tiny duration of brief instants. Neither experience—which is fleeting—nor reason—which is but a psycholog-ical sense of seeming connections where there are none—can reach beyond experience. Since the relation of cause and effect is the foundation of all our beliefs about everything that we are not right now at this instant of our lives experi-encing, the entire world built up by common sense as well as by science *is a construction, an elaborate fiction, without any reason behind it.* All the traditions have just gone up in Pyrrhonean flames:

☙

When we run over libraries, persuaded of these principles, what havoc must we make? If we take in our hand any volume—of divinity or school metaphysics, for instance—let us ask, *Does it contain any abstract reasoning concerning quantity or number?* No. *Does it contain any experimental reasoning concerning matter of fact and existence?* No. Commit it then to the flames, for it can contain nothing but sophistry and illusion.

☙

Hume is not merely denying Aristotelian teleology or Platonic formalism. He is conceiving the most horrible and darkest thing that could possibly be conceived, a truth more horrible than any other. Existence is *utter chaos* all the way down, with *nothing* keeping everything the way it is rather than some other way. *Nothing* in charge. *Nothing* guiding *anything*. *Nothing*.

Socrates had his own God, Heraclitus his Logos. Even the Stoics and Pyrrhonean Skeptics had their inner peace. Hume's enlightenment came in absolute darkness, the penultimate awakening: it was no less than the beginning of the death of God.

15.5 The Death of God

In his famous *Dialogues Concerning Natural Religion,* Hume mounts a detailed and searing attack on all the major arguments for the existence of God and presents a devastating version of the argument from evil against God's existence. Bowing to pressure from his friends who feared for his life, he left it to be published posthumously.

Consider the proposition, "God exists." Is it analytic? Well, Anselm, Descartes, and Spinoza all accepted some version of the so-called *ontological argument* for the existence of some version of God, according to which God exists *necessarily*. So the proposition, "It is not the case that God exists" is, in their view, ultimately self-

contradictory. So they would consider the proposition "God exists" to be analytic. Hume's response, in a nutshell, is that in that case the proposition is tautological and tells us nothing about reality, any more than the true sentence "A necessarily existent being exists necessarily" tells us whether there is actually such a necessarily existent being.

In his third Meditation, Descartes relied on the idea of God to reinstate his beliefs about an external world and other minds; otherwise, he would be left in the Cartesian circle of solipsism, in which all he could be certain of is his own existence. Berkeley used the idea of God to retain his notion of a world and its objects existing even when conscious human egos are not observing them; what you don't see, God sees, and so the existence of things unseen by you persists. Thus, not only the Berkeleyian and Cartesian worlds, but also the worlds of earlier thinkers such as Aquinas, Anselm, Augustine, and their philosophical avatar Aristotle, hang on the question of whether it is reasonable to believe that God exists.

Hume has no need for such a hypothesis. His interest is not edification but truth at all costs, even if it means losing the world. Indeed, as we shall see in the next section, solipsism, which so often is regarded with such dread, as if it were the end of the world, is the discovery of a whole heavenly choir as far as Hume is concerned! For Hume affirms even his own *nonexistence:* the self is nothing but a self-deceptive illusion.

Descartes's argument for the existence of God hinged on his premise that the idea of God, which he found among his other ideas when he examined, through introspection, the contents of his mind, *could not have come from himself.* Hume, already in his *Inquiry,* argues as follows:

The idea of God, as meaning an infinitely intelligent, wise and good Being, arises from reflecting on the operations of our own mind, and augmenting, without limit, those qualities of goodness and wisdom.

In other words, man has made God in man's idealized image of man. Likewise,

Our ideas reach no further than our experience. We have no experience of divine attributes and operations. I need not conclude my syllogism. You can draw the inference yourself.

So how do we come to have an idea of God, when we have no experience of divine attributes? Our idea of God has its origin in impressions having to do with ourselves. It is entirely *anthropomorphic*. I have an impression of myself as a being who, to a certain limited degree, can do certain things; I then extrapolate to an unlimited being that can do all things. I have an impression of myself as a being who, to a certain limited degree and in a certain relative sense, can know some things; I then extrapolate to an unlimited being that can know all things absolutely. I have an impression of myself as being to a certain degree good; I then extrapolate to an all-good being. And so on. This extrapolation is made possible because we have the impressions of *more* and *less*; combining the impression of *more* with our impression of power, intelligence, and moral goodness, we can form an idea of ourselves being more powerful, wiser, and better than we are. We then augment, without limit, this process until we form an idea of God.

The most popular arguments for the existence of God during the so-called Age of Enlightenment, however, came not from such medieval scholastic methods but from a new emphasis on experience. Indeed, the universe—its existence (the cosmological argument) as well as its order (the argument from design)—came to be regarded as the supreme evidence for the existence of God. Let us now turn to Hume's *Dialogues Concerning Natural Religion* to see how he handles the first of these, and then discuss the rest.

⚒

The argument, replied Demea, which I would insist on is the common one. Whatever exists must have

---

From David Hume, *Dialogues Concerning Natural Religion* (London, 1779).

a cause or reason of its existence, it being absolutely impossible for anything to produce itself or be the cause of its own existence. In mounting up, therefore, from effects to causes, we must either go on in tracing an infinite succession, without any ultimate cause at all, or must at last have recourse to some ultimate cause that is *necessarily* existent. Now that the first supposition is absurd may be thus proved. In the infinite chain or succession of causes and effects, each single effect is determined to exist by the power and efficacy of that cause which immediately preceded; but the whole eternal chain or succession, taken together, is not determined or caused by anything, and yet it is evident that it requires a cause or reason, as much as any particular object which begins to exist in time. The question is still reasonable why this particular succession of causes existed from eternity, and not any other succession or no succession at all. If there be no necessarily existent being, any supposition which can be formed is equally possible; nor is there any more absurdity in *nothing's* having existed from eternity than there is in that succession of causes which constitutes the universe. What was it, then, which determined *something* to exist rather than *nothing,* and bestowed being on a particular possibility, exclusive of the rest? *External causes,* there are supposed to be none. *Chance* is a word without a meaning. Was it *nothing?* But that can never produce anything. We must, therefore, have recourse to a necessarily existent Being who carries the *reason* of his existence in himself, and who cannot be supposed not to exist, without an express contradiction. There is, consequently, such a Being—that is, there is a Deity.

I shall not leave it to Philo, said Cleanthes, though I know that the starting objections is his chief delight, to point out the weakness of this metaphysical reasoning. It seems to me so obviously ill-grounded, and at the same time of so little consequence to the cause of true piety and religion, that I shall myself venture to show the fallacy of it.

I shall begin with observing that there is an evident absurdity in pretending to demonstrate a matter of fact, or to prove it by any arguments *a priori*. Nothing is demonstrable unless the contrary implies a contradiction. Nothing that is distinctly conceivable implies a contradiction. Whatever we conceive as existent, we can also conceive as nonexistent. There is no being, therefore, whose non-existence implies a contradiction. Consequently there is no being whose existence is demonstrable. I propose this argument as entirely decisive, and am willing to rest the whole controversy upon it.

It is pretended that the Deity is a necessarily existent being; and this necessity of his existence is attempted to be explained by asserting that, if we knew his whole essence or nature, we should perceive it to be as impossible for him not to exist, as for twice two not to be four. But it is evident that this can never happen, while our faculties remain the same as at present. It will still be possible for us, at any time, to conceive the non-existence of what we formerly conceived to exist; nor can the mind ever lie under a necessity of supposing any object to remain always in being; in the same manner as we lie under a necessity of always conceiving twice two to be four. The words, therefore, *necessary existence* have no meaning or, which is the same thing, none that is consistent.

But further, why may not the material universe be the necessarily existent Being, according to this pretended explication of necessity? We dare not affirm that we know all the qualities of matter; and, for aught we can determine, it may contain some qualities which, were they known, would make its non-existence appear as great a contradiction as that twice two is five. I find only one argument employed to prove that the material world is not the necessarily existent Being; and this argument is derived from the contingency both of the matter and the form of the world. "Any particle of matter," it is said, "may be *conceived* to be annihilated, and any form may be *conceived* to be altered. Such an annihilation or alteration, therefore, is not impossible." But it seems a great partiality not to perceive that the same argument extends equally to the Deity, so far as we have any conception of him, and that the mind can at least imagine him to be non-existent or his attributes to be altered. It must be some unknown, inconceivable qualities which can make his non-existence appear impossible or his attributes unalterable; and no reason can be assigned why these qualities may not belong to matter. As they are altogether unknown and inconceivable, they can never be proved incompatible with it.

Add to this that in tracing an eternal succes-sion of objects it seems absurd to inquire for a general cause or first author. How can anything that exists from eternity have a cause, since that relation implies a priority in time and a beginning of existence?

In such a chain, too, or succession of objects, each part caused by that which preceded it, and causes that which succeeds it. Where then is the difficulty? But the *whole*, you say, wants a cause. I answer that the uniting of these parts into a whole, like the uniting of several distinct countries into one kingdom, or several distinct members into one body, is performed merely by an arbitrary act of the mind, and has no influence on the nature of things. Did I show you the particular causes of each individual in a collection of twenty particles of matter, I should think it very unreasonable should you afterwards ask me what was the cause of the whole twenty. This is sufficiently explained in explaining the cause of the parts.

Though the reasonings which you have urged, Cleanthes, may well excuse me, said Philo, from starting any further difficulties, yet I cannot forbear insisting still upon another topic. It is observed by arithmeticians that the products of 9 compose always either 9 or some lesser product of 9 if you add together all the characters of which any of the former products is composed. Thus, of 18, 27, 36, which are products of 9, you make 9 by adding 1 to 8, 2 to 7, 3 to 6. Thus 369 is a product also of 9; and if you add 3, 6, and 9, you make 18, a lesser product of 9. To a superficial observer so wonderful a regularity may be admired as the effect either of chance or design; but a skilful algebraist immediately concludes it to be the work of necessity, and demonstrates that it must for ever result from the nature of these numbers. Is it not probable, I ask, that the whole economy of the universe is conducted by a like necessity, though no human algebra can furnish a key which solves the difficulty? And instead of admiring the order of natural beings, may it not happen that, could we penetrate into the intimate nature of bodies, we should clearly see why it was absolutely impossible they could ever admit of any other disposition? So dangerous is it to introduce this idea of necessity into the present question! and so naturally does it afford an inference directly opposite to the religious hypothesis!

This is just the opening salvo of Hume's *Dialogues,* in which the arguments for the existence of God are divided into *anthropomorphic* (the ontological, cosmological, and design arguments) and *mystical.* Together, these categories are meant to be mutually exhaustive, that is, they contain all possible types of arguments for God. Hume destroys them all, starting with the cosmological argument (also sometimes called the *first cause* argument, or "argument from the first cause"). It is a perfect example of the application of Hume's method, discussed in the previous sections.

The bare logical structure of the argument as presented by Demea can be sketched as follows:

1. The universe exists.

2. "*Q* exists" implies "*P* exists," where *P* is the cause of *Q.*

Therefore, 3. The cause of the universe exists.

Propositions 1 and 2 are the premises, and 3 is the conclusion. But right away we notice that *God* is conspicuously absent from the conclusion, which establishes, at best, the existence of the cause of the universe. What would then be needed is another argument establishing that the cause of the universe is God. But, first, does this argument even establish the conclusion?

No. We have already seen in great detail Hume's criticisms of the concept of causality. We don't know that premise 2 is true. How do we know that everything must have a cause? Is it *self-contradictory* to suppose that there exists an event without a cause? No. The argument fails.

But suppose we did somehow know that every event has a cause. What then? Would the argument then work? The answer would still be no, unless we knew, also, that the word *universe* is not merely the name of an endless series of events, each of which is a cause of the next, but refers to *an event.* That is, we would need to know, first, that the universe had a beginning in time. But even that is not enough. We would also have to know that the universe is not the sort of thing that could exist without a cause or else have somehow caused itself to exist. In other words, for the cosmological argument to work,

we would have to know that the universe is not the sort of thing that can exist without a cause or be its own cause.

Demea suggests that God, unlike the universe, exists necessarily. Cleanthes responds, first, by arguing that the idea *necessary existence* is meaningless—literally, nonsense—and, second, that even if it weren't and if such a concept applied to something real, we could never know that the universe is not that sort of thing. How, after all, does the theologian know what the universe can or cannot do? Furthermore, in conceiving of something that exists without an external cause, premise 2 is denied. Indeed, if it were possible to conceive of a being that exists without an external cause, then *the cosmological argument would be self-contradictory.* The theologian could try to argue, again, that only God, not the universe, has this special property. But this evokes, without any reason (after all, what is the *evidence?*), a double standard: one standard for God, one standard for the universe.

In other words, if God caused the universe, what caused God? To answer, "God exists without an external cause," is, first, to deny that nothing can exist without a cause (premise 2), and it evokes without sufficient reason a double standard. After all, none of us has ever seen *this* universe come into existence, much less a *number* of universes, which would be required in order to be able to claim that we know whether universes are the sorts of things that bring themselves into existence or not.

In short, there are so many things wrong with the cosmological argument for the existence of God that one wonders how anyone could ever have come to believe in God on the basis of it. Hume would remind us, of course, that people making such arguments are not reasoning but *rationalizing,* trying to explain their nonrational beliefs as if they were rational. The real "cause" for people's belief in God is *bad logic, fear,* and the wish to repress others. But nobody wants to see that in themselves so they invent religions to justify their shortcomings and hide their flaws.

The argument from design is just like the cosmological argument and contains the same flaws that are obvious once one sees them but invisible as long as one is blinded by unreflective acceptance. It goes something like this:

1. "*Q* is well ordered" implies the existence of a well-ordered *P* that gave rise to *Q*.
2. The universe is well ordered.

Therefore, 3. There exists a well-ordered something that gave rise to the universe.

Once again, there is no way to link the evidence—the existence of a well-ordered universe—to the existence of God. First, the conclusion does not lead to the existence of God but, at best, to the existence of "a well-ordered something." We would thus again need a second argument to convince us that the only sort of well-ordered something that could have given rise to the universe is God. Second, to suppose that something with a very high degree of order can exist without an external designer is to contradict premise 2 of the argument from design. For, if God designed the universe, what (who) designed God? To answer that God is so well ordered, not through the effects of an external designer but by God's own nature, is once again to contradict premise 2. Third, to suppose that the existence of such a being is possible evokes the same fallacious double standard as before.

What, then, are we to make of religion? Here is Cleanthes' answer:

⚹

All religious systems, it is confessed, are subject to great and insuperable difficulties. Each disputant triumphs in his turn, while he carries on an offensive war, and exposes the absurdities, barbarities, and pernicious tenets of his antagonist. But all of them, on the whole, prepare a complete triumph for the *sceptic*, who tells them that no system ought ever to be embraced with regard to such subjects: for this plain reason than no absurdity ought ever to be assented to with regard to any

subject. A total suspense of judgment is here our only reasonable resource. And if every attack, as is commonly observed, and no defense among theologians is successful, how complete must be *his* victory who remains always, with all mankind, on the offensive, and has himself no fixed station or abiding city which he is ever, on any occasion, obliged to defend?

⚹

15.6 I Do Not Exist

So what about the world, the *external* world, the world in which I supposedly exist as an individual being among many? We have alluded to Hume's dissolution of the idea of the world but have not focused specifically on his account of external existence. In one section of the *Treatise*, "Of the Ideas of Existence and of External Existence" (immediately preceding the "Of Personal Identity" section), he addresses directly the idea of external existence:

⚹

A like reasoning will account for the idea of *external existence*. We may observe, that 'tis universally allow'd by philosophers, and is besides pretty obvious of itself, that nothing is ever really present with the mind but its perceptions or impressions and ideas, and that external objects become known to us only by those perceptions they occasion. To hate, to love, to think, to feel, to see; all this is nothing but to perceive.

Now since nothing is ever present to the mind but perceptions, and since all ideas are deriv'd from something antecedently present to the mind; it follows, that 'tis impossible for us so much as to conceive or form an idea of any thing specifically different from ideas and impressions. Let us fix our attention out of ourselves as much as possible: Let us chace our imagination to the heavens, or to the utmost limits of the universe; we never really advance a step beyond ourselves, nor can conceive any kind of existence, but those perceptions, which have appear'd in that narrow compass. This is the universe of the imagination, nor have we any idea but what is there produc'd.

⟡

So here you are, inside the *universe of the imagination*. And where, exactly, is that? Where are these appearances that you are right now having? So what are you? *Who* are you? As we are about to find out, you are literally a *nowhere man* in the middle of *nowhere*. In what sense, then, do you even exist? Hume's answer: you don't.

"Of Personal Identity," a section in the *Treatise*, contains his famous denial of the self; the following passages are among the most often quoted in the whole of philosophy:

⟡

There are some philosophers, who imagine we are every moment intimately conscious of what we call our SELF; that we feel its existence and its continuance in existence; and are certain, beyond the evidence of a demonstration, both of its perfect identity and simplicity. The strongest sensation, the most violent passion, say they, instead of distracting us from this view, only fix it the more intensely, and make us consider their influence on *self* either by their pain or pleasure. To attempt a farther proof of this were to weaken its evidence; since no proof can be deriv'd from any fact, of which we are so intimately conscious; nor is there any thing, of which we can be certain, if we doubt this.

Unluckily all these positive assertions are contrary to that very experience which is pleaded for them, nor have we any idea of *self*, after the manner it is here explain'd. For from what impression cou'd this idea be deriv'd? This question 'tis impossible to answer without a manifest contradiction and absurdity; and yet 'tis a question, which must necessarily be answer'd, if we wou'd have the idea of self pass for clear and intelligible. It must be some one impression, that gives rise to every real idea. But self or person is not any one impression, but that to which our several impressions and ideas are suppos'd to have a reference. If any impression gives rise to the idea of self, that impression must continue invariably the same, thro' the whole course of our lives; since self is sup-

From David Hume, *A Treatise of Human Nature*, 1738.

pos'd to exist after that manner. But there is no impression constant and invariable. Pain and pleasure, grief and joy, passions and sensations succeed each other, and never all exist at the same time. It cannot, therefore, be from any of these impressions, or from any other, that the idea of self is deriv'd; and consequently there is no such idea.

But farther, what must become of all our particular perceptions upon this hypothesis? All these are different, and distinguishable, and separable from each other, and may be separately considered, and may exist separately, and have no need of any thing to support their existence. After what manner, therefore, do they belong to self; and how are they connected with it? For my part, when I enter most intimately into what I call *myself*, I always stumble on some particular perception or other, of heat or cold, light or shade, love or hatred, pain or pleasure. I never can catch *myself* at any time without a perception, and never can observe any thing but the perception. When my perceptions are remov'd for any time, as by sound sleep; so long am I insensible of *myself*, and may truly be said not to exist. And were all my perceptions remov'd by death, and cou'd I neither think, nor feel, nor see, nor love, nor hate after the dissolution of my body, I shou'd be entirely annihilated, nor do I conceive what is farther requisite to make me a perfect non-entity. If any one upon serious and unprejudic'd reflexion, thinks he has a different notion of *himself*, I must confess I can reason no longer with him. All I can allow him is, that he may be in the right as well as I, and that we are essentially different in this particular. He may, perhaps, perceive something simple and continu'd, which he calls *himself*; tho' I am certain there is no such principle in me.

But setting aside some metaphysicians of this kind. I may venture to affirm of the rest of mankind, that they are nothing but a bundle or collection of different perceptions, which succeed each other with an inconceivable rapidity, and are in a perpetual flux and movement. Our eyes cannot turn in their sockets without varying our perceptions. Our thought is still more variable than our sight; and all our other senses and faculties contribute to this change; nor is there any single power of the soul, which remains unalterably the same, perhaps for one moment. The mind is a kind of theatre, where several perceptions successively make their appearance; pass, re-pass, glide away, and mingle in an infinite variety of postures and situations. There is properly no *simplicity* in it at one time, nor *identity* in different; whatever natural propension we may have to imagine that simplicity and identity. The comparison of the theatre must not mislead us. They are the successive perceptions only, that constitute the mind; nor have we the most distant notion of the place, where these scenes are represented, or of the materials, of which it is compos'd.

What then gives us so great a propension to ascribe an identity to these successive perceptions, and to suppose ourselves possest of an invariable and uninterrupted existence thro' the whole course of our lives? In order to answer this question, we must distinguish betwixt personal identity, as it regards our thought or imagination, as it regards our passions or the concern we take in ourselves. The first is our present subject; and to explain it perfectly we must take the matter pretty deep, and account for that identity, which we attribute to plants and animals; there being a great analogy betwixt it, and the identity of a self or person.

We have a distinct idea of an object, that remains invariable and uninterrupted thro' a suppos'd variation of time; and this idea we call that of *identity or sameness.* We have also a distinct idea of several different objects existing in succession, and connected together by a close relation; and this to an accurate view affords as perfect a notion of *diversity,* as if there was no manner of relation among the objects. But tho' these two ideas of identity, and a succession of related objects be in themselves perfectly distinct, and even contrary, yet 'tis certain, that in our common way of thinking they are generally confounded with each other. That action of the imagination, by which we consider the uninterrupted and invariable object, and that by which we reflect on the succession of related objects, are almost the same to the feeling, nor is there much more effort of thought requir'd in the latter case than in the former. The relation facilitates the transition of the mind from one object to another, and renders its passage as smooth as if it contemplated one continu'd object. This resemblance is the cause of the confusion and mistake, and makes us substitute the notion of identity, instead of that of related objects. However at one instant we may consider the related succession as variable or interrupted, we are sure the next to ascribe to it a perfect iden-

tity, and regard it as invariable and uninterrupted. Our propensity to this mistake is so great from the resemblance above-mention'd, that we fall into it before we are aware; and tho' we incessantly correct ourselves by reflexion, and return to a more accurate method of thinking, yet we cannot long sustain our philosophy, or take off this bias from the imagination. Our last resource is to yield to it, and boldly assert that these different related objects are in effect the same, however, interrupted and variable. In order to justify to ourselves this absurdity, we often feign some new and unintelligible principle, that connects the objects together, and prevents their interruption or variation. Thus we feign the continu'd existence of the perceptions of our senses, to remove the interruption, and run into the notion of a *soul,* and *self,* and *substance,* to disguise the variation. But we may farther observe, that where we do not give rise to such a fiction, our propension to confound identity with relation is so great, that we are apt to imagine something unknown and mysterious, connecting the parts, beside their relation; and this I take to be the case with regard to the identity we ascribe to plants and vegetables. And even when this does not take place, we still feel a propensity to confound these ideas, tho' we are not able fully to satisfy ourselves in that particular, nor find any thing invariable and uninterrupted to justify our notion of identity.

Thus the controversy concerning identity is not merely a dispute of words. For when we attribute identity, in an improper sense, to variable or interrupted objects, our mistake is not confin'd to the expression, but is commonly attended with a fiction, either of something invariable and uninterrupted, or of something mysterious and inexplicable, or at least with a propensity to such fictions. What will suffice to prove this hypothesis to the satisfaction of every fair enquirer, is to shew from daily experience and observation, that the objects, which are variable or interrupted, and yet are suppos'd to continue the same, are such only as consist of a succession of parts, connected together by resemblance, contiguity, or causation. For as such a succession answers evidently to our notion of diversity, it can only be by mistake we ascribe to it an identity; and as the relation of parts, which leads us into this mistake, is really nothing but a quality, which produces an association of ideas, and an easy transition of the imagination from one to another, it can only be from the resemblance, which this act of the mind bears to that, by which we contemplate one continu'd object, that the error arises. . . .

We may also consider the two following phænomena, which are remarkable in their kind. The first is, that tho' we commonly be able to distinguish pretty exactly betwixt numerical and specific identity, yet it sometimes happens, that we confound them, and in our thinking and reasoning employ the one for the other. Thus a man, who hears a noise, that is frequently interrupted and renew'd, says, it is still the same noise; tho' 'tis evident the sounds have only a specific identity or resemblance, and there is nothing numerically the same, but the cause, which produc'd them. In like manner it may be said without breach of the propriety of language, that such a church, which was formerly of brick, fell to ruin, and that the parish rebuilt the same church of free-stone, and according to modern architecture. Here neither the form nor materials are the same, nor is there any thing common to the two objects, but their relation to the inhabitants of the parish; and yet this alone is sufficient to make us denominate them the same. But we must observe, that in these cases the first object is in a manner annihilated before the second comes into existence; . . .

We now proceed to explain the nature of *personal identity,* which has become so great a question in philosophy. . . . And here 'tis evident, the same method of reasoning must be continu'd, which has so successfully explain'd the identity of plants, and animals, and ships, and houses, and of all the compounded and changeable productions either of art or nature. The identity which we ascribe to the mind of man, is only a fictitious one, and of a like kind with that which we ascribe to vegetables and animal bodies. It cannot, therefore, have a different origin, but must proceed from a like operation of the imagination upon like objects.

But lest this argument shou'd not convince the reader; tho' in my opinion perfectly decisive; let him weigh the following reasoning, which is still closer and more immediate. 'Tis evident, that the identity, which we attribute to the human mind, however perfect we may imagine it to be, is not able to run the several different perceptions into one, and make them lose their characters of distinction and difference, which are essential to

them. 'Tis still true, that every distinct perception, which enters into the composition of the mind, is a distinct existence, and is different, and distinguishable, and separable from every other perception, either contemporary or successive. . . .

The only question, therefore, which remains, is, by what relations this uninterrupted progress of our thought is produc'd, when we consider the successive existence of a mind or thinking person. And here 'tis evident we must confine ourselves to resemblance and causation, and must drop contiguity, which has little or no influence in the present case.

To begin with *resemblance*; suppose we cou'd see clearly into the breast of another, and observe that succession of perceptions, which constitutes his mind or thinking principle, and suppose that he always preserves the memory of a considerable part of past perceptions; 'tis evident that nothing cou'd more contribute to the bestowing a relation on this succession amidst all its variations. For what is the memory but a faculty, by which we raise up the images of past perceptions? And as an image necessarily resembles its object, must not the frequent placing of these resembling perceptions in the chain of thought, convey the imagination more easily from one link to another, and make the whole seem like the continuance of one object? In this particular, then, the memory not only discovers the identity, but also contributes to its production, by producing the relation of resemblance among the perceptions. The case is the same whether we consider ourselves or others.

As to *causation*; we may observe, that the true idea of the human mind, is to consider it as a system of different perceptions or different existences, which are link'd together by the relation of cause and effect, and mutually produce, destroy, influence, and modify each other. Our impressions give rise to their correspondent ideas; and these ideas in their turn produce other impressions. One thought chaces another, and draws after it a third, by which it is expell'd in its turn. In this respect, I cannot compare the soul more properly to any thing than to a republic or commonwealth, in which the several members are united by the reciprocal ties of government and subordination, and give rise to other persons, who propagate the same republic in the incessant changes of its parts. And as the same individual republic may not only change its members, but also its laws and constitutions; in like manner the same person may vary his character and disposition, as well as his impressions and ideas, without losing his identity. Whatever changes he endures, his several parts are still connected by the relation of causation. And in this view our identity with regard to the passions serves to corroborate that with regard to the imagination, by the making our distant perceptions influence each other, and by giving us a present concern for our past or future pains or pleasures.

As memory alone acquaints us with the continuance and extent of this succession of perceptions, 'tis to be consider'd, upon that account chiefly, as the source of personal identity. Had we no memory, we never shou'd have any notion of causation, nor consequently of that chain of causes and effects, which constitute our self or person. But having once acquir'd this notion of causation from the memory, we can extend the same chain of causes, and consequently the identity of our persons beyond our memory, and can comprehend times, and circumstances, and actions, which we have entirely forgot, but suppose in general to have existed. For how few of our past actions are there, of which we have any memory? Who can tell me, for instance, what were his thoughts and actions on the first of *January* 1715, the 11th of *March* 1719, and the 3d of *August* 1733? Or will he affirm, because he has entirely forgot the incidents of these days, that the present self is not the same person with the self of that time; and by that means overturn all the most establish'd notions of personal identity? In this view, therefore, memory does not so much *produce* as *discover* personal identity, by shewing us the relation of cause and effect among our different perceptions. 'Twill be incumbent on those, who affirm that memory produces entirely our personal identity, to give a reason why we can thus extend our identity beyond our memory.

The whole of this doctrine leads us to a conclusion, which is of great importance in the present affair, *viz.* that all the nice and subtle questions concerning personal identity can never possibly be decided and are to be regarded rather as grammatical than as philosophical difficulties. Identity depends on the relations of ideas; and these relations produce identity, by means of that easy transition they occasion. But as the relations, and the easiness of the transition may diminish by insensible degrees, we have no just standard, by which

we can decide any dispute concerning the time, when they acquire or lose a title to the name of identity. All the disputes concerning the identity of connected objects are merely verbal, except so far as the relation of parts gives rise to some fiction or imaginary principle of union, as we have already observ'd.

What I have said concerning the first origin and uncertainty of our notion of identity, as apply'd to the human mind, may be extended with little or no variation to that of *simplicity*. An object, whose different co-existent parts are bound together by a close relation, operates upon the imagination after much the same manner as one perfectly simple and indivisible, and requires not a much greater stretch of thought in order to its conception. From this similarity of operation we attribute a simplicity to it, and feign a principle of union as the support of this simplicity, and the center of all the different parts and qualities of the object.

✦

Let us see if we can take stock of Hume's argument. We have already become familiar with his bundle theory of the mind. What is the mind? A bundle of perceptions. Perceptions come in two varieties: impressions and ideas. The life of individual perceptions, whether they are impressions or ideas, is short; flickering in and out of existence, "they succeed each other with an inconceivable rapidity." His argument against the existence of the self begins with the statement that

✦

There are some philosophers, who imagine that we are every moment intimately conscious of what we call our SELF; that we feel its existence and its continuance in existence; and are certain, beyond the evidence of a demonstration, both of its perfect identity and simplicity.

✦

By *identity*, Hume means persistence without change *over time*. By *simplicity*, he means existence as a unity—an individual thing rather than as a collection—*at a time*. Thus, from what impression indeed could the idea of self—that is, the experience of unity at a time and identity over time—be derived? The term *self* is supposed to represent an idea of our personal unity at a time that continues unchanged over time. If it is a *meaningful* term and not just an empty noise standing for nothing, there must be some impression of which it is a representation. And the problem is that *there simply is no such impression*. Therefore, there cannot even exist any *idea* of a self! Can you see this? It is a truly incredible thing to see. The idea of *self* is not even a *misrepresentation* of an impression; it is but an insubstantial ghost—literally a figment of the imagination.

But *whose* imagination? Nobody's.

Let me repeat: Hume is not merely proving the nonexistence of the self; he is making the much more radical claim that *we do not even have any idea of such a thing!* It is an empty word, like "God," that refers to nothing. Thus, technically speaking, Hume is not so much *denying* the existence of the self as he is claiming that to affirm or to deny the existence of the self is to speak utter nonsense. This has rarely been understood properly, even by philosophers.

Let us now see why, exactly, Hume claims that there is no impression that corresponds to the (imaginary, fictive) idea of the self. In the preceding passage, he is applying his own introspective method of paying close attention to the phenomena of his own experience without theorizing about it or framing any hypothesis that goes beyond the immediate data of his experience. Now, he isn't *just* looking; he is looking *for* something: a simple, unchanging impression that persists over time. All he finds are individual sensations, emotions, and thoughts. He invites us to try for ourselves; after all, maybe you and I are different. So let's not just read this and blindly accept it; let us see if we can do any better than Hume.

Right now you're reading this book. Probably you're sitting down. Do you feel the pressure of the chair against your rear? Focus your attention on that feeling of pressure. *That's* an impression.

Call it i_1. It occurs at a particular time. Call it t_1. You're reading words. These words. Now these. As you read, you hear the words in your head as a sequence of mental whispers, auditory images, sounds in your mind. Pause now a moment, close your eyes, and repeat ten times the sentence "I am an auditory image." That is an auditory image and so is *this* sound that you are hearing right now as you read *these* words. You now know what the phrase "auditory image" refers to. It refers to those impressions that you just heard . . . *NO, NO, NO!* Not to *those*. To *these!* The impressions that you are *now* hearing are the ones that exist *now; those* previous ones (which occurred a few moments ago when you were reading four lines up) are no longer here. They no longer exist as you read these lines. *Those* impressions are *then*. These impressions are *now. Those* past impressions can now only be represented, at best, if at all, as *ideas* (when you *recall* them in this, the new, present).

Impressions come and go. They vanish into nothing almost instantly. They can be "recalled" as ideas ("recalled" being in quotes because you're not bringing back the past moments in which those impressions came and went). *Ideas* do not have the same identity as the impressions of which they are representations; they are not one and the same impression. These words that you are right now hearing in your head are, likewise, new impressions.

Let us call the impressions when you first said the phrase "I am an auditory image" i_2. Let us call whatever moment of time this new moment is t_2. Let us suppose that you're also hungry at the moment. You have a sensation of hunger. That too is an impression. Call it i_3; it exists during some brief interval of time, t_3. This impression might appear as a grumbling in your stomach, a feeling of emptiness, or a conglomerate of these. Suppose, on the other hand, that you now say to yourself, "Damn, I'm hungry." That phrase is experienced not as a tactile image (grumbling in your stomach) but as an auditory image (the sound of words in your head). It too is an impression. Call it i_4. It exists at t_4.

Let us suppose you're getting curious about

how this section will play itself out, how it will end; this feeling of curiosity, a sensation of wonder, is also an impression, call it i_5. It exists at t_5. What about the light you see? That too is a sensation. The page you see may be glowing with a reflected light, or there may be what appears to be sunlight in the window, and so on. Focus on your sensation of light reflected from the page of the book you are right now reading. That visual image is also an impression. Call it i_6 at time t_6.

Now, focus on the pressure of the chair against your rear. There it is again, that same impression, i_1—NO, NO, NO! *This* one, the impression that you feel as the tactile image of the pressure of the chair against your rear, the one that is going on *right now*; impressions exist only in the present. This new impression began at the top of this paragraph and it will last awhile until it disappears into the cascade of new impressions. *This* feeling of pressure, the impression you feel now (is it even the same one you felt at the top of the paragraph?)? Let us call it i_7. It exists at whatever the time is now; let us refer to this moment of time as t_7.

Here, then, is the *identity* question: is impression i_1 the very same impression as i_7? Hume is *not* asking whether i_1 and i_7 are *similar*. He is asking whether they are one and the same entity. And the answer is *no, $i_1 \neq i_7$! They are not the same perceptual object*. Why? First, i_1 exists at time t_1, which is in the past from time t_7, when i_7 popped into existence. Second, *impression i_1 did not exist continuously from time t_1 to time t_7*.

You might think that the impression caused by the pressure of the chair against your rear existed even when you weren't experiencing it. Do you see why Hume would object? He would say that *no*, an *impression* is a perceptual object that exists as a mental entity, requiring consciousness to exist. No conscious experience, no mind; after all, if we put some machine to register the pressure of the chair at regular intervals, that machine would not have any *impressions* unless it had, also, a conscious mind.

Well, but what about the fact that impression i_1 and i_7, even though they are separated in time and even though there is a big discontinuous gap in their existences, seem more alike than do i_1 and i_2? That is, the impression of the chair against your rear at time t_1 is much more like the impression of the chair against your rear at time t_2, even if they are not one and the same object (this one is now; that one was then). Then it was like the impression of the sound in your head when you repeat the phrase "I am an auditory image." Hume would not deny this (though he might ask you how you think you can know that any two impressions, which are not before the mind at the same time, are alike). Hume would agree that i_1 and i_7 are *qualitatively similar*, whereas i_1 and i_2 are qualitatively dissimilar. But *qualitative similarity does not identity make*. In other words, what Hume is saying here is that two things that *look* alike are not, therefore, by virtue of looking similar to one another, one and the same, numerically identical thing! Suppose my silver 2001 Honda Odyssey looks just like your silver 2001 Honda Odyssey. We can say, in a purely verbal sense, that we have "the same car," but that is *not* to say that my car is your car. That is Hume's point about differentiating between mere verbal claims of similarity and the strict logical claim of identity. Our *two* cars are made by the same manufacturer, they are the same model, and so on, but *two* things are *not one* thing! The identity of the object in my garage begins and ends in my garage and does not in any way extend into your garage.

And that, by analogy, is what Hume is saying about our individual impressions. As I sit at my computer typing these words that you are right now reading (*ah—but are these words that I am right now typing the very ones that you are reading? Think about it!*), I feel the pressure of the chair against my rear. This impression of mine might be as similar to your impression going on right now there wherever (and whoever) you are, sitting and reading, as my car is similar to your car; but just as my car is not your car, no matter how similar the two physical objects may be, my impression is not your impression—regardless of how *similar* the two mental events might be.

But that's just the start of it. It's far worse than that. Look now what happens without my ever having to talk about you or anybody else! The *me* that is *here and now*—is this the *me* that began this book? Is this person sitting here and now typing these very words even the *me* that began this chapter, this section, this page? Hume's answer is a resounding *No!* The problem is that the word *me* does not have the reference that we ordinarily (in our unreflective and unphilosohical consciousness), falsely think it does: it does not refer to a *self*. There simply is no such self, no unity at a time that continues to exist with identity over time. There is no unity at a time because of the disjointed cascade of individual impressions flickering in and out of existence. There is no identity at a time because these individual flickerings do not last very long; their duration is "unimaginably brief," not even a few seconds.

Thus, for instance, when I say, "I am cold," it is like saying "It is raining." To what does the word *It* refer? The sky? Hardly. The sky is not raining. The clouds? No. The weather? Hardly. Perhaps I should say instead (although it is more cumbersome) "Raining is going on." There are just the individual raindrops. There is no one thing that is "rain," likewise with impressions. There is no "self" that is the sum total of them. There are just the individual little psychological drops falling, briefly in and then quickly out, of existence. Thus, in the case of "I am cold," the reference of the word *I* is, at best, directed to a bundle of perceptions. Perceptions consist of two things: impressions and ideas. There is not even an *idea* corresponding to a self. There are only the impressions. So there is no personal identity over time. In other words, I am as *nonidentical* to "myself" as I am to you! I may be much more *qualitatively similar* to myself over time than I am to you, but, again, *qualitative similarity does not personal identity make*. It only fosters an illusion.

Let us take another, especially poignant example. Suppose Descartes says to Hume, "I think, therefore I am." Hume would ask Descartes how he knows that the first instance of the word *I* and the second instance of the word *I* have the same reference. There you are, Descartes, sitting in the dark. *That's* an impression, a black phenomenal impression (assuming I am in total darkness) with some white flickerings. (When you are in complete darkness, or have your eyes completely shut, that is what you see: the "blackness" is anything but uniform. Try it.) If Descartes is sitting in a chair, he feels pressure against his rear. Even if he's in an isolation tank and doesn't feel any such feelings of pressure against any part of his body, there is then the series of sensations that are still going on at each moment, such as the feeling of floating, *even the feeling that he is nowhere*, or *in limbo*. Those too are impressions (try going into an isolation tank and you will see exactly what I mean).

So then Descartes has the thought "I think, therefore I am." Does the first impression of *I*—vaguely, the feeling of one's own existence—last for the entire duration of the speaking of that sentence, without any interruption? Hume, like Buddha, would claim that by his own experience the answer to even that question is no. We are like the fire, each flame briefly flickering in and then quickly out of existence. But let us not quibble with the first and second instances of the use of the word *I* in Descartes's famous sentence! Let us just call that entire auditory image—the cognitive image "I think, therefore I am"—an impression. All right, now, go ahead and say that phrase to yourself: I think, therefore I am. That's an impression, call it i_8. It happened at this time—call it t_8—which is in the future relative to t_1–t_7. We can add i_8 to our numbered series of impressions.

Focus now on the pressure of the chair: i_9. Now scratch your head: i_{10}. Now say once more to yourself, "I think, therefore I am." That's impression i_{11}. So, is i_{11} *the same auditory image* as i_8? Are they one and the same mental object? No, i_{11} is a different impression from i_8 and i_1 is a different impression from i_7. In both cases what we have is qualitative similarity, not numerical identity. Figure 15.1 is a picture of the various sensations, emotions, and thoughts, the impressions and ideas that come and go, flickering in and out of existence with such rapidity and in such multitudes that the gaps are never noticed.

Our existence consists in just such flickerings. Memories, theories, ideas, all come and go; no permanence, no identity—all is flux. Going in and out of existence, individual perceptions (both as impressions and as ideas) have no persistent identity over time, except perhaps for very short Buddha instants. The self in Hume's sharp analysis is like a story we keep telling ourselves in each and every instant as we die. But who is telling it? No one.

Or, if you like, a ghost. In Hume's dark labyrinth time is not just a thief, it is a cosmic Jack the Ripper with a sharp, quick scalpel that never stops cutting. Time dismembers experience and we talk about *re*membering ourselves in the future, but that is but a ghost's empty dream. Nothing lasts. Nothing persists. Not even a world. Ours is but a brief series of brief tales told by a series of brief, disintegrating idiots, full of sound and fury, signifying nothing.

Such dark and dreary thoughts, so full of dread, yet Hume did not fear his woeful ruminations. Why? Because he realized that, by his own dispositions, something from within himself would in the end draw him back out into the world. All it took was a rousing game of backgammon. And then he was out of it. For a while. Until he missed it! And then he would return, once more, to the heart of darkness:

⚐

The *intense* view of these manifold contradictions and imperfections in human reason has so wrought upon me, and heated my brain, that I am ready to reject all belief and reasoning, and can look upon no opinion even as more probable or likely than another. Where am I, or what? From what causes do I derive my existence, and to what condition shall I return? Whose favour shall I court, and whose anger must I dread? What beings surround me? and on whom have I any influence, or who have any influence on me? I am confounded with all these questions, and begin to fancy myself in the most deplorable condition imaginable, inviron'd with the deepest darkness, and utterly depriv'd of the use of every member and faculty.

Most fortunately it happens, that since reason is incapable of dispelling these clouds, nature herself suffices to that purpose, and cures me of this philosophical melancholy and delirium, either by relaxing this bent of mind, or by some avocation, and lively impression of my senses, which obliterate all these chimeras. I dine, I play a game of backgammon, I converse, and am merry with my friends; and when after three or four hours' amusement, I wou'd return to these speculations, they appear so cold, and strain'd, and ridiculous,

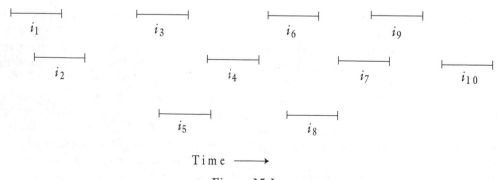

Time ⟶

Figure 15.1

that I cannot find in my heart to enter into them any farther.

Here then I find myself absolutely and necessarily determin'd to live, and talk, and act like other people in the common affairs of life. But notwithstanding that my natural propensity, and the course of my animal spirits and passions reduce me to this indolent belief in the general maxims of the world, I still feel such remains of my former disposition, that I am ready to throw all my books and papers into the fire, and resolve never more to renounce the pleasures of life for the sake of reasoning and philosophy. For those are my sentiments in that splenetic humour, which governs me at present. I may, nay I must yield to the current of nature, in submitting to my senses and understanding; and in this blind submission I shew most perfectly my sceptical disposition and principles. But does it follow, that I must strive against the current of nature, which leads to indolence and pleasure; that I must seclude myself, in some measure, from the commerce and society of men, which is so agreeable: and that I must torture my brain with subtilities and sophistries, at the very time that I cannot satisfy myself concerning the reasonableness of so painful an application, nor have any tolerable prospect of arriving by its means at truth and certainty. Under what obligation do I lie of making such an abuse of time? And to what end can it serve either for the service of mankind, or for my own private interest? No: If I must be a fool, as all those who reason or believe anything *certainly* are, my follies shall at least be natural and agreeable. Where I strive against my inclination, I shall have a good reason for my resistance; and will no more be led a wandering into such dreary solitudes, and rough passages, as I have hitherto met with.

These are the sentiments of my spleen and indolence; and indeed I must confess, that philosophy has nothing to oppose to them, and expects a victory more from the returns of a serious good-humor'd disposition, than from the force of reason and conviction. In all the incidents of life we ought still to preserve our scepticism. If we believe, that fire warms, or water refreshes, 'tis only because it costs us too much pains to think otherwise. Nay if we are philosophers, it ought only to be upon sceptical principles, and from an inclination, which we feel to the employing ourselves after that manner. Where reason is lively, and mixes itself with some propensity, it ought to be assented to. Where it does not, it never can have any title to operate upon us.

At the time, therefore, that I am tired with amusement and company, and have indulg'd a *reverie* in my chamber, or in a solitary walk by a river-side, I feel my mind all collected within itself, and am naturally *inclin'd* to carry my view into all those subjects, about which I have met with so many disputes in the course of my reading and conversation. I cannot forbear having a curiosity to be acquainted with the principles of moral good and evil, the nature and foundation of government, and the cause of those several passions and inclinations, which actuate and govern me. I am uneasy to think I approve of one object, and disapprove of another; call one thing beautiful, and another deform'd; decide concerning truth and falsehood, reason and folly, without knowing upon what principles I proceed. I am concern'd for the condition of the learned world, which lies under such a deplorable ignorance in all these particulars. I feel an ambition to arise in me of contributing to the instruction of mankind, and of acquiring a name by my inventions and discoveries. These sentiments spring up naturally in my present disposition; and shou'd I endeavour to banish them, by attaching myself to any other business or diversion. I *feel* I shou'd be a loser in point of pleasure; and this is the origin of my philosophy.

Part V ⚹ Kant and the Golden Age of German Philosophy

16 ✿ Kant

16.0 Kant (1724–1804)

Immanuel Kant was born at Königsberg in East Prussia (today's Russia), where his grandfather had emigrated from Scotland. The school he attended raised children according to the tenets of Pietism, a seventeenth-century Christian evangelical movement emphasizing devotional meetings, Bible study, and personal religious experience. His mother, who had no formal education, and his father, who made saddles for a living, wanted him to have a college education and so in 1740, when he was sixteen, they enrolled him in the University of Königsberg. At the time, the philosophy of Leibniz and the science of Newton dominated not only the university but much of continental Europe; many, perhaps most, scholars had come to believe that philosophy, science, and mathematics would soon integrate into one complete system of knowledge.

By all accounts Kant was extremely studious and competent but showed no particular flair or originality; certainly his teachers had no idea that he would one day be regarded as one of the most important thinkers of modern times. After graduating he got no offer from the university. He supported himself over the next ten years by hiring himself out as a private tutor in science, mathematics, and philosophy. In 1755, the University of Königsberg offered him a job, a position as a lowly instructor without any official title. For the next fifteen years he dutifully stayed in this post without any promotion until 1770 when, at the age of forty-six, he was finally promoted to professor of logic and metaphysics.

At one point he was reprimanded for the "distortion of many leading and fundamental doctrines of holy writ and Christianity," by no less than the Prussian king, Frederick William II. The king ordered Kant not to lecture or write further on such topics. Kant dutifully obeyed the king's orders until the day the king died, at which point Kant promptly resumed.

His personal life was anything but illustrious. He never married. He did not socialize, though he was known for his extreme politeness and graciousness. Not once during his entire life did he venture outside of town. The only time he went out was for his daily walk at half past four, when he walked up and down his little street exactly eight times. He would give his lectures; he would come home; he would go for his walk. His neighbors considered him a charming, if rather reclusive, eccentric.

Then, when Kant was fifty-seven, he published his first philosophy book. At first the reception was mixed. Some claimed it made no sense and was practically unreadable. Others thought it was nonsense. Some thought that it was the greatest single work in philosophy ever written.

The book, *Critique of Pure Reason*, turned out to be beyond any doubt one of the major achievements in philosophy. Published in 1781, it brought Kant instant fame. Philosophers all over Europe suddenly began proclaiming themselves "Kantians," while others continued criticizing his work as derivative of Leibniz; still others, especially those steeped in Romanticism, claimed Kant did not fully understand the logical implications of his own views. In any case, it became the book every philosopher was talking and writing about. And then, two years later, in 1783, Kant published *Prolegomena to Any Future Metaphysics*, followed by *Principles of the Metaphysics of Ethics* in 1785, *Metaphysical First Principles of Natural Science* in 1786, a revision of *Critique of Pure Reason* in 1787, *Critique of Practical Reason* in 1788, *Critique of Judgment* in 1790, *Religion Within the Limits of Mere Reason* in 1793, and *Perpetual Peace* in 1795. Philosophy would never be the same again.

Contemporary philosopher Anthony Flew refers to Kant's *Critique of Pure Reason* as "one of the greatest masterpieces of philosophy, although also one of the most unreadable." Kant would not object. Kant called the *Critique* "dry, obscure, contrary to all ordinary ideas, and on top of that prolix." As a remedy he wrote the *Prolegomena to Any Future Metaphysics*. Designed for the use not of students but of teachers, the much shorter and more easily accessible *Prolegomena* provides the groundwork for understanding the *Critique of Pure Reason*. But the *Critique*, "which discusses the pure faculty of reason in its whole compass and bounds, will remain the foundation, to which the *Prolegomena*, as a preliminary exercise, refer; for critique as a science must first be established as complete and perfect before we can think of letting metaphysics appear on the scene or even have the most distant hope of attaining it."

16.1 Awakening from Dogmatic Slumbers

In the introduction to his *Prolegomena*, Kant explains the role of David Hume in the development of his own philosophy:

⚹

Since the Essays of Locke and Leibnitz, or rather since the origin of metaphysics so far as we know its history, nothing has ever happened which was more decisive to its fate than the attack made upon it by David Hume. He threw no light on this species of knowledge, but he certainly struck a spark from which light might have been obtained, had it caught some inflammable substance and had its smoldering fire been carefully nursed and developed.

Hume started from a single but important concept in Metaphysics, viz., that of Cause and Effect (including its derivatives force and action, etc.). He challenges reason, which pretends to have given birth to this idea from herself, to answer him by what right she thinks anything to be so constituted, that if that thing be posited, something else also must necessarily be posited; for this is the meaning of the concept of cause. He demonstrated irrefutably that it was perfectly impossible for reason to think *a priori* and by means of concepts a combination involving necessity. We cannot at all see why, in consequence of the existence of one thing, another must necessarily exist, or how the concept of such a combination can arise *a priori*. Hence he inferred, that reason was altogether deluded with reference to this concept, which she erroneously considered as one of her children, whereas in reality it was nothing but a bastard of imagination, impregnated by experience, which subsumed certain representations under the Law of Association, and mistook the subjective necessity of habit for an objective necessity arising from insight. Hence he inferred that reason had no power to think such combinations, even generally, because her concepts would then be purely fictitious, and all her

From Immanuel Kant, *Prolegomena to Any Future Metaphysics*, Paul Carus, trans. (La Salle, IL: Open Court, 1902), with emendations by the author.

pretended *a priori* cognitions nothing but common experiences marked with a false stamp. In plain language there is not, and cannot be, any such thing as metaphysics at all. . . .

The question was not whether the concept of cause was right, useful, and even indispensable for our knowledge of nature, for this Hume had never doubted; but whether that concept could be thought by reason *a priori,* and consequently whether it possessed an inner truth, independent of all experience, implying a wider application than merely to the objects of experience. This was Hume's problem. It was a question concerning the *origin,* not concerning *the indispensable need* of the concept. Were the former decided, the conditions of the use and the sphere of its valid application would have been determined as a matter of course.

But to satisfy the conditions of the problem, the opponents of the great thinker should have penetrated very deeply into the nature of reason, so far as it is concerned with pure thinking,—a task which did not suit them. They found a more convenient method of being defiant without any insight, viz., the appeal to *common sense.* It is indeed a great gift of God, to possess right, or (as they now call it) plain common sense. But this common sense must be shown practically, by well-considered and reasonable thoughts and words, not by appealing to it as an oracle, when no rational justification can be advanced. To appeal to common sense, when insight and science fail, and no sooner—this is one of the subtle discoveries of modern times, by means of which the most superficial ranter can safely enter the lists with the most thorough thinker, and hold his own. But as long as a particle of insight remains, no one would think of having recourse to this subterfuge. For what is it but an appeal to the opinion of the multitude, of whose applause the philosopher is ashamed, while the popular charlatan glories and confides in it? I should think that Hume might fairly have laid as much claim to common sense as Beattie, and in addition to a critical reason (such as the latter did not possess), which keeps common sense in check and prevents it from speculating, or, if speculations are under discussion restrains the desire to decide because it cannot satisfy itself concerning its own arguments. By this means alone can common sense remain sound. Chisels and hammers may suffice to work a piece of wood, but for steel-engraving we require an engraver's needle. Thus common sense and speculative understanding are each serviceable in their own way, the former in judgments which apply immediately to experience, the latter when we judge universally from mere concepts as in metaphysics where sound common sense, so called in spite of the inapplicability of the word, has no right to judge at all.

I openly confess, the suggestion of David Hume was the very thing, which many years ago first interrupted my dogmatic slumber, and gave my investigations in the field of speculative philosophy quite a new direction.

⟡

First, what does Kant mean by *metaphysics?* The term is an arbitrary title, invented around 70 B.C.E. by Andronicus of Rhodes and given to a collection of Aristotle's writings that came after his *Physics,* meaning after (meta) the physics. Since then, however, the term has come to be used as a general one having to do with that aspect of philosophy which happened to be covered in that collection, "the study of being as such." Recall Descartes's discussion of the piece of wax (Section 10.5). First, Descartes notices that every one of *its* properties changes; to what, then, does the *it* refer, actually? Not the shape. Not the color. That which has shape and color. And what is that? All that remains the same across the changes is its "extension" (the thing does not cease to take up space), but neither space nor extension is itself an *object of perception*: all you ever see are colored shapes and figures. So the idea of there being something "beneath" all of the changes is the idea of *sub*stance, meaning, literally, "standing beneath," which, from the time of the ancient Greeks, came to be closely associated with the idea of reality, based on the notion that ultimate reality was permanent and unchanging (Parmenides, Section 1.10). But, furthermore, even if space or the idea of extension were the object of our perception, it would then be no different from any other aspect of the wax as it is represented in perception, since the perception I have of it is a case not of vision or touch or imagination . . . but of purely mental scrutiny.

Likewise for all objects that immediately appear before you right now—the book you hold in your hands, the light you see reflecting off the objects, all the things you see, smell, taste, and touch:

> I now know that even bodies are not strictly perceived by the senses or the faculty of the imagination but by the intellect alone, and that this perception derives not from their being touched or seen but from their being understood.

This, of course, is just the first principle of our notion of philosophical enlightenment: the awareness that our eyes are not windows—the one point that, according to Hume, all philosophers universally accept. Descartes, Hume, and Kant certainly accept it. But, in that case, how are we ever to have knowledge of the wax as it exists in reality, independently of our own understanding—knowledge of substance, of "being in itself"? Descartes's answer, and the answer of all so-called rationalist philosophers, is that the mind can have knowledge of physical substance through *pure reason*. It is possible for us to thus go beyond what is given to us in our own minds, as Spinoza and Leibniz also argued, using rational tools such as mathematics to polish the mind into perfection.

Apparently Kant, too, assumed that such a thing could be possible until he read Hume's criticisms of a priori necessary truths (found in the domain of "relations of ideas" vs. "matters of fact")—not that there aren't any, but that they are merely empty tautologies. The only possibly real content would have to come from a posteriori synthetic truths, which come to the mind in the form of perceptions; but, as Hume showed, these exist only as momentary, flickering sensations, or—even worse—as fictional abstract ideas in the mind. So how can we have knowledge of things in themselves? For Kant, this is not only the central problem for *metaphysics* but for the whole of philosophy.

16.2 Transcendental Idealism

Reflecting on the whole history of philosophy before him, Kant laments that every attempt to solve the problem of metaphysics thus far has been thwarted, not so much by *lack* of available solutions but by the presence of *too many* solutions. For every philosophical system there is a contrary philosophical system; for every solution to the problem of metaphysics, there is a competing solution in terms of a completely different method for acquiring true knowledge of reality:

> It seems almost ridiculous, while every other science is continually advancing, that in this, which pretends to be Wisdom incarnate, for whose oracle every one inquires, we should constantly move round the same spot, without gaining a single step.

What we need, then, is to be able to take the all-important first step in the right direction—but which way could that possibly be, asked Kant, when every attempt to solve the problem of metaphysics ends in a dead-end? Rationalist systems of pure reason, built using a priori analytic truths, give rise to dogmatic beliefs such as Berkeley's Omniperceiving God and Descartes's Self and Nondeceiving God. Empiricist systems of pure experience, built using a posteriori synthetic truths, give rise to skeptical doubts, such as Hume's No-Self, No-God, No-World. So Kant set out to find an alternative to both empiricism and rationalism as a way of avoiding both dogmatism and skepticism.

Recall Hume's analytic/synthetic distinction (pp. 317–320). Analytic propositions (like "All bachelors are married," where the predicate is already contained in the subject) are known a priori (that is, "independent of experience, and even of all sensuous expressions"), and synthetic propositions (like "The cat is hungry," where the predicate is not already contained in the subject) are known a posteriori (that is, by sense experience). Rationalists took the former path; empiricists took the latter. This brought us to Hume's fork (Section 15.2); both roads are a dead end. But what if there is a path between the two paths—one so narrow that every great philosopher had thus far missed it—and it took a scrupulous, methodical pedant like Kant to find it? "The path to truth is thin as a razor," warns an ancient proverb from the East. "Few can cross it without being divided." Kant will now attempt to walk that razor's edge.

He finds it in the thin and narrow, apparently self-contradictory, path that Hume failed to notice: the way of the *synthetic a priori*. It is possible, claims Kant, to make meaningful statements about the world that are derived from experience (but not in the way Hume and other empiricists thought), whose truth is known a priori—independently of any experience! This, then, becomes Kant's metaphysical path to knowledge, the way of synthetic a priori truths:

⟟

[M]etaphysics is properly concerned with synthetical propositions *a priori*, and these alone constitute its end, for which it indeed requires various dissections of its concepts, viz., of its analytical judgments, but wherein the procedure is not different from that in every other kind of knowledge, in which we merely seek to render our concepts distinct by analysis. But the generation of *a priori* cognition by concrete images as well as by concepts, in fine of synthetical propositions *a priori* in philosophical cognition, constitutes the essential subject of metaphysics. . . .

⟟

This is where Kant proceeds to forge a new philosophical path, at the juncture of Hume's fork, right at the point of contact between synthetic truth and analytic truth. According to Hume, Locke, Berkeley, Descartes, Leibniz, and every philosopher before Kant, there is no such point of contact between the two for the simple reason that there *can't* be. Yet Kant does not reject his predecessors; he begins, as Plato, Descartes, Locke, Berkeley, and Hume all did before him, with an acknowledgment of what we have been calling the first philosophical insight—the realization that our eyes are not windows. Thus far, he says it has led

either to Humean and other varieties of Skepticism or to Berkeleyan and other varieties of Idealism. Kant does not deny the single main insight of the whole history of philosophy, but he uses it in a different and unexpected way.

Kant, like Hume, points out that all philosophers agree that you do not directly experience objects out there in the world as they exist in themselves, independently of the mind. All you experience directly are objects of your own mind. These Kant calls *representations*—not of *impressions,* as Hume thought. That would lead either to Berkeleyan idealism, the view that there is no world beyond the mind, since the "representations" are themselves representing mental (phenomenal) objects. To view the phenomenal world (the world of your experience) as consisting in representations of phenomena is to be an idealist, pure and simple. Hence Berkeley's "to be is to be perceived" makes knowledge possible by making metaphysics—in the sense of knowing things in themselves as they exist beyond or outside our experience—*unnecessary*. But, in Berkeley's case, it requires the dogma of abstract ideas like God or, as Hume points out, the Self, which are mere fictions, and so without the weight of metaphysics the idealist system evaporates. In the case of materialist philosophies, it requires abstract ideas like cause and effect, or material substance, that then collapses under the weight of their metaphysics, leaving an unbridgeable gap between the phenomenal world of appearances and what Kant calls the *noumenal* world of things in themselves (discussed in detail in the next section). This name is the one he gives to the real world as it is in itself, independently of our representations, which he admits we can know absolutely nothing about *except* that it exists *as such* because all we are ever directly aware of is the activity of our own minds; all we ever have access to is our own representations of things and not the things in themselves. How can we know things in themselves, when our experience connects us, ultimately, not to things in themselves but only to ourselves and—if Hume is correct—not even to ourselves? How can such a mind-independent world ever be *reachable* given that there is no path into the mind from such a world, and no way from the mind out into the world?

We've already noted the similarity between an aspect of Augustine's philosophical system, built in the fourth century, and that of Descartes, especially in terms of Augustine's argument that his own existence could be known by him with absolute certainty (Section 5.2). Now we note another similarity—with Kant. For, like Augustine, Kant's elaborate metaphysics is predicated on a threefold division of the mind, three "faculties" which he calls *intuition, understanding,* and *reason.* He then performs what he calls a *transcendental analysis* of each of these faculties. That is Kant in a nutshell. But let us see what is involved.

First, let us get clear on what Kant means by *intuitions.* This is potentially confusing, for what he means is really the same thing that Hume meant by the terms *impressions* and *perceptions.* All the things you are seeing right now are, in Kant's vocabulary, your own intuitions of things, not things in themselves. Readers are often confused because they think of the word *intuition* in its vernacular English sense of hunches, thoughts, or gut feelings. What Kant means is *perception,* but his concern is not with a Humean introspective analysis of the phenomena of perception; rather, the key question for Kant is *how is perception possible?*

⁂

[S]ensuous perception represents things not at all as they are, but only the mode in which they affect our senses, and consequently by sensuous perception appearances only and not things themselves are given to the understanding for reflexion. After this necessary corrective, an objection rises from an unpardonable and almost intentional misconception, as if my doctrine turned all the things of the world of sense into mere illusion.

When an appearance is given us, we are still quite free as to how we should judge the matter. The appearance depends upon the senses, but the judgment upon the understanding, and the only

From Kant, *Prolegomena.*

question is, whether in the determination of the object there is truth or not. But the difference between truth and dreaming is not ascertained by the nature of the representations, which are referred to objects (for they are the same in both cases), but by their connexion according to those rules, which determine the coherence of the representations in the concept of an object, and by ascertaining whether they can subsist together in experience or not. And it is not the fault of the appearances if our cognition takes illusion for truth, i.e., if the intuition, by which an object is given us, is considered a concept of the thing or of its existence also, which the understanding can only think. The senses represent to us the paths of the planets as now progressive, now retrogressive, and herein is neither falsehood nor truth, because as long as we hold this path to be nothing but appearance, we do not judge of the objective nature of their motion. But as a false judgment may easily arise when the understanding is not on its guard against this subjective mode of representation being considered objective, we say they appear to move backward; it is not the senses however which must be charged with the illusion, but the understanding, whose province alone it is to give an objective judgment on appearances.

Thus, even if we did not at all reflect on the origin of our representations, whenever we connect our intuitions of sense (whatever they may contain), in space and in time, according to the rules of the coherence of all cognition in experience, illusion or truth will arise according as we are negligent or careful. It is merely a question of the use of sensuous representations In the understanding, and not of their origin. In the same way, if I consider all the representations of the senses, together with their form, space and time, to be nothing but appearances, and space and time to be a mere form of the sensibility, which is not to be met with in objects out of it, and if I make use of these representations in reference to possible experience only, there is nothing in my regarding them as appearances that can lead astray or cause illusion. For all that they can correctly cohere according to rules of truth in experience. Thus all the propositions of geometry hold good of space as well as of all the objects of the senses, consequently of all possible experience, whether I consider space as a mere form of the sensibility, or as something cleaving to the things themselves. In the former case however I comprehend how I can know *a priori* these propositions concerning all the objects of external intuition. Otherwise, everything else as regards all possible experience remains just as if I had not departed from the vulgar view.

But if I venture to go beyond all possible experience with my notions of space and time, which I cannot refrain from doing if I proclaim them qualities inherent in things in themselves (for what should prevent me from letting them hold good of the same things, even though my senses might be different, and unsuited to them?), then a grave error may arise due to illusion, for thus I would proclaim to be universally valid what is merely a subjective condition of the intuition of things and sure only for all objects of sense, viz., for all possible experience; I would refer this condition to things in themselves, and do not limit it to the conditions of experience.

My doctrine of the ideality of space and of time, therefore, far from reducing the whole sensible world to mere illusion, is the only means of securing the application of one of the most important cognitions (that which mathematics propounds *a priori*) to actual objects, and of preventing its being regarded as mere illusion. For without this observation it would be quite impossible to make out whether the intuitions of space and time, which we borrow from no experience, and which yet lie in our representation *a priori*, are not mere phantasms of our brain, to which objects do not correspond, at least not adequately, and consequently, whether we have been able to show its unquestionable validity with regard to all the objects of the sensible world just because they are mere appearances.

Secondly, though these my principles make appearances of the representations of the senses, they are so far from turning the truth of experience into mere illusion, that they are rather the only means of preventing the transcendental illusion, by which metaphysics has hitherto been deceived, leading to the childish endeavor of catching at bubbles, because appearances, which are mere representations, were taken for things in themselves. Here originated the remarkable event of the antimony of Reason which I shall mention by and by, and which is destroyed by the single observation, that appearance, as long as it is employed in experience, produces truth, but the moment it transgresses the bounds of experience, and consequently becomes transcendent, produces nothing but illusion.

Inasmuch, therefore, as I leave to things as we obtain them by the senses their actuality, and only limit our sensuous intuition of these things to this, that they represent in no respect, not even in the pure intuitions of space and of time, anything more than mere appearance of those things, but never their constitution in themselves, this is not a sweeping illusion invented for nature by me. My protestation too against all charges of idealism is so valid and clear as even to seem superfluous, were there not incompetent judges, who, while they would have in old name for every deviation from their perverse though common opinion, and never judge of the spirit of philosophic nomenclature, but cling to the letter only, are ready to put their own conceits in the place of well-defined notions, and thereby deform and distort them. I have myself given this my theory the name of transcendental idealism, but that cannot authorise any one to confound it either with the empirical idealism of Descartes (indeed, his was only an insoluble problem, owing to which he thought every one at liberty to deny the existence of the corporeal world, because it could never be proved satisfactorily), or with the mystical and visionary idealism of Berkeley, against which and other similar phantasms our Critique contains the proper antidote. My idealism concerns not the existence of things (the doubting of which, however, constitutes idealism in the ordinary sense), since it never came into my head to doubt it, but it concerns the sensuous representation of things, to which space and time especially belong. Of these [viz., space and time], consequently of all appearances in general, I have only shown, that they are neither things (but mere modes of representation), nor determinations belonging to things in themselves. But the word "transcendental," which with me means a reference of our cognition, i.e., not to things, but only to the cognitive faculty, was meant to obviate this misconception. Yet rather than give further occasion to it by this word, I now retract it, and desire this idealism of mine to be called critical. But if it be really an objectionable idealism to convert actual things (not appearances) into mere representations, by what name shall we call him who conversely changes mere representations to things? It may, I think, be called "dreaming idealism," in contradistinction to the former, which may be called "visionary," both of which are to be refuted by my transcendental, or, better, critical idealism.

※

The previous passage begins with, "sensuous perception represents things not at all as they are, but . . . appearances only and not things themselves are given to the understanding for reflection." That's our "eyes are not windows" point. Again, it is the one point Hume identified as being the only proposition that is

※

universally allowed by philosophers, and is besides pretty obvious of itself, that nothing is ever really present with the mind but its perceptions or impressions and ideas, and that external objects become known to us only by those perceptions they occasion. To hate, to love, to think, to feel, to see; all this is nothing but to perceive.

※

The point that eyes are not windows may be obvious "in itself," once one has thought about it, but it certainly is not obvious to an unreflective mind not steeped in philosophy. Kant insists that this fact should not be overlooked because he takes it to be a very important piece of information that these phenomena—all the things we feel and see—are themselves automatically interpreted by us, by the very thing that gives rise to them, not as *phenomena,* but as *things.* Hume had already said that this point is obvious, and by now it should seem at the very least *familiar* to you. But notice that things don't look any different once you know this! Knowing that your eyes are not windows does not change the quality of your perceptions in any way; they still don't start *seeming* to you like perceptions, mental phenomena, products of the imagination, dreams, or anything like that; the "things" you see still look to you like *things.* In other words, what is *not* obvious, at least not to an unreflective mind, is that what the mind is looking at are its own representations; once it is revealed that the things we

see are falsely (and quite automatically) interpreted by us as objects existing outside our minds, *this insight does not in any way alter the character of the phenomena.*

Let's make sure we understand. Look around. The objects you see don't *look* like visual phenomena, they don't *look* like mental images, they don't *look* like mere mental representations of things. Well, but that's not quite right. As we made clear at various points with exercises such as crossing your eyes or bringing things so close they are out of focus, the things you see can be made to *look* very much like what they are: images. When you cross your eyes and see two chairs where you once saw one, your visual experience very much *looks like* the sort of phenomenon you would expect from a mental apparition (you do not have the power to divide physical objects in two by crossing your eyes). But *even then* we interpret what we are looking at to be mind-independent physical objects, things in themselves (though again, Kant notes, this interpretation is not something we do but something that happens to us; that is, it is done for us by our own cognitive faculties). Thus, when Kant says that "the difference between truth and dreaming is not ascertained by the nature of the representations, which are referred to objects," Kant means just this: phenomena are *referred to objects* whether we are dreaming or awake; that is, referred to objects are taken to denote things like tables and chairs. In a manner of speaking, when you are dreaming your mind *becomes,* if you are dreaming about a chair, a phenomenal representation of a chair; likewise, when you are awake and in the presence of a chair, your mind again *becomes* a phenomenal representation of a chair. There's no *phenomenal* difference between the two states. What then *is* the difference?

The key difference is, remarkably and paradoxically, as similar to Descartes's method as it is different from it. Recall that Descartes forged a new (though, again, Augustine-inspired) path to certainty by doubting. Specifically, he discovered that *in the act of maximal doubting,* while realizing that he might be deceived about everything, he could then see the one thing he could not be deceived of, and see it with absolute certainty: his own existence. In Kant's transcendental analysis, the focus is not on one's existence per se. Rather, it goes like this. You realize that the things you are looking at when you are experiencing phenomena are not things in themselves but, at best, representations of those things. You realize that you never see outside yourself, that everything you will ever know, or can ever know through the having of experience, are only your own mental states as such. Then, and only then, in the very midst of this realization that what you are looking at is not reality as it exists in itself but only your own representation of it, you realize that there is and must be something making it possible for you to have representations as such *and that this is known by you with absolute certainty*. At one point, Kant illustrates with the paradigm example of the planets:

᛭

The senses represent to us the paths of the planets as now forward, now backward, and herein is neither falsehood nor truth, because as long as we hold this path to be nothing but appearance, we do not judge of the objective nature of their motion. But as a false judgment may easily arise when the understanding does not carefully guard against this subjective mode of representation being considered objective, we say they appear to move backward; it is not the senses however which are charmed with the illusion, but the understanding, whose province alone it is to give an objective judgment on the phenomenon.

᛭

In other words, it is not the fault of our phenomena that they are phenomena! What else but phenomena can they be? If actual physical chairs entered our brains we would die. You can't put *real*, objective objects into the mind. So the source of error lies not in the phenomena but in our understanding of the phenomena. Ordinarily, we don't understand that phenomena are

phenomena. We don't *experience* the process by which phenomena are created. All we experience is the effect: the objects we see. We don't see how they're constructed by our own minds. We don't consciously know how this is happening. In our own *subjectivity* we understand the phenomena to be things in themselves, whereas *objectivity* requires us to understand that the phenomena are phenomena.

Experience will always have this illusory aspect to it. That is, the structuring of the objects of perception as if they were other than what they are is not a flaw in the mind to be fought against or removed but is itself *a necessary condition for the having of experience*. Do you see the subtle simplicity of this realization by Kant? To expect or look for a "direct" experience of reality is like trying to invent a language that consists, not of words (which are not things but only symbols standing for things), but of things. *Things do not a language make*.

You need nonthings, which are *not* rocks or chairs or tables or atoms or whatever is really out there (careful—those are just *words*, after all), but which are themselves *immaterial*, which is exactly what words are, and you need grammar, syntax, interpretation schemes, and so on. *Without language you just have an inert world of matter.* Likewise, *without phenomena you just have an inert world of "   ,"* whatever it is that *exists, things in themselves.*

We can carry this analogy with language even further. Already implicit in Hume's philosophy was the radical idea that *meaning* is up to a point man-made. Certain disputes, such as ones about the self, were purely verbal. Others, such as ones about identity, were not: they were truly meaningful, their meaning being a sort of midway interface between ideas, which are mental representations of impressions, and impressions. It was, for Hume, a proper sort of relation rather than a fictive one. Kant carries this one step further, to a meta-level. As we shall see, it is not just meaning (a linguistic phenomenon) but *objects* that are, in part, man-made. Which is *not* to say that Kant is espousing idealism:

⚹

These my principles, because they make phenomena of the representations of the senses, are so far from turning the truth of experience into mere illusion, that they are rather the only means of preventing the transcendental illusion, by which metaphysics has hitherto been deceived, and led to the childish endeavor of catching at bubbles, while phenomena, which are mere representations, were taken for things in themselves.

⚹

To see why representations—phenomena—are taken for things in themselves, we must understand what Kant means by the "transcendental illusion." He means just this: the illusion that your eyes are windows, that what you are seeing—the phenomena themselves, which are but your mind's representations, consisting of visual and tactile intuitions—are things existing outside you, independently of the mind. It is this illusion that gives rise to the various "antinomies of reason," contradictory systems by which philosophies flip flop back and forth, like a Necker cube, between materialism and idealism, dogmatism and skepticism, atheism and theism, deism and pantheism, a one-self view to a no-self view, and so on. All such antinomies, Kant argues, are "destroyed by the single observation, that *phenomenon*, as long as it is used in experience, produces truth, but the moment it transgresses the bounds of experience, and consequently becomes transcendent, produces nothing but illusion."

Think again in terms of our analogy with language. As long as we are perfectly clear about what words are and what they are not, then *the mere fact that words exist and can do what they do* can be used to distinguish the true from the false. But not just in the domain of language. It is more like the world itself has a grammar and a syntax, a logic by which it operates, and these structure both language, which is a representation of the world, and that which is represented by language.

But let us continue to proceed slowly, step by step, making sure that we understand exactly what Kant is doing *and how he is doing it*. For Kant is the all-important figure for much of the philosophy that follows, both as an inspiration for it and as a sort of metaphysical sounding board against which many will try to build opposing systems.

The passage we read ends with Kant saying that what in *Critique of Pure Reason* he called "transcendental idealism" he now wishes to call "critical" or "visionary" idealism. The all-important point is that when he called his philosophy "transcendental," he did not mean to imply that it was somehow possible to transcend the phenomena and thereby reach the things in themselves. This would be akin, in his view, to trying *really hard* to use the word *dog* until it becomes a dog. The word never will become the object (and if it does, you've lost your mind; that is, then you know you're *really* dreaming!). Rather, what he means is that his critical method of transcendental analysis can be used to transcend phenomena, *not for the purposes of reaching the noumenal world,* which is impossible, but for reaching *the three cognitive faculties of the mind.*

Before we go into even more detail to see exactly what this means, let us pause to address the revolution in thought that is here unfolding. For therein lies the whole secret behind Kant's metaphysics.

16.3 Kant's "Copernican Revolution"

We've already touched upon one of the major assumptions underlying not just the Newtonian worldview but nearly every view ever held of the relationship between our minds and reality: namely, the assumption that our minds are passive perceivers of reality and not in any way the creators of it. This assumption also seems too obvious to question! To question it seems to move us away from the domain of philosophy into the world of myth, magic, and shamanism of the most blatant and superstitious kind. After all, to find such beliefs one would have to go all the way back to prehistoric pagans, who believed that things like wishing, human emotions, and beliefs could affect reality! Someone might put a curse on you, or you might have to appease some ancient spirit lest the weather destroy you, and so on. But of course, if you think about it, such beliefs have nevertheless persisted into the modern period through the idea of a God who, as essentially a *mind* or *spirit,* affects not just individual aspects of reality but the *whole* of reality. Today many people believe that while their own minds cannot turn thoughts into reality simply by wishing, they can express their wishes to some "divine" mind that *can* then affect reality in exactly that way. Likewise, there have always been stories about certain special individuals who have unique powers to influence or bring about, through their thoughts and wills alone, real events beyond their minds: people who bend spoons, make accidents happen (or not), and so on. But what if such a "link" between mind and reality exists, not just in the domain of religion and magic, but in the very underpinnings of the world itself, *within you?* What if it was operating right now, everywhere, and at all times, even *within you?*

Such an idea may seem the stuff of weird science fiction or the twilight zone, but in some ways this is exactly Kant's claim. Transcend the phenomena by recognizing them as such and you reach the realm of the cognitive faculties— the Kantian threefold division of the mind into *intuition* (perception), *understanding,* and *reason.* And what are they, really, these cognitive faculties? What powers do they have? Not just the power to create the phenomena we see; that is obvious from the fact that we experience phenomena as such. Our cognitive faculties, Kant argues, also affect the objects. They are not, as Hume and other empiricist philosophers have thought, purely passive. In a way, Kant is reversing Locke's idea of (primary and secondary) qualities (Section 13.1) that we explained in terms of *powers* of objects in the real world

(things in themselves) to affect our minds, which are passive receivers, blank slates, and so on. He is ascribing such active powers not to inanimate things but to the cognitive faculties, the powers of the mind.

Thus, it is the faculty of the understanding that gives an order and regularity to "the phenomena which we call nature." And where do the so-called laws of nature come from? *It is we who are their source.* For, as he concludes in the following selection from his *Critique of Pure Reason,* "However exaggerated therefore and absurd it may sound, that the understanding is itself the source of the laws of nature, and of its formal unity, such a statement is nevertheless correct and in accordance with experience":

⚖

It is we therefore who carry into the phenomena which we call nature, order and regularity, nay, we should never find them in nature, if we ourselves, or the nature of our mind, had not originally placed them there. For the unity of nature is meant to be a necessary and a *priori* certain unity in the connection of all phenomena. And how should we a *priori* have arrived at such a synthetical unity, if the subjective grounds of such unity were not contained a *priori* in the original sources of our knowledge, and if those subjective conditions did not at the same time possess objective validity, as being the grounds on which alone an object becomes possible in our experience? . . .

However exaggerated therefore and absurd it may sound, that the understanding is itself the source of the laws of nature, and of its formal unity, such a statement is nevertheless correct and in accordance with experience. It is quite true, no doubt, that empirical laws, as such, cannot derive their origin from the pure understanding, as little as the infinite manifoldness of phenomena could be sufficiently comprehended through the pure form of sensuous intuition. But all empirical laws are only particular determinations of the pure laws

---

From Immanuel Kant, *Critique of Pure Reason,* F. Max Muller, trans. (London, 1881), with emendations by the author.

of the understanding, under which and according to which the former become possible, and phenomena assume a regular form, quite as much as all phenomena, in spite of the variety of their empirical form, must always submit to the conditions of the pure form of sensibility.

⚖

First, lest you think that this idea is just plain crazy, consider this: how much crazier is the idea that an *inanimate, lifeless* object has such powers over *you*? In other words, which is more bizarre—that lifeless, inert matter can affect the mind, or that the you, a mind, consisting not just in phenomena but in cognitive faculties producing them (already recognized by anyone who has thought about it as a great power), can affect *them*, the inert lifeless things in themselves?

Second, you may get a clearer sense of what Kant is here doing if you think back once again to our analogy with language. What do dogs, cats, tables, and chairs have to do with the existence of the words dog, cat, table, and chair within our language? The answer isn't just "nothing." If there weren't any such things in any sense of the word, the cognitive apparatus through which language emerges would not have responded by inventing such sounds and giving them references. And, likewise, what do these words have to do with the things? Here you may be tempted to answer "nothing," but clearly in the cases of tables and chairs and other man-made objects that is not true. Words have a lot to do with the existence of those things. But in the case of *phenomena*, the connection is even stronger. What Kant is saying is that the cognitive apparatus through which phenomena appear in us is itself something that functions in the world as such and is operating under the same laws.

Put the two together and you may begin to gain a glimpse into what Kant is saying about reality. Think of how many actual human experiences come about because of the generation, within our minds, of new phenomena and new words with which to interpret them. Concepts affect percepts, percepts affect concepts; Kant will extend this sort of relationship into the domains of space, time, and causality. For example, how is it possible that we can express true sentences about the height of a mountain, if Hume and the empiricists are right in claiming that we never perceive space? According to Hume, perceptions consist only in ideas and impressions; impressions come in discrete bundles of sense-data, and ideas are merely representations of them, so we never really perceive space. Likewise, Kant asks, how is it possible that we can make true statements about how long it takes, say, to get from Berlin to Frankfurt, if Hume and the empiricists are correct in claiming that we never perceive time—only discrete impressions and ideas—which are their representations?

Kant's solution hinges on his ability to explain foundations of the faculty of perception through transcendental analysis. A posteriori sentences like "Mt. Everest is more than three feet tall" presuppose the truth of the sentence "Objects exist in space and time." But the fact is, Kant argues, that sometimes we can know that a sentence like "Mt. Everest is more than three feet tall" is true, *but such a sentence cannot be true unless the second sentence is also true.* However, the second sentence is not analytically true (it is not a contradiction to deny it), nor is it known to be true a posteriori (there is no impression of space or time on the basis of which an idea could form a legitimate representation). *So it must be a synthetic a priori truth.*

This statement is the crux of the new understanding of reality that Kant gave to the world. Many of the ideas behind twentieth-century scientific "revolutions" in thought, in which the boundary between mind and reality dissolves in exactly this way, such as Einstein's theory of relativity and the subsequent advent of quantum mechanics, can be found in Kant. Indeed, Albert Einstein said that reading Kant's *Critique of Pure Reason* and *Prolegomena to Any Future Metaphysics* had the greatest impact on him of all philosophical works and helped him in his development of relativity. (Think of Einstein's "frames of reference," of how *time slows down or speeds up relative to the motions of the observers,* and so on, and you will begin to understand the nature of the link.) It was Kant who first showed in what sense space, time, and causality—the very fabric of existence—are not mere figments of our imagination, as Hume supposed, nor are they fully objective realities, as Newton supposed. Rather, the entire phenomenal world in which we exist as phenomenal beings is an interface, a fulcrum between that which exists only in the mind and in reality as it exists in itself, independently of the mind.

This interface, then, is part of Kant's philosophical revolution, which he likened to a second "Copernican revolution," his revolution being not in natural philosophy (physics) but within the innermost core of *any* knowledge-seeking enterprise, without which no knowledge in any area can be possible: namely, epistemology. It is a reversal of the traditional epistemological question. Instead of asking how objects in the world affect the mind, Kant asks how the mind affects the objects of knowledge: "We must make trial whether we may not have more success in the tasks of metaphysics, if we suppose that objects must conform to our knowledge." This is how he creates a philosophical synthesis between the empiricism of Locke, Berkeley, and Hume and the rationalism of Descartes and Leibniz.

The world is real and it is not silent. Its language is not mathematics, not reason, not even logic. Objects are the illuminated words of the world, not shadows; they are speech itself.

16.4 The Phenomenal and Noumenal Worlds

The phenomenal world is *not* an illusion. It is real. So if it is true, then, that the phenomenal world is a collaboration between the three faculties of the mind and the noumenal world, it follows that *real* objects are partially constituted,

as real objects, by the mind. To understand how it is possible that such a constitution takes place requires Kant's method of analysis, which he called *transcendental deduction.* It transcends direct observation. It gets behind or underneath the phenomena to discover the necessary conditions of experience. We thereby look reflectively behind the phenomenal world of appearance and glimpse into the cognitive machinery that makes the phenomenal world possible.

Again, in calling this glimpsing behind the appearances *transcendental,* Kant does not mean that philosophical inquiry can reach outward into the world of things in themselves. Rather, it reaches back into itself, into the functional activities of the mind. How is the mind able to create, or structure, such a phenomenon? As we've just seen, it is because space and time are not features of external, noumenal reality but are themselves features of the structure of the mind.

The human mind analyzes *and synthesizes* the impressions it receives in terms of the categories of space and time. Space and time are our *two-way* "irremovable lenses" through which the phenomenal world is created. It would be wrong to say merely that we perceive the world through the lenses of space and time; that would be to take a Cartesian-Lockean-Berkelyan-Humean passive view of the mind. Anyway, what would "the world" in such a case refer to? We'd be right back with Humean fictions (or, at best, some theoretical construction). Rather, space and time both *inform the mind* and, in turn, *inform the phenomenal world.*

Think about a game of chess. The pieces are things. So is the board! Kant is *not* saying that space and time are like the board. Rather, he is saying that space and time are like the rules according to which the game of chess is played, without which the game of chess would cease to exist. What we call reality is a game of chess and each of us is an active player.

Or, take our old example of the chair. You see a chair. Forget about the chair "out there." Forget about the idea of atoms. *How is it possible that you are having this experience?* Remember, if you get confused, that the existence of a chair "out there" is not *necessary* for you to be having an experience of the chair. This is an extremely important thing to realize! Dreams are a quick proof. If you can experience phenomena such as a chair in a dream, this is an albeit indirect but vivid proof that the existence of physical chairs is not a necessary condition for there to exist the phenomenon of a chair. Do you see the point? Well, but what then makes it possible for you to have an experience of a chair, whether an imaginary chair that exists only in your imagination or an imaginary chair that exists as a representation of some real chair? Do you see what Kant is asking?

One thing that should bother you is that *you don't know the answer to that question*. The reason this should bother you is that now the focus and the burden are not on what is beyond you or outside you but on what is within you. Whether the chair you see exists *only* in the mind, and there is *nothing* out there of which it is an accurate (or inaccurate) representation, or whether the chair is a perfect representation, *you can't see how you're doing that*. Do you see why Kant is so concerned about transcending the phenomena, not to get to the "outside" noumenal world, but to get *inside ourselves*, to our own faculties of cognition? To put it colloquially: *that's* where the action is.

Another thing to notice is that *what we've just done* is to learn something not *by* experience but *through* experience; that is, we've just learned something by attending to our experience, not in terms of what it is *of* but what, in and of itself, it is like, and then inquiring into the question of how it could be like that. And this is how we got to the categories of space and time as being necessary conditions for the having of experience.

Besides the perceptual faculty—the having of *intuitions*—there is the faculty of understanding and the faculty of reason. Both of these, too, are reachable through transcendental deductions. It is the faculty of understanding that makes it possible for us to understand, not just facts about the world (the phenomenal world, that is) but all the things we've just been talking about:

⚮

We have before given various definitions of the understanding, by calling it the spontaneity of knowledge (as opposed to the receptivity of the senses), or the faculty of thinking, or the faculty of concepts or of judgments; all of these explanations, if more closely examined, coming to the same. We may now characterise it as *the faculty of rules*. This characteristic is more significant, and approaches nearer to the essence of the understanding. The senses give us forms (of intuition), the understanding rules, being always busy to examine phenomena, in order to discover in them some kind of rule.

Rules, so far as they are objective (therefore necessarily inherent in our knowledge of an object), are called laws. Although experience teaches us many laws, yet these are only particular determinations of higher laws, the highest of them, to which all others are subject, springing *a priori* from the understanding; not being derived from experience, but, on the contrary, imparting to the phenomena their regularity, and thus making experience possible. The understanding therefore is not only a power of making rules by a comparison of phenomena, it is itself the lawgiver of nature, and without the understanding nature, that is, a synthetical unity of the manifold of phenomena, according to rules, would be nowhere to be found, because phenomena, as such, cannot exist without us, but exist in our sensibility only. This sensibility, as an object of our knowledge in any experience, with everything it may contain, is possible only in the unity of apperception, which unity of apperception is the transcendental ground of the necessary order of all phenomena in an experience. The same unity of apperception with reference to the manifold of representations (so as to comprehend it in one) forms what we call the rule, and the faculty of these rules I call the understanding. As possible experience therefore, all phenomena depend in the same way *a priori* on the understanding, and receive their formal possibility from it as, when looked upon as mere intuitions, they depend on sensibility, and become possible through it, so far as their form is concerned.

The pure understanding is therefore in the categories the law of the synthetical unity of all phenomena, and thus makes experience, so far as its form is concerned, for the first time possible. This, and no more than this, we were called upon to prove in the transcendental deduction of the categories, namely, to make the relation of the understanding to our sensibility, and through it to all objects of experience, that is the objective validity of the pure concepts of the understanding, conceivable *a priori*, and thus to establish their origin and their truth.

⚹

Recall the sense in which the answer to the question, "What am I seeing the objects of my perceptions *with*?" is *not* "the eyes!" At most, for philosophers like Descartes, Locke, and Berkeley, the eyes bring in *nonperceptual* information (wavelengths of light, and so on) to the body. Rather, it is the *understanding* by which they all meant (in various ways) something like the "mind's eye." Kant goes into this eye; it is for him, to use a horribly bad but rather appropriate phrase, the phenomenal eye of the soul. Remember, when you're dreaming, What do you see the dream *with*? Not your eyes! But the same phenomenon is going on right now, Kant would remind you, as when you dream. The only difference is that the phenomena you experience in dreams are *not* real, whereas the phenomena you experience in waking life (a sort of "waking dream," if you like) *are* real. And so for Kant it is the faculty of the understanding that not only passively apprehends phenomena (as it does for Descartes, Locke, and Berkeley), but actively imbues them with the meanings that they have in all the various ways in which meaning occurs—not only in the phenomenal and intellectual realms but even, as we shall see in the next section, in the moral realms.

By peering into the understanding, Kant analyzes it into "the categories of the understanding," which he identifies as unity/plurality/totality, causality, and substantiality. These concepts are *not* deduced from reality—neither from the noumenal world nor from the phenomenal world—by the mind; that is, they are not themselves, in any sense, phenomenal representations, and they are not noumenal things in themselves.

Rather, such categories are structural/functional rules *for phenomena and meaning formation* which the mind brings to the phenomena and imparts to the real world. That is why Hume could not find them when he looked for them! They do not exist out there in the world. Sentences such as "Every event has a cause," which are neither analytic nor synthetic according to Hume, are paradigms of *synthetic a priori truths* according to Kant.

In some ways this concept can be seen as a philosophical evolution of the doctrine of Plato's forms or Descartes's doctrine of innate ideas. The big difference is that, in Kant's view, these categories of the understanding are not ideas that we are born with; rather, the mind is structured in such a way that it analyzes its own data in terms of a priori rules of thought. These rules are like the operating system on a computer, nowhere apparent but everywhere essential. For instance, computers use an operating system to structure *everything* within them; the categories are thus like the permanent part of the mind's operating system that produce ideas when either the senses or the cognitive apparatus of the mind provides information. That is how the mind makes sense of the world, using concepts such as time, space, substantiality, and causality. We are thus programmed, for instance, to see the world as consisting of things, each of which has "thingness," although there exists nothing "out there," in the noumenal world, that is itself a *thing* in the sense of any type of *substance*. Likewise, the mind is forced by its very programming at the most fundamental level to conceive of things in terms of cause and effect, even though nothing exists out there in the noumenal world that is the cause of anything. Thus, we may now be in a position to understand Kant's famous phrase: thoughts without content are empty; intuitions without concepts are blind.

For Kant, then, there are two distinct realities: the *phenomenal world* of appearance and representation, and the *noumenal world* of things in themselves. The noumenal world cannot be known by the mind; we can know the world only as it is interpreted and structured through the mind's categories and represented as phenomena. The key to his "transcendental" philosophy consists in the mind's coming to be aware that the phenomenal world of appearances consists not of things in the world as they exist in themselves but the mind's own representations of things as interpreted through and structured by its own categories. This means that when I open my eyes and am confronted by all the visible objects in my field of vision, I must learn to recognize that what I am looking at is a sort of virtual reality, a world of my own ideas, representations of objects in the world, and not the objects in the world as they exist in themselves. And yet Kant claims not to be an idealist (at least not in Berkeley's sense) because a phenomenon experienced as a representation of an object—say, the chair I see—is in fact the product of two causes: the mind and the chair in itself. In other words, as a phenomenal object the chair represented to me as a phenomenon exists as an interface between the mind and the world. Kant's phenomenal world is, therefore, *real*. He explicitly shuns the title of idealism, which he says should better be put on the ordinary, naive view of reality that takes what are in fact phenomena and treats them as things in themselves—what he calls "dreaming idealism" in contrast to his enlightened, *transcendental*, or *critical*, idealism.

What about the third Kantian faculty of the mind, the faculty of reason? It is the faculty of reason that produces the *pure* concepts—those concepts that are "uncontaminated" by the senses—the domain of *pure reason*. What are those concepts? And are they real?

Given the title of his most famous work, *Critique of Pure Reason*, the answer should not be surprising, although many found it devastating. The paradigms of pure concepts are "God" and "soul." The question then becomes: Are there any synthetic a priori grounds for believing in God or the soul? Kant's notorious answer is an unmitigated, absolute, resounding *no.*

What about other pure concepts, such as freedom and *justice*?

Here Kant spawned a second sort of revolution, one that led to the subsequent varieties of a very influential movement within philosophy known as *pragmatism*. Although we cannot predicate any sort of metaphysical necessity to any aspect of the ethical and moral realms, we can find there a sort of *practical,* what he calls *moral,* necessity. Before we turn to Kant's moral realm, we would do well to take a brief detour to the one philosopher who here influenced Kant more than any other: Rousseau.

16.5 Rousseau (1712–1778): The Romantic Legacy

In Kant's study, directly above his desk, next to a large picture window that opened out into the street, hung a portrait of Jean-Jacques Rousseau, whom Kant called "the Newton of the moral world."

Rousseau was born in Geneva, Switzerland. His father, a watchmaker, had to raise him alone after his mother died a few days after his birth. Instead of a formal education his father gave him a variety of novels along with the works of Plutarch (46–119), whose *Parallel Lives,* an extensive biography of great Greek and Roman figures, tries to elucidate the universal ideas of human greatness through formal comparisons of different individuals paired by similarities of deeds and strengths of character. At the age of ten his father put him in the care of an aunt and uncle who sent him off to boarding school where "we were to learn . . . all the insignificant trash that has obtained the name of education," as he wrote in his *Confessions.* He objected so vehemently that they apprenticed him to an engraver, which he despised even more than boarding school, and so in 1728 he ran away to France where he met an older noblewoman, Madame de Warens, who virtually adopted him and eventually became his lover.

Warens tried to have young Rousseau formally educated at various institutions, including the Hospice of the Holy Spirit in Turin (a

Lazarist seminary) where he converted from orthodox Calvinism to Catholicism (he would later convert again, to Protestantism), and then the choir school of the cathedral at Annecy. Still unhappy with his schooling, Rousseau tried his hand at a variety of jobs, including engraving, copying music, and giving music lessons. In the seven years he was Warens's live-in lover, Rousseau spent his time composing music and studying Plato, Montaigne, Pascal, Virgil, and Horace, as well as reading the works of the contemporary French Enlightenment movement: Voltaire (1694–1778); Montesquieu (1689–1755); Diderot (1713–1784), who became his close friend; and Condorcet (1743–1794). During this time Rousseau invented a new scheme of musical notation and wrote an opera, a play, and even a collection of poems. Though he had little success with any of these early projects, his ballet, *les Muses Galantes,* was performed at the Paris Opera in 1747 but its reception was lukewarm. When Warens took on a younger lover, Rousseau began an affair with a servant in a hotel, with whom he had five children; although he eventually married her, he sent all their children to orphanages.

At the age of thirty-seven, Rousseau entered a Dijon academy essay contest on the question of whether the revival of the arts and sciences had purified or corrupted morals. Opposing the church's view that humans are by nature sinners who need orthodox institutions to make them good, Rousseau argued in his essay, *Discourse on the Arts and Science,* that it is the institutions of learning that make human beings bad. The arts and the sciences, he claimed, are themselves the worst corrupters because they mold our behavior and condition us away from the brute, primordial passions we had in a state of nature: by conditioning our speech, our thoughts, and our emotions away from what we really feel and think, the arts and sciences bribe us with promises of wealth and luxury, corrupting us into living false, artificial lives of self-deception.

Not only did his essay win first prize, almost overnight Rousseau became famous throughout Europe. Within a year, his operetta, *Le Devin du Village,* was performed before the court of King Louis XV and his comedy, *Narcisse,* played at the prestigious Theatre Francais. One success followed another. In 1755 he published his *Discourse on What Is the Origin of the Inequality Among Men and Is It Authorized by Natural Law?,* a more thorough version of the arguments presented in the prize-winning Dijon essay. His novel, *Julie, ou la Nouvelle Heloise* (1761) became the most celebrated novel of the eighteenth century and helped launch the romantic movement in literature; he followed it a year later with *Emile,* a fictional account of his provocative new approach to education.

His most famous work, also published that year, *The Social Contract,* begins with the famous words, "Man is born free; and everywhere he is in chains," and goes on to describe the transition from the original "state of nature," in which all human beings once lived, to the modern "civil state." The lasting influence of Plutarch, who had been initiated in the mystical rites of Dionysus and inspired by the Stoics, Pythagoreans, and Peripatetics (except Epicurus), is evident throughout; many footnotes refer explicitly to details found in Plutarch.

⚘

The Social Contract

Subject of the First Book

Man is born free; and everywhere he is in chains. One thinks himself the master of others, and still remains a greater slave than they. How did this change come about? I do not know. What can make it legitimate? That question I think I can answer.

If I took into account only force, and the effects derived from it, I should say: "As long as a people is compelled to obey, and obeys, it does well; as

---

From Jean-Jacques Rousseau, *The Social Contract,* G. H. H. Cole, trans. (New York: E. P. Dutton, 1913), with emendations by the author.

soon as it can shake off the yoke, and shakes it off, it does still better; for, regaining its liberty by the same right as took it away, either it is justified in resuming it, or there was no justification for those who took it away." But the social order is a sacred right which is the basis of all rights. Nevertheless, this right does not come from nature, and must therefore be founded on conventions. . . .

The Social Compact

I suppose men to have reached the point at which the obstacles in the way of their preservation in the state of nature show their power of resistance to be greater than the resources at the disposal of each individual for his maintenance in that state. That primitive condition can then subsist no longer; and the human race would perish unless it changed its manner of existence.

But, as men cannot engender new forces, but only unite and direct existing ones, they have no other means of preserving themselves than the formation, by aggregation, of a sum of forces great enough to overcome the resistance. These they have to bring into play by means of a single motive power, and cause to act in concert.

This sum of forces can arise only where several persons come together: but, as the force and liberty of each man are the chief instruments of his self-preservation, how can he pledge them without harming his own interests, and neglecting the care he owes to himself? This difficulty, in its bearing on my present subject, may be stated in the following terms:

"The problem is to find a form of association which will defend and protect with the whole common force the person and goods of each associate, and in which each, while uniting himself with all, may still obey himself alone, and remain as free as before." This is the fundamental problem of which the *Social Contract* provides the solution.

The clauses of this contract are so determined by the nature of the act that the slightest modification would make them vain and ineffective; so that, although they have perhaps never been formally set forth, they are everywhere the same and everywhere tacitly admitted and recognized, until, on the violation of the social compact, each regains his original rights and resumes his natural liberty, while losing the conventional liberty in favor of which he renounced it.

These clauses, properly understood, may be reduced to one—the total alienation of each associate, together with all his rights, to the whole community; for, in the first place, as each gives himself absolutely, the conditions are the same for all; and, this being so, no one has any interest in making them burdensome to others.

Moreover, the alienation being without reserve, the union is as perfect as it can be, and no associate has anything more to demand: for, if the individuals retained certain rights, as there would be no common superior to decide between them and the public, each, being on one point his own judge, would ask to be so on all; the state of nature would thus continue, and the association would necessarily become inoperative or tyrannical.

Finally, each man, in giving himself to all, gives himself to nobody; and as there is no associate over which he does not acquire the same right as he yields others over himself, he gains an equivalent for everything he loses, and an increase of force for the preservation of what he has.

If then we discard from the social compact what is not of its essence, we shall find that it reduces itself to the following terms:

"Each of us puts his person and all his power in common under the supreme direction of the general will, and, in our corporate capacity, we receive each member as an indivisible part of the whole."

At once, in place of the individual personality of each contracting party, this act of association creates a moral and collective body, composed of as many members as the assembly contains voters, and receiving from this act its unity, its common identity, its life, and its will. This public person, so formed by the union of all other persons, formerly took the name of city, and now takes that of *Republic* or *body politic;* it is called by its members *State* when passive, *Sovereign* when active, and *Power* when compared with others like itself. Those who are associated in it take collectively the name of *people,* and severally are called *citizens,* as sharing in the sovereign power, and *subjects,* as being under the laws of the State. But these terms are often confused and taken one for another: it is enough to know how to distinguish them when they are being used with precision.

⚓

Like all of Rousseau's other works, *The Social Contract* is critical not only of Christianity but also of rationality and philosophical skepticism. Subsequently, in the end the French authorities took offense and issued a warrant for his arrest. He escaped and spent his remaining years as a fugitive, condemned by both church and state authorities. With the help of David Hume he lived in exile in England for sixteen months. Convinced that his enemies were still out to get him, however, he apparently began to suffer from paranoia and accused even Hume of conspiring against him. He returned to France using the pseudonym "M. Renou." A few years later he took his own name back so that he could publicly defend himself against his enemies; the authorities, however, had by then apparently decided it was best to leave him alone. His candid autobiography, *Confessions,* which details his tumultuous life, appeared shortly after his death.

Although Rousseau is often regarded by some as being an unsystematic and nonrigorous philosopher, and although many others regard his views as deeply inconsistent, his influence has been tremendous. He has been called the originator of the romantic movement, mainly because of the powerful appeal he made on behalf of the sensibility of the heart. His emphasis on equality, liberty, and the supremacy of individual citizens inspired the leaders of the French Revolution and the builders of republican democracies, but he influenced many authoritarian movements as well. His assertions that human beings realize their true nature only through society, along with the idea that the individual is under the complete domination and control of the sovereign, supposedly inspired the Hegelians with the idea of national spirit. Along similar lines, others have suggested that Rousseau made possible the suppression of freedom in the name of freedom through his idea that the true road to freedom lies in the social contract, entered theoretically at some point in the historic past—that is, by trading your natural liberty for civil liberty. In doing so,

"each of us puts his persona and all his power in common under the supreme direction of the general will, and, in our corporate capacity, we receive each member as an indivisible part of a whole." Anyone who does not obey this "general will" may be forced to do so; hence Rousseau's famous contention that through the social contract man is "forced to be free." Thus Bertrand Russell, for instance, calls Rousseau "the inventor of the political philosophy of pseudodemocratic dictatorships as opposed to traditional absolute monarchies. Ever since his time, those who considered themselves reformers have been divided into two groups, those who followed him and those who followed Locke. . . . At the present time, Hitler is an outcome of Rousseau; Roosevelt and Churchill, of Locke."[1]

In Rousseau's view, the will of the political leader is the incarnation of the general will, which reflects the sum of the individual wills of all the citizens. Kant, as we are about to see, drew much inspiration from Rousseau, especially his claim that if each individual citizen was given enough information and the freedom to choose, all citizens would, independently of each other—since they are all directed to the same will to do the common good—arrive at the general will for the good of all humankind.

16.6 The Moral Law Within

Kant's *Foundations of the Metaphysics of Morals* (1785), from which the following selection is taken, gives his widely influential deontological (rule-based) ethical theory, which centers on his categorical imperative, "Act only on that maxim which you can at the same time will to become a universal law." As the universal moral test of right principles of action, the categorical imperative according to Kant makes us all duty-bound to obey certain principles in the same way that objects in nature are bound to act according to the laws of nature.

⚘

Foundations of the Metaphysics of Morals

The Good Will

Nothing can possibly be conceived in the world, or even out of it, which can be called good, without qualification, except a Good Will. Intelligence, wit, judgment, and the other *talents* of the mind, however they may be named, or courage, resolution, perseverance, as qualities of temperament, are undoubtedly good and desirable in many respects; but these gifts of nature may also become extremely bad and mischievous if the will which is to make use of them and which, therefore, constitutes what is called *character,* is not good. It is the same with the *gifts of fortune.* Power, riches, honour, even health, and the general well-being and contentment with one's conditions which is called *happiness,* inspire pride, and often presumption, if there is not a good will to correct the influence of these on the mind, and with this also to rectify the whole principle of acting, and adapt it to its end. The sight of a being who is not adorned with a single feature of a pure and good will, enjoying unbroken prosperity, can never give pleasure to an imperial rational spectator. Thus a good will appears to constitute the indispensable condition even of being worthy of happiness.

There are even some qualities which are of service to this good will itself, and may facilitate its action, yet which have no intrinsic unconditional value, but always presuppose a good will and this qualifies the esteem that we justly have for them, and does not permit us to regard them as absolutely good. Moderation in the affections and passions, self-control, and calm deliberation are not only good in many respects, but even seem to constitute part of the intrinsic worth of the person; but they are far from deserving to be called good without qualification, although they have been so unconditionally praised by the ancients. For without the principles of a good will, they may become extremely bad; and the coolness of a villain not only makes him far more dangerous, but also directly makes him more abominable in our eyes than he would have been without it.

From Immanuel Kant, *Foundations of the Metaphysics of Morals*, T. K. Abbot, trans. (London, 1873), with emendations by the author.

A good will is good not because of what it performs or effects, not by its aptness for the attainment of some proposed end, but simply by virtue of the volition, that is, it is good in itself, and considered by itself to be esteemed much higher than all that can be brought about by it in favour of any inclination, nay, even of the sum-total of all inclinations. Even if it should happen that, owing to special disfavour of fortune, or the niggardly provision of a step-motherly nature, this will should wholly lack power to accomplish its purpose, if with its greatest efforts it should yet achieve nothing, and there should remain only the good will (not, to be sure, a mere wish, but the summoning of all means in our power), then, like a jewel, it would still shine by its own light, as a thing which has its whole value in itself. Its usefulness or fruitlessness can neither add to nor take away anything from this value. It would be, as it were, only the setting to enable us to handle it the more conveniently in common commerce, or to attract to it the attention of those who are not yet connoisseurs, but not to recommend it to true connoisseurs, or to determine its value.

The First Proposition of Morality

. . . it is always a matter of duty that a trader not overcharge an inexperienced purchaser; and whenever there is much commerce the prudent tradesman does not overcharge, but keeps a fixed price for everyone, so that a child buys of him as well as any other. Men are thus *honestly* served; but this is not enough to make us believe that the tradesman has so acted from duty and from principles of honesty: his own advantage required it; it is out of the question in this case to suppose that he might besides have a direct inclination in favour of the buyers, so that, as it were, from love he should give no advantage to one over another. Accordingly the action was done neither from duty nor from direct inclination, but merely with a selfish view.

On the other hand, it is a duty to maintain one's life; and, in addition, everyone has also a direct inclination to do so. But on this account the often anxious care which most men take for it has no intrinsic worth, and their maxim has no moral import. They preserve their life *as duty requires,* no doubt, but not *because duty requires.* On the other hand, if adversity and hopeless sorrow have completely taken away the relish for life; if the unfortunate one, strong in mind, indignant at his fate rather than desponding or dejected, wishes for death, and yet preserves his life without loving it—not from inclination or fear, but from duty—then his maxim has a moral worth.

The Second Proposition of Morality

The second proposition is: That an action done from duty derives its moral worth, *not from the purpose* which is to be attained by it, but from the maxim by which it is determined, and therefore does not depend on the realization of the object of the action, but merely on the *principle of volition* by which the action has taken place, without regard to any object of desire. It is clear from what precedes that the purposes which we may have in view in our actions, or their effects regarded as ends and springs of the will, cannot give to actions any unconditional or moral worth. In what, then, can their worth lie, if it is not to consist in the will and in reference to its expected effect? It cannot be anywhere but in the *principle of the will* without regard to the ends which can be attained by the action. For the will stands between its *a priori principle,* which is formal, and its *a posteriori* spring, which is material, as between two roads, and as it must be determined by something, it follows that it must be determined by the formal principle of volition when an action is done from duty, in which case every material principle has been withdrawn from it.

The Third Proposition of Morality

The third proposition, which is a consequence of the two preceding, I would express thus: *Duty is the necessity of acting from respect for the law.* I may have *inclination* for an object as the effect of my proposed action, but I cannot have *respect* for it, just for this reason, that it is an effect and not an energy of will. Similarly, I cannot have respect for inclination, whether my own or another's; I can at most, if my own, approve it; if another's, sometimes even love it; *i.e.* look on it as favourable to my own interest. It is only what is connected with my will as a principle, by no means as an effect—what does not subserve my inclination, but overpowers it, or at least in case of choice excludes it from its calculation—in other words, simply the law of itself, which can be an object of respect, and hence a command. Now an action done from

duty must wholly exclude the influence of inclination, and with it every object of the will, so that nothing remains which can determine the will except objectively the *law,* and subjectively *pure* respect for this practical law, and consequently the maxim that I should follow this law even to the thwarting of all my inclinations.

The Supreme Principle of Morality: The Categorical Imperative

But what sort of law can that be, the conception of which must determine the will, even without paying any regard to the effect expected from it, in order that this will may be called good absolutely and without qualification? As I have deprived the will of every impulse which could arise to it from obedience to any law, there remains nothing but the universal conformity of its actions to law in general, which alone is to serve the will as a principle, *i.e.* I am never to act otherwise than so *that I could also will that my maxim should become a universal law.* Here, now, it is the simple conformity to law in general, without assuming any particular law applicable to certain actions, that serves the will as its principle, and must so serve it, if duty is not to be a vain delusion and a chimerical notion. The common reason of men in its practical judgments perfectly coincides with this, and always has in view the principle here suggested.

First Formulation of the Categorical Imperative: Universal Law

In this problem we will first inquire whether the mere conception of a categorical imperative may not perhaps supply us also with the formula of it, containing the proposition which alone can be a categorical imperative; for even if we know the tenor of such an absolute command, yet how it is possible will require further special and laborious study, which we postpone to the last section.

When I conceive a hypothetical imperative, in general I do not know beforehand what it will contain until I am given the condition. But when I conceive a categorical imperative, I know at once what it contains. For as the imperative contains besides the law only the necessity that the maxims shall conform to this law, while the law contain no conditions restricting it, there remains nothing but the general statement that the maxim of the action should conform to a universal law, and it is this conformity alone that the imperative properly represents as necessary.

There is therefore but one categorical imperative, namely, this: *Act only on that maxim whereby thou canst at the same time will that it should become a universal law.*

Now if all imperatives of duty can be deduced from this one imperative as from their principle, then, although it should remain undecided whether what is called duty is not merely a vain notion, yet at least we shall be able to show what we understand by it and what this notion means.

Since the universality of the law according to which effects are produced constitutes what is properly called *nature* in the most general sense (as to form), that is the existence of things so far as it is determined by general laws, the imperative of duty may be expressed thus: *Act as if the maxim of thy action were to become by thy will a universal law of nature.*

⁂

Let us begin by getting clear about what Kant means by *will.* The concept is extremely important, not just in Kant but in many Kant-inspired later philosophers (such as, most notably, Schopenhauer, Chapter 17), and yet it has been almost universally misunderstood. The biggest and most common mistake is to confuse your *will* with your *wishing.* Allow me to illustrate. You're sitting in front of the television, wishing that you weren't watching television; you would rather be doing something else. But you can't! You're stuck. Maybe that other thing is even something you would love to do, and yet you're doing something completely different, wishing that you were doing that other thing! *Your wishing doesn't get you there.* That's what Kant means by distinguishing actions done from mere *inclination* rather than by the will. And the foundation of morality consists in having a *good will:*

There is no possibility of thinking of anything at all in the world, or even out of it, which can be regarded as good without qualification, except a *good will.*

Notice how different this conception of moral goodness is from Plato, Aristotle, Epicurus, and Augustine, all of whom understood morality in terms of happiness—in their case, one's own. Later so-called *utilitarians,* such as Mill (Chapter 19), also use happiness as their moral foundation, in opposition to Kant, though not just in terms of one's own happiness but that of everyone's.

Next, Kant distinguishes two kinds of *imperatives.* An imperative is *hypothetical* when it is of the form: "If you wish (or want, or would like) *x* in circumstances *y*, do action *a.*" The *categorical* imperative, on the other hand, makes no reference to your wishes, wants, or desires. It is independent of any utilitarian concerns having to do with consequences or goals. It simply says, "If you are in circumstance *y*, do *a.*" Period. Regardless of what you want, that is what you must do.

His reasoning is rather straightforward. Since the moral law is a rule for choosing among rules—that is, a rule for distinguishing between right and wrong rules—it cannot refer to the *content* of rules. It must therefore refer only to their *form*: that is why it must be a *categorical,* rather than *hypothetical,* imperative. It has the same form as scientific laws of nature; that is, it has a *universal form.* Think, for instance, of Newton's law $F = Ma$ (force equals mass times acceleration). If this is to be a law of nature, it must apply everywhere and at all times; it can have no exceptions. That is what it means to say that something is a law of *nature.* It applies universally. And so Kant's "supreme principle of morality" is this:

Act only according to that maxim [rule] whereby you can at the same time will that it should become a universal law.

Notice that it is synthetic; if you deny it no contradiction results. Because it has no empirical content, it is a priori. *Therefore, it is a paradigm of pure reason at work in the moral realm.*

Suppose you are about to take a test. You haven't studied, so you consider cheating. Should you cheat? What would Kant say? The answer is clear. Simply check whether you could universalize your action into a universal principle. How do you do that? Well, you ask yourself what would happen if everyone who did not study for an exam cheated. Could there be a universal law: "Everyone ought to cheat on exams"? First, notice that you might think this law would not be such a good idea if you were going in for open heart surgery and wanted a reputable doctor who had passed all the necessary exams! But the situation is more clear-cut than that. Kant would tell you that "Everyone ought to cheat on exams" would be *an impossible law,* because if everyone complied with it, there would be no need for exams. Exams, as such, would cease to exist.

Likewise, think of lying, stealing, and killing. "Everyone ought always to lie." Impossible! You couldn't even state the law without breaking it. "Everyone ought always to steal." This would destroy the notion of property and thereby invalidate the concept of *stealing,* as such. And so on. But there is an equally important second aspect to the categorical imperative:

> So act as to treat humanity, whether in your own person or in that of any other, always at the same time as an end and never simply as a means only.

In saying that we should treat others as ends in themselves and not merely as a means, Kant is saying that we ought not to *use* other people as a means to our own ends. But it applies as much to ourselves as it does to others; it is, in fact, the very source of our ability to choose the way of freedom because the moral law, in terms of the categorical imperative, arises from, and is known through, pure reason. It says, "Choose your rules according to whether they can be universalized." But notice that since this is a principle of *pure* reason, and since I am a rational being, I am not merely a subject to this law! *I am also in part its author.* In other words, just as the objects of the phenomenal world are in part created (constituted into reality) by my own mind, so too the moral law is itself in part my own creation:

> The will is thus not merely subject to the law but is subject to the law in such a way that it must be regarded also as legislating for itself and only on this account as being subject to the law of which it can regard itself as the author.

Hence, quite fully in the spirit of Rousseau, it is when we act from duty with respect to the moral law that each of us exists as a fully and absolutely *autonomous* being:

⚑

The will is a kind of causality belonging to living beings insofar as they are rational; freedom would be the property of this causality that makes it effective independent of any determination by alien causes. . . . [F]reedom is certainly not lawless, even though it is not a property of will in accordance with laws of nature. It must, rather, be a causality in accordance with immutable laws, which, to be sure, is of a special kind. . . . What else, then, can freedom of the will be but autonomy, i.e., the property that the will has of being a law to itself? The proposition that the will is in every action a law to itself expresses, however, nothing but the principle of acting according to no other maxim than that which can at the same time have itself as a universal law for its object. Now this is precisely the formula of the categorical imperative and is the principle of morality. Thus a free will and a will subject to moral laws are one and the same.

⚑

NOTE

1. Bertrand Russell, *History of Western Philosophy* (New York: Simon and Schuster, 1945), pp. 484–485.

17 ✤ Hegel and the German Idealists

17.0 Fichte (1762–1814): The Subjective Idealist

Johann Gottlieb Fichte was born in Rammenau, a village in Upper (Saxon) Lusatia, the son of a farmer and linen-maker. He attended the universities of Jena and Leipzig and then worked as a tutor in Zürich. Although his first work, "Aphorisms on Religion and God" (1790), owed much to Spinoza's determinism, he was mainly influenced by Kant, whom he visited in Königsberg. Kant agreed to read Fichte's next manuscript, *Essay Toward a Critique of All Revelation* (1792). Deeply impressed, Kant sent the manuscript to a publisher on Fichte's behalf. Due to a printer's error, the book appeared without Fichte's name or preface, and everyone assumed it had been written by Kant! Kant published a retraction stating that the work was Fichte's, not his, adding that the book just happens to solve a major problem with Kant's system that Kant had found insoluble. Fichte's reputation was instantly secured.

The problem with his own work, as Kant saw it, was this. His *Critique of Pure Reason* puts speculative theology in a completely negative light. Yet his *Critique of Practical Reason* puts the moral law, so central to Kant's thought, as the absolute content, or substance, of any religion. This inconsistency left open the puzzling question of the conditions under which religious belief was possible. In his *Critique of All Revelation,* Fichte bridges the gap between Kant's two monumental works by showing how the absolute requirements of the moral law supply the necessary conditions that make revealed religion possible.

His reputation thus established, Fichte became professor of philosophy at the University of Jena in 1794. In the same year, he published *On the Concept of the Science of Knowledge, or So-called Philosophy* (1794) and *Fundamental Principles of the Science of Knowledge* (1794), from which our selection is taken. In it, he departs from Kantian philosophy in a direction that paved the way for three related and subsequent extremely important movements in philosophy: absolute idealism, phenomenology, and existentialism, each of which we shall study in due course. Especially influential was Fichte's analysis of the ego as a self-affirming primitive act of consciousness that constructs the objective world, not in tandem with "things in themselves," as Kant supposed, but solely out of its own appearances.

⅄

Fundamental Principles of the Science of Knowledge

Attend to yourself; turn your glance away from all that surrounds you and upon your own innermost self. Such is the first demand which philosophy makes of its disciples. We speak of nothing that is without you, but wholly of yourself.

In the most fleeting self-observation every one must perceive a marked difference between the various immediate determinations of his consciousness, which we may also call representations. Some of them appear entirely dependent upon our freedom, and it is impossible for us to believe that there is anything without us corresponding to them. Our imagination, our will, appears to us as free. Others, however, we refer to a truth, as their model, which is held to be established, independent of us; and in the attempt to determine such representations, we find ourselves conditioned by the necessity of their harmony with this truth. In the knowledge of their contents we do not consider ourselves free. In brief, we can say, some of our representations are accompanied by the feeling of freedom, others by the feeling of necessity.

The question cannot reasonably arise: Why are the representations, which are directly dependent upon our freedom, determined in precisely this manner and not otherwise? For when it is affirmed that they are dependent upon our freedom, all application of the conception of a ground is dismissed; they are thus, because I have so determined them, and if I had determined them otherwise, then they would be different. But it is

From Johann Fichte, *The Science of Knowledge*, B. Rand, trans., with emendations by the author.

certainly a question worthy of reflection: What is the ground of the system of those representations which are accompanied by the feelings of necessity and of that feeling of necessity itself? To answer this question is the task of philosophy; and, in my opinion, nothing is philosophy but the science which solves this problem. The system of those representations which are accompanied by the feeling of necessity is also called *experience*: internal as well as external experience. Philosophy has therefore—to express the same thing in other words—to discover the ground of all experience. . . . There are three ways in which the object can be related to consciousness. Either the object appears to have been produced by the representation, or as existing without its aid; and in the latter case, either also as determined in regard to its structure, or as present merely with respect to its existence, but determinable in regard to its structure by the free intelligence.

The first relation applies merely to an imaginary object, whether with or without purpose; the second applies to an object of experience; and the third applies only to an object, which we shall forthwith describe.

I can determine myself by freedom to think this or that; for example, the thing-in-itself of the dogmatist. Now if I abstract from the thought and look simply upon myself, then I myself become the object of a particular representation. That I appear to myself as determined in precisely this manner and not otherwise, *e.g.*, as thinking, and among all possible thoughts as thinking just the thing-in-itself, is in my opinion to depend upon my freedom of self-determination: I have made myself such an object of my own free will. I have not, however, made myself, but I am compelled to presuppose myself as determinable through this self-determination. I am therefore myself my own object, the determinate character of which depends under certain conditions altogether upon intelligence, but the existence of which must always be presupposed.

Now this very I in itself is the object of Idealism. The object of this system does not occur actually as something real in consciousness, as a *thing in itself,*—for then idealism would cease to be what it is, and would be transformed into dogmatism,—but it does appear as *I in itself*. It occurs not as object of experience,—for it is not determined, but is solely determinable through me, and without this determination it would be nothing at all,—but it appears as something raised above all experience. . . .

The dispute between the idealist and the dogmatist is precisely the question whether the independence of the Ego is to be sacrificed to that of the thing, or *vice versa*.

Now the representation of the independence of the Ego and that of the thing can exist certainly together; but not the independence itself of both. Only one can be the first, the beginning, the independent; the second, by the very fact of being second, is necessarily dependent upon the first, with which it is to be connected.

Now which of the two is to be made the first? Reason affords no ground for a decision; for the question does not relate to the connecting of one link with another, where alone the grounds of reason extend; but to the beginning of the entire succession, which as an absolute first act is wholly dependent upon the freedom of thinking. The decision is therefore entirely arbitrary; and since the arbitrariness must have a cause, the decision is dependent upon *inclination* and *interest*. The last ground of the distinction between the dogmatist and the idealist is consequently the difference of their interest.

The highest interest, and hence the ground of all other interest, is that *for ourselves.* Thus with the philosopher. Not to lose his Self in his reasoning, but to retain and to assert it, this is the interest which unconsciously guides all his thinking. Now, there exist two grades of mankind; and in the progress of our race, before the last grade has been universally attained, two chief classes of men. The one class consist of those who have not raised themselves to the full feeling of their freedom and of absolute independence, but who are merely conscious of themselves in the representations of outward things. These have only a desultory self-consciousness, bound up with outward objects, and collected from their manifoldness. The image of their Self is reflected to them only from the things, as from a mirror. If the latter be taken from them, then they lose the Self at the same time. For their own sake, they cannot give up the belief in the independence of things, since they exist only together with these things. Whatever they are they have actually become through the external world. Whosoever is only a product of the things will never view himself in any other manner, and he is

entirely correct, so long as he speaks merely of himself and of those like him. The principle of the dogmatist is: belief in the things for their own sake; hence, a mediated belief in his own desultory Self, as merely the result of the things.

But whosoever becomes conscious of his self-existence and independence from all outward things—and this one can only become by making something of one's self, by means of one's own self, independently of all external things—needs no longer the things in support of his Self, and cannot use them, because they destroy his self-existence and transform it into an empty appearance. The Ego, which he possesses, and which interests him, destroys that belief in the things; he believes in his independence from inclination, and lays hold of it with affection. His belief in himself is immediate.

⁂

Fichte's philosophy thus begins with an antinomy-like conflict between the inner sense of free will and the external sense that the world is completely determined: "In immediate consciousness, I appear to myself as free; by reflection on the whole of Nature, I discover that freedom is absolutely impossible." And yet, the only knowledge of which any one of us is capable is that of our own minds: "In all perception you perceive only your own state." Thus, in a way that Hume might well have responded to Kant's rebuttal to his argument against causality, the idea of things in themselves is *itself* but a projection of the mind and therefore not something to which consciousness is bound.

In other words, just as many later existentialists will claim, the boundary by which we distinguish between self and other, based on what we can consciously control, is deeply bogus. Just about all subsequent idealists will make a great deal of this. Think of dream states. You're being chased by dogs. You don't consciously *want* to be chased by dogs, you're consciously afraid, and so on. *But what is the cause of the movement of the dogs, the chase, the fear?* In the case of the dream it is your own mind. Only you are not, as the conscious ego, conscious of the mechanisms by which the world of your dreams is run by you.

Something like that is going on in the case of the world. Our failure to realize this leads non-idealists to accept the notion of things in themselves over which we have no power. But this, argues Fichte, is like supposing, "What I consciously control is me, what I do not consciously control is a thing in itself." Such reasoning is invalid. Think, again, of your dream states; the dogs chasing you in the dream are *not* material things; they are *not* things in themselves. Why can't you just wish them away? As the nineteenth-century American idealist philosopher Josiah Royce (Chapter 20) will argue, it is because the mind is far more resilient and stubborn than any concept of inert matter! Thus, in Fichte's view,

⚹

A finite rational being has nothing beyond experience; it is this that comprises the entire staple of his thought. The philosopher is necessarily in the same position; it seems, therefore, incomprehensible how he could raise himself above experience . . . the thing-in-itself is a pure invention and has no reality whatsoever. It does not occur in experience for the system of experience is nothing other than thinking . . . nothing else but the totality of relations unified by the imagination, and that all these relations constitute the thing; the object is surely the original synthesis of all these concepts. Form and matter are not separate items; the totality of form is the matter.

⚹

In other words, for something, say our proverbial chair, to be *objectively real* simply means, in Fichte's philosophy, that it consists of all possible experiences that it can generate in the mind of a potential observer. Take the chair apart or don't take it apart; look at it from above and below or not. The point is that you can do so because the chair is a containing space of all (perhaps infinite) possibilities of the relation of that object.

Lest this strike you as a philosophical flight

of fancy utterly removed from our contemporary scientific worldview, this view became the metaphysical foundation of early twentieth-century quantum mechanics, in which what it means for something to be real at the physical level is that the equation describing the object allows you to list all the possible solutions that it can generate: beyond that range of possibility there is no mind-independent actuality. Albert Einstein, of course, famously rejected the absolute idealism of quantum physicists like Niels Bohr in favor of a Kantian transcendental idealism; Einstein defended the idea of the thing-in-itself, a mind-independent reality, against other leading physicists.[1]

In Fichte's subjective idealist world, as in Berkeley's, everything is thought. But what, then, is thought? According to Fichte, it

⚹

has no *being* proper, no subsistence, for this is the result of an interaction and there is nothing . . . with which the intellect could be set to interact [because, for Fichte, there is no noumenal world of the thing in itself]. The intellect, for idealism, is an *act,* and absolutely nothing more; we should not even call it an active something, for this expression refers to something subsistent in which activity inheres.

⚹

In some ways this anticipates and lays a metaphysical foundation for the functionalist theories developed by twentieth-century computer scientists and cognitive philosophers,[2] in which reality and its simulation are viewed as one and the same: the universe is viewed as an abstract program, or Absolute Idea, which is functionally equivalent to the human intellect, or program. Fichte's notion of an *act* as an undefined fundamental property of the human intellect is thus an avatar of the idea that human consciousness is a key ingredient in the universal algorithm through which reality unfolds from one state to the next.

In his lifetime Fichte was recognized as one of the three successors to Kant (the other two were his contemporaries Hegel and Schelling). An extremely dynamic and popular lecturer at Jena, he commanded a large following among his students as well as the public, but this did not work out to his advantage. After a prolonged conflict with the Jena administration over academic freedom, he was forcibly dismissed from his position. Apparently, Fichte's philosophy was regarded as so highly dangerous that he had been asked not to publish his views; he refused, arguing that a philosopher had not only the right but the moral duty to expound his thoughts, including and especially the philosophy of religion (one of the leading bones of contention with both the university and public authorities). After his dismissal, Fichte continued to publish and even increased the number of his public lectures, becoming one of the leading figures in Berlin. There, during the French occupation, shortly after Napoleon had arrived in 1806, Fichte delivered his famous *Addresses to the German Nation* (1807), inspiring his fellow Germans to moral regeneration through national unity and political reform. Four years later, in 1810, Fichte helped found the new University of Berlin where he remained for the rest of his life.

17.1 Schelling (1775–1854): The Objective Idealist

Born in Leonberg, a small town of Würtemberg in Germany, Friedrich Wilhelm von Schelling was educated first at the cloister school where his father was chaplain and professor and then at the theological seminary at Tübingen, where he studied Spinoza, Kant, and especially Fichte. There he met and befriended fellow student G. W. F. Hegel, with whom he edited a philosophy journal. In 1798 he was invited to become philosophy professor at the famous University of Jena by its rector, the duke Charles Augustus; three years later Hegel joined the illustrious

department that included Fichte, Hegel, Schelling, Schlegel,[3] and Schiller.[4] Although his transcendental form of idealism clearly owes much to Kant, Fichte, and Hegel, Schelling's greatest original contribution was to romanticism, the eighteenth- and nineteenth-century philosophical movement opposed to both rationalism and empiricism. Reacting against both continental rationalism and British Empiricism, Schelling's philosophy centers on the self, transcendentalism, and the power of imagination and art. Generally regarded as the leading romantic of the period, Schelling inspired the great English romantic poets, including Wordsworth and Shelley and on through the writings of Samuel Coleridge (1772–1834).

Schelling's main work, *System of Transcendental Idealism,* is a treatise on the philosophy of nature, epistemology, and ethics, in which he tries to unify objective and subjective thought. His so-called philosophy of identity is an elaborate system in which subject and object coincide in the Absolute, a conscious mystical state that can be reached through intellectual intuition. Whereas for Kant and Fichte the purpose of philosophical thought is morality, for Schelling the ultimate culmination is in the creative act of the artist expressed in the special relation of identity between the subjective self and the objective world: although the only immediate object of knowledge is consciousness, knowledge of the objective world presents itself as a limiting condition of the dynamic evolutionary process from consciousness to self-consciousness. According to Schelling, only in art can the mind become fully aware of its own existence; the ultimate pinnacle of philosophical reflection is thus the production of great and profound art.

Like Fichte, Schelling's distinction between nature (the external, objective world) and spirit (mind, the internal, subjective world) is based on the concept of a third, higher reality, the Absolute. It is neither conscious nor unconscious; like Kant's Noumenal Self, it transcends the categories of thought. But for unknown reasons it seeks or desires to become conscious.

This it can do only by positing the existence of a material, inanimate, nonconscious world which it then uses to distinguish itself into becoming a conscious mind. In other words, the Absolute, in opposition to its own concept of itself, becomes the relative, phenomenal world, without loss of identity:

⚹

Nature and spirit are fundamentally the same. . . . That which is posited *out of* consciousness is in its very essence the same as that which is posited *in* consciousness. . . . [T]he known must itself bear the impression of the knower. . . . The ground of nature and spirit, the absolute, is the identity of the real and the ideal.

⚹

Like Spinoza, Schelling thereby establishes two kinds of knowledge: the *philosophical knowledge* of the rational faculties and the *confused knowledge* of the imagination. These give rise to two forms of existence: the infinite, undivided existence of the absolute, and the finite existence of individual things. The self-developing things of the phenomenal world arise in thought alone and possess no true reality; as with Leibniz, while things appear particular to our inadequate representations of them, the philosopher can view them *sub specie aeterni* (from God's point of view, see Section 12.4), in their totality, as ideas. Thus, to construe things as such is to present them to ourselves as they are in the totality of the world-soul, wherein all things are a Parmenidean One. In the Absolute—by which all the absolute idealists mean *the sum total of the whole of existence considered as such*—all is absolute, eternal, infinitude.

Furthermore, like Giordano Bruno, by whom he was also greatly influenced,[5] Schelling thought the finitude of the individual things in the world is broken up into a plurality of self-developing individual existences, among which is you, but within which the essential unity of all things is not entirely lost: each one of us is a def-

inite expression of the absolute, and to the absolute as such the character of identity belongs, though in a diminished degree and mingled with difference (Bruno's and Leibniz's monads). In its ultimate reality the world is absolute, the individual things relative, and nothing exists that is purely objective or purely subjective. There is identity in both individuality and totality; everything is both objective and subjective. It is only from any particular perspective that one or the other is always dominant. Schelling thus argues that the phenomena of nature, like the phenomena of the mind, are a unity not of matter and spirit but of the real and the ideal, the objective and the subjective, only that in the former realms there is a preponderance of the real—in the latter a preponderance of the ideal.

In the following passage from his *System of Transcendental Idealism*, he begins with a Cartesian-like certainty in the proposition *I Am* and shows how the transcendental proposition "There are things outside of me" can also be known with the same absolute certainty. Keep in mind, however, that whereas for Kant the transcendental process reaches beyond the phenomenal world of appearance, *not* to the noumenal world of the thing in itself but only to the cognitive faculties of the mind, according to Schelling the object reached is the objective, absolute world itself.

⚹

System of Transcendental Idealism

[T]here exists nothing immediately certain except the affirmation *I am*, which, since it loses all significance outside of immediate consciousness, is the most individual of all truths, and the absolute prejudice, which must be assumed, if anything else is to be made certain. The affirmation *There are things outside of us,* will therefore be certain for the transcendental philosopher, solely because of

---

From F. W. von Schelling, *System of Transcendental Idealism*, Benjamin Rand, trans., 1908 with emendations by the author.

its identity with the affirmation *I am*; and its certainty will also only be equal to the certainty of the affirmation from which it derives its own.

According to this view transcendental knowledge would be distinguished from common knowledge in two particulars.

First.—That for it the certainty of the existence of external things is a mere prejudice, which it transcends, in order to investigate the grounds of it. (It can never be the task for transcendental philosophy to prove the existence of things in themselves, but only to show that it is a natural and necessary prejudice to assume external objects as real.)

Second.—That it separates the two affirmations, *I am* and *There are things outside of me,* which run together in the ordinary consciousness, and places the one before the other, in order to prove their identity and that immediate connection which in the other is only felt. By this act of separation, when it is completed, one transports one's self in the transcendental act of contemplation, which is by no means a natural, but an artificial one.

3. If the subjective alone has reality for the transcendental philosopher he will also make only the subjective directly his object. The objective will be for him only indirectly an object, and, whereas, in ordinary knowledge, knowledge itself—the act of knowing—disappears in the object, in transcendental knowledge, on the contrary, the object as such disappears in the act of knowing. Transcendental knowledge is therefore a knowledge of knowing, in so far as it is purely subjective.

Thus, for example, in intuition it is the objective only that reaches the ordinary consciousness; the act of intuition is itself lost in the object; whereas on the contrary the transcendental mode of observation gets only a glimpse of the object of intuition by the act of intuition. Thus the ordinary thinking is a mechanism, in which ideas prevail, without, however, being distinguished as ideas; whereas the transcendental act of thought interrupts this mechanism, and in becoming conscious of the idea as an act, rises to the idea of the idea. In ordinary action, the acting is itself forgotten in the object of the action; philosophizing is also an action, but not an action only. It is likewise a continued self-intuition in this action.

The nature of the transcendental mode of thought must consist, therefore, in general in this: that, in it, that which in all other thinking,

knowing, or acting escapes the consciousness, and is absolutely non-objective, is brought into consciousness, and becomes objective. In brief, it consists in a continuous act of becoming an object to itself on the part of the subjective.

The transcendental art will therefore consist in the ability to maintain one's self constantly in this duplicity of acting and thinking.

⁂

Thus, in marked contrast with Fichte's subjective idealism, Schelling paves the way for his absolute idealism, which is still idealism but radically different from its previous incarnations, including, and especially, Fichte's:

⁂

Fichte could side with idealism from the point of view of reflection. I, on the other hand, took the viewpoint of production with the principle of idealism. To express this contrast most distinctly, idealism in the subjective sense had to assert, the ego is everything, while conversely idealism in the objective sense had to assert: Everything = ego and nothing exists but what = ego. These are certainly different views, although it will not be denied that both are idealism.

⁂

In marked contrast with Berkeley's idealism, in which an external and separate God (one not identical to the universe) sustains the nonrational order in the universe when no rational ego through observation projects the requisite order to make it real, both Fichte and Schelling argue that reality is constructed internally from itself, as a coherent universal system where the absolute (God) is identical to the phenomenal, relative level. But whereas Fichte argued that the subjective, which is primary, posits the objective, Schelling argued the opposite—that the objective posits the subjective. That is, for Fichte, as for Kant, a necessary condition for experience is that what is experienced is interpreted to be other than mental phenomena; in other words, our point that "eyes are not windows" must be obscured within consciousness in order for experience to be possible. Schelling, on the other hand, says that

🟊

I posit God, as the first and the last, as the Alpha and the Omega; but as Alpha he is not what he is as Omega, and in so far as he is only the one—God "in an eminent sense"—he cannot be the other God, in the same sense, or in strictness, be called God. For in that case, let it be expressly said, the unevolved God, *Deus implicitus,* would already be what, as Omega, the *Deus explicitus* is.

🟊

But then why does God not remain as it is in itself, the objective Absolute Being? Why does infinite unity give rise to the separations in which we exist in our present, multiperspectival reality? This is analogous to the theological question of why God is not content to stay God, why God gives rise to a world in the first place. Schelling's original answer, which he puts forth in his *Bruno,* reverses the traditional religious concept of "the fall." In an absolute act of freedom, the origin of the phenomenal, relative world comes about so that we, as creative agents, actualize the world through our consciousness; it is the individual mind—an obscure, unconscious impulse toward self-representation—that adds the crucial ingredient that solidifies all this that you see around you from the realm of mere possibility into actuality. The human faculty of the understanding *is* the Logos, the Word, the Absolute— God—as revealed to self.

Unlike Spinoza's deterministic God, however, Schelling's God makes choice and freedom possible within the real world through the presence of individual conscious beings, each of which is the actualizing, creative power of the Absolute. According to Schelling the creator of the world is thus not anything like the sort of Judeo-Christian creator who created the world to be inhabited by individual souls; rather, it is we who

are the true artists of reality. This leads him to the exact opposite conclusion from Plato's view of art; indeed, he elevates the philosophy of art into the highest branch of the discipline.

🟊

Preliminary Division of Transcendental Philosophy

This division is preliminary, because the principles of the division can be derived only from the science itself.

We return to the idea of science.

Transcendental philosophy has to explain how knowledge is possible at all, assuming that the subjective in it is accepted as the ruling, or first element.

It is therefore, not a single part, nor a special object of knowledge, but knowledge itself, and knowledge in general, that it takes for its object.

Now all knowledge can be reduced to certain original convictions or original prejudices. These different convictions transcendental philosophy must trace to one original conviction. This ultimate conviction from which all others are derived, is expressed in the first principle of this philosophy, and the task of finding such is none other than to find the absolutely certain by which all other certainty is attained.

The division of transcendental philosophy is determined through those original convictions, whose validity it affirms. These convictions must, in the first place, be sought in the common understanding. If, therefore, we go back to the standpoint of the ordinary view, we find the following convictions deeply engraven in the human understanding:

A. That not only does there exist a world of things independent of us, but also that our representations agree with them in such a manner that there is nothing else in the things beyond what we represent by them. The necessity in our objective representations is explained by the belief that the things are unalterably determined, and that by this determination of things our representations appear to be mediately determined. By this first and most original conviction, the first problem of philosophy is determined, *viz.*: to explain how representations can absolutely agree with objects which exist entirely independent of them. Since it is upon the assumption that things are exactly as we represent them, and that we therefore certainly know things as they are in themselves, that the possibility of all experience rests (for what would experience be, and where would physics, for example, stray to, without that presupposition of the absolute identity of being and seeming?), the solution of this problem is identical with theoretical philosophy, which has to investigate the possibility of experience.

B. The second equally original conviction is, that representations which originate in us freely and without necessity can pass over from the world of thought into the real world, and attain objective reality.

This conviction is opposed to the first. According to the first, it is assumed that objects are unalterably determined, and our representations by them; according to the other, that objects are changeable, and that, too, by the causality of representations in us. According to the first conviction, a transition takes place within us from the real world into the world of representations, or a determining of the representations by the objective, according to the second, a transition takes place from the world of representations into the world of reality, or a determining of the objective by a (freely conceived) representation in us.

By this second conviction, a second problem is determined, *viz.* how, by something merely thought, an objective is changeable, so as entirely to correspond with that something thought.

Since the possibility of all free action rests upon that assumption, the solution of this problem is practical philosophy.

C. But with these two problems we find ourselves involved in a contradiction. According to B, the supremacy of thought (the ideal) over the world of sense is demanded. But how is such supremacy conceivable, if (according to A) the idea in its origin is already only the slave of the objective? On the other hand, if the real world is something wholly independent of us, and is something with which our ideas must conform as their pattern (by A), then it becomes inconceivable how, on the other hand, the real world can conform to the ideas in us (by B). In brief, in the theoretical certainty we lose the practical; in the practical we lose the theoretical. It is impossible that at the same time there should be truth in our knowledge and reality in our volition.

This contradiction must be solved, if there is to be a philosophy at all. The solution of this problem, or the answering of the question: How can ideas be conceived as conforming to objects, and at the same time objects as conforming to ideas?—is not the first, but is the chief task of transcendental philosophy.

It is easy to see that this problem cannot be solved either in theoretical or practical philosophy, but in a higher one, which is the connecting link of both, and is neither theoretical nor practical, but both at the same time.

How at the same time the objective world conforms to representations in us, and representations in us conform to the objective world, cannot be conceived, unless there exists a preëstablished harmony between the two worlds of the ideal and the real. But this preëstablished harmony is itself not conceivable unless the activity by which the objective world is produced, is originally identical with that which displays itself in volition, and *vice versa*.

Now it is certainly a *productive* activity which manifests itself in volition. All free action is productive, but productive only with consciousness. If, then, since the two activities are only one in principle, we suppose that the same activity which is productive *with* consciousness in free action, is productive *without* consciousness in the production of the world, this preëstablished harmony is a reality, and the contradiction is solved. If we suppose that all this is actually the case, then that original identity of the activity which is engaged in the production of the world, with that which exhibits itself in volition, must manifest itself in the productions of the former, and these must necessarily appear as the productions of an activity at once conscious and unconscious.

Nature, as a whole, no less than in its different productions, will of necessity appear as a work produced with consciousness and yet at the same time as the production of the blindest mechanism. It is the result of purpose without being explainable as such. The philosophy of the aims of nature, or teleology, is therefore the required point of union of theoretical and practical philosophy.

D. Heretofore, we have posited only in general terms the identity of the unconscious activity which has produced nature and the conscious activity which manifests itself in volition, without having decided where the principle of this activity lies, whether in nature or in us.

But now the system of knowledge can be regarded as complete only when it reverts to its principle. Transcendental philosophy would therefore be completed only when it also could demonstrate that identity—the highest solution of its entire problem—in its principle (the *Ego*).

It is therefore postulated, that activity, at once conscious and unconscious, can be shown in the subjective, that is in consciousness itself.

Such an activity can be no other than the *æsthetic,* and every work of art can only be conceived as the product of such. The ideal work of art and the real world of objects are therefore products of one and the same activity. The meeting of the two (of the conscious and the unconscious) gives *without* consciousness the real, *with* consciousness the œsthetic world.

The objective world is only the original still unconscious poetry of the soul. The universal organum of philosophy—the keystone of its entire arch—is the philosophy of art.

⚐

In case you're wondering what he means by the *universal organum* of philosophy, an *organum* is a polyphonic voice part accompanying the *cantus firmus,* the plainsong or simple Gregorian melody sung in unison (usually at a fourth, fifth, or octave above or below), note for note. Thus, by equating the objective world with "the still unconscious poetry of the soul" and philosophy as the "universal organum," Schelling is providing the metaphysical scaffolding for Hegel's subsequent notion that it is not the study of *nature* that allows us to glimpse into the mind of God, as Kepler, Galileo, and the New Scientists thought, but the study of *philosophy*. In studying the evolution of philosophy we are experiencing, and taking part in, the birth of God.

17.2 Hegel (1770–1831): The Absolute Idealist

Georg Wilhelm Friedrich Hegel was born into an upper-middle-class family in Stuttgart, Germany. The views that would make him the leading philosopher of the nineteenth century grew out of all-night conversations with fellow students at the seminary at the University of Tübingen, including the philosopher Schelling (Section 17.1) and the poet Johann Christian Friedrich Hölderlin. After graduation he worked for seven years as a private tutor before he received his first teaching appointment, in 1801, as a lecturer at the University of Jena. In 1805 he was appointed professor of philosophy, but the following year, with Napoleon's victory at Jena and the French occupation, he lost his position. He moved to Bamberg and supported himself for a while as a newspaper editor, then as a school principal in Nuremberg. In 1816 he was reappointed professor of philosophy, first in Heidelberg and then in 1818 in Berlin where he remained for the rest of his life.

In Chapter 16 we saw Kant's development of what he called "critical" or "transcendental" idealism based on his distinction between the phenomenal, knowable world of appearances and the unknowable, noumenal world of things in themselves. Both are *real* but, just as Berkeley before him would have argued, an epistemologically inaccessible noumenal reality can hardly be called *reality* and ought better to be called *conjecture* or *theory* or, as Hume did call it, a fiction. So Hegel's philosophy, like Fichte's and Schelling's, developed in reaction to Kant's notion of a nonmental reality that is utterly unknowable. In Kant, the objects of the phenomenal world—all the objects you see around you—are actively processed by the faculties of your mind into existence. Since these faculties are in part the effect of the noumenal world, the objects thereby constituted are created partly (and indirectly) by the noumenal reality and partly (and directly) by your own mental faculties. In Hegel, as in Fichte and Schelling, there is just one world—one world whose objects are created *completely* by the mind *whose own faculties* are created through its own (historical, evolutionary) oppositions against itself. With Kantian thoroughness, Hegel thus builds an elaborate metaphysical system in which the mind does not merely structure and regulate reality but wholly generates and constitutes it, up to and including itself. What he calls "the Absolute," the world as it exists in itself, is mind or spirit.[6] That is, the world in itself is a self-thinking thought, such that the entire process of existence in time is the teleological (goal-directed) movement[7] of the universe becoming aware of itself, a process of "the Absolute realizing itself."

In other words, in marked contrast to Kant's transcendental (or critical) idealism and Berkeley's subjective idealism, both of which are pluralistic,[8] Hegel conceives of the Absolute in terms of a monistic system in which the whole of existence is one substance that is itself a spirit, or mind: everything that is, was, or will be is an evolving form within the world-mind, where the forces of evolution are driven, not by events in the past or present, but by the still uncreated future. In this way, the Kantian noumenal reality, nowhere present among the phenomenal world of appearances, becomes as yet undeveloped domains of future possibility toward which everything evolves. The history of philosophy is itself part of this evolution. The events of history are not merely a succession of various physical *things* rearranged into different positions, nor a series of ideas and views each of which turns out to be false when it is replaced by a new view. Rather, historical developments in thought from, say, Plato to Hegel, are themselves changes in the way the world is. In other words, philosophy is not merely a passive intellectual activity, the result of human philosophers at work grappling with the enigma of existence; rather, the stages of philosophy represent the absolute mind going through various stages of the thinking process in its own metaphysical development.

In a sense, Hegel one-ups Kant's Copernican revolution. Recall how Kant conceived the mind's engagement with real objects, not in passive terms where impressions and ideas are the effects of the object, but in active terms where the objects are in part the effects of the mind. But *this whole process* is, for Kant, a static thing: the mind does what it does to the phenomenal world using the faculties that it has; the noumenal world does what it does to the faculties of the mind and that's the way it is. Hegel now dislodges even the concept behind these relationships from its privileged position, arguing that the entire process is actively created by the mind! But how can that be, if the mind is everything that there is? Where is the impetus for its being if there is not some transcendental mind behind it, empowering it to constitute its objects as they are? Kant's answer in terms of a fixed noumenal world is, for Hegel, just another "earth-centered" prejudice, this time not predicated on the phenomena but on the entire conceptual framework all the way down to the very logic of thought.

In Hegel, *nothing* stands still, not even metaphysics. In Kant's philosophy the active process of reality creation on the part of the *mind* is a passive fact about the way the world is. The phenomenal-noumenal totality, including the ego and the transcendental ego, are all there all at once, together in their totality, implying, ultimately, the noumenal world is the given fixed place around which everything centers, a Godlike, otherworldly absolute ground of being. Hegel pushes Kant's reasoning beyond its own limits. According to Hegel, the drawing of the boundary between the unknowable thing in itself and the knowable phenomena is not conceived in terms of a static horizontal (albeit fuzzy) line *between* (phenomenal and noumenal) worlds, but as an ever-receding vertical line *within* the world, drawn between the past and the future. And what is this line? Where is it? It is here; it is now; it is the ever-receding present moment of existence: the future, the not-yet realm of infinite possibility *as unreachable and inaccessible from the present* as Kant's noumenal world is from the phenomenal realm, draws us with ever-increasing detail and richness into reality. The point of contact is time.

Thus we might think of the world as conceived by the absolute idealists as a natural evolution from the Kantian culmination of previous philosophical perspectives as follows. Kant, as we saw, conceives of space and time as categories of the mind. But, as such, they are different categories and not themselves aspects of the world as it exists in itself in the noumenal realm. We've already discussed the sense in which Kant's transcendental idealism influenced the revolutionary development of the relativistic space and time theories of Einstein, where the observer's own "reference frame" (itself conceived in terms of a Cartesian coordinate system of many dimensions) imparts its own structure[9] onto the real world. Now we shall see how Hegel's absolute idealism, built upon the subjective idealism of Fichte and the objective idealism of Schelling, becomes an avatar for subsequent developments in which Kant's concept of a mind-independent, noumenal reality, even as developed by Einstein, gives way to the strange world of quantum mechanics, where all our most mind-boggling philosophies become integrated into the most fundamental of all sciences: "physics."

But even *this*—the evolutionary changes in our ways of thinking about ourselves and the world—is not just the result of philosophers, scientists, and mathematicians at work, but the world trying to understand itself. And this, Hegel argues, cannot be understood by the philosophers, scientists, and mathematicians unless there is a thorough knowledge of all these developing stages of thought as represented by the history of philosophy. It is a testament to the brilliance of Hegel's often maligned mind that he then sets out to write one.

In reading the history of thought, we are not viewing just the intellectual struggles of individual thinkers; we are experiencing birthing stages in the evolution of the consciousness of the world. The individuals, as such, are but cogs in the cosmic wheel of the Absolute. Contemporary writer Umberto Eco[10] puts such an idea most poetically when he writes,

⚓

Now, I realized that not infrequently books speak of books: it is as if they spoke among themselves. In the light of this reflection, the library seemed all the more disturbing to me. It was then the place of long, centuries-old murmuring, an imperceptible dialogue between one parchment and another, a living thing, a receptacle of powers not to be ruled by a human mind, a treasure of secrets emanated by many minds, surviving the death of those who had produced them or had been their conveyors.

⚓

Starting from within a Kantian framework, like Fichte, Hegel discards Kant's notion of mind-independent reality, the "thing-in-itself," as ultimately unintelligible. He begins with Kant's notion of necessary truths that are not logically necessary (the synthetic a priori), the linchpin requiring the mind to exist not in a passive relation to its objects but, up to a point, as an active participant in the construction of objects. Beyond that point, for Kant, the objects in the world exist as mind-independent things-in-themselves, contributing something to the phenomenal objects in the same way that the mind contributes to them, and that is why the phenomenal world exists as a sort of superposition of the effects of objects as things-in-themselves and the effects of the faculties of the knowing mind. Hegel also puts similar great emphasis on necessary truths that are not necessary in the logical sense. But instead of positing any mind-independent things-in-themselves that exist beyond experience, affecting objects in a way that necessarily involves the possibility of experience as discoverable by the natural sciences, *Hegel's necessity comes from within the mind* and such necessities are *expressed by the laws of history*. In this way the unseen is brought (and itself created) into view, where it can then be explored, examined, and further developed.

According to Hegel, the laws of history follow a necessary process, and so a structure is thereby imposed upon consciousness in the same way that for Kant things-in-themselves impose it. Thus, for Hegel as for Kant, necessary truths are mind-dependent and not logically necessary; but for Hegel, as for all subsequent absolute idealists, these truths do not depend in any way on some sort of substance beyond the reach of mind. All that exists is the mental: one thinking substance, the thinking subject. Truth therefore depends not on some correspondence between a mind-independent reality and its representation in the mind but, rather, on coherence within a complete system of thought. "The true is the whole." A complete system in Hegel's sense thus does not *correspond* to any objective reality; it *is*, itself, objective reality. Again, this Hegelian whole is *not* a static thing existing beyond, or transcendental to, the world but is immanent in it as an evolutionary, developing process existing within the world itself, accessible to the philosopher through Hegel's theory of dialectic.

Hegel's theory of dialectic begins with the thesis, an initial proposition that turns out to be false or inadequate. The thesis then generates a contradictory proposition, its antithesis, which also turns out to be false or inadequate. This then leads to a rationality-preserving and irrationality-canceling synthesis of the two initially contradictory propositions, which he calls "sublation" (*Aufhebung*). This in turn leads to a new thesis and the process continues indefinitely.

Hegel outlines this process in his third published work, *The Encyclopedia of the Philosophical Sciences in Outline* (1817), a manual written for his students explaining his entire philosophical system, starting with the notion that all is mind. Yet, as Kant had already pointed out, this is not how things *seem* to the mind. We seem to ourselves to be minds existing in an objective material world, surrounded by material objects that exist independently of our thoughts. This, what Kant called the "transcendental illusion," is an illusion that Hegel calls "estrangement," or "alienation" (*Entfremdung*). The difference is not just a matter of semantics. Hegel uses this language to imply that the illusion is grounded, not in an ontological boundary between the mental and nonmental world but wholly created within the mind by the mind; it is the mind's drawing a false boundary

within itself against itself. But, as in Kant, the awareness, or recognition, of this illusion is the first step to reaching the next stage of philosophical progress; that is, the mind's overcoming of the illusion that what is before the mind is not mind but mind-independent material objects (not by *ending* the illusion but merely, as in Kant, *recognizing* it) is the first part of the thesis-antithesis-synthesis process that culminates, ultimately, in the mind's "return to itself." These three stages of the development of thought are presented in the *Encyclopedia* in three parts. The first part is called "Logic," by which Hegel means not formal logic but what he called "the science of thought." Here he argues that since only thought exists, logic should be viewed as metaphysics; logic according to Hegel and the subsequent generation of absolute idealist philosophers is the study of "the idea in and for itself." Thus, he would proclaim to his students: "The Living Being is a syllogism whose very moments are syllogisms." The second part of his *Encyclopedia* is the Philosophy of Nature, the study of "the idea in its otherness"; and the third part, the Philosophy of Mind, is the study of the "idea come back to itself out of that otherness."

One can easily imagine that in the hands of a lesser philosopher Hegel's attempt to provide a systematic account of absolute reality as a whole might have ended up merely as an elaborate series of counterarguments to Kant's transcendental arguments in which Kant tried to show that reason's attempt to transcend the understanding and thereby grasp noumenal reality results in unresolvable antinomies. This approach, as we saw, was in large part the one taken by Schelling, for whom reality remains, as for Kant, an incomprehensible mystery. But Hegel is not content merely to argue *against* Kant; he insists that the true philosopher, as a stage in the development of the world-soul, must proceed beyond mere criticism and counterargument (which mirror the *antithesis* stage of the philosophical evolution of the universe) to evolve the system to its next level. *If* our only means for grasping the whole universe—the Absolute—were with the Kantian faculty of understanding, this would be impossible because the understanding is limited to its own divisive, contradictory concept pairs like "finite and infinite," "freedom and determinism," and so on. Such opposite concepts could never present to the mind reality as it exists in its totality, since *that absolute totality* is *not* divided. The universe would in that case remain, as it does for Kant and Schelling, ultimately incomprehensible and *statically* mysterious. Hegel, however, uses reason to transcend, not just the phenomenal world as a means of reaching the active faculties of the mind involved in the construction of the phenomena, but even beyond those faculties, to "transcend the understanding" and thereby "contain the opposites." In this way, the whole universe in its totality, the Absolute—Being itself—the "mystical" becomes inaccessible to *dialectical* thought which leads not to unresolvable antinomies but to the resolution of the contradictions. How?

Kant and Schelling both failed to pay sufficient attention to "the tremendous power of the negative." Typically, in our self-alienated, transcendental illusionary stage of consciousness, when we encounter deep contradiction and paradox in our thinking, we experience an unhappy dread. Seeking to avoid this state of mental confusion, reason is moved by the force of its own negativity toward its negativity to sublate its previous conception and to thereby progress to the next, higher stage, where it is free of the previous contradiction but will more than likely encounter another, even deeper and more perplexing one. Again, this is not merely some intellectual process in which philosophers engage but the very life and source of reality: "Being is thought" and "What is actual is rational." Nor is it a static process; the concept of *being,* as a thesis, gives rise to the opposite concept, its antithesis, *nonbeing.* With these opposites the mind is then perplexed to create a new sublation of these two into the concept that is their synthesis, *becoming;* the mind thus continues to extend itself beyond its own limits to create *a higher* or *expanded consciousness.*

In some ways, to use a crude contemporary analogy from computer science, Hegel is in a sense trying to increase the mind's "RAM" space. In fact, the analogy with computers is actually rather appropriate in our attempt to understand absolute idealism within a contemporary framework. Although one must always be cautious in using such analogies, it is a fact that many computer theorists, including philosophical logicians and cognitive philosophers, conceive of the entire universe as a computer program being run on an *abstract* rather than a physical computer. (Recall that our understanding of the concept of abstractness is in terms of something that does not exist in space and time.) Indeed, it is quite easy to see that the universe as a whole must be an abstract object in that it does not exist in space and time. Once you think about this a little it loses its mystery. What, after all, does it mean to be *somewhere*? It means to have a location. Location, in turn, is conceived in terms of having a containing space. Right now, for instance, I'm in my study, which is in my house, which is in New York, which is on the East Coast, which is on planet Earth, which is in the solar system, which is in the Milky Way galaxy, which is in the universe, which is . . . Well, where *is* the universe? Where *could* it be? If by universe we mean, as Hegel does, the totality of all existence, including the whole of space and time, the universe cannot be *in* any space. For in talking of the Absolute, Hegel is talking about the universe of all universes, such that even if there are other "super" and "hyper" spaces, the sum whole of all these types of spaces cannot be *in* any space.

So the universe must be nowhere. How, after all, did I provide location in each of the preceding series, from my room to the galaxies? In every case, I gave the larger map, the containing space. The universe conceived as the Absolute totality cannot, by definition, have a containing space. It is, therefore, *necessarily nowhere.* That's not just true, it *has* to be true! Likewise for time; this moment is now, which is today, which is within this week of this month of this year in this century in this millennium at the tail end of the universe's fifteen-billion-year history. But when does all this time take place? Again, to speak of the universe in Absolute terms, the absolute answer is *never*. This is because the universe contains not only all of space but also all of time. Thus the universe, which is nowhere, never happens! It has neither a place (position) where it exists nor a time in which it occurs. Thus the universe of universes, the Absolute, is more like *the set of all numbers*. And what, after all, are numbers? Recall our detailed discussion of numbers (on pages 41–46). Numbers are abstract entities. And the universe thus conceived as an abstract entity makes it amenable to the same kinds of analyses as mathematical objects.

We have seen this sort of metaphysical move brewing for centuries, both in the work of philosophers and the mathematically inspired scientists. It is so central to understanding the various revolutions in thought during our own century that it behooves us to go a bit further into it. Furthermore, it is deeply ironic that Hegel's system and the subsequent absolute idealist movements in the nineteenth century have often been regarded as somehow not being central to subsequent developments in philosophy, mathematics, physics, and computer science. Nothing could be further from the truth. What happened, historically, is that while philosophers descended (meant *literally*, not pejoratively) into the domain of logical analyses and reductions of thought to language, the development of the ideas of Kant and the nineteenth-century absolute idealists were carried forth by physicists like Einstein and Niels Bohr, whereas mathematicians like Alan Turing and logicians like Kurt Gödel and Alonzo Church dissolved the distinction between representation and reality to a new level of logical rigor, encodeable into the types of algorithmic processes that, when embedded in physical processes, became the universal machines now known as computers. Let us see if we can catch a glimpse of this process, which is perhaps itself a paradigm of the Hegelian process.

According to Hegel and the absolute idealists, *everything is thought*. But what is thought? We've discussed this question at various points using several different philosophical systems to get at this question.[11] Using methods that we should by now be familiar with, we can (when we attend to our own thoughts) very quickly come to realize that in the intellectual domain (meaning other than the perceptual representations—the visual impressions and ideas) thoughts exist as *auditory* images which themselves consist, in turn, of strings of words. Likewise, the *rational* thinking process, or insofar as it is rational, consists in stringing together *propositions*. Once we see this we can perhaps understand what is generally regarded as one of the most cryptic remarks of Hegel's, namely, that "the living being is a syllogism whose very moments are syllogisms."

Typically, such assertions by Hegel have been ridiculed as nonsensical. But, as has so often been the case, there may be far more to the statements of a great philosopher than what first meets the understanding. Perhaps truths about reality cannot fit into the limited and limiting mind space of our ordinary, commonsense understanding. Hegel and many subsequent philosophers to whom he was avatar believed that ordinary (natural) languages are inadequate in their present form and that their conceptual base must somehow be enhanced. In any case, here we have a statement like "Everything is made of water," which at first glance seems preposterous but may contain the seed of some great, as yet unblooming, insight: "Everything is a string of syllogisms." How could that be? A string of syllogisms, after all, is a string of *propositions*, which are the molecules making up a complex tautology strung together by *logic*.

But this is exactly the sort of process that happens in a computer program, except that the propositions have been further reduced to numbers. What is a computer program, philosophically speaking? Abstractly, a program can be represented as a map $f: N \to N$, where N is the set of natural numbers mapped onto N—that is, a map into itself. Given some input, which is just an integer or string of integers, the program can then use this number to generate another number as output. Contemporary computer theory is a decision procedure for determining what constitutes an *effective* procedure (a way of going on; a "rule") and describing its attributes (what states it is in and what states it can get to—its "memory bank"). Today, not only can we model (represent) the human mind using a computer program but also the entire universe by using a formal language in which the universe evolves deterministically from an initial state into a final state.[12] If you think of "formal" languages as related to Plato's forms, you will not be far off the mark; the term refers to languages such as logic and mathematics that are used to talk, not about actual particular objects in the world, such as "All Swedes are persons" and "My sweater is pretty," but the general forms of grammar and syntax underlying them, such as "All *S* are *P*" and "Some *S* are *P*," and so on. The same holds, less obviously, for mathematics.

What absolute idealists do in equating reality with the process of thought is remarkably analogous to what a computer scientist does in viewing the universe as equivalent to its simulation,[13] conceived as a Universal Program. Likewise, within the general Universal Program human beings are conceived as subprograms that act in exactly the same way in the "simulation" as "real" human beings do in the "real" universe. Suppose you ask: But how could operations consisting not of the sensations of happiness and sadness, dryness, and wetness, and so on, but of electrical impulses in computer wiring, be the same as real human thought? Well, then you have to ask yourself what things like the experience of sadness and the experience of rain— mental events in what you call the "real" world—consist in? *In the firing of neurons* (happiness) and *in the activities of clouds* (rain)? But what are neurons? What are clouds and rain? These all consist in the movement of molecules which are neither happy nor wet. H_2O is just a constellation of three little round atoms that are *not* wet! Likewise, a sequence of neurons is a sequence of neurons and *not*, itself, happy or sad!

Thus, starting from an absolute idealist perspective, the question would have to be reversed: How can "real wires," "real computers," "real rocks, rivers, and hurricanes," and so on, consist not in *physical* things but in *mental* things? Hegel's elaborate answer comes in the form, not just of a metaphysical theory but a logical procedure for carrying out such a program into the faculties of human understanding, thereby increasing the logical space of the understanding. Once this happens the philosopher is in a position to see why the mind's "models" of reality are, themselves, reality: because, in a nutshell, in Hegel's world there is no underlying substantive thing in itself. Thoughts are themselves not only the objects of our experience but also the elements of reality.

In other words, and more explicitly, the Hegelian process of enlightenment consists not in transcending beyond the phenomenal world outwardly, to things in themselves, nor inwardly, to the mental faculties of the understanding, but in breaking through the logical categories. That is, Hegel wants to use the old logic of Aristotle to move into the realm of a higher logic in which contradictions are not errors (irrationalities) but a method of cognitive evolution. When the mind evolves to this higher level, the ontological distinction between concept pairs like "being, nonbeing," "something, nothing," "imaginary, real," "subjective, objective," "phenomenal, noumenal," "mental, physical," "perceptual, conceptual," "representational, presentational," "simulational, actual," and so on, disappears such that all distinctions derived from the false dichotomy between empiricist and rationalist systems of thought dissolve.

To put it in contemporary computer language: the universal simulation does not *need* to run on an "actual" computer to be exactly what it is. Rather, the universal simulation is to be regarded as an abstract sequence of mappings, meaning that it does not need to exist in space and time. This is reminiscent of Plato's forms except that you may recall why, for Hegel as for Berkeley and Kant, to be an object in space and time *means simply to be a mental event*. Follow this through to its ultimate conclusion and you will get the whole, complicated upshot of Hegel's almost incomprehensible system, which we might put as follows: *To be a mental event, a mental event does not need to be a mental event!*

That last statement may well be the sum and substance of what has since evolved into the revolution in thought that we are presently undergoing. It is, of course, too soon to tell.

In any case, this statement is sufficient for our purposes of giving you some access to the idea that the actual universe in which we live can be properly regarded as a representation of the abstract universal program *in exactly the way that the numeral "3" is a representation of the number 3* (as we discussed in our sections on the systems of Pythagoras and Plato).[14] In other words—and this is the new additional step in computer theory that parallels the move made by the absolute idealists—*the actual physical computer is itself a representation of an abstract program.*[15]

Staying with our analogy with computers, we can continue to make sense of Hegel's system as follows. Individual minds like yours and mine, as rational subroutines living in (functioning within) the universal program, cannot distinguish between the abstract running of the universal program and the physically real evolution of the universe. Such a universe would be a Kantian noumenal thing-in-itself, which is excluded not just by the absolute idealists but also by the twentieth-century logical systems of the type invented by Kurt Gödel and Alonzo Church. Models of what a real computer program is and a real computer program *are identical objects* in exactly the way that Hegel envisioned. The Universe, regarded as an abstract program, is an Absolute Idea. It has exactly the same nature as our individual human minds, the programs or subroutines running within it. The absolute idealists' conception of individual intellectual *acts,* none of which are substances or things in themselves but rather abstract objects

(see Section 17.0), is thus analogous to the fundamental map (procedure or program) that takes the universe (the universal program) from one state into the next. Reality can thus be viewed as a series of operations of an abstract universal machine.

In this view, the real universe is an abstract entity that is an unimaginably complex program that forms subprograms, the most important of which is a model of itself as a subprogram—the world presented as objective reality—and a subprogram for studying this subprogram—the human mind, or consciousness. But that's not all. As it turns out, the famous incompleteness theorems of Kurt Gödel show that an exact model of such a process involving all processes is impossible—even for infinite machines such as the universal Turing machine.[16] Thus, the various approaches of the subjective and objective idealists can today be further explained using these contemporary terms, as follows.

A subjective idealist system such as Fichte's starts with the finite rational subprograms of individual human egos as the foundation. It then constructs a representation of the universal program, using the logical functions inherent in the rational operations of our own individual conscious minds, whereas an *objective idealist system* such as Schelling's starts with the universal program as the foundation and then constructs individual rational minds as parts inherent in the very nature of the universal program, necessary elements for making the whole not just a whole but *real. An absolute idealist system* such as Hegel's takes yet a third approach. Basically, in a Hegelian evolving system neither the Fichte- or Schelling-type idealisms are real options to be discovered; rather, the philosophies are part of the construction. In other words, the universe—the whole of reality—is presently writing itself into existence!

But, if anything like this is really true, and we *are* that, why don't we see it? Why don't we understand it? Why is philosophy so difficult?

One way of putting it, and the way on which subsequent phenomenologists such as Heidegger will build their systems, would be this: a necessary condition for comprehensibility is incomprehensibility. Such developments will parallel advances made in mathematics, where it turns out that the most difficult theorems can be proven once it is proven that no proof exists; this allows a proof to be made! Recall Fichte's contention, derived from Kant's analysis of the necessary conditions for the having of experience, that in order to be conscious a mind must necessarily interpret some of its own activities as other than its own activities. Put in physicalist language: the neurons of a properly functioning brain must function so as to tell one another, at some point, "I am not a neuron," or "I am not a neural firing," or, "I am not an event in the brain." You see a chair, after all, and even on the most basic physical understanding of the brain, seeing a chair means that a part of the brain (somewhere in the calcarine fissure, according to the latest neurophysiological theory, where the active neural processing of perceptual events takes place as such) is interpreted by another part of the brain as not being part of the brain! This, in a nutshell, is a very stripped down version of a very difficult to understand twentieth-century theorem, which we've already referred to, known as Gödel's theorem. In effect, as we are here presenting it, such an insight says that any system must, in order to be a properly functioning system, *lie to itself*. Translating this into a computer language vocabulary, we could say that a computer program can be conscious only if it is embedded as a subroutine in a larger program containing many such subroutines that are interpreted by each subroutine, not as subroutines in a program but as an external world. Furthermore, not only must the Universal Program give rise to self-conscious subprograms, but these must in turn continue to evolve toward becoming one. *Only at that point does the Universal Program actually come into existence as such.* In other words, the problem is that the world is not *yet* fully comprehensible! Such Hegelian thinking, involving a bootstrap metaphysics

where the future brings about the past, is exactly of the sort found in recent quantum models of the universe, such as that of John Archibald Wheeler. According to Wheeler, we live in a "participatory universe"[17] in which our own acts of consciousness actualize reality retroactively. Such thinking comes out of the so-called measurement problem in quantum mechanics, and this was already quite explicitly anticipated by Hegel.

※

Logic

Measure is the qualitative quantum, in the first place as immediate,—a quantum, to which a determinate being or a quality is attached.

Measure, where quality and quantity are in one, is thus the completion of Being. Being, as we first apprehend it, is something utterly abstract and characterless: but it is the very essence of Being to characterise itself, and its complete characterisation is reached in Measure. Measure, like the other stages of Being, may serve as a definition of the Absolute: God, it has been said, is the measure of all things. It is this idea which forms the groundnote of many of the ancient Hebrew hymns, in which the glorification of God tends in the main to show that He has appointed to everything its bound: to the sea and the solid land, to the rivers and mountains; and also to the various kinds of plants and animals. To the religious sense of the Greeks the divinity of measure, especially in respect of social ethics, was represented by Nemesis. That conception implies a general theory that all human things, riches, honour, and power, as well as joy and pain, have their definite measure, the transgression of which brings ruin and destruction.

※

In the conscious mind such discreet, *quantum* measurement states *are the reality* necessary to bring the world into being. Prior to such acts of

From *The Logic of Hegel*, William Wallace, trans. (Oxford, 1842), with emendations by the author.

consciousness, all events subsisted in a weird superposition of ghostly possibilities that came into a state of *being* only through the process of measurement.

The fundamental philosophical basis for such thinking emerges from Hegel's notion of the universe in terms of ultimately self-thinking thought, where philosophy can be viewed as *the evolving software of an abstract universal machine, the universe.* But then we must remember that philosophy is not yet a done act! The entire process of human history, as presented in Hegel's system of thought, is the evolving *struggle* of the universe to become aware of itself. This incredible idea is laid out in great detail in the first and most difficult of Hegel's systematic works; published in 1807, *The Phenomenology of Mind* describes the stages that consciousness must necessarily undergo in its evolution from naive common-sense notions of reality to a truly philosophical, synthetic view and full self-consciousness, in which the universe not only fully realizes that it exists but therein creates itself through "the consciousness of its own freedom." Starting with the "unhappy consciousness" stage—a subjectively idealistic, abstract, and dualistic view of truth that represents itself in our conscious psychologies as a lonely, religious quest for some remote, "changeless," deified, consciousness—it begins the slow process of awakening into its final, absolute stage. The process of Hegelian enlightenment is thus not just the process of our trying to become lovers of wisdom, though it *is* that. It is also the enlightenment of the world entire, of being itself, through a process whose machinery can be studied. That process is history.

Armed with some glimpses into Hegel's elaborate philosophical thought, let us thus turn to the following selection from his posthumously published *Lectures on the Philosophy of History* (1837), which Hegel delivered between 1822 and 1831, and which were supplemented with two sets of notes by students. Here Hegel gives an account of "the philosophical history of the world," by which he means not observations on history or the study of records and facts, nor even reflections on history, but the "universal history" of the evolutionary unfolding of thought itself, the absolute world-mind trying to realize itself.

⚓

Lectures on the Philosophy of History

[T]he Greek Anaxagoras was the first to enunciate the doctrine that nous, Understanding in general, or Reason, governs the world. It is not intelligence as self-conscious Reason, not a spirit as such, that is meant; and we must clearly distinguish these from each other. The movement of the solar system takes place according to unchangeable laws. These laws are Reason, implicit in the phenomena in question. But neither the sun nor the planets that revolve around it according to these laws can be said to have any consciousness of them.

A thought of this kind—that Nature is an embodiment of Reason; that it is unchangeably subordinate to universal laws—appears nowise striking or strange to us. We are accustomed to such conceptions, and find nothing extraordinary in them. And I have mentioned this extraordinary occurrence partly to show how history teaches that ideas of this kind, which may seem trivial to us, have not always been in the world; that on the contrary, such a thought marks an epoch in the annals of human intelligence. Aristotle says of Anaxagoras, as the originator of the thought in question, that he appeared as a sober man among the drunken. Socrates adopted the doctrine from Anaxagoras, and it forthwith became the ruling idea in Philosophy—except in the school of Epicurus, who ascribed all events to chance. "I was delighted with the sentiment," Plato makes Socrates say, "and hoped I had found a teacher who would show me Nature in harmony with Reason, who would demonstrate in each particular phenomenon its specific aim, and in the whole, the grand object of the Universe. I would not have surrendered this hope for a great deal. But how very much was I disappointed, when, having zealously applied myself to the writings of Anaxagoras, I found that he adduces only external causes, such as Atmosphere, Ether, Water, and the like." It is evident that the defect Socrates complains of respecting Anaxagoras' doctrine does not concern the principle itself but the shortcoming of the propounder in applying it to Nature in the concrete. Nature is not deduced from that principle: the latter remains in fact a mere abstraction, inasmuch as the former is not comprehended and exhibited as a development of it—an organization produced by and from Reason. I wish, at the very outset, to call your attention to the important difference between a conception, a principle, a truth limited to an *abstract* form and its determinate application and concrete development. This distinction affects the whole fabric of philosophy; and among other bearings of it there is one to which we shall have to revert at the close of our view of Universal History, in investigating the aspect of political affairs in the most recent period.

(2) We have next to notice the rise of this idea—that Reason directs the world—in connection with a further application of it, well known to us: in the form, viz. of the religious truth that the world is not abandoned to chance and external contingent causes, but that a Providence controls it. I stated above that I would not make a demand on your faith with regard to the principle announced. Yet I might appeal to your belief in it, in this religious aspect, if, as a general rule, the nature of philosophical science allowed it to attach authority to presuppositions. To put it in another form, this appeal is forbidden, because the science of which we have to treat proposes itself to furnish the proof (not indeed of the abstract Truth of the doctrine, but) of its correctness as compared with facts. The truth, then, that a Providence (that of God) presides over the events of the World, consorts with the proposition in question; for Divine Providence is Wisdom endowed with an infinite Power, which realizes its aim, viz. the absolute rational design of the World. Reason is Thought conditioning itself with perfect freedom. But a difference—rather a contradiction—will manifest itself, between this belief and our principle, just as was the case in reference to the demand made by Socrates in the case of Anaxagoras' dictum. For that belief is similarly indefinite; it is what is called a belief in a general Providence, and is not followed out into definite application, or displayed in its bearing on the grand total—the entire course of human history. But to *explain* History is to depict the passions of mankind, the genius, the active powers, that play their part on the great stage; and the providentially determined process that these exhibit constitutes what is generally called the "plan" of Providence. Yet it is

this very plan which is supposed to be concealed from our view: which it is deemed presumption even to wish to recognize. The ignorance of Anaxagoras as to how intelligence reveals itself in actual existence was ingenuous. Neither in his consciousness nor in that of Greece at large had that thought been further expanded. He had not attained the power to apply his general principle to the concrete, so as to deduce the latter from the former. It was Socrates who took the first step in comprehending the union of the Concrete with the Universal. Anaxagoras, then, did not take up a hostile position towards such an application. The common belief in Providence *does*; at least it opposes the use of the principle on the large scale, and denies the possibility of discerning the plan of Providence. In isolated cases this plan is supposed to be manifest. Pious persons are encouraged to recognize in particular circumstances something more than mere chance, to acknowledge the guiding hand of God—*e.g.* when help has unexpectedly come to an individual in great perplexity and need. But these instances of providential design are of a limited kind, and concern, the accomplishment of nothing more than the desires of the individual in question. But in the history of the World, the Individuals we have to do with are Peoples, totalities that are States. We cannot, therefore, be satisfied with what we may call this "peddling" view of Providence, to which the belief alluded to limits itself. Equally unsatisfactory is the merely abstract, undefined belief in a Providence, when that belief is not brought to bear upon the details of the process which it conducts. On the contrary our earnest endeavor must be directed to the recognition of the ways of Providence, the means it uses, and the historical phenomena in which it manifests itself; and we must show their connection.

⚓

17.3 Schopenhauer (1788–1860): The Will of the World

Arthur Schopenhauer was born in the free city of Danzig; when Prussia took over in 1793, his father, a successful and liberal-minded merchant, moved the family to Hamburg. At the age of nine Schopenhauer was sent for two years to Le Havre to learn French and then for four years to a boarding school in Hamburg. As a teenager he traveled for two years through England, France, Switzerland, and Austria, until his father made him go to work at a merchant's office. Schopenhauer was only seventeen when his father committed suicide by throwing himself into a canal.

Schopenhauer moved with his mother, a novelist, to Weimar and studied literature until 1809 when he enrolled at the University of Göttingen. He began studying medicine but two years later moved to the University of Berlin to study with Fichte. He completed his doctorate in philosophy at Jena.

Deeply influenced by Plato and Kant, for whom he had the highest regard, Schopenhauer's own philosophy developed out of the idealism espoused by Kant, Fichte, and Hegel, the latter whom he despised. He blended elements of the Kantian and Platonic views of ideas, Oriental mysticism (especially Indian philosophy), Goethe's (whom he met through his mother) romanticism, the views of Fichte and Schelling, as well as the British empiricists (especially Locke and Hume). When at the age of thirty he published his most important work, *The World as Will and Idea* (also translated as *The World as Will and Representation*), he expected it would cause a great stir, but for the next thirty years it was almost universally ignored. The book did, however, help him to get a teaching position in philosophy at the University of Berlin at the same time as Hegel, whose ideas had already begun to dominate German philosophy. Although their philosophies had much in common, both systems of thought having been developed from a Kantian framework, Schopenhauer vehemently and openly opposed Hegel's use of the concept of reason as the basic force of the world, arguing instead that what is most fundamental to the world is *will*. He tried to compete with Hegel by scheduling his own lectures at the same time; much to his disappointment, he never managed to achieve any following among the students, while Hegel's influence continued to spread throughout the whole of Europe. Schopenhauer left Berlin, bitter and dejected. Here is what he had to say about his colleague:

Hegel, installed from above by the powers that be as the certified Great Philosopher, was a flat-headed, insipid, nauseating, illiterate charlatan, who reached the pinnacle of audacity in scribbling together and dishing up the craziest mystifying nonsense.

His view of most other philosophers, with the exception of Plato and Kant, was not much better; he referred to them as "windbags."

Although he continued to write for the rest of his life, it was only after issuing a second edition of *The World as Will and Idea* in 1844 along with fifty supplementary chapters that he began to attract attention. Then in his sixties, he suddenly found himself the center of a rapidly growing international following of philosophers, psychologists, writers, and musicians who had discovered him. His reputation quickly spread by word of mouth. Some of his most famous and devoted adherents included Friedrich Nietzsche, Richard Wagner, Leo Tolstoy, Joseph Conrad, Marcel Proust, Thomas Mann, and Sigmund Freud.

In *The World as Will and Idea,* from which the following selection is taken, Schopenhauer takes as his starting point that everything you are right now experiencing and have ever experienced—the world entire—*is you*. Everything you do, everyone you've ever known, every object you have ever seen or touched, is all, literally, your dream: "The world is my idea." But that is only the half of it. The dark twist is yet to come.

The World as Will and Idea

The World as Idea

"The world is my idea":—this is a truth which holds good for everything that lives and knows, though

From *Die Welt als Willie und Volstellung*, Leipzig, 1810; 3. Aufl. 1859. Reprinted here from A. Schopenhauer's *The World as Will and Idea*, translated by R. B. Haldane and J. Kemp, London, Trübner & Co., 1883, vol. i, with emendations by the author.

man alone can bring it into reflective and abstract consciousness. If he really does this, he has attained to philosophical wisdom. It then becomes clear and certain to him that what he knows is not a sun and an earth, but only an eye that sees a sun, a hand that feels an earth; that the world which surrounds him is there only as idea, *i.e.,* only in relation to something else, the consciousness, which is himself. If any truth can be asserted *a priori,* it is this: for it is the expression of the most general form of all possible and thinkable experience: a form which is more general than time, or space, or causality, for they all presuppose it; and each of these, which we have seen to be just so many modes of the principle of sufficient reason, is valid only for a particular class of ideas; whereas the antithesis of object and subject is the common form of all these classes, is that form under which alone any idea of whatever kind it may be, abstract or intuitive, pure or empirical, is possible and thinkable. No truth therefore is more certain, more independent of all others, and less in need of proof than this, that all that exists for knowledge, and therefore this whole world, is only object in relation to subject, perception of a perceiver, in a word, idea. This is obviously true of the past and the future, as well as of the present, of what is farthest off, as of what is near; for it is true of time and space themselves, in which alone these distinctions arise. All that in any way belongs or can belong to the world is inevitably thus conditioned through the subject, and exists only for the subject The world is idea.

The truth is by no means new. It was implicitly involved in the sceptical reflections from which Descartes started. Berkeley, however, was the first who distinctly enunciated it, and by this he has rendered a permanent service to philosophy, even though the rest of his teaching should not endure. Kant's primary mistake was the neglect of this principle, as is shown in the appendix. How early again this truth was recognised by the wise men of India, appearing indeed as the fundamental tenet of the Vedânta philosophy. . . .

In this first book, then, we consider the world only from this side, only so far as it is idea. The inward reluctance with which any one accepts the world as merely his idea, warns him that this view of it, however true it may be, is nevertheless one-sided, adopted in consequence of some arbitrary abstraction. And yet it is a conception from which he can never free himself. The defectiveness of this view will be corrected in the next book by means of a truth which is not so immediately certain as that from which we start here; a truth at which we can arrive only by deeper research and more severe abstraction, by the separation of what is different and the union of what is identical. This truth, which must be very serious and impressive if not awful to every one, is that a man can also say and must say, "The world is my will."

In this book, however, we must consider separately that aspect of the world from which we start, its aspect as knowable, and therefore, in the meantime, we must, without reserve, regard all presented objects, even our own bodies (as we shall presently show more fully), merely as ideas, and call them merely ideas. By so doing we always abstract from will (as we hope to make clear to every one further on), which by itself constitutes the other aspect of the world. For as the world is in one aspect entirely *idea,* so in another it is entirely *will.* A reality which is neither of these two, but an object in itself (into which the thing in itself has unfortunately dwindled in the hands of Kant), is the phantom of a dream, and its acceptance is an *ignis fatuus* in philosophy.

That which knows all things and is known by none is the subject. Thus it is the supporter of the world, that condition of all phenomena, of all objects which is always presupposed throughout experience; for all that exists, exists only for the subject. Every one finds himself to be subject, yet only in so far as he knows, not in so far as he is an object of knowledge. But his body is object, and therefore from this point of view we call it idea. For the body is an object among objects and is conditioned by the laws of objects, although it is an immediate object. Like all objects of perception, it lies within the universal forms of knowledge, time and space, which are the conditions of multiplicity. The subject, on the contrary, which is always the knower, never the known, does not come under these forms, but is presupposed by them; it has therefore neither multiplicity nor its opposite unity. We never know it, but it is always the knower wherever there is knowledge.

So then the world as idea, the only aspect in which we consider it at present, has two fundamental, necessary, and inseparable halves. The one half is the object, the forms of which are space and time, and through these multiplicity. The other half is the subject, which is not in space and time, for it is present, entire and undivided, in every percipient being. So that any one percipient being, with the object, constitutes the whole world as idea just as fully as the existing millions could do; but if this one were to disappear, then the whole world as idea would cease to be. These halves are therefore inseparable even for thought, for each of the two has meaning and existence only through and for the other, each appears with the other and vanishes with it. They limit each other immediately; where the object begins the subject ends. The universality of this limitation is shown by the fact that the essential and hence universal forms of all objects, space, time, and causality, may, without knowledge of the object, be discovered and fully known from a consideration of the subject, *i.e.,* in Kantian language, they lie *a priori* in our consciousness. That he discovered this is one of Kant's principal merits, and it is a great one. . . .

So far as we have considered the question of the reality of the outer world, it arises from a confusion which amounts even to a misunderstanding of reason itself, and therefore thus far, the question could be answered only by explaining its meaning. After examination of the whole nature of the principle of sufficient reason, of the relation of subject and object, and the special conditions of sense perception, the question itself disappeared because it had no longer any meaning. There is, however, one other possible origin of this question, quite different from the purely speculative one which we have considered, a specially empirical origin, though the question is always raised from a speculative point of view, and in this form it has a much more comprehensible meaning than it had in the first. We have dreams; may not our whole life be a dream? or more exactly: is there a sure criterion of the distinction between dreams and reality? between phantasms and real objects? The assertion that what is dreamt is less vivid and distinct than what we actually perceive is not to the point, because no one has ever been able to make a fair comparison of the two; for we can only compare the recollection of a dream with the present reality. Kant answers the question thus: "The connection of ideas among themselves, according to the law of causality, constitutes the difference between real life and dreams." But in dreams, as well as in real life, everything is connected individually at any rate, in accordance with the principle of sufficient

reason in all its forms, and this connection is broken only between life and dreams, or between one dream and another. Kant's answer therefore could only run thus: —the *long* dream (life) has throughout complete connection according to the principle of sufficient reason; it has not this connection, however, with *short* dreams, although each of these has in itself the same connection: the bridge is therefore broken between the former and the latter, and on this account we distinguish them.

But to institute an enquiry according to this criterion, as to whether something was dreamt or seen, would always be difficult and . . . it must for ever remain uncertain whether an event was dreamt or really happened. Here, in fact, the intimate relationship between life and dreams is brought out very clearly, and we need not be ashamed to confess it, as it has been recognised and spoken of by many great men. The Vedas and Puranas have no better simile than a dream for the whole knowledge of the actual world, which they call the web of Mâyâ, and they use none more frequently. Plato often says that men live only in a dream; the philosopher alone strives to awake himself. . . . beside which most worthily stands Shakespeare:—

> We are such stuff
> As dreams are made of, and our little life
> Is rounded with a sleep.
> —*Tempest,* Act IV, Sc. 1.

Lastly, Calderon was so deeply impressed with this view of life that he sought to embody it in a kind of metaphysical drama—"Life a Dream."

After these numerous quotations from the poets, perhaps I also may be allowed to express myself by a metaphor. Life and dreams are leaves of the same book. The systematic reading of this book is real life, but when the reading hours (that is, the day) are over, we often continue idly to turn over the leaves, and read a page here and there without method or connection: often one we have read before, sometimes one that is new to us, but always in the same book. Such an isolated page is indeed out of connection with the systematic study of the book, but it does not seem so very different when we remember that the whole continuous perusal begins and ends just as abruptly, and may therefore be regarded as merely a larger single page.

Thus although individual dreams are distinguished from real life by the fact that they do not fit into that continuity which runs through the whole of experience, and the act of awaking brings this into consciousness, yet that very continuity of experience belongs to real life as its form, and the dream on its part can point to a similar continuity in itself. If, therefore, we consider the question from a point of view external to both, there is no distinct difference in their nature, and we are forced to concede to the poets that life is a long dream.

᛭

Often, when people start out reading Schopenhauer they get an uplifting, positive sense of enlightenment; your life is a dream, the world is a dream—what could be better than that? But Schopenhauer's philosophy now turns on a subtle and dark twist. For there is a second part to the equation. *If everything is a dream, why is there so much suffering, despair, violence? Why is the world so horrible?* Here is Schopenhauer's dark answer: "The World is my will." In other words, things are as you willed them. What does that reveal about you?

Let us go back to Schopenhauer's starting point, the Kantian distinction between phenomena (appearances) and noumena (things-in-themselves) and apply it to our own intimate experience of ourselves. We saw why Kant claimed the noumenal world of things-in-themselves would forever have to remain beyond reach of the phenomena and even of reason. The noumenal world according to Kant remains unknowable. But according to Schopenhauer that noumenal world of the thing in itself is very much involved in every aspect of every experience. It is none other than the will.

What is the will? This is not some abstract notion. You can *see* the will. Your body. The tables and chairs. All the things you see, feel, and experience. It is all the active construction of the will at work.

This is explained in the next section. Schopenhauer begins by pointing out that you are to yourself a phenomenal object in the same way as a table, rock, or tree. Yet, your self-consciousness reveals that you are much more than that: the perceivable body extended in space and time does not just respond and react to its environment; it is, itself, an embodiment of *will*.

᛭

The World as Will

. . . . What now impels us to inquiry is, that we are not satisfied with knowing that we have ideas, that they are such and such, and that they are connected according to certain laws, the general expression of which is the principle of sufficient reason. We wish to know the significance of these ideas; we ask whether this world is merely idea; in which case it would pass by us like an empty dream or a baseless vision, not worth our notice; or whether it is also something else, something more than idea, and if so, what. Thus much is certain, that this something we seek for must be completely and in its whole nature different from the idea; that the forms and laws of the idea must therefore be completely foreign to it; further, that we cannot arrive at it from the idea under the guidance of the laws which merely combine objects, ideas, among themselves, and which are the forms of the principle of sufficient reason.

Thus we see already that we can never arrive at the real nature of things from without. However much we investigate, we can never reach anything but images and names. We are like a man who goes round a castle seeking in vain for an entrance, and sometimes sketching the façades. And yet this is the method that has been followed by all philosophers before me.

In fact, the meaning for which we seek of that world which is present to us only as our idea, or the transition from the world as mere idea of the knowing subject to whatever it may be besides this, would never be found if the investigator himself were nothing more than the pure knowing subject (a winged cherub without a body). But he is himself rooted in that world; he finds himself in it as an *individual*, that is to say, his knowledge, which is the necessary supporter of the whole world as idea, is yet always given through the medium of a body, whose affections are, as we have shown, the starting-point for the understanding in the perception of that world. His body is, for the pure knowing subject, an idea like every other idea, an object among objects. Its movements and actions are so far known to him in precisely the same way as the changes of all other perceived objects, and would be just as strange and incomprehensible to him if their meaning were not explained for him in an entirely different way. Otherwise he would see his actions follow upon given motives with the constancy of a law of nature just as the changes of other objects follow upon causes, stimuli, or motives. But he would not understand the influence of the motives any more than the connection between every other effect which he sees and its cause. He would then call the inner nature of these manifestations and actions of his body which he did not understand a force, a quality, or a character, as he pleased, but he would have no further insight into it. But all this is not the case; indeed the answer to the riddle is given to the subject of knowledge who appears as an individual, and the answer is *will*. This and this alone gives him the key to his own existence, reveals to him the significance, shows him the inner mechanism of his being, of his action, of his movements. The body is given in two entirely different ways to the subject of knowledge, who becomes an individual only through his identity with it. It is given as an idea in intelligent perception, as an object among objects and subject to the laws of objects. And it is also given in quite a different way as that which is immediately known to every one, and is signified by the word *will*. Every true act of his will is also at once and without exception a movement of his body. The act of will and the movement of the body are not two different things objectively known, which the bond of causality unites; they do not stand in the relation of cause and effect; they are one and the same, but they are given in entirely different ways,— immediately, and again in perception for the understanding. The action of the body is nothing but the act of the will objectified, *i.e.*, passed into perception. It will appear later that this is true of every movement of the body, not merely those which follow upon motives, but also involuntary movements which follow upon mere stimuli, and, indeed, that the whole body is nothing but objectified will, *i.e.*, will become idea. All this will be proved and made quite clear in the course of this

work. In one respect, therefore, I shall call the body the *objectivity of will*; as in the previous book, and in the essay on the principle of sufficient reason, in accordance with the one-sided point of view intentionally adopted there (that of the idea), I called it *the immediate object*. Thus in a certain sense we may also say that will is the knowledge *a priori* of the body, and the body is the knowledge *a posteriori* of the will. Resolutions of the will which relate to the future are merely deliberations of the reason about what we shall will at a particular time, not real acts of will. Only the carrying out of the resolve stamps it as will, for till then it is never more than an intention that may be changed, and that exists only in the reason *in abstracto*. It is only in reflection that to will and to act are different; in reality they are one. Every true, genuine, immediate act of will is also, at once and immediately, a visible act of the body. And, corresponding to this, every impression upon the body is also, on the other hand, at once and immediately an impression upon the will. As such it is called pain when it is opposed to the will; gratification or pleasure when it is in accordance with it. The degrees of both are widely different. It is quite wrong, however, to call pain and pleasure ideas, for they are by no means ideas, but immediate affections of the will in its manifestation, the body; compulsory, instantaneous willing or not-willing of the impression which the body sustains. There are only a few impressions of the body which do not touch the will, and it is through these alone that the body is an immediate object of knowledge, for, as perceived by the understanding, it is already an indirect object like all others. These impressions are, therefore, to be treated directly as mere ideas, and excepted from what has been said. The impressions we refer to are the affections of the purely objective senses of sight, hearing, and touch, though only so far as these organs are affected in the way which is specially peculiar to their specific nature. This affection of them is so excessively weak an excitement of the heightened and specifically modified sensibility of these parts that it does not affect the will, but only furnishes the understanding with the data out of which the perception arises, undisturbed by any excitement of the will. But every stronger or different kind of affection of these organs of sense is painful, that is to say, against the will, and thus they also belong to its objectivity. Weakness of the nerves shows itself in this, that the impressions which have only such a degree of strength as would usually be sufficient to make them data for the understanding reach the higher degree at which they influence the will, that is to say, give pain or pleasure, though more often pain, which is, however, to some extent deadened and inarticulate, so that not only particular tones and strong light are painful to us, but there ensues a generally unhealthy and hypochondriacal disposition which is not distinctly understood. The identity of the body and the will shows itself further, among other ways, in the circumstance that every vehement and excessive movement of the will, *i.e.*, every emotion, agitates the body and its inner constitution directly, and disturbs the course of its vital functions. This is shown in detail in "'Will in Nature," p. 27 of the second edition and p. 28 of the third.

Lastly, the knowledge which I have of my will, though it is immediate, cannot be separated from that which I have of my body. I know my will, not as a whole, not as a unity, not completely, according to its nature, but I know it only in its particular acts, and therefore in time, which is the form of the phenomenal aspect of my body, as of every object. Therefore the body is a condition of the knowledge of my will. Thus, I cannot really imagine this will apart from my body. In the essay on the principle of sufficient reason, the will, or rather the subject of willing, is treated as a special class of ideas or objects. But even there we saw this object become one with the subject; that is, we saw it cease to be an object. We there called this union the miracle, and the whole of the present work is to a certain extent an explanation of this. So far as I know my will specially as object, I know it as body. . . .

. . . [C]onsequently every individual act, and also its condition, the whole body itself which accomplishes it, and therefore also the process through which and in which it exists, are nothing but the manifestation of the will, the becoming visible, *the objectification of the will*. Upon this rests the perfect suitableness of the human and animal body to the human and animal will in general, resembling, though far surpassing, the correspondence between an instrument made for a purpose and the will of the maker, and on this account appearing as design, *i.e.*, the teleological explanation of the body. The parts of the body must, therefore, completely correspond to the principal desires through which the will manifests itself; they must be the visible

expression of these desires. Teeth, throat, and bowels are objectified hunger; the organs of generation are objectified sexual desire; the grasping hand, the hurrying feet, correspond to the more indirect desires of the will which they express. As the human form generally corresponds to the human will generally, so the individual bodily structure corresponds to the individually modified will, the character of the individual, and therefore it is throughout and in all parts characteristic and full of expression. It is this application of reflection alone that prevents us from remaining any longer at the phenomenon, and leads us to the *thing in itself.* Phenomenal existence is idea and nothing more. All Idea, of whatever kind it may be, all *object,* is *phenomenal* existence, but the *will* alone is a *thing in itself.* Now, all this is very well, but to me, when I consider the vastness of the world, the most important point is this, that the thing-in-itself, whose manifestation is the world—whatever else it may be—cannot have its true self spread out and dispersed after this fashion in boundless space, but that this endless extension belongs only to its manifestation. The thing-in-itself, on the contrary is present entire and undivided in every object of nature and in every living being. Therefore we lose nothing by standing still beside any single individual thing, and true wisdom is not to be gained by measuring out the boundless world, or, what would be more to the purpose, by actually traversing endless space. It is rather to be attained by the thorough investigation of any individual thing, for thus we seek to arrive at a full knowledge and understanding of its true and peculiar nature.

The subject which . . . has, doubtless, already presented itself to the mind of every student of Plato, is, that these different grades of the objectification of will which are manifested in innumerable individuals, and exist as their unattained types or as the eternal forms of things, not entering themselves into time and space, which are the medium of individual things, but remaining fixed, subject to no change, always being, never becoming, while the particular things arise and pass away, always become and never are,—that these *grades of the objectification of will* are, I say, simply *Plato's Ideas*. I make this passing reference to the matter here in order that I may be able in future to use the word *Idea* in this sense. In my writings, therefore, the word is always to be understood in its true and original meaning given to it by Plato, and has absolutely no reference to those abstract productions of dogmatising scholastic reason, which Kant has inaptly and illegitimately used this word to denote, though Plato had already appropriated and used it most fitly. By Idea, then, I understand every definite and fixed grade of the objectification of will, so far as it is thing-in-itself, and therefore has no multiplicity. . . .

⁂

We can use the example of dreams to try to understand what Schopenhauer is saying. You're in a dream. Say you're dreaming that you're running away from an enemy. So you are running, legs and arms moving, your body straining to get away . . . but wait. *That* body, the body in the dream, the one from within which you seem to be experiencing the dream at the exclusion of all other phenomenal points in the dream, how is it constituted? *You are willing that those phenomena appear as a body.* You, of course, don't experience that in the dream, but there nevertheless is the will at work, *your* will (whose else's? The dream is not being beamed into your head from Mars). Now, your legs and arms in the dream move by what appears, while you are dreaming, as immediate acts of will on your part. *But that too is elaborate self-deception.* The *real* will must in Schopenhauer's philosophy be distinguished from the *apparent* will. This is not often understood properly and is the cause of much misconception about Schopenhauer's philosophy.

Thus, when Schopenhauer speaks of the will he does not mean the *apparent* will. To suppose that when you are being mugged you are willing this seems utterly absurd—you *want* to get away, you *want* to overpower the muggers, and so on—but *wishing* and the *appearance* of willing are not at all the thing-in-itself behind the appearances—the will, that is the ultimate, dark, driving force of everything. That is why Schopenhauer refers to your *body* as the direct manifestation of will, not your phenomenal psychological "wishing states" or "ruminations." Do you see the point? Forget about your ordinary frame of mind about living in a "real," "mind-independent, physical world" and keep

your focus on Schopenhauer's use of the analogy of dreams and you will see exactly what he means. *Even then*, in your dream, when you (now, from the perspective of your "waking" state) are obviously *in your own world* (when Schopenhauer's statement, "The world is my idea," is obviously true), there is something projecting your consciousness into one part of the dream (your phenomenal body) and excluding it from another (the phenomenal bodies of, say, the dream muggers). *That something is the will.* Once you see this, you are just one step from seeing what Schopenhauer is saying about the world entire, the waking world, all the "real" events as they unfold. *Those too are the constructions of the will, of your will, for there is no other.*

As developed by Schopenhauer, the concept of will becomes the fulcrum for the understanding of the entire world, the missing bridge between phenomena and noumena which Kant had not been able to unveil. Thus, what is ultimately real for Schopenhauer is not any sort of rational world-*mind*, as it was for Hegel, but a nonrational world-*will*, the vile and inexorable force, the blind momentum of existence. In its insatiable craving the will creates all and destroys all, unrelentingly.

It is this will that drives the world. It is not some benevolent God, not even any sort of rational force! Hiding behind the veil of appearance so as to be utterly invulnerable to the prying glances of its own creatures created to satiate its insatiable cravings, which become objectified as sex, violence, greed, war, and domination, lies the eternal, dark, metaphysical world-will: blind, insatiable, absolutely purposeless in its infinite hunger. It is here that Sigmund Freud would create the psychoanalytic foundations that influenced much of twentieth-century thought about ourselves and the world from a psychological perspective; his notion of the id (Latin for "it") refers to the same noumenal force as Schopenhauer's will. As Freud would one day admit, "We have unwittingly steered our course into the harbor of Schopenhauer's philosophy." Freud's highly influential *Analysis of Dreams* was itself an elaborate attempt for ourselves as individual phenomenal beings to try to communicate with the dark, irrational forces behind all our actions. But this can never be fully achieved, and it is this that drove Schopenhauer to despair, for the negative power of self-deception is such that we are always led by our own thoughts to believe that we act from conscious and rational deliberation, when the truth is that our intellects rationalize only the blind, unconscious actions of the underlying will. The very notion of truth in some rational sense is at best an elaborate self-deception.

In other words, we are so constructed as to forever be imprisoned in a cocoon of our own self-deception, even regarding our own view of ourselves and the world. The will is completely hidden from us as it passes through the conceptual framework of the categories.[18] Even our desires and wishes for states of happiness are but so much illusion, a malevolent pipe dream. The will cares nothing for our happiness—the proof is that when they are not pretending otherwise nearly everyone everywhere is always suffering, living an estranged life in which the only real force is reproduction. The whole of human culture is nothing but one more experiment of the will in which optimism, hope, and psychological feelings of happiness are part of the way the will deceives us about what is really going on behind the veil of appearances. It is all a grand illusion: art, religion, morality, politics, law, science, and even philosophy. These are but rationalizations of the will.

And yet in the center of this dark vision Schopenhauer finds one glimmer of hope. There is a secret passageway. As we are about to see in this final selection, Schopenhauer, like Schelling, finds in art a unique possibility to escape the sphere of the will through art.

⚓

Third Book. The World as Idea

It follows from our consideration of the subject, that, for us, Idea and thing-in-itself are not entirely one and the same, in spite of the inner agreement between Kant and Plato, and the identity of the aim they had before them or the conception of the world which roused them and led them to philosophise. The Idea is for us rather the direct, and therefore adequate, objectivity of the thing-in-itself, which is, however, itself the *will*—the will as not yet objectified, not yet become idea. For the thing-in-itself must, even according to Kant, be free from all the forms connected with knowing as such; and it is merely an error on his part that he did not count among these forms, before all others, that of being object for a subject, for it is the first and most universal form of all phenomena, *i.e.*, of all idea; he should therefore have distinctly denied objective existence to his thing-in-itself, which would have saved him from a great inconsistency that was soon discovered. The Platonic Idea, on the other hand, is necessarily object, something known, an idea, and in that respect is different from the thing-in-itself, but in that respect only. It has merely laid aside the subordinate forms of the phenomenon, all of which we include in the principle of sufficient reason, or rather it has not yet assumed them; but it has retained the first and most universal form, that of the idea in general, the form of being object for a subject. It is the forms which are subordinate to this (whose general expression is the principle of sufficient reason) that multiply the Idea in particular transitory individuals, whose number is a matter of complete indifference to the Idea.

. . . and here lies the ground of the great agreement between Plato and Kant, although, in strict accuracy, that of which they speak is not the same. . . .

In order to gain a deeper insight into the nature of the world, it is absolutely necessary that we should learn to distinguish the will as thing-in-itself from its adequate objectivity, and also the different grades in which this appears more and more distinctly and fully, *i.e.*, the Ideas themselves, from the merely phenomenal existence of these Ideas in the forms of the principle of sufficient reason, the restricted method of knowledge of the individual. We shall then agree with Plato when he attributes actual being only to the Ideas, and allows only an illusive, dream-like existence to things in space and time, the real world for the individual. Then we shall understand how one and the same Idea reveals itself in so many phenomena, and presents its nature only bit by bit to the individual, one side after another. Then we shall also distinguish the Idea itself from the way in which its manifestation appears in the observation of the individual, and recognise the former as essential and the latter as unessential. . . . But what kind of knowledge is concerned with that which is outside and independent of all relations, that which alone is really essential to the world, the true content of its phenomena, that which is subject to no change, and therefore is known with equal truth for all time, in a word, the *Ideas*, which are the direct and adequate objectivity of the thing-in-itself, the will? We answer, *Art*, the work of genius. It repeats or reproduces the eternal Ideas grasped through pure contemplation, the essential and abiding in all the phenomena of the world; and according to what the material is in which it reproduces, it is sculpture or painting, poetry or music. Its one source is the knowledge of Ideas; its one aim the communication of this knowledge. While science, following the unresting and inconstant stream of the fourfold forms of reason and consequent, with each end attained sees further, and can never reach a final goal nor attain full satisfaction, any more than by running we can reach the place where the clouds touch the horizon; art, on the contrary, is everywhere at its goal. For it plucks the object of its contemplation out of the stream of the world's course, and has it isolated before it. And this particular thing, which in that stream was a small perishing part, becomes to art the representative of the whole, an equivalent of the endless multitude in space and time, It therefore pauses at this particular thing; the course of time stops; the relations vanish for it; only the essential, the Idea, is its object. We may, therefore, accurately define it as the way *of viewing things independent of the principle of sufficient reason,* in opposition to the way of viewing them which proceeds in accordance with that principle, and which is the method of experience and of science. This last method of considering things may be compared to a line infinitely extended in a horizontal direction, and the former to a vertical line which cuts it at any point. The method of viewing things which proceeds in accordance with the principle of sufficient reason is the rational method, and it alone is valid and of use in practical life and in science. The method which looks away from the content of this principle is the method of genius, which is only valid and of use in art. The first is the method of Aristotle; the second is, on the whole, that of Plato.

The first is like the mighty storm, that rushes along without beginning and without aim, bending, agitating, and carrying away everything before it; the second is like the silent sunbeam, that pierces through the storm quite unaffected by it. The first is like the innumerable showering drops of the waterfall, which, constantly changing, never rest for an instant; the second is like the rainbow, quietly resting on this raging torrent. Only through the pure contemplation described above, which ends entirely in the object, can Ideas be comprehended; and the nature of *genius* consists in pre-eminent capacity for such contemplation. Now, as this requires that a man should entirely forget himself and the relations in which he stands, *genius* is simply the completest *objectivity, i.e.,* the objective tendency of the mind, as opposed to the subjective, which is directed to one's own self—in other words, to the will. Thus genius is the faculty of continuing in the state of pure perception, of losing oneself in perception, and of enlisting in this service the knowledge which originally existed only for the service of the will; that is to say, genius is the power of leaving one's own interests, wishes, and aims entirely out of sight, thus of entirely renouncing one's own personality for a time, so as to remain *pure knowing subject,* clear vision of the world; and this not merely at moments, but for a sufficient length of time, and with sufficient consciousness, to enable one to reproduce by deliberate art what has thus been apprehended, and "to fix in lasting thoughts the wavering images that float before the mind." It is as if, when genius appears in an individual, a far larger measure of the power of knowledge falls to his lot than is necessary for the service of an individual will; and this superfluity of knowledge, being free, now becomes subject purified from will, a clear mirror of the inner nature of the world. This explains the activity, amounting even to disquietude, of men of genius, for the present can seldom satisfy them, because it does not fill their consciousness. This gives them that restless aspiration, that unceasing desire for new things, and for the contemplation of lofty things, and also that longing that is hardly ever satisfied, for men of similar nature and of like stature, to whom they might communicate themselves; whilst the common mortal, entirely filled and satisfied by the common present, ends in it, and finding everywhere his like, enjoys that peculiar satisfaction in daily life that is denied to genius. . . .

⚓

The role of the genius is to deliver the archetypal ideas and permanent, essential forms of reality to the masses who are themselves blinded to metaphysics by the mundane concerns of everyday life. Schopenhauer thus presents the extreme end of the romantic conception of art as essentially antithetical to all practical concerns: art is a metaphysical bridge between the phenomenal world of appearance and noumenal world of the will. Since the will, which is not rational, controls everything, the world cannot be understood by rational thought or by empirical science. So true understanding, if it is at all possible, can be found only through the aesthetic experience of art, in some transcendental realm of "will-less" perception. Thus, what for Plato is the very problem with art is, for Schopenhauer, the solution to the problem of existence. *Because* art is not subservient to science and rational thinking (which are subservient to the will), art provides the highest form of true understanding and thereby even makes room, albeit very slight room, for freedom.

But there is a catch. Whereas for Schelling artistic creation in general and the whole experience of art are the highest and purest form of contemplation, Schopenhauer accepts only *music.* And not just any music! Only very purely formal music, which does not rely on words or images, can for brief moments free us from the tyranny of the will. Escape can be found only through the elaborate, tortuous, self-referential labyrinths of baroque music, constructed out of pure mathematical formalism.

Neither Plato, nor Kant, nor even Christ or Buddha ever found a way out of Plato's cave. Only Bach.

NOTES

1. For a detailed discussion see my "Quantum Cosmology, the Anthropic Principle, and Why Is There Something Rather Than Nothing?" in *The Experience of Philosophy,* 3d ed., Kolak and Martin, eds. (Belmont, CA: Wadsworth, 1996).

2. See, for instance, *The Mind's I* by Douglas R. Hofstadter and Daniel C. Dennett (New York: Basic Books, 1984ts).

3. Friedrich Von Schlegel (1772–1829), German writer, philosopher, and critic, was one of the originators of the German romantic movement. He transformed Fichte's transcendental philosophy into a philosophy of imaginative creation.

4. Friedrich Schiller (1759–1805), German idealist philosopher, playwright, and poet, was one of the greatest German dramatists of the time. His works express the view that the mind can attain freedom through art.

5. One of his early works was *Bruno, or on the Divine and Natural Principle of Things,* 1803.

6. There is no word for "mind" in Germanic and Slavic languages; the word Hegel used was *geist,* which has, as its root, the concept of ghost or spirit.

7. The easiest way to understand the Aristotelian concept of teleology is as opposed to mechanism, which explains the present and the future in terms of the past; teleology explains the past and the present in terms of the future.

8. That is, they involve more than one substance: Noumenal and Phenomenal reality for Kant; the human mind and the spiritual mind of God for Berkeley.

9. In terms of its own quantitative and qualitative yardsticks, such as provided by the topological concept of a metric.

10. Professor of semiotics at the University of Bologna and author of the best-selling philosophical novels *The Name of the Rose* and *Foucault's Pendulum*. This passage is from the latter. Semiotics is the term coined by philosopher C. S. Peirce (Section 20.0) to refer to the general theory of *signs.*

11. See, for instance, Sections 13.1, 15.7, and 17.3.

12. For many excellent articles on this topic, see Hofstadter and Dennett, *The Mind's I*, Basic Books 1981.

13. Provided, of course, that the simulation can meet certain specific conditions in terms of functional equivalence, isomorphism, and so on.

14. See Sections 1.3 and 2.4.

15. For good, clear presentations of some of these concepts, see F. S. Beckman, *Mathematical*

Foundations of *Programming* (London: Addison-Wesley, 1980); M. Machtey and P. Young, *An Introduction to the General Theory* of *Algorithms* (Amsterdam: Elsevier North-Holland, 1978.
16. Discussed in more detail in *Mathematical Thought*.

17. See my "Quantum Cosmology" in *The Experience of Philosophy* (Wadsworth, 1996).
18. Discussed in Kant, Chapter 16.

18 ✿ Kierkegaard and Nietzsche

18.0 Kierkegaard (1813–1855): Prelude to Subjectivity

Søren Kierkegaard was born in Copenhagen, Denmark. At age seventeen he went to study theology at the University of Copenhagen but spent most of his time reading literature and philosophy, both of which were under the influence of contemporary Hegelian philosophy. He liked the works of Plato and the romantics, but although he admired Hegel he found himself deeply critical of Hegel's work. Upon hearing Schelling's criticisms of Hegel in Berlin, Kierkegaard commented, "If Hegel had written the whole of his Logic and then said . . . that it was merely a joke, then he could certainly have been the greatest thinker who ever lived. As it is, he is himself merely a joke." Kierkegaard saw Hegel's rendering of the whole of reality as deeply ironic, in that not only had he failed to capture what Kierkegaard saw as its most important aspect—individual human existence as such—but even went so far as to deny it. Kierkegaard presented his criticisms of Hegel in a brilliant master's thesis, *The Concept of Irony*. He went on to publish an enormous number of

highly original books before his untimely death at age forty-two.

Critical both of established philosophy and all institutional religion, especially the Danish state church, in his voluminous writings Kierkegaard went on to argue for the primacy of *existence* which he saw in radically individualistic terms, diametrically opposed both to abstract thought and to all group social systems. He claimed that authentic individuality can come about only through a relationship of commitment and engagement with the world through choice, involving despair and dread toward the unknown. This relationship cannot be achieved with logic and reason, which are incapable of approaching the ultimate, unknowable unknown, which Kierkegaard called God; it can be attained only through self-actualization, which meant experiencing the direct awareness of existence as an unknown and then within that despair affirming one's own individual existence, the self-creation of a true, inner self.

For Hegel, thought and existence are identical; according to Kierkegaard, it is not even possible to relate to existence via thought. In Kierkegaard's Platonic view of meaning, existence is itself unthinkable; thought is but an abstraction limited to concepts within general categories. Thinking only removes us from the direct experience of existence and instead imprisons us in language, itself an abstraction. Likewise, although Kierkegaard admired Descartes for trying to base philosophy in the self, he saw Descartes as making the same mistake as Hegel: namely, equating the self with thought. According to Kierkegaard, "I think, therefore I am," is the ultimate mistake in philosophy! We can think *about* ourselves but this involves us only in our outward roles. We cannot through thinking experience existence, for in thinking we are moving away from the existential core of our own being, hiding ourselves from ourselves through abstraction. Existence must be lived and experienced with full passion, decision, action. Kierkegaard thus laid the foundations for the highly influential existentialist movement in philosophy, of which he is widely regarded as the originating founder.

Although Kierkegaard's views arose in opposition to Hegel's, they owe a lot to his system. The very titles of some of Kierkegaard's most important works were direct attacks on Hegel. *Either/Or* (1843), from which the first selection is taken, is a satire of what Kierkegaard saw as a depersonalization of human existence in Hegel's departure from traditional logic, which had been erected by Aristotle upon three fundamental principles: (1) the principle of identity, (2) the principle of noncontradiction, and (3) the principle of the excluded middle. The first says that everything is identical to itself: $A = A$. The second says that nothing both is and is not the case; for instance, no proposition (such as "Socrates exists") is both true and false: $\sim(p \wedge \sim p)$. The third says that anything either is or is not the case; for instance, "Socrates exists" is either true or false: $p \vee \sim p$. Rejecting all three principles, Hegel's dialectical logic makes everything its own opposite, $A = \sim A$, and so the second and third Aristotelian principles, both of which stand on the more basic principle of identity, are invalidated in Hegel's system. Kierkegaard saw this as an abomination: without the

principle of identity the individual ceases to exist; without the excluded middle all decision making and with it freedom are denied—leading to the state described in the selection from *Either/Or*, one of the most amusing in all of philosophy.

⁂

Either/Or

An Ecstatic Lecture

If you marry, you will regret it; if you do not marry, you will also regret it; if you marry or do not marry, you will regret both; whether you marry or do not marry, you will regret both. Laugh at the world's follies, you will regret it; weep over them, you will also regret that; laugh at the world's follies or weep over them, you will regret both; whether you laugh at the world's follies or weep over them, you will regret both. Believe a woman, you will regret it, believe her not, you will, also regret that; believe a woman, or believe her not, you will regret both; whether you believe a woman or believe her not, you will regret both. Hang yourself, you will regret it; do not hang yourself, and you will also regret that; hang yourself or do not hang yourself, you will regret both; whether you hang yourself or do not hang yourself, you will regret both. This, gentlemen, is the sum and substance of all philosophy.

⁂

In the next selection, taken from one of Kierkegaard's most important works, *Concluding Unscientific Postscript* (1846), he distinguishes subjective thought, which concerns itself with the *how*, from objective thought, which concerns itself with the *what*, a distinction central to Kierkegaard's philosophy.

⁂

From Søren Kierkegaard, *Either/Or*, D. F. Swenson and L. M. Swenson, trans. (Princeton, NJ: Princeton University Press, 1944).

Concluding Unscientific Postscript

. . . Not for a single moment is it forgotten that the subject is an existing individual, and that existence is a process of becoming, and that therefore the notion of the truth as identity of thought and being is a chimera of abstraction, in its truth only an expectation of the creature not because the truth is not such an identity, but because the knower is an existing individual for whom the truth cannot be such an identity as long as he lives in time. Unless we hold fast to this, speculative philosophy will immediately transport us into the fantastic realism of the I-am-I, which modern speculative thought has not hesitated to use without explaining how a particular individual is related to it; and God knows, no human being is more than such a particular individual.

If an existing individual were really able to transcend himself, the truth would be for him something final and complete; but where is the point at which he is outside himself? The I-am-I is a mathematical point which does not exist, and in so far there is nothing to prevent everyone from occupying this standpoint; the one will not be in the way of the other. It is only momentarily that the particular individual is able to realize existentially a unity of the infinite and the finite which transcends existence. This unity is realized in the moment of passion. Modern philosophy has tried anything and everything in the effort to help the individual to transcend himself objectively, which is a wholly impossible feat; existence exercises its restraining influence, and if philosophers nowadays had not become mere scribblers in the service of a fantastic thinking and its preoccupation, they would long ago have perceived that suicide was the only tolerable practical interpretation of its striving. But the scribbling modern philosophy holds passion in contempt; and yet passion is the culmination of existence for an existing individual—and we are all of us existing individuals. In passion the existing subject is rendered infinite in the eternity of the imaginative representation, and yet he is at the same time most definitely himself. The fantastic I-am-I is not an identity of the infinite and the finite since neither the one nor the other is real.

From Søren Kierkegaard, *Concluding Unscientific Postscript*, D. F. Swenson, trans. (Princeton, NJ: Princeton University Press, 1941).

⚹

The idea is this. Thought cannot grasp pure existence, but it must be used to interpret existence. That is how *subjective* thought allows individuals to create themselves existentially: the subjective thinker is defined not by studying or observing truth but by living it. The Kierkegaardian individual becomes the truth; he *exists it*. Once again, Hegel's objective history, objective reflection, objective existence, and so on, are the soundingboards against which Kierkegaard launches his own view: the Hegelian individual, defined by the state, exists in a system of objective thought in which the individual's own existence is absurdly and comically excluded because all he has at his disposal for self-understanding are abstract, universal, and timeless categories. The individual's concrete, particular existence in time is thereby appropriated into the crowd, the group, the system until the individual exists no more. Indeed, Kierkegaard suggests that in a fully Hegelian world the individual has literally and completely ceased to exist:

⚹

One must therefore be very careful in dealing with a philosopher of the Hegelian school, and, above all, to make certain of the identity of the being with whom one has the honor to discourse. Is he a human being, an existing human being? Is he himself *sub specie aeterni*, even when he sleeps, eats, blows his nose, or whatever else a human being does? Is he himself the pure "I am I" . . . Does he in fact exist?

⚹

Kierkegaard's philosophy thus opened a path for the radical subjectivity that became the cornerstone of existential thought in which the concrete individual is primary and existence itself is understood, ultimately, in concrete individualistic terms. Since no objective system is possible, the subjective thinker is doomed to exist in perpetual uncertainty. According to Kierkegaard recognizing this as our fate is the key to an authentic life. The unique category of the individual (*Enkelte*) is for Kierkegaard so central that he had it inscribed on his tombstone.

In taking his own views to heart, Kierkegaard went to such extreme lengths that none of his works is presented as a system, not even as his. Instead of writing in the objective voice used by nearly all other philosophers (except perhaps to a certain degree Plato, who as far as we know wrote only dialogues through the voices of characters other than himself), all of Kierkegaard's works are presented through the individual eyes of distinct characters. Perhaps recognizing that the idea of the author as an objective, external observer was itself a construction (as the later deconstructionists would insist), Kierkegaard created vivid characters with their own distinctive psychologies, ideas, beliefs, and writing styles. He wrote his works not in "his own" voice but from within the subjective voice of the created persona. Thus, for instance, *Either/Or* is presented as a correspondence between a young aesthete and an older man named Judge Wilhelm; the *Either*, written by the young man, is lyrical and poetic, whereas the *Or*, written by the old man, is dry and pedantic. But Kierkegaard goes even further and puts both books within the persona of yet another pseudonym, an imaginary editor named Victor Eremita. Among the many other personas that Kierkegaard created for his voluminous works are Johannes de Silentio, Constantin Constantius, Johannes Climacus, Nicolaus Notabene, Vigilius Hafniensis, Anti-Climacus, and Hilarius Bogbinder.

18.1 Nietzsche (1844–1900): The Philosopher as Superman

Friedrich Nietzsche was born in Röcken, Prussia. Since his father and both his grandfathers were Lutheran ministers, his family fully expected that he too would become a man of the cloth. Not only did he reject the religion, he became one of the most radical, influential, and outspoken critics of religion of all time, rejecting all its traditional morality and values, especially as espoused by Christianity and Judaism. It is Nietzsche who coined the famous slogan, "God is dead."

When he was only four his father died, leaving him to be raised solely by a clan of women—his mother, grandmother, sister, and two maiden aunts—and so his family worried that Nietzsche had no father figure and no strong male role models. It is once again ironic that Nietzsche originated one of the most masculine philosophies—the superman.

As a young man at the famous *Schulpforta* he excelled in classics, religion, literature, and philosophy; he was moved most by the works of Plato. At the University of Bonn he found the students and professors so shallow that after one year he transferred to Leipzig, where he discovered the philosophy of Schopenhauer and the music of Richard Wagner. He published some exceptional papers and was such a brilliant student that before he completed his doctorate at Leipzig, the University of Basel in Switzerland offered him a professorship and he accepted. The following year, while he was still only twenty-four, Leipzig awarded him the doctorate in philosophy without any examination.

At Basel, Nietzsche met and befriended Richard Wagner who had a lasting influence on him. Nietzsche taught there for ten years and then resigned to devote full attention to his writing. Among the most important of his fourteen highly original and provocative books, many of which are widely admired not only for their philosophy but also as brilliant and original prose poems, are *Thus Spake Zarathustra* (1883, 1884, and 1885, published in three installments), *Beyond Good and Evil* (1886), *The Genealogy of Morals* (1887), *The Antichrist* (1895), and *The Will to Power* (published posthumously in 1901).

In *Beyond Good and Evil*, excerpted in the first selection, Nietzsche argues that the concepts "good," "bad," "evil," and so on, arose out of what he calls a "transvaluation of classical values" by meek, lowly, and degenerate people. Especially guilty are Jewish and Christian priests who, philosophically blind and with a deep contempt, "transvalued" the most basic biological, psychological, and philosophical aspects of life. Nor does Nietzsche spare the philosophers, whom he sees as overly intellectual and whose pursuit of the chimera of "objective knowledge" blinds them, as surely as the concept of God blinds Christians, to the subjective, perspectival nature of truth which must be created by the strongest, through the will to power.

⚒

Beyond Good and Evil

Supposing that Truth is a woman—what then? Is there not ground for suspecting that all philosophers, in so far as they have been dogmatists, have failed to understand women—that the terrible seriousness and clumsy importunity with which they have usually paid their addresses to Truth, have been unskilled and unseemly methods for winning a woman? Certainly she has never allowed herself to be won; and at present every kind of dogma stands with sad and discouraged mien—*if*, indeed, it stands at all! For there are scoffers who maintain that it has fallen, that all dogma lies on the ground—nay more, that it is at its last gasp. But to speak seriously, there are good grounds for hoping that all dogmatising in philosophy, whatever solemn, whatever conclusive and decided airs it has assumed, may have been only a noble puerilism and tyronism; and probably the time is at hand when it will be once and again understood *what* has actually sufficed for the basis of such imposing and absolute philosophical edifices as the dogmatists have hitherto reared: perhaps some popular superstition of immemorial time (such as the soul-superstition, which, in the form of subject- and ego-superstition, has not yet ceased doing mischief). . . .

*

From Friedrich Nietzsche, *Beyond Good and Evil*, Helen Zimmern, trans., in *The Complete Works of Friedrich Nietzsche*, translated under Oscar Levy, 1909.

The falseness of an opinion is not for us any objection to it: it is here, perhaps, that our new language sounds most strangely. The question is, how far an opinion is life-furthering, life-preserving, species-preserving, perhaps species-rearing; and we are fundamentally inclined to maintain that the falsest opinions (to which the synthetic judgments *a priori* belong), are the most indispensable to us; that without a recognition of logical fictions, without a comparison of reality with the purely *imagined* world of the absolute and immutable, without a constant counterfeiting of the world by means of numbers, man could not live—that the renunciation of false opinions would be a renunciation of life, a negation of life. *To recognise untruth as a condition of life:* that is certainly to impugn the traditional ideas of value in a dangerous manner, and a philosophy which ventures to do so, has thereby alone placed itself beyond good and evil.

*

That which causes philosophers to be regarded half-distrustfully and half-mockingly, is not the oft-repeated discovery how innocent they are—how often and easily they make mistakes and lose their way, in short, how childish and childlike they are,—but that there is not enough honest dealing with them, whereas they all raise a loud and virtuous outcry when the problem of truthfulness is even hinted at in the remotest manner. They all pose as though their real opinions had been discovered and attained through the self-evolving of a cold, pure, divinely indifferent dialectic (in contrast to all sorts of mystics, who, fairer and foolisher, talk of "inspiration"); whereas, in fact, a prejudiced proposition, idea or "suggestion," which is generally their heart's desire abstracted and refined, is defended by them with arguments sought out after the event. They are all advocates who do not wish to be regarded as such, generally astute defenders, also, of their prejudices, which they dub "truths,"—and *very* far from having the conscience which bravely admits this to itself; very far from having the good taste of the courage which goes so far as to let this be understood, perhaps to warn friend or foe, or in cheerful confidence and self-ridicule. The spectacle of the Tartuffery of old Kant, equally stiff and decent, with which he entices us into the dialectic by-ways that lead (more correctly mislead) to his "categorical imperative"—makes us fastidious ones smile, we who find no small amusement in spying out the subtle tricks of old moralists and ethical preachers. Or, still more so, the hocus-pocus in mathematical form, by means of which Spinoza has as it were clad his philosophy in mail and mask—in fact, the "love of *his* wisdom," to translate the term fairly and squarely—in order thereby to strike terror at once into the heart of the assailant who should dare to cast a glance on that invincible maiden, that Pallas Athene:—how much of personal timidity and vulnerability does this masquerade of a sickly recluse betray!

*

It seems to me that there is everywhere an attempt at present to divert attention from the actual influence which Kant exercised on German philosophy, and especially to ignore prudently the value which he set upon himself. Kant was first and foremost proud of his Table of Categories; with it in his hand he said: "This is the most difficult thing that could ever be undertaken on behalf of metaphysics." Let us only understand this "could be"! He was proud of having *discovered* a new faculty in man, the faculty of synthetic judgment *a priori*. Granting that he deceived himself in this matter; the development and rapid flourishing of German philosophy depended nevertheless on his pride, and on the eager rivalry of the younger generation to discover if possible something—at all events "new faculties"—of which to be still prouder!"—But let us reflect for a moment—it is high time to do so. "How are synthetic judgments *a priori possible?*" Kant asks himself—and what is really his answer? *"By means of a means (faculty)"*—but unfortunately not in five words, but so circumstantially, imposingly, and with such display of German profundity and verbal flourishes, that one altogether loses sight of the comical *niaiserie allemande* involved in such an answer. People were beside themselves with delight over this new faculty, and the jubilation reached its climax when Kant further discovered a moral faculty in man—for at that time Germans were still moral, not yet dabbling in the "Politics of hard fact." Then came the honeymoon of German philosophy. All the young theologians of the Tübingen institution went immediately into the groves—all seeking for "faculties." And what did they not find—in that innocent, rich, and still youthful period of the German spirit, to which Romanticism, the malicious fairy, piped and sang, when one could not yet distinguish between

"finding" and "inventing"! Above all a faculty for the "transcendental"; Schelling christened it, intellectual intuition, and thereby gratified the most earnest longings of the naturally pious-inclined Germans. One can do no greater wrong to the whole of this exuberant and eccentric movement (which was really youthfulness, notwithstanding that it disguised itself so boldly in hoary and senile conceptions), than to take it seriously, or even treat it with moral indignation. Enough, however—the world grew older, and the dream vanished. A time came when people rubbed their foreheads, and they still rub them to-day. People had been dreaming, and first and foremost—old Kant. "By means of a means (faculty)"—he had said, or at least meant to say. But, is that—an answer? An explanation? Or is it not rather merely a repetition of the question? How does opium induce sleep? "By means of a means (faculty)," namely the *virtus dormitiva,* replies the doctor in Molière . . .

But such replies belong to the realm of comedy, and it is high time to replace the Kantian question, "How are synthetic judgments *a priori* possible?" by another question, "Why is belief in such judgments *necessary?*"—in effect, it is high time that we should understand that such judgments must be *believed* to be true, for the sake of the preservation of creatures like ourselves; though they still might naturally be *false* judgments! Or, more plainly spoken, and roughly and readily—synthetic judgments *a priori* should not "be possible" at all; we have no right to them; in our mouths they are nothing but false judgments. Only, of course, the belief in their truth is necessary, as plausible belief and ocular evidence belonging to the perspective view of life. . . .

*

There are still harmless self-observers who believe that there are "immediate certainties"; for instance, "I think," or as the superstition of Schopenhauer puts it, "I will "; as though cognition here got hold of its object purely and simply as the "thing in itself," without any falsification taking place either on the part of the subject or the object. I would repeat it, however, a hundred times, that "immediate certainty," as well as "absolute knowledge" and the "thing in itself," involve a *contradictio in adjecto;* we really ought to free ourselves from the misleading significance of words! The people on their part may think that cognition is knowing all about things, but the philosopher must say to himself: "When I analyse the process that is expressed in the sentence, 'I think,' I find a whole series of daring assertions, the argumentative proof of which would be difficult, perhaps impossible: for instance, that it is *I* who think, that there must necessarily be something that thinks, that thinking is an activity and operation on the part of a being who is thought of as a cause, that there is an 'ego,' and finally, that it is already determined what is to be designated by thinking—that I *know* what thinking is. For if I had not already decided within myself what it is, by what standard could I determine whether that which is just happening is not perhaps 'willing' or 'feeling'? In short, the assertion 'I think,' assumes that I *compare* my state at the present moment with other states of myself which I know, in order to determine what it is; on account of this retrospective connection with further 'knowledge,' it has at any rate no immediate certainty for me."—In place of the "immediate certainty" in which the people may believe in the special case, the philosopher thus finds a series of metaphysical questions presented to him. . . . "From whence did I get the notion of 'thinking'? Why do I believe in cause and effect? What gives me the right to speak of an 'ego,' and even of an 'ego' as cause, and finally of an 'ego' as cause of thought?" He who ventures to answer these metaphysical questions at once by an appeal to a sort of *intuitive* perception, like the person who says, "I think, and know that this, at least, is true, actual, and certain"—will encounter a smile and two notes of interrogation in a philosopher nowadays. "Sir," the philosopher will perhaps give him to understand, "it is improbable that you are not mistaken, but why should it be the truth?"

*

With regard to the superstitions of logicians, I shall never tire of emphasising a small, terse fact, which is unwillingly recognised by these credulous minds—namely, that a thought comes when "it" wishes, and not when "I" wish; so that it is a *perversion* of the facts of the case to say that the subject "I" is the condition of the predicate "think." *One* thinks; but that this "one" is precisely the famous old "ego," is, to put it mildly, only a supposition, an assertion, and assuredly not an "immediate certainty." After all, one has even gone too far with this "one thinks"—even the

"one" contains an *interpretation* of the process, and does not belong to the process itself. One infers here according to the usual grammatical formula—"To think is an activity; every activity requires an agency that is active; consequently" . . . It was pretty much on the same lines that the older atomism sought, besides the operating "power," the material particle wherein it resides and out of which it operates—the atom. More rigorous minds, however, learnt at last to get along without this "earth-residuum," and perhaps some day we shall accustom ourselves, even from the logician's point of view, to get along without the little "one" (to which the worthy old "ego" has refined itself).

*

It is certainly not the least charm of a theory that it is refutable; it is precisely thereby that it attracts the more subtle minds. It seems that the hundred-times-refuted theory of the "free will" owes its persistence to this charm alone; some one is always appearing who feels himself strong enough to refute it.

*

Philosophers are accustomed to speak of the will as though it were the best-known thing in the world; indeed, Schopenhauer has given us to understand that the will alone is really known to us, absolutely and completely known, without deduction or addition. But it again and again seems to me that in this case Schopenhauer also only did what philosophers are in the habit of doing—he seems to have adopted a *popular prejudice* and exaggerated it. Willing—seems to me to be above all something *complicated,* something that is a unity only in name—and it is precisely in a name that popular prejudice lurks, which has got the mastery over the inadequate precautions of philosophers in all ages.

So let us for once be more cautious, let us be "unphilosophical": let us say that in all willing there is firstly a plurality of sensations, namely, the sensation of the condition *"away from which* we go," the sensation of the condition *"towards which* we go," the sensation of this *"from"* and *"towards"* itself, and then besides, an accompanying muscular sensation, which, even without our putting in motion "arms and legs," commences its action by force of habit, directly we "will" anything. Therefore, just as sensations (and indeed many kinds of sensations) are to be recognised as ingredients of the will, so, in the second place, thinking is also to be recognised; in every act of the will there is a ruling thought;—and let us not imagine it possible to sever this thought from the "willing," as if the will would then remain over! In the third place, the will is not only a complex of sensation and thinking, but it is above all an *emotion,* and in fact the emotion of the command. That which is termed "freedom of the will" is essentially the emotion of supremacy in respect to him who must obey: "I am free, 'he' must obey"—this consciousness is inherent in every will; and equally so the straining of the attention, the straight look which fixes itself exclusively on one thing, the unconditional judgment that "this and nothing else is necessary now," the inward certainty that obedience will be rendered—and whatever else pertains to the position of the commander. A man who *wills* commands something within himself which renders obedience, or which he believes renders obedience. But now let us notice what is the strangest thing about the will,—this affair so extremely complex, for which the people have only one name. Inasmuch as in the given circumstances we are at the same time the commanding *and* the obeying parties, and as the obeying party we know the sensations of constraint, impulsion, pressure, resistance, and motion, which usually commence immediately after the act of will; inasmuch as, on the other hand, we are accustomed to disregard this duality, and to deceive ourselves about it by means of the synthetic term "I": a whole series of erroneous conclusions, and consequently of false judgments about the will itself, has become attached to the act of willing—to such a degree that he who wills believes firmly that willing *suffices* for action. Since in the majority of cases there has only been exercise of will when the effect of the command—consequently obedience, and therefore action—was to be *expected,* the *appearance* has translated itself into the sentiment, as if there were there a *necessity of effect;* in a word, he who wills believes with a fair amount of certainty that will and action are somehow one; he ascribes the success, the carrying out of the willing, to the will itself, and thereby enjoys an increase of the sensation of power which accompanies all success. "Freedom of Will"—that is the expression for the complex state of delight of the person exercising volition, who commands and at the same time identifies himself with the executor of the order—who, as such, enjoys also the triumph over obstacles, but thinks within himself that it was really his own will that overcame them. . . . It is

nothing more than a moral prejudice that truth is worth more than semblance; it is, in fact, the worst proved supposition in the world. *So* much must be conceded: there could have been no life at all except upon the basis of perspective estimates and semblances; and if, with the virtuous enthusiasm and stupidity of many philosophers, one wished to do away altogether with the "seeming world"— well, granted that *you* could do that,—at least nothing of your "truth" would thereby remain! Indeed, what is it that forces us in general to the supposition that there is an essential opposition of "true" and "false"? Is it not enough to suppose degrees of seemingness, and as it were lighter and darker shades and tones of semblance—different *valeurs,* as the painters say? Why might not the world *which concerns us—be* a fiction? And to any one who suggested: "But to a fiction belongs an originator?" —might it not be bluntly replied: *Why?* May not this "belong" also belong to the fiction? Is it not at length permitted to be a little ironical towards the subject, just as towards the predicate and object? Might not the philosopher elevate himself above faith in grammar? All respect to governesses, but is it not time that philosophy should renounce governess-faith? . . .

*

Supposing that nothing else is "given" as real but our world of desires and passions, that we cannot sink or rise to any other "reality" but just that of our impulses—for thinking is only a relation of these impulses to one another:—are we not permitted to make the attempt and to ask the question whether this which is "given" does not *suffice,* by means of our counterparts, for the understanding even of the so-called mechanical (or "material") world? I do not mean as an illusion, a "semblance," a "representation" (in the Berkeleyan and Schopenhauerian sense), but as possessing the same degree of reality as our emotions themselves—as a more primitive form of the world of emotions, in which everything still lies locked in a mighty unity, which afterwards branches off and develops itself in organic processes (naturally also, refines and debilitates)—as a kind of instinctive life in which all organic functions, including self-regulation, assimilation, nutrition, secretion, and change of matter, are still synthetically united with one another—as *a primary form* of life?—In the end, it is not only permitted to make this attempt, it is commanded by the conscience of *logical method.* Not to assume several kinds of causality, so long as the attempt to get along with a single one has not been pushed to its furthest extent (to absurdity, if I may be allowed to say so): that is a morality of method which one may not repudiate nowadays—it follows "from its definition," as mathematicians say. The question is ultimately whether we really recognise the will as *operating,* whether we believe in the causality of the will; if we do so—and fundamentally our belief *in this* is just our belief in causality itself—we *must* make the attempt to posit hypothetically the causality of the will as the only causality. "Will" can naturally only operate on "will"—and not on "matter" (not on "nerves," for instance): in short, the hypothesis must be hazarded, whether will does not operate on will wherever "effects" are recognised—and whether all mechanical action, inasmuch as a power operates therein, is not just the power of will, the effect of will. Granted, finally, that we succeeded in explaining our entire instinctive life as the development and ramification of one fundamental form of will—namely, the Will to Power, as *my* thesis puts it; granted that all organic functions could be traced back to this Will to Power, and that the solution of the problem of generation and nutrition—it is one problem—could also be found therein: one would thus have acquired the right to define *all* active force unequivocally as *Will to Power.* The world seen from within, the world defined and designated according to its "intelligible character"—it would simply be "Will to Power," and nothing else.

*

"What? Does not that mean in popular language: God is disproved, but not the devil?"—On the contrary! On the contrary, my friends! And who the devil also compels you to speak popularly! . . .

Thus, there are no gods and no devils, no things-in-themselves—not even *things* as such—no pure being of any kind (neither noumenal nor phenomenal), no Platonic ideas; there is but a chaotic Heraclitean flux, stripped even of the Logos, upon which we impose our will. Epistemology is as dead as God. Nietzsche deconstructs philosophy back into its Sophist form, where the only rule is that of the powerful imposing their will upon the weak as espoused by Thrasymachus (Section 1.12). To "know" is to *invent* and the only authentic invention known to man is to lie. Nietzsche's thinking here is not just outright paradoxical; inauthentic lying, in which one lies "traditionally," using the terms and methods of established traditions such as religious, political, and educational institutions, is an elaborate form of *self*-deception. "Authentic lying" is "creative." Invention subjugates others to one's own "Will to Power." Using one's own creative might, the mouldable clay of reality is forced into a shape to which others must then bend. But only the few and the brave can retain enough original creative power while passing through the self-destructive gauntlet of "normalization," previous lies imposed upon us through institutions that are but the decaying remnants of others' will to power.

These insidious processes cut deep, not only into our biological and psychological makeups but into the very structure of thought and language, the vehicles not of truth but self-deception. Language works by lying. Our very words deny what is real, the perpetual flux of ephemeral things, by presenting to the mind fictitious similarities among the appearances through the repetitive noises we make at the world. Thus, for instance, we identify ourselves as part of the same group by willfully ignoring and thereby suppressing from our consciousness the primordial fact that *no* two persons are alike; a false identity is imposed upon us by the various religions, clubs, organizations, racial classes, and so on—institutions through which people deceive themselves into having a sense of identity where in fact there is none. But whereas Kierkegaard argued for the radical identity of the true individual, Nietzsche's destruction goes even deeper, forcing us to realize that there is not even any authentic personal being that any of us are, that this too is a lie and a deception. The only *authentic* move left to us is the willful construction of *masks* with which to further exert unto the insubstantial world our own will to power:

⚓

Everything that is profound loves the mask; the profoundest things have a hatred even of figure and likeness. Should not the *contrary* only be the right disguise for the shame of a God to go about in? A question worth asking!—it would be strange if some mystic has not already ventured on the same kind of thing. There are proceedings of such a delicate nature that it is well to overwhelm them with coarseness and make them unrecognisable; there are actions of love and of an extravagant magnanimity after which nothing can be wiser than to take a stick and thrash the witness soundly: one thereby obscures his recollection. Many a one is able to obscure and abuse his own memory, in order at least to have vengeance on this sole party in the secret: shame is inventive. They are not the worst things of which one is most ashamed: there is not only deceit behind a mask—there is so much goodness in craft. I could imagine that a man with something costly and fragile to conceal, would roll through life clumsily and rotundly like an old, green, heavily-hooped wine-cask: the refinement of his shame requiring it to be so. A man who has depths in his shame meets his destiny and his delicate decisions upon paths which few ever reach, and with regard to the existence of which his nearest and most intimate friends may be ignorant; his mortal danger conceals itself from their eyes, and equally so his regained security. Such a hidden nature, which instinctively employs speech for silence and concealment, and is inexhaustible in evasion of communication, *desires* and insists that a mask of himself shall occupy his place in the hearts and heads of his friends; and supposing he does not desire it, his eyes will some day be opened to the fact that there is nevertheless a mask of him there—and that it is well to be so. Every profound spirit needs a mask; nay, more, around every profound spirit there continually grows a mask, owing to the constantly false, that is to say, *superficial* interpretation of every word he utters, every step he takes, every sign of life he manifests. . . . Every philosophy also *conceals* a philosophy; every opinion is also a *lurking-place,* every word is also a *mask.*

⚓

Language is but another tyrannical mask imposed upon us "as a condition of life," which becomes the source of new creative possibilities because of the fact that it *must* by its very nature lie. Language is a "mobile army of metaphors, metonyms and anthropomorphisms." A metaphor is a figure of speech in which a term is transposed from its original concept to another, thereby establishing—*falsely*—a sort of likeness or analogy between them. We say "the ship plows the sea." In *reality* there is no similarity; the likeness is imparted to the objects of the world by our language.

This concept applies just as much to ourselves! We "see solutions" to problems. Jones is a "brilliant" student. That philosopher is "clear," that one "fuzzy," "dull," or "obscure." All these words are but metaphors. We "approach" a problem from a certain "viewpoint." We "grapple" with the various "solutions." And so on. Do you see that just about every word we use to refer to our own mental states is itself a metaphor built upon tissues of metaphors? But there are also metonyms. A *metonym* is a figure of speech in which you use the name of one thing as a substitute for something else with which it is associated; but this "association," Nietzsche points out, exists only as a linguistic entity; it is thereby created by your language. So, you say "I spent last night reading *Nietzsche,*" "In the interest of the United States . . .", "By the will of God," and so on. In every case what you say is literally a lie (think about it). Finally, there are anthropomorphisms, figures of speech in which we project human "traits" (and what are *they?*) onto what is not human. For instance, "The tree *strives* to reach the sky" (which consists of a set of unconscious metaphors).

From his early training as a philologist, Nietzsche was well familiar with how *all* language is metaphoric, metonymic, and anthropomorphic in origin; that is, that all language originally had the same origin and function as *poetry.* Nietzsche viewed the subsequently imposed division between the "literal," "scientific," and "logical" nature of language, on the one hand,

and its "metaphoric," "figurative," or "poetic" nature on the other, as a wholly artificial division and the leading cause of error among philosophers. Like Heidegger after him (Section 21.2), Nietzsche tried by his writings to return language and thereby philosophy to its original, primordial function as poetry. Indeed, Nietzsche referred to his own major philosophical works as elaborate "poems" (something that even Ludwig Wittgenstein will do, as we'll see in Chapter 23), explaining that terms such as "Will to Power," "the Death of God," and the "Superman," are but the products of the metaphorical/metonymical/anthropomorphic process. For Nietzsche such terms are *not* to be regarded as philosophical insights into being itself, some "*true reality*"! Rather, as interpretations—*poetical* interpretations—of being, they are the artistic forces of self-creation acting in the world.

Nietzsche is quick to warn, however, that not all interpretations are created equal. Those rare and powerful poetic lies that "affirm life"—what following Thrasymachus he calls truly *noble* lies—are regarded by him as *true*. Nietzsche condemns common lies, such as those found in both Platonism and Christianity ("Platonism for the masses,"), as bad poetry consisting of ignoble lies, for both Platonism and Christianity (as social, intellectual, or emotional *movements*) deny reality as it is—a chaotic flux to be molded in the image of each Will. They both set up a false and unfulfillable longing for another world (Platonic Ideas, Heaven, and so on). What these otherworldly philosophical and religious congregations truly long for are *nothingness* and *death*. They are not life-affirming but life-denying. This, in Nietzsche's view, makes them utterly decrepit and false.

Again, keep in mind that by the words *true* and *false* Nietzsche does not mean what the logician means; for him poetic truth, aesthetic truth, is the only truth there is because, like Schopenhauer and Kierkegaard, Nietzsche claims that our reasoning and even our individual thoughts—indeed, the very language in which thought consists in words—are but manifestations of the will to power, leading us into self-deception. In showing, like Kierkegaard, that language functions precisely by lying, he is in a way doing to words what Kant did to the appearances: explaining why their being not what they seem is not an epistemological *problem* but its very *solution*. Taking our lies, pretensions, and self-deceptions for what they are allows us to face the chaotic flux of reality in a creative way so that it can be molded, like a great work of art, into something noble through the will to power.

Nor is the Will to Power the dark Schopenhaurian notion of the World Will; rather, it is of Dionysian character, marked by laughter, dancing, and life-affirmation culminating, ultimately, in what Nietzsche calls the "Superman," an enlightened individual who represents the triumph of the Will to Power. Such a person must, first and foremost, teach and impose "the Death of God." What Nietzsche means by this cryptic phrase is to bring about *the end of all traditional forms of authority:* not only religious but historical, political, moral, and any kind of *textual* authority. This notion is in part influenced by his early philological studies, where he recognized (what is generally held secret from the public at large) that the foundational books for all the major world religions—such as the New Testament, the Old Testament, the *Vedas,* the *Upanishads,* and so on—consist of multiple indirect translations of multiple existing documents, compilations of fragments of deeply conflicting evidence derived from a multitude of sources. None of these books exists in anything like a truly "authoritative edition," nor are they based on any truly "original text." These so-called holy books are merely the result of decisions to let some particular subjective interpretation of a scattered and fragmentary series of texts stand as the "official" and "holy" version. (For instance, in the case of the New Testament, none of the so-called gospels were written by eyewitnesses, and there are dozens of other gospels, even more contradictory, some of which are even older, which were kept hidden from the general public by church authorities.[1]) Indeed, Nietzsche's philosophical approach can be seen as an extension of his philological insights from the textual into the ontological and epistemological domains, where the whole of existence—Being—comes to be viewed, not as something to be described in language but as consisting in the form of an elaborate text. (Recall our discussions on Hegel and the quote from Umberto Eco on p. 376, Chapter 17.)

Nietzsche thus presents a sort of philosophical fulcrum between Hegel and a subsequent twentieth-century intellectual movement in philosophy, literary theory, and criticism known as *deconstructionism,* which systematically challenges all the fixed orthodoxical hierarchies central to Western thought and culture based on exactly the sort of dissolution between formerly antithetical concepts we explored in the work of the nineteenth-century idealists (Chapter 17). The major additional development is that instead of the dissolution of the distinction between *object* and its *representation* conceived in noumenal/phenomenal terms, the analysis moves on to more technical examinations of the elements of language, experience, and thought, each conceived in terms of *signs.* When ordinarily we think of signs, we think of symbols used to represent objects, a way of bringing before our consciousness something that is not otherwise fully present to consciousness. Thus, in talking about reality, we use signs and gestures as if these were of secondary importance and the reality behind the signs (the thing in itself signified?) as primary. But this is just the old primary–secondary qualities distinction rearing its ugly head again; the claims made by (absolute-idealist-inspired) contemporary continental philosophers like Jacques Derrida are thus deeply inspired by Nietzsche. Derrida, who challenges what he calls "the metaphysics of presence," claims that there are no beings and events that exist apart from the signs. (Recall, again, the quote from Umberto Eco on p. 376.) Thus in claiming, "There is nothing outside of the texts," the twentieth-century deconstructionists are echoing

Nietzsche, as another passage from *Beyond Good and Evil* makes "clear":

⁂

Let me be pardoned, as an old philologist who cannot desist from the mischief of putting his finger on bad modes of interpretation, but "Nature's conformity to law," of which you physicists talk so proudly, as though—why, it exists only owing to your interpretation and bad "philology." It is no matter of fact, no "text," but rather just a naively humanitarian adjustment and perversion of meaning, with which you make abundant concessions to the democratic instincts of the modern soul! "Everywhere equality before the law—Nature is not different in that respect, nor better than we:" a fine instance of secret motive, in which the vulgar antagonism to everything privileged and autocratic—likewise a second and more refined atheism—is once more disguised. *"Ni dieu, ni maître"*—that, also, is what you want; and therefore "Cheers for natural law!"—is it not so? But, as has been said, that is interpretation, not text; and somebody might come along, who, with opposite intentions and modes of interpretation, could read out of the same "Nature," and with regard to the same phenomena, just the tyrannically inconsiderate and relentless enforcement of the claims of power—an interpreter who should so place the unexceptionalness and unconditionalness of all "Will to Power" before your eyes, that almost every word, and the word "tyranny" itself, would eventually seem unsuitable, or like a weakening and softening metaphor—as being too human; and who should, nevertheless, end by asserting the same about this world as you do, namely, that it has a "necessary" and "calculable" course, *not,* however, because laws obtain in it, but because they are absolutely *lacking,* and every power effects its ultimate consequences every moment. Granted that this also is only interpretation—and you will be eager enough to make this objection?—well, so much the better.

⁂

Let us now turn to some concrete examples of Nietzsche's attacks on traditional forms of authority, starting with morality:

⚓

In a tour through the many finer and coarser moralities which have hitherto prevailed or still prevail on the earth, I found certain traits recurring regularly together, and connected with one another, until finally two primary types revealed themselves to me, and a radical distinction was brought to light. There is *master-morality* and *slave-morality;*—I would at once add, however, that in all higher and mixed civilisations, there are also attempts at the reconciliation of the two moralities; but one finds still oftener the confusion and mutual misunderstanding of them, indeed, sometimes their close juxtaposition—even in the same man, within one soul. The distinctions of moral values have either originated in a ruling caste, pleasantly conscious of being different from the ruled—or among the ruled class, the slaves and dependents of all sorts. In the first case, when it is the rulers who determine the conception is "good," it is the exalted, proud disposition which is regarded as the distinguishing feature, and that which determines the order of rank. The noble type of man separates from himself the beings in whom the opposite of this exalted, proud disposition displays itself: he despises them. Let it at once be noted that in this first kind of morality the antithesis "good" and "bad" means practically the same as "noble" and "despicable";—the antithesis "good" and *"evil"* is of a different origin. The cowardly, the timid, the insignificant, and those thinking merely of narrow utility are despised; moreover, also, the distrustful, with their constrained glances, the self-abasing, the dog-like kind of men who let themselves be abused, the mendicant flatterers, and above all the liars:—it is a fundamental belief of all aristocrats that the common people are untruthful. "We truthful ones"—the nobility in ancient Greece called themselves. It is obvious that everywhere the designations of moral value were at first applied to *men,* and were only derivatively and at a later period applied to *actions;* it is a gross mistake, therefore, when historians of morals start with questions like, "Why have sympathetic actions been praised?" The noble type of man regards *himself* as a determiner of values; he does not require to be approved of; he passes the judgment: "What is injurious to me is injurious in itself"; he knows that it is he himself only who confers honour on things; he is a *creator of values.* He honours whatever he recognises in himself: such morality is self-glorification. In the foreground there is the feeling of plenitude, of power, which seeks to overflow, the happiness of high tension, the consciousness of a wealth which would fain give and bestow:—the noble man also helps the unfortunate, but not—or scarcely—out of pity, but rather from an impulse generated by the super-abundance of power. The noble man honours in himself the powerful one, him also who has power over himself, who knows how to speak and how to keep silence, who takes pleasure in subjecting himself to severity and hardness, and has reverence for all that is severe and hard. . . .

The ability and obligation to exercise prolonged gratitude and prolonged revenge—both only within the circle of equals,—artfulness in retaliation, *raffinement* of the idea in friendship, a certain necessity to have enemies (as outlets for the emotions of envy, quarrelsomeness, arrogance—in fact, in order to be a good *friend):* all these are typical characteristics of the noble morality, which, as has been pointed out, is not the morality of "modern ideas," and is therefore at present difficult to realise, and also to unearth and disclose.—It is otherwise with the second type of morality, *slave-morality.* Supposing that the abused, the oppressed, the suffering, the unemancipated, the weary, and those uncertain of themselves, should moralise, what will be the common element in their moral estimates? Probably a pessimistic suspicion with regard to the entire situation of man will find expression, perhaps a condemnation of man, together with his situation. The slave has an unfavourable eye for the virtues of the powerful; he has a scepticism and distrust, a *refinement* of distrust of everything "good" that is there honoured—he would fain persuade himself that the very happiness there is not genuine. On the other hand, *those* qualities which serve to alleviate the existence of sufferers are brought into prominence and flooded with light; it is here that sympathy, the kind, helping hand, the warm heart, patience, diligence, humility, and friendliness attain to honour; for here these are the most useful qualities, and almost the only means of supporting the burden of existence. Slave-morality is essentially the morality of utility. Here is the seat of the origin of the famous antithesis "good" and *"evil":*—power and dangerousness are assumed to reside in the evil, a certain dreadfulness, subtlety, and strength, which do not admit of being despised. According to slave-morality, therefore, the "evil" man arouses fear; according to master-morality, it is precisely the "good" man who arouses fear and seeks to arouse it, while the bad man is regarded as the despicable being. The contrast attains its maximum when, in accordance with the logical consequences of slave-morality, a shade of depreciation—it may be slight and well-intentioned—at last attaches itself even to the "good" man of this morality; because, according to the servile mode of thought, the good man must in any case be the *safe* man: he is good-natured, easily deceived, perhaps a little stupid, *un bonhomme.* Everywhere that slave-morality gains the ascendancy, language shows a tendency to approximate the significations of the words "good" and "stupid."—A last fundamental difference: the desire for *freedom,* the instinct for happiness and the refinements of the feeling of liberty belong as necessarily to slave-morals and morality, as artifice and enthusiasm in reverence and devotion are the regular symptoms of an aristocratic mode of thinking and estimating.—Hence we can understand without further detail why love *as a passion*—it is our European specialty—must absolutely be of noble origin; as is well known, its invention is due to the Provençal poet-cavaliers, those brilliant ingenious men of the *"gai saber,"** to whom Europe owes so much, and almost owes itself.

***

In stating that "Slave-morality is essentially the morality of utility," Nietzsche is explicitly referring to the utilitarian systems of morality, in particular that of John Stuart Mill (which we shall discuss again in more detail in Section 19.3).

To see how Nietzsche's "turning values upside down" plays itself out in the religious domain where he shows how slave-morality can take over the master-morality, we turn to the most celebrated example of Nietzsche's attack on traditional forms of authority: Christianity. In his book the *Will to Power,* he launches the greatest single attack on Christianity since Marcus Aurelius (Section 4.2), calling it the most "fatal

and seductive lie that has ever yet existed" for the suppression of humanity, urging everyone to declare "open war with it."

***

The Will to Power

I regard Christianity as the most fatal and seductive lie that has ever yet existed—as the greatest and most *impious* lie: I can discern the last sprouts and branches of its ideal beneath every form of disguise. I decline to enter into any compromise or false position in reference to it—I urge people to declare open war with it.

The morality of paltry people as the measure of all things: this is the most repugnant kind of degeneracy that civilisation has ever yet brought into existence. And this *kind of ideal* is hanging still, under the name of "God," over men's heads!!

However modest one's demands may be concerning intellectual cleanliness, when one touches the New Testament one cannot help experiencing a sort of inexpressible feeling of discomfort; for the unbounded cheek with which the least qualified people will have their say in its pages, in regard to the greatest problems of existence, and claim to sit in judgment on such matters, exceeds all limits. The impudent levity with which the most unwieldy problems are spoken of here (life, the world, God, the purpose of life), as if they were not problems at all, but the most simple things which these little bigots *know all about*!!!

This was the most fatal form of insanity that has ever yet existed on earth:—when these little lying abortions of bigotry begin laying claim to the words "God," "last judgment," "truth," "love," "wisdom," "Holy Spirit," and thereby distinguishing themselves from the rest of the world; when such men begin to transvalue values to suit themselves, as though they were the sense, the salt, the standard, and the measure of all things; then all that one should do is this: build lunatic asylums for their incarceration. To *persecute* them was an egregious act of antique folly: this was taking them too seriously; it was making them serious.

---

* Gay science.

From Friedrich Nietzsche, *The Will to Power,* A. M. Ludovici, trans., in *The Complete Works of Friedrich Nietzsche,* translated under Oscar Levy, 1909.

The whole fatality was made possible by the fact that a similar form of megalomania was already *in existence, the Jewish* form (once the gulf separating the Jews from the Christian-Jews was bridged, the Christian-Jews *were compelled* to employ those self-preservative measures afresh which were discovered by the Jewish instinct, for their own self-preservation, after having accentuated them); and again through the fact that Greek moral philosophy had done everything that could be done to prepare the way for moral-fanaticism, even among Greeks and Romans, and to render it palatable. . . . Plato, the great importer of corruption, who was the first who refused to see Nature in morality, and who had already deprived the Greek gods of all their worth by his notion *"good,"* was already tainted with *Jewish bigotry* (in Egypt?). . . .

This was the case, for example, when Buddha appeared among a people that was both peaceable and afflicted with great intellectual weariness.

This was also the case in regard to the first Christian community (as also the Jewish), the primary condition of which was the absolutely *unpolitical* Jewish society. Christianity could grow only upon the soil of Judaism—that is to say, among a people that had already renounced the political life, and which led a sort of parasitic existence within the Roman sphere of government. Christianity goes a step *farther*: it allows men to "emasculate" themselves even more; the circumstances actually favour their doing *so.—Nature* is *expelled* from morality when it is said, "Love ye your enemies": for *Nature's* injunction, "Ye shall *love* your neighbour and *hate* your enemy," has now become senseless in the law (in instinct); now, even *the love a man feels for his neighbour* must first be based upon something (*a sort of love of God*). *God* is introduced everywhere, and *utility* is withdrawn; the natural *origin* of morality is denied everywhere: the *veneration of Nature,* which lies in *acknowledging a natural morality,* is *destroyed* to the roots. . . .

Whence comes the *seductive charm* of this emasculate ideal of man? Why are we not *disgusted* by it, just as we are disgusted at the thought of a eunuch? . . . The answer is obvious: it is not the voice of the eunuch that revolts us, despite the cruel mutilation of which it is the result; for, as a matter of fact, it has grown sweeter. . . . And owing to the very fact that the "male organ" has been amputated from virtue its

voice now has a feminine ring, which, formerly, was not to be discerned.

On the other hand, we have only to think of the terrible hardness, dangers, and accidents to which a life of manly virtues leads—the life of a Corsican, even at the present day, or that of a heathen Arab (which resembles the Corsican's life even to the smallest detail: the Arab's songs might have been written by Corsicans)—in order to perceive how the most robust type of man was fascinated and moved by the voluptuous ring of this "goodness" and "purity." . . . A pastoral melody . . . an idyll . . . the "good man": such things have most effect in ages when tragedy is abroad.

The *Astuteness of moral castration.*—How is war waged against the virile passions and valuations? No violent physical means are available; the war must therefore be one of ruses, spells, and lies—in short, a "spiritual war."

First recipe: One appropriates virtue in general, and makes it the main feature of one's ideal; the older ideal is denied and declared to be *the reverse of all ideals.* Slander has to be carried to a fine art for this purpose.

Second recipe: One's own type is set up as a general *standard;* and this is projected into all things, behind all things, and behind the destiny of all things—as God.

Third recipe: The opponents of one's ideal are declared to be the opponents of God; one arrogates to oneself a *right* to great pathos, to power, and a right to curse and to bless.

Fourth recipe: All suffering, all gruesome, terrible, and fatal things are declared to be the results of opposition to *one's* ideal—all suffering is *punishment* even in the case of one's adherents (except it be a trial, etc.).

Fifth recipe: One goes so far as to regard Nature as the reverse of one's ideal, and the lengthy sojourn amid natural conditions is considered a great trial of patience—a sort of martyrdom; one studies contempt, both in one's attitudes and one's looks towards all "natural things."

Sixth recipe: The triumph of anti-naturalism and ideal castration, the triumph of the world of the pure, good, sinless, and blessed, is projected into the future as the consummation, the finale, the great hope, and the "Coming of the Kingdom of God."

I hope that one may still be allowed to laugh at this artificial hoisting up of a small species of man to the position of an absolute standard of all things?

To what extent psychologists have been corrupted by the moral idiosyncrasy!—Not one of the ancient philosophers had the courage to advance the theory of the non-free will (that is to say, the theory that denies morality);—not one had the courage to identify the typical feature of happiness, of every kind of happiness ("pleasure"), with the will to power: for the pleasure of power was considered immoral;—not one had the courage to regard virtue as a *result of immorality* (as a result of a will to power) in the service of a species (or of a race, or of a *polis*); for the will to power was considered immoral.

In the whole of moral evolution, there is no sign of truth: all the conceptual elements which come into play are fictions; all the psychological tenets are false; all the forms of logic employed in this department of prevarication are sophisms. The chief feature of all moral philosophers is their total lack of intellectual cleanliness and self-control: they regard "fine feelings" as arguments: their heaving breasts seem to them the bellows of godliness. . . . Moral philosophy is the most suspicious period in the history of the human intellect.

The first great example: in the name of morality and under its patronage, a great wrong was committed, which as a matter of fact was in every respect an act of decadence. Sufficient stress cannot be laid upon this fact, that the great Greek philosophers not only represented the decadence of *every kind of Greek ability,* but also made it *contagious.* . . . This "virtue" made wholly abstract was the highest form of seduction; to make oneself abstract means to *turn one's back on the world.*

The moment is a very remarkable one: the Sophists are within sight of the first *criticism* of morality, the first *knowledge* of morality:—they classify the majority of moral valuations (in view of their dependence upon local conditions) together; —they lead one to understand that every form of morality is capable of being upheld dialectically: that is to say, they guessed that all the fundamental principles of a morality must be *sophistical*—a proposition which was afterwards proved in the grandest possible style by the ancient philosophers from Plato onwards (up to Kant);—they postulate the primary truth that there is no such thing as a "moral *per se,*" a "good *per se,*" and that it is madness to talk of "truth" in this respect.

Wherever was *intellectual uprightness* to be found in those days?

The Greek culture of the Sophists had grown out of all the Greek instincts; it belongs to the culture of the age of Pericles as necessarily as Plato does not: it has its predecessors in Heraclitus, Democritus, and in the scientific types of the old philosophy; it finds expression in the elevated culture of Thucydides, for instance. And—it has ultimately shown itself to be right: every step in the science of epistemology and morality has *confirmed the attitude* of the Sophists. . . . Our modern attitude of mind is, to a great extent, Heraclitean, Democritean, and Protagorean . . . to say that it is *Protagorean* is even sufficient: because Protagoras was in himself a synthesis of the two men Heraclitus and Democritus.

⚒

Along with a call to arms against Christianity, Nietzsche here presents his perspectivist analysis of truth and an instrumentalist theory of knowledge. "Against positivism," he wrote, "which halts at phenomena—'There are only facts'—I would say: No, facts are precisely what there are not, only interpretations." According to Nietzsche, it is impossible to separate facts from values, even in the most rigorous science; no observation can exist without theory. Though initially dubbed as "irrationalism" by some, in the end his criticism of logical positivist science would reemerge later in the twentieth century through such influential philosophers of science as Thomas Kuhn and Paul Feyerabend. "Physics, too," Nietzsche wrote, "is only an interpretation and exegesis of the world. . . . Behind all logic and its seeming sovereignty of movement, there also stand valuations or, more clearly, physiological demands for the preservation of a certain type of life." He explains this in the following passage on the universe:

⚒

. . . And do you know what "the universe" is to my mind? Shall I show it to you in my mirror? This universe is a monster of energy, without beginning or end; a fixed and brazen quantity of energy that grows neither bigger nor smaller, does not consume itself, but only alters its face; as a whole its bulk is immutable, it is a household without either losses or gains, but likewise without increase and without sources of revenue, surrounded by nonentity as by a frontier. It is nothing vague or wasteful, it does not stretch into infinity; but is a definite quantum of energy located in limited space, and not in space that would be anywhere empty. It is rather energy everywhere, the play of forces and force-waves, at the same time one and many, agglomerating here and diminishing there, a sea of forces storming and raging in itself, forever changing, forever rolling back over incalculable ages to recurrence, with an ebb and flow of its forms, producing the most complicated things out of the most simple structures; producing the most ardent, most savage, and most contradictory things out of the quietest, most rigid, and most frozen material, and then returning from multifariousness to uniformity, from the play of contradictions back into the delight of consonance, saying Yea unto itself, even in this homogeneity of its courses and ages; forever blessing itself as something which recurs for all eternity—a becoming that knows not satiety, or disgust, or weariness—this, my Dionysian world of eternal self-creation, of eternal self-destruction, this mysterious world of twofold voluptuousness; this, my "Beyond Good and Evil," without aim, unless there is an aim in the bliss of the circle, without will, unless a ring must by nature keep good will to itself—would you have a name for my world? A *solution* of all your riddles? Do you also want a light, you most concealed, strongest and most undaunted men of the blackest midnight?—This *world is the Will to Power—and nothing else!* And even you yourselves are this Will to Power—and nothing else!

I fancy I have divined some of the things that lie hidden in the soul of the highest man; perhaps every man who has divined so much must go to ruin. But he who has seen the highest man must do all he can to make him *possible.*

Fundamental thought: we must make the future the standard of all our valuations—and not seek the laws for our conduct behind us.

Not "mankind," but *Superman,* is the goal.

And what is this Nietzschean philosophical Superman like? He is "the genius of heart," a true lover of wisdom:

A philosopher: that is a man who constantly experiences, sees, hears, suspects, hopes, and dreams extraordinary things; who is struck by his own thoughts as if they came from the outside, from above and below, as a species of events and lightning-flashes *peculiar to him;* who is perhaps himself a storm pregnant with new lightnings; a portentous man, around whom there is always rumbling and mumbling and gaping and something uncanny going on. A philosopher: alas, a being who often runs away from himself, is often afraid of himself—but whose curiosity always makes him "come to himself" again.

Nietzsche's voluminous writings have continued to attract a wide and ever-widening influential following, including George Bernard Shaw, Thomas Mann, Hermann Hesse, Karl Jaspers, Martin Heidegger, Sigmund Freud, Jean-Paul Sartre, H. L. Mencken, Jacques Derrida, and Michel Foucault. What his own writings meant to him he reveals to us at the conclusion of his *Will to Power,* where he writes an ode to his own words:

Alas! what are you, after all, my written and painted thoughts! Not long ago you were so variegated, young, and malicious, so full of thorns and secret spices, that you made me sneeze and laugh—and now? You have already doffed your novelty, and some of you, I fear, are ready to become truths, so immortal do they look, so pathetically honest, so tedious! And was it ever otherwise? What then do we write and paint, we mandarins with Chinese brush, we immortalisers of things which *lend* themselves to writing, what are we alone capable of painting? Alas, only that which is just about to fade and begins to lose its odour! Alas, only exhausted and departing storms and belated yellow sentiments! Alas, only birds strayed and fatigued by flight, which now let themselves be captured with the hand—with *our* hand! We immortalise what cannot live and fly much longer, things only which are exhausted and mellow! And it is only for your *afternoon,* you, my written and painted thoughts, for which alone I have colours, many colours perhaps, many variegated softenings, and fifty yellows and browns and greens and reds;—but nobody will divine thereby how ye looked in your morning, you sudden sparks and marvels of my solitude, you, my old, beloved— evil thoughts!

NOTE

1. See, for instance, The *Gnostic Gospels* by Elaine Pagels (New York: Random House, 1979), key sections of which are reprinted in Kolak and Martin, *Self, Cosmos, God* (Harcourt Brace Jovanovich, 1993). Her argument is that the reason the early Christians chose the texts they did was to establish a male hierarchy and authority structure.

Part VI ⚘ The Social Philosophers

19 ✿ The Social Philosophers: Wollstonecraft, Comte, Bentham, Mill, and Marx

19.0 The Shift to the Social Arena

The naive realist believes (1) in a mind-independent real world and (2) that this mind-independent real world is directly experienced. Naive realism is the view children come to naturally. We might call it "folk philosophy." We have seen various philosophers take a stand for or against (1) but none who accepts (2)—although in the next chapter we *will* see some who accept (2). Among the various responses to (1), idealists deny the existence of any such mind-independent world, whereas *representationalists*, most notably Kant, argue that the real world is in part created by the mind (the phenomenal world) and in part created by things-in-themselves (the noumenal world).

Notice, however, that such views have thus far been predicated on the notion that *if* there is such a two-way relation between real objects and the mind, it is a case of *individual* minds affecting *the same public reality*.[1] There is just one world; we are each participators *in that world*. Thus, objective reality is created. But we've already seen Schopenhauer begin to move in a

new direction, one followed both by Kierke-gaard and Nietzsche. In arguing that the *thing-in-itself* is *the will* and that the will is *the body*, Schopenhauer implies the possibility of transcending subjectivity *in the social arena*. That is, there is already in Schopenhauer the implicit possibility of *verifying* whether an experience is "real," whether an object is "real," whether an event is "real," whether an idea is "real," and so on, by seeing to what extent there is agreement among minds. More than that: given the active view of the powers of the mind taken by Kant, Hegel, Fichte, Schelling, Kierkegaard, and Nietzsche, *it now seems possible that the ego can create reality, which otherwise is out of reach of its prying insubstantiality, by convincing, seducing, or forcing other minds to think as you do.* This reality *is* thus directly manipulatable.

Just about all subsequent philosophies have been influenced by that line of thinking in certain aspects and in varying degrees. Thus, both Comte's positivism and the logical positivism of a century later could be based in part on the notion that *public ("social") verification is a necessary condition for truth and meaning.* Likewise, the shift in Kierkegaard, Nietzsche, and Marx from the search for new and better epistemologies and metaphysical systems to building, instead, a new kind of human individual, is largely predicated, not on new critiques of reason but—especially in Nietzsche and Marx—on critiques of social institutions. Indeed, the entire basis for Marx's famous call to arms—"The philosophers have only *interpreted* the world in various ways: the point however is to *change* it"—is predicated on his belief not that *individual consciousness makes reality* but, rather, *that social reality makes individual consciousness.*

From such a vantage point, the entire so-called Industrial Revolution, a term used by the English economic historian Arnold Toynbee (1889–1975) to describe Europe's economic development from 1760 to 1840, can be seen as the result, literally, of a philosophical shift in *thought*. Traditionally, the end goal of philosophy—it's "product"—was thought. In the process of philosophical enlightenment we went from having *those* (false, wrong, misguided) thoughts to having *these* (true, correct, learned) thoughts. The philosopher had certain thoughts that the nonphilosopher didn't. Occasionally, as in the Epicurean and Stoic periods, there were shifts in emphases from a search for the right *cognitive* states to a search for the right *emotive* states. But now if the world is my idea—or, more broadly, if by "idea," "perception," "phenomenon," and so on, I mean all these things that are at this moment before my eyes—it is only a matter of time before I draw the conclusion as to what the activity of philosophy—traditionally imbued into the human intellect as the study, manipulation, construction, improvement, and so on, of *ideas*—should now become! The building of "bridges," "roads," and the proverbial "pillars of knowledge" becomes, literally, the building of bridges, roads, and pillars, along with a study, understanding, and general improvement of the means of their production. If my theory is correct, the fact that the European Industrial Revolution corresponds to the time of Kant (1724–1804), Fichte (1762–1814), Hegel (1770–1831), Schelling (1775–1854), Schopen-

hauer (1788–1860), Comte (1798–1857), Mill (1806–1873), Kierkegaard (1813–1855), and Marx (1818–1883) is no accident, for it is precisely in these philosophers that this *literal* shift in thought occurs.

In other words, although the nineteenth-century shift of philosophy into the social arena has often been misunderstood as a shift away from traditional concerns with epistemology and metaphysics toward social engineering, it can be viewed as a shift in focus concerning the question of where and what the stuff of reality *is*. The common misunderstanding is partly the fault of the nineteenth- and early twentieth-century philosophers who so openly *talked* against metaphysics when in reality what they conceived of themselves as doing was not just studying the "noumenal" world by manipulating thought, but bringing the real world into existence—constructing and then ultimately improving it. One does not have to "turn Hegel upside down," as in Marx's dialectical materialism, and peek up socialism's skirt to see this; it is already evident in Schopenhauer. After all, where, in Schopenhauer's view, are those mysterious "things-in-themselves"? Where is the *will*? Hold up your hand! There it is. Look all around you. You're in the belly of the beast.

In this chapter, we shall examine the shift of philosophy as an *introspective* activity to philosophy as a *social, political,* and—what was the ultimate outcome of this line of thought, through the work of Hegel's most famous and influential student, Karl Marx—*economic* activity.

19.1 Wollstonecraft (1759–1797): The Rights of Women

Mary Wollstonecraft was born in London to an unhappy family; her father, a violent drunkard, squandered the money left to him by his own father and took out his frustrations on his wife and children. Mary, the oldest of seven children, tried her best to protect her mother and siblings from his wrath. Her oldest brother, Edward, instead of trying to help, actually made matters even worse by stealing what little money was left. For most of her life, Mary took on the burden of supporting her mother and siblings, which she tried to do by writing. Because women were not given the same opportunities for education as men, she educated herself by reading and also took it upon herself to educate her sisters and younger brothers. Her sense of injustice and alienation inspired her to write numerous letters, articles, and essays, which drew much attention from the London intelligentsia because of their bold and direct style. She became known as a gifted young rebel with a cause: the rights of women. Her first published work was *Thoughts on the Education of Daughters*.

Wollstonecraft did not believe in traditional marriage, and after a tumultuous affair with an American writer she gave birth out of wedlock to her first daughter, Fanny. As she was raising Fanny she met and fell in love with a well-known political anarchist, William Godwin, and she became pregnant again. By this time her book, *A Vindication of the Rights of Women*, from which our selection is taken, had established her reputation as a brilliant literary and philosophical talent. Life seemed to have turned for the better when complications from her second delivery ended her life prematurely; she died at the age of 38.

The story, however, does not end there. Godwin was heartbroken at her death and devoted himself to raising her children. He wrote a book of memoirs, praising his life with Wollstonecraft, openly admitting that both her first child and the one he fathered were illegitimate. Their daughter, Mary Godwin, thus grew up under great public scandal that in the end inspired her, in turn, to a career in writing. She married the poet Percy Bysshe Shelley and went on to write one of the great novels, *Frankenstein*, whose scathing criticism of male-dominated society is well hidden in one of the most famous allegories ever written. It is about how men, because they cannot give birth, time and again produce nothing but various technological and scientific monstrosities.

In the following selection from *A Vindication of the Rights of Women*, Wollstonecraft argues persuasively that women should not be encultur-ated by society into positions of weakness and dependency. Her brilliant argument, which is meant to persuade men who are in power to rethink the roles of women, is that liberating women would ultimately be in the best interests of men. This liberation became a battle cry, not only for the first feminists but also for the many men who were persuaded and inspired to this day by the power of her prose.

⚘

A Vindication of the Rights of Women

Moralists have unanimously agreed, that unless virtue be nursed by liberty, it will never attain due strength—and what they say of man I extend to mankind, insisting that in all cases morals must be fixed on immutable principles; and, that the being cannot be termed rational or virtuous, who obeys any authority, but that of reason.

To render women truly useful members of society, I argue that they should be led, by having their understandings cultivated on a large scale, to acquire a rational affection for their country, founded on knowledge, because it is obvious that we are little interested about what we do not understand. And to render this general knowledge of due importance, I have endeavoured to shew that private duties are never properly fulfilled unless the understanding enlarges the heart; and that public virtue is only an aggregate of private. But, the distinctions established in society under-mine both, by beating out the solid gold of virtue, till it becomes only the tinsel-covering of vice; for whilst wealth renders a man more respectable than virtue, wealth will be sought before virtue; and, whilst women's persons are caressed, when a child-ish simper shews an absence of mind—the mind will lie fallow. Yet, true voluptuousness must proceed from the mind—for what can equal the sensations produced by mutual affection, sup-ported by mutual respect? What are the cold, or feverish caresses of appetite, but sin embracing death, compared with the modest overflowings of

---

From *A Vindication of the Rights of Women* by Mary Wollstonecraft. London: 1792.

a pure heart and exalted imagination? Yes, let me tell the libertine of fancy when he despises understanding in woman—that the mind, which he disregards, gives life to the enthusiastic affection from which rapture, short-lived as it is, alone can flow! And, that, without virtue, a sexual attachment must expire, like a tallow candle in the socket, creating intolerable disgust. To prove this, I need only observe, that men who have wasted great part of their lives with women, and with whom they have sought for pleasure with eager thirst, entertain the meanest opinion of the sex.— Virtue, true refiner of joy!—if foolish men were to fright thee from earth, in order to give loose to all their appetites without a check—some sensual wight of taste would scale the heavens to invite thee back, to give a zest to pleasure!

That women at present are by ignorance rendered foolish or vicious, is, I think, not to be disputed; and, that the most salutary effects tending to improve mankind might be expected from a REVOLUTION in female manners, appears, at least, with a face of probability, to rise out of the observation. For as marriage has been termed the parent of those endearing charities which draw man from the brutal herd, the corrupting intercourse that wealth, idleness, and folly, produce between the sexes, is more universally injurious to morality than all the other vices of mankind collectively considered. To adulterous lust the most sacred duties are sacrificed, because before marriage, men, by a promiscuous intimacy with women, learned to consider love as a selfish gratification—learned to separate it not only from esteem, but from the affection merely built on habit, which mixes a little humanity with it. Justice and friendship are also set at defiance, and that purity of taste is vitiated which would naturally lead a man to relish an artless display of affection rather than affected airs. But that noble simplicity of affection, which dares to appear unadorned, has few attractions for the libertine, though it be the charm, which by cementing the matrimonial tie, secures to the pledges of a warmer passion the necessary parental attention; for children will never be properly educated till friendship subsists between parents. Virtue flies from a house divided against itself—and a whole legion of devils take up their residence there.

The affection of husbands and wives cannot be pure when they have so few sentiments in common, and when so little confidence is established at home, as must be the case when their pursuits are so different. That intimacy from which tenderness should flow, will not, cannot subsist between the vicious.

Contending, therefore, that the sexual distinction which men have so warmly insisted upon, is arbitrary, I have dwelt on an observation, that several sensible men, with whom I have conversed on the subject, allowed to be well founded; and it is simply this, that the little chastity to be found amongst men, and consequent disregard of modesty, tend to degrade both sexes; and further, that the modesty of women, characterized as such, will often be only the artful veil of wantonness instead of being the natural reflection of purity, till modesty be universally respected.

From the tyranny of man, I firmly believe, the greater number of female follies proceed; and the cunning, which I allow makes at present a part of their character, I likewise have repeatedly endeavoured to prove, is produced by oppression.

Were not dissenters, for instance, a class of people, with strict truth, characterized as cunning? And may I not lay some stress on this fact to prove, that when any power but reason curbs the free spirit of man, dissimulation is practised, and the various shifts of art are naturally called forth? Great attention to decorum, which was carried to a degree of scrupulosity, and all that puerile bustle about trifles and consequential solemnity, which Butler's caricature of a dissenter, brings before the imagination, shaped their persons as well as their minds in the mould of prim littleness. I speak collectively, for I know how many ornaments to human nature have been enrolled amongst sectaries; yet, I assert, that the same narrow prejudice for their sect, which women have for their families, prevailed in the dissenting part of the community, however worthy in other respects; and also that the same timid prudence, or headstrong efforts, often disgraced the exertions of both. Oppression thus formed many of the features of their character perfectly to coincide with that of the oppressed half of mankind; or is it not notorious that dissenters were, like women, fond of deliberating together, and asking advice of each other, till by a complication of little contrivances, some little end was brought about? A similar attention to preserve their reputation was conspicuous in the dissenting and female world, and was produced by a similar cause.

Asserting the rights which women in common

with men ought to contend for, I have not attempted to extenuate their faults; but to prove them to be the natural consequence of their education and station in society. If so, it is reasonable to suppose that they will change their character, and correct their vices and follies, when they are allowed to be free in a physical, moral, and civil sense. [72]

[72] I had further enlarged on the advantages which might reasonably be expected to result from an improvement in female manners, towards the general reformation of society; but it appeared to me that such reflections would more properly close the last volume.

Let woman share the rights and she will emulate the virtues of man; for she must grow more perfect when emancipated, or justify the authority that chains such a weak being to her duty.—If the latter, it will be expedient to open a fresh trade with Russia for whips; a present which a father should always make to his son-in-law on his wedding day, that a husband may keep his whole family in order by the same means; and without any violation of justice reign, wielding this sceptre, sole master of his house, because he is the only being in it who has reason:—the divine, indefeasible earthly sovereignty breathed into man by the Master of the universe. Allowing this position, women have not any inherent rights to claim; and, by the same rule, their duties vanish, for rights and duties are inseparable.

Be just then, O ye men of understanding! and mark not more severely what women do amiss, than the vicious tricks of the horse or the ass for whom ye provide provender—and allow her the privileges of ignorance, to whom ye deny the rights of reason, or ye will be worse than Egyptian task-masters, expecting virtue where nature has not given understanding!

19.2 Comte (1798–1857): The Founder of Sociology and Positivism

Born in Montpelier, France, Isidore Auguste Marie François Comte was the son of a tax collector. After studying at the École Polytechnique in Paris for two years, he took part in a student rebellion that closed the school. He stayed in

Paris and supported himself giving private lessons in mathematics while studying philosophy. In 1833 when the École Polytechnique reopened, he was hired as an entrance examiner, but two years later, when it was discovered that he had taken part in the revolution, he was fired. He had by then, however, attracted the support of many admirers, among them John Stuart Mill in England, who regarded him as the most "original and bold new thinker" of his time.

During the end of the nineteenth century, Comte's voluminous philosophical writings turned out to be a major source of inspiration for the subsequent shift in philosophy from a metaphysical to a "scientific" orientation, where "scientific" is broadly construed within its implicit (and usually covertly hidden) *social* aspects— what we might even term "social epistemology." This is a key new direction—an explicitly different grounding of certainty away from the Cartesian notion of *I think, therefore I am*— where all certainty is grounded through an individual's relation to the truth, to an interpersonal, social realm.

In his main philosophical work, *Cours de Philosophie Positive (Course of the Positive Philosophy*, in six volumes, published from 1842–1854), from which the following selection is taken, Comte presents his theory of the law of the three "theoretical conditions" of the intellectual development of human thought.

Course of the Positive Philosophy

From the study of the development of human intelligence, in all directions, and through all times, the discovery arises of a great fundamental law, to which it is necessarily subject, and which has a solid foundation of proof, both in the facts of our organization and in our historical experience. The law is this:—that each of our leading concep-

From the *Cours de Philosophie Positive*, Paris, 1830–1842. Reprinted from Comte's *The Positive Philosophy*, London, 1853, vol. I, ch. I.

tions,—each branch of our knowledge,—passes successively through three different theoretical conditions: the Theological, or fictitious; the Metaphysical, or abstract; and the Scientific, or positive. In other words, the human mind, by its nature, employs in its progress three methods of philosophizing, the character of which is essentially different, and even radically opposed: viz., the theological method, the metaphysical, and the positive. Hence arise three philosophies, or general systems of conceptions on the aggregate of phenomena, each of which excludes the others. The first is the necessary point of departure of the human understanding; and the third is its fixed and definitive state. The second is merely a state of transition.

In the theological state, the human mind, seeking the essential nature of beings, the first and final causes (the origin and purpose) of all effects,—in short, Absolute knowledge,—supposes all phenomena to be produced by the immediate action of supernatural beings.

In the metaphysical state, which is only a modification of the first, the mind supposes, instead of supernatural beings, abstract forces, veritable entities (that is, personified abstractions) inherent in all beings, and capable of producing all phenomena. What is called the explanation of phenomena is, in this stage, a mere reference of each to its proper entity.

In the final, the positive state, the mind has given over the vain search after Absolute notions, the origin and destination of the universe, and the causes of phenomena, and applies itself to the study of their laws,—that is, their invariable relations of succession and resemblance. Reasoning and observation, duly combined, are the means of this knowledge. What is now understood when we speak of an explanation of facts is simply the establishment of a connection between single phenomena and some general facts, the number of which continually diminishes with the progress of science.

The Theological system arrived at the highest perfection of which it is capable when it substituted the providential action of a single Being for the varied operations of the numerous divinities which had been before imagined. In the same way, in the last stage of the Metaphysical system, men substitute one great entity (Nature) as the cause of all phenomena, instead of the multitude of entities

at first supposed. In the same way, again, the ultimate perfection of the Positive system would be (if such perfection could be hoped for) to represent all phenomena as particular aspects of a single general fact;—such as Gravitation, for instance.

The importance of the working of this general law will be established hereafter. At present, it must suffice to point out some of the grounds of it.

There is no science which, having attained the positive stage, does not bear marks of having passed through the others. Some time since it was (whatever it might be) composed, as we can now perceive, of metaphysical abstractions; and, further back in the course of time, it took its form from theological conceptions. We shall have only too much occasion to see, as we proceed, that our most advanced sciences still bear very evident marks of the two earlier periods through which they have passed.

The progress of the individual mind is not only an illustration, but an indirect evidence of that of the general mind. The point of departure of the individual and of the race being the same, the phases of the mind of a man correspond to the epochs of the mind of the race. Now, each of us is aware, if he looks back upon his own history, that he was a theologian in his childhood, a metaphysician in his youth, and a natural philosopher in his manhood. All men who are up to their age can verify this for themselves.

Besides the observation of facts, we have theoretical reasons in support of this law.

The most important of these reasons arises from the necessity that always exists for some theory to which to refer our facts, combined with the clear impossibility that, at the outset of human knowledge, men could have formed theories out of the observation of facts. All good intellects have repeated, since Bacon's time, that there can be no real knowledge but that which is based on observed facts. This is incontestable, in our present advanced stage; but, if we look back to the primitive stage of human knowledge, we shall see that it must have been otherwise then. If it is true that every theory must be based upon observed facts, it is equally true that facts cannot be observed without the guidance of some theory. Without such guidance, our facts would be desultory and fruitless; we could not retain them: for the most part we could not even perceive them.

Thus, between the necessity of observing facts

in order to form a theory, and having a theory in order to observe facts, the human mind would have been entangled in a vicious circle, but for the natural opening afforded by Theological conceptions. This is the fundamental reason for the theological character of the primitive philosophy. This necessity is confirmed by the perfect suitability of the theological philosophy to the earliest researches of the human mind. It is remarkable that the most inaccessible questions,—those of the nature of beings, and the origin and purpose of phenomena,—should be the first to occur in a primitive state, while those which are really within our reach are regarded as almost unworthy of serious study. The reason is evident enough:—that experience alone can teach us the measure of our powers; and if men had not begun by an exaggerated estimate of what they can do, they would never have done all that they are capable of. Our organization requires this. At such a period there could have been no reception of a positive philosophy, whose function is to discover the laws of phenomena, and whose leading characteristic it is to regard as interdicted to human reason those sublime mysteries which theology explains, even to their minutest details, with the most attractive facility. It is just so under a practical view of the nature of the researches with which men first occupied themselves. Such inquiries offered the powerful charm of unlimited empire over the external world,—a world destined wholly for our use, and involved in every way with our existence. The theological philosophy, presenting this view, administered exactly the stimulus necessary to incite the human mind to the irksome labour without which it could make no progress. We can now scarcely conceive of such a state of things, our reason having become sufficiently mature to enter upon laborious scientific researches, without needing any such stimulus as wrought upon the imaginations of astrologers and alchemists. We have motive enough in the hope of discovering the laws of phenomena, with a view to the confirmation or rejection of a theory. But it could not be so in the earliest days; and it is to the chimeras of astrology and alchemy that we owe the long series of observations and experiments on which our positive science is based. Kepler felt this on behalf of astronomy, and Berthollet on behalf of chemistry. Thus was a spontaneous philosophy, the theological, the only possible beginning, method, and pro-

visional system, out of which the Positive philosophy could grow. It is easy, after this, to perceive how Metaphysical methods and doctrines must have afforded the means of transition from the one to the other.

The human understanding, slow in its advance, could not step at once from the theological into the positive philosophy. The two are so radically opposed, that an intermediate system of conceptions has been necessary to render the transition possible. It is only in doing this, that Metaphysical conceptions have any utility whatever. In contemplating phenomena, men substitute for supernatural direction a corresponding entity. This entity may have been supposed to be derived from the supernatural action: but it is more easily lost sight of, leaving attention free for the facts themselves, till, at length, metaphysical agents have ceased to be anything more than the abstract names of phenomena. It is not easy to say by what other process than this our minds could have passed from supernatural considerations to natural; from the theological system to the positive.

The Law of human development being thus established, let us consider what is the proper nature of the Positive Philosophy.

As we have seen, the first characteristic of the Positive Philosophy is that it regards all phenomena as subjected to invariable natural *Laws*. Our business is,—seeing how vain is any research into what are called *Causes*, whether first or final,—to pursue an accurate discovery of these Laws, with a view to reducing them to the smallest possible number. By speculating upon causes, we could solve no difficulty about origin and purpose. Our real business is to analyse accurately the circumstances of phenomena, and to connect them by the natural relations of succession and resemblance. . . .

The Positive Philosophy, which has been rising since the time of Bacon, has now secured such a preponderance, that the metaphysicians themselves profess to ground their pretended science on an observation of facts. They talk of external and internal facts, and say that their business is with the latter. This is much like saying that vision is explained by luminous objects painting their images upon the retina. To this the physiologists reply that another eye would be needed to see the image. In the same manner, the mind may observe all phenomena but its own. It may be said that a man's intellect may observe his passions, the seat of the reason being somewhat apart from that of the emotions in the brain; but there can be nothing like scientific observation of the passions, except from without, as the stir of the emotions disturbs the observing faculties more or less. It is yet more out of the question to make an intellectual observation of intellectual processes. The observing and observed organs are here the same, and its action cannot be pure and natural. In order to observe, your intellect must pause from activity; yet it is this very activity that you want to observe. If you cannot effect the pause, you cannot observe: if you do effect it, there is nothing to observe. The results of such a method are in proportion to its absurdity. After two thousand years of psychological pursuit, no one proposition is established to the satisfaction of its followers. They are divided, to this day, into a multitude of schools, still disputing about the very elements of their doctrine. This interior observation gives birth to almost as many theories as there are observers. We ask in vain for any one discovery, great or small, which has been made under this method. The psychologists have done some good in keeping up the activity of our understandings, when there was no better work for our faculties to do; and they may have added something to our stock of knowledge. If they have done so, it is by practicing the Positive method—by observing the progress of the human mind in the light of science; that is, by ceasing, for the moment, to be psychologists.

The view just given in relation to logical Science becomes yet more striking when we consider the logical Art.

The Positive Method can be judged of only in action. It cannot be looked at by itself, apart from the work on which it is employed. At all events, such a contemplation would be only a dead study, which could produce nothing in the mind which loses time upon it. We may talk for ever about the method, and state it in terms very wisely, without knowing half so much about it as the man who has once put it in practice upon a single particular of actual research, even without any philosophical intention. Thus it is that psychologists, by dint of reading the precepts of Bacon and the discourses of Descartes, have mistaken their own dreams for science. . . .

This, then, is the first great result of the Positive Philosophy—the manifestation by experiment of the laws which rule the Intellect in the investiga-

tion of truth; and, as a consequence the knowledge of the general rules suitable for that object.

The Positive Philosophy offers the only solid basis for that Social Reorganization which must succeed the critical condition in which the most civilized nations are now living.

It cannot be necessary to prove to anybody who reads this work that Ideas govern the world, or throw it into chaos; in other words, that all social mechanism rests upon Opinions. The great political and moral crisis that societies are now undergoing is shown by a rigid analysis to arise out of intellectual anarchy. While stability in fundamental maxims is the first condition of genuine social order, we are suffering under an utter disagreement which may be called universal. Till a certain number of general ideas can be acknowledged as a rallying-point of social doctrine, the nations will remain in a revolutionary state, whatever palliatives may be devised; and their institutions can be only provisional. But whenever the necessary agreement on first principles can be obtained, appropriate institutions will issue from them, without shock or resistance; for the causes of disorder will have been arrested by the mere fact of the agreement. It is in this direction that those must look who desire a natural and regular, a normal state of society.

Now, the existing disorder is abundantly accounted for by the existence, all at once, of three incompatible philosophies,—the theological, the metaphysical, and the positive. Any one of these might alone secure some sort of social order; but while the three co-exist, it is impossible for us to understand one another upon any essential point whatever. If this is true, we have only to ascertain which of the philosophies must, in the nature of things, prevail; and, this ascertained, every man, whatever may have been his former views, cannot but concur in its triumph. The problem once recognized cannot remain long unsolved; for all considerations whatever point to the Positive Philosophy as the one destined to prevail. It alone has been advancing during a course of centuries, throughout which the others have been declining. The fact is incontestable. Some may deplore it, but none can destroy it, nor therefore neglect it but under penalty of being betrayed by illusory speculations. This general revolution of the human mind is nearly accomplished. We have only to complete the Positive Philosophy by bringing Social phenomena within its comprehension, and afterwards consolidating the whole into one body of homogeneous doctrine. The marked preference which almost all minds, from the highest to the commonest, accord to positive knowledge over vague and mystical conceptions, is a pledge of what the reception of this philosophy will be when it has acquired the only quality that it now wants—a character of due generality. When it has become complete, its supremacy will take place spontaneously, and will re-establish order throughout society.

⚼

The first of Comte's three stages of knowledge, the primitive "theological or fictitious" stage, relies on supernatural beings and supernatural explanations. The second "metaphysical" stage is merely an intermediary modification of the theological stage, with the replacement of the supernatural entities with abstract notions. In the third and final "positive" stage, the mind has freed itself from its vain search for "Absolute notions" and relies instead on reason and observation.

In turning away from introspective philosophy, in which the apperception of one's own psychological states is taken as an epistemological yardstick, toward the public "sociological" realm of cross-verification and "social facts," he is in the domain of what we shall call, in its broadest sense, *scientific*.

Comte argues that his theory should be applied not just to our search for knowledge about the world but to the human social realm as well. For the first time he began the process of establishing in a systematic fashion the social science to which he gave the name "sociology." In the early part of the twentieth century, his thinking helped pave the way for both the social, political, and moral philosophy of John Stuart Mill and the scientism of the logical positivists. And, like Nietzsche and Marx, he makes a radical break with traditional religion.

Arguing that positive philosophy has no room for traditional religion, he calls for its eradication

on the grounds that it obfuscates not only the truth but also our essential role in its creation, and thus religion obstructs the natural progress of humanity. In lieu of traditional religion, he calls for the establishment of a new "religion of humanity," whose new priesthood would consist of scientists, businesspeople, politicians, and a "calendar of saints" that would include such persons as Adam Smith, Dante, and Shakespeare.

19.3 Bentham (1748–1832): The Moral Utilitarian

Comte's philosophical successor, who carried on both his phenomenalist and presentationalist philosophy into the social arena of politics and ethics, was John Stuart Mill. But first we must turn to an even greater influence on Mill's views, one of the leading radical reformers of the nineteenth century, Jeremy Bentham.

Born in London, the son of a leading attorney, Bentham was a child prodigy who began studying history and Latin at the age of three. At twelve he entered Queen's College in Oxford and earned his B.A. in three years and his M.A. two years later at the age of seventeen. His father expected him to become a practicing lawyer, but Bentham was far more interested in the philosophical foundations of ethics, morality, and legal theory. He traveled widely throughout Europe and wrote his first essay on economics in Russia. In 1792 he became a citizen of France.

Bentham's main philosophical influences were Locke and Hume. When he read Hume's *Treatise on Human Nature* he said it was "as if scales fell" from his eyes. He went on to publish several books on political and legal theory, but it was his *Introduction to the Principles of Morals and Legislation* (1789) that made him a powerful and influential international figure. In his *Principles* he laid the groundwork for utilitarianism; as developed by Mill (whom we shall consider in the next section), his theory is still today one of the leading moral theories in the world.

Bentham defines his principle of utility as

that property in any object whereby it tends to produce pleasure, good or happiness, or to prevent the happening of mischief, pain, evil or unhappiness to the party whose interest is considered.

According to Bentham, this principle takes account of the two main motives for all human action—pain and pleasure. Governments, social, political, and legal institutions, as well as individual citizens, should follow the Greatest Happiness Principle: choose that course of action that leads to the greatest happiness for the greatest number of people. His utilitarianism, designed to free people from oppressive laws and to make governing bodies moral, provided a foundation to many democratic societies. Since leaders as well as individuals are thus morally bound to follow the same universal principle and one that is readily accessible to everyone—we all know what pain and pleasure are—there can be no manipulation, through rhetoric, of the weak by the powerful. In Bentham's system we are each our own best judge as to how best to live and attain happiness.

His *Principles* drew much attention and praise throughout Europe and the United States. When he became a French citizen in 1792, he continued to work on establishing the codes for laws that could be applied in all countries wishing to follow his utilitarian principles. Deeply critical of established political and legal institutions, he condemned as evil the legal judges who

made the common law. Do you know how they make it? Just as a man makes laws for his dog. When your dog does anything you want to break him of, you wait till he does it and then beat him . . . this is the way judges make laws for you and me.

Bentham's utilitarianism is designed to break this repressive structure of laws imposed, under the guise of morality, on people by corrupt and exploitive leaders. He openly called for the rejection of all monarchies and established churches, claiming that "all government is in itself one vast evil." The only justification for putting such evil into place would be to prevent some greater evil; governments should therefore never stray from the principle of utility—the greatest happiness for the greatest number. Among Bentham's many disciples, the most famous is John Stuart Mill, who further developed utilitarianism but along rather different lines.

When Bentham died at the age of eighty-five he bequeathed his fortune to University College in London under the following conditions: his body should be dissected in the presence of his friends, his head mummified and replaced with a wax replica. These instructions were faithfully carried out, along with Bentham's final proviso: his dressed corpse with his mummified head alongside it continues to attend all board of trustees' meetings.

19.4 John Stuart Mill (1806–1873): Utilitarianism

John Stuart Mill was born in London. Educated by his father—a prominent philosopher, historian, and economist—Mill began to study Greek at age three. By the age of eight he had read all the major works of Plato in the original and began to study Latin, Euclid, and algebra. By age twelve he had read Aristotle's logical treatises, and within the next two years he turned to logic, mathematics, and world history. It was all part of his father's "educational experiment." The effect, in Mill's own words, was that "through the training bestowed on me by my father, I started, I may fairly say, with an advantage of a quarter century over my contemporaries."

At age twenty-five he experienced an emotional burnout: "[T]he habit of analysis has a tendency to wear away the feelings . . . I was thus, as I said to myself, left stranded at the commencement of my voyage, with a well equipped ship and a rudder, but no sail." He apparently found his sail in Mrs. Harriet Taylor, with whom he formed a lasting friendship; they married after her husband died. According to Mill, not only did she inspire him emotionally, but she should be credited as the coauthor of his most important works: *A System of Logic* (1843), *The Principles of Political Economy* (1848), and *On Liberty* (1859).

Having been raised by his father on the utilitarian doctrines of Jeremy Bentham and the "philosophical radicals," Mill ended up revolutionizing their ideas in his most widely influential book *Utilitarianism* (1863), from which the first selection is taken.

⚹

Utilitarianism

Our moral faculty, according to all those of its interpreters who are entitled to the name of thinkers, supplies us only with the general principles of moral judgments; it is a branch of our reason, not of our sensitive faculty; and must be looked to for the abstract doctrines of morality, not for perception of it in the concrete. The intuitive, no less than what may be termed the inductive, school of ethics insists on the necessity of general laws. They both agree that the morality of an individual action is not a question of direct perception, but of the application of a law to an individual case. They recognize also, to a great extent, the same moral laws but differ as to their evidence and the source from which they derive their authority. According to the one opinion, the principles of morals are evident *a priori,* requiring nothing to command assent except that the meaning of the terms be understood. According to the other doctrine, right and wrong, as well as truth and falsehood, are questions of observation and experience. But both hold equally that morality must be deduced from principles; and the intuitive school affirm as strongly as the inductive that there is a science of morals. Yet they seldom attempt to make out a list of the *a priori* principles which are to serve as the premises of the science; still more rarely do they make any effort to reduce those various principles to one first principle, or common ground of obligation. They either assume the ordinary precepts of morals as of *a priori* authority, or they lay down as the common

From J. S. Mill, *Utilitarianism.* First published in 1863.

groundwork of those maxims, some generality much less obviously authoritative than the maxims themselves, and which has never succeeded in gaining popular acceptance. Yet to support their pretensions there ought either to be some one fundamental principle or law at the root of all morality, or, if there be several, there should be a determinate order of precedence among them; and the one principle, or the rule for deciding between the various principles when they conflict, ought to be self-evident.

To inquire how far the bad effects of this deficiency have been mitigated in practice, or to what extent the moral beliefs of mankind have been vitiated or made uncertain by the absence of any distinct recognition of an ultimate standard, would imply a complete survey and criticism of past and present ethical doctrine. It would, however, be easy to show that whatever steadiness or consistency these moral beliefs have attained has been mainly due to the tacit influence of a standard not recognized. Although the nonexistence of an acknowledged first principle has made ethics not so much a guide as a consecration of men's actual sentiments, still, as men's sentiments, both in favor and of aversion, are greatly influenced by what they suppose to be the effect of things upon their happiness, the principle of utility, or, as Bentham latterly called it, the greatest happiness principle, has a large share in forming the moral doctrines even of those who most scornfully reject its authority. Nor is there any school of thought which refuses to admit that the influence of actions on happiness is a most material and even predominant consideration in many of the details, of morals, however unwilling to acknowledge it as the fundamental principle of morality and the source of moral obligation. I might go much further and say that to all those *a priori* moralists who deem it necessary to argue at all, utilitarian arguments are indispensable. It is not my present purpose to criticize these thinkers; but I cannot help referring, for illustration, to a systematic treatise by one of the most illustrious of them, the *Metaphysics of Ethics* by Kant. This remarkable man, whose system of thought will long remain one of the landmarks in the history of philosophical speculation, does, in the treatise in question, lay down a universal first principle as the origin and ground of moral obligation; it is this: "So act that the rule on which thou actest would admit of being adopted as a law by all rational beings." But when he begins to deduce from this precept any of the actual duties of morality, he fails, almost grotesquely, to show that there would be any contradiction, and the logical (not to say physical) impossibility, in the adoption by all rational beings of the most outrageously immoral rules of conduct. All he knows is that the *consequences* of their universal adoption would be such as no one would choose to incur. . . .

On the present occasion, I shall, without further discussion of the other theories, attempt to contribute something towards the understanding and appreciation of the "utilitarian" or "happiness" theory, and towards such proof as it is susceptible of. It is evident that this cannot be proof in the ordinary and popular meaning of the term. Questions of ultimate ends are not amenable to direct proof. Whatever can be proved to be good must be so by being shown to be a means to something admitted to be good without proof. The medical art is proved to be good by its conducing to health; but how is it possible to prove that health is good? The art of music is good, for the reason, among others, that it produces pleasure; but what proof is it possible to give that pleasure is good? If, then, it is asserted that there is a comprehensive formula, including all things which are in themselves good, and that whatever else is good is not so as an end but as a means, the formula may be accepted or rejected, but is not a subject of what is commonly understood by proof. We are not, however, to infer that its acceptance or rejection must depend on blind impulse, or arbitrary choice. There is a larger meaning of the word "proof," in which this question is as amenable to it as any other of the disputed questions of philosophy. The subject is within the cognizance of the rational faculty; and neither does that faculty deal with it solely in the way of intuition. Considerations may be presented capable of determining the intellect either to give or withhold its assent to the doctrine; and this is equivalent to proof.

What Utilitarianism Is

A passing remark is all that needs be given to the ignorant blunder of supposing that those who stand up for utility as the test of right and wrong use the term in that restricted and merely colloquial sense in which utility is opposed to pleasure. An apology is due to the philosophical opponents of utilitarianism, for even the momentary appear-

ance of confounding them with anyone capable of so absurd a misconception; which is the more extraordinary, inasmuch as the contrary accusation, of referring everything to pleasure, and that, too, in its grossest form, is another of the common charges against utilitarianism: and, as has been pointedly remarked by an able writer, the same sort of persons and often the very same persons, denounce the theory "as impracticably dry when the word 'utility' precedes the word 'pleasure,' and as too practically voluptuous when the word 'pleasure,' precedes the word "utility'." Those who know anything about the matter are aware that every writer, from Epicurus to Bentham, who maintained the theory of utility, meant by it, not something to be contradistinguished from pleasure, but pleasure itself, together with exemption from pain; and instead of opposing the useful to the agreeable or the ornamental have always declared that the useful means these, among other things. Yet the common herd, including the herd of writers, not only in newspapers and periodicals, but in books of weight and pretension, are perpetually falling into this shallow mistake. Having caught up the word "utilitarian," while knowing nothing whatever about it but its sound, they habitually express by it the rejection or the neglect of pleasure in some of its forms: of beauty, of ornament, or of amusement. Nor is the term thus ignorantly misapplied solely in disparagement, but occasionally in compliment, as though it implied superiority to frivolity and the mere pleasures of the moment. And this perverted use is the only one in which the word is popularly known, and the one from which the new generation are acquiring their sole notion of its meaning. Those who introduced the word, but who had for many years discontinued it as a distinctive appellation, may well feel themselves called upon to resume it if by doing so they can hope to contribute anything towards rescuing it from this utter degradation.

The creed which accepts as the foundation of morals "utility" or the "greatest happiness principle" holds that actions are right in proportion as they tend to promote happiness, wrong as they tend to produce the reverse of happiness. By happiness is intended pleasure, and the absence of pain; by unhappiness, pain, and the privation of pleasure. To give a clear view of the moral standard set up by the theory, much more requires to be said; in particular, what things it includes in the ideas of pain and pleasure; and to what extent this is left an open question. But these supplementary explanations do not affect the theory of life on which this theory of morality is grounded—namely, that pleasure and freedom from pain are the only things desirable as ends, and that all desirable things (which are as numerous in the utilitarian as in any other scheme) are desirable either for the pleasure inherent in themselves, or as means to the promotion of pleasure and the prevention of pain.

Now such a theory of life excites in many minds, and among them in some of the most estimable in feeling and purpose, inveterate dislike. To suppose that life has (as they express it) no higher end than pleasure—no better and nobler object of desire and pursuit—they designate as utterly mean and groveling; as a doctrine worthy only of swine, to whom the followers of Epicurus were, at a very early period, contemptuously likened; and modern holders of the doctrine are occasionally made the subject of equally polite comparisons by its German, French, and English assailants.

When thus attacked, the Epicureans have always answered that it is not they, but their accusers, who represent human nature in a degrading light, since the accusation supposes human beings to be capable of no pleasures except those of which swine are capable. If this supposition were true, the charge could not be gainsaid, but would then be no longer an imputation; for if the sources of pleasure were precisely the same to human beings and to swine, the rule of life which is good enough for the one would be good enough for the other. The comparison of the Epicurean life to that of beasts is felt as degrading, precisely because a beast's pleasures do not satisfy a human being's conceptions of happiness. Human beings have faculties more elevated than the animal appetites and, when once made conscious of them, do not regard anything as happiness which does not include their gratification. I do not, indeed, consider the Epicureans to have been by any means faultless in drawing out their scheme of consequences from the utilitarian principle. To do this in any sufficient manner, many Stoic, as well as Christian, elements require to be included. But there is no known Epicurean theory of life which does not assign to the pleasures of the intellect, of the feelings and imagination, and of the moral sentiments, a much higher value of pleasures than to those of mere sensation. It must be admitted,

however, that utilitarian writers in general have placed the superiority of mental over bodily pleasures chiefly in the greater permanency, safety, uncostliness, etc., of the former—that is, in their circumstantial advantages rather than in their intrinsic nature. And on all these points utilitarians have fully proved their case; but they might have taken the other and, as it may be called, higher ground with entire consistency. It is quite compatible with the principle of utility to recognize the fact that some kinds of pleasure are more desirable and more valuable than others. It would be absurd that, while, in estimating all other things, quality is considered as well as quantity, the estimation of pleasures should be supposed to depend on quantity alone.

If I am asked what I mean by difference of quality in pleasures, or what makes one pleasure more valuable than another, merely as a pleasure, except its being greater in amount, there is but one possible answer. Of two pleasures, if there be one to which all or almost all who have experience of both give a decided preference, irrespective of a feeling of moral obligation to prefer it, that is the more desirable pleasure. If one of the two is, by those who are competently acquainted with both, placed so far above the other that they prefer it even though knowing it to be attended with a greater amount of discontent, and would not resign it for any quantity of the other pleasure which their nature is capable of, we are justified in ascribing to the preferred enjoyment a superiority in quality so far outweighing quantity as to render it, in comparison, of small account.

Now it is an unquestionable fact that those who are equally acquainted with and equally capable of appreciating and enjoying both, do give a most marked preference to the manner of existence which employs their higher faculties. Few human creatures would consent to be changed into any of the lower animals for a promise of the fullest allowance of a beast's pleasures; no intelligent human being would consent to be a fool, no instructed person would be an ignoramus, no person of feeling and conscience would be selfish and base, even though they should be persuaded that the fool, the dunce, or the rascal is better satisfied with his lot than they are with theirs. They would not resign what they possess more than he for the most complete satisfaction of all the desires which they have in common with him. If they ever fancy they would, it is only in cases of unhappiness so extreme that to escape from it they would exchange their lot for almost any other, however undesirable in their own eyes. A being of higher faculties requires more to make him happy, is capable probably of more acute suffering, and certainly accessible to it at more points, than one of an inferior type; but in spite of these liabilities, he can never really wish to sink into what he feels to be a lower grade of existence. We may give what explanation we please of this unwillingness; we may attribute it to pride, a name which is given indiscriminately to some of the most and to some of the least estimable feelings of which mankind are capable: we may refer it to the love of liberty and personal independence, an appeal to which was with the Stoics one of the most effective means for the inculcation of it; to the love of power or to the love of excitement, both of which do really enter into and contribute to it; but its most appropriate appellation is a sense of dignity, which all human beings possess in one form or other, and in some, though by no means in exact, proportion to their higher faculties, and which is so essential a part of the happiness of those in whom it is strong that nothing which conflicts with it could be otherwise than momentarily an object of desire to them. Whoever supposes that this preference takes place at a sacrifice of happiness—that the superior being, in anything like equal circumstances, is not happier than the inferior—confounds the two very different ideas of happiness and content. It is indisputable that the being whose capacities of enjoyment are low has the greatest chance of having them fully satisfied; and a highly endowed being will always feel that any happiness which he can look for, as the world is constituted, is imperfect. But he can learn to bear its imperfections, if they are at all bearable; and they will not make him envy the being who is indeed unconscious of the imperfections, but only because he feels not at all the good which those imperfections qualify. It is better to be a human being dissatisfied than a pig satisfied; better to be Socrates dissatisfied than a fool satisfied. And if the fool, or the pig, are of a different opinion, it is because they only know their own side of the question. The other party to the comparison knows both sides.

It may be objected that many who are capable of the higher pleasures occasionally, under the influence of temptation, postpone them to the lower. But this is quite compatible with a full appreciation of the intrinsic superiority of the higher. Men often, from infirmity of character, make their election for the nearer good, though they know it to be the less valuable; and this no less when the choice is between two bodily pleasures than when it is between bodily and mental. They pursue sensual indulgences to the injury of health, though perfectly aware that health is the greater good. It may be further objected that many who begin with youthful enthusiasm for everything noble, as they advance in years, sink into indolence and selfishness. But I do not believe that those who undergo this very common change voluntarily choose the lower description of pleasures in preference to the higher. I believe that, before they devote themselves exclusively to the one, they have already become incapable of the other. Capacity for the nobler feelings is in most natures a very tender plant, easily killed, not only by hostile influences, but by mere want of sustenance; and in the majority of young persons it speedily dies away if the occupations to which their position in life has devoted them, and the society into which it has thrown them, are not favorable to keeping that higher capacity in exercise. Men lose their high aspirations as they lose their intellectual tastes, because they have not time or opportunity for indulging them, and they addict themselves to inferior pleasures, not because they deliberately prefer them, but because they are either the only ones to which they have access, or the only ones which they are any longer capable of enjoying. It may be questioned whether any one who has remained equally susceptible to both classes of pleasures, ever knowingly and calmly preferred the lower, though many, in all ages, have broken down in an ineffectual attempt to combine both.

I have dwelt on this point, as being a necessary part of a perfectly just conception of utility or happiness considered as the directive rule of human conduct. But it is by no means an indispensable condition to the acceptance of the utilitarian standard; for that standard is not the agent's own greatest happiness, but the greatest amount of happiness altogether; and if it may possibly be doubted whether a noble character is always the happier for its nobleness, there can be no doubt that it makes other people happier, and that the world in general is immensely a gainer by it. Utilitarianism, therefore, could only attain its end by the general cultivation of nobleness of character, even if each individual were only benefited by the nobleness of others, and his own, so far as happiness is concerned, were a sheer deduction from the benefit. But the bare enunciation of such an absurdity as this last renders refutation superfluous.

According to the greatest happiness principle, as above explained, the ultimate end, with reference to and for the sake of which all other things are desirable—whether we are considering our own good or that of other people—is an existence exempt as far as possible from pain, and as rich as possible in enjoyments, both in point of quantity and quality; the test of quality and the rule for measuring it against quantity being the preference felt by those who, in their opportunities of experience, to which must be added their habits of self-consciousness and self-observation, are best furnished with the means of comparison. This, being, according to the utilitarian opinion, the end of human action, is necessarily also the standard of morality, which may accordingly be defined "the rules and precepts for human conduct," by the observance of which an existence such as has been described might be, to the greatest extent possible, secured to all mankind; and not to them only, but, so far as the nature of things admits, to the whole sentient creation.

⚹

Here we see the major modification of Bentham's ethical theory. Whereas Bentham had defined his utility principle in terms of avoiding pain and securing pleasure, Mill argues that such self-interest is an inadequate criterion of moral goodness. What is missing in Bentham's moral calculus is a qualitative distinction between pleasures. Bentham had defined pains and pleasures using seven categories:

1. Intensity: How strong is the sensation (of pain or pleasure)?
2. Duration: How long does it last?
3. Certainty: How clear and distinct is it?
4. Proximity: How soon will it be experienced?
5. Fecundity: What other sensations of pleasure or pain will follow?

6. Purity: How free from pain is the pleasure, and vice versa?
7. Extent: How many persons will be affected by it, one way or another?

Thus, if a law would produce a very intense pleasure very briefly for just a few individuals while inducing great pain for a long time for a great number, it is a bad law. But whereas Bentham does not distinguish between various *types* of pleasure sensations and various *types* of pain sensations—stating that "quantity of pleasure being equal, pushpin is as good as poetry." Mill wants to differentiate sensations in terms not just of quantity but also quality, so he adds an eighth category to the list: Quality, which he defined in the passage in terms of the "higher faculties." Thus the famous quote, "better to be Socrates dissatisfied than a fool satisfied."

But who is to say who is wise and who the fool? It depends on whom you ask! This problem takes Bentham's "moral calculus" out of the scientific domain. Such qualitative judgments are subjective. Mill's solution ties his moral theory to his political theory; he says that such judgments must be decided *democratically*, through majority rule.

In the next selection, taken from his equally popular *On Liberty* (1859), he argues that the fundamental utilitarian principle—the greatest amount of happiness for the greatest number of people—would best be achieved by allowing all individuals unrestricted freedom of thought and action as long as it did not cause actual harm to others. The work was particularly influential in the further development of democracy in the United States.

⚹

On Liberty

The object of this Essay is to assert one very simple principle, as entitled to govern absolutely the dealings of society with the individual in the way of

---

From J. S. Mill, *On Liberty* (London: 1859).

compulsion and control, whether the means used be physical force in the form of legal penalties, or the moral coercion of public opinion. That principle is, that the sole end for which mankind are warranted, individually or collectively, in interfering with the liberty of action of any of their number, is self-protection. That the only purpose for which power can be rightfully exercised over any member of a civilized community, against his will, is to prevent harm to others. His own good, either physical or moral, is not a sufficient warrant. He cannot rightfully be compelled to do or forbear because it will be better for him to do so, because it will make him happier, because, in the opinions of others, to do so would be wise, or even right. These are good reasons for remonstrating with him, or reasoning with him, or persuading him, or entreating him, but not for compelling him, or visiting him with any evil in case he do otherwise. To justify that, the conduct from which it is desired to deter him must be calculated to produce evil to some one else. The only part of the conduct of anyone, for which he is amenable to society, is that which concerns others. In the part which merely concerns himself, his independence is, of right, absolute. Over himself, over his own body and mind, the individual is sovereign.

It is perhaps hardly necessary to say that this doctrine is meant to apply only to human beings in the maturity of their faculties. We are not speaking of children, or of young persons below the age which the law may fix as that of manhood or womanhood. Those who are still in a state to require being taken care of by others, must be protected against their own actions as well as against external injury. . . .

It still remains to speak of one of the principal causes which make diversity of opinion advantageous, and will continue to do so until mankind shall have entered a stage of intellectual advancement which at present seems at an incalculable distance. We have hitherto considered only two possibilities: that the received opinion may be false, and some other opinion consequently true; or that, the received opinion being true, a conflict with the opposite error is essential to a clear apprehension and deep feeling of its truth. But there is a commoner case than either of these: when the conflicting doctrines, instead of being one true and the other false, share the truth between them; and the nonconforming opinion is needed to supply the remainder of the truth, of which the received doctrine embodies only a part. Popular opinions, on subjects not palpable to sense, are often true, but seldom or never the whole truth. They are a part of the truth; sometimes a greater, sometimes a smaller part, but exaggerated, distorted, and disjointed from the truths by which they ought to be accompanied and limited. Heretical opinions, on the other hand, are generally some of these suppressed and neglected truths, bursting the bonds which kept them down, and neither seeking reconciliation with the truth contained in the common opinion, or fronting it as enemies, and setting themselves up, with similar exclusiveness, as the whole truth. The later case is hitherto the most frequent, as, in the human mind, one-sidedness has always been the rule, and many-sidedness the exception. Hence, even in revolutions of opinion, one part of the truth usually sets while another rises. . . .

Such being the reasons which make it imperative that human beings should be free to form opinions, and to express their opinions without reserve; and such the baneful consequences to the intellectual, and through that to the moral nature of man, unless this liberty is either conceded, or asserted in spite of prohibition; let us next examine whether the same reasons do not require that men should be free to act upon their opinions—to carry these out in their lives, without hindrance, either physical or moral, from their fellow-men, so long as it is at their own risk and peril. . . .

. . . Genius can only breathe freely in an *atmosphere* of freedom. Persons of genius are, *ex vi termini* [by the force of the term], more individual than any other people—less capable, consequently, of fitting themselves, without hurtful compression, into any of the small number of molds which society provides in order to save its members the trouble of forming their own character. If from timidity they consent to be forced into one of these molds, and to let all that part of themselves which cannot expand under the pressure remain unexpanded, society will be little the better for their genius. If they are of a strong character, and break their fetters, they become a mark for the society which has not succeeded in reducing them to commonplace, to point out with solemn warning as "wild," "erratic," and the like; much as if one should complain of the Niagara river for not flowing smoothly between its banks like a Dutch canal.

I insist thus emphatically on the importance of genius, and the necessity of allowing it to unfold itself freely both in thought and in practice, being well aware that no one will deny the position in theory, but knowing also that almost everyone, in reality, is totally indifferent to it. People think genius a fine thing if it enables a man to write an exciting poem, or paint a picture. But in its true sense, that of originality in thought and action, though no one says that it is not a thing to be admired, nearly all, at heart, think that they can do very well without it. Unhappily this is too natural to be wondered at. Originality is the one thing which unoriginal minds cannot feel the use of. . . . exceptional individuals, instead of being deterred, should be encouraged in acting differently from the mass. In other times there was no advantage in their doing so, unless they acted not only differently but better. In this age, the mere example of nonconformity, the mere refusal to bend the knee to custom, is itself a service. Precisely because the tyranny of opinion is such as to make eccentricity a reproach, it is desirable, in order to break through that tyranny, that people should be eccentric. Eccentricity has always abounded when and where strength of character has abounded; and the amount of eccentricity in a society has generally been proportional to the amount of genius, mental vigor, and moral courage it contained. That so few now dare to be eccentric marks the chief danger of the time.

⚓

Plato thought Democracy the worst form of government; having seen the wisest person in the land die by the vote of the unwise majority, he wanted rule by philosopher-kings. Twenty-two centuries later, Mill comes to the opposite conclusion. His reasoning, as articulated, is that, first, if we have learned anything from the past it is that no one has a monopoly on truth. Second, and even worse, it seems all we ever manage to capture, even with our best efforts, are partial truths. Third, essential to the well-being of a society is *growth* and *change*, lest we end up like the Byzantine and Roman empires—with singularity of purpose and leadership, death through stagnation. Fourth, and perhaps most important, if the wisest are the rulers of the land, then the rest of society will look up to them. This too leads to stagnation, for then the "truths" are simply passed down from generation to generation, and there is no attempt to generate the new. A society should therefore encourage individuality and even rebellion.

In the final analysis, what matters most in Mill's view is the originality generated by individuals through whom new ideas are born into the world. The more eccentric, the better. How tolerant is the majority toward the minorities? How tolerant are the wise toward those whom they regard as unwise? Originality is the key not only to a healthy, evolving society but also to a moral one in which the greatest happiness for the greatest number can actually be achieved.

Mill applied his theories to many causes. In *The Subjection of Women* (1861), he put forth the then-radical idea that women should be allowed to vote and have careers. He spoke out on discrimination against women, helped found the first women's suffrage society, and was one of the first advocates of birth control.

Mill never held an academic post. During most of his life he worked for the East India Company, where he started at age seventeen as a clerk and quickly rose to the highest post in his department. When he retired from the company in 1865, he was invited to run for Parliament and was elected; during his term in office he achieved sweeping reforms for the British working class, fought on behalf of exploited Jamaicans, and argued for fair redistribution of land in Ireland. His revealing and detailed *Autobiography* was published after his death.

19.5 Marx (1818–1883): The Birth of Communism

Karl Marx was born in the town of Trèves (Trier, Germany) in what was then Prussia. He studied history and philosophy at the universities of Berlin and Bonn and received his Ph.D. in philosophy at the University of Jena. His doctoral dissertation was on the Greek atomism espoused by Democritus and Epicurus. The influence of Hegel's philosophy was so widespread in Germany during this time that most philosophers divided themselves into two differing camps: the Hegelian right—consisting mainly of older, more conservative philosophers who gave an orthodox reading of Hegel's views of religion and morality—and the Hegelian left—consisting mainly of younger, more radical philosophers. Marx belonged to the latter group, whose members called themselves "the Young Hegelians." They took Hegel's views on social and political issues as literally false but full of hidden truths that implied the very opposite of what Hegel had originally thought. Indeed, Marx would go on to claim that his own system of materialistic dialectic was Hegel's upside-down idealistic dialectic turned right-side up.

Although Marx worked for a while as a newspaper editor for the Cologne *Rheinische Zeitung* and as a reporter in London for the *New York Tribune,* for most of this life he was unemployed and extremely poor. Several of his children died because of his extreme poverty. Supported by his friend and coauthor of the *Communist Manifesto,* Friedrich Engels, Marx nevertheless managed to produce an extremely influential body of work; he is generally recognized as the most important figure in the history of socialist thought.

Like many Hegelian critics at the time, Marx rejected Hegel's system on grounds that it posited transcended entities up to and including the Absolute world-mind. The greatest influence on Marx came from Ludwig Feuerbach, whose *Essence of Christianity* was a sort of bible for the Young Hegelian leftists. Feuerbach argued that since the time of Plato the human mind has been corrupted by its own ideal images of universal values, which are in reality unattainable. In craving its own idealizations, human consciousness thus becomes alienated from itself, transferring its desires onto an imaginary ideal being, God. In doing so, human consciousness prevents its own ascension to the ideal and will forever be prevented from doing so as long as it is imprisoned by religion. Feuerbach thus argued, as Marx would later, that religious imagery must be abolished from the human psyche so that true peace, happiness, and self-illumination could finally be attained. Marx, however, went further. In his *Theses on Feuerbach* (1886), he criticized Feuerbach on grounds that bringing about changes in the actual human family could not be attained by changing or manipulating ideas and images; unlike Feuerbach's "speculative" materialism, Marx's "practical materialism" called for a change in the actual material relationships and structures of the human family. Thus, just as he reversed Hegel, he took Descartes's apocryphal statement from *Meditations* about how the purpose of philosophy is not to change the world but to change yourself and wrote, "The philosophers have only *interpreted* the world in various ways, the point however is to *change* it." Thus the *Communist Manifesto,* from which the first selection is taken, became the rallying cry for world-revolution involving a class struggle between the "bourgeoisie"—the capitalist employers of wage labor who owned the means of production—and the "proletariat"—wage laborers who had no means of production and were thus forced to sell their labor in order to live.

☙

Communist Manifesto

The history of all hitherto existing society is the history of class struggles.

Free man and slave, patrician and plebeian, lord and serf, guild master and journeyman, in a word, oppressor and oppressed, stood in constant opposition to one another, carried on an uninterrupted, now hidden, now open fight, a fight that each time ended either in a revolutionary reconstitution of society at large or in the common ruin of the contending classes.

From Karl Marx and Friedrich Engels, *Communist Manifesto*, trans. Samuel Moore, 1888.

In the earlier epochs of history we find almost everywhere a complicated arrangement of society into various orders, a manifold gradation of social rank. In ancient Rome we have patricians, knights, plebeians, slaves; in the Middle Ages, feudal lords, vassals, guild masters, journeymen, apprentices, serfs; in almost all of these classes, again, subordinate gradations.

The modern bourgeois society that has sprouted from the ruins of feudal society has not done away with class antagonisms. It has but established new classes, new conditions of oppression, new forms of struggle in place of the old ones.

The distinguishing feature of communism is not the abolition of property generally, but the abolition of bourgeois property. But modern bourgeois private property is the final and most complete expression of the system of producing and appropriating products that is based on class antagonisms, on the exploitation of the many by the few.

In this sense the theory of the communists may be summed up in the single sentence: Abolition of private property.

We communists have been reproached with the desire of abolishing the right of personally acquiring property as the fruit of a man's own labor, which property is alleged to be the groundwork of all personal freedom, activity, and independence.

In bourgeois society, therefore, the past dominates the present; in communist society the present dominates the past. In bourgeois society capital is independent and has individuality, while the living person is dependent and has no individuality.

And the abolition of this state of things is called by the bourgeois abolition of individuality and freedom! And rightly so. The abolition of bourgeois individuality, bourgeois independence, and bourgeois freedom is undoubtedly aimed at.

By freedom is meant, under the present bourgeois conditions of production, free trade, free selling and buying.

But if selling and buying disappear, free selling and buying disappear also. This talk about free selling and buying, and all the other "brave words" of our bourgeoisie about freedom in general, have a meaning, if any, only in contrast with restricted selling and buying, with the fettered traders of the Middle Ages, but have no meaning when opposed to the communistic abolition of buying and selling, of the bourgeois conditions of production, and of the bourgeoisie itself.

You are horrified at our intending to do away with private property. But in your existing society private property is already done away with for nine tenths of the population; its existence for the few is solely due to its non-existence in the hands of those nine tenths. You reproach us, therefore, with intending to do away with a form of property the necessary condition for whose existence is the non-existence of any property for the immense majority of society.

In one word, you reproach us with intending to do away with your property. Precisely so; that is just what we intend.

From the moment when labor can no longer be converted into capital, money, or rent, into a social power capable of being monopolized, i.e., from the moment when individual property can no longer be transformed into bourgeois property, into capital, from that moment, you say, individuality vanishes.

You must, therefore, confess that by "individual" you mean no other person than the bourgeois, than the middle-class owner of property. This person must, indeed, be swept out of the way and made impossible.

Communism deprives no man of the power to appropriate the products of society; all that it does is to deprive him of the power to subjugate the labor of others by means of such appropriation.

It has been objected that upon the abolition of private property all work will cease and universal laziness will overtake us.

According to this, bourgeois society ought long ago have gone to the dogs through sheer idleness, for those of its members who work acquire nothing and those who acquire anything do not work. The whole of this objection is but another expression of the tautology that there can no longer be any wage labor when there is no longer any capital.

All objections urged against the communistic mode of producing and appropriating material products have, in the same way, been urged against the communistic modes of producing and appropriating intellectual products. Just as, to the bourgeois, the disappearance of class property is the disappearance of production itself, so the disappearance of class culture is to him identical with the disappearance of all culture.

That culture, the loss of which he laments, is, for the enormous majority, a mere training to act as a machine.

But don't wrangle with us so long as you apply, to our intended abolition of bourgeois property, the standard of your bourgeois notions of freedom, culture, law, etc. Your very ideas are but the outgrowth of the conditions of your bourgeois production and bourgeois property, just as your jurisprudence is but the will of your class made into a law for all, a will whose essential character and direction are determined by the economic conditions of existence of your class.

The selfish misconception that induces you to transform into eternal laws of nature and of reason the social forms springing from your present mode of production and form of property—historical relations that rise and disappear in the progress of production—this misconception you share with every ruling class that has preceded you. What you see clearly in the case of ancient property, what you admit in the case of feudal property you are of course forbidden to admit in the case of your own bourgeois form of property.

Abolition of the family! Even the most radical flare up at this infamous proposal of the communists.

On what foundation is the present family, the bourgeois family, based? On capital, on private gain. In its completely developed form this family exists only among the bourgeoisie. But this state of things finds its complement in the practical absence of the family among the proletarians, and in public prostitution.

The bourgeois family will vanish as a matter of course when its complement vanishes, and both will vanish with the vanishing of capital.

Do you charge us with wanting to stop the exploitation of children by their parents? To this crime we plead guilty.

But, you will say, we destroy the most hallowed of relations when we replace home education by social.

And your education! Is not that also social, and determined by the social conditions under which you educate, by the intervention, direct or indirect, of society, by means of schools, etc.? The communists have not invented the intervention of society in education; they do but seek to alter the character of that intervention, and to rescue education from the influence of the ruling class.

The bourgeois claptrap about the family and education, about the hallowed co-relation of parent and child, becomes all the more disgusting,

the more, by the action of modern industry, all family ties among the proletarians are torn asunder and their children transformed into simple articles of commerce and instruments of labor.

"But you communists would introduce community of women," screams the whole bourgeoisie in chorus.

The bourgeois sees in his wife a mere instrument of production. He hears that the instruments of production are to be exploited in common and, naturally, can come to no other conclusion than that the lot of being common to all will likewise fall to the women.

He has not even a suspicion that the real point aimed at is to do away with the status of women as mere instruments of production.

For the rest, nothing is more ridiculous than the virtuous indignation of our bourgeois at the community of women which, they pretend, is to be openly and officially established by the communists. The communists have no need to introduce community of women; it has existed almost from time immemorial.

Our bourgeois, not content with having the wives and daughters of their proletarians at their disposal, not to speak of common prostitutes, take the greatest pleasure in seducing each other's wives.

Bourgeois marriage is in reality a system of wives in common and thus, at the most, what the communists might possibly be reproached with is that they desire to introduce, in substitution for a hypocritically concealed, an openly legalized community of women. For the rest, it is self-evident that the abolition of the present system of production must bring with it the abolition of the community of women springing from that system, i.e., of prostitution, both public and private. . . .

The charges against communism made from a religious, a philosophical, and, generally, from an ideological standpoint are not deserving of serious examination.

⁂

Marx's criticism of capitalism and existing social, political, economic, and religious structures owes much to Hegelian dialectic, especially the way various capitalist theses lead to their opposites: competition leads to monopoly and the lack of competition, unemployment is solved by creating more money, which leads to inflation which in turn is fixed in capitalism by increasing unemployment, and so on. The end result of the communist revolution would be to bring about the collapse of capitalism, replacing it with a temporary "dictatorship of the proletariat" in which the workers would begin the process of abolishing the class-structured society in order to create a true communist democracy in place of a false capitalist democracy. In the end the new revolutionary leaders would have to resign so that history—as defined by Marx in terms of class struggle—would come to an end.

According to Marx the communist revolution would best be achieved by eliminating private property, empowering the working class, and banishing what he called "alienated labor." Our freedom lies in our ability to do and make things, to create, so as to be fashioned by our products. In other words, the Cartesian self begins not as a given individual but is in part a social construction through engagement with the world. When we do not control the process and means of production for the things we produce, we are alienated from them and never become true individuals; we are under the domination of those who control the means of production, subtly but permanently imprisoned in ways described in the next selection, *Alienation:*

⚹

Political economy proceeds from the fact of private property, but it does not explain it to us. It expresses in general, abstract formulae the *material* process through which private property spends himself, the more powerful the alien objective world becomes which he creates over-against himself, the poorer he himself—his inner world—becomes, the less belongs to him as his own. It is the same in religion. The more man puts into God, the less he retains in himself. The worker puts his

life into the object; but now his life no longer belongs to him but to the object. Hence, the greater this activity, the greater is the worker's lack of objects. Whatever the product of his labor is, he is not. Therefore the greater this product, the less is he himself. The *alienation* of the worker in his product means not only that his labor becomes an object, an *external* existence, but that it exists *outside him,* independently, as something alien to him, and that it becomes a power on its own confronting him; it means that the life which he has conferred on the object confronts him as something hostile and alien.

Let us now look more closely at the *objectification,* at the production of the worker, and therein at the *estrangement,* the *loss* of the object, his product.

The worker can create nothing without *nature,* without the *sensuous external world.* It is the material on which his labor is manifested, in which it is active, from which and by means of which it produces.

But just as nature provides labor with the *means of life* in the sense that labor cannot *live* without objects on which to operate, on the other hand, it also provides the *means of life* in the more restricted sense—i.e., the means for the physical subsistence of *the worker* himself.

Thus the more the worker by his labor *appropriates* the external world, sensuous nature, the more he deprives himself *of means of life* in the double respect: first, that the sensuous external world more and more ceases to be an object belonging to his labor to be his labor's *means of life;* and secondly, that it more and more ceases to be *means of life* in the immediate sense, means for the physical subsistence of the worker.

Thus in this double respect the worker becomes a slave of his object, first, in that he receives an *object of labor,* i.e., in that he receives *work;* and secondly, in that he receives *means of subsistence.* Therefore, it enables him to exist, first, as a *worker;* and, second, as a *physical subject.* The extremity of this bondage is that it is only as a *worker* that he continues to maintain himself as a *physical subject,* and that it is only as a *physical subject* that he is a *worker.*

(The laws of political economy express the estrangement of the worker in his object thus: the more the worker produces, the less he has to

From Karl Marx, *Economic and Philosophic Manuscripts of 1844,* Martin Milligan, trans., 1888.

consume; the more values he creates, the more valueless, the more unworthy he becomes; the better formed his product, the more deformed becomes the worker; the more civilized his object, the more barbarous becomes the worker; the mightier labor becomes, the more powerless becomes the worker; the more ingenious labor becomes, the duller becomes the worker and the more he becomes nature's bondsman.)

Political economy conceals the estrangement inherent in the nature of labor by not considering the direct relationship between the worker (labor) *and production.* It is true that labor produces for the rich wonderful things—but for the worker it produces privation. It produces palaces—but for the worker, hovels. It produces beauty—but for the worker, deformity. It replaces labor by machines—but some of the workers it throws back to a barbarous type of labor, and the other workers it turns into machines. It produces intelligence—but for the worker idiocy, cretinism. . . .

What, then, constitutes the alienation of labor?

First, the fact that labor is *external* to the worker, i.e., it does not belong to his essential being, that in his work, therefore, he does not affirm himself but denies himself, does not feel content but unhappy, does not develop freely his physical and mental energy but mortifies his body and ruins his mind. The worker therefore only feels himself outside his work, and in his work feels outside himself. He is at home when he is not working, and when he is working he is not at home. His labor is therefore not voluntary, but coerced; it is *forced labor*. It is therefore not the satisfaction of a need; it is merely a *means* to satisfy needs external to it. Its alien character emerges clearly in the fact that as soon as no physical or other compulsion exists, labor is shunned like the plague. External labor, labor in which man alienates himself, is a labor of self-sacrifice, of mortification. Lastly, the external character of labor for the worker appears in the fact that it is not his own, but someone else's, that it does not belong to him, that in it he belongs, not to himself, but to another. Just as in religion the spontaneous activity of the human imagination, of the human brain and the human heart, operates independently of the individual—that is, operates on him as an alien, divine or diabolical activity—in the same way the worker's activity is not his spon-

taneous activity. It belongs to another; it is the loss of his self.

⚓

The worst culprit of such alienation is capitalism. Again, the key to understanding Marx's thought is that human consciousness is less the cause of such social processes than it is an effect; in his *Contribution to the Critique of Political Economy*, he wrote:

⚓

In the social production of their life, men enter into definite relations that are indispensable and independent of their will, relations of production which correspond to a definite stage of development of their material productive forces. The sum total of these relations of production constitutes the economic structure of society, the real foundation, on which rises a legal and political superstructure and to which correspond definite forms of social consciousness. The mode of production of material life conditions the social, political, and intellectual life process in general. It is not the consciousness of men that determines their social being, but, on the contrary, their social being that determines their consciousness.

⚓

Once the ruthless competition and other capitalistic evils were removed from society, human consciousness would in Marx's view evolve to a more enlightened state. The true individual would emerge from the cocoon of society, and the world would become a utopia.

What prevents this? The chief problem is that in the condition of alienated labor, the natural needs of human beings become utterly perverted. In the following passage from "The Power of Money," he explains why:

⚓

. . . what I *am* and *am capable* of is by no means determined by my individuality. I am ugly, but I can buy for myself the most *beautiful* of women. Therefore I am not *ugly,* for the effect of *ugliness*—its deterrent power—is nullified by money. I, in my character as an individual, am *lame,* but money furnishes me with twenty-four feet. Therefore I am not lame. I am bad, dishonest, unscrupulous, stupid; but money is honored, and therefore so is its possessor. Money is the supreme good, therefore its possessor is good. Money, besides, saves me the trouble of being dishonest: I am therefore presumed honest. I am *stupid,* but money is the *real mind* of all things and how then should its possessor be stupid? Besides, he can buy talented people for himself, and is he who has power over the talented not more talented than the talented? Do not I, who thanks to money am capable of *all* that the human heart longs for, possess all human capacities? Does not my money therefore transform all my incapacities into their contrary?

If *money* is the bond binding me to *human* life, binding society to me, binding me and nature and man, is not money the bond of all *bonds?* Can it not dissolve and bind all ties? Is it not, therefore, the universal *agent of divorce?* It is the true *agent of divorce* as well as the true *binding agent—the* [universal]* *galvano-chemical* power of Society.

Shakespeare stresses especially two properties of money:

(1) It is the visible divinity—the transformation of all human and natural properties into their contraries, the universal confounding and overturning of things: it makes brothers of impossibilities. (2) It is the common whore, the common pimp of people and nations.

The overturning and confounding of all human and natural qualities, the fraternization of impossibilities—the *divine* power of money—lies in its *character* as men's estranged, alienating and self-disposing *species-nature.* Money is the alienated *ability of mankind.*

That which I am unable to do as a *man,* and of which therefore all my individual essential powers are incapable, I am able to do by means of *money.* Money thus turns each of these powers into something which in itself it is not—turns it, that is, into its *contrary.*

If I long for a particular dish or want to take the mail-coach because I am not strong enough to go by foot, money fetches me the dish and the mail-coach: that is, it converts my wishes from something in the realm of imagination, translates them from their meditated, imagined or willed existence into their *sensuous, actual* existence—from imagination to life, from imagined being into real being. In effecting this mediation, money is the *truly creative* power.

No doubt *demand* also exists for him who has no money, but his demand is a mere thing of the imagination without effect or existence for me, for a third party, for the others, and which therefore remains for me *unreal* and *objectless.* The difference between effective demand based on money and ineffective demand based on my need, my passion, my wish, etc., is the difference between *being* and *thinking,* between the imagined which *exists* merely within me and the imagined as it is for me outside me as a *real object.*

If I have no money for travel, I have no *need*—that is, no real and self-realizing need—to travel. If I have the *vocation* for study but no money for it, I have *no* vocation for study—that is, no *effective,* no *true* vocation. On the other hand, if I have really *no* vocation for study but have the will *and* the money for it, I have an *effective* vocation for it. Being the external, common *medium* and *faculty* for turning an *image* into *reality* and *reality* into a mere *image* (a faculty not springing from man as man or from human society as society), *money* transforms the *real essential powers of man and nature* into what are merely abstract conceits and therefore *imperfections—into* tormenting chimeras—just as it transforms *real imperfections and chimeras*—essential powers which are really impotent, which exist only in the imagination of the individual—into *real powers* and *faculties.*

In the light of this characteristic alone, money is thus the general overturning of *individualities* which turns them into their contrary and adds contradictory attributes to their attributes.

Money, then, appears as this *overturning* power both against the individual and against the bonds of society, etc., which claim to be *essences* in themselves. It transforms fidelity into infidelity, love into hate, hate into love, virtue into vice, vice into virtue, servant into master, master into servant, idiocy into intelligence and intelligence into idiocy.

Since money, as the existing and active concept of value, confounds and exchanges all things, it is the general *confounding* and *compounding* of all

---

*An end of the page is torn out of the manuscript.

things—the world upside-down—the confounding and compounding of all natural and human qualities.

He who can buy bravery is brave, though a coward. As money is not exchanged for any one specific quality, for any one specific thing, or for any particular human essential power, but for the entire objective world of man and nature, from the standpoint of its possessor it therefore serves to exchange every property for every other, even contradictory, property and object: it is the fraternization of impossibilities. It makes contradictions embrace.

Assume *man* to be *man* and his relationship to the world to be a human one: then you can exchange love only for love, trust for trust, etc. If you want to enjoy art, you must be an artistically-cultivated person; if you want to exercise influence over other people, you must be a person with a stimulating and encouraging effect on other people. Every one of your relations to man and to nature must be a *specific expression,* corresponding to the object of your will, of your *real individual* life. If you love without evoking love in return—that is, if your loving as loving does not produce reciprocal love; if through *a living expression* of yourself as a loving person you do not make yourself a *loved person,* then your love is impotent—a misfortune.

⚵

NOTE

1. On one interpretation of Leibniz each individual monad is part creator of its own individual world, such that each of us exists in our own world of which there are an infinite number. In any case, such a view is very different from the social reality view here being developed.

Part VII ❧ The 20th Century

20 ⚶ The American Experience: Peirce, James, Dewey, and Royce

20.0 Peirce (1839–1914): The American Pragmatist

Charles Sanders Peirce was born in Cambridge, Massachusetts. Educated from a young age mainly by his father, a Harvard mathematician, Peirce graduated from Harvard University at the bottom of his class. He taught logic at the Johns Hopkins University from 1879 to 1884 and gave a few philosophical lectures at Harvard and the Lowell Institute in Boston, but he was unable to secure a permanent teaching position. Subsequently, the only job he could get was with the U.S. Coast and Geodetic Survey. He continued, however, to produce an impressive body of original philosophy and fundamentally influenced the thought of the other leading American philosophers of the time, including William James, John Dewey, and Josiah Royce.

Peirce had begun to develop his ideas at the "metaphysical club" in Cambridge, an informal discussion group that included William James and Oliver Wendell Holmes. His metaphysics grew out of his close study of Kant, Hegel, and the recent evolutionary theory of Charles

Darwin (1809–1882). According to Peirce the entire universe is one mind moving toward a *rational* end but its driving force is *love*. We saw Kierkegaard and Nietzsche develop Hegel's absolute idealism toward an understanding of the world entire, not as a thing but as itself consisting in words and symbols, a sort of symbolic text or program, and Peirce carried this process to its logical conclusion and became the founder of the view that the whole of reality is to be viewed as consisting in *signs*. As he put it:

> I am, as far as I know, a pioneer, or rather a backwoodsman, in the work of clearing and opening up what I call *semiotic,* that is the doctrine of the essential nature and fundamental varieties of possible *semiosis.**

Peirce coined the term *semiosis* to refer to any "sign action" or "sign process," by which he meant that signs have a force or will of their own. And what is a "sign"? The term goes all the way back to the medievals, particularly to Duns

---

* *Collected Papers of Charles Peirce*, C. Hartshore and P. Weiss, eds. (Cambridge, MA: Harvard University Press, 1931–1958).

Scotus, who defined it as *aliquid stat pro aliquo,* meaning, literally, *something that stands for something else.* Symbols—letters, numerals, pictures—icons, myths, texts, and so on, are all signs or sets of signs. The prevalent view at the time was developed by one of the greatest linguists of all times, the Swiss Ferdinand De Saussure (1857–1913). He saw a sign as an accidental and arbitrary correlation between a *signifier* and a *signified.* In the passage we shall read from Peirce, he will use the example of an acoustic image (a "sound wave") as the *signifier* and the corresponding concept thereby encoded (a Humean impression, such as for instance a "thump" of a particular magnitude, frequency, and intensity). This is an explicitly *dyadic* model of signs, meaning simply that it is a paired relation between two terms, the signifier and the signified. But Peirce, largely due to his understanding of the systems of Kant and the subsequent Hegelian-inspired idealists, insisted—no doubt enlightened by Nietzsche's understanding of language—that as the ultimate elements of his cosmos, signs were to be conceived in *triadic* terms. Thus, there is the sign—the symbol—that stands for something, called its *object,* which generates *another* sign, called its *interpretant.* In other words, the signs generate further signs, and so on, in a cosmic process that is the textual evolution of existence. In this way, Peirce lay the philosophical foundations for the discipline known today as *semiotics.* "The entire universe," wrote Peirce, "is perfused with signs."

Prior to Kant, Hegel, and Nietzsche, it was commonly believed that signs were but the inert and ineffectual instruments we used to make meaning out of the world. In Peirce's elaborate system, inspired by Kant, Hegel, absolute idealism, and Nietzsche, it is the other way around; the world is made, *as are we ,* by signs, which are themselves logical functions and thus, like numbers, do not need to be created in order to exist. Fichte's *act* (see Section 17.0) is crucial for an understanding of Peirce's meaning, as well as Hume's analysis of the mind. One way to try to combine such differing analyses of our mental states (the Kantian-Rationalist-Idealist versus the Humean-Empirical-Skeptical perspective) is to interpret Peirce's theory of the mind as analogous to Hume's bundle theory, except that the *individual* perceptions are *themselves* active in exactly the way that Kant thought the faculties were. In other words, Peirce's highly original and groundbreaking interpretation, for which he is rarely given sufficient credit, is that of viewing the elements of the mind as having the active functional structure that Kantian-type theories require transcendental deductions to achieve. Such a move, of course, owes a lot, as well, to Leibniz's concept of the monad.

Semiotics today is still a flourishing and highly evolving philosophical discipline[1] that reaches into many other areas—including linguistics, computer science, logic, and phenomenology—almost as if the various rifts among some of these disciplines had never happened. Remarkably, however, this was not Peirce's only contribution, for he also initiated the movement in American philosophy known as *pragmatism.* Peirce's pragmatism, also developed from his close study of Kant and Hegel, paved the way for a completely new understanding of the concept of truth, based on one's own personal experience and the *practical* significance of statements. According to this conception of truth philosophy must turn to the "clarification of thought" according to the central "principle of clarification," which Peirce called "the pragmatic principle":

> Consider what effects, that conceivably might have practical bearings, we conceive the object of our conception to have. Then our conception of these effects is the whole of our conception of the object.[*]

According to Peirce, beliefs are but habits that predispose us to a readiness to respond in certain ways to certain situations—either by producing physical movement or psychological expectation. Beliefs are either stable or unstable. In "The Fixation of Belief," one of his most famous arti-

---

[*] *Collected Papers.*

cles, he identifies four basic ways that habits, customs, traditions, and "folkways," ranging from personal convictions to metaphysically fashionable philosophical systems, come to be "fixed" in our minds:

⬧

That which determines us, from given premises, to draw one inference rather than another, is some habit of mind, whether it be constitutional or acquired. The habit is good or otherwise, according as it produces true conclusions from true premises or not; and an inference is regarded as valid or not, without reference to the truth or falsity of its conclusion specially, but according as the habit which determines it is such as to produce true conclusions in general or not. The particular habit of mind which governs this or that inference may be formulated in a proposition whose truth depends on the validity of the inferences which the habit determines; and such a formula is called a *guiding principle* of inference. . . .

We generally know when we wish to ask a question and when we wish to pronounce a judgment, for there is a dissimilarity between the sensation of doubting and that of believing.

But this is not all which distinguishes doubt from belief. There is a practical difference. Our beliefs guide our desires and shape our actions. The Assassins, or followers of the Old Man of the Mountain, used to rush into death at his least command, because they believed that obedience to him would insure everlasting felicity. Had they doubted this, they would not have acted as they did. So it is with every belief, according to its degree. The feeling of believing is a more or less sure indication of there being established in our nature some habit which will determine our actions. Doubt never has such an effect.

Nor must we overlook a third point of difference. Doubt is an uneasy and dissatisfied state from which we struggle to free ourselves and pass into the state of belief; while the latter is a calm and satisfactory state which we do not wish to avoid, or to change to a belief in anything else. On the contrary, we cling tenaciously, not merely

From Charles Sanders Peirce, "The Fixation of Belief," *Popular Science Monthly,* 1877.

to believing, but to believing just what we do believe.

Thus, both doubt and belief have positive effects upon us, though very different ones. Belief does not make us act at once, but puts us into such a condition that we shall behave in a certain way, when the occasion arises. Doubt has not the least effect of this sort, but stimulates us to action until it is destroyed. This reminds us of the irritation of a nerve and the reflex action produced thereby; while for the analogue of belief, in the nervous system, we must look to what are called nervous associations—for example, to that habit of the nerves in consequence of which the smell of a peach will make the mouth water.

The irritation of doubt causes a struggle to attain a state of belief. I shall term this struggle *inquiry,* though it must be admitted that this is sometimes not a very apt designation.

The irritation of doubt is the only immediate motive for the struggle to attain belief. It is certainly best for us that our beliefs should be such as may truly guide our actions so as to satisfy our desires; and this reflection will make us reject any belief which does not seem to have been so formed as to insure this result. But it will only do so by creating doubt in the place of that belief. With the doubt, therefore, the struggle begins, and with the cessation of doubt it ends. Hence, the sole object of inquiry is the settlement of opinion. We may fancy that this is not enough for us, and that we seek, not merely an opinion, but a true opinion. But put this fancy to the test, and it proves groundless; for as soon as a firm belief is reached we are entirely satisfied, whether the belief be false or true. And it is clear that nothing out of the sphere of our knowledge can be our object, for nothing which does not affect the mind can be a motive for mental effort. The most that can be maintained is that we seek for a belief that we shall *think* to be true. But we think each one of our beliefs to be true, and, indeed, it is mere tautology to say so.

That the settlement of opinion is the sole end of inquiry is a very important proposition. It sweeps away, at once, various vague and erroneous conceptions of proof. A few of these may be noticed here.

1. Some philosophers have imagined that to start an inquiry it was only necessary to utter a question or set it down on paper, and have even

recommended us to begin our studies with questioning everything! But the mere putting of a proposition into the interrogative form does not stimulate the mind to any struggle after belief. There must be a real and living doubt, and without this all discussion is idle.

2. It is a very common idea that a demonstration must rest on some ultimate and absolutely indubitable propositions. These, according to one school, are first principles of a general nature; according to another, are first sensations. But, in point of fact, an inquiry, to have that completely satisfactory result called demonstration, has only to start with propositions perfectly free from all actual doubt. If the premises are not in fact doubted at all, they cannot be more satisfactory than they are.

3. Some people seem to love to argue a point after all the world is fully convinced of it. But no further advance can be made. When doubt ceases, mental action on the subject comes to an end; and, if it did go on, it would be without a purpose.

If the settlement of opinion is the sole object of inquiry, and if belief is of the nature of a habit, why should we not attain the desired end by taking any answer to a question, which we may fancy, and constantly reiterating it to ourselves, dwelling on all which may conduce to that belief, and learning to turn with contempt and hatred from anything which might disturb it? This simple and direct method is really pursued by many men. I remember once being entreated not to read a certain newspaper lest it might change my opinion upon free trade. "Lest I might be entrapped by its fallacies and misstatements," was the form of expression. "You are not," my friend said, "a special student of political economy. You might, therefore, easily be deceived by fallacious arguments upon the subject. You might, then, if you read this paper, be led to believe in protection. But you admit that free trade is the true doctrine; and you do not wish to believe what is not true." I have often known this system to be deliberately adopted. Still oftener, the instinctive dislike of an undecided state of mind, exaggerated into a vague dread of doubt, makes men cling spasmodically to the views they already take. The man feels that, if he only holds to his belief without wavering, it will be entirely satisfactory. Nor can it be denied that a steady and immovable faith yields great peace of mind. It may, indeed, give rise to inconveniences,

as if a man should resolutely continue to believe that fire would not burn him, or that he would be eternally damned if he received his *ingesta* otherwise than through a stomach-pump. But then the man who adopts this method will not allow that its inconveniences are greater than its advantages. He will say, "I hold steadfastly to the truth and the truth is always wholesome." And in many cases it may very well be that the pleasure he derives from his calm faith overbalances any inconveniences resulting from its deceptive character. Thus, if it be true that death is annihilation, then the man who believes that he will certainly go straight to heaven when he dies, provided he has fulfilled certain simple observances in this life, has a cheap pleasure which will not be followed by the least disappointment. A similar consideration seems to have weight with many persons in religious topics, for we frequently hear it said, "Oh, I could not believe so-and-so, because I should be wretched if I did." When an ostrich buries its head in the sand as danger approaches, it very likely takes the happiest course. It hides the danger, and then calmly says there is no danger; and, if it feels perfectly sure there is none, why should it raise its head to see? A man may go through life systematically keeping out of view all that might cause a change in his opinions, and if he only succeeds—basing his method, as he does, on two fundamental psychological laws—I do not see what can be said against his doing so. It would be an egotistical impertinence to object that his procedure is irrational, for that only amounts to saying that his method of settling belief is not ours. He does not propose to himself to be rational, and, indeed, will often talk with scorn of man's weak and illusive reason. So let him think as he pleases.

But this method of fixing belief, which may be called the method of tenacity, will be unable to hold its ground in practice. The social impulse is against it. The man who adopts it will find that other men think differently from him, and it will be apt to occur to him in some saner moment that their opinions are quite as good as his own, and this will shake his confidence in his belief. This conception, that another man's thought or sentiment may be equivalent to one's own, is a distinctly new step, and a highly important one. It arises from an impulse too strong in man to be suppressed without danger of destroying the human species. Unless we make ourselves hermits, we shall necessarily influence each other's opinions, so that the problem becomes how to fix belief, not in the individual merely, but in the community.

Let the will of the state act, then, instead of that of the individual. Let an institution be created which shall have for its object to keep correct doctrines before the attention of the people, to reiterate them perpetually, and to teach them to the young; having at the same time power to prevent contrary doctrines from being taught, advocated, or expressed. Let all possible causes of a change of mind be removed from men's apprehensions. Let them be kept ignorant, lest they should learn of some reason to think otherwise than they do. Let their passions be enlisted, so that they may regard private and unusual opinions with hatred and horror. Then, let all men who reject the established belief be terrified into silence. Let the people turn out and tar-and-feather such men, or let inquisitions be made into the manner of thinking of suspected persons, and, when they are found guilty of forbidden beliefs, let them be subjected to some signal punishment. When complete agreement could not otherwise be reached, a general massacre of all who have not thought in a certain way has proved a very effective means of settling opinion in a country. If the power to do this be wanting, let a list of opinions be drawn up, to which no man of the least independence of thought can assent, and let the faithful be required to accept all these propositions, in order to segregate them as radically as possible from the influence of the rest of the world.

This method has, from the earliest times, been one of the chief means of upholding correct theological and political doctrines, and of preserving their universal or catholic character. In Rome, especially, it has been practiced from the days of Numa Pompilius to those of Pius Nonus. This is the most perfect example in history; but wherever there is a priesthood—and no religion has been without one—this method has been more or less made use of. Wherever there is an aristocracy, or a guild, or any association of a class of men whose interests depend, or are supposed to depend, on certain propositions, there will be inevitably found some traces of this natural product of social feeling. Cruelties always accompany this system; and when it is consistently carried out, they become atrocities of the most horrible kind in the eyes of any rational man. Nor should this occasion surprise, for the officer of a society does not feel justified in surrendering the interests of that society for the sake of mercy, as he might his own private interests. It is natural, therefore, that sympathy and fellowship should thus produce a most ruthless power.

In judging this method of fixing belief, which may be called the method of authority, we must, in the first place, allow its immeasurable mental and moral superiority to the method of tenacity. Its success is proportionately greater; and, in fact, it has over and over again worked the most majestic results. The mere structures of stone which it has caused to be put together—in Siam, for example, in Egypt, and in Europe—have many of them a sublimity hardly more than rivalled by the greatest works of Nature. And, except the geological epochs, there are no periods of time so vast as those which are measured by some of these organized faiths. If we scrutinize the matter closely, we shall find that there has not been one of their creeds which has remained always the same; yet the change is so slow as to be imperceptible during one person's life, so that individual belief remains sensibly fixed. For the mass of mankind, then, there is perhaps no better method than this. If it is their highest impulse to be intellectual slaves, then slaves they ought to remain.

But no institution can undertake to regulate opinions upon every subject. Only the most important ones can be attended to, and on the rest men's minds must be left to the action of natural causes. This imperfection will be no source of weakness so long as men are in such a state of culture that one opinion does not influence another—that is, so long as they cannot put two and two together. But in the most priest-ridden states some individuals will be found who are raised above that condition. These men possess a wider sort of social feeling; they see that men in other countries and in other ages have held to very different doctrines from those which they themselves have been brought up to believe; and they cannot help seeing that it is the mere accident of their having been taught as they have, and of their having been surrounded with the manners and associations they have, that has caused them to believe as they do and not far differently. Nor can their candor resist the reflection that there is no reason to rate their own views at a higher value than those of other nations and other centuries; thus giving rise to doubts in their minds.

They will further perceive that such doubts as these must exist in their minds with reference to every belief which seems to be determined by the caprice either of themselves or of those who originated the popular opinions. The willful adherence to a belief, and the arbitrary forcing of it upon others, must, therefore, both be given up. A different new method of settling opinions must be adopted, that shall not only produce an impulse to believe, but shall also decide what proposition it is which is to be believed. Let the action of natural preferences be unimpeded, then, and under their influence let men, conversing together and regarding matters in different lights, gradually develop beliefs in harmony with natural causes. This method resembles that by which conceptions of art have been brought to maturity. The most perfect example of it is to be found in the history of metaphysical philosophy. Systems of this sort have not usually rested upon any observed facts, at least not in any great degree. They have been chiefly adopted because their fundamental propositions seemed "agreeable to reason." This is an apt expression; it does not mean that which agrees with experience, but that which we find ourselves inclined to believe. Plato, for example, finds it agreeable to reason that the distances of the celestial spheres from one another should be proportional to the different lengths of strings which produce harmonious chords. Many philosophers have been led to their main conclusions by considerations like this; but this is the lowest and least developed from which the method takes, for it is clear that another man might find Kepler's theory, that the celestial spheres are proportional to the inscribed and circumscribed spheres of the different regular solids, more agreeable to *his* reason. But the shock of opinions will soon lead men to rest on preferences of a far more universal nature. Take, for example, the doctrine that man only acts selfishly—that is, from the consideration that acting in one way will afford him more pleasure than acting in another. This rests on no fact in the world, but it has had a wide acceptance as being the only reasonable theory.

This method is far more intellectual and respectable from the point of view of reason than either of the others which we have noticed. But its failure has been the most manifest. It makes of inquiry something similar to the development of taste; but taste, unfortunately, is always more or less a matter of fashion, and accordingly metaphysicians have never come to any fixed agreement, but the pendulum has swung backward and forward between a more material and a more spiritual philosophy, from the earliest times to the latest. And so from this, which has been called the *a priori* method, we are driven, in Lord Bacon's phrase, to a true induction. We have examined this *a priori* method as something which promised to deliver our opinions from their accidental and capricious element. But development, while it is a process which eliminates the effect of some casual circumstances, only magnifies that of others. This method, therefore, does not differ in a very essential way from that of authority. The government may not have lifted its finger to influence my convictions; I may have been left outwardly quite free to choose, we will say, between monogamy and polygamy, and, appealing to my conscience only, I may have concluded that the latter practice is in itself licentious. But when I come to see that the chief obstacle to the spread of Christianity among a people of as high culture as the Hindus has been a conviction of the immorality of our way of treating women, I cannot help seeing that, though governments do not interfere, sentiments in their development will be very greatly determined by accidental causes. Now, there are some people, among whom I must suppose that my reader is to be found, who, when they see that any belief of theirs is determined by any circumstance extraneous to the facts, will from that moment not merely admit in words that that belief is doubtful, but will experience a real doubt of it, so that it ceases in some degree to be a belief.

To satisfy our doubts, therefore, it is necessary that a method should be found by which our beliefs may be caused by nothing human, but by some external permanency—by something upon which our thinking has no effect. Some mystics imagine that they have such a method in a private inspiration from on high. But that is only a form of the method of tenacity, in which the conception of truth as something public is not yet developed. Our external permanency would not be external, in our sense, if it was restricted in its influence to one individual. It must be something which affects, or might affect, every man. And, though these affections are necessarily as various as are individual conditions, yet the method must be such that the ultimate conclusion of every man shall be the same. Such is the method of science. Its fundamental hypothesis, restated in more familiar language, is this: There are Real things, whose characters are entirely independent of our opinions about them; those realities affect our senses according to regular laws, and, though our sensations are as different as are our relations to the objects, yet, by taking advantage of the laws of perception, we can ascertain by reasoning how things really are; and any man, if we have sufficient experience and he reason enough about it, will be led to the one True conclusion. The new conception here involved is that of Reality. It may be asked how I know that there are any realities. If this hypothesis is the sole support of my method of inquiry, my method of inquiry must not be used to support my hypothesis. The reply is this: 1. If investigation cannot be regarded as proving that there are Real things, it at least does not lead to a contrary conclusion; but the method and the conception on which it is based remain ever in harmony. No doubts of the method, therefore, necessarily arise from its practice, as is the case with all the others. 2. The feeling which gives rise to any method of fixing belief is a dissatisfaction at two repugnant propositions. But here already is a vague concession that there is some *one* thing to which a proposition should conform. Nobody, therefore, can really doubt that there are realities, for, if he did, doubt would not be a source of dissatisfaction. The hypothesis, therefore, is one which every mind admits. So that the social impulse does not cause men to doubt it. 3. Everybody uses the scientific method about a great many things, and only ceases to use it when he does not know how to apply it. 4. Experience of the method has not led us to doubt it, but, on the contrary, scientific investigation has had the most wonderful triumphs in the way of settling opinion. These afford the explanation of my not doubting the method or the hypothesis which it supposes; and not having any doubt, nor believing that anybody else whom I could influence has, it would be the merest babble for me to say more about it. If there be anybody with a living doubt upon the subject, let him consider it. . . .

This is the only one of the four methods which presents any distinction of a right and a wrong way. If I adopt the method of tenacity, and shut myself out from all influences, whatever I think necessary to doing this, is necessary according to

that method. So with the method of authority: the state may try to put down heresy by means which, from a scientific point of view, seem very ill-calculated to accomplish its purposes; but the only test *on that method* is what the state thinks; so that it cannot pursue the method wrongly. So with the *a priori* method. The very essence of it is to think as one is inclined to think. All metaphysicians will be sure to do that, however they may be inclined to judge each other to be perversely wrong. Hegel's system of Nature represents tolerably the science of that day; and one may be sure that whatever scientific investigation has put out of doubt will presently receive *a priori* demonstration on the part of the metaphysicians. But with the scientific method the case is different. I may start with known and observed facts to proceed to the un-known; and yet the rules which I follow in doing so may not be such as investigation would approve. The test of whether I am truly following the method is not an immediate appeal to my feelings and purposes, but, on the contrary, itself involves the application of the method. Hence it is that bad reasoning as well as good reasoning is possible; and this fact is the foundation of the practical side of logic.

It is not to be supposed that the first three methods of settling opinion present no advantage whatever over the scientific method. On the contrary, each has some peculiar convenience of its own. The *a priori* method is distinguished for its comfortable conclusions. It is the nature of the process to adopt whatever belief we are inclined to, and there are certain flatteries to the vanity of man which we all believe by nature, until we are awakened from our pleasing dream by rough facts. The method of authority will always govern the mass of mankind; and those who wield the various forms of organized force in the state will never be convinced that dangerous reasoning ought not to be suppressed in some way. If liberty of speech is to be untrammelled from the grosser forms of constraint, then uniformity of opinion will be secured by a moral terrorism to which the respectability of society will give its thorough approval. Following the method of authority is the path of peace. Certain non-conformities are permitted; certain others (considered unsafe) are forbidden. These are different in different countries and in different ages; but, wherever you are, let it be known that you seriously hold a tabooed belief, and you may be perfectly sure of being treated with a cruelty less brutal but more refined than hunting you like a wolf. Thus, the greatest intellectual benefactors of mankind have never dared, and dare not now, to utter the whole of their thought; and thus a shade of *prima facie* doubt is cast upon every proposition which is considered essential to the security of society. Singularly enough, the persecution does not all come from without; but a man torments himself and is oftentimes more distressed at finding himself believing propositions which he has been brought up to regard with aversion. The peaceful and sympathetic man will, therefore, find it hard to resist the temptation to submit his opinions to authority. But most of all I admire the method of tenacity for its strength, simplicity, and directness. Men who pursue it are distinguished for their decision of character, which becomes very easy with such a mental rule. They do not waste time in trying to make up their minds what they want, but, fastening like lightning upon whatever alternative comes first, they hold it to the end, whatever happens, without an instant's irresolution. This is one of the splendid qualities which generally accompany brilliant, unlashing success. It is impossible not to envy the man who can dismiss reason, although we know how it must turn out at last.

Such are the advantages which the other methods of settling opinion have over scientific investigation. A man should consider well of them; and then he should consider that, after all, he wishes his opinions to coincide with the fact and that there is no reason why the result of those three methods should do so. To bring about this effect is the prerogative of the method of science. Upon such considerations he has to make his choice—a choice which is far more than the adoption of any intellectual opinion, which is one of the ruling decisions of his life, to which, when once made, he is bound to adhere. The force of habit will sometimes cause a man to hold on to old beliefs, after he is in a condition to see that they have no sound basis. But reflection upon the state of the case will overcome these habits, and he ought to allow reflection its full weight. People sometimes shrink from doing this, having an idea that beliefs are wholesome which they cannot help feeling rest on nothing. But let such persons suppose an analogous though different case from their own. Let them ask themselves what they

would say to a reformed Mussulman who should hesitate to give up his old notions in regard to the relations of the sexes; or to a reformed Catholic who should still shrink from reading the Bible. Would they not say that these persons ought to consider the matter fully, and clearly understand the new doctrine, and then ought to embrace it, in its entirety? But, above all, let it be considered that what is more wholesome than any particular belief is integrity of belief, and that to avoid looking into the support of any belief from a fear that it may turn out rotten is quite as immoral as it is disadvantageous. The person who confesses that there is such a thing as truth, which is distinguished from falsehood simply by this, that if acted on it will carry us to the point we aim at and not astray, and then, though convinced of this, dares not know the truth and seeks to avoid it, is in a sorry state of mind indeed.

Yes, the other methods do have their merits: a clear logical conscience does cast something—just as any virtue, just as all that we cherish, costs us dear. But we should not desire it to be otherwise. The genius of a man's logical method should be loved and reverenced as his bride, whom he has chosen from all the world. He need not condemn the others; on the contrary, he may honor them deeply, and in doing so he only honors her the more. But she is the one that he has chosen, and he knows that he was right in making that choice. And having made it, he will work and fight for her, and will not complain that there are blows to take, hoping that there may be as many and as hard to give, and will strive to be the worthy knight and champion of her from the blaze of whose splendors he draws his inspiration and his courage.

⚒

So the four ways in which the human mind can come to have a fixed belief about some subject matter are actually used both for settling opinions and resolving doubt. They are *tenacity, authority,* the *a priori method,* and the *method of science.* The first is the impoverished domain of common sense. The second comes about through military, governmental, and church organizations conditioning us against willful disobedience. The third, practiced by rationalists from Plato to Descartes, is better than the first two but ultimately the use of reason in philosophy has, according to Peirce, amounted to little more than an elaborate form of *rationalization*. While these three methods may have their social and institutional functions, the only reliable method is the "self-corrective" way of what he calls the "scientific method," where one does not know in advance where one is going. This concept is *not* as easy to understand as it may sound; it is closely aligned with Darwin's analysis of how evolution works. *Evolution works precisely because there is nothing guiding it.*

By way of explanation, let me suggest to you what in my view are areas of similar domain: *probability, logic,* and *geometry.* Although we haven't the space to explore this in much detail here, if you think about it a little you will realize that the reason probability works in the way it does is *because there is nothing directing the way the world goes.* If there were "forces" guiding the behavior of probabilistic events, one would not see the patterns that one sees—for instance, with fair coins, bell curves, and so on. Likewise with logic. Logic works as it does *because there is nothing imposing itself upon the terms as such.* "Validity," "soundness," "implication," and so on, *are relations among terms.* It is already implicit in such concepts that the connectives "of no connectives," if you like, leads ultimately to a completely stable, functional, and incontrovertible system of operations. Likewise for space. Space is, let us say, just nothing, emptiness. That is why it has the structure it has—*that* is why it has what is called a "geometry." And so on. Now, of course, I am speaking rather metaphorically here, but the idea may help you to see what is inspiring Peirce and subsequent thinkers along the directions leading up to today's exciting and mind-boggling developments, which few people are in a position to understand because so few have taken the time to trace our ideas back into their originating sources.

Indeed, one can even go so far as to relate what is being said here all the way back to the very beginning of this book where we started with Socrates and his desired relationship with

the unknown, wisdom, via *love*. Philosophers spend a great deal of time on the concept of wisdom, appropriately so, but very little on the other half of the equation. Peirce's concept of love, rarely studied nowadays, has a function in his philosophy very close to that of Socrates.

So how should one proceed, according to Peirce? It is a path few have dared to tread. In the East such cryptic phrases as "There is no path to truth; one must be free of all paths to find it," and "The Tao (way) that can be named is not the Tao," and so on, are in effect saying much the same thing. But what Peirce called for is utter spontaneity at the *end* of a process of acquiring the known, in order that the next step can occur; in some ways, it is a reversal of the Cartesian procedure of starting by doubting everything. One must start, rather, by learning everything and *then* . . . and then what? We then proceed by a new method

✿

by which our beliefs may be caused by nothing human, but by some external permanency—by something upon which our thinking has no effect. . . . It must be something which affects, or might affect, every man. And, though these affections are necessarily as various as are individual conditions, yet the method must be such that the ultimate conclusion of every man shall be the same. Such is the method of science. Its fundamental hypothesis, restated in more familiar language is this: There are real things, whose characters are entirely independent of our opinions about them; those realities affect our senses according to regular laws, and, though our sensations are as different as our relations to the objects, yet, by taking advantage of the laws of perception, we can ascertain by reasoning how things really are, and any man, if he have sufficient experience and reason enough about it, will be led to the one true conclusion.

✿

In this way Peirce sought to develop a new scientific method in which our beliefs are a *response* to something utterly independent of ourselves, both in terms of our desires and our opinions. Second, this is a *publicly verifiable* method markedly influenced by the positivist philosophy of Comte (Section 19.2) and already a call to arms to subsequent logical positivists; that is, our method for acquiring beliefs must be independent of any personal peculiarities; it must have nothing to do with *unique* experiences that only some few special people can have. Everyone must be equally affected or at least equally affectable by the results of the method.

But how does Peirce know that there actually is a reality independent of our thinking, perceiving, willing, of which we can form correct beliefs? Peirce's answer is that philosophy makes it possible for us to understand in what ways a belief "is not a momentary code of consciousness." Rather, according to Peirce, to truly believe some proposition X is to be behaviorally disposed to act as if X were true. This belief provides the psychological confidence that allows you to behave in a certain way in the world. On the other hand, to truly doubt some proposition X is to be in an uncertain state about it. You lack a settled habit and don't know what to do when a given situation in which X becomes relevant to making a decision actually comes up. That is precisely the reason why we work so hard to avoid doubt, because it is psychologically painful, an anxious and irritating state. The effort we make to escape our doubt by acquiring a belief is what Peirce defines to be the process of *inquiry*. It is really, at bottom line, a psychological concept, an attempt to recover the stoic calm that we experience when we know what to do.

Peirceian inquiry requires three things: (1) a *stimulus,* the experience of *doubt;* (2) an *end,* the settlement of opinion; and (3) a *method,* which is science. Thus, as with all pragmatists after him, not just inquiry in particular but thinking in general must become a *felt problem*. If you don't feel that there is a problem, if you are not puzzled, if you are not in a state of doubt, you are *not* capable of inquiry. Your mind is closed. In the following selection taken from his "How to Make Our Ideas Clear," a follow-up to his

"Fixation of Belief," he begins with a criticism of Descartes's notion of clear and distinct ideas, which he claims is *itself* not clear and distinct:

⸙

When Descartes set about the reconstruction of philosophy, his first step was to (theoretically) permit scepticism and to discard the practice of the schoolmen of looking to authority as the ultimate source of truth. That done, he sought a more natural fountain of true principles, and professed to find it in the human mind; thus passing, in the directest way, from the method of authority to that of a priority, as described in my first paper. Self-consciousness was to furnish us with our fundamental truths, and to decide what was agreeable to reason. But since, evidently, not all ideas are true, he was led to note, as the first condition of infallibility, that they must be clear. The distinction between an idea *seeming* clear and really being so, never occurred to him. Trusting to introspection, as he did, even for a knowledge of external things, why should he question its testimony in respect to the contents of our own minds? But then, I suppose, seeing men, who seemed to be quite clear and positive, holding opinions upon fundamental principles, he was further led to say that clearness of ideas is not sufficient, but that they need also to be distinct, *i.e.*, to have nothing unclear about them. What he probably meant by this (for he did not explain himself with precision) was, that they must sustain the test of dialectical examination; that they must not only seem clear at the outset, but that discussion must never be able to bring to light points of obscurity connected with them.

Such was the distinction of Descartes, and one sees that it was precisely on the level of his philosophy. It was somewhat developed by Leibniz. This great and singular genius was as remarkable for what he failed to see as for what he saw. That a piece of mechanism could not do work perpetually without being fed with power in some form, was a thing perfectly apparent to him; yet he did not understand that the machinery of the mind can

From Charles S. Peirce, "How to Make Our Ideas Clear," *Popular Science Monthly*, 1878.

only transform knowledge, but never originate it, unless it be fed with facts of observation. He thus missed the most essential point of the Cartesian philosophy, which is, that to accept propositions which seem perfectly evident to us is a thing which, whether it be logical or illogical, we cannot help doing. Instead of regarding the matter in this way, he sought to reduce the first principles of science to formulas which cannot be denied without self-contradiction, and was apparently unaware of the great difference between his position and that of Descartes. So he reverted to the old formalities of logic, and, above all, abstract definitions played a great part in his philosophy. It was quite natural, therefore, that on observing that the method of Descartes labored under the difficulty that we may seem to ourselves to have clear apprehensions of ideas which in truth are very hazy, no better remedy occurred to him than to require an abstract definition of every important term. Accordingly, in adopting the distinction of *clear* and *distinct* notions, he described the latter quality as the clear apprehension of everything contained in the definition; and the books have ever since copied his words. There is no danger that his chimerical scheme will ever again be overvalued. Nothing new can ever be learned by analyzing definitions. Nevertheless, our existing beliefs can be set in order by this process, and order is an essential element of intellectual economy, as of every other. It may be acknowledged, therefore, that the books are right in making familiarity with a notion the first step toward clearness of apprehension, and the defining of it the second. But in omitting all mention of any higher perspicuity of thought, they simply mirror a philosophy which was exploded a hundred years ago. That much-admired "ornament of logic"—the doctrine of clearness and distinctness—may be pretty enough, but it is high time to relegate to our cabinet of curiosities the antique *bijou*, and to wear about us something better adapted to modern uses.

The very first lesson that we have a right to demand that logic shall teach us is, how to make our ideas clear; and a most important one it is, depreciated only by minds who stand in need of it. To know what we think, to be masters of our own meaning, will make a solid foundation for great and weighty thought. It is most easily learned by those whose ideas are meager and restricted; and far happier they than such as wallow helplessly in a rich mud of conceptions. A nation, it is true, may, in the course of generations, overcome the disadvantage of an excessive wealth of language and its natural concomitant, a vast, unfathomable deep of ideas. We may see it in history, slowly perfecting its literary forms, sloughing at length its metaphysics, and, by virtue of the untirable patience which is often a compensation, attaining great excellence in every branch of mental acquirement.

. . . the action of thought is excited by the irritation of doubt, and ceases when belief is attained; so that the production of belief is the sole function of thought. All these words, however, are too strong for my purpose. It is as if I had described the phenomena as they appear under a mental microscope. Doubt and Belief, as the words are commonly employed, relate to religious or other grave discussions. But here I use them to designate the starting of any question, no matter how small or how great, and the resolution of it. If, for instance, in a horse-car, I pull out my purse and find a five-cent nickel and five coppers, I decide, while my hand is going to the purse, in which way I will pay my fare. To call such a question Doubt, and my decision Belief, is certainly to use words very disproportionate to the occasion. To speak of such a doubt as causing an irritation which needs to be appeased, suggests a temper which is uncomfortable to the verge of insanity. Yet, looking at the matter minutely, it must be admitted that, if there is the least hesitation as to whether I shall pay the five coppers or the nickel (as there will be sure to be, unless I act from some previously contracted habit in the matter), though irritation is too strong a word, yet I am excited to such small mental activity as may be necessary to deciding how I shall act. Most frequently doubts arise from some indecision, however momentary, in our action. Sometimes it is not so. I have, for example, to wait in a railway-station, and to pass the time I read the advertisements on the walls, I compare the advantages of different trains and different routes which I never expect to take, merely fancying myself to be in a state of hesitancy, because I am bored with having nothing to trouble me. Feigned hesitancy, whether feigned for mere amusement or with a lofty purpose, plays a great part in the production of scientific inquiry. However the doubt may originate, it stimulates the mind to an activity which may be slight or energetic, calm or turbulent. Images pass rapidly through consciousness, one incessantly melting into another, until at last, when all is over—it may be in a fraction of a second, in an hour, or after long years—we find ourselves decided as to how we should act under such circumstances as those which occasioned our hesitation. In other words, we have attained belief. . . .

And what, then, is belief? It is the demicadence which closes a musical phrase in the symphony of our intellectual life. We have seen that it has just three properties: First, it is something that we are aware of; second, it appeases the irritation of doubt; and, third, it involves the establishment in our nature of a rule of action, or, say, for short, a *habit*. As it appeases the irritation of doubt, which is the motives for thinking, thought relaxes, and comes to rest for a moment when belief is reached. But, since belief is a rule for action, the application of which involves further doubt and further thought, at the same time that it is a stopping-place, it is also a new starting-place for thought. That is why I have permitted myself to call it thought at rest, although thought is essentially an action. The *final* upshot of thinking is the exercise of volition, and of this thought no longer forms a part; but belief is only a stadium of mental action, an effect upon our nature due to thought, which will influence future thinking.

The essence of belief is the establishment of a habit, and different beliefs are distinguished by the different modes of action to which they give rise. If beliefs do not differ in this respect, if they appease the same doubt by producing the same rule of action, then no mere differences in the manner of consciousness of them can make them different beliefs, any more than playing a tune in different keys is playing different tunes. Imaginary distinctions are often drawn between beliefs which differ only in their mode of expression;—the wrangling which ensues is real enough, however. To believe that any objects are arranged as in Figure 1, and to believe that they are arranged [as] in Figure 2, are one and the same belief; yet it is conceivable that a man should assert one proposition and deny the other. Such false distinctions do as much harm as the confusion of beliefs really different, and are among the pitfalls of which we ought constantly to beware, especially when we are upon metaphysical ground. One singular deception of this sort, which often occurs, is to mistake the sensation produced by our own unclearness of thought for a character of the object we are thinking. Instead of perceiving

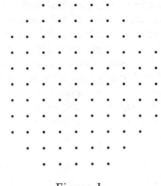

Figure 1

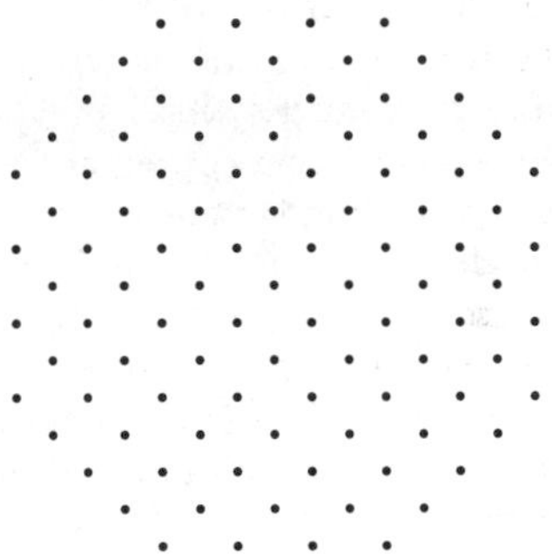

Figure 2

that the obscurity is purely subjective, we fancy that we contemplate a quality of the object which is essentially mysterious; and if our conception be afterward presented to us in a clear form we do not recognize it as the same, owing to the absence of the feeling of unintelligibility. So long as this deception lasts, it obviously puts an impassable barrier in the way of perspicuous thinking; so that it equally interests the opponent of rational thought to perpetuate it, and its adherents to guard against it.

Another such deception is to mistake a mere difference in the grammatical construction of two words for a distinction between the ideas they express. In this pedantic age, when the general mob of writers attend so much more to words than to things, this error is common enough. When I just said that thought is an *action,* and that it consists in a relation, although a person performs an action but not a relation, which can only be the result of an action, yet there was no inconsistency in what I said, but only a grammatical vagueness.

From all these sophisms we shall be perfectly safe so long as we reflect that the whole function of thought is to produce habits of action; and that whatever there is connected with a thought, but irrelevant to its purpose, is an accretion to it, but no part of it. If there be a unity among our sensations which has no reference to how we shall act on a given occasion, as when we listen to a piece of music, why, we do not call that thinking. To develop its meaning, we have, therefore, simply to determine what habits it produces, for what a thing means is simply what habits it involves. Now, the identity of a habit depends on how it might lead us to act, not merely under such circumstances as are likely to arise, but under such as might possibly occur, no matter how improbable they may be. What the habit is depends on *when* and *how* it causes us to act. As for the when, every stimulus to action is derived from perception; as for the how, every purpose of action is to produce some sensible result. Thus, we come down to what is tangible and conceivably practical, as the root of every real distinction of thought, no matter how subtle it may be; and there is no distinction of meaning so fine as to consist in anything but a possible difference of practice.

Let us now approach the subject of logic, and consider a conception which particularly concerns it, that of *reality.* Taking clearness in the sense of familiarity, no idea could be clearer than this. Every child uses it with perfect confidence, never dreaming that he does not understand it. As for clearness in its second grade, however, it would probably puzzle most men, even among those of a reflective turn of mind, to give an abstract definition of the real. Yet such a definition may perhaps be reached by considering the points of difference between reality and its opposite, fiction. A figment is a product of somebody's imagination; it has such characters as his thought impresses upon it. That whose characters are independent of how you or I think is an external reality. There are, however, phenomena within our own minds, dependent upon our thought, which are at the same time real in the sense that we really think them. But though their characters depend on how we think, they do not depend on what we think those characters to be. Thus, a dream has a real existence as a menu phenomenon, if somebody has really dreamt it; that he dreamt so and so does not depend on what anybody thinks was dreamt, but is completely independent of all opinion on the subject. On the other hand, considering not the fact of dreaming but the thing dreamt, it retains its peculiarities by virtue of no other fact than that it was dreamt to possess them. Thus we may define the real as that whose characters are independent of what anybody may think them to be.

But, however satisfactory such a definition may be found, it would be a great mistake to suppose that it makes the idea of reality perfectly clear. Here, then, let us apply our rules. According to them, reality, like every other quality, consists in the peculiar sensible effects which things partaking of it produce. The only effect which real things have is to cause belief, for all the sensations which they excite emerge into consciousness in the form of beliefs. The question therefore is, how is true belief (or belief in the real) distinguished from false belief (or belief in fiction).

. . . Now, as we have seen in the former paper, the ideas of truth and falsehood, in their full development, appertain exclusively to the scientific method of settling opinion. A person who arbitrarily chooses the propositions which he will adopt can use the word truth only to emphasize the expression of his determination to hold on to his choice. Of course, the method of tenacity never prevailed exclusively; reason is too natural to men for that. But in the literature of the dark ages we find some fine examples of it. When Scotus Erigena is commenting upon a poetical passage in which hellebore is spoken of as having caused the death of Socrates, he does not hesitate to inform the inquiring reader that Helleborus and Socrates were two eminent Greek philosophers, and that the latter having been overcome in argument by the former took the matter to heart and died of it! . . .

The real spirit of Socrates, who I hope would have been delighted to have been "overcome in argument," because he would have learned something by it, is in curious contrast with the naive idea of the glossist, for whom discussion would seem to have been simply a struggle. When philosophy began to awake from its long slumber, and before theology completely dominated it, the practice seems to have been for each professor to seize upon any philosophical position he found unoccupied and which seemed a strong one, to intrench himself in it, and to sally forth from time to time to give battle to the others.

. . . Since the time of Descartes, the defect in

the conception of truth has been less apparent. Still, it will sometimes strike a scientific man that the philosophers have been less intent on finding out what the facts are, than on inquiring what belief is most in harmony with their system. It is hard to convince a follower of the *a priori* method by adducing facts; but show him that an opinion he is defending is inconsistent with what he has laid down elsewhere, and he will be very apt to retract it. These minds do not seem to believe that disputation is ever to cease; they seem to think that the opinion which is natural for one man is not so for another, and that belief will, consequently, never be settled. In contenting themselves with fixing their own opinions by a method which would lead another man to a different result, they betray their feeble hold of the conception of what truth is. . . .

They may at first obtain different results, but, as each perfects his method and his processes, the results will move steadily together toward a destined center. So with all scientific research. Different minds may set out with the most antagonistic views, but the progress of investigation carries them by a force outside of themselves to one and the same conclusion. This activity of thought by which we are carried, not where we wish, but to a foreordained goal, is like the operation of destiny. No modification of the point of view taken, no selection of other facts for study, no natural bent of mind even, can enable a man to escape the predestinate opinion. This great law is embodied in the conception of truth and reality. The opinion which is fated to be ultimately agreed to by all who investigate, is what we mean by the truth, and the object represented in this opinion is the real. That is the way I would explain reality. . . . though the object of the final opinion depends on what that opinion is, yet what that opinion is does not depend on what you or I or any man thinks. Our perversity and that of others may indefinitely postpone the settlement of opinion; it might even conceivably cause an arbitrary proposition to be universally accepted as long as the human race should last. Yet even that would not change the nature of the belief, which alone could be the result of investigation carried sufficiently far; and if, after the extinction of our race, another should arise with faculties and disposition for investigation, that true opinion must be the one which they would ultimately come to. "Truth crushed to earth

shall rise again," and the opinion which would finally result from investigation does not depend on how anybody may actually think. But the reality of that which is real does depend on the real fact that investigation is destined to lead, at last, if continued long enough, to a belief in it.

🔾

Peirce's complaint against Descartes's idea is that it relies solely on the a priori method which he rejects on grounds that it appeals, ultimately, to nonverifiable self-evidence. This is but the *first level* of clarity, not itself sufficient. Similarly, he rejects Leibniz's method of abstract definition on the grounds that "nothing new can ever be learned by analyzing definitions." This is but the *second* level of clarity, also not sufficient. Peirce thus calls for a third grade of clearness, predicated upon and identical with his pragmatic maxim, which renders as meaningless any terms or concepts that go beyond the possible effects on observable objects: beliefs must be judged solely by the habits they produce, the practical rules of action that they govern. His system thus comes full circle and completes itself.

One must be careful to not psychologize what we might call Peirce's *pragmatic semiotic philosophy*, which is nevertheless often done even though he so vehemently opposed this psychologizing tendency on the part of other so-called pragmatists that at one point he opted to distance himself from them by calling his system "pragmaticism." Indeed, the pragmatists have often been accused by subsequent twentieth-century philosophers of somehow being "unphilosophical" (accusations also levied at Nietzsche, Schopenhauer, Hegel, and others), in that they are replacing the notion of truth with a psychological notion of practicality. But such misunderstandings are based, in part, on an insufficient understanding of Peirce's semiotics. The other part has to do with Peirce's choice of words with regard to the term *habit*. Let us see why.

As stated, his theory of signs involves a triadic structure. Instead of simply saying "*A* means *B*," we must instead say that "*A* means *B* to *C*," where *A* is the original sign, *B* is its object, and *C* is the interpretant. The rules in a language for relating the various signs, *A, B, C . . .* , to each other—the set of possible "word-word" relations—is called *syntax*. The relation between the words and what they are about—their designated objects, what they "stand" for, the "word-world" relation—is called *semantics*. The way that words (or, more accurately, the signs) affect their users and hearers is called *pragmatics*. As we saw in Peirce's analysis, there can be three ways that a sign can be related to its designated object: (1) causality, which Peirce calls *indexes*; (2) resemblance, which he calls *icons*; and (3) conventionality (arbitrarily), which he calls *symbols*. Smoke is a sign of fire (way 1), the bust of Plato resembles a man (way 2), the word *dog* stands for a dog (way 3), and so on. Just about all of the words in our language are like "dog"; they in no way are *caused* by their designated objects nor do they in any way *resemble* them. This is extremely important. "Red" is not red by any sense of the word! So how did these "symbols" come to represent what they represent? Purely by convention; it is arbitrary.

Now this is quite an amazing similarity to the moves we have seen made before by other philosophers in other areas of inquiry. Nietzsche found a way to use language to attain what he called "truth," which is predicated on the realization that language is, at each and every step of the way, a lie, a fabrication, the result of elaborate self-deception. Kant achieved the transcendental deduction through the realization that what is before the mind *is not real* and thereby ascends to knowledge of what is real, even of transcending the phenomena to what is their cause. Through doubting and in fact making a thorough method of doubt Descartes attained a method of knowledge. And so on. Peirce is noting that the noises we make at the world are really not in any way related to the things in the world *and therein he sees the solution to the problems of knowledge, reality, and the puzzling nature of language and thought*. One may even notice here a startling resonance with the ancient Pythagoreans' discovery

that their framework of numbers did not work—that there was a gap, that their mathematics was grossly inadequate and conceptually misguided all the way down—as a means of providing a method for the subsequent development and rigorous advances in mathematics!

Peirce's great insight is that words *as symbols* stand for things, not because they are related to things but because they are related to their designated objects *only through their interpretants*. A sign is itself meaningless. It is a brute and uninterpreted fact, purely arbitrarily arrived at through the random and chaotic processes of events. It is the interpretant that gives the sign meaning. And by way of making it perfectly clear in what sense Peirce was not merely psychologizing the notion of truth, let us be clear that he distinguishes three different *kinds* of interpretants of signs.

Some words, like *God, love, freedom, death,* and so on, produce a lot of intense feeling when heard or uttered, whereas others—such as *orange juice, toe,* and *doormat,* do not. Now, what are these feelings? They themselves are *not* brute facts, meaningless. They are signs; they themselves are significant. Thus, the emotional feeling of pride at seeing a flag is a sign having a reference to one's country, just as much as the flag is.

Second, there are *energetic* interpretants. He gives an example of a drill sergeant barking out the order, "Ground arms!" The troop's movement to lower the muskets to the ground is an *energetic* interpretant of the command.

The third and most important interpretant is the *logical* interpretant, *which is a sign having the same meaning as the sign it interprets*. For example, suppose you look up the word *halcyon* in the dictionary, and you find it defined as "pleasingly or idyllically calm or peaceful: serene." Next, you look up *serene,* and you find it defined as "lighthearted carefree episode having simplicity and charm." So then you look up *lighthearted* . . . and so on. Unless you're already quite familiar with a language, the dictionary is quite useless. As Peirce points out, in the logical case there is no interpretant that can serve as the final or ultimate interpretant because it is itself a sign and thereby calls for further interpretations of exactly the same kind, which require still others, and so on *forever!*

But *not* forever. There is, according to Peirce, an *ultimate* interpretant. *It is habit.* Yet if we recall, from the preceding passages, that this fact is predicated on his third level of clearness, we may be in a position to understand the full meaning and implication of his profound system of thought. For the third level of clearness is given by a set of "if-then" sentences specifying a series of operations together with the results that will occur if you perform them. This means that a linguistic or conceptual sign can function as a sign provided that there is already in operation a fully *functional* system of such signs. The *habits* in Peirce's system are nothing less than programs encoded into the signs.

Think, after all, about the way you learned language. If you don't speak a word of English, the English dictionary will be useless; you need to have some way of translating at least some words into your own language to get you started. But in the case of your own native language, or with English if you are a native speaker, there was never a translation into some previously known native language because you didn't yet know a language! So how did you ever learn to speak a language?

Peirce's answer, and the answer of the subsequent semioticians, is that you *couldn't* have and you *didn't;* just as the British did not invent the British language, and the Germans did not invent German, and so on, no native speakers invented their language; the native speakers are, themselves, the "inventions" of the language. That is anything but a psychological interpretation! Let us recall again the beautiful and cryptic words of Umberto Eco:

⚓

Now, I realized that not infrequently books speak of books: it is as if they spoke among themselves. In the light of this reflection, the library seemed all the more disturbing to me. It was then the place of long, centuries-old murmuring, an imperceptible dialogue between one parchment and another, a living thing, a receptacle of powers not to be ruled by a human mind, a treasure of secrets emanated by many minds, surviving the death of those who had produced them or had been their conveyors.

⚓

20.1 James (1842–1910): The Radical Empiricist

William James, brother of the novelist Henry James, was born in New York City. He studied science and medicine, first at the Lawrence Scientific School and then at Harvard Medical School. He interrupted his studies to accompany the famous explorer Louis Agassiz on an expedition to unknown parts of the Amazon and then spent a year at a medical school in Germany before returning to Harvard. Early on, James apparently had a mystical experience that changed his life:

⚓

I went one evening into a dressing-room in the twilight to procure some article that was there; when suddenly there fell upon me without any warning, just as if it came out of the darkness, a horrible fear of my own existence. . . . it was as if something hitherto solid within my breast gave way entirely, and I became a mass of quivering fear. After this the universe was changed for me altogether. I awoke morning after morning with a horrible dread at the pit of my stomach, and with a sense of the insecurity of life that I never knew before, and that I have never felt since. It was like a revelation . . . for months I was unable to go out into the dark alone. In general I dreaded to be left alone. I remember won-

From *The Writings of William James*, quoted in *The Experience of Philosophy*, 3rd ed., Kolak and Martin, eds. (Belmont, CA: Wadsworth, 1996).

dering how other people could live, how I myself had ever lived, so unconscious of that pit of insecurity beneath the surface of life.

⟟

James's lifelong search for meaning and understanding of his own existence and the existence of the world took him across a variety of disciplines; after his initial work in medical physiology he made profound and important contributions to psychology and several areas of philosophy, including epistemology, the philosophy of mind, and the philosophy of religion.

After receiving his M.D. in 1869 James became an instructor in comparative physiology at Harvard and then taught physiology and psychology at Johns Hopkins University in Baltimore. He returned to Harvard in 1880 to join its illustrious philosophy department, which at that time included Josiah Royce and graduate student George Santayana (1863–1952). Although James directed Santayana's doctoral thesis the relationship was not a happy one; James called the dissertation "the perfection of rottenness."

In 1890 James published his famous *Principles of Psychology,* the first textbook on psychology. A huge and instant success, it provided a philosophical foundation for the newly developing science of psychology; subsequently, James helped found the American Psychological Association and served as its first president.

Six years later, at a combined meeting of the philosophy clubs of Yale and Brown Universities, James delivered a famous and controversial lecture, "The Will to Believe," in which he defended the rationality, under certain conditions, of believing in the existence of God in the absence of adequate arguments or evidence for God's existence. Although still regarded as a live philosophical issue today and sometimes defended even by atheists, James's thesis has been criticized as an example of how badly a philosopher can go awry if he gives up the notion of objective truth.

⟟

The Will to Believe

Let us give the name of *hypothesis* to anything that may be proposed to our belief; and just as the electricians speak of live and dead wires, let us speak of any hypothesis as either *live* or *dead*. A live hypothesis is one which appeals as a real possibility to him to whom it is proposed. If I ask you to believe in the Mahdi, the notion makes no electric connection with your nature—it refuses to scintillate with any credibility at all. As an hypothesis it is completely dead. To an Arab, however (even if he be not one of the Mahdi's followers), the hypothesis is among the mind's possibilities: it is alive. This shows that deadness and liveness in an hypothesis are not intrinsic properties, but relations to the individual thinker. They are measured by his willingness to act. The maximum of liveness in an hypothesis means willingness to act irrevocably. Practically, that means belief; but there is some believing tendency wherever there is willingness to act at all.

Next, let us call the decision between two hypotheses an *option*. Options may be of several kinds. They may be —first, *living* or *dead;* secondly, *forced* or *avoidable;* thirdly, *momentous* or *trivial;* and for our purposes we may call an option a genuine option when it is of the forced, living, and momentous kind.

1. A living option is one in which both hypotheses are live ones. If I say to you: "Be a theosophist or be a Mohammedan," it is probably a dead option, because for you neither hypothesis is likely to be alive. But if I say: "Be an agnostic or be a Christian," it is otherwise: trained as you are, each hypothesis makes some appeal, however small, to your belief.

2. Next, if I say to you: "Choose between going out with your umbrella or without it," I do not offer you a genuine option, for it is not forced. You can easily avoid it by not going out at all. Similarly, if I say, "Either love me or hate me," "Either call my theory true or call it false," your option is avoidable. You may remain indifferent to me, neither loving nor hating, and you may decline to offer any judgment as to my theory. But if I say,

An address to the Philosophical Clubs of Yale and Brown Universities. Published in the *New World,* June 1896.

"Either accept this truth or go without it," I put on you a forced option, for there is no standing place outside of the alternative. Every dilemma based on a complete logical disjunction, with no possibility of not choosing, is an option of this forced kind. . . .

⚜

Bertrand Russell (Chapter 23) criticizes James's principle, "If the hypothesis of God works satisfactorily in the widest sense of the word, it is true," on the grounds that "This simply omits as unimportant the question whether God really is in His heaven; if He is a useful hypothesis, that is enough." Ironically, even the pope—who would have had little on which to agree upon with Bertrand Russell—condemned the pragmatic defense of religion.

Part of James's motivation in the essay was to try and develop a coherent version of a pragmatic theory of truth as inspired by Peirce and Dewey (who both disassociated themselves from James's version of pragmatism). Whereas Peirce and Dewey modeled their pragmatism on scientific thinking and the scientific method, James's analysis at this point in his development relied primarily on religious and moral considerations: "An idea is 'true' so long as to believe it is profitable to our lives." In saying that truth is but something that "happens to an idea," James was reacting against modern representationalist views of truth, according to which an idea "represents" reality and is true insofar as it is a good facsimile of what exists "out there" in the "objective world." Bertrand Russell, who otherwise greatly admired James, especially for his work in psychology and the philosophy of mind, labeled James's theory of truth "subjectivist madness."

James spent the next five years ignoring his critics and working on his *Varieties of Religious Experience* (1902), a synergistic blend of philosophical psychology, philosophy of religion, and the philosophy of mysticism. Unlike many of his contemporaries, he tried to put mysticism in a positive light; today the work is widely regarded as a definitive study of mystical experience. After its publication, James decided to respond to his earlier critics with an effort to provide a solid philosophical basis for his pragmatic theory of truth. In 1907 he succeeded to a certain degree with *Pragmatism: A New Name for Some Old Ways of Thinking*. In it, James broadened his approach and presented the roots of his version of pragmatism in the context of certain European philosophers. This is something other American pragmatists were also already doing; thus, James's book was dedicated to John Stuart Mill, Dewey paid tribute to Hegel, whereas Peirce acknowledged the deep influence of Kant. In his attempt to make pragmatism philosophically more respectable, James finally ended up developing a new theory of mind, based on a subtle and precise analysis of percepts and concepts using many of the introspective techniques he had developed during his former forays into mysticism. This new philosophical method, which has since come to be known, following his own label, as *radical empiricism*, turned out to be James's crowning achievement in philosophy.

In many ways a psychological version of logical positivism, James's radical empiricism grew out of an attempt to wed the basic tenets of his earlier version of pragmatism with a new emphasis on experience along the lines espoused by the increasingly influential logical positivist movement, itself derived from the earlier positivism of August Comte (Section 19.2). Thus, in James's new and improved version of (his *own* former version of) a pragmatic theory of truth and also of meaning, a proposition is true or false depending *not* on "what difference it makes to you and me," as he had claimed earlier, but on whether it *succeeds or fails to predict new sense experience*. This was a radical and profound departure for James, and it transformed his entire philosophical system by tying it closely with the nature of experience in such a way that the entire world itself comes to be viewed as consisting entirely of experience. Propositions that do not successfully make any such predictions one way or the other are meaningless. This then led James to his alternative to both traditional forms of idealism and materialism, what he called "neutral monism," according to which *neither* matter *nor* consciousness exists!

⚓

Does "Consciousness" Exist?

"Thoughts" and "things" are names for two sorts of object, which common sense will always find contrasted and will always practically oppose to each other. Philosophy, reflecting on the contrast, has varied in the past in her explanations of it, and may be expected to vary in the future. At first, "spirit and matter," "soul and body," stood for a pair of equipollent substances quite on a par in weight and interest. But one day Kant undermined the soul and brought in the transcendental ego, and ever since then the bipolar relation has been very much off its balance. The transcendental ego seems nowadays in rationalist quarters to stand for everything, in empiricist quarters for almost nothing. . . .

[T]he spiritual principle attenuates itself to a thoroughly ghostly condition, being only a name for the fact that the "content" of experience *is known*. It loses personal form and activity—these passing over to the content—and becomes a bare *Bewusstheit* [consciousness] or *Bewusst-sein überhaupt* [consciousness in general], of which in its own right absolutely nothing can be said.

I believe that "consciousness," when once it has evaporated to this estate of pure diaphaneity, is on the point of disappearing altogether. It is the name of a nonentity, and has no right to a place among first principles. Those who still cling to it are clinging to a mere echo, the faint rumor left behind by the disappearing "soul" upon the air of philosophy. . . . For twenty years past I have mistrusted "consciousness" as an entity; for seven or eight years past I have suggested its non-existence to my students, and tried to give them its pragmatic equivalent in realities of experience. It seems to me that the hour is ripe for it to be openly and universally discarded.

To deny plumply that "consciousness" exists seems so absurd on the face of it—for undeniably "thoughts" do exist—that I fear some readers will follow me no farther. Let me then immediately explain that I mean only to deny that the word

stands for an entity, but to insist most emphatically that it does stand for a function. There is, I mean, no aboriginal stuff or quality of being, contrasted with that of which material objects are made, out of which our thoughts of them are made; but there is a function in experience which thoughts perform, and for the performance of which this quality of being is invoked. That function is *knowing*. "Consciousness" is supposed necessary to explain the fact that things not only are, but get reported, [that they] are known. Whoever blots out the notion of consciousness from his list of first principles must still provide in some way for that function's being carried on.

1.

My thesis is that if we start with the supposition that there is only one primal stuff or material in the world, a stuff of which everything is composed, and if we call that stuff "pure experience," then knowing can easily be explained as a particular sort of relation towards one another into which portions of pure experience may enter. The relation itself is a part of pure experience; one of its "terms" becomes the subject or bearer of the knowledge, the knower, the other becomes the object known. This will need much explanation before it can be understood. The best way to get it understood is to contrast it with the alternative view; and for that we may take the recentest alternative, that in which the evaporation of the definite soul-substance has proceeded as far as it can go without being yet complete. If neo-Kantism has expelled earlier forms of dualism, we shall have expelled all forms if we are able to expel neo-Kantism in its turn.

For the thinkers I call neo-Kantian, the word consciousness to-day does no more than signalize the fact that experience is indefeasibly dualistic in structure. It means that not subject, not object, but object-plus-subject is the minimum that can actually be. The subject-object distinction meanwhile is entirely different from that between mind and matter, from that between body and soul. Souls were detachable, had separate destinies; things could happen to them. To consciousness as such nothing can happen, for, timeless itself, it is only a witness of happenings in time, in which it plays no part. It is, in a word, but the logical correlative of "content" in an Experience of which the peculiarity is *that fact comes to light* in it, that *awareness of content* takes place. Consciousness as such is entirely

From the *Journal of Philosophy, Psychology, and Scientific Methods*, Vol. I, No. 18, September, 1904.

impersonal—"self" and its activities belong to the content. To say that I am self-conscious, or conscious of putting forth volition, means only that certain contents, for which "self" and "effort of will" are the names, are not without witness as they occur.

Thus, for these belated drinkers at the Kantian spring, we should have to admit consciousness as an "epistemological" necessity, even if we had no direct evidence of its being there.

But in addition to this, we are supposed by almost every one to have an immediate consciousness of consciousness itself. When the world of outer fact ceases to be materially present, and we merely recall it in memory, or fancy it, the consciousness is believed to stand out and to be felt as a kind of impalpable inner flowing, which, once known in this sort of experience, may equally be detected in presentations of the outer world. . . .

This supposes that the consciousness is one element, moment, factor—call it what you like—of an experience of essentially dualistic inner constitution, from which, if you abstract the content, the consciousness will remain revealed to its own eye. Experience, at this rate, would be much like a paint of which the world pictures were made. Paint has a dual constitution, involving, as it does, a menstruum (oil, size or what not) and a mass of content in the form of pigment suspended therein. We can get the pure menstruum by letting the pigment settle, and the pure pigment by pouring off the size or oil. We operate here by physical subtraction; and the usual view is, that by mental subtraction we can separate the two factors of experience in an analogous way—not isolating them entirely, but distinguishing them enough to know that they are two.

2.

Now my contention is exactly the reverse of this. *Experience, I believe, has no such inner duplicity; and the separation of it into consciousness and content comes, not by way of subtraction, but by way of addition*—the addition, to a given concrete piece of it, of other sets of experiences, in connection with which severally its use or function may be of two different kinds.

The paint will also serve here as an illustration. In a pot in a paint-shop, along with other paints, it serves in its entirety as so much saleable matter. Spread on a canvas, with other paints around it, it represents, on the contrary, a feature in a picture and performs a spiritual function. Just so, I maintain,

does a given undivided portion of experience, taken in one context of associates, play the part of a knower, of a state of mind, of "consciousness"; while in a different context the same undivided bit of experience plays the part of a thing known, of an objective "content." In a word, in one group it figures as a thought, in another group as a thing. And, since it can figure in both groups simultaneously we have every right to speak of it as subjective and objective both at once. The dualism connoted by such double-barrelled terms as "experience," "phenomenon," "datum," *"Vorfindung"*—terms which, in philosophy at any rate, tend more and more to replace the single-barrelled terms of "thought" and "thing"—that dualism, I say, is still preserved in this account, but reinterpreted, so that, instead of being mysterious and elusive, it becomes verifiable and concrete. It is an affair of relations, it falls outside, not inside, the single experience considered, and can always be particularized and defined.

The entering wedge for this more concrete way of understanding the dualism was fashioned by Locke when he made the word "idea" stand indifferently for thing and thought, and by Berkeley when he said that what common sense means by realities is exactly what the philosopher means by ideas. Neither Locke nor Berkeley thought his truth out into perfect clearness, but it seems to me that the conception I am defending does little more than consistently carry out the "pragmatic" method which they were the first to use.

If the reader will take his own experiences, he will see what I mean. Let him begin with a perceptual experience, the "presentation," so called, of a physical object, his actual field of vision, the room he sits in, with the book he is reading as its centre; and let him for the present treat this complex object in the commonsense way as being "really" what it seems to be, namely, a collection of physical things cut out from an environing world of other physical things with which these physical things have actual or potential relations. Now at the same time it is just *those self-same things* which his mind, as we say, perceives; and the whole philosophy of perception from Democritus's time downwards has been just one long wrangle over the paradox that what is evidently one reality should be in two places at once, both in outer space and in a person's mind. "Representative" theories of perception avoid the logical paradox, but on the other hand they violate the reader's sense of life, which knows no intervening mental image but seems to see the room and the book immediately just as they physically exist.

The puzzle of how the one identical room can be in two places is at bottom just the puzzle of how one identical point can be on two lines. It can, if it be situated at their intersection; and similarly, if the "pure experience" of the room were a place of intersection of two processes, which connected it with different groups of associates respectively, it could be counted twice over, as belonging to either group, and spoken of loosely as existing in two places, although it would remain all the time a numerically single thing.

Well, the experience is a member of diverse processes that can be followed away from it along entirely different lines. The one self-identical thing has so many relations to the rest of experience that you can take it in disparate systems of association, and treat it as belonging with opposite contexts. In one of these contexts it is your "field of conscious-ness"; in another it is "the room in which you sit," and it enters both contexts in its wholeness, giving no pretext for being said to attach itself to con-sciousness by one of its parts or aspects, and to outer reality by another. What are the two processes, now, into which the room-experience simultaneously enters in this way?

One of them is the reader's personal biography, the other is the history of the house of which the room is part. The presentation, the experience, the *that* in short (for until we have decided *what* it is it must be a mere *that*) is the last term of a train of sensations, emotions, decisions, movements, classifications, expectations, etc., ending in the present, and the first term of a series of similar "inner" operations extending into the future, on the reader's part. On the other hand, the very same *that* is the *terminus ad quem* of a lot of pre-vious physical operations, carpentering, papering, furnishing, warming, etc., and the *terminus a quo* of a lot of future ones, in which it will be con-cerned when undergoing the destiny of a physical room. The physical and the mental operations form curiously incompatible groups. As a room, the experience has occupied that spot and had that environment for thirty years. As your field of consciousness it may never have existed until now. As a room, attention will go on to discover endless new details in it. As your mental state merely, few new ones will emerge under attention's eye. As a

room, it will take an earthquake, or a gang of men, and in any case a certain amount of time, to destroy it. As your subjective state, the closing of your eyes, or any instantaneous play of your fancy will suffice. In the real world, fire will consume it. In your mind, you can let fire play over it without effect. As an outer object you must pay so much a month to inhabit it. As an inner content, you may occupy it for any length of time rent-free. If, in short, you follow it in the mental direction, taking it along with events of personal biography solely, all sorts of things are true of it which are false, and false of it which are true if you treat it as a real thing experienced, follow it in the physical direction, and relate it to associates in the outer world.

3.

So far, all seems plain sailing, but my thesis will probably grow less plausible to the reader when I pass from percepts to concepts, or from the case of things presented to that of things remote. I believe, nevertheless, that here also the same law holds good. If we take conceptual manifolds, or memories, or fancies, they also are in their first intention mere bits of pure experience, and, as such, are single *thats* which act in one context as objects, and in another context figure as mental states. By taking them in their first intention, I mean ignoring their relation to possible perceptual experiences with which they may be connected, which they may lead to and terminate in, and which then they may be supposed to "represent." Taking them in this way first, we confine the problem to a world merely "thought-of" and not directly felt or seen. This world, just like the world of percepts, comes to us at first as a chaos of expe-riences, but lines of order soon get traced. We find that any bit of it which we may cut out as an example is connected with distinct groups of asso-ciates, just as our perceptual experiences are, that these associates link themselves with it by different relations, and that one forms the inner history of a person, while the other acts as an impersonal "objective" world, either spatial and temporal, or else merely logical or mathematical, or otherwise "ideal."

The first obstacle on the part of the reader to seeing that these non-perceptual experiences have objectivity as well as subjectivity will probably be due to the intrusion into his mind of *percepts,* that third group of associates with which the non-perceptual experiences have relations, and which, as a whole, they "represent," standing to them as thoughts to things. This important function of the non-perceptual experiences complicates the question and confuses it; for, so used are we to treat percepts as the sole genuine realities that, unless we keep them out of the discussion, we tend altogether to overlook the objectivity that lies in non-perceptual experiences by themselves. We treat them, "knowing" percepts as they do, as through and through subjective, and say that they are wholly constituted of the stuff called consciousness, using this term now for a kind of entity, after the fashion which I am seeking to refute.

Abstracting, then, from percepts altogether, what I maintain is, that any single non-perceptual experience tends to get counted twice over, just as a perceptual experience does, figuring in one context as an object or field of objects, in another as a state of mind: and all this without the least internal self-diremption on its own part into consciousness and content. It is all consciousness in one taking; and, in the other, all content. . . .

And yet, just as the seen room (to go back to our late example) is *also* a field of consciousness, so the conceived or recollected room is *also* a state of mind; and the doubling-up of the experience has in both cases similar grounds.

The room thought-of, namely, has many thought-of couplings with many thought-of things. Some couplings are inconstant, others are stable. In the reader's personal history the room occupies a single date—he saw it only once perhaps, a year ago. Of the house's history, on the other hand, it forms a permanent ingredient. Some couplings have the curious stubbornness, to borrow Royce's [see next section] term of fact; others show the fluidity of fancy—we let them come and go as we please. Grouped with the rest of its house, with the name of its town, of its owner, builder, value, decorative plan, the room maintains a definite foothold, to which, if we try to loosen it, it tends to return, and to reassert itself with force. With these associates, in a word, it coheres, while to other houses, other towns, other owners, etc., it shows no tendency to cohere at all. The two collections, first of its cohesive, and, second, of its loose associates, inevitably come to be contrasted. We call the first collection the system of external realities, in the midst of which the room, as "real,"

exists; the other we call the stream of our internal thinking, in which, as a "mental image," it for a moment floats. "The room thus again gets counted twice over. It plays two different roles, being thought-of-an-object, and the object-thought-of, both in one; and all this without paradox or mystery, just as the same material thing may be both low and high, or small and great, or bad and good, because of its relations to opposite parts of an environing world.

As "subjective" we say that the experience represents; as "objective" it is represented. What represents and what is represented is here numerically the same; but we must remember that no dualism of being represented and representing resides in the experience *per se*. In its pure state, or when isolated, there is no self-splitting of it into consciousness and what the consciousness is "of." Its subjectivity and objectivity are functional attributes solely, realized only when the experience is "taken," *i.e.*, talked-of, twice, considered along with its two differing contexts respectively, by a new retrospective experience, of which that whole past complication now forms the fresh content.

The instant field of the present is at all times what I call the "pure" experience. It is only virtually or potentially either object or subject as yet. For the time being, it is plain, unqualified actuality, or existence, a simple *that*. In this *naïf* immediacy it is of course *valid;* it is *there,* we *act* upon it; and the doubling of it in retrospection into a state of mind and a reality intended thereby, is just one of the acts. The "state of mind," first treated explicitly as such in retrospection, will stand corrected or confirmed, and the retrospective experience in its turn will get a similar treatment; but the immediate experience in its passing is always "truth," practical truth, *something to act on*, at its own movement. If the world were then and there to go out like a candle, it would remain truth absolute and objective, for it would be "the last word," would have no critic, and no one would ever oppose the thought in it to the reality intended.

I think I may now claim to have made my thesis clear. Consciousness connotes a kind of external relation, and does not denote a special stuff or way of being. *The peculiarity of our experiences, that they not only are, but are known, which their "conscious" quality is invoked to explain, is better explained by their relations—these relations themselves being experiences—to one another.*

⚱

James's theory is both phenomenalistic and yet reminiscent of naive realism. The basic but radical innovation, though in many ways extremely subtle, is this: ideas are the only existent *given,* but that does not mean necessarily that they are *mental.* In other words, James accepts as true certain basic aspects of absolute idealism while rejecting as false the existence of an intrinsically subjective consciousness. The result is a sort of "pan-objectivism" in which, contra Berkeley and Bradley, *all* essential relations in the universe are *external* relations.

James's statement of these views as presented in the selection from "Does 'Consciousness' Exist?" establishes his radical empiricist position of neutral monism through a detailed analysis of consciousness, leading up to the conclusion that what we ordinarily call consciousness *does not exist.* What there is, instead, is "pure experience." In some ways, on this point James's philosophy can be seen as a synthesis of previous developments in the philosophy of mind and a precursor of the conceptual revolutions in twentieth-century physics and mathematics pioneered by Einstein, Russell, and Bohr, in which the mind is seen, not just as a passive observer of reality but more along Kantian and Leibnizian lines—that is, as having a pivotal role in the structuring of reality. One major difference between James and Kant is that according to James, as for the absolute idealist reactions to Kant, there is no "thing-in-itself" existing independently of experience.

More than two decades after the preceding article appeared, Bertrand Russell wrote:

⚱

Twenty-three years have elapsed since William James startled the world with his article entitled, "Does 'Consciousness' Exist?" In this article . . . he

set out the view that "there is only one primal stuff or material in the world," and that the word "consciousness" stands for a function, not an entity. He holds that there are "thoughts," which perform the function of "knowing," but that thoughts are not made of any different "stuff" from that of which material objects are made. He thus laid the foundations for what is called "neutral monism," a view advocated by most American realists.

⚱

As we shall see in Chapter 23, Russell too was an advocate of neutral monism, in which the mind–body problem as originally posed by Descartes is resolved through an analysis in which mind and physical matter are but different constructions of the same basic type of elements, neither strictly mental nor strictly physical. James's idea is that the real world is, ultimately, as he entitled the follow-up article, "a world of pure experience."[2] According to James, the proper concept that captures what the world in and of itself is (rather than how it "merely" appears or how it "truly" is independently of our phenomenal states) is *experience.* James's notion of what *experience* is, however, must be understood against the backdrop of what he said about consciousness.

In denying the existence of consciousness—a claim that he acknowledged is apt to strike his readers as utterly absurd—James is *not* denying the existence of *thoughts!* He is denying, rather, that the word *consciousness* denotes or refers to any entity. Consciousness is not a "thing," nor is it just *nothing.* Likewise, "things" are not *things* either, in the sense of being physical objects or anything like that conceived in terms of some sort of *substance.* Rather, the proper reference of the term "consciousness" is to a specific type of *function,* and this function is an *act*—in the Fichtean-Peircean sense of "act"—an act *of knowing.*

Thus, in exactly the same way that Peirce's semiotics is impersonal, the field of knowledge is both active and yet *impersonal:* that "Consciousness as such is entirely impersonal" is exactly how he put it in the reading. Further-

---

Bertrand Russell, quoted in *Plato to Wittgenstein: The Historical Foundations of Mind,* Daniel Kolak (Belmont, CA: Wadsworth, 1994).

more, once we understand that the traditional separation between *consciousness* and *content* is bogus—that this is an illusion which the mind adds to the experience of reality—we are in a position to see an object of perceptual experience, not as a representation of a nonmental object but, as he calls it, a *presentation*. It makes an *external* relation out of the functional activity of consciousness.

In other words, subjectivity, which has traditionally been regarded as the very essence of conscious states, is thereby removed from James's system of thought. His neutral monism is thus an attempt to transcend *in language itself* the entire subjective-objective distinction. This philosophical move will be carried out further by John Dewey through his Darwin-inspired theory in which James's program of conceiving not just the mind but the human being and the world entire as interactions among *natural* processes becomes the foundation for the widely influential twentieth-century movement known as naturalism. Breaking down the boundary between knowers and what is known (but within a strictly positivistic outlook) leads to a completely *naturalized epistemology*. We shall see this in the next section.

20.2 Dewey (1859–1952): Epistemology Naturalized

John Dewey was born in Burlington, Vermont, the son of a grocer. At his mother's urging and apparently against his own wishes, he entered the University of Vermont. He had little interest in intellectual pursuits, viewing them as unnecessary abstractions from the practical concerns of reality, until his senior year, when he took some philosophy courses. Impressed both by the "Scottish empirical realism" and "German rational idealism"—especially Leibniz, Kant, and Hegel—he also studied the evolutionary views of T. H. Huxley. After graduation, he taught high school for two years in Pennsylvania but then decided to go to graduate school in philosophy at Johns Hopkins University. In only two years

he received his doctoral degree for his dissertation, "The Psychology of Kant." Six years later he published a little known but seminal work on the philosophy of Leibniz, *Leibniz's New Essays Concerning Human Understanding: A Critical Exposition* (1888), from which we already read a selection (Section 12.1).

Throughout this early period Dewey was a Hegelian, especially with regard to the view that individuals do not exist in isolation from history, culture, and environment. Although this remained a central aspect of Dewey's later philosophy of education, he later modified his idealism into a unique version of pragmatism following Kant (who was the first to use the word *pragmatishe* in the sense employed by Dewey, James, and other American pragmatists). Yet still he remarked that Hegel had "left a permanent deposit in my thinking." His philosophy began to change even more drastically away from German idealism after reading William James's *Principles of Psychology* (1890). In an essay, "The Development of American Pragmatism," Dewey credits James's *Principles* with awakening him to the idea of pragmatism and the development of a theory of experience according to which the perceiving mind directly apprehends reality:

It is not experience which is experienced, but nature—stones, plants, animals, diseases, health, temperature, electricity, and so on. Things interacting in certain ways *are* experience; they are what is experienced. Linked in certain other ways with another natural object—the human organism—they are *how* things are experienced as well. Experience thus reaches down into nature; it has depth. It also has breadth and to an indefinitely elastic extent. It stretches. That stretch constitutes inference.

"The Development of American Pragmatism," *The Middle Works* (Southern Illinois University Press, 1977).

In thus naturalizing epistemology, Dewey is making the whole category of thought as it relates to both philosophical as well as scientific inquiry an aspect of *problem solving*. This is still very much a pragmatic notion:

⚘

The function of reflective thought is to transform a situation in which there is experienced obscurity, doubt, conflict, disturbance of some sort, into a situation that is clear, coherent, settled, harmonious.

⚘

This constitutes the essence of the *philosophical* as well as the *scientific* problem. But it does *not* delegate either activity into the realm of the personal because, in Dewey's view, we as knowers are not spectators of the world! Just as Kant, Hegel, and the idealists have argued, the relation between knowers and the known is itself an *act* and, as such, it is a participatory existence.

Second, as Dewey makes clear in the next selection, from his *Quest for Certainty* (1929), knowledge is not to be understood, as it has been traditionally from the time of Descartes, as a quest for certainty. The correctness of our beliefs depends not entirely on *present* activities of consciousness but is in part determined by future tests. Anyone's claims to a state of certainty *now* can be known to be false because *any* claim to certainty as an attained state experienced in the present moment must be, at best, the derivative of an abstract illusion. *Everything* is open to revision.

Thus, like Hegel, Dewey sees the whole of philosophy, science, and even mathematics and logic—all our methods, concepts, and tools—as being a part of history. Explicitly unlike Hegel, however, and very much like Kierkegaard (Section 18.0), Dewey sees no such thing as a completion of the process—no attainment of the absolute or of absolute knowledge.

As in James's system, the whole gamut of human knowledge-seeking is an aspect of nature in its various forms. His "naturalized epistemology" is not a call to *scientism*, of which he is deeply critical:

⚘

Only when the older theory of knowledge and metaphysics is retained, is science thought to inform us that nature in its true reality is but an interplay of masses in motion, without sound, color, or any quality of enjoyment and use. What science actually does is to show that any natural object we please may be treated in terms of relations upon which its occurrence depends, or as an event, and that by so treating it we are enabled to get behind, as it were, the immediate qualities the object of direct experience presents, and to regulate their happening, instead of having to wait for conditions beyond our control to bring it about. Reduction of experienced objects to the form of relations, which are neutral as respects qualitative traits, is a prerequisite of ability to regulate the course of change, so that it may terminate in the occurrence of an object having desired qualities. . . . Thus, "science," meaning physical knowledge, became a kind of sanctuary. A religious atmosphere, not to say an idolatrous one, was created. "Science" was set apart; its findings were supposed to have a privileged relation to the real. In fact the painter may know colors as well as the meteorologist; the statesman, educator and dramatist may know human nature as truly as the professional psychologist; the farmer may know soils and plants as truly as the botanist and mineralogist. For the criterion of knowledge likes in the method used to secure consequences and not in metaphysical conceptions of the nature of the real. . . . That "knowledge" has many meanings follows from the operational definition of conceptions. There are as many conceptions of knowledge as there are distinctive operations by which problematic situations are resolved.

⚘

"The Development of American Pragmatism," *The Middle Works* (Southern Illinois University Press, 1977).

From *The Quest for Certainty*, 1929 (New York: Putnam's Sons, 1960).

This opens up a cosmic multiperspectival outlook on our epistemologies that is more in sync with the multiplicity of nature; Dewey is here, of course, closely following the insights of Leibniz and the concept of infinitude worlds within worlds. Recall, again, his remarks about Leibniz (Section 12.1).

Like Kant, Dewey conceives of his version of pragmatism (itself derived from Kant) as another "Copernican revolution" in philosophical, social, moral, and economic thought. The key shift in perspective is laid out for us in the following selection from *The Quest for Certainty*.

⚐

The theory of knowing is modeled after what was supposed to take place in the act of vision. The object refracts light to the eye and is seen; it makes a difference to the eye and to the person having an optical apparatus, but none to the thing seen. The real object is the object so fixed in its regal aloofness that it is a king to any beholding mind that may gaze upon it. A spectator theory of knowledge is the inevitable outcome. There have been theories which hold that mental activity intervenes, but they have retained the old premise. They have therefore concluded that it is impossible to know reality. Since mind intervenes, we know, according to them, only some modified semblance of the real object, some "appearance." It would be hard to find a more thoroughgoing confirmation than this conclusion provides of the complete hold possessed by the belief that the object of knowledge is a reality fixed and complete in itself, in isolation from an act of inquiry which has in it any element of production of change.

All of these notions about certainty and the fixed, about the nature of the real world, about the nature of the mind and its organs of knowing, are completely bound up with one another, and their consequences ramify into practically all important ideas entertained upon any philosophic question. They all flow—such is my basic thesis—from the separation (set up in the interest of the quest for absolute certainty) between theory and practice, knowledge and action. . . .

⚐

Dewey criticizes the traditional philosophical emphasis on "certainty" as an outdated remnant of ancient Greek thinking, based on the same basic presuppositions found in religion—a hopeless "doctrine of escape from the vicissitudes of existence by means of measures which do not demand an active coping with conditions." Thus, according to Dewey, the quest for certainty from Aristotle to the present has wrongly emphasized the theoretical and ideal rather than the practical and useful. It is this intellectual alienation away from practical experience that led philosophers time and again to overestimate the power of pure reason for comprehending reality and to underestimate the true cognitive significance of ordinary experience. Dewey thus tries to unite reflective and concrete experience in a way that makes philosophy more "relevant" to the world as it is conceived *out of experience* rather than as something transcendent to, or the cause of, experience.

In *Democracy and Education* (1916), Dewey applies his methods to education, arguing for the central importance of practical experience to any type of thinking. As he points out,

⚐

an experience, a very humble experience, is capable of generating and carrying any amount of theory (or intellectual content), but a theory apart from an experience cannot be definitely grasped even as a theory.

⚐

By this crucial point he has abandoned all hopes for a Kantian-type transcendental deduction that is supposed to go beyond experience and has adopted instead a type of Humean primacy of the empirical. The real purpose of thought and therefore of philosophy, he argues, is not to make *distinctions* but to make *connections*—among both our actions and their consequences. Ultimately, for Dewey, thinking is not to be understood in terms of the intellect but is itself a type of experience, albeit a reflective one.

Dewey taught at the University of Michigan for ten years before he became chairman of the Department of Philosophy, Psychology, and Education at the University of Chicago, where he designed and ran his "Laboratory School." This was an experimental learning environment where he tried out his unorthodox methods of teaching on children from ages four to fifteen. In 1905 he moved to New York to join the philosophy department at Columbia University and remained there for the rest of his life, exerting a tremendous influence on subsequent American philosophers.

20.3 Royce (1855–1916): The American Idealist

Josiah Royce was born in Grass Valley, a California mining town. After studying engineering at the then newly opened University of California, he went to Germany to study philosophy at Leipzig and Göttingen, where he came under the influence of the Hegelian idealists. Upon his return to the United States he became one of the first fellows at Johns Hopkins University, along with William James and Charles Peirce. After receiving his Ph.D. in philosophy from Johns Hopkins at the age of twenty-three, he taught briefly at the University of California and then settled at Harvard.

Of the great American philosophers, Royce is virtually the only one who, in the grand Hegelian style, attempted to construct a complete system encompassing the whole of reality. Although he has much in common with Peirce, Dewey, and James in terms of making a *philosophy of experience,* in marked contrast to his colleagues' pragmatism Royce became the first and foremost American idealist. Also, like his American contemporaries and unlike his German and British counterparts, especially F. H. Bradley (1846–1924), Royce's version of absolute idealism is uniquely *individualistic.* Against both the British and German absolute idealists' conception of the Absolute as being beyond the categories of thought and hence inaccessible to the individual mind, Royce argues that complete

knowledge is possible via an "Absolute experience to which all facts are known and for which all facts are subject to universal law."

In his *Spirit of Modern Philosophy* (1892), from which the following selection is taken, he begins where Berkeley's idealism ended, by identifying each and every aspect of the world around him as the immediate presence of the world-soul, known and revealed not through faith but logic and even agnosticism.

⚹

The Spirit of Modern Philosophy

My reason for believing that there is one absolute World-Self, who embraces and is all reality, whose consciousness includes and infinitely transcends our own, in whose unity all the laws of nature and all the mysteries of experience must have their solution and their very being,—is simply that the profoundest agnosticism which you can possibly state in any coherent fashion, the deepest doubt which you can any way formulate about the world or the things that are therein, already presupposes, implies, demands, asserts, the existence of such a World-Self. The agnostic, I say, already asserts this existence—unconsciously, of course, as a rule, but none the less inevitably. For, as we shall find, there is no escape from the infinite Self except by self-contradiction. Ignorant as I am about first causes, I am at least clear, therefore, about the Self. If you deny him, you already in denying affirm him. You reckon ill when you leave him out. "Him when you fly, he is the wings." He is the doubter and the doubt. You in vain flee from his presence. The wings of the morning will not aid you. Nor do I mean all this now as any longer a sort of mysticism. This truth is, I assure you, simply a product of dry logic. When I try to tell you about it in detail, I shall weary you by my wholly unmystical analysis of commonplaces. Here is, in fact, as we shall soon find, the very presupposition of presuppositions. You cannot stir, nay, you cannot even stand still in thought without it. Nor is it an unfamiliar idea. On the contrary, philosophy finds trouble in bringing it to your consciousness merely *because* it is so famil-

From Josiah Royce, *The Spirit of Modern Philosophy* (Boston: Houghton Mifflin Co., 1892).

iar. When they told us in childhood that we could not see God just *because* he was everywhere, just because his omnipresence gave us no chance to discern him and to fix our eyes upon him, they told us a deep truth in allegorical fashion. The infinite Self, as we shall learn, is actually asserted by you in every proposition you utter, is there at the heart, so to speak, of the very multiplication table. The Self is so little a thing merely guessed at as the unknowable source of experience, that already, *in* the very least of daily experiences you unconsciously know him as something present. This, as we shall find, is the deepest tragedy of our finitude, that continually he comes to his own, and his own receive him not, that he becomes flesh in every least incident of our lives; whilst we, gazing with wonder upon his world, search here and there for first causes, look for miracles, and beg him to show us the Father, since that alone will suffice us. No wonder that thus we have to remain agnostics. "Hast thou been so long time with me, and yet hast thou not *known* me?" Such is the eternal answer of the Logos to every doubting question. Seek him not as an outer hypothesis to explain experience. Seek him not anywhere yonder in the clouds. He is no "thing in itself." But for all that, experience contains him. He is the reality, the soul of it. "Did not our heart burn within us while he talked with us by the way? And, as we shall see, he does not talk merely to our hearts. He reveals himself to our coolest scrutiny.

⁂

The method by which he constructed his elaborate system starts with the fundamental insight that we have been calling the first step to philosophical enlightenment: the point, used to various advantages by different philosophers, that your eyes are not windows; or, as Royce so eloquently puts it in the following passage, that we are "such stuff as ideas are made of."

⁂

. . . This idealistic analysis consists merely in a pointing out, by various devices, that the world of your knowledge, whatever it contains, is through and through such stuff as ideas are made of, that you never in your life believed in anything defin-

able *but* ideas, that, as Berkeley put it, " this whole choir of heaven and furniture of earth" is nothing for any of us but a system of ideas which govern our belief and our conduct. Such idealism has numerous statements, interpretations, embodiments: forms part of the most various systems and experiences, is consistent with Berkeley's theism, with Fichte's ethical absolutism. . . .

The other aspect of idealism is the one which gives us our notion of the absolute Self. To it the first is only preparatory. This second aspect is the one which from Kant, until the present time, has formed the deeper problem of thought. Whenever the world has become more conscious of its significance, the work of human philosophy will be, not nearly ended (Heaven forbid an end), but for the first time fairly begun. For then, in critically estimating our passions, we shall have some truer sense of whose passions they are.

I begin with the first and the less significant aspect of idealism. Our world, I say, whatever it may contain is such stuff as ideas are made of.

Here, then, is our so real world of the senses, full of light and warmth and sound. If anything could be solid and external, surely, one at first will say, it is this world. Hard facts, not mere ideas, meet us on every hand. Ideas any one can mould as he wishes. Not so facts. In idea socialists can dream out Utopias, disappointed lovers can imagine themselves successful, beggars can ride horses, wanderers can enjoy the fireside at home. In the realm of facts, society organizes itself as it must, rejected lovers stand for the time defeated, beggars are alone with their wishes, oceans roll drearily between home and the wanderer. Yet this world of fact is, after all, not entirely stubborn, not merely hard. The strenuous will can mould facts. We can form our world, in part, according to our ideas. Statesmen influence the social order, lovers woo afresh, wanderers find the way home. But thus to alter the world we must work, and just because the laborer is worthy of his hire, it is well that the real world should thus have such fixity of things as enables us to anticipate what facts will prove lasting, and to see of the travail of our souls when it is once done. This, then, is the presupposition of life, that we work in a real world, where housewalls do not melt away as in dreams, but stand firm against the winds of many winters, and can be felt as real. We do not wish to find facts wholly plastic; we want them to be stubborn, if only the stubbornness be not altogether unmerciful. Our will makes constantly a sort of agreement with the world, whereby, if the world will continually show some respect to the will, the will shall consent to be strenuous in its industry. Interfere with the reality of my world, and you therefore take the very life and heart out of my will.

The reality of the world, however, when thus defined in terms of its stubbornness, its firmness as against the will that has not conformed to its laws, its kindly rigidity in preserving for us the fruits of our labors,—such reality, I say, is still something wholly unanalyzed. In what does this stubbornness consist? Surely, many different sorts of reality, as it would seem, may be stubborn. Matter is stubborn when it stands in hard walls against us, or rises in vast mountain ranges before the path-finding explorer. But minds can be stubborn also. The lonely wanderer, who watches by the seashore the waves that roll between him and his home, talks of cruel facts, material barriers that, just because they *are* material, and not ideal, shall be the irresistible foes of his longing heart. "In wish," he says, "I am with my dear ones, but alas, wishes cannot cross oceans! Oceans are material facts, in the cold outer world. Would that the world of the heart were all!" But alas! to the rejected lover the world of the heart *is* all, and that is just his woe. Were the barrier between him and his beloved only made of those stubborn material facts, only of walls or of oceans how lightly might his will erelong transcend them all! Matter stubborn! Outer nature cruelly the foe of ideas! Nay, it is just an idea that now opposes him,—just an idea, and that, too, in the mind of the maiden he loves. But in vain does he call this stubborn bit of disdain a merely ideal fact. No flint was ever more definite in preserving its identity and its edge than this disdain may be. Place me for a moment, then, in an external world that shall consist wholly of ideas,—the ideas, namely, of other people about me, a world of maidens who shall scorn me, of old friends who shall have learned to hate me, of angels who shall condemn me, of God who shall judge me. In what piercing north winds, amidst what fields of ice, in the labyrinths of what tangled forests, in the depths of what thickwalled dungeons, on the edges of what tremendous precipices, should I be more genuinely in the presence of stubborn and unyielding facts than in that conceived world of ideas! So, as one sees, I by no means deprive my world of stubborn reality, if I merely call it a world of ideas. On the contrary, as every teacher knows, the ideas of the people are often the most difficult of facts to influence. We were wrong, then, when we said that whilst matter was stubborn, ideas could be moulded at pleasure. Ideas are often the most implacable of facts. Even my own ideas, the facts of my own inner life, may cruelly decline to be plastic to my wish. The wicked will that refuses to be destroyed,—what rock has often more consistency for our senses than this will has for our inner consciousness!

⚓

This passage ends with the famous remark referred to by William James (Section 20.1), in which Royce asserts a simple and obvious response to the simple and obvious objection often levied, not only against idealism but representationalist and even presentationalist theories (such as James's *neutral monism,* a "world of pure experience"). If reality consists not of *material* stuff but some sort of *mind* stuff, made up of experiential or symbolic components, as in the philosophies of Peirce and James, or idealistic components, as in Royce, *why are so many aspects of reality fixed and impenetrable?* In other words, if the world of my experience, as Schopenhauer claimed, is my idea, or if it is a series of signs, as Peirce claimed, or even a representation, as in Kant's philosophy, why can't I just wish whatever I want into my experience, my thoughts, my symbols, my ideas, and thereby affect existence? Why can I not seem to affect reality with my thoughts, ideas, symbols, experiences? Royce's response is that ideas, whether conceived in purely experiential terms or in symbolic terms— even though they are *immaterial*—can be more "stubborn" and "resilient" than the firmest concept of matter:

⚓

This system of ideas we can't change by our wish; it is for us as overwhelming a fact as guilt, or as the bearing of our fellows towards us, but we know it only *as* such a system of ideas. And we call it the world of matter.

⚹

Guilt is not such stuff as rocks are made of. Guilt is such stuff as ideas are made of. Guilt is a mental phenomenon consisting of mental sensations, emotions, and thoughts. Why, then, when you are in the grips of such a phenomenon, itself consisting of mental events in your own mind, are you in its power? Why can you not simply wish it away?

We've encountered and engaged in this sort of reasoning before. For instance, in your dreams you encounter situations in which you realize (now that you are awake, of course) that what is before you while the dream is happening—the entire "world" in which you exist while the dream is going on—is a mental, idealist world, one of your mind's own concoction. So then why can't you, in your dreams, simply wish the dream images to go as you want? Royce's point isn't so much that you should be able to answer that question; he merely wants to direct your attention to the fact that when you are in the grip, literally, of an idea—even if that idea, as in the case of dreams, consists of visual apparitions—you do not move *it* around with your wishes; rather, it moves *you*. His thinking here is influenced in part by Peirce's semiotic analysis of signs, insofar as the phenomenal elements in which the world consists have, just as do symbols, their own relations among themselves, which function in certain lawlike ways. Ideas can be impenetrable to our prying into them, which is really their own prying into themselves (that is, the Absolute Idea can be impenetrable to the prying of the experiential bundle, within itself, that is the individual ego). Royce is not saying that this cannot be altered in any way, merely that our individual minds as such have not yet attained sufficient knowledge to do so. To put it slightly differently; there exist, within the world-soul, *imperspicuous ideas* that correspond, within a materialistic framework, to impenetrable matter.

Royce thus evokes a key distinction between *epistemological* idealism—the claim that our knowledge of the world is ultimately subjective—and *metaphysical* idealism—the claim that the world is ultimately a mental, or spiritual, entity. In defending *metaphysical* idealism in the tradition of Fichte, Schelling, and Hegel against both materialist realism and empiricism, he argues that *metaphysical idealism is the only system that makes genuine knowledge possible*. This, he claims, is a great improvement over all nonidealist philosophers who conceive of the world in terms of some ultimately nonmental substance such as physical atoms or material "things in themselves" that sever the mind from the world and make the world ultimately *unknowable*.

To see exactly what Royce means, let us look at a particularly revealing passage, whose depth of meaning would have escaped even its own author! The most common sort of criticism levied against idealism relies on the primacy in our language of commonly accepted terminology from current science which *seems*, at least on the surface, to be inconsistent with the idealist perspective as Royce construes it. Like Berkeley, he acknowledges how difficult it is to accept the *idea* that the world consists of ideas once you have the *idea* of matter rooted in the very language in terms of which your understanding operates. He writes:

⚹

And here you have trouble. Is the outer world, as it exists outside of your ideas, or of anybody's ideas, something, having shape, filling space, possessing solidity, full of moving things? That would in the first place seem evident. The sound isn't outside of me, but the sound-waves, you say, are. The colors are ideal facts; but the ether waves don't need a mind to know them. Warmth is an idea, but the physical fact called heat, this playing to and fro of molecules, is real, and is there apart from any mind. But once more, *is* this so evident? What do I *mean* by the shape of anything, or by the size of anything? Don't I mean just the idea of shape or of size that I am obliged to get under certain circumstances? What is the meaning of any property that I give to the real outer world? How can I express that property except in case I think it in terms of my ideas? As for the sound-waves and the ether waves, what are they but things ideally conceived to explain the facts of nature? The conceptions have doubtless their truth, but it is an ideal truth. What I mean by saying that the things yonder have shape and size and trembling molecules, and that there is air with sound-waves, and ether with light-waves in it,—what I *mean* by all this is that experience forces upon me, directly or indirectly, a vast system of ideas, which may indeed be founded in truth beyond me, which in fact *must* be founded in such truth if my experience has any sense, but which, like my ideas of color and of warmth, are simply expressions of how the world's order must appear to me, and to anybody constituted like me. Above all, is this plain about space. The real things, I say, outside of me, fill space, and move about in it. But what do I mean by space? Only a vast system of ideas which experience and my own mind force upon me. Doubtless these ideas have a validity. They have *this* validity, that I, at all events, when I look upon the world, am bound to see it in space, as much bound as the king in Hamlet was, when he looked within, to see himself as guilty and unrepentant. But just as his guilt was an idea,—a crushing, an irresistible, an overwhelming idea,—but still just an idea, so, too, the space in which I place my world is one great formal idea of mine. That is just why I can describe it to other people. "It has three dimensions," I say, "length, breadth, depth." I describe each. I form, I convey, I construct, an idea of it through them. I know space, as an idea, very well. I can compute all sorts of unseen truths about the relations of its parts. I am sure that you, too, share this idea. But, then, for all of us alike it is just an idea; and when we put our world into space, and call it real there, we simply think one idea into another idea, not voluntarily, to be sure. but inevitably, and yet without leaving the realm of ideas.

Thus, all the reality that *we* attribute to our world, in so far as *we* know and can tell what we mean thereby, becomes ideal. There is, in fact, a certain system of ideas, forced upon us by experience, which we have to use as the guide of our conduct. This system of ideas we can't change by our wish; it is for us as overwhelming a fact as guilt, or as the bearing of our fellows towards us, but we know it only *as* such a system of ideas. And we call it the world of matter. John Stuart Mill very well expressed the puzzle of the whole thing, as we have now reached the statement of this puzzle,

when he called matter a mass of "permanent possibilities of experience" for each of us. Mill's definition has its faults, but it is a very fair beginning. You know matter as something that either now gives you this idea or experience, or that would give you some other idea or experience under other circumstances. A fire, while it burns, is for you a permanent possibility of either getting the idea of an agreeable warmth, or of getting the idea of a bad burn, and you treat it accordingly. A precipice amongst mountains is a permanent possibility of your experiencing a fall, or of your getting a feeling of the exciting or of the sublime in mountain scenery. You have no experience just now of the tropics or of the poles, but both tropical and polar climates exist in your world as permanent possibilities of experience. When you call the sun 92,000,000 miles away, you mean that between you and the sun (that is, between your present experience and the possible experience of the sun's surface) there would inevitably lie the actually inaccessible, but still numerically conceivable series of experiences of distance expressed by the number of miles in question. In short, your whole attitude towards the real world may be summed up by saying: "I have experiences now which I seem bound to have, experiences of color, sound, and all the rest of my present ideas; and I am also bound by experience to believe that in case I did certain things (for instance, touched the wall, traveled to the tropics, visited Europe, studied physics), I then should get, in a determinate order, dependent wholly upon *what* I had done, certain other experiences (for instance, experiences of the wall's solidity, or of a tropical climate, or of the scenes of an European tour, or of the facts of physics)." And this acceptance of actual experience, this belief in possible experience, constitutes all that you mean by your faith in the outer world.

But, you say, Is not, then, all this faith of ours after all well founded? Isn't there really something yonder that corresponds in fact to this series of experiences in us? Yes, indeed, there no doubt is. But what if this, which so shall correspond without us to the ideas within us, what if this hard and fast reality should itself be a system of ideas, outside of our minds but not outside of every mind? As the maiden's disdain is outside the rejected lover's mind, unchangeable so far for him, but not on that account the less ideal, not the less a fact in a mind, as, to take afresh a former fashion of illustration, the price of a security or the objective existence of this lecture is an ideal fact, but real and external for the individual person,—even so why might not this world beyond us, this "permanent possibility of experience" be in essence itself a system of ideal experiences of some standard thought of which ours is only the copy? Nay, must it not be such a system in case it has any reality at all? For, after all, isn't this precisely what our analysis brings us to? Nothing whatever can I say about my world yonder that I do not express in terms of mind. *What* things are, extended, moving, colored, tuneful, majestic, beautiful, holy, *what* they are in any aspect of their nature, mathematical, logical, physical, sensuously pleasing, spiritually valuable, all this must mean for me only something that I have to express in the fashion of ideas. The more I am to know my world, the more of a mind I must have for the purpose. The closer I come to the truth about the things, the more ideas I get. Isn't it plain, then, that *if* my world yonder is anything knowable at all, it must be in and for itself essentially a mental world? Are my ideas to *resemble* in any way the world? Is the truth of my thought to consist in its *agreement* with reality? And am I thus capable, as common sense supposes, of *conforming* my ideas to things? Then reflect. What can, after all, so well agree with an idea as another idea? To what can things that go on in my mind conform unless it be to another mind? If the more my mind grows in mental clearness, the nearer it gets to the nature of reality, then surely the reality that my mind thus resembles must be in itself mental.

After all, then, would it deprive the world here about me of reality, nay, would it not rather save and assure the reality and the knowableness of my world of experience, if I said that this world, as it exists outside of my mind, and of any other human minds, exists in and for a standard, an universal mind, whose system of ideas simply constitutes the world? Even if I fail to prove that there is such a mind, do I not at least thus make plausible that, as I said, our world of common sense has no fact in it which we cannot interpret in terms of ideas, so that this world is throughout such stuff as ideas are made of? To say this, as you see, in no wise deprives our world of its due share of reality. If the standard mind knows now that its ideal fire has the quality of burning those who touch it, and if I in my finitude am bound to conform in my experiences to the thoughts of this standard mind, then in case I

touch that fire I shall surely get the idea of a burn. The standard mind will be at least as hard and fast and real in its ideal consistency as is the maiden in her disdain for the rejected lover; and I, in presence of the ideal stars and the oceans, will see the genuine realities of fate as certainly as the lover hears his fate in the voice that expresses her will.

⁂

Consider, for instance, your view of, say, the shape and size of a chair. How different would the very *shape and size* of that "thing" you are looking at *be* if you were a different size—for example, the size of a flea or an atom? Clearly, the apparent "primary" qualities of the chair are themselves perspectival. What is the size and shape of that "thing" when you move a hundred feet away from it? Well, you say, its *atoms* don't change, its *spatial* properties don't change, and so on. Ah—but what are *atoms*? What is *space*? But hold on, that's not the whole of it. There is something subtle going on here that we are at this moment in a position to make perfectly clear. When we use the words *atom* and *space* today, these words have a completely different meaning from what they did in the time of Royce, which after all was not so long ago. The nineteenth-century conception of atoms has very little, if anything at all, in common with today's quantum mechanical model. Likewise, our conception of space has changed in unimaginably drastic ways with the reformulations of non-Euclidean geometries and Einsteinian spacetime relativity. If ever there was an opportunity for you to experience such "scientific" terms as *ideas*, it is here, with Royce's use of the term "ether."

At the time Royce was writing (1892), space was conceived of in terms of an all-pervasive ether, a perfectly continuous, gaseous-like material substance that stretched across the whole universe, literally the "fabric" of space. Now, when his contemporaries read the preceding passage, their minds passed without trouble over the term *ether*, just as yours do over the terms *atom* and *space*. And Royce went to great lengths to try to get them to realize—hard as it may be to try to believe, he readily acknowledged—that these very terms do not refer to mind-independent realities but are themselves, after all, ideas. It is as if Royce had difficulty at this point *imagining how it could be possible that the ether is just an idea in his mind.* You see the point? This is not a point about *skepticism* but about *ontology*. In going to such great lengths to try to convince his readers of 1892 that terms like *hardness, molecules,* and so on are predicated upon ideas, he unwittingly threw in the scientific term *ether* in the way that you or I today might throw in the words *atom* or *quark* or *quantum state* in order to sound scientific. How can *quarks* be just ideas? They are the very foundation of our currently best explanation of physical reality! But the same was once true of the ether!

There is an incredible irony here. *Ether* waves? Royce was, in effect, saying to his readers: look, I know this is absolutely preposterous—that something as scientifically incontrovertible and foundational as the *ether* does not, as a term, refer to anything real—but try to go along with me! It is as if he, too, had a hard time with that one. And yet since Einstein's time science has given up the notion of an ether. Like the concept "phlogiston," used once to explain combustion, the term "ether" in the final analysis refers to *nothing.* Not an experience. Not a thing. It is a fiction in exactly the way that David Hume claimed that all the terms of science are elaborate fictions.

But note, again, that Royce was not trying to make a skeptical point about science. His solution to the problem of knowledge, like all the idealists, was not to be attained at the scientific level at all! It was not like saying, to a frightened child, all right, how do you know that ghosts and goblins really exist, what evidence do you have for them, have you ever really seen one, and so on. Rather, it is like saying to the child look, these are just ideas in your head, and then engaging with *that* question. *One does not go to the closet or under the bed to look. It is not a scientific issue. It is a philosophical one.*

In other words, Royce's method did not go

beyond the realm of ideas as they are known in experience. We should also note that Royce was not merely content with putting forth his own idealist views in opposition to nonidealist, materialistic views. Rather, he put idealism in the context of a historical evolution, very much along the lines Hegel had attempted, by distinguishing four different stages, which he described in his *The World and the Individual* (1899), in terms of his "four historical conceptions of Being": Realism, Mysticism, Critical Rationalism, and what we might call "Teleological Idealism." The first three can be encapsulated, respectively, as the view that *to be is to be independent,* that *to be is to be immediate,* and *to be is to be valid,* and although each ultimately involves self-contradiction, Royce claimed to capture what is best and most appealing from each in the formation of his fourth conception, which he summarized with the ancient mystic's chant, "That art thou." This, according to Royce, is the only consistent view of reality.

⚹

The World and the Individual

There is an ancient doctrine that whatever is, is ultimately something Individual. Realism early came to that view; and only Critical Rationalism has ever explicitly maintained that the ultimate realities are universals, namely, valid possibilities of experience, or mere truths as such. Now at the close of the last lecture, after analyzing the whole basis of Critical Rationalism, the entire conception of the Real as merely valid, we reinstated the Individual as the only ultimate form of Being. In so far we returned to a view that, in the history of thought, Realism already asserted. But we gave a new reason of our own for this view. Our reason was that the very defect of our finite ideas which sends us seeking for Being lies in the fact that whether we long for practical satisfaction, or think of purely theoretical problems, we, as we now are, are always seeking another object than what is yet present to our ideas. Now any ultimate reality, for

From Josiah Royce, *The World and the Individual* (New York: Macmillan, 1899).

us while as finite thinkers we seek it, is always such another fact. Yet this other object is always an object for our thought only in so far as our thought already means it, defines it, and wills it to be our object. But what is for us this other? In its essence it is already defined even before we undertake to know it. For this other is precisely the fulfilment of our purpose, the satisfaction of the will now imperfectly embodied in our ideas, the completion of what we already partially possess in our finite insight. This completion is for us another, solely because our ideas, in their present momentary forms, come to us as general ideas,—ideas of what is now merely a kind of relative fulfilment and not an entire fulfilment. Other fulfilment of the same general kind is needed before we can face the whole Being that we seek. This kind of fulfilment we want to bring, however, to some integral expression, to its own finality, to its completeness as a whole fact. And this want of ours, so I asserted, not only sets us looking for Being, but gives us our only ground and means for defining Being.

Being itself we should directly face in our own experience only in case we experienced finality, *i.e.* full expression of what our finite ideas both mean and seek. Such expression, however, would be given to us in the form of a life that neither sought nor permitted another to take its own place as the expression of its own purpose. Where no other was yet to be sought, there alone would our ideas define no other, no Being, of the type in question, lying yet beyond themselves, in the direction of their own type of fulfilment. The other would be found, and so would be present. And there alone should we consequently stand in the presence of what is real. Conversely, whoever grasps only the nature of a general concept, whoever merely thinks of light or colors, or gravitation, or of man, whoever lacks, longs, or in any way seeks another, has not in his experience the full expression of his own meaning. Hence it is that he has to seek his object elsewhere. And so he has not yet faced any ultimate Being. He has upon his hands mere fragments, mere aspects of Being. Thus an entire instance of Being must be precisely that which permits your ideas to seek no other than what is present. Such a being is an Individual. Only, for our present conception of Being, an individual being is not a fact independent of any experience, nor yet a merely valid truth, nor yet a merely

immediate datum that quenches ideas. For all these alternatives we have already faced and rejected. On the contrary an individual being is a Life of Experience fulfilling Ideas, in an absolutely final form. And this we said is the essential nature of Being. The essence of the Real is to be Individual, or to permit no other of its own kind, and this character it possesses only as the unique fulfilment of purpose.

Or, once more, as Mysticism asserted, so we too assert of your world, *That art thou.* Only the Self which is your world is your completely integrated Self, the totality of the life that at this instant you fragmentarily grasp. Your present defect is a matter of the mere form of your consciousness at this instant. Were your eyes at this instant open to your own meaning, your life as a whole would be spread before you as a single and unique life, for which no other could be substituted without a less determinate expression of just your individual will. Now this complete life of yours, is. Only such completion can be. Being can possess no other nature than this. And this, in outline, is our Fourth Conception of Being.

⚹

Royce thus leads us full circle into the heart of the philosophical tumult where each of us, as a corridor, opens up into every other, a multiperspectival cosmic labyrinth that is the one self of the world-soul, everywhere all at once, always everyone. That is how in his brilliant and original conception of idealism he avoids the problem of solipsism, in which your mind is the only mind that exists: by in effect saying that all individual minds are the same mind, that *I am you.*

We have encountered this proposition before, as for example in the works of Averroës—where it went on to become one of the *forbidden propositions*—and Giordano Bruno, who in 1600 was burned at the stake for asserting it. And Spinoza was censored and banished for merely implying it. At the dawn of the twentieth century Royce reawakened the thought, philosophically legitimizing it into the American philosophical experience. Similar eruptions can be experienced in many poetical and literary works of the time, most notably in Mark Twain's *Mysterious*

Stranger and as a centerpiece in one of the greatest poems ever written, *Song of Myself* by Walt Whitman.

We ought also, in the interest of preparing ourselves for the subsequent developments in twentieth-century analytic philosophy, to pay careful attention to Royce's argument concerning the role of *meaning*. Like Ludwig Wittgenstein (Chapter 23), Royce argued that the notion of an *x* that is a pure unknowable would literally be nonsense:

⚹

Only ideas are knowable. And nothing absolutely unknowable can exist. For the absolutely unknowable, the *x* pure and simple, the Kantian thing in itself, simply cannot be admitted. The notion of it is nonsense.

⚹

Such notions having to do with the role and nature of meaning will be discussed by Wittgenstein, Russell, and Quine—debates whose outcomes had a lot to do with the structuring of twentieth-century philosophy. For our present purposes, let us close with the following section where Royce establishes the sovereignty of his idealism by default, via the notion that a nonidealistic worldview is not merely *false* but, in fact, *meaningless:*

⚹

But with this result we come in presence of a final problem. All this, you say, depends upon my assurance that there is after all a real and therefore an essentially knowable and rational world yonder. Such a world would have to be in essence a mind, or a world of minds. But after all, how does one ever escape from the prison of the inner life? Am I not in all this merely wandering amidst the realm of my own ideas? *My* world, of course, isn't and can't be a mere *x*, an essentially unknowable thing,

From Josiah Royce, *The World and the Individual* (New York: Macmillan, 1899).

just because it *is my* world, and I have an idea of it. But then does not this mean that *my* world is, after all, forever just *my* world, so that I never get to any truth beyond myself? Isn't this result very disheartening? My world is thus a world of ideas, but alas! how do I then ever reach those ideas of the minds beyond me?

The answer is a simple, but in one sense a very problematic one. You, in one sense, namely, never *do* or can get beyond your own ideas, nor ought you to wish to do so, because in truth all those other minds that constitute your outer and real world are in essence one with your own self. This whole world of ideas is essentially *one* world, and so it is essentially the world of one self and *That art Thou.*

The truth and meaning of this deepest proposition of all idealism is now not at all remote from us. The considerations, however, upon which it depends are of the dryest possible sort, as commonplace as they are deep.

Whatever objects you may think about, whether they are objects directly known to you, or objects infinitely far removed, objects in the distant stars, or objects remote in time, or objects near and present—such objects, then, as a number with fifty places of digits in it, or the mountains on the other side of the moon, or the day of your death, or the character of Cromwell, or the law of gravitation, or a name that you are just now trying to think of and have forgotten, or the meaning of some mood or feeling or idea now in your mind,—all such objects, I insist, stand in a certain constant and curious relation to your mind whenever you are thinking about them,—a relation that we often miss because it is so familiar. What is this relation? Such an object, while you think about it, needn't be, as popular thought often supposes it to be, the *cause* of your thoughts concerning it. Thus, when you think about Cromwell's character, Cromwell's character isn't just now *causing* any ideas in you,— isn't, so to speak, doing anything to you. Cromwell is dead, and after life's fitful fever his character is a very inactive thing. Not as the *cause*, but as the *object* of your thought is Cromwell present to you. Even so, if you choose now to think of the moment of your death, that moment is somewhere off there in the future, and you can make it your object, but it isn't now an active cause of your ideas. The moment of your death has no present physical existence at all, and just now causes nothing. So, too, with the mountains on the other side of the moon. When you make them the object of your thought, they remain indifferent to you. They do not affect you. You never saw them. But all the same you can think about them.

Yet this thinking *about* things is, after all, a very curious relation in which to stand to things. In order to think *about* a thing, it is *not* enough that I should have an idea in me that merely resembles that thing. This last is a very important observation. I repeat, it is *not* enough that I should merely have an idea in me that resembles the thing whereof I think. I have, for instance, in me the idea of a pain. Another man has a pain just like mine. Say we both have toothache; or have both burned our finger-tips in the same way. Now my idea of pain is just like the pain in him, but I am not on that account necessarily thinking about *his* pain, merely because what I am thinking about, namely my own pain, resembles his pain. No; to think about an object you must not merely have an idea that resembles the object, but you must *mean* to have your idea resemble that object. Stated in other form, to think of an object you must consciously aim at that object, you must pick out that object, you must already in some measure possess that object enough, namely, to identify it as what you mean. But how can you *mean*, how can you *aim at,* how can you *possess,* how can you *pick out,* how can you *identify* what is not already present in essence to your own hidden self? Here is surely a deep question. When you aim at yonder object, be it the mountains in the moon or the day of your death, you really say, "I, as my real self, as my larger self, as my complete consciousness, already in deepest truth possess that object, have it, own it, identify it. And that, and that alone, makes it possible for me in my transient, my individual, my momentary personality, to mean yonder object, to inquire about it, to be partly aware of it and partly ignorant of it." You can't mean what is utterly foreign to you. You mean an object, you assert about it, you talk about it, yes, you doubt or wonder about it, you admit your private and individual ignorance about it, only in so far as your larger self, your deeper personality, your total of normal consciousness already *has* that object. Your momentary and private wonder, ignorance, inquiry, or assertion, about the object, implies, asserts, presupposes, that your total self is in full and immediate possession of the object. This, in fact, is the

very nature of that curious relation of a thought to an object which we are now considering. The self that is doubting or asserting, or that is even feeling, its private ignorance about an object, and that still, even in consequence of all this, is *meaning,* is *aiming at* such object, is in essence identical with the self for which this object exists in its complete and consciously known truth.

So paradoxical seems this final assertion of idealism that I cannot hope in one moment to make it very plain to you. . . . But what I intend by thus saying that the self which thinks about an object, which really, even in the midst of the blindest ignorance and doubt concerning its object still means the object,—that this self is identical with the deeper self which possesses and truly knows the object,—what I intend hereby I can best illustrate by simple cases taken from your own experience. You are in doubt, say, about a name that you have forgotten, or about a thought that you just had, but that has now escaped you. As you hunt for the name or the lost idea, you are all the while sure that you mean just one particular name or idea and no other. But you don't yet know what name or idea this is. You try, and reject name after name. You query, "Was this what I was thinking of, or this?" But after searching you erelong find the name or the idea, and now at once you *recognize* it. "Oh, that," you say, "was what I meant all along, only—I didn't know what I meant." Did you know? Yes, in one sense you knew all the while,— that is, your deeper self, your true consciousness knew. It was your momentary self that did not know. But when you found the long-sought name, recalled the lost idea, you recognized it at once, because it was all the while your own, because you, the true and larger self, who owned the name or the idea and were aware of what it was, now were seen to include the smaller and momentary self that sought the name or tried to recall the thought. Your deeper consciousness of the lost idea was all the while there. In fact, did you not presuppose this when you sought the lost idea? How can I mean a name, or an idea, unless I in truth am the self who knows the name, who possesses the idea? In hunting for the name or the lost idea, I am hunting for my own thought. Well, just so I know nothing about the far-off stars in detail, but in so far as I mean the far-off stars at all, as I speak of them, I am identical with that remote and deep thought of my own that already knows the stars. When I study the stars, I am trying to find out what I really mean by them. To be sure, only experience can tell me, but that is because only experience can bring me into relation with my larger self. The escape from the prison of the inner self is simply the fact that the inner self is through and through an appeal to a larger self. The self that inquires, either inquires without meaning, or if it has a meaning, this meaning exists in and for the larger self that knows.

Here is a suggestion of what I mean by Synthetic Idealism. No truth, I repeat, is more familiar. That I am always meaning to inquire into objects beyond me, what clearer fact could be mentioned? That only in case it is already I who, in deeper truth, in my real and hidden thought, *know* the lost object yonder, the object whose nature I seek to comprehend, that only in this case I can truly *mean* the thing yonder,—this, as we must assert, is involved in the very idea of *meaning*. That is the logical analysis of it. You can mean what your deeper self knows; you cannot mean what your deeper self doesn't know. To be sure, the complete illustration of this most critical insight of idealism belongs elsewhere. Few see the familiar. Nothing is more common than for people to think that they mean objects that have nothing to do with themselves. Kant it was, who, despite his things in themselves, first showed us that nobody really means an object, really knows it, or doubts it, or aims at it, unless he does so by aiming at a truth that is present to his own larger self. Except for the unity of my true self, taught Kant, I have no objects. And so it makes no difference whether I know a thing or am in doubt about it. So long as I really *mean* it, that is enough. The self that *means* the object is identical with the larger self that possesses the object, just as when you seek the lost idea you are already in essence with the self that possesses the lost idea.

In this way I suggest to you the proof which a rigid analysis of the logic of our most commonplace thought would give for the doctrine that in the world there is but *one* Self, and that it is *his* world which we all alike are truly meaning, whether we talk of one another or of Cromwell's character or of the fixed stars or of the far-off æons of the future. The relation of my thought to its object has, I insist, this curious character, that *unless* the thought and its object are parts of one larger thought I can't even be *meaning* that object yonder, can't even be in error about it, can't even doubt its existence. You, for instance, are part of one larger self with me, or else I can't even be meaning to address you as outer beings. You are part of one larger self along with the most mysterious or most remote fact of nature, along with the moon, and all the hosts of heaven, along with all truth and all beauty. Else could you not even intend to speak of such objects beyond you. For whatever you speak of you will find that your world is meant by you as just your world. Talk of the unknowable, and it forthwith becomes your unknowable, your problem, whose solution, unless the problem be a mere nonsense question, your larger self must own and be aware of. The deepest problem of life is, "What is this deeper self?" And the only answer is, *It is the self that knows in unity all truth.* This, I insist, is no hypothesis. It is actually the presupposition of your deepest doubt. And that is why I say: Everything finite is more or less obscure, dark, doubtful. Only the Infinite Self, the problem-solver, the complete thinker, the one who knows what we mean even when we are most confused and ignorant, the one who includes us, who has the world present to himself in unity, before whom all past and future truth, all distant and dark truth is clear in one eternal moment, to whom far and forgot is near, who thinks the whole of nature, and in whom are all things, the Logos, the world-possessor,—only his existence, I say, is perfectly sure.

⁂

NOTES

1. The best textbook ever written on the subject, by my lights, is Umberto Eco's *A Theory of Semiotics* (Indiana University Press, 1979). This is the same Umberto Eco who wrote the best-selling novels *The Name of the Rose,* which was turned into a movie, and *Foucault's Pendulum.*

2. "A World of Pure Experience," William James, *Journal of Philosophy, Psychology and Scientific Methods,* Vol. 1, No. 20 (1904), reprinted in Daniel Kolak, *From Plato to Wittgenstein: The Historical Foundations of Mind* (Belmont, CA: Wadsworth, 1994.)

21 ⚘ The European Experience: Brentano, Husserl, Heidegger, and Sartre

21.0 Brentano (1838–1917): The Intentional Philosopher

Franz Brentano was born in 1838 in Marienberg, Germany. His father, Christian Brentano, was a noted romantic writer, as were his uncle Clemens Brentano and his sister Bettina von Armin. He attended the Royal Bavarian Gymnasium in Aschaffenburg, where at age seventeen he began to experience grave religious doubts that tormented him for the rest of his life. At the University of Munich he studied theology, focusing on Aquinas and Aristotle. In 1862, at the age of twenty-four, he published his first book: *On the Several Senses of Being in Aristotle*, earning his doctorate from the University of Tübingen. He was ordained as a priest in 1864.

Two years later, Brentano became a *Privatdozen* in philosophy at the University of Würzburg, where he presented a paper to the faculty entitled, "Exposition and Critique of Schelling's Teaching in his Three Phases," for which he received much praise. He followed with "The Psychology of Aristotle, in Particular his Doctrine of *Nous Poietikos*," in which he pre-

sented not only a new interpretation of Aristotle but also a new method for understanding philosophers. The idea was to study the philosopher's views and to immerse oneself into the character of his spirit, to take on the self or personality of the philosopher as a modern actor might take on a role by "becoming" that person. In this way one should, through the process of identification, become in effect identical to the philosopher one is studying, thereby bringing the ideas to life under the same thought patterns that originally gave rise to them.

Besides trying to revive within himself the minds of Aristotle and Aquinas, Brentano immersed himself in the philosophies and characters of Descartes, Leibniz, and Kant. Subsequently, his lectures on metaphysics, logic, psychology, and the history of philosophy were regarded by faculty and students alike as the best they had ever heard. He had a powerful and lasting influence on his students, many of whom—such as Carl Stumpf, Anton Marty, and Edmund Husserl (see next section)—went on to great success.

According to Brentano, the history of philosophy can be seen as evolving in four stages, based on the theory of the three phases of human development according to Auguste Comte (see pp. 420–424). Brentano saw Comte as a great realist critic of the leading German idealist philosophies of the time (led by Fichte, Schelling, and Hegel) which Brentano regarded as "decadent mysticism." Such idealisms must, according to Brentano, give way to a scientific positivism—related to the anti-metaphysical trend of the "positive" philosophy of the Vienna Circle but much more closely aligned with positivism as espoused by Comte.

In 1870 Brentano made a formal break from the Catholic Church, based on his published criticism of the dogma of papal infallibility. He claimed that the infallibility doctrine contradicts three major source—the Gospels, the teaching of the Church fathers, and the complete history of the Church. He not only left the priesthood but also resigned his professorship. A year later he received a professorship at the University of Vienna and published his greatest work, *Psychology from an Empirical Starting Point*, in which he developed the view of intentionality that has become central in philosophy to this day.

Through his students, Brentano was influential in giving rise to several of the most important philosophical movements of the twentieth century, which were led by philosophers such as Edmund Husserl, who founded phenomenology, and Alexius Meinong, who founded the School of Graz. Other students of his exerted great political influence in Europe; his disciples von Hertling and Masaryk became great enemies during the First World War; von Hertling as the chancellor of Germany, and Masaryk as the president of Czechoslovakia. Other great philosophers, as diverse as Martin Heidegger and Bertrand Russell, said that Brentano was one of the most important influences in their own work.

21.1 Husserl (1859–1938): The Founder of Phenomenology

Edmund Husserl was born at Prossnitz in Moravia of Jewish parents. He studied mathematics

in Leipzig, Berlin, and finally Vienna where, in 1884, he attended Brentano's lectures, which had a profound effect on him: "Without Brentano I should have written not a word of philosophy." It was after hearing these lectures that Husserl decided to give up mathematics for philosophy. He subsequently taught in Halle, Göttingen, and Freiburg im Breisgau.

Brentano's views were rooted in the Aristotle-inspired scholastic theory of "intentional inexistence," which he called "immanent objectivity," a phrase used to distinguish mental from physical phenomena. In "Intentionality" he explains:

⚹

Every mental phenomenon is characterized by what the Scholastics of the Middle Ages called the intentional (or mental) inexistence of an object, and what we might call, though not wholly unambiguously, reference to a content, direction toward an object (which is not to be understood here as meaning a thing), or immanent objectivity. Every mental phenomenon includes something as object within itself, although they do not all do so in the same way. In presentation something is presented, in judgment something is affirmed or denied, in love loved, in hate hated, in desire desired and so on.

⚹

Brentano's notion of intentionality not only was the starting point for Husserl's philosophy but also influenced many analytic philosophers in their analysis of meaning, reference, and the relation between mind and language.

As the founder of the influential European philosophical tradition to which he gave the name *phenomenology* (from the Greek *phainomenon*, "appearance," thus "the study of appearances"), Husserl's goal was to create a pure, non-

---

From Franz Brentano, "Intentionality," in *Psychology from an Empirical Standpoint*, original German edition 1924 (London: Routledge, 1973).

empirical science for describing and defining the genuine essence (*eidos*) of conscious data within the domain of formal logic and mathematics. Although phenomenology has sometimes been construed as developing in marked opposition to logical positivism and the originators of analytic philosophy, Husserl corresponded with and was highly influenced by Frege,[1] who in turn was influenced in his view of mathematics by Husserl. Also, the founders of the twentieth-century mathematical movement known as *intuitionism* owe a lot to Husserl's work, particularly his shift from a Kantian emphasis on the fundamentality of the a priori nature of space to taking the a priori nature of time as being more basic and fundamental to an analysis of the structure and content of the mind.

Like Descartes, Husserl takes consciousness to be the foundation of all philosophy, but instead of building theories to get from the mind to the world, or evoking as Descartes and Berkeley did the notion of God, Husserl focuses on a purely descriptive and nontheoretical account of consciousness to try to see directly how the world appears, or "reveals itself," to consciousness. This revelation, for Husserl, means the real world of everyday experience, free of theoretical philosophy and science. The purpose is to get "behind" the *content* of consciousness, where the deep structure of the world can reveal itself through the *structure* of consciousness. The method—similar to Descartes's method of doubt, which Husserl calls "phenomenological reduction" or *epoché* (Greek for "suspension of belief")—is to "bracket" an experience. This means describing experience purely in experiential terms without the usual assumptions and presuppositions surrounding it. This way one can "illuminate" the objects of intentionality by which Husserl means the ordinary objects in conscious experience.

Such a phenomenological reduction reveals consciousness as it presents itself. Here, for instance, is an example of a phenomenological reduction from his *Phenomenology of Internal Time-Consciousness:*

⚹

Let us look at a piece of chalk. We close and open our eyes. We have two perceptions, but we say of them that we see the same piece of chalk twice. We have, thereby, contents which are separated temporally. We also can see a phenomenological, temporal apartness, a separation, but there is no separation in the object. It is the same. In the object there is duration, in the phenomenon, change. Similarly, we can also subjectively sense a temporal sequence where Objectively a coexistence is to be established. The lived and experienced content is "Objectified," and the Object is now constituted from the material of this content in the mode of apprehension. The object, however, is not merely the sum or complexion of this "content," which does not enter into the object at all. The object is more than the content and other than it. Objectivity belongs to "experience," that is, to the unity of experience, to the lawfully experienced context of nature. Phenomenologically speaking, Objectivity is not even constituted through "primary" content but through characters of apprehension and the regularities which pertain to the essence of these characters. It is precisely the business of the phenomenology of cognition to grasp this fully and to make it completely intelligible.

⚹

Husserl applied his method to what in his view is the essential manifold of the real world, our conscious experience of time—an idea that is further developed in Heidegger's masterpiece, *Being and Time* (which we shall look at in the next section).

Such phenomenological reductions can also be performed on an act of consciousness itself. This reduction allows the philosopher to peek behind ordinary appearance into the pure consciousness of the "transcendental ego," to see directly into the heart of the hidden self—that

From Edmund Husserl, *Phenomenology of Internal Time-Consciousness*, Martin Heidegger, ed., James Churchill, trans. (Bloomington: Indiana University Press, 1964).

authentic consciousness behind the mask. Moreover, like the Cartesian "I think," Husserl's phenomenological reduction is supposed to provide an absolutely certain foundation for knowledge.

Husserl distinguishes *natural thinking* in science and everyday life, which to him are both aspects of naive realism. In both natural science and in our ordinary, day-to-day thinking, we are "untroubled by the difficulties concerning the possibility of cognition." This sort of thought— the type done in ordinary, unreflective life and in the most sophisticated science and mathematics—is contrasted with what he calls *philosophical thought,* which he defined by "one's position toward the problems concerning the possibility of cognition." In other words, how does science arise in the first place and how is it practiced, if not by disregarding just about all the deep philosophical questions we have raised? Say the scientist starts performing experiments with inclined planes, or even thinking theoretically about inertia, momentum, and so on. The scientist does this *without ever being concerned with the questions of what makes an experience possible and what makes a thought possible.* In Husserl's view this lack leads to

⚹

Absurdity: to begin with, when we think naturally about cognition and fit it and its achievements into the natural ways of thinking which pertains to the sciences we arrive at theories that are appealing at first. But they end in contradiction or absurdity, inclining one to open skepticism.

⚹

What does it mean to think "naturally"? It means merely to think as thinking happens, without doing anything special. Philosophy in general and phenomenology in particular are, in that sense, *un*natural. They don't arise *naturally* in one's own daily life.

There is a deep subtlety here, one that has often been misunderstood by philosophers

attempting to comprehend Husserl. Some of them are confused by his call to the study of the experience objects unencumbered by theory and interpretation from a theoretical perspective. Think of logic and mathematics as opposed to *natural* language and you will understand the essence of Husserl's point; just as logic and mathematics are *formal* rather than *natural* languages, so phenomenology is *formal* rather than *natural* experience. And just as a formal language tool like logic can be instrumental to the study of natural language, so a formal experiential tool like phenomenology can be instrumental to the study of natural experience. Therefore it should not be surprising that phenomenology is extremely technical, like logic. Indeed, in his early work that has not been translated into English, Husserl equated his technique of phenomenology with using the concept of *pure logic,* through which one could achieve a *seeing of the fundamental logical forms themselves, that is, the categories of thought.* The task of pure phenomenology is then to test the genuineness and range of this logical "seeing" by distinguishing it from ordinary ways *of being conscious.*

As he sets out to explain in *The Idea of Phenomenology* lectures he delivered in Göttingen in 1907, the method is not

⚹

about perception or having a vague intension or idea of it. Instead, perception itself stands open to my inspection as actually or imaginatively given to me. And the same is true of every intellectual process, of every form of thinking and cognizing.

I have here put on the same level the "seeing" [act of] reflective perception and [the "seeing" act of reflective] imagination. If one followed the Cartesian view, one would have to emphasize perception first; it would in some measure correspond to the so-called inner perception of traditional epistemology, though this is an ambivalent concept.

William Alston and George Nakhnikian, trans. (The Hague: Martinus Nijhoff, 1973).

Every intellectual process and indeed every mental process whatever, while being enacted, *can be made the object of a pure "seeing" and under-standing, and is something absolutely given in this "seeing."* It is given as something that is, that is here and now, and whose being cannot be sensibly doubted. To be sure, I can wonder what sort of being this is and how this mode of being is related to other modes. It is true I can wonder what given-ness means *here*, and reflecting further I can "see" the "seeing" itself in which this givenness, or this mode of being, is constituted. But all the same I am now working on an absolute foundation: namely, this perception is, and remains as long as it lasts, something absolute, something here and now, something that in itself is what it is, something by which I can measure as by an ultimate standard what being and being given can mean and here must mean, at least, obviously, as far as the sort of being and being given is concerned which a "here and now" exemplifies. And that goes for all specific ways of thinking, whenever they are given. All of these, however, can also be data in imagination; they can "as it were" stand before our eyes and yet not stand before them as actualities, as actually accomplished perceptions, judgments, etc.; even then, they are, in a certain sense, data. They are there *open to intuition.* We talk about them not in just vague hints and empty intention. We inspect them, and while inspecting them we can observe their essence, their constitution, their intrinsic char-acter, and we can make our speech conform in a pure measure to what is "seen" in its full clarity.

※

This process can be performed by the phe-nomenologist either on the object of intention-ality, such as a piece of chalk, or *on an act of con-sciousness.* It is this second step in the phenome-nological reduction, the *epoché,* that moves the field of consciousness back from its normal state to an enlightened pure consciousness, reaching its own transcendental ego, the Transcendental Self behind the self. Like the Cartesian *I am,* only more deeply real, this marks the new, Husserlian starting point for *philosophical,* as opposed to merely scientific, knowledge.

Husserl's phenomenology, his descriptive

method, and his theory of intentionality became the source of the phenomenological movement in philosophy, while his further development of Brentano's theory of intentionality—the view that all consciousness is essentially referential, that is, consciousness *of* something—was incor-porated both by "phenomenologists" and "ana-lytic" philosophers. In Germany, Husserl's phi-losophy continued most notably in the work of Martin Heidegger; in France its two leading pro-ponents were Maurice Merleau-Ponty and Husserl's most famous pupil, Jean-Paul Sartre, who used phenomenology to create another widely influential movement, existentialism.

21.2 Heidegger (1889–1976): In Search of Being

Martin Heidegger was born in Messkirch in the Black Forest. At the University of Freiburg he studied philosophy with Edmund Husserl, whose phenomenological method for inquiry into the immediate data of experience exerted a lasting influence on Heidegger's own highly original work. In 1923 Heidegger became pro-fessor at Marburg. Five years later he succeeded his former mentor Husserl (to whom *Being and Time* is dedicated) at Freiburg, where he was then elected rector (president) of the university. Although Heidegger did not consider himself an existentialist, he inspired the great French exis-tentialist Jean-Paul Sartre as well as many philosophers in both the phenomenological and analytic traditions. He also drew his share of both philosophical and personal criticism. In a famous 1932 article, "The Elimination of Metaphysics," the logical positivist Rudolf Carnap used Heidegger as a supposed example of "philosophical nonsense," and he was also criticized for being a Nazi sympathizer. More recently, in the influential *Philosophy and the Mirror of Nature* (1979), Richard Rorty called Heidegger one of the three most important philosophers of the twentieth century (along with Dewey and Wittgenstein).

Like Husserl, Heidegger regarded as essential the "bracketing," or disregarding, of all preconceived epistemological and logical assumptions ordinarily used to distinguish consciousness from the external world. According to Heidegger existence must be apprehended directly via the analysis of human *Dasein,* by which he means individual "being there," the conscious agent of participation and involvement with the events of experience:

⊥

Dasein is an entity which does not just occur among other entities. Rather it is . . . distinguished by the fact that, in its very Being, that Being is an *issue* for it. But in that case, this is a constitutive state of Dasein's Being, and this implies that Dasein, in its Being, has a relationship towards that Being—a relationship which itself is one of Being. And this means further that there is some way in which Dasein understands itself in its Being, and that to some degree it does so explicitly. It is peculiar to this entity that with and through its Being, this Being is disclosed to it. Understanding of Being is itself a definite characteristic of Dasein's Being. Dasein is . . . distinctive in that it is ontological.

⊥

In Being and Time (1927), from which this passage is taken, Heidegger uses language expressly for the purpose of moving beyond the limitations of language so as to have a philosophically direct and intimate relation with Being. To understand what he is after here we must make sure we understand the three-level distinction in his use of the concept of *being.*

Consider the world—whatever it really is— as the totality of facts. A fact is something that is the case (whether we know it or not, let us say), so there is the totality of the way things are, making up the world (as a totality). Presumably, if one made a list of all the facts, one would in principle have a map of the entire world. But how do you *list* facts? You can, at best, list sentences that express propositions.

What, then, is the relationship between a proposition and a fact? Well, some propositions are false. Others are true. Facts, as such, aren't "true" or "false." They just *are.* You see the problem facing Heidegger (and us)? Well, what *are* these facts? What do they consist of? Matter? Ah—by now we should realize that this won't work, any more than the concept of "mind" will work. For if everything consists of matter, then there is the fact that matter exists *and this is not a piece of matter.* Or, if everything consists of ideas, then there is the fact that ideas exist *and this is not a piece of an idea. Well, what then are such things?*

Such talk may be empty and meaningless as some philosophers have charged, or it may be profound. But in any case Heidegger is trying to reach *the facts, not propositions as represented in language, but even beyond them.* The whole process may indeed be empty and meaningless, but that does not make the effort any less profound.

Thus, Heidegger distinguishes entities that make up the world—the individual existent beings—and Being itself, the "fact that the world itself exists," not the *existence of the world* as such but *that* the world exists. The obscurity of this thinking process that we are at this moment engaging in is, according to Heidegger, itself the result of our being in the world, "being too close to being" to see it. To use a visual metaphor, think of the eye not seeing the eye—why doesn't it? At this moment why do your eyes not see the eyes? Well, if you think about it, you will realize that the eye needs to be some *distance* from anything that it is looking at; the closer the object is, the blurrier, until—to speak in terms of a phenomenological reduction—the thing being looked at becomes unseeable as the object that it is. In this way the eye (again, still phenomenologically speaking) must by necessity disappear from itself in order to see. (Part of Heidegger's overall philosophical program is to give us some *distance* from being in order to see being—a paradox that some have used to liken Heidegger's philosophy to a certain aspect of Zen Buddhism.)

Thus far, then, we have the first two-level distinction between being—or, being-as-entity in the world—and Being, the fact of the existence of the entire world. The third, crucial, Heideggerian distinction is not between being and Being but an identification, among all the individual entities, of the one unique type of being, described in the preceding passage: Dasein. That identification is why he says that "Dasein is an entity which does not just occur among other entities." It is also why, instead of just talking about "I" or "consciousness" or "being," he uses as a technical term the German word *Dasein*. I, as Dasein, *this being here in the world,* exist not just as a being having a certain physical boundary, a size, certain personal and cultural psychological characteristics, and so on; nor do I, as Dasein, merely use language as a specific type of tool when I think, will, experience fear, and so on. Rather, it is that in my own being, my very presence in the world, I do not merely exist; my very existence is "an *issue.*" This issue he defines, again by using an ordinary German word in a technical way, as *existence.* When Heidegger speaks of existence, he is speaking of the unique characteristic of Dasein: Dasein *exists.* This existence involves, in part, always projecting itself beyond the given present into the not-yet-present future possibilities.

In other words, by being aware of the present moment, its existence within us, in light of what it has been—the past—and what it could become—the future—we escape the confinement in which beings that are *not* Dasein do not have: for instance, spiders, snakes, birds, and bees. They are beings who are mere automata; the bird never asks, "Why am I a bird and not an elephant?" Making what is not there present to consciousness is the unique aspect of human consciousness that makes us *uniquely* and *radically* free. Thus in Heidegger's view the world is structured into different regions of existential modalities dispersed through an environment consisting of accessible and utilizable objects so that human knowledge *and* human existence cannot be divorced from human action. In this

way he is paving the way for the development of the philosophical movement known as *existentialism* (which we shall explore in detail in the next section), carried to its fruition by Jean-Paul Sartre.

In his masterpiece, *Being and Time* (1927), Heidegger continues to trace the fundamental question of metaphysics back to Plato and Aristotle and then sets out to discover the very *meaning* of all being. This discovery cannot be achieved through sophisticated theories using concepts like substance and cause but, rather, must be attained through the philosophical investigation of Dasein, one's own individual human presence, the "being there" of the world as it concerns itself with its own basic situation and aims through active participation and involvement with the rest of being. And just as the fundamental question for each individual Dasein is "Why do I exist?" (or "Why was I ever born?" or "Why did I ever come to be rather than never having existed?")—that too is the question for the entire world. This question leads Heidegger into an analysis of the most fundamental question of being: Why is there something rather than nothing?

Heidegger devoted an entire book, his *Introduction to Metaphysics* (1959), to this question. He explains why this question cannot properly be addressed either by science or by religion but only by philosophy:

⋆

It is perfectly true that we cannot talk about nothing, as though it were a thing like the rain outside or a mountain or any object whatsoever. In principle, nothingness remains inaccessible to science. 'The man who wishes truly to speak about nothing must of necessity become unscientific. But this is a misfortune only, so long as one supposes that scientific thinking is the only authentic rigorous thought, and that it alone can and must be made into the standard of philosophical thinking.

From Martin Heidegger, *Introduction to Metaphysics* (New Haven, CT: Yale University Press, 1959).

But the reverse is true. All scientific thought is merely a derived form of philosophical thinking, which proceeded to freeze into its scientific cast. . . . To speak of nothing will always remain a horror and an absurdity for science. . . . Authentic speaking about nothing always remains extraordinary. It cannot be vulgarized. It dissolves if it is placed in the cheap acid of a merely logical intelligence.

⚓

It has been said that there are two sorts of persons: those for whom this question arises at some point in their lives, and those for whom it does not. Have you ever asked this question of yourself? All this—why does it exist? Why is there something rather than nothing? This question is the biggest one of all. It extends to everything. It asks: Why existence? Why does anything exist? Why isn't there just nothing?

Heidegger uses this question to remove the borders among all things before us, to reduce the many to an undifferentiated one and to ask: *why being rather than nonbeing?* If we do not discriminate among things, the question extends to everything. It lumps all the things in the world into one and asks: Why is there a world, any world, rather than no world? By ignoring the quantity, quality, and types of existent things, we bring the question of the brute fact of existence into sharp focus. Why existence rather than nonexistence?

The oldest answer to the biggest question is *God*. The reason there is something rather than nothing is that God created it. And the reason God exists is that God has always existed. God is eternal, and the reason God is eternal is that that is God's nature.

One thing nearly all religions have in common is their shared belief in some sort of noncontingent being—a being which exists *necessarily* and which they call *God*. However, if we have understood Heidegger's question properly, *the question of whether God exists is ontologically irrelevant.* It's not that God is the *wrong* answer; God is not even *an* answer. To offer God as an answer is just a very fancy existential bait and switch.

Question: Why is there something rather than nothing?

Answer: Because a Big Something made the little something!

This is not an answer. Heidegger's question asks why *anything,* why *any sort* of anything exists—material, spiritual, neutral monistical, you name it whatever you want—rather than nothing? God is not nothing. God is also something. The question asks about God too. From the point of view of Heidegger's question, a world without God is no less mysterious than a world *with* God. In fact, if God exists, then the biggest question of all time has grown even bigger. *Why is there a (material) world and an immaterial world (God) rather than nothing?* If a world consisting of *contingent* material somethings is puzzling, how much more puzzling is it to find ourselves in a world containing contingent material somethings *plus* a *non*contingent immaterial something? *Why is there something— any type of something, contingent or noncontingent, material or spiritual—rather than nothing?*

Realizing that the question does not have an answer, that it can't possibly have an answer, that it must apply to any existent thing and to any world regardless of what there is, leads to the further realization that the "most" unanswerable question is also the most *meaningful.* It is the presence of this unanswerable possibility of absolute nothing that our own existence negates without any ultimate cause, reason, or explanation, that brings Being most close at hand to consciousness:

⚓

What about this Nothing? . . . Where do we seek the Nothing? How do we find the Nothing? . . . We know the Nothing. . . . What about this Nothing? The Nothing itself nothings. *Anxiety reveals the nothing.*

⚓

Here Heidegger takes an unexpected turn. Instead of an answer, he finds an experience—a deep, profound, *awful* experience in the primordial and etymological sense of *awful*—"filled with awe." But the experience is too much; it reveals the "too muchness" of existence to existence, causing deep existential dread to awaken the Dasein to the presence of the whole of Being. This is not mere fear. Fear always has an *object,* some entity or state. The existential anxiety of which Heidegger speaks reveals the most general form of Dasein's Being. It is not directed at any particular entity in the world, which would amount to one part of the world (for instance, you) relating to another (for instance, an enemy chasing you) but the whole of Being confronting the whole of Being at its fulcrum, which is Dasein: "that in the face of which one has anxiety is Being-in-the-world as such." Being-in-the-world is, itself, the most fundamental existential characteristic of Dasein. This brings us to the final pinnacle of Heidegger's entire philosophy. Dasein is anxious-in-the-face-of *itself.* Ordinarily, Dasein is hidden, absorbed, "alienated" in the various aspects of its living in the world as individual human beings. It is in a state of "fallenness." Awakened to its own presence in the world, catching sight of itself, *the One* that is the everyday Dasein trembles:

꙳

Anxiety thus takes away from Dasein the possibility of understanding itself, as it falls, in terms of the "world" and the way things have been publicly interpreted. Anxiety throws Dasein back upon that which it is anxious about—its authentic potentiality-for-Being-in-the-world. Anxiety individualizes Dasein. . . . Anxiety makes manifest in Dasein its *Being towards* its ownmost potentiality-for-Being—that is, its *Being-free* for the freedom of choosing itself and taking hold of itself.

꙳

In this way Being becomes *forlorn;* it individualizes itself, breaking apart into the many, and experiences itself not as itself, the clearest ontological manifestation of this within you. The

Dasein that you are, at the present moment is the existential division between *self and other.* The clearest existential manifestation of it is anxiety, or the degree to which you feel that deepest, darkest dread of being. Ask someone suffering from anxiety, What do you fear? The answer: *nothing.*

No one has ever illustrated this state better than the great American existentialist writer Ernest Hemingway, in his short story, "A Clean, Well-Lighted Place."

꙳

"Last week he tried to commit suicide," one waiter said.

"Why"

"He was in despair."

"What about?"

"Nothing."

"How do you know it was nothing?"

"He has plenty of money." . . .

"Come on. Stop talking nonsense and lock up."

"I am of those who like to stay late at the café," the older waiter said. He was now dressed to go home. "It is not only a question of youth and confidence although those things are very beautiful. Each night I am reluctant to close up because there may be some one who needs the café."

"Hombre, there are bodegas open all night long."

"You do not understand. This is a clean and pleasant café. It is well lighted. The light is very good and also, now, there are shadows of the leaves."

"Good night," said the younger waiter.

"Good night," the other said. Turning off the electric light he continued the conversation with himself. It is the light of course but it is necessary that the place be clean and pleasant. You do not want music. Certainly you do not want music. Nor can you stand before a bar with dignity although that is all that is provided for these hours. What did he fear? It was not fear or dread. It was a

---

Ernest Hemingway, "A Clean, Well-Lighted Place," in *The Short Stories of Ernest Hemingway* (Charles Scribner's, 1938).

nothing that he knew too well. It was all a nothing and a man was nothing too. It was only that and light was all it needed and a certain cleanness and order. Some lived in it and never felt it but he knew it all was nada y pues nada y nada y pues nada. Our nada who art in nada, nada be thy name thy kingdom nada thy will be nada in nada as it is in nada. Give us this nada our daily nada and nada us our nada as we nada our nadas and nada us not into nada but deliver us from nada, pues nada. Hail nothing full of nothing, nothing is with thee. He smiled and stood before the bar with a shining steam pressure coffee machine.

"What's yours?" asked the barman.

"Nada."

⚓

21.3 Sartre (1905–1980): The French Existentialist

French philosopher, playwright, and novelist Jean-Paul Sartre was born in Paris to an illustrious family. His father was a decorated naval officer, his mother the cousin of the famous theologian and jungle doctor, Albert Schweitzer. Orphaned at a young age, Sartre was raised by his grandfather, in whose rich library he "found my religion: nothing seemed to me more important than a book. I regarded the library as a temple." He went on to study philosophy at the prestigious École Normale Supérieure and then at Göttingen under the direction of Husserl. He taught philosophy for a few years at Le Havre in Paris but then resigned to pursue a full-time writing career.

During World War II Sartre joined the French Army but spent most of his time working on a novel and two plays, often typing in front of his commanding officers, for which he was frequently reprimanded. Captured by the Germans, he was a prisoner of war for eight months during which time he put on plays and gave lectures to the officers on the history of German philosophy from Kant to Husserl; he escaped using papers

that the German officers had forged for him! He returned to the French resistance and promptly resumed his writing and finished two plays—*The Flies* and *No Exit*—both widely regarded as masterpieces. The latter, which has become a paradigm of existentialist drama, contains the famous line, "Hell is other people."

When Sartre's massive philosophical work *Being and Nothingness* appeared in 1943, it was instantly heralded as a new philosophical classic. By war's end, he became the famous proponent of his atheistic brand of existentialism and a world-renowned leader of left-wing intellectuals. In 1964 he won the Nobel Prize but refused to accept it on the grounds that Nobel, who had made his fortune by inventing and selling dynamite, had profited from human suffering and that the prize was but another political tool of the military-industrial complex.

What *is* existentialism? "Most people who use the word," wrote Sartre, "would be embarrassed if they had to explain it, since, now that the word is all the rage, even the work of a musician or painter is being called existentialist." The term refers, as Sartre put it, to the most *austere* of all philosophical doctrines. Before we give his explanation, let us return briefly to Aristotle's concept of essence.

In a nutshell: even though Platonic and Aristotelian philosophies evolved along different, often opposing, lines, Aristotle and Plato both took it as an incontrovertible given that *essence precedes existence*. Think about Plato's ideas; there is the abstract, eternal idea of, say, the triangle, which exists nowhere in the world (but has "Being," in a Parmenidean-Heideggerian sense). Before there can exist an actual, physical representation of a triangle there must be that antecedent idea, or essence; otherwise, the very concept of a representation does not make sense. For Aristotle, everything that exists exists for a purpose; there is some end for which everything is designed by nature to strive. Nature is teleological. The essence of the thing, its defining characteristic, is part of its being in the world—the very core of its individuality. Even in

Leibniz's work, according to which this is the best of all possible worlds, the concept of something existing without any reason is incomprehensible, meaningless; his principle of sufficient reason is one of the foundational principles of reality. In religious contexts, such as Christianity ("Platonism for the masses"), prior to the existence of *anything* in the world, indeed, prior to the existence of the world entire, there is God, in whose mind the essence of all things precedes their arrival on the scene in the world of God's creation. God doesn't just randomly throw stuff into existence; there is purpose and design in God's plan, and so on.

Sartre turns all this upside down. Instead of essence preceding existence, in his view it is the other way around: *existence precedes essence*. This view, then, is the *starting point* as well as the *end point* of the philosophy known as existentialism, but it does not apply to all beings. Just as we saw the special role played by Dasein in Heidegger's analysis, so human existence is the very fulcrum of existentialism. Unlike most other things in the world, it is true in the sphere of human existence; even if everything else in the world were prefabricated and predetermined, we would still be free, according to Sartre, *radically* so.

He asks us to compare our existence with that of a fabricated object such as a paper cutter. In the case of the paper cutter, the concept, the need, the essence, preceded its existence. There was a need in the world for paper cutters, some craftsperson had an idea to make one, he or she came up with several designs until the best one was found, and then made one according to the conception. In our case, however, we are thrown into the world, forlorn, purposeless. Indeed, were God to exist, some of the problem of our own existence would thereby be alleviated (for us, that is, but not for God, for whom the problem would be even worse!). *But God is dead.*

The death of God, says Sartre, which other philosophers have tried to pass over quietly so as not to disturb the public and to leave religion alone on the supposition (false, in Sartre's view) that faith in God is necessary for our well being

(in fact it is the cause of much of our suffering), is itself a cause for great alarm and dread. It is the very source of our forlornness.

⚓

Existentialism

When we speak of forlornness, a term Heidegger was fond of, we mean only that God does not exist and that we have to face all the consequences of this. The existentialist is strongly opposed to a certain kind of secular ethics which would like to abolish God with the least possible expense. . . . The existentialist, on the contrary, thinks it very distressing that God does not exist, because all possibility of finding values in a heaven of ideas disappears along with Him. . . . Nowhere is it written that the Good exists, that we must be honest, that we must not lie . . . Dostoievsky said, "If God didn't exist, everything would be possible." That is the very starting point of existentialism. Indeed, everything is permissible if God does not exist, and as a result man is forlorn, because neither within him nor without does he find anything to cling to. He can't start making excuses for himself. If existence really does precede essence, there is no explaining things away by reference to a fixed and given human nature. . . . we have no excuse behind us, nor justification before us. We are alone, with no excuses.

⚓

Again Sartre's famous "existence precedes essence" formula is not true for most objects in the world; in the case of tables, chairs, and paper cutters, "essence"—what they essentially are and what they are for—precedes their existence. The idea comes first, as a concept or notion in the mind, and then the object is created following the preconceived blueprint. Human existence has no blueprint, no designer, no creator. God does not exist and so no antecedent idea of human nature exists; there is no given purpose to life, no

From Jean-Paul Sartre, *Existentialism*, Bernard Frechtman, trans. (Philosophical Library, 1957).

essence that precedes human existence. Only after we emerge into the universe as existent entities do we define our own essence, arbitrarily, but through choice. Because there is no God there can be no prefabricated meaning; human beings are forlorn. We are each condemned to be free since we cannot ever do otherwise than choose who and what we are. Nothing is given except that nothing is given. We are fully and radically responsible for our lives.

But there is a deeper level—even if God exists—*so what?*

⚹

Existentialism isn't so atheistic that it wears itself out showing that God doesn't exist, that would change nothing. There you've got our point of view. Not that we believe that God exists, but we think that the problem of His existence is not the issue. In this sense existentialism is optimistic, a doctrine of action.

⚹

The problem is that we do not allow ourselves to really see our own inescapable freedom because we fear it. Just as in Heidegger's notion of anxiety, *fear of freedom* is not a fear of any object, but a fear of a lack of direction, a lack of certainty, a lack of there being some way that things have to be or must be. We don't want to have to choose. We shield ourselves from the fact that it is we who make up meaning by pretending that we are what we are, that we have a fixed nature, when really it's all made up.

You die and find yourself in heaven before someone claiming to be God. Maybe this apparent entity appears to work miracles, explains things to you, and so on. Is anything now fixed, determined, settled? Nothing. Is this God? *How do you know?* Ultimately, you still have to decide. Is it the devil playing tricks? Is it some aspect of your own mind? A priori, there are an infinity of possible worlds perfectly consistent with the world you see. Of these interpretations, many are equally preposterous (or equally plausible).

There will *always,* Sartre is careful to point out, be a multitude of interpretations of anything—which viewpoint has sometimes been called the "hermeneutic circle."[2]

But Sartre does not view this multiplicity of interpretations as something negative, since it makes human beings the true artists of themselves and their world. Going about looking for the meaning of life, Sartre might say, is like staring at a blank canvas, looking for the greatest painting. Searching misses the point. The blankness is not horrible, any more than having always to choose from among many equally plausible colors and brushes is horrible; it is not the end of the world, but the beginning, for now there is room for an infinity of possibilities. What we choose to paint and how we choose to paint it are arbitrary, but paintings are not arbitrary.

In his famous novel, *Nausea,* Sartre describes the feeling of realizing that there is no necessity in the world, that everything is radically *contingent:*

⚹

This moment was extraordinary. I was there, motionless and icy, plunged in a horrible ecstasy. But something fresh had just appeared in the very heart of this ecstasy; I understood the Nausea, I possessed it. To tell the truth, I did not formulate my discoveries to myself. But I think it would be easy for me to put them in words now. The essential thing is contingency. I mean that one cannot define existence as necessity. To exist is simply *to be there*; those who exist let themselves be encountered, but you can never deduce anything from them. I believe there are people who have understood this. Only they tried to overcome this contingency by inventing a necessary, causal being. But no necessary being can explain existence: contingency is not a delusion, a probability which can be dissipated; it is the absolute, consequently, the perfect free gift. All is free, this park, this city and myself. When you realize that, it turns your heart upside down and everything begins to float.

—————————

Jean-Paul Sartre, *Nausea,* Lloyd Alexander, trans. (New Directions, 1964).

In his major philosophical work, *Being and Nothingness*, building upon themes developed by Hegel, Kierkegaard, Husserl, Heidegger, Peirce, and Freud, Sartre presents a phenomenological study of being, nothingness, consciousness, the self, and emotion. He begins by distinguishing two different categories of being: *being-in-itself*, fully complete and determinate, independent of everything else, without relation to anything—not even itself—versus *being-for-itself*, the fully indeterminate and open domain of human consciousness characterized by freedom. He then goes on to examine the related and apparently opposite phenomena of *bad faith* and *sincerity*, arguing that these are both tools of self-deception by which we blind ourselves to the fact that we have no fixed natures, and that is how we hide ourselves from our freedom and our freedom from our true, self-created selves.

He uses an example of a young man and woman who go out on a date. He asks her if she wants to go to a movie, as if this is what he is after! He needs *her* to go to the movie, he wants some companionship, whatever—and she, pretending to not know what he is after, accepts. She wants to be "nice," she doesn't want him to have to go alone, and so on. The movie is now over. They're in the car. He reaches for her hand. She pretends that she did not anticipate him taking her hand; she allows it. Or not. The game begins. The game is called self-deception. Sartre has a term for it—*bad faith.*

Being and Nothingness

We shall say that this woman is in bad faith. But we see immediately that she uses various procedures in order to maintain herself in this bad faith. She has disarmed the actions of her companion by

---

From J. P. Sartre, *Being and Nothingness* (Philosophical Library, 1956).

reducing them to being only what they are; that is, to existing in the mode of the in-itself. But she permits herself to enjoy his desire, to the extent that she will apprehend it as not being what it is, will recognize its transcendence. Finally while sensing profoundly the presence of her own body—to the point of being aroused, perhaps—she realizes herself as *not being* her own body, and she contemplates it as though from above as a passive object to which events can *happen* but which can neither provoke them nor avoid them because all its possibilities are outside of it. What unity do we find in these various aspects of bad faith? It is a certain art of forming contradictory concepts which unite in themselves both an idea and the negation of that idea. The basic concept which is thus engendered utilizes the double property of the human being, who is at once a *facticity* and a *transcendence*. These two aspects of human reality are and ought to be capable of a valid coordination. But bad faith does not wish either to coordinate them or to surmount them in a synthesis. Bad faith seeks to affirm their identity while preserving their differences. It must affirm facticity as *being* transcendence and transcendence as *being* facticity, in such a way that at the instant when a person apprehends the one, he can find himself abruptly faced with the other.

The way that we thus shield ourselves from our fear of freedom is by pretending that we have a fixed nature that limits it. Both bad faith—self-deception—and even *sincerity* are, according to Sartre, elaborate ways of refusing to face the fact that we have no fixed natures. "I promise to be yours forever." How can you make such a promise, if not in bad faith? How do you know what you will feel ten years from now, ten months, ten days, ten minutes? It does no good to say to yourself that it is the making of the commitment to something or someone that matters. This is just another way of trying to convince yourself that there is some way that you can make yourself out to be when the truth is that at any moment you are capable of doing and being just about anything.

⊥

Let us consider this waiter in the café. His movement is quick and forward, a little too precise, a little too rapid. He comes toward the patrons with a step a little too quick. He bends forward a little too eagerly; his voice, his eyes express an interest a little too solicitous for the order of the customer. Finally there he returns, trying to imitate in his walk the inflexible stiffness of some kind of automaton while carrying his tray with the recklessness of a tight-rope-walker by putting it in a perpetually unstable, perpetually broken equilibrium which he perpetually reestablishes by a light movement of the arm and hand. All his behavior seems to us a game. He applies himself to chaining his movements as if they were mechanisms, the one regulating the other; his gestures and even his voice seem to be mechanisms; he gives himself the quickness and pitiless rapidity of things. He is playing, he is amusing himself. But what is he playing? We need not watch long before we can explain it: he is playing at *being* a waiter in a café. There is nothing there to surprise us. The game is a kind of marking out and investigation. The child plays with his body in order to explore it, to take inventory of it; the waiter in the café plays with his condition in order to *realize* it. This obligation is not different from that which is imposed on all tradesmen. Their con-dition is wholly one of ceremony. The public demands of them that they realize it as a ceremony; there is the dance of the grocer, of the tailor, of the auctioneer, by which they endeavour to persuade their clientele that they are nothing but a grocer, an auctioneer, a tailor. A grocer who dreams is offensive to the buyer, because such a grocer is not wholly a grocer. Society demands that he limit himself to his function as a grocer, just as the soldier at attention makes himself into a soldier-thing with a direct regard which does not see at all, which is no longer meant to see, since it is the rule and not the interest of the moment which determines the point he must fix his eyes on (the sight "fixed at ten paces"). There are indeed many precautions to imprison a man in what he is, as if we lived in perpetual fear that he might escape from it, that he might break away and suddenly elude his condition.

⊥

NOTES

1. See Section 22.1.
2. *Hermeneutics* is a term derived from the name of Hermes, the Greek messenger god, meaning "theory of interpretation."

22 ⚹ The New Metaphysicians: Bradley, Bergson, and Whitehead

22.0 Bradley (1846–1924): The Absolute Idealist

Frances Herbert Bradley was born in Clapham, Surrey (now London), one of twenty-two children fathered by an Evangelical preacher. After graduating from University College, Oxford, he was elected to a fellowship at Merton College. His unique brand of absolute idealism grew out of opposition both to the past British empiricists (Locke, Berkeley, and Hume) and to the then-current empiricism of J. S. Mill. Like most post-Kantian idealist metaphysicians, Bradley conceived the totality of what really exists in terms of "the Absolute," an essentially whole world-mind similar to Hegel's and Schelling's conceptions, except that Bradley's more atheistic system does not involve any type of God.

The Absolute as conceived by Bradley requires us to transcend all the fundamental categories of human thought; quality and relation, substance and cause, subject and object, time and space, and so on, are but mere appearances. Neither one nor many, the Absolute is a "unity in diversity." Individuals, who are not collections of attributable properties, get their unity and character from the relations of their properties. This means that in Bradley's view there are no "external" relations: all relations are internal.

Suppose an individual named Socrates has a property—say, that of being a teacher—by virtue of which he has a relation R to some other individual or individuals; in that case, R is an internal relation of Socrates. Socrates is a teacher; the relation of being someone's teacher is one of Socrates' internal relations. An external relation is one where there is no property by virtue of which an individual is necessarily R-related to anyone else. For instance, if Socrates is taller than Plato, this relation is external. Now, since according to Bradley and other British absolute idealists (most notably T. H. Green and B. Bosanquet) all relations are internal, this means that any individual has relations to absolutely all other individuals; to assert any truth about Socrates is thus to assert a truth about the Absolute (the whole world of actually existing things). In other words, to say anything at all about any individual part of the universe is really to say something about the whole universe.

In his most famous work, *Appearance and*

Reality, excerpted below, Bradley presents his unique brand of absolute idealism devoid of religious metaphysics and grounded in a logic distinct from both psychology and physics. According to his absolute idealism, all that exists is the mind, to which the absolute reveals itself directly; the absolute is, in that sense, *immanent*. He argues, however, that this absolute reality as it exists in the mind must be understood, not as a *system* of appearances but as the container of that system, such that each appearance is itself an essential constituent of reality; appearance thus *is* reality. Bertrand Russell was greatly influenced by Bradley's views, first by agreement and then through opposition, and so was G. E. Moore. Even while rejecting Bradley's positive theses, both Moore and Russell remained under the influence of Bradley's sharply critical dialectic as well as the approach to logic he developed in *The Principles of Logic* (1883; 2nd ed., 1922, corrected 1928). Three months before his death, Bradley became the first philosopher to be appointed to the Order of Merit.

⚝

Appearance and Reality

Book II: Reality

CHAPTER XXVI: THE ABSOLUTE AND ITS APPEARANCES

. . . All is appearance, and no appearance, or any combination of these, is the same as Reality. This is half the truth, and by itself it is a dangerous error. We must turn at once to correct it by adding its counterpart and Supplement. The Absolute *is* its appearances, it really is all and every one of them. That is the other half-truth which we have already insisted on, and which we must urge once more here. And we may remind ourselves at this point of a fatal mistake. If you take appearances, singly or all together, and assert barely that the Absolute is

From F. H. Bradley, *Appearance and Reality: A Metaphysical Essay* (London: George Allen & Unwin Ltd.; New York: Macmillan, 1893; 2nd ed., 1897).

either one of them or all—the position is hopeless. Having first set these down as appearance, you now proclaim them as the very opposite; for that which is identified with the Absolute is no appearance but is utter reality. But we have seen the solution of this puzzle, and we know the sense and meaning in which these half-truths come together into one. The Absolute is each appearance, and is all, but it is not any one as such. And it is not all equally, but one appearance is more real than another. In short the doctrine of degrees in reality and truth is the fundamental answer to our problem. Everything is essential, and yet one thing is worthless in comparison with others. Nothing is perfect, as such, and yet everything in some degree contains a vital function of Perfection. Every attitude of experience, every sphere or level of the world, is a necessary factor in the Absolute. Each in its own way satisfies, until compared with that which is more than itself. Hence appearance is error, if you will, but not every error is illusion. At each stage is involved the principle of that which is higher, and every stage (it is therefore true) is already inconsistent. But on the other hand, taken for itself and measured by its own ideas, every level has truth. It meets, we may say, its own claims, and it proves false only when tried by that which is already beyond it. And thus the Absolute is immanent alike through every region of appearances. There are degrees and ranks, but, one and all, they are alike indispensable.

We can find no province of the world so low but the Absolute inhabits it. Nowhere is there even a single fact so fragmentary and so poor that to the universe it does not matter. There is truth in every idea however false, there is reality in every existence however slight; and, where we can point to reality or truth, there is the one undivided life of the Absolute. Appearance without reality would be impossible, for what then could appear? And reality without appearance would be nothing, for there certainly is nothing outside appearances. But on the other hand Reality (we must repeat this) is not the sum of things. It is the unity in which all things, coming together, are transmuted, in which they are changed all alike, though not changed equally. And, as we have perceived, in this unity relations of isolation and hostility are affirmed and absorbed. These also are harmonious in the Whole, though not of course harmonious as such, and while severally confined to their natures as separate. Hence it would show blindness to urge, as an objection against our view, the opposition found in ugliness and in conscious evil. The extreme of hostility implies an intenser relation, and this relation falls within the Whole and enriches its unity. The apparent discordance and distraction is overruled into harmony, and it is but the condition of fuller and more individual development. But we can hardly speak of the Absolute itself as either ugly or evil. The Absolute is indeed evil in a sense and it is ugly and false, but the sense, in which these predicates can be applied, is too forced and unnatural. Used of the Whole each predicate would be the result of an indefensible division, and each would be a fragment isolated and by itself without consistent meaning. Ugliness, evil, and error, in their several spheres, are subordinate aspects. They imply distinctions falling, in each case, within one subject province of the Absolute's kingdom; and they involve a relation, in each case, of some struggling element to its superior, though limited, whole. Within these minor wholes the opposition draws its life from, and is overpowered by the system which supports it. The predicates evil, ugly, and false must therefore stamp, whatever they qualify, as a mere subordinate aspect, an aspect belonging to the province of beauty or goodness or truth. And to assign such a position to the sovereign Absolute would be plainly absurd. You may affirm that the Absolute *has* ugliness and error and evil, since it owns the provinces in which these features are partial elements. But to assert that it *is* one of its own fragmentary and dependent details would be inadmissible.

It is only by a licence that the subject-systems, even when we regard them as wholes, can be made qualities of Reality. It is always under correction and on sufferance that we term the universe either beautiful or moral or true. And to venture further would be both useless and dangerous at once.

If you view the Absolute morally at all, then the Absolute is good. It cannot be one factor contained within and overpowered by goodness. In the same way, viewed logically or aesthetically, the Absolute can only be true or beautiful. It is merely when you have so termed it, and while you still continue to insist on these preponderant characters, that you can introduce at all the ideas of falsehood and ugliness. And, so introduced, their direct application to the Absolute is impossible. Thus to identify the supreme universe with a partial system may, for some end, be admissible. But to take it as a single

character within this system, and as a feature which is already overruled, and which as such is suppressed there, would, we have seen, be quite unwarranted. Ugliness, error, and evil, all are owned by, and all essentially contribute to the wealth of the Absolute. The Absolute, we may say in general, has no assets beyond appearances; and again, with appearances alone to its credit, the Absolute would be bankrupt. All of these are worthless alike apart from transmutation. But, on the other hand once more, since the amount of change is different in each case, appearances differ widely in their degrees of truth and reality. There are predicates which, in comparison with others, are false and unreal.

To survey the field of appearances, to measure each by the idea of perfect individuality, and to arrange them in an order and in a system of reality and merit—would be the task of metaphysics. This task (I may repeat) is not attempted in these pages. I have however endeavoured here, as above, to explain and to insist on the fundamental principle. And, passing from that, I will now proceed to remark on some points of interest. There are certain questions which at this stage we may hope to dispose of.

Let us turn our attention once more to Nature or the physical world. Are we to affirm that ideas are forces, and that ends operate and move there? And, again, is Nature beautiful and an object of possible worship? On this latter point, which I will consider first, I find serious confusion. Nature, as we have seen, can be taken in various senses. We may understand by it the whole universe, or again merely the world in space, or again we may restrict it to a very much narrower meaning. We may first remove everything which in our opinion is only psychical, and the abstract residue—the primary qualities—we may then identify with Nature. These will be the essence, while all the rest is accessory adjective, and, in the fullest sense, is immaterial. Now we have found that Nature, so understood, has but little reality. It is an ideal construction required by science, and it is a necessary working fiction. And we may add that reduction to a result, and to a particular instance, of this fiction, is what is meant by a strictly physical explanation. But in this way there grows up a great confusion. For the object of natural science is the full world in all its sensible glory, while the essence of Nature lies in this poor fiction of primary qualities, a fiction believed not to be idea but solid fact. Nature then, while unexplained, is still left in its sensuous splendor, while Nature, if explained, would be reduced to this paltry abstraction. On one side is set up the essence—the final reality—in the shape of a bare skeleton of primary qualities; on the other side remains the boundless profusion of life which everywhere opens endlessly before our view. And these extremes then are confused, or are conjoined, by sheer obscurity or else by blind mental oscillation. If explanation reduces facts to be adjectives of something which they do not qualify at all, the whole connection seems irrational, and the process robs us of the facts. But if the primary essence after all *is* qualified, then its character is transformed. The explanation, in reducing the concrete, will now also have enriched and have individualized the abstract, and we shall have started on our way towards philosophy and truth. But of this latter result in the present case there can be no question. And therefore we must end in oscillation with no attempt at an intelligent unity of view. Nature is, on the one hand, that show whose reality lies barely in primary qualities. It is, on the other hand, that endless world of sensible life, which appeals to our sympathy and extorts our wonder. It is the object loved and lived in by the poet and by the observing naturalist. And, when we speak of Nature, we have often no idea which of these extremes, or indeed what at all, is to be understood. We in fact pass, as suits the occasion, from one extreme unconsciously to the other.

‎🟉

22.1 Bergson (1859–1941): The Spiritual Metaphysician

Henri Bergson (1859–1941) was born in Paris to Jewish immigrants; his father was a musician from Poland, his mother from England. At the prestigious École Normale Supérieure his studies turned from mathematics, in which he had shown early prodigal abilities, to science and then finally to philosophy. By the time he became a professor of philosophy at the Collège de France in 1900, after having taught at a variety of places, he was already famous in philo-

sophical circles for his doctoral dissertation, published in 1889 as *Essai sur les donnés immédiates de la conscience* (*Essay on the immediate data of consciousness*). In his *Essay* he argued that experience will forever be beyond the reach of the intellect because experience is an indivisible continuum (in the mathematical sense) and therefore cannot ever be adequately represented as a succession of demarcated conscious states (as required by the intellect).

Like Husserl, Bergson drew a sharp distinction between the concept of time and the experience of time; real time is not the static (abstract) time of being but the dynamic time of becoming as given in experience. Experiential time is apprehended solely by intuition as duration, which ultimately is inaccessible to the conceptual objectifications of the intellect. From this initial work Bergson came to reject all mechanistic and scientific reductionisms of the human mind to any sort of mechanistic explanation. By the turn of the century, his philosophy of "dynamism" extended beyond philosophical and scientific circles and attracted a wide public following through his lectures on human freedom and spirituality against the growing scientific determinism. His method and unique style is presented most clearly in his *An Introduction to Metaphysics* (1903), from which the following selection is taken.

‎🟉

An Introduction to Metaphysics

A comparison of the definitions of metaphysics and the various conceptions of the absolute leads to the discovery that philosophers, in spite of their apparent divergencies, agree in distinguishing two profoundly different ways of knowing a thing. The first implies that we move round the object; the second that we enter into it. The first depends on the point of view at which we are

From Henri Bergson, *An Introduction to Metaphysics*, trans. T. E. Hulme (New York: Putnam, 1912).

placed and on the symbols by which we express ourselves. The second neither depends on a point of view nor relies on any symbol. The first kind of knowledge may be said to stop at the *relative*; the second, in those cases where it is possible, to attain the *absolute*.

Consider, for example, the movement of an object in space. My perception of the motion will vary with the point of view, moving or stationary, from which I observe it. My expression of it will vary with the systems of axes, or the points of reference, to which I relate it: that is, with the symbols by which I translate it. For this double reason I call such motion *relative*: in the one case, as in the other, I am placed outside the object itself. But when I speak of an *absolute* movement, I am attributing to the moving object an interior and, so to speak, states of mind; I also imply that I am in sympathy with those states, and that I insert myself in them by an effort of imagination. Then, according as the object is moving or stationary, according as it adopts one movement or another, what I experience will vary. And what I experience will depend neither on the point of view I may take up in regard to the object, since I am inside the object itself, nor on the symbols by which I may translate the motion, since I have rejected all translations in order to possess the original. In short, I shall no longer grasp the movement from without, remaining where I am, but from where it is, from within, as it is in itself. I shall possess an absolute.

Consider, again, a character whose adventures are related to me in a novel. The author may multiply the traits of his hero's character, may make him speak and act as much as he pleases, but all this can never be equivalent to the simple and indivisible feeling which I should experience if I were able for an instant to identify myself with the person of the hero himself. Out of that indivisible feeling, as from a spring, all the words, gestures, and actions of the man would appear to me to flow naturally. They would no longer be accidents which, added to the idea I had already formed of the character, continually enriched that idea, without ever completing it. The character would be given to me all at once, in its entirety, and the thousand incidents which manifest it, instead of adding themselves to the idea and so enriching it, would seem to me, on the contrary, to detach themselves from it, without, however, exhausting it or impoverishing its essence. All the things I am told about the man provide me with so many points of view from which I can observe him. All the traits which describe him, and which can make him known to me only by so many comparisons with persons or things I know already, are signs by which he is expressed more or less symbolically. Symbols and points of view, therefore, place me outside him; they give me only what he has in common with others, and not what belongs to him and to him alone. But that which is properly himself, that which constitutes his essence, cannot be perceived from without, being internal by definition, nor be expressed by symbols, being incommensurable with everything else. Description, history, and analysis leave me here in the relative. Coincidence with the person himself would alone give me the absolute.

It is in this sense, and in this sense only, that *absolute* is synonymous with *perfection*. Were all the photographs of a town, taken from all possible points of view, to go on indefinitely completing one another, they would never be equivalent to the solid town in which we walk about. Were all the translations of a poem into all possible languages to add together their various shades of meaning and, correcting each other by a kind of mutual retouching, to give a more and more faithful image of the poem they translate, they would yet never succeed in rendering the inner meaning of the original. A representation taken from a certain point of view, a translation made with certain symbols, will always remain imperfect in comparison with the object of which a view has been taken, or which the symbols seek to express. But the absolute, which is the object and not its representation, the original and not its translation, is perfect, by being perfectly what it is.

It is doubtless for this reason that the *absolute* has often been identified with the *infinite*. Suppose that I wished to communicate to someone who did not know Greek the extraordinarily simple impression that a passage in Homer makes upon me; I should first give a translation of the lines, I should then comment on my translation, and then develop the commentary; in this way, by piling up explanation on explanation, I might approach nearer and nearer to what I wanted to express; but I should never quite reach it. When you raise your arm, you accomplish a movement of which you have, from within, a simple perception; but for me, watching it from the outside, your arm passes through one point, then through another, and between these two there will be still other points; so that, if I began to count, the operation would go on for ever. Viewed from the inside, then, an absolute is a simple thing; but looked at from the outside, that is to say, relatively to other things, it becomes, in relation to these signs which express it, the gold coin for which we never seem able to finish giving small change. Now, that which lends itself at the same time both to an indivisible apprehension and to an inexhaustible enumeration, is, by the very definition of the word, an infinite.

It follows from this that an absolute could only be given in an *intuition,* while everything else falls within the province of *analysis.* By intuition is meant the kind of *intellectual sympathy* by which one places oneself within an object in order to coincide with what is unique in it and consequently inexpressible. Analysis, on the contrary, is the operation which reduces the object to elements already known, that is, to elements common both to it and other objects. To analyze, therefore, is to express a thing is a function of something other than itself. All analysis is thus a translation, a development into symbols, a representation taken from successive points of view from which we note as many resemblances as possible between the new object which we are studying and others which we believe we know already. In its eternally unsatisfied desire to embrace the object around which it is compelled to turn, analysis multiplies without end the number of its points of view in order to complete its always incomplete representation, and ceaselessly varies its symbols that it may perfect the always imperfect translation. It goes on, therefore, to infinity. But intuition, if intuition is possible, is a simple act.

Now it is easy to see that the ordinary function of positive science is analysis. Positive science works, then, above all, with symbols. Even the most concrete of the natural sciences, those concerned with life, confine themselves to the visible form of living beings, their organs and anatomical elements. They make comparisons between these forms, they reduce the more complex to the more simple; in short, they study the workings of life in what is, so to speak, only its visual symbol. If there exists any means of possessing a reality absolutely instead of knowing it relatively, of placing oneself within it instead of looking at it from outside points of view, of having the intuition instead of

making the analysis: in short, of seizing it without any expression, translation, or symbolic representation—metaphysics is that means. *Metaphysics, then, is the science which claims to dispense with symbols.*

There is one reality, at least, which we all seize from within, by intuition and not by simple analysis. It is our own personality in its flowing through time—our self which endures. We may sympathize intellectually with nothing else, but we certainly sympathize with our own selves.

When I direct my attention inward to contemplate my own self (supposed for the moment to be inactive), I perceive at first, as a crust solidified on the surface, all the perceptions which come to it from the material world. These perceptions are clear, distinct, juxtaposed, or juxtaposable one with another; they tend to group themselves into objects. Next, I notice the memories which more or less adhere to these perceptions and which serve to interpret them. These memories have been detached, as it were, from the depth of my personality, drawn to the surface by the perceptions which resemble them; they rest on the surface of my mind without being absolutely myself. Lastly, I feel the stir of tendencies and motor habits—a crowd of virtual actions, more or less firmly bound to these perceptions and memories. All these clearly defined elements appear more distinct from me, the more distinct they are from each other. Radiating, as they do, from within outwards, they form, collectively, the surface of a sphere which tends to grow larger and lose itself in the exterior world. But if I draw myself in from the periphery toward the center, if I search in the depth of my being that which is most uniformly, most constantly, and most enduringly myself, I find an altogether different thing.

There is, beneath these sharply cut crystals and this frozen surface, a continuous flux which is not comparable to any flux I have ever seen. There is a succession of states, each of which announces that which follows and contains that which precedes it. They can, properly speaking, only be said to form multiple states when I have already passed them and turn back to observe their track. While I was experiencing them they were so solidly organized, so profoundly animated with a common life, that I could not have said where any one of them finished or where another commenced. In reality no one of them begins or ends, but all extend into each other.

✼

With the publication of *Creative Evolution* in 1907, Bergson became world-renown. William James called the work "a pure classic in point of form." In it, Bergson argues that the inner creative urge, a vital principle, or *élan vital,* is the teleological force behind evolution, rather than the (blind) natural selection envisioned by the Darwinists. He presents reality as an integrated whole and yet undetermined in a way that allows individual minds to play an active role. The ultimate goal of human existence, according to Bergson, is to enter into a mystical union with the ultimate, a state beyond all rationality. This enlightened experience is the culmination of the *élan vital,* the key ingredient in Bergson's dynamic universe of becoming; at its pinnacle, the human mind joins mystic intuition with scientific experiment, thereby taking an active and central role in "the essential function of the universe, which is a machine for the making of gods."

Bergson was elected to the Council of the Legion of Honor, the French Academy, the Academy of Sciences, and served as president of the League of Nations Committee for Intellectual Cooperation. In 1928 he won the Nobel Prize for literature.

22.2 Whitehead (1861–1947): The Process Philosopher

Alfred North Whitehead (1861–1947) was born in England at Ramsgate, Kent. His grandfathers were both schoolmasters, his father a parson. As a boy he played along the grim walls of Richborough Castle, built by the Romans, and nearby at Ebbes Fleet beach Augustine had once preached his first sermon. He spent his adolescence at Sherborne, a 1,200-year-old school, studying in an abbot's cell in whose bells he says he heard "the living voices of past centuries." The lessons and books were in Latin and Greek. At age nineteen, he entered Cambridge. At that time the education there was distinctly Platonic, consisting of freewheeling conversations with professors and other students. Later when he was a professor at Harvard he was once asked how he could have finished his *Science and the Modern World* in one semester while carrying a full teaching load, he referred back to his years of study, replying that "Everything in the book had been talked over for the previous forty years."

While still only twenty-four (in 1885) Whitehead became a fellow of Trinity College, Cambridge, which was then generally considered one of the greatest universities in the world; it openly boasted that two centuries ago under its auspices Sir Isaac Newton had discovered all the fundamental laws of the universe. Although Whitehead would do groundbreaking work in both philosophy and mathematics, his formal study at Trinity was in the latter discipline because "Mathematics must be studied; philosophy should be discussed." His first and in many ways his most important contribution appeared in his famous collaboration with Bertrand Russell on *Principia Mathematica* (1910–1913, in 3 vols.), a monumental and comprehensive work on the foundations of mathematics. This work was the first attempt to build a complete axiom system of logic; in contrast to Euclid and Newton, the axioms are stripped bare of any concrete content, with no reference to spatial reality or any kind of transcendental, or extrasensory, reality as in Plato's theory of Ideas.

Indeed, in Whitehead's view of things, atoms—the sorts of ultimately "real" things of which Newtonian-inspired physicists imagined the world to be constructed—are themselves "intellectual abstractions" that have no actual existence independent of the mind. In the tradition of Berkeley, Mach, Royce, and James, Whitehead replaced the Democritan and Newtonian inert atoms with the atomic constituents of reality that, like Leibnizian monads, exist as processes in relation to the human experience. He said these actual entities, or "actual occasions," are key to the understanding of metaphysics, freed from the Cartesian dualism and the mind–body problem. For Whitehead, as for Aristotle, there is but one insubstantial substance undergoing perpetual change: what appears, what is given in direct perception, is real. Nothing exists beyond what is present in the direct experience of the perceiving subject, which itself exists in relation to its object.

As in the Heraclitean flux, Whitehead's universe has no static concepts or substances, only an interconnected network of events. These events are actual extensions, spatiotemporal unities, giving rise within the flux to organisms sensitive to the existences of all others. The relations between them are experiences as a kind of feeling. Every actual entity consists of all its active relations with other things, which he terms its "prehensive occasion," as well as its "negative prehension," determined by the exclusion of everything that it is not. Unlike Leibniz's monads, Whitehead's "actual entities" have no permanent identity or history; they exist perpetually in the process of becoming. Death and the perishing of actual entities is but the creativity of the universe moving on to the next birth, such that the actual occasion loses its uniqueness but is preserved in the flow of process.

In this way, nothing can ever be completely understood, for everything is always changing. The great mistake made throughout the history of thought, according to Whitehead, is what he called the "fallacy of misplaced concreteness," which results from our mistaking intellectual abstractions for actual entities. The only permanence in the world is not in the realm of actuality but in the realm of possibility; possibilities themselves are what he calls "eternal objects," reminiscent of Plato's Ideas. The relation between actualities and possibilities he calls *ingression*, by which he means that a possibility has made itself manifest upon actuality; it has *ingressed* through the subject into the object: "the functioning of an eternal object in the self-creation of an actual entity is the 'ingression' of the eternal object in the actual entity." In this way, past actualities—events that have occurred in the past—achieve "objective immorality" because the actual entities are forever involved in the process of actuality, into which eternal objects ingress from universals whose selection is necessary to the existence of actual entities. The entire system thus remains in perpetual flux, incomplete, unresolvable, unknowable except as momentary influxes into the process.

Asked once what he thought the ancient philosophers would have to say about the twentieth century, Whitehead replied:

⚘

Aristotle would be inexpressibly shocked at the way his generalizations have gone overboard. Mind you, I don't say his ideas . . . haven't proved vastly useful. Aristotle discovered all the half-truths which were necessary to the creation of science. . . . Plato's ideas . . . tend, in comparison to be vague. But I prefer the vagueness. I prefer Plato. He seems to me to have been the one man in the ancient world who would not have been surprised at what has happened, because his thought constantly took into account the unpredictable, the limitless possibilities of things. There is always more chance of hitting something valuable when you aren't too sure what you want to hit upon . . . am I right in thinking that [scholars] are quite wrong in trying to identify Plato with some explicit conclusion in his *Dialogues*, with some single speaker and a final point of view? It seems to me that was just what he was trying to avoid. Take his letters: assuming that he wrote them, and even if he didn't, they would state a prevailing frame of mind in ancient times about his work: namely, that there *is* no Platonic system of philosophy. What he did was explore various aspects of a problem and then leave us with them. . . . He seems to me to have had, more than anyone else, a supreme sense of the limitless possibilities of the universe.

⚘

At the age of sixty-three, Whitehead was invited to join the philosophy department at Harvard University. His work in mathematics and logic, which had a profound influence on symbolic logic, had been completed and his phi-

_____

From *Dialogues of Alfred North Whitehead*, recorded by Lucian Price, 1954.

losophy of education was widely influential in England, so he set out to create a comprehensive philosophical system. His most important works from this time are *Science and the Modern World* (1925), *Process and Reality* (1929) and *Adventures of Ideas* (1933). For all their scope and brilliance, the works are often criticized as being too vague and open ended, to which Whitehead openly replied, "In philosophical discussion, the merest hint of dogmatic certainty as to finality of statement is an exhibition of folly."

It was actually Whitehead who first admired another rather mysterious figure in philosophy, a young student of his and Russell's from Vienna named Wittgenstein. Russell remarked:

⊥

Whitehead described to me the first time that Wittgenstein came to see him. He was shown into the drawing-room during afternoon tea. He appeared scarcely aware of the presence of Mrs. Whitehead, but marched up and down the room for some time in silence, and at last said explosively: "A proposition has two poles. It is *apb*." Whitehead, in telling me, said: "I naturally asked what are *a* and *b*, but I found that I had said quite the wrong thing. "*a* and *b* are indefinable," Wittgenstein answered in a voice of thunder.

⊥

After their pioneering work together, Whitehead and Russell had a great philosophical falling out. Their disagreement came about in part because of the tumultuous upheaval in science at the turn of the century, with the ending of the Newtonian worldview and developments that heralded the coming of Einstein's relativity:

⊥

We supposed that nearly everything of importance about physics was known. Yes, there were a few

obscure spots, strange anomalies . . . which physicists expected to be cleared up by 1900. They were. But in so being, the whole science blew up, and the Newtonian physics, which had been supposed to be fixed as the Everlasting Seat, were gone. Oh, they were and still are useful as a way of looking at things, but regarded as a final description of reality, no longer valid. Certitude was gone.*

⊥

Whitehead's philosophical response was unpopular not just with Russell but with most of the logical positivists at the time, who sided with the new physics. Indeed, Russell was so impressed by the current state of the physics that he used it as an epistemoloigcal foundation in his philosophy. Whitehead, on the other hand, was singularly unimpressed by the new scientific certitude. He said,

⊥

The Universe is vast. Nothing is more curious than the self-satisfied dogmatism with which mankind at each period of its history cherishes the delusion of the finality of its existing modes of knowledge. Skeptics and believers are all alike. At this moment scientists and skeptics are the leading dogmatists. Advance in detail is admitted; fundamental novelty is barred. This dogmatic common sense is the death of philosophic adventure. The Universe is *vast*.[†]

⊥

Although he and Russell remained friends (even though Whitehead was, politically, an extreme conservative and Russell was an extreme liberal), as Russell veered to the side of mathematics and science, Whitehead, the mathematician, turned deeply philosophical. Lamenting the uncertainty of those philosophers who, like

---

From *The Autobiography of Bertrand Russell*, 1951, Atlantic Monthly Press.

---

* From *Dialogues of Alfred North Whitehead*, recorded by Lucien Price, 1954.
[†] Ibid.

Whitehead, were skeptical of the new certainty of physicists and mathematicians, Russell wrote,

⚘

The people I don't trust are the philosophers, including Whitehead. They are cautious and constitutionally timid; nine out of ten hate me personally, not without reason; they consider philosophical research a foolish pursuit. . . . Before the war I fancied that quite a lot of them thought philosophy important; now I know that most of them resemble Professors Hanky and Panky in *Erewhon Revisited*.[*]

⚘

Meanwhile, Whitehead put his position in no uncertain terms when he says that

⚘

Let me speak personally for a moment. I had a good classical education, and when I went up to Cambridge early in the 1880's my mathematical training was continued under good teachers. Now nearly everything was supposed to be known about physics that could be known—except a few spots, such as electromagnetic phenomena, which remained (or so it was thought) to be co-ordinated with the Newtonian principles. But, for the rest, physics was supposed to be nearly a closed subject.

Those investigations to co-ordinate went on through the next dozen years. By the middle of the 1890's there were a few tremors, a slight shiver as of all not being quite secure, but no one sensed what was coming. By 1900 the Newtonian physics were demolished, done for! Still speaking personally, it had a profound effect on me; I have been fooled once, and I'll be damned if I'll be fooled again! Einstein is supposed to have made an epochal discovery. I am respectful and interested, but also sceptical. There is no more reason to suppose that Einstein's relativity is anything final, than Newton's *Principia*. The danger is dogmatic thought; it plays the devil with religion, and science is not immune from it.[†]

⚘

Whitehead of course turned out to be right; the Einsteinian world view has since given way dramatically to the strange new world of the quantum. According to the latest physical science the reality we live in now would have seemed utterly absurd to just about anyone except, perhaps, some extreme nineteenth-century idealists and a quiet old ex-mathematician who broke ranks to become chairman of the philosophy department at Harvard.

After waiting in the wings for more than three millennia, the Heraclitean flux swallowed the soul of Parmenides with a vengeance.

---

[*]From *The Autobiography of Bertrand Russell*, op.cit.

[†]From *Dialogues of Alfred North Whitehead*, op. cit

23 ✦ The Birth of Analytic Philosophy: Frege, Russell, Wittgenstein, and Quine

23.0 The Legacy of Frege (1848–1925): Sense and Reference

Gottlob Frege was born at Wismar, Germany. After studying at the famous universities of Jena and Göttingen, he became a lecturer and then a professor of mathematics at Jena. His lifelong interests and contributions, however, were always deeply philosophical; he founded modern mathematical logic, philosophy of mathematics, and philosophy of language. In the introduction to his groundbreaking *Grundgesetze der Arithmetik* (*Basic Laws of Arithmetic,* 1884), for instance, he warns that "Mathematicians reluctant to venture into the labyrinths of philosophy are requested to leave off reading."

We've seen some fundamental contributions to mathematics made by some of the greatest philosophers, such as Pythagoras, Descartes, and Leibniz. Plato, after all, wrote at the entrance to his Academy, "Let no one ignorant of mathematics enter here" because he regarded it as the highest possible form of human knowledge; mathematics comes closest to giving us

direct access to the forms. The concept of mathematical truths conceived as synthetic a priori was pivotal in the philosophy of Kant and others. To Frege, as to many other logically and mathematically minded philosophers then and today, it seemed puzzling that the majority of philosophers continued doing philosophy as if the formal languages of mathematics and logic were some technical appendage to the heart of philosophy, which was to be done using *natural* language.

Indeed, even Descartes, who invented analytic geometry, and Leibniz, who invented calculus, did not state their *philosophy* in the language of mathematics but in French, Latin, German, and so on. Why? Even the logicians presented the most technical subject matter, logic—what it is, what it's for, how it works—in natural language. And even in cases such as Spinoza, whose whole system is modeled on a rigorous axiomatic system such as is found in Euclidean geometry, the symbols he used are the symbols of a natural language, not the symbols of mathematics (except by way of example).

By and large the influence of Gottlob Frege

(mainly through his leading philosophical disciple Bertrand Russell) redirected many philosophers, if not to mathematics, toward an attempt to achieve technically rigorous levels of sophistication within philosophy in terms of its use of languages and logics beyond their merely given, natural, forms. In his *Basic Laws of Arithmetic,* a major landmark in thought, Frege put forth his philosophy of what would become known as *logicism:* the view that all of mathematics reduces to pure logic, a view that would be developed further by Bertrand Russell. But that is only part of it. Another part, nowhere directly stated in Frege but a prevalent background theory that had been brewing for many centuries, since the time of Leibniz, attained a notable peak in Bertrand Russell: that all languages, including English, German, and French, are reducible to logic. Nor is that the whole of it! Already developing at the time, and a view still being formulated today, is that the mind is a logical-mathematical entity. As Bertrand Russell remarked briefly and mysteriously in his introduction to his own groundbreaking *Principles of Mathematics,* a sort of "oh, and by the way":

⚹

Philosophy asks of Mathematics: What does it mean? Mathematics in the past was unable to answer, and Philosophy answered by introducing *the totally irrelevant notion of mind.* But now Mathematics is able to answer, so far at least as to reduce the whole of its propositions to certain fundamental notions of logic. At this point, the discussion must be resumed by Philosophy.

⚹

We shall study Russell in the next section. It is Frege who argued that proofs in mathematics must be constructed using a completely perspic-

---

From Bertrand Russell, *Principles of Mathematics,* 1903.

uous machinery, where every demonstration is clear and distinct, not just mathematically (what would that even *mean*) but *philosophically,* heralding a new level of deductive rigor; each step must be absolutely explicit, nothing must be left to intuition or psychology. Well, what then does *that* mean? Where is the clearness and distinctness to be attained, if not in some psychological sensation of clearness and distinctness?

In Plato's *Meno* we read the paradigm of the slave boy experiencing an "aha, yes" illumination when he saw the Pythagorean theorem. We saw Descartes's attempt to further develop such a psychologically special state of mind into the basis for a rigorous epistemology where the *rational intuition* mind-state is a sort of interface, or point of intersection, between the noumenal truth and our conscious experience. This attempt, in turn, influenced Kant's notion of the synthetic a priori. In Frege's view, propositions of arithmetic and analysis are not synthetic a priori, as Kant thought, nor empirical, as John Stuart Mill thought. Rather, they are pure a priori expressions of logic. The technical apparatus for his theory, developed in his *Begriffsschrift* (1879), was the development of a new formal language with a specific vocabulary and specified modes of construction, much along the lines of the *calculus philosophicus et ratiocinator,* exactly of the type envisioned centuries earlier by Leibniz. Frege invented the notions of quantifiers and variables, symbolic constructions that allow us to take the first steps toward the formalization of natural languages. He went on to develop a revolutionary analysis of sense and meaning in terms of the primacy of reference (*Bedeutung*) that influenced philosophers as varied as Bertrand Russell, Edmund Husserl, and Martin Heidegger.

In his *Basic Laws of Arithmetic* (1884), Frege takes a vehement stand against subjective idealism and also against psychologism, the view that psychology and introspection are the foundation of philosophy and that introspection is the primary method of inquiry.

⁎

Basic Laws of Arithmetic

It is important that we make clear at this point what definition is and what can be attained by means of it. It seems frequently to be credited with a creative power; but all it accomplishes is that something is marked out in sharp relief and designated by a name. Just as the geographer does not create a sea when he draws boundary lines and says: the part of the ocean's surface bounded by these lines I am going to call the Yellow Sea, so too the mathematician cannot really create anything by his defining. Nor can one by pure definition magically conjure into a thing a property that in fact it does not possess—save that of now being called by the name with which one has named it. But that an oval figure produced on paper with ink should by a definition acquire the property of yielding one when added to one, I can only regard as a scientific superstition. One could just as well by a pure definition make a lazy pupil diligent. It is easy for unclarity to arise here if we do not distinguish sufficiently between concept and object. If we say: "a square is a rectangle in which the adjacent sides are equal," we define the concept *square* by specifying what properties a thing must have in order to fall under this concept. These properties I call "characteristic marks" of the concept. But these characteristic marks of a concept, properly understood, are not the same as its properties. The concept *square* is not a rectangle; only such objects as may fall under this concept are rectangles, just as the concept *black cloth* is neither black nor a cloth. Whether there are any such objects is not known immediately from the definition. Now suppose one defines, for instance, the number zero, by saying: it is something which yields one when added to one. In so doing one has defined a concept, by specifying what property an object must have in order to fall under the concept. But this property is not a property of the concept defined. People frequently seem to fancy that by the definition something has been created that yields one when added to one. A great delusion!

From Gottlob Frege, *Basic Laws of Arithmetic*, M. Furth, trans. (Berkeley and Los Angeles: University of California Press, 1964).

The number one, for instance, is not easily taken to be actual, unless we are disciples of John Stuart Mill. On the other hand, it is impossible to ascribe to every person his own number one; for in that case we should first have to investigate the extent to which the properties of these ones agreed, and if one person said "one times one is one" and the next said "one times one is two," we could only register the difference and say: your one has one property, mine has another. There could be no question of any argument as to who was right, or of any attempt to correct anyone; for they would not be speaking of the same object. Obviously this is totally contrary to the sense of the word "one" and the sense of the sentence "one times one is one." Since the number one, being the same for everyone, stands apart from everyone in the same way, it can no more be researched by making psychological observations than can the moon. Whatever ideas there may be of the number one in individual souls, they are still to be as carefully distinguished from the number one, as ideas of the moon are to be distinguished from the moon itself. Because the psychological logicians fail to recognize the possibility of there being something objective that is not actual, they take concepts to be ideas and thereby consign them to psychology.

If we could not grasp anything but what was within our own selves, then a conflict of opinions (based on) a mutual understanding would be impossible, because a common ground would be lacking, and no idea in the psychological sense can afford us such a ground. There would be no logic to be appointed arbiter in the conflict of opinions.

⁎

Frege's proof for his contention that the individual mind can indeed have access to something beyond itself is a model of technical precision. It is based on a distinction between the *meaning* of a term, what Frege calls its *Sinn*—translated from the German, typically, as "sense"—and its *Bedeutung*—translated from the German, typically, as "reference"—although here there has been an unusually wide latitude, at the extreme end of which is "Nominatum" (Feigl). Frege whittles his entire thesis to perfection by demonstrating that two terms having *different meanings* can have *the same reference*.

This is made clear in his famous paper "Über Sinn und Bedeutung" ("On Sense and Reference"). It is rather more technical than the previous selection, but the clarity is increased, not decreased, if only one takes time to let the presentation do the work. Let us therefore first read a key passage from the beginning and then represent it to ourselves as an explanation (make sure to actually draw, for yourself, the figure that he describes).

⚹

On Sense and Reference

Let a, b, c be straight lines which connect the corners of a triangle with the midpoints of the opposite sides. The point of intersection of a and b is then the same as that of b and c. Thus we have different designations of the same point and these names ('intersection of a and b,' 'intersection of b and c') indicate also the manner in which these points are presented. Therefore the sentence expresses a genuine cognition.

Now it is plausible to connect with a sign (name, word combination, expression) not only the designated object, which may be called the reference of the sign, but also the sense (connotation, meaning) of the sign in which is contained the manner and context of presentation. Accordingly, in our examples the reference of the expressions 'the point of intersection of a and b' and 'the point of intersection of b and c' would be the same;—not their senses. The reference of 'evening star' and 'morning star' is the same but not their senses.

⚹

Here is the figure:

Herbert Feigl, trans., in *Readings in Philosophical Analysis,* Feigl and Sellars, eds. (New York: Appleton-Century-Crofts, 1949), with emendations by the author.

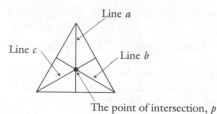

The point of intersection, *p*

What this shows in no uncertain terms is that the *A*, "the point of intersection between *a* and *b*," and *B*, "the point of intersection between *b* and *c*," have *the same reference* but *different senses*. The reference of *A* and *B* is one and the same particular point: that one where the lines intersect. Let us call it "*p*, the point of intersection." But *A* and *B* express different cognitions; they have a different sense, or meaning, that is revealed by the fact that when you went through the cognitive process of constructing them, the construction of *A* was *different* from—not the same mental event as—the construction of *B*.

Likewise for the terms *morning star* and *evening star*. One appears in the morning, at daybreak, in the east. Then, as the sun rises, it vanishes. The second appears at the end of the day, at the dusk of twilight. The two phenomenal images look very different; the crepuscular light of dawn is not the iridescence of twilight. Someone who does not know that the "morning star" is not a star but the planet Venus, and that the "evening star" is also that same planet, Venus, would not even *realize* consciously that by using those names he is referring to one and the same designated object—that in *reality* those two terms *with very different meanings* have one and the same *reference*.

Frege's technically precise distinction is pivotal for understanding the first of two very different approaches—within the history of philosophy—to the nature, function, and role of *language*. According to the first approach—which we have seen epitomized by philosophers like Plato, Aquinas, Spinoza, Leibniz, Kant, Hegel, and Royce—meaning is a relation between language and the world.

According to the second approach—which we

have seen epitomized by philosophers like Protagoras, William of Ockham, Hobbes, Locke, Hume, Comte, James, and Russell—meaning is understood in terms of acts performed by speakers of ordinary language in everyday contexts. In the former, the ultimate tools of analysis are mathematics, logic, and formal languages; in the latter, which views the first approach in terms of analysis of relations between "language and world" as a source of metaphysical confusion, the main tool is natural language. Frege's technical apparatus provided a much-needed impetus to the first approach as philosophy entered the twentieth century. His propositional calculus and quantification theory not only inspired Bertrand Russell to attempt the full reduction of mathematics to logic in the gargantuan *Principia Mathematica,* but also led Russell, after reading Frege's work, to discover the famous paradox that now bears his name and which, together with *Principia,* had an immense influence on some of the most important intellectual achievements in the twentieth century, including Gödel's famous incompleteness theorem. However, Russell's paradox, which he pointed out to Frege, brought an end to Frege's efforts to develop his own system further, about which Russell remarked,

⟟

As I think about acts of integrity and grace, I realize that there is nothing in my knowledge to compare with Frege's dedication to truth. His entire life's work was on the verge of completion, much of his work had been ignored to the benefit of men infinitely less capable, his second volume was about to be published, and upon finding that his fundamental assumption was in error, he responded with intellectual pleasure clearly submerging any feelings of personal disappointment. It was almost superhuman and a telling indication of that of which men are capable if their dedication is to creative work and knowledge instead of cruder efforts to dominate and be known.

From *The Autobiography of Bertrand Russell* (Atlantic Monthly Press, 1951).

⟟

Ironically, Russell experienced a similar fate with his own star pupil, Wittgenstein.

23.1 Russell (1872–1970): Upon the Wings of Logic

Bertrand Russell was born in Monmouthshire, England. His parents, Lord and Lady Amberley, both died while Russell was still a child, leaving him in the charge of his grandfather, Lord John Russell. At age eighteen Russell entered Cambridge University to study mathematics and philosophy. Under the tutelage of Frances Herbert Bradley (1846–1924) (see Chapter 22) he became a Hegelian idealist.

Following Frege (see the previous section) Russell broke from Bradley's views by establishing the logical reality of external relations—thereby extending Leibniz's notions of monads.

After spending eight years studying with Bradley, under the influence of his friend and fellow pupil G. E. Moore (1873–1958) Russell rejected both Hegelianism and idealism, first in favor of Moore's commonsense philosophy and then his own original brand of realism that was even more radically opposed to Moore's commonsense view of things than it was to Bradley's views. As a fellow at Trinity College, Cambridge, Russell in his early views espoused both mind-matter dualism and realism about the existence of universals, which he saw as irreducible to particulars.

Russell was inspired by Frege even though he disagreed with him. In *The Principles of Mathematics* (1903), Russell's first major work, he equated meaning and reference by arguing that meaningful terms must have real entities as references—even mathematical terms like numbers, points, and lines. Over the following decade he collaborated with mathematician Alfred North Whitehead (1861–1947) on the monumental *Principia Mathematica* (three volumes, 1910–1913). Starting from irreducible logical concepts and axioms and using rigorously logical steps in the sense Frege had called for, Russell and Whitehead tried to derive the whole content of mathematics from pure logic. In reducing mathematics to logic they relied on Russell's theory of logical constructions to show how the foundations of mathematics could be established using the method of analysis or "contextual definition," in which mathematical concepts are translated into their logical equivalents. Chief among Russell's many innovations from this period were the axiom of infinity, the set theory paradox that now bears his name, and the theory of types, which revolutionized the way philosophy was done.

In 1911, as a professor at Cambridge, Russell discovered and became mentor to another of the greatest philosophers of the twentieth century, Ludwig Wittgenstein. Wittgenstein, in turn, came to have a lasting influence on Russell, especially regarding his views on logic and the philosophy of language. In subsequent decades Russell went on to extend his original logical-analytic method to virtually all areas of philosophy, even to physics and psychology.

Russell was also a lifelong critic of religion. In the 1957 preface to his famous *Why I Am Not a Christian* (the title essay which was first delivered in 1927), he wrote:

⚹

I think all the great religions of the world— Buddhism, Hinduism, Christianity, Islam and Communism—both untrue and harmful. It is evident as a matter of logic that, since they disagree, not more than one of them can be true. With very few exceptions, the religion which a man accepts is that of the community in which he lives, which makes it obvious that the influence of environment is what has led him to accept the religion in question. It is true that the Scholastics invented what professed to be logical arguments proving the existence of God, and that these arguments, or

From Bertrand Russell, *Why I Am Not a Christian* (New York: Watts & Co., 1957).

others of a similar tenor, have been accepted by many eminent philosophers, but the logic to which these traditional arguments appealed is of an antiquated Aristotelian sort which is now rejected by practically all logicians except such as are Catholics. . . . The question of the truth of a religion is one thing, but the question of its usefulness is another. I am as firmly convinced that religions do harm as I am that they are untrue. The harm that is done by a religion is of two sorts, the one depending on the kind of belief which it is thought ought to be given to it, and the other upon the particular tenets believed. As regards the kind of belief: it is thought virtuous to have Faith—that is to say, to have a conviction which cannot be shaken by contrary evidence. . . . The conviction that it is important to believe this or that, even if a free inquiry would not support the belief, is one which is common to almost all religions and which inspires all systems of state education. The consequence is that the minds of the young are stunted and are filled with fanatical hostility both to those who have other fanaticisms and, even more virulently, to those who object to all fanaticisms.

⚹

Russell's outspoken criticisms not only of religion but also of traditional morality, orthodox education, and militarism made him unpopular with a variety of authorities. During World War I he was fired from his teaching position in England for being a pacifist. In 1940 he was prevented from accepting a teaching position at the College of the City of New York, supposedly because of his liberal views on sex. He was jailed many times in his life, as late as the age of eighty-nine when he was arrested for protesting against nuclear arms.

A prolific writer, Russell published so much— more than seventy books and hundreds of articles and essays on virtually every topic—that even a cursory description of the Russell library would take a whole volume.

In 1949 Russell was awarded the Order of Merit, Britain's most prestigious award to civilians, and in 1950 he won the Nobel Prize for Literature. He once remarked, however, that no philosopher could receive a greater public honor than the welcome accorded him upon his arrival in the United States to accept a teaching position at the City University of New York, when Bishop Manning of the Protestant Episcopal Church wrote to every New York newspaper denouncing the appointment of "a man who is a recognized propagandist against both religion and morality, and who specifically defends adultery. . . . Can anyone who cares for the welfare of our country be willing to see such teaching disseminated with the countenance of our colleges and universities?" State councilman Charles Keegan likewise declared, "if we had an adequate system of immigration, that bum could not land within a thousand miles." Senator Phelps Phelps (sic) went on record stating that Russell "is an unfit person to hold an important post in the educational system of our state at the expense of the taxpayers." Former city magistrate Joseph Goldstein claimed that Russell "is not a philosopher . . . not a lover of wisdom . . . all his alleged doctrines which he calls philosophy are just cheap, tawdry, worn-out, patched-up fetishes." Martha Byrnes, the registrar of New York County, demanded that Russell be "tarred and feathered and driven out of the country." The matter was finally settled by the New York Supreme Court when Judge McGeehan, after no doubt a careful reading of Russell's many books, in his official judgment wrote that "It is not necessary to detail here the filth which is contained in the books. . . . The court therefore holds that Bertrand Russell *is not qualified to teach*." Mayor La Guardia, on the off-chance that Judge McGeehan's ruling might be overruled at the federal level, promptly struck the appointed position from the state budget. As a result, Russell went to Harvard.

In the following selection, taken from *Our Knowledge of the External World* (1914), Russell argues for his Frege-inspired view that logic is the essence of philosophy. He also refutes the adequacy of traditional subject-predicate logic and presents his theory of the twofold nature of logic. These revolutionary views culminated in

his original version of logical atomism. Unlike the "old logic" that put "thought in fetters," this "new logic gives it wings."

⊥

Our Knowledge of the External World

. . . The first serious advance in real logic since the time of the Greeks was made independently by Peano and Frege—both mathematicians. They both arrived at their logical results by an analysis of mathematics. Traditional logic regarded the two propositions, "Socrates is mortal" and "All men are mortal," as being of the same form; Peano and Frege showed that they are utterly different in form. The philosophical importance of logic may be illustrated by the fact that this confusion—which is still committed by most writers—obscured not only the whole study of the forms of judgment and inference, but also the relations of things to their qualities, of concrete existence to abstract concepts, and of the world of sense to the world of Platonic ideas. Peano and Frege, who pointed out the error, did so for technical reasons, and applied their logic mainly to technical developments; but the philosophical importance of the advance which they made is impossible to exaggerate.

Not only Frege's theory of number . . . but the whole theory of physical concepts which will be outlined in our next two lectures, is inspired by mathematical logic, and could never have been imagined without it.

In every proposition and in every inference there is, besides a particular subject-matter concerned, a certain *form*, a way in which the constituents of the proposition or inference are put together. If I say, "Socrates is mortal," "Jones is angry," "The sun is hot," there is something in common in these three cases, something indicated by the word "is." What is in common is the *form* of the proposition, not an actual constituent. If I say a number of things about Socrates—that he was an Athenian, that he married Xantippe, that he drank the hemlock—there is a common constituent,

From Bertrand Russell, *Our Knowledge of the External World* (London: Allen & Unwin, 1914).

namely Socrates, in all the propositions I enunciate, but they have diverse forms. If, on the other hand, I take any one of these propositions and replace its constituents, one at a time, by other constituents, the form remains constant, but no constituent remains. Take (say) the series of propositions, "Socrates drank the hemlock," "Coleridge drank the hemlock," "Coleridge drank opium," "Coleridge ate opium." The form remains unchanged throughout this series, but all the constituents are altered. Thus form is not another constituent, but is the way the constituents are put together. It is forms, in this sense, that are the proper object of philosophical logic.

It is obvious that the knowledge of logical forms is something quite different from knowledge of existing things. The form of "Socrates drank the hemlock" is not an existing thing like Socrates or the hemlock, nor does it even have that close relation to existing things that drinking has. It is something altogether more abstract and remote. . . . We say "this thing is bigger than that," we are not assigning a mere quality of "this," but a relation of "this" and "that." We might express the same fact by saying "that thing is smaller than this," where grammatically the subject is changed. Thus propositions stating that two things have a certain relation have a different form from subject-predicate propositions, and the failure to perceive this difference or to allow for it has been the source of many errors in traditional metaphysics.

The existing world consists of many things with many qualities and relations. A complete description of the existing world would require not only a catalogue of the things, but also a mention of all their qualities and relations. We should have to know not only this, that, and the other thing, but also which was red, which yellow, which was earlier than which, which was between which two others, and so on. When I speak of a "fact," I do not mean one of the simple things in the world; I mean that a certain thing has a certain quality, or that certain things have a certain relation. Thus, for example, I should not call Napoleon a fact, but I should call it a fact that he was ambitious, or that he married Josephine. Now a fact, in this sense, is never simple, but always has two or more constituents. When it simply assigns a quality to a thing, it has only two constituents, the thing and the quality. When it consists of a relation between two things, it has three constituents, the things

and the relation. When it consists of a relation between three things, it has four constituents, and so on. The constituents of facts, in the sense in which we are using the word "fact," are not other facts, but are things and qualities or relations. When we say that there are relations of more than two terms, we mean that there are single facts consisting of a single relation and more than two things. I do not mean that one relation of two terms may hold between A and B, and also between A and C, as, for example, a man is the son of his father and also the son of his mother. This constitutes two distinct facts: if we choose to treat it as one fact, it is a fact which has facts for its constituents. But the facts I am speaking of have no facts among their constituents, but only things and relations. For example, when A is jealous of B on account of C, there is only one fact, involving three people; there are not two instances of jealousy, but only one. It is in such cases that I speak of a relation of three terms, where the simplest possible fact in which the relation occurs is one involving three things in addition to the relation. And the same applies to relations of four terms or five or any other number. All such relations must be admitted in our inventory of the logical forms of facts: two facts involving the same number of things have the same form, and two which involve different numbers of things have different forms.

Given any fact, there is an assertion which expresses the fact. The fact itself is objective, and independent of our thought or opinion about it; but the assertion is something which involves thought, and may be either true or false. An assertion may be positive or negative: we may assert that Charles I. was executed, or that he did *not* die in his bed. A negative assertion may be said to be a *denial*. Given a form of words which must be either true or false, such as "Charles I. died in his bed," we may either assert or deny this form of words: in the one case we have a positive assertion, in the other a negative one. A form of words which must be either true or false I shall call a *proposition*. Thus a proposition is the same as what may be significantly asserted or denied. A proposition which expresses what we have called a fact, *i.e.* which, when asserted, asserts that a certain thing has a certain quality, or that certain things have a certain relation, will be called an atomic proposition, because, as we shall see immediately, there are other propositions into which atomic propositions enter in a way analogous to that in which atoms enter into molecules. Atomic propositions, although, like facts, they may have any one of an infinite number of forms, are only one kind of propositions. All other kinds are more complicated. In order to preserve the parallelism in language as regards facts and propositions, we shall give the name "atomic facts" to the facts we have hitherto been considering. Thus atomic facts are what determine whether atomic propositions are to be asserted or denied.

Whether an atomic proposition, such as "this is red," or "this is before that," is to be asserted or denied can only be known empirically. Perhaps one atomic fact may sometimes be capable of being inferred from another, though I do not believe this to be the case; but in any case it cannot be inferred from premises no one of which is an atomic fact. It follows that, if atomic facts are to be known at all, some at least must be known without inference. The atomic facts which we come to know in this way are the facts of sense-perception; at any rate, the facts of sense-perception are those which we most obviously and certainly come to know in this way. If we knew all atomic facts, and also knew that there were none except those we knew, we should, theoretically, be able to infer all truths of whatever form.[*] Thus logic would then supply us with the whole of the apparatus required. But in the first acquisition of knowledge concerning atomic facts, logic is useless. In pure logic, no atomic fact is ever mentioned: we confine ourselves wholly to forms, without asking ourselves what objects can fill the forms. Thus pure logic is independent of atomic facts; but conversely, they are, in a sense, independent of logic. Pure logic and atomic facts are the two poles, the wholly *a priori* and the wholly empirical. But between the two lies a vast intermediate region, which we must now briefly explore.

"Molecular" propositions are such as contain conjunctions—*if, or, and, unless,* etc.—and such words are the marks of a molecular proposition.

---

*This perhaps requires modification in order to include such facts as beliefs and wishes, since such facts apparently contain propositions as components. Such facts, though not strictly atomic, must be supposed included if the statement in the text is to be true.

Consider such an assertion as, "If it rains, I shall bring my umbrella." This assertion is just as capable of truth or falsehood as the assertion of an atomic proposition, but it is obvious that either the corresponding fact, or the nature of the correspondence with fact, must be quite different from what it is in the case of an atomic proposition. Whether it rains, and whether I bring my umbrella, are each severally matters of atomic fact, ascertainable by observation. But the connection of the two involved in saying that *if* the one happens, *then* the other will happen, is something radically different from either of the two separately. It does not require for its truth that it should actually rain, or that I should actually bring my umbrella; even if the weather is cloudless, it may still be true that I should have brought my umbrella if the weather had been different. Thus we have here a connection of two propositions, which does not depend upon whether they are to be asserted or denied, but only upon the second being inferable from the first. Such propositions, therefore, have a form which is different from that of any atomic proposition.

Such propositions are important to logic, because all inference depends upon them. If I have told you that if it rains I shall bring my umbrella, and if you see that there is a steady downpour, you can infer that I shall bring my umbrella. There can be no inference except where propositions are connected in some such way, so that from the truth or falsehood of the one something follows as to the truth or falsehood of the other. It seems to be the case we can sometimes know molecular propositions, as in the above instance of the umbrella, when we do not know whether the component atomic propositions are true or false. The *practical* utility of inference rests upon this fact.

The next kind of propositions we have to consider are *general* propositions, such as "all men are mortal," "all equilateral triangles are equiangular." And with these belong propositions in which the word "some" occurs, such as "some men are philosophers" or "some philosophers are not wise." These are the denials of general propositions, namely (in the above instances), of "all men are non-philosophers" and "all philosophers are wise." We will call propositions containing the word "some" *negative* general propositions, and those containing the word "all" *positive* general propositions. These propositions, it will be seen, begin to have the appearance of the propositions in logical text-books. But their peculiarity and complexity are not known to the text-books, and the problems which they raise are only discussed in the most superficial manner.

When we were discussing atomic facts, we saw that we should be able, theoretically, to infer all other truths by logic if we knew all atomic facts and also knew that there were no other atomic facts besides those we knew. The knowledge that there are no other atomic facts is positive general knowledge; it is the knowledge that "all atomic facts are known to me," or at least "all atomic facts are in this collection"—however the collection may be given. It is easy to see that general propositions, such as "all men are mortal," cannot be known by inference from atomic facts alone. If we could know each individual man, and know that he was mortal, that would not enable us to know that all men are mortal, unless we *knew* that those were all the men there are, which is a general proposition. If we knew every other existing thing throughout the universe, and knew that each separate thing was not an immortal man, that would not give us our result unless we *knew* that we had explored the whole universe, *i.e.* unless we knew "all things belong to this collection of things I have examined." Thus general truths cannot be inferred from particular truths alone, but must, if they are to be known, be either self-evident, or inferred from premises of which at least one is a general truth. But all *empirical* evidence is of *particular* truths. Hence, if there is any knowledge of general truths at all, there must be *some* knowledge of general truths which is independent of empirical evidence, *i.e.* does not depend upon the data of sense.

The above conclusion, of which we had an instance in the case of the inductive principle, is important, since it affords a refutation of the older empiricists. They believed that all our knowledge is derived from the senses and dependent upon them. We see that, if this view is to be maintained, we must refuse to admit that we know any general propositions. It is perfectly possible logically that this should be the case, but it does not appear to be so in fact, and indeed no one would dream of maintaining such a view except a theorist at the last extremity. We must therefore admit that there is general knowledge not derived from sense, and that some of this knowledge is not obtained by inference but is primitive.

Such general knowledge is to be found in logic. Whether there is any such knowledge not derived from logic, I do not know; but in logic, at any rate, we have such knowledge. It will be remembered that we excluded from pure logic such propositions as, "Socrates is a man, all men are mortal, therefore Socrates is mortal," because *Socrates* and *man* and *mortal* are empirical terms, only to be understood through particular experience. The corresponding proposition in pure logic is: "If anything has a certain property, and whatever has this property has a certain other property, then the thing in question has the other property." This proposition is absolutely general: it applies to all things and all properties. And it is quite self-evident. Thus in such propositions of pure logic we have the self-evident general propositions of which we were in search.

A proposition such as "If Socrates is a man, and all men are mortal, then Socrates is mortal," is true in virtue of its *form* alone. Its truth, in this hypothetical form, does not depend upon whether Socrates actually is a man, nor upon whether in fact all men are mortal; thus it is equally true when we substitute other terms for *Socrates* and *man* and *mortal.* The general truth of which it is an instance is purely formal, and belongs to logic. Since it does not mention any particular thing, or even any particular quality or relation, it is wholly independent of the accidental facts of the existent world, and can be known, theoretically, without any experience of particular things or their qualities and relations.

Logic, we may say, consists of two parts. The first part investigates what propositions are and what forms they may have; this part enumerates the different kinds of atomic propositions, of molecular propositions, of general propositions, and so on. The second part consists of certain supremely general propositions, which assert the truth of all propositions of certain forms. This second part merges into pure mathematics, whose propositions all turn out, on analysis, to be such general formal truths. The first part, which merely enumerates forms, is the more difficult, and philosophically the more important; and it is the recent progress in this first part, more than anything else, that has rendered a truly scientific discussion of many philosophical problems possible.

The problem of the nature of judgment or belief may be taken as an example of a problem whose solution depends upon an adequate inventory of logical forms. We have already seen how the supposed universality of the subject-predicate form made it impossible to give a right analysis of serial order, and therefore made space and time unintelligible. But in this case it was only necessary to admit relations of two terms. The case of judgment demands the admission of more complicated forms. If all judgments were true, we might suppose that a judgment consisted in apprehension of a *fact*, and that the apprehension was a relation of a mind to the fact. From poverty in the logical inventory, this view has often been held. But it leads to absolutely insoluble difficulties in the case of error. Suppose I believe that Charles I. died in his bed. There is no objective fact "Charles I.'s death in his bed" to which I can have a relation of apprehension. Charles I. and death and his bed are objective, but they are not, except in my thought, put together as my false belief supposes. It is therefore necessary, in analysing a belief, to look for some other logical form than a two-term relation. Failure to realise this necessity has, in my opinion, vitiated almost everything that has hitherto been written on the theory of knowledge, making the problem of error insoluble and the difference between belief and perception inexplicable.

Modern logic, as I hope is now evident, has the effect of enlarging our abstract imagination, and providing an infinite number of possible hypotheses to be applied in the analysis of any complex fact. In this respect it is the exact opposite of the logic practised by the classical tradition. In that logic, hypotheses which seem *prima facie* possible are professedly proved impossible, and it is decreed in advance that reality must have a certain special character. In modern logic, on the contrary, while the *prima facie* hypotheses as a rule remain admissible, others, which only logic would have suggested, are added to our stock, and are very often found to be indispensable if a right analysis of the facts is to be obtained. The old logic put thought in fetters, while the new logic gives it wings.

⚹

In Russell's view, the only real entities in the world are *logical atoms,* which are analogous to Leibniz's monads except they have evolved to a technically precise rendition in language such that, in a sense, metaphorically and poetically speaking, we might say: Russell compressed logic into a diamond drill with which to open the windowless monads. What we then see, by glimpsing into reality using Russell's logical apparatus, is that just about all the objects that we ordinarily take to be real turn out to be nothing more than elaborate fictions, in exactly the way that David Hume had supposed. Not only does the term *fiction* apply to the whole universe, *Russell shows it applies even to the logical structure of such a concept.* Indeed, this unique blend of Russell the cosmic mystic and Russell the technical, rationally precise logician is nowhere more apparent than in his *explicit proof* of the *logical impossibility* of the existence of the world—the entire universe—conceived as a whole! For Russell here constructed *the* paradox of the twentieth century, which still today bears the name "Russell's Paradox."

We shall compare Russell's Paradox with Zeno's Paradox (Section 1.11). You may recall how Zeno's Paradox plunged us into the abyss of the very, very small, showing that the whole cannot be understood as consisting of individual parts. Three thousand years later, Russell's Paradox goes in the other direction and shows that the paradox at the most minuscule lower bound of the universe reappears, in reverse and *doubly* paradoxical, at the outermost bounds!

Lest the paradox sound overly mystical, we should note that it is a precisely formed antinomy within the branch of mathematics known as set theory. Informally speaking, sets are well-defined collections of objects of any sort whatsoever, designated either by a property that all the things have in common or by a list of the things. Thus, (1) "the books in Kolak's library" is a set. So is (2) "all even numbers greater than 12," and so is (3) "coffee cup, table, chair," and likewise for (4) "a, b, c," and so on. Sets (1) and (2) are defined the first way, by a property, whereas (3) and (4) are defined the second way, by a list. Some sets, such as (2), are infinite, whereas others, such as (1), (3), and (4) are finite. Now, if you think about it a little, all the things in the universe can be talked about, or conceived of, in terms of sets when we want to refer to them as wholes consisting of parts; for instance, your physical body would consist in the set of all your physical atoms, each of the atoms in your body would consist in the set of all their quantum particles, and so on. Likewise for non-physical things. Your mind, for instance, can be conceived as the set of all your sensations, emotions, and thoughts, including your memories, and so on; a particular perception can be conceived as a set of its individual impressions and ideas (a la Hume). Now, let us simply take the set of all sets and call it, "Universe," or U for short. What could be simpler than that? Individual things exist, we might not know what they are but we can see *that* they are, and we can certainly see that there are lots and lots of them, and so therefore there must be some whole sum total of all the things that there are, of all the varieties of things that there are—whether perceptual, conceptual, physical, mental, spiritual, zwabongial, whatever there is, even the unknowns (for instance, we can conceive of the set of all unknown things). After all, when we think of the world—and even when we don't think of it, the concept is there, in the back of our minds—we think of the totality of all that exists. You can even be mystical, if you like, and call it the "Tao."

Thinking along these lines, Russell notices an interesting fact. Some sets contain themselves as members, whereas others do not. Compare, for instance, the word *word* with the word *dog*. The word *word* is a word but the word *dog* is not a dog. That's about as simple a version of the idea as you can imagine to get you started. All you need is one simple piece of symbolic notation. To indicate that the number 3 is a member of the set of integers, I, we write $3 \in I$, and to indicate that the number 3 is not a member of the set of all even numbers, E, we write $3 \notin E$. In general, "$x \in y$" means "x is a member of set y," or, equivalently, "y contains x as a member." Thus, if y is the set of all citizens of the United States and x is Syphax McCune, then $x \in y$.

Now, some sets contain themselves as members, which we can express as $x \in x$, and some do not, which we can express by $x \notin x$. Thus, the set of all the things mentioned on this page is a member of itself (we just mentioned it). Whereas the set of all sets that contain more than three members does not contain itself, since there are more than three such sets. Likewise, the set of all sets is itself a set and so it, too, is a member of itself.

Most sets do not have this self-referential property. The set of all even numbers, for instance, does not contain itself because this set is not, itself, an even number; similarly, the set of all citizens of the United States is not a member of itself, since this set is not, itself, a citizen. And so on.

By Q let us denote the set of all sets that contain themselves as members, and by Z let us denote the set of all sets that do not contain themselves as members. Thus,

{all even numbers} $\in Z$
{all citizens} $\in Z$
{all sets containing more than three members} $\in = Z$

whereas

{all things mentioned on this page} $\in Q$
{the set of all sets} $\in Q$

Even more generally, we can write that for any set x, $x \in Q$ if and only if $x \in x$, whereas for any set x, $x \in Z$ if and only if $x \notin$ x. Now, is the set Z a member of itself or not?

Well, let's see. Suppose that it is: $Z \in Z$. In that case, we know by definition that $Z \notin Z$. But if $Z \notin Z$, then by definition $Z \in Z$! Thus, *Z is a member of itself if and only if it is not a member of itself.* This contradiction is the very heart of Russell's paradox. It shows us that there is something fundamentally wrong with the very concept of a collection of things—a set—but it does not merely tell us something about set theory! It tells us something about the whole universe.

To see why, let us return to our set U, which is the set of all the things that there are. This is very similar, if not identical, to the concept of the set of all sets. The only reason we think it's not identical is that *universe* is supposed to refer to a *real object* whereas *set* is supposed to refer to just a mathematical concept—a term in a theory that has no existence outside our conceptual framework. But now Russell has shown—and this is the subtle part of the paradox—that (1) the concept *universe* has the same ontological status as the concept *set,* and (2) insofar as the latter is a theoretical construction, then so is the former.

It is meditating on this perplexity, combined with studying Russell and Whitehead's *Principia Mathematica,* that Kurt Gödel (1906–1978) formulated one of the most groundbreaking theorems of all time, his famous "incompleteness theorem," proving in no uncertain terms the existence of what are called "formally undecidable propositions" in any formal system such as arithmetic. More formally, it says that for any formal system *S,* there will be a sentence *P* of the language of *S* such that if *S* is consistent, neither *P* nor its negation can be proved in *S.* In proving this ultimate black hole in the universe of thought, Gödel showed how to translate the syntax of *S* itself into arithmetic, making *S* capable of representing its own syntax. This can then be used to show that there must necessarily exist a sentence *P* in *S* that can be interpreted as meaning "I am not provable." The coding system that he invented to show these things made it possible to translate everything you are reading right now into 0's and 1's so that it can be encoded into a universal machine such as the computer that I am right now writing on.

To get a sense of what is involved, consider the concept of a "Complete Pictorial Catalogue of the Universe." It's very big, of course. It contains a picture of everything in the universe—every cat, dog, snail, plant, atom, subatomic particle, point in space, conglomeration of points, locations, perspectives, and so on. Now, does it contain a picture of itself—a picture of all pictures? Imagine a giant collage of all the pictures—of everything. You take a picture of that. You now have a picture of all pictures—but wait! What about that picture that you are now

holding? *There's one picture that's not in the picture.* The picture of all pictures tells you: "I'm not a picture in the picture."

We can now compare Russell's paradox to Zeno's Paradox as follows. In Russell's Paradox the parts—sets that do not contain themselves as members—are there but the whole—the set of all such sets—is not. In Zeno's Paradox, the separation between Achilles and the wall, or between any point *a* and any other point *b,* is there, and also the point of contact is there (after Achilles has reached the wall) *but the moment of making contact is never there.* It is as if the parts that are there cannot be put together into the whole. In some fundamental sense everything that we are seeing and thinking at each instant of our experience must not be as it appears, up to and including our conception of, and our experience of, the entire world. We must ultimately be dealing not with reality but with fictions.

Unlike David Hume, who was distressed by his conclusions about the fictional nature both of his own self and the world and ran off to play backgammon, and unlike Heidegger's anxiety and Sartre's nausea, Russell experienced through the activity of philosophy a "strangeness and wonder lying just below the surface even in the commonest things of daily life." You don't have to go as far as the outer reaches of the universe to feel it. Consider, for instance, an ordinary table:

(1) Is there a real table at all? (2) If so, what sort of object can it be? Now both Berkeley and Leibniz admit that there is a real table, but Berkeley says it is certain ideas in the mind of God, and Leibniz says it is a colony of souls. Thus both of them answer our first question in the affirmative, and only diverge from the views of ordinary mortals in their answer to our second question. In fact, almost all philosophers seem to be agreed that there is a real table: they almost all agree that, however much our sense-data—colour, shape, smoothness, etc.—may depend upon us, yet their occurrence is

a sign of something existing independently of us, something differing, perhaps, completely from our sense-data, and yet to be regarded as causing those sense-data whenever we are in a suitable relation to the real table.

Now obviously this point in which the philosophers are agreed—the view that there *is* a real table, whatever its nature may be—is vitally important, and it will be worth while to consider what reasons there are for accepting this view before we go on to the further question as to the nature of the real table. Our next chapter, therefore, will be concerned with the reasons for supposing that there is a real table at all.

Before we go farther it will be well to consider for a moment what it is that we have discovered so far. It has appeared that, if we take any common object of the sort that is supposed to be known by the senses, what the senses *immediately* tell us is not the truth about the object as it is apart from us, but only the truth about certain sense-data which, so far as we can see, depend upon the relations between us and the object. Thus what we directly see and feel is merely 'appearance,' which we believe to be a sign of some 'reality' behind. But if the reality is not what appears, have we any means of knowing whether there is any reality at all? And if so, have we any means of finding out what it is like?

Such questions are bewildering, and it is difficult to know that even the strangest hypotheses may not be true. Thus our familiar table, which has roused but the slightest thoughts in us hitherto, has become a problem full of surprising possibilities. The one thing we know about it is that it is not what it seems. Beyond this modest result, so far, we have the most complete liberty of conjecture. Leibniz tells us it is a community of souls: Berkeley tells us it is an idea in the mind of God; sober science, scarcely less wonderful, tells us it is a vast collection of electric charges in violent motion.

Among these surprising possibilities, doubt suggests that perhaps there is no table at all. Philosophy, if it cannot *answer* so many questions as we could wish, has at least the power of *asking* questions which increase the interest of the world, and show the strangeness and wonder lying just below the surface even in the commonest things of daily life.

According to Russell, to experience such strangeness and wonder of reality is, in part, "the point of philosophy." As he makes perfectly clear in his famous *Mysticism and Logic*, it is not the goals of mysticism to which his logical atomism is opposed but rather mysticism's depreciation of the cosmic power of rational knowledge to bring about not just a *fictive* or *religious* but *real* "form of union of Self and not-Self."

Like Leibniz, Russell firmly believed in the infinite greatness of the world entire, such that through its union between Self and not-Self,

> the mind also is rendered great, and becomes capable of that union with the universe which constitutes its highest good.

In this same work Russell also makes perfectly clear how his logical atoms differ from the concept of physical atoms by presenting in no uncertain terms a devastating problem for any naive realist conception of physical reality that is based on physical science verifying truths through direct experience.

Mysticism and Logic

Physics is said to be an empirical science, based upon observation and experiment.

It is supposed to be verifiable, i.e. capable of calculating beforehand results subsequently confirmed by observation and experiment.

What can we learn by observation and experiment?

Nothing, so far as physics is concerned, except immediate data of sense: certain patches of colour, sounds, tastes, smells, etc., with certain spatio-temporal relations.

The supposed contents of the physical world are *prima facie* very different from these: molecules have no colour, atoms make no noise, electrons have no taste, and corpuscles do not even smell.

If such objects are to be verified, it must be solely through their relation to sense-data: they must have

From *Mysticism and Logic* (London: Longman's, Green Co., 1918).

some kind of correlation with sense-data, and must be verifiable through their correlation *alone*.

But how is the correlation itself ascertained? A correlation can only be ascertained empirically by the correlated objects being constantly *found* together. But in our case, only one term of the correlation, namely, the sensible term, is ever *found*: the other term seems essentially incapable of being found. Therefore, it would seem, the correlation with objects of sense, by which physics was to be verified, is itself utterly and for ever unverifiable.

There are two ways of avoiding this result.

(1) We may say that we know some principle *a priori*, without the need of empirical verification, e.g. that our sense-data have *causes* other than themselves, and that something can be known about these causes by inference from their effects. This way has been often adopted by philosophers. It may be necessary to adopt this way to some extent, but in so far as it is adopted physics ceases to be empirical or based upon experiment and observation alone. Therefore this way is to be avoided as much as possible.

(2) We may succeed in actually defining the objects of physics as functions of sense-data. Just in so far as physics leads to expectations, this *must* be possible, since we can only *expect* what can be experienced. And in so far as the physical state of affairs is inferred from sense-data, it must be capable of expression as a function of sense-data. The problem of accomplishing this expression leads to much interesting logico-mathematical work.

In physics as commonly set forth, sense-data appear as functions of physical objects: when such-and-such waves impinge upon the eye, we see such-and-such colours, and so on. But the waves are in fact inferred from the colours, not vice versa. Physics cannot be regarded as validly based upon empirical data until the waves have been expressed as functions of the colours and other sense-data.

Thus if physics is to be verifiable we are faced with the following problem: Physics exhibits sense-data as functions of physical objects, but verification is only possible if physical objects can be exhibited as functions of sense-data. We have therefore to solve the equations giving sense-data in terms of physical objects, so as to make them instead give physical objects in terms of sense-data.

Russell thus gives up mind–body dualism in favor of a version of the thesis that the ultimate elements of the world are neither physical nor mental "things" but, rather, logical particulars— the logical atoms—and their external relations. He extends his logical-analytic method to the question of the relation between sense perception and physical objects. By combining his theory of descriptions in which meaning and reference are equated with his logical construction principle (the substitution, wherever possible, of constructions out of known entities for inference to unknown ones), he shows how even the symbols of physics—points in space, moments in time (instants), physical particles, and so on— can be analyzed (translated) into their propositional contexts—that is, into logical statements about empirical entities.

Thus, like the early James, Russell became an advocate of a type of "neutral monism," resolving the mind–body problem raised by Descartes through an analysis in which mind and physical matter are viewed as different constructions out of the same, basic *logical* elements. Russell didn't offer a merely metaphysical claim, however, about how the world must therefore be understood as neither mental nor physical but *logical*. The key concept is a synthesis of the best from many previous views of what the ultimate elements of existence are, whether construed as material, idealistic, mathematical, or logical elements. Using his extraordinary intellect and his extensive knowledge of mathematics, logic, science, and the history of philosophy, Russell came up with a model of the mind as a logically operating system of *data processing*. The key concept here is his notion of *sense-data*:

⊥

When I speak of a "sense-datum," I do not mean the whole of what is given in sense at one time. I mean rather such a part of the whole as might be singled out by attention: particular patches of colour, particular noises, and so on. There is some difficulty in deciding what is to be considered *one* sense-datum: often attention causes divisions to

⊥

appear where, so far as can be discovered, there were no divisions before. An observed complex fact, such as that this patch of red is to the left of that patch of blue, is also to be regarded as a datum from our present point of view: epistemo-logically, it does not differ greatly from a simple sense-datum as regards its function in giving knowledge. Its *logical* structure is very different, however, from that of sense: *sense* gives acquaintance with particulars, and is thus a two-term relation in which the object can be *named* but not asserted, and is inherently incapable of truth or falsehood, whereas the observation of a complex fact, which may be suitably called perception, is not a two-term relation, but involves the propositional form on the object-side, and gives knowledge of a truth, not mere acquaintance with a particular. This logical difference, important as it is, is not very relevant to our present problem; and it will be convenient to regard data of perception as included among sense-data for the purposes of this paper. It is to be observed that the particulars which are constituents of a datum of perception are always sense-data in the strict sense.

Concerning sense-data, we know that they are there while they are data, and this is the epistemological basis of all our knowledge of external particulars. (The meaning of the word "external" of course raises problems which will concern us later.) We do not know, except by means of more or less precarious inferences, whether the objects which are at one time sense-data continue to exist at times when they are not data. Sense-data at the times when they are data are all that we directly and primitively know of the external world; hence in epistemology the fact that they are *data* is all-important. But the fact that they are all that we directly know gives, of course, no presumption that they are all that there is. If we could construct an impersonal metaphysic, independent of the accidents of our knowledge and ignorance, the privileged position of the actual data would probably disappear, and they would probably appear as a rather haphazard selection from a mass of objects more or less like them. In saying this, I assume only that it is probable that there are particulars with which we are not acquainted. Thus the special importance of sense-data is in relation to epistemology, not to metaphysics. In this respect, physics is to be reckoned as metaphysics: it is impersonal, and nominally pays no

special attention to sense-data. It is only when we ask how physics can be *known* that the importance of sense-data re-emerges.

⚹

Thus, just as the mind's cognitive function—thought, mathematics, and logic—consists in logical atoms, so its perceptual function—seeing, feeling, smelling, emoting, and so on—consists in their atomic form as individual sense-data. And, as Russell clearly states, "I regard sense-data as not mental." Ultimately, they consist in external relations. In his article "Some Explanations in Reply to Mr. Bradley" (*Mind* 1910), he explained the realistic interpretation and central role in his system of external relations:

⚹

I maintain that there are such facts as that *x* has the relation R to *y*, and that such facts are not in general reducible to, or inferable from, a fact about *x* only and a fact about *y* only [i.e., internal relations]: they do not imply that *x* and *y* have any complexity, or any intrinsic property distinguishing them from a *z* and a *w* which do not have the relation R. This is what I mean when I say that relations are external. But I maintain also . . . that whenever we have two terms *x* and *y* related by a relation R, we have also a complex, which we may call "*xRy*," consisting of the two terms so related. This is the simplest example of what I call a "complex" or a "unity." What is called analysis consists in the discovery of the constituents of a complex. A complex differs from the mere aggregate of its constituents, since it is one, not many, and the relation which is one of its constituents enters into it as an actually relating relation, and not merely as one member of an aggregate.

⚹

In taking such a functional approach to both mind and matter, Russell helped pave the way toward a purely logico-mathematical model of mind and reality. The key passage (which we already referred to in the previous section) appears in his *Principles of Mathematics*:

Philosophy asks of Mathematics: What does it mean? Mathematics in the past was unable to answer, and Philosophy answered by introducing the totally irrelevant notion of mind. But now Mathematics is able to answer, so far at least as to reduce the whole of its propositions to certain fundamental notions of logic. At this point, the discussion must be resumed by Philosophy.

In Russell's pioneering work on the foundations of mathematics, logic, and language we thus see the beginnings of a purely formal and functional analysis of the elements of thought. Later in the twentieth century this analysis will help make possible the invention of mechanical minds and artificial intelligence by translating human language and the elements of experience, including the activity of thinking and reasoning, into a logical form that can in turn be translated into a purely logical machine language. Russell's detailed and explicitly precise analyses of logic, language, and mathematical reasoning, including his reduction of mathematics to logic in *Principia Mathematica*,[1] were thus instrumental in paving the way for many of the later developments that eventually led to the computer.

On the other, less technical side, his philosophy of philosophy—what it is for, what it is about, and how it ought to be done—helped bring together a tumultuous variety of activities under one rubric. In the concluding chapter of his *Problems of Philosophy* (1912), Russell points out that unlike other disciplines, such as physics and medicine, whose value you can experience without knowing them or partaking in them (for instance, you have the benefit of their technology), philosophy has no direct utility outside of the lives of those who partake in what he takes to be both the true value of philosophy and the highest good of humanity: the attainment of "union with the universe."

Problems of Philosophy

Having now come to the end of our brief and very incomplete review of the problems of philosophy, it will be well to consider, in conclusion, what is the value of philosophy and why it ought to be studied. It is the more necessary to consider this question, in view of the fact that many men, under the influence of science or of practical affairs, are inclined to doubt whether philosophy is anything better than innocent but useless trifling, hair-splitting distinctions, and controversies on matters concerning which knowledge is impossible.

This view of philosophy appears to result, partly from a wrong conception of the ends of life, partly from a wrong conception of the kind of goods which philosophy strives to achieve. Physical science, through the medium of inventions, is useful to innumerable people who are wholly ignorant of it; thus the study of physical science is to be recommended, not only, or primarily, because of the effect on the student, but rather because of the effect on mankind in general. Thus utility does not belong to philosophy. If the study of philosophy has any value at all for others than students of philosophy, it must be only indirectly, through its effects upon the lives of those who study it. It is in these effects, therefore, if anywhere, that the value of philosophy must be primarily sought. . . .

The value of philosophy is, in fact, to be sought largely in its very uncertainty. The man who has no tincture of philosophy goes through life imprisoned in the prejudices derived from common sense, from the habitual beliefs of his age or his nation, and from convictions which have grown up in his mind without the co-operation or consent of his deliberate reason. To such a man the world tends to become definite, finite, obvious; common objects rouse no questions, and unfamiliar possibilities are contemptuously rejected. As soon as we begin to philosophize, on the contrary, we find . . . that even the most everyday things lead to problems to which only very incomplete answers can be given. Philosophy, though unable to tell us with certainty what is the true answer to the doubts which it raises, is able to suggest many possibilities which enlarge our thoughts and free them from the tyranny of custom. Thus, while diminishing our feeling of certainty as to

From Bertrand Russell, *Problems of Philosophy*, 1912.

what things are, it greatly increases our knowledge as to what they may be; it removes the somewhat arrogant dogmatism of those who have never travelled into the region of liberating doubt, and it keeps alive our sense of wonder by showing familiar things in an unfamiliar aspect. . . .

The mind which has become accustomed to the freedom and impartiality of philosophic contemplation will preserve something of the same freedom and impartiality in the world of action and emotion. It will view its purposes and desires as parts of the whole, with the absence of insistence that results from seeing them as infinitesimal fragments in a world of which all the rest is unaffected by any one man's deeds. The impartiality which, in contemplation, is the unalloyed desire for truth, is the very same quality of mind which, in action, is justice, and in emotion is that universal love which can be given to all, and not only to those who are judged useful or admirable. Thus contemplation enlarges not only the objects of our thoughts, but also the objects of our actions and our affections: it makes us citizens of the universe, not only of one walled city at war with all the rest. In this citizenship of the universe consists man's true freedom, and his liberation from the thraldom of narrow hopes and fears.

Thus, to sum up our discussion of the value of philosophy; Philosophy is to be studied, not for the sake of any definite answers to its questions, since no definite answers can, as a rule, be known to be true, but rather for the sake of the questions themselves; because these questions enlarge our conception of what is possible, enrich our intellectual imagination and diminish the dogmatic assurance which closes the mind against speculation; but above all because, through the greatness of the universe which philosophy contemplates, the mind also is rendered great, and becomes capable of that union with the universe which constitutes its highest good.

⁂

23.2 Wittgenstein (1889–1951): Philosophy's Blind Spot

Ludwig Wittgenstein was one of eight children born to a prominent Viennese family of Jewish origin that had converted to Roman Catholicism. His father, who owned the largest steel company in Austria, used his considerable resources to make their home a cultural mecca for Viennese artists, musicians, and writers. Everyone in the family played at least one musical instrument superbly and participated actively in the family's many cultural events.

Educated at home until the age of fourteen, Wittgenstein enrolled at the *Realschule* in Linz the same year Adolph Hitler graduated. For two years he studied mainly mathematics and physics before going on to Berlin to get a degree in engineering. At age nineteen he moved to England with the idea of further studying aeronautical engineering (the forerunner of aerospace engineering) at the University of Manchester. His growing interest in the foundations of mathematics, however, took him instead to Cambridge University where he met Bertrand Russell. In his autobiography, Russell describes his fateful meeting with Wittgenstein on the eve of World War I. While studying engineering mathematics Wittgenstein apparently became extremely perplexed about what it was about the world and the mind that made mathematics possible. Not finding any answer in his mathematics books, he asked whom he should see. Russell says:

⁂

Somebody mentioned my name, and he took up his residence at Trinity. He was perhaps the most perfect example I have ever known of genius as traditionally conceived, passionate, profound, intense, and dominating. He had a kind of purity which I have never known equalled except by G. E. Moore. I remember taking him once to a meeting of the Aristotelian Society, at which there were various fools whom I treated politely. When we came away he raged and stormed against my immoral degradation in not telling these men what fools they were. His life was turbulent and troubled, and his personal force was extraordinary.

From *The Autobiography of Bertrand Russell* (Atlantic Monthly Press, 1951).

. . . He used to come to see me every evening at midnight, and pace up and down my room like a wild beast for three hours in agitated silence. Once I said to him: "Are you thinking about logic or about your sins?" "Both," he replied, and continued his pacing. I did not like to suggest that it was time for bed, as it seemed probable both to him and me that on leaving me he would commit suicide. At the end of his first term at Trinity, he came to me and said: "Do you think I am an absolute idiot?" I said: "Why do you want to know?" He replied: "Because if I am I shall become an aeronaut, but if I am not I shall become a philosopher." I said to him: "My dear fellow, I don't know whether you are an absolute idiot or not, but if you will write me an essay during the vacation upon any philosophical topic that interests you, I will read it and tell you." He did so, and brought it to me at the beginning of the next term. As soon as I read the first sentence, I became persuaded that he was a man of genius, and assured him that he should on no account become an aeronaut.

★

When Russell asked G. E. Moore what he thought of Wittgenstein, Moore replied that he thought very well of him "Because at my lectures he looks puzzled, and nobody else ever looks puzzled."

When World War I broke out Wittgenstein interrupted his studies with Russell to fight on the side of the Germans. He left Cambridge and became an officer in the Austrian army. While in the trenches he began writing what would be his doctoral dissertation and one of the most influential philosophy books of the twentieth century. He completed it in an Italian prison camp. The work, *Tractatus Logico-Philosophicus*, from which the first selection is taken, was the only work published in his lifetime, but it helped to create a revolution in philosophy, leading to the development of logical positivism, linguistic analysis, and semantics. Wittgenstein's profound effect on many aspects of twentieth-century philosophy cannot be overstated; the noted Oxford philosopher P. F. Strawson has called Wittgen-

stein, "the preeminent philosopher of this century." In an intimate letter to a woman friend, Russell describes hauntingly the influence his most famous student had on him:

★

Do you remember that at the time when you were seeing Vittoz I wrote a lot of stuff about Theory of Knowledge, which Wittgenstein criticized with the greatest severity? His criticism, though I don't think you realized it at the time, was an event of first-rate importance in my life, and affected everything I have done since. I saw he was right, and I saw that I could not hope ever again to do fundamental work in philosophy. My impulse was shattered, like a wave dashed to pieces against a breakwater. I became filled with utter despair.

★

In the *Tractatus*, Wittgenstein tries to make clear the relationship between language and thought by delineating the limit of language as the expression of thought and by showing how the mind is able to "hook" onto reality by using language; language is the medium of representation as to how things are in the world. Just as Kant tried to show the necessary conditions that would make experience-as-representation possible, Wittgenstein tries to show the necessary conditions that would make language-as-representation possible by claiming that the world consists, ultimately, not of things but of Russellian "atomic facts" made in part accessible by the propositional logic as developed by Russell. Atomic propositions are the linguistic counterparts of atomic facts, to which they are related as pictures are to the things they depict, in virtue of what Wittgenstein calls their "logical form."

The *Tractatus* begins with the famous proposition (1) "The world is all that is the case." What Wittgenstein means by "world," however,

From *The Autobiography of Bertrand Russell* (Atlantic Monthly Press, 1951).

is given by proposition 1.1: "The world is the totality of facts, not of things." This of course is in direct and perhaps shocking contradiction to the commonsense view that the world is made of *things*. But let us put this in the context of where we began, with the pre-Socratic puzzlement about what everything is made of, and perhaps we may not be so shocked. What Wittgenstein is saying goes well with other views expressing the idea that the world—the totality of everything—is not made of some physical, material stuff but of something entirely different in nature. Indeed, it will also help us to compare Wittgenstein's assertion with Schopenhauer's, which in point of fact greatly influenced Wittgenstein: "The world is my idea." Schopenhauer's point, itself evolved from and influenced by Kant's analysis of the categories of thought and the nature of the mind, is that what the mind has direct access to is not things as they exist independently of the mind (as conceived in materialist metaphysics) but its own items: perceptions, thoughts, and language. However, we must be careful to note that here Wittgenstein is *not* denying the existence of *things* in any of the straightforward senses of the idealists (whether of the subjective, objective, or critical variety). If he were, the statements in the *Tractatus*, in which he constantly uses the word "thing" (*ding*), would turn out to be exactly the sort of nonsense that Wittgenstein most definitely thinks he is *not* writing, namely, non-illuminating nonsense; for although there is a tension in many of his sentences that play on contradiction to make their philosophical "showings" clear, it is supposed to be the sort of illuminating "nonsense" that sentences in logic express.

Indeed, in that respect we might think of Wittgenstein's philosophy as a sort of "linguistic idealism," provided that it is understood in the critical rather than the subjective form, because the form of experience for Wittgenstein, as for Kant, is subjective in the transcendental sense because the subject is the *metaphysical subject* and not the empirical subject as conceived in psychology, which is part of the world describ-

able in language. Thus Wittgenstein says in 5.6 that "*The boundary of my language* is the boundary of my world." For the boundaries of language themselves determine the boundaries of the world of the metaphysical subject's "logical space" of possible worlds. And yet, as for Schopenhauer, this world is nevertheless *my* world, as he declares in 5.62: "That the world is *my* world reveals itself in the fact that the boundary of language (the language that I alone understand) is the boundary of *my* world."

But what does he mean in claiming that everything—the world—is made of *facts*? What is a Wittgensteinian *fact*? Wittgenstein construes facts, not in some *standard* type of realism but as "states of affairs" (*Sachverhalten*), such that he really meant that any particular *Sachverhalt* may or may not be the case. Indeed, in that regard he talks about positive and negative facts, where a positive fact is the existence of a particular state of affairs and a negative fact is the non-existence of a particular state of affairs. Thus, for instance, "The Eiffel tower is taller than Mt. Everest" is a negative fact and "Mt. Everest is taller than the Eiffel Tower" is a positive fact. Indeed, he says of facts (in 1.21) that "Each one can be the case or not be the case while all else remains the same," which establishes for him the distinction between that which Wittgenstein thinks the world is made of—facts—from what common sense says it is made of—things. It should be noted, however, that one major difference between things as ordinarily understood, especially by German-speaking philosophers, is that "If one thing changes its qualities, this can have an effect upon another thing. Things affect each other and resist each one another. . . . This description of things and their interdependence corresponds to what we call the "natural conception of the world" (Heidegger, *What Is a Thing* [South Bend, Indiana: Regnery/Gateway, 1967, p33]." Notice that here Heidegger, who is as wildly antithetical to any natural conception as Wittgenstein (although in a different way), nicely and no doubt unintentionally illustrated for us why Wittgenstein would have wanted to insist (and did) that the *world did not consist of such items* (things) but of items that are implicitly *not* linked into a cosmos as conceived in natural science.

Let us apply this concept to a familiar situation. "Kolak is in his study," is at this moment a true simple declarative sentence. It describes a particular state of affairs. Likewise, "Kolak is sitting in a chair," is also true. It describes a different particular state of affairs. "Kolak is writing," is also true and describes yet another particular state of affairs. These three states of affairs just described using the above three sentences are all related by virtue of a *fact*. It is difficult, perhaps impossible, to say exactly what this fact is, even to specify its boundaries or to enumerate it (i.e., count it) in relation to other facts about the world. In an important sense, we don't know how many facts the world consists of because we cannot specify their borders—only the boundary of the world (something that the whole *Tractatus* sets out to delineate.) In that sense facts are thus as elusive to the mind as Kant's things-in-themselves (*ding-an-sich*). However, unlike facts, sentences—which are their linguistic representatives—can be enumerated, and there exists the totality of true statements within a language, and so on. So in speaking of particular states of affairs, Wittgenstein is alluding to the fact that, for instance, it can be observed or seen that Kolak is in his study, sitting in a chair, writing, and so on—particular states of affairs all of which can be described via the content of simple declarative sentences (I just did it), "information bundles" packaged either in linguistic terms (sentences describing observed situations) or in experiential terms (items in a visual field). Often, but not always, it may help our understanding to think of "states of affairs" as synonymous to what is available to the perceiving subject in a particular visual field, in terms of the relations of the objects present in that visual field. Indeed, it is in saying that we cannot talk about anything beyond what is present in such states of affairs that Wittgenstein made himself so useful to the logical positivists and members of the Vienna circle. Likewise, it

sometimes helps to think of "states of affairs" as a synonym for *statements*. (Below I discuss the sense in which both visual events and linguistic events can be seen as the mind's "statements to itself" [my terminology, not Wittgenstein's].)

Wittgenstein offers a subtle and brilliant solution to the problematic nature of the relation in philosophy between [phenomenal] objects to things [in themselves, in Kant's sense], in terms of what he conceives the true meaning of the word to *be*. In speaking of x as a *thing*, collection of *things* or *somethings*, and so on, Wittgenstein—like many a philosopher from Kant to Heidegger—is trying to refer to *x* in the most neutral way possible. The "object" already is specific; it has a direction. (The German *Gegenstand* means, literally, "against" [*gegen*] + "stand" [*stand*]). That which it stands against is of course the *subject*, and we have ourselves borne witness to the long philosophical tradition—not just in idealism but in a variety of radical empiricisms, phenomenalisms, and presentationalisms—in which it is held that in order to exist, objects as such require a subject. *Thing*, on the other hand, implies something that can stand on its own, independently of being directed at (or, in some views [Fichte's, Schelling's, Schopenhauer's] *from*) a subject. This view minimizes one Wittgensteinian tension only to leave us with the problem of how we should then interpret his claim that "The world is the totality of facts, not of things." For although Wittgenstein's view of what the world is—like Schopenhauer's—is that the world is, literally, *his* world and no one else's, the items of which it is composed and that stand independently of the ego are not things but facts. And this, again, moves us away from the kind of linkage presented in scientific theories to the unique type of Wittgensteinian linkage.

Let me then restate what we have considered thus far; according to Wittgenstein, the *world* (*Die Welt*) is the totality of *facts* (*Tatsachen*), which consist of *elementary facts* (*Sachverhalte*) which, in turn, consist of configurations of *objects* (*Gegenstande*). He uses the word *thing* to emphasize that he is trying to refer to "a something" in as simple and generic a way as possible to mean "a something, an any sort of something," that (in this case) constitutes (is a constituent of) an elementary fact.[2] Language itself provides the means by which something (the objects of the world) are referenced through symbolization, such that existence is implied. That is, the objects themselves are expressed in symbolic form and thus, by studying the forms, we study the objects themselves. Since the world is the totality of facts, not things by *substance* (i.e., that which exists independently), it is not the concept of *matter* but *logical form* that is for Wittgenstein the most "real" existence (it is permanent, necessary, and unalterable). And yet he uses the word *form* in several different ways. It can mean *shape*, as in the "form of a spot," *type* or *kind*, as in "form of independence," or *content,* as in "the form of the visual field," or any combination thereof to show the way in which the world is collectively organized into a coherent whole. In a rather mystical sense, the medium *is* itself the message; language and world "*entsprechen,*" which can be translated as "correspond," but which has an extremely revealing etymology that is in accord with Wittgenstein's overall theory: it means, literally, "to speak for." The world is not silent; it speaks. Experiences are its sayings. That's what Wittgenstein had in mind while building his bridge between sentences and facts.

The key representing relation by which language makes contact with reality is, itself, part of the picture. That is, a picture does not need to resemble what it depicts, so that we can somehow depict this resemblance to ourselves. The idea is that nothing stands between our language and our application of that language to the world; they are already in contact.

According to Wittgenstein, to think is to form mental pictures. What is not possible is not thinkable. Therefore, in Wittgenstein's view, (meaningful) sentences are thoughts expressed in a communicable way. It will help here to think of a projection in geometry, where say a 3-D cube is projected onto a 2-D coordinate system. This illuminating image takes us all the way back to Plato's

ideal forms, where the relation of an elementary sentence to an elementary fact is like a projected shadow of an ideal form. That is the sense in which the "world" you presently see around you is a pictorial statement—your mind talking to itself with pictures. What I think Wittgenstein means is that the objects you see presently before you (say, this book) are, literally, concepts illuminated into actual presence by the mind; they are phenomenal and they are a veneer (and, in *that* sense an illusion or a false showing) but ones that are ultimately revealing. (One might playfully add, "What cannot be seen must not be looked at," and think of visual phenomena as *perceptual notation.*)

In 4 of the *Tractatus* Wittgenstein makes the radical claim that, "A sentence that makes sense is a thought." This can be taken in two different ways, one which we might think of as the conservative, *linguistic* sense and the other which we might think of as the radical, *semiotic* sense. In the radical, semiotic sense we can understand him to mean that a sentence that makes sense *is* what a thought is; in other words, minds or consciousness as conceived in some super-linguistic (i.e., supernatural) terms are absolutely not required. The early Wittgenstein, just as we saw in Russell and Peirce, can thus be seen as intuiting a computational approach to the problem of consciousness, where the computations are logical processes and the items processed are linguistic objects. On the related matter of what we might think of as "the linguistic extraction of truth from the logical structure of the world," we might by analogy say, "Given that I have 10 things, I have two things," "Given that I have 100 things, I have two things," and, most perspicuously, "Given that I have $\aleph_0$ things I have n things," where n is any number I choose. This concept is telling because for Wittgenstein there are in fact $\aleph_0$ "things" of which the world is comprised, except they are not things but facts. It is extremely illuminating to conceive of the relation of a particular fact to the world in toto as conceptually mirrored in the relation of a particular number, say 3, to $\aleph_0$. What I like about this view is that you cannot in fact remove any number from $\aleph_0$, and in that sense all numbers are *necessarily* a part of $\aleph_0$, just as each and every fact is necessarily a part of the world, except the nature of the connection is negative. Hence there is a Buddhist-like centrality in the *Tractatus* and in Wittgenstein's thought in general of the operation of *negation*. It is a unique point of contact, the blind spot in the mirror—the point at which the particulars of sentential language and the statements out of which the facts of which the world is comprised connect. After all, the blind spot is what makes vision possible; it is where the optic "nerve" connects the eye to the brain. That is the sense in which the concept of negation is unique; it is the central black hole in Wittgenstein's negative of the cosmos, in that it not only expresses the common rule for *all logical operations* but also forms the foundation for the *general form of truth function*, the *general form of an operation*, and the *general form of a sentence*.

Beyond this structure, and within it, is the mystical: "(6.44) It's not *how* the world is that is mystical but *that* it is. (6.45) To view the world *sub specie aeterni* is the view of it as a—bounded—whole. The feeling of the world as a bounded whole is the mystical feeling. (6.5) If the answer cannot be put into words the question, too, cannot be put into words. *The riddle* does not exist. . . . (6.522) The inexpressible indeed exists. This *shows* itself. It is the mystical. . . . (6.54) My sentences are illuminating in the following way: to understand me you must recognize my sentences—once you have climbed out through them, on them, over them—as senseless. (You must, so to speak, throw away the ladder, after you have climbed up on it.) You must climb out through my sentences; then you will see the world correctly. (7) Of what we cannot speak we must be silent."

The *Tractatus* gave much impetus to the antimetaphysical views of the logical positivists, and yet, ironically, it is also a call to a unique type of mysticism. In trying to say what can properly be only "shown," Wittgenstein claims he is

trying to stand outside language. According to his own view, however—since sense exists only within the limits of language—everything he is saying in the *Tractatus* is therefore, strictly speaking, "nonsense." Acknowledging that it is nonsense, he claims that his book is a very special type of illuminating nonsense.

It is illuminating to read Wittgenstein's own notes about the meaning of his text. At Harvard, one student of Russell's who served as his teaching assistant happened to keep a copy of Wittgenstein's original "Notes on Logic," dated September 1913, to help him deal with the puzzled students who came to see him. He writes:

❧

In the spring of 1914 Bertrand Russell came to Harvard as a visiting lecturer. One of his two courses was on logic, and I was assigned to assist him with it. He was late in arriving, and I gave two or three weeks of lectures, mostly on how to read the symbolism of the *Principia Mathematica*. His lectures also largely followed the *Principia*. He assigned Frege's *Foundations of Arithmetic* to be read—in German. He also had with him some notes and excerpts, giving the opinions of a brilliant student of his, named Ludwig Wittgenstein, who had been recommended by Frege to come to him. I copied this manuscript, dated September, 1913.

It is Wittgenstein's theory of that time about propositions. I may say, as a first approximation of my own, a proposition is not the words of a statement, but it is *what the statement says*. It is the same proposition, whether it is asserted or denied, believed, considered, referred to, emoted over. In a sense it is intended as a description of fact, but you can understand it without knowing the fact, if you know *what would be the case if the proposition were true, and what the case if it were false*. It always has a contradictory, only one of them true, the other false. It and its contradictory, have a complementary "sense" (*Sinn*), and the same "meaning" (*Bedeutung*), the meaning being the external fact, the fact meant, and they have only one fact between them. The two thus referring to

From Harry Costello, "Logic in 1914 and Now," *Journal of Philosophy*, April 1957.

the same fact, says Wittgenstein, are really only one proposition with two poles. You are able to verify the proposition as true when you observe that the pole you have asserted fits the fact. But it remains the statement of two alternative possibilities, of which you now know which alternative is true. The verified proposition is still double and symbolic, and does not fuse with the corresponding fact and disappear—as it did, for instance, in Royce's Hegelian "inner meaning and outer meaning of an idea." If you deny a proposition instead of asserting it, you reverse the polarity, and two such denials bring you back where you started. Russell indicated this on the blackboard by an arrow, which you might reverse and reverse again.

⚚

Wittgenstein was known to get extremely angry whenever anyone would analyze his work; at one point he screamed at a roomful of eminent philosophers, telling them that he had written a beautiful poem, which was not meant to be dissected by them!

The initial reception of the *Tractatus* was mixed. In his introduction to the book, Russell called it an "important event in the philosophical world." But another important twentieth-century philosopher, Clarence Irving (C. I.) Lewis, who also did foundational work in logic, wrote in a letter to the editor of the prestigious *Journal of Philosophy*:

> Have you looked at Wittgenstein's new book yet? I am much discouraged by Russell's foolishness in writing the introduction to such nonsense. I fear it will be looked upon as what symbolic logic leads to. If so, it will be the death of the subject.*

Lewis apparently changed his mind a decade later when he claimed that "the nature of logical

*See Lewis's cover letter to his "A Pragmatic Conception of the A Priori," in *The Journal of Philosophy* 20 (1923) 169–177: quoted in Burton Dreben and Juliet Floyd, "Tautology: how Not to Use a Word," Synthese 87 (1991) 23–49.

truth itself has become more definitely understood, largely through the discussions of Wittgenstein."[3]

The *Tractatus* contains seven propositions, numbered 1 through 7, along with secondary propositions that are observations of the first, 1.1, 2.1, and so on, each of which is followed by tertiary propositions that are observations of the observations, 1.11, 2.11, and so on.

⚚

Tractatus Logico-Philosophicus

1 The world is all that is the case.

1.1 The world is the totality of facts, not of things. . . .

1.12 For the totality of facts determines all that is the case and also all that is not the case. . . .

1.13 The facts in logical space are the world.

2 What is the case—a fact—is the existence of elementary facts.

2.01 An elementary fact is a combination of objects (items, things).

2.02 Objects are simple.

2.03 In an elementary fact the objects hang in one another like the links of a chain. . . .

2.063 The sum total of reality is the world.

2.1 We make pictures of facts to ourselves.

2.11 Such a picture represents an elementary fact in logical space, the existence and nonexistence of elementary facts.

2.12 Such a picture is a model of reality.

2.13 To the objects correspond, in such a picture, the elements of the picture. . . .

2.2 A picture must have the logical form of representation in common with what it depicts.

2.21 Such a picture agrees with reality or not; it is right or wrong, true or false.

2.22 Such a picture represents what it represents independently of its truth or falsity, via its representational form.

2.221 What this picture represents is its sense.

2.222 Its truth or falsity consists in the agreement or disagreement of its sense with reality.

From *Wittgenstein's Tractatus*, translated by Daniel Kolak (Mountain View, CA: Mayfield, 1998).

3.0 A thought is a logical picture of a fact.

3.01 The totality of all true thoughts is a picture of the world. . . .

3.1 In a sentence the thought expresses itself perceptibly.

3.11 We use a sentence (spoken or written, etc.) as a projection of a possible fact.
The method of projection is our thinking the sense of the sentence. . . .

4 A sentence that makes sense is a thought.

4.01 A sentence is a picture of reality.

A sentence is a model of reality as we think it is.

4.02 This we see from the fact that we understand the sense of a sentence without having had it explained to us.

4.021 A sentence is a picture of reality, for if I understand the sentence I know the fact represented by it. And I understand the sentence without its sense having been explained to me. . . .

5.6 *The boundary of my language* is the boundary of my world.

5.61 Logic fills the world: the boundary of logic is also the boundary of the world.

So in logic we cannot say, "The world has this in it and this, but not that."

For apparently presuppose that some possibilities were thereby being excluded, which cannot possibly be the case, since this would require that logic should extend beyond the boundary of the world; for only then could it have a view from the other side of the boundary.

What we cannot think, that we cannot think: we cannot therefore *say* what we cannot think.

5.62 This thought itself shows how much truth there is in solipsism.

What the solipsist intends to say is absolutely correct. The problem is that the truth cannot speak but only shows itself.

That the world is *my* world reveals itself in the fact that the boundary of language (the language that I alone understand) is the boundary of *my* world.

5.621 The world and life are one.

5.63 1 am my world. (The microcosm.)

5.631 The thinking, perceiving subject does not exist.

If I were to write a book, *The World as I Found It,* I would also have to include an account of my body in it, and report which parts are subject to my will and which not., etc. This then would be

a method of isolating the subject, or rather of showing that in an important sense there is no subject; that is to say: of it alone in this book mention could *not* be made.

5.632 The subject does not belong to the world but is the boundary of the world.

5.633 Where *in* the world could a metaphysical subject be? You say this is just like the case with the eye and the visual field. But you do *not* really see the eye.

And there is nothing *in the visual field* to let you infer that it is being seen through an eye.

5.64 Here we can see that solipsism thoroughly thought out coincides with pure realism. The *I* in solipsism shrinks to an extensionless point and there remains the reality coordinated with it.

5.641 Thus there really is a sense in which philosophy can speak about the self in a non-psychological way.

The *I* occurs in philosophy through the fact that the "world is my world."

The philosophical *I* is not the human being, not the human body, nor the human soul with which psychology deals. The philosophical self is the metaphysical subject, the boundary—nowhere in the world. . . .

6.1 The sentences of logic are tautologies.

6.11 The sentences of logic therefore say nothing. (They are analytic sentences.)

6.12 The fact that the sentences of logic are tautologies shows the formal—logical—properties of language, of the world.

6.13 Logic is not a theory about the world but a reflection of it, its mirror-image.

Logic is transcendent. . . .

6.41 The meaning of the world must lie outside the world. In the world everything is as it is, everything happens as it does happen; there is no value *in* it—if there were any, the value would be worthless.

For a value to be worth something, it must lie outside all happening and outside being this way or that. For all happening and being this way or that is accidental.

The non-accidental cannot be found in the world, for otherwise this too would then be accidental.

The value of the world lies outside it.

6.42 Likewise, there can be no sentences in ethics. Sentences cannot express anything higher.

6.421 Clearly, ethics cannot be put into words. Ethics is transcendent.

(Ethics and esthetics are one.)

6.422 As soon as we set up an ethical law having the form "thou shalt . . .," our first thought is: So then what if I don't do it? But clearly ethics has nothing to do with punishment and reward in the ordinary sense. The question about the consequences of my action must therefore be irrelevant. At least these consequences will not be events. For there must be something right in that formulation of the question. There must be some sort of ethical reward and ethical punishment, but this must lie in the action itself.

6.423 We cannot speak of the will as if it were the ethical subject.

And the will as a phenomenon is only of interest to psychology.

6.43 If good or bad willing changes the world, it only changes the boundaries of the world, not the facts; not the things that can be expressed in language.

6.431 In death, too, the world does not change but only ceases.

6.4311 Death is not an event in life. Death is not lived through.

If by *eternity* we mean not endless temporal duration but timelessness, then to live eternally is to live in the present.

In the same way as our visual field is without boundary, our life is endless.

6.4312 The temporal immortality of the human soul—its eternal survival after death—is not only without guarantee, this assumption could never have the desired effect. Is a riddle solved by the fact that I survive forever? Is eternal life not as enigmatic as our present one? The solution of the riddle of life in space and time lies *outside* of space and time.

(Certainly it does not involve solutions to any of the problems of natural science.)

6.432 *How* the world is, is completely indifferent to what is higher. God does not reveal himself in the world.

6.4321 The facts all belong to the setting up of the problem, not to its solution.

6.44 It's not *how* the world is that is mystical but that it is.

6.45 To view the world *sub specie aeterni* is the view of it as—bounded—whole.

The feeling of the world as a bounded whole is the mystical feeling.

6.5 If the answer cannot be put into words the question, too, cannot be put into words.

The riddle does not exist.

If a question can be put at all, then it *can* also be answered.

6.51 Skepticism is *not* irrefutable, only nonsensical, in so far as it tries to raise doubts about what cannot be asked.

For doubt can only exist provided there is a question; a question can exist only provided there is an answer, and this can only be the case provided something *can* be *said*.

6.52 We feel that even if *all possible* scientific questions were answered, the problems of life would still not have been touched at all. To be sure, there would then be no question left, and just this is the answer.

6.521 The vanishing of this problem is the solution to the problem of life.

(Is this not the very reason why people to whom after long bouts of doubt the meaning of life became clear, could not then say what this meaning is?)

6.522 The inexpressible indeed exists. This *shows* itself. It is the mystical.

6.53 The right method in philosophy would be to say nothing except what can be said using sentences such as those of natural science—which of course has nothing to do with philosophy—and then, to show those wishing to say something metaphysical that they failed to give any meaning to certain signs in their sentences. Although they would not be satisfied—they would feel you weren't teaching them any philosophy—*this* would be the only right method.

6.54 My sentences are illuminating in the following way: to understand me you must recognize my sentences—once you have climbed out through them, on them, over them—as senseless. (You must, so to speak, throw away the ladder, after you have climbed up on it.)

You must climb out through my sentences; then you will see the world correctly.

7 Of what we cannot speak we must be silent.

Wittgenstein's picture theory of language and his austere tone of logical rigor sever what can be said—sense—from what cannot be said—the mystical—with explicit statements to the effect that philosophy must remain completely silent about that which is beyond language. This view led the logical positivists, who thought that the traditional philosophical domain of metaphysics was bankrupt, to welcome the *Tractatus* as their bible. Wittgenstein regarded the positivists' interpretation of his work as too narrow and missing the essential point of the mystical allusions. Overall, however, Wittgenstein was fully satisfied with his work; he felt certain that he had successfully answered all of philosophy's main questions and thus abandoned the profession in favor of teaching elementary school in the Austrian Alps. Shunning what he considered the trappings of wealth, Wittgenstein had by then given away his share of the family fortune, and so when he grew disillusioned with teaching elementary school he worked as a gardener in a nearby monastery, taking time off to design a house for one of his sisters.

Seven years later, in 1929, Russell arranged for Wittgenstein to be awarded a doctorate in philosophy on the basis of the *Tractatus.* Wittgenstein thus returned to Cambridge and remained there as lecturer. In 1937, he succeeded G. E. Moore in the chair of philosophy. He shunned academic life, however, and lectured mostly in his own rooms, spontaneously, and without notes, in an effort to always create something new by his method of "philosophizing out loud." Although he wrote much and circulated some of his writings among his students, he did not allow any of them to be published during his lifetime. In 1947, he resigned from Cambridge and spent the rest of his life in seclusion, working on various unfinished manuscripts and occasionally visiting his former students.

It has often been said that Wittgenstein is unique in the history of philosophy for having inspired two very different and in many ways antithetical philosophical movements. Just as the *Tractatus* inspired a whole generation of logical positivists, his *Philosophical Investigations* (1953), published two years after his

death, was instrumental in advancing ordinary language philosophy. In the preface, Wittgenstein writes:

⚓

the thoughts which I publish in what follows are the precipitate of philosophical investigations which have occupied me for the last sixteen years. They concern many subjects: the concepts of meaning, of understanding, of a proposition, of logic, the foundations of mathematics, states of consciousness, and other things. I have written down all these thoughts as *remarks,* short paragraphs, of which there is sometimes a fairly long chain about the same subject, while I sometimes make a sudden change, jumping from one topic to another.

⚓

Philosophical Investigations begins with a criticism of his former picture theory of language and of the *Tractatus* as a whole, with an Augustinelike confession regarding his previous views: "I have been forced to recognize grave mistakes in what I wrote." He claimed that the *Tractatus* had captured only one of the many uses of language. The other legitimate uses can be found in ordinary language through meanings derived from social, tribal, cultural, scientific, and psychological contexts. Thus, according to his new and improved theory, "the meaning of a word is its use in the language." In his *Investigations,* Wittgenstein puts forth his new game theory of language, according to which the rules of the game change from one game to another. For instance, he uses the example of pain to argue that mental concepts do not refer to inner private states; uncovering the "logical grammar of pain" reveals that our sensations, thoughts, and experiences cannot be understood using a private language. Language

---

From *Philosophical Investigations*, trans. G. E. M. Anscombe (Oxford: Blackwell, 1953).

exists through usage defined by social constructions; correct language use cannot be stipulated by private rules of application.

⚹

Excerpts from Wittgenstein's Philosophical Investigations

69. How should we explain to someone what a game is? I imagine that we should describe *games* to him, and we might add: "This *and similar things* are called 'games'." And do we know any more about it ourselves? Is it only other people whom we cannot tell exactly what a game is?—But this is not ignorance. We do not know the boundaries because none have been drawn. To repeat, we can draw a boundary—for a special purpose. Does it take that to make the concept usable? Not at all! (Except for that special purpose.) . . .

129. The aspects of things that are most important for us are hidden because of their simplicity and familiarity. (One is unable to notice something—because it is always before one's eyes.) The real foundations of his enquiry do not strike a man at all. Unless *that* fact has at some time struck him.—And this means: we fail to be struck by what, once seen, is most striking and most powerful. . . .

371. *Essence* is expressed by grammar.

372. Consider: "The only correlate in language to an intrinsic necessity is an arbitrary rule. It is the only thing which one can milk out of this intrinsic necessity into a proposition."

373. Grammar tells what kind of object anything is. (Theology as grammar.) . . .

426. A picture is conjured up which seems to fix the sense *unambiguously*. The actual use, compared with that suggested by the picture, seems like something muddied. Here again we get the same thing as in set theory: the form of expression we use seems to have been designed for a god, who knows what we cannot know; he sees the whole of each of those infinite series and he sees into human consciousness. For us, of course, these forms of expression are like pontificals which we may put on, but cannot do much with, since we

lack the effective power that would give these vestments meaning and purpose.

In the actual use of expressions we make detours, we go by sideroads. We see the straight highway before us, but of course we cannot use it, because it is permanently closed. . . .

454. "Everything is already there in. . . . " How does it come about that [an] arrow *points*? Doesn't it seem to carry in it something besides itself?— "No, not the dead line on paper; only the psychical thing, the meaning, can do that."—That is both true and false. The arrow points only in the application that a living being makes of it.

This pointing is *not* a hocus-pocus which can be performed only by the soul. . . .

464. My aim is: to teach you to pass from a piece of disguised nonsense to something that is patent nonsense. . . .

504. But if you say: "How am I to know what he means, when I see nothing but the signs he gives?" then I say: "How is *he* to know what he means, when he has nothing but the signs either?" . . .

512. It looks as if we could say: "Word-language allows of senseless combinations of words, but the language of imagining does not allow us to imagine anything senseless.—Hence, too, the language of drawing doesn't allow of senseless drawings? Suppose they were drawings from which bodies were supposed to be modelled. In this case some drawings make sense, some not.—What if I imagine senseless combinations of words? . . .

562. But how can I decide what is an essential, and what an inessential, accidental, feature of the notation? Is there some reality lying behind the notation, which shapes its grammar? Let us think of a similar case in a game: in [checkers] a king is marked by putting one piece on top of another. Now won't one say it is inessential to the game for a king to consist of two pieces? . . .

564. So I am inclined to distinguish between the essential and the inessential in a game too. The game, one would like to say, has not only rules but also a *point* . . . .

574. A proposition, and hence in another sense a thought, can be the 'expression' of belief, hope, expectation, etc. But believing is not thinking. (A grammatical remark.) The concepts of believing, expecting, hoping are less distantly related to one another than they are to the concept of thinking. . . .

From *Philosophical Investigations*, trans. G. E. M. Anscombe (Oxford: Blackwell, 1953).

635. "I was going to say . . . "—You remember various details. But not even all of them together show your intention. It is as if a snapshot of a scene had been taken, but only a few scattered details of it were to be seen: here a hand, there a bit of a face, or a hat—the rest is dark. And now it is as if we knew quite certainly what the whole picture represented. As if I could read the darkness. . . .

655. The question is not one of explaining a language-game by means of our experiences, but of noting a language-game.

⚓

Although Wittgenstein's *Investigations* exemplifies his philosophical shift, on the one hand, from a pictorial to a descriptive view of language and, on the other, from logical atomism to linguistic pluralism, the task of Wittgensteinian philosophy remains in many ways the same. Philosophy according to Wittgenstein is still the "battle against the bewitchment of our intelligence by means of language," whose ultimate purpose is to show "the fly the way out of the flybottle."

23.3 Quine (1908–): The Boundary Dissolves

Willard Van Orman Quine was born in Akron, Ohio. While still in high school he showed an aptitude for both formal mathematics and the grammar and etymology of natural language. At the same time, he says he saw the "implausibility of the home religion" and tried to convert his friends from "their Episcopalian faith to atheism." What inspired him most of all to do philosophy was his fascination with Edgar Allan Poe's "Eureka," a poem that "for all its outrageousness fostered the real thing: the desire to understand the universe. So did the antireligious motive."

As an undergraduate at Oberlin, Quine concentrated on mathematics and mathematical philosophy, especially the works of Peano,[4] Russell, and Whitehead. He went on to study philosophy at Harvard, where he received a doctorate in only two years. In his second year, a visit from Russell during which Whitehead (who chaired the department) and Russell shared the podium to give a joint talk—his "most dazzling exposure to greatness"—moved Quine to write his dissertation on *The Logic of Sequences: A Generalization of "Principia Mathematica,"* later published as his first book, *A System of Logic.* In it, Quine presents an original view of logic in "kinship with the most general and systematic aspects of natural science, farthest from observation. Mathematics and logic are supported by observation only in the indirect way that those aspects of natural science are supported by observation; namely, as participating in an organized whole which, way up at its empirical edges, squares with observation."

After earning his doctorate, Quine accepted a series of postdoctoral fellowships in Vienna, Prague, and Warsaw, where he met and studied with Moritz Schlick, who founded the logical positivist group known as the Vienna Circle, the philosopher of science Hans Reichenbach, as well as the logical positivist Rudolf Carnap and the great mathematician and logician Adolph Tarski. Upon his return to the United States in 1936, Quine went back to Harvard as an instructor in philosophy. Over the next several years he published *Mathematical Logic* (1940) and *Elementary Logic* (1941) at a time during which "Germans massacred Jews, Germans swarmed over France, Japanese bombed Hawaii. Logic seemed off the point." So he joined the navy and worked for radio intelligence in Washington. After the war he returned to Harvard and became a full professor in 1948.

At a lecture delivered at Yale and published a few years later in *The Review of Metaphysics,* Quine addressed the age-old problem of "ontological commitment"—the fundamental question of how to decide philosophical disputes over *what there is.*

⚓

On What There Is

The physical conceptual scheme simplifies our account of experience because of the way myriad scattered sense events come to be associated with single so-called objects; still there is no likelihood that each sentence about physical objects can actually be translated, however deviously and complexly, into the phenomenalistic language. Physical objects are postulated entities which round out and simplify our account of the flux of experience, just as the introduction of irrational numbers simplifies laws of arithmetic. From the point of view of the conceptual scheme of the elementary arithmetic of rational numbers alone, the broader arithmetic of rational and irrational numbers would have the status of a convenient myth, simpler than the literal truth (namely, the arithmetic of rationals) and yet containing that literal truth as a scattered part. Similarly, from a phenomenalistic point of view, the conceptual scheme of physical objects is a convenient myth, simpler than the literal truth and yet containing that literal truth as a scattered part.

Now what of classes or attributes of physical objects, in turn? A platonistic ontology of this sort is, from the point of view of a strictly physicalistic conceptual scheme, as much a myth as that physicalistic conceptual scheme itself is for phenomenalism. This higher myth is a good and useful one, in turn, in so far as it simplifies our account of physics. Since mathematics is an integral part of this higher myth, the utility of this myth for physical science is evident enough. In speaking of it nevertheless as a myth, I echo that philosophy of mathematics to which I alluded earlier under the name of formalism. But an attitude of formalism may with equal justice be adopted toward the physical conceptual scheme, in turn, by the pure aesthete or phenomenalist.

The analogy between the myth of mathematics and the myth of physics is, in some additional and perhaps fortuitous ways, strikingly close. Consider, for example, the crisis which was precipitated in the foundations of mathematics, at the turn of the century, by the discovery of Russell's paradox and other antinomies of set theory. These contradic-

tions had to be obviated by unintuitive, *ad hoc* devices; our mathematical myth-making became deliberate and evident to all. But what of physics? An antinomy arose between the undular and the corpuscular accounts of light; and if this was not as out-and-out a contradiction as Russell's paradox, I suspect that the reason is that physics is not as out-and-out as mathematics. Again, the second great modern crisis in the foundations of mathematics—precipitated in 1931 by Gödel's proof that there are bound to be undecidable statements in arithmetic—has its companion piece in physics in Heisenberg's indeterminacy principle.

In earlier pages I undertook to show that some common arguments in favor of certain ontologies are fallacious. Further, I advanced an explicit standard whereby to decide what the ontological commitments of a theory are. But the question what ontology actually to adopt still stands open, and the obvious counsel is tolerance and an experimental spirit. Let us by all means see how much of the physicalistic conceptual scheme can be reduced to a phenomenalistic one; still, physics also naturally demands pursuing, irreducible *in toto* though it be. Let us see how, or to what degree, natural science may be rendered independent of platonistic mathematics; but let us also pursue mathematics and delve into its platonistic foundations.

From among the various conceptual schemes best suited to these various pursuits, one—the phenomenalistic—claims epistemological priority. Viewed from within the phenomenalistic conceptual scheme, the ontologies of physical objects and mathematical objects are myths. The quality of myth, however, is relative; relative, in this case, to the epistemological point of view. This point of view is one among various, corresponding to one among our various interests and purposes.

⚹

Is the universe a mental object? A material object? Does consciousness exist? Influenced by pragmatism, by Russell, and by Ockham's razor, Quine tries to solve disputes over the "old Platonic riddle of nonbeing" in an ingenious way, by arguing for relativity; different, even opposing, philosophical stances, such as phenomenalism and physicalism, should best be viewed as essentially different but equally funda-

From Quine, "On What There Is," *Review of Metaphysics*, Vol. 2 (1948).

mental points of view, whose preference must be determined depending on one's practical purposes. Ultimately, "the ontological controversy should tend into controversy over language." That is, the issue of what exists resolves itself into the question of what some statement or doctrine *says* exists. Such "ontological relativity" would later be even further developed by Quine in his *Ontological Relativity*.

The following famous lecture, delivered in 1951 to the American Philosophical Association, became an instant classic. Entitled "Two Dogmas of Empiricism," it was published subsequently as the second chapter of *From a Logical Point of View*. In it, Quine presents a challenge to the fundamental, age-old distinction between analytic and synthetic truth by claiming that "a boundary between analytic and synthetic statements simply has not been drawn." That there is such a distinction to be drawn at all is an unempirical dogma of empiricists, a metaphysical article of faith.

⚹

Two Dogmas of Empiricism

Modern empiricism has been conditioned in large part by two dogmas. One is a belief in some fundamental cleavage between truths which are *analytic*, or grounded in meanings independently of matters of fact, and truths which are *synthetic*, or grounded in fact. The other dogma is *reductionism*: the belief that each meaningful statement is equivalent to some logical construct upon terms which refer to immediate experience. Both dogmas, I shall argue, are ill-founded. One effect of abandoning them is, as we shall see, a blurring of the supposed boundary between speculative metaphysics and natural science. Another effect is a shift toward pragmatism.

1. Background for Analyticity

Kant's cleavage between analytic and synthetic truths was foreshadowed in Hume's distinction between relations of ideas and matters of fact, and

in Leibniz's distinction between truths of reason and truths of fact. Leibniz spoke of the truths of reason as true in all possible worlds. Picturesqueness aside, this is to say that the truths of reason are those which could not possibly be false. In the same vein we hear analytic statements defined as statements whose denials are self-contradictory. But this definition has small explanatory value; for the notion of self-contradictoriness, in the quite broad sense needed for this definition of analyticity, stands in exactly the same need of clarification as does the notion of analyticity itself. The two notions are the two sides of a single dubious coin.

Kant conceived of an analytic statement as one that attributes to its subject no more than is already conceptually contained in the subject. This formulation has two shortcomings: it limits itself to statements of subject-predicate form, and it appeals to a notion of containment which is left at a metaphorical level. But Kant's intent, evident more from the use he makes of the notion of analyticity than from his definition of it, can be restated thus: a statement is analytic when it is true by virtue of meanings and independently of fact. Pursuing this line, let us examine the concept of *meaning* which is presupposed.

Meaning, let us remember, is not to be identified with Frege's example of 'Evening Star' and 'Morning Star,' and Russell's of 'Scott' and 'the author of *Waverley*,' illustrate that terms can name the same thing but differ in meaning. The distinction between meaning and naming is no less important at the level of abstract terms. The terms '9' and 'the number of the planets' name one and the same abstract entity but presumably must be regarded as unlike in meaning; for astronomical observation was needed, and not mere reflection on meanings, to determine the sameness of the entity in question.

The above examples consist of singular terms, concrete and abstract. With general terms, or predicates, the situation is somewhat different but parallel. Whereas a singular term purports to name an entity, abstract or concrete, a general term does not; but a general term is *true of* an entity, or of each of many, or of none. The class of all entities of which a general term is true is called the *extension* of the term. Now paralleling the contrast between the meaning of a singular term and the entity named, we must distinguish equally between the meaning of a general term and its

---

From *Philosophical Review*, 1951.

extension. The general terms 'creature with a heart' and 'creature with kidneys,' for example, are perhaps alike in extension but unlike in meaning.

Confusion of meaning with extension, in the case of general terms, is less common than confusion of meaning with naming in the case of singular terms. It is indeed a commonplace in philosophy to oppose intension (or meaning) to extension, or, in a variant vocabulary, connotation and denotation.

The Aristotelian notion of essence was the forerunner, no doubt, of the modern notion of intension or meaning. For Aristotle it was essential in men to be rational, accidental to be two-legged. But there is an important difference between this attitude and the doctrine of meaning. From the latter point of view it may indeed be conceded (if only for the sake of argument) that rationality is involved in the meaning of the word 'man' while two-leggedness is not; but two-leggedness may at the same time be viewed as involved in the meaning of 'biped' while rationality is not. Thus from the point of view of the doctrine of meaning it makes no sense to say of the actual individual, who is at once a man and a biped, that his rationality is essential and his two-leggedness accidental or vice versa. Things had essences, for Aristotle, but only linguistic forms have meanings. Meaning is what essence becomes when it is divorced from the object of reference and wedded to the word.

For the theory of meaning a conspicuous question is the nature of its objects: what sort of things are meanings? A felt need for meant entities may derive from an earlier failure to appreciate that meaning and reference are distinct. Once the theory of meaning is sharply separated from the theory of reference, it is a short step to recognizing as the primary business of the theory of meaning simply the synonymy of linguistic forms and the analyticity of statements; meanings themselves, as obscure intermediary entities, may well be abandoned.

The problem of analyticity then confronts us anew. Statements which are analytic by general philosophical acclaim are not, indeed, far to seek. They fall into two classes. Those of the first class, which may be called *logically true,* are typified by:

(1) No unmarried man is married.

The relevant feature of this example is that it not merely is true as it stands, but remains true under any and all reinterpretations of 'man' and 'married.' If we suppose a prior inventory of *logical*

particles, comprising 'no,' 'un-,' 'not,' 'if,' 'then,' 'and,' etc., then in general a logical truth is a statement which is true and remains true under all reinterpretations of its components other than the logical particles.

But there is also a second class of analytic statements, typified by:

(2) No bachelor is married.

The characteristic of such a statement is that it can be turned into a logical truth by putting synonyms for synonyms; thus (2) can be turned into (1) by putting 'unmarried man' for its synonym 'bachelor.' We still lack a proper characterization of this second class of analytic statements, and therewith of analyticity generally, inasmuch as we have had in the above description to lean on a notion of "synonymy" which is no less in need of clarification than analyticity itself. . . .

A natural suggestion, deserving close examination, is that the synonymy of two linguistic forms consists simply in their interchangeability in all contexts without change of truth value—interchangeability, in Leibniz's phrase, *salva veritate.* Note that synonyms so conceived need not even be free from vagueness, as long as the vaguenesses match.

But it is not quite true that the synonyms 'bachelor' and 'unmarried man' are everywhere interchangeable *salva veritate.* Truths which become false under substitution of 'unmarried man' for 'bachelor' are easily constructed with the help of 'bachelor of arts' or 'bachelor's buttons'; also with the help of quotation, thus:

'Bachelor' has less than ten letters.

Such counterinstances can, however, perhaps be set aside by treating the phrases 'bachelor of arts' and 'bachelor's buttons' and the quotation "bachelor" each as a single indivisible word and then stipulating that the interchangeability *salva veritate* which is to be the touchstone of synonymy is not supposed to apply to fragmentary occurrences inside of a word. This account of synonymy, supposing it acceptable on other counts, has indeed the drawback of appealing to a prior conception of "word" which can be counted on to present difficulties of formulation in its turn. Nevertheless some progress might be claimed in having reduced the problem of synonymy to a problem of wordhood. Let us pursue this line a bit, taking "word" for granted.

The question remains whether interchangeability *salva veritate* (apart from occurrences within words) is a strong enough condition for synonymy, or whether, on the contrary, some heteronymous expressions might be thus interchangeable. Now let us be clear that we are not concerned here with synonymy in the sense of complete identity in psychological associations or poetic quality; indeed no two expressions are synonymous in such a sense. We are concerned only with what may be called *cognitive* synonymy. Just what this is cannot be said without successfully finishing the present study; but we know something about it from the need which arose for it in connection with analyticity in §1. The sort of synonymy needed there was merely such that any analytic statement could be turned into a logical truth by putting synonyms for synonyms. Turning the tables and assuming analyticity, indeed, we could explain cognitive synonymy of terms as follows (keeping to the familiar example): to say that 'bachelor' and 'unmarried man' are cognitively synonymous is to say no more nor less than that the statement:

(3) All and only bachelors are unmarried men is analytic.

What we need is an account of cognitive synonymy not presupposing analyticity——if we are to explain analyticity conversely with help of cognitive synonymy as undertaken in §1. And indeed such an independent account of cognitive synonymy is at present up for consideration, namely, interchangeability *salva veritate* everywhere except within words. The question before us, to resume the thread at last, is whether such interchangeability is a sufficient condition for cognitive synonymy. We can quickly assure ourselves that it is, by examples of the following sort. The statement:

(4) Necessarily all and only bachelors are bachelors

is evidently true, even supposing 'necessarily' so narrowly construed as to be truly applicable only to analytic statements. Then, if 'bachelor' and 'unmarried man' are interchangeable *salva veritate,* the result:

(5) Necessarily all and only bachelors are unmarried men

of putting 'unmarried man' for an occurrence of 'bachelor' in (4) must, like (4), be true. But to say that (5) is true is to say that (3) is analytic, and

hence that 'bachelor' and 'unmarried man' are cognitively synonymous.

Let us see what there is about the above argument that gives it its air of hocus-pocus. The condition of interchangeability *salva veritate* varies in its force with variations in the richness of the language at hand. The above argument supposes we are working with a language rich enough to contain the adverb 'necessarily,' this adverb being so construed as to yield truth when and only when applied to an analytic statement. But can we condone a language which contains such an adverb? Does the adverb really make sense? To suppose that it does is to suppose that we have already made satisfactory sense of 'analytic.' Then what are we so hard at work on right now?

Our argument is not flatly circular, but something like it. It has the form, figuratively speaking, of a closed curve in space. . . .

4. Semantical Rules

Analyticity at first seemed most naturally definable by appeal to a realm of meanings. On refinement, the appeal to meanings gave way to an appeal to synonymy or definition. But definition turned out to be a will-o'-the-wisp, and synonymy turned out to be best understood only by dint of a prior appeal to analyticity itself. So we are back at the problem of analyticity.

I do not know whether the statement 'Everything green is extended' is analytic. Now does my indecision over this example really betray an incomplete understanding, an incomplete grasp of the "meanings," of 'green' and 'extended? I think not. The trouble is not with 'green,' or 'extended,' but with 'analytic.'

It is often hinted that the difficulty in separating analytic statements from synthetic ones in ordinary language is due to the vagueness of ordinary language and that the distinction is clear when we have a precise artificial language with explicit "semantical rules." This, however, as I shall now attempt to show, is a confusion.

The notion of analyticity about which we are worrying is a purported relation between statements and languages: a statement *S* is said to be *analytic* for a language *L*, and the problem is to make sense of this relation generally, that is, for variable '*S*' and '*L*.' The gravity of this problem is not perceptibly less for artificial languages than for natural ones. The problem of making sense of the idiom 'S is analytic for L,' with variable 'S' and 'L,' retains its stubbornness even if we limit the range of the variable 'L' to artificial languages.

From the point of view of the problem of analyticity the notion of an artificial language with semantical rules is a *feu follet par excellence*. Semantical rules determining the analytic statements of an artificial language are of interest only in so far as we already understand the notion of analyticity; they are of no help in gaining this understanding.

Appeal to hypothetical languages of an artificially simple kind could conceivably be useful in clarifying analyticity, if the mental or behavioral or cultural factors relevant to analyticity—whatever they may be—were somehow sketched into the simplified model. But a model which takes analyticity merely as an irreducible character is unlikely to throw light on the problem of explicating analyticity.

It is obvious that truth in general depends on both language and extralinguistic fact. The statement 'Brutus killed Caesar' would be false if the world had been different in certain ways, but it would also be false if the word 'killed' happened rather to have the sense of 'begat.' Thus one is tempted to suppose in general that the truth of a statement is somehow analyzable into a linguistic component and a factual component. Given this supposition, it next seems reasonable that in some statements the factual component should be null; and these are the analytic statements. But, for all its a priori reasonableness, a boundary between analytic and synthetic statements simply has not been drawn. That there is such a distinction to be drawn at all is an unempirical dogma of empiricists, a metaphysical article of faith.

※

The second dogma of empiricists is reductionism, according to which every meaningful statement can be translated into a statement about immediate experience. But any conceptual scheme we bring to it "is a man-made fabric which impinges on experience only along the edges." Since according to Quine there are no analytic truths (propositions that can be known to be true a priori just in virtue of their meaning), he concludes that "no statement is immune to revision."

In his book *Ontological Relativity* (1969), Quine presents the thesis that two of his most important philosophical theses about meaning—the indeterminacy of translation and the inscrutability of reference—lead to the conclusion that one cannot truly say what a language is about, not even a scientific and formal language. Like scientific theories, theories of meaning are underdetermined by the available data; different competing and mutually exclusive theories can all account for the data. Which theory does a better job in terms of its ontological claims is itself ultimately relative,, depending on what purposes the theory is supposed to serve; we cannot say what the objects of the world are independently of the conceptual schemes in which they occur as terms in a language. Since there are always competing alternative theories within a number of conflicting conceptuals schemes, one must always make room for the possibility of new views improved according to established scientific principles. Though Quine ultimately agrees with Wittgenstein that it is not possible to have a private language, communication gives us access to each other's conceptual schemes, thereby making possible what Quine calls "semantic ascent." This involves developing a more inclusive conceptual scheme in which the users of the language can make intelligent "ontic decisions" about what they are talking about, even though they know that the translation of meanings must forever remain, like ourselves and the world, ultimately indeterminate.

NOTES

1. Indeed, it is possible to view the entire three volumes as the first attempt to write a program—a set of algorithmic procedures—for the algorithmic procedure known as deductive mathematics. It is, I have been told by its inventors, no accident that the most sophisticated mathematics software today in use by mathematics professors and students is called *Mathematica*.

2. The German word is *Sachlage*, which has most often been translated as "state of affairs," while *Sachverhalt* is rendered in English as "*atomic* or *particular* state of affairs." We should also keep in mind that, unlike in English, *Sache* (fact, a something), *Tatsache* (fact), *Sachverhalte* (particular states of affairs), and *Sachlage* (state of affairs) all have the word *Sach* in common.

3. Quoted in Dreben and Floyd, p. 23.

4. Giuseppe Peano (1858–1932), Italian mathematician, whose mathematical logic was a bridge between the old algebra of logic and newer methods inspired by Frege and Russell.

24 ⚘ The Postmodernists: Gadamer, Merleau-Ponty, Foucault, and Derrida

24.0 Gadamer (1900–): The Philosopher's Apprentice and the Birth of Hermeneutics

Hans-Georg Gadamer was born in Marburg, Germany, and grew up in the Silesian town of Breslaw (now Wroclaw, Poland). As a young man he was fascinated by the Prussian army and everyone thought he would enter the military. At the University of Marburg, however, he discovered philosophy. The two works that influenced him most were Kierkegaard's *Either/Or* and Kant's *Critique of Pure Reason*. In 1922 he contracted polio but this did not prevent him from earning his doctoral dissertation the following year, at the age of 23. He received a junior teaching position at Freiburg, where he met both Husserl and Heidegger. In *Philosophical Apprenticeships* he describes meeting Heidegger as

⚘

a basic event, not only for me but for all of the Marburg of those days. He demonstrated a well-integrated spiritual energy laced with such a plain power of verbal expression and such a radical simplicity of questions that the habitual and more or less mastered games of wit and categories or modalities quickly left me.

⚘

It was as Heidegger's apprentice that he developed his system of philosophical hermeneutics:

⚘

As I was attempting to develop a philosophical hermeneutic, it followed from the previous history of hermeneutics that the interpretive (*verstehenden*) sciences provided my starting point. But to these was added a hitherto neglected supplement. I am referring to the experience of art. For both art and the historical sciences are modes of experiencing in which our own understanding of existence comes directly into play. . . .My starting point was thus the critique of Idealism and its Romantic traditions. It was clear to me that the forms of consciousness of our inherited and acquired historical education—aesthetic consciousness and historical consciousness—presented alienated forms of our true historical being. The primordial experiences that are transmitted through art and history are not to be grasped from the points of view of these forms of consciousness.*

⚒

During the next five years, while serving as Heidegger's apprentice and teaching assistant, he completed his second doctorate—his "habilitation," the second dissertation traditionally required of all teachers in German universities—on Plato under Heidegger's direction. He remained in Marburg as a *Privatdozent* teaching philosophy. When the Nazis came to power Gadamer lost his job and was sent to a "rehabilitation camp," after which he became "extraordinary professor" in 1937 at Marburg.

In 1939 he moved on to Leipzig, where he taught philosophy throughout World War II. When the war ended and Russian forces occupied the area, the Russians made him rector of the University, which he ran for several years before accepting a position at the University of Frankfurt and then Heidelberg, where he wrote his most famous work, *Truth and Method* (1960), from which our selection is taken.

The main focus of the work is what Gadamer calls "philosophical hermeneutics." Hermeneutics is the art of interpretation and understanding texts. The word itself is derived from the Greek word that means "to interpret," itself derived from *Hermes*, the tricky messenger of the Gods. One could never be quite sure, from Hermes' message, what the Gods truly intended—or, at least, one had to be careful and wise in interpreting Hermes' message. According to Greek mythology, it was Hermes who invented language and writing for the purpose of making communication possible between us and the Gods.

Throughout history, the goal of hermeneutics has been to find some sort of objective method for interpreting authoritative texts that always seemed extremely amenable to multiple interpretations. This was a major problem in theology, where multiple interpretations of scriptures produced wide disagreement among theologians as to the true meaning and understanding of "God's word." In theology, hermeneutics involved the search for a method of interpreting scriptures that would produce the one true and correct meaning. Gadamer set out to construct such a heremeneutic for philosophy.

The problem, as Gadamer sees it, is that any theory is caught in the *hermeneutic circle*. Consider a sentence. To understand a sentence, you must first be able to understand the individual words in the sentence. However, the meanings of individual words are themselves both vague and ambiguous and thus cannot be understood without understanding the larger context of the sentence within which they occur. According to Heidegger, the hermeneutical circle

⚒

is not to be reduced to the level of a vicious circle, or even of a circle which is merely tolerated. In the circle is hidden a positive possibility of the most primordial kind of knowing, and we genuinely grasp this possibility only when we have understood that our first, last, and constant task in interpreting is never to allow our fore-having, fore-sight, and fore-conception to be presented to us by fancies and popular conceptions, but rather to make the scientific theme secure by working out these fore-structures in terms of the things themselves.

⚒

This "primordial kind of knowing" begins by the interpreter acknowledging the *fore-structures* that exist both in the mind and in language that determine any particular interpretation. These Gadamer calls *prejudices*, by which he "means a

---

*From *Philosophical Apprenticeships*, trans. Robert R. Sullivan (Cambridge, MA: MIT Press, 1985).

From Heidegger, *Being and Time*, J. Macquarrie and E. Robinson, trans. (Harper & Row, 1962).

judgment that is rendered before all the elements that determine a situation have been finally examined." We must seek out and bring to light the "hidden prejudices" that make us "deaf to what speaks to us in tradition."

According to Gadamer, "all understanding is interpretation." This would seem to lead to radical subjectivity, since interpretations differ radically among individuals, but Gadamer argues that not all interpretation is subjective in the sense of being the product of a single, solitary subject who does the interpreting. Interpreting is not something that we do; it is something that happens to us. "Language is the universal medium in which understanding itself is realized." And "it is always a past that allows us to say, 'I have understood,'" not because meaning and understanding reside in the past but because "the essential nature of the historical spirit consists not in the restoration of the past but in thoughtful mediation with contemporary life."

In *On Gadamer*, contemporary philosopher Patricia Johnson presents the main thesis of *Truth and Method* in the following terms:

⚹

In *Truth and Method*, Gadamer develops philosophical hermeneutics, emphasizing that all understanding is self-understanding. Through the rehabilitation of the concept of aesthetic consciousness, he begins to develop a philosophical position that overcomes the sense of alienation that results from Enlightenment thinking, especially from the distinction of subject from object. He examines the experience of art, moving to the insight that we belong to our world in an integral manner.

In rehabilitating the concept of historical consciousness, he further develops this experience of belonging. It becomes evident that understanding is a process in which each finite human participates. We enter a particular point in that process and so are affected by what has gone before us, We have certain prejudices because we are part of this

process. These prejudices form and make possible our understandings. Yet, as finite humans, we can still develop interpretive distance and so filter prejudices. We cannot remove ourselves from the situation to which we belong, but we can move around within that situation and so change our horizons. In this process we experience the fusion of horizons. We are not beings alienated and isolated from the past. Rather, we are a living part of an ongoing conversation. We are active participants in a dialogue with the past that will carry on into the future. This dialogue is mediated through the medium of language.

The third part of *Truth and Method* turns to an examination of language. Gadamer writes, "The guiding idea of the following discussion is *that the fusion of horizons that takes place in understanding is actually the achievement of language*" (TM 378). He begins the discussion of language with a quotation from Schleiermacher, "Everything presupposed in hermeneutics is but language." In the process of his own analysis of language he writes, *"Being that can be understood is language"* (TM 474). The examination of language is, therefore, central and fundamental to Gadamer's philosophical position. It retains this position in his thinking for the rest of his career.

In the third part of *Truth and Method*, Gadamer examines language as what he calls the medium of human experience. This examination is a further development of the fusion that he first notes in aesthetic consciousness and develops more fully in the analysis of historical consciousness. He traces the history of the emergence of the concept of language in order to demonstrate that he is not imposing something on language. This follows his approach in the first two parts of *Truth and Method*. He emphasizes that the concept of language as he sets it out is part of the process of the historical emergence of a concept of language. Finally, he sets out a concept of language as the horizon of a hermeneutic ontology. We are situated within language and in that situation we understand everything that is, including ourselves.

⚹

The central role of language and our place within the hermeneutic exerted a wide influence on many writers and thinkers over the past four

---

From Pat Johnson, *On Gadamer* (Belmont, CA: Wadsworth, 1999).

decades and continues to this day. In the following passage from *Truth and Method* Gadamer explains the hermeneutic circle and its development from Heidegger's philosophy.

⚒

Truth and Method (in part)

Part II: The Extension of the Question of Truth To Understanding in the Human Sciences

SECTION II: ELEMENTS OF A THEORY OF HERMENEUTIC EXPERIENCE

CHAPTER 1: THE ELEVATION OF THE HISTORICITY OF UNDERSTANDING TO THE STATUS OF A HERMENEUTIC PRINCIPLE

(A) THE HERMENEUTIC CIRCLE AND THE PROBLEM OF PREJUDICES

(1) HEIDEGGER'S DISCLOSURE OF THE FORE-STRUCTURE OF UNDERSTANDING

Heidegger entered into the problems of historical hermeneutics and critique only in order to explicate the fore-structure of understanding for the purposes of ontology. Our question, by contrast, is how hermeneutics, once freed from the ontological obstructions of the scientific concept of objectivity, can do justice to the historicity of understanding. Hermeneutics has traditionally understood itself as an art or technique. This is true even of Dilthey's expansion of hermeneutics into an organon of the human sciences. One might wonder whether there is such an art or technique of understanding—we shall come back to the point. But at any rate we can inquire into the consequences for the hermeneutics of the human sciences of the fact that Heidegger derives the circu-

From Hans-Georg Gadamer, *Truth and Method*, 2nd revised edition, translation revised by Joel Weinsheimer and Donald G. Marshall (London: Sheed and Ward, 1989).

lar structure of understanding from the temporality of Dasein. These consequences do not need to be such that a theory is applied to practice so that the latter is performed differently—i.e., in a way that is technically correct. They could also consist in correcting (and refining) the way in which constantly exercised understanding understands itself—a process that would benefit the art of understanding at most only indirectly.

Hence we will once more examine Heidegger's description of the hermeneutical circle in order to make its new fundamental significance fruitful for our purposes. Heidegger writes, "It is not to be reduced to the level of a vicious circle, or even of a circle which is merely tolerated. In the circle is hidden a positive possibility of the most primordial kind of knowing, and we genuinely grasp this possibility only when we have understood that our first, last, and constant task in interpreting is never to allow our fore-having, fore-sight, and fore-conception to be presented to us by fancies and popular conceptions, but rather to make the scientific theme secure by working out these fore-structures in terms of the things themselves" (*Being and Time*, p. 153).

What Heidegger is working out here is not primarily a prescription for the practice of understanding, but a description of the way interpretive understanding is achieved. The point of Heidegger's hermeneutical reflection is not so much to prove that there is a circle as to show that this circle possesses an ontologically positive significance. The description as such will be obvious to every interpreter who knows what he is about. All correct interpretation must be on guard against arbitrary fancies and the limitations imposed by imperceptible habits of thought, and it must direct its gaze "on the things themselves" (which, in the case of the literary critic, are meaningful texts, which themselves are again concerned with objects). For the interpreter to let himself be guided by the things themselves is obviously not a matter of a single, "conscientious" decision, but is "the first, last, and constant task." For it is necessary to keep one's gaze fixed on the thing throughout all the constant distractions that originate in the interpreter himself. A person who is trying to understand a text is always projecting. He projects a meaning for the text as a whole as soon as some initial meaning emerges in the text.

Again, the initial meaning emerges only because he is reading the text with particular expectations in regard to a certain meaning. Working out this fore-projection, which is constantly revised in terms of what emerges as he penetrates into the meaning, is understanding what is there.

This description is, of course, a rough abbreviation of the whole. The process that Heidegger describes is that every revision of the fore-projection is capable of projecting before itself a new projection of meaning; rival projects can emerge side by side until it becomes clearer what the unity of meaning is; interpretation begins with fore-conceptions that are replaced by more suitable ones. This constant process of new projection constitutes the movement of understanding and interpretation. A person who is trying to understand is exposed to distraction from fore-meanings that are not borne out by the things themselves. Working out appropriate projections, anticipatory in nature, to be confirmed "by the things" themselves, is the constant task of understanding. The only "objectivity" here is the confirmation of a fore-meaning in its being worked out. Indeed, what characterizes the arbitrariness of inappropriate fore-meanings if not that they come to nothing in being worked out? But understanding realizes its full potential only when the fore-meanings that it begins with are not arbitrary. Thus it is quite right for the interpreter not to approach the text directly, relying solely on the fore-meaning already available to him, but rather explicitly to examine the legitimacy—i.e., the origin and validity—of the fore- meanings dwelling within him.

⚓

24.1 Merleau-Ponty (1908–1961): Many Worlds, Many Selves

Maurice Merleau-Ponty was born in Rochefort-sur-mer, France. Like many other French philosophical luminaries of the twentieth century, he studied philosophy at the École Normale Supérieure in Paris. As a student he was most attracted to the ideas of Husserl and Heidegger. Ironically, just as the mutual philosophical collaboration and influence between German phenomenologists and French existentialists was

reaching its peak, the two nations found themselves at war.

Merleau-Ponty's first book, *The Structure of Behavior*, had just been published when World War II broke out. He immediately enlisted as an officer in the French Army. When the French surrendered a year later, he returned to academic life under the German occupation. He taught at the Lycee Carnot in Paris, where he and his former classmate Jean-Paul Sartre formed a resistance group, *Socialism and Liberty*. After the war his collaboration with both Sartre and Simone de Beauvoir continued and they published the highly influential journal, *Les Temps Modernes*.

The ending of the war coincided with the publication of Merleau-Ponty's second and most influential book, *Phenomenology of Perception* (1945). It was highly acclaimed throughout postwar Europe and earned him teaching positions at the University of Lyon and then at the Sorbonne. In 1952 he was awarded the prestigious Chair of Philosophy at the College de France, a position he held for the rest of his life.

Merleau-Ponty's thought was influenced both by philosophy and by recent developments in the new science of psychology. Like most of his contemporaries, his philosophical development was inspired by German phenomenology and driven to a large extent by a reaction against the moderns in general and Descartes in particular—this in spite of the fact that throughout his life Merleau-Ponty's philosophical focus remained on Descartes. He tried to present a radical new reinterpretation of Cartesian thought that went well beyond the *cogito*:

⚓

The *Cogito* was the coming to self-awareness of this inner core. But all meaning was *ipso facto* conceived as an act of thought, as the work of a pure *I*, and although rationalism easily refuted empiri-

From Maurice Merleau-Ponty, *Phenomenology of Perception* (New York: Humanities Press, 1962), p. 147.

cism, it was itself unable to account for the variety of experience, for the element of senselessness in it, for the contingency of contents. Bodily experience forces us to acknowledge an imposition of meaning which is not the work of a universal constituting consciousness, a meaning which clings to certain contents. My body is that meaningful core which behaves like a general function, and which nevertheless exists, and is susceptible to disease.

᭡

In developing a neo-Cartesian theory of mind, Merleau-Ponty drew on *Gestalt* theory in psychology as well as behaviorism even while being highly critical of both movements. Likewise, the central problem with the Cartesian viewpoint, he argues, is that

> Descartes . . . detached the subject, or consciousness, by showing that I could not possibly apprehend anything as existing unless I first of all experienced myself as existing in the act of apprehending it.

In *The Structure of Behavior* (1942), Merleau-Ponty presents, in opposition to the behaviorists, what he calls a "dialectical" conception of behavior. The main idea is that as organisms evolve over time, higher "forms" of behavior transform the life of the organism with new capacities. These new powers are not mere additions to a particular neurophysiology. Rather, through the process of "dialectical" assimilation, these new capacities bring changes to the way the organism is able to function by restructuring the underlying neurophysiology. Thus to a certain degree he anticipates the advent of neurobiological explanations of mental functioning that have been the hallmark of recent work in cognitive science.

Central to Merleau-Ponty's thought is the idea of human consciousness as a *body-subject*—an irreducible composite of body and mind. This is the phenomenological body, which exists as a projection into and an amalgam of phenomenological space. Think, for instance, of your body in a dream; this body—not just some disembodied Cartesian Ego—is the central focus of your conscious experience, that to which all the objects in the dream are directed, a focal point of self-awareness and intentionality. In waking states you are likewise situated in a body that is a phenomenological projection into phenomenological space, except that the space you are in is now one in which other subjects are publicly situated, each tied to its own representational world and thereby to each other: "to be a body is to be tied to a certain world . . . our body is not primarily in space: it is of it." In other words, the body itself is to be understood as a mind, having intentional qualities—an embodied mind situated within a mind presenting itself to itself not as mind but as world.

This focus on the body as a situated intentional subject of conscious cognition is a radical departure from the existentialists and phenomenologists of the time, especially and most notably Sartre, for whom intentionality is attributed to pure consciousness alone. According to Merleau-Ponty this attribution is a mistake because it abstracts consciousness away from its actual presentation to itself as physical object (the phenomenological body, what we perceive as our body). In this way Merleau-Ponty was much closer in his thinking to Husserl, who had called for a philosophical embargo on abstraction and a return to the "things themselves."

Nor does Merleau-Ponty dissociate the (phenomenological) body—what in cognitive science today we would call the body image—from its surrounding phenomenological space. Surrounding the body is what he called an "intentional arc," the locus of intellectual and perceptive experiences defined by the possibilities of directing consciousness in divergent directions; like a projector that can be turned in all directions, our consciousness spreads itself into an "intentional arc" all around us, creating and situating us in our world. Furthermore, this intentional arc—what, ordinarily and naively we would simply call the world all around—is an amalgam of our past, present, and future, along with our entire philosophical, scientific, and moral outlooks. It brings to life these aspects of our own minds as centers of meaning. That is, the "intentional arc" of experience weaves an ongoing tapestry of meaning, stitching together the discrete moments of our lives into a unity, thereby providing the basis of our personal identity.

In this way Merleau-Ponty completely rejects the Cartesian dualism under which the mind–body is conceived. The body exists in the mental and the mental exists in the body; the relationship between these two intentional modes must, he argues, itself be understood ultimately in dialectical terms:

⚹

there is no question here of a duality of substances. In other words, the concepts 'soul' and 'body' must be rendered relative. There is, first, the body as a mass of chemical combinations which constantly interact; then, the body as the dialetics of the living being and its environment; also the body as the dialetics of the social subject with its group; even all our habits may pass as an untouchable body for the 'I' of every moment. Each of these grades is 'soul' with respect to the lower grades, and 'body' with respect to the higher grades. The body in general is a whole of already established paths, already acquired powers, it is the acquired dialectic soil on which higher formation takes shape, and the soul is the new meaning that comes into existence.

⚹

Merleau-Ponty suggests that Husserl's phenomenology paved the way out of the old metaphysical mind–body dualism. The goal of phenomenology is to provide a comprehensive account of the totality of the world of our experience—the "phenomenological horizon"—by describing the phenomena of human consciousness out of which our experience is constituted. In this way philosophy can return itself to "the things them-

From Remy C. Kwant's translation of pp. 226–227 of *La structure de comportement*, as seen in his *The Phenomenological Philosophy of Merleau-Ponty* (Pittsburgh, PA: Duquesne University Press, 1963), pp. 46–47.

selves"—not to the noumenal "things-in-themselves" (*ding-an-sich*) as Kant showed to be absolutely unreachable—but to the "things" experienced in the everyday world of our experience. This may sound like a new and lofty exercise in strangeness, perhaps, but consider how closely this philosophical movement is aligned with the radical empiricism of William James (20.1). But under Merleau-Ponty's analysis James would still be considered steeped in and hindered by the Cartesian paradigm of the perceiving subject as situated from within the mind–body, rather than as the body in phenomenal space in the way that Merleau-Ponty conceives it. For the "world of experience" is itself a projection from the subject, which has, in Merleau-Ponty's phrase, motility—the capacity to project the phenomenal field in any direction, with itself at the center. In Merleau-Ponty's philosophy this notion of the projectors is sometimes considered as an idealistic sort of metaphor, but he means it literally. He is a realist about what is going on when the subject becomes the phenomenal body and thereby situates itself in a world of its own projection, becoming the *body-subject*. Furthermore, this phenomenal world projected through the situated subject who is, at once, both generator and seer of the phenomena, is not something constructed from atomic phenomenal-psychological elements. This construction was Hume's mistake. Hume claimed that our ideas (the perceived objects) are constructed out of sensations—the psychological elements of experience—conjoined by association and conjunction, glued together in memory. Instead, Merleau-Ponty claims that our perceptions themselves arise as phenomenological wholes, complete gestalts (*Gestalten*), *phenomenal fields*.

What is a phenomenal field? Look around you. Everything you see is a phenomenal field. It may seem as if what you are looking at is static, a fixed set of things in space, a fixed set of passive objects that persist in your visual field into which they arrive via light rays projected from them to you, the perceiving subject. But in fact, claims

Merleau-Ponty, what you are looking at is an active projection *from out of yourself, the body-subject*. In this way the Cartesian *cogito*, the *I think*, is replaced by the body-subject that is both the receiver and giver of the objects of perception, which exist as phenomenological textures within the phenomenal field.

⚓

What Is Phenomenology?

It is a matter of describing, not of explaining or analysing. Husserl's first directive to phenomenology, in its early stages, to be a "descriptive psychology," or to return to the "things themselves," is from the start a rejection of science. I am not the outcome or the meeting-point of numerous causal agencies which determine my bodily or psychological make-up. I cannot conceive myself as nothing but a bit of the world, a mere object of biological, psychological or sociological investigation. I cannot shut myself up within the realm of science. All my knowledge of the world, even my scientific knowledge, is gained from my own particular point of view, or from some experience of the world without which the symbols of science would be meaningless. The whole universe of science is built upon the world as directly experienced, and if we want to subject science itself to rigorous scrutiny and arrive at a precise assessment of its meaning and scope, we must begin by reawakening the basic experience of the world of which science is the second order expression. Science has not and never will have, by its nature, the same significance *qua* form of being as the world which we perceive, for the simple reason that it is a rationale or explanation of that world. I am, not a "living creature" nor even a "man," nor again even "a consciousness" endowed with all the characteristics which zoology, social anatomy or inductive psychology recognize in these various products of the natural or historical process—I am the absolute source, my existence does not stem from my antecedents, from my physical and social environment; instead it moves out towards them and sustains them, for I alone bring into being for myself (and therefore into being in the only sense that the word can have for me) the tradition which I elect to carry on, or the horizon whose distance from me would be abolished—since that distance is not one of its properties—if I were not there to scan it with my gaze. Scientific points of view, according to which my existence is a moment of the world's, are always both naive and at the same time dishonest, because they take for granted, without explicitly mentioning it, the other point of view, namely that of consciousness, through which from the outset a world forms itself round me and begins to exist for me. To return to things themselves is to return to that world which precedes knowledge, of which knowledge always *speaks*, and in relation to which every scientific schematization is an abstract and derivative sign-language, as is geography in relation to the countryside in which we have learnt beforehand what a forest, a prairie or a river is.

⚓

In Merleau-Ponty's philosophy that we each exist as a body-subject situated in our own phenomenal world is an overarching idea that can help us to understand one of the central differences between so-called "continental" philosophy and philosophy in the so-called "anglo-saxon" analytic tradition. In the former, we each exist in our own world. In the latter, we all exist in one and the same world, conjoined by perceptions and a web of beliefs into a network of meaning. In both cases language plays a fundamental role as communicator among the many selves in the many worlds, providing a holistic system of conjoined selves. It is this latter notion—the real self—that comes under attack in the subsequent philosophy of Michel Foucault.

Maurice Merleau-Ponty, *Phenomenology of Perception*, trans. by Colin Smith (London: Routledge and Kegan Paul, Ltd., 1967).

24.2 Foucault (1926–1984): The Death of the Self

Michel Foucault was born in Poitiers, France, to a prominent medical family; both parents were children of prominent doctors. His father was a surgeon and professor of anatomy. Like many of the best upper-class children at the time, he attended the prestigious École Normale Supérieure in Paris (just as Sartre had a generation before him) where he studied philosophy. These early years were extremely difficult and traumatic for him, starting with the experiences of World War II.

🜍

The menace of war was our background, our framework of existence. . . . Much more than the activities of family life, it was these events concerning the world which are the substance of our memory. . . . Maybe that is the reason why I am fascinated by history and the relationship between personal experience and those events of which we are a part.

🜍

A loner deeply alienated from his classmates, he tried to commit suicide several times. The school doctor suggested that "these troubles resulted from an extreme difficulty in experiencing and accepting his homosexuality." In any case, the question of what madness is and its relation, not just to "sanity" but to all aspects of power, politics, and the self, became the central focus of all his subsequent philosophizing. His doctoral dissertation, which he wrote at the Maison Francaise in Uppsala, Sweden, became the basis for his first, highly influential work, *Madness and Civilization* (1961). Here he argues that most human institutions are organized like a prison system designed to suppress "Madness"—a state of mind derived from the Greek *daimon* that once was thought to be divinely inspired—by shifting it to the concept of mental illness. According to Foucault madness is a great creative force—reminiscent of Nietzsche's *Will to*

Power—that the institutional traditions of Western society have repressed:

🜍

Perhaps some day we will no longer really know what madness was. Its face will have closed upon itself, no longer allowing us to decipher the traces it may have left behind. Will these traces themselves have become anything to the unknowing gaze but simple black marks? Or will that the most have become part of the configurations that we others now cannot sketch but that in the future would constitute the indispensable grids through which we and our culture become legible? Artaud will belong to the foundation of our language, not to its rupture: the neuroses will belong among the constitutive forms (and not the deviations) of our society. Everything we experience today in the mode of a limit, or as foreign, or as intolerable will have returned to the serenity of the positive.

Only the enigma of this exteriority will remain. What was, then, this strange demarcation, one will ask, that was at work from the heart of the Middle Ages until the twentieth century and possibly beyond? Why did Western culture cast from its field that in which it might just as well have recognized itself, where in fact it had recognized itself obliquely? Why has it formulated so clearly since the nineteenth century, but in a way already since the classical age, that madness was the truth of the human laid bare while nevertheless placing it in a space, neutralized and pale, where it was as it were canceled? What was the point of collecting the texts of Nerval or Artaud? Why discover oneself in their utterances and not in themselves? So the sharp image of reason will wither in flames. . . .

🜍

Nietzsche's influence on Foucault is apparent throughout his work, which in many ways is a continuation and evolution of Nietzsche's philosophy. Foucault agrees with Nietzsche that things have no essence—that essence is a human

From Michel Foucault, *Politics, Philosophy, Culture: Interviews and Other Writings, 1077–1984* (New York: Routledge, 1988).

From "Madness, the Absence of Work" by Michel Foucault, translated by Peter Stastny and Denis Sengel.

fabrication—and that therefore truth and knowledge are themselves human fabrications as a result of the quest for power. Foucault turns this thinking inward, however, arguing that power resides neither in human subjects nor in our social and political institutions; rather, power is distributed throughout society, indeterminate, ineffable, without any apparent origin.

⚹

"Truth and Power"

. . . In societies like ours, the "political economy" of truth is characterised by five important traits. "Truth" is centred on the form of scientific discourse and the institutions which produce it; it is subject to constant economic and political incitement (the demand for truth, as much for economic production as for political power); it is the object, under diverse forms, of immense diffusion and consumption (circulating through apparatuses of education and information whose extent is relatively broad in the social body, not withstanding certain strict limitations); it is produced and transmitted under the control, dominant if not exclusive, of a few great political and economic apparatuses (university, army, writing, media); lastly, it is the issue of a whole political debate and social confrontation ("ideological" struggles).

It seems to me that what must now be taken into account in the intellectual is not the "bearer of universal values." Rather, it's the person occupying a specific position—but whose specificity is linked, in a society like ours, to the general functioning of an apparatus of truth. In other words, the intellectual has a three-fold specificity: that of his class position (whether as petty-bourgeois in the service of capitalism or "organic" intellectual of the proletariat); that of his conditions of life and work,

From "Truth and Power," translated by Colin Gordon, in *Power/Knowledge: Selected Interviews and Other Writings 1972–77*, edited by Colin Gordon (New York: Pantheon, 1972), pp. 131–33. Copyright © 1972, 1975, 1976, 1977 by Michel Foucault. Collection copyright © 1980 by the Harvester Press, a division of Random House, Inc.

linked to his condition as an intellectual (his field of research, his place in a laboratory, the political and economic demands to which he submits or against which he rebels, in the university, the hospital, etc.); lastly, the specificity of the politics of truth in our societies. And it's with this last factor that his position can take on a general significance and that his local, specific struggle can have effects and implications which are not simply professional or sectoral. The intellectual can operate and struggle at the general level of that regime of truth which is so essential to the structure and functioning of our society. There is a battle "for truth," or at least "around truth"—it being understood once again that by truth I do not mean "the ensemble of truths which are to be discovered and accepted," but rather "the ensemble of rules according to which the true and the false are separated and specific effects of power attached to the true," it being understood also that it's not a matter of a battle "on behalf" of the truth, but of a battle about the status of truth and the economic and political role it plays. It is necessary to think of the political problems of intellectuals not in terms of "science" and "ideology," but in terms of "truth" and "power." And thus the question of the professionalisation of intellectuals and the division between intellectual and manual labour can be envisaged in a new way.

. . .

"Truth" is to be understood as a system of ordered procedures for the production, regulation, distribution, circulation and operation of statements.

"Truth" is linked in a circular relation with systems of power which produce and sustain it, and to effects of power which it induces and which extend it. A regime of truth.

This regime is not merely ideological or superstructural; it was a condition of the formation and development of capitalism. . . .

The essential political problem for the intellectual is not to criticise the ideological contents supposedly linked to science, or to ensure that his own scientific practice is accompanied by a correct ideology, but that of ascertaining the possibility of constituting a new politics of truth. The problem is not changing people's consciousnesses—or what's in their heads—but the political, economic, institutional regime of the production of truth.

It's not a matter of emancipating truth from every system of power (which would be a chimera, for truth is already power) but of detaching the power of truth from the forms of hegemony, social, economic and cultural, within which it operates at the present time.

The political question, to sum up, is not error, illusion, alienated consciousness or ideology; it is truth itself. Hence the importance of Nietzsche.

⚓

Foucault thus rejects outright those aspects of modern philosophy that describe the human being as both the subject and object of knowledge, in which thinking exists as something separate from the empirical world, rooted in some sort of a priori categories. According to Foucault even the concept of rationality is an artificial illusion perpetrated by invisible forces external to the individual, over which the individual has no control. Indeed, to Nietzsche's famous slogan, "God is dead," Foucault would add: "So also man, the self: the individual is dead." He thus concludes his *Archaeology of Knowledge* (1969) with this ode to Nietzsche: "You may have killed God beneath the weight of all that you have said; but don't imagine that, with all that you are saying, you will make a man that will live longer than he."

To understand the significance of Foucault and his immense influence on so many twentieth-century thinkers, we have to appreciate the impact of a central claim to his philosophy, namely, that "language is a species of writing." The main characteristic of writing to which he is drawing our attention is the "inner monologue" in which we hear ourselves speak and then imagine someone who is the originator of the speech, and that someone is of course taken to be us, ourselves, the self as the author of thinking and speaking. But notice, first, that when you think or write there is a strange and subtle illusion at play. The illusion makes it seem as if you are controlling the flow of speech, the choice of words, the intention of what is being said, and so on. The "you" here refers to the conscious self, the subject of experience, the *I* that you take yourself to be. But if you pay close attention you will see that you—the conscious self—do not so much *cause* or *control* the choice and sequence of words as *hear* them as an audi-

ence does. You merely and immediately identify the words as your own, the voice as yourself, but you are not in charge. It is all occurring "behind the scenes," so to speak.

Like Heidegger—who also influenced him though not to the extent that Nietzsche did—Foucault, like Derrida (see next section), is hereby attacking "the metaphysics of presence." This is the notion that there exist definite things—entities that ground our thinking, speaking, acting, and so on—that exist independently of and outside our language. But—similar in some ways to Wittgenstein—there is no getting beyond or outside language, and all efforts to find some "transcendental signified" are doomed to failure. Indeed, like many subsequent naturalists—such as, most notably, Quine, and Davidson—Foucault insists that words cannot have meaning by standing for things (entities, images, etc.) that are somehow directly present to consciousness. Not even "mental experiences" are signified by the signs of language. In other words, not only can we never reach the transcendental world outside the mind by language or experience, but we can never reach the transcendental world of our own selves by language or experience. The human mind as giver and repositor of mental life, the Kantian faculties, the thinker who thinks—all these metaphysical entities are nonexistent chimeras. For us who exist within language there is neither a real world present in our words nor a real mind; no*thing* is present, and that this *seems* so obviously *not* to be the case is an illusion.

Thus, to understand Foucault, we must understand his claim that all language is but a species of writing in light of his deeper underlying claim that there is no author. This claim should strike you, at the very least, as an extremely unnerving idea—especially in view of everything that we have undertaken thus far in our quest for the great lovers of wisdom! But this claim is one of the central tenets of the philosophical movement known as *postmodernism*, of which Foucault is one of the originators. We have been studying Plato, Hume, Descartes, Kant, and so on as if these great, enlightened selves wrote all those wonderful, enlightening works. For postmodernist thinkers, there is a great deception in all this, namely, that in conceiving in our minds of these selves who wrote these works, we are creating the illusion of "subject-centered reason." We are as guilty of make-believe as those who, upon reading the Bible, ascribe the words to its great spiritual author, God. And it's not just that the philosophical bibles, so to speak, were written by non-divine, ordinary human beings. It's that these non-divine, ordinary human beings lacked any central subject of mental discourse—a unified, intelligent author who communicated through words some great hidden truths. For these reasons it is not surprising that, for the postmodernists, not only is the self out of the question, but philosophy itself must necessarily come to an end. Why? Because, strictly speaking, there are no philosophers. The great lovers of wisdom must go the way of the gods. They are imaginary fictions.

Foucault makes this radical idea clear in "What Is an Author?" from which our next selection is taken.

⋆

What Is an Author?

The coming into being of the notion of "author" constitutes the privileged moment of *individualization* in the history of ideas, knowledge, literature, philosophy, and the sciences. Even today, when we reconstruct the history of a concept, literary genre, or school of philosophy, such categories seem relatively weak, secondary, and superimposed scansions in comparison with the solid and fundamental unit of the author and the work. . . .

This usage of the notion of writing runs the risk of maintaining the author's privileges under the protection of writing's a priori status: it keeps alive, in the gray light of neutralization, the interplay of those representations that formed a particular

image of the author. The author's disappearance, which, since Mallarmé, has been a constantly recurring event, is subject to a series of transcendental barriers. There seems to be an important dividing line between those who believe that they can still locate today's discontinuities [*ruptures*] in the historico-transcendental tradition of the nineteenth century, and those who try to free themselves once and for all from that tradition.*

It is not enough, however, to repeal the empty affirmation that the author has disappeared. For the same reason, it is not enough to keep repeating (after Nietzsche) that God and man have died a common death. Instead, we must locate the space left empty by the author's disappearance, follow the distribution of gaps and breaches, and watch for the openings that this disappearance uncovers. . . .

. . . the author is not an indefinite source of significations which fill a work; the author does not precede the works; he is a certain functional principle by which, in our culture, one limits, excludes, and chooses; in short, by which one impedes the free circulation, the free manipulation, the free composition, decomposition, and recomposition of fiction. In fact, if we are accustomed to presenting the author as a genius, as a perpetual surging of invention, it is because, in reality, we make him function in exactly the opposite fashion. One can say that the author is an ideological product, since we represent him as the opposite of his historically real function. (When a historically given function is represented in a figure that inverts it, one has an ideological production.) The author is therefore the ideological figure by which one marks the manner in which we fear the proliferation of meaning.

In saying this, I seem to call for a form of culture in which fiction would not be limited by the figure of the author. It would be pure romanticism, however, to imagine a culture in which the fictive would operate in an absolutely free state, in which fiction would be put at the disposal of everyone and would develop without passing through something like a necessary or constraining figure. Although, since the eighteenth century, the author has played the role of the regulator of the fictive, a role quite

*[For discussion of the notions Of discontinuity and historical tradition see Foucault's *Les Mots et les choses* (Paris: Gallimard, 1966), translated as *The Order of Things* (New York: Pantheon, 1971).—Ed.]

characteristic of our era of industrial and bourgeois society, of individualism and private property, still, given the historical modifications that are taking place, it does not seem necessary that the author function remain constant in form, complexity, and even in existence. I think that, as our society changes, at the very moment when it is in the process of changing, the author function will disappear, and in such a manner that fiction and its polysemic texts will once again function according to another mode, but still with a system of constraint—one which will no longer be the author, but which will have to be determined or, perhaps, experienced.

All discourses, whatever their status, form, value, and whatever the treatment to which they will be subjected, would then develop in the anonymity of a murmur. We would no longer hear the questions that have been rehashed for so long: "Who really spoke? Is it really he and not someone else? With what authenticity or originality? And what part of his deepest self did he express in his discourse?" Instead, there would be other questions, like these: "What are the modes of existence of this discourse? Where has it been used, how can it circulate, and who can appropriate it for himself? What are the places in it where there is room for possible subjects? Who can assume these various subject functions?" And behind all these questions, we would hear hardly anything but the stirring of an indifference: "What difference does it make who is speaking?"

⚹

Who—*what*—is the author of a book? Take, for instance, Shakespeare's *Hamlet*. Here we take Shakespeare to be the particular individual who gives unity and intention to *Hamlet*—it's design, meaning, and significance. Clearly, Shakespeare thus conceived exists as a being, an entity, transcendent to the text. This belief is a mistake for several reasons. First of all, "criticism and philosophy took note of the disappearance—or death—of the author some time ago." We have seen this in various cases, such as, for instance, in the work of Buddha in the east and Hume in the west. Second, and even more importantly, just as belief in God can draw

attention away from the world itself, so belief in an author draws attention away from the text itself. In other words, everything I am saying here right now in talking about Foucault simply draws your attention away from the text excerpted above. It gets you thinking about Foucault's intentions, his philosophy, his meaning, and what deep and profound aspects of his thinking he may have been trying to express. All this is, according to Foucault, a waste and a destruction. Attend, instead, only to the works themselves. "What difference," he asks, "does it make who is speaking?"

Foucault's radical ideas did not prevent him from becoming, perhaps ironically, a central authoritative figure. He held several notable positions, serving as chair of the philosophy departments at the University of Clermont-Ferrand and at Vincennes. He became famous throughout the world and lectured in the United States, Canada, Japan, and Brazil. He lived openly with his lover, Daniel Defert, and was involved in everything from the Iranian revolution to Maoist communism, to the French communist party, as well as to anti-communist movements. He was an avid participant in the drug and gay bathhouse scene in San Francisco until his premature death, in 1984, from AIDS.

24.3 Derrida (1930–   ): The Art of Deconstruction

Jacques Derrida was born to Jewish parents in Algiers. As a young boy he hated school so much that in 1942, when he and other Jewish children were forbidden to go to school because of the German Nazi occupation, he thought the Nazis were doing him a personal favor. Nevertheless, he read and studied on his own and taught himself philosophy so well that seven years later, at the age of nineteen, he was admitted to arguably the best school for philosophy in Paris, the prestigious École Normale Supérieure.

There he stayed and taught philosophy to a small and devoted group of students. Although an early essay on Husserl's work on geometry won a prize, he taught and lived in relative obscurity until 1966, when he suddenly became a figure of world renown.

The occasion was a conference at Johns Hopkins University on the new structuralism that was then all the philosophical rage in Paris. Derrida made a profound leap beyond anything the structuralists were doing, so much beyond that his talk there is usually heralded as the birth of "post-structuralism." Derrida concluded that talk with a remark that should by now be familiar to us: "I don't believe there is any perception."

To understand Derrida's thought we must begin with the movement that he was both reacting against and emerging from, namely, structuralism, which had itself arisen in reaction to and evolved out of the work of Saussure and C. S. Peirce (see pp. 442–451). Structuralism appealed to many academicians in the politically turbulent 1960s because it gave a semblance of scientific objectivity to literary studies. Instead of looking at meanings in particular linguistic usages and subjective/cultural interpretations, the structuralists studied the structure of a system in the abstract. Thus a structuralist reading of a particular text—whether literary or a work of philosophy—ignores all notions of a writer's history, culture, purpose, and so on, and treats the work as if what it says is but a pattern produced by impersonal forces, not the result of a personal subject of experience in the deliberative action of composing thoughts. Personal, subjective individuality is thus replaced by the study of objective patterns, systems, and structures. These structures, in turn, are analyzed as the result of particular and perhaps random variations on certain fundamental universal narrative patterns.

We can easily see how structuralism influenced Foucault and Derrida, each of whom in his own way wanted to remove the notion of the author as subject. In their view the text is not the product of any individual; it is not subjective. But whereas for the structuralists, and to a certain degree for Foucault, the text is a product of a system, Derrida strips the system of any causal power. Systems and individuals are both the products of language—that is, for all these thinkers, we don't speak a language; language speaks *us*. Everything is made up of the "already written." Thus, according to Levi-Strauss, one of the leading structuralists, history becomes completely irrelevant because the structures that matter are universal and timeless.

In this way the entire so-called "postmodernist" movement, from structuralism to deconstruction, which is usually presented as a radical departure from classical and modern thinking, can be seen as a natural evolution of the most important philosophical insights that preceded it. Its revolution is merely a shift from talk about metaphysics, ontology, and epistemology to language. Thus, the naïve notions that there is a "real world" that exists "out there" indepen-dently of the human mind—a world that can either be perceived correctly via experience or intuited via rationality—are demolished by postmodernism because what was previously learned by philosophers about experience and rationality is now seen to apply just as well to language. Language cannot depict any "real world" that exists independently of the mind, nor can it give us access to any true or inner self. It is the structure of language that produces what we call "reality." All our perceptions are themselves framed within and structured by language.

Enter Derrida. According to the leading structuralists of the time, meaning was to be found in the signs and grammars governing language. Although meaning is not derived from individuals, the system within which individuals exist governs the meanings under which the individuals function and interpret their worlds. Thus structuralism was a sort of linguistic version of the Copernican revolution; instead of the individual being at the center of meaning, it is the structure of language that provides the unifying center from which meaning emanates and illuminates the entire system. Derrida removes any notion of a center at all. It is a radical sort of relativity; just as Einstein showed that there is no center to the universe, no absolute point of reference, Derrida argues that there is no center to language, thought, and meaning. According to Derrida, this belief in a center is where philosophy has been in error; time and again it has posited a center from which everything—existence, meaning, knowledge, etc.—comes. Whether that center is God, or the self, or the mind, or the collective unconscious, or rationality, or science, or language, the problem is in each case the same. So how do we get out of this predicament that Derrida dubs the *logo*centric in *Of Grammatology*? In a word: *deconstruction*.

According to Derrida, here is how deconstruction works. First we must locate what has been posited as the center—the point of origin—of a particular system or structure. This is logocentrism: the false presupposition that there is, so to speak, a gravitational center of gravity around which languages revolve, an absolute pull toward certainty. Second, within this system we locate the set of binary pairs or oppositions—two terms placed in relation to each other—that provide the dynamic tension of discourse within that system. Third, we find which of the two terms is "positive" in each case and which is "negative." Take, for instance, the notion of good/evil. Good is taken as the positive value; evil as the negative. The former is valued over the latter. Likewise for other such pairs of terms: male/female, right/left, scientific/unscientific, rational/irrational, light/dark, truth/fiction, reality/appearance, thought/language, signified/signifier, center/margin, objective/ subjective, and so on. In traditional West-ern thought the first term is always valued over the second. In the act of deconstruction, we don't destroy or rebuild it; rather, we "reread it" to change it through a process of intellectual identification

by making it our own; it becomes part of our own vision. This change is achieved, first of all, by reversing the preceding polarities—not for the purpose of creating an opposing counter-system but, rather, to completely subvert and destabilize a system that was constructed arbitrarily, usually by politically motivated considerations. "Deconstruction does not consist in passing from one concept to another, but in overturning and displacing a conceptual order, as well as the nonconceptual order with which the conceptual order is articulated."

In the act of deconstruction we analyze how the fundamental units of a particular structure or systems—its binary pairs of opposites—functions within that system. Again, the goal is not to reverse the polarities to create an anti-system—i.e., to value evil over good, dark over light, irrationality over rationality, nonbeing over being, etc.—but *to erase the borders between them*. In other words, each term of a binary term is not a polar opposite of the other but part of one concept. The structure of opposition that which kept them apart—the slash—is erased. The system has been deconstructed because its fundamental units contradict their own logic.

In his most famous work, *Of Grammatology*, Derrida analyzes the opposition pair, "speech/writing." Speech has always been taken as more important than writing because, traditionally, it is assumed that speech came first and that writing is just the transcription of speech. Derrida argues that speech has been given the privileged position because it is associated with exactly the sort of *metaphysical presence* that he—like Foucault, following Heidegger—claims is the universal mistake in all previous thinking. (We might add to our "eyes are not windows" locution, "*words are not tunnels*.") The previous idea was that for spoken language to exist, the subject must exist; there must be someone who is speaking. But in the philosophy of Foucault, this belief is false.

The false belief that the speech guarantees a speaker reinforces the illusion that there exists a real self within whom and from whom the speech act originates. According to Derrida, this is the central falsehood of the metaphysics of presence that was the driving force, not just in modern philosophy but all the way from the beginning of Western philosophy, at least as far back as Plato.

In "Signature, Event, Context," from which our next selection is taken, Derrida begins by deconstructing the philosophies of Condillac, Husserl (see Section 21.1); and John Austin to reach the conclusion that writing itself does not exist.

⊥

Signature, Event, Context

To conclude this very dry* discussion:

1. as writing, communication, if we retain that word, is not the means of transference of meaning, the exchange of intentions and meanings *[vouloir-dire]*, discourse and the "communication of consciousnesses." We are witnessing not an end of writing that would restore, in accord with McLuhan's ideological representation, a transparency or an immediacy to social relations; but rather the increasingly powerful historical expansion of a general writing, of which the system of speech, consciousness, meaning, presence, truth, etc., would be only an effect, and should be analyzed as such. It is the exposure of this effect that I have called elsewhere logocentrism;

2. the semantic horizon that habitually governs the notion of communication is exceeded or split by the intervention of writing, that is, by a dissemination irreducible to *polysemy.* Writing is read; it is not the site, "in the last instance," of a hermeneutic deciphering, the decoding of a meaning or truth;

3. despite the general displacement of the classical, "philosophical," occidental concept of

Trans. by Sam Weber and Jeff Mehlman from *Glyph* 1, 1977.
*[The French word for dry here is sec which combines the initial letters of Derrida's three word title: Signature, Event, Context.)

writing, it seems *necessary to* retain, provisionally and strategically, the old name, This entails an entire logic of *paleonymics* that I cannot develop here.** Very schematically: an opposition of metaphysical concepts (e.g., speech/writing, presence/absence, etc.) is never the confrontation of two terms, but a hierarchy and the order of a subordination. De-construction cannot be restricted or immediately pass to a neutralization: it must, through a double gesture, a double science, a double writing—put into practice a reversal of the classical opposition *and* a general *displacement* of the system. It is on that condition alone that deconstruction will provide the means of *intervening* in the field of oppositions it criticizes and that is also a field of nondiscursive forces. Every concept, moreover, belongs to a systematic chain and constitutes in itself a system of predicates. There *is* no concept that is metaphysical in itself. There is a labor—metaphysical or not—performed on conceptual systems. Deconstruction does not consist in moving from one concept to another, but in reversing and displacing a conceptual order as well as the nonconceptual order with which it is articulated. For example, writing, as a classical concept, entails predicates that have been subordinated, excluded, or field in abeyance by forces and according to necessities to be analyzed. It is those predicates (I have recalled several of them) whose force of generality, generalization, and generativity is liberated, grafted onto a "new" concept of writing that corresponds as well to what has always *resisted* the prior organization of forces, always constituted the *residue* irreducible to the dominant force organizing the hierarchy that we may refer to, in brief as logocentric. To leave to this new concept the old name of writing is tantamount to maintaining the structure of the *graft,* the transition and indispensable adherence to an effective *intervention* in the constituted historical field. It is to give to everything at stake in the operations of deconstruction the chance and the force, the power of *communication.*

But this will have been understood, as a matter of course, especially in a philosophical colloquium: a disseminating operation removed from the presence (of being) according to all its modifications; writing, if there is any, perhaps communicates, but

**Cf. La dissémination and Positions.

]certainly does not exist. Or barely, hereby, in the form of the most improbable signature.

(Remark: the—written—text of this—oral—communication was to have been addressed to the *Association of French Speaking Societies of Philosophy* before the meeting. Such a missive therefore had to be signed. Which I did, and counterfeit here. Where? There. J.D.)

J. DERRIDA

Index